lonely planet

Eastern USA

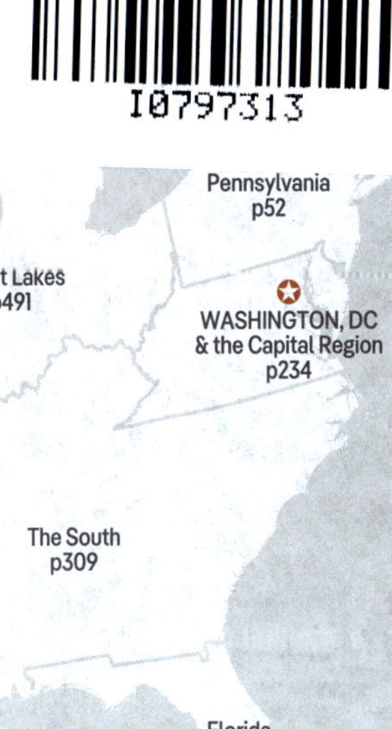

Ann Babe, Mary Fitzpatrick, John Garry, Regis St Louis,
Jesse Scott, Karla Zimmerman

AHPIX/SHUTTERSTOCK

Arlington National Cemetery (p295)

CONTENTS

Plan Your Trip

The Journey Begins Here 4
Eastern USA Map 8
Our Picks 10
Regions & Cities 22
Itineraries 24
When to Go 34
Get Prepared 36
The Food Scene 38
The Outdoors 42
National Parks 46
Epic Road Trips 48

The Guide

New York, New Jersey & Pennsylvania 52
Find Your Way 54
Plan Your Time 56
New York City 58
New York State 98
New Jersey 120
Pennsylvania 130
Places We Love to Stay 150

New England 153
Find Your Way 154
Plan Your Time 156
Boston 158
Massachusetts 176
Rhode Island 186
Connecticut 193
Vermont 202
New Hampshire 214
Maine 221
Places We Love to Stay 232

Washington, DC & the Capital Region 234
Find Your Way 236
Plan Your Time 238
Washington, DC 240
Delaware 263
Maryland 272
Virginia 285
West Virginia 298
Places We Love to Stay 306

The South 309
Find Your Way 310
Plan Your Time 312
North Carolina 314
South Carolina 333
Tennessee 345
Kentucky 358
Georgia 366
Alabama 380
Mississippi 389
Arkansas 397
New Orleans 407
Louisiana 420
Places We Love to Stay 424

Florida 426
Find Your Way 428
Plan Your Time 430
Miami 432
Everglades & Biscayne National Park 444
Florida Keys & Key West 450
Southeast Florida 456
Orlando & Walt Disney World® 464
Space Coast 471
Northeast Florida 476
Tampa Bay & Southwest 482
Places We Love to Stay 488

Great Lakes 491
Find Your Way 492
Plan Your Time 494
Chicago 496
Illinois 509
Indiana 516
Ohio 525
Michigan 536
Wisconsin 552
Minnesota 564
Places We Love to Stay 578

Toolkit

Arriving 582
Getting Around 583
Travel by Train 584
Money 585
Accommodations 586
Family Travel 587
Food, Drink & Nightlife 588
Responsible Travel 590
Health & Safe Travel 592
LGBTIQ+ Travelers 593
Accessible Travel 594
Nuts & Bolts 595

Storybook

A History of Eastern USA in 15 Places 598
Introducing Eastern USA 602
How the US Got Its Groove 604
Southern Barbecue 606
Birthplace of the Revolution 608
The Cherokee 611
The Birth of America's Summer Vacation 614

LIFE LOOKS/SHUTTERSTOCK

Cape Cod (p183)

EASTERN USA

THE JOURNEY BEGINS HERE

My first job post-college required traveling around the US by bus. Before hitting the road, the America I knew was limited to my one-stoplight hometown in the Catskill Mountains, the nonstop bustle of NYC and childhood vacations – touring Newport's gilded mansions and Florida's shell-strewn beaches. I didn't realize how vast and varied everything else could be – how Maine's rough-cut cliffs give way to Cape Cod's dunes in hours; how those salty Atlantic sands mirror the freshwater shorelines of Michigan. I'd yet to see the blue haze above the Smokies or the synchronous fireflies of Congaree. I didn't know New Orleans felt like a nation unto itself. I'd never considered how growing up on bagels instead of biscuits might shape a person. Dialects change faster than the coastline across the Eastern USA, its 29 states brimming with cultures as colorful as the seasons.

John Garry

@garryjohnfrancis

John is a writer, teacher, urban wanderer, mountain hiker and museum lover who eats out too much in Brooklyn, where he lives.

My favorite experience is climbing **Mt Beacon** (p107). On clear days, views stretch along the mountain-flanked Hudson to NYC's skyline, flickering 60 miles downriver – a grand diorama of America's diverse landscapes.

WHO GOES WHERE

Our writers and experts choose the places which, for them, define Eastern USA.

LASSE HOLST HANSEN/SHUTTERSTOCK

Call me biased – I grew up in Wisconsin so I totally am – but **Superior** (pictured; p549) just might be the most beautiful lake on the planet. At over 31,000 sq miles, it's so vast it could be mistaken for an ocean, and its rocky, rugged shoreline is a watercolor dream. I love it.

Ann Babe
annbabe.com
Ann writes about travel, culture and belonging.

JON BILOUS/SHUTTERSTOCK

Maryland (pictured; p272) is especially lovely around its edges, with the Eastern Shore a highlight. Secluded coves shelter picturesque waterside towns, quiet marshlands echo with the calls of ospreys, brilliant sunsets paint the skies and unique traditions endure, centered around the work of local watermen and the moods of the Chesapeake Bay (pictured; p275). When you cross the Bay Bridge, you'll almost immediately feel slower-paced rhythms taking over, a oneness with the tides and the seasons, and a sense of tranquility and muted beauty.

Mary Fitzpatrick
Mary is an Africa-based writer with roots along the East Coast, where she returns frequently for visits.

WEIDMAN PHOTOGRAPHY/SHUTTERSTOCK

I have fond memories of visiting the **Great Smoky Mountains** (pictured; p329) as a young boy and experiencing the thrill of nature for the first time: thundering waterfalls, towering old-growth poplar trees, and fern-lined streams full of salamanders. Years later, after returning with my own children, I realized these biologically rich forests have lost none of their magic. The Smokies have so many different facets it's hard not to be filled with wonder after a trip here.

Regis St Louis

@regisstlouis

The son of two Coloradans, Regis has spent half a lifetime exploring the world's wild places. He is the author of more than 100 Lonely Planet guides.

BOOGICH/GETTY IMAGES

My home base of **Fort Lauderdale** (pictured; p456) truly lives up to its 'Venice of America' nickname. Within a five-minute coast along its Las Olas Boulevard artery, you can be gawking at superyachts coasting along the Intracoastal Waterway and neighboring canals; strolling a stretch of designer boutiques; and dipping your toes in the Atlantic Ocean. Beyond its white-sand-heaven reputation, I love how Fort Lauderdale's artistic edge is becoming more visible, too, with the Flagler Village neighborhood now rivaling Miami's Wynwood in terms of graffiti-art-draped pizzazz.

Jesse Scott

@jesserobertscott

A Fort Lauderdale resident and the founder of browardist.com, Jesse has been writing about entertainment, food, travel and their intersections for 20-plus years.

ELESI/SHUTTERSTOCK

Chicago (p496) is my favorite place. That's why I've lived here for 35 years! The skyline still amazes me. Every time I take the L toward downtown, it's like the buildings suddenly pop up and expand storybook-style. I love blue-green Lake Michigan spilling over the horizon, and old-school baseball at Wrigley Field. Then there are the beer gardens (pictured), free outdoor concerts at Millennium Park, and water-squirting public art. Still not bored after all this time!

Karla Zimmerman

@karlazimmerman

Karla writes about travel and oddball sights when she's not eating donuts and yelling at the Cubs at home in Chicago. She wrote part of the Great Lakes (Chicago, Illinois, Wisconsin, Minnesota).

CONTRIBUTING WRITERS

Amy C Balfour
Ray Bartlett
Rachel Chang
Gregor Clark
Julekha Dash
Sarah Etinas
Caroline Eubanks
David Gibb
Michael Grosberg
Brian Healy
Carolyn Heller
Robert Isenberg
Lauren Keith
Emily Matchar
Marisa Paska
Kevin Raub
Britany Robinson
Jason Ruffin
Maya Stanton
Meena Thiruvengadam
Caroline Trefler
Mara Vorhees
Terry Ward

Chicago
Midwest epicenter for arts, eats and architecture (p490)
Detroit
The Motor City is restarting its cultural engine (p537)
Niagara Falls
See North America's most voluminous cascade (p118)
Newport
Gilded Age mansions rise along the Atlantic (p190)
Boston
Uncover the port city's revolutionary streak (p158)
Acadia National Park
Craggy cliffs and wave-bashed beaches (p228)
New York City
The USA's electric cultural empire (p58)
New River Gorge National Park
Whitewater raft down an ancient river (p300)
CANADA
MAINE
NH
VT
MA
CT
RI
NEW YORK
NEW JERSEY
PENNSYLVANIA
DELAWARE
MARYLAND
VIRGINIA
WEST VIRGINIA
OHIO
INDIANA
ILLINOIS
MICHIGAN
WISCONSIN
MINNESOTA
IOWA
Lake Superior
Lake Michigan
Lake Huron
Lake Erie
Lake Ontario
Lake St Clair
Georgian Bay
Saginaw Bay
Green Bay
Lake Champlain
Gulf of Maine
Vermillion Lake
Mille Lacs Lakes
Mississippi
Illinois
Kankakee
Grand Forks
Fargo
Wahpeton
Sioux Falls
Sioux City
Duluth
St Cloud
Buffalo
St Paul
Rochester
La Crosse
Ashland
Ironwood
Houghton
Rice Lake
Wausau
Madison
Dubuque
Davenport
Iron Mountain
Marquette
Green Bay
Oshkosh
Milwaukee
Racine
Chicago
Champaign
Sault Ste Marie
Mackinaw City
Midland
Grand Rapids
Lansing
Flint
Jackson
Detroit
South Bend
Toledo
Findlay
Indianapolis
Dayton
Columbus
Cleveland
Akron
Cambridge
Youngstown
Pittsburgh
Bridgeport
Charleston
Erie
Niagara Falls
Buffalo
Rochester
Binghamton
Scranton
Allentown
Harrisburg
Philadelphia
Baltimore
WASHINGTON, DC
Dover
Atlantic City
Trenton
New York City
Long Beach
New Haven
Syracuse
Watertown
Massena
Albany
Springfield
Worcester
Providence
Newport
Boston
Provincetown
Manchester
Portsmouth
Concord
Montpelier
Portland
Augusta
Bangor
Lincoln

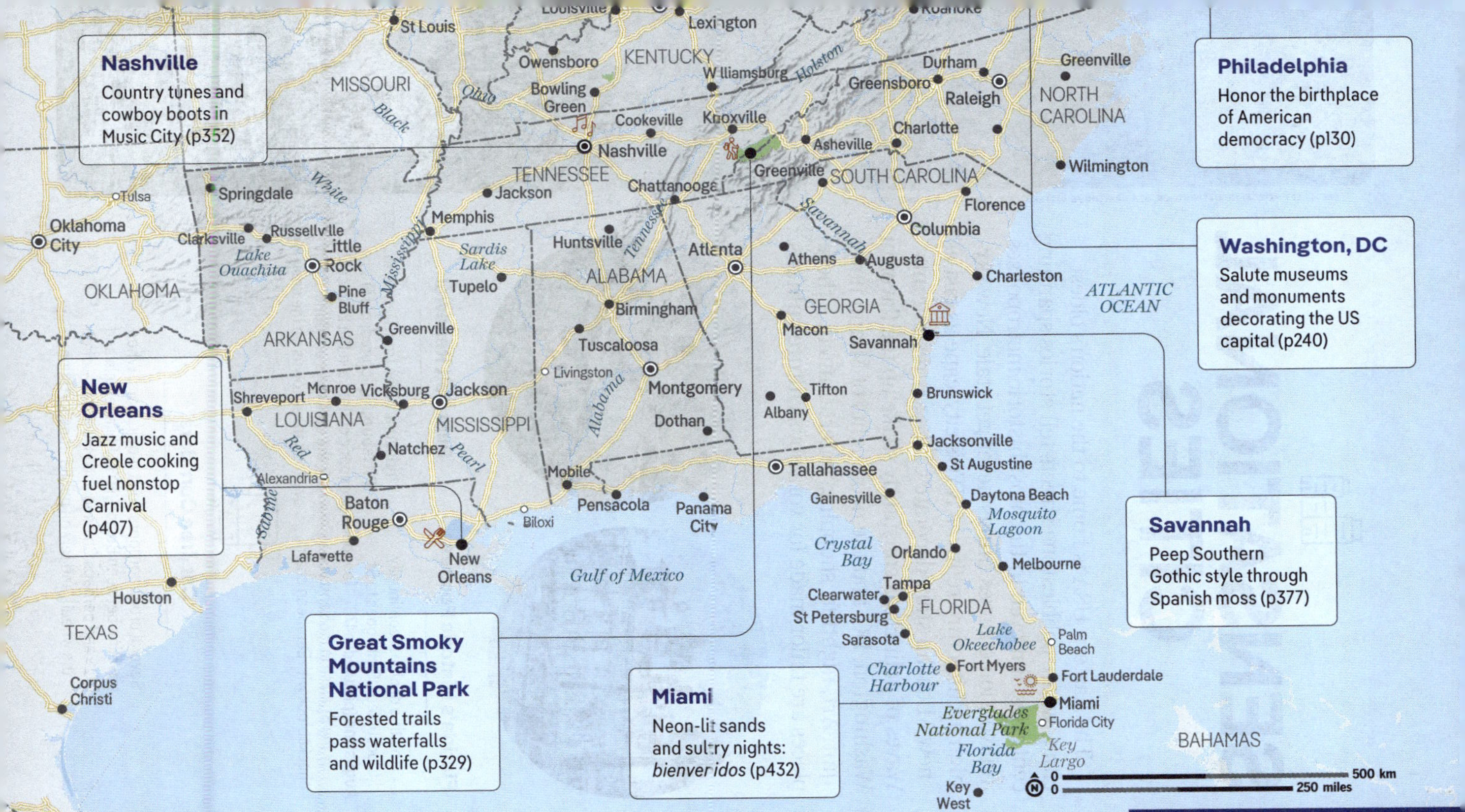

Nashville
Country tunes and cowboy boots in Music City (p352)

New Orleans
Jazz music and Creole cooking fuel nonstop Carnival (p407)

Great Smoky Mountains National Park
Forested trails pass waterfalls and wildlife (p329)

Miami
Neon-lit sands and sultry nights: *bienvenidos* (p432)

Philadelphia
Honor the birthplace of American democracy (p130)

Washington, DC
Salute museums and monuments decorating the US capital (p240)

Savannah
Peep Southern Gothic style through Spanish moss (p377)

SENSATIONAL CITIES

The Eastern USA is home to the nation's oldest cities, where cobblestone streets tell stories spanning centuries. But even in the most historic metropolises, reinvention ensures things never get stale. New sky-high architecture redraws NYC's cityscape as fast as new Michelin stars decorate Chicago's restaurants. Waves of politicians constantly shake up the flavor in Washington, DC, and the neon lights of Miami never quit. Art, nightlife, shopping, entertainment – these places are tailor-made for voracious culture vultures.

Florida's Historic Fortress

The title of oldest continually occupied US city goes to **St Augustine** (pictured; p478) – founded by the Spanish in 1565 and still chockablock with European charm.

Rust Belt Renewal

Industrial cities from Detroit to **Pittsburgh** (pictured; p146) saw economic collapse in the 20th century, but the dark days are done. Don't overlook these towns on the upswing.

Car-free Corridors

Several urban corridors don't require cars. When traveling between Boston, NYC, Philadelphia and DC – and perhaps Chicago and Milwaukee – ditch the wheels and rely on public transportation.

FROM LEFT: KOSOFF/SHUTTERSTOCK, SEAN PAVONE/SHUTTERSTOCK, SEAN PAVONE/SHUTTERSTOCK

Cherry blossoms (p249) near Washington Monument (p244)

BEST CITY EXPERIENCES

Hop between the ❶ **East Village's** restaurants and entertainment venues to eat and experience what NYC's trendy crowds are enjoying right now. (p70)

Take an ❷ **architecture boat tour** in Chicago, birthplace of the skyscraper, to appreciate the Windy City's stunning steel-and-stone canyons. (p499)

Stroll Washington, DC's ❸ **Tidal Basin** around April, when cherry trees dress the nation's hard-nosed political epicenter in soft pink petals. (p249)

Wander through Miami's ❹ **Wynwood**, where muralists and graffiti artists have transformed countless blocks into an alfresco art gallery. (p437)

Poke around Atlanta's ❺ **Midtown**: peep at High Museum art, lunch in Colony Square and walk through sprawling Piedmont Park. (p81)

HIGHLIGHTS OF HISTORY

The USA's forefathers built the nation's foundation on the East Coast – along waterways linking European colonists to the country's interior and on battlefields where they raged against Great Britain. This is where brothers fought in the Civil War, where defining social movements found their voice and where every US President called the shots. The landscapes have their own stories to share too, in ancient rivers and hidden tunnels, sculpted by nature over millions of years. Prepare to time travel.

Let Freedom Ring

Philadelphia (p130), dubbed the 'cradle of liberty,' planted seeds for the American Revolution (1775–83) and provides insight into the pivotal war at dozens of local sites.

History Lesson

Get a crash course in US history at the free-to-visit **Smithsonian museums** (p240) in Washington, DC, where galleries explore national politics, nature and African American culture.

Original Residents

People have occupied the East Coast for 12,000 years, possibly longer. Remnants of ancient civilizations like Georgia's **Ocmulgee Mounds** (p374) tell tales of complex Indigenous societies.

FROM LEFT: JOHN_SILVER/SHUTTERSTOCK, MIA2YOU/SHUTTERSTOCK, SEAN PAVONE/SHUTTERSTOCK

Old State House on the Freedom Trail (p164), Boston

BEST HISTORY EXPERIENCES

Wind through Ithaca's ❶ **gorges**, lined with sedimentary rocks deposited 400 million years ago when the area was an inland ocean. (p113)

Follow the nation's founding footsteps along Boston's red-brick ❷ **Freedom Trail**, exploring the city's role in the American Revolution. (p164)

Pay your respects at ❸ **Gettysburg National Military Park**, the Civil War battle site where over 50,000 died or were injured. (p144)

Glimpse Gilded Age opulence by ogling the gold-trimmed mansions of ❹ **Newport**, constructed as elite 19th-century summer escapes. (p192)

Unearth the nation's dark history of slavery in ❺ **Montgomery, Alabama**, through memorials that confront the past and inspire reflection. (p386)

COASTAL TREASURES

Quiet fishing villages, boisterous boardwalks, salt-swept cities and mangrove canals – coastlines along the Eastern USA have it all. The Atlantic stretches from Maine's craggy cliffs to the tropical Keys. The Gulf Coast's warm breezes kiss southern beaches and bayous from Florida to Louisiana. Then there are the Great Lakes, spanning over 94,000 sq miles – vast inland seas rimmed with dunes, sprinkled with islands and peppered with storybook towns. Don't forget your beach towel.

Coastal Queen

Florida (p426) has more coastline than any other state in the contiguous US, including 825 miles of sugar-sand beaches and 350 miles of coral reefs.

Shark Tales

Over 50 shark species call the East Coast's Atlantic waters home, but encounters are extremely rare – despite horrors evoked by *Jaws*, filmed on Martha's Vineyard.

Dynamic Dunes

The Great Lakes boast the world's largest collection of freshwater sand dunes – most prominent around Lake Michigan, home to a 400ft sandy peak at **Sleeping Bear Dunes National Lakeshore** (p545).

Wild horses on Assateague Island National Seashore (p279)

BEST COASTAL EXPERIENCES

Cruise along Cape Cod's ❶ **Old King's Highway**, once an Indigenous route, now a bayside thoroughfare linking historic towns. (p183)

Swim, snorkel, paddle or dive around Florida Keys reefs at ❷ **John Pennekamp Coral Reef State Park**, the nation's first underwater park. (p450)

Spot herds of wild horses trotting between dunes dotting ❸ **Assateague Island National Seashore** in Maryland. (p278)

Beeline for ❹ **Cape May** during autumn's migration season, when peregrine falcons and monarch butterflies funnel through New Jersey's southernmost tip. (p122)

Jump into Lake Michigan from ❺ **Door County, Wisconsin** – a remote 80-mile-long peninsula where wild waves crash along limestone cliffs. (p560)

ENTERTAINMENT CAPITALS

All Eastern USA is a stage and each region plays a starring role. The sonic landscape shifts from swinging rhythms in jazzed-up New Orleans to banjo-twanging Appalachia and country crooning Nashville. NYC's Broadway gave birth to musical theater, exported across state lines with touring shows and regional productions. Theme parks dazzle with thrill rides and fireworks. Sports arenas coax fans to cheer for the home team. Join the roaring crowds.

FROM LEFT: RBLFMR/SHUTTERSTOCK, MELISSA HERZOG/SHUTTERSTOCK, MIKE LIU/SHUTTERSTOCK

Distinguishing Broadway

To be considered a Broadway production, the show must play in a 500-plus seat house located in NYC's Theater District. Venues with 100-499 seats are Off-Broadway.

Heart of Rock 'n' Roll

Rock 'n' roll has many roots: **Memphis** (p347) is its birthplace; Cleveland holds the **Hall of Fame** (pictured; p526); Bethel, NY, hosted legendary rock concert **Woodstock** (p109).

Athletic Adversaries

Heading to Boston's **Fenway Park** (p171) for a Red Sox game? Ditch any New York Yankees swag – the baseball teams have been rivals since 1919.

Wrigley Field (p503), Chicago

BEST ENTERTAINMENT EXPERIENCES

Let your ears guide you down Nashville's ❶ **Honky Tonk Highway**, where live musicians earn the town its 'Music City' moniker. (p353)

Go avant-garde in NYC by seeing what's on at ❷ **Playwrights Horizons**, an Off-Broadway theater heralding up-and-coming drama makers. (p82)

Sing quintessential baseball tune 'Take Me Out to the Ball Game' during the 7th-inning stretch of a Chicago Cubs game at ❸ **Wrigley Field**. (p503)

Drink around the world at EPCOT, race Harry Potter at Universal Studios and meet aquatic creatures at SeaWorld while touring ❹ **Orlando**. (p464)

Stomp and sway through ❺ **Clarksdale's juke joints**, where the soulful sounds of blues musicians echo across the Mississippi Delta. (p393)

FABULOUS FESTIVALS

From small-town parades to citywide blowouts, festivals showcase idiosyncratic pockets of creativity, community and culture. These aren't just parties – they're peak season experiences worth planning a trip around. Whether honoring identity, celebrating history or dancing under the summer sun at a major music fest, each event provides a glimpse of the loud, proud American spirit.

BEST FESTIVAL EXPERIENCES

Dance through the glitter-soaked streets of New Orleans as brass bands blare and Carnival season crescendos into its finale: ❶ **Mardi Gras**. (p407)

Load up the picnic basket for a summer night of memorable music at ❷ **Tanglewood**, tucked into the Berkshire Mountains. (p184)

Clink beer steins at ❸ **Oktoberfest Zinzinnati**, the nation's largest Oktoberfest celebration, honoring Ohio's German heritage with plenty of oom-pah-pah. (p530)

Learn about cultural traditions across the country during the two-week ❹ **Smithsonian Folklife Festival**, with performances and demonstrations in Washington, DC. (p251)

Spend three weekends grooving to the rhythms of Milwaukee's ❺ **Summerfest** – dubbed 'The World's Largest Music Festival,' going strong since 1968. (p555)

Independence Day

The Fourth of July commemorates the Declaration of Independence with barbecues, processions and fireworks – particularly splendid in **Washington, DC** (p234), where marching bands parade down Constitution Ave.

Pride Month

Cities and small towns fly rainbow flags at parties and parades throughout June. The biggest celebration is in **NYC** (p58), birthplace of the modern LGBTIQ+ rights movement.

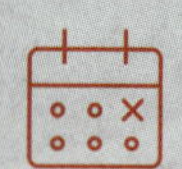

Federal Holidays

Check the calendar before making plans. On federal holidays, including US-specific holidays like Thanksgiving and Memorial Day, many businesses shut down, particularly in rural regions.

PLANT WIZARD/SHUTTERSTOCK

Henry Mercer's Fonthill Castle (p140)

BEST OFFBEAT EXPERIENCES

Hike through 500 acres of forests and fields at ❶ **Storm King Art Center**, admiring massive modern sculptures rooted in upstate New York. (p104)

Dive into the genius mind of ❷ **Henry Mercer** – the maximalist Renaissance man who constructed a concrete castle in Doylestown. (p140)

Wind through West Virginia's wooded mountains in search of museums dedicated to the mythical ❸ **Mothman and Bigfoot**. (p302)

Wait for the full moon at Kentucky's ❹ **Cumberland Falls**, when planetary alignment and mist form a moonbow – a rare after-dark rainbow. (p365)

Dig deep and dream big at ❺ **Crater of Diamonds State Park** in Arkansas, where lucky visitors can keep whatever sparkling gems they find. (p402)

OFFBEAT WONDERS

Leave the well-trod path behind to uncover the weirdest and wildest corners of these 29 states. Under-the-radar destinations may take extra effort to reach, but even a tiny detour reaps big rewards: outdoor art installations, roadside folk monuments, oddball museums, surreal landscapes – and, sometimes, a chance to escape the crowds.

National vs State Parks

Federally recognized national parks get all the glory, attracting swarms of visitors, but lesser-known state parks can rival their beauty. Give these underdog destinations a try.

Roadside Attractions

Drive through Minnesota to find some of the nation's quirkiest stop-and-gawk sights, including the world's largest ball of twine and the pork-praising **Spam Museum** (p572).

SPECTACULAR SMALL TOWNS

Skip down Eastern USA's Main Sts to experience the slow-lane locales. Small towns have long occupied a big place in the national imagination – symbols of simplicity, nostalgia and neighborly pride. Across the region, they deliver on those promises, proving cities aren't the country's only cultural sanctuaries. Tight-knit art communities, mom-and-pop restaurants and streets leading to mountain trailheads and pristine lakes: in these quiet corners, charm gets served in bite-size portions.

Vermont in Autumn

The Green Mountain State turns red, orange and yellow for leaf-peeping season. Wow at the arboreal bounty while driving between tiny villages (pictured Stowe; p206) on **Scenic Route 100** (p210).

Out in the Ozarks

Fall in love with Arkansas by road tripping from college town **Fayetteville** (pictured; p402) to museum-anchored **Bentonville** (p405) and ending at pretty-as-a-postcard **Eureka Springs** (p404).

The Catskills in Summer

When weather is warm, trace the Delaware River Scenic Byway hugging NY's **Western Catskills** (p110) to trade quaint downtown strips for a hop in the refreshing water.

FROM LEFT: STEVE HEAP/SHUTTERSTOCK, SHUTTERSV/SHUTTERSTOCK, MARGARET.WIKTOR/SHUTTERSTOCK

Brevard (p327)

BEST SMALL TOWN EXPERIENCES

Follow the Hudson River from Beacon to ❶ **Hudson**, two art-packed upstate New York towns surrounded by mountain trails and farmland. (p104)

Chase over 250 cascades in ❷ **Brevard, North Carolina**, known as the 'Land of Waterfalls,' then celebrate your finds at a local brewery. (p327)

Inspect the paintings at ❸ **Grand Marais Art Colony** to see how the Minnesota hamlet's Lake Superior setting inspired a century of creativity. (p575)

Wander from antique stores to art galleries around ❹ **Lambertville, NJ** (p129), and **New Hope, PA** (p141) – sister cities divided by the Delaware River.

Hop between Maryland, Virginia and West Virginia while visiting historic ❺ **Harpers Ferry**, its federalist facades an ode to 19th-century architecture. (p304)

REGIONS & CITIES

Find the places that tick all your boxes.

Great Lakes

OVERLOOKED BEAUTY IN THE USA'S HEARTLAND

Chicago reigns over this region, with its glittering skyline, electric arts scene and deep-dish Midwestern pride. Five mighty lakes link everything else – their coasts covered in gold dunes, moose-tracked forests, and cities like Milwaukee and Detroit in mid-Renaissance revival. Everything from quirky roadside attractions to pristine canoe paths through the wilderness await.

New York, New Jersey & Pennsylvania

SPRAWLING CITIES, HISTORIC HAMLETS AND NATURAL WONDERS

New York is packed with superlatives, ruled by cultural capital NYC – the nation's most populous city – and home to America's largest mountain-studded state park and the continent's most powerful waterfall. The rest of the region swings between seaside boardwalks, serene river towns and bucolic farms, and toward Rust Belt cities on the rise.

New England

QUAINT VILLAGES, COLONIAL HISTORY AND ATLANTIC SHORELINE

Maine's rugged coast, Cape Cod's dune-framed peninsula and Rhode Island's white-sand beaches: New England's lobster-loving seaside is a summer oasis. Mountains crawl across the inland landscape, dotted with farms supporting a locavore food scene, vibrant in Vermont, epicenter of autumn leaf-peeping. It's all anchored by scholarly, sports-crazed Boston, built by America's revolutionaries.

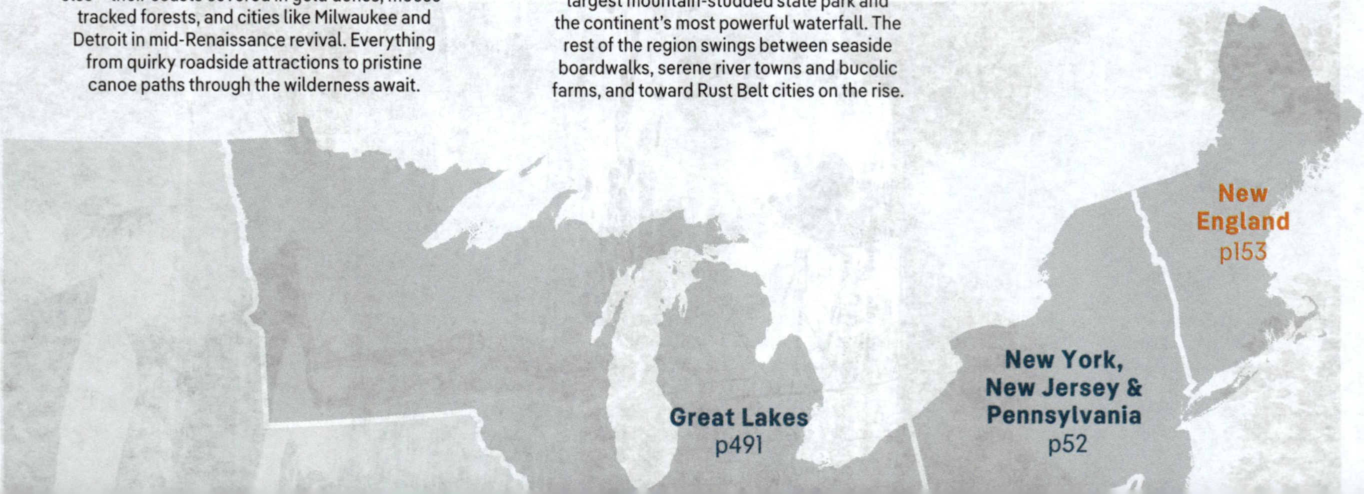

Washington, DC & the Capital Region

US CAPITAL, MUSEUMS, BEACHES AND MOUNTAINS

'DC' is America's political powerhouse, adorned with monuments, parks and museums. Maryland and Delaware sit north, where salty shores connect to wooded mountains and diversity makes life blue-crab-meat sweet. Virginia is south, home of presidents, Civil War battlefields and the mountain-climbing Blue Ridge Parkway. West Virginia spreads across Appalachia's wild wonderland.

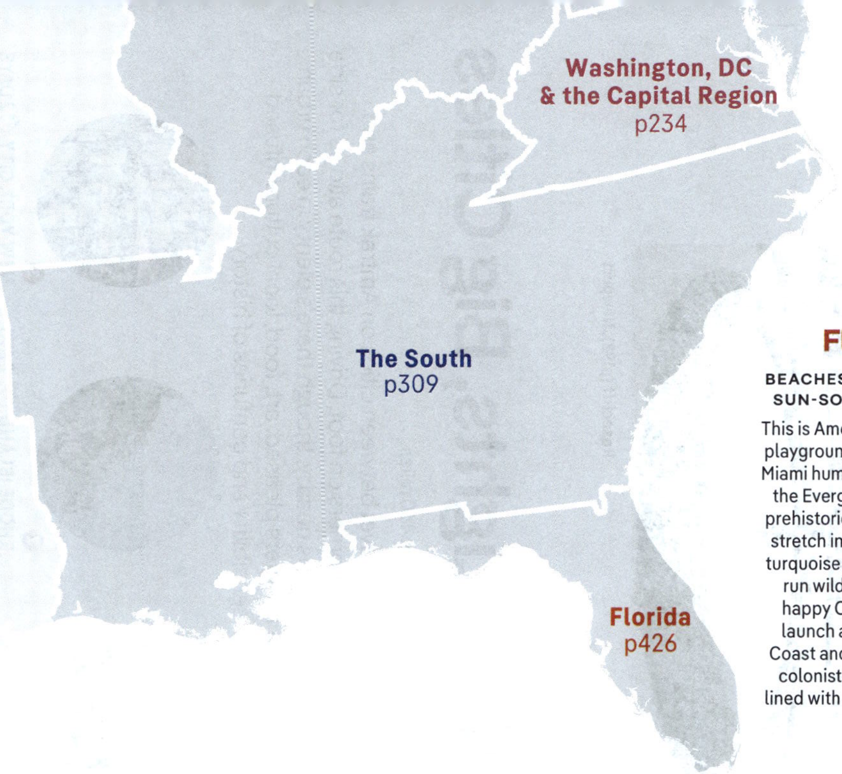

The South

BIRTHPLACE OF AMERICAN MUSIC AND CIVIL RIGHTS

The South's syncopated rhythms echo from Atlantic sand bars to colonial coastal cities, up Appalachian mountain trails and along Gulf Coast bayous. It rings out in New Orleans jazz clubs and Nashville honky-tonks; in crackling Memphis barbecues and bars pouring Kentucky bourbon. It's steeped in legend, both glorious and grim, central to America's soul.

Washington, DC & the Capital Region p234

The South p309

Florida p426

Florida

BEACHES, CULTURE AND SUN-SOAKED TROPICS

This is America's sun-soaked playground, where art-deco Miami hums with Latin flavor, the Everglades pulse with prehistoric life and the Keys stretch into a coral-dotted turquoise sea. Imaginations run wild in theme-park-happy Orlando, rockets launch along the Space Coast and tales of Spanish colonists linger in towns lined with moss-laden oaks.

FELIX LIPOV/SHUTTERSTOCK

Rosecliff (p192), Newport

ITINERARIES

Bright Lights, Big Cities

Allow: 10 days **Distance:** 460 miles

No car? No problem. Travel between cities on Amtrak trains and explore their coolest corners on foot. Driving this route allows for side trips to exceptional sites nearby, though there's plenty in each urban hub to keep train travelers pleased: art, food, local culture infused with international sensibility and centuries of history.

FROM LEFT: JOSEPH SOHM/SHUTTERSTOCK, YINGNA CAI/SHUTTERSTOCK, MOHANNAD KHATIB/SHUTTERSTOCK

1 BOSTON 2 DAYS

Steep yourself in history in the American Revolution's birthplace. Begin by following colonial footsteps on the **Freedom Trail** (p164), appreciating architecture along the way. Pace yourself: you'll need energy to admire John Singer Sargent paintings at the **Museum of Fine Arts** (p169) and catch a baseball game at **Fenway Park** (pictured; p171).

Detour: Ride the ferry to postcard-pretty LGBTIQ+ haven ***Provincetown*** *(p179), located on Cape Cod's dune-trimmed tip. 1½ hrs.*

2 RHODE ISLAND 2 DAYS

Train to the nation's smallest state for big-time adventures. Start in Providence, Rhode Island's culinary capital, to sample seafood at **Dune Brothers Seafood** (p188) before **kayaking** (p188) through downtown along the Providence River. Devote day two to uppercrust Newport. Arrive by Seastreak ferry (one hour) or car (40 minutes) to wander **Gilded Age mansions** (p192) and hike the **Cliff Walk** (pictured; p190), waves crashing on rocky beaches.

3 NEW YORK CITY 2 DAYS

Stick to Manhattan for a quick trip to NYC. Follow immigrant footsteps on **Ellis Island** (p64), glimpse New York's colonial past in the **Financial District** (p62) then order global cuisine around **Chinatown** (pictured; p63) and the **East Village** (p73). Day two is about culture: see art collections at magnificent museums, amble along **Hudson River Park** (p78), applaud a **theater performance** (p80) or treat yourself to a Michelin-star meal.

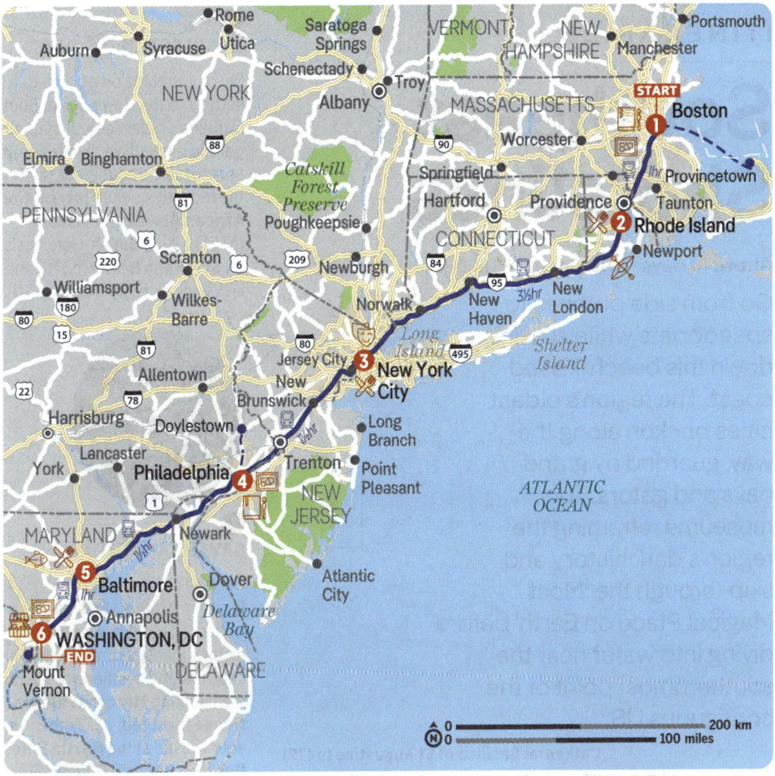

4 PHILADELPHIA ⏱ 1 DAY

Choose from colonial history, world-class art and entertainment on a Philly overnight. Walk the hallowed halls of **Independence National Historical Park** (p134), peer at the **Barnes Foundation's** (p138) impressionist paintings, applaud **Gayborhood drag performers** (p132) or eat your way through **Reading Terminal Market** (pictured; p136).

***Detour:** Zip to Doylestown to see **Henry Mercer's** concrete castle and madcap collection of preindustrial objects (p140). 🚆 1½ hrs.*

5 BALTIMORE ⏱ 1 DAY

Some call it DC's scrappy little sister, but Baltimore wasn't nicknamed Charm City for nothing. Watch playful puffins splash around one of the nation's top-ranked **aquariums** (pictured; p279), step aboard a 19th-century warship, then set sail to **Fort McHenry** (p282), where Francis Scott Key wrote verses that eventually became the national anthem. Don't leave without gobbling a meaty Maryland-style crab cake, perhaps from **Faidley Seafood** (p281).

6 WASHINGTON, DC ⏱ 2 DAYS

The nation's sophisticated capital is inundated with enough **National Mall monuments** (pictured Lincoln Memorial; p250), art exhibits and science centers to keep crowds endlessly entertained. There's also **Dupont Circle's** (p259) boutiques and restaurants, the **U Street Corridor's** (p255) Black heritage and immigrant enclaves all over. Not everything here is politics.

***Detour:** Glimpse the life of first US president George Washington at his **Mount Vernon** home (p297). 🚗 40 mins.*

FROM LEFT: REPORT/SHUTTERSTOCK, ANDREI MEDVEDEV/SHUTTERSTOCK, V_E/SHUTTERSTOCK

ITINERARIES

Southeast Shorelines

Allow: 10 days **Distance:** 795 miles

Go from side porches to speedboats while slinking down this beach-kissed coast. The region's oldest cities beckon along the way, guarded by grand oaks and gators. Tour museums reframing the region's dark history and skip through the 'Most Magical Place on Earth' before diving into water near the southernmost point of the contiguous US.

Cathedral Basilica of St Augustine (p479)

NAGEL PHOTOGRAPHY/SHUTTERSTOCK

1 CHARLESTON 2 DAYS

Savor sweet tea on a porch to settle into the slow pace of South Carolina's oldest city. Just don't get too relaxed: you'll need ample time to learn about Black history at the recently opened **International African American Museum** (p355), visit a Gullah-Geechee site on **St Helena Island** (p340) and kick back on **Folly Beach** (p341).

2 SAVANNAH 1 DAY

Georgia's oldest city drips Southern Gothic style, its moss-bedecked oak trees lending each historic mansion a mysterious air. Lean into the aesthetic by touring the haunting **Mercer-Williams House** (pictured; p377), then wet your whistle at the **Myrtle & Rose Rooftop Bar** (p377), cocktail in hand, and reserve a table at the **Grey** (p377), formerly a 1930s bus terminal.

Detour: *Kayak the tidal creeks of* ***Jekyll Island*** *(p379) between Savannah and St Augustine. 1 hr 45 mins.*

3 ST AUGUSTINE 1 DAY

The nation's oldest continuously occupied European settlement mixes old-world allure with modern American culture. Stroll St George St for a taste, noshing on a salty pretzel while eyeing an **18th-century cathedral** (pictured; p479). Next, take a **trolley tour** (p122) to see where Ponce de Léon searched in vain for the fountain of youth, then ponder how well St Augustine defies time's passage at **Castillo de San Marcos** (p481), a 17th-century relic.

FROM LEFT: ROLF_52/SHUTTERSTOCK, BRIAN LOGAN PHOTOGRAPHY/SHUTTERSTOCK

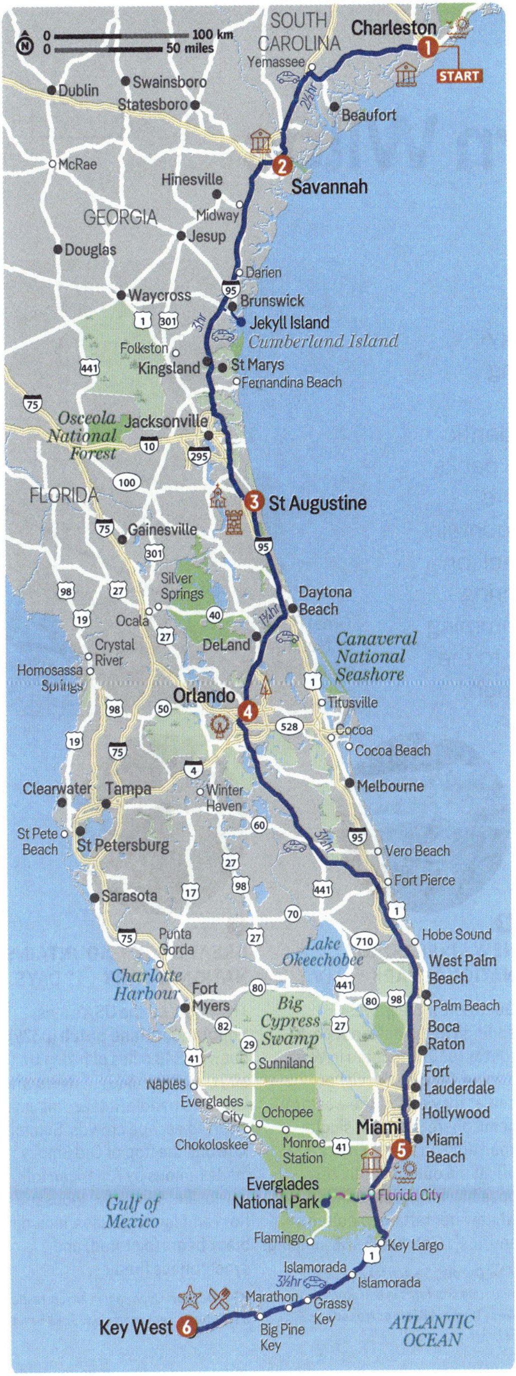
0 100 km
0 50 miles
SOUTH CAROLINA
Charleston
1
START
Yemassee
2½hr
Beaufort
Dublin
Swainsboro
Statesboro
McRae
Hinesville
2
Savannah
GEORGIA
Midway
Jesup
Douglas
Darien
Waycross
95
Brunswick
1
301
3hr
Jekyll Island
Cumberland Island
Folkston
441
Kingsland
St Marys
Fernandina Beach
75
Osceola National Forest
Jacksonville
10
295
100
FLORIDA
3
St Augustine
75
Gainesville
301
95
Silver Springs
98
27
Daytona Beach
19
Ocala
40
1¼hr
27
DeLand
Crystal River
Canaveral National Seashore
Homosassa Springs
1
Orlando
Titusville
98
50
4
528
19
Cocoa
75
Cocoa Beach
4
Clearwater
Tampa
Melbourne
Winter Haven
St Pete Beach
St Petersburg
60
95
3¼hr
Vero Beach
27
Fort Pierce
98
Sarasota
17
441
1
70
75
Punta Gorda
27
Hobe Sound
Lake Okeechobee
710
West Palm Beach
Charlotte Harbour
Fort Myers
80
441
80
98
Palm Beach
Big Cypress Swamp
82
27
Boca Raton
29
41
Sunniland
Fort Lauderdale
Naples
Everglades City
Ochopee
Hollywood
Chokoloskee
Monroe Station
41
Miami
5
Miami Beach
Everglades National Park
Florida City
Gulf of Mexico
Flamingo
Key Largo
1
Islamorada
3½hr
Islamorada
Marathon
Grassy Key
Key West
6
Big Pine Key
ATLANTIC OCEAN

4

ORLANDO 2 DAYS

Disney (p467) isn't such a 'small world' – budget a day or more to make the most of the Mouse's lair and don't leave without riding Guardians of the Galaxy: Cosmic Rewind. With more time, venture beyond the roller coasters: spot manatees wintering at **Blue Spring State Park** (p466), canoe the turquoise trails of **Wekiwa Springs** (p466) and wow at flowers blooming around **Leu Gardens** (p468).

5

MIAMI 2 DAYS

Melt into the powder sands of Miami Beach for several days or explore what makes this city electric. Admire South Beach's **art-deco architecture** (p434), go on a *Miami Vice*-style **speedboat ride** (p437), sample Cuban treats in **Little Havana** (pictured below; p440) and learn the basics of graffiti before appreciating **Wynwood Walls**' magnificent outdoor murals (p437).

***Detour:** Seek out alligators, turtles and aquatic birds sunning around **Everglades National Park** (p444). 1 hr.*

Azúcar!

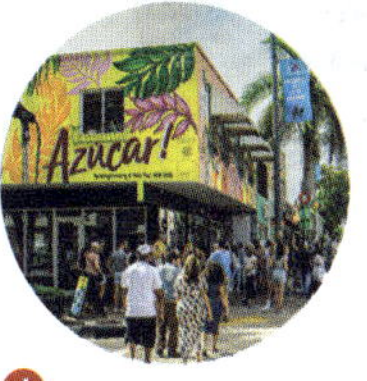

6

KEY WEST 2 DAYS

Cruise down the Overseas Highway to reach this coral cay archipelago. On Key Largo, dive to the undersea gardens at **John Pennekamp State Park** (p450), then refuel with conch fritters and a slice of key lime pie. Feed tank-size tarpons at **Robbie's Marina** (p452) en route to **Key West** (p450), and end by raising a cocktail as the tangerine sun drops into the ocean beyond Mallory Sq.

ITINERARIES

Southern Wilds

Allow: A week or more
Distance: 1040 miles

Trade skyscrapers for sky-piercing peaks by snaking through the Southern Appalachians toward Atlantic Ocean sands. This route packs in three national parks and North Carolina's cool mountain capital before kicking back on barrier islands. Go for spring wildflowers, summer swimming or autumn leaves. Flying to the region? Use DC as your hub.

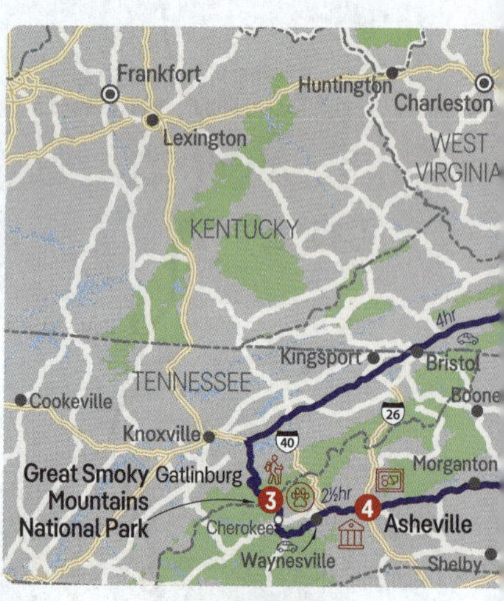

1 SHENANDOAH NATIONAL PARK ⏱1 DAY

Seek out Blue Ridge Mountains views while driving or hiking around this **park's** 197,439 acres (p292). In summer, climb through **Old Rag Mountain's** granite boulder maze, a strenuous hike affording 360-degree panoramas of tree-topped hillsides. When autumn arrives, join leaf-peepers admiring the arboreal splendor along the 105-mile **Skyline Drive**.

Detour: *Spend the night in Charlottesville, near former US president Thomas Jefferson's storied* ***Monticello estate*** *(p292). 1 hr.*

2 NEW RIVER GORGE NATIONAL PARK ⏱1 DAY

Get to know the newest addition to the **national park roster** (p300), located in West Virgina. Stop by the visitor center for views of the western hemisphere's longest single-span arch bridge, then tick off all the outdoor activities possible: hiking, climbing, skiing, whitewater rafting (pictured), and, if it's October, BASE jumping.

Detour: *Search for mythical mountain creatures in and around the* ***West Virginia Bigfoot Museum*** *(p302). 1 hr.*

3 GREAT SMOKY MOUNTAINS NATIONAL PARK ⏱2 DAYS

This might be the USA's most **popular parkland patch** (p329), but with 848 miles of hiking trails and over 2100 miles of rivers where kayakers paddle, it takes minimal effort to escape crowds. Summit **Kuwohi**, the 'top of Old Smoky' made famous by American folk music, and search for thousands of flora and fauna species, including black bears (pictured) and synchronous fireflies.

Detour: *Overnight in kitsch-tastic* ***Gatlinburg****, Tennessee (p355). 5 mins.*

FROM LEFT: VLADIMIR GRABLEV/SHUTTERSTOCK, STEVE HEAP/SHUTTERSTOCK, BEN MCMURTRAY/SHUTTERSTOCK

4

ASHEVILLE ⏱2 DAYS

Head east to Asheville, a liberal enclave in the Blue Ridge Mountains ruled by hippie-dippie mountain folk and creative entrepreneurs. Art fiends find their tribe around the **River Arts District** (p326), hikers take to trails in the surrounding hills, and there's enough award-winning restaurants and craft breweries to please all palates. Don't miss **Biltmore** (pictured; p326) – an 8000-acre estate and ode to the Vanderbilt family fortune.

5

DURHAM ⏱1 DAY

Dip into **Durham** (p323) for a night-long stopover between North Carolina's mountains and coast. Plan ahead: book reservations at the **Duke Lemur Center** (pictured; p323) to greet ring-tailed primates as they hop around an 85-acre wooded sanctuary. Spend the rest of your time ambling through downtown. Factories built during Durham's tobacco empire days have been rehabbed as restaurants, breweries and boutiques – integral to the city's revitalization.

6

CAPE HATTERAS NATIONAL SEASHORE ⏱1 DAY

Unwind on this wild stretch of North Carolina's Outer Banks, clinking along Hatteras and Ocracoke Islands for 70 miles. Start in Hatteras with tales of shipwrecks at the **Graveyard of the Atlantic Museum** (p318), then search for birds among the salt marsh at the **Hatteras Island Ocean Center** (p319). Finish by ferrying to **Ocracoke** (p319) – a former pirate haunt where ponies roam freely along the shore.

FROM LEFT: KONSTANTIN L/SHUTTERSTOCK, DANITA DELIMONT/SHUTTERSTOCK, WILDNERDPIX/SHUTTERSTOCK

ITINERARIES

America's Musical Heartland

Allow: 7 Days **Distance:** 1160 miles

Trace the nation's sonic landscape from Louisiana to Lake Michigan, visiting cities where the first downbeats of jazz, blues, rock 'n' roll and Motown rang out. After wandering backroads and bars where musical legends found their sound, sop up barbecue sauces, bourbon flights and Southern soul food: the cuisine will make you sing.

Motown Museum (p539), Detroit

SCHAGER/SHUTTERSTOCK

1 NEW ORLEANS 2 DAYS

Bourbon St? Sure – imbibe down the famous thoroughfare with impunity – but get drunk on the city's spirit elsewhere. Start in the French Quarter, where Royal St's buskers play by day and **Preservation Hall's** (pictured; p411) brass band swings by night. Join the jazz fest on **Frenchmen** (p415), shop down **Magazine** (p418) and greet the permanent residents of an **above-ground necropolis** (p412). NOLA's voodoo magic hits fast.

2 CLARKSDALE 1 DAY

Groove to singer-songwriter Muddy Waters while driving into Mississippi, his home state, and find the beat in Clarksdale – a city soundtracked by the blues. Learn about legends at the **Delta Blues Museum** (p391), then catch live sets at jiving juke joints **Ground Zero** and **Cat Head** (p392).

***Detour:** Before reaching Clarksdale, visit the **Highway 61 Blues Museum** and **BB King Museum** (p391) to applaud more Mississippi icons. 1 hr.*

3 MEMPHIS 1 DAY

Fall in love with Memphis soul, made of blues and barbecue. Start at the **Rock 'n' Soul Museum** (p347), genuflect at Elvis Presley's **Graceland** (p349), chill out to vinyl at the **Memphis Listening Lab** (p350) or let **Beale Street's** live bands (p349) carry you into the night. Before leaving, fill up on **Charlie Vergos' Rendezvous'** dry-rub ribs (p347) and the **The Four Way**'s fried green tomatoes (p347): a delicious Memphis encore.

FROM LEFT: ADAM MCCULLOUGH/SHUTTERSTOCK, ALEXEY STIOP/SHUTTERSTOCK

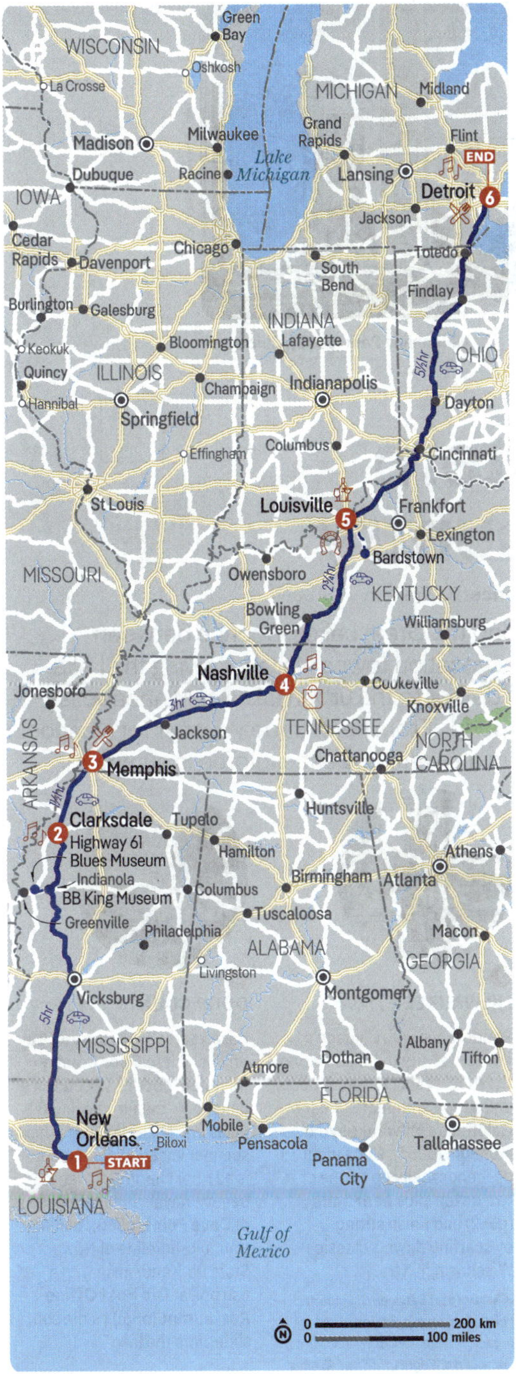

4 NASHVILLE 1 DAY

It's honky-tonk time. After picking up the requisite cowboy boots at **Boot Country** (p353), part of the Nashville uniform, catch a guitar guru at the **Grand Ole Opry** (p353) then follow **Lower Broadway's** (p353) blazing lights into a beer-swilling bastion for live country tunes. With more time, hunt for vintage souvenirs around **East Nashville** (p353) and get a local history lesson at the **Tennessee State Museum** (p352).

5 LOUISVILLE 1 DAY

Bourbon, baseball bats and horse racing: these are Louisville's biggies. Taste Kentucky's honey-colored liquor along **Whiskey Row** (p360) and see how the Louisville slugger gets made at its eponymous museum and factory. The Kentucky Derby's horses run at **Churchill Downs** (pictured; p360) in May, but you can honor the prestigious competition at the connected museum year-round.

***Detour:** Book a designated driver to tour **Bardstown's** distilleries (p361). 1 hr.*

6 DETROIT 1 DAY

Head to Detroit, birthplace of Motown, for a grand musical finale. Hum a Stevie Wonder tune while bopping through the **Motown Museum** (p539), then grab a seat at **Baker's Keyboard Lounge** (p539), the world's oldest continually operating jazz club. Nosh on artisanal treats from **Eastern Market** (p539) while spotting nearby street art, then bike the **Dequindre Cut Greenway** to **Belle Isle** (p541), soaking in the city's sounds.

LUCKY-PHOTOGRAPHER/SHUTTERSTOCK

Millennium Park (p498), Chicago

ITINERARIES

Midwestern Lake Country

Allow: 8 days or more **Distance:** 835 miles

Get ready to splash around the Great Lakes. Bounce between cultured cities and quaint vacation towns while following the Lake Michigan shoreline, then detour to the urban lakes of Minneapolis before reaching Lake Superior. From here, trade your car for a canoe: the wild Boundary Waters are waiting, best explored in summer.

1

CHICAGO 2 DAYS

Spend a day getting acquainted with the city. Hop on a **Chicago Architecture Center** (p499) boat tour, meander to **Millennium Park** (p498) to view the skyline's reflection in the *Bean*, zoom to **Willis Tower's** (p501) 103rd floor to see everything from above, then dig into **deep-dish pizza** (pictured; p496) for dinner. Day two: praise impressionist paintings at the **Art Institute** (p497), catch an **improv show** (p503) and order a **Michelin-rated meal** (p502).

2

MILWAUKEE 1 DAY

Rendezvous with Chicago's cool sister city to traipse along the **RiverWalk** (pictured; p555) and scope architect Santiago Calatrava's **Milwaukee Art Museum** (p555). Once night descends, belly up to one of two dozen-plus **beer halls** (p552) and finish strong by scarfing down a classic Wisconsin fish fry.

***Detour:** Between Chicago and Milwaukee, stop in **Racine** to see the organic architecture of Wisconsin-born Frank Lloyd Wright (p556). 45 mins.*

3

DOOR COUNTY 1 DAY

Base yourself in **Sturgeon Bay** on this visit to **Door County** (pictured; p560) – Wisconsin's limestone 'thumb' sticking 80 miles into Lake Michigan. This summer vacation destination is all rural charm with natural beauty. Kayak around the cliffs of **Cave Point** (p560), trek the tranquil shoreline of Newport State Park and finish with a fish boil at **Old Post Office Restaurant** (p561) as the sun slides into the lake.

FROM LEFT: SUPITCHAMCSDAM/GETTY IMAGES, BIG JOE/SHUTTERSTOCK, KENNETH KEIFER/SHUTTERSTOCK

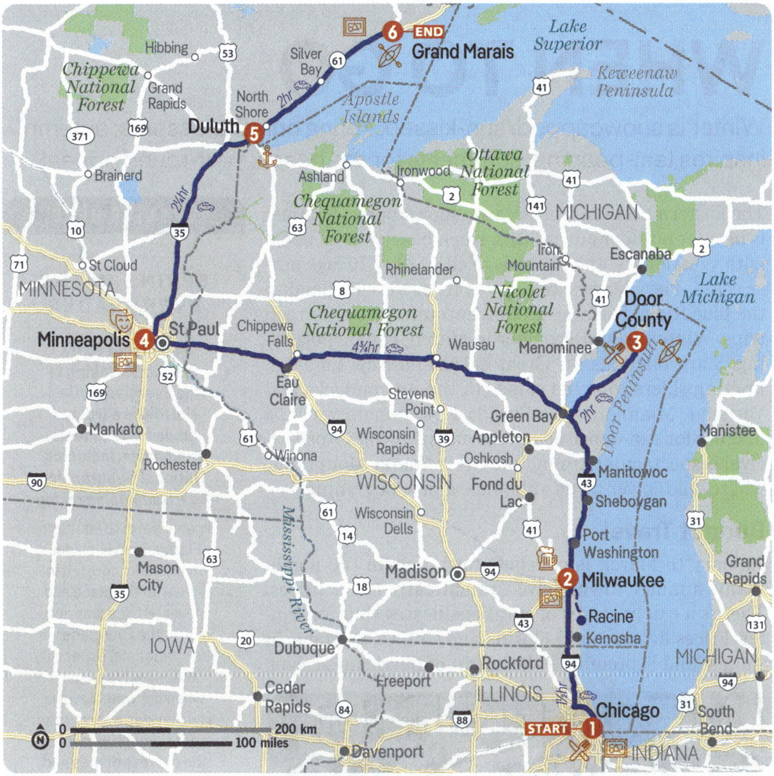

4

MINNEAPOLIS 1 DAY

Break from the Great Lakes to see the 'City of Lakes,' lapped by some 22 pools. Stretch your legs along winding waterfront paths on **Lake of the Isles** (p569), then gorge on the cultural offerings: the **Walker Art Center** (pictured; p565) and its neighboring sculpture garden, plates of modern Indigenous fare at **Owamni** (p566), theater performances at the **Guthrie** (p569) and local breweries, numbering over 30.

5

DULUTH 1 DAY

See what the fuss is about in 'climate-proof **Duluth**' (p572) – a nickname bestowed upon the town in 2019, attracting migrants moving from flooding coastlines. Duluth has its own 'ocean' – Lake Superior, the world's largest freshwater lake by surface area. Stroll the Duluth Lakewalk, spot massive freighters at the **Aerial Lift Bridge** (pictured; p572) and dip your toes in the chilly waters along a slender 7-mile-long sandbar.

6

GRAND MARAIS 2 DAYS

Stay in artistically inclined **Grand Marais** (p574), gateway to Minnesota's magnificent lake-scape. After getting a load of the galleries in town, check out nature's handiwork by driving along the **Gunflint Trail** (pictured; p575) or renting a canoe and paddling into the **Boundary Waters** (p575). This ancient superhighway, once an important navigational route for Indigenous travelers, is now the second largest wilderness east of the Rockies, covering one million acres.

FROM LEFT: CHECUBUS/SHUTTERSTOCK, JL JAHN/SHUTTERSTOCK, TAMMI MILD/GETTY IMAGES

WHEN TO GO

Winter is snowcapped/sun-kissed, spring brings blossoms, autumn inspires leaf-peeping, summer is for the beach: year-round appeal.

The Eastern USA is a multi-season showstopper. Summer is best for outdoor adventures, when beach towns boom with vacationers, and festivals in cities like Chicago never cease. Fiery leaves ignite trees from New England to the Blue Ridge Parkway around autumn, scenic for road trips. Winter, from December to March, can be polarizing. Snow blankets the Great Lakes and New England, inviting skiers to shred slopes in the Adirondacks and Vermont. Miami and the Florida Keys remain warm, a magnet for sun-deprived northerners. Spring's April arrival is spectacular around the Great Smoky Mountains, where wildflower fields announce a new beginning.

Budget Travel

January to March is cheapest for hotels in the north; many summer towns have dramatically lower prices. There's a catch: scores of rural businesses shut for winter. Prices drop around Florida and Gulf Coast states in August and September – the height of hurricane season.

Mermaid Parade (p97)

I LIVE HERE

SPRING IN THE EVERGLADES

Founder of Garl's Coastal Kayaking in the Everglades, Garl Harrold is a trusted guide for top media companies, including National Geographic. *@garlscoastalkayaking*

I came down to southern Florida from Michigan many years ago, fell in love with the place and never left. It's amazing to visit the Everglades in the springtime, especially in April or May. That's when the water level is at its lowest, and you can spot so much wildlife in the cypress domes and freshwater ponds.

NORTHEAST LEAF-PEEPING

Fall's arboreal color fest starts around September and lasts through early November. *Yankee* Magazine *(newengland.com)* publishes foliage maps; I LOVE NY *(iloveny.com)* issues weekly reports, compiling observations from on-location 'leaf spotters.'

Weather through the Year

   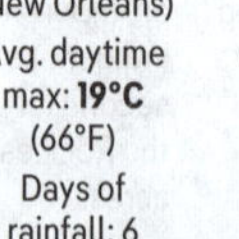    

JANUARY (Miami)	FEBRUARY (New Orleans)	MARCH (Wash, DC)	APRIL (Nashville)	MAY (Boston)	JUNE (NYC)
Avg. daytime max: **25°C** (77°F)	Avg. daytime max: **19°C** (66°F)	Avg. daytime max: **13°C** (56°F)	Avg. daytime max: **22°C** (72°F)	Avg.daytime max: **19°C** (66°F)	Avg. daytime max: **26°C** (79°F)
Days of rainfall: 7	Days of rainfall: 6	Days of rainfall: 11	Days of rainfall: 12	Days of rainfall: 13	Days of rainfall: 11

FLORIDA'S GULF VS OCEAN

Florida's Gulf Coast has warmer water temperatures in summer and cooler temperatures in winter than the Atlantic. Swimming off Marco Island in February means entering chilly water hovering around 69°F (21°C), while Miami's balmy coast averages a more tolerable 76°F (24°C).

Historic Events & Parades

St Patrick's Day A local plumbers' union dyes the Chicago River shamrock green – using a nontoxic, plant-based powder – just in time for a parade celebrating all things Irish in the Windy City. **March**

Kentucky Derby Festival (p360) Five Kentucky 'princesses' preside over this two-week, party-packed, marathon-running, firework-exploding lead-up to America's longest continuously held sporting event where bold hats abound. **April–May**

Halloween (p97) Autumn witch tours in Massachusetts and the **Great Jack O'Lantern Blaze** in Sleepy Hollow (p111): preludes to All Hallows' Eve, when New Yorkers get sartorially spooky for the **Village Halloween Parade**. **October**

Thanksgiving (p97) The US president pardons a turkey in DC days before Philadelphia kicks off this traditional food fest with the nation's oldest Thanksgiving Day parade, one of many across the region. **November**

Wacky & Wonderful Festivals

Tulip Time (p546) Visit Holland, Michigan, to see millions of tulips during a nine-day flower fest, with traditional clog dancing and a parade showered in petals. **May**

Mermaid Parade (p97) Glitter-soaked merfolk meander down Coney Island's Surf Ave in a party that skews more Mardi Gras than Walt Disney to celebrate summer's solstice. **June**

Chincoteague Pony Penning (p295) 'Saltwater Cowboys' herd a horde of semi-feral swimming ponies into Virginia's Assateague Channel, then auction the foals on Chincoteague Island. Also called the 'Pony Swim.' **July**

Bean Fest (p401) After eating bowls of beans prepared in pots by local chefs, a parade of outlandishly-outfitted outhouses compete for the 'fastest privy' prize in the Ozarks. **October**

I LIVE HERE

A MAN FOR ALL SEASONS

Garrett Miller cofounded Finger Lakes Cider House – a New York cidery, restaurant and farm. *@flxciderhouse*

The Northeast has striking seasonality. I love settling into summer's groove by swimming in Cayuga Lake. Temperatures cool for fall. After harvesting pumpkins and apples, I look forward to winter's dark months. We call spring 'green up' – grass is growing, calves and lambs are born, the orchard blooms.

S'NOWHERE TO BE FOUND

NYC snow feels like a forecast from the past; though the average accumulation hovers around 29in annually, New Yorkers experienced a 702-day dry spell between 2022 and 2024. Looking for white wonder? Try New Hampshire's Mt Washington: it sees 280in yearly.

JULY (Cape May) Avg. daytime max: **29°C** (85°F) Days of rainfall: 10

AUGUST (Chicago) Avg. daytime max: **28°C** (83°F) Days of rainfall: 4

SEPTEMBER (Charleston) Avg. daytime max: **30°C** (86°F) Days of rainfall: 10

OCTOBER (Burlington) Avg. daytime max: **14°C** (58°F) Days of rainfall: 12

NOVEMBER (Philadelphia) Avg. daytime max: **13°C** (56°F) Days of rainfall: 8

DECEMBER (Minneapolis) Avg. daytime max: **-3°C** (27°F) Days of rainfall: 8

FROM LEFT: MARGARET.WIKTOR/SHUTTERSTOCK, PLAN B ENTERTAINMENT/MOVIESTORE COLLECTION LTD/ALAMY

Blue Ridge Parkway (p292)

GET PREPARED FOR EASTERN USA

Useful things to load in your bag, your ears and your brain.

Clothes

Casual threads Many rural establishments/ small cities cater to jeans-and-T-shirt crowds.

Smart, upscale attire NYC style leans toward looser silhouettes; DC toward buttoned-up sophistication; Miami clubs require style.

Layers Bring options, no matter the season. Northern winters require hats, jackets and gloves. Spring and fall are temperamental. Summer days might start sweaty but finish brisk. Even in the balmy south, frigid air conditioning can make a light sweater worthwhile.

Sneakers Forget heels for urban outings. Your feet will thank you after slogging around uneven sidewalks and museums.

Hiking shoes Serious mountain trails require waterproof boots ready to tackle all terrain.

Manners

Talking to strangers Keep to yourself on city streets, especially in Chicago and NYC. Expect a 'hello' in small towns.

Southern charm Locals in states like South Carolina and Georgia are the paragon of politeness. Don't be alarmed when a stranger strikes up a conversation.

Sidewalks In cities, pedestrian traffic sticks to the right. Don't dawdle.

READ

The Devil in the White City (Erik Larson; 2003) An architect and a serial killer pull focus at Chicago's 1893 World's Fair.

North Woods (Daniel Mason; 2023) One plot of land in western Massachusetts bears witness to centuries of haunting stories.

Vanishing New York (Jeremiah Moss; 2017) Nonfiction dive into socioeconomic forces and gentrification in NYC's historic neighborhoods.

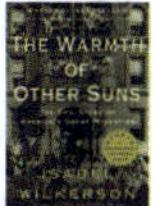

The Warmth of Other Suns (Isabel Wilkerson; 2010) Detailed account of millions of Black Americans moving north during the Great Migration.

Words

Bless your heart A southern expression with multiple meanings – an expression of sympathy/judgement for foolish behavior. Context is key.

DMV For locals around DC, it's the 'DC-Maryland-Virginia' area – not the Department of Motor Vehicles.

The L Short for 'elevated,' referring to Chicago's train system – even when it's underground.

MTA Abbreviation for the Metropolitan Transit Authority – the company responsible for NYC's subways and buses.

POTUS Acronym meaning President of the United States – likely seen or heard while exploring DC's political arena.

Snowbird A person who lives in Florida part-time during winter to escape the cold weather up north.

Soda The East Coast name for a sugary fizzy drink. Midwesterners often call it 'pop.' Southerners may call it 'coke,' regardless of brand.

Wicked New England slang for 'extremely,' eg 'that's wicked cool.'

Yankee Used by the Confederate South to demonize Union soldiers during the Civil War. Today, it's a regional epithet occasionally heard in the South, referencing New Englanders and East Coasters from places like New York and Pennsylvania. Also NYC's baseball team.

Y'all The South's plural 'you' (you all), used to address a group of people. In western Pennsylvania, 'y'all' becomes 'yinz' (or 'yunz').

WATCH

A Streetcar Named Desire (Elia Kazan; 1951) Tennessee Williams' tale of a fragile Southern belle crumbling in New Orleans.

The Departed (Martin Scorsese; 2006) Undercover cop and a mole play cat and mouse amid Boston's Irish mob.

Lincoln (Steven Spielberg; 2012) Biopic of Abe Lincoln and his attempts to abolish slavery in 1863.

Moonlight (Barry Jenkins; 2016; pictured) The struggles of a gay Black man in a rough Miami neighborhood.

Paris is Burning (Jennie Livingston; 1991) Dazzling, intimate NYC documentary of 1980s drag-ball culture.

LISTEN

1619 (Nikole Hannah-Jones; 2019) A six-episode podcast chronicling the enduring dark shadow of slavery in the US.

Born to Run (Bruce Springsteen; 1975) New Jersey's 'Boss' sings about the 'runaway American dream' with blue-collar angst.

Hamilton (Lin-Manuel Miranda; 2015) The USA's forefathers rap for democracy through the hip-hop-ified lens of musical theater.

Jolene (Dolly Parton; 1974) The Tennessee-born queen of country gives voice to female vulnerability and strength in a male-dominated art form.

JACEK CHABRASZEWSKI/SHUTTERSTOCK

Gumbo (p419)

THE FOOD SCENE

International plates attract epicurean eaters; seafood and farm fare appease devout locavores; mom-and-pop or Michelin-starred, there's something for all.

Hopping between states can be a foodie's thrill ride. Scarf down street eats that taste like a million bucks, then dine on 10-course meals created by award-winning chefs.

Differences in regional menus highlight locally grown ingredients – be it New England's crustaceans plucked from the Atlantic or Florida's oranges picked from sunny groves. Go for bud-to-bottle, bay-to-tray and farm-to-table experiences – the tastiest way to explore each landscape.

Dig into the nation's kitchen cabinets and you'll find that the most popular food here arrived with immigrants. No place encapsulates this melting-pot culture quite like New York City, which serves a global array of tastes at more than 25,000 restaurants across five boroughs. It's possible to find nearly all the Eastern USA flavors here, too – the city covers all the cuisines you can imagine.

Still, each region crafts a specialty best enjoyed on home turf – and when it comes to comparing favorites, everyone's a critic. Be it Manhattan boiled bagels or Carolina barbecues, locals debate preferences like they're at a congressional showdown in DC.

New England: Freshly Caught & Farm-grown

New England's coastline is seafood central. Chilly North Atlantic waters offer up clams, mussels, cod and monster-sized lobsters. Maine is America's lobster capital,

BEC
An on-the-go NYC bodega breakfast: bacon, egg and cheese.

BISCUIT
The South's scone: fluffy, buttery and possibly served with gravy, ham or jam.

CRABCAKE
Maryland's delicacy: crabmeat bound with bread crumbs, mayonnaise, mustard and seasonings.

producing 90% of the nation's supply. Slap on a bib to enjoy the crustacean's classic preparation: boiled or steamed, cracked open and then dipped in butter. Summers from Rhode Island to Maine are synonymous with clambakes – listen to Rodgers and Hammerstein's 1945 musical *Carousel* for proof. 'This was a real nice clambake,' sings a cast stuffed with shellfish that's been steamed over seaweed in a seaside fire pit with sweet corn, chicken and sausage. It's sometimes served alongside more regional staples, be it clam chowder (a creamy, milk-white soup) or blueberry pie.

Inland Vermont produces the most maple syrup in the US and is also known for its exceptional cheese. The state even has a cheese trail *(vtcheese.com)*, linking visitors to over 40 dairy farms that churn out butter and ice cream.

FROM LEFT: THE IMAGE PARTY/SHUTTERSTOCK, WANGKUN JIA/SHUTTERSTOCK

Mid-Atlantic: Brine, Berries, Diners & Delis

From New York to Virginia, the Mid-Atlantic goes coo-coo for crustaceans and mollusks. In Maryland, it's all about blue crabs, harvested in Chesapeake Bay. Oysters are equally popular, with connoisseurs slurping these aphrodisiac appetizers like fine wine.

Fried chicken

Farms here are famous for their fruit – and in summer, fruit-picking programs invite visitors to pluck their berries of choice. Autumn brings apples, baked into pies and pressed into ciders and sauces.

Maine Lobster Festival (p225)

FOODIE FESTIVALS

National Cherry Festival (p546; late June–early July) The terroir in Michigan's Traverse City produces exceptional cherries, central to this nine-day celebration that sees a carnival, parade, concerts and plenty of cherry pie.

Picklesburgh (p146; July) Pittsburgh's three-day, dill-icious pickled palooza, featuring the infamous pickle-drinking contest.

Maine Lobster Festival (p225; late July–early August) Feast on the state's beloved crustaceans for five days in the seaside town of Rockland.

Kentucky Bourbon Festival (p361; September) Bardstown – the 'Bourbon Capital of the World' – imbibes for three days straight.

Maryland Crab Cake Festival (p279; October) Savor all the crabmeat cakes you can, then see which one is crowned the state's best.

Bowen's Wharf Seafood Festival (p192; October) Coastal Newport goes bonkers for brine during this two-day eat-a-thon with chowder, lobster rolls and oysters galore.

FISH FRY
Wisconsin's tradition: deep-fried freshwater fish served with fries, coleslaw and tartar sauce.

GUMBO
Louisiana's savory stew: meat or shellfish, veggies and herbs.

HOT CHICKEN
Nashville's fried chicken: coated in a cayenne pepper sauce.

SCRAPPLE
Dutch Pennsylvania loaf: pig-scrap mush, bound with cornmeal and flour.

SHRIMP & GRITS
From South Carolina's Lowcountry: shrimp mixed with creamy stone-ground grits.

Asheville beer (p326)

FROM LEFT: ALEX BAHR/SHUTTERSTOCK, NEVADA.CLAIRE/SHUTTERSTOCK

CRAFTY CONCOCTIONS

Fermentation aficionados in the US whet their palates with locally made beverages. Chicago and Asheville compete for the title of 'city with the most craft breweries per capita'; Vermont has more per capita than any other state; and New York and Pennsylvania have the second- and third-most hop houses in the nation – more than 500 apiece.

Virginia is the 'birthplace of American wine,' and New York's wine scene is underrated no more, thanks to the grape-gleaming Finger Lakes and Long Island. Pennsylvania claims birthrights to American whiskey: roughly 70 distillers fill barrels with brown libations, while Kentucky is the bourbon king, producing 95% of the world's supply.

No alcohol options also abound. In the South, you can enjoy 'sweet tea' – black iced tea with sugar. NYC celebrates third-wave coffee culture at cafes where baristas treat pour-overs like chemistry experiments, and in New England, there's apple cider – refreshingly cool in autumn and heated in winter as a warming treat.

They're particularly popular in New York, the nation's second largest apple producer.

New Jersey is the spiritual home of the all-American diner: a 'greasy spoon' with all-day breakfasts, sandwiches, pies and other affordable fare. The region is also dotted with delis selling cold cuts, sliced cheeses and cured meats piled onto sandwiches.

The South: Down-home Cooking

Slow-cooked, deep-fried and simmering with soul: the South serves the nation's best comfort food. Barbecue is ubiquitous, and pig is usually central to the meal – be it a pulled-pork sandwich in Memphis, TN, or a chopped whole hog dipped in vin-egar sauce around eastern North Carolina. At barbecue joints, side dishes can steal the show: mac 'n' cheese, cornbread, fried okra, collard greens, potato salad or candied yams. Some of this filling fare represents 'soul food' – a cuisine initially crafted by enslaved Africans in the Southeastern USA who made do with what was available, and now a celebration of Black traditions in America.

The region's most distinctive cuisine originates in Louisiana. There's bayou-born Cajun (deemed 'country food') – a flavorful fusion of Indigenous ingredients and French roots, spiced with African, Caribbean and Spanish influences. In New Orleans, there's Creole (Cajun's aristocratic cousin) – slightly less spicy than Cajun, often incorporating tomatoes and shrimp. Both styles utilize the holy trinity of diced onion, celery and green bell pepper – found in dishes like gumbo and jambalaya.

Florida favors fish (grouper, snapper, mahi mahi) – and hits a home run with fruit. The state is one of the nation's top producers of oranges, grapefruits, limes, mangoes and more.

Great Lakes: Big Plates & City Accolades

'Cornfed' is a term often associated with well-nourished Midwesterners – particularly in Illinois and Minnesota, states that are part of the grain-producing Corn Belt. But corn isn't the only reason these folks stay sated. The Great Lakes region leans toward ample portions of unfussy foods, captured in Minnesota's classic 'hotdish' – a casserole with some type of starch, meat and veggies, often topped with crispy tater tots. Wisconsin is 'America's Dairyland,' one of the nation's leading milk producers, best known for cheese curds – squeaky pieces of fresh, popcorn-sized cheese. Lakeside diets lean into freshwater fish, be it walleye or perch.

Chicago stands apart from the pack, where hole-in-the-wall eateries sit alongside fine-dining restaurants adorned with Michelin stars. Hulu's TV dramedy *The Bear* – released in 2022 – captures the city's diverse food scene, with cameos from beloved local restaurants.

Specialties

Pizza

Introduced to the US by Italian immigrants in the late 19th century, this affordable treat – often made with dough, sauce and mozzarella – takes many forms in cities across the US.

NYC, NY A hand-tossed pie cut into triangular slices; has a thin, foldable crust but also ranges from square-cut Sicilian pillows to sourdough crusts and soupy Neapolitan discs.

Chicago, IL The deep-dish has a thick, buttery crust topped with layers of chunky tomato sauce and cheese; the cousin of a casserole or quiche.

Detroit, MI Rectangular pies with airy crusts and crispy cheese that's caramelized at the corners.

New Haven, CT Home of the 'apizza' – thin-crusted, coal-fired, Neapolitan-style pizza with charred edges and a chewy texture.

Scranton, PA Rectangular 'trays' – not circular pies – served in what's unofficially proclaimed the 'pizza capital of the world' – a hotly contested title.

Sandwich, Katz's delicatessen (p69)

Regional Sandwiches

Philadelphia Cheesesteak
Grilled steak, onions and gooey cheese on a roll.

New Orleans Po'Boy Roast beef or fried seafood piled with toppings such as lettuce and tomatoes, served between two remoulade-slathered pieces of French bread.

Florida Cuban Ham, roast pork, cheese, mustard and pickles on a buttered, grilled baguette – served in Florida by way of Cuba.

NYC Pastrami A Jewish deli staple: thinly sliced, smoked and cured beef stacked between rye bread and coated in yellow mustard.

MEALS OF A LIFETIME

Kasama (p502; Chicago, IL) Queue up for Filipino breakfast sandwiches and sweets by day; splurge on the 13-course fine-dining tasting menu by night.

Thai Diner (p67; NYC, NY) Slide into a booth for this Bangkok-meets-Big Apple mash-up – an edible example of NYC's melting pot.

Legal Seafoods – Harborside (p173; Boston, MA) Three floors with three different menus showcasing seafood's possibilities, plus harbor island views from the roof deck.

Grey (p377; Savannah, GA) Mashama Bailey, winner of the James Beard Foundation Award for Outstanding Chef, elevates traditional Black recipes in a formerly segregated Greyhound bus station.

Dooky Chase (p414; New Orleans, LA) Fried chicken and Creole-style gumbo so good it fueled the Civil Rights movement.

THE YEAR IN FOOD

SPRING

March is sugaring-off season in Vermont, when freshly harvested maple syrup flows. Down South is a crawfish commotion: Louisiana harvests around 110 million pounds of the critters between March and May.

SUMMER

The scent of burgers announces barbecue season up north. Expect ocean-side lobster rolls, sea bass and clams. July is best for blueberries and cherries in the Mid-Atlantic and New England; August delivers peaches and corn.

AUTUMN

Harvest season arrives in the north. Apples hang heavy, waiting to be picked. Patches of pumpkins get carved up for pies. Hunting season brings venison and turkey to tables. Florida oranges ripen from October to June.

WINTER

The holidays invite decadence: crack open a red Long Island wine to pair with country ham, a Christmas-dinner staple in Appalachia. Oysters are at their tastiest down South. Strawberries are prime for plucking in the Everglades.

FROM LEFT: JULIA BOGDANOVA/SHUTTERSTOCK, KYLE COONEY/SHUTTERSTOCK, JORGE SALCEDO/SHUTTERSTOCK, KIT LEONG/SHUTTERSTOCK

FROM LEFT: BARRY WINIKER/GETTY IMAGES, JAMES KIRKIKIS/SHUTTERSTOCK

Shining Sea Bikeway (p178), Falmouth

THE OUTDOORS

Salty shores sparkle along the coast, while rolling mountains rise inland. There's winter skiing, summer swimming and urban parks to explore year-round. Get ready to wear out those hiking boots.

Counting every serpentine inlet and cove, over 40,000 miles of Atlantic-lapped coastline stretch from Louisiana to Maine. The Appalachian Mountains cross over a dozen states, with creeks and rivers sculpting their wild subranges from the Smokies to the Catskills. Five Great Lakes link Minnesota to New York – a vast land-locked sea between the US and Canada. More than 100,000 smaller lakes dot the countryside, with over 35,000 in Florida alone. Forget amusement parks – the Eastern USA is already a vast adventure zone.

Hike & Stroll

Trails cater to all levels of outdoor expertise. Wheelchair users roll above South Florida swamps on **boardwalks** (p447), and urban wanderers explore manicured green spaces like NYC's **Central Park** (p92). Hardcore hikers can trek through 14 states on the Appalachian Trail (AT) – the world's longest hiking-only footpath, stretching 2194 miles from Georgia's Springer Mountain to Maine's Mt Katahdin. No need to conquer the whole route: there are plenty of AT day hikes, particularly scenic around the **Great Smoky Mountains** (p329) and New Hampshire's White Mountains, especially around the **Kancamagus Highway** (p220). More top-tier eastern USA trails summit **Mt Mansfield** (p208) in Vermont's Green Mountains and New York's **Adirondacks** (p109).

Hiking in the northern states is best between May and October. Winter's ice and snow require crampons or snowshoes on high-elevation trails, while spring's melt-off makes conditions muddy, though waterfalls gush with gusto. Most routes are

Outdoor Thrills

SKIING
Rip down the East Coast's largest vertical drop on **Whiteface Mountain** (p112), the snowy slopes of the Adirondacks where Olympians have raced.

SCUBA DIVING
Flip your fins to see coral reefs and a shipwreck waiting underwater at Florida's **Biscayne National Park** (p444).

SANDBOARDING
Soar from a North Carolina sand dune at **Jockey's Ridge State Park** (p320), near the spot where the Wright Brothers took flight.

FAMILY ADVENTURES

Count rainbows while sailing aboard the **Maid of the Mist** (p119), a sopping-wet thrill ride at New York's Niagara Falls. Search the seas off Cape Cod for breaching whales and shark fins with **Dolphin Fleet Whale Watch** (p180); kids four and under ride free.

Turn on your headlamp to tour the subterranean karst wonderland of **Mammoth Cave National Park** (p363) in Kentucky.

Take a break from building sandcastles to savor ice cream and amusement rides at **Morey's Piers** (p123), along New Jersey's Wildwood boardwalk.

Look for alligators and turtles on a guided boat ride through the Swamp Creatures Area at Georgia's **Okefenokee National Wildlife Refuge** (p375).

Get soaked at **Shipwreck Island Waterpark** (p476), then dry off while racing go-karts at Florida's **Adventure Landing Jacksonville Beach** (p476).

well maintained and easy to follow. Download the **AllTrails app** *(alltrails.com)* as a handy navigational tool.

Swim, Surf & Paddle

Florida's seascape is synonymous with aquatic adventure – and its southern tip is blessed with warm water for year-round swimming. The state's coast also holds the largest coral reef system in the continental US – most magical around **John Pennekamp Coral Reef State Park** (p450), a diver's delight. For the rest of the region, nautical recreation picks up between May and September, when bracing ocean waters become ideal for dunking. If you want to try surfing, this is the time to do it – best at beaches with consistent swells, such as **Ditch Plains Beach** (p99) in Montauk, NY.

Freshwater lakes and rivers reach top temperatures in July and August – the perfect time for splashing around the **beaches** (p508) of Chicago's Lake Michigan, jumping in the swimming holes and waterfalls of New York State's **Finger Lakes** (p113) or tubing down Philadelphia's stretch of the **Delaware River** (p109). Then there's Minnesota, nicknamed the 'Land of 10,000 Lakes' (though there are actually 11,842), where paddle pros can take to some 1500 miles of canoe routes through the untamed **Boundary Waters** (p575).

ACTION AREAS

See p44 for more activities

US National Whitewater Center (p322)

Cycle

Urban cycling has ever-expanding bike-share programs in NYC, Chicago, and Washington, DC, make it easy to find wheels – and an acceleration in e-bike usage means riders can go faster and farther. Smaller cities, like South Carolina's Greenville, are catching on, too, with the 22-mile **Swamp Rabbit Trail** (p343) – an old railroad corridor reimagined as a cycling greenway.

Long-distance cyclists can zip between beaches on the 26-mile **Cape Cod Rail Trail** *(mass.gov/locations/cape-cod-rail-trail)*, pedal between 45 Atlanta neighborhoods on the soon-to-be-22-mile **BeltLine** (p373), or roll between DC and Pittsburgh on the **C&O Canal Towpath** (p284).

BIRDING
Aim binoculars skyward above New Jersey's **Cape May** (p122) as 400 avian species flap along the Atlantic Flyway during migration season.

WHITE-WATER RAFTING
Thrash down frothy, white-capped, Class II–IV rapids that rage through the **US National Whitewater Center** (p322) in Charlotte, NC.

KAYAKING
Cruise Vermont's Lake Champlain on a kayak with Burlington's **Community Sailing Center** (p205) and camp at one of the 600-plus lakeside spots.

HOUSEBOATING
Rent an easy-to-operate houseboat with **Ebel's Voyageur Houseboats** (p576) and adventure amid the pristine islands of Voyageurs National Park.

ACTION AREAS

Where to find Eastern USA's best outdoor activities.

Walking/Hiking

1. Kaaterskill Falls (p108)
2. Kuwohi (p331)
3. Mammoth Cave National Park (p363)
4. Mt Katahdin (p230)
5. Old Rag Mountain (p292)
6. Smugglers Notch (p207)

Animals/Wildlife

1. Assateague Island National Seashore (p279)
2. Cajun Country Swamp Tours (p423)
3. Everglades National Park (p444)
4. Indiana Dunes National Park (p521)
5. Isle Royale National Park (p549)
6. Okefenokee National Wildlife Refuge (p375)
7. Smithsonian's National Zoo (p257)

Cycling
1 D & R Canal (p129)
2 Lakefront Trail (p507)
3 Shark Valley (p444)
4 Slaughter Pen (p405)
5 Swamp Rabbit Trail (p343)
Swimming/Beaches
1 Asbury Park (p124)
2 Cape Hatteras National Seashore (p318)
3 Ditch Plains Beach (p99)
4 John Pennekamp Coral Reef State Park (p450)
5 Sleeping Bear Dunes National Lakeshore (p545)
6 South Beach (p432)
Kayaking/Boating
1 Apostle Islands National Lakeshore (p562)
2 Biscayne National Park (p448)
3 Boundary Waters (p575)
4 Congaree National Park (p344)
5 Lake George (p111)
6 New River Gorge National Park (p300)
KANSAS
MISSOURI
KENTUCKY
VIRGINIA
NORTH CAROLINA
SOUTH CAROLINA
TENNESSEE
ARKANSAS
OKLAHOMA
TEXAS
LOUISIANA
MISSISSIPPI
ALABAMA
GEORGIA
FLORIDA
BAHAMAS
ATLANTIC OCEAN
Gulf of Mexico
St Louis
Frankfort
Lexington
Roanoke
Durham
Greenville
Raleigh
Owensboro
Bowling Green
Williamsburg
Greensboro
Springfield
Joplin
Vinita
Tulsa
Springdale
Nashville
Cookeville
Knoxville
Asheville
Charlotte
Fayetteville
Wilmington
Jackson
Chattanooga
Greenville
Florence
Myrtle Beach
Oklahoma City
Clarksville
Russellville
Little Rock
Memphis
Huntsville
Columbia
Athens
Augusta
Atlanta
Charleston
Tupelo
Birmingham
Macon
Pine Bluff
Greenville
Tuscaloosa
Savannah
Fort Worth
Dallas
Shreveport
Monroe
Vicksburg
Jackson
Livingston
Montgomery
Tifton
Brunswick
Albany
Dothan
Jacksonville
St Augustine
Natchez
Waco
Alexandria
Baton Rouge
Mobile
Tallahassee
Gainesville
Daytona Beach
Opelousas
Biloxi
Pensacola
Panama City
Austin
Lafayette
Houston
New Orleans
Orlando
Melbourne
Tampa
Clearwater
St Petersburg
Sarasota
Palm Beach
Fort Myers
Fort Lauderdale
Miami
Key West
Corpus Christi
Lake Tawakoni
Toledo Bend Reservoir
Lake Livingston
Lake Ouachita
Sardis Lake
Lake Pontchartrain
Crystal Bay
Mosquito Lagoon
Lake Okeechobee
Charlotte Harbour
Florida Bay
Ohio
Black
White
Mississippi
Red
Sabine
Pearl
Alabama
Tennessee
Cumberland
Holston
Appalachian Mountains
Chattahoochee
Savannah
Altamaha
Saint Johns
Cape Fear
500 km
250 miles

Elk, Great Smoky Mountains (p329)

TRIP PLANNER

NATIONAL PARKS

Over a dozen national parks dot the Eastern USA, stretching from coral reefs off Florida's coast to a moose-stalked island in Michigan. Each park offers a unique snapshot of America's untamed corners, where visitors can camp, hike, swim, drive or raft around the landscape. Pick your passion and run wild.

If You Like...

FANTASTIC FLORA & FAUNA

Travel from misty hilltops to coastal swamps to experience the breadth of Eastern USA biodiversity. Over 19,000 plant and animal species reside within the **Great Smoky Mountains** (p329) – more than any other US national park. Visit in spring when wildflowers paint green hillsides with pastel blooms. Bring binoculars to Florida's **Everglades** (p444), where alligators and manatees swim among mangrove waterways and aquatic birds soar above the scene. At **Congaree** (p344) in South Carolina, synchronous fireflies light up forests around May, and the floodplain teems with turtles and river otters year-round.

GEOLOGICAL WONDERS

Cloud-piercing mountains and underground cathedrals: the East Coast showcases millions of years' worth of nature's handiwork. Maine's **Acadia** (p228) pairs hikes up granite cliffs with Atlantic Ocean vistas, most magical on Cadillac Mountain – the tallest peak on the eastern seaboard. **Shenandoah's** (p292) 105-mile Skyline Drive traces the Blue Ridge Mountains, where boulder-strewn hikes lead to panoramas of Virginia's rolling hills. Beneath Kentucky's forest floor, **Mammoth Cave** (p363) stretches over 400 miles – the world's longest cave system, featuring the stunning stalactites of Frozen Niagara.

PARKS APPS & PODCASTS

National Park Service *(nps.gov)* The NPS app features maps, self-guided tours, accessibility information and updates on park conditions.

AllTrails *(alltrails.com)* Lists of trails with user reviews, current conditions and real-time tracking while hiking. It's worth paying for AllTrails+: download maps offline and get wrong-turn alerts.

Recreation.gov Reserve campsites, permits and day-use passes for national parks and other federal areas.

GuideAlong *(guidealong.com)* Self-guided audio tours – ideal for road-tripping through the Smokies and Shenandoah.

National Park After Dark *(npadpodcast.com)* Two friends investigate the dark underbelly of America's natural treasures, with fascinating histories, tragic events and firsthand anecdotes.

ADVENTURES ON THE WATER

Minnesota's **Voyageurs** (p576) is nearly 40% water, with 40 named lakes home to 54 fish species. At West Virginia's **New River Gorge** (p300), rafting season begins around April, but daredevils don't arrive until September, ready to take on Class V rapids along the Gauley River. **Biscayne** (p444), near Miami, trades roads for reefs – 95% of the park is underwater, tempting snorkelers to take a plunge.

SMALL CROWDS & SOLITUDE

Remote national parks are unreachable by roads. Michigan's **Isle Royale** (p549), accessible by boat or seaplane, receives fewer annual visitors than the Smokies see in a day. Expert campers can overnight to explore the island's boreal forests, home to moose and wolves, overlooking Lake Superior. Florida's Dry Tortugas lies 70 miles off Key West's coast, where day-trippers snorkel among coral, and overnight campers get beaches to themselves.

Mammoth Cave National Park (p363)

KNOW BEFORE YOU GO

Fees & Reservations

- Entrance fees vary from free to $35 per vehicle. If you want to visit multiple parks and other federal recreational lands within 12 months, consider purchasing the America the Beautiful pass *($80; store.usgs.gov/pass)*, which provides access for four adults and all children under 16 at over 2000 federal recreation areas across the US. Some campgrounds, such as Dry Tortugas, require reservations. Start planning nine to 12 months in advance – spots fill fast. Others are first come, first served, including sites on Isle Royale.

What to Pack

- Pack lightweight, moisture-wicking layers and sturdy footwear. Weather can change quickly, so bring extra clothing reflecting any potential extremes. Wear plenty of sunscreen and bring glasses and a hat. Pack plenty of water and fueling snacks (fruits, nuts). Long-distance hikers, backpackers and campers should have a first-aid kit, fire-starting materials, a portable charger and an emergency shelter (a tent, tarp or space blanket). Flashlights and headlamps illuminate dark nights.

Safety Tips

- Consult a park ranger before tackling long trails. Always leave details of your route and expected return time with a responsible party. It's not wise to wander off alone. Day hikers: allow ample time to complete a trail before nightfall.

BILANOL/SHUTTERSTOCK

Blue Ridge Parkway (p292)

TRIP PLANNER

EPIC ROAD TRIPS

Fall in love with America's many landscapes from the driver's seat. Scenic byways and linear parks stitch the region together with cement, creating a grand collage of tiny towns, historic sites, neon-lit cities and serene state forests. Whether you've got two days or 10, there's a route here worth roaming.

Choose Your Trip

DRAMATIC SCENERY

The **Blue Ridge Parkway** (p292) ditches highway billboards for natural beauty while snaking from Virginia's Shenandoah National Park to North Carolina's Smokies. The speed limit never tops 45 mph, giving drivers time to contemplate the roadside vistas while cruising to towns like crafty Asheville, NC. Blast bluegrass tunes, stretch your legs on mountain trails and fuel up at folksy log diners for a taste of Southern hospitality.

COLORFUL AMERICANA

The **Great River Road** *(experiencemississippiriver.com)* traces the Mississippi through 10 states along federal, state and county routes. Start in Minnesota's pinewood forests, end beneath Louisiana's moss-mired oaks and discover America's beating heart in between: there's *Fargo*-famed Brainerd, MN; Mormon pilgrimage magnet Nauvoo, IL; then BBQ-smoked **Memphis** (p347), TN; and jazzed-up **New Orleans** (p407), LA.

SOUTHERN HISTORY

The **Natchez Trace Parkway** (p396) drifts from Nashville's honky-tonks to Natchez's Victorian mansions along a quiet two-lane road that follows an Indigenous route through Tennessee, Alabama and Mississippi. The roadway is a visual textbook of Southern heritage, passing an ancient ceremonial mound, Civil War battlefields, the alligator-laden Cypress Swamp and Tupelo – the birthplace of rock-and-roll king, Elvis Presley.

ROAD TRIP CHECKLIST

Join an Automobile Association Some international automobile associations have reciprocal agreements with their US counterparts: check if you can bring a member card from home. Associations such as the AAA provide 24-hour emergency roadside assistance and discounts on lodging and attractions.

Pack Repair Tools Make sure your vehicle has a spare tire and tool kit (including a jack, jumper cables, ice scraper and tire pressure gauge) and emergency equipment (including flashers).

Bring Maps Don't rely solely on GPS – it might not work in remote areas. A good map comes in handy when cell service fails.

Carry Your Driver's License and Proof of Insurance Never get behind the wheel without them.

THE OVERSEAS HIGHWAY

Curving beneath Southern Florida are the Florida Keys: a 106-mile-long archipelago of mangrove and sandbar islands, teal waters and magnificent sunsets. A memorable journey down the **Overseas Highway** (p453) takes you from the bustle of Key Largo to Key West, passing arts-loving villages, old-fashioned roadside eateries and stretches of verdant hardwood forest, crossing some 42 bridges along the way (including one that stretches 7 miles across open waters).

LAKESIDE SUMMERS

Highway 61 (p573) connects Louisiana and Canada, part of the Great River Road, but the prettiest section rolls through Minnesota, also called the North Shore All-American Scenic Drive. Play Bob Dylan's 1965 album *Highway 61 Revisited* while soaking up the sights. There's Duluth (Dylan's birthplace), the world's most inland port city, where grassy sand dunes stretch into Lake Superior. A rocky coastline follows, passing eight state parks before reaching the Canada border. Chase waterfalls, spot lighthouses, dine on freshwater fish and enjoy the sun on public beaches.

MIA2YO/SHUTTERSTOCK

Overseas Highway (p453)

PLAN YOUR TIME

Blue Ridge Parkway

Start: Front Royal, VA. **End:** Cherokee, NC. **Distance:** 469 miles. **Duration:** 2–5 days.

- Visit between April and October, when most park facilities open. October is prime for peeping fall foliage; May brings bursts of wildflowers.

Great River Road

Start: Itasca State Park, MN.
End: New Orleans, LA.
Distance: 2000 miles.
Duration: 6–10 days.

- Take the trip between May and October, avoiding the wintry conditions of the northern states. Spring and autumn are best, as summer down South can be brutally hot.

Natchez Trace Parkway

Start: Nashville, TN. **End:** Natchez, MS. **Distance:** 444 miles. **Duration:** 2–3 days.

- Spring and autumn are lovely. Avoid summer's swelter and know that winter can be chilly.

Overseas Highway

Start: Key Largo, FL. **End:** Key West, FL. **Distance:** 106 miles. **Duration:** 1–3 days.

- There's no bad time to make this trip, though be aware of sky high prices from December through February, and pay close attention to weather forecasts if traveling during hurricane season (June to November).

Highway 61

Start: Duluth, MN.
End: Grand Portage, MN.
Distance: 154 miles. **Duration:** 2–3 days.

- This drive is best in balmy summer weather. A dip in Lake Superior is refreshing after a long drive or strenuous hike.

EASTERN USA

THE GUIDE

New England p153

New York, New Jersey & Pennsylvania p52

Great Lakes p491

WASHINGTON, DC & the Capital Region p234

The South p309

Florida p426

Chapters in this section are organised by hubs and their surrounding areas. We see the hub as your base in the destination, where you'll find unique experiences, local insights, insider tips and expert recommendations. It's also your gateway to the surrounding area, where you'll see what and how much you can do from there.

Liberty Bell (p135)

SEAN PAVONE/SHUTTERSTOCK

Written and curated by John Garry

New York, New Jersey & Pennsylvania

CITIES, HISTORIC HAMLETS & NATURAL WONDERS

These three neighboring states mix big-city riches with small-town simplicity. They're like an everything bagel – that iconic NYC treat – sprinkled with something for all tastes.

New York City – America's cultural capital – is the East Coast's focal point, with an origin story that echoes across state lines. Initially the Indigenous Lenape's stomping ground, the island they called 'Manahatta' saw its first shady real-estate transaction when the Dutch purchased the area in 1626, dubbing it New Amsterdam. The British barged in next, renamed it New York and vacated after losing the Revolutionary War. There was good reason to fight for the land. With its superior port and eventual waterway link to the Great Lakes, New York became the United States' financial and industrial powerhouse. Immigrants followed, lured by promises of prosperity, and the population boomed. It's no wonder NYC is called 'the city that never sleeps': density transformed it into a creative pressure cooker. There's something new to do on every corner.

Things might be sleepier outside NYC, but they're no less exciting. In New York State, mountains and rivers provide the backdrop for creative towns where a locavore food scene flourishes. In Pennsylvania, wild woodlands link Pittsburgh, the former 'Steel City' experiencing a rebirth, to Philadelphia, the heartbeat of colonial American history. New Jersey's farmsteads run from Pennsylvania's border to the Atlantic Ocean – a summertime fun zone lined with beaches and boardwalks.

The possibilities here are as diverse as the seasons: ever-changing and always ready with a colorful palette of adventures.

WOODSNORTHPHOTO/SHUTTERSTOCK

THE MAIN AREAS

NEW YORK CITY
The USA's electric cultural empire.
p58

NEW YORK STATE
Rivers and mountains link artsy enclaves.
p98

NEW JERSEY
Atlantic coastline and Ivy League pedigree.
p120

PENNSYLVANIA
Forests connect cities amid a renaissance.
p130

For places to stay in New York, New Jersey & Pennsylvania, see p150

MASSIMO SALESI/SHUTTERSTOCK

Left: Clayton House (p148) Pittsburgh; Above: the High Line (p77), New York City

Find Your Way

NYC and Philadelphia, linked together by trains, are best explored by foot and public transport. Nearly everywhere else requires a car. There's no better way to reach the region's serene mountain towns, state parks and sandy beaches.

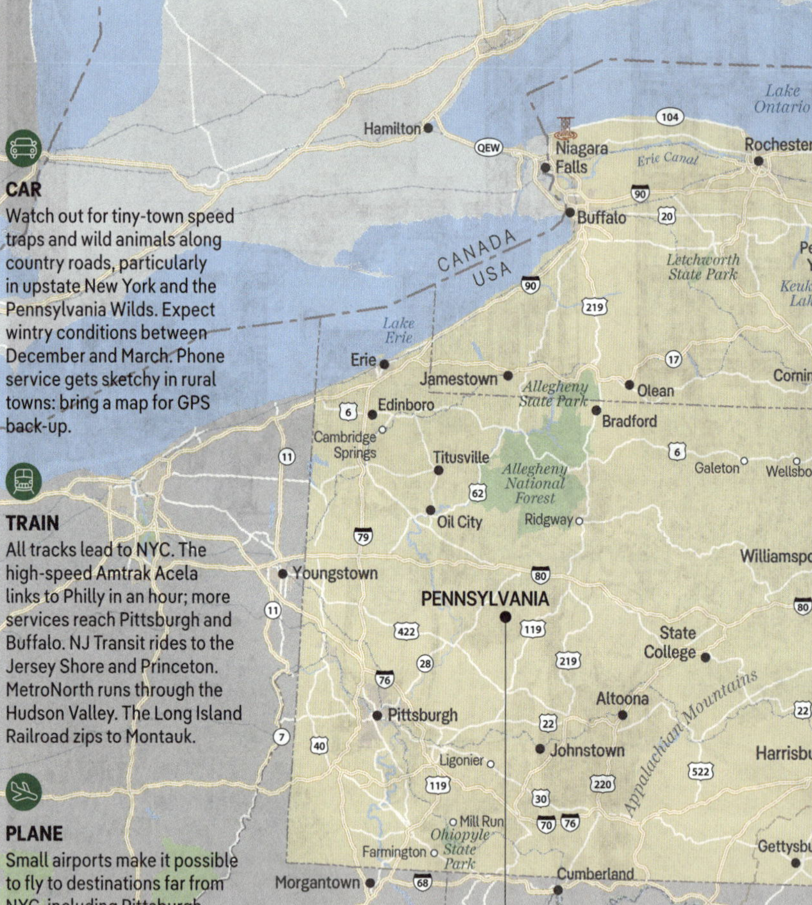

CAR

Watch out for tiny-town speed traps and wild animals along country roads, particularly in upstate New York and the Pennsylvania Wilds. Expect wintry conditions between December and March. Phone service gets sketchy in rural towns: bring a map for GPS back-up.

TRAIN

All tracks lead to NYC. The high-speed Amtrak Acela links to Philly in an hour; more services reach Pittsburgh and Buffalo. NJ Transit rides to the Jersey Shore and Princeton. MetroNorth runs through the Hudson Valley. The Long Island Railroad zips to Montauk.

PLANE

Small airports make it possible to fly to destinations far from NYC, including Pittsburgh, Buffalo and NY state capital Albany near the Adirondacks. Flying cuts down dramatically on driving time, especially on trips to Buffalo and Pittsburgh, over six hours away.

Pennsylvania, p130

Forested parks fill gaps between edgy Philadelphia's historic sites, revitalized Pittsburgh's big-time museums, bucolic Lancaster's Amish country and the untamed Pocono Mountains.

New York State, p98
Well-heeled Manhattanites summer in the Hamptons. Outdoor adventures await in upstate mountains. Gorges delight around the vineyard-laced Finger Lakes and Niagara Falls.
New York City, p58
Lady Liberty stands guard over the nation's largest city, delivering on the promise of its name by always having something 'new' to explore.
New Jersey, p120
Highways studded with greasy-spoon diners lead to beachfront boardwalks. Migrating birds fly above Cape May. Revolutionary War sites await in Central Jersey.
NEW YORK
NEW JERSEY
VERMONT
MASSACHUSETTS
CONNECTICUT
RHODE ISLAND
DELAWARE
ATLANTIC OCEAN
New York City
Albany
Syracuse
Utica
Rome
Binghamton
Ithaca
Watertown
Plattsburgh
Burlington
Saratoga Springs
Poughkeepsie
Newburgh
Hartford
Providence
New Haven
New London
Philadelphia
Trenton
Princeton
Atlantic City
Ocean City
Wildwood
Cape May
Baltimore
Annapolis
Dover
Scranton
Wilkes-Barre
Allentown
Bethlehem
Easton
Reading
Lancaster
York
Hershey
Stroudsburg
Adirondack Park
Catskill Forest Preserve
Long Island
Long Island Sound
Mohawk Valley
Hudson R
Lake Champlain
St Lawrence River
Delaware Water Gap National Recreation Area
Pocono Mtns
Pinelands National Reserve
Wharton State Forest
Brendan T Byrne State Forest
Barnegat Peninsula
Delaware Bay
Whiteface Mountain (4867ft)
Montauk
Southampton
Westhampton Beach
0 200 km
0 100 miles

Plan Your Time

The region's size can overwhelm. Each state is a mini universe; every city is a distinct planet. Stick to a geographic region based on your interests or explore it all on a whirlwind road trip.

MOHANNAD KHATIB/SHUTTERSTOCK

Ellis Island (p64)

A Long NYC Weekend

- Spend your first day exploring Lower Manhattan. Follow immigrant footsteps on **Ellis Island** (p64), order global cuisine around **Chinatown** (p63), shop through the **SoHo** (p67), then dine and drink around the Lower East Side's **cocktail bars** (p72).

- Go uptown on day two. Start with a history crash course at the **Museum of the City of New York** (p87), skip through the **Met** (p88) to admire world-class art, then ramble across **Central Park** (p92) for pizza from **Mama's TOO!** (p90). Once satiated, hop on a **Citi Bike** (p63), roll down the Hudson River to Midtown and end the night with innovative theater at **Playwrights Horizons** (p82).

- Travel to Brooklyn for day three. Ogle NYC's skyline from **Brooklyn Bridge Park** (p91), then hop around **Williamsburg breweries** (p95) and dance 'til dawn at **Elsewhere** (p95).

Seasonal Highlights

Summer is action packed and autumn makes for fantastic road trips. Many rural regions and coastal treasures hibernate throughout winter, aside from upstate New York's ski-happy mountain towns. NYC perpetually buzzes.

JANUARY

Skiers hit slopes around Lake Placid and Hunter Mountain, while chilly weather in cities like NYC and Philly inspires indoor trips to museums. Budget travelers can find hotel deals throughout winter.

JUNE

Rainbow-splashed **Pride marches** in Philly and NYC bookend this festival-packed month. Nautical costumes flood Coney Island for the **Mermaid Parade** and Livingston Manor gets fishy mid-month for the **Trout Parade**.

JULY

Crowds bombard Jersey Shore boardwalks in Asbury Park and Wildwood. Surfers catch waves around Montauk. Hikers trace the gorge trails around Ithaca, jumping into cascade-splashed swimming holes as a post-trek reward.

Five Days from Philly to the Coast

● Choose from colonial history and contemporary culture during a short Philadelphia stint. Walk the halls of **Independence National Historical Park** (p134), peer at the **Barnes Foundation's** (p138) impressionist paintings and applaud the Gayborhood's **drag performers** (p132). With more time, eat around **Reading Terminal Market** (p136) and admire the mosaics at **Philadelphia's Magic Gardens** (p139).

● Drive to sister towns **New Hope** (p141) and **Lambertville** (p129) for a quiet afternoon of antiquing along the Delaware River.

● The Jersey Shore comes next. Explore Asbury Park first: traipse down the mile-long **boardwalk** (p124), dip your toes in the Atlantic and hear rock bands jam at the **Stone Pony** (p125).

● Finish at Cape May: tour **Victorian architecture** (p122) and peep at **birds along the beachscape** (p122).

A Week Driving Around New York State

● Zip north of NYC for outdoor adventures between spring and autumn. Hike around **Storm King's** outdoor sculptures (p104) and stroll Beacon's quaint **Main Street** (p105). Reserve a day for nearby Hudson: shop along **Warren Street** (p105), stop by art-packed **Olana** (p107) then see **Kaaterskill Falls** (p108), New York's tallest two-tiered cascade.

● The Adirondacks beckon next, with high-octane trekking to the peak of **Buck Mountain** (p111), a historic steamboat cruise along **Lake George** (p111) and Olympics history around **Lake Placid** (p112).

● Zoom to the Finger Lakes for a day or two, best spent **wine tasting** (p114) and at watering holes around the region's **gorges** (p114).

● Detour to the wondrous waterfalls of **Letchworth State Park** (p115) en route to **Niagara Falls** (p118) – the exclamation point on a week packed with captivating cascades.

AUGUST

Summer's dog days invite vacationers around the Poconos and Catskills to hop in tubes and float down the Delaware River. Swimmers, kayakers and cruisers all bob around Lake George.

SEPTEMBER

Harvest season unfolds with foodie festivals throughout the region, including weekend markets at Bethel Woods. Twitchers flock to Cape May as migratory birds soar above its beaches. Sunflowers color Kane's fields gold.

OCTOBER

Leaf-peepers fawn over fiery forests in the Catskills and Adirondacks – but nothing burns brighter than the **Great Jack O'Lantern Blaze** in Hudson Valley spooktown Sleepy Hollow. Thousands gather in NYC for the **Village Halloween Parade**.

DECEMBER

NYC gets into the holiday spirit with Christmas markets, outdoor skating rinks and twinkling decorations. The jolly jamboree culminates in **Times Square's ball drop**, ringing in the new year.

New York City

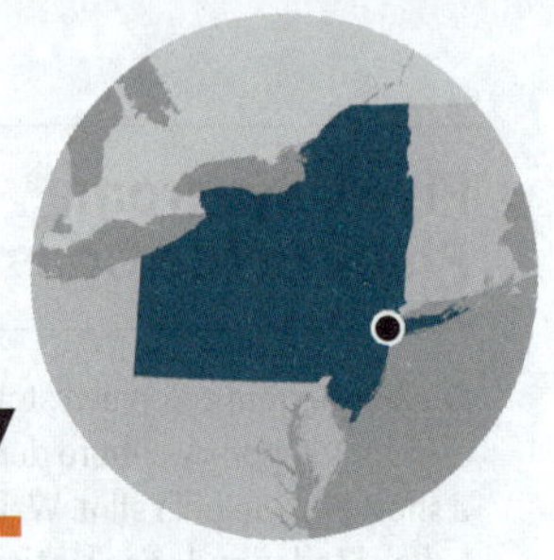

ARTISTIC EXCELLENCE | ENDLESS ENERGY | MELTING-POT MAGIC

GETTING AROUND

NYC is a pedestrian town, and strolling is a fantastic way to see the sites – as long as you follow the unspoken sidewalk rules: keep right, walk no more than two people across, and if you need to pause, step aside. Prefer speed? Cycle the city's 1500 miles of interconnected bike lanes using Citi Bike, NYC's bikeshare program. For longer distances, hop on the subway (run by the MTA; *mta.info*), zipping 1.4 million passengers daily between 462 stations spread across 665 miles of track. It's cheap, efficient and operates 24/7. Tap a smartphone or contactless bank card to go. Buses, also run by the MTA, are best for people with limited mobility.

Skyscraper canyons. Honking cabs. Rattling trains. Massive museums. Michelin-starred restaurants. The bright lights of Broadway. The list doesn't stop; New York doesn't either. It's the most populous metropolis in the United States, with 8.4 million residents. You'll find more subway stations here than in any other city worldwide, and you might hear 800 languages: NYC is the most linguistically diverse destination on Earth. This modern-day Babel boasts biblically tall towers, including One World Trade Center, the Western Hemisphere's highest building. There are 170-plus museums, 2300 green spaces and more than 20,000 restaurants spread across five boroughs. Many visitors start by exploring Manhattan, where the city's most captivating histories reveal themselves. From Indigenous Lenape land to Dutch settlement to global melting pot, NYC has remained resilient through wars, epidemics, economic crises and riots. Take a bite of the Big Apple and you'll barely scratch the surface. Spend a lifetime here and you'll still find yourself surprised.

Sail Away to Governors Island

MAP P60

Escape lower Manhattan's incessant buzz

Car-free, glamp-ready and laced with paths for strolling and cycling, **Governors Island** *(govisland.com)* might be a five-minute ferry ride from Manhattan's southern tip, but it's energetically worlds away. Choose your own adventure on this 172-acre pleasure pad, shaped like an ice-cream cone and sprinkled with activities for all palates.

To see the sites quickly, cycle the island's 7 miles of trails for panoramas of Lower Manhattan's skyline. Rent wheels from **Blazing Saddles** *(blazingsaddles.com/new-york; from $21)*, or use one of three Citi Bike stations around the island.

Art enthusiasts can spend an afternoon admiring mammoth outdoor sculptures, such as the indigenous fruit trees populating the living *Open Orchard* earthwork. Kids can get

Brooklyn Bridge

a thrill zooming down the city's longest slide, a 57ft screamer on aptly named **Slide Hill**. When hunger calls, head to **Liggett Tce's food trucks** or a waterfront restaurant with New York Harbor views. To decompress, book a session at a Roman-style spa at **QC NY** *(qcny.com; from $98)*, where guests unwind in saunas and steam rooms, and soak up city views from a heated outdoor infinity pool.

Governors Island has seen tremendous transformations since Indigenous tribes fished here in the 1500s. It's now 100 acres larger, having been bulked up in 1912 with debris from the Lexington Ave subway excavation, and decorated with architectural remnants from two centuries as a military stronghold. **Fort Jay** and **Castle Williams**, completed in the early 19th century, are the most impressive – both served as prisons for Confederate soldiers during the Civil War.

Ferries depart from Lower Manhattan's **Battery Maritime Building** daily. Adult tickets cost $5; on weekends, all passengers ride free until 11am.

Stroll the Brooklyn Bridge

MAP P60

Architectural icon with breeze-buffeted views

When this marvel of modern engineering opened in 1883, it was the world's first steel suspension **bridge** *(nyc.gov)* and the first land link between Manhattan and Brooklyn, spanning 1596ft across the East River.

Longer NYC bridges have since snatched the spotlight, but this 1-mile-plus journey still inspires awe. Its elevated pedestrian path is like an open-air cathedral, with granite stones forming neo-Gothic arches that point toward the heavens, while at sunset, the latticework of steel-wire cables seems like stained glass. Reach the bridge's apex for picture-perfect frames of Manhattan's skyscrapers and Brooklyn's waterfront.

TOP TIP

Improvising last-minute plans is possible – but it will limit your options. Book tickets to Broadway shows weeks or months in advance; reserve tables at trendy or high-end restaurants several weeks prior; schedule timed tickets to museums a week or so before arrival.

VIEWS FROM NEW YORK HARBOR

Captain Jonathan Boulware, president and CEO of South Street Seaport Museum. *@seaportmuseum*

New York is a maritime town. It was a port before it was a city, and its identity as a global destination is rooted in its port-ness. Until the middle of the 20th century, the first sight of New York that greeted new arrivals was from the harbor, looking at the lower end of Manhattan. It's possible to see that historic vista from two **South Street Seaport Museum** vessels: the 1885 *Pioneer* schooner, and the last surviving New York–built wooden tugboat, *WO Decker*. Trips last a couple of hours, starting at Pier 16 *($10-50)*.

HIGHLIGHTS
1 Brooklyn Bridge

SIGHTS
2 African Burial Ground National Monument
3 Battery
4 Lovelace Tavern foundation
5 National Museum of the American Indian
6 National September 11 Memorial
7 National September 11 Memorial Museum
8 Oculus Center
9 One World Trade Center
10 Slave Market Historical Marker
11 South Street Seaport Museum
12 Trinity Church

EATING
13 Fraunces Tavern
14 Manhatta
15 Tin Building
16 Tiny's & the Bar Upstairs

DRINKING & NIGHTLIFE
17 Dead Rabbit
18 Overstory
19 Split Eights

SHOPPING
20 CityStore
21 McNally Jackson
22 Philip Williams Posters

TRANSPORT
23 Battery Maritime Building

For a soul-stirring jaunt to Brooklyn, start at the bridge entrance at Manhattan's City Hall Park. The Brooklyn side has two exits: the first leads to Dumbo, with easy access to Brooklyn Bridge Park (p91); the second ends where leafy Brooklyn Heights meets Downtown Brooklyn. Expect large crowds from late morning to early evening, particularly in good weather.

Constructing the Brooklyn Bridge was no walk in the park. An estimated 27 people died during the 14-year process, including designer John Roebling, who contracted tetanus after his foot was crushed at Fulton Landing in the early stages of work. His son, Washington Roebling, took the baton, only to become bedridden with the bends (decompression sickness) after toiling away in underwater caissons used to excavate the riverbed for the bridge's towers. His wife, Emily, supervised most of the construction and became the first person to cross the bridge in a carriage, holding a rooster as a sign of victory.

See NYC from One World Observatory MAP P60

Soar to great downtown heights

The World Trade Center site's 16-acre campus is a symbol of NYC's resilience. There's the **National September 11 Memorial** and a connected **museum** *(911memorial.org; adult/youth $24/36)*, a somber tribute honoring victims of the deadliest terror attack on US soil, alongside amazing modern architecture, including Santiago Calatrava's gleaming cream **Oculus**. The greatest testament to the city's recovery from 9/11 is **One World Trade Center** (aka Freedom Tower), which soars 1776ft above the plaza like a phoenix, claiming the title of tallest building in the Western Hemisphere.

The shimmering 104-floor spectacle is impressive from below, but wait until you reach the observation decks *(oneworld observatory.com/tickets; from $54)* on levels 100 to 102. Floor-to-ceiling windows showcase a 360-degree panorama of all five boroughs and three adjoining states. If you need help identifying landmarks, interactive mobile tablets programmed in multiple languages are available, included in a combo ticket for a well-spent extra $10.

Purchase tickets online to avoid long queues and consider arriving early to beat the crowds (sunsets on clear days are particularly busy). The experience is more 'theme-park glam' than 'NYC grit,' but if you can stomach snaking security lines and wide-eyed visitors, it's worth the trip.

See SoHo's Artsy Side MAP P66

Free galleries and sidewalk surprises

Today's fashionistas lust over flagship stores around SoHo (South of Houston, pronounced 'How-stown'), but in the 1960s, many New Yorkers considered the area a wasteland – unless they were among the artists living and working in its industrial loft spaces. By the 1980s, these creative crowds turned the neighborhood into NYC's arty epicenter. Look beyond the storefronts for a couple of hours to spot SoHo's stylish origins

UNIQUE NEW YORK SOUVENIRS

Fishs Eddy: Come to this Union Sq store for bold NYC-themed kitchenware, be it a 'Don't touch my nuts' squirrel dish or Lady Liberty mug. *(fishseddy.com)*

Only NY: This LES fashion shop's line of city-themed merch drips with local swagger. *(onlyny.com)*

CityStore: Find authentic-looking taxi medallions and FDNY tees inside the Manhattan Municipal Building. *(nyc.gov/site/dcas/about/citystore)*

Philip Williams Posters: Time flies while scanning museum-worthy stacks piled with 100,000 printed pieces in Tribeca, including vintage New Yorker covers. *(postermuseum.com)*

Quimby's Bookstore: In Williamsburg, leaf through boxes stuffed with locally made zines covering everything from Barbie's queer subtext to Aleister Crowley's unforgettable quotes. *(quimbys.com)*

EATNG IN LOWER MANHATTAN: BEST MEALS MAPS P60, P66

Tin Building: Celebrated restaurateur Jean-Georges Vongerichten attracts crowds to this marketplace with 53,000 sq ft of food counters. *8am-10pm* $$

Manhatta: Splurge on the tasting menu or sip a cocktail bar-side – what's most important are the 60th-floor views. *hours vary* $$$

Frenchette: This contemporary French bistro is more Left Bank Paris than West Side Manhattan. *noon-10pm Mon-Fri, from 11am Sat, 11am-9:30pm Sun* $$$

Tiny's & the Bar Upstairs: American classics get doused with modern pizzazz at this pretty-in-pink 1810 townhouse. *hours vary* $$$

UNCOVER LOWER MANHATTAN'S COLONIAL PAST

In a city known for its relentless drive to be 'New,' a trove of old-world history hides in plain sight.

START	END	LENGTH
Battery	African Burial Ground National Monument	2 miles; 3 hours

Start at the ❶ **Battery's** waterfront, facing Lady Liberty, to consider how her lofty ideals compare with the city's complicated origins. Stop by the ❷ **National Museum of the American Indian** *(free)* on the park's eastern side to learn about 'Turtle Island' land before European takeover. Trace the park to ❸ **Pearl St**, the city's original shoreline before landfill expanded it outward, and jog east to ❹ **Fraunces Tavern** *(museum adult/child $10/5)*, where George Washington famously threw back a few pints. Across the street, look for the bones of ❺ **Lovelace Tavern's foundation**, buried beneath the sidewalk. Next stop is ❻ **Stone St**, which became the city's first cobblestone-paved passage in the 17th century. Three blocks northeast is a plaque marking the site of New York's ❼ **slave market**, opened in 1711. Slavery was introduced to the city in 1626; by 1730, 42% of the free population owned enslaved people. Walk west on ❽ **Wall St** (an actual defence wall in the 17th century) toward ❾ **Trinity Church** (resting place of Alexander Hamilton) and north along ❿ **Broadway** (built on an old Lenape route). End at the ⓫ **African Burial Ground National Monument** *(free)*, a memorial and museum honoring the estimated 15,000 African souls interred on-site. The mass grave is a reminder of the backs on which New York was built.

The African burial ground was unearthed in 1991 during construction of an office building.

Before Henry Hudson arrived in 1609, the Lenape paddled here in wood-carved canoes.

Built in 1670 and burned down in 1706, Lovelace Tavern wasn't rediscovered until 1979.

Begin at the **Leslie-Lohman Museum of Art** *(leslielohman.org; free)*, the world's first museum dedicated to LGBTIQ+ themes. Charles Leslie and the late Fritz Lohman started showcasing their gay-centric art collection from a SoHo loft in 1969 – an assemblage that rapidly expanded as they rescued works by dying artists during the 1980s AIDS pandemic. Nearby, you'll find the **Drawing Center** *(drawingcenter.org; free)*, a nonprofit institute focused solely on drawings. Founded in 1977 as SoHo's art scene took shape, the free-to-visit museum is now a neighborhood fixture that's featured everyone from Michelangelo to Richard Serra.

Continue to the 2nd floor of 141 Wooster St to see the work of artist Walter de Maria – a room filled with 280,000lb of dirt. This is the **New York Earth Room** *(diaart.org; free; open noon-3pm & 3:30pm-6pm Wed to Sun)*, on view since 1980. It's a heady experience,. Finally, watch where you step while walking over the northwest corner of Prince St and Broadway (outside Prada) and you'll spot the work of sculptor Ken Hiratsuka, who carved roughly 40 sidewalks after moving to NYC in 1982. This design took about five hours of actual work, though its completion took two years (1983–84), as police patrols often disrupted Hirasuka's illegal chiseling.

Eat Everything in Chinatown

MAP P66

Dumplings, rolls, buns and bao

The most rewarding way to visit Chinatown is through your taste buds. Follow this 1-mile food tour past dangling duck roasts, paper lanterns and simple storefronts where food is the main attraction. Begin inside the East Broadway Mall, a largely abandoned shopping center beneath the Manhattan Bridge. Look past the grungy vestibules and let your nose lead you downstairs to **Fu Zhou Wei Zhong Wei Jia Xiang Feng Wei**, which roughly translates to 'The tastiest Fuzhou hometown-flavor restaurant.' Order the dumplings and decide if the food lives up to the name. Next stop is **Mei Lai Wah** *(@meilaiwahcoffeeshop)*, famous for pineapple buns with roast pork. There's often a line snaking outside this tiny shop. Once it's your turn, place an order at the digital kiosk inside and watch the kitchen staff prep to-go bags for ravenous hordes. Give your belly a break from the food frenzy in **Columbus Park**, once a part of Five Points – NYC's first tenement slums. Today, entering the leafy oasis is like a trip to Shanghai: spy spirited mah-jongg meisters, slow-motion tai-chi practitioners

(continues on p67)

CYCLE THE CITY

Citi Bike *(citibikenyc.com)*, NYC's ubiquitous bikeshare program, offers single passes ($4.99 for 30 minutes) and day passes ($25 for unlimited 30-minute rides), allowing users to unlock bikes at one station and drop them off at any other station around the city. You can purchase day passes at station kiosks, but download the Citi Bike app for a better user experience. If you're new to urban biking, get your bearings along the Hudson River Greenway – a north–south bike path that rolls along Manhattan's west side. There are around 20 Citi Bike kiosks surrounding the laneway, so you can dock and explore the borough's pretty riverside parks. New Yorkers use this path for commuting. Act accordingly: obey traffic lights; slower traffic sticks to the right.

DRINKING IN LOWER MANHATTAN: BEST COCKTAILS

MAPS P60, P66

Overstory: This lofty lounge on the 64th floor is best for marveling at the city's sparkling lights. Reserve an outdoor table ($75 minimum spend). *5:45pm-midnight*

Dead Rabbit: It's tough beating this three-floor bar named after a 19th-century Irish American gang – the Irish coffee is a knockout. *11am-2am, Sun-Thu to 3am Fri & Sat*

Split Eights: Let the bartender decide what you should imbibe at this moody bi-level hang out where buttoned-up crowds let loose. *4:30pm-2am*

Smith & Mills: Former carriage house turned cocktail bar and restaurant. Don't leave without seeing the loo, inside a 1902 cage elevator. *4-11pm Sun & Mon, to 1am Tue-Sat*

LET GO MEDIA/SHUTTERSTOCK

Liberty Island's museum

TOP EXPERIENCE

Statue of Liberty & Ellis Island

'Lady Liberty' is New York's most enduring icon, her torch shining high above the harbor since 1886. A one-woman welcoming committee for millions of immigrants, 'Liberty Enlightening the World' (her official name) is an international symbol of freedom, justice and opportunity. Nearby is Ellis Island, America's immigration epicenter from 1892 to 1924, from where 40% of the US population can trace their ancestry.

DID YOU KNOW?

Lady Liberty was intended as an icon of emancipation, celebrating the end of slavery in the US, not immigration. Ellis Island didn't open its 'golden door' until six years after the statue was unveiled. The original idea was replaced by the sentiment of Emma Lazarus' 1883 poem 'The New Colossus,' on the pedestal, which welcomes 'huddled masses yearning to breathe free.'

Ride the Ferry

Start your journey along the water-splashed Battery, where crowds congregate for the 15-minute ferry ride to Liberty Island. Expect airport-style security screenings at the boarding station, with 30- to 90-minute waits during summer's high season. Once on board, grab a seat by the lower-level windows or on the upper-level railings for views of Governors Island (p58), the Verrazzano-Narrows Bridge and Manhattan's jagged skyline.

PRACTICALITIES

- cityexperiences.com/new-york/city-cruises/statue
- adult/child $25.50/16.50
- 1st ferry departs the Battery 9am
- last ferry departs Ellis Island 5:15pm

Visit the Museum

Step into Liberty Island's free museum – a 26,000-sq-ft complex completed in 2019 – for a riveting introduction. The statue's original torch, removed in 1984, is the visual pièce de résistance, while the most engaging exhibit digs into the statue's hypocrisy. In 1886, 'universal liberty' was a dream deferred for many Americans – women didn't have the right to vote and African Americans suffered through racist government policies during post–Civil War reconstruction. Even today, America maintains a complicated relationship with Lady Liberty's ideals.

Gaze at the Goddess

While staring at Lady Liberty's sea-green copper sheen, consider the fantastic feats it took to bring her to America. Designer Frédéric-Auguste Bartholdi's 450,000lb giantess was constructed in Paris between 1881 and 1884, with help from French engineer Alexandre Gustave Eiffel (of the eponymous tower), using 300 copper sheets, each about 7.8ft wide. She was transported to New York across the treacherous Atlantic in 214 crates, reassembled from 350 pieces over four months, then placed on a granite pedestal designed by architect Richard Morris Hunt, bringing her total height to 305ft.

Sail to Ellis Island

Traveling to Ellis Island begins as it did for roughly 12 million immigrants – on the water. The 27.5-acre plot of land is only accessible by ferry, which leaves from Liberty Island, sailing for 15 minutes to the National Immigration Museum. Get your camera ready: the trip from Liberty Island is particularly scenic.

Understand the United States

Immerse yourself in the complex tapestry of US immigration prior to Ellis Island's debut around the Main Building's 1st-floor museum. *Journeys: The Peopling of America, 1550–1890* traces the movement of people to and through the US as they built the blocks of the nation's foundation. Stories of displaced Native Americans, enslaved Africans and optimistic immigrants illuminate America's ongoing struggles with identity.

See an Immigrant's Point of View

On the Main Building's 2nd floor, you can visit *Through America's Gate*, an exhibition chronicling the step-by-step process for newly arrived immigrants on Ellis Island. Begin in the 338ft-long Registry Room, where thousands of hopefuls once gathered daily to wade through the tape of American bureaucracy. From here, wander through halls to learn about medical and legal inspections necessary to gain admittance to the US, including the 29 questions that would determine a person's future. While 98% of immigrants eventually made it into the country, 2% of people faced the personal and financial pain of rejection – which could account for more than 1000 people per month. Take a moment to examine pieces of salvaged walls, scrawled on by immigrants desperate to make their mark on America.

OYSTERS TO ELLIS

Native Americans called Ellis Island 'Kioshk' (Gull Island). The Dutch called it Oyster Island for its mass of mollusks. It was then dubbed Gibbet Island when criminals were hanged here in the 1760s. Today's name comes from Samuel Ellis, a merchant who took ownership in the 1770s. He unsuccessfully tried to rid himself of the property while alive. The upside? Now his name is famous.

TOP TIPS

- Statue Cruises is the only company that sells tickets to Liberty and Ellis islands; the box office operates inside the Battery's Castle Clinton and New Jersey's Liberty State Park. Book online to avoid queues.
- If you want to see the Statue of Liberty and Ellis Island in one day, hop on a ferry before 2pm.
- Liberty Island's food is expensive and mediocre. Pack lunch or snacks to enjoy on-site instead.
- Head to Ellis Island's lobby to check the schedule for free tours, to watch screenings of the 35-minute film *Island of Hope, Island of Tears,* and to pick up a free audio guide.

HIGHLIGHTS
1 Elizabeth Street Garden

SIGHTS
2 Basilica of St Patrick's Old Cathedral
3 Chinatown Fair Family Fun Center
4 Columbus Park
5 Drawing Center
6 Hudson River Park
7 Judd Foundation
8 Leslie-Lohman Museum of Art
9 New York Earth Room

SLEEPING
10 Crosby Street Hotel

EATING
11 Frenchette
12 Golden Steamer
13 Lombardi's
14 Mei Lai Wah
15 Raoul's
16 Rubirosa
17 Thai Diner
18 Yi Ji Shi Mo

DRINKING & NIGHTLIFE
19 Cafe Integral
20 Ear Inn
21 Fanelli Cafe
22 Felix Roasting Company
23 Jimmy
24 Smith & Mills

SHOPPING
25 Bloomingdale's
26 Canal Street Market
27 Corridor
28 IF Boutique
29 Olfactory NYC
30 Oroboro
31 R Swiader

(continued from p63)

and aunties gossiping over homemade dumplings. Continue to Elizabeth St's **Yi Ji Shi Mo**, a tiny counter famous for rice rolls. End your food tour with Chinatown's tastiest *bao* (steamed buns) at **Golden Steamer** on Grand St. Order the pumpkin – if they haven't already run out.

Expect Great Performances at the Public Theater

MAP P74

Downtown theater and cabaret

Broadway isn't the only place to see great theater. See what's playing at the **Public** *(publictheater.org)*, a legendary Off-Broadway house founded in 1954 that launched some of New York's biggest hits, including *Hamilton* in 2015. Today, you'll find a lineup of new works and reimagined classics, with Shakespeare on heavy rotation. Speaking of the bard, the Public also stages star-studded Shakespeare in the Park performances during the summer – free, if you can get tickets (try the TodayTix lottery: *todaytix.com*), and located in Central Park.

Next door is **Joe's Pub**, named for Public Theater founder Joseph Papp. Part bar, part cabaret venue, the intimate space serves up top-shelf entertainers, ranging from downtown icon Joey Arias to Broadway's biggest divas and heavy hitters (Adele even sang here). Take a chance on lesser-known names. Who knows? They might be New York's next big thing.

Shop 'til You Drop

MAP P66

Pop into SoHo's boutiques

Soho and its surrounds burst at the seams with sartorial splendor. Spend an afternoon following NYC's style fiends to the neighborhood's trendiest shops. Start by strutting down Broadway for global chains from Adidas to Zara and everything in between – including **Bloomingdale's** *(bloomingdales.com)*, a department store beloved by big spenders. Zigzag west toward West Broadway to try on designer labels at spots like **IF Boutique** *(ifsohonewyork.com)*, a SoHo fashion stalwart since 1978.

In Nolita (North of Little Italy), jewel-box boutiques sell unique threads, kicks and fragrances. Don't miss **Oroboro** (upscale-casual womenswear; *oroborostore.com*), **R Swiader** (gender-optional clothes plus a salon; *rswiader.com*) and **Corridor** (thick-knit plaids for gents; *corridornyc.com*).

HALF-SHELL HISTORY

Long before pizza became the cheap-eat treat for famished New Yorkers, a salty sea candy reigned supreme on the streets: oysters. Their thick beds lined the city's estuaries, plucked by the Indigenous Lenape then pillaged by European colonizers. NYC earned a reputation as the world's oyster capital, and some biologists estimate that New York Harbor contained half the world's supply. But by 1927, pollution and overharvesting killed the masses of meaty mollusks. Today, Hudson River Park is dedicated to repopulating their defunct reefs. In 2021, 11.2 million larval oysters were added to the Hudson River Park's Estuarine Sanctuary, and the Billion Oyster Project plans to restore one billion oysters back to New York Harbor by 2035.

EATING IN SOHO & CHINATOWN: BEST MEALS

MAP P66

Thai Diner: Classic NY-diner style (chrome stools, spacious booths), retooled with Southeast Asian flavors. *11am-10:30pm Mon-Wed, to 11:30pm Thu-Sat, from 10am Sat & Sun* $$

Raoul's: Cool kids started lining up for Raoul's French-bistro classics in 1975. Order the peppercorn-crusted burger – if it's available. *5-11pm Mon-Fri, 11am-2:30pm Sat & Sun* $$$

Lombardi's: Opened in 1905 when Little Italy dominated the area, this Neapolitan-style parlor claims to be America's first pizzeria. *noon-10pm Sun-Thu, to midnight Fri & Sat* $$

Golden Diner: Trek to this Manhattan Bridge haunt for surprising takes on greasy-spoon grub, including Asian influences. *10am-10pm Tue-Sun* $$

SNAKE DOWN DOYERS ST

In a city dominated by an orderly grid, Doyers St – a curved block in Chinatown – refuses to conform. Named after Hendrick Doyer, an 18th-century Dutch immigrant who owned a distillery here, Doyers became the epicenter of Chinatown as it took shape in the late 1800s. By the end of the century, the street earned new monikers, including the 'Bloody Angle' – a reference to criminal activity. Throughout the early 20th century, warring tongs (Chinese gangs) attacked rivals by hiding behind the street's sharp bend – a cause for concern among anyone visiting nearby tenement buildings packed with gambling parlors and opium dens. Today, it's a peaceful pedestrian promenade; a colorful mural decorates the formerly blood-splattered street.

HERE NOW/SHUTTERSTOCK

For fantastic street vendors, skip to the stands on Prince St (between Mulberry and Mott) to see handmade jewelry and art. Searching for scents? Stop by **Olfactory NYC** *(olfactorynyc.com)*.

You don't need to be a fashionista to enjoy the consumer circus. Bookstores such as **McNally Jackson** *(mcnallyjackson.com)* cater to literati, and you can choose between shopping and eating thanks to local vendors at **Canal Street Market** *(canalstreet.market)*.

Find Solitude in a Secret Garden

MAP P66

Nolita's hidden public park

Cement-smacked SoHo and Nolita are largely devoid of green space, save for **Elizabeth Street Garden** *(elizabethstreetgarden.com; 11am-6pm)*, a hidden oasis between Prince and Spring Sts. It started in 1991, when an antiques dealer leased the abandoned lot from the city, added landscaping and sprinkled its acre with outdoor sculptures. This whimsical spot is now a serene refuge for shop-weary New Yorkers. Grab a coffee from nearby **Cafe Integral** *(cafeintegral.com)* to sip in the shade of garden trees.

DRINKING IN SOHO: BEST BARS & CAFES

MAP P66

Ear Inn: See how SoHo looked before fashionistas took over at this 18th-century house-turned-drinking-den built for James Brown, George Washington's African aide. *11:30am-4am*

Jimmy: Tipsy patrons spill onto the open deck at this sky-high hangout atop ModernHaus SoHo. *5-11pm Sun & Mon, to 1am Tue & Wed, to 2am Thu-Sat*

Fanelli Cafe: A saloon from 1847, Fanelli bridges SoHo's past and present. The corner table looking down Prince and Mercer Sts is the envy of TikTok. *11am-late*

Felix Roasting Company: Contemporary cafe culture meets Gilded Age at the Greenwich St branch of this java chain fit for an Astor. *7am-10pm*

Elizabeth Street Garden

Explore the Tenement Life of Immigrants

MAP P70

Big stories in tiny apartments

Stand in one of the tenement apartments alongside eight or 10 fellow visitors on the popular tours at the **Tenement Museum** *(tenement.org; $30)*, and you'll get an idea of what it was like living in these cramped quarters. Depending on which tour you choose, a docent will lead you through various rooms of the historically restored buildings and tell you the stories of people who lived there in the 19th and 20th centuries. The 'Tenement Women: 1902' tour, for instance, will take you into the small three-room apartment of the Levine family – where Jewish immigrant Jennie Levine managed the household while her husband ran a garment factory in the front room. Other tours explore the stories of immigrants from Germany, Puerto Rico, Italy and China, among other places, who lived here at various points. Tours are the only way to experience the museum, and they sell out daily, so book tickets in advance.

Taste NYC's Beloved Pastrami

MAP P70

Sandwiches at Katz's Delicatessen

Eating a pastrami sandwich on rye bread is one of those quintessential NYC experiences, and **Katz's** (established 1888; *katzsdelicatessen.com*) is the number-one place to do it. This kosher-style deli has all the trappings – neon signs, table seating, gruff but kind-hearted staff and usually a line out the door. (Movie buffs: this is where Meg Ryan faked her famous orgasm in the 1989 film *When Harry Met Sally*.) Get a ticket when you walk in and proceed to the various counters to order your meal. Keep that ticket to pay after you eat. You might be surprised by the prices *(around $28)*, but the sandwiches are huge and best shared.

WHEN LITTLE ITALY WAS BIG

Mulberry St, named after the mulberry trees that once lined its sidewalks, became synonymous with Italy in the late 19th and early 20th centuries as millions of Italian immigrants funneled into the country. By 1910, roughly 10,000 Italian Americans crammed themselves into a 2-mile radius of tenement buildings that Jacob Riis called the 'foul core of New York's slums.' After WWII, the community began a mass exodus and, as Chinatown expanded, Little Italy went from a brash boot to a slim sandal. But wiping out the Italian heritage is impossible: restaurants such as **Rubirosa** *(rubirosanyc.com)* ensure Mulberry St remains soaked in red sauce, and September's 11-day festival for the **Feast of San Gennaro** *(sangennaronyc.org)* revives its red, white and green glory.

EAST VILLAGE & THE LOWER EAST SIDE

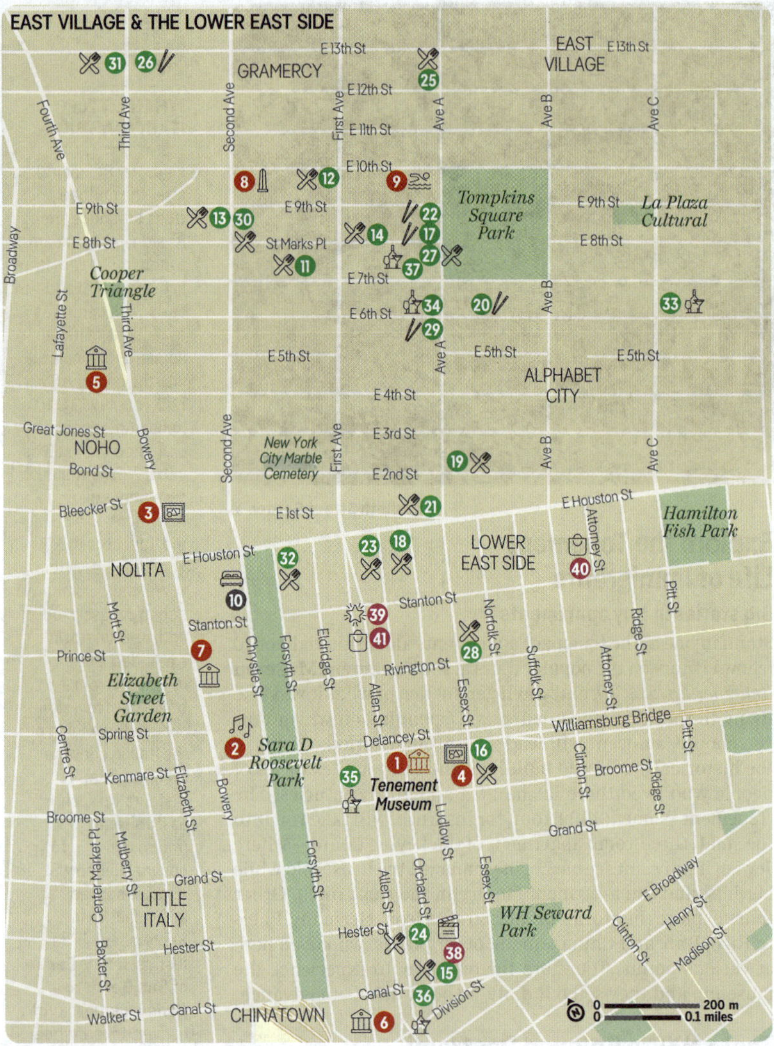

HIGHLIGHTS
1 Tenement Museum

SIGHTS
2 Bowery Ballroom
3 Hole
4 International Center of Photography
5 Merchant's House Museum
6 Museum at Eldridge Street
7 New Museum
8 Yiddish Walk of Fame
9 Russian & Turkish Baths

SLEEPING
10 Public Hotel

EATING
11 Abraço
12 Apollo Bagels
13 B&H Dairy
14 Cafe Mogador
15 Dimes
16 Essex Market
17 Hanoi House
18 Katz's Delicatessen
19 Little Myanmar
20 Nowon
21 Punjabi Grocery & Deli
22 Rosella
23 Russ & Daughters
24 Scarr's Pizza
25 Smør
26 Soothr
27 Superiority Burger
28 Supermoon Bakehouse
29 Takahachi
30 Veselka
31 Yellow Rose
32 Yonah Schimmel's Knish Bakery

DRINKING & NIGHTLIFE
33 Accidental Bar
34 Amor y Amargo
35 Attaboy
36 Lobby Lounge
37 Ruffian

ENTERTAINMENT
38 Metrograph
39 Slipper Room

SHOPPING
40 Only NY
41 Orchard Corset

Kvell over Jewish History

MAP P70

From knishes to temples

In the 19th and 20th centuries, about two million Jews left Europe for the US in response to anti-Jewish sentiment – and about 75% of them ended up in NYC. Most settled around the Lower East Side's tenements, which became the capital of Jewish life in America. Their descendants might've moved elsewhere, but their cultural impact remains. Spend a couple hours following their footsteps.

Start by looking for faded stars in the pavement on the **Yiddish Walk of Fame's** southeast corner (E 10th St and Second Ave) to spot names of Jewish thespians who thrived here pre-WWII. Back then, Second Ave was known as 'Yiddish Broadway.' Clock the Chase Bank that takes up the corner – it was once a Jewish deli.

Next, slip inside **B&H Dairy** *(bandhdairykosher.com)*, a slender greasy spoon open since the late 1930s, for a taste of a time when Second Ave was the land of milk and honey. Polish Catholic Ola Abdelwahed now runs the Jewish Kosher luncheonette with her Muslim Egyptian husband Fawzy, churning out Yiddish comfort classics (blintzes, matzo ball soup), arguably better than a *bubbe*.

Save some appetite for **Yonah Schimmel's Knish Bakery** *(knishery.com)*, which started selling its namesake Jewish dough pockets from a Coney Island pushcart in the 1890s. By 1910, the store opened on the LES, where it continues selling knishes stuffed with potatoes, cabbage, blueberry cheese and more.

Walk off your meal en route to the **Museum at Eldridge Street** *(eldridgestreet.org; adult/child $15/8)*, a landmark synagogue built in 1887 and the center of Jewish life for decades. The high-ceilinged sanctuary must have felt like a reprieve for the tenement-dwelling neighborhood residents of yore. Join a docent-led tour to appreciate the stunning stained glass (added in 2010) or explore on your own.

Pop into Orchard Street Storefronts

MAP P70

Shopping and strolling through the LES

In the early 1700s, there was actually an orchard on **Orchard St**, but in the late 1800s this became the Lower East Side's main shopping strip, with garment workers packed into tenement buildings and storefronts selling textiles. Nowadays, Orchard St is the hippest part of the neighborhood,

UNDERSTAND THE EAST VILLAGE & LOWER EAST SIDE

The East Village and Lower East Side (LES) are integral to NYC's multicultural melting pot, home to successive waves of immigrant communities, remnants of which linger around every corner. This is also where all the cool stuff happened – where the Beat Generation gravitated in the 1950s, the hippies came in the '60s, and where CBGB kick-started careers of punk and new-wave musicians including the Ramones. Things got sketchy in the '70s, coming to a head in the late 1980s with riots in Tompkins Square Park. The neighborhoods continue changing, but they remain Manhattan's most eclectic, creative places to be. New restaurants, cocktail bars and fashion boutiques now vie for attention amid the old-school delis and dives.

EATING IN EAST VILLAGE: BEST RESTAURANTS

MAP P70

Superiority Burger: The best veggie burger in town, plus mouthwatering pies and flavor-packed sides. *hours vary* **$$**

Veselka: This vestige of the area's Ukrainian past has been serving handmade *varenyky* (pierogis), borscht and goulash since 1954. *8am-midnight Mon-Sat, to 11pm Sun* **$$**

Rosella: Sustainably minded sushi earns this Japanese restaurant an A+. The menu features locally caught fish, all approved by Seafood Watch or NOAA. *5-10pm Wed-Sun* **$$$**

Yellow Rose: Flour tortillas give Tex-Mex taquerias their north-of-the-border flair at this outpost, far north of Texas. *noon-10pm Tue-Fri, 10am-4pm & 5-10pm Sat & Sun* **$$**

TOP SPOTS FOR DOWNTOWN NOSTALGIA

Merchant's House Museum: Tour this red-brick mansion from 1832 for an authentic look at 19th-century life.

Judd Foundation: Admire minimalist artist Donald Judd's five-story, cast-iron home, purchased in 1968 for a now-unthinkable $68,000.

Basilica of St Patrick's Old Cathedral: Descend into the catacombs on a guided tour of the Gothic Revival basilica, a 19th-century Irish Catholic stronghold.

Chinatown Fair Family Fun Center: This Mott St arcade has been going strong since 1940, delivering childhood sentimentality with Ms Pac-Man and more.

Metrograph: Serious cinephiles catch oldies and rare archival films at this LES throwback movie theater with an on-site restaurant and bar.

BRIAN LOGAN PHOTOGRAPHY/SHUTTERSTOCK

Essex Market

especially the stretch between Houston and Canal Sts, which is lined with indie boutiques, happening restaurants such as **Scarr's Pizza** *(scarrspizza.com)* and upstart art galleries. Wander this seven-block strip and you'll still find some yesteryear holdouts, including **Orchard Corset**, which opened in 1968 and caters to everyone from Orthodox Jews to trans women – all with the aspirations of Victorian silhouettes.

Sweat It out at the Russian & Turkish Baths

MAP P70

Spa day in a townhouse basement

Locals have been schvitzing at this slightly cramped downtown **spa** *(russianturkishbaths.com; $60)* since 1892. These days, it draws an eclectic mix of actors, students, couples, singles, Russian regulars and old-school locals. Everyone strips down to their skivvies or bathing suits (towels, cotton shorts and sandals are provided) and moves between steam rooms, saunas, an ice-cold plunge pool, the sun deck and the restaurant. Most hours are coed (clothing required), but there are blocks of men- and women-only hours (clothing optional). Massages, scrubs and Russian oak-leaf treatments are available, too. The cafe serves specials such as Polish sausage and blinis.

DRINKING IN THE VILLAGE & LOWER EAST SIDE: OUR PICKS

MAP P70

Attaboy: Speakeasy vibes and bespoke cocktails – tell the barkeep what you like and they'll whip up the concoction of your dreams. Expect to wait. *5pm-3am*

Amor y Amargo: 'Love and Bitters' is a cocktail chemistry lab showcasing its namesake amaro selection. Bartenders offer advice on flavors. *3pm-midnight*

Accidental Bar: The sake sommeliers behind this Japanese juice joint with a hilariously descriptive menu to inspire indulgence. *5-11pm Sun, Tue & Wed, to midnight Thu-Sat*

Ruffian: If you're into funky orange wines, grab a stool at this intimate vino joint to taste Eastern European grapes and mostly vegetarian fare. *5pm-midnight Mon-Sat, 3-11pm Sun*

Grab a Snack at Essex Market

MAP P70

An LES food market

Street vendors have come together at what's known as the **Essex Market** *(essexmarket.nyc)* since 1818, though its newest location only opened in 2019. The most recent Grand St incarnation is a wide-ranging representation of the neighborhood with stalls selling everything from cheese, groceries, spices and Dominican food to ceviche, rice balls and more. Legendary lunch counter **Shopsin's** serves its wide-ranging menu of inventive diner fare in a tiny sit-down space. Downstairs, the **Market Line** food court has outposts of local institutions like Veselka (p71), as well as pizza, ramen, pho and sushi. If you're ordering counter food, head upstairs to dine in sunny, open-atrium seating. This makes a sensible pit stop while walking down Orchard St (p71), located two blocks west.

Sample NYC's Melting Pot

MAP P70

Gorge on global cuisine in the East Village

The diversity of worldwide cuisines in the East Village is jaw-dropping. Find what tickles your taste buds, then tour the world through food. **Nowon** *(nowonusa.com)* is a favorite for American Korean 'drinking food,' and some people say the northern-style pho at **Hanoi House** *(hanoihousenyc.com)* is better than anything in Vietnam. Nibble Nordic delicacies at **Smør** *(smornyc.com)* and its adjoining bakery, which serves freshly baked cardamom buns and egg sandwiches on fluffy brioche. Try Burmese specialties at **Little Myanmar** *(littlemyanmar.nyc)*, and if you like spicy Thai food, go to **Soothr** (pronounced 'sood'; *soothrnyc.com*). Meanwhile, **Cafe Mogador** *(cafemogador.com)* has been turning out Moroccan favorites since 1983 and **Takahachi** *(takahachi.net)* has been a stalwart for sushi and Japanese noodles since 1991. For quick, cheap eats, follow the cab drivers to **Punjabi Grocery & Deli** *(@punjabidelinyc)* for delectable vegetarian fare.

Admire the Whitney Museum's Permanent Collection

MAP P74

America's modern art masters

The **Whitney Museum of American Art** *(whitney.org; adult/25 & under $30/free)* opened as a showcase for homegrown artists in a W 8th St townhouse in 1930. After successive

(continues on p76)

EDGY ART, MUSIC & CINEMA

New Museum: Work by emerging and established contemporary artists inside a futuristic fortress that looks like a giant's Tetris game.

Hole: Art openings attract rowdy crowds at this bi-coastal gallery known for performances and special events.

Bowery Ballroom: Audiences adore this concert venue's intimate feel and great sound system. Head downstairs for drinks and mingling.

International Center of Photography: Rotating exhibits celebrate the humanitarian and political documentary work of world-class photographers.

Slipper Room: Squeeze in tight for hit-or-miss shows featuring comics, magicians, burlesque dancers and circus performers, often worth the gamble.

EATING IN THE VILLAGE & LOWER EAST SIDE: BREAKFAST & COFFEE

MAP P70

Abraço: Sip espresso while inhaling the dangerously addictive olive-oil cake inside this ground-level cafe. *8am-6pm Tue-Thu & Sun, to 9pm Fri & Sat* $

Supermoon Bakehouse: Lines of laminated pastries, including cruffins, look like designer jewelry at this shop where flavors change weekly. *10am-6pm Thu-Mon* $

Russ & Daughters: Feast on bagels and the city's best smoked salmon at this diner extension of a long-running Jewish delicatessen. *8:30am-2:30pm Mon-Thu, to 3:30pm Fri-Sun* $$

Apollo Bagels: Classic NY bagel texture (crispy exterior, chewy interior) with a twist: these are made with slightly tangy sourdough. *7am-5pm* $

WEST VILLAGE & CHELSEA
W 29th St
W 28th St
28th St
W 27th St
Chelsea Park
W 26th St
Eleventh Ave
W 25th St
Seventh Ave
W 24th St
W 23rd St
23rd St
W 22nd St
Tenth Ave
Ninth Ave
Eighth Ave
W 21st St
CHELSEA
W 20th St
W 19th St
Pier 60
W 18th St
18th St
Pier 59
W 17th St
W 16th St
W 15th St
Pier 57
8th Ave-14th St
14th St
Hudson River Park
W 14th St
W 13th St
Jackson Sq
WEST VILLAGE
Little Island
Little W 12th St
Greenwich Ave
Horatio St
Whitney Museum of American Art
High Line
Hudson St
Jane St
Bank St
Hudson River Park
Bethune St
See Enlargement
W 10th St
Christopher St
Christopher St-Sheridan Sq
West Side Hwy
Perry St
Barrow St
Grove St
Charles St
Hudson River
Bleecker St
Hudson River Park
Leroy St
Barrow St
Morton St

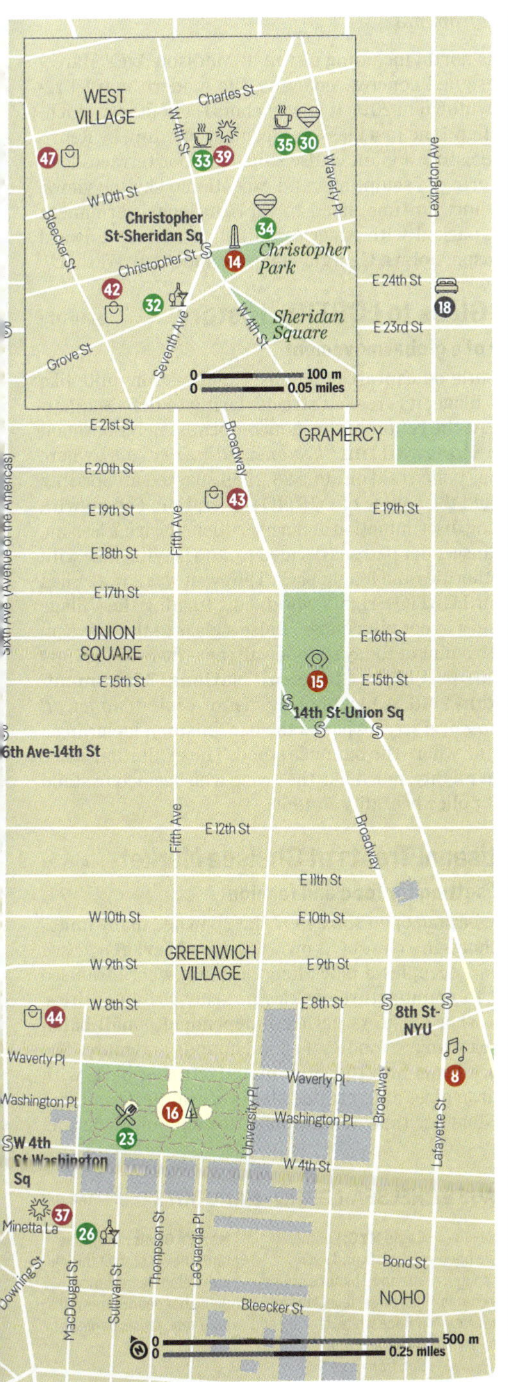

HIGHLIGHTS

1 High Line
2 Whitney Museum of American Art

SIGHTS

3 520 W 28th Street
4 Dia Chelsea
5 Gagosian
6 Gansevoort Peninsula
7 High Line Nine
8 Joe's Pub
9 Little Island
10 Pace Gallery
11 Paula Cooper Gallery
12 Pier 45
13 Pier 57
14 Stonewall National Monument
15 Union Square
16 Washington Square Park

ACTIVTIES

17 Chelsea Piers Complex

SLEEPING

18 Freehand
19 Hotel Chelsea
20 Jane Hotel

EATING

21 Anixi
22 L'Industrie
23 NY Dosas
24 Semma
25 Shukette

DRINKING & NIGHTLIFE

26 124 Old Rabbit Club
27 Cubbyhole
28 Eagle NYC
29 Employees Only
30 Julius'
31 Le Bain
32 Marie's Crisis
33 St Jardim
34 Stonewall Inn
35 Té Company

ENTERTAINMENT

36 Atlantic Theater Company
37 Comedy Cellar
38 Lucille Lortel Theatre
see 8 Public Theater
39 Smalls
40 Village Vanguard

SHOPPING

41 Chelsea Market
42 Cueva
43 Fishs Eddy
44 Goods for the Study
45 Printed Matter, Inc
46 Screaming Mimis
47 Zuri

NYC'S HIPPEST MICRO-HOOD?

Is Dimes Sq the hippest new micro-hood in NYC? Does it even exist? Media coverage has debated whether this small Lower East Side corner around Division and Canal Sts is a publicity joke or a real thing, and talking about it has brought it into being. What we know for sure: **Dimes** *(dimesnyc.com)* was an immediate restaurant hot spot for cool downtown kids when it opened in 2013. We're still happy to hang out there if we can get a table. Dine elsewhere with the in-crowd at one of the area's fashionable bars and restaurants, including the chic **Lobby Lounge** inside **Nine Orchard Hotel** *(nineorchard.com)*. It might be a media-made gimmick, but it's cool – like the rest of the Lower East Side.

(continued from p73)

expansions north, including a stint at Madison Ave's Marcel Breuer–designed concrete colossus, the modern marvel returned downtown in 2015. It now anchors the southern reaches of the High Line in a glass-and-cement building by Renzo Piano, suggesting a giant cruise ship. Outdoor terraces lead to a smattering of sculptures and exceptional skyline views. If you're short on time, head to the 7th floor's permanent collection, packed with American all-stars such as Edward Hopper, Jasper Johns, Georgia O'Keeffe and Andy Warhol.

Raise a Glass to LGBTIQ+ History

MAP P74

Epicenter of a global movement

No neighborhood captures the queer imagination quite like the West Village, its crooked streets daring to defy Manhattan's grid. At the center of this nonconformist neighborhood stands the **Stonewall Inn** *(thestonewallinnnyc.com)*, where an infamous police raid on June 28, 1969 sparked an uprising that changed the course of LGBTIQ+ liberation. Fed up with never-ending discrimination and persecution, the bar's lesbian, gay and transgender patrons decided to stop playing nice with bigoted authorities and fought back. The event was a watershed moment for LGBTIQ+ rights worldwide, turning the Village into a place of queer pilgrimage. Raise a glass to the brave pioneers with a pint at today's Stonewall (next door to the 1969 incarnation), part of the **Stonewall National Monument**, designated in 2016. A neighboring visitor center *(stonewall visitorcenter.org; free)* explores the bar's history, including a silver outline where the bar once stood. The exhibition space is small but mighty, much like the group who decided to stand up against police brutality in 1969.

Find Artisanal Treats at Chelsea Market

MAP P74

Industrial setting for food and fashion

This urban bazaar, open since 1997, has spawned many imitators but belongs in a class of its own. **Chelsea Market** *(chelsea market.com)* occupies a block-long building where Nabisco once used to manufacture cookies in army-size quantities. Today, it's where visitors peruse independent, small-batch delicacies catering to foodies, fashion hounds and more. The architecture leans into the site's manufacturing past, with huge cast-iron pipes and serrated blocks of granite. Over three dozen vendors ply their temptations throughout, including

DRINKING IN THE WEST VILLAGE & CHELSEA: LGBTIQ+ HANGOUTS — MAP P74

Julius': One of NYC's longest-running gay joints, this cozy dive, famous for a 1966 civil rights 'Sip In,' is refreshingly unpretentious. *hours vary*

Cubbyhole: Femme-forward crowds have been cramming into this snug spot to play jukebox tunes since 1994. *4pm-2am Mon-Thu, to 4am Fri, 2pm-4am Sat, 2pm-2am Sun*

Eagle NYC: Leather fetishists and jock-strapped himbos cruise this three-level sleaze palace while dancing and drinking. *10pm-4am Mon-Sat, from 5pm Sun*

Marie's Crisis: The show tunes never stop at this all-are-welcome basement piano bar near Stonewall. *4pm-late, music begins at 5:30pm*

MARCOBRIVIOPHOTO.COM/SHUTTERSTOCK

Lobster Place

Miznon (Israeli street food), the Lobster Place (good luck resisting its rolls), Fat Witch Bakery (brownies and other decadent hits) and Los Tacos No 1 (authentic Mexican tacos). Head to the covered sidewalk tables for outdoor seating. Once you've had your fill, check out Artists & Fleas, a small market where local artists sell their wares. It makes a great pit stop while wandering the High Line.

Skip down the High Line

MAP P74

Chelsea's elevated train-track park

Snaking between the Meatpacking District to Hudson Yards, 30ft above street level, the **High Line** *(thehighline.org)* is a fabulous example of industrial reuse. Once a 20th-century freight line linking slaughterhouses along the Hudson River, it's now an art-strewn pedestrian ribbon running between galleries, modern high-rises and swanky shopping centers.

The High Line's story began in the early 20th century, when the west side's booming industrial enterprises were served by perilous street-level tracks, earning Tenth Ave the nickname 'Death Avenue.' A two-story-high railway became the expensive solution, and the 'West Side Elevated Line' ran its first train in 1933. It wasn't long before the train line became a money pit and fell into disuse; in the 1990s, demolition was mooted. Enter

A VILLAGE THEORY

The Village's compact streets are chockablock with charm. To find out why this neighborhood beguiles, read *The Death and Life of Great American Cities*, a 1961 tome by urban-planning guru Jane Jacobs. Inspired by Greenwich Village, Jacobs was the first to expound ideas that are now commonplace: density spurs commerce and community, and city life takes place outdoors in a 'sidewalk ballet.' Her greatest adversary? Urban planner Robert Moses, a political Goliath who fought to build a highway through Jacobs' beloved neighborhood. While Moses transformed much of NYC's landscape, you can see who won this particular battle: the late Jacobs is immortalized with a plaque at 555 Hudson St ('Jane Jacobs Way').

DRINKING IN THE VILLAGE: BEST BARS & CAFES

MAP P74

Employees Only: This divine speakeasy-style bar ushered in a new era of haute mixology when it served its first egg-white cocktail in 2004. *6pm-4am*

St Jardim: Perched on a lively Village side street, this all-day cafe and natural wine bar is perfect for people-watching. *hours vary*

124 Old Rabbit Club: The reward for finding this craft-beer haunt (look for the word 'Rabbit') is rare brews and local ales. *6pm-2am Mon-Sat, 4pm-midnight Sun*

Té Company: Loose-leaf teas from Taiwanese farmers served alongside sweets so pretty they belong in a Wes Anderson film. *noon-6pm Tue-Fri, from 11am Sat & Sun*

FASHION, JOURNALS & ZINES IN THE VILLAGE & CHELSEA

Screaming Mimis: This funtastic shop carries an excellent selection of vintage, designer and flamboyant costume threads.

Cueva: Eclectic designs rotate inside this seasonally curated international menswear collection.

Zuri: Colorful racks of one-style-fits-all dresses made from ethically sourced fabrics from Kenya.

Goods for the Study: Hardcore journalers and sketch-pad savants go ga-ga for this assortment of paper and writing utensils.

Printed Matter, Inc: Trim shelves hide thousands of ideas packed into strange zines and artist monographs.

FIIPHOTO/SHUTTERSTOCK

Jersey City skyline from Little Island

the Friends of the High Line, with a vision of an elegant park. Years of activism resulted in the jewel we enjoy today: a pedestrian catwalk, planted with 500-plus native species, wending its way above former factories and plenty of top-dollar real estate.

Begin your one- or two-hour journey near **Hudson Yards** (enter at 30th or 34th Sts), with super-tall skyscrapers shining eastward. Plant-packed railroad tracks evoke the industrial wilderness that preceded the park's creation. As the path narrows, you'll see tons of contemporary constructions, including starchitect Zaha Hadid's futuristic glass-and-metal apartment complex at **520 W 28th Street**.

For a bird's-eye view of Tenth Ave, sit on the amphitheater-style seats at 17th or 26th Sts and watch as cabs whiz by. If you prefer serene scenery, snag a train-wheel-tracked chaise longue on the Diller-von Furstenberg Sundeck – named after fashion queen Diane von Furstenberg and her billionaire husband Barry Diller, the pockets behind this entire project.

The High Line ends at the foot of the Whitney Museum (p73) and near a few other noteworthy areas, including Hudson River Park and the West Village's winding streets.

MEET THOSE DANCIN' FEET

Consider yourself a theater buff? Grab drinks alongside chorus kids at some of their favorite Midtown haunts and don't miss the **Museum of Broadway** (p82), a love letter to NYC show business.

Head up Hudson River Park MAPS P66, P74

The west side's green ribbon

Hudson River Park is the 550-acre shining star of Manhattan's modern green spaces, and its most popular sections hug the Village and Chelsea. Spend a sunny afternoon roaming around the waterfront.

Start at **Pier 45** (also called Christopher St Pier and beloved by queer crowds), where Speedo-clad gaggles gather to worship the sun – and each other. Walking north, there's **Gansevoort Peninsula**, completed in 2023 and billed as Manhattan's first public beach. Lounge in Adirondack chairs and admire David Hammons' ghostly *Day's End*, a skeletal art installation evoking the docks that once populated the riverfront.

Up next is **Little Island** *(littleisland.org)*, which appeared like a surrealist dream in 2021: 132 concrete pods shoot from the water like tulips, crowned by undulating green hills. Stroll the 2.4-acre folly's footpaths to enjoy gentle breezes and expansive views, or check the seasonal event schedule for live performances.

Pier 57 rounds out the park with its range of offerings, including City Winery's live music and Market 57's food vendors curated by the James Beard Foundation. (This is a great spot to try dim sum from Nom Wah Tea Parlor, a popular Chinatown restaurant.) Don't miss the rooftop – perfect for picnics and panoramas, including the best view you'll get of Little Island, backed by One World Trade Center.

QUEER PIER PAST

Ken Lustbader, co-founder and co-director of the NYC LGBT Historic Sites Project, explores the Greenwich Village waterfront's 20th-century history. *@nyclgbtsites*

This was one of the country's busiest ports, comprised of piers and beaux-arts-style shipping terminals. Eventually, those piers were abandoned and became urban ruins, which were appropriated by men who had sex with men, as well as gay artists who used the decrepit, deteriorating pier structures for public artwork and open-air sexual experimentation. Artist David Wojnarowicz was at the piers regularly, taking photographs, and even said, 'This is the real MoMA.' If you go there now, it's a sanitized version of a waterfront, without any of this history discernible in the current landscape.

Meet the Locals in Washington Square Park

MAP P74

A slice of Village life

Grab a seat in Greenwich Village's unofficial **town square** *(nycgovparks.com)* and you'll see it all: NYU students scurrying between classes, street vendors selling handmade clothes, fearless squirrels, socializing canines, speed-chess pros, brassy buskers, barefoot children splashing around the fountain – and possibly ghosts.

Centuries ago, this site was a marshy area crossed by Minetta Creek. Dutch colonists granted land rights (for a price) to settlers of African descent, who created a community known as Little Africa. Later, the plot became a public cemetery for the unidentified deceased. When the burial grounds turned into a space for military parades in the 1830s, real-estate developers followed and some of the city's toniest homes sprouted on the park's north border. Today, the park is dominated by the Stanford White–designed Washington Square Arch – 73ft of gleaming white Tuckahoe marble. Originally made of wood to celebrate the centennial of George Washington's inauguration in 1889, it proved so popular that it was replaced with stone six years later.

Head to the park's northwest corner to see an English elm considered one of Manhattan's oldest trees. Known as Hangman's Elm, its branches were used (according to legend) to hang traitors during the American Revolution.

EATING IN THE VILLAGE: RESERVATIONS RECOMMENDED

MAP P74

Semma: Experience summer in South India with the spicy chutneys and sauces on Michelin-starred Semma's menu (if you can snag a reservation). *5-10pm Mon-Sat* **$$$**

Shukette: The fluffy pita is an enticing teaser for what's to come: bites of delicious, shareable Middle Eastern delicacies. *5-11pm Mon-Sat, 4-10pm Sun* **$$**

Anixi: This faux-meat fortress is dressed to impress, with velvet curtains and crystal chandeliers as fancy as its Mediterranean-inspired menu. *hours vary* **$$**

L'Industrie: Wait in line for a pizza slice smothered in burrata and a cream-filled maritozzo, then bring it next door to Talea and pair it with a beer flight. *noon-10pm* **$**

APPLAUD PERFORMING ARTS

Village Vanguard: Turn a quiet Monday night into a big-band jamboree by seeing the Vanguard Jazz Orchestra at this prestigious jazz club.

Comedy Cellar: Talented regulars, including up-and-coming TV writers and personalities, have tested new material inside this chuckle den since the 1980s.

Atlantic Theater Company: This Off-Broadway house knows how to pick 'em: numerous shows here went on to win Best Musical Tony Awards.

Lucille Lortel Theatre: Clock the sidewalk stars in front of this Off-Broadway playhouse, including theater wordsmiths such as Neil LaBute and Charles Busch.

Smalls: Intimate basement jazz den that winks at Prohibition-era speakeasies.

If hunger calls, grab food from **NY Dosas** *(@nydosas; 11am-3pm Mon-Sat)*, Sri Lanka–born Thiru Kumar's South Indian pushcart near the dog run. Chow down while taking it all in.

Ogle Art at Chelsea's Galleries

MAP P74

DIY contemporary-art crawl

Zigzagging through far-west Chelsea is like visiting a free contemporary-art museum. The area is home to NYC's densest concentration of galleries; most open to the public from 10am to 6pm Tuesday to Saturday. Spend a couple of hours seeing what's on view. A perfect starting point is **High Line Nine** *(highlinenine.org)*. This thin strip mall linking 27th and 28th Sts is a gallery space where collectors spot up-and-coming artists. The eight floors of the **Pace Gallery** *(pacegallery.org)* showcase work by leading contemporary artists. Don't miss its smaller 4000-sq-ft space at 510 W 25th St – inside one of the many auto garages that once populated the area. Seeing exhibits at global chain **Gagosian** *(gagosian.com)* is akin to spinning around the Guggenheim – except everything is for sale. Check the website to see what's showing – perhaps Jeff Koons or Nam June Paik. The massive pieces inside the 20,000-sq-ft **Dia Chelsea** *(diaart.org)* would dwarf most jewel-box Manhattan galleries. Marvel at their size before perusing the picture-perfect art bookshop. End at **Paula Cooper Gallery** *(paulacoopergallery.com)*, the eponymous founder of which started SoHo's gallery explosion in 1968, then moved to Chelsea in the 1990s before it became cool.

Climb Higher than King Kong

MAP P81

Tour Midtown's Empire State Building

There's a reason King Kong chose this tower above the rest. One World Trade Center might be taller. The Chrysler Building might be prettier. But when it comes to skyline landmarks, the **Empire State Building** (*esbnyc.com; adult/child from $44/38*) is NYC's queen. Built in a frenzied 410 days, this steel-framed, limestone-and-granite-clad art-deco emblem opened in 1931 as the world's tallest building – a title it held until 1970, when the Twin Towers eclipsed its height. Take the vertiginous elevator ride to spectacular city views.

The main observation deck on the 86th floor is outdoors. There's also a tiny room with floor-to-ceiling windows on the 102nd floor ($35 extra). While on the 86th floor, train binoculars on the nearby Chrysler Building to admire its deco details.

EATING IN MIDTOWN: BEST RESTAURANTS

MAP P81

Le Bernardin: French-born chef Eric Ripert has spent decades steering this restaurant to deceptively simple seafood heaven. Michelin agrees. Book ahead. *hours vary* **$$$**

Barbetta: Linger at this gorgeous Restaurant Row time warp for Piedmontese specialties such as gnocchi and risotto. *4:30-11pm Tue-Sat, plus noon-2pm Wed & Sat* **$$$**

Mercado Little Spain: Celebrity chef José Andrés brings the Iberian peninsula to the Hudson Yards mall, where kiosks and sit-downs serve Spanish cuisine. *11am-9pm* **$$**

Ace's Pizza: When hunger strikes around Rockefeller Center, head here for rectangular Detroit-style pizza slices. *11:30am-7pm Mon-Fri, to 6pm Sat & Sun* **$**

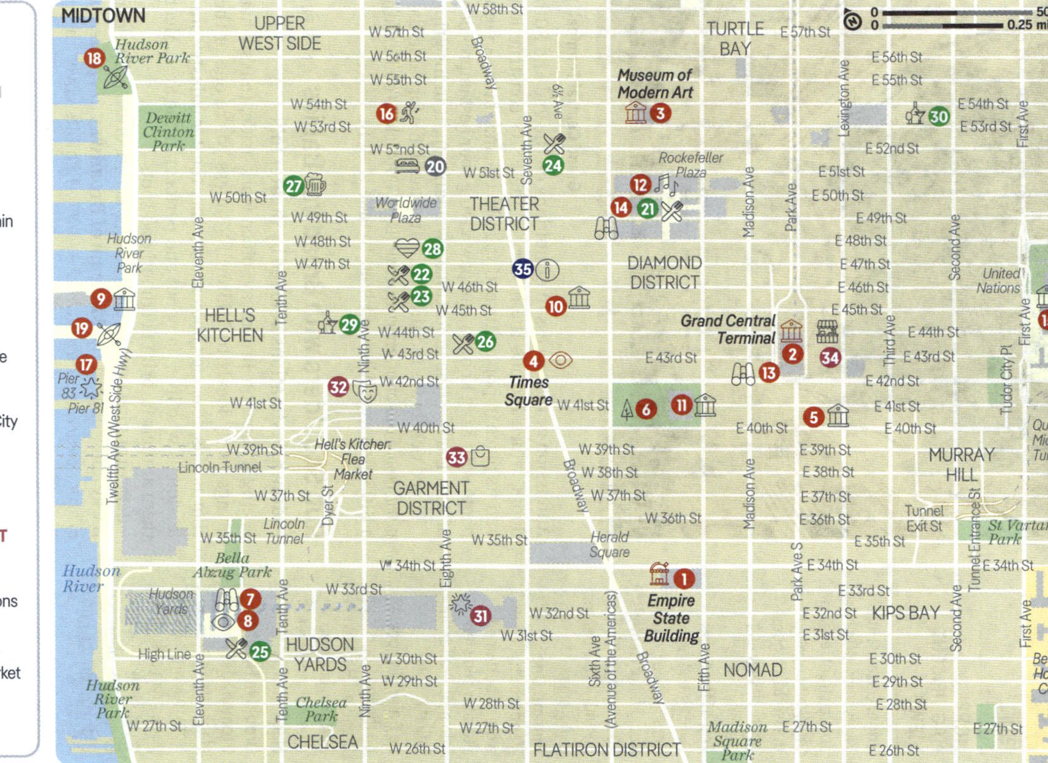

★ **HIGHLIGHTS**
1 Empire State Building
2 Grand Central Terminal
3 Museum of Modern Art
4 Times Square

SIGHTS
5 AKC Museum of the Dog
6 Bryant Park
7 Edge
8 Hudson Yards
9 Intrepid Sea, Air & Space Museum
see 6 Le Carrousel
10 Museum of Broadway
11 New York Public Library
12 Radio City Music Hall
13 Summit One Vanderbilt
14 Top of the Rock
15 United Nations

ACTIVITIES
16 54 Below
17 Circle Line Boat Tours
18 Manhattan Community Boathouse
19 Manhattan Kayak Co

SLEEPING
20 Romer

EATING
21 Ace's Pizza
22 Barbetta
see 6 Bryant Park Grill
see 2 Grand Central Oyster Bar & Restaurant
23 Joe Allen
24 Le Bernardin
25 Mercado Little Spain
26 Sardi's

DRINKING & NIGHTLIFE
27 As Is
see 23 Bar Centrale
see 11 Bryant Park Cafe
see 2 Campbell
28 Dickens
see 2 Grand Central City Winery
see 14 Pebble Bar
29 Rudy's Bar & Grill
30 Tomi Jazz

ENTERTAINMENT
31 Madison Square Garden
32 Playwrights Horizons

SHOPPING
33 Drama Book Shop
34 Grand Central Market

INFORMATION
35 TKTS Booth

MORE MAGNIFICENT VIEWS

Edge: Gaze at Hudson Yards from 100 floors above street level, or test your nerves on the world's highest open-air building ascent.

Top of the Rock: Get a blockbuster perspective from Rockefeller Center's 70th floor, 850ft in the air with a 360-degree panorama.

Summit One Vanderbilt: Ride a glass-bottomed elevator and step into a city-reflecting infinity room.

Le Bain: Sip cocktails on the top floor of the Standard Hotel while partying in a club overlooking lower Manhattan.

Brooklyn Heights Promenade: Wow at Manhattan's skyline from this eight-block pedestrian strip atop the Brooklyn–Queens Expressway near Brooklyn Bridge Park.

TOMML/GETTY IMAGES

Grand Central Terminal

Admission grants access to exhibitions on the 2nd and 80th floors, which include the history of the ESB's construction and its place in pop culture. If you like cinema shtick, snag a photo with King Kong's giant paw, giving your best impression of Ann Darrow (the unfortunate woman caught in his grip).

Timed tickets are required and often available for same-day purchase. Sunset offers exquisite light, but tickets come with a $10 surcharge. Allow an hour to take it all in.

Rub Shoulders with Broadway Babies MAP P81

Midtown destinations beloved by theater folk

Seeing a show on Broadway: office work aside, that's what brings many locals to Midtown – unless you're one of the chorus kids, seasoned hoofers and other theater industry professionals who live, hang out and perform in the area. Meet them at their favorite neighborhood spots.

Before running into the theater cognoscenti, brush up on your B'way knowledge at the **Museum of Broadway** *(themuseumofbroadway.com; adult/child $43/35)*. Exhibits cover three centuries of razzmatazz with artifacts, costumes and props highlighting everything from *Annie* to *Oklahoma* and beyond. Visitors also get a peek behind the curtain with a 1st-floor exhibit showcasing the soup-to-nuts making of a Broadway show.

After learning your Do-Re-Mi, skip to the **Drama Book Shop** *(dramabookshop.com)* – designed by *Hamilton's* scenic designer – to pick up scripts and other theater-related paraphernalia.

When it comes to seeing theater, plenty of non-Broadway stages welcome the industry's biggest names – and you'll likely sit in the audience with local thespians. Off-Broadway company **Playwrights Horizons** *(playwrightshorizons.org)* produces some of New York's most innovative productions, each a celebration of contemporary American writers. Theater fans should also consider a cabaret and dinner at **54 Below** *(54below.org)*, where everyone from Tony Award winners to New York's up-and-coming stars belt the night away.

For a taste of old-school insider Broadway, stop by **Sardi's** *(sardis.com)* – a restaurant with walls covered in caricatures of famous patrons. After curtain call, you might spot actors clinking glasses at **Bar Centrale** *(barcentrale.com)* or **Joe Allen** *(joeallenrestaurant.com)*.

Time Travel at the Museum of Modern Art MAP P81

Admire art-world stars in Midtown

Name a notable artist from the 19th century onward – Van Gogh, Matisse, Picasso, Kahlo, Rothko, Warhol, Bourgeois – and **MoMA** *(moma.org; adult/child $30/free)* probably shows some of their best work among its 200,000-piece collection. For aesthetes, it's an encounter with the sublime; for the uninitiated, a cultural crash course. Attempting to see everything in MoMA's 630,000-sq-ft space could take half a day or more – a surefire way to experience museum fatigue. Instead, go through the collection chronologically, ensuring a glimpse of the big names on display. Pieces rotate through the galleries at least once a year, which means first-timers might miss some famous works, but repeat visitors will get a fresh experience.

Work your way down: floor 5 covers the 1880s–1940s. Count on seeing Van Gogh's swirling *Starry Night*, Monet's Impressionist water lilies and, if you're lucky, Frida Kahlo's gender-bending *Self Portrait with Cropped Hair*. Floor 4 tackles the 1940s–70s, with Jackson Pollock and Andy Warhol leading the charge. Don't miss Faith Ringgold's 1967 response to Picasso's *Guernica* in the shocking *American People Series #20: Die*. On floor 2 (1970s–present), there's Richard Serra's *Equal*, composed of 80-ton steel stacks, and works by NYC painter Jean-Michel Basquiat.

Timed tickets are required to guarantee museum entry; book online in advance.

Slow down at Grand Central Terminal MAP P81

Relive the railroad's golden age

Don't rush through this 1913 beaux-arts station hall like Metro-North's commuters. **Grand Central Terminal** *(grandcentral terminal.com)* evokes the romance of rail travel and it's worth

THEATER TICKET DISCOUNTS

Broadway tickets often have three-digit prices, but there are ways to score fabulous seats at a fraction of the cost. For the most options, visit the Theatre Development Fund's **TKTS Booth** under the red steps in Times Square's Father Duffy Sq, offering up to 50% off same-day shows and next-day matinees (lines can be long). Most shows hold lotteries, allowing select winners to purchase choice seats at bargain prices. Many productions also have rush tickets, slashing seat prices on a first-come, first-served basis – visit *playbill.com* for a show-by-show guide. The TodayTix app *(todaytix.com)* offers discounted pricing in all forms, including digital lotteries – the most convenient way to grab tickets before arriving in NYC. Want to avoid online fees? Purchase tickets directly from the box office.

DRINKING IN MIDTOWN: BEST BARS MAP P81

Pebble Bar: This townhouse bar has done the unthinkable: create a cool cocktail scene in kitschy Rockefeller Center. *4pm-midnight Sun-Wed, to 2am Thu-Sat*

Tomi Jazz: Stumble into this Japanese jazz den after 6pm, when whiskey flows as freely as an improvised sax solo. *5pm-1am Sun-Thu, to 3am Fri & Sat*

As Is: Hell's Kitchen's beer heads agree – this hops den is tops, with 20 beers on tap. *3pm-late Mon-Fri, from noon Sat & Sun*

Dickens: Dine and drink inside this posh four-floor LGBTIQ+ palace, an elevated answer to Hell's Kitchen cramped gay dens. *hours vary*

MIDTOWN TOURS & QUIRKY MUSEUMS

New York Public Library: Visit the magnificent Rose Reading Room to see its celestially painted coffered ceiling on a 15-minute tour.

Radio City Music Hall: Join the 60-minute Stage Door Tour for the inside scoop on the famous performance complex.

Madison Square Garden: Can't make it to a Knicks NBA or Rangers NHL game? Tour the complex instead.

AKC Museum of the Dog: The airy 1st-floor galleries contain paintings of dogs, and an upstairs library carries books on every breed.

United Nations: Go international on a tour through Le Corbusier and Oscar Niemeyer's mid-century masterpiece.

spending at least an hour falling in love with its treasures. Start by strolling across the marble-trimmed concourse to gaze at the vaulted aquamarine ceiling depicting the night sky's constellations. The starry wonder isn't original – it's a 1944 copy covering water damage in the first fresco designed by French painter Paul Cesar Helleu. A 1990s renovation added twinkling lights (part of Helleu's plan) and cleaned the ceiling. Follow Cancer's claws to the northwest corner to a tiny black rectangle: an original patch of soot, approximately 9 by 5 inches, caused by decades of air pollutants. While admiring the work, examine the layout. The zodiac is actually backwards. After its unveiling, railroad officials swatted away critics, saying it was painted from the perspective of God. For more hidden wonders, head to the Whispering Gallery (p247) between the Main Concourse and Vanderbilt Hall, where an acoustic quirk allows people to stand on opposite gallery corners and carry a conversation sotto voce. There's plenty to eat and drink, too – try **Grand Central Market** (fast casual), **Grand Central Oyster Bar & Restaurant** (fine dining), **Grand Central City Winery** and the **Campbell**, which features live jazz on weekend evenings.

Light up at Midnight

MAP P81

Times Square's nightly art show

There isn't a dimmer switch – **Times Square** *(timessquarenyc.org)* perpetually shines. It's a splash of Vegas, a soupçon of Disney and a digital deluge of American commercialism. Love it or loathe it, it's hard not to be mesmerized by the lights – particularly around midnight, when crowds thin out and the blinking billboards momentarily transform from ads into an immersive art experience.

Midnight Moment, the world's largest digital public art program, synchronizes 92 digital displays between 41st and 49th St for a three-minute, immersive contemporary art spectacle starting at 11:57pm. Works change monthly, featuring well-known names like Andy Warhol and contemporary boundary-breakers in the digital-art ecosystem. For the most mesmerizing view, climb the 27 red steps above the TKTS Booth at 47th St and watch art appear all around.

End the light show with a nightcap – perhaps a $4 draught from **Rudy's Bar & Grill** *(rudysbarnyc.com)* or a fancy cocktail from Pebble Bar (p83), both within walking distance.

Take a Break in Bryant Park

MAP P81

Eat, shop, skate and stroll

European coffee kiosks, alfresco chess games and outdoor events for the whole family make leafy, Parisian-style **Bryant Park** *(bryantpark.org)* a whimsical break from Midtown's mayhem. Office workers stream in at lunchtime, competing for tables with skyscraper views. There's also **Bryant Park Grill**, with a patio ideal for twilight cocktails, and neighboring **Bryant Park Cafe**, an alfresco hangout from mid-April

UPPER WEST SIDE & UPPER EAST SIDE

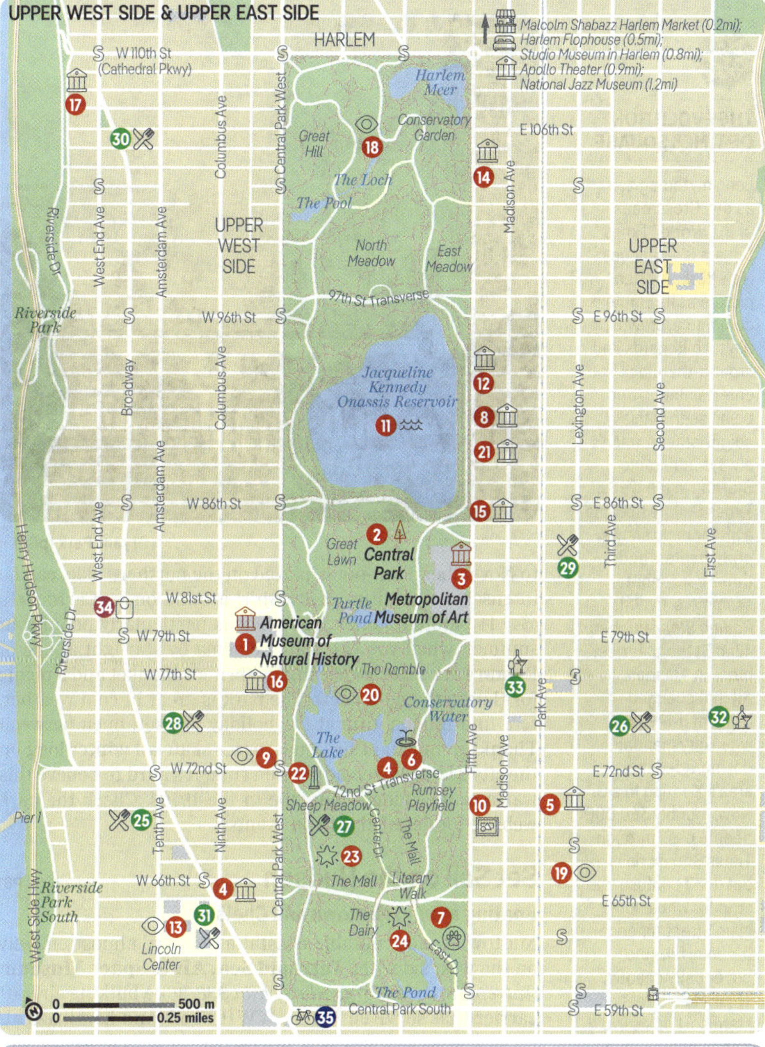

★ **HIGHLIGHTS**
1 American Museum of Natural History
2 Central Park
3 Metropolitan Museum of Art

● **SIGHTS**
4 American Folk Art Museum
5 Asia Society & Museum
6 Bethesda Fountain
7 Central Park Zoo
8 Cooper-Hewitt Smithsonian Design Museum
9 Dakota Building
10 Frick Collection
11 Jacqueline Kennedy Onassis Reservoir
12 Jewish Museum
13 Lincoln Center
14 Museum of the City of New York
15 Neue Galerie
16 New-York Historical Society
17 Nicholas Roerich Museum
18 North Woods
19 Park Avenue Armory
20 Ramble
21 Solomon R Guggenheim Museum
22 Strawberry Fields

● **ACTIVITIES**
23 Sheep Meadow
24 Wollman Skating Rink

● **EATING**
25 Cafe Luxembourg
see 15 Café Sabarsky
26 JG Melon
27 Le Pain Quotidien
28 Levain
29 Lexington Candy Shop
30 Mama's TOO!
31 Tatiana

● **DRINKING & NIGHTLIFE**
32 2nd Floor Bar & Essen
33 Bemelmans Bar

● **SHOPPING**
34 Zabar's

● **TRANSPORT**
35 Central Park Bike Tours

THE EVOLUTION OF TIMES SQUARE

Long mythologized as the 'Crossroads of the World,' Times Square is what non-New Yorkers often picture as its emblem: commerce, crowds, digital billboards and around-the-clock entertainment. But being seen in this neighborhood wasn't always admirable. Starting in the 1960s, Times Square became a pit for peep shows, porn theaters and three-card-monte scammers. In 1981, *Rolling Stone* dubbed 42nd St the 'sleaziest block in America.' All that changed in the mid-1990s when city mandates downgraded the area's X-rating to a G. Now, roughly 360,000 people pass through Times Square daily – but don't confuse this strip for wholesome Main Street America. It's colorful, sure, but equally chaotic. Think Main Street on steroids. Locals avoid it at all costs.

LANAG/SHUTTERSTOCK

Bryant Park (p84)

to November. Ping-pong, played on the northern side, can be intensely competitive. Kids whirl around on Le Carrousel's *($4)* 14 painted ponies. The scene is particularly popular in summer, when you can watch cinema by starlight at one of Bryant Park's free movie nights (bring a blanket and a picnic for thorough enjoyment). The park is great in cold weather, too: find unique gifts at the holiday market, open between Thanksgiving and Christmas, or ice skate all winter long on the city's largest free-admission rink. It's hard to believe this was a crime-ridden hellscape in the 1970s. Check the park website for detailed info on events.

Set Sail on the Hudson

MAP P81

Boating around Midtown and Chelsea

Midtown's most notable coastal assets are almost entirely on the west side. The **Intrepid Sea, Air & Space Museum** *(intrepidmuseum.org; adult/child $38/28),* a hulking aircraft carrier that survived both a WWII bomb and kamikaze attacks, houses an impressive interactive military museum with videos, historical artifacts and frozen-in-time living quarters. The flight deck features fighter planes and military helicopters, which might inspire you to try the museum's high-tech flight simulators. On a pier just to the Intrepid's south, board a Circle Line tour for a floating perspective of the city's profile. The 90-minute Landmarks cruise *(circleline.com; from $43)* is essential for New Yorkers eager to see the skyline from afar. Next door to Circle Line, on Pier 94 (at 44th St), **Manhattan Kayak Co** *(manhattankayak.com; rentals $12)* offers a variety of kayaking and stand-up paddleboarding classes and tours. To try out kayaking on the Hudson for free, in a more limited area, head north to Pier 96 (at 55th St) and the **Manhattan Community Boathouse** *(hudsonriverpark.org).*

There's also an exceptional architecture tour run by Classic Harbor Line, which teams up with the American Institute of Architects for a fun, informative, three-hour cruise aboard a 1920s-style commuter yacht that circumnavigates Manhattan *(sail-nyc.com; adult/student $112/88)*. Expert guides narrate tales about riverfront towers while motoring underneath bridges and circling the Statue of Liberty. Tickets include a complimentary drink. Boats depart from **Chelsea Piers**.

Visit Austria at the Neue Galerie

MAP P85

Art and food with Viennese flair

Austrian and German art from 1890–1940 take center stage inside this Upper East Side **mansion** *(neuegalerie.org; adult/student $28/15)* from 1914 designed by Carrère and Hastings (the architects behind the New York Public Library and the Frick). The museum's most prized collection is a series of sketches and paintings by Gustav Klimt, including his gold-flecked 1907 *Portrait of Adele Bloch-Bauer 1,* acquired for a cool $135 million by cosmetics magnate and museum founder Ronald Lauder. (The 2015 film *Woman in Gold* recounts the painting's fascinating history, which includes looting Nazis, a feisty Bloch-Bauer heir and the obstinate Austrian government.) A connected bookstore is a museum unto itself, decorated with artist monographs and coffee-table books.

For an immersive Austrian experience, reserve a table at Vienna-style **Café Sabarsky**. With dishes such as goulash soup, roasted bratwurst and *topfentorte* (quark cheesecake), you might mistake the Upper East Side for Europe's Eastern Alps.

Cover Centuries of NYC History

MAP P85

Museum dedicated to local stories

The **Museum of the City of New York** *(mcny.org; adult/child $23/free),* housed in a Georgian Colonial Revival–style building near the top of Central Park, artfully illustrates the past, present and future of this ever-evolving city. At a minimum, spare 28 minutes to watch *Timescapes,* a multiscreen documentary that chronicles NYC's past 400 years from tiny Dutch trading center to international powerhouse. Other permanent exhibits explore centuries of social activism and feature notable New Yorkers such as poet Walt Whitman and urbanist Jane Jacobs.

MORE MAGNIFICENT UES MUSEUMS

Solomon R Guggenheim Museum: Architect Frank Lloyd Wright's iconic inverted ziggurat spirals up from Fifth Ave.

Cooper-Hewitt Smithsonian Design Museum: Andrew Carnegie's 64-room Georgian mansion devotes itself to historical and contemporary interior design.

Jewish Museum: Housed in a 1908 French Gothic chateau, this 30,000-piece collection spans 4000 years of Jewish culture.

Park Avenue Armory: This Gothic Revival behemoth features a 55,000-sq-ft performance space, plus designs by the likes of Stanford White.

Asia Society & Museum: One of America's preeminent institutions for pan-Asian art: Chola-period Indian bronzes, modern Japanese paintings etc.

EATING & DRINKING ON THE UES: OUR PICKS

MAP P85

JG Melon: No-frills, cash-only pub serving one of NYC's best burgers since 1972. Wash it down with a beefy Bloody Mary. *11:30am-3am* $

Lexington Candy Shop: Order an egg cream at New York's oldest family-run luncheonette, serving diner delights since 1925. *7am-6pm Mon-Fri, 8am-6pm Sat, to 4pm Sun* $

Bemelmans Bar: Sip Manhattans and admire murals by *Madeleine* illustrator Ludwig Bemelmans as pianists tinkle the ivories. *hours vary*

2nd Floor Bar & Essen: Down creative drinks and shtetl-style bar bites in this speakeasy-esque hangout above a kosher deli. *5pm-midnight Tue-Thu, to 2am Fri & Sat*

BRESTER IRINA/SHUTTERSTOCK

TOP EXPERIENCE

Metropolitan Museum of Art

This stately, two-million-sq-ft museum, founded in 1870, is an encyclopedic bastion of world-class art, celebrating 5000 years of human creativity. The Met's one-million-plus objects cover all corners of the globe with artifacts, paintings, sculptures, textiles and even an Egyptian tomb guarded by a moat. It's the Western Hemisphere's largest museum, overflowing with must-see treasures. Dive in.

DON'T MISS

- Temple of Dendur
- Leon Levy and Shelby White Roman Sculpture Court
- Van Gogh's *White Field with Cypresses*
- Damascus Room
- Leutze's *Washington Crossing the Delaware*
- Charles Engelhard Court
- Benton's *America Today*
- Cantor Rooftop Garden Bar

Egyptian Art

Time-travel through Egypt's history in 39 galleries covering the Paleolithic to Roman eras (c 300,000 BCE to 400 CE). Start at the **Tomb of Perneb**, a limestone burial chamber with intricately painted reliefs (Gallery 100). Next, after walking past pyramid pieces and funerary statues, pause at Gallery 136's mysterious *Fragment of a Queen's Face* (c 1390–1336 BCE) to appreciate the sculptor's laser-like precision. If you only see one thing, make it the **Temple of Dendur** (Gallery 131). This is the Western Hemisphere's only complete Egyptian temple, built over 2000 years ago on the banks of the Nile.

PRACTICALITIES

- metmuseum.org
- adult/student $30/17
- 10am-5pm Sun-Tue & Thu, to 9pm Fri & Sat

Greek & Roman Art

With more than 30,000 individual pieces, this is North America's most comprehensive assemblage of toga-wearing trophies. Start south of the **Great Hall** to gape at chiseled gods preening under a vaulted beaux-arts ceiling. All this eye candy might inspire staying put, but even greater treasures await in the sunlit **Leon Levy and Shelby White Roman Sculpture Court** (Gallery 162). Bonus points for spotting the headless **Three Graces** of Greek mythology – Beauty, Mirth and Abundance.

European Paintings

From Giotto to Gauguin, the Met has it all: religious iconography from the 13th century, every Dutch master you can name and a sweeping selection of 19th-century French Impressionists. Unlike *Starry Night* at MoMA (p83), you won't contend with crowds to see Vincent van Gogh's paintings here. Stand before his *White Field with Cypresses* (Gallery 822) to imagine a blustery day in Saint-Rémy-de-Provence. Don't leave without viewing self-taught artist Henri Rousseau's *The Repast of the Lion* (Gallery 825).

Islamic Art

Objects sacred and secular fill these 15 galleries dedicated to the Arabian Peninsula, Turkey, and Central and South Asia. The glazed-tile **mihrab** (prayer niche; Gallery 455) is a vision in blue, framed by the five pillars of Islam, written in Kufic. If you're a fan of interiors, stop by Gallery 461 to wow over gold-leaf embellishments in the 18th-century **Damascus Room**.

American Wing

This two-floor collection in the museum's northwest corner covers everything from colonial times to the early 20th century, including Emanuel Luetze's iconic *Washington Crossing the Delaware*, which looms large over Gallery 760. If you need a pick-me-up, stop by the American Wing Cafe in the **Charles Engelhard Court** – a glass garden filled with American-made sculptures and framed by a marble facade that once graced Wall St. Visit on Friday or Saturday for Date Night (5pm to 9pm), when live music sets a romantic scene.

Modern & Contemporary Art

Georgia O'Keeffe, Edward Hopper, Pollock, Dalí – the museum's southwestern corner is a who's who of art-world titans from the late 19th century onward. Particularly impressive is Thomas Hart Benton's *America Today* (Gallery 909), a room-sized mural depicting the US at the Great Depression's onset.

Special Events at the Met

Visit on Friday or Saturday evening, when the museum stays open until 9pm and live music drifts through the halls. Enjoy the aural art with drinks at the American Wing Cafe or Petrie Court Cafe. If you're here in summer, see the Costume Institute's spring fashion exhibit, following the annual celebrity-studded Met Gala – always a hit.

AN ANCIENT EMBLEM

Stop by Gallery 136 to meet William, a blue faience hippopotamus with an essential museum job: mascot. Discovered in an Egyptian tomb in 1910 and acquired by the Met in 1917, the hippo quickly became the museum's quirky frontman, earning his name from a British humor magazine. Ancient Egyptians feared the aggressive hippo, but here, little Billy is cute as a button.

TOP TIPS

- Beat the Great Hall's snaking ticket line by entering at 81st St.
- Don't try to see everything in one visit. Pick a few galleries or a handful of pieces and immerse yourself.
- Upon entering, join the virtual queue via QR code for temporary exhibits. These artist retrospectives and cultural deep-dives are often some of the city's most fantastic museum shows.
- Stream the Met's free audio guide, which includes a Highlights Tour – an exceptional resource available on your smartphone. Visit *metmuseum.org/audio-guide*.
- Docents offer free guided tours of specific galleries. Check the website or at the information desk for details.

GET CULTURED ON THE UPPER WEST SIDE

Lincoln Center: This travertine complex is home to renowned performance venues such as the Metropolitan Opera and New York City Ballet.

Nicholas Roerich Museum: A townhouse turned art temple featuring rich Tibetan landscape paintings by Russian-born Roerich (1874–1947).

Zabar's: Cheese, meats and freshly baked knishes: a bastion of gourmet kosher foodie-ism since 1934.

New-York Historical Society: NYC's oldest museum (1804) showcases 60,000-plus quirky and fascinating objects.

American Folk Art Museum: Kaleidoscopic quilts, hand-carved decoy ducks and other art celebrates homegrown, self-taught makers.

Step Inside a Gilded Age Jewel Box

MAP P85

Fantastic art at the Frick

When industrialist Henry Clay Frick made plans to build an Indiana limestone mansion along Fifth Ave in the early 20th century, he intended to turn it into a museum after his death. You'll be glad he made good on his promise. Walk through the **Frick Collection's** palatial rooms *(frick.org; $30, no under 10s)*, fresh off a $220-million makeover completed in 2025, to find gilt-framed masterpieces by Western European artists like Bellini, Goya, Rembrandt, Turner and Vermeer. Unlike the Met's massive collection, this is the kind of place you can zoom around in an hour, before Gilded Age envy sets in.

Geek out over Bones & Bugs

MAP P85

American Museum of Natural History

You could spend a lifetime (or at least a couple of hours) exploring this **cutting-edge science center** *(amnh.org; adult/child $25/14)* and can't-miss hit for kids. From the main entrance on Central Park West, enter the soaring Theodore Roosevelt Rotunda to spot skeletons of a barosaurus and allosaurus frozen in combat. The astounding Milstein Family Hall of Ocean Life contains interactive lessons about marine food chains – all under a suspended, 94ft-long replica of a blue whale. Budding entomologists should make a beeline for the David Family Butterfly Vivarium in the new Gilder Center, where fluttering specimens land on outstretched arms. Armchair astronauts will appreciate the Rose Center for Earth & Space, its spherical theater transporting visitors to faraway galaxies. And don't forget the hundreds of dinosaur fossils – they're on the top floor.

Feel the Pulse of Harlem's Soul

MAP P85

Highlights of the Harlem Renaissance and beyond

Ever since the Harlem Renaissance jazzed up New York in the early 20th century, Harlem has been a cradle of Black culture, birthing talents and trends with global appeal. This is where Billie Holiday crooned, where Romare Bearden pieced together collages and where Langston Hughes penned his explosive poetry. Walk these streets and hear them sing.

In the 1920s, the rhythmic baton of Duke Ellington led Harlem's Jazz Age jamboree. Pay your respects to the big-band maestro at the tiny **National Jazz Museum** *(jmih.org; free)*

EATING ON THE UWS: OUR PICKS

MAP P85

Levain: The original location of this cookie chain remains its most charming. Each dough ball is a 6oz lesson in decadence. Get the chocolate-chip walnut. *8am-8pm* **$**

Mama's TOO!: You'll understand why people crowd outside this bite-sized pizza shop after tearing into the Angry Nonna (a square slab of hot honey-drizzled pepperoni). *noon-11pm* **$**

Tatiana: Good luck getting a table at this Afro-Caribbean-inspired restaurant in David Geffen Hall, featured on nearly every NYC 'best' list. *5-10pm Mon-Sat* **$$$**

Cafe Luxembourg: Upper-crust locals have been knocking back cocktails and nibbling steak tartare at this French bistro since the 1980s. *hours vary* **$$$**

MARIS PUKITIS/SHUTTERSTOCK

American Museum of Natural History

– a one-room, Smithsonian-affiliated love letter to improvisational tunes. Ellington's cream-white baby grand piano sits up front.

Harlem's heart beats loudest on 125th St, home to the **Apollo Theater**, where Ella Fitzgerald got her start. Skip the live performances – you're here instead for the **Studio Museum in Harlem** *(studiomuseum.org; free)*. This incubator for promising artists of African descent is set to unveil a new five-story building in late 2025. Come here to spot the art world's next big thing.

End your Harlem tour by trawling **Malcolm Shabazz Harlem Market** on 116th St for its colorful African goods. Textiles, jewelry and musical instruments represent countries like Nigeria, Kenya and Ghana. The canopied bazaar is the heart of Little (or 'Le Petit') Senegal – home to scores of francophone immigrants who began building a community here around the 1980s.

Spend an Afternoon on Brooklyn's Waterfront

MAP P94

See NYC from Brooklyn Bridge Park

Jaw-dropping views and recreational activities, plus restaurants, stores and performance spaces: **Brooklyn Bridge Park** *(brooklynbridgepark.org)* is a one-stop shop for urban leisure. Devote a few hours to this 85-acre green space hugging the East River.

For a breezy introduction to Brooklyn's historic waterfront, hop on a Manhattan ferry *(ferry.nyc; $4.50)* at Midtown's 34th St or Fidi's Pier 11, sailing across the river like writer Walt Whitman in the 19th century. You'll land at **Fulton Ferry Landing**, where lines from his 1856 poem 'Crossing the Brooklyn Ferry' are engraved on the guard rails.

(continues on p95)

NEIGHBORHOOD BODEGAS

Some call them delis. Others call them convenience stores. If you're a New Yorker, the proper term is 'bodega' – an embodiment of the 'city never sleeps,' often open 24/7. A bodega is technically a store with no more than two cash registers that sells milk and mostly food – and isn't a specialty store, like a butcher. At their core, these corner shops are more like neighborhood lifelines for groceries, beer, cleaning supplies, lottery tickets, ATMs and the beloved BEC (bacon, egg and cheese). Bodegas first appeared in the early 20th century, opened by Puerto Rican and Cuban immigrants to serve their communities. Now, there are roughly 13,000 around town, mainly run by Dominican, Mexican, Yemeni and East Asian immigrants – and occasionally guarded by a resident 'bodega cat.'

FRANCESCO BONINO/SHUTTERSTOCK

Bethesda Fountain

TOP EXPERIENCE

Central Park

With 843 acres of meadows, ponds and woodlands, Central Park seems like Manhattan in its raw state. But every inch was built by human hands. And thank goodness it was: the majestic merger of nature and art provides a welcome respite from urban jungle living. Spend half a day getting lost on its curving pathways – deliberately designed as a break from Manhattan's grid.

DON'T MISS

- Central Park Zoo
- Sheep Meadow
- Strawberry Fields
- Bethesda Fountain
- Ramble
- Jacqueline Kennedy Onassis Reservoir
- North Woods
- Central Park Conservancy's guided tours

A Grand Project

In the early 1850s, this area of Manhattan was occupied by pig farms, a garbage dump, a bone-boiling operation and Seneca Village, the largest community of African American property owners in pre–Civil War New York. All that changed in 1858, when plans created by landscape designer Frederick Law Olmstead and architect Calvert Vaux began taking shape. Today, this people's park has over 18,000 trees, 136 acres of woodland, 21 playgrounds, seven bodies of water and more than 40 million visitors a year.

PRACTICALITIES

- centralparknyc.org
- free
- 6am-1am

Tour the South End

Most visitors enter Central Park from its southern edge at W 59th St. Walk along the **pond** at the southeast corner to spot ducks and geese flapping in the blue. In winter, crowds ice skate at **Wollman Skating Rink**, where Midtown's soaring skyscrapers provide a dramatic backdrop.

Continue northeast to the small but mighty **Central Park Zoo** *(adult/child $22.95/16.95)*, near E 64th St, the pavilions of which house penguins, grizzly bears, tropical birds and even a snow leopard. Kids (and most adults) will love petting goats in the children's area and watching sea lions sing for their supper.

Perhaps most popular in this part of the park is **Sheep Meadow** (near W 67th St), a 15-acre lawn where thousands picnic, toss Frisbees and bare their skin in summer. Spending a few hours people-watching here is a quintessential city experience.

A skip north is **Strawberry Fields** (near W 72nd St), a tear-shaped garden and moving memorial for John Lennon, assassinated in front of his home at the **Dakota** in 1980. It contains a grove of stately elms and a tiled mosaic that says simply, 'Imagine.'

Amble around Mid Park

Work your way east to **Bethesda Fountain**, then cross picture-perfect **Bow Bridge** to enter one of the park's most transporting sections. The **Ramble**, a 36-acre forest, features waterfalls, rocky outcroppings and unpaved paths through thickets of trees. Don't be surprised to see people pointing binoculars at nearby branches: this is a beloved birding destination. Central Park, located along the Atlantic Flyway (an important route for migrating birds), acts as a resting pad for weary winged travelers. Twitchers can spot more than 200 avian species resting among the leaves in spring and autumn.
Continue north and you'll arrive at the **Jacqueline Kennedy Onassis Reservoir**, stretching between 86th and 96th Sts. The 6.1-mile gravel path along its perimeter is the domain of runners, who navigate the loop in a strictly clockwise direction. Exercise deference if you walk the loop to snap a pic of skyscrapers reflected on the water's glassy surface.

Wind through the North End

Crowds thin out as you head uptown, making a wander through the **North Woods** particularly magical. This 40-acre arcadia on the upper reaches of Central Park feels more like the Adirondacks than the heart of Manhattan. Amble along the waterfall-linked **loch**, a gentle tree-hugged stream (accessible via the Glen Span Arch near W 103rd St), to spot scampering chipmunks and the occasional raccoon. If you wander deep enough, skyscrapers disappear and traffic becomes but a murmur.

EXPERT GUIDES

If navigating the park alone seems Sisyphean, join a tour led by the **Central Park Conservancy** *(centralparknyc.org; adult/child $33/ free)*. Guided walks cover everything from woodland ecology to little-known park histories and iconic landmarks. Most tours (aside from low-cost, family-geared offerings) start around 10am and last roughly 1½ hours. Check the website for schedules; advanced booking is required.

TOP TIPS

- Speed through the park by cycling its 6.1-mile loop. For rentals, try **Central Park Bike Tours** *(centralparkbiketours.com; from $17)*. There's also **Citi Bike**, though the docking system makes it difficult to park and explore.
- If you didn't pack a picnic, dine alfresco near Sheep Meadow at casual **Le Pain Quotidien** *(lepainquotidien.com)*, or stop by a food cart for snacks and drinks (be prepared with cash).
- Turned around? Check the numbers at the base of park lamp posts. The first two digits indicate nearby cross streets; the second two note if you're east or west (even numbers mean you're on the park's east side).

HIGHLIGHTS
1 Brooklyn Bridge Park
2 Coney Island

SIGHTS
3 Avant Gardner
4 Brooklyn Heights Promenade
5 City Reliquary
6 Deno's Wonder Wheel Park
7 Elsewhere
8 Empire Stores
9 Jane's Carousel

SLEEPING
10 Pod Brooklyn
11 Wythe Hotel

EATING
12 Bonnie's
13 Fornino at Pier 6
14 Laser Wolf
15 Lilia
16 Nathan's Famous
17 Smorgasburg

DRINKING & NIGHTLIFE
18 18th Ward Brewing
19 3 Dollar Bill
20 Brooklyn Brewery
21 Grimm Artisanal Ales
22 House of Yes
23 Long Island Bar
24 Maison Premiere
25 Mood Ring
26 Pilot
27 SEY Coffee
28 Talea

ENTERTAINMENT
29 Luna Park
30 Mermaid Parade

SHOPPING
31 Quimby's Bookstore NYC

TRANSPORT
32 Fulton Ferry Landing

(continued from p91)

Like so much of NYC, this landscape differs greatly from the time when Whitman wrote '...Brooklyn of ample hills was mine.' In the following decades, the Brooklyn and Manhattan Bridges became Big Apple landmarks. Red-brick buildings shot up along the waterfront, home to companies that manufactured goods such as cardboard boxes and Brillo pads. Commercial production didn't last long: by the 1970s, businesses left and the waterfront became a wasteland. Industrial facades, cobblestone streets and antique railroad tracks remain today, but the waterfront is otherwise transformed in a triumph of urban renewal.

Venture north of Fulton Ferry to soak in an East River panorama. For 360-degree views, spin around **Jane's Carousel** *(janescarousel.com; $3)*, a vintage 1922 treasure housed in a Pritzker Prize–winning acrylic box. Behind the carousel is **Empire Stores**, which houses the **Time Out Market** *(timeout.com)*, a collection of bustling food stalls and bars, plus a selection of retail chains.

Crowds thin out south of Fulton Ferry. If you're willing to hoof it, stop by Pier 6 for alfresco eating options, including **Fornino** (unfussy wood-fired pizza; *fornino.com*) and **Pilot** (oysters and cocktails on a wooden schooner; *crew.fun/pilot; May-Oct*).

Feast Your Eyes on Quirky Relics

MAP P94

Williamsburg's kooky mini-museum

Walk through an antique subway turnstile into **City Reliquary** *(cityreliquary.org; adult/child $10/free)*, a tiny museum dedicated to Big Apple ephemera. The three-room collection contains an oddball mix of memorabilia: Lady Liberty figurines, Second Ave Deli signage and a shrine honoring Brooklyn Dodgers star Jackie Robinson. Seeing the jam-packed space takes 20 to 30 minutes tops – a bit steep at the ticket price, but worth it if you like marching to the offbeat. Check its online events calendar to catch occasional readings, burlesque shows and junk craft classes in the art-filled backyard.

Sip Craft Beer at Brooklyn Breweries

MAP P94

Williamsburg tap tour

When it comes to craft chemistry, Brooklyn is NYC's go-to scientist. Over a dozen breweries cater to all tastes, whether you prefer floral IPAs or tart goses. Spend a night hopping between Williamsburg and Bushwick to see which hops you like best.

THE BEST NIGHTLIFE VENUES IN BROOKLYN & QUEENS

Elsewhere: Rap, rock and rave music are just a few styles you'll hear inside this furniture factory turned concert venue in East Williamsburg.

Avant Gardner: Dust off your dance shoes before seeing a show at East Williamsburg's 80,000-sq-ft EDM palace.

3 Dollar Bill: Brooklyn's biggest queer bar packs its 10,000-sq-ft space with fantastic performances and a colorful crowd.

Nowadays: Transcendental tunes fly through the air during Mister Sunday, a May-to-October alfresco dance party beloved by techno heads.

House of Yes: Burlesque performers, drag artists and circus acts set the stage at this all-inclusive warehouse club.

DRINKING IN BROOKLYN: BEST BARS & CAFES

MAP P94

Maison Premiere: Visiting the green fairy at this absinthe-forward oyster-and-cocktail bar is like traveling to 19th-century New Orleans. *2pm-1am Mon-Fri, from noon Sat & Sun*

Mood Ring: Tattooed 20-somethings with a zeal for the zodiac get sweaty at this ultra-inclusive astrology-themed club. *6pm-2am Sun-Wed, to 3am Thu, to 4am Fri & Sat*

Long Island Bar: This retro 1951 juice joint is always abuzz with cool-cat clientele, sipping cocktails crafted by Cosmo inventor Toby Cecchini. *5pm-midnight Tue-Fri, from 2pm Sat & Sun*

SEY Coffee: A mad-scientist attention to detail ensures this Nordic-style coffee roaster produces impeccable brews. *7am-5pm Mon-Fri, from 8am Sat & Sun*

BROOKLYN'S HEADY HISTORY

Brooklyn is no stranger to beer. As German immigrants flooded New York in the 19th century, breweries sprang up around the borough, turning Kings County into Lager Elysium. By the turn of the 20th century, Brooklyn was home to nearly 50 breweries, and a 12-block stretch linking Williamsburg and Bushhwick earned the nickname 'Brewer's Row' thanks to its near-dozen suds-focused establishments. But as the decades marched on, business dried up. By 1976, all of Brooklyn's beer makers were gone. It took more than a decade to turn the tap back on and now Brooklyn is once again the leader of NYC's pint-sized revolution. In addition to Williamsburg, the Gowanus neighborhood is known for producing exceptional brews inside industrial spaces. Sop up the scene at **Threes Brewing** *(threesbrewing.com)*.

SWELLEN AZEVEDO/GETTY IMAGES

Begin at **Brooklyn Brewery** *(brooklynbrewery.com)* – the granddad of Brooklyn's contemporary beer boom, open since 1996. Soak up suds in the taproom or book a guided tasting *($32.66)* – reserve your spot online. Next up is **Talea** *(taleabeer.com)* – New York's first women-owned brewery. Head to the original Williamsburg location to try fruit-forward beers in the pastel-tiled interior. **18th Ward Brewing** *(18thwardbrewing.com)* gets pretty packed whenever there's a concert at nearby Brooklyn Steel, but it's worth wading through the crowds to sample easy-drinking ales. End with bold flavors from **Grimm Artisanal Ales** *(grimmales.com)*. It's nearly impossible to decide between the experimental IPAs, barrel-aged sours and chocolatey lagers. Order a flight to sample them all, best enjoyed on the rooftop terrace.

Get Topsy Turvy at Coney Island

MAP P94

Amusement rides on Brooklyn's 'riviera'

Tattooed mermaids, vintage roller coasters and greasy-food stands await at this gritty-glamorous escape along the Brooklyn waterfront. A one-hour trip from Midtown, **Coney Island** became a democratized day-tripper destination in turn-of-the-20th-century New York, promising sugar-sand beaches and cotton-candy clouds. Spend half a day admiring its charms.

The official season for this summer escape is Memorial Day to Labor Day, when you can expect big weekend crowds. Start by skipping down **Riegelmann Boardwalk**, a 2.5-mile waterfront promenade from 1923, to pass a sea of colorful characters, along with whirling carnival rides.

Riegelmann Boardwalk

Fancy getting flung into the air at 90mph? The Sling Shot awaits at **Luna Park** *(lunaparknyc.com; day pass from $48.60 or pay per ride $10)*. Perhaps the 56mph race around the 2233ft-long Thunderbolt is more your speed. Or you can go old-school – New Yorkers started shrieking down the wooden Cyclone's 85ft plunge in 1927, and the drop still thrills riders.

At **Deno's Wonder Wheel Park** *(denoswonderwheel.com; pay per ride)*, you can hop on the Wonder Wheel (*$10*). Around since 1920, Coney Island's oldest ride is also its most romantic: sweeping views from 150ft above ground are bound to make your heart pitter-pat.

If your stomach survives the thrills and spills, get a taste of tradition by biting into one of **Nathan's Famous** hotdogs at the flagship location on Surf and Stillwell *(nathansfamous.com)*. The beefy frank, snuggled in a toasted bun, has been a Coney classic since 1916.

WACKY & WONDERFUL FESTIVALS & EVENTS

Mermaid Parade: Artsy, eclectic crowds don nautical costumes to flip their fins down Surf Ave on Coney Island for June's summer solstice.

NYC Pride March: All of June is a rainbow-splashed extravaganza, culminating in one of the world's largest LGBTIQ+ celebrations.

Village Halloween Parade: Thousands of outlandishly costumed ghouls stalk Sixth Ave during this spooky street fest on October 31.

Macy's Thanksgiving Day Parade: Massive helium-filled balloons float above high-kicking Rockettes and adoring throngs in November.

New Year's Eve: An army of merrymakers descend on Times Square to ring in the new year and see the iconic ball drop.

EATING IN WILLIAMSBURG: OUR PICKS

MAP P94

Lilia: This pasta restaurant in a former auto shop cranks out some of the best noodles in town. Getting reservations is notoriously tough. *4-10pm* **$$$**

Laser Wolf: Everything here is a feast: mezze appetizers, Israeli-style skewers and views of Manhattan from the Hoxton Hotel's terrace. *5-11pm Sun-Wed, to 1am Thu-Sat* **$$$**

Bonnie's: A Cantonese-American marriage of flavors, plus a rowdy wedding-party-style scene, especially if you're drinking the Long Island iced tea pot with eight servings. *5-10pm* **$$**

Smorgasburg: Every Saturday from April to October, foodies file into Marsha P Johnson State Park to sample hand-held treats at this open-air culinary bazaar. *11am-6pm* **$$**

New York State

CULTURED ENCLAVES | FARMSTEADS | FORESTS

Places

Long Island p98
Hudson Valley p104
The Catskills p108
The Adirondacks p109
Finger Lakes p113
Letchworth State Park p115
Buffalo p116
Niagara Falls p118

GETTING AROUND

New York spans 54,554 sq miles. While buses and trains travel across large swaths of the state, covering a land mass this size requires a car. Renting wheels is cheaper outside NYC; take a train elsewhere to pick up a vehicle.

New York is more than its eponymous metropole. NYC accounts for 40% of the state's population, but it covers less than 1% of its area. Over half the state is blanketed in forests – a leafy universe lit by constellations of tiny towns, midsize cities and 180 state parks.

NYC residents consider anything north of NYC 'upstate' – a distinction hotly contested by everyone else. Follow the Hudson River north for the Hudson Valley, a network of arty towns and rural farmland. The Catskill Mountains rise west, with eccentric communities of outdoor enthusiasts. Jet northeast to the Hudson's source to reach the Adirondacks, home of the largest publicly protected park in the contiguous United States. Central New York sparkles with the Finger Lakes. Western New York draws crowds thanks to Niagara Falls, next to Buffalo, undergoing a Rust Belt revival. Downstate and east of NYC is Long Island, where suburban sprawl gives way to ritzy summer escapes lapped by the Atlantic.

Long Island

MAP P102

Views from Montauk Point Lighthouse

New York's **first lighthouse** *(montaukhistoricalsociety.org; adult/child $15/5)* is the exclamation point on Long's Island's eastern edge, standing 110ft above the sea-battered coast since 1796. Originally commissioned by President George Washington to warn sailors of the rocks below, it's now the photogenic heart of **Montauk Point State Park** *(parks.ny.gov; summer car fee $8)*, an 862-acre expanse of wooded trails and bluff-backed beaches. A small museum, located in the keepers' house from 1860, provides historical insight, and climbing the tower's 137 iron steps leads to 360-degree views. Stop by around sunrise or sunset (outside of museum hours) when the candy-colored tower gets painted burnt sienna by the light. For exquisite views from afar, head to **Camp Hero State Park** *(parks.ny.gov; summer car fee $8)* and hike east

ALWAYSSUNNYALWAYSREAL/SHUTTERSTOCK

Montauk Point Lighthouse

along the seaside bluffs – the lighthouse shines as a distant maritime beacon.

Surf with Montauk's pros

Montauk is the holy land of East Coast surfing, and catching waves at **Ditch Plains Beach** is akin to attending church. Unlike typical Atlantic Ocean waves that break quickly over sandy shores, Ditch Plains waves cascade over cobblestones, offering surfers minute-long rides to fine-tune their surfing skills. Seasonal variations add to the allure: summer brings gentle waves, while fall and winter unveil majestic swells fit for serious board disciples. There's a blend of clean and consistent surf, making it paradise for both beginners and experts. As a result, Montauk teems with seasoned surfers – and knowledgeable teachers – who genuflect before their boards year-round.

If you're eager to join this spiritual communion, **Sunset Surf Shack** *(sunsetsurfshack.com; from $100)* offers hour-long lessons complete with wetsuit, surfboard and instructor. Bring a towel, some water and a can-do attitude: hanging ten can be tough, but the promise of a wave riding revelation can't be beaten.

DIVE INTO MONTAUK

Montauk sizzles like a summer romance, burning hot from Memorial Day to Labor Day, then cooling off as winter's population shrinks from 40,000 to 4000. Falling in love with this Long Island escape is easy: the peninsula is kissed by beaches and wrapped with six state parks. It's New York's easternmost point – nicknamed 'The End' – and the state's last stop before jumping into the Atlantic, far from NYC's towers. The hamlet has seen its share of suitors: the Indigenous Montaukett, followed by English colonizers, fisherfolk and eventually Carl G Fisher, who tried turning Montauk into the 'Miami Beach of the North' in the 1920s. Although his plan failed, future generations succeeded, opening swanky restaurants serving summer's moneyed masses.

EATING & DRINKING IN MONTAUK: OUR PICKS

Bird on the Roof: Aussie-inspired brunch transitions to American-style dinner with pastas, curries, fish and inventive cocktails. *8am-2pm Sat & Sun, 5-11pm Thu-Sat* **$$**

Duryea's: Seasonal spot to catch the sunset while slurping oysters and sipping rosé. Connected to a market and boutique. *hours vary May-Sep* **$$$**

Montauket: Ideal location for soaking up sunsets with seafaring locals. Come early for window-facing seats. Seafood served in summer. *2pm-late, from noon Sat & Sun*

Montauk Brewing Company: Red-barn bastion for beer, founded by three local buds. Chill vibes. *2-6pm Mon, Thu & Fri, from noon Sat & Sun*

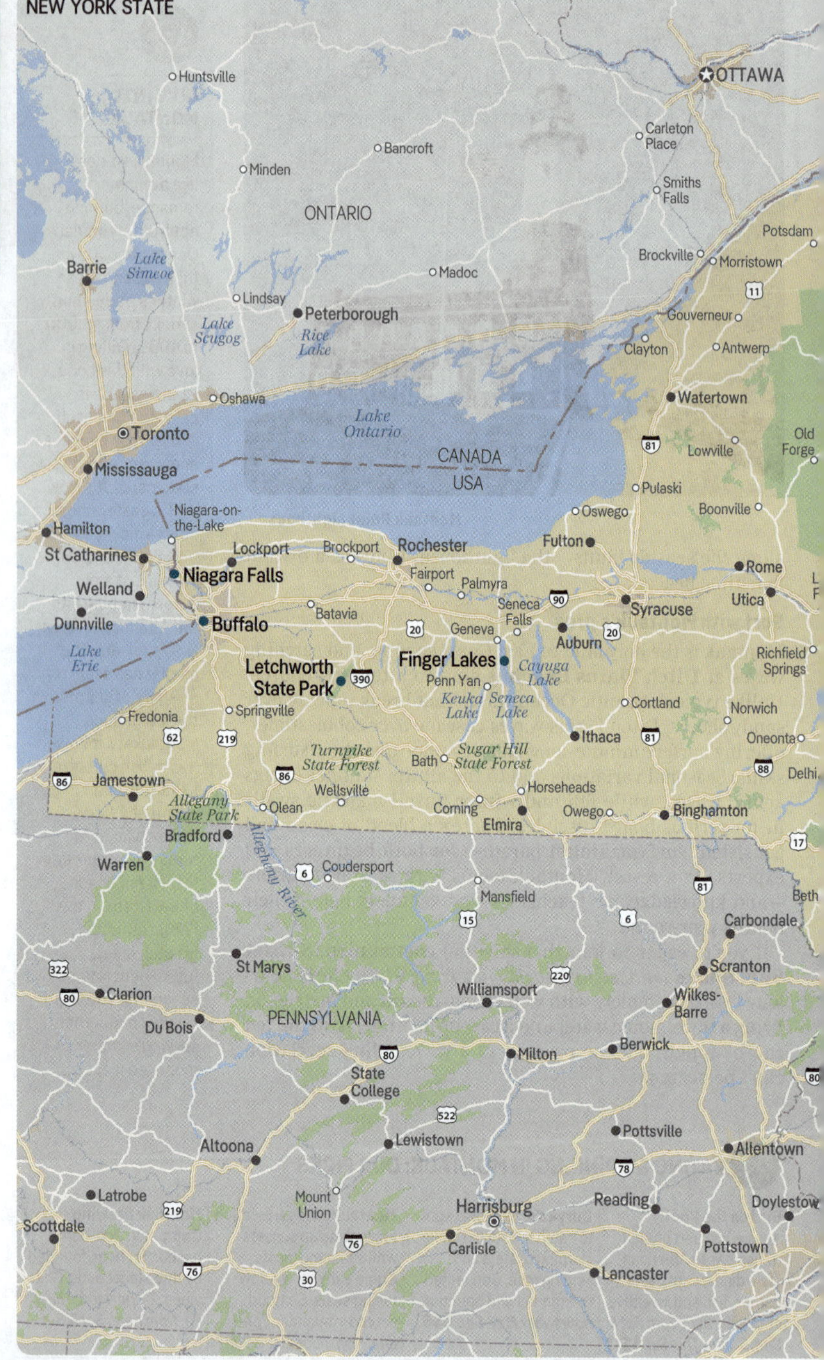
NEW YORK STATE
OTTAWA
Huntsville
Carleton Place
Bancroft
Minden
Smiths Falls
ONTARIO
Potsdam
Brockville
Morristown
Barrie
Lake Simcoe
Madoc
Lindsay
Peterborough
Lake Scugog
Rice Lake
Gouverneur
Clayton
Antwerp
Oshawa
Lake Ontario
Watertown
Toronto
CANADA
USA
Lowville
Old Forge
Mississauga
Pulaski
Niagara-on-the-Lake
Oswego
Boonville
Hamilton
Fulton
St Catharines
Lockport
Brockport
Rochester
Rome
Niagara Falls
Fairport
Welland
Palmyra
Utica
Seneca Falls
Syracuse
Dunnville
Batavia
Buffalo
Geneva
Auburn
Lake Erie
Finger Lakes
Cayuga Lake
Richfield Springs
Letchworth State Park
Penn Yan
Keuka Lake
Seneca Lake
Cortland
Norwich
Fredonia
Springville
Ithaca
Oneonta
Turnpike State Forest
Sugar Hill State Forest
Bath
Jamestown
Delhi
Wellsville
Horseheads
Allegany State Park
Olean
Corning
Owego
Binghamton
Elmira
Bradford
Allegheny River
Warren
Coudersport
Mansfield
Beth
Carbondale
St Marys
Scranton
Clarion
Williamsport
Wilkes-Barre
Du Bois
PENNSYLVANIA
Milton
Berwick
State College
Pottsville
Altoona
Lewistown
Allentown
Latrobe
Mount Union
Harrisburg
Reading
Doylestown
Scottdale
Carlisle
Pottstown
Lancaster

TOP TIP

If NYC is your base and you're traveling sans car, visiting Beacon, Hudson and Montauk is possible via Metro-North and Long Island Rail Road *(mta.info)*. Metro-North trips along the Hudson River are splendid in fall, chugging past crayon-colored woodlands. **Amtrak** *(amtrak.com)* serves Buffalo; rideshares are easy to find upon arrival.

LONG ISLAND

HIGHLIGHTS
1 Cherry Grove
2 Ditch Plains Beach
3 Montauk Point Lighthouse

SIGHTS
4 Amsterdam Beach Trailhead
5 Big Duck
6 Camp Hero State Park
7 Channing Daughters
see 1 Cherry Grove Community House and Theater
8 Dia Bridgehampton
9 Hither Hills State Park
10 Kirk Park Beach
11 LongHouse Reserve
12 Montauk Point State Park
13 Pollock-Krasner House
14 Sag Harbor Village Marina
see 14 Sag Harbor Whaling & Historical Museum
15 Shadmoor State Park
16 South Edison Beach
17 Sunken Forest

ACTIVITIES
18 Fire Island Pines
see 16 Sunset Surf Shack

SLEEPING
19 Breakers
see 16 Daunt's Albatross Motel

EATING
see 8 Almond
20 Amber Waves Farm
see 16 Bird on the Roof
21 Doubles
22 Duryea's
see 14 Sag Pizza

DRINKING & NIGHTLIFE
see 18 Blue Whale
see 1 Ice Palace
23 Montauk Brewing Company
see 22 Montauket
see 18 Sip-n-Twirl

ENTERTAINMENT
see 14 Sag Harbor Cinema

SHOPPING
see 14 Sag Harbor Books

TRANSPORT
24 Sayville Ferry Service

Sag Harbor's whaling past and wealthy present

The 'un-Hampton': until a decade ago, that's how locals fancied Sag Harbor. While well-heeled Manhattanites reshaped towns such as East Hampton with status-symbol shops (Gucci, Rolex etc), Sag Harbor maintained its charm with locally owned boutiques and a dedication to historic preservation. Although some of the magic is waning (everything here is expensive), stroll down Main St to see why Sag Harbor remains a South Fork standout. Start at the **Sag Harbor Whaling & Historical Museum** *(sagharborwhalingmuseum.org; adult/child $8/3)*, erected in 1845 for a whaling tycoon. Whale blubber, used to make oil, earned locals big bucks throughout the 1830s and '40s, but the rush was brief. By the 1850s, overfishing sank the whale-oil market just as kerosene and petroleum gained popularity. Continue north to Main St's three-block shopping center and you'll see that money found its way back to town. Stop for slices at **Sag Pizza** *(sagpizza.com)*, snap a picture of art-deco **Sag Harbor Cinema** *(sagharborcinema.org)* and pop into **Sag Harbor Books** *(southamptonsagharborbooks.com)* to leaf through *Moby Dick* (author Herman Melville gives the village a shout-out). Sag Harbor's **marina** punctuates Main St's history. In summer, mansion-sized yachts line the docks – a nod to Sag's seafaring origins and recent wealthy upswing.

Find freedom on Fire Island

Muscular architecture, maritime forests and sweeping dunes lapped by the Atlantic: between May and September, there are myriad reasons to board the **Sayville Ferry** for a day trip to Fire Island, a slender sandbar off Long Island's coast. But the main draw? LGBTIQ+ crowds.

Cherry Grove became 'America's first gay and lesbian town' around the 1930s and 1940s. Pay your respects at the **Cherry Grove Community House and Theater** *(artsprojectcg.org)*, where openly LGBTIQ+ residents played important roles in civic life decades before the US elected queer politicians to office. Summer evenings center around the **Ice Palace** *(ice palace.club)*, a club and performance space graced by the likes of Liza Minelli, Patti LuPone and scantily clad men who come for Friday night's Underwear Party. If you prefer low-key to late night, take a detour to the **Sunken Forest** *(nps.gov)*. A 1.5-mile boardwalk loops through its 300-year-old collection of American holly trees, sassafras and juneberry, 'sunken' beneath protective dunes.

While Cherry Grove welcomes mixed LGBTIQ+ crowds, including a strong sapphic contingency, neighboring **Fire Island Pines** is predominantly gay. Join the boys strutting its boardwalks to ogle eye-candy architecture. Many of the modernist homes were designed by architect Horace Gifford in the 1960s and '70s, using cedar and glass to complement the natural surroundings. The facade of **252 Bay Walk** looks like a proscenium arch for a seductive stage play; **482 Tarpon** boasts a deck that hovers above its neighbors – a voyeur's delight.

MONTAUK BEACH ACCESS

The secret is out – Montauk is spoiled with spectacular beaches, and though they're all open to the public, parking is usually restricted to permits issued by the Town of East Hampton. This includes beloved Ditch Plains. Permits for non-residents cost $500 – a steep price for a weekend getaway – though some beaches have reasonable day passes, such as **Kirk Park Beach** *($35)* and **Hither Hills State Park** *($10)*. Don't defy local laws – cops sniff out illegally parked cars like sharks smelling blood. Prefer free parking? Consider booking a hotel near popular **South Edison Beach** so you can walk to the seashore (try **Daunt's Albatross Motel**; p150), or hike the easy 1.5-mile trail to **Amsterdam Beach**.

MORE LGBTIQ+ BEACH HAVENS

Fire Island is one of many communities that historically cater to queer summer crowds. There's also Ogunquit, Maine (p221), Provincetown on Cape Cod (p179), Asbury Park along the Jersey Shore (p120) and Rehoboth Beach, Delaware (p268).

SPECTACULAR SIGHTS IN THE HAMPTONS

Shadmoor State Park: Montauk trails thick with black cherry trees lead to WWII bunkers and oceanside bluffs.

Pollock-Krasner House: Explore the paint-splattered studio and home of husband-and-wife abstract expressionists Jackson Pollock and Lee Krasner. Open May–October; reservations required.

Dia Bridgehampton: This shingle-style 1908 house has served as fire station, Baptist church and, now, exhibition space for minimalist Dan Flavin's fluorescent artwork.

Big Duck: Quirky detour where the North and South Forks split. Step inside the 20ft-tall Pekin duck from 1931.

LongHouse Reserve: More than 60 sculptures, including works by Yoko Ono and Willem de Kooning, sprout from this 16-acre garden.

All boardwalks here eventually lead to the **Blue Whale** *(pinesfi.com),* where gaggles gather around 5pm to babble over cocktails at 'Low Tea.' At 8pm, crowds flow to the adjacent pool deck for 'High Tea.' The final stop is **Sip-n-Twirl**, where music pulses until dawn.

Hudson Valley

Lose yourself in Beacon's steel canyons

Manhattan day-trippers arrive via Metro-North to drool over NYC's most sought-after commodity: space, superabundant at contemporary-art institution **Dia Beacon**. Roughly 300,000 sq ft of this former Nabisco box-printing factory devotes itself to minimalist paintings and mammoth sculptures that wouldn't fit through an NYC doorway. The most transportive works feel less 'contemporary art museum' and more 'aesthete's playground.' Winding through Richard Serra's rust-red *Torqued Ellipses* feels like hiking Arizona's Antelope Canyon, the sweet scent of Meg Webster's 8ft-tall *Wall of Beeswax* recalls a buzzy honey farm, and barbed-wire walls by Melvin Edwards add a tinge of danger while walking about. Free guided tours take place on Saturday and Sunday at noon and 1:30pm, though it's best to experience the museum at your own pace. Gliding through the galleries, lit by 34,000 sq ft of skylights, is a meditative experience. An on-site cafe serves treats; the gift shop is stacked with interesting art tomes.

Cornwall's outdoor sculpture park

Storm King Art Center *(welcome.stormking.org; adult/youth $25/15; open Apr-Nov)* marries what the Hudson Valley does best – nature and art. Hike around this pastoral park's 500 acres and you might wonder where one ends and the other begins. Colossal pieces sprout from manicured lawns and pop among the woodlands. Site-specific works also mimic the landscape, such as Maya Lin's *Storm King Wavefield,* an 11-acre earthwork undulating like a miniature Hudson Highlands.

Budget a few hours to adequately explore. Start by trekking around the North Woods, then walk counterclockwise, stopping by Menashe Kadishman's gravity-defying *Suspended* on your way to the top of Museum Hill, the park's highest point. Here you'll find the museum's shop and gallery space, housed in a Normandy-style château. Finish by meandering among native grasslands, creeks and allées, where you might spot white-tailed deer, box turtles and cottontail rabbits crawling

EATING & DRINKING IN THE HAMPTONS: OUR PICKS

Amber Waves Farm: Charming roadside cafe and market on a working farm in Amagansett. Peep the goats, pick produce, sit swing-side. Great for kids. *8am-2pm* $$

Almond: Bridgehampton's boisterous French-style bistro, where white-collar crowds dine on roast chicken and raw bar delicacies. *from 5pm Tue-Sat, closing hours vary* $$$

Doubles: Amagansett's outpost for Caribbean-influenced food, including doubles (fried dough topped with a curried chickpea concoction). *11:30am-8pm* $$

Channing Daughters: The South Fork's most inventive boutique winery serves flights patio-side, overlooking 33 acres of vine-wrapped trellises. *11am-5pm*

WIRESTOCK CREATORS/SHUTTERSTOCK

Shadmoor State Park

around works by Roy Lichtenstein, Alexander Calder and Mark di Suvero.

If you want to zip through the park quickly, rent a bicycle *($20 to $30)* or hop on the wheelchair-accessible tram loop. Getting here is easiest by car (25 minutes from Beacon), though it's possible to take a free museum shuttle from Beacon's train station (summer only) or catch a Coach bus (*coachusa.com*) from Manhattan. Plan a trip around leaf-peeping season (mid-September to early November), when trees put on an arboreal art show rivaling the sculptures.

Hudson's trendy heart

Uber-hip Hudson is beloved by NYC weekenders, who travel by car or train to cruise Warren St's antique stores, boutiques, galleries and restaurants. Join the crowds for a 1-mile stroll.

Start by snacking on a sourdough croissant from **Mel the Bakery** *(melthebakery.com)*, or rev up your engine with java from **MOTO Coffee Machine** *(motocoffeemachine.com)*, a coffee-and-motorcycle shop. You'll spot more than 10 art galleries along Warren St, including **Carrie Haddad's** *(carriehaddadgallery.com)* collection of notable locals. Peep the hidden upstairs hallway dedicated to Mark Beard's athletic nudes. There's an eclectic collection of upcycled decor at **LikeMindedObjects** *(likemindedobjects.com)*, vintage home

ALL ABOUT BEACON

Bohemian Beacon's unofficial nickname is 'Brooklyn North' – a nod to the influx of people from NYC who've spent two decades transforming it into King's County's upstate cousin. Walk down Main St and all the Brooklyn-as-brand signifiers are present: artisanal boutiques, small-batch breweries, avant-garde art galleries and farm-to-table restaurants. But Beacon is more than NYC's facsimile. Sandwiched between the Hudson River and Hudson Highlands, it's a jump-off point for outdoor adventures, including a collection of heart-pumping mountain hikes. This small town is a perfect NYC getaway: take the 1½-hour train ride from Grand Central via Metro-North, then hoof it to Main St or hop on the Beacon Free Loop bus rolling through town.

EATING & DRINKING IN BEACON: OUR PICKS

Roundhouse: Standard seasonal fare served inside this hat factory-turned-hotel is just an appetizer for the views of a gushing Fishkill Creek waterfall. *hours vary* $$$

Noble Pies: The Hudson Valley apple pie is a salute to Americana, served with other sweet and savory selections at this regional chain. *9am-8pm Sun-Thu, to 9pm Fri & Sat* $

Hudson Valley Brewery: Lavender, dandelions and sour candy are a few flavors found in these funky ales – arguably Beacon's best. *noon-8pm Sun & Mon, to 10pm Thu-Sat*

Big Mouth Coffee Roasters: First-rate third-wave coffee, with art-adorned walls (for sale), ample seating and on-site bean roasting. *7am-6pm Mon-Fri, 8am-7pm Sat, to 5pm Sun*

GREAT HUDSON VALLEY MUSEUMS & GALLERIES

Boscobel House & Gardens: This 19th-century Federalist home showcases how the fledgling US remained tethered to British influence.

Art Omi: Wander 120 acres of outdoor sculptures among fields and forests in Ghent.

Magazzino Italian Art: Bold postwar Italian art fills this beautiful brutalist space. Wave to the museum's 14 Sardinian donkeys.

KuBe Art Center: Edgy 'Kunsthalle Beacon' transforms a former high school into an art gallery with cheeky rotating exhibits.

Kykuit: Four generations of oil-rich Rockefellers inhabited this Gilded Age mansion atop historic Sleepy Hollow.

FELIX LIPOV/SHUTTERSTOCK

furnishings at well-curated **FINCH Hudson** *(finchhudson.com)* and high fashion with an outdoorsy edge at **Meridian** *(meridian.vision)*. The antiques game is strong here, too. Pop into **Red Chair on Warren** *(redchair-antiques.com)* for Swiss, Belgian and French finds from the 17th, 18th and 19th centuries. At **Spotty Dog Books & Ale** *(thespottydog.com)*, you can thumb through novels while sipping beer. Throughout the journey, admire Hudson's beautiful bones. Warren St is chockablock with 19th-century architecture, including Federal, Queen Anne and Victorian homes.

America's first major art movement

Rapid industrialization and westward expansion captured the imaginations of most 19th-century Americans. But painter Thomas Cole (1801–48), an émigré from soot-smothered England, saw power in preservation. His prescient viewpoint became the canvas for America's first significant artistic fraternity – the Hudson River School, coined in the 1870s to classify a group of landscape artists who depicted the country's wild frontier as sublime. The Hudson Valley and Catskills served as Cole's local muses, and paintings of places such as Kaaterskill Falls (p108) became his artistic form of proto-environmentalism. Visit his art-filled property in Catskill – the **Thomas Cole National Historic Site** *(thomascole.org)*,

EATING & DRINKING IN HUDSON: OUR PICKS

Lil' Deb's Oasis: Home to Hudson's avant garde, who gobble trendy takes on Mexican food while sipping from goblets of wine. *5-10pm Thu-Sun* **$$**

BackBar: Pack into a picnic table at this relaxed indoor-outdoor hangout for Southeast Asian plates and cocktails. *5-10pm Thu, noon-10pm Fri & Sat, noon-8pm Sun* **$$**

Quinnie's: Equal parts coffee shop, bakery, specialty market, sandwich shop and cocktail bar inside a lovingly renovated 1700s farmhouse on six grassy acres. *9am-4pm Fri-Tue* **$**

Half Moon: One-stop shop for last call (local beer), late-night munchies (pizza) and the occasional concert. *4pm-midnight Mon-Thu, to 1am Fri & Sat* **$**

Olana mansion

a 10-minute drive from Hudson. The three-building compound showcases Cole's work inside his Federal-style home, framing distant mountains. Strolling the grounds is free; guided tours cost $20.

After seeing Cole's work, drive across the Rip Van Winkle Bridge to **Olana** *(olana.org)*, a Gothic-Moorish mansion owned by Cole's protégé, Frederic Edwin Church (1826–1900). Church studied with Cole from 1844–1846 before making a name for himself with romantic landscapes of the Andes Mountains, icebergs and more distant landscapes most New Yorkers would never see in real life. Paintings aside, Church's standout work is this fairy-tale castle (completed in 1872), which he designed in collaboration with Central Park architect Calvert Vaux. Wandering the 250-acre estate, free and open to the public daily from 8am to sunset, is like stepping into one of his oil paintings. More than 5 miles of carriage roads roll from meadows to an artificial lake and on to expansive views of the Hudson River and Catskill Mountains. The home is even more impressive, with exterior brickwork and ceramic tiles nodding to the international curios displayed inside. Tours of the landscape *($12)*, house interior *($20)*, or a combo of the two *($40)* enhance the experience. Book tickets in advance.

TOP HUDSON VALLEY HIKES

Download the AllTrails app *(alltrails.com)* for detailed info on each route.

Mt Beacon: Scale Mt Beacon's 1600-ft summit on a 4-mile return journey to breathtaking views of the Hudson Highlands.

Bull Hill: Trek past scenic overlooks and mysterious ruins on this 5.4-mile loop trail near Beacon.

Breakneck Ridge: Brace yourself for rocky scrambles and steep ascents on this 3.2-mile hike, accessible on summer weekends via Metro-North. Closed for maintenance until 2027.

Storm King Mountain: Circle the crown of this 1300ft peak on a 2.4-mile trail, different from the same-named art park.

Walkway over the Hudson: Stroll or roll across the world's longest elevated pedestrian bridge, a 1.3-mile link between Poughkeepsie and Highland.

EATING & DRINKING AROUND WOODSTOCK: OUR PICKS

Phoenicia Diner: Greasy-spoon aesthetics (chrome, terrazzo) and creative Catskills takes on classics, like po'boys with cornmeal-crusted trout. *8am-6pm Thu-Tue* **$$**

Silvia: An unpretentious take on farm-to-fine dining. Start with the horseradish-spiced mushroom lentil pâté; finish with a wood-smoked pork chop. *hours vary* **$$$**

Good Night: Slide into a plush velvet banquette for upscale Southeast Asian-inspired plates with plenty of crunch, spice and tang. *hours vary* **$$$**

West Kill Brewing: Sip beer made with locally grown and foraged ingredients on a historic 127-acre farm. Cinematic scenery. *noon-7pm Fri & Sat, to 6pm Sun*

COME TO THE CATSKILLS

The Catskill Mountains are a vast collection of rolling plateaus, including 600,000-acre Catskill Park, sculpted by streams, lakes and forests. The Hudson and Delaware Rivers frame the landscape, speckled with sleepy main streets where a cultural renaissance is underway, steadily moving westward across the region with rustic-chic resorts and a formidable art scene. If you're staying in the region, base yourself in or around the eastern Catskills town of Woodstock – not to be confused with the concert that rocked America's psyche in 1969, which took place in Bethel, 60 miles west. Woodstock blossomed from an art colony formed in 1902 and retains its creative edge. Wander along Tinker St for a taste – galleries, tchotchke shops and inventive restaurants.

STEVEN GROUP/SHUTTERSTOCK

Kaaterskill Falls

The Catskills

Stand in awe at Kaaterskill Falls

New York's **tallest cascade** *(catskillsvisitorcenter.org; free)* – a two-tiered stunner 90ft higher than Niagara Falls (p118) – has inspired artists for centuries. Washington Irving described its 'feathery foam' in *Rip Van Winkle*, and poet William Cullen Bryant evoked its 'palace of ice' in wintertime. Today, 100,000-plus annual visitors attempt to capture the 260ft local icon on camera. Follow their lead: if you only take one hike in the Catskills, this should be it.

Start at the Laurel House Rd parking lot and choose from routes catering to novice and experienced hikers alike. Take the easy 1000yd round-trip trail to the **Falls Viewing Platform** to see the glorious gusher from above. The 1.4-mile round-trip jaunt to the lower falls will get your blood pumping with its steep staircase (unsuitable in icy conditions). Tack on an extra mile by following the Kaatskills Creek downstream to **Bastion Falls**, or head to the Escarpment Trail for a 4.8-mile loop leading to **Inspiration Point**, where you can see Kaaterskill Clove, a slender cleft in the Catskills sculpted by glaciation and the persistence of Kaaterskill Creek.

EATING & DRINKING IN THE WESTERN CATSKILLS: OUR PICKS

Heron: Nearby farms provide most ingredients at this Narrowsburg spot for southern-inspired American fare. Sublime outdoor-terrace views. *hours vary* $$

Cochecton Fire Station: Former pyro police pad turned contemporary cocktail joint with wood-fired pub grub. *3-8pm Mon & Tue, to 9pm Fri, noon-9pm Sat, noon-8pm Sun*

Katskeller: Sit at outdoor picnic tables to savor Neapolitan pizza and sides in Livingston Manor. Try the brook trout rillettes, a local creek delicacy. *hours vary* $$

Catskill Brewery: This Livingston Manor beer hang is famous for the bitter pinewood finish of its Devil's Path IPA. *hours vary*

America's modern Stonehenge

Quarrying bluestone was a profitable enterprise in the 19th-century Catskills. Cities from Albany to NYC used the durable, slate-blue sandstone for sidewalks until the 20th century, when cement took over. Many quarrying companies folded as a result, leaving square-cut scars across the landscape. Self-taught sculptor Harvey Fite turned some of those scars into the Catskills' most captivating artwork. After purchasing property surrounded by abandoned quarries, Fite started a 37-year project: **Opus 40** (1939–76), a whimsical 6.5-acre handcrafted earthwork, visible on his property-turned-sculpture-park from late March through late December *(opus40.org; adult/child $16/5, guided tours $31)*. Fite adapted Mayan stone-working techniques to create his serpentine structure – an open-air monument to Indigenous design and the majestic Catskill Mountains.

Feel Woodstock's beat in Bethel

In the summer of 1969, America was at war. Nixon commanded the Oval Office, LGBTIQ+ patrons revolted against police brutality at Stonewall and soldiers lost their lives in Vietnam. But on Max Yasgur's dairy farm, nearly half a million people found peace – unless they tripped on the bad acid supposedly going around. This was the Woodstock Music and Art Fair, a three-day hippie happening that took the sleepy town of Bethel by surprise. Rock legends including Janis Joplin, the Grateful Dead and Santana electrified crowds. Jimi Hendrix riled audiences with a rousing rendition of 'The Star Spangled Banner,' turning the national anthem into a guitar hero's protest.

Though the crowds have long gone – save a few white-haired hippies who never left – the spirit lingers. Yasgur's farm is now **Bethel Woods Center for the Arts** *(bethelwoodscenter.org)*, where you can revive Woodstock's memory at outdoor summer concerts. There's also the seasonal **Museum at Bethel Woods** *(adult/child $22.69/5, cheaper if booked in advance; Apr-Dec)* bursting with music and images from Woodstock. For the full summer of '69 experience, consider booking a campsite during one of the shows. (Unlike Woodstock, where visitors camped for free on mud-slick farmland, this sanitized and markedly grassier version starts at $82 per night.) There's are also a weekend harvest festival throughout September and October, with plenty of artisans, food trucks and live music on display.

If you can't attend a summer concert, drive by to pay your respects. While lingering before the coffin-shaped monument near the field where history sang, commiserate with Joni Mitchell by listening to her wail 'Woodstock.' She missed the cultural capstone, too.

The Adirondacks

Climb every Adirondack mountain

Over 2000 miles of hiking trails weave their way through the Adirondacks, with options for all levels of outdoor enthusiasm.

MORE OUTDOOR ADVENTURES IN THE CATSKILLS

Overlook Mountain: Pass the charred remains of a 19th-century hotel on this 4.6-mile hike to views above Woodstock.

Delaware River: Tube, raft or kayak down gentle rapids with **Lander's River Trips**.

Sam's Point Area: Climb the Shawangunk Ridge on this 7-mile trek to panoramic overlooks, ice caves and 187ft-high Verkeerderkill Falls.

Peekamoose Blue Hole: Cool off during summer's dog days by braving Roundout Creek's icy, Caribbean-blue water.

Hunter Mountain: Shred slopes from late November to early April on 67 trails spread across 320 acres.

MORE WONDERFUL WATERFALLS

If you love chasing waterfalls, head to Ithaca, a Finger Lakes city graced with more than 100 gushing cataracts, including the East Coast's tallest single-drop waterfall, Taughannock Falls (p113).

TOUR THE WESTERN CATSKILLS' CUTEST TOWNS

The Catskills' revival as 'hickster' haven is most apparent while driving between tiny Delaware River towns where forests give way to walkable main streets.

START	END	LENGTH
Narrowsburg	Upward Brewing Company	22 miles; 3-4 hours

Begin on Main St in ❶ **Narrowsburg**, perched on a bluff above the Delaware. Breakfast sandwiches from Tusten Cup fuel some light shopping. Stop in River Gallery (landscape paintings), Narrowsburg Proper (market snacks) and One Grand Books (lit hand-picked by famous creatives). In summer, swimmers jump into the river from rocks below the sea-green Narrowsburg–Darbytown Bridge.

Drive along a portion of the Upper Delaware Scenic Byway (Rte 97) as it snakes along Pennsylvania's border toward ❷ **Callicoon**. The town's name, derived from the Dutch 'Kollikoonkill,' meaning 'Wild Turkey Creek,' is still fitting for a place resembling the set for a cowboy flick. Sample whiskey at distiller Catskill Provisions and peek inside Farmhouse Project, an elegant artisan shop and cocktail parlor. The town seems to quadruple in population for Sunday's farmers' market *(11am to 2pm)*, where local vendors hock honey, jam, baked goods, pottery and piles of organic fruit.

❸ **Livingston Manor**, unfurling along Willowemoc Creek, is the liveliest town of the bunch. Walk Main St to peruse shops and grab food: eye Homestedt's cabin-core collection; gobble biscuits from the Walk In, then drive to ❹ **Upward Brewing Company** to sip craft beer on its 120 acres, complete with ski-mountain-inspired chalet.

The trip takes 45 minutes without stopping, but plan a whole day to enjoy each town's offerings.

Cap off the day by hiking to the peak of Upward Brewing Company's property, aptly named Beer Mountain.

For a gentler swim spot, head to Skinners Falls, 10 minutes north, where giant boulders create serene river pools.

Experienced hikers in the Lake George area will appreciate the 6.5-mile return route to **Buck Mountain**, which shoots 2000ft above Lake George's eastern banks. Crawl across granite slopes knotted with tree roots, littered with boulders and cut by gentle creeks to a spectacular view of the island-dotted lake below. Bonus points if you can spot the Sagamore Resort, a historic horseshoe-shaped hotel on the edge of Green Island. Use AllTrails for more info.

If you'd rather roll to picture-perfect panoramas, put the pedal to the metal on **Prospect Mountain** *(dec.ny.gov)*. Between late May and early November, drivers pay $10 to reach the summit, where views extend 100 miles on clear days. Hikers who tackle the arduous 3.2-mile woodland trail (steep and rocky with scrambles) reach the summit for free. Park along Smith St to access the trailhead.

Superlative paths near Lake Placid offer similar levels of accessibility. The 10-plus-mile trail to **Indian Head** leads to a low summit with a photogenic long shot of the Ausable River. From May to October, it's necessary to make parking reservations with **Adirondack Mountain Reserve** *(hikeamr.org; free)*. For views from the comfort of your car, drive up Whiteface Mountain, New York's fifth-highest peak (4867ft), on the **Whiteface Veterans' Memorial Highway** *(whiteface.com; $10)*, open from late spring to fall.

Be prepared to contend with ice and snow while hiking outside of summer. Most trails require crampons or snowshoes in winter.

Swim, kayak and cruise on Lake George

While touring the Adirondacks in 1791, Thomas Jefferson wrote, 'Lake George is without comparison, the most beautiful water I ever saw.' Spend a few hours floating around the lake and it's hard to disagree. In summer, join families on the 51-acre **Million Dollar Beach** *(dec.ny.gov; parking $10)* and wade into crystal-clear waters under the protective eye of a lifeguard. Water tends to reach 70°F to 75°F, with peak temperatures around late July and August.

If you'd rather explore the lake's wild shores without crowds, rent a kayak, canoe or stand-up paddleboard from **Lake George Kayak Co** *(lakegeorgekayak.com; per hour/half-day $35/75)*. There are tons of boat-rental companies around the lake, too, though not all are reputable and costs can be prohibitive. At **FR Smith & Sons** *(frsmithandsonsmarina.com)*

AMERICAN MYTHOLOGY

If you know the stories 'Rip Van Winkle' (the Catskills man who hit a 20-year snooze button) or 'The Legend of Sleepy Hollow' (Ichabod Crane's ill-fated meet-up with the Headless Horseman), you know Washington Irving, America's first celebrated wordsmith. Both tales, published in 1819, feature one of his favorite locations – the Hudson Valley – where he transformed a stone Dutch house with eclectic architectural styles. The property, **Sunnyside** *(hudsonvalley.org; adult/child $18/13)* is tour-worthy, as is the nearby town of Sleepy Hollow, renamed in 1996 to capitalize on his ghoulish account, sewn into American mythology. Visit around Halloween to see Van Cortlandt Manor's **Great Jack O'Lantern Blaze** *(pumpkinblaze.org; $20)*, when thousands of pumpkins light up the night.

EATING & DRINKING AROUND THE ADIRONDACKS: OUR PICKS

Hitching Post & Tavern: It's all about cheese at this restaurant and market run by Nettle Meadow Farms, a purveyor of fantastic goat *fromage*. *hours vary* $$

Deer's Head Inn: The Adirondacks' oldest tavern (1808) serves American classics utilizing local ingredients, modernized with international zest. *5-9pm Wed-Sun* $$$

Capisce Coffee & Espresso Bar: Strong java, sandwiches and a small selection of local art and vintage clothes. *6am-4pm Mon, Tue & Thu-Sat, to noon Wed & Sun* $

Paradox Brewery: Sample craft beer made with pristine water from Adirondack Park's granite bedrock. *noon-8pm Wed & Thu, to 9pm Fri & Sat, to 6pm Sun*

TROUT TOWN, USA

When spring blossoms erupt around the Catskills, fly fishers pull out their poles to catch trout. Fly fishing is a local tradition dating back to the 1890s, thanks to Theodore Gordon – 'Father of American Dry Fly Fishing' – who revolutionized the sport with new techniques (dubbed 'Catskill style') in rivers and creeks around Roscoe and Livingston Manor. Today, both towns wear their fishy history with pride. Roscoe calls itself 'Trout Town, USA' (find tackle shops along Old Rte 17), and Livingston Manor celebrates local legends at the **Catskill Fly Fishing Center & Museum** *(cffcm.com; $12).* In June, Livingston Manor dons its best river drag for the wacky and wonderful **Trout Parade** *(livingston manorny.com),* led by marching bands and giant trout puppets.

JACK AIELLO/SHUTTERSTOCK

in Bolton Landing, a full-day affair on a four-person boat costs $522 – a price worth the pleasure of speeding off to a private cove. For a uniquely Lake George experience, see the sights from one of **Lake George Steamboat Company's** *(lakegeorgesteamboat.com)* historic cruise vessels, docked along the lake's south side. The most adorable of the bunch is ***Minnie-Ha-Ha*** *(adult/child $24.50/$12.50; May-Oct),* one of America's last steam paddle-wheel ships, which toot-toots along the lake during an informative, family-friendly, one-hour tour. A calliope – the boat's 32-whistle steam organ – belts classic tunes between journeys from the top deck.

Go for gold in Lake Placid

Lake Placid, two-time host of the Winter Olympics, doesn't need snow to celebrate seasonal sports – the alpine village wears its athletic heritage like a badge of honor year-round. Spend a day following in the ski tracks of global champions at sites in and around town. Start at the **Lake Placid Olympic Museum** *(lakeplacidolympicmuseum.org; adult/youth $15/12),* a small but mighty look at the 1932 and 1980 Games. The museum holds a little something for everyone: plenty of history, graphic and fashion designs from Olympics past, and a riveting video chronicling one of the most legendary Olympic upsets – the underdog US ice-hockey team's 1980 victory over the Soviet Union. There's also an interactive section where visitors can hop into a bobsled for a virtual thrill ride. Adrenaline junkies who prefer a real-life rush should soar to the **Olympic Jumping Complex** *(olympicjumpingcomplex.com),* where ski jumpers zoom down steep ramps before taking flight. Take a similar (and safer) journey on the high-speed **Sky Flyer Zipline** *($45).* Your final stop is **Whiteface Mountain** *(whiteface.com),* where Olympic slalom stars raced for

Taughannock Falls

gold in 1980. Between the end of November and mid-April, visitors can purchase a day pass *($129)* and rent equipment *($71)* to test their skills on the East Coast's biggest vertical drop (3430ft). In summer, take the 15-minute **Cloudsplitter Gondola** *(adult/youth $30/25)* ride to the top of Little White Face, gliding above grassy slopes to a majestic view of Lake Placid and nearby Lake Champlain.

Finger Lakes

Trails to powerful plunges near Ithaca

More than 150 waterfalls grace gorges in a 10-mile radius around Ithaca, beating heart of the Finger Lakes region, with more gushers dazzling further afield. The most wow-worthy of the bunch is **Taughannock Falls** *(parks.ny.gov; per car $9)*, the East Coast's tallest single-drop waterfall, shooting 215ft into a canyon of gun-metal-gray shale. Follow the well-groomed and largely flat 1.8-mile out-and-back Gorge Trail to feel its power from below, then drive to the Taughannock Park Rd viewing platform to appreciate the landscape from above.

LAKE GEORGE: GATEWAY TO THE ADIRONDACKS

Lake George, the 'Queen of American Lakes,' is royal indeed. Crowned by pine-packed peaks and bejeweled with over 170 islands, humans have spent centuries admiring the 32-mile-long, spring-fed stunner. The Indigenous Haudenosaunee (or Iroquois Confederacy) and Mohicans came first and called it 'Andia-ta-roc-te' (lake that shuts itself in), followed by the French, then pushed out by the British, who renamed it after King George II in 1755. Gilded Age travelers built grand cabins here throughout the 19th century, and these days, summertime tourists descend upon the lake between Memorial and Labor Days. Along the queen's southern shores sits the village of Lake George, gateway to Adirondack Park – a 6-million-acre preserve with 46 mountains over 4000ft high.

EATING AROUND ITHACA: OUR PICKS

Moosewood: America's longest-running vegetarian restaurant planted seeds for a farm-to-table revolution in 1973 and remains top tier. *11:30am-9pm Wed-Mon* **$$**

Hazelnut Kitchen: Regional ingredients get dressed to impress, but this dining room in Trumansburg remains casual and quaint. *5-8:30pm Thu-Sat* **$$$**

Creekside Cafe: Snug, low-key operation for breakfast sandwiches and sweets, located at the heart of Trumansburg's Main St. *9am-2pm Fri & Sat, to 1pm Sun* **$**

Cayuga Lake Creamery: Divert from vineyards for experimental homemade ice-cream flavors such as jalapeño popper, apple-cider sorbet and maple bacon. *hours vary* **$**

FUN IN THE FINGER LAKES

Look at a map of Central New York and you'll see 11 spindly bodies of water splayed out like a giant's hands. These are the glacier-gouged Finger Lakes, adorned with farmsteads and tiny towns. At the bottom of 39-mile-long Cayuga Lake, the hand's longest appendage, sits hippie-dippie Ithaca, bookended by Cornell University and Ithaca College. The city's academic underpinnings make it a magnet for free-spirit thinkers who dine and drink around the Commons, Ithaca's pedestrian strip below Cornell's campus. The city's tourism slogan since the 1970s, 'Ithaca is Gorges,' plays on the region's abundance of geological showstoppers: narrow canyons carved by creeks and lashed by some of the East Coast's most magnificent waterfalls.

For spectacular gorge trails, **Watkins Glen State Park** sets the gold standard. This 3-mile out-and-back trail climbs 832 stone steps to 19 cascades that appear plucked from the pages of a Tolkien tale. Closer to Ithaca, there's **Robert H Treman State Park**, which has a dozen cascades on its 4.5-mile Gorge and Rim Trail loop. **Buttermilk Falls State Park** packs 10 waterfalls into a similar 1.6-mile loop. Both showcase natural swimming holes at the base of frothy cataracts – perfect for a refreshing post-hike dip in summer. All state parks cost $10 per car.

In downtown Ithaca, you can drive by **Ithaca Falls**, a 150ft-tall, 175ft-wide powerhouse visible from Lake St, or hike through **Cascadilla Gorge** *(cornellbotanicgardens.org; free)*, passing six feathery falls on a 1.2-mile round-trip path linked to Cornell.

To hike all the gorge trails, visit between late May and October. Taughannock Falls remains open year-round, but many paths close between winter and spring.

Unwind at verdant vineyards

Drive the pastoral perimeter of Cayuga and Seneca Lakes, decorated with neat rows of grape vines. Nearly 150 winemakers call the Finger Lakes home – a tradition that flowered in the 1960s when Ukrainian refugee Dr Konstantin Frank successfully planted vinifera grapes near Keuka Lake. While the region is best known for German-style rieslings, plucky vintners have recently shown potential for cultivating reds such as cabernet franc and pinot noir. Quality here varies drastically, so instead of hopping on one of the area's touted wine trails for an improvised tour, choose your stops judiciously. **Six Eighty Cellars** *(sixeightycellars.com)* is Cayuga Lake's west-coast-cool kid, with knowledgeable staff espousing the virtues of bubbly pét-nats and smoky chardonnays. Tastings come with a charcuterie board, which you can enjoy in the whitewashed tasting room or in an outdoor Adirondack chair overlooking Cayuga Lake. At **Forge Cellars** *(forgecellars.com)*, located on a steep hill with heavenly Seneca Lake views, it's all about the local terroir. Sample rieslings that differ in only one way – the site upon which the grapes were grown. A map of local growing sites accompanies flights. **Lakewood Vineyards** *(lakewoodvineyards.com)* is best for budgets, with $5 flights – choose between samples of sweet or dry wines. Don't sleep on **Heart & Hands Wine Co's** *(heartandhandswine.com)* pinot noir, either. Need a chauffeur to usher you

DRINKING IN ITHACA: BEER, COCKTAILS & COFFEE

Personal Best Brewing: Come to this industrial, yeast-scented brewhouse for hop-forward suds; stay for the full-sized shuffleboard courts and board games. *hours vary*

Ithaca Beer Co: Flower Power IPAs grace taps in 15 states, but you'll only find kegs of its experimental ales here. *4-9pm Wed & Thu, from noon Fri-Sun*

Bar Argos: While Cornell's party crowds down shots around the Commons, sophisticated sippers head to Argos Inn's Victorian-style lobby for quiet cocktail contemplation. *4-10pm*

Press Cafe: Ithaca's coffee-fueled undergraduate digerati clack away on keyboards inside this bright, bohemian two-room cafe showcasing local art. *8am-6pm*

PQK/SHUTTERSTOCK

Lakewood Vineyards

between vineyards? Hire a ride through **Main St Drivers** *(mainstreetdrivers.com; from $48 per hour, 4hr minimum).*

Letchworth State Park

Gaze into the Grand Canyon of the East

The Genesee River has spent thousands of years carving Letchworth Gorge – the shale-and-sandstone centerpiece of 17-mile-long **Letchworth State Park** *(parks.ny.gov; per car $10),* dubbed the 'Grand Canyon of the East,' one hour east of Buffalo by car. While the comparison to Arizona's stony celebrity is flattering, it belies the singular beauty on view here: 600ft-high cliffs topped by woodlands thick with hemlock, oak and sugar maple trees – a spectacular sight in fall. There are also three major cascades – the Upper, Middle (most magnificent) and Lower Falls. Though they are not as powerful as Niagara Falls, the park is less crowded and more wild, making it a worthwhile detour between Buffalo and Ithaca.

To experience the park on foot, follow the 14-mile out-and-back **Gorge Trail**. Don't be alarmed by the mileage – this is more of a steady stroll than a heart-pounding hike, following the gorge's scenic western rim.

The park also prioritizes accessibility. Parking lots and pull-outs for cars are near all the top sights, and the **Autism Nature Trail** *(autismnaturetrail.com),* a 1-mile route with eight sensory-friendly stations, provides autistic individuals a safe space to experience the great outdoors.

BEST OF THE REST AROUND THE FINGER LAKES

Corning Museum of Glass: Ancient Egyptian glassmaking, Dale Chihuly creations and glass-blowing demonstrations.

Town of Aurora: Century-old mansions line this manicured 2-mile strip along Cayuga Lake. Grab a walking tour brochure from **Inns of Aurora** (p150).

Women's Rights National Historical Park: Honor the First Women's Rights Convention in 1848, birthing a gender-equality movement.

Sunset View Creamery: 'Cow cuddling' with three to four gentle calves inside a hay-covered pen.

Finger Lakes Cider House: Swill ciders on a hillside farm or take a tour *($24)* to learn about bud-to-bottle production.

BUFFALO'S BACKSTORY

Its winters may be harsh, but Buffalo is a city in spring. After economic turmoil in the late 20th century, artists, preservationists and a squad of local cheerleaders are planting the seeds for Western New York's Rust Belt revitalization. Incorporated in 1832, Buffalo owes its origins to the Erie Canal, linking to NYC. When the artificial waterway opened in 1825, the city overflowed with riches and became an industrial boomtown. By 1901, it boasted more millionaires per capita than any American metropole. But after WWII, industries vanished, leaving behind their brick-and-cement skeletons. These bones are now the bedrock of Buffalo's rebirth, with visionaries turning abandoned buildings into breweries, museums, restaurants and parks.

PIERRE WILLIOT/SHUTTERSTOCK

Buffalo

Tour Buffalo's historic architecture

Buffalo's architectural landscape glimmers with riches from its industrial past. From the 19th century, there's **Delaware Park** *(bfloparks.org)*, designed by Frederick Law Olmsted (of Central Park and Niagara Falls fame), and the neighboring **Richardson Olmsted Campus** *(richardson-olmsted.com; guided tours from $20)*, featuring the Romanesque Revival Buffalo State Asylum for the Insane, now a boutique hotel. There's also downtown's **Buffalo City Hall** *(buffalony.gov; free)* from 1931: after enjoying its art-deco details from Niagara Sq, take an elevator to the 25th floor and walk up three flights for panoramic city views.

Thanks to local preservationists, Buffalo is also the greatest sanctuary, outside of Chicago, for Frank Lloyd Wright's organic architecture. The 1906, Prairie-style **Martin House** *(martinhouse.org; 75min tour of main structures $25, full 2hr tour $45)*, commissioned by self-made millionaire Darwin Martin, is most magnificent – even Wright called it 'a well-nigh perfect composition.' Book a guided tour to see interiors on the 30,000-sq-ft grounds. Exploring the building's Roman brick exterior and gardens is free, though a $15 audio tour enhances the experience. The interwar **Graycliff Estate** *(experiencegraycliff.org; adult/child $38/23)*, constructed as a Lake Erie summer home for the Martin family, awaits 30 minutes' drive south in Derby, NY. Standard 90-minute tours examine the property.

MORE RESPLENDENT WRIGHTS

Fans of Frank Lloyd Wright will fawn over **Fallingwater** (p148), his masterful creation outside Pittsburgh, Pennsylvania. For more Wright in NY, head to NYC's **Guggenheim** (p87), a circular departure from the city's blocky buildings.

Richardson Olmsted Campus

Wander Buffalo's waterfront

Efforts to rinse off Buffalo's Rust Belt image are most apparent throughout Canalside, a district transformed from bustling Erie Canal terminus to late-20th-century wasteland and now a recreation-packed park. Spend an hour exploring the area, or plan an adventure that lasts half a day.

Roaming around is half the fun: historical placards provide Erie Canal insight and *Shark Girl*, the 'fish out of water' statue by Casey Riordan, begs passersby to snap a selfie. Throughout summer, visitors can paddle around Elevator Alley (a stretch of river flanked by towering grain elevators) with rentals from **BFLO Harbor Kayak** *(bfloharborkayak.com; per hour $25)* or hop on the **Queen City Bike Ferry** *(queencityferry.com; $1)* for access to Lake Erie's serene Outer Harbor. Ride the **Buffalo Heritage Carousel** from 1924 *(buffaloheritagecarousel.org; $3)*, skate around New York's largest outdoor winter rink, **Ice at Canalside** *(buffalowaterfront.com; adult/child $8/5, skate rental $5)*, or cruise Lake Erie on a two-hour **Spirit of Buffalo** schooner tour *(buffaloboattours.com; adult/child $39/19)*. From this point of view, Buffalo's renaissance has arrived.

MORE BUFFALO MUSEUMS & TOURS

Buffalo AKG Art Museum: Modern and contemporary art inside a 1905 neoclassical temple, 1962 modernist addition and 2023 glass-walled wing.

Burchfield Penney Art Center: Admire dreamy landscapes by local watercolorist Charles Ephraim Burchfield.

Buffalo History Museum: Covers 12,000 years of local history.

Silo City Ground and Vertical Tours: **Explore Buffalo** leads seasonal 1½-hour explorations of abandoned and repurposed grain silos.

Buffalo Transportation Pierce-Arrow Museum: Revs up motorheads with its collection of vintage vehicles and local history.

EATING & DRINKING IN BUFFALO: OUR PICKS

West Side Bazaar: Immigrant and refugee chefs show off their skills at this food hall featuring Congolese, Jamaican, Korean and more international eats. *11am-8pm Tue-Sat* **$**

Dapper Goose: The goose is debonair indeed, with smart takes on shareable American plates and meaty mains served under pressed-tin ceilings. *5-9pm Tue-Sun* **$$$**

Gabriel's Gate: The city's spicy, deep-fried Buffalo wings were invented at Anchor Bar (1964) but perfected here. *11:30am-midnight Mon-Fri, to 1am Sat & Sun* **$$**

duende: Ghostly grain silos and gardens surround this industrial indoor-outdoor bar pouring drinks inside a 1940s American Malting Company office building. *hours vary*

ALIZADASTUDIOS/GETTY IMAGES

Prospect Point Observation Tower

TOP EXPERIENCE

Niagara Falls

Prepare to be mystified: North America's most powerful falls dump roughly 700,000 gallons of water over three distinct cascades every second, plunging into the Niagara Gorge at 25mph. Their immensity is hypnotic, attracting conservationists, industrialists and thrill-seekers to the boundary between the US and Canada for centuries. Join thousands of onlookers, electrified by nature's spectacle each day.

DON'T MISS

- Maid of the Mist
- Prospect Point Observation Tower
- Luna Island
- Three Sisters Islands
- Goat Island
- Cave of the Winds
- Niagara Falls Underground Railroad Heritage Center

Celebrate Niagara's Sculptors

Begin your journey at **Prospect Point**, overlooking the crest of the American Falls. More than 12,000 years in the making, Niagara's story begins with receding glaciers from the last ice age, which carved the Great Lakes, unleashed a deluge of melting ice and formed the Niagara River linking Lake Erie and Lake Ontario.

The verdant crown atop the park owes its existence to the Free Niagara movement, a cadre of 19th-century environmentalists appalled by industrial abuse of the natural wonder. Their fiery advocacy culminated in the establishment of Niagara

PRACTICALITIES

- niagarafallsstatepark.com
- 24hr
- prices and hours vary by activity

Falls as the nation's first state park in 1885. Follow the park's sinuous pathways, designed by Calvert Vaux and Frederick Law Olmsted, to experience the falls for free.

Feel the Powerful Falls

Though walking above the falls is pretty, sailing into the thundering cascades is the best way to appreciate their force. On the **Maid of the Mist** *(maidofthemist.com; adult/child $30.25/19.75; enter at Prospect Point)* boat tour, operating since 1846, visitors brave the water's icy embrace on a half-hour ride. Despite the experience's theme-park trappings (long entrance lines; exit through a gift shop), the ride provides heart-pumping, must-see perspectives. Be sure to don the blue ponchos provided and store your phone somewhere safe – floating near Horseshoe Falls, the largest waterfall, can be like cruising into a tempest. Tickets include access to the **Prospect Point Observation Tower** ($1.25 when sold separately, but a sensible post-ride pitstop), which extends over the gorge for panoramic views.

Find Your Favorite Viewpoint

From Prospect Point, follow Goat Island Rd to an archipelago above the gorge. On tiny **Luna Island**, peer over railings to gasp at the brink of Bridal Veil Falls. **Three Sisters Islands** offers a glimpse of the park's untamed origins, spread across rocky tufts lapped by whitecaps. **Goat Island** is the largest of the collection, featuring **Cave of the Winds** *(adult/child $21/17)*, a hurricane-worthy waterfall encounter 175ft down into the gorge. Instead of a cave (it collapsed in the 1950s), visitors walk along a series of wooden boardwalks built 20ft from Bridal Veil Falls' nonstop torrents. The entire boardwalk is only installed during summer, though thousands of nesting seagulls make it a worthwhile sight out of season

You can partially admire Horseshoe Falls from Goat Island's **Terrapin Point**, but for unobstructed views, consider traversing the **Rainbow Bridge** *(ezbordercrossing.com; cars $6, pedestrians $1)* to Canada (passports required). While parts of Canada's Niagara suffer from over-commercialization, the scenery from **Queen Victoria Park** *(niagaraparks.com)* is tops.

Dive into Local History

Niagara Falls' proximity to Canada, which abolished slavery three decades before the US, made it a haven for freedom-seeking enslaved African Americans in the 19th century. Crossing the Niagara Gorge became a promising path to liberty, turning Niagara Falls into a crucial stop along the Underground Railroad. To learn more about the town's abolitionist past, head to the **Niagara Falls Underground Railroad Heritage Center** *(niagarafallsundergroundrailroad.org; adult/child $15/10)*, five minutes north by car, which centers stories of self-emancipating freedom seekers in its immersive exhibit *One More River to Cross*.

DAREDEVIL DAMSEL

Annie Edson Taylor celebrated her 63rd birthday in 1901 by climbing into a barrel and plunging over Niagara Falls. She became the first person to survive the death-wish journey, escaping with but a cut on her head. The stunt, she hoped, would solve her financial woes. It didn't, and her fame lasted as long as the ride – just over 15 minutes.

TOP TIPS

- Arrive early to park near Prospect Point ($10 Monday to Thursday, $15 Friday to Sunday) or on Goat Island.
- If walking isn't your speed, hop on the Niagara Scenic Trolley – a vintage hop-on, hop-off bus that cruises around the park April to December *(adult/child $5/3)*.
- Cycle around Niagara Falls using the bikeshare Reddy program or **Sight See Rentals** *(sightseerentals.com; per day $25)*.
- Food sold around the park is mediocre and overpriced. Bring snacks or hold out for a meal at **Savor** *(sunyniagara.edu/nfci/savor)*, prepared by Niagara Falls Culinary Institute students.
- Purchase timed-entry tickets for Cave of the Winds in advance.
- Wear shoes you can get wet – waterproof is best.

New Jersey

BEACHFRONT ESCAPES | SUMMERTIME BOARDWALKS | HISTORIC TOWNS

Places

Cape May p122
Wildwood p123
Asbury Park p124
Long Beach Island p124
Sandy Hook p125
Princeton p126
Lambertville p129

TOP TIP

Weekend traffic along the Jersey Shore can be heinous. Get an early start to avoid highway pile-ups. If you're spending most of your time along the coast, know that many communities charge a beach-access fee. You'll have to pay between Long Beach Island north to Sandy Hook. Atlantic City and Wildwood are free.

Don't be fooled by everything you've seen on TV. Sure, some things from *The Real Housewives of New Jersey* and *The Sopranos* ring true – namely the thick Jersey accents (lose the 'New' to sound local). But it's not all McMansions and mobsters. Look beyond northern Jersey's labyrinthine highways and you'll see why it's called the Garden State. Farmland and green parks bloom between two important waterways: the Delaware River to the west and the Atlantic Ocean to the east, lapping 127 miles of coastline.

The state's hurricane of history goes from Indigenous Lenape territory to British colony to important battleground during the American Revolutionary War. After WWII, it became a destination for African Americans moving north, and industrial cities bolstered the country's economy. Most people come here to visit the Jersey Shore – running from super-sized boardwalks to tranquil summer towns – though inland hamlets steeped in history are equally worth exploring.

GETTING AROUND

The most common way to navigate Jersey is with a car. Don't get caught off guard at the gas station: this is the only US state where you can't pump fuel – an attendant will do it for you. Trains connect much of the state to NYC via **NJ Transit** *(njtransit.com)*. The North Jersey Coast Line stops at seaside towns including Asbury Park, while the Northeast Corridor Line runs through Princeton and links to Philadelphia. Ferries are also an option: ride the pedestrian-only **Seastreak** *(seastreak.com)* from NYC to Sandy Hook, or the **Cape May–Lewes ferry** *(capemaylewesferry.com)* to Lewes, near Rehoboth Beach, Delaware.

NEW JERSEY
Goshen
Milford
Monroe
Peekskill
Hudson River
Promised Land State Park
Gouldsboro State Park
Childs State Forest Park
Sussex
Wallkill River
Warwick
NEW YORK
Bushkill
Franklin
Surprise Lake
Newton
White Plains
Stroudsburg
Lake Hopatcong
New Rochelle
Paterson
Yonkers
Mt Vernon
PENNSYLVANIA
Bangor
Dover
Palmerton
Morristown
Newark
New York City
Washington
Jersey City
Easton
Elizabeth
Round Valley Reservoir
Allentown
Bethlehem
Plainfield
Frenchtown
Raritan River
New Brunswick
Sandy Hook
Quakertown
East Greenville
Lambertville
Hopewell
Red Bank
Princeton
Doylestown
Long Branch
Freehold
Pottstown
Trenton
Asbury Park
Schuylkill River
Lakewood
West Chester
Philadelphia
Camden
Beachwood
Brendan T Byrne State Forest
Barnegat Bay
Delaware River
Pinelands National Reserve
Wilmington
Wharton State Forest
New Castle
Long Beach Island
Tuckerton
NEW JERSEY
Salem
Beach Haven
Vineland
Middleton
Bridgeton
Millville
Pleasantville
Atlantic City
Ocean City
Dover
Delaware Bay
Stone Harbor
ATLANTIC OCEAN
Wildwood
Cape May
Milford
0 40 km
0 20 miles
DELAWARE
Lewes

JERSEY VINO

New Jersey's wine industry, youthful and growing, can trace its origins to Cape May's farmlands, blessed as they are with a long, frost-free growing season. But it was the 1981 New Jersey Wine Act, which stamped out restrictive Prohibition-era rules about winemaking, that allowed the industry to grow. The **New Jersey Wine Grower's Association** *(newjerseywines.com)* provides a wine 'passport' you can get stamped at some three dozen stops.

One of the seven wineries in Cape May County worth visiting is brother-run **Hawk Haven** *(hawkhaven vineyard.com)*. They began growing grapes on their grandparents' farmland where lima beans once sprouted, experimenting and figuring out what the grapes naturally wanted to do. There's a food truck out back and live music on Friday nights in summer.

Cape May

See Victorians by the shore

Cape May, located on New Jersey's southern tip, is the only place in the state where the sun rises and sets over the water. It's idyllic. It should be no surprise, then, that it became one of the nation's first seaside resorts in the mid-18th century. Climb the 199 steps to the lookout at **Cape May Lighthouse** *(capemaymac.org; adult/child $12/8)* to understand what those early vacationers were after: sweeping gold beaches tumbling into the blue Atlantic.

Much of the lavish architecture built to house those trend-setting beach bums burned down in an 1878 fire, sweeping through 35 acres across town. When Cape May rebuilt, it was the height of the Victorian era – a style that characterizes today's landscape.

Take a **Cape May MAC trolley tour** *(capemaymac.org; adult/child $20/15)* for an overview of Cape May's architectural legacy. The guide points out Italianate and Queen Anne towers, shingled mansard roofs and distinctive Victorian colors, with asides about the town's history. The pastel-painted gingerbread homes, with wraparound porches and filigree trim, are outliers along the Shore – otherwise known for generic, contemporary condos.

If you're raring to see a historic home's interior, head to the whimsically designed **Emlen Physick Estate** from 1879 *(capemaymac.org; adult/child $20/15)*, where 45-minute guided tours by volunteers provide details about how Cape May's upper class once lived.

Look to the sea and sky

Philadelphians and Jerseyites aren't the only ones who flock 'down the shore' (local lingo for heading to Jersey's coastline). Birds, butterflies and bottlenose dolphins also bum-rush Cape May throughout the year.

The town's peninsula is an important migratory crossroads – best appreciated in spring and autumn, when birds on the Atlantic Flyway pass through. If you're new to birding, get your bearings at the **Cape May Bird Observatory** *(njaudubon.org/centers/cape-may-bird-observatory)*. Pick up binoculars and field guides in the bookstore, then hop on the observatory's mile-long loop trail in search of winged wonders.

If you're already a big-time bird-watcher, consider visiting in September and October, when Cape May's skies are ruled by peregrine falcons – predatory birds known for being some of the

EATING IN CAPE MAY: OUR PICKS

Uncle Bill's Pancake House: Drawing crowds hungry for butter-drenched flapjacks since the 1960s. *8am-1pm* **$**

Taco Caballito: This open-air beachfront tequileria and taco joint has especially good service. Try the short-rib banh mi. *noon-10pm, to 11pm Fri & Sat* **$**

Mad Batter: Eat fluffy oat pancakes or rich clam chowder in this white Victorian B&B beloved for brunch. Live music nightly. *8am-9pm* **$$**

Lobster House: A classic waterfront seafood experience. Order from the raw bar or takeout window, or grab a wharfside table for a full-blown lobster. *11:30am-3pm & 4:30-10pm* **$$$**

AGENTSNAP/SHUTTERSTOCK

Cape May Lighthouse

world's fastest animals. Head to **Cape May Point State Park** *(nj.gov/dep/parksandforests)* to watch them swoop through the air.

Autumn is also a fantastic time to spot monarch butterflies, which undertake the longest migration of any North American butterfly species, flitting from Canada to Mexico in six to eight months. Their arrival in Cape May can turn the landscape into a fluttering orange kaleidoscope.

In spring and summer, you might spot New Jersey's most iconic endangered bird – the piping plover. This migratory shorebird requires sandy beaches with few disturbances. Some areas have symbolic fencing with informational signs, marking nesting sites and reminding people to keep their distance. Be quiet and listen attentively – you might hear one peep (or 'pipe') before you see it.

As for marine life, bottlenose dolphins and migrating whales arrive around spring. Several companies run cruises out of the marina to spot them flipping their fins. Set sail with **Cape May Whale Watch & Research Center** *(capemaywhalewatch.com; 2hr Dolphin & Bird Watch tour from $40)*.

Wildwood

The Big Daddy of boardwalks

Wildwood's boardwalk is summer on steroids. **Morey's Piers** *(moreyspiers.com; packages from $45)*, probably the best and biggest of all the Jersey Shore's parks, takes up vast chunks of boardwalk real estate, with three amusement piers and two water parks. Locals debate whose is the better slice of pizza on the beach: **Sam's** *(samswildwood.com)* thin crust or **Mack's** doughy? **Wildwood's Honky Tonk** *(honkytonkww.com)*, a huge country bar with live music, is housed in a former boardwalk arcade. And since 1949, a miniature rubber-tired **tram** *(wildwood.com; $5)* runs the boardwalk's length, chirping 'Watch the tram car, please.' Cycling can also be fun – a

CINEMATIC JERSEY MOBSTERS

New Jersey's glittering shoreline has attracted centuries of beach bums – along with crime bosses, particularly in the 1920s, when rum runners used its coastal inlets, rivers and bays to offload illegal liquor during Prohibition, a phenomenon explored in the TV series *Boardwalk Empire* (2010–14). The show was inspired by real-life Atlantic City-based gangster Enoch 'Nucky' Johnson, who controlled and influenced politicians, businessmen and the heads of organized-crime families. He even helped host the Atlantic City Conference – the first-ever national meeting of the American mob. The end of Prohibition marked the end of Atlantic City's allure as a 'den of iniquity' – though it remains a gambler's Gomorrah.

BOAT RIDES ALONG THE SHORE

Tiki Bar Boat: Book a 1½-hour trip on the dry-grass-covered pontoon in Beach Haven. BYOB.

Miss Beach Haven: Join a three-hour fluke fishing tour several miles from Beach Haven.

Black Pearl Pirate Tours: Kids can go full Jack Sparrow, shooting water cannons at an accompanying boat.

Atlantic City Cruises: Dolphin-watching tours with a money-back guarantee of success; the captain provides background on wildlife.

Seastreak: Tours are run on four winter Saturdays; a wildlife expert educates passengers on a variety of birds and seals.

EQROY/SHUTTERSTOCK

Convention Hall

12-mile bike path runs along the oceanfront. Pick up wheels from **Crest Bike Rental** *(crestbikerental.com; adult single-speeds from $15)*.

For those interested in solitude, head to the beach access point at Rambler Rd, south of the boardwalk. There's free street parking nearby, plus clean bathrooms. For even more tranquility, visit **Hereford Lighthouse** (pronounced *heh-ford; herefordinletlighthouse.com; free*) from 1874, situated at the northern end of North Wildwood with a pretty garden.

Visit on Friday evenings to end your Wildwood day with a bang: fireworks light up the night sky.

Asbury Park

Relive the Jersey Shore's Jazz Age

Artsy and edgy Asbury Park is the Jersey Shore's jewel of renewal – a once-derelict haunt that's undergone a bohemian rebirth over the past decade, attracting a diverse crowd of artsy couples, young families and LGBTIQ+ folks who arrive via New Jersey Transit from NYC. Mosey along the historic seaside boardwalk at the center of the renaissance.

Kicks things off by admiring the architecture. Enter the boardwalk near Fifth Ave to see **Convention Hall**, built between 1928 and 1930 by the same designers behind Manhattan's Grand Central Terminal. Continue south past sizzling food stands to see the gutted beaux-arts casino and carousel – ghostly reminders of the town's Jazz Age heyday.

Along your stroll, join retired pinball wizards rediscovering their youth at **Silverball Retro Arcade** *(silverballmuseum.com/asbury-park; 1/6hr $17.50/20)*. There are over 160 restored arcade games – including a 'rotary merchandiser' from the 1930s. Placards above machines offer historical context.

If you want to join the beach brigade, you'll need to book a beach pass *(apbeachpasses.com; weekdays $7, weekends & holidays $10)* from Memorial Day to Labor Day.

Rock out in Asbury Park

Bruce Springsteen put this beach town on the map with his 1973 debut album *Greetings from Asbury Park* – and 50 years later, the locals still love grooving to 'The Boss.' Follow Springsteen's path to fame by heading to the **Stone Pony** *(stoneponyonline.com; tickets from $35)*, a boardwalk-adjacent rock club where he honed his sound in the '70s. Check the venue's Summer Stage schedule to see big-name acts perform under the stars from May through September. If you don't like the line-up, see who's playing at **Wonder Bar** *(wonderbarasburypark.com; tickets from $28)*, where up-and-coming acts rip through sets of rock, pop and punk.

Long Beach Island

Try Jersey's 'Chowda'

One of the best off-season times to visit Beach Haven is in early October for the **Chowda Cookoff** *(bhchowdercookoff.com)*, formerly known as the Chowda Fest. During this event, local restaurants go head to head, competing to have the best red or white chowder on Long Beach Island (or the best 'Jersey chowder,' a combo of red and white). There's usually a 'most unique chowder' category; one past noteworthy winner was clam-chowder ice cream – a fishy yet refreshing take on the summer dessert. The opening and closing ceremonies attract large crowds – it's often the last weekend when summer-home owners head 'down the shore.'

Sandy Hook

The Jersey Shore's northern tip

It's hard to believe Sandy Hook is only a 40-minute **ferry ride** *(seastreakferry.com; adult/child $49/22)* from NYC's Financial District. This stretch of the Jersey Shore's northern peninsula is a far cry from city life: from here, NYC's skyscrapers appear toy-sized.

Cyclists cruise along the peninsula's 7-mile multi-use path, while history buffs tour **Fort Hancock** *(nps.gov; day pass $20)* – an old army base, home to America's oldest operating **lighthouse**, built in 1764 (park rangers provide tours from 1pm to 4:30pm April to October). The most popular reason to venture here is for pristine beaches. For family-friendly fun, stick to Beaches B, C, D and E. North Beach tends toward the quiet side.

JOYOUS JERSEY FESTIVALS

Red, White & Blueberry Festival: Hammonton, the birthplace of the American blueberry, kicks off this June celebration with a massive pancake breakfast.

Atlantic City Air Show: Half a million people fly to AC in mid-August; come on warm-up day before to avoid the throngs.

Mutzfest: Fill up on mozzarella at Hoboken's most famous April festival. Have more room? Go pastry crazy.

Barefoot Country Music Festival: Wildwood books A-listers for beachfront performances on the third weekend in June.

Shadfest: Lambertville's April shindig honors fishing for shad (the largest in the herring family) with music, food and fun.

EATING AROUND ASBURY PARK: OUR PICKS

Ada's Gojjo: A curious combination of Dominican and Ethiopian in Asbury Park, with dishes from both cultures on the same menu. *noon-8pm Sun & Tue-Thu, to 9pm Fri & Sat* **$**

Starving Artist: Casual Ocean Grove spot with a large outdoor patio for breakfast, grilled fare and fried seafood; ice cream is available at the adjacent shop. *8am-2pm Thu-Tue* **$**

Heirloom at the St Laurent: One-of-a-kind mouthwatering dishes innovatively combining flavors and ingredients. *11am-2pm & 5-10pm Wed-Mon* **$$$**

Moonstruck: Has views of Wesley Lake, dividing Asbury and Ocean Grove, and an extensive, Italian-leaning menu. It's romantically lit up at night. 4-9pm Wed-Sun **$$$**

SURFING THE JERSEY SHORE

Chris Sciarra, co-owner of Kona Surf Company in Wildwood. *@konasurfcompany*

We have beginner-friendly waves that can get really good, even 10ft to 15ft during hurricane season. The lowest swell is during the summer season. Generally, the further north, the better and bigger the waves are, around Belmar and spots in Monmouth County. The area's best breaks are Cape May's Cove and Poverty beaches; in Wildwood; at 10th and 2nd Sts in North Wildwood and at Diamond Beach south of Wildwood Crest.

Beginners: check out Jason Reagan's Cape May surf school *(jasonreagansurf school.com)*, Randazzo surf school and camps *(randazzosurf.com)* in Margate and North Wildwood, and Tim Kaye's Surftopia *(thesurftopia.com)* in Wildwood for rentals and lessons.

If you want to throw caution (and your swimsuit) to the wind, head to **Gunnison Beach** – a naturist oasis on Sandy Hook's curved shaft. Locals say it's been a skinny-dipping sensation since Fort Hancock's army troop days, and now, on top of being a time-honored tradition, it's New Jersey's only legal clothing-optional shore. LGBTIQ+ travelers take note – the beach's south side is a favorite among gay men, who bring elaborate beach set-ups for day-long fiestas. As for the rules, there are two to hold dear: this isn't a peep show, so don't stare, and if you don't want to get naked, get lost. As for packing – a towel, sunblock, water and snacks are musts. Bring an umbrella – shade is a hot commodity.

Princeton

Half a day with the Ivy League

Perfectly coiffed Princeton is packed with elegant architecture and anchored by its top-tier Ivy League university. The university's Nassau Hall, built in the mid-1700s, became one of the largest stone structures in the American colonies and briefly served as the nation's capital when the Continental Congress arrived in 1783. Like most seats of learning, Princeton is flush with brewpubs and chic boutiques – though it skews more 'bougie upper-crust' than 'penny-pinching collegiate.' Spend half a day studying its streets.

Start by following the footsteps of Princeton's smart set around the Collegiate Gothic **campus** on a self-guided tour. Head to *visitour.io/princeton-university* and choose the free standard Orange Key guide – a one-hour trip to 11 destinations around the campus's immaculate landscaping.

It's also worth peeking inside the **Princeton University Art Museum** *(artmuseum.princeton.edu; free)*, slated to reopen in a new, modern complex in fall 2025. The collection is like a mini version of NYC's Metropolitan Museum of Art, with 117,000 artworks spanning over 5000 years of global creativity. Budget an hour.

Once you're ready to graduate from college life, head to nearby Palmer Sq, edged with preppie stores, and stroll the surrounding streets for light shopping. Vinyl and CD lovers may lose track of time flipping through **Princeton Record Exchange's** *(prex.com)* 100,000 non-digitized musical selections. Bibliophiles and casual readers can make like a Princeton English major and wander the two floors of **Labyrinth Books** *(labyrinthbooks.com)*.

EATING IN PRINCETON: OUR PICKS

MAP P127

Chuck's Spring Street Cafe: Wings are the thing at Chuck's: you can order up to 100 of these twice-cooked tangy buffalo-style ones at a time. *11am-9pm Tue-Sun* $

Little Chef Pastry Shop: The Haitian-born pastry chef here has been spinning out decadent croissants, napoleons and eclairs since 2003. *9:30am-3:30pm* $

Winberie's Restaurant & Bar: Aka 'the Princeton Pub'; has the town's best fried chicken, as well as other upscale comfort food. *11:30am-11pm* $

Mistral: Serves three- to four-course brunches and dinners, with flavors ranging from the Caribbean to Scandinavia. *5-9pm Mon-Fri, 11:30am-2pm & 4-10pm Sat & Sun* $$$

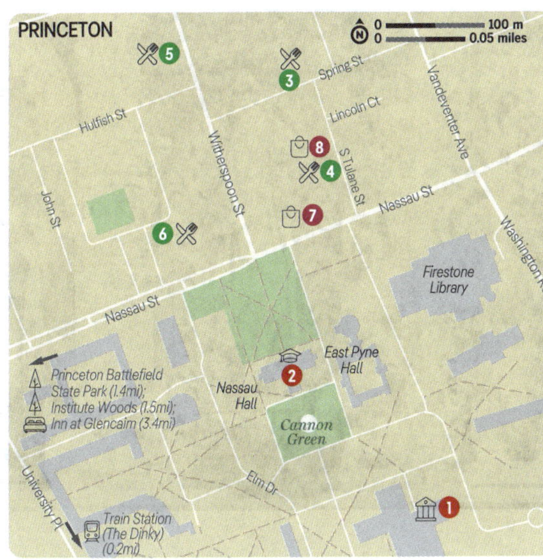

SIGHTS
1 Princeton University Art Museum
2 Princeton University

EATING
3 Chuck's Spring Street Cafe
4 Little Chef Pastry Shop
5 Mistral
6 Winberie's Restaurant & Bar

SHOPPING
7 Labyrinth Books
8 Princeton Record Exchange

Walk through Revolutionary woods

Princeton Battlefield State Park *(nj.gov/dep/parksandforests; free)* is mostly a grassy field with some plaques and a historic house – but use your imagination, and a bloody scene unfolds. On January 3, 1777, General George Washington and his ill-equipped troops won a decisive battle here against British forces, the world's most powerful army at the time. Hundreds of men lost their lives. It's widely regarded as a turning point in the fight for American independence.

Sharing the same parking lot is **Institute Woods** *(ias.edu/about/campus-and-lands)* – a 600-acre slice of forested countryside. Washington and his troops marched through these woods before the Battle of Princeton. Later, Robert Oppenheimer, Albert Einstein and John Nash (to name a few intellectual luminaries) found the forest a beneficial refuge for contemplation. These days, the pathways are beloved for strolling and birding – it's an important stop for warblers during spring migration, when the number of avian species jumps from 42 to 200.

MORE AMERICAN REVOLUTION HISTORY

Follow George Washington's path to victory outside **Lambertville** (p129), where he crossed the Delaware River before coming to Princeton, and see the spot where he trained soldiers at Pennsylvania's **Valley Forge** (p140).

EATING IN DINERS BEYOND PRINCETON: OUR PICKS

White Mana Diner: For Jersey kids, sitting at the circular linoleum counter is still a rite of passage at this pioneer of the fast-food hamburger. *8am-11pm* $

Tick Tock Diner: Aka 'The Tick,' this legendary diner in Clifton serves classics like disco fries covered in mozzarella and brown gravy. *7am-10pm* $

Shut up and Eat!: This Tom's River spot adds a dose of Jersey attitude with pajama-clad waitresses, snappy repartee and a cornucopia of kitsch. *6:30am-3:30pm* $

Summit Diner: Grab a swivel stool to chow down on traditional diner breakfasts and sandwiches at this railroad-car-designed greasy spoon. *5:30am-4pm* $

DINER DEMOCRACY

The diner is a chrome-covered bastion of Americana – an affordable, egalitarian 'greasy spoon' serving all-day breakfast alongside sandwiches, pies, wings and sides. Menus are novels. Coffees are bottomless. They're immortalized in Edward Hopper's *Nighthawks* painting and Suzanne Vega's song 'Tom's Diner.' Roughly 450 of these swivel-stool sanctuaries call New Jersey home – more than any other US state, making it the world's diner capital. In the past decade, however, many nostalgia-stuffed restaurants shuttered – victims of rising expenses and changing tastes. But the diner isn't done – it's adapting to the times. New additions to the scene incorporate international flavors, like **Golden Diner** (p67) in NYC; others celebrate locavore movements, like **Phoenicia Diner** (p107) in the Catskills.

ANN KAPUSTINA/SHUTTERSTOCK

America's magnificent Hindu temple

The 200ft spires of the **BAPS Swaminarayan Akshardham** *(usa.akshardham.org; free; timed reservations required for weekends and holidays)*, one hour south of Princeton, rise from green fields like limestone mountains – a modern echo of ancient Angkor Wat. Completed in 2023, this is the largest Hindu temple complex outside of India, with roughly 1.9 million cu ft of interlocking granite, marble and more decorative stones sourced worldwide. Its multiple buildings sprawl over nearly 180 acres and showcase some 10,000 statues – including the 49ft gold deity Nilkanth Varni, the child-yogi form of Bhagwan Swaminarayan, balanced on one leg. (According to followers, he held this yogic position for 2½ months in a Himalayan winter.)

New Jersey has one of the nation's largest Hindu populations, and the temple serves as an important place of pilgrimage. Within the Akshardham – which means 'divine abode' – you'll find intricate carvings depicting moments from Swaminarayan's life. Other Hindu deities have separate altars, and according to the scriptures and principles, they're fed, clothed and 'put to rest' several times daily.

There's also a secular edge to the site, with quotes from Martin Luther King Jr and Albert Einstein. In fact, it's a visitor-friendly experience, welcoming plenty of tourists more interested in architecture than spiritual experiences. Guided tours provide context, offered hourly on Monday, Wednesday, Thursday and Friday between 10am and 5pm; advanced booking recommended. Wearing shorts or sleeveless tops isn't permitted (sarongs are provided if needed). For food, drop into **Shayona Café** *(11am-8pm)*, serving excellent vegetarian Indian fare.

Though the site is awe-inspiring, its construction was clouded in controversy. In 2021, the organization was accused of using forced labor to complete the complex – which required

BAPS Swaminarayan Akshardham

an estimated 4.7 million hours of work across 15 years. The plaintiffs withdrew their lawsuit in 2023, but not before the allegations attracted widespread news coverage.

Lambertville

Antique treasures on the Delaware

Lambertville, perched on the eastern banks of the Delaware River, is an antiques oasis, with half a dozen top-quality shops in town, along with art galleries and home-furnishing stores with mid-century-modern flair. You'll find most of the action around North Union St – though the area's biggest and oldest operation is 2 miles south on Rte 29 – the **Golden Nugget Antique Flea Market** *(gnflea.com)*, open since 1967. The outdoor tables and 20-plus specialist indoor stores are a haphazard cornucopia of potential *Antiques Roadshow* treasures. Haggle to your heart's content with vendors hawking furniture, books and a thousand other collectibles.

People often pair a trip to Lambertville with neighboring New Hope, PA (p141) – its sister town on the Delaware's western side.

Cycle through history

The 70-mile **D & R Canal trail** *(dandrcanal.org)* traces the 19th-century Delaware and Raritan Canal, built as an industrial shipping route. Now a linear parkway through Central New Jersey, it's a sensational spot for cycling. Rent bikes from **Pure Energy Cycling & Java House** in Lambertville *(pure energycycling.com; per hour from $18)* then pedal 7 miles south to tour **Washington Crossing State Park** *(nj.gov; free)*, commemorating the site where George Washington and his men snuck across the Delaware in 1776. Wander the grounds to soak up the history, then head further south or loop back to Lambertville for a hearty meal.

BEST STATE FORESTS & PARKS

Visit *nj.gov/dep/parksandforests* for more park info.

High Point State Park: The state's highest point (1803ft), with views of the Delaware River and surroundings; great for camping and hiking.

Norvin Green State Forest: Awesomely isolated 5000-acre forest near the New York border; trails from moderate to difficult, with spectacular views.

Cheesequake State Park: A blend of pine barrens, salt- and freshwater swamps and forest. Choose between four easy to moderate trails, swimming and kayaking.

Kittatinny Valley State Park: Home to lakes with campsites, hiking and cycling paths. Part of the Appalachian Trail runs along the ridge.

Wharton State Forest: New Jersey's largest single tract of parkland forest in the Pine Barrens.

Pennsylvania

REVOLUTIONARY HISTORY | ARTS & CULTURE | RIVER TOWNS

Places

Philadelphia p130
Brandywine Valley p139
Valley Forge p140
Doylestown p140
New Hope p141
The Poconos p142
Lancaster p143
Gettysburg p144
Pennsylvania Wilds p144
Pittsburgh p146
Laurel Highlands p148

Sprawling Pennsylvania (PA) sits at an American crossroads, linking the East Coast's end to the Midwest's beginning. The Mason–Dixon line runs along its southern border – a symbolic divide between northern and southern sensibilities. In Philadelphia, colonial architecture from the American Revolution shares the skyline with contemporary skyscrapers. In Lancaster, sports cars whizz by horse-drawn buggies guided by Amish farmers. The Civil War's deadliest battle once raged in Gettysburg, now a peaceful park. Steel factories that fueled Pittsburgh's industrial days stand dormant as the Rust Belt city rises from the ashes. Between it all, patchworks of forests and rushing rivers link mountains and rural hamlets, where elk herds and eagles sometimes outnumber people. On top of covering some 46,000 sq miles, PA captures a diverse spectrum of American culture. It's got world-class art and outdoor adventures, queer communities and conservative towns. Equal parts Philly cheesesteak and Pennsylvania Dutch scrapple, the Keystone State defies tidy labels.

GETTING AROUND

Philadelphia is accessible from NYC and DC via Amtrak train and easy to navigate sans car. The rest of the state is sprawling: you need a set of wheels to see it all. GPS service can be sketchy away from major towns; a hard-copy map is a good backup. Gas station chains (Sheetz, Wawa, Rutter's) might be your best bet for food in remote regions.

Philadelphia

MAP P133

Discover world-changing documents

In the shadow of Independence Hall, the **National Constitution Center** *(constitutioncenter.org; adult/youth $19/15)* stands as a pilgrimage site for those seeking to understand democracy's roots and the challenges it faces.

The museum does a fantastic job dramatizing the US Constitution – an otherwise dry, dense document outlining the government's structure and the rights of citizens. Visits start with a theater-in-the-round presentation by a single actor explaining the evolution of the political experiment. 'The Story of We the People' exhibit narrates a captivating journey through the US Constitution. Interactive displays and multimedia presentations dive into detail about the founding

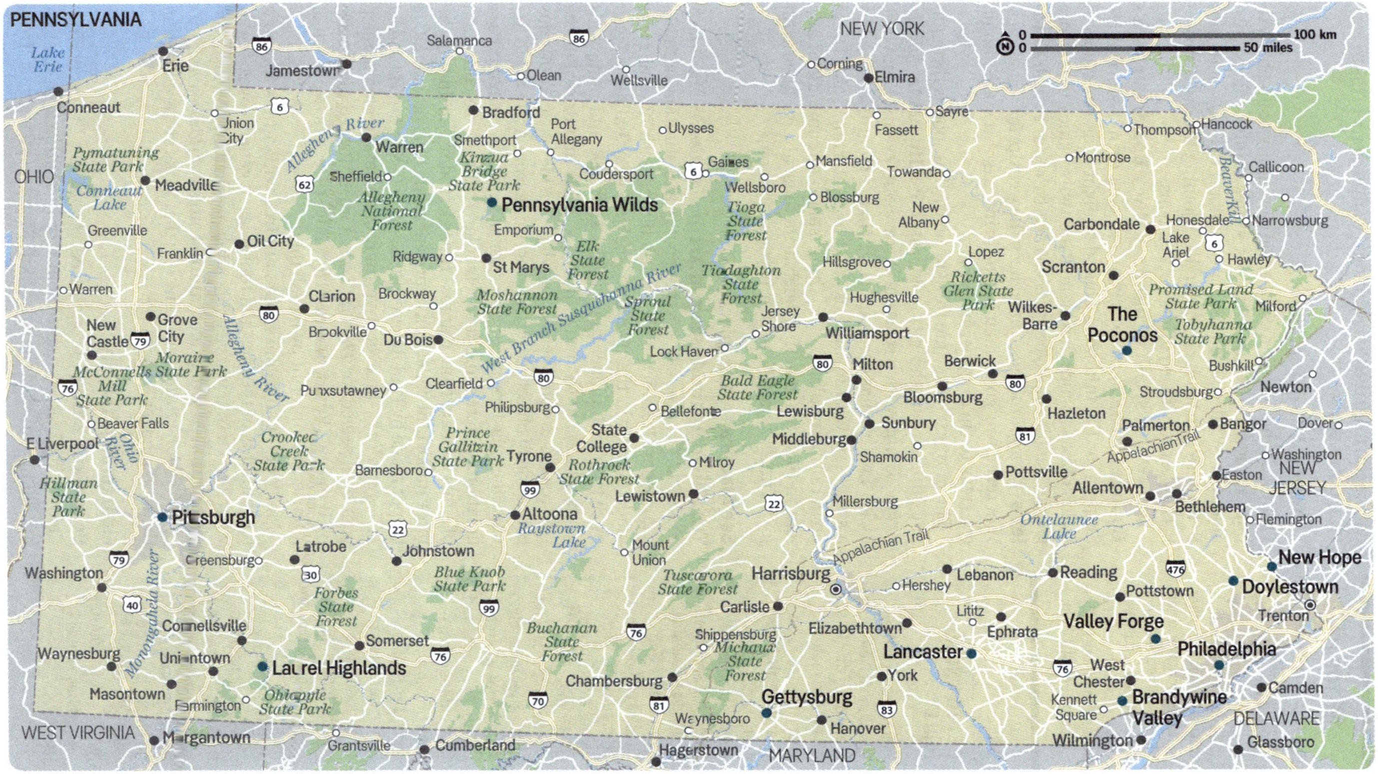
PENNSYLVANIA
Lake Erie
NEW YORK
OHIO
WEST VIRGINIA
MARYLAND
NEW JERSEY
DELAWARE
0 100 km
0 50 miles
Erie
Conneaut
Jamestown
Salamanca
Olean
Wellsville
Corning
Elmira
Sayre
Fassett
Ulysses
Bradford
Union City
Warren
Allegheny River
Smethport
Port Allegany
Kinzua Bridge State Park
Coudersport
Gaines
Mansfield
Towanda
Thompson
Hancock
Montrose
Callicoon
Beaverkill
Pymatuning State Park
Conneaut Lake
Meadville
Sheffield
Allegheny National Forest
Pennsylvania Wilds
Wellsboro
Blossburg
Tioga State Forest
New Albany
Carbondale
Honesdale
Narrowsburg
Lake Ariel
Hawley
Greenville
Franklin
Oil City
Ridgway
Emporium
St Marys
Elk State Forest
Tiadaghton State Forest
Hillsgrove
Lopez
Scranton
Warren
Clarion
Brockway
Moshannon State Forest
West Branch Susquehanna River
Sprout State Forest
Jersey Shore
Hughesville
Ricketts Glen State Park
Wilkes-Barre
Promised Land State Park
Milford
Tobyhanna State Park
The Poconos
New Castle
Grove City
Allegheny River
Brookville
Du Bois
Lock Haven
Williamsport
Milton
Berwick
Bushkill
Moraine State Park
McConnells Mill State Park
Punxsutawney
Clearfield
Philipsburg
Bellefonte
Bald Eagle State Forest
Lewisburg
Bloomsburg
Hazleton
Stroudsburg
Newton
Beaver Falls
Ohio River
State College
Sunbury
Middleburg
Shamokin
Palmerton
Bangor
Dover
E Liverpool
Crooked Creek State Park
Prince Gallitzin State Park
Tyrone
Rothrock State Forest
Milroy
Barnesboro
Appalachian Trail
Washington
Hillman State Park
Pottsville
Easton
Allentown
Bethlehem
Flemington
Pittsburgh
Altoona
Raystown Lake
Lewistown
Millersburg
Ontelaunee Lake
Latrobe
Johnstown
Greensburg
Mount Union
Appalachian Trail
New Hope
Washington
Monongahela River
Blue Knob State Park
Forbes State Forest
Tuscarora State Forest
Harrisburg
Hershey
Lebanon
Reading
Pottstown
Doylestown
Trenton
Connellsville
Carlisle
Lititz
Ephrata
Valley Forge
Waynesburg
Uniontown
Laurel Highlands
Somerset
Buchanan State Forest
Shippensburg
Michaux State Forest
Elizabethtown
Lancaster
Philadelphia
Masontown
Farmington
Ohiopyle State Park
Chambersburg
York
West Chester
Camden
Gettysburg
Kennett Square
Brandywine Valley
Morgantown
Grantsville
Cumberland
Waynesboro
Hanover
Hagerstown
Wilmington
Glassboro
6
62
80
79
76
86
22
99
30
40
70
81
83
476

TOP TIP

Prepare for the Philadelphia dialect. 'Water' sounds like 'wooder,' 'youse' is the plural 'you,' a 'hoagie' is a sandwich (usually a roll with meat and other accoutrements) and 'jeet yet?' is someone asking if you've had food. If you haven't, ask them for a recommendation: Philly is foodie central. Dig in.

GET TO KNOW PHILLY

Philadelphia is the USA's most American metropolis thanks to it's art and melt-in-your-mouth cuisine, though it's the city's prominence in US history that usually steals the spotlight. Founded by idealistic 17th-century English Quaker William Penn, Philadelphia's name comes from ancient Greek, meaning 'brotherly love.' Philly, as it's affectionately known, was where the colonies declared their independence from Britain and served as the first US capital. It later developed into a leading industrial town, then fell on hard times in the mid-20th century. The economic boom, bust and 21st-century rebirth molded it into a scrappy survivor – no longer the middle child between NYC and DC, but a cultural powerhouse holding its own.

document, from the Constitutional Convention of 1787 to contemporary debates.

Show your LGBTIQ+ pride

Philly's Gayborhood – a compact area roughly bound by Walnut, Spruce, Broad and 11th Sts – flies rainbow flags with abandon. While there are plenty of non-LGBTIQ+ activities to do here (particularly for foodies), joining the queer crowd is the best way to experience its charms.

Start with a splash of history at divey **Bob & Barbara's Lounge** *(bobandbarbaras.com)*, serving drinks since 1969. Stop by for the infamous Thursday night drag show hosted by Lisa Lisa ('so nice they named her twice') since 1995. More gender-bending lip-sync assassins death drop at **Frank Bradley's** *(frankybradleys.com)*; check the website for showtimes. Wherever you go, remember to bring cash: it's a common courtesy to tip drag performers.

The most exciting time to visit the Gayborhood is throughout June, when the city celebrates **Philly Pride** *(philly pride365.org)* with a series of extravagant events. Festivities kick off with a massive march early in the month, followed by a street fair with food trucks and live entertainment. Dress up in rainbow-colored everything, splash on some glitter and join in the fun (sometimes debaucherous, always filled with joy). This is a party where everyone's welcome.

See American masterpieces

The **Philadelphia Museum of Art** *(philamuseum.org; adult/child $30/free)*, the city's premier cultural institution, occupies a gorgeous Grecian temple–style building with 72 stone steps made famous in the 1976 film *Rocky:* Rocky Balboa (played by Sylvester Stallone) runs up the staircase and pumps his arms triumphantly. You'll likely see a few imitators. But the real reason to come here is for what's inside – a 200,000-plus collection of objects covering everything from Asian art to Renaissance masters, post-impressionist work and contemporary creations. There's also a spectacular 12,000-piece collection of American art from colonial times to today – including the most important collection of presidential china outside DC, a teapot made by Paul Revere and Georgia O'Keeffe's *Two Calla Lilies on Pink* – an evocative study of flowers in bloom. Keep your eyes peeled for *The Life Line*, a water-logged nightmare by Winslow Homer, and *Interior,* Edgar Degas's depiction of a tense encounter lit by lamplight.

Many of the museum's tours are free with admission; join a Highlights of the Museum tour to get a general overview of what's on view. If you've got headphones handy, try one of the museum's free self-guided **audio tours** *(philamuseum.org/visit/visitor-guide)*, including one that looks at the collection through a queer lens.

Float through the city

Schuylkill Banks (pronounced *skool*-kill), lining Philly's Center City West, is a scenic outdoor recreation area stretching along 8 miles of the Schuylkill River's eastern bank, from

(continues on p136)

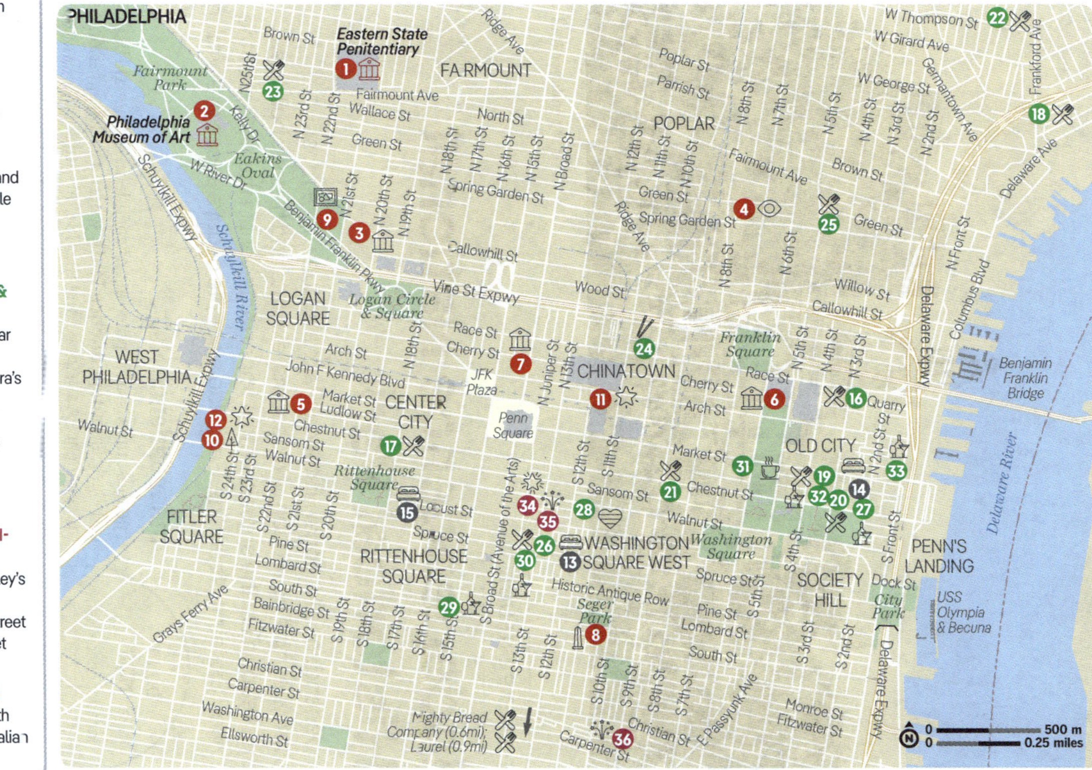

![Highlights] **HIGHLIGHTS**
1 Eastern State Penitentiary
2 Philadelphia Museum of Art

SIGHTS
3 Barnes Foundation
4 Edgar Allan Poe National Historic Site
5 Mütter Museum
6 National Constitution Center
7 Pennsylvania Academy of the Fine Arts
8 Philadelphia's Magic Gardens
9 Rodin Museum
10 Schuylkill Banks

ACTIVITIES
11 City Food Tours
12 Hidden River Outfitters

SLEEPING
13 Alexander Inn
14 Apple Hostels
15 Franklin on Rittenhouse

EATING
16 Cafe Ole
17 Cleavers
see 17 Dandelion
18 Elwood
19 Fork
20 Forsythia
21 High Street Philadelphia
22 Laser Wolf
23 Little Pete's
24 Nan Zhou Hand Drawn Noodle House
25 Silk City
26 Vetri Cucina

DRINKING & NIGHTLIFE
27 48 Record Bar
28 Bike Stop
29 Bob & Barbara's Lounge
30 Dirty Franks
31 La Colombe
32 National Mechanics
33 Panorama

ENTERTAINMENT
34 Franky Bradley's
35 Philly Pride
36 South 9th Street Italian Market Festival

SHOPPING
see 36 South 9th Street Italian Market

FIIPHOTO/SHUTTERSTOCK

Independence Hall

TOP EXPERIENCE

Independence National Historical Park

Independence National Historical Park is a stunning, almost overwhelming collection of museums, exhibits and historic buildings that keeps alive the arguably most important event in the history of the United States: its founding. Set aside a couple of days to see everything.

DON'T MISS

- Independence Hall
- Museum of the American Revolution
- Liberty Bell Center
- Congress Hall
- Benjamin Franklin Museum
- Franklin Court
- President's House Site

Independence Hall

The most unmissable place at Independence National Historical Park is **Independence Hall**, where the Declaration of Independence was signed and the US Constitution was written – two documents that enshrined the concept of democratic rule. Entry to this World Heritage site, a Georgian building that also served as the Pennsylvania State House, is by tour only. Inside, you'll visit the **Supreme Court Chamber**, which has been restored to look much as it did in those hallowed days of the country's founding.

PRACTICALITIES

- nps.gov/inde/index.htm
- hours vary by building; check the website
- free
- timed tickets required for tours; book ahead at nps.gov/inde/planyourvisit/fees.htm

Across the hall is the **Assembly Room**, with its photogenic green felt tabletops and hardwood chairs, where most of the building's notable events took place. The Declaration of Independence was approved here on July 4, 1776. George Washington sat in the chair at the center; Abraham Lincoln's body lay here in state for two days following his assassination in 1865.

Museum of the American Revolution

Enter this impressive, multimedia-rich **museum** *(amrev museum.org)* and virtually 'participate' in the American Revolution through interactive dioramas and 3D experiences, taking visitors from contentment with British rule to the eventual rejection of it. Learn about the events, people, cultures and religions that participated in one of the world's most important events. Lots of hands-on displays and video stories mean kids will have as much fun as adults. All entry tickets are timed; reserve them early online. A prime attraction is George Washington's battle tent, dramatically revealed after an engrossing presentation about it. Actors dramatize period scenes as well, though schedules vary. Check the website for details.

Liberty Bell Center

Originally called the State House Bell, the Liberty Bell was made in 1751 to commemorate the 50th anniversary of Pennsylvania's constitution. Mounted in Independence Hall, it tolled on the first public reading of the Declaration of Independence. The crack developed in the 19th century. The bell was retired in 1846 and now sits as the star attraction of the **Liberty Bell Center**.

Congress Hall

Near Independence Hall, **Congress Hall** served as the seat of the United States Congress from 1790 to 1800. It's where George Washington was inaugurated for his second term as president and John Adams took the oath of office as the nation's second president.

Franklin Court

The peaceful **Franklin Court**, accessible from Market and Chestnut Sts, is where Benjamin Franklin's home once stood. The house was demolished in 1812, but you can still get a good impression of its dimensions from the tubular steel 3D outline of the building designed by the architectural firm Venturi, Rauch and Scott Brown in 1976.

Benjamin Franklin Museum

The **Benjamin Franklin Museum** features a diverse collection of exhibits and artifacts related to his life and achievements. Explore interactive displays showcasing Franklin's inventions, scientific experiments and writings, including his famous Poor Richard's Almanack and contributions to the field of electricity. The exhibition, divided into five areas that focus on one of Franklin's traits, is cleverly laid out with interactive elements and plenty of famous quotations. In the courtyard, park rangers demonstrate the printing process Franklin would have used.

PRESIDENT'S HOUSE SITE

Across from the Liberty Bell Center, the **President's House Site** shows where the first two US presidents, George Washington and John Adams, had their presidential offices. Partially built redbrick walls mark the outlines of where the building once stood and frame a series of exhibits and archaeological remains that offer a window into the lives of the enslaved people who lived and worked here.

TOP TIPS

- Time your visit carefully to avoid crowds; weekday mornings are best.
- Consider bringing games for kids as lines can be long, including those for bathrooms.
- Bring snacks and plenty of water.
- You will be walking a lot, both inside the buildings and from spot to spot.
- Some exhibits (such as George Washington's tent) are only viewable as part of hourly timed viewings (every hour on the hour), but general admission includes this opportunity.
- The National Park Service can provide wheelchairs for loan.
- Check *nps.gov/inde* for any alerts and information.

GETTING AROUND PHILLY

Ditch the car: traffic and limited parking can make navigating the city nightmarish. The Old City's colonial-era streets are a pedestrian paradise. Take note: numbered streets generally run north-south; streets with tree names ('Walnut' etc) generally run east-west. For far distances, ride **SEPTA** *(septa.org)* – the city's bus, subway and trolley network. Purchase a day pass or SEPTA Key (a reusable, contactless card) to access the transport system. If you pay in cash, bring exact change. Philly also has a bikeshare program, **Indego** *(rideindego.com; unlocking fee $4.50, plus 30¢ per ride, 24hr pass $15, plus 20¢ per ride)*, with options for single rides. Download the app to purchase passes, then cruise through town on over 200 miles of cycling lanes.

REPORT/SHUTTERSTOCK

(continued from p132)

below the Fairmount Dam through a surprising location for a park: Philadelphia's tower-studded center.

One of the best ways to explore this urban oasis is on a guided kayak tour. Paddle with **Hidden River Outfitters** *(hiddenriveroutfitters.com; from $40)* to learn about the river's history and ecology from a seasoned guide. Prefer to float without effort? Riverboat tours are also available – check **Schuylkill Banks** *(schuylkillbanks.org/events/riverboat-tours; adult/child $25/12)* for dates.

Taste Philly's flavors

Reading Terminal Market *(readingterminalmarket.org)* isn't just a fancy grocer – it's a city institution dating back to 1893. The stalls attract everyone from blue-collar workers to billionaires, lured in by Philly's cultural melting pot of flavors. There are nearly 100 stalls – which may be overwhelming. Start with some favorites, then explore with your taste buds.

Dutch Eating Place sells Amish baked goods. **Hershel's East Side Deli** hocks juicy corned-beef sandwiches. **Pearl's Oyster Bar** serves freshly shucked oysters and snapping turtle soup. **Miller's Twist** is known for buttery pretzels. **Bassetts** is the country's oldest ice-cream company, established in 1861. If you wind up at **Sweet Nina's**, order the banana pudding. Note that Amish and Mennonite stalls are closed on Sundays.

EATING & DRINKING IN THE OLD CITY: BREAKFAST & LUNCH

MAP P133

Cafe Ole: The sunshine-yellow decor makes the great muffins, pastries and sandwiches taste even better. Great coffees, lattes and teas as well. *8am-6pm* **$$**

High Street Philadelphia: Fancy mushroom bowls, non-grain pasta and other delicious fare. *8am-5pm Mon, to 9pm Tue-Thu, to 9:30pm Fri & Sat, 10am-3pm Sun* **$$**

Fork: Seasonal, locally sourced ingredients are crafted into innovative dishes, and paired with a sophisticated atmosphere and excellent service. *11am-3:30pm & 5-9pm Tue-Sun* **$$$**

Forsythia: A French-inspired spot with plating as stunning to behold as it is to eat. Weekend brunch is sublime. *10:30am-2:30pm Sat & Sun, 5-10pm Mon-Sat, to 9pm Sun* **$$$**

Reading Terminal Market

You could also snack while listening to Philly food lore on a 45-minute visit with **City Food Tours** *(phillysfoodtour.com; $25)*. Tours begin at 10:30am and 2pm, starting with a snack and ending with an additional something to savor. During the tour, guests learn about the market's history as a guide spins colorful food-related yarns.

Eat tantalizing Italian in South Philly

In the late 19th century, Italian immigrants began settling in Philadelphia, mostly on 9th between Wharton and Fitzwater Sts. They brought with them culinary traditions, including a love for fresh produce, meats and cheeses.

As the Italian community grew, so did this **South 9th Street Italian Market** *(italianmarketphilly.org)*, which became a hub for locals to purchase authentic Italian ingredients and goods. The market's fame expanded in the 1970s when it gained national attention through movies like *Rocky* and *Philadelphia*. It's also expanded beyond Italian goods and now includes shops from around the world. It even has a section known as Little Vietnam.

Today, visitors to the South 9th Street Italian Market can explore streets lined with vendors selling produce, seafood, meats, cheeses and pastries. Visit in mid-May for the annual **South 9th Street Italian Market Festival**. Highlights include the Procession of Saints and team attempts

A TASTE OF READING TERMINAL HISTORY

Philadelphia has always been a market city – but they weren't always indoors. So many outdoor markets once sprouted here that by the mid-1800s, residents complained about noise and unsanitary conditions. As a result, markets either closed or moved inside. The current Reading Terminal Market is the combined descendant of two markets once located on Market St's 1100 block. When the block was purchased by the Reading Railway, merchants refused to leave. After heated meetings between railway brass and merchant spokespeople, both sides reached a compromise: the vendors could stay. The market served Philadelphians for a century, until a decline in the 1970s forced closure. A newfound interest in farmer-grown fare rejuvenated the market to its current glory.

DRINKING IN THE OLD CITY: BEST COCKTAILS, WINE & COFFEE

MAP P133

48 Record Bar: More casual than some of the Old City standbys, with a music-first vibe, friendly bartenders and creative cocktails. *5pm-2am, Tues-Sun*

National Mechanics: In the former Mechanics National Bank, now plying liquid gold – cocktails. *noon-10pm Mon & Tue, to midnight Wed, to 2am Thu & Fri, 10am-2am Sat, 10am-10pm Sun*

Panorama: Wine-focused restaurant with an extensive list of Italian wines, craft cocktails, classic Italian dishes and gorgeous city views. *5-9pm Tue-Thu, to 10pm Fri, 3-10pm Sat, to 9pm Sun*

La Colombe: A Philly chain gone big, La Colombe offers great specialty coffees, a signature 'draft latte' and excellent indie vibes. *7am-6pm*

FANTASTIC PHILLY MUSEUMS

Barnes Foundation: A reproduction of art collector Albert C Barnes' mansion holds a trove of work by Cézanne, Van Gogh and other European stars.

Rodin Museum: The only institution outside Paris devoted to French sculptor Auguste Rodin showcases 140 career-spanning pieces.

Mütter Museum: Dedicated to odd and disturbing medical conditions, this museum is not for the squeamish.

Pennsylvania Academy of the Fine Arts: Victorian Gothic architecture nearly overshadows what's inside: works by Winslow Homer, Andy Warhol, Mary Cassatt and more.

Edgar Allan Poe National Historic Site: Descend to the cellar of this small museum, which inspired Poe to write *The Black Cat* while living here.

ZACK FRANK/SHUTTERSTOCK

Al Capone's cell, Eastern State Penitentiary

at climbing a 30ft pole greased with lard, with treats and money at the top.

Get spooked in a former prison

Eastern State Penitentiary *(easternstate.org; adult/child $21/17, cheaper if booked in advance)* is eerie year-round, but especially during Halloween, when the former prison transforms into a haunted attraction. It's worth a trip no matter the season. Beyond the spine-chilling setting, exhibits tackle issues like racial prejudice and overcrowding in the US, problems the nation continues to confront.

When it opened in 1829, the penitentiary was seen as a paragon of modern incarceration – praised by politicians, police officers and prison reformers alike. It offered something no other prison did at the time: solitary confinement, then seen as a miraculous solution to the unsafe practice of housing prisoners in dorms. But it was as costly as it was impressive, and as views on solitary confinement shifted, so did the prison's fortunes.

Though it housed infamous inmates like Al Capone and other high-profile criminals, Eastern State Penitentiary fell out of favor and began closing in 1960; it finally shuttered in 1971. Today, the empty cells, peeling paint and rusted bars

EATING IN CHINATOWN & THE GAYBORHOOD: OUR PICKS

MAP P133

Nan Zhou Hand Drawn Noodle House: At this popular noodle shop, everything is good, but the bowls of cut noodles in savory broth are best. *11am-10pm* **$**

Vetri Cucina: One of Philly's priciest meals, this spectacular spot has a gourmet prix fixe that's divine. The wine pairings are highly recommended. *5-9pm* **$$$**

Dirty Franks: Friendly neighborhood bar with cheap drinks, dartboards and even reverse BYOB – bring your own food to eat with a beer from the bar. *1pm-2am Wed-Sun, from 4pm Mon & Tue*

Bike Stop: At this leather-and-chains gay biker bar, a Philly icon, it's not uncommon to see dudes walking around in a harness and little else. *4pm-2am Mon-Sat, from 2pm Sun*

are hauntingly photogenic – the kind of place that can pull you in for hours.

Marvel at mosaics

Philadelphia's Magic Gardens *(phillymagicgardens.org; adult/child $15/8)* is a South Philly folk-art wonderland that will mystify, mesmerize and perhaps even baffle. It's the on-going life's work of mosaic mural artist Isaiah Zagar, who started beautifying the South St area with public installations in the 1960s. He started work on the Magic Gardens in 1994; the riot of artsy flotsam now covers half a block.

Zagar's psychedelic mirror murals, bottle walls and sculptures can be seen around the city; visiting the Magic Gardens helps you know what style to look for elsewhere. This spot also puts on small exhibitions of other artists' work, with a focus on mosaic and folk art by self-taught creatives. Guided tours *($25)* offer deeper insight into the museum itself, murals on surrounding blocks, or Zagar's 10,000-sq-ft Magic Gardens Studio – a mosaic-mired masterpiece about 25 minutes away on foot.

Brandywine Valley

Flowers and fountains in Kennett Square

The choreographed water-fountain shows at **Longwood Gardens** *(longwoodgardens.org; adult/youth $32/17, reservations required)*, one of North America's largest and most spectacular petal palaces, blows even the Bellagio in Las Vegas away. Longwood occupies 1100 acres (400 open to the public) just outside the town of Kennett Square, an hour drive west of Philadelphia. Its superlatives include having the largest tulip collection outside the Netherlands, but no need to wait for spring blossoms. With one of the world's largest greenhouses and 11,000 kinds of plants, something is always in bloom.

Pierre du Pont, the great-grandson of the DuPont chemical-company founder, began designing this property in 1906 with the grand gardens of Europe in mind, especially those in France and Italy. In 2024, Longwood pumped $250 million into a new 17-acre makeover project, including the Mediterranean-inspired 'crystal palace,' designed to look like it's floating on water. The estate now has around 5 acres of glass-protected gardens, perfect for year-round exploration.

Horticulture heads will need a minimum of two hours to take it all in. Tickets don't allow you to leave and re-enter, so grab snacks and drinks at one of Longwood's eateries.

SEGREGATED CITY

Philadelphia is one of the most diverse cities in the US. It's also one of the most segregated. Among the nation's 30 biggest cities, Philly is second to Chicago in its level of residential segregation between Black and white residents, according to data collected by Brown University in 2021. In 2020, the Black Lives Matter movement brought renewed attention to these divisions. One of its targets was the statue of controversial former mayor and police commissioner Frank Rizzo, whose tough stance on crime led to deep rifts along racial lines. Activist Asa Khalif voiced the feelings of the wider Black community when he said the statue represented decades of oppression and violence. In 2020, the statue was removed from its prominent location facing City Hall.

EATING IN PHILLY: BRUNCH & LUNCH

MAP P133

Cleavers: Devour tasty cheesesteaks and a lot more at this popular sandwich spot using artisanal ingredients. *11am-9pm Sun-Wed, to 10pm Thu-Sat* $$

Little Pete's: Come to this spot near the Museum of Art for some of the finest Philly cheesesteaks in town, sold at reasonable prices. *7am-9pm* $

Silk City: A Spring Garden St fixture since the 1950s outfitted with classic diner booths and chrome. *4-10pm Mon-Wed, to 11pm Thu, to 2am Fri, 11am-2am Sat, to 10pm Sun* $$

Mighty Bread Company: Order to go and eat in nearby Columbus Square Park. The orange ricotta teacake is spectacular. *8am-6pm Mon, Thu & Fri, from 9am Sat & Sun* $

'SHROOM TOWN

That putrefying organic matter you smell around the Kennett Square area? It's the scent of money to mushroom farmers. Essentially a liquified manure and compost mix, it's the fertilizer that makes this area the 'mushroom capital of the world.' Legend says mushroom farming started here around 1880s, when two Quaker flower growers brought back some spores from Europe. These days, the region produces 60% to 64% of the country's mushrooms. Locals say they get used to the smell, but, periodically, their complaints lead to campaigns that pressure the industry to make changes. Mushrooms are fungi, so they're not grown outside like plants, but instead cultivated year-round inside 'mushroom houses.' **The Mushroom Cap** *(themushroomcap.com)* in Kennett Square sells locally produced mushrooms and mushroom-themed gifts.

Valley Forge

Washington's war refuge

Valley Forge National Historic Park *(nps.gov; free)* commemorates the 'birthplace of the Continental Army.' This is where, after the British occupation of Philadelphia, George Washington trained a rag-tag, short-term militia of nearly 12,000 into a cohesive force. It's also where 2000 continental soldiers died of disease and exposure during the famously devastating winter of 1777–78. That winter, Washington and the Continental Congress changed their recruitment strategy: they offered land and more money for those who'd commit to fight to the end.

Today, paths for cyclists and walkers border the park's 5.5 sq miles of rural beauty. Before taking to the trails or doing the self-guided audio tour, stop by the visitor center for some historical context. The scene is incongruously only minutes from the massive King of Prussia mall, which is about 45 minutes northwest of Philly. A 30-mile cycling path along the Schuylkill River connects Valley Forge to Philadelphia.

Doylestown

Museums dedicated to Henry Mercer

Henry Mercer was an archaeologist, ceramicist, amateur historian, inveterate traveler and polymath. He was also heir to his wealthy aunt's fortune, allowing him to indulge his passions and leave a lasting, eccentric and utterly fascinating legacy in Doylestown, an hour's drive north of Philly. His idiosyncratic architectural vision led to the construction of the 19,000-sq-ft, 44-room Gothic-Romanesque-Byzantine **Fonthill Castle** *(mercermuseum.org; adult/youth $20/10)*, where Mercer lived as a bachelor for 18 years until his death in 1930. The hour-long guided house tours reveal how every feature reflects Mercer's obsessive scholarly mind – like the 'main study,' with four working desks positioned for various periods of the day.

Next door, at the **Moravian Tile Factory** *(thetileworks.org; 30min tours from $15)*, is where Mercer established himself as 'America's foremost arts and crafts tile maker,' after fearing that pottery skills (and most others) were disappearing. The Spanish mission–style building houses a workshop with apprenticeships and residencies. It's also open to the public for enthusiastic tours, perfect for kids interested in playing with and molding clay *($75)*.

EATING IN PHILLY: UPSCALE DINNERS

MAPS P94, P133

Dandelion: Great cocktails, a homey bar and excellent food like Welsh rarebit salutes the Union Jack. *11:30am-11pm Mon-Thu, to midnight Fri, 10am-midnight Sat, to 10pm Sun* **$$**

Laser Wolf: One of the neighborhood's top dining experiences in hip-and-happening Fishtown, with bold flavors and expertly crafted Middle Eastern dishes. *5-10pm* **$$$**

Laurel: Fancy French doesn't get much better, with menu options like black onion poached cod and duck with knotweed. Desserts look as spiffy as they taste. *5-10pm Tue-Sat* **$$$**

Elwood: Unique farm-to-table Pennsylvania Dutch dishes, like shad roe served on fine porcelain. Join weekends-only high tea. *5-9:30pm Thu & Fri, 11am-2pm & 5-9:30pm Sat & Sun* **$$$**

Valley Forge National Historic Park

But it's the one-of-a-kind **Mercer Museum** *(mercermuseum.org; adult/youth $20/10)*, only a short drive away, that encapsulates Mercer's primary concern: postindustrial Americans were losing the knowledge and skills in how things were made. Look up upon entering the main building's six-story light-filled central hall. It's like a vision out of a Dr Seuss story, with every manner of object hanging from the walls and ceiling. Throughout, niches dedicated to every imaginable craft, from candlemaking to gunsmithing to beekeeping, are filled with tools and explanatory text on the crafts' history and evolution.

New Hope

Old charms in New Hope

Like its sister town Lambertville (p129), located across the Delaware River, New Hope is a quaint town that's overrun with visitors gorging at its cafes, ice-cream shops and restaurants between May and September. It all started as an artists' colony; Broadway playwright Moss Hart and lyricist Oscar Hammerstein both spent time here. Their influence lives on at the **Bucks County Playhouse** *(bcptheater.org)*, a jewel-box theater presenting main-stage musicals and smaller cabarets

BEST WINERIES AROUND PHILLY

Penns Woods Winery: A family-run place with European-style blends and tastings paired with artisanal cheeses and meats.

Chaddsford Winery: Housed in a 17th-century dairy barn with a festive outdoor scene on weekends. Check out Brandywine River Museum nearby.

Va La Vineyards: A highly regarded and small-batch artisanal producer with more than two dozen varietals – mostly Italian, some fairly unique.

Wycombe Vineyards: A family-owned farm since the 1920s, it's relatively new to winemaking and offers friendly, personable attention during tastings.

Bishop Estate Vineyard & Winery: A charming farm-and-vineyard, with over two dozen varieties offered at tastings. Stay for the fire pits and live music.

DRINKING IN PHILLY: MORE BARS

Ranstead Room: Look for the red lantern above a doorway, place your name on the reservations list, then wait to be escorted inside. *7pm-midnight Mon-Wed, to 2am Thu-Sat*

Harp & Crown: Upstairs has a long horseshoe bar; downstairs is a two-lane bowling alley and cozy gentleman's club-like space with leather armchairs. *4pm-midnight*

Monk's Cafe: Hops fans crowd this mellow wood-paneled place for Belgian and American craft beer – one of the best selections in the city. *11:30am-11:45pm Tue-Sun*

Philadelphia Distilling: Imbibe while learning how to craft great cocktails at this distillery and teaching lab. *4-10pm Thu, to 11pm Fri, 1-11pm Sat, to 9pm Sun*

WHERE TO SHOP IN NEW HOPE

Peddler's Village: Walk the lovely grounds of this outdoor 'mall,' lined with 60 boutiques and shops, many locally owned.

George Nakashima Woodworkers Studio: There are guided tours and floor pieces for sale at this internationally renowned furniture designer/craftsman's workshop.

Rice's Market: Flea market with indoor and outdoor spaces selling nearly everything, including antiques, clothing and fresh food.

Love Saves the Day: This smorgasbord of secondhand clothing, one-of-a-kind objects and other ephemera was formerly an East Village, NYC, mainstay.

Avigail Adam: This magical wonderland of a shop sells hand-crafted, ornately designed whimsical 'goddess' jewelry.

ALIZADA STUDIOS/SHUTTERSTOCK

Central Market, Lancaster

throughout the year. Located between NYC and Philly, New Hope's abundance of sophisticated B&Bs makes it a favorite weekend getaway and a low-key alternative for LGBTIQ+ travelers who aren't into party-hard Fire Island (p103). It's also ideal for a day trip: wander Main St to take it all in.

The Poconos

River tubing and waterfalls

The Pocono Mountains were once associated with cheesy TV ads featuring resorts with heart-shaped hot tubs for honeymooners. No longer. Today, charming towns like Milford, Hawley and Honesdale draw tourists from NYC and Philly, who flock to its idyllic forest trails and waterways. In summer, one of the best things to do here is tube down the Delaware River, rushing between NY's Catskills and PA's Poconos.

Tubing outfits like **Adventure Sports** *(adventuresport.com; from $53)* and **Kittatinny Canoes** *(kittatinny.com; from $40)* can drive you to a river-access point, rent you a tube, then pick you up further downstream. The current can be slow, which means you'll have to contend with some paddling. Expect to share the river with the occasional group of beer-chugging weekenders. Start early, set aside half a day and apply more sunblock than you think you should.

EATING IN KENNETT SQUARE: OUR PICKS

La Michoacana: This place has been doling out homemade Mexican ice cream and popsicles for several decades. *noon-8pm* $

Market at Liberty Place: An excellent food court with Korean, Mediterranean, fried chicken and vegan offerings. *7am-10pm Sun-Thu, to 11pm Fri & Sat* $

Trattoria La Tavola: Exceptional Italian pastas, pizza, fish and meaty mains, along with tasty mushroom soup and fantastic service. *11:45am-9pm Sun-Thu, to 10pm Fri & Sat* $$

Talula's Table: This gourmet takeout cafe serves a highly sought-after eight-course tasting menu at dinnertime (booked out many months in advance). *7am-6pm* $$$

For dry land fun, it's easy to access several impressive waterfalls on PA's side of the Delaware. Most impressive is **Dingmans Falls**, the second tallest PA waterfall. The 130ft gusher comes into focus towards the end of a woodland walk along Dingmans Creek Trail, a 0.8-mile out-and-back boardwalk route.

Eat Scranton pizza

Often trotted out as shorthand for former President Joe Biden's working-class PA roots, Scranton – the largest city in the Poconos – is also known as the 'pizza capital of the world.' (Think twice before mentioning this to residents of NYC or New Haven, CT.) Some of the best spots are in Old Forge, just outside Scranton. Sample **Revello's** *(revellos.com)*, **Salerno's** *(salernoscafe.com)* or **Arcaro & Genell** *(arcaroandgenell.com)*, with its double-crusted white pizza that's a grilled cheese–pizza hybrid. In Exeter, a 20-minute drive from Scranton, taste test two very different styles: **Pizza L'Oven** *(pizzalovenexeter.com)* serves cheesy pan-fried Sicilian squares; **Sabatini's** *(sabatinis.com)* is more traditional, with a slightly sweet sauce.

In Scranton proper, try **Maroni's Pizza** *(maronispizza.com)* – a family-run favorite since 1982. For fans of *The Office* (set in Scranton), stop by **Alfredo's Cafe** *(alfredoscafe.com)* – it's referenced as the 'good pizza place' on the TV show.

Lancaster

Fun on the farm

The Amish are farmers, so it's no wonder the best things to do around lovely Lancaster relate to eating and enjoying the bucolic landscape's bounty. Spend a day getting your fill. For food, stop by Lancaster's **Central Market** *(centralmarketlancaster.com)* – the nation's oldest continually run farmers market, open since 1730. While not all vendors are Amish, nearly everyone has an interesting story to tell. Groff's Vegetables has been around for over seven decades. Kauffman Orchards is run by the family's fourth generation. Long's Horseradish has used the same grinder since 1889. S Clyde Weaver won awards for the best cheddar at the 2023 World Cheese Championship in Norway.

Learn more about the Pennsylvania Dutch simple life at **Amish Experience** *(amishexperience.com; adult/child from $26.95/19.95)* – a big operation along Old Philadelphia Pike. Choose your adventure: perhaps the informative guided

THE US NATIONAL BIRD

Look up while cruising the Delaware River and you might spot a bald eagle gliding above the treetops. With its white-feathered head, bright yellow beak and a wingspan sometimes reaching over 7ft, the bald eagle has symbolized American independence and strength since landing on the Great Seal in 1782. But by the mid-20th century, habitat loss and pesticide use brought the species to the brink of extinction. Thankfully, after decades of intensive restoration efforts, their numbers are once again soaring. Around 150 to 200 eagles winter in the Upper Delaware region, and every year, more stick around to rear their young throughout summer. They're not the only raptors enamored with the waterway: hawks, ospreys, kestrels and vultures all migrate through the area in spring and autumn.

EATING IN DOYLESTOWN & NEW HOPE: OUR PICKS

Sprig & Vine: New Hope's all-vegan cafe serves innovative dishes like an oyster mushroom po'boy wrap and jerk-grilled tofu. *4-8:30pm Wed-Sat, 10am-2:30pm Sun* **$$**

Hattery Stove & Grill: Doylestown Inn's restaurant offers tacos, burgers, rack of lamb and a delicious pistachio-crusted salmon. *hours vary* **$$**

Terrain Cafe: Part of a Doylestown high-end garden center; offers a great daily 'brunch' and dinner complemented by an extensive wine selection. *11am-9pm Mon-Thu, 9am-10pm Fri-Sun* **$$**

Bowman's Tavern: This New Hope place has burgers and other elevated pub grub, along with live music nightly. *11:30am-9pm Tue-Sun* **$$**

BEST ARTISANAL SHOPS AROUND LANCASTER

Pennsylvania Guild of Craftsmen: Real-deal, well-curated Pennsylvania Dutch artisanal goods in Lancaster, with furniture, home decor, fabrics and kitchen goods.

Dutchland Galleries: High-quality original paintings by local artists, plus prints by well-known names, in Intercourse's Kitchen Kettle Village.

Mount Hope Wine Gallery: Join a tasting to sample its products, including Rumspringa craft beer and hard ciders.

Stoltzfus Meats: Specialty smoked meats, sausages and homemade bakery items.

Old Country Store: Locally handmade crafts (pillows, art, embroidery, quilts) and edibles like jam and canned goods.

minibus tour along backcountry roads or, our favorite, a visit to a working farmstead and home where you can chat and ask questions.

At **Old Windmill Farm** *(oldwindmillfarm.com; from $22),* 20 minutes from Lancaster, you can pet animals, milk a cow, go on a hayride and jump around a ball-pit-style barn filled with corn.

Gettysburg

The Civil War's bloodstained battlefield

This tranquil town, surrounded by rolling hills 55 miles west of Lancaster, is synonymous with one of the bloodiest conflicts in American history: the Civil War's 1863 Battle of Gettysburg. Over 50,000 people lost their lives, and the southern state–led Confederacy never recovered. Historians consider it the war's turning point. Later that year, President Abraham Lincoln delivered one of his most eloquent and powerful speeches – the 'Gettysburg Address' ('Four score and seven years ago...') – reinforcing the Union's mission of equality.

Tours of the **Gettysburg National Military Park** *(gettysburgmuseum.com; tours up to 6 people from $82)* last two to three hours, best done privately in your car with a licensed guide. The expert drives and talks, telling a detailed account of the fighting. Other options are downloadable audio tours and bus tours with guides.

The **museum** *(adult/child $18/9)* at the visitor center is a must-see, chronicling the war from its onset to Lincoln's assassination. Set aside a couple hours. Rangers also lead several free tours daily, including a 'history hike' and a cemetery visit. Check the visitor center's digital board for details.

Pennsylvania Wilds

Wow over Pennsylvania's Grand Canyon

The PA Wilds is a collection of deep forests, winding rivers and ancient mountains stretching over 3100 sq miles across the state's northern boundary. It's sparsely dotted with tiny, self-sufficient towns and the occasional lodge for hunting and fishing. It's worth passing through between spring and autumn to see Pine Creek Gorge – a 45-mile-long chasm plunging to depths of 1500 ft – dubbed the 'Grand Canyon of Pennsylvania.'

Views from behind the gorge's western side, near the visitor center at **Leonard Harrison State Park** *(pa.gov),* are more

EATING IN HONESDALE & HAWLEY: OUR PICKS

Be Kind Bakehouse: Casey Zier, Honesdale's best baker, makes inventive sweets from scratch, like pine needle cookies and blueberry-lavender cream pies. *9am-4pm Wed-Sat* **$**

Scarfalloto's Town House Diner: A popular Honesdale place with classic diner menu, portions and decor, with a toy train running throughout near the ceiling. *6am-8pm Wed-Mon* **$**

Dyberry Forks: This chef-run bistro in Honesdale has a wide-ranging menu, from chicken parma and burgers to sushi and ramen. *5-9pm Wed-Sun* **$$**

Glass: Eat out on the deck for stunning waterfall views in Hawley while enjoying anything from a porterhouse to a variety of small dishes. *5-9pm* **$$$**

RONALDL/SHUTTERSTOCK

Leonard Harrison State Park

panoramic than what you'll see on the east. To admire the gorge, hike the short-but-challenging Turkey Trail, a 2-mile out-and-back trek starting to the right of Leonard Harrison's visitor center. It descends to the valley floor, passing several waterfalls. At the bottom of the gorge is the **Pine Creek Rail Trail**, a mostly flat 62-mile former railroad bed that's good for cycling, hiking and even a kid-friendly **Ole Covered Wagon ride** *(olecoveredwagon.com; adult/child $40/20)*. Stop by **Pine Creek Outfitters** *(pinecrk.com)* on Rte 6 near the park's visitor center: it's a one-stop-shop for all outdoor needs, including bike, kayak and canoe rentals.

See what's blooming in Kane

The quaint town of Kane, two hours between Pine Creek Gorge and Pittsburgh by car, is all mom-and-pop shops hidden in the Allegheny National Forest. Civil War General Thomas Kane founded the town in 1863 and built the Georgian Revival–style **Kane Manor Inn** *(kanemanorinn.com)* – an 18,000-sq-ft mansion from 1896, now a gorgeous B&B and the best place to stay in town.

These days, **Wilds Sonshine Factory** is putting Kane on the map as one of the world's few producers of sunflower spirits *(wildssonshinefactory.org)* – an earthy, honey-hinted liquor.

GETTYSBURG'S GREATEST FESTIVALS

Gettysburg Festival of Races: An April weekend of long-distance running through the battlefield's roads and fields.

Gettysburg Bluegrass Festival: Mid-May and mid-August weekends of top-flight contemporary and traditional bluegrass, in a farmland location.

Battle of Gettysburg Anniversary: The first week of July sees book signings, talks and other events.

National Apple Harvest Festival: Held on the first two weekends in October in Biglerville; celebrates apples with great food and live music.

Remembrance Day & Dedication Day: There's a history reenactors parade, talks and more on November 11 and 19 (the latter being the anniversary of Lincoln's cemetery address)

EATING AROUND GETTYSBURG: OUR PICKS

Hollabaugh Bros: Stop by this lovely farmers market in Biglerville for sandwiches, pastries and fresh produce. *9am-5pm Mon-Sat, from noon Sun* **$**

Blessing: Slip into a comfy booth for a variety of Mexican dishes. The juicy birria tacos are a must. *10:30am-8:30pm Wed-Mon* **$**

Dobbin House: Gettysburg's oldest building houses this atmospheric restaurant, offering hefty portions of crab cakes and strip steaks. *11:30am-9pm* **$$$**

Hickory Bridge Farm Restaurant: Reserve a table for family-size portions of country-style fare at this B&B restaurant outside Gettysburg. *4pm-8pm Fri & Sat, 11:30am-3pm Sun* **$$$**

THAT'S SO PITTSBURGH

From slang like 'jag-off' (idiot) and 'yinz' (you all) to its singular food culture, Pittsburgh is proudly and defiantly distinct. One of its most iconic food offerings is the Primanti sandwich: two pieces of Mancini Italian bread stuffed with pastrami or roast beef, french fries and coleslaw. Its origins are labor related – it was basically a way for truck and train drivers to grab a full meal on the go without stopping work, as it could be held and eaten with one hand. Then there's the pickle-making Heinz legacy, which lives on in **Picklesburgh** *(picklesburgh.com)*. This downtown July festival is dedicated to all things pickled: pickle pizza, pickle beer and even pickle doughnuts. Plastic vomit bags are kept on standby during the pickle-juice drinking contest. You've been warned.

A visitor center describes how sustainability and natural-resource conservation guided the project.

Stop by at night or weekends for a specialty cocktail at the bar and tasting room. The bar boasts the world's longest table made from a single piece of wood, carved from Pennsylvania's state tree, the Eastern hemlock. Ask to check out the nearby fields between mid-August and September, when sunflowers typically bloom.

Pittsburgh

MAP P147

Meet the Yinzers

Get to know Yinzers (a nickname for Pittsburghers) at this Smithsonian-affiliated **Heinz History Center** *(heinzhistorycenter.org; adult/youth $20/11)* with galleries spread across a six-story former ice warehouse. Interactive exhibits explore the classic PBS children's show *Mister Rogers*, filmed in town, and Heinz, the home-grown company behind the iconic ketchup. History buffs will appreciate galleries tracing the French and Indian War, which raged here in the 1700s, and a ground-floor exhibit honoring prominent local women. Sports fans: head straight to the floor with memorabilia celebrating Pittsburgh's beloved Steelers, Penguins and Pirates.

Feast on the Strip

Eating around Pittsburgh's Strip is a must-taste experience. This half-square-mile district north of downtown is peppered with dining institutions, offering an edible history of Pittsburgh's working-class comfort food. Visit on weekends, when it's the liveliest place in town.

One of the strip's anchor restaurants is **Primanti Bros** *(primantibros.com)*, a Great Depression–era stalwart famous for adding fries to sandwiches. It's nearly impossible to grab a table when one of the city's sports teams is playing. **Jimmy & Nino Sunseri Co** *(sunserisinthestrip.com)*, open since 1985, boasts the best pepperoni roll in the city. The spot gets so crowded in summer that the rolls are sold on the street; ask for the pepper-stuffed 'atomic roll.' Bubblegum-pink **Pamela's Diner** *(pamelasdiner.com)* is a favorite of former President Obama, known for its fruit-flavored pancakes.

The specialty markets and food halls are also worth sampling: there's **Novo Asian Food Hall** *(novoasianfoodhall.com)* for Japanese, Korean and more and **Wholey Fish Market**

EATING IN KANE: OUR PICKS

Texas Hot Lunch: A family-run place since 1914, with classic diner fare and Greek dishes like souvlaki and pita sandwiches. *7am-9pm* $

Bell's Meat & Poultry: Cobble together a lunch from this market's variety of cheeses and sausages, or Swedish specialities like pickled herring and crispbreads. *9am-5pm* $

Table 105: A casual, upscale eatery with artisanal pizza, juicy steaks and creatively conceived fish dishes. Sushi on Wednesday nights. *11am-9pm* $$

Flickerwood Wine Cellars: Thursday is pasta night; otherwise it's appetizers, charcuterie and subs served with the made-in-house wine. *noon-5pm Mon-Thu, 11am-9pm Fri & Sat, noon-6pm Sun* $$

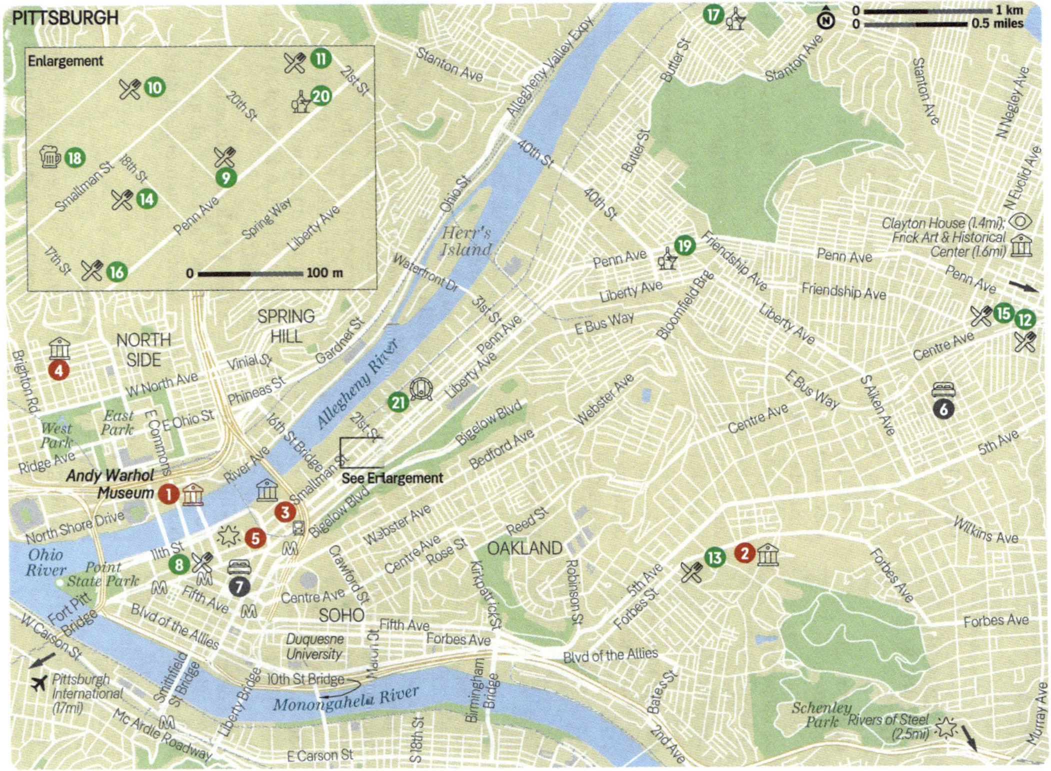

PITTSBURGH

HIGHLIGHTS
1 Andy Warhol Museum

SIGHTS
2 Carnegie Museums
3 Heinz History Center
4 Mattress Factory

ACTIVITIES
5 Walk the Burgh Tours

SLEEPING
6 Inn on Negley
7 Monaco

EATING
8 Con Alma
9 Jimmy & Nino Sunseri Co
10 Novo Asian Food Hall
11 Pamela's Diner
12 Paris 66
13 Porch at Schenley
14 Primanti Bros
15 Square Café
16 Wholey Fish Market

DRINKING & NIGHTLIFE
17 Allegheny Wine Mixer
18 Aslin Brewery
19 Brillobox
20 Lefty's
21 Wigle Whiskey Distillery

FANTASTIC PITTSBURGH MUSEUMS & TOURS

Mattress Factory: Once a mattress warehouse, this contemporary art museum now houses works like Yayoi Kusama's infinity rooms.

Carnegie Museums of Pittsburgh: With 44,000 art objects and 22 million scientific specimens, it takes a few hours to explore.

Rivers of Steel: Tours explore the Rust Belt remnants of Pittsburgh's coal-fueled industrial past and postindustrial rebirth.

'Burgh Bits & Bites Food Tours: Culinary walking tours of a number of 'hoods; the Strip is deservedly most popular.

Walk the Burgh Tours: A wide variety of tours and themes, including films, history and whiskey, led by longtime locals.

(wholeyscurbside.com) for seafood and sushi. If you're here in the evening, cap it all off with beer from **Aslin Brewery** *(aslinbeer.com)* or a sip the 'daddy juice'.

Peep Pittsburgh's Warhols

Pittsburgh has two internationally known exports: steel (hence its nickname, Steel City) and its prodigal pop-art son, Andy Warhol. Most people are familiar with Warhol's bold-color screen prints of celebrities like Marilyn Monroe, but Warhol was more than an image-duplicating dynamo. He was the ultimate taste maker – predicting a future where everyone has 15 minutes of fame, documenting his friends' lives like a modern-day influencer, critiquing mass consumerism and celebrating queerness. And though he left Pittsburgh for NYC in 1949 at the age of 21, there's no better place to learn about Warhol's art and life. The **Andy Warhol Museum** *(warhol.org; adult/child $25/13)* holds the world's largest collection of his work, exhibited over seven floors. It's the largest museum dedicated to one artist in North America. Budget at least an hour.

The house that steel built

Gilded Age steel baron Henry Clay Frick (1849–1919) was a titan of Pittsburgh industry who controlled an enormous chunk of the American economy. Taking the 75-minute 'Gilded, Not Golden' tour of the 22-room **Clayton House** *(thefrickpittsburgh.org/clayton; adult/youth $22/12)*, where he lived for 20 years, provides enlightening insight into Frick's complicated legacy while exploring the travails of working-class men who toiled in his factories. It's a tricky balance, handled with aplomb by talented guides who describe Frick's uncompromising opposition to organized labor – which led to the deaths of 16 people during the 1892 Homestead Strike.

While on site, visit the free **Frick Art Museum** to spot works from the likes of Vermeer and Monet, along with Chinese porcelains, Flemish tapestries and bronze statuettes.

Laurel Highlands

Fall in love with Fallingwater

Fallingwater *(fallingwater.org)* is one of architect Frank Lloyd Wright's best-known creations, completed in 1938 as a weekend retreat for the Kaufmanns, owners of a Pittsburgh

EATING IN PITTSBURGH: OUR PICKS MAP P147

Square Café: Sunny East Liberty cafe with elevated diner food like brussels sprouts hash, banana foster waffles and strawberry Nutella crepes. *7am-3pm Wed-Mon* $

Con Alma: Equally notable for its Latin-inspired menu and its top-flight jazz musicians. Sip excellent cocktails while savoring it all. *5-10pm Mon-Sat, 4-9pm Sun* $$

Porch at Schenley: Ingredients from local gardens get served with flair in a casual-chic setting with a weekday happy hour. *7am-10pm Mon-Fri, from 10am Sat & Sun* $$

Paris 66: Order top-end French fare like *coq au vin* and steak frites while sitting in this cozy bistro. *3-9pm Wed-Fri, from noon Sat, 10am-2pm Sun* $$$

Andy Warhol Museum

department store. Tucked between two ridges of the Allegheny Mountains, 90 minutes south of Pittsburgh near Ohiopyle State Park, Wright wanted the home to look like it sprouted from the surrounding forest. Concrete cantilevers appear as continuations of rocky outcroppings over a waterfall, audible in every room. An ice-cold plunge pool, steps down from the living room, sits in a pristine trout stream. It's the epitome of Wright's organic architecture, blending human life with the natural world. Standard guided tours last an hour; reservations should be made far in advance. Tours of the grounds cost $18; the must-do architecture tour is $39. The house is closed in January, February and the beginning of March. An on-site cafe serves drinks and snacks.

Kentuck Knob *(kentuckknob.com; adult/student $30/18)*, another Wright house, is also worth a visit, located 7 miles southwest of Fallingwater. Designed in 1953 and built into the side of a rolling hill, it's notable for its hexagonal design and honeycomb skylights. After a guided house tour, check out the panoramic views of the Youghiogheny River gorge and take the woodland trail passing around 30 sculptural works.

BEST HIKES IN OHIOPYLE STATE PARK

Visit *pa.gov* for more park info.

Ferncliff Trail: A short loop trail that's just over the bridge from Ohiopyle village, on the peninsula's and river's edge, with views of falls.

Great Gorge Trail: A popular 1.8-mile loop easily accessible from Ohiopyle, partly along old train tracks, with river views and spring wildflowers.

Baughman & Sugarloaf Trail Loop: Combining two routes into a 5.3-mile adrenaline pumper with a relatively steep ascent and descent. Do it for views from the overlook.

Old Mitchell Loop: A peaceful, meandering 2.2 miles through forests, past waterfalls and along meadows good for birding.

Laurel Highlands Hiking Trail: Overnight at shelters every 10 miles while hiking 70 miles along the Youghiogheny River from Ohiopyle to the Conemaugh Gorge.

DRINKING IN PITTSBURGH: OUR PICKS

Lefty's: The city's dingiest dive bar has cup holders nailed to the wall. Crowds spill out onto the street in warm weather. *12:30pm-midnight*

Allegheny Wine Mixer: This high-end Lawrenceville wine bar has an extensive menu, smart staff and tasty nibbles. *5pm-midnight Tue-Thu & Sun, to 1am Fri & Sat*

Wigle Whiskey Distillery: Come to this North Side whiskey maker to sample the honey-colored liquor. *11am-7pm Mon & Tue, to 9pm Wed & Thu, to 10pm Fri & Sat, to 4pm Sun*

Brillobox: A busy Lawrenceville spot with live music, open-mic events and DJs, plus vegetarian-friendly food and a decent beer selection. *5pm-2am Tue-Sat*

Places We Love to Stay

$ Budget $$ Midrange $$$ Top End

New York City

MAPS P66, P70, P74, P81, P85, P94

Jane Hotel (West Village) **$** Ship-cabin-sized rooms were initially constructed for sailors in 1908; *Titanic* survivors stayed here in 1912. Now it's a haunt for out-of-town hipsters.

Freehand (Midtown) **$** Arty, affordable and located between Union Square and Midtown. Save bucks by bunking four to a room, or spread out with a king.

Harlem Flophouse (Harlem) **$** Old-school style works its charm inside this Victorian brownstone, 15 minutes' walk north of Central Park. Most rooms share a bathroom, complete with antique claw-foot tubs.

Pod Brooklyn (Williamsburg) **$** The perfect crash pad after a Brooklyn all-nighter.

Romer (Midtown) **$$** It's a skip to Broadway, Central Park and Ninth Ave's glut of international restaurants. The best part: sage-green rooms provide a tranquil escape from Midtown mayhem.

Public Hotel (Lower East Side) **$$** Studio 54's disco days are over, but you can still stay up all night in the neon glow of club co-founder Ian Schrager's slick, minimalist digs.

Hotel Chelsea (Chelsea) **$$$** This iconic bohemian hang for big-name artists (Hendrix, Mapplethorpe, Madonna) got a plush 2022 revamp. Raise a glass to their ghosts in the Lobby Bar.

Crosby Street Hotel (SoHo) **$$$** Vibrant patterns and colorful splashes adorn every room, making this serene hotel seem like it was plucked from a glossy fashion magazine.

Wythe Hotel (Williamsburg) **$$$** With fab on-site French brasserie Le Crocodile, this factory-turned-upscale-hotel brings Parisian elegance to an industrial space.

New York State

MAP P102

Nest Hudson (Hudson) **$** Rooms inside this 1920s arts-and-crafts-style building are tiny, but you'll likely spend your time strolling around Hudson's main drag, two blocks away.

Urban Cowboy Lodge (Central Catskills) **$$** Step inside a Pendleton ad at this creekside lodge with a hearty on-site restaurant, forest footpath, wood sauna and antlers galore.

Herwood Inn (Woodstock) **$$** All four rooms in this cheery lodge pay tribute to iconic female musicians (Joni Mitchell, Stevie Nicks etc); a 15-minute stroll from Woodstock's epicenter.

Daunt's Albatross Motel (Montauk) **$$** Spartan but stylish: slate-gray floors, sea-green tiles and blonde wood like fine sand, designed to match Montauk's South Edison Beach two blocks away. Fantastic value.

Breakers (Montauk) **$$** Whitewashed walls seem sun-bleached, just like the surrounding landscape as it spills into the ocean. Private cottages give 'summer camp' vibes. Walkable to Montauk restaurants.

Lodge at Schroon Lake (The Adirondacks) **$$** Hotel rooms, private chalets and glamp sites nod to the region's 19th-century Great Camps above this lesser known, but no less stunning, Adirondacks lake.

Firelight Camps (Finger Lakes) **$$** Glamp on the edge of Buttermilk Falls State Park in safari-style tents with plush bedding, balconies and electric heaters for cool nights.

Richardson Hotel (Buffalo) **$$** Don't worry about ghosts inside this Gothic fortress, originally built as a 19th-century insane asylum – contemporary comforts ensure everyone sleeps soundly.

DeBruce (Western Catskills) **$$$** It's hard to choose between Foster Supply Hospitality's five idyllic retreats, each catering to various budgets. Plus points here: exceptional food and Livingston Manor proximity.

Roundhouse (Beacon) **$$$** With minimalist rooms overlooking Fishkill Creek and Main St, it's hard to believe this serene space once whirred with 19th-century manufacturing equipment.

Sagamore Resort (The Adirondacks) **$$$** An icon of Lake George luxury since 1883, comprising a Colonial Revival mansion and multi-unit lodges perched on Green Island.

Inns of Aurora (Finger Lakes) **$$$** This campus of historic homes revamped as cozy, museum-worthy accommodations is the pearl of Cayuga Lake; serene spa and top-tier restaurants included.

New Jersey

Hugh Inn (Cape May) **$$** The eight individually designed rooms here have a mix of Victorian original detail and contemporary glam with bold colors. A sophisticated French bistro is attached.

Pan American Hotel (Wildwood) **$$** Every room in this stylish retro air-travel-themed hotel has a balcony and sea views. There's a new restaurant, heated outdoor pool and fire pit.

St Laurent Social Club (Asbury Park) **$$** The stylish rooms here feature fold-down beds and designer surfboards. There's a pool and bar, and the restaurant is one of the best around.

Inn at Glencairn (Princeton) **$$** Five serene rooms in a renovated Georgian manor with old-world style and modern amenities.

Lambertville House (Lambertville) **$$** The rooms here creak with age, but the four-poster beds, immaculate wooden furniture and lobby bar make up for it. Located in the heart of town.

Pennsylvania MAPS P133, P147

Apple Hostels (Philadelphia) **$** The apple-green color scheme fits the name, but this Hosteling International-affiliated place is also strong on details such as kitchens, lounges and power outlets in lockers.

Alexander Inn (Philadelphia) **$** Impeccably kept rooms have a subdued, slightly vintage style; some have old-fashioned half-size tubs. Original architectural details, including stained-glass windows, oak moldings and marble-tiled floors, add to the atmosphere.

Monaco (Pittsburgh) **$$** This good downtown choice has exceptionally stylish room decor and a recommended basement restaurant.

Inn on Negley (Pittsburgh) **$$** A Shadyside place with all the amenities and first-name-basis friendliness of a quiet B&B.

Porches on the Towpath (New Hope) **$$** This cozy Victorian is relatively secluded, with porches, canal views and uniquely designed main-house rooms and others in an atmospheric 19th-century carriage house.

Darby (Poconos) **$$** This stylish boutique lodging is located just over a bridge and the Delaware River from Narrowsburg, NY.

Rough Cut Lodge (PA Wilds) **$$** Conveniently close to the PA 'Grand Canyon,' this place has homey room suites on one side of the road and more lodge-style riverside options on the other.

Red Caboose Motel (PA Dutch Country) **$$** A fun novelty hotel between Lancaster and Philly, these motel rooms are wedged into a colorful collection of caboose cars.

Gettysburg Battlefield B&B (Gettysburg) **$$** This atmospheric Civil War–era farmhouse has a wide variety of room configurations, morning 'history talks' and evening 'ghost talks.'

Franklin on Rittenhouse (Philadelphia) **$$$** This 1911 mansion is a fine choice for small and local luxury. The place mixes old-world sophistication with contemporary touches, and its location can't be beat.

LEONARD ZHUKOVSKY/SHUTTERSTOCK

Wythe Hotel (p94), Williamsburg

For places to stay in New England, see p232

ROLF_52/SHUTTERSTOCK

Above: Plimoth Patuxet Museum (p175); Right: Freedom Trail (p164)

THE MAIN AREAS

BOSTON
Revolutionary history and innovative artistry.
p158

MASSACHUSETTS
Dune-backed beaches, whale-watching and the Berkshire Mountains.
p176

RHODE ISLAND
Where land and sea are intertwined.
p186

Written and curated by
Mary Fitzpatrick

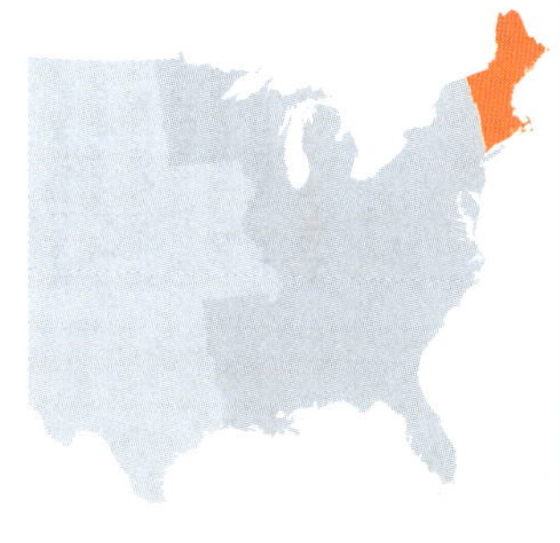

New England

QUAINT VILLAGES, COLONIAL HISTORY AND ATLANTIC SHORELINE

Whether hiking amid spectacular fall foliage, spotting whales along the coast, exploring cosmopolitan Boston or immersing yourself in the region's past, New England never fails to captivate.

In the beginning were the Wampanoag, Abenaki and other First American peoples. Then came the Pilgrims at Plymouth Rock, the Revolutionary War's minute men, abolitionist heroes, enslaved people seeking sanctuary along the Underground Railroad, and free-spirited thinkers and immigrants from almost every corner of the globe. Today, all these and more make up New England's rich cultural and historical mosaic. The region's history is the USA's history, and its images – of single-spired churches on manicured town greens, wave-battered lighthouses, cobbled streets and lobster pots stacked on wooden piers – have become iconic images of the country.

The musings of New England's poets and philosophers and its unparalleled collection of universities underpin a long tradition of progressive thinking and independent minds. Its museums and urban architecture showcase a dynamic artistic and cultural diversity. And then there is the scenery, which alone would be worth a visit. On the coast are small harbors, sandy coves, graceful windjammers, rugged islands and myriad kayaking spots. Inland are lively towns, rolling hills dotted with a patchwork of farms and orchards, winding lanes with old covered bridges and the Adirondack Mountains, beckoning outdoor adventure with their jagged peaks, blazing foliage and wealth of hiking paths and ski trails. Picturesque inns and B&Bs, and a thriving farm-to-table dining culture featuring abundant produce, locally made cheese and fresh seafood, make overnighting and eating a delight too.

WILLIAM SILVER/SHUTTERSTOCK

CONNECTICUT
Charming shoreline, river valleys and vibrant cities.
p193

VERMONT
Four-season celebration of nature.
p202

NEW HAMPSHIRE
Mountains, lakes and historic town centers.
p214

MAINE
North America's dramatic coastline.
p221

Find Your Way

New England packs so much into a relatively compact area. Pick a base or two and explore from there. Trains, buses and even ferries reach some major highlights, but you'll need a car to discover the region in-depth.

Vermont, p202
Lake Champlain and the Green Mountains provide a splendid backdrop for Vermont's historic villages, small farms and year-round opportunities for outdoor recreation.

New Hampshire, p214
It's easy to fall for the Granite State, a gem of small, vibrant towns; expansive state parks and New England's highest mountains.

Maine, p221
Much more than a land of lobsters and lighthouses, Maine has enchanting seaside towns, remote island getaways and plentiful adventures on land and sea.

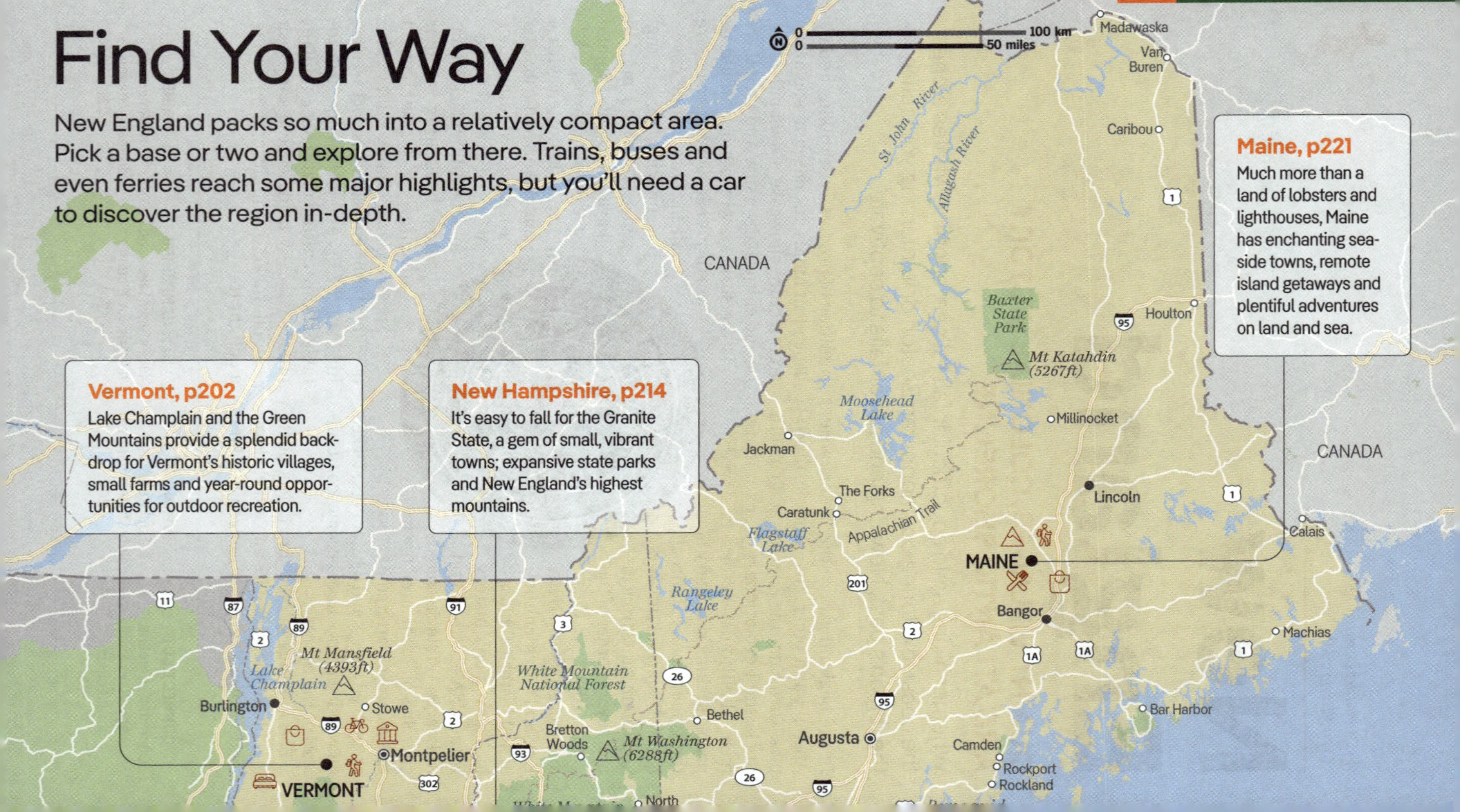

Massachusetts, p176
Visit Cape Cod, New England's premier seaside destination, and explore central and western Massachusetts' artful mix of cultural, cosmopolitan, rural and rustic.

Boston, p158
With its rich history, grand architecture and world-renowned academic and cultural institutions, Boston makes a big splash for a mid-sized city.

Connecticut, p193
Follow meandering rock walls – first laid in the late 18th century to clear farmland – to historic cities, quaint coastal towns and industrial hubs.

Rhode Island, p186
The country's smallest state inspires big passion for local seafood, history and innovation, and 400 miles of coastal adventures.

TRAIN

You'll find trains along the coastal corridor and a few scenic routes in rural areas. **Amtrak**'s *(amtrak.com)* **Downeaster** runs from Boston's North Station to Brunswick (Maine) via Exeter (New Hampshire) and Portland (Maine); its **Lake Shore Limited** and **Vermonter** trains serve destinations in Massachusetts, Rhode Island, Connecticut and Vermont.

BUSES, TAXIS & RIDESHARES

The T is Boston's subway/underground system. City buses also provide transportation – within Boston and in other big cities. Some areas have regional bus lines. Taxis and Uber are common in the largest cities, but you'll probably have to phone a cab in smaller towns.

BUS

Greyhound *(greyhound.com)* and regional carrier **Peter Pan** *(peterpanbus.com)* provide services within New England. Other bus companies plying routes within the region include **Concord Coach Lines** *(concordcoachlines.com)*, with services from Boston to destinations in New Hampshire and Maine.

Plan Your Time

Summer is wonderful, but visiting in spring or late fall helps to avoid congested coastal roads and crowds. Away from the ski resorts, note that many places close in the winter off-season.

AIMINTANG/GETTY IMAGES

Cadillac Mountain (p228)

Pressed for Time

With less than a week in New England, split your time between Boston and Cape Cod. In **Boston** (p158), begin with a dip into the region's past by walking along the **Freedom Trail** (p164) and discovering the **Black Heritage Trail** (p167) before visiting the **Museum of Fine Arts** (p169) and the **Boston Athenaeum** (p167); the city has plenty more great museums to sample. Afterwards, find more Revolutionary history around **Concord and Lexington** or visit storied **Plymouth** (p174), where the **Plimoth Patuxet Museum** (p175) takes you back to the US's early days. Then take the **ferry** (p176) to Cape Cod's Provincetown for views from the **Pilgrim Monument** (p179), some **whale-watching** (p180) and your fill of salty sea air.

Seasonal Highlights

Summertime brings the crowds but also ample outdoor adventures and generally fine weather. Fall's fiery landscapes are a highlight, while winter offers skiing and snowboarding; spring brings buds and flowers.

JANUARY

Temperatures are chilly but New England's crisp, snowy panoramas are a highlight. Away from the busy ski resorts in the mountains, some hotels close, while others slash their prices in the off-season.

APRIL

Spring in New England can take a long time to arrive, but when it does come, it's lovely. Travel in this season can be ideal, with greening-up landscapes and fewer people.

MAY

May is a perfect travel month. Sights and hikes throughout the region remain less crowded, it's generally drier than in April, and whale-watching season begins along the coast.

More Than One Week

More than a week lets you take in three of New England's best mountain hikes. Start in Vermont's **Stowe** (p206) to get your bearings before heading off for a walk on **Mt Mansfield** (p208), the state's highest peak. From here, make your way into New Hampshire's White Mountains, basing yourself in **North Conway** and getting an early start for the ascent up **Mt Washington** (p218), New England's highest summit. If hiking up it doesn't appeal, you can drive up or take a cog train. No matter what you choose, the views are stunning. Finish with some time in Maine's **Acadia National Park** (p228), where you can hike (or drive) up the 1530ft **Cadillac Mountain** (p228).

A New England Road Trip

With several weeks, do a south-to-north road trip, spending a few days in **Connecticut** (p193) and **Rhode Island** (p186) before carrying on to Massachusetts. **Boston** (p158) will take as much reward as you can give it, but also visit other parts of **Massachusetts** (p176), including Cape Cod and the Berkshires. **Vermont** (p202) is a highlight, where driving the **Scenic Route 100** (p210) makes for a good introduction and puts you within range of **Smugglers Notch** (p207). In **New Hampshire** (p214), take in the White Mountains' scenery along the **Kancamagus Highway** (p220) before finishing in **Maine** (p221), perhaps taking a **windjammer cruise** (p225), driving the **Blue Hill Peninsula** (p226) and hiking **Mt Katahdin** (p230).

JULY

July – especially the weekend of July 4 – marks the start of the main tourist season, with summer festivals, beach weather, ice cream, barbecues and busy coastal roads.

SEPTEMBER

From mid-September into October, New England's famous, blazing fall foliage is at its prime. Check **Yankee Magazine** *(newengland.com)* for leaf-peeping maps, although it's guaranteed beautiful almost everywhere.

OCTOBER

October is full of traditional regional scenes. Farmers markets are laden with fresh fruits and other produce from New England's bountiful harvest, and farm-to-table dining is at its best.

DECEMBER

Cozy lodges, quiet landscapes and snowy ski trails make it easy to forget the cold. Many hotels have peak-season pricing from late December into early January, but watch for discounts in early December.

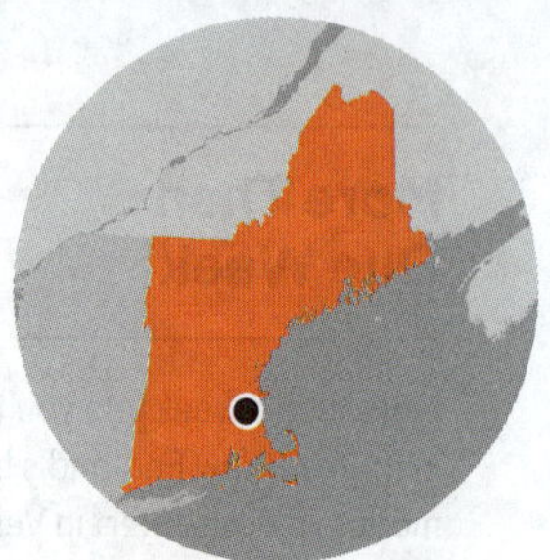

Boston

REVOLUTIONARY HISTORY | INNOVATIVE ARTISTRY | CHARLES RIVER

GETTING AROUND

From any airport terminal, take the silver-line bus to the Seaport District or **South Station** to connect with red-line subway trains, or take the free shuttle bus to the blue-line Airport Station, from where you can ride the subway into central Boston. Downtown is compact and walkable, with T stations everywhere. To reach **Faneuil Hall** (p165), take any line (except red) to Haymarket, State or Government Center. The blue-line Aquarium stop offers the easiest waterfront access. **Blue Bikes** *(bluebikes.com)* is Boston's bikeshare program, with hundreds of stations and bikes around the city and surrounding towns. Pay per half-hour or get an all-day pass.

It was the Puritans who set out in search of religious freedom and founded Boston as their 'shining city on a hill.' In the following century, the Sons of Liberty were born in Boston, where they caroused and rabble-roused until the colonies found themselves in the midst of the War of Independence. A hundred years later, it was Boston's writers and philosophers who were leading a cultural revolution, pushing progressive causes such as abolitionism and transcendentalism.

Today, innovation and higher education shape the city, with it's universities attracting scholars, scientists, philosophers and writers who feed off and contribute to the evolving culture and economy.

Besides being young, the residents of Boston are also diverse, with non-Hispanic whites making up almost half the population. The result is a rich cultural landscape, with music, food and festivals representing every corner of the world.

Boston packs a lot in. Plan your days, but leave time for detours (literally and figuratively).

Flowers, Fountains & Food Trucks

MAP P160

Find your way along the Greenway

A multilane elevated highway once separated downtown Boston from its scenic waterfront. Fortunately, it was relocated underground and replaced with the **Rose Kennedy Greenway** *(rosekennedygreenway.org)*. This 1.5-mile linear park weaves a green, garden-filled path from the North End to Chinatown. Stroll along the Greenway to explore pollinator gardens, observe beehives (cautiously), patronize food trucks and admire an evolving array of public art.

At the northern end, residents and workers picnic on the lawn, while kiddos cool off in the Canal Fountains. For a more meditative experience, walk the **Labyrinth** in the Armenian Heritage Park further south. Nearby, young visitors make a beeline for the hand-carved sea turtles, peregrine falcons and other creatures on the whimsical **Greenway Carousel**. For

JONGPOL JUJAROEN/SHUTTERSTOCK

Chinatown Gate

lunch, food trucks often park at nearby **Dewey Sq Parks**, while **Trillium Garden** serves cold local drafts. Check the Greenway website for events throughout the year, such as the annual Boston Local Food Festival or the Winter Sauna Village.

Ocean Adventures

MAP P160

See the creatures of the sea

The **New England Aquarium** *(neaq.org; adult/child $39/30)* highlights marine life from around the region and across the globe. The centerpiece is the four-story Giant Ocean Tank, a Caribbean coral reef environment teeming with vibrant tropical fish. Additionally, there are penguins, sea lions, a giant octopus and more. Look also for exhibits about conservation efforts and sustainable seafood.

Of course, the best place to see the creatures of the sea (and all creatures, really) is in the wild. Whale-watching tours set off from Long Wharf to journey out to Stellwagen Bank, a breeding ground for whales, dolphins and marine birds. Whale sightings are practically guaranteed.

Art & Culture in Chinatown

MAP P160

More than delicious dining

Flanked by two marble lions, the **Chinatown Gate** marks the entrance to Boston's historically Chinese district, a neighborhood that still retains much of its cultural identity.

Chinese immigrants began arriving in Boston in the 1870s. Some of these early migrants pitched their tents in Ping On Alley, a narrow lane off Essex St; and as recently as the 1950s, this alley held a communal roasting oven that all the local residents and restaurants used.

While the original immigrants came from southern China, today the neighborhood is home to people with roots from all

(continues on p162)

TOP TIP

Boston is a compact city that's wonderful for walking or cycling, with its main sights and activities contained within an area that's only about 3 sq miles. Otherwise, most of the main attractions are accessible by subway. Driving is not usually recommended due to bad traffic, tricky navigation and ornery Boston drivers.

HIGHLIGHTS

1 Boston Common
2 Freedom Trail Foundation
3 Museum of African American History
4 Rose Kennedy Greenway

SIGHTS

5 Boston Children's Museum
6 Boston Fire Museum
7 Boston Tea Party Ships & Museum
8 Brewer Fountain
9 Bunker Hill Monument
10 Castle Island & Fort Independence
11 Charlestown Navy Yard
12 Chinatown Gate
13 Copp's Hill Burying Ground
14 Dewey Sq Parks
15 Faneuil Hall
16 Granary Burying Ground
17 Greenway Carousel
18 Institute of Contemporary Art
19 King's Chapel & Burying Ground
20 Labyrinth
21 Make Way for Ducklings Statue
22 Massachusetts State House
23 Nichols House Museum
24 Old Corner Bookstore
25 Old North Church
26 Old South Meeting House
27 Old State House
28 Pao Arts Center
29 Park Street Church
30 Paul Revere House
31 Paul Revere Mall
32 Public Garden
33 Robert Gould Shaw Memorial

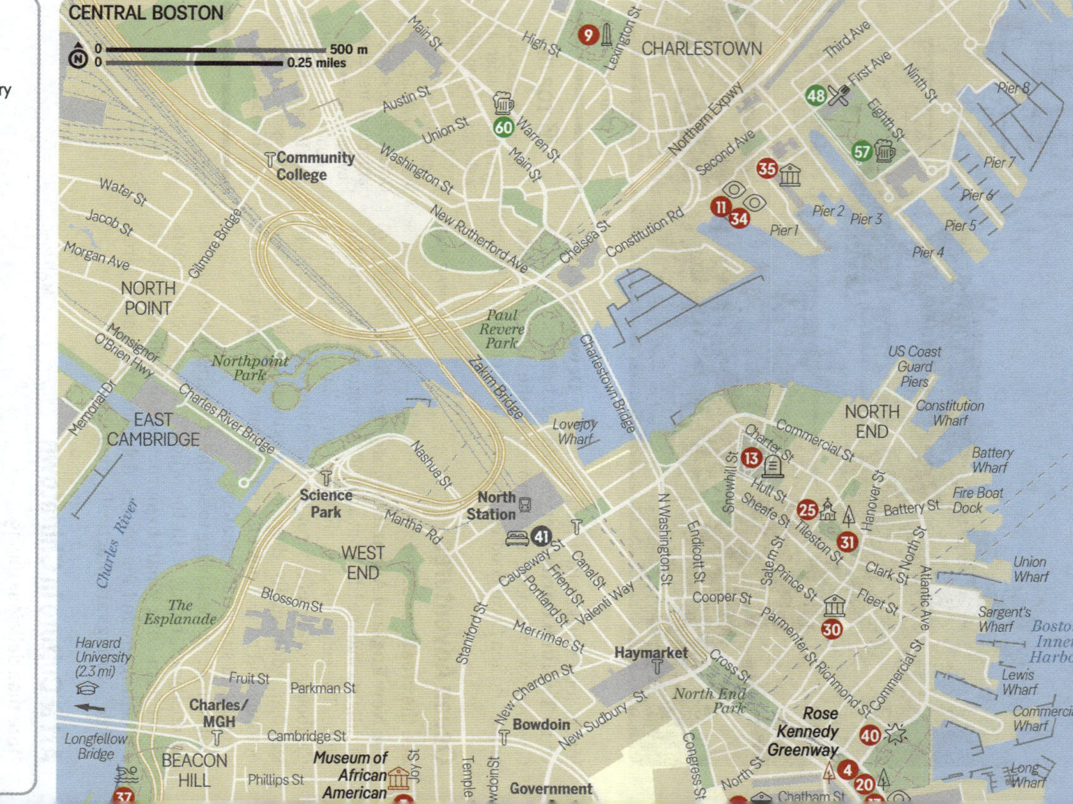

34 USS Constitution
35 USS Constitution Museum

ACTIVITIES & TOURS
see 33 Black Heritage Trail
36 Boston Athenaeum
37 Community Boating
38 Martin's Park
39 New England Aquarium
40 Urban AdvenTours

SLEEPING
41 CitizenM North Station
42 College Club
43 Godfrey Hotel
44 HI Boston Hostel

EATING
45 75 Chestnut
46 Beacon Hill Books & Cafe
47 Cobblestones
48 Dovetail
49 Dumpling King
50 Hei La Moon
51 Legal Seafoods - Harborside
52 Row 34
53 Somenya
54 Tatte
55 Yankee Lobster Co
56 Zhi Wei Cafe

DRINKING & NIGHTLIFE
57 The Anchor
58 Trillium Brewing
59 Trillium Garden
60 Warren Tavern

TRANSPORT
61 South Station Bus Terminal

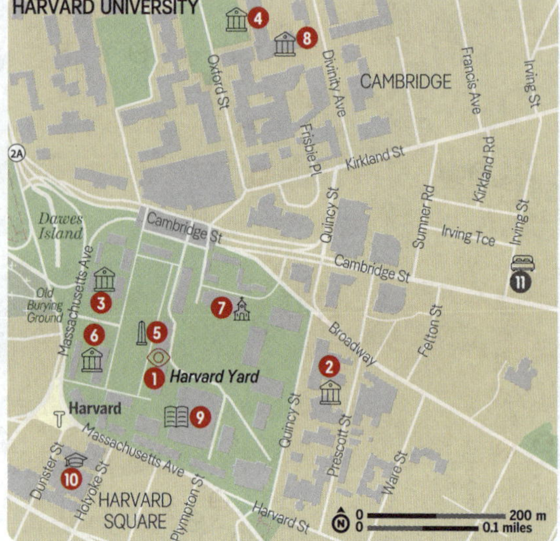

HIGHLIGHTS
1 Harvard Yard

SIGHTS
2 Harvard Art Museums
3 Harvard Hall
4 Harvard Museum of Natural History
5 John Harvard Statue
6 Massachusetts Hall
7 Memorial Church at Harvard University
8 Peabody Museum of Archaeology & Ethnology
9 Widener Library

ACTIVITIES
10 Smith Campus Center

SLEEPING
11 Irving House at Harvard

INFORMATION
see 10 Harvard University Information Center

(continued from p159)
across China and Asia, including Hong Kong, Taiwan, Vietnam and Cambodia. A hub for Chinatown arts, the **Pao Arts Center** *(paoartscenter.org)* aims to celebrate Asian American Pacific Islander (AAPI) culture and exhibits works by artists across the diaspora.

An Uncommon Park

MAP P160

Boston's green heart

The United States oldest public park, the **Boston Common** dates to 1634, when Puritan arrivals set aside pastures for grazing on the unceded territory of the Indigenous Massachusett Nation. Today, the Common is a leafy refuge in the urban center. Kids splash around on the Frog Pond, and food trucks provide lunch near the **Brewer Fountain**.

The Common pays tribute to past and recent history with its many sculptures and monuments. You can't miss the newest landmark, *The Embrace*. Unveiled in 2023, this 20ft-tall bronze sculpture of intertwining arms celebrates Martin Luther King Jr and his wife Coretta Scott King, who met as students at Boston University in the 1950s.

Blooms & Boats

MAP P160

The Public Garden's peaceful appeal

West of the Boston Common, the more formal and manicured **Public Garden** *(friendsofthepublicgarden.org; free)* opened in 1837 as the country's first public botanical garden. In 1877, entrepreneur Robert Paget started offering boat rides on the lagoon, on a boat driven by pedals and decorated with a swan.

(continues on p166)

EXPLORING CHINATOWN

Cynthia Woo, Director of the Pao Arts Center *(@paoartscenter)*, says 'There's more to Asian identity than traditional lion dances.'

Every autumn, Experience Chinatown organizes a mural festival, as well as other musical performances, gallery shows and arts events year-round.

Check out neighborhood murals, such as *Where We Belong*, painted by artist Ponnapa Prakkamaku near 79 Essex St.

TOP EXPERIENCE

Harvard University

Founded in 1636 to educate men for the ministry, Harvard is the country's oldest university, and remains one of its most prestigious. Alumni of the original Ivy League school include eight US presidents and dozens of Nobel laureates and Pulitzer Prize winners. For visitors, the campus contains some historic buildings clustered around Harvard Yard, as well as impressive architecture and excellent museums.

Johnston Gate

Touring the Grounds

While Harvard now occupies vast areas in Cambridge and Allston, its geographic and historic heart remains **Harvard Yard**. Flanking the main entrance at **Johnston Gate** are the two oldest buildings on campus. South of the gate, **Massachusetts Hall** (1720) houses the offices of the President of the University. North is **Harvard Hall** (1766). The focal point of the yard is the **John Harvard Statue**, where every Harvard hopeful has a photo taken (and touches the statue's shiny shoe for good luck).

The most imposing building in the Yard is **Widener Library** (closed to the public), which contains more than 5 miles of books. The **Memorial Church** was built in 1932 to honor the students and alums who died in World War I. Museums on the university's grounds include the **Harvard Art Museums** *(harvardartmuseums.org; free)*, the **Peabody Museum of Archaeology & Ethnology** *(peabody.harvard.edu; adult/child $15/10)* and the **Harvard Museum of Natural History** *(hmnh.harvard.edu; adult/child $15/10)*, which is famed for its botanical galleries, featuring some 3000 pieces of hand-blown, intricately crafted glass flowers and plants.

TOP TIPS

- Stop by the **Smith Campus Center**, where the lobby is lush with thousands of plants growing on the living walls.
- Free campus tours depart from the **Information Center** inside the Smith Campus Center.
- Get a self-guided tour booklet or download the mobile app from the website.

PRACTICALITIES

Scan this QR code for prices and opening hours

BORISVETSHEV/SHUTTERSTOCK

Old South Meeting House

TOP EXPERIENCE

Freedom Trail

Summon your inner Paul Revere and follow the redbrick road of the Freedom Trail, from the Boston Common to the Bunker Hill Monument. This 2.5-mile walking route is the best introduction to revolutionary Boston, tracing the locations of the events that earned the town its status as the 'Birthplace of the Revolution.'

DON'T MISS

- Boston Massacre Monument
- Granary Burying Ground
- Faneuil Hall
- Old North Church
- Copp's Hill Burying Ground
- Bunker Hill Monument

Walking the Trail

The Freedom Trail kicks off at the **Boston Common** (p162), the USA's oldest public park. Don't miss the memorial to Union officer **Robert Gould Shaw** and the all-Black 54th Regiment, who fought for the Union in the Civil War. Overlooking the Common is the **Massachusetts State House**, on land that was previously part of John Hancock's cow pasture. Go inside for a free tour.

PRACTICALITIES

Scan this QR code for an audio tour of the Freedom Trail, plus links to written information about each stop.

Next is **Park Street Church**, whose soaring spire has been a landmark since 1809. The church earned the moniker 'Brimstone Corner,' both for its usage as a gunpowder storage spot during the War of 1812 and for its fiery preaching. Next door, a pair of Egyptian Revival gates open to the **Granary Burying Ground**, the final resting place for revolutionary hero Paul Revere and many other Sons of Liberty, as well as the victims of the Boston Massacre.

At the corner of School St, the Georgian **King's Chapel** overlooks its adjacent burying ground – the oldest in the city. Check out its large bell, crafted by Paul Revere, and the governor's pew, once occupied by George Washington. On School St, a plaque commemorates the site of the country's first public school (1635). Note the statue of Benjamin Franklin, the school's most famous dropout. On the corner is the **Old Corner Bookstore**, the mid-19th century home of Ticknor & Fields, an influential publishing house that helped shape US literature. Just south is the **Old South Meeting House**, which saw the beginnings of the Boston Tea Party, one of the Revolution's most vociferous protests.

Turning north, walk to the **Old State House**, a striking redbrick edifice. Outside, gaze up at the balcony where the Declaration of Independence was first read to Bostonians in 1776; the cobblestone circle marks the site of the 1770 **Boston Massacre**, the Revolution's first violent conflict. Inside, peruse historic artifacts and listen to firsthand accounts of revolutionary events.

Just beyond is historic **Faneuil Hall** (1770), Boston's original market and public meeting place. Don't miss the insightful Boston Slavery Exhibit.

Now make your way across the Rose Kennedy Greenway and into North End to reach charming North Sq, home to Paul Revere. Tours of the **clapboard house** shed light on Revere's work and family life. North on Hanover St, **Paul Revere Mall** has a statue of the patriot and views of your next destination, the **Old North Church**. Boston's oldest house of worship, the 1723 church played a crucial role in revolutionary events. About 500ft further on, **Copp's Hill Burying Ground** is home to some of the city's oldest gravestones and is the resting place of Daniel Malcolm, one of the Sons of Liberty – British soldiers used his headstone for target practice.

Now cross the Charlestown Bridge to the **Charlestown Navy Yard** (p173), home to the world's oldest commissioned warship, the **USS Constitution** (p173). Board for a tour of the upper decks.

Finish the Freedom Trail by climbing the 294 steps to the top of the **Bunker Hill Monument** – a 220ft granite obelisk – for views of the city, the harbor and beyond.

BEST GUIDED TOURS

Freedom Trail Foundation *(thefreedomtrail.org)* Guides in period costume cover the main Freedom Trail sites (not including Charlestown).

Boston by Foot *(bostonbyfoot.org)* 'Boston by Little Feet' is a truncated Freedom Trail tour designed for kids.

Ye Olde Tavern Tours *(yeoldetaverntours.com)* Combines education and libation at Boston's historic sites and pubs.

Photo Walks *(photowalks.com)* Covers the first 11 Freedom Trail sites, with plenty of time for pictures. Also offers custom-designed scavenger hunts for interactive explorations.

TOP TIPS

- The self-guided tour is excellent; scan the QR code on the previous page to access it.
- Pick up information and maps from the Boston Common information kiosk or the visitor center in Faneuil Hall.
- Many of the sites are free of charge; you can visit the Old State House and the Old South Meeting House with one ticket.
- The Freedom Trail Foundation offers seasonal tours, such as spooky lantern-lit tours in October and festive holiday tours in December.

DUCKS ON PARADE

In addition to the Swan Boats, the Public Garden has another waterbird landmark: sculptor Nancy Schön's **Make Way for Ducklings** statue, a whimsical parade of eight bronze ducklings following their mother, Mrs Mallard. Installed in 1987, the artwork pays tribute to Robert McCloskey's classic children's book of the same title – first published in 1941 – which tells the story of a duck family who came to live in the Public Garden.

See if you can quickly say the ducklings' names three times: Jack, Kack, Lack, Mack, Nack, Ouack, Pack and Quack.

The ducklings often get dressed up for special occasions, such as public holidays and Red Sox victories.

HEIDI BESEN/SHUTTERSTOCK

(continued from p162)
The design for the Swan Boats was inspired by the Wagner opera *Lohengrin* (1848), in which a heroic knight crosses a river in a boat pulled by a swan. Paget's descendants continue to operate this beloved Boston seasonal attraction, and the Swan Boats are still pedal-powered. In summer, the Friends of the Public Garden lead free one-hour tours of the blooms and artwork.

Genteel Beacon Hill

MAP P160

Local life in days gone by

Boston's Beacon Hill neighborhod, in the shadow of the golden dome of Massachusetts State House, is known for its celebrated history of Black activism and literary achievement, its political vibes and its narrow cobblestone streets lined with brick townhouses and gas lanterns. Take a tour here of the **Nichols House Museum** *(nicholshousemuseum.org; adults/students/children $16/8/free)* to admire the elegant interior of the 1804 townhouse and learn about the Nichols family who lived here. The star of the tour is former resident Rose Standish Nichols, who was a landscape designer, suffragette and all-round crafty woman. Her work is on display around the house.

EATING IN CHINATOWN: OUR PICKS

MAP P160

Hei La Moon: A top choice for dim sum, featuring everything from shrimp hargow to baked pork buns to custardy egg tarts. *11am-8pm Mon-Fri, from 10am Sat & Sun* $

Dumpling King: This takeout stall in the minuscule Avana Mall serves one thing – dumplings – and they're delicious. *10am-6pm* $

Zhi Wei Cafe: Lanzhou-style beef noodle soup is the specialty of this modern Leather District Chinese eatery. *11am-9pm Mon-Thu, to 10pm Fri & Sat, noon-9pm Sun* $$

Somenya: With or without soup, housemade soba and udon are highlights at this serene Japanese noodle shop. *noon-10pm Sun-Thu, to 10:30pm Fri & Sat* $$

Public Garden (p162)

Established in 1807, the **Boston Athenaeum** *(boston athenaeum.org; day pass $40)* is one of the oldest libraries in the country, with extensive collections of rare books and artworks. Reserve a spot on the one-hour guided Art & Architecture Tour to learn more about the building's cultural heritage, or purchase a day pass to commune with the spirits of Louisa May Alcott, Nathaniel Hawthorne and other literary forebears.

Beacon Hill's Black History

MAP P160

Black community in Boston

In the 18th and 19th centuries, a vibrant, free Black community lived on the north slope of Beacon Hill. The neighborhood's Abiel Smith School, dating to 1835, was the first public school for Black students in the United States. The building, now the **Museum of African American History** *(maah.org; adult/child $15/8)*, houses changing exhibits about Boston's Black heritage, with many items drawn from the museum's collection of over 3000 artifacts.

Next door, the African Meeting House (also part of the museum) is the oldest Black church in the US. Many anti-slavery activists spoke here, including newspaper publisher and

BLACK HERITAGE TRAIL

Delve deeper into the history of Beacon Hill on the **Black Heritage Trail** *(nps.gov/boaf)*, a route that connects sites related to the abolitionist movement, the Underground Railroad and other landmarks from the Black community who resided here in the 18th and 19th centuries.

Download the National Park Service (NPS) app *(nps.gov/subjects/digital/nps-apps.htm)* for an audio tour of the 1.6-mile route around Beacon Hill. Or take a free guided tour led by NPS park rangers. The trail begins at the bronze memorial opposite the Massachusetts State House (p164). The Robert Gould Shaw and Massachusetts 54th Regiment Memorial, sculpted by Augustus Saint-Gaudens and located opposite the State House, honors one of the first units of Black soldiers to serve in the US Civil War.

EATING IN BEACON HILL: OUR PICKS

MAP P160

Cobblestones: Stop into this Charles St storefront for breakfast, sandwiches and several varieties of soups. *8am-6pm* $

Tatte: Take a break for coffee and pastries at this local bakeshop's Charles St branch. *7am-8pm Mon-Sat, to 7pm Sun* $

Beacon Hill Books & Cafe: Tiny bookshop cafe offering a small but creative breakfast and lunch menu, plus prix-fixe suppers ($$$). *9am-9pm Tue-Sat, 11am-5pm Sun* $$

75 Chestnut: Longstanding neighborhood eatery known for its seafood and steaks. *5-11pm Mon-Fri, from 10:30am Sat & Sun* $$

CHARLES RIVER BIKE PATH

The Charles River Esplanade is part of a longer cycling circuit that runs along both sides of the Charles River, between the Charles River Dam (at the Museum of Science) and the Mt Auburn St bridge at Watertown Sq, 5 miles west of Cambridge. The paved, off-road route provides a wonderful overview of Boston, offering glimpses of working waterfronts, spectacular cityscapes, inviting parklands and historic college campuses. The round trip is 17 miles, but 10 bridges in between offer ample opportunities to shorten the excursion.

Get a bicycle from Boston's bikeshare program, **Blue Bikes** *(bluebikes.com)*, or rent from **Urban AdvenTours** *(urbanadventours.com)*. If you're nervous about navigating on two wheels, the latter also offers guided bike rides along the route.

abolitionist William Lloyd Garrison, abolitionist leader Frederick Douglass and women's rights and anti-slavery advocate Maria W Stewart. Guided tours walk visitors through the history of Boston's Black community and its fight for rights and justice.

The Museum of African American History is the final stop on the Black Heritage Trail (p167).

Life on the Charles

MAP P170

Experience Boston's other waterfront

In the late 1880s, landscape architect Frederick Law Olmsted designed 'Charlesbank,' a riverside promenade featuring the region's first free outdoor gym. But it wasn't until Boston's river was dammed in 1910 that the parkland was transformed to a scenic recreation area. In the 1930s, Olmsted disciple Arthur Shurcliff expanded it, creating the foundation for the park now known as the **Charles River Esplanade** *(esplanade.org)*.

With riverfront walking and cycling paths, the Esplanade extends from the Charles River dam to the Boston University Bridge and makes for a leafy location to walk, run or cycle, with river and city views.

Community Boating *(community-boating.org)* offers various ways to explore the river; they rent sailboats, kayaks and stand-up paddleboards to visitors between April and October, and it's a wonderful way to escape the crowds and see Boston from a different perspective. The dockmaster will briefly interview sailors to ensure they have prior experience before going out on the water.

Jazzy Beats & Good Eats

MAP P170

Black History in the South End

There was a time when the intersection of Mass Ave and Columbus Ave had a music club on every corner. This was the heyday of jazz – in the 1940s and 1950s – when a quarter of Boston's Black population lived in the South End. The only club remaining from this era is **Wally's Cafe**, which has been holding its own since 1947. Wally's was the first nightclub in Boston with an African American owner – one Joseph Walcott. Nowadays, Walcott's great-grandchildren run the place. Nothing fancy going on here, just pure live music – blues, jazz and funk – every night of the week.

The peak of jazz's popularity was also the era of segregated restaurants and hotels. History has it that visiting jazz musicians knew they could get a good meal up the street at **Charlie's Sandwich Shoppe**. This old-school diner has changed owners but still retains its welcoming atmosphere and retro decor. Photos and memorabilia record the many famous visitors over the years. It's only open for breakfast and lunch.

VLAD G/SHUTTERSTOCK

Museum of Fine Arts

Art on the Avenue

MAP P170

Admire art through the ages

Boston's premier art venue, the **Museum of Fine Arts** *(MFA; mfa.org; adult/child from $27/10)* occupies a handsome neoclassical building overlooking the Fens (aka the Back Bay Fens, a picturesque parkland). The museum's holdings encompass all periods, making it truly encyclopedic in scope (though there are a few genres where the museum excels). There's too much to see in one visit, so choose a wing or two to explore and enjoy at your leisure.

Art of the Americas: The pride of the museum is the four-story Americas wing, which includes 53 galleries with art from the pre-Columbian era (lower level) up through the 20th century (top level). On the first level, you'll find some treasures from colonial-era Boston, as well as an incomparable collection of paintings by John Singleton Copley. On the second level, a highlight is the gallery dedicated to John Singer Sargent.

European Art: The collection of European art in the museum's northern wing also covers all periods, with highlights from the Italian Renaissance. You'll find an impressive display of impressionists and postimpressionists, including one of the largest collections of Monet paintings this side of Paris.

GETTING AROUND FENWAY-KENMORE

Using public transportation, it can be quite tricky to get around the Fenway-Kenmore area to the west and southwest of central Boston, as the green line of the T forks into four branches. To stay on the right route, pay attention not only to the color of your subway train, but also its letter (B, C, D or E). To reach either Kenmore Sq or Fenway Park, take any of the green-line subway trains – except the E branch – to the Kenmore T station. Sights along Huntington Ave in Fenway are accessible from the E-branch (the Museum of Fine Arts stop) or from the orange line (Ruggles Station). The Massachusetts Bay Transportation Authority (MBTA) website *(mbta.com)* has a helpful trip planner.

EATING & DRINKING NEAR THE WATER: OUR PICKS

MAP P160

The Anchor: Pleasant waterfront beer garden in Charlestown, with occasional live music and events. Open weekends only in winter (with igloos to keep you warm). *4-9pm Mon-Fri, to 9pm Sat-Sun* **$**

Warren Tavern: A historic tavern on Charlestown's Main St that dates to 1780 and is named for revolutionary war hero Joseph Warren. Local beers and modern pub grub. *11am-1am* **$**

Dovetail: Hidden among the Navy Yard's granite warehouses, this is a delightful stop for lunch or dinner, featuring seafood and pasta. *hours vary* **$$**

Trillium Brewing: Sample brews in the tap room, eat in the dining room or chill on the rooftop at Trillium Brewing's Fort Point location. *noon-11pm Mon-Sat, to 10pm Sun* **$$**

FENWAY-KENMORE

SIGHTS
1 Berklee Performance Center
2 Boston Symphony Orchestra
3 Charles River Esplanade
4 David Ortiz Drive
5 Fenway Park
6 House of Blues
7 Museum of Fine Arts
8 New England Conservatory
9 Red Room at Cafe 939

SLEEPING
10 Charlesmark Hotel
11 Copley Square Hotel
12 Oasis Guest House

EATING
13 Audubon
14 Charlie's Sandwich Shoppe
15 Kenmore
16 Phinista
17 Saltie Girl
18 Time Out Market

DRINKING & NIGHTLIFE
19 Bleacher Bar

ENTERTAINMENT
20 Wally's Cafe

The MFA has recently opened a new center of Netherlandish art, along with seven galleries showcasing Dutch and Flemish fabulousness. Feast your eyes on some 100 paintings by Golden Age masters, including five by Rembrandt.

Asia and the Ancient World: In the southwestern wing, the collection of Asian art includes exhibits in the serene Buddhist Temple room. In the southeastern wing, wide-ranging displays of ancient art include two rooms of mummies in the Egyptian galleries.

Contemporary Art: The Linde Wing for Contemporary Art is full of surprises. The pieces change regularly, with plenty of room given over to video, multimedia and other experiments. Look out for the remarkable *Black River*, a huge tapestry of discarded bottle caps by the Ghanaian artist El Anatsui.

Fenway Park, Inside & Out

MAP P170

America's oldest baseball park

Home of the Boston Red Sox since 1912, **Fenway Park** *(redsox.com)* is the oldest operating ballpark in the country and an obligatory pilgrimage site for baseball fans. The best way to experience it is to watch the Olde Towne Team do their stuff, from April through October. You can also learn about Fenway's history by taking a tour (year-round), where you visit the press box, the visiting team's locker room and the Green Monster seats.

Alternatively (or additionally), take a walk around the outside of Fenway Park to pick up some fun facts and local lore. Start at Gate A, the main entrance on Lansdowne St. The street is lined with bars, but the coolest place to pre-game is the **Bleacher Bar**. You enter from the street, but the bar is tucked beneath the bleachers, with a big window looking out onto center field.

Around the corner, outside of Gate B, is a series of statues of Red Sox legends. The touching sculpture *Teammates* depicts Ted Williams, Johnny Pesky, Bobby Doerr and Dom DiMaggio – four Hall-of-Famers who were teammates for seven years and friends for life.

West of the ballpark is **David Ortiz Drive**, named for the beloved Red Sox slugger in 2017. His big, red number 34 is also here, along with the retired numbers of other Red Sox greats.

BOSTON'S BEST MUSIC VENUES

Boston Symphony Orchestra: The queen of Boston cultural institutions successfully entertains listeners at the spectacular Symphony Hall.

New England Conservatory: The country's oldest music school and primary feeder to the Boston Symphony Orchestra. Students and faculty perform at Jordan Hall.

Berklee Performance Center: The main venue at the Berklee College of Music, where programs focus on contemporary music, especially jazz and modern American music.

Red Room at Cafe 939: This all-ages club is a more intimate Berklee venue.

House of Blues: The bigger, glossier successor to the very first House of Blues that Dan Aykroyd opened in Cambridge in 1992.

EATING IN FENWAY KENMORE: NEIGHBORHOOD FAVORITES

MAP P170

Phinista: A delightful French-Vietnamese cafe serving sweet crepes and savory *banh mi* (sandwiches). *8am-5pm, to 9pm Wed-Sun* $

Kenmore: The rare kitchen that is open late night (until at least 11:30pm). Best burgers in the 'hood. *10am-1am Sun, 11am-1am Mon-Wed, to 2am Thu-Sat* $

Time Out Market: The Landmark Center houses this excellent food hall with 15 eateries and two bars from local chefs and restaurateurs. *8.30am-10pm Mon-Thu, till 11pm Fri, 9am-10pm Sat & Sun* $$

Audubon: A sophisticated take on a 'local,' with great food and class but casual ambiance. *11:30am-1am Mon-Wed, to 2am Thu-Sat, to midnight Sun* $$

SEAPORT DISTRICT FOR KIDS

Boston Children's Museum: A multistory multimedia museum on the waterfront. Whether it's experimenting with bubbles, ball launchers or turtles, kids have plenty to challenge their minds and bodies. *(bostonchildrensmuseum.org; $24)*

Boston Fire Museum: Exhibits document firefighting through the centuries. There are antique firetrucks (great photo ops), firefighting equipment and displays of devastating blazes. *(bostonsparks.com/boston-fire-museum; free)*

Martin's Park: A shady oasis along the harbor walk with a replica wooden ship, timber maze and climbing sphere. The park honors Martin Richard, the youngest victim of the 2013 Boston Marathon bombings. *(martinsparkboston.org; free)*

Castle Island: Neither an island nor a castle, this historic site is actually a cape jutting out into Pleasure Bay with walking trails, fishing piers, family-friendly beaches, sea breezes and wonderful views. *(nps.gov/places/castle-island.htm; free)*

WANGKUN JIA/SHUTTERSTOCK

USS Constitution

Join the Revolution

MAP P160

Welcome to the tea party

On December 16, 1773, a gang of colonists snuck onto three ships moored at Griffin's Wharf and threw their precious cargo of tea into the Boston Harbor. This act of rebellion – to protest unfair taxes – became known as the Boston Tea Party, a key event that led to the Revolutionary War.

Full-scale replicas of two of these ships now comprise the **Boston Tea Party Ships & Museum** *(bostonteapartyship.com; adult/child from $36/26)*. After learning about the political climate at the time, visitors can board the vessels and throw crates of tea into the harbor in solidarity with their ancestors. The story continues inside the museum, with talking portraits and other presentations.

Art with a View

MAP P160

A dramatic setting for distinctive pieces

The **Institute of Contemporary Art** *(ICA; icaboston.org; adult/child $20/15)* is as notable for its waterfront architecture as for its collections. Designed by Diller Scofidio + Renfro, the building is cantilevered over the water, and its translucent spaces glow. Outside, sit on the wooden steps with views out to sea; inside, the glass-enclosed Founders Gallery offers even more expansive vistas.

Look for specially curated digital exhibits in the Mediathèque. This unusual gallery is suspended below the cantilever at a seemingly precarious angle. The result is a view of the water and nothing else – no land, no horizon, no context. It's at once mesmerizing and disorienting.

The ICA's permanent collection includes many 20th- and 21st-century art innovators, including photographer Robert Mapplethorpe, pop artist Yayoi Kusama and multimedia artist Paul Chan.

Sailing Vessels & Battleships

MAP P160

Discover the Charlestown Navy Yard

For nearly two centuries, the **Charlestown Navy Yard** *(nps.gov/bost/learn/historyculture/cny.htm; free)* was a hub of industry and innovation in the realm of shipbuilding and seafaring. Nowadays, this busy spot is a sort of living museum: the National Park Service (NPS) visitor center is a good place to start your explorations.

The main attraction is the 1797 ***USS Constitution*** *(nps.gov/bost/learn/historyculture/ussconst.htm; free)*, the country's oldest Navy ship. US Navy crew members give free tours of the historic ship (fondly termed 'Old Ironsides'), telling of its greatest feats and direst tragedies. Photo ID is required for security purposes.

Learn more about Old Ironsides at the **USS Constitution Museum** *(ussconstitutionmuseum.org; suggested donation from $10)*. Exhibits explore the birth of the US Navy during the Barbary Wars and the War of 1812, and a unique exhibit gives kids (or anyone) a chance to experience a sailor's life by scrubbing the boatdeck and furling a sail. The museum is also the headquarters of the USS Constitution Model Shipwright Guild.

The USS *Cassin Young* is a Fletcher-class WWII destroyer that was built right here in Charlestown. It participated in the 1944 Battle of Leyte Gulf, as well as the 1945 invasion of Okinawa. In season, guided tours explore the ins and outs of the battleship, or you can wander around the main deck independently.

Although most of the shipyard buildings are not open to the public, many of the old granite structures are still standing. The oldest building in the yard is the imposing Federal-style Commandant's House, dating to 1805.

Revolutionary Beginnings

The American Revolution's first battles

Students of history and lovers of liberty can trace the events of the fateful day – April 19, 1775 – that started a revolution. Follow the footsteps of the British troops and colonial minutemen who tromped out to Lexington to face off at sunrise on the village green, now known as **Battle Green**. The *Lexington Minuteman* statue stands guard at the southeastern end of Battle Green, honoring the bravery of the 77 minutemen who met the British here in 1775, and the eight who died.

SEAFARING IN MINIATURE

Paul Schmitt, Admiral of the USS Constitution Model Shipwright Guild *(usscmsg.org)*, talks about a unique museum experience.

The USS Constitution Museum is home to one of the largest ship-modeling clubs in the world, the USS Constitution Model Shipwright Guild. Members share a passion for maritime history and building fine scale models of all types.

On the museum's 1st floor, the club maintains a working model shop in which volunteer members demonstrate ship modeling to visitors, and in which we keep our extensive library of modeling books and plans. The museum and guild co-sponsor an annual ship model exhibit and competition, timed to coincide with the local winter school vacation.

EATING IN AND AROUND THE SEAPORT DISTRICT: SEAFOOD

MAP P160

Yankee Lobster Co: A seafood shack that has been specializing in the eponymous crustaceans since the 1950s. *11am-8pm Tue-Thu, to 8:30pm Fri & Sat, to 7pm Sun* $$

Row 34: A bustling seafood hall in a former warehouse. Snack on oyster sliders, smoked seafood spreads and (pricey) lobster rolls. *11:30am-10pm Mon-Sat, to 9pm Sun* $$$

Legal Seafoods - Harborside: Two words: roof deck. Come for the clam chowder, grilled fish, steamed lobster and sea views. *11am-10pm Sun-Thu, to 11pm Fri & Sat* $$$

Saltie Girl: Serves up seafood towers, lobster rolls and other specialties of the sea. *11am-10pm Mon-Wed, till 11pm Thu-Sat, till 9pm Sun* $$$

A REVOLUTIONARY RIDE

Starting near Alewife Station in Cambridge, the **Minuteman Bikeway** *(minutemanbikeway.org)* rail trail runs 6.5 miles from Cambridge to historic Lexington, skirting the shady woodlands and flat marshlands of Great Meadows. The route then traverses an additional 3.5 miles of idyllic scenery, terminating in the rural suburb of Bedford. At the end of the trail is Depot Park, which contains a vintage diesel car and an information center in the old freight house.

The unpaved Reformatory Branch extends the trail by an additional 4 miles, from Bedford to the Old North Bridge in Concord. Ride back along Battle Rd or take the commuter rail back to Cambridge or Boston.

Rent your bicycle from **Urban AdvenTours** (p168) or **Blue Bikes** *(bluebikes.com)*.

JAY YUAN/SHUTTERSTOCK

Overlooking the green, **Buckman Tavern** *(lexingtonhistory.org; adult/child $14/8)* was the minutemen's headquarters.

From here, the regulars marched west toward Concord. This whole area has been preserved as the **Minute Man National Historical Park** *(nps.gov/mima; free)*. The visitor center at the eastern end of the park shows an informative multimedia presentation depicting Paul Revere's ride from Boston to warn his compatriots about the British advance, as well as the ensuing battles. Within the park, Battle Road is a 5-mile wooded trail that connects the historic sites related to the battles, including Paul Revere's capture site and Hartwell Tavern.

Further west, the **Old North Bridge** *(nps.gov/mima; free)* is the site of the 'shot heard around the world' (as Ralph Waldo Emerson wrote in his poem, 'Concord Hymn'). This is where enraged minutemen fired on British troops and forced them to retreat to Boston. Daniel Chester French's first statue, *Minute Man*, presides over the park. Stop into the visitor center to see a video about the battle and admire the Hancock, the Revolutionary War brass cannon.

Lexington is about 12 miles west of downtown Boston, and Concord center is another 6 miles west. The Massachusetts Bay Transportation Authority (MBTA) operates buses 62 and 76 run from Alewife Station in Cambridge to Lexington; the MBTA commuter rail runs from North Station in Boston to Concord. There's no public transportation between the two towns.

Time Travel in Plymouth

Visit a 17th-century colonial village

During the winter of 1620–21, after arriving on the shores of Massachusetts, half of the Plymouth colonists died of disease,

Old North Bridge

privation and exposure to the elements. But new arrivals joined the survivors the following year, and by 1627 – just before an additional influx of settlers founded the colony of Massachusetts Bay – Plymouth Colony was on the road to prosperity.

The **Plimoth Patuxet Museum** *(plimoth.org; adult/child from $35/20)* have recreated the English Village with exacting authenticity. Everything here – costumes, implements, vocabulary, artistry, recipes and crops – has been painstakingly researched and remade. Historic interpreters, in costume and in character, explain the details of daily life and answer your questions as they work and play. And yes, you will be invited to participate. A highlight is the Craft Center, where you can help artisans as they weave baskets, throw pottery and build furniture using the techniques and tools of the early 17th century.

At the nearby **Historic Patuxet Homesite**, Indigenous people demonstrate the lifestyle of the Wampanoag Native Americans during the 17th century. You can go inside a *wetu* (traditional dome-shaped hut covered in bark), check out the furs (many) and furnishings (limited), observe cooking and growing techniques, and see the construction of a *mishoon* (dugout canoe). Unlike the actors at the English Village, these individuals are not acting as historic characters: they are Indigenous people speaking from a modern perspective. The large, open-air complex is open from late March through Thanksgiving Day.

Plymouth & Brockton *(p-b.com)* buses depart every hour from South Station (p161) for the one-hour trip to Plymouth. The bus stop in Plymouth is at the Park & Ride lot at Exit 13. From here, it's 15 minutes on the GATRA Mayflower Link to either Plymouth Center or the Plimoth Patuxet Museum. Allow at least half a day, if not a full day, to explore these sites.

MORE PLIMOTH PATUXET MUSEUMS

There are two additional living-history sites in Plymouth that are part of Plimoth Patuxet Museum.

The **Mayflower II** *(plimoth.org; adult/child $19/13)* is a replica of the small ship in which the Pilgrims made their fateful voyage from England to the New World, where 102 people lived together for 66 days as the ship sailed the stormy North Atlantic. Actors in period costume are on board, recounting harrowing tales from the journey. The ship is docked at State Pier.

A half-mile south on Town Brook, the **Plimoth Grist Mill** *(plimoth.org; adult/child $11/8)* is a working duplicate of an actual gristmill that was constructed in 1636. See how the water wheel powers the mill to grind corn, and take home a bag of freshly ground cornmeal to sample.

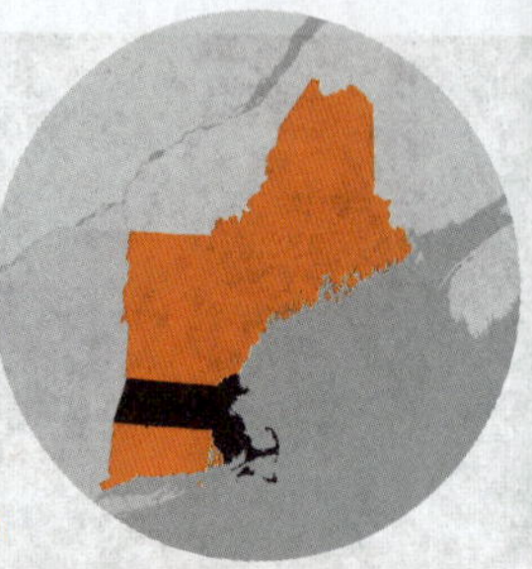

Massachusetts

DUNE-BACKED BEACHES | WHALE-SPOTTING | BERKSHIRE MOUNTAINS

Places

Falmouth p178
Sandwich p178
Provincetown p179
Nantucket Island p181
Sturbridge p181
Springfield & Around p182
The Berkshires p184

TOP TIP

If your time in Massachusetts is limited, get the essence of Olde Cape Cod by driving east along the historic **6A** (p183), known as the Old King's Highway, while beelining toward **Provincetown** (p179). To the west, a weekend in the **Berkshires** (p184) is a highlight.

Massachusetts – New England's most populous state – packs a lot into a small area. To the east are Cape Cod's lighthouses, dune-backed beaches, tranquil marshes and salty air – all far removed in feel from Boston's fast pace. Home to the USA's oldest continuous art colony and longest-running professional summer theater, the Cape continues to attract talented artisans of all types. Hikers and cyclists are drawn to the miles of pristine trails, while boaters, fishers, nature lovers and whale- and seal-watchers converge along the shore.

Turning westwards, the mighty Connecticut River cuts through central Massachusetts for more than 60 miles, connecting a series of appealing college towns. Further west, the Berkshire Mountains line up along the New York border, offering stunning panoramas and outdoor adventure. Eating and drinking is also a highlight in these parts, thanks to the area's delicious farm-to-table dining scene, supplied by bountiful farms and complemented by world-class summer festivals.

GETTING AROUND

A car is hands down the best way to get around. Budget, Avis and Enterprise all have local outlets. The **Cape Cod Regional Transit Authority** *(CCRTA; capecodrta.org)* operates buses throughout all 15 Cape municipalities, in addition to their **Dial-A-Ride Transportation** (DART), a door-to-door shared-ride service (Monday to Saturday). Check online for maps and schedules.

The **Steamship Authority** *(steamship authority.com)* runs several car and passenger ferries, and the **Bay State Cruise Company** *(baystatecruisecompany.com)* has a daily Boston-Provincetown ferry (May to October). The **Berkshire Transit Authority** *(BRTA; berkshirerta.com)* runs buses between Lenox and the other Berkshire towns.

MASSACHUSETTS
VERMONT
NEW HAMPSHIRE
NEW YORK
CONNECTICUT
RHODE ISLAND
ATLANTIC OCEAN
0 50 km
0 25 miles
Bennington
Wilmington
Brattleboro
Connecticut River
Milford
Nashua
Lawrence
Lowell
Williamstown
North Adams
Mt Greylock (3491ft)
Northfield
Greenfield
Athol
Gardner
Fitchburg
Leominster
Wilmington
Plum Island
Ipswich Bay
Concord
Onota Lake
Dalton
Pittsfield
The Berkshires
Goshen
South Deerfield
Quabbin Reservoir
Barre
Wachusett Reservoir
Hudson
Waltham
Cambridge
Boston
Massachusetts Bay
Lenox
Haydenville
Amherst
Northampton
Paxton
Marlborough
Newton
Framingham
Dedham
Quincy
Stockbridge
Lee
Chester
Goose Pond
Otis
Belchertown
Spencer
Worcester
Great Barrington
Holyoke
Brookfield
Auburn
Milford
Walpole
Pembroke
Provincetown
Cape Cod
Housatonic River
Pioneer Valley
Westfield
Chicopee
Springfield
Sturbridge
Southbridge
Webster
Woonsocket
Foxboro
Truro
New Boston
Canaan
Union
Plymouth
Plympton
Cape Cod Bay
Nauset Marsh
Windsor Locks
Putnam
Chepachet
Pawtucket
Taunton
Eastham
Orleans
Providence
West Wareham
Sandwich
Brewster
Dennis
Harwich Port
Torrington
Hartford
Manchester
Willimantic
Somerset
Bourne
Yarmouth Port
Chatham
Warwick
Fall River
Buzzards Bay
Mashpee
Hyannis
South Yarmouth
Monomoy Island
Prudence Island
Voluntown
Woods Hole
Falmouth
Nantucket Sound
Waterbury
Norwich
Richmond
Westport
Elizabeth Islands
Oak Bluffs
Chappaquiddick Island
Charlestown
Martha's Vineyard
Edgartown
New London
Rhode Island Sound
Vineyard Sound
Muskeget Island
Nantucket Island
Danbury
New Haven
Groton
Westerly
Chilmark
Nantucket

THE WAMPANOAG TRIBE

Considered the 'New World' by Pilgrims, the Wampanoag (meaning 'People of the First Light') looked at Cape Cod a bit differently. They'd toiled here for over 12,000 years, building villages, cultivating crops, and hunting and fishing the region's ecological mosaic, nurturing the land they called 'Patuxet.'

Once 40,000 strong, the Wampanoag people now number around 4500, within two federally recognized tribes: the Mashpee Wampanoags and the Wampanoags of Gay Head (in Martha's Vineyard).

Learn more about their cultural heritage by visiting the **Mashpee Wampanoag Museum** *(mashpeewampanoagtribe-nsn.gov/museum; adult/child $15/10)*, just outside Falmouth, where artifacts, relics and a replica of a traditional Wampanoag dwelling depict the tribe's history and emphasize their enduring legacy on the Cape's landscape.

Falmouth

Biking, hiking and village shop-hopping

Falmouth boasts Gilded Age mansions fronting 68 miles of white-sand beaches along Buzzards Bay and Vineyard Sound. Cyclists can explore it on the **Shining Sea Bikeway** *(falmouthma.gov/1362/The-Shining-Sea-Bikeway)*, a 10.7-mile, multiuse, coastal rail trail running from North Falmouth to Woods Hole, past peaceful cranberry bogs, salt marshes, ponds and rivers. For bike rental, try **Corner Cycle** in Falmouth or **Bike Zone Rentals** in North Falmouth.

Nature lovers will enjoy the easy, quarter-mile path winding through sandy pine forests at **The Knob** – a jetty of land extending into Buzzards Bay in neighboring Woods Hole. Hikers are rewarded with a breathtaking vista of Quissett Harbor's crystal-clear waters after climbing 16 gently sloping steps at the tip of the peninsula. The Knob is closed at night, and bikes are forbidden; parking is limited (with aggressive ticketing).

A namesake of the woodland hideaway's original creators, **Spohr Gardens** *(spohrgardens.org; free/donations only)* is a colorful, six-acre botanical wonderland. Twisting paths lined with daffodils and other bright perennials lead to Oyster Pond, where 13 rusting 18th-century anchors, collected by patriarch Charles Spohr, line its rock-trimmed shore. The gardens are open from 8am to 8pm.

The undersea world

The tiny fishing village of **Woods Hole**, just southwest of Falmouth, is home to the Woods Hole Oceanographic Institution (WHOI), which has spawned many Nobel laureates, as well as the country's oldest public aquarium. The **Woods Hole Science Aquarium** *(fisheries.noaa.gov/about/woods-hole-science-aquarium; free)* has been researching North Atlantic marine life and ecosystems since 1885, with about 140 species currently on display – including crabs, urchins, starfish and lobsters. Touch tanks allow children to safely encounter selected sea life, and don't miss Bubba, the lonely harbor seal born into captivity who loves attention and basks outdoors in his retirement glory.

Head over to WHOI's Ocean Science Discovery Center to learn more about the marine research taking place, and its global impact. Interactive exhibits highlight daring ocean explorations, including the *Titanic* discovery. Open May to October.

Sandwich

The ancient art of glassmaking

Located in the Upper Cape region, the picture-perfect town of Sandwich, founded in 1637, is Cape Cod's oldest, and its **Sandwich Glass Museum** *(sandwichglassmuseum.org; adult/child $14/3)* seldom disappoints.

Deming Jarves shook this established farming and fishing community in 1825 when he opened the Sandwich Glass

JON BILOUS/SHUTTERSTOCK

Provincetown

Manufactory. Employing 500 workers, it quickly became one of the US' largest glass factories. Today, the packed gallery showcases over 10,000 pieces sculpted by factory artisans, including exquisite beehive designs and decorated glassware rarely seen in today's conveyor-belt production lines.

Watch a brief documentary on the history of glassmaking, then witness a live glass-blowing demonstration as a sculptor creates a tabletop masterpiece in front of you. The museum is closed January.

Provincetown

Towering vistas and compelling history

Muster your energy and climb 116 steps and 60 ramps to the top of Provincetown's 252ft **Pilgrim Monument** *(pilgrim-monument.org; adult/child including Provincetown Museum $21/12)* for panoramic views of the picturesque town below, and the beaches and ocean waters stretching to the horizon. Built in 1910 to commemorate the first landing of the Mayflower Pilgrims in 1620 (and subsequent signing of the Mayflower Compact, a predecessor to the Constitution), it's the tallest all-granite tower in the country. The plaque in **Pilgrims' First Landing Park**, at the western terminus of

EATING AROUND FALMOUTH: BEST FEASTS & TREATS

Betsy's Diner: Step back into simpler times with throwback pricing at this '50s-themed 1957 Mountain View diner. Great breakfasts and gluten-free options, too. *7am-2pm* $

Epic Oyster: Lip-smacking local oysters and fresh-from-the-waves seafood in a 1922 Tierney dining car: a fave Bob Dylan chill spot. *5-9pm Tue-Fri, from noon Sat* $$

Polar Cave Ice Cream Parlour: Embrace your inner child at this ice-cream parlor straight from a fairy tale. Dare to try the 'Death By Chocolate.' *hours vary* $

Ben & Bill's Chocolate Emporium: Decadent chocolates and ice cream, with gluten and lactose-free options. Try their summertime lobster-flavored cone. *hours vary* $$

TRAVELING ON A BUDGET

Pinching pennies? Vacationing in Cape Cod isn't cheap, but deals and discounts can still be scored. Try these tips.

Pitch a tent, rent a yurt or choose homestays with kitchens to prepare meals yourself. Eating out gets expensive, fast. Shop for groceries at Market Basket and buy booze from Trader Joe's to save on cash.

Prioritize free, outdoor activities: bring/rent bikes and hit beautiful trails and gardens, or beachcomb for treasures (but avoid parking at the beach).

Take advantage of highly discounted off-season rates, when lodging costs drop big-time. Check *capecoddailydeal.com* for special discounts and promotions.

VADIM 777/SHUTTERSTOCK

Whale-watching

Commercial St, marks the historic spot where the Pilgrims first stepped aground.

At the base of the tower, the ADA-compliant **Provincetown Museum** highlights the chronology of the town's evolution. From its First Nations, the Wampanoags, and their encounters with the Pilgrims, to its development as a predominantly Portuguese fishing port and eventual emergence as a free-spirited arts, theater and LGBTIQ- embracing tourist hub, its story is celebrated with pride and reverence. The museum is open April to November (closed Mondays and Tuesdays), and there's plenty of parking.

On the **Town Green**, near the inclined elevator (an accessible uphill conveyance to the monument), the **Bas Relief** – an impressive 16ft-by-9ft bronze plaque erected in 1920 – marks the 300th anniversary of the Pilgrims signing the Mayflower Compact.

Whale-watching around Provincetown

The Cape's best whale-watching expeditions launch from **MacMillan Pier**, steps from Commercial St, with **Dolphin Fleet Whale Watch** *(whalewatch.com; adult/child/aged 4 and under $75/50/free)* a leading favorite. Each 3–4-hour excursion, running up to 10 times daily during peak season, is narrated and supervised by an experienced naturalist – who's

EATING IN PROVINCETOWN: OUR PICKS

Tin Pan Alley: Our runaway favorite. Outstanding service, mouthwatering comfort foods and rockin' themed specials. A neighborhood eatery where you're part of their community. *11:30am-12:30am* $$

The Canteen: Cozy place with tasty comfort food. Don't miss the garlic-marinated pickles. *11am-4pm Sun-Thu, to 8pm Fri & Sat* $$

Relish: Great breakfast and lunch sandwiches, plus a bakery and salad bar. Best chicken salad sandwich, ever. *hours vary* $$

Fanizzi's: Wide views overlooking the bay. Don't miss their all-you-can-eat Sunday brunch smorgasbord. *11:30am-3:30pm & 4:15-9:30pm* $$

busy collecting and sharing data from each trip with scientific and educational institutions that support whale conservation efforts. You'll head 6 miles off coast to the **Stellwagen Bank National Marine Sanctuary** – a protected marine habitat home to whales, dolphins, seals and sharks – where you're virtually guaranteed to see acrobatic humpbacks breaching the waters next to your boat. Bring binoculars and sunblock – and be ready to get wet. The tours run April to October, and reservations are recommended. Breakfast, lunch and cocktails are available.

Explore beaches, forests and bogs

Bike, hike or skate the paved, 5.45-mile **Province Lands Trail** *(nps.gov/caco)* through pine forests, sandy dunes and marshy bogs for stunning views of Cape Cod Bay and the Atlantic Ocean. It's an intermediate-level challenge.

Start at the **Province Lands Visitor Center** (open May to October), where there's ample parking and ocean views from the observatory deck (open year-round) – watch for spouting and breaching whales in the distance. Begin the trail loop to the left, leading past **Provincetown Municipal Airport** toward **Race Point Beach** and then on toward **Herring Cove Beach**, where you can try to spot right whales during their spring and summer migration. Complete your loop to finish back at the visitor center.

Nantucket Island

Harpoons, whale tales and commanding views

About 30 miles south of Cape Cod is Nantucket Island, where the highlight is the **Whaling Museum** *(nha.org; adult/child $20/5)*. Covering the island's storied and proud heritage as whaling capital of the world, the museum is housed in a circa-1846 whale-oil candle factory, where exhibits depict life during the late-1700s peak of the once cutting-edge, financially lucrative whaling industry. Banned since 1986, commercial whalers previously supplied a much-coveted product used in lamp oil, candles, paint, soap, textiles, toys and rope. Nowadays, efforts continue across Cape Cod to protect whale species, promoting the resurgence of local populations. Don't miss the awesome views from the rooftop deck. The museum is open Monday to Saturday (and Sundays in summer), mid-February to December.

Sturbridge

Step back into 19th-century New England

Once you've explored the coast, turn your sights inland, where **Old Sturbridge Village** *(osv.org; adult/child $27/12, discounts available)* – about a 30-minute drive from Worcester in central Massachusetts – takes you back into a rural New England hamlet from the 1830s, complete with houses, shops, churches, schools and mills, all of which were transported from around the region. The museum covers some 240 acres, with houses and shops surrounding a green in the center, and

LONG POINT DREAMING

Ed Macri, co-owner of the exquisite Land's End Inn *(landsendinn.com)* B&B, shares a favorite activity.

One of Provincetown's most magical excursions is to **Long Point Beach**, a strip of sand ending the spiral of Cape Cod. There, you might share the beach with only seals, stand just yards from passing boats and enjoy breathtaking views of town. The easiest way to get there is via the Flyer's Shuttle at MacMillan Pier. Or trek across the breakwater, a short walk from our inn in the West End. After the 40-minute journey across, turn right and follow the beach until you reach Wood End Lighthouse. Just be sure to pack plenty of water and check the tides – the breakwater becomes impassable at high tide.

BEST CENTRAL MASSACHUSETTS HIKES

Scenic mountain ranges rise steeply on either side of the Connecticut River, offering moderate hikes with great panoramic rewards.

The **Mt Tom State Reservation** protects the Mt Tom Range on the west side of the river. Start near the visitor center for the challenging 4-mile hike up Mt Tom (990ft), or the easier 1.7-mile hike up to **Goat Peak**, which is topped with a lookout tower.

You can drive to the top of Mt Holyoke (942ft), in **Skinner State Park**, from May to September. Thankfully the 1.5-mile hike is not too strenuous, providing summiteers with expansive vistas over the Connecticut River Valley.

working farms and water-powered mills in the surrounding countryside.

Visitors are invited to wander and explore independently. Along the way, you'll meet 'interpreters' – historians dressed in period garb – who are hard at work tending their homes, farms and shops. The interpreters stay in character as they explain their tasks and tools. Check the schedule of daily events for possible cooking demonstrations, school lessons, house tours and more. Incredible handiwork is on display here, as the craftspeople demonstrate cabinetry, pottery, basket-weaving, blacksmithing and more. It's also interesting to see the farm animals – all 'heritage' breeds that are similar to the historical breeds from the 19th century.

Old Sturbridge Village is open year-round, Wednesday through Sunday, plus holiday Mondays. In December, it's open on select evenings only (for a Christmas by Candlelight program) but closed during its regular operating hours. It's best to avoid the village on weekdays from the end of April until mid-June, as this is a popular time for school field-trips.

Springfield & Around

An immersion in children's literature

If you're travelling with Dr Seuss fans, consider making a detour to visit the **Amazing World of Dr Seuss** *(seussinspringfield.org; adult/child $25/13)* in Springfield. The museum celebrates the life and work of Theodor Seuss Geisel (aka Dr Seuss), who was born and raised here. It offers hands-on kid's activities, original artwork displays and a moving collection of letters. Outside, the Dr Seuss Memorial Sculpture Garden includes bronze depictions of his most beloved characters.

Just 25 miles north on I-91, in Amherst, is the **Eric Carle Museum of Picture Book Art** *(carlemuseum.org; adult/child $15/8)*, co-founded by Eric Carle, the author and illustrator of *The Very Hungry Caterpillar* (and about 70 other books). This superb spot displays book illustrations from around the world and the permanent collection of Carle's own vibrant work. Read-aloud story times and hands-on art projects engage visitors of all ages.

Both museums have excellent bookstores, but if you don't find what you're looking for, head 9 miles west to **High Five Books** *(highfivebooks.org)* in Florence (a village of Northampton).

DRINKING AROUND STURBRIDGE & WORCESTER: BEST BREWERIES

Rapscallion Pub: Beers from the brewery in Spencer are served in this cozy Sturbridge pub along with snacky food and live music. *4-10pm Mon-Thu, from noon Fri & Sat, to 8pm Sun*

Tree House Brewing Company: Highly touted New England IPAs and other beers are brewed and sold only on-site, 5 miles east of Sturbridge. *11am-8pm Mon-Thu, to 9pm Fri & Sat, noon-8pm Sun*

Wachusett Brewing Co: This Westminster outfit makes and serves ales and lagers in a brewhouse in the shadow of its namesake mountain. *noon-9pm Mon-Thu, to 10pm Sat, to 7pm Sun*

Jack's Abby: Winning awards for craft lagers since 2011, sample beers and wood-fired pizzas at this Framingham brewery, between Boston and Worcester. *noon-9pm Sun & Tue-Thu, to 11pm Fri & Sat*

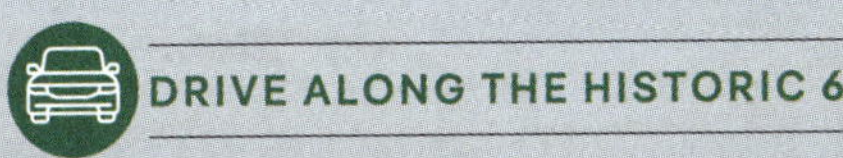

DRIVE ALONG THE HISTORIC 6A

Known as the Old King's Highway, this scenic road dissects villages that evoke the spirit of Olde Cape Cod, with galleries, antique shops, museums and charming historical properties.

START	END	LENGTH
Sturgis Library	Brewster Store	15 miles; 2 hours

Begin your journey at ❶ **Sturgis Library** in Barnstable. Dating to c 1644, it's the USA's oldest building housing a library – and holds a first-edition *Moby Dick*. Head east to ❷ **Old Jail**, a wooden prison that's held infamous pirates and is believed to be haunted. Admire historic captains' homes while driving east toward ❸ **Edward Gorey House**, a museum in Yarmouth Port once home to the delightfully twisted author, who was also an illustrator for Lewis Carroll and HG Wells. A bit further on, hang a left onto Center St for ❹ **Gray's Beach** in Dennis. Back on the Old King's Highway, continue east, turn right onto Scargo Hill Rd and follow signs to ❺ **Scargo Tower**. Climb atop this century-old, 30ft cobblestone tower for commanding views. Drive a mile back to 6A and park at ❻ **Cape Cinema**, an operating vintage theater and site of the 1939 world premiere of *The Wizard of Oz* thanks to Margaret Hamilton (the Wicked Witch), who'd played summer theater in the same arts complex at ❼ **Cape Playhouse**. This 540-seat, velvet-draped venue has been hosting Broadway-quality performances since 1927. Next door, ❽ **Cape Cod Museum of Art** presents established and up-and-coming Cape artists in a variety of media. Push on 5 miles east along 6A. ❾ **Cape Cod Museum of Natural History** in Brewster features compelling presentations on the region's geographic transformation, showcasing much of its colorful fauna. End your trip at ❿ **Brewster Store**, an 1866 general store that time has forgotten.

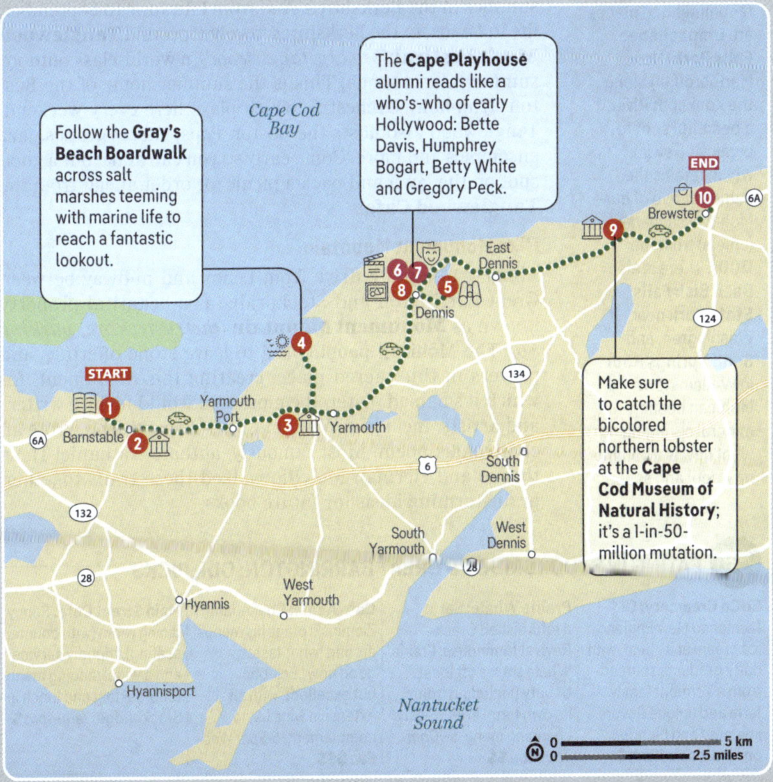

Follow the **Gray's Beach Boardwalk** across salt marshes teeming with marine life to reach a fantastic lookout.

The **Cape Playhouse** alumni reads like a who's-who of early Hollywood: Bette Davis, Humphrey Bogart, Betty White and Gregory Peck.

Make sure to catch the bicolored northern lobster at the **Cape Cod Museum of Natural History**; it's a 1-in-50-million mutation.

NATIVE AMERICAN HERITAGE

Bonney Hartley is the Historic Preservation Manager of the Stockbridge-Munsee Tribe *(mohican.com)*.

Mohican people are 'people of the waters that are never still,' and our Berkshire homelands reflect this quality of our heritage. The landscape is abundant with rivers, waterfalls and natural springs that our ancestors knew and loved. Some recommended places are **Umpachenee Falls Park** (New Marlborough) along the Konkapot River, a beautiful spot to picnic and swim, which retains the names of two of our Mohican *sachems* (chiefs) from the 1700s. There is also **Bash Bish Falls State Park** near Mt Washington, and **Sand Springs Pool** in Williamstown – a Mohican healing mineral spring filling what now is a community pool and sauna.

GIOTHEPHOTOGRAPHER/SHUTTERSTOCK

The Berkshires

Music under the stars

An evening of alfresco entertainment is one of the delights of summer in the Berkshires. And from late June to September, life in Lenox, in the Berkshires, revolves around **Tanglewood Music Festival** *(bso.org/tanglewood)*, a world-class outdoor summer music venue. This is the summer home of the Boston Symphony Orchestra, which plays here every weekend. Tanglewood also hosts the Boston Pops, choral groups, jazz ensembles and more. Come early so you can stake out a good spot on the lawn and pack a picnic (or order ahead from the **Tanglewood Cafe**).

Hike Monument Mountain

About a 15-minute drive from Lenox and midway between Great Barrington and Stockbridge is a beautiful property known as **Monument Mountain** *(thetrustees.org; parking $6)*. The Mohican people used to leave stone offerings and prayers in this sacred place, creating the 'monument' for which it's named. Later, the mountain would inspire writers and artists, including William Cullen Bryant, who wrote an eponymous poem. Most famously, authors Nathaniel Hawthorne and Herman Melville walked these trails together, brainstorming ideas for future books.

EATING IN STOCKBRIDGE & GREAT BARRINGTON: OUR PICKS

SoCo Creamery: Old-fashioned New England ice cream at its best, with dairy products sourced from a Vermont family farm and unique flavors invented and blended on-site. *noon-10pm* $

Prairie Whale: Set in a refurbished Greek Revival farmhouse, Prairie Whale shows off local bounty (including from its own farm) in its weekly changing menu. *5-10pm Thu-Mon* $$

Cafe Adam: Chef Adam Zieminski plans his menus around 'what tastes good now.' Eclectic but excellent, with an extensive wine list to complement. *5-9pm Wed-Sun* $$$

Main Street Cafe: Sunny dining room (with counter seating), friendly service and a wide-ranging menu for breakfast and lunch in Stockbridge. *7am-4pm* $

Mt Greylock

You, too, might find inspiration at Monument Mountain, with its 3-mile hiking route to/from the summit at Squaw Peak (1642ft) via the Hickey Trail and a lookout at Devil's Pulpit. On a clear day, you'll see all the way to **Mt Greylock** (Massachusetts' highest peak) in the northwest and the Catskills in the east.

Visit a living museum

The Shakers were an 18th-century religious sect that practiced communal living, gender and racial equality, pacifism and celibacy (the latter explaining why they have all but disappeared). Their worship often included ecstatic trembling, which inspired their moniker, and they were also renowned for their work ethic and artistry.

In the late 18th century, Shaker communities sprouted up throughout the northeast, including the **Hancock Shaker Village** *(hancockshakervillage.org; adult/child $20/8)* in Pittsfield, which today remains as a living museum with original buildings, Shaker furniture and exhibits about community life (though no Shakers live here anymore). It's open daily from mid-April through October.

FARMS FOR EVERY SEASON

Berkshire Grown *(berkshiregrown.org)* is a guide to locally grown food, including pick-your-own, farmers markets, events and farm-to-table restaurants. Some of our favorites:

Windy Hill Farm: Come for blueberries in summer and apples in fall.

Lakeview Orchard: Pick your own sweet and tart cherries, raspberries, plums, redcurrants, blueberries and 15 varieties of apples.

High Lawn Farm: A dairy farm where you can purchase fresh-from-the-cow milk and cream, farmstead cheese, slow-churned butter and – yes! – dense ice-cream.

Hilltop Orchards: A traditional apple orchard, with pick-your-own apples and fresh cider. The Furnace Brook Winery is on-site.

EATING IN LENOX: OUR PICKS

Chocolate Springs Cafe: This cozy cafe is filled with chocolate treats, from 'serious' hot chocolate to gelato, truffles and more. Also, see the chocolatiers at work. *9am-7pm* $

Haven Cafe & Bakery: With ingredients sourced from local farms, Haven offers a refined menu of fancy egg dishes for breakfast and sophisticated sandwiches for lunch. *8am-2pm Thu-Mon* $$

Bistro Zinc: A slick, modern setting (with a zinc bar) for decadent French classics, from *moules frites* to beef bourguignon. *11:30am-3pm & 5-9pm* $$$

Alta: Head to this classy eatery for decadent delights such as seared duck in salty caramel sauce or chipotle-braised pork cheeks. *5-9pm Sun, Mon, Wed & Thu, to 10pm Fri & Sat* $$$

Rhode Island

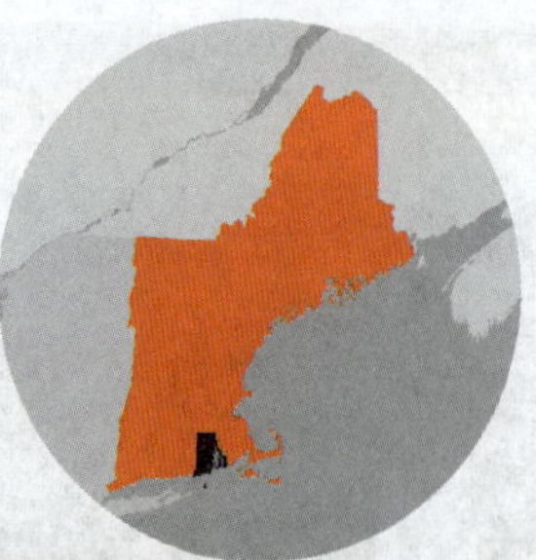

WATERSIDE WALKS | MUSEUMS | STATELY HOMES

Places

Providence p188
Newport p190

TOP TIPS

You can drive almost anywhere in Rhode Island in under an hour. But give yourself time – those 1034 sq miles are dense with things to see and do. Also factor in extra time for navigating around inlets and across Narragansett Bay.

Puritan minister and theologian Roger Williams landed in what would become Rhode Island after he was banished from Massachusetts for his belief in the separation of church and state – opinions that officials deemed 'new and dangerous.' Williams and his wife fled to the tip of Narragansett Bay, where they befriended Native Americans and purchased a portion of their land, which they declared a place of religious freedom. Relationships with area tribes became more complicated as colonists continued arriving with big plans and an individualistic outlook. While conflict between neighboring colonies and tribes sowed chaos across Rhode Island for much of the 17th century, the colony's commitment to religious freedom opened up the waterways to a steady flow of both newcomers and commerce.

Today, the state holds on to that underdog energy. Between its shiny resort exteriors and a proud, ocean-worn heart is a willingness to try new things, innovate and welcome new ideas.

GETTING AROUND

It's helpful to have four wheels in Rhode Island, where major highways connect most destinations. Check out at least one of the state's nine designated scenic roadways. Parking is plentiful in Providence, but can be crowded in Newport. Both cities are enjoyably walkable and in Newport, popular attractions can be reached by the city's trolley, which offers a free hop-on-hop-off service from May through October, departing from the Newport Transportation Center.

From June to October, you can board the **Seastreak Ferry** *(seastreak.com)* to travel between Providence, Bristol and Newport. It's a slow but fun way to see three significant destinations.

RHODE ISLAND
Webster
Douglas
Uxbridge
Franklin
Foxboro
Mansfield
Easton
Woonsocket
Blackstone River Valley
Burrillville
Pascoag Reservoir
Oakland
Cumberland
West Glocester
Chepachet
Smithfield
Attleboro
Glocester
Lincoln
North Foster
Greenville
Pawtucket
North Providence
North Dighton
Killingly
Johnston
Rehoboth
Danielson
Providence
Foster Center
Scituate
Scituate Reservoir
Seekonk
Dighton
Cranston
Somerset
Barrington
Swansea
Warren
West Warwick
Coventry
Greene
Warwick
Fall River
Mt Hope Bay
Flat River Reservoir
Bristol
East Greenwich
West Greenwich
Escoheag
Prudence Island
Tiverton
Portsmouth
Narragansett Bay
Voluntown
Exeter
Wickford
Pachaug State Forest
North Kingstown
Adamsville
Middletown
Jamestown
Little Compton
Richmond
Kingston
Newport
Hopkinton
Carolina
South Kingstown
Sakonnet
Shannock
Narragansett
Sakonnet Point
South County
Wakefield
Narragansett Pier
Charlestown
Matunuck
Westerly
Galilee
Trustom Pond
Point Judith
Rhode Island Sound
Misquamicut
Weekapaug
Watch Hill
ATLANTIC OCEAN
Block Island Sound
New Shoreham
Old Harbor
0
20 km
0
10 miles

STILL HERE MURAL

Across the river from College Hill stands the *Still Here* mural. It's a striking depiction of Narragansett tribe member Lynsea Montanari holding a photograph of the late Princess Red Wing, of the Narragansett/Niantic and Pokanoket tribes, who led the fight for the federal government to recognize the Narragansett Nation. The mural was painted by Baltimore artist Andrew Pisacane *(@Gaiastreetart)* in partnership with the **Tomaquag Museum** *(tomaquagmuseum.org; adult/child $6/3)* and Avenue Concept. The piece is meant to bring awareness to the erasure of Native American history and the continuing existence of Indigenous people in Providence. It's become an iconic, though temporary, element of the Providence skyline – a reminder that Indigenous people have always been here and will continue to be.

Providence

MAP P189

Paddle downtown in Providence

You'll likely spend time alongside the Providence River while exploring the city's downtown, but slipping *into* the water gives you a whole new view of the state capital. **Providence Kayak Co** *(providencekayak.com)* – located inside the **Landing Cafe** – offers single and tandem rentals for 45- and 75-minute trips, the perfect amount of time to paddle up and down the main stretch of the river. Rentals sell out quickly in the summer months, so make a reservation if you can.

Marvel at WaterFire's dancing flames

All three rivers running through downtown Providence glow and flicker gold on WaterFire nights, when over 100 bonfires are lit on the surface of the waterways. These floating flames are part of a mesmerizing art installation by Brown graduate Barnaby Evans. The first installation took place in 1994 in an effort to reinvigorate Providence as a destination. Today, it's hard to imagine the cultural and aesthetic charm of the state's capital was ever in question, but **WaterFire** *(waterfire.org)* played a significant role in attracting visitors, alongside the river relocation plan, which made it physically possible for people to enjoy the waterfront.

The bonfires are lit by torchbearers in gondolas, and musical performances take place in the parks along the rivers. Thousands of visitors descend on downtown to take it all in. You'll want to get here early to find parking and claim a spot along the water. Lightings typically start around sunset, and the fires burn until midnight. WaterFire takes place from May through November, on roughly two Saturday evenings each month.

Experience design and creativity

Providence is nicknamed the 'Creative Capital' for its eclectic community of thinkers and makers, with the **Rhode Island School of Design** (RISD) at its heart. It was founded in 1877 by a group of women – before women had the right to vote – with a focus on progressive thinking and curiosity. You can visit the **RISD Museum of Art** *(risdmuseum.org; $20),* located between the river and Brown University. The stunning collections range from ancient Greek and Egyptian to the 21st century, with over 100,000 items on display. If you love art, plan to spend a few hours here. The museum is free on Sundays and Thursday evenings; reserve tickets in advance on those days.

EATING IN PROVIDENCE: OUR PICKS

MAP P189

Dune Brothers Seafood: Food cart serving sustainable seafood. Try the two local favorites: chowder and clam cakes. *11am-7pm Wed-Sat, to 5pm Sun* $$

Los Andes: Peruvian and Bolivian food served in this always-packed spot with a leafy patio. Don't miss the ceviche. *hours vary* $$

Nicks on Broadway: Upscale diner experience with an extensive but fresh menu. Book ahead, especially for brunch. *10am-8pm Wed-Sat, to 4pm Sun* $

Al Forno: Classic Providence restaurant serving up rustic Italian dishes in a sophisticated atmosphere since 1980. *5-10pm Tue-Fri, from 4pm Sat* $$

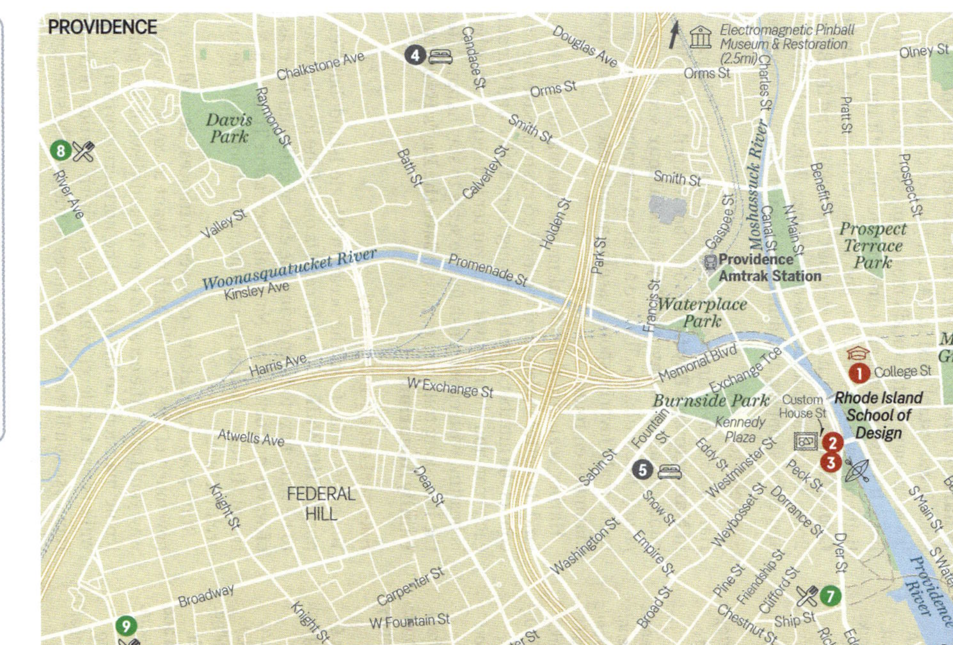

HIGHLIGHTS
1 Rhode Island School of Design

SIGHTS
see 1 RISD Museum of Art
2 Still Here mural

ACTIVITIES
3 Providence Kayak Co.

SLEEPING
4 Esperanto
5 Dean Hotel

EATING
6 Al Forno
7 Dune Brothers Seafood
8 Los Andes
9 Nicks on Broadway

DRINKING & NIGHTLIFE
see 3 Landing Cafe

RHODE ISLAND MUSEUMS FOR RAINY DAYS

Living Sharks Museum: *(living sharks.org; free)* A Westerly museum dedicated to 'shark history and shark future.'

Newport Car Museum *(newport carmuseum.org; adult/child $20/10)*: Collection of 100+ automobiles.

International Tennis Hall of Fame: *(tennis fame.com; adult/child $20/free)* National Historic Landmark, first opened in 1880.

Newport Art Museum: *(newport artmuseum.org; adult/child $15/free)* Over 3000 artworks, from the 18th century to the present.

Sailing Museum & National Sailing Hall of Fame: *(the sailingmuseum.org; adult/child $18/12)* The history of sailing.

Electromagnetic Pinball Museum and Restoration: *(electro magneticpinball museum.com; $10 including free pinball)* Learn about the craft behind pinball machines.

Newport

MAP P191

Stroll Newport's historic wharf

At the ocean end of Newport's Pelham St is a lively marina lined with shopping, dining and boat slips. **Bannister's Wharf** *(bannistersnewport.com)* has been a hub of activity since it was established in 1742, and as a deep water marina, it's seen some of the world's most impressive yachts moored here. It's also a bustling tourist attraction with the authenticity of a working marina, and home to the iconic **Clarke Cooke House**, which includes the Candy Store and the Boom Boom Room, a popular basement dance club. Stroll the pier and enjoy shopping and dinner on a warm summer evening.

Say hello to seals

Harbor seals love winter's chill, and over 400 of them hang out in **Narragansett Bay** from November to April. To see them, bundle up and join **Save the Bay** for a **seal tour** *(savebay.org/family-fun/seals)*. You'll board a boat in Newport to cruise out to the seals' favorite spots, learning about these semi-aquatic mammals en route.

Harbor seals are the official marine animal of Rhode Island. To better understand the local ecosystem, Save the Bay counts the number of seals arriving from Maine and Canada each year, and their arrival each winter is a sign that the bay is healthy, with enough fish for the seals to stay happy. After the hour-long tour, you can visit **Save the Bay's Hamilton Family Aquarium**.

Hike past ocean and history

You're never far from the ocean in Rhode Island, but Newport's **Cliff Walk** *(cliffwalk.com)* is one of the loveliest ways to be right next to it, enjoying the caw of gulls and the crash of waves on rocks. This National Recreation Trail in a National Historic District is a unique tour of both wildlife and architecture.

Start your walk at one of seven entrances, depending on how much of the 3.5-mile path you want to cover. Along the way, you'll enjoy the ocean to one side and views of Newport's iconic mansions to the other. The northern portion of the walk is flat and level, while the southern portion becomes rocky , so you'll want steady shoes to traverse the sometimes slippery surfaces.

EATING IN NEWPORT: SCRUMPTIOUS BREAKFASTS

MAP P191

Corner Cafe: A cozy spot for all-day breakfast. House specials like the Jimmy Pesto Especial are worth the wait. *hours vary* **$$**

Cru Cafe: The locally sourced menu rotates seasonally at this trendy cafe. Breakfast served all day. Bonus: BYOB. *8am-3pm* **$$**

Annie's: The best breakfast deal is right on Bellevue Ave. The classic diner menu includes budget basics and decadent options such as crab-cake Benedict. *7am-3pm* **$**

Coffee Grinder: For a light breakfast, enjoy an authentic Italian espresso coffee and a pastry with views of Newport Harbor. *7am-6pm Sun-Thu, to 7pm Fri & Sat* **$**

NEWPORT

HIGHLIGHTS
1 Bannister's Wharf
2 Cliff Walk
3 The Breakers

SIGHTS
4 International Tennis Hall of Fame
5 Marble House
6 Newport Art Museum
7 Rosecliff
8 The Elms
9 Sailing Museum & National Sailing Hall of Fame

ACTIVITIES
10 Save the Bay's Hamilton Family Aquarium

SLEEPING
11 Mill Street Inn

EATING
12 Annie's
13 Clarke Cooke House
14 Corner Cafe
15 Cru Cafe
16 Scales & Shells
17 The Red Parrot

DRINKING & NIGHTLIFE
18 Coffee Grinder

ENTERTAINMENT
19 Bowen's Wharf Seafood Festival

NEWPORT'S BELOVED FESTIVALS

Newport Folk Festival: Started in 1959, the summer event takes place on a peninsula in Fort Adams State Park.

Newport Jazz Festival: A multiday music fest that includes jazz and genre-defying artists, both well-known and up-and-coming; also in Fort Adams State Park.

Newport Oyster Festival: For one weekend in May, oyster growers and vendors gather at Bowen's Wharf for visitors to sample the local variety.

Bowen's Wharf Seafood Festival: In October, historic Bowen's Wharf hosts a cornucopi of local seafood along with live music.

Newport Pride: The annual June Pride march includes a bike parade, live performances and an inclusive, loving atmosphere.

CARL BEUST/SHUTTERSTOCK

Newport Folk Festival

Discover gilded-age extravagance

In the late 19th century, when robber barons were rolling in untaxed wealth, Newport became the most stylish summer destination. The wealthiest of New York and Philadelphia spent millions building extravagant mansions on rolling estates with views of the Atlantic Ocean. Today you can tour a handful of these opulent homes for a look inside the Gilded Age. Highlights include the **Breakers** – a Vanderbilt family property built in the Italian Renaissance style; **Rosecliff**, featuring a heart-shaped staircase and Newport's largest ballroom; **Marble House**; and **The Elms**. Regular house tours are self-guided, and you can download the Newport Mansions app *(newportmansions.org)* for an audio tour of each. If you're interested in going deeper, book a guided tour, like 'Beneath the Breakers', where you'll explore the subterranean levels of the house, or the 'Servant Life Tour' to see how 'the help' kept things running.

EATING IN NEWPORT: SEAFOOD FAVORITES

MAP P191

Flo's Clam Shack: Established in 1936, this casual spot serves scrumptious fried seafood from two locations: Middletown and Portsmouth. *11am-9pm* **$**

Scales & Shells: Exclusively serving seafood, this popular eatery sources locally. Snag a seat on the balcony for views of Thames St. *hours vary* **$$**

Clarke Cooke House (p190)**:** Refined dishes served with classic maritime elegance, on Bannister's Wharf with harbor views. *1:30pm-midnight Mon-Sat, from 11am Sun* **$$$**

Red Parrot: Lobster is the star of the Red Parrot's extensive menu, served on three levels with festive, family-friendly vibes. *11:30am-9:30pm Sun-Thu, to 10:30pm Fri & Sat* **$$**

Connecticut

CHARMING SHORELINE | RIVER VALLEYS | VIBRANT CITIES

Connecticut, perhaps more than any other New England state, is cloaked in clichés as a moneyed place where New Yorkers come to play tennis and ride horses. But people who know the state know of its grit, history and charm, from the dense woods where gnarled trees grow through 19th-century farm equipment to industry towns that have risen, fallen and risen again with the evolution of goods and technology.

Prior to the arrival of Dutch fur traders and English Puritan settlers, the Pequots, Mohegans, Paugussets and Schaghticokes called this land home. Despite a devastating genocide known as the Pequot War, surviving Pequots have maintained their culture and now own the famous Foxwoods Casino and other major businesses. While colonial history dominates, there are many opportunities to learn about the people who have been here for thousands of years while exploring a state dotted with picturesque coastal towns, rolling hills, covered bridges and medium-sized cities full of nightlife and culture.

Places

New Haven p195
Guilford & Madison p197
Essex p197
Mystic p198
Hartford p199
Northeastern Connecticut p201

TOP TIP

New Haven was the United States' first city designed on a grid. While this layout should make it easy to navigate, one-way streets can make driving a frustrating endeavor. Take the train or ditch the car ASAP and explore on foot. Elsewhere, most towns have a walkable green or central district, but you'll want to drive to reach other areas of interest.

GETTING AROUND

Driving makes it easier to get to the central and northern parts of the state. I-95 will bring you up and down the coast, while I-91 is the main thoroughfare north. Take the scenic routes if you have time.

The **Metro-North Railroad** *(mta.info)* services the shoreline, from New York's Grand Central Terminal to New Haven. From there, you can continue along the coast via Shoreline East all the way to New London. The **Hartford Line** *(hartfordline.com)* connects central Connecticut to the coast.

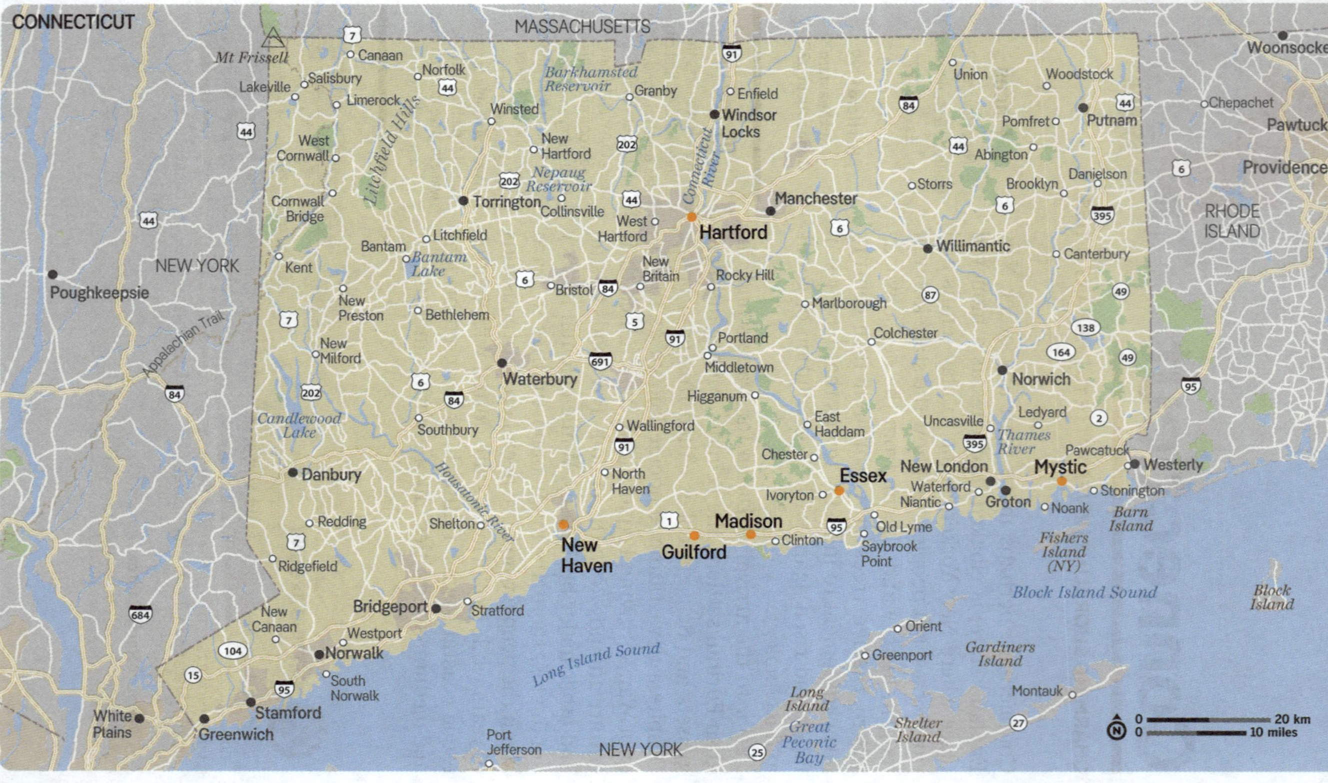
CONNECTICUT
MASSACHUSETTS
NEW YORK
RHODE ISLAND
Mt Frissell
Canaan
Salisbury
Lakeville
Limerock
Norfolk
Litchfield Hills
West Cornwall
Cornwall Bridge
Kent
Bantam
Litchfield
Bantam Lake
Winsted
Barkhamsted Reservoir
Granby
New Hartford
Nepaug Reservoir
Torrington
Collinsville
West Hartford
Enfield
Windsor Locks
Connecticut River
Hartford
Manchester
Union
Woodstock
Pomfret
Putnam
Abington
Storrs
Brooklyn
Danielson
Willimantic
Canterbury
Chepachet
Woonsocket
Pawtucket
Providence
Poughkeepsie
Appalachian Trail
New Preston
Bethlehem
Bristol
New Britain
Rocky Hill
Marlborough
Colchester
Portland
Middletown
New Milford
Waterbury
Southbury
Candlewood Lake
Danbury
Higganum
Wallingford
East Haddam
Norwich
Uncasville
Ledyard
Thames River
Pawcatuck
Westerly
Chester
Essex
New London
Mystic
Ivoryton
Waterford
Niantic
Groton
Noank
Stonington
Barn Island
North Haven
Housatonic River
Redding
Shelton
Madison
Clinton
Old Lyme
Saybrook Point
New Haven
Guilford
Fishers Island (NY)
Block Island Sound
Block Island
Ridgefield
Bridgeport
Stratford
New Canaan
Westport
Norwalk
South Norwalk
Long Island Sound
Orient
Greenport
Gardiners Island
Montauk
Long Island
Great Peconic Bay
Shelter Island
White Plains
Stamford
Greenwich
Port Jefferson
0 20 km
0 10 miles

New Haven

MAP P196

Line up for pizza

New Haven pizza is a family affair. **Frank Pepe** opened his pizzeria *(pepespizzeria.com)* on Wooster Street in 1925. His nephew opened Pepe's long-standing rival, **Sally's Apizza** *(sallys apizza.com)*, on the same street in 1938. **Modern Apizza** *(modernapizza.com)* was already on the scene in 1934, and the three cemented the city's status as a pizza destination with a uniquely New Haven style: Neapolitan with an extra thin crust that's fired to a crispy, black char (don't call it burnt).

A visit to Pepe's or Sally's means lining up, even before they open, and then declaring yourself committed to one or the other. Don't expect an expansive menu of sides and drinks. All three serve the white clam pie pizza, invented by Pepe's and embraced by all.

The 'newest' pizza spot is **BAR** *(barnightclub.com)*, a restaurant-club-pub which opened in 1996 to serve a younger, hipper crowd; it's famous for the mashed potato pie.

All four are within a mile or two of each other, and walking between them is a great way to see the Wooster and East Rock neighborhoods.

Climb above the city

If you're looking for a bird's eye view of New Haven and some green reprieve from the city streets, **East Rock Park** is your spot. The summit, standing 350ft above Mill River, was formed 200 million years ago when molten rock erupted between stress cracks in the region's sandstone bedrock, then cooled and hardened into dolomite. The surrounding sandstone was softer, and erosion carved it down through the centuries, eventually making East Rock a distinguished rock face.

Climb the **Giant Steps Trail** to the summit, where you'll find the *Soldiers and Sailors* monument, commemorating New Haven residents who died in various wars. Enjoy the views over New Haven as it stretches to the Long Island Sound.

Go back in time at the Peabody

The dinosaur skeletons got a bit older during the four years that New Haven's **Yale Peabody Museum** *(peabody.yale.edu; free)* was closed for major renovations and expansion – but in that time, they found lots of new friends. The renowned natural history museum reopened in March 2024 with new

NEW HAVEN TRAIN STATIONS

New Haven has two train stations: **Union Station** and **State Street Station**.

Union Station is the larger of the two, with Amtrak, Metro-North and CTrail services, along with many bus and shuttle lines. The station itself is a bustling, beautiful hub of transportation, with classic wooden benches and a high ornamental ceiling. The ride from Union Station to Grand Central in New York City is just under two hours and runs regularly. Expect crowded trains at rush hour and around the holidays.

State Street is a smaller, newer station with only local service.

If you're heading to a train station in New Haven, make sure you know which one!

EATING IN NEW HAVEN: BEYOND PIZZA

MAP P196

Meat & Co.: Grab a thick, decadent sandwich at Meat & Co. and bring it next door for beer at East Rock Brewery. *11:30am-8:30pm Sun-Thu, to 9:30pm Fri & Sat* $

Camacho Garage: Housed in an old Shell gas station, this Westville favorite serves contemporary Mexican street food. *hours vary* $$

Heirloom: Located in The Study at Yale, the menu at this place is an exciting exploration of local seafood and farm-fresh produce. *7am to 9pm* $$

Junzi Kitchen: Healthy, filling meals prepared to order with authentic Chinese flavors – and made extra tasty with their signature chili oil. *11am-9pm* $

NEW HAVEN

HIGHLIGHTS
1 Frank Pepe
2 Yale Peabody Museum

SLEEPING
3 Blake Hotel

EATING
4 Heirloom
5 Junzi Kitchen
6 Modern Apizza
7 Sally's Apizza

DRINKING & NIGHTLIFE
8 BAR

TRANSPORT
9 Union Station

spaces, exhibits and an increased focus on accessibility. The cathedral-like building's two-story great hall was built to house the giant skeletons of extinct reptiles, including a beloved brontosaurus, and they continue to be a major draw. Today, the new and improved Peabody includes 14 million specimens and objects that map the history of life on Earth.

Guilford & Madison

A Connecticut shoreline sampler

Dive into a books and beaches theme when exploring Guilford and Madison, adjacent shoreline towns where you'll find thoughtfully curated independent bookstores and peaceful coastal spots to read. In Guilford, **Breakwater Books** *(breakwaterbooks.net)* sits on a vibrant town green with a row of boutiques, restaurants, a coffee shop and a chocolatier. Once you've picked your read, enjoy it on nearby **Jacobs Beach**.

From Guilford, take Rte 1 to the main strip of downtown Madison and **RJ Julia Booksellers** *(rjjulia.com)*. This cozy shop is packed with just about any genre you can imagine, and there's a cafe. If the sun is out, bring your book to nearby **Hammonasset Beach State Park**, with a 2-mile stretch of sand and water access.

You might also venture down one of the nature trails through the park's tidal marsh habitat. The National Audubon Society named Hammonasset a Globally Significant Bird Area for its high concentration of rare and endangered birds.

Essex

A turning point in travel

About a 40-minute drive from New Haven is Essex, where you can experience a slice of travel history by riding a **steam train** *(essexsteamtrain.com)* and riverboat for a tour of the Connecticut River Valley. Board a vintage coach pulled by a steam locomotive at Essex Station for the narrated 90-minute trip, during which you'll chug through thick forest and small towns, with a beautiful landscape gliding by your window.

At Deep River Landing, leave the train to board the *Becky Thatcher* riverboat to cruise along the Connecticut River. There are multiple open-air decks from which can view the riparian habitat of blue herons, egrets, cormorants and red-winged blackbirds. From February to March, you're likely to spot bald eagles as they migrate to the region from Canada.

THE OLD STONE HOUSE

About halfway between the Guilford Town Green and the marina sits the oldest house in Connecticut, set back from the road on a gently rolling lawn, and easy to miss as you drive by. Now officially called the **Henry Whitfield State Museum** (and also known as the Stone House), it was built in 1639 by Reverend Henry Whitfield, who lived there with his wife and children. The land was taken over by the Whitfields as part of an agreement with the Menunkatuck band of the Quinnipiac tribe; the settlers also used it as a defensive building, and it marked the start of tensions and the eventual displacement of the native people of coastal Connecticut.

EATING ON THE CONNECTICUT SHORELINE: SEAFOOD

Lenny & Joe's Fish Tale: Lenny and Joe's is a festive summer favorite, thanks to the big patio with a merry-go-round and ice-cream shack. *11:30am-8:30pm Sun-Thu, to 9pm Fri & Sat* **$$**

Shell & Bones Oyster Bar & Grill: Decadent small plates and dinners are served on a beautiful waterfront patio in New Haven. *noon-10pm Mon-Thu, 11am-11pm Fri-Sun* **$$$**

Bill's Seafood: The perfect place to celebrate summer, with seafood and live music. Their Rhode Island and New England clam chowders are both delicious. *11am-9pm* **$**

Dog Watch Cafe: Sit on a dock in Stonington or play yard games in Mystic. Both locations have distinct vibes and scrumptious seafood. *11:30am-9pm* **$$**

PROTECTIVE SALT MARSHES

Salt marshes cover about 15,000 acres along Connecticut's shoreline, marking the transition from ocean to land. But the salt marshes have shrunk significantly in the past century. To ensure the state maintains this vital foraging habitat for birds, breeding habitat for saltwater fish and flood protection for coastal communities, **Audubon Connecticut** *(audubon.org)* is working on salt-marsh restoration up and down the Connecticut coast. Efforts include removing invasive plants and using dredged soil to rebuild target elevations that have suffered from erosion. You can enjoy the lively beauty of salt marshes from the Guilford Salt Meadows Audubon Sanctuary, Hammonasse Beach State Park, and the Stewart B. McKinney National Wildlife Refuge.

ACTIUM/SHUTTERSTOCK

Choose between coach, 1st class or the caboose for the train. First-class passengers are able to purchase alcohol and nonalcoholic beverages. The boat is open seating/standing.

Mystic

Climb aboard wooden ships

About an hour's drive from New Haven is the **Mystic Seaport Museum** *(mysticseaport.org; adult/child $32/22)* – a hands-on exploration of Connecticut's maritime history, focused on the 1800s, when Mystic's whaling industry was thriving. But you won't just look at pictures and read placards about rigging wooden ships and forging iron harpoons; you'll watch people actually *do* these things. Come prepared for an indoor/outdoor experience: start with the indoor museum, which includes an art gallery and rotating exhibits on maritime history. Then wander the replica seaport village and the shipyard, where you can visit their historic ships.

The *Charles W Morgan* is the museum's most famous vessel. Built in 1841, this whaling ship once traversed much of the globe, breaking through sea ice in the Arctic circle and rounding Cape Horn to bring back the whale oil that fueled lamps and greased countless innovations of the Industrial Revolution. Today it's the only remaining wooden whaling ship in the world, and it sits out of the water at Mystic Seaport, meaning visitors can clamber aboard and glimpse what it would have been like to live onboard for months at a time.

It's easy to spend several hours at the museum. To make a full day of it, opt for the Mystic Seapass, which includes

Mystic Seaport Museum

entrance to both the Mystic Seaport Museum and the **Mystic Aquarium** *(mysticaquarium.org; adult child from $34/26)* just down the street.

Hartford

Tour Mark Twain's family home

Mark Twain was a man of big dreams and strong opinions, and visitors to the **Mark Twain House & Museum** *(marktwainhouse.org; adult/child $28/15)* in Hartford get a feel for that. All of the words he wrote and thought about travel, politics, racism, imperialism, public schools and more bounce timelessly between these walls that preserve his legacy.

The home was built in 1873, and Sam Clemens (Mark Twain was his pen name) moved in with his wife Olivia in 1874. It was their dream home, and the author later called the years they spent there with their daughters the family's happiest. He wrote some of his most popular books in the Hartford house, including *The Adventures of Tom Sawyer* (1876), *Adventures of Huckleberry Finn* (1884) and *A Connecticut Yankee in King Arthur's Court* (1889).

EATING IN HARTFORD: OUR PICKS

Max's Trumbull Kitchen: A global menu paired with a long list of seasonal cocktails offers endless possibilities at this downtown location. *hours vary* $$

Black-Eyed Sally's Southern Kitchen & Bar: Award-winning Southern staples are served in a lively atmosphere with live music. *noon-8pm, bar open late* $$

Rockin Chicken: Succulent chicken is cooked in a charcoal rotisserie oven from Peru and served alongside other authentic Peruvian favorites. *11am-8pm* $$

Max Downtown: Upscale steakhouse classics. There's a dress code for the main dining area. *11:30am-9pm Mon-Thu, to 10pm Fri, from 5pm Sat* $$$

THE OLDEST NEWSPAPER

The ***Hartford Courant*** was first published in 1764, before the founding of the US. When the second owner died of smallpox, his widow, Hannah Bunce Watson, took over, becoming the country's first female publisher. For many years, the paper ran ads to aid in the capture of fugitive enslaved people. The northern state's early pro-slavery sentiments reflects a dark and often-overlooked aspect of Connecticut's history.

The ads ended in 1848 when the state officially outlawed slavery, but the paper remained a significant political voice. Around 1870, Samuel Clemens (Mark Twain) sought (unsuccessfully) to become a shareholder. Today, the *Hartford Courant* is the oldest continuously running newspaper in the country and it prints daily. The online version *(courant.com)* is a great resource for news and events.

He and his family loved Hartford, too. It was a city of intellectuals, with Harriet Beecher Stowe, author of *Uncle Tom's Cabin* (1852), their neighbor. 'All I should get for it would be the pleasure of living in Hartford among a most delightful society, and one in which [Livy] and I both would be supremely satisfied,' he once said, according to the Mark Twain House and Museum.

The only way to visit the house is on a tour, which is well worth it. They're offered seven days a week and sell out several days ahead of time, so book yours early.

Traverse art history

Any visit to downtown Hartford should include at least a couple hours at the **Wadsworth Atheneum** *(thewadsworth.org; adult/child $20/free)*, an art museum that's sprawling in both space and coverage. A cultural hub since the 19th century, the collection includes 50,000 pieces spanning 5000 years. While the original proposal was for an art 'gallery,' founder and Hartford native Daniel Wadsworth decided to make it an 'atheneum' instead – a cultural center dedicated not just to the preservation of fine art but also to history and education. Don't miss the Morgan Great Hall, where powerful American and European paintings from the 16th to 19th centuries climb deep blue walls to reach an arched white ceiling with dazzling skylights.

Roseland Park, Woodstock, in the Last Green Valley

Northeastern Connecticut

Enjoy fall foliage with Walktober

Connecticut's northeastern 'Quiet Corner' is also known as the **Last Green Valley** *(thelastgreenvalley.org)*. This region is a National Heritage Corridor, a wilderness more than 10 times bigger than Acadia National Park. In October, the area comes to life with fall colors and activities, including **Walktober**, a local event that's been taking place for over 34 years. Throughout the month, you can join dozens of guided walking tours in many of the Last Green Valley's 35 Connecticut towns. Tours range from historical walking tours and ghost tours to farm visits and river paddles.

FEAST ON FARM PRODUCE

Litchfield County, in the Berkshire foothills, is home to over 85,205 acres of farmland that produces fresh fruit and vegetables, as well as eggs, meat and dairy. For the freshest food, go straight to the farms or farmers markets in the area, where you can meet the growers and enjoy unique agricultural experiences. On Saturdays, the **Litchfield Hills Farm Fresh Market** *(litchfieldfarmersmarket.org)* is open indoors at the Litchfield Community Center from October through May. In July, pick your own berries at **Evergreen Berry Farm** *(evergreenberryfarm.com)* in Watertown. At **Lindell Flower Farm** *(lindellflowerfarm.com)*, admire rows of color and bring home your own bouquet; the farm store is open daily from 10am to 6pm.

EATING IN LITCHFIELD COUNTY: ALFRESCO DINING

Down the Hatch: Vacation vibes are strong at the only restaurant on Candlewood Lake. Enjoy fresh seafood and cocktails. *11:30am-midnight, Tue-Sun* **$$**

White Horse: British-inspired pub food next to the East Aspetuc River. Savor award-winning cooking on one of the four patios. *11:30am-9pm Mon-Thu, to 10pm Fri & Sat, 11am-8:30pm Sun* **$$**

West Shore Seafood: *The* place in Litchfield County for fried fish, shrimp baskets and lobster rolls. Pick up food at the window and enjoy in their all-weather tent or on the lawn. *hours vary* **$**

Hopkins Inn: Austrian fine dining, sitting above the shore of Lake Waramaug. Try the traditional Wiener schnitzel. *hours vary* **$$$**

Vermont

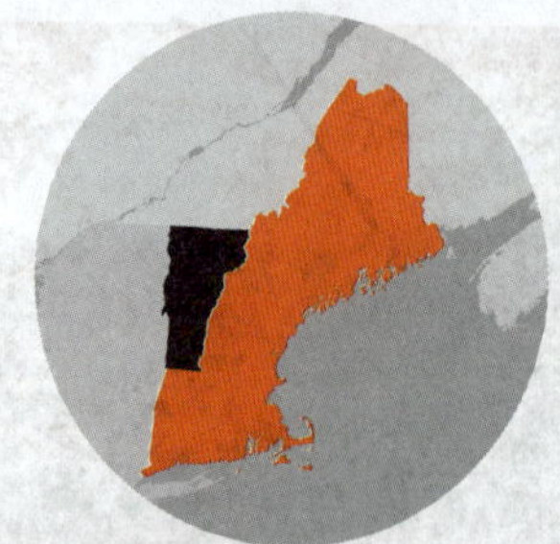

LAKE CHAMPLAIN | GREEN MOUNTAINS | HISTORIC VILLAGES

Places

Burlington p204

Middlebury & Around p205

Stowe & Around p206

Montpelier p209

East Burke p212

Peacham p213

Bennington p213

TOP TIP

Travel in Vermont is slower than you'd expect from the state's diminutive size, which maxes out at 150 miles north to south, and 90 miles east to west. Allow extra time to navigate the mountainous terrain and rural roads.

With its blend of bucolic farmland, serene mountains and picturesque villages, Vermont is one of the country's most uniquely appealing destinations. Here in the nation's second-least-populous state, where the capital city (Montpelier) only has 8000 residents, and the largest (Burlington) tallies just shy of 45,000, nature always feels close at hand. Hikers, bikers, skiers and boaters flock year-round to Vermont's Green Mountain slopes, the expansive waters of Lake Champlain and the impressive network of parks and recreation trails.

Travelers invariably notice something different when they cross the state line. For starters, there's Vermont's total lack of billboards; you'll also see more mom-and-pop businesses, fewer big box stores and considerably less urban sprawl than in other parts of the country.

In a world where breakneck growth often prevails, Vermont takes a certain pride in its nonconformist approach and remains a haven for quirky creativity and community-mindedness. It's a bastion of the 'small is beautiful' aesthetic.

GETTING AROUND

Two superhighways serve Vermont. I-91 traces the state's eastern edge from Massachusetts to Canada, while I-89 cuts a diagonal swath northwest from New Hampshire to Lake Champlain and the Québec border. Western Vermont's main thoroughfare is US Hwy 7. Elsewhere, two-lane state highways and remote backroads prevail.

Amtrak *(amtrak.com)* operates two Vermont-bound trains: the **Ethan Allen Express**, running from New York City through the Hudson Valley to Rutland, Middlebury and Burlington; and the **Vermonter**, connecting Philadelphia, New York City, Connecticut, Massachusetts and Washington, DC, with nine Vermont stations between Brattleboro and St Albans.

Vermont Translines *(vttranslines.com)* and **Greyhound** *(greyhound.com)* offer long-distance bus services from Albany and Montréal, while **Dartmouth Coach** *(dartmouthcoach.com)* runs from Boston and New York City to neighboring New Hampshire. Within the state's borders, various regional operators provide shorter distance connections around places such as Burlington, Montpelier and Brattleboro.

VERMONT
CANADA
QUÉBEC
0 40 km
0 20 miles
Alburg
North Troy
Newport
Enosburg Falls
Coventry
Brownington
Island Pond
North Hero
St Albans
Lake Willoughby
Barton
Mt Pisgah (1443ft)
Glover
Grand Isle
Cambridge
Jeffersonville
Craftsbury Common
Caspian Lake
West Burke
East Burke
South Hero
Mt Mansfield (4393ft)
Underhill State Park
Smuggler's Notch
Lyndonville
Lake Champlain
Burlington
Stowe
Northeast Kingdom
St Johnsbury
Shelburne
Waterbury Center
Peacham
Waterbury
Charlotte
Mad River Glen
Montpelier
Groton
Waitsfield
Vergennes
Bristol
Warren
Addison
Middlebury
Bradford
East Middlebury
Ripton
Green Mountain National Forest
Randolph
Shoreham
Goshen
Talcville
Brandon
Bethel
Pittsfield
White River Junction
Killington
Quechee
Lebanon
Woodstock
Rutland
Whitehall
East Poultney
Plymouth Notch
Hartland
Windsor
Ludlow
Claremont
Pawlet
Danby
Weston
Merck Forest
Dorset
Grafton
Mt Equinox (3848ft)
Manchester
Bellows Falls
Walpole
Arlington
Shaftsbury
Newfane
Putney
Dover
Keene
Bennington
Wilmington
Marlboro
Brattleboro
Williamstown
North Adams
Readsboro
Colrain
Northfield
MASSACHUSETTS
Erving
Gardner
Fitchburg
Greenfield
NEW YORK
NEW HAMPSHIRE
Connecticut River
White Mountain National Forest
Warren
Appalachian Trail
Bristol
Concord

CHAMP, VERMONT'S LOVABLE LAKE MONSTER

A dinosaur relic or Ice Age proto-whale? A tree trunk? A really, really big fish? Lake Champlain's beloved lake monster, **Champ**, has long captivated the imaginations of local residents. Known to the Abenaki First Nation as Tatoskok, Champ was reportedly sighted by French explorer Samuel de Champlain in 1609. He described seeing a fish-like creature up to 10ft long with two rows of sharp, dangerous teeth.

Indulge your curiosity with a visit to the Champ Monument at Burlington's Perkins Pier, or spot the Champ display at Burlington's **Echo Leahy Center for Lake Champlain**. Better yet, attend a **Vermont Lake Monsters** *(vermontlakemonsters.com)* minor league baseball game, where a lovable green-costumed Champ mascot dances on the dugout roof between innings.

Burlington

Explore the waterfront on foot or by bike

Burlington's waterfront is an inviting sight, with Lake Champlain's sparkling waters juxtaposed against the distant profile of New York's Adirondack Mountains.

The waterfront area, anchored by the leafy greenery and flowering shrubs of **Waterfront Park**, includes a scenic promenade, a pier for Lake Champlain boat trips, a kids' playground and the family-friendly aquarium at the **Echo Leahy Center for Lake Champlain** *(echovermont.org; adult/child $20/16.50)*. Historical markers posted about the park tell tales of bygone days, from the launching of the country's second commercial steamboat here in 1808 to the world's first international ice hockey tournament in 1886. Presiding over it all is **Union Station**, where a daily train service to New York City, aboard Amtrak's *Ethan Allen Express*, was reintroduced in mid-2022 after a nearly 70-year hiatus.

South of the station, Burlington's bicycle advocacy organization, **Local Motion** *(localmotion.org)*, rents bikes from its Trailside Center. The **Burlington Greenway**, a paved recreation path for walking, biking, in-line skating and general perambulating, runs for 8 miles along the waterfront and feeds into the Island Line Trail, a gravel path that culminates in a scenic arc of causeway extending 2.7 miles into the middle of Lake Champlain. From late May to early October, Local Motion operates a bike ferry from the path's far end to South Hero on the Champlain Islands.

Cruise Lake Champlain

For the ultimate aquatic experience, get out on Lake Champlain – affectionately known to Vermonters as North America's sixth Great Lake.

Burlington's hub for boat cruises is the **Burlington Community Boathouse**, a popular hangout fashioned after the city's original 1900s' yacht club – easy to spot from the waterfront recreational path. From May to October, the *Spirit of Ethan Allen* plies the lake with scenic 1½-hour day cruises, lunch trips and dinner excursions, and 2½-hour sunset voyages. For a more immersive experience, sail around Lake Champlain on the *Friend Ship* and *Wild Rose*, a pair of classic New England sailing sloops operated by the **Whistling Man Schooner Company** *(whistlingman.com)*. The captains are knowledgeable about the area, and they encourage passengers to bring food and drink on board.

EATING IN BURLINGTON: OUR PICKS

Grey Jay: Trendy Mideast-influenced breakfast and lunch spot just off Church St Marketplace. *9am-2pm* **$**

Pho Hong: Locals line up for superb, authentic Vietnamese fare at this family-run spot in Burlington's North End. *3-9pm Tue-Thu, 11am-3pm & 5-9pm Fri & Sat* **$$**

Spot on the Dock: The Lake Champlain views are unbeatable from this waterfront resto-bar. Best at sunset when colorful reflections dance across the water. *11am-9pm May-Sep* **$$**

Santiago's: Cuban spot serving empanadas, *lechón* (roast pork), *ropa vieja* (shredded beef) and Cuban sandwiches, both traditional and vegan. *5-9pm Tue-Thu, to 10pm Fri & Sat* **$$**

Lake Champlain

Burlington's **Community Sailing Center** *(communitysailingcenter.org)* rents out kayaks, canoes and paddleboards by the hour.

Serious paddlers with their own boats can explore dozens of miles of shoreline north and south of the city on the **Lake Champlain Paddlers' Trail**. There's no finer way to enjoy the water than on a multiday excursion, overnighting at one or more of the 600-plus camping spots around the lake.

Middlebury & Around

Walk the Robert Frost Trail

For nearly four decades, Robert Frost (1874–1963), the Poet Laureate of Vermont, spent the summer and fall near Middlebury (about an hour's drive from Burlington), growing apple trees, teaching and writing much of his poetry in a log cabin in **Ripton**, a beautiful hamlet set in the Green Mountains. For a taste of the landscape he loved and the poetry it inspired, take a walk on the **Robert Frost Interpretive Trail** *(fs.usda.gov)*, 10 miles southeast of Middlebury on VT 125. The roughly 0.75-mile loop traverses a wetland on boardwalks, then crosses the Middlebury River and loops through forests and meadows. Along the way, plaques display half a dozen of Frost's poems.

VERMONT'S BEST FARMSTANDS

Cedar Circle Farm: Shop this East Thetford farmstand for fruit and veggies, or pick your own in expansive fields stretching down to the Connecticut River.

Champlain Orchards: Renowned apple-cider producer southwest of Middlebury hosting pick-your-own-fruit-and-berries sessions, plus seasonal events.

Brattleboro Farmers Market: Folks gather here weekly to buy direct from farmers and enjoy live music beside the tree-shaded Whetstone Brook.

Jubilee Farmstand: This gargantuan barn in Huntington with a Camel's Hump mountain backdrop epitomizes Vermont's time-honored self-serve system (choose your produce, leave money in the cashbox).

Pete's Greens: Four-season organic farm selling direct to customers daily (May to October) in charming Craftsbury village.

EATING BEYOND BURLINGTON: OUR PICKS

Middlebury Bagel & Deli: Family-run Middlebury institution specializing in homemade donuts, bagel sandwiches and made-to-order breakfasts. *6am-1pm, closed Thu & Sun* $

Rustic Roots: Delightful breakfast and lunch spot in an old gray farmhouse near the center of Shelburne village. *9am-2pm Wed-Sun* $$

Shelburne Farms Inn: Pioneering farm-to-table eatery serving breakfast and dinner in a lakeside mansion on a gorgeous historic estate. *8-11am & 5-8:30pm* $$$

Blue Paddle Bistro: Popular dinner spot on the Champlain Islands offering everything from burgers to lobster, plus a great Sunday brunch. *5-8pm Thu-Sat, 9:30am-1pm Sun* $$$

BEST FALL FOLIAGE SPOTS

Mt Mansfield: Head to Stowe, Jeffersonville, Cambridge, Smugglers Notch or Underhill State Park for panoramic views of the fiery foliage and (sometimes) snow-dusted summit of Vermont's highest peak.

Lake Willoughby: Enjoy the technicolor majesty of changing maples on the precipitous slopes of this fjord-like lake.

Mad River Valley: Gawk at gorgeous colors from VT 100, the backroads on the opposite side of the valley, or Mad River Glen's iconic single chairlift.

Merck Forest: Take in breathtaking Taconic Mountain vistas from Merck's barn meadow.

Grafton: Grafton's white clapboard houses are especially photogenic when contrasted against blazing maples and a brilliant blue October sky.

WANGKUN JIA/SHUTTERSTOCK

Trapp Family Lodge

A quarter mile further east, National Forest Rd 396 leads from the Robert Frost Wayside picnic area up to Frost's former cabin; today it's viewable from the outside only, but the lovely mountain views from here are well worth the detour. Continue east up VT 125 to find the distinctive yellow-frame buildings of the **Bread Loaf School of English** *(middlebury.edu/blse)*, which Frost helped found while teaching at Middlebury College. In winter, Bread Loaf transforms itself into the **Rikert Outdoor Center** *(rikertoutdoor.com)*, whose Frost Fields loop trail allows skiers to experience the poet's cabin in all its wintry glory.

Stowe & Around

Ski the USA's oldest Nordic trails

Among Vermont's 30 Nordic skiing venues, nothing compares to a day at **Trapp Family Lodge** *(vontrappresort.com)*, 4 miles west of Stowe. Founded by the Von Trapp family of *The Sound of Music* fame, America's oldest cross-country center features 40 miles of groomed trails for every skill level; the Austrian-inspired eating and drinking options make for a dreamy all-day skiing experience.

For a delightful loop, start with an easy glide through snow-covered forest on Sugar Rd, then huff and puff your way

EATING IN STOWE: OUR PICKS

Piecasso: Stowe's go-to choice for pizza, après-ski or following a summer outing on the adjacent Stowe Recreation Path. *11am-10pm Fri & Sat, to 9pm Sun-Thu* **$$**

Bistro at Ten Acres: On a hillside west of town, this cozy spot serves soups, salads and mains, from veggie curry to meat and fish specials. *5-10pm Fri-Tue* **$$$**

Harrison's: Steaks, grilled pork chops, roast lamb, venison and seafood rule the menu at this traditional favorite in the heart of Stowe village. *4:30-8:30pm Wed-Sat* **$$$**

Michael's on the Hill: Gourmet choice in a sweet 19th-century hilltop farmhouse 6 miles south of Stowe. *5-9pm Wed-Mon* **$$$**

up the Parizo Trail to a junction with the Cabin Trail. From here, a more gentle climb leads to **Slayton Pasture Cabin**, where you can warm yourself by the fire with hot chocolate, homemade soup or chili.

Now comes the fun part! At the far end of Slayton Pasture, begin the ridiculously long and gradual descent down Haul Rd. At the bottom, you can pick up the Luce Trail to loop back to the lodge – but for a longer, even more blissful day out, cross Trapp Hill Rd and continue descending through open pastures to Lager Lane, home to the **Von Trapp Bierhall**. Here you can feast on bratwurst, schnitzel, sauerkraut mashed potatoes and roasted veggies, all accompanied by the Von Trapp's European-styled homebrews and finished off with Austrian desserts like Sachertorte.

Afterwards, Sleigh Rd is your gateway to several scenic (albeit uphill) loops back to the lodge.

Explore Vermont's most captivating mountain pass

Just 10 miles northwest of Stowe via VT 108, **Smugglers Notch** (2170ft) is one of Vermont's most scenic mountain passes. Named for the smugglers who used this route to transport goods between Vermont and British Canada prior to the War of 1812, it's the jumping-off point for numerous hiking trails, including the **Long Trail**, which runs for 272 miles between the Massachusetts and Québec borders.

The road up is an adventure in itself. Near the summit, cliffs and boulders encroach on the roadway from both sides, narrowing the state highway to a strip of asphalt barely wide enough for two vehicles. An obligatory stop en route is the **Barnes Camp Visitors Center**, where the recently constructed Smugglers Notch Boardwalk allows visitors in wheelchairs or with strollers to follow a short section of the Long Trail through a montane wetland to a viewpoint with lovely perspectives on the notch. Plaques along the way offer insights about the ecology and natural history. Hiking destinations from the notch include Sterling Pond and Elephant's Head to the northeast, and Mt Mansfield (p208) to the southwest.

Enjoy legendary ice-cream

In 1978, Ben Cohen and Jerry Greenfield took over an abandoned gas station in Burlington and, with a modicum of training, launched the outlandish flavors that forever changed America's ice-cream culture. Nearly half a century later, a tour of **Ben & Jerry's Ice Cream Factory** *(benjerry.com/about-us/factory-tours; adult/child $6/1)* – 1 mile north of

ROADS LESS TRAVELED

For a scenic adventure, try these less-traveled, unpaved Green Mountain crossings.

Hazens Notch Rd: This Revolutionary War-era route crosses a glacier-scoured notch, passing pretty wetlands and beautiful views of Jay Peak.

Lincoln Gap Rd: The 16-mile road from Bristol to Warren climbs ridiculously steeply through Lincoln Gap (2428ft). When closed in winter, it's popular with daredevil sledders.

Mt Tabor Rd: Surrounded by Green Mountain National Forest, the 15-mile journey from Danby to Landgrove grants access to the Appalachian Trail and White Rocks National Recreation Area.

Kelley Stand Rd: Stretching from East Arlington to Stratton, this 14-mile road climbs steeply up the Battenkill River's Roaring Branch before leveling into a landscape of high altitude ponds.

DRINKING IN STOWE: OUR PICKS

Alchemist Beer Cafe: Enjoy a draft Heady Topper with Jamaican fare at Vermont's renowned Alchemist Brewery. *11am-6pm*

Von Trapp Bierhall: Authentic Alpine food and German-style lagers are served under the soaring ceiling at this ski-in trailside beerhall. *11:30am-9pm*

Stowe Cider: Sample crisp, hard ciders in the tasting room, or pair them with a meal at the adjacent Shakedown Street BBQ. *4-9pm Wed & Thu, noon-9pm Fri & Sat, to 8pm Sun*

WhistlePig Pavilion: Sip Vermont's finest rye whiskey and cocktails après-ski or during the summer concert series at Stowe's Spruce Peak. *noon-7pm Sun-Thu, to 9pm Fri & Sat*

VERMONT'S LONG-DISTANCE HIKING & SKIING TRAILS

Long Trail: The USA's first long-distance hiking trail was built between 1912 and 1930. It traces the Green Mountains' ridgeline for 272 miles from Massachusetts to Canada. The **Green Mountain Club** (GMC; *greenmountainclub.org*) maintains more than 60 rustic lodges and lean-tos en route; for more info, visit GMC's headquarters south of Stowe. The Long Trail served as inspiration for the Appalachian Trail, and these two venerable routes coincide for nearly 100 miles in southern Vermont.

Catamount Trail: Running the length of Vermont from Readsboro to North Troy, the 300-mile Catamount Trail is the country's longest cross-country ski route. Its magnificent meander through the Green Mountains encompasses 11 ski touring centers, including some that offer lodging.

Waterbury off I-89 and about a 15-minute drive from Stowe – remains an obligatory stop. Half-hour tours start with a campy video that follows the company's long, strange trip to corporate gianthood; next, you'll head to a special glassed-in room to glimpse the production line in action. After chowing (very teeny) free scoops, linger a while to admire the informational displays about Ben & Jerry's efforts to change the world through community building and environmental leadership, one scoop at a time. In summer, cows roam among the solar panels and pastures outside.

Before you leave, make sure to climb the grassy knoll above the upper parking lot to see Ben & Jerry's Flavor Graveyard. Ringed by a neat white picket fence and framed by a grand purple archway, this tongue-in-cheek tribute to four-dozen ice-cream flavors that flopped features neat rows of headstones that honor forgotten concoctions like Dastardly Mash, Divinity Bovinity and Vermonty Python. Each memorial is lovingly inscribed with the flavor's brief lifespan on the grocery shelves of this Earth and a poem in tribute.

Admire 360-degree views of Vermont

Vermont's tallest mountain may look small by world standards, but a climb to the summit here is an unforgettable experience. **Mt Mansfield** (4393ft) encompasses a larger swath of above-the-treeline terrain than any place in Vermont, yielding spectacular views west to Lake Champlain and the Adirondacks, south along the Green Mountains' rugged spine, east to the White Mountains and north into Québec on a clear day. The peak's profile resembles a human face, as reflected in the anthropomorphic names (Adam's Apple, Chin, Nose, Forehead) shown on local trail maps. Mansfield is also home to 200 acres of fragile alpine tundra, the largest such expanse in Vermont. Stowe makes a fine base for Mt Mansfield.

Two classic approaches to the mountain are via the **Long Trail South** from Barnes Camp (p207) or the **Hell Brook Trail** from Smugglers Notch (p207; look for both trailheads west of Stowe on VT 108); however, the steep ascents here (2700ft over roughly 2 miles) are not for the faint of heart.

For a more moderate climb (2600ft over 3.3 miles) with awesome nonstop views, head for **Underhill State Park** (*vtstateparks.com/underhill.html*) on Mt Mansfield's western flank. Start with a gentle 1-mile climb on the CCC Rd, then bear left into the forest, cross several bridges and begin climbing in earnest on the **Sunset Ridge Trail**. Partway up the mountain, a worthwhile detour leads to Cantilever Rock,

EATING BEYOND STOWE: OUR PICKS

Red Hen Bakery: Roadside pit stop between Waterbury and Montpelier that's beloved for its delectable pastries, sandwiches and hearty organic bread. *7am-3pm* **$**

Warren Store: Enjoy breakfast and lunchtime goodies on the deck or the steps overlooking the sculpted rocks and swimming hole below. *7:30am-5pm Fri & Sat, 8am-3pm Sun-Thu, closed Tue* **$**

American Flatbread: Wood-fired pizzas and locally sourced salads served beside a roaring fire in winter or at picnic tables with mountain views in summer. *4-9pm Thu-Sun* **$$**

Hen of the Wood: Waterbury's iconic gourmet eatery, featuring farm-to-table and wild-sourced ingredients. *5-10pm Wed-Mon* **$$$**

Vermont State House

where you can pause for a snack on massive stone slabs. Back on the main trail, you'll soon emerge above the treeline. The summit looks deceptively close, but you've still got a solid hour of steady climbing; no worries – the jaw-dropping vistas offer ample compensation. You'll know you're getting close when you reach junctions with the Laura Cowles and Long Trail and begin crossing boardwalks through the tundra. From here, it's a short scramble to reach the 360-degree panoramas up top. Allow five to six hours for the round trip.

Montpelier

Visit the country's smallest capital city

With only 8000 inhabitants, Montpelier is the country's smallest capital city, and the only one without a McDonald's. Towering above town, the golden dome of the **Vermont State House** *(statehouse.vermont.gov; free)* is Montpelier's unmissable landmark. On weekdays, visitors can take a tour (docent- or self-guided, depending on whether the legislature is in session). In the lobby, look for the fossils of ancient sea creatures embedded in the 'black marble' (actually limestone) floor, quarried from an ancient reef on Isle La Motte in the Champlain Islands.

(continues on p212)

GETTING AROUND IN NORTH-CENTRAL VERMONT

Exploring north-central Vermont is easier with your own vehicle, as public transit is limited, with Burlington the most economical place to arrange rentals. If you don't have your own car, **Amtrak**'s once-daily *Vermonter* train to/from Washington, DC and New York City has stops in Montpelier and Waterbury. The **RCT** *(Rural Community Transportation; riderct.org)* bus 100 runs from Waterbury to Stowe. The **GMT** *(Green Mountain Transit; ridegmt.com)* bus 83 – the Waterbury Commuter – connects Waterbury with Montpelier (20 to 30 minutes), and bus 86 (the Montpelier Link Express) offers service from Montpelier and Waterbury to Burlington. From late December through March, GMT also runs a seasonal ski shuttle from Waitsfield to Mt Snow's Lincoln Peak.

DRINKING BEYOND STOWE: OUR PICKS

Lawson's Finest Liquids: Iconic Vermont brewery serving pints and pub grub around outdoor firepits and under the high ceilings of its Waitsfield brewpub. *noon-7pm Sun-Thu, 11am-8pm Fri & Sat*

Prohibition Pig: Waterbury microbrewery with an on-site restaurant specializing in scrumptious barbecue and Southern fare. *4-9pm Mon-Fri, from noon Sat & Sun*

Three Penny Taproom: Excellent cocktails and an ever-evolving assortment of top-notch beers on tap in downtown Montpelier. *11am-9pm Mon-Thu, to 10pm Fri & Sat*

Capitol Grounds: Montpelier's go-to spot for an early-morning java jolt; near the Vermont State House. *6:15am-2pm Mon-Fri, from 7am Sat & Sun*

DRIVING TOUR

Drive Vermont's Scenic Route 100

Weaving along the base of the Green Mountains through the rural heart of Vermont, VT 100 is one of New England's quintessential road trips. The route rambles past cow-speckled pastures, tiny villages with country stores and white-steepled churches, and verdant mountainsides crisscrossed with hiking trails and ski slopes. Even if your time is limited, don't miss the scenic 45-mile stretch between Stockbridge and Waterbury, an easy detour off I-89.

1 Wilmington

Nestled in the upper Deerfield Valley, historic Wilmington was chartered by New Hampshire governor Benning Wentworth in 1751. These days, it's best known as the access point for **Mt Snow** *(mountsnow.com)*, one of southern Vermont's best ski resorts and a summertime mountain-biking and golfing destination.

The Drive Head 44 miles north on VT 100, passing through the pretty villages of Jamaica and Londonderry.

2 Weston

The picture-postcard village of Weston (population 566) is renowned for its **Vermont Country Store**, run by five generations of the Orton family. This browsers' paradise is packed with vintage games, flannel nighties, Vermont-made cheeses, maple products, penny candies and more. Across the town green, catch a show at **Weston Theater Company** *(westontheater.org)*, Vermont's oldest professional theater.

The Drive A quick 10-mile hop up VT 100 brings you to Ludlow.

3 Ludlow

On the Green Mountains' eastern slopes, low-key Ludlow is home to family-friendly **Okemo Mountain Resort** *(okemo.com)*. With 100-plus trails, the east's longest superpipe, excellent snowmaking and

ACTIUM/SHUTTERSTOCK

Plymouth Cheese Corporation

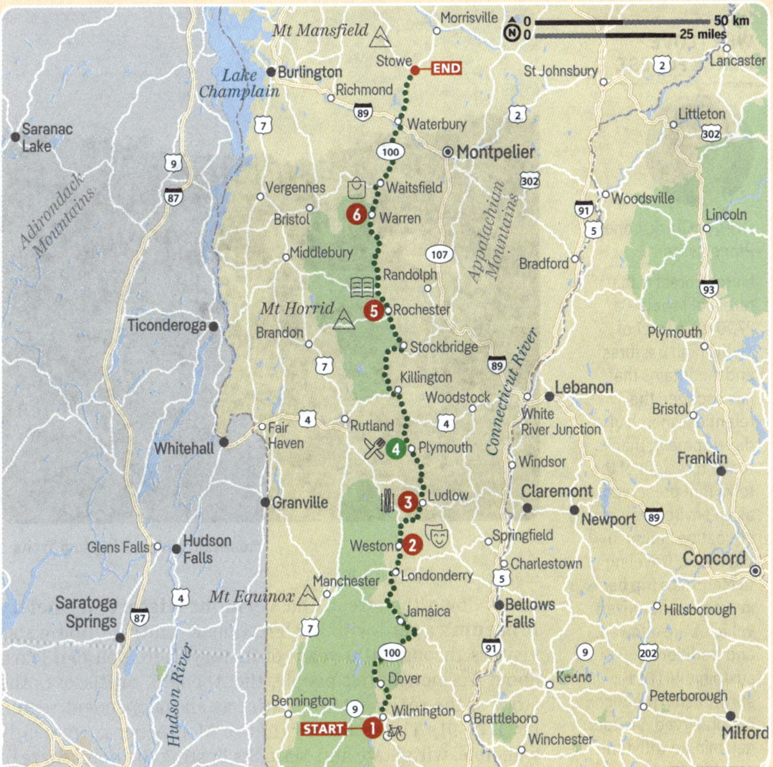

high-speed lifts, Okemo appeals to skiers and snowboarders of all levels.

The Drive VT 100 snakes north past a series of lakes to Plymouth Notch, where a one-mile detour on VT 100A leads to the **President Calvin Coolidge State Historic Site**.

4 Plymouth

President Calvin Coolidge's boyhood home of Plymouth is a Vermont village frozen in time, with its one-room schoolhouse, general store and barns gracefully arrayed among old maples on a bucolic hillside. Sample the venerable Vermont cheddar produced on-site at **Plymouth Cheese Corporation** *(plymouthcheese.com)*.

The Drive VT 100 doglegs west past Killington ski area, then resumes a northward course through the wide-open White River Valley.

5 Rochester

Cradled between two Green Mountain ridges, Rochester is another classic Vermont village with a tidy town green. Settle in for home-baked snacks and browse the shelves at **Sugar Mama's** and **The Bookery**, a cozy spot spread across two historic farmhouses.

The Drive Continue 19 miles on VT 100, passing pretty **Moss Glen Falls** and watching for moose in Granville Gulf, the gateway to the Mad River Valley.

6 Warren

Warren's blink-and-you'll-miss-it village center revolves around the **Warren Store** (p208), a creaky-floored edifice boasting two levels of shopping bliss. Head upstairs for clothing, Vermont crafts and kids' games, or grab snacks and drinks from the downstairs deli's vintage ice chest, best enjoyed on the sunny deck overlooking the sculpted rocks along Freeman Brook; the mini-gorge here is perfect for a summertime dip. North of town, giant barns, covered bridges and old farmhouses dot the landscape on your 29-mile journey up the Mad River Valley to **Stowe** (p206).

WHY I LOVE MERCK FOREST

Gregor Clark, Lonely Planet writer

Merck Forest is that rarest of jewels – a 2700-acre tract of idyllic high pastures and mountains that has escaped the relentless march of development, thanks to the foresight of the folks that preserved it as an environmental education center in the 1950s. Traveling to Merck is a trip back in time; no motorized vehicles are allowed, and traditional, sustainable land stewardship practices are observed. Visitors can mingle with farm animals and admire sweeping Taconic Mountain vistas just 10 minutes from the parking lot, or travel deep into the forest on Merck's extensive trail network for overnights at rustic backcountry cabins. As a 16-year-old, I volunteered here with the Student Conservation Association, and totally fell in love – 20 years later, Merck inspired my move to Vermont.

MICHAEL LAMONICA/SHUTTERSTOCK

Mountain biking, Kingdom Trails

(continued from p209)

Just down the street, the **Vermont Historical Society Museum**'s award-winning 'Freedom & Unity' exhibit walks visitors through 400 years of history. Here you can learn about Vermont's first people, the Abenaki, or discover the story of the region's 14-year stint as an independent republic (1777–91). The rest of downtown Montpelier is eminently walkable, with State and Main Sts hosting the lion's share of shops and restaurants.

East Burke

Mountain bike the Kingdom Trails

Passing through century-old farms and forest floors dusted with pine needles, the award-winning **Kingdom Trails** *(kingdomtrails.com)* network offers one of New England's best mountain-biking experiences. In winter, its dozens of miles of singletrack, doubletrack and dirt roads are also a magnet for cross-country skiing, snowshoeing and fat biking. Trail passes are available online; a day pass costs US$20/15 per adult/child.

One of the network's most striking sections any time of year is the high ridgeline along Darling Hill Rd, where miles of trail command far-reaching views over the Northeast Kingdom's mountains and meadows. From May to October, buy trail passes at the **Kingdom Trails Welcome Center** in **East Burke**. From December to March, head uphill to the **Nordic Adventure Center**. Trails are typically closed in April and November.

Peacham

Historic village and autumn foliage

One great joy of traveling in Vermont is the serene beauty of its historic villages. One such place is Peacham, founded in the late 1700s along the then-bustling Bayley-Hazen Military Rd. These days, the town's privileged hilltop setting and the pastoral beauty of its surrounding farmland remain largely untouched by modern development, making this a wonderful spot for aimless wandering – especially in early October, when blazing maples contrast with the lush, rolling fields. From Peacham's town center, scenic dirt roads fan out in all directions. Pull out your Vermont road atlas and build a loop of any length; pretty options include Academy Hill Rd, Green Bay Loop, County Rd, Town Rd South and Old Cemetery Rd.

Bennington

Get folksy with Grandma Moses

Bennington's standout **museum** *(benningtonmuseum.org; adult/child $16/free)* houses the world's largest public collection of works by Anna Mary Robertson Moses, aka 'Grandma' Moses, who spent most of her life on a farm just across the state line in Eagle Bridge, NY, and attained international fame as a folk artist in her later years, from ages 70 to 101. The Grandma Moses gallery – recently renovated, expanded and reopened to the public – displays the artist's trademark paintings of rural life, alongside textiles and furniture. The remainder of the museum showcases three centuries worth of Vermont paintings, decorative arts and folk art. Don't miss the extensive collection of local pottery, and the vintage Martin Wasp, a showstopper of a 1925 luxury car manufactured right here in Bennington.

VERMONT'S BEST COVERED BRIDGES

Vermont has more covered bridges per square mile than any other state. Here's a pontist's guide to our favorites:

Montgomery: The seven covered bridges in Montgomery village represent the densest concentration anywhere in Vermont.

Three-in-a-Row Bridges, Northfield: On Cox Brook Rd off VT 12, cross the Station, Lower and Upper Bridges within just 0.3 miles.

Cornish-Windsor Bridge: This 449ft span from Windsor, VT, to Cornish, NH, is the country's longest covered bridge.

Fisher Railroad Bridge, Wolcott: Off VT 15 is a bridge replete with a cupola, designed to disperse smoke from the steam engines that once rumbled through.

Bartonsville: This bridge has been resurrected by the community after floodwaters swept away its 19th-century predecessor in 2011.

EATING IN & BEYOND BENNINGTON: OUR PICKS

Blue Benn Diner: A Bennington classic since 1948, this iconic diner boasts individual jukeboxes in every booth. *6am-3pm Tue, Wed, Sat & Sun, to 8pm Thu & Fri* **$**

Pangaea: Cozy North Bennington resto-bar with half-formal, half-casual seating and a beautiful patio overlooking the river out back. *5-9pm Tue-Sat* **$$**

Phelps Barn Pub: Enjoy paella, duck breast or classic pub fare by the fireside in this comfy eatery. *5-8pm Tue-Sat* **$$**

TJ Buckley's: Brattleboro's intimate eight-table bistro, in a converted railway dining car, is famed for its gourmet, seasonal, farm-to-table cuisine. *6-9pm Thu-Sun* **$$$**

New Hampshire

MOUNTAINS | LAKES | HISTORIC TOWN CENTERS

Places

Portsmouth p216
Mt Washington p218
White Mountains p220
Franconia p220

Jagged mountains, serene valleys and island-dotted lakes lurk in every corner of New Hampshire. The whole state begs for exploration, whether looking for loons near Winnipesaukee or trekking the upper peaks surrounding Mt Washington. Each season yields a bounty of adrenaline and activity: skiing and snowshoeing in winter (many slopes are open into spring), magnificent walks and drives through fall's fiery colors, and swimming in crisp mountain streams in summer.

Jewel-box historical settlements such as Portsmouth set a sophisticated tone, while small-town culture lives on in pristine villages like Peterborough and Littleton. There's even a bit of beach action, with the state making the most of its 18-mile shoreline.

Named in 1629 after the eponymous English county New Hampshire was one of the first American colonies to declare its independence from Britain in 1776. These days, it's known for its libertarian tendencies and one of the country's best-known mottos: 'Live Free or Die.'

TOP TIPS

If your time in New Hampshire is limited, check out Portsmouth and the beaches, then head north to **Mt Washington** (p218) for year-round adventures (hiking, train rides, scenic drives and skiing).

GETTING AROUND

Historic town centers like Portsmouth are quite walkable, but to get between destinations, a car is very handy in this part of New England. You can often get the best rental rates in Manchester.

Concord Coach Lines *(concordcoachlines.com)* provide service between Boston (South Station and the airport) and various key towns in New Hampshire, including Concord and North Conway. There's also **Dartmouth Coach** *(dartmouthcoach.com)*, with quick service between Boston and Hanover.

For the White Mountains, Concord Coach Lines travel daily from Boston's South Station to North Conway (about 3¾ hours). US302 and NH16 run through the valley, joining in North Conway (where there's free parking) as the White Mountain Hwy.

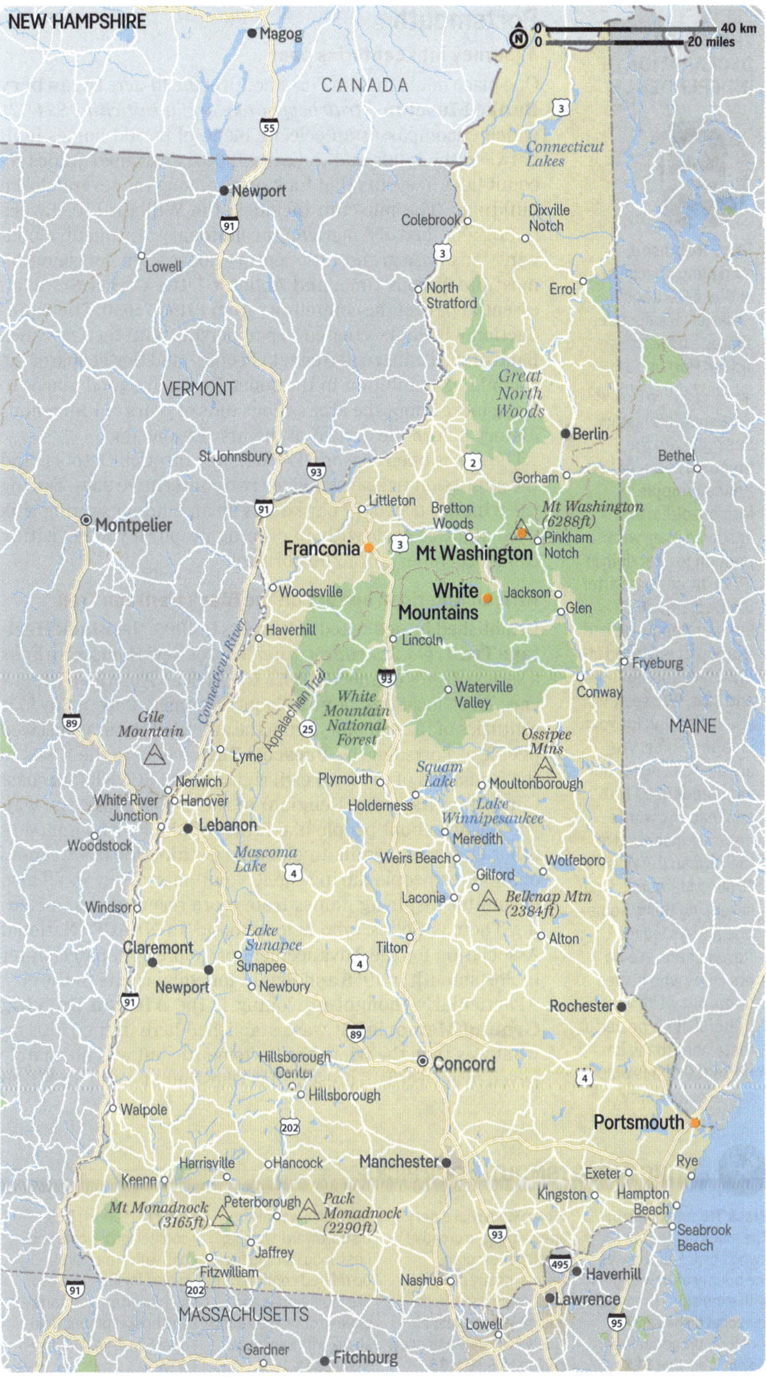
NEW HAMPSHIRE
0 40 km
0 20 miles
Magog
CANADA
Newport
Lowell
VERMONT
St Johnsbury
Montpelier
Colebrook
Connecticut Lakes
Dixville Notch
North Stratford
Errol
Great North Woods
Berlin
Bethel
Gorham
Littleton
Bretton Woods
Mt Washington (6288ft)
Pinkham Notch
Franconia
Mt Washington
White Mountains
Jackson
Glen
Woodsville
Haverhill
Lincoln
Fryeburg
Connecticut River
Appalachian Trail
White Mountain National Forest
Waterville Valley
Conway
MAINE
Gile Mountain
Lyme
Ossipee Mtns
Squam Lake
Plymouth
Moultonborough
Norwich
White River Junction
Hanover
Holderness
Lake Winnipesaukee
Lebanon
Meredith
Woodstock
Mascoma Lake
Weirs Beach
Wolfeboro
Gilford
Laconia
Belknap Mtn (2384ft)
Windsor
Alton
Lake Sunapee
Tilton
Claremont
Sunapee
Newport
Newbury
Rochester
Hillsborough Center
Concord
Hillsborough
Walpole
Portsmouth
Harrisville
Hancock
Manchester
Rye
Keene
Exeter
Kingston
Hampton Beach
Mt Monadnock (3165ft)
Peterborough
Pack Monadnock (2290ft)
Seabrook Beach
Jaffrey
Fitzwilliam
Nashua
Haverhill
Lawrence
MASSACHUSETTS
Lowell
Gardner
Fitchburg

THE OTHER DECLARATION OF INDEPENDENCE

Terry Robinson, marketing specialist at Black Heritage Trail New Hampshire, shares a little known side of Portsmouth. *@blackheritagetrailnh*

Portsmouth's history ties right into the founding of our nation. Prince Whipple, a former soldier and enslaved man, wrote a petition for freedom in 1779 – three years after the Declaration of Independence. He and a group of enslaved individuals got together and said, 'We see that you're fighting for your independence. We are also asking for our independence.' You can read the words he wrote inscribed at the African Burying Ground Memorial. One surprising thing: someone always leaves flowers here. We do not know who leaves them, but we're very grateful. It's a powerful testament to the importance of this place to the community.

Portsmouth

A journey into centuries past

One place not to miss in Portsmouth is the 10-acre **Strawbery Banke Museum** *(strawberybanke.org; adult/child $24/12)*, which encompasses an eclectic blend of period homes built between the 1690s and the early 1800s. Costumed guides recount tales of events that took place among the several dozen buildings. The museum includes: the William Pitt Tavern (1766), a hotbed of American revolutionary sentiment; Goodwin Mansion, a grand 19th-century house from Portsmouth's most prosperous time; and Abbott's Little Corner Store, an essential part of the community from 1919 to 1950. The reproduction wigwam – created in partnership with the Cowasuck Band of the Pennacook-Abenaki People – and the 'People of the Dawnland' exhibition in the Jones House are good places to learn more about the area's thousands of years of Indigenous history before the arrival of the first Europeans.

The site is open seasonally from May through October, and the admission ticket is good for two consecutive days. During the winter, Strawbery Banke sets up an outdoor skating rink – a delightful spot (with an evening firepit) if you're visiting from December through February.

African American history on the Black Heritage Trail

Established by dedicated volunteers in 1995, the **Black Heritage Trail** *(blackheritagetrailnh.org)* of New Hampshire links a series of sites connected with the African American experience. At 23 locations, bronze plaques commemorate nearly four centuries of Black history, from the arrival of the first enslaved people at Portsmouth's **Prescott Park** wharf in the 1680s to the formation of the local civil rights group SCORR (Seacoast Council on Race and Religion) in the 1960s. Along the way, you'll learn about people like Prince Whipple, who joined 18 other enslaved men in an eloquent petition for the freedom of all Black people during the Revolutionary War. You'll also encounter inspiring names from more recent times, including Thomas Cobbs, who helped found an NAACP (National Association for the Advancement of Colored People) chapter in Portsmouth in 1958 and fought for equal rights in the city.

Particularly thought-provoking is the **African Burying Ground Memorial**. It was established here in the 1700s on what was then the fringes of Portsmouth, but was ultimately paved over to create present-day Chestnut St – and forgotten

EATING IN PORTSMOUTH: OUR PICKS

Black Trumpet Bistro: The much lauded chef-owned bistro showcases the bounty of New England with exquisitely prepared seasonal dishes and locally sourced seafood. *5-9pm Wed-Sun* **$$$**

Moxy: Convivial eatery specializing in creative small plates: crab fritters, crispy pork belly, mushroom carbonara and other hits that pair nicely with well-balanced cocktails. *5-9pm* **$$**

Cure: In a warmly lit bistro, award-winning chef Julie Cutting fires up refined comfort fare like lobster mac and cheese or braised lamb shank with cassoulet. *5-9pm* **$$$**

Hearth Market: Deli counter, pizza, cafe and bar, with armchairs and tables for lingering over satisfying crepes, tarts and brisket plates. *8am-8pm Sun-Thu, to 10pm Fri & Sat* **$**

HISTORIC PORTSMOUTH ON FOOT

Peel back the centuries while taking the pulse of present-day Portsmouth on a walk amid the town's old lanes.

START	END	LENGTH
Market Square	Pier	1.5 miles; 30 min

Start in picturesque 1 **Market Square**, Portsmouth's hub since the mid-1700s. The white spire of the 2 **North Church** soars above the square's southeast side. It was built in 1854 to replace a meeting house built in 1713.

A few blocks southwest of there, the 3 **African Burying Ground Memorial** is an impressive work that pays homage to the town's African and African American community, with many members laid to rest here between 1705 and 1803.

Wind your way past the 4 **South Meeting-house**, a fine Italianate design from the 19th century. Stop to admire the fresh catch of the day at 5 **Sanders Fish Market**. Loop back along the 6 **waterside lane** (Mechanic St), taking in the tranquil views to nearby Peirce Island. At the 7 **Point of Graves Burial Ground**, peruse finely carved gravestones from the early 1800s.

Cross 8 **Trial Gardens** and walk out onto the 9 **pier**, where you can see a constant flurry of activity at the Portsmouth Naval Shipyard, going strong since 1800. From here, look for boats sailing under the movable Memorial Bridge, completed in 2013. The ribbon-cutting ceremony was led by Eileen Foley. At 95, the beloved former mayor reprised her role from 1923, when she cut the silk ribbon for the opening of the first Memorial Bridge as a five-year-old.

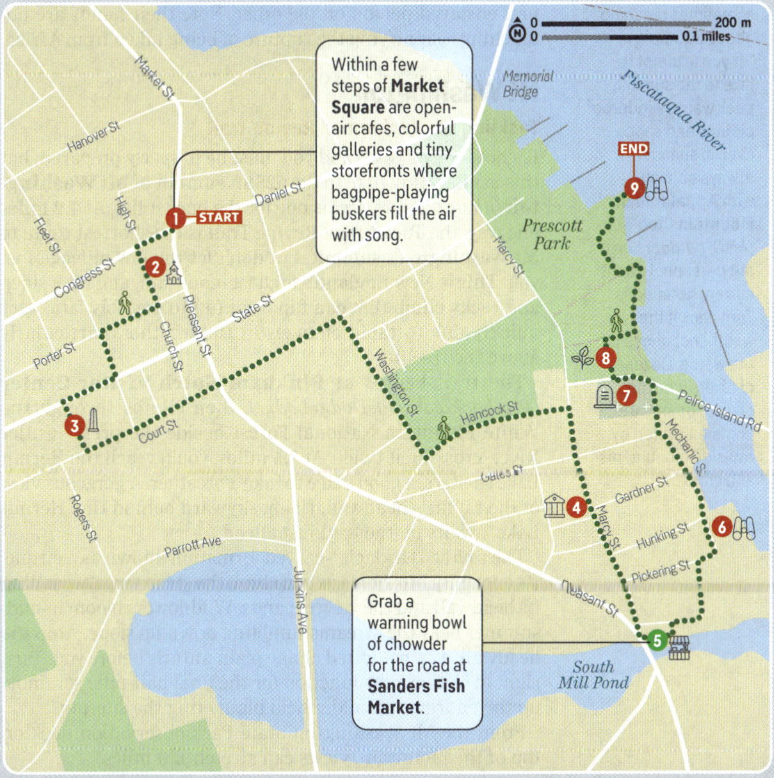

Within a few steps of **Market Square** are open-air cafes, colorful galleries and tiny storefronts where bagpipe-playing buskers fill the air with song.

Grab a warming bowl of chowder for the road at **Sanders Fish Market**.

FRAME CRAFT 8/SHUTTERSTOCK

as the city grew. The powerful statue anchoring the north end of the memorial represents Mother Africa on one side and the first enslaved person on the other. Note their hands are not touching – signifying the rupture of being taken from Africa.

Mt Washington

Tackling the Tuckerman Ravine Trail

It's not for everyone, and you must be properly prepared, but this exhilarating hike to the 6288ft summit of **Mt Washington** *(nhstateparks.org)* is one for the bucket list. At 4.2 miles one way, the Tuckerman Ravine Trail is the shortest route to Mt Washington's summit, but don't let the low mileage fool you. This is New England's highest mountain, and it's a steep and rocky climb that can flip from fun to possibly fatal very quickly due to rapid changes in the weather, particularly above the tree line.

The trail begins at **Pinkham Notch Visitor Center** *(facebook.com/JoeDodgeLodge)*, then climbs through the White Mountain National Forest beside the pretty Cutler River, crossing it twice. At 2.5 miles, you'll reach the Hermit Lake shelters, a good place to take a breather. A gorgeous view of the ravine's headwall, rising skyward behind tiny Hermit Lake, awaits on the trail just ahead.

The ravine is a glacier-carved formation known as a cirque. Its enormity hits home as you climb the steep steps ascending its headwall and the view expands. Wildflowers bloom in midsummer near the streams tumbling down its slope. Atop the headwall, a cairn-dotted alpine plain unfurls before you. Turn right at Tuckerman Junction for the final half-mile scramble up the enormous boulder field blanketing the summit.

From the Mt Washington State Park observation deck on top of the mountain, views can stretch 130 miles.

MT WASHINGTON: KNOW BEFORE YOU GO

The mountain is renowned for frighteningly bad weather – the average temperature on the summit is 26.5°F (-3°C), while the mercury has fallen as low as -47°F (-43°C), but only risen as high as 72°F (22°C). Over 21ft of snow falls each year, and the climate can mimic Antarctica's. Hurricane-force winds blow every three days or so on average, sometimes reaching above 200mph.

If you attempt to hike to the summit, pack warm, windproof clothes and shoes, even in summer. Always consult with **Appalachian Mountain Club** *(AMC; outdoors.org)* hut personnel about current conditions. Turn back if the weather changes for the worse. Dozens of hikers who died on the summit are commemorated by trailside monuments and crosses.

Mt Washington Cog Railway

Train to the summit

Purists walk and the lazy drive, but the quaintest way to reach Mt Washington's summit is via the **Mt Washington Cog Railway** *(thecog.com; adult/child from $84/61)*. From 1869 until 2008, coal-fired, steam-powered locomotives traveled the scenic 3-mile track up the mountainside. In more recent times, the coal-burning engines have been largely replaced by cleaner biodiesel locomotives, though the railway still operates two vintage steam engines in the warmer months.

Train lovers will undoubtedly enjoy the unique ride (and views), with an average grade of 25%, reaching 38% just below the tree line on the world's second steepest railroad trestle (the steepest is at Mt Pilatus, Switzerland). The round trip takes roughly three hours, with about one hour spent at the summit.

The train operates year-round but only goes as high as Waumbek Station (elevation 4000ft) from late fall through early spring.

Driving a legendary road

One of New England's top adventures, the serpentine drive up the 7.6-mile **Mt Washington Auto Road** *(mt-washington.com/drive-yourself; adult/child $36/15)* is not for the faint of heart. This private, narrow, alpine toll road gains more than 1000ft in elevation as it travels from the Pinkham Notch area to the parking lot just below the 0200ft summit. There are pull-offs along the way to admire the view (and cool your brakes on the descent). The priceincludes entry to the weather-focused Extreme Mount Washington Museum. 'This car climbed Mt Washington' bumper stickers are sold in the summit gift shop. For a guided audio tour, download the free Mt Washington Auto Road app before you arrive.

TOP OUTDOOR ADVENTURES

Rock Climbing: Go rock- or ice-climbing in White Mountain National Forest with **Eastern Mountain Sports Climbing School** *(@easternmntnsports)*.

River Trips: Conway-based **Saco Bound** *(sacobound.com)* offer tubing and canoeing, from easygoing one-hour paddles to multi-day camping trips.

Skiing & Snowboarding: Appealing winter resorts include **Cranmore** *(cranmore.com)*, with 56 trails and seven lifts; a mile east of North Conway.

Cross-country Skiing & Snowshoeing: Jackson XC *(jacksonxc.org)* is legendary: 60 miles of Nordic ski trails and 40 miles of snowshoeing.

Aerial Adventures: In addition to skiing, **Wildcat Mountain** *(skiwildcat.com)* rusn a summertime Ziprider – a chair suspended high above the ground, where you'll glide 45mph.

KANCAMAGUS PRACTICALITIES

The **Saco Ranger District Office** (Conway), the **White Mountains Visitor Center** (Woodstock) and the smaller **Lincoln Woods Visitor Center** are all good places to get maps and up-to-date info on trail conditions. Serious hikers will want to purchase a detailed map, such as the excellent, locally produced *Exploring NH's White Mountains* waterproof top map.

A day-use pass *($5)* is required any time you leave your car. Passes are sold at visitor centers and at self-pay kiosks. US National Parks passes (and other federal passes) are also accepted. Place your pass on your dashboard.

Camping is first-come, first-served at five of six campgrounds along the Kancamagus Highway; reserve ahead at **Covered Bridge Campground**. Backcountry camping is free, but restrictions apply.

If you'd rather not drive, you can take a two-hour guided van tour, which allows a full hour on the summit. In summer, one-way shuttles for hikers are available on a first-come, first-served basis – but don't assume you'll nab a spot. The road may be closed in severe weather (even in summer).

White Mountains

Driving the Kancamagus Highway

One of New Hampshire's prettiest driving routes, the **Kancamagus Highway** immerses you in the forested beauty of the **White Mountains**. Winding for 35 miles between Lincoln and Conway, and paved only in 1964, the 'Kanc' is still unspoiled by commercial development. It offers easy access to US Forest Service (USFS) campgrounds, hiking trails and fantastic scenery.

Among the most popular spots to tramp through the forest is the **Lincoln Woods Trail**. Here you can head off on short hikes or multi-day treks into 'the Pemi' (the Pemigewasset Wilderness).

Wherever you're heading, the journey begins by crossing a suspension bridge. The Lincoln Trail then continues another 1.4 miles along an abandoned railway that parallels a mountain stream. Make it even more rewarding by going all the way to Franconia Falls (around 6.8 miles round trip). There are plenty of other options if you want to keep going. You'll find the trailhead about 5 miles east of Lincoln.

A 0.3-mile one-way stroll on the popular **Sabbaday Brook Trail** ends at **Sabbaday Falls**, a gorge waterfall that zigzags through narrow granite walls into lovely pools. Steps lead to overlooks with mesmerizing views of the flume. The trailhead is about 16 miles west of the Saco Ranger District Office in Conway, and the trail is accessible for people with disabilities.

Franconia

Visiting Robert Frost's farmhouse

In the mid-20th century, Robert Frost (1874–1963) was the USA's most renowned and best-loved poet. For several years he lived with his family on a farm near Franconia (about an hour's drive from North Conway), now known as the **Frost Place** *(frostplace.org; adult/child $7/free)*. The years spent here were some of the most productive and inspired of his life.

The farmhouse has been kept as faithful to the period as possible, with numerous exhibits of memorabilia. In the forest behind the house is a 0.5-mile nature trail, with some of Frost's poems displayed along the way.

Maine

ACADIA NATIONAL PARK | SEASIDE TOWNS | ADVENTURES

New England's largest state boasts hundreds of miles of coastline encompassing sea cliffs, sandy beaches and craggy, wave-kissed shores. Offshore, there are countless islands for exploring, with scenic walks amid empty coves and misty, forested shorelines, while villages nearby boast year-round populations that fail to reach the triple digits. Inland, Maine has vast tracts of wilderness, with thick forests, mirror-like lakes and treeless, boulder-strewn peaks. Such a magnificent landscape offers near-countless adventures, and you can spend the day cycling along winding shore roads, kayaking beside curious harbor seals or hiking up above falcon nests to lofty mountaintop overlooks.

Given all that wilderness, it's not surprising that Maine residents are known for being independent and hardy. The state's history reaches back to the earliest Paleo-Indians, who hunted and fished here for thousands of years. The rugged, glacier-carved landscape was a serious challenge for early European colonists, and the region has remained sparsely populated up to the present.

Places

Portland p223
Boothbay Harbor p225
Rockland p225
Bar Harbor & Acadia National Park p228
Quoddy Head State Park p230
Baxter State Park p230

TOP TIP

Take in the beaches of southern Maine, then work your way up the coast, stopping in harbor towns and the famous **Acadia National Park** (p228). With extra time, detour to the mountainous wilderness of **Baxter State Park** (p231).

GETTING AROUND

The **Downeaster**, operated by **Amtrak** *(amtrak.com)*, runs five times daily between Boston and Portland, a journey of about 2½ hours. The train also stops in Wells on the coast, a 15-minute drive to Ogunquit and a 20-minute drive to York.

Having your own wheels is essential if you want to explore beyond Portland (where several rental agencies, including Enterprise and Budget, have bases). **Concord Coach Lines** *(concordcoachlines.com)* has several stops in Maine on its routes between New York, Boston and Portland. The US 1 hwy parallels the coastline and offers scenic travel but can be quite slow (and gridlocked in the summer).

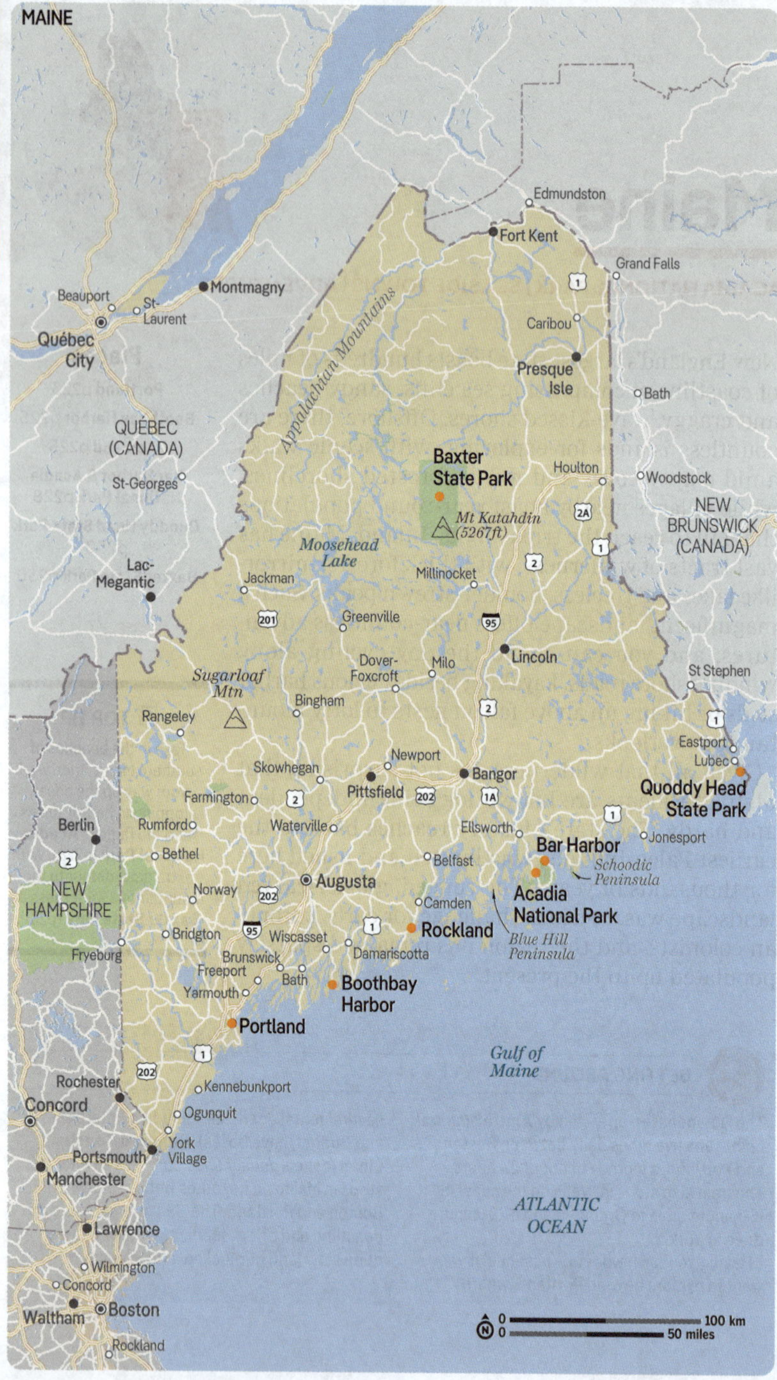
MAINE
Beauport
St-Laurent
Montmagny
Québec City
QUÉBEC (CANADA)
St-Georges
Lac-Megantic
Appalachian Mountains
Edmundston
Fort Kent
Grand Falls
Caribou
Presque Isle
Bath
Baxter State Park
Mt Katahdin (5267ft)
Houlton
Woodstock
NEW BRUNSWICK (CANADA)
Moosehead Lake
Jackman
Millinocket
Greenville
Lincoln
Dover-Foxcroft
Milo
St Stephen
Sugarloaf Mtn
Rangeley
Bingham
Eastport
Lubec
Newport
Skowhegan
Pittsfield
Bangor
Quoddy Head State Park
Farmington
Berlin
Rumford
Waterville
Ellsworth
Jonesport
Bethel
Belfast
Bar Harbor
Schoodic Peninsula
NEW HAMPSHIRE
Norway
Augusta
Acadia National Park
Camden
Fryeburg
Bridgton
Wiscasset
Rockland
Blue Hill Peninsula
Brunswick
Damariscotta
Freeport
Bath
Boothbay Harbor
Yarmouth
Portland
Gulf of Maine
Kennebunkport
Rochester
Concord
Ogunquit
York Village
Portsmouth
Manchester
ATLANTIC OCEAN
Lawrence
Wilmington
Concord
Waltham
Boston
Rockland
0 100 km
0 50 miles

Portland

Adventures on Casco Bay

Gulls shriek overhead as the scent of the sea drifts through the streets like the fog off Casco Bay, and everywhere the salt-laced wind licks your skin. Portland – Maine's largest city – has capitalized on the gifts of its port history to become one of New England's most vibrant small cities. Its famous ferry service, **Casco Bay Lines** *(cascobaylines.com)*, heads out to six different islands year-round, delivering mail, freight and visitors. It's a picturesque journey no matter where you go. **Peaks Island**, just 17 minutes from Portland, is a popular day-trip destination for walking and cycling. A five-minute stroll from the dock, **Brad's Bike Rental** hires out two-wheelers and tandems for scenic spins around the island. There's a selection of scenic cruises, too – the three-hour mailboat run is a great way to see the bay's sights.

The trail of Henry Wadsworth Longfellow

The revered American poet Henry Wadsworth Longfellow (1807–82) grew up in Portland in a Federal-style house, built in 1785 by his Revolutionary War-hero grandfather. Open only during the summer (Tuesday to Saturday, June though October), the **Wadsworth-Longfellow House** *(mainehistory.org; adult/child $18/12)* has been impeccably restored to look as it did in the 1800s, complete with original furniture, artifacts and a lovely garden.

One part of the complex features the galleries of the **Maine Historical Society** *(mainehistory.org)*, included with admission to the Wadsworth-Longfellow house. Here you'll find some of Portland's best exhibits looking at life in the state. Recent topics focused on photojournalism and the 1936 flood, the early roots of Maine music and the building of the International Appalachian Trail. The galleries are open Tuesday to Saturday, February through December.

Epicenter of fine art

Founded in 1882, the **Portland Museum of Art** *(PMA; portlandmuseum.org; adult/child $20/free)* houses an outstanding collection of American works. Maine artists, including Winslow Homer, Edward Hopper, Louise Nevelson and Andrew Wyeth, are particularly well-represented. You'll also find a few works by European masters, including Monet, Degas, Picasso and Renoir. The temporary exhibitions are among the best in the state and often blaze new trails, such as the 2024 show *Jeremy Frey: Woven*, which was the first-ever major retrospective

PORTLAND'S BEST TOURS

Lucky Catch Cruises: *(luckycatch.com)* Live the life of a lobsterman or lobsterwoman – if only for 90 minutes – as a passenger aboard a commercial lobster boat.

Maine Island Kayak Co: *(maineislandkayak.com)* From its base on Peaks Island, this well-run outfitter offers fun half-day, full-day and sunset paddling trips.

Portland Schooner Company: *(portlandschooner.com)* Take a two-hour tour on an elegant early-20th-century schooner.

Summer Feet Cycling: *(summerfeet.net)* Combine cycling with sightseeing and local history on various tours (with lobster-roll stops thrown in for good measure).

Maine Day Ventures: *(mainedayventures.com)* Delve deeper on a guided walking tour: there are foodie excursions, history outings and working waterfront walks.

EATING IN PORTLAND: OUR PICKS

Scales: Cavernous dockside warehouse serving some of Portland's best seafood. Feast on Bangs Island mussels, seared scallops and pan-roasted halibut. *4:30-9:30pm* **$$$**

Central Provisions: Choose from masterfully prepared small plates that range from sea urchin to bone marrow toast. *11am-2pm & 5-9:30pm* **$$**

Green Elephant: Even carnivores shouldn't miss the vegetarian fare at this Zen-chic, Asian-inspired bistro with hits like king oyster mushroom tempura. *11:30am-2:30pm & 5-9:30pm* **$$**

Eventide Oyster Co: Portland's most celebrated raw bar has scrumptious Maine oysters and shellfish, shucked to order, plus an enticing menu of creative small plates. *11am-11pm* **$$$**

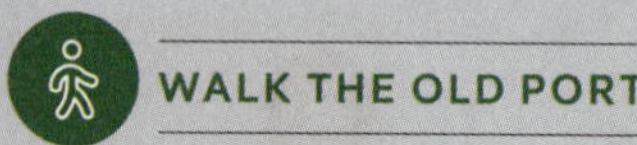

Stroll Portland's Old Port district and take in the history, cuisine, ambiance and views.

START	END	LENGTH
Bread & Friends	Portland Observatory	1.5 miles; 30 min

Fuel up for a day's walk in vibrant Portland with a stop at the charming neighborhood cafe and bakery 1 **Bread & Friends**. Nearby, take a look at the bronze 2 **statue** dedicated to local-boy-turned-movie-director John Ford. Find your way to 3 **Wharf Street**, whose brick buildings and cobblestone paving embodies the historic yet unpolished allure of the Old Port District – there's even a brewpub here called 4 **Gritty's**.

Near the corner of Fore and Moulton is the three-story building known as 5 **Mariners' Church**, which dates back to 1829; it held a 3rd-floor chapel that catered to waterfront workers. In the basement, Daniel Colesworthy ran a bookshop and printer.

You'll soon spot the seagulls as you walk down to 6 **Long Wharf**, which is dotted with bobbing vessels and a few curiosities on dry land. These include a giant slab of the 7 **Berlin Wall**, complete with a Soviet hammer and sickle on one section. Two piers over, you can take in the bounty of the sea at the iconic 8 **Harbor Fish Market**. Next door, head into the very first 9 **Sea Bags** store, which takes old sail cloth and upcycles it into bags and totes. If you're not ready to call it a day, head up to the quiet East End and climb up the 10 **Portland Observatory**. The seven-story brick tower, built in 1807, offers views over Casco Bay.

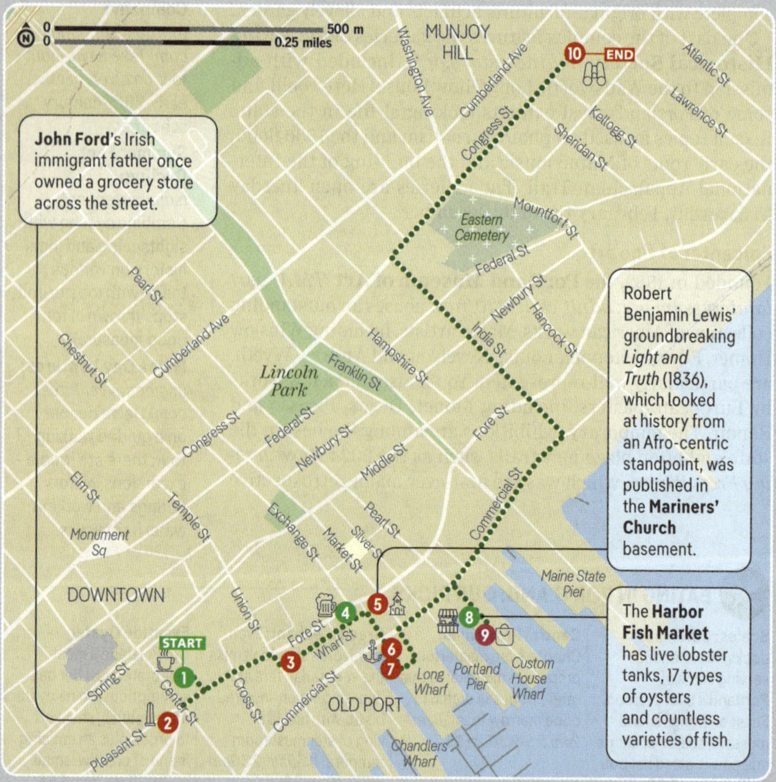

John Ford's Irish immigrant father once owned a grocery store across the street.

Robert Benjamin Lewis' groundbreaking *Light and Truth* (1836), which looked at history from an Afro-centric standpoint, was published in the **Mariners' Church** basement.

The **Harbor Fish Market** has live lobster tanks, 17 types of oysters and countless varieties of fish.

of a Wabanaki artist in a fine art museum in the US. The collections are spread across three separate buildings, with the majority of works in the postmodern Charles Shipman Payson building, designed by the firm of famed architect IM Pei. Check online for events throughout the year, including curator talks and family days with hands-on art activities. Admission is free Friday evenings (from 4pm to 8pm).

Boothbay Harbor

Paddling Boothbay's waterways

Once a beautiful little seafarers' village on a wide blue bay, Boothbay Harbor is now an extremely popular tourist resort in the summer, when its narrow and winding streets are packed with visitors. Still, there's good reason to join the holiday masses in this picturesque place. Overlooking a pretty waterfront, the large, well-kept Victorian houses crown the town's many knolls, and a wooden **footbridge** ambles across the harbor.

Maine Kayak rent out single and tandem kayaks for taking out on the water. The coast and secluded islands nearby make fine settings for spotting ospreys, harbor seals, bald eagles and plenty of other wildlife. A good destination is **Burnt Island**, about a 2-mile paddle south of Boothbay and set with rocky shores, maritime forest and an 1821 lighthouse. Pack a picnic and enjoy some downtime.

Rockland

Rock a bib at the Maine Lobster Festival

Boasting a large fishing fleet and a proud year-round population, the former shipbuilding center of Rockland has a vibrancy lacking in some of Maine's other mid-coast towns. Lobster fanatics won't want to miss the five-day **Maine Lobster Festival** *(mainelobsterfestival.com)*, held here in late July or early August. It's not just a homage to the crusty crustacean, however. There's also plenty of live music, parades, an art show and a fun run. Accommodations get booked up for many miles surrounding Rockland, so reserve well ahead.

Sail the High Seas

Although traveling by schooner largely went out of style at the dawn of the 20th century, adventurers can still explore the untamed Maine coast the old-fashioned way – aboard fast sailing ships, or windjammers. Nine of these multi-masted vessels anchor at **Rockland** and **Camden** and offer outings ranging from an overnight to nine days around Penobscot Bay and beyond. Travelers explore towns and islands along the way, stopping for hiking, sightseeing and shopping. They also take their meals on the boat (expect sunset dinners and plenty of lobster; the food is generally excellent). Four- to six-day cruises are the most common. For details of schooners, schedules and prices, visit the **Maine Windjammer Association** *(mainewindjammerfleet.com)*.

TOP FOUR BOOTHBAY HARBOR TOURS

Cap'n Fish's Cruises: *(boothbayboattrips.com)* Offers a big menu of boat trips, from whale-watching to scenic excursions to Eastern Egg Rock in search of puffins.

Balmy Days Cruises: *(balmydayscruises.com)* Balmy Days run sunrise trips, sailing adventures and mackerel fishing.

Maine Kayak: *(mainekayak.com)* Based in New Harbor, this outfit provides two-hour jaunts along the coast, as well as up Johns River to an oyster farm.

Boothbay Sailing: *(boothbaysailing.com)* Boothbay run two-hour sailing trips (including a sunset voyage) aboard one of two impressive schooners.

DRIVING TOUR

Drive the Blue Hill Peninsula

If you're looking for the soul of coastal Maine, head to the Blue Hill Peninsula. You'll find charming seaside villages, pretty walks through forest and along shoreline, and a vibrant artisan food scene. South of the peninsula lies Deer Isle, actually a collection of islands joined by causeways and linked to the mainland by a pretty suspension bridge. Old lobster towns, island walks and idyllic countryside views are all part of the allure.

1 Blue Hill

Start off in Blue Hill, a petite coastal town that's home to a number of artists and writers. Pick up an espresso from **Bucklyn Coffee**, check out artwork and Maine titles (or play chess or board games) at the **Blue Hill Public Library** *(bhpl.net; free)*. Head just north of town to reach Blue Hill's eponymous **mountain** *(bluehillheritage trust.org)*, which, at 934ft, offers a fine vantage point over the peninsula. Several well-marked trails lead up to the summit, including the **Osgood Trail** (0.9 miles).

The Drive It's a 20-minute journey along forest-lined roads to Brooklin, with occasional glimpses of the Mt Desert Narrows off to the left.

2 Brooklin

The sleepy settlement of Brooklin in the southeastern corner of the Blue Hill Peninsula has some surprising finds. Don't miss the **Brooklin Candy Company**, a whimsical store with sweet treats from around the globe. Try heavenly Swedish elderflower candy, Australian Tim Tams or chocolate bars made with real crickets. Just up the

EARL D WALKER/SHUTTERSTOCK

Stonington

road, you'll find more goodies (snacks, coffee, ceramics) at the **Brooklin General Store**. Next door, **Leaf & Anna** has loads of Maine-centric gift ideas, including stationery, market bags and bath products.

The Drive The 45-minute journey winds to Castine through forest and past white-washed churches, then skirts the Bagaduce River, with occasional glimpses of the wide waterway.

3 Castine

One of Maine's prettiest villages, Castine has a handsome town common ringed with historic buildings and a pleasant waterfront overlooking Penobscot Bay. Get a dose of local history at the **Castine Historical Society** *(castinehistoricalsociety.org)*, visit the small anthropological collection at the **Wilson Museum** *(wilsonmuseum.org; free)* and take a stroll in **Witherle Woods** *(mcht.org)*. Pick up a snack and some new literature from the much-loved **Compass Rose Books**.

The Drive It's a little under an hour to Deer Isle, and you'll have some fine views of Penobscot Bay along the way, particularly from Deer Isle Bridge.

4 Nervous Nellie's Jams & Jellies

Famous for its jams made from Maine's berries, **Nervous Nellie's** is a shop but also a sprawling fantasyland. Wander the vivid installations of the *Wild West*, *Camelot* and the *Deep South*, the imaginative creations of artist Peter Beerits.

The Drive The 15-minute trip to Stonington follows the eastern shore, passing pockets of greenery and remote homesteads before reaching the southern edge of the island.

5 Stonington

Deer Isle's main town, Stonington, is a quaint settlement where lobster fisherfolk and artists live side by side. Wander the tiny Main St overlooking the water, and peek in shops and galleries, like the family-owned **Dry Dock**, with its pottery, artwork and clothing.

ACADIA NATIONAL PARK ESSENTIALS

Layout: Mt Desert Island covers the bulk of the national park. Other parts of the park are on the Schoodic Peninsula and Isle au Haut.

Entry Fee: A one-week vehicle pass costs $35.

Visitor Centers: Three miles northwest of Bar Harbor, Acadia's main gateway is **Hulls Cove Visitor Center**, which has maps, info and park passes. When Hulls Cove is closed (November to mid-April), head to the **Bar Harbor Chamber of Commerce**.

Navigating the Park: The 27-mile-long **Park Loop Rd** circumnavigates the eastern section of Mt Desert Island, passing many trailheads and points of interest. It's one-way in places.

Opening Days: The park is open year-round, although many roads (including the Park Loop Rd) close from around late November to mid-April.

JAMES KIRKIKIS/SHUTTERSTOCK

Acadia National Park

Bar Harbor & Acadia National Park

Learn about the Wabanaki

In the waterfront town of Bar Harbor, the **Abbe Museum** *(abbe museum.org; adult/child $18/10)* contains a fascinating collection of cultural artifacts related to Maine's Native American heritage – particularly the Wabanaki people, who inhabited Mt Desert Island for thousands of years before the Europeans arrived. You can see pottery, tools, combs and fishing implements spanning the last 2000 years. Contemporary pieces include finely wrought wood carvings, birch-bark containers and baskets.

Grand views over Acadia

The only national park in all of New England, **Acadia National Park** *(nps.gov/acad; one-week entry per person/vehicle $20/35)* offers unrivaled coastal beauty and numerous activities, from hiking and cycling woodland trails to rock climbing and kayaking. The gateway to the park is Bar Harbor, where you'll find elegant B&Bs, along with inviting restaurants, taverns and boutiques – particularly along Main St and Cottage St. Adventure outfitters here offer a wide range of gear and tours that allow visitors to make the most of the scenic spendor.

Don't leave the park without driving – or hiking – to the 1530ft summit of **Cadillac Mountain**. For panoramic views of Frenchman Bay, walk the paved 0.5-mile summit loop of the mountain. It's a popular place in the early morning, as it's touted as the first spot in the US to see the sunrise.

There are numerous paths to the top, leading from north, south, east and west. The easiest to access is the **Cadillac North Ridge Trailhead**, located about 3 miles southwest of central Bar Harbor (and about 3.5 miles south of **Hulls Cove Visitor Center**). From the trailhead, it's a moderate 2.2-mile (one-way) climb to the summit, with fine views of Eagle Lake to the west on the way up.

To avoid the hassle of driving, use Bar Harbor's free shuttle system, the **Island Explorer** *(exploreacadia.com)*; it runs from late June to mid-October.

Acadia's prettiest pond

On clear days, the glassy waters of the 176-acre **Jordan Pond** reflect the image of Penobscot Mountain like a mirror. A stroll around the pond and its surrounding forests and flower meadows is one of Acadia National Park's most popular and family-friendly activities. (Sorry, no swimming allowed.) Follow the 3-mile self-guided nature trail around the pond before stopping for refreshments at the **Jordan Pond House**.

There are numerous trails leading off from the lake, some easy, others strenuous. For a short but challenging climb up to a viewpoint overlooking the water, take the trail up to **South Bubble**, located in the northeast corner of the pond. It's steep, but it's only about 0.4 miles to **Bubble Rock**, a massive boulder that seems quite precariously perched over the mountain's ledge.

Hiking the wave-battered coast

Jutting out to sea on the eastern side of Acadia's **Sand Beach** is the forested headland known as **Great Head**. A 1-mile trail loops around the headland, providing spectacular views of the craggy coastline and the pounding surf hitting against the rocks below. It's a fairly easy hike through forest, then out along the exposed rock face.

Wild Gardens' flower power

Wander a serene trail and breathe in the heady aroma of the pine-scented air while exploring the national park's acre-sized **Wild Gardens of Acadia** *(nps.gov/places/wild-gardens-of-acadia.htm)*. Despite the small size, the gardens boast 13 of Acadia's biospheres in miniature, from bog and coniferous woods to meadow and heath. In all, over 400 plant species are present.

Hiking on the Schoodic Peninsula

About 45 minutes by boat from Bar Harbor across Frenchman Bay is the **Schoodic Peninsula**, which contains a quieter, less visited portion of Acadia National Park. From here, you can hike various trails (ranging from half a mile to 3 miles one-way) and enjoy great views of Cadillac Mountain and other high points of Mt Desert Island. There are also some 8 miles of packed gravel paths ideal for cycling. Although you can drive here in an hour, it's more enjoyable (and faster) to take the ferry operated by **Downeast Windjammer** *(downeast windjammer.com)*, who have five departures daily (late May

TOP LOCAL TOURS

Acadia Mountain Guides Climbing School: *(acadia mountainguides.com)* The highly regarded outfitter and climbing school leads half- and full-day rock-climbing adventures in Acadia.

Acadian Boat Tours: *(acadianboattours.com)* Look for whales, porpoises, bald eagles, seals and more on a narrated two-hour nature cruise.

Maine State Sea Kayak: *(mainestate kayak.com)* Runs highly regarded half-day tours down the quieter west side of the island, with scenic paddling and downtime on a beach.

Lulu Lobster Boat: *(lululobsterboat.com)* Brush up on your lobster knowledge aboard a lobster boat while combining sightseeing and seal-watching.

Diver Ed's Dive-In Theater: *(diveintheater.com)* A family favorite, this adventure provides a boat trip with live viewing of undersea life, followed by hands-on interactions with small sea creatures.

EATING & DRINKING IN BAR HARBOR: OUR PICKS

Blaze: Warm, welcoming Blaze has wood-fired pizzas and high-end pub fare, plus outstanding jerk pork chops (the chef is Jamaican). *11:30am-8:30pm* $$

Thirsty Whale: A wood-lined tavern that draws locals and out-of-towners, who come for satisfying seafood, including delicious fried haddock sandwiches. *11am-midnight* $$

Barnacle: Much-loved local haunt with numerous Maine craft brews on tap, plus creative cocktails (try the spicy ghost pepper margarita) and oysters. *4pm-1am Wed-Sun* $$

Brasserie Le Brun: Dress up for this elegant bistro. Think French classics made with Maine ingredients: lobster bouillabaisse, duck breast cassoulet and roasted cauliflower. *4-10pm* $$$

to mid-October) between Bar Harbor and Winter Harbor. At the latter, the Island Explorer (p229) provides a free shuttle service looping around the southern end of the peninsula. You can take bikes aboard the ferry.

OTHER ACADIA GATEWAYS

Apart from Bar Harbor, there are several other settlements on and near Mt Desert Island that make quieter bases for exploring the park. On the east side of Somes Sound, **Northeast Harbor** overlooks a waterfront sprinkled with yachts, and its tiny Main St is dotted with galleries and cafes, while the hillsides are lined with Gilded Age mansions and fantastical gardens.

Across the Sound, **Southwest Harbor** is a less upscale community that's home to a commercial fishing harbor. The heart of town is the intersection of Main St and Clark Point Rd, with its shops and restaurants.

About 10 miles north of Mt Desert Island, the bigger town of **Ellsworth** is further from the action, but has ample lodging and dining options.

Quoddy Head State Park

Dramatic coastal trails

Anchoring the easternmost point in Maine (and thus the contiguous US), **Quoddy Head State Park** *(maine.gov/quoddyhead; day pass adult/child $4/1)* is best known for its jagged sea cliffs that offer unique views along the coast – at least when the weather is cooperating. Fog often blankets this lush peninsula, making for some cinematic shots of the historic, red-and-white striped **West Quoddy Head Lighthouse** *(westquoddy.com)*. There are various trails in the 541-acre park, most of which are fairly level but require constant vigilance while negotiating the uneven, sometimes slippery terrain. Follow the rocky shoreline along the **Coastal Trail**, then loop back through conifer woods, lichens and mosses along the **Thompson Trail**. It's worth making a short detour to the **Bog Trail**, a boardwalk that passes unusual flora, including carnivorous pitcher plants.

Baxter State Park

Views from the Mt Katahdin summit

Reaching the summit of Baxter Peak, better known as **Mt Katahdin** *(baxterstatepark.org; park entry per person $20)*, is on the bucket list of many New England hikers – and for good reason. Ascending Maine's highest peak – at an elevation of 5267ft – is one of the most challenging and rewarding day hikes in the state, particularly if you get here via the harrowing **Knife Edge Trail**.

Don't underestimate this hike, as there have been fatal accidents over the years (most from falls or lightning strikes), so make sure you're in good shape and adequately prepared. On the morning of the ascent, check the weather report at the ranger station; if rain or high winds are forecast, don't go. Start out early, as you'll need eight to 12 hours to complete the hike.

There are several ways to the top; all are rated by the park as 'very strenuous' and require scrambling over boulders above the tree line.

The most popular route is the **Hunt Trail** (also the final section of the Appalachian Trail), which leads up from Katahdin

EATING NEAR ACADIA: DESTINATION DINING

Thurston's Lobster Pound: Super fresh lobster and crab are the headliners at this waterfront lobster pound. Tie on a bib and dive in. *noon-8pm, late May-mid-Oct* $$

Aragosta at Goose Cove: Delicious, painstakingly prepared dishes sourced locally from farm and sea. The waterfront setting (with patio) is magical. Reservations essential. *hours vary* $$$

Islesford Dock Restaurant: Book ahead for this beautifully sited spot on Little Cranberry Island that serves lobster, mussels, oysters, veggie dishes and more. *hours vary* $$$

Tinder Hearth: Munch phenomenal pizzas in a weathered barn or out on the garden-fringed lawn. There are also morning croissants. Reserve ahead. *hours vary* $$

Penobscot River

Stream. This 5.2-mile (one way) hike past the scenic Katahdin Stream Falls involves a 4188ft elevation gain.

The hardest way to the top means taking the 3.2-mile **Helon Taylor Trail** (starting at Roaring Brook) up to Pamola Peak and continuing via the Knife Edge for the final 1.1 miles. This last bit lives up to its name, as you'll be walking along a narrow rocky traverse (4ft wide in parts), with steep drop-offs on both sides. It's more of a technical hike, and you'll need focus and agility. Those afraid of heights should steer clear.

Be sure to register at the gatehouse before setting out on the hike, and after you've returned safely. Also note that if you plan to hike from any of the Katahdin trailheads, be sure to make a day-use parking reservation (DUPR) online *(baxterstatepark.org; $5)* up to two weeks before your visit.

Canoeing on serene ponds

Most people come to Baxter to hike, but it's also a great place for idyllic paddling. You can spend the morning on mirror-like waters against the backdrop of mountain peaks, with the chance to spy beavers, moose and bald eagles. The park rents out canoes for a mere $1 per hour (or $8 per day). These are available at over two-dozen locations, including **Daicey Pond**. Check with park rangers (some canoes require a key) for availability when you arrive.

World-class rafting on the Penobscot

The white water draws adventure-seekers to the **Penobscot River**, which churns through Baxter State Park, within view of soaring Mt Katahdin. You can join an epic rafting trip with **North County Rivers** *(northcountryrivers.com)*, spending six hours on the Penobscot and traveling 12 miles as you navigate class IV rapids and a few stretches of class V. The season runs from mid-May through mid-September. Trips meet at the **Big Moose Inn**, roughly halfway between the town of Millinocket and the entrance to Baxter State Park.

BAXTER STATE PARK ESSENTIALS

Gateways: The town of Millinocket is a handy base for exploring Baxter if you're staying in the park. It has a handful of simple hotels, cafes and restaurants, as well as places selling hiking gear.

Visitor Centers: In Millinocket, the **Baxter State Park Authority Headquarters** doles out information and has essential hiking maps for sale.

Entry Fee: One-day entry costs $20, a season pass costs $50.

Overnighting in the Park: There are 11 campgrounds, plus bunkhouses and basic cabins, and numerous backcountry sites. Make reservations up to four months in advance.

Lodges: There are also various private campgrounds and lodges, ranging from rustic to high-end.

TRAVELLING TO BAXTER

If you're traveling without a car, you can take an evening bus from Bangor to Medway (70 minutes), operated by **Cyr Bus Line** *(johntcyrandsons.com)*. From there, the **Appalachian Trail Hostel** (p233) runs a shuttle to their location in Millinocket, located 30 minutes' drive outside Baxter State Park.

Places We Love to Stay

$ Budget $$ Midrange $$$ Top End

Boston

MAPS P160, P162, P170

HI Boston Hostel $ The private rooms with en suite baths, the enormous guest kitchen and the ample hanging-out space highlight this modern 430-bed urban hostel near Chinatown.

CitizenM North Station $ You'd have to sleep on the hockey rink to be closer to TD Garden events; this cheeky, high-tech hotel is in the North Station complex.

Charlesmark Hotel $ The pocket-sized rooms in this narrow six-story hotel don't have much light, but they're smartly designed, and the Copley Square location couldn't be more central.

College Club $ Part private club and part B&B (open to all), this traditional 1864 townhouse has six cozy singles sharing hall baths, plus six spacious en suite doubles.

Irving House at Harvard $ Right behind Harvard Yard, this warm and welcoming inn offers smart rooms. Top marks for the excellent breakfast. Inquire about shared bathrooms to save money.

Godfrey Hotel $$ Only a block from the Boston Common, this 242-room downtown hotel has a bike share program, a George Howell coffee shop and service-centered staff.

Copley Square Hotel $$ In Boston's second oldest continuously operating hotel, the traditional guest rooms have been smartly updated. Guests can help themselves to coffee in the communal kitchen.

Oasis Guest House $$ This Euro-style guesthouse occupies four bow-front townhouses on a tree-lined lane in Back Bay. Rooms are modest but comfortable, including cheapies with shared bathrooms.

Longfellow's Wayside Inn $$ Operating since 1716, this wonderfully old-fashioned inn was the setting for Longfellow's collection of poems, *Tales of a Wayside Inn*. Located west of Concord in Sudbury.

3 Waves $$ Promises a relaxing stay, with six lovely rooms, incredible service and some unique wellness amenities, plus easy access to the beach; in Plymouth.

Massachusetts

Cornell Inn (Lenox) $ Unbeatable value for designer rooms, impeccable service and a prime location overlooking a picturesque pond; a few blocks from the town center.

AutoCamp Cape Cod (Cape Cod) $ Boutique camping. Fully equipped Airstream trailers and accessible cabins, near Cape Cod's Shining Sea Bikeway. Clubhouse has an indoor fire pit, tuck shop and restaurant.

Dunes' Edge Campground (Provincetown) $ Family-friendly RV/tent sites and rustic bungalows on 17 acres of pines and dunes near Provincetown. Close to National Seashore. Busy, so book early. Mid-May to September.

Masthead Resort (Provincetown) $$ Historic inn with rustic cottages and renovated suites. Lounge on Adirondack chairs overlooking the bay. Year-round value.

Woods Hole Inn (Woods Hole) $$ Nineteenth-century beauty, with downhome charm and comfort, complemented by upscale decor, offering 14 bright rooms. Mornings start with scrumptious home-cooked breakfasts, served with a smile.

Rhode Island

MAPS P189, P191

Dean Hotel (Providence) $ A design-focused boutique hotel, the Dean features a beer hall, karaoke bar and cocktail den.

Esperanto (Providence) $ A backpackers' hostel with private rooms and shared dorms with up to five beds. The staff are friendly and helpful.

Mill Street Inn (Newport) $ Exposed brick and high ceilings harken back to its former mill days. Studio and one-bedroom suites are great value.

Atlantic Beach Hotel Newport (Newport) $$ Clean, modern rooms sitting right on Easton's Beach. The rooftop sundeck is a nice place to lounge.

Connecticut

MAP P196

Quiet Corner Inn (Brooklyn) $ Budget accommodation in northeast Connecticut that doesn't cut corners. The rooms are simple, clean and comfortable.

Inn at Mystic (Mystic) $ Overlooking Mystic Harbor, this quaint inn includes some little luxuries, such as rooms with ocean views and fireplaces.

Simsbury 1820 House (Hartford) $$ A historic country inn with modern amenities. Hotel bikes are available for riding the Rail Trail.

Blake Hotel (New Haven) $$ This boutique hotel offers downtown luxury in apartment-style rooms with kitchens.

Vermont

Inn at Long Trail (Killington) $ Rustic hikers' lodge smack in the middle of Vermont's illustrious Long Trail, and convenient if you're driving the scenic Route 100.

Hostel Tevere (Stowe) $ Charming four-room hostel in an old farmhouse a stone's throw from the Mad River Valley ski slopes.

Burton Island State Park (St Albans City) $ Book early for the simple lean-tos and cabins lining the lakeshore at this family-friendly state park on an island in the middle of Lake Champlain.

Stowe Motel & Snowdrift (Stowe) $ Halfway between Stowe village and the slopes, this well-priced motel on the Stowe Recreation Path has swimming, lawn games and free bikes and snowshoes for guests.

Green Mountain Inn (Stowe) $$ Relax in a front porch rocker and watch the world go by from this historic inn in the heart of Stowe village.

Lang House (Burlington) $$ Long-established B&B in a Victorian home perched on the hillside between downtown Burlington and the University of Vermont.

Trapp Family Lodge (p206) (Stowe) $$$ High on a hillside above Stowe, this Austrian-inspired lodge lures guests with beautiful mountain views and a world-class Nordic ski center.

New Hampshire

Colonial Motel (North Conway) $ Budget-friendly family-run motel offers good value for its simple but well-maintained rooms, less than a mile south of North Conway's center.

Sailmaker's House (Portsmouth) $$ Breezy blue accents, crisp white linens and hardwood floors set a maritime vibe at this 10-room boutique inn near Strawbery Banke in Portsmouth.

Hotel Portsmouth (Portsmouth) $$ A short walk from the town center, the 32-room Queen Anne-style inn dates from 1881 and has beautiful rooms and common areas.

Cranmore Inn (North Conway) $$ Decor is classic but feels modern at this central three-story North Conway option; the seasonal pool is the perfect antidote to a day of hiking.

Spruce Moose Lodge (North Conway) $$ A short walk from town, Spruce Moose has charming rooms set inside a spruce-green 1850s home, plus fabulous home-cooked breakfasts.

Kearsarge Inn (North Conway) $$ Just off Main St, this lovely choice evokes a bygone era, with rooms kitted out with antique-style furnishings and gas fireplaces.

Maine

Appalachian Trail Hostel (Baxter State Park) $ A favorite of thru-hikers, this welcoming spot in Baxter State Park has a mix of shared and private accommodations, plus a room in a converted school bus.

Seawall Campground (Mt Desert Island) $ Our pick of Acadia's three campgrounds, Seawall is on the quieter side of Mt Desert Island and has 200 shaded sites, including a handful of walk-ins.

Black Elephant Hostel (Portland) $ Portland's first (and currently only) hostel has vibrantly colorful interiors and a friendly social vibe that's ideal for meeting other travelers.

Inn at St John (Portland) $$ Portland's oldest continuously operating inn (opened 1897) has a European vibe, with attractive accommodations, including budget-friendly vintage rooms with shared bathrooms.

Tugboat Inn (Boothbay) $$ You can't get much closer to the water without sleeping with the fishes at this pleasant motel-style inn in the heart of Boothbay.

LimeRock Inn (Rockland) $$ This eight-bedroom mansion in Rockland, built in 1890, has been lovingly furnished with a tasteful mix of antique and modern furniture.

Little Fig Hotel (Bar Harbor) $$$ Friendly Bar Harbor inn with spacious rooms in a contemporary style and grab-and-go tea, coffee and snacks available around the clock.

Copley Square Hotel (p170), Boston

Written and curated by
Mary Fitzpatrick

Washington, DC & the Capital Region

US CAPITAL, MUSEUMS, BEACHES AND MOUNTAINS

From cosmopolitan Washington, DC to West Virginia's remote mountain towns, DC and the Capital Region pack incredible diversity into a relatively small and easily explored area.

There are few places in the US where the juxtaposition of bustling urban centers and quiet rural byways is as stark as in Washington, DC and the Capital Region. Within a few hours' drive of the nation's capital, with its world-class museums, African American history, monuments, theaters, markets and restaurants, you'll find winding backroads, expansive estates and rolling wine country. Throughout, the attractions are almost limitless. Wander the cobbled streets of Annapolis. Move on to the Eastern Shore, where watermen make a living from the bounty of the Chesapeake Bay. Carry on further to walk for hours on long Delaware beaches around Rehoboth, before turning inland to follow in the footsteps of Harriet Tubman and the underground railroad, or to learn about Native American history. To the west, visit Civil War battlefields, and to the south, step back into the colonial era at Virginia's Mount Vernon and Colonial Williamsburg. Visit Revolutionary-era mansions in Fredericksburg and chateau-like estates in Delaware's Brandywine Valley, and then follow those twisting, turning West Virginia mountain roads past forested slopes and fast-flowing rivers, taking in the views and seeing why the state is 'almost heaven.' All the while, you'll experience the Capital Region's unique mix of gracious southern hospitality and bustling northern practicality while gathering enough road-trip memories to last a lifetime.

KYLE J LITTLE/SHUTTERSTOCK

THE MAIN AREAS

WASHINGTON, DC
Capital of the USA.
p240

DELAWARE
Beaches, art and history.
p263

MARYLAND
Eastern Shore waterways and colonial history.
p272

VIRGINIA
Beach walks and mountain drives.
p285

WEST VIRGINIA
Heart of Appalachia.
p298

For places to stay in Washington, DC & the Capital Region, see p306

ORHAN ÇAM/SHUTTERSTOCK

Left: Virginia Beach (p293); Above: US Capitol Building (p246)

Find Your Way

The Capital Region, sandwiched between Atlantic beaches, Chesapeake Bay coves and Appalachian mountain valleys, packs so much into every corner. Start in one of its hubs and revel in exploring.

West Virginia, p298

Raft wild rivers, hike shady trails and lose yourself in the forests and small towns of this resilient state.

CAR

Driving is often the only way to reach out-of-the-way destinations and to enjoy the region's many scenic roads. Within urban areas, heavy traffic and parking challenges make walking, bikeshares, local bus and taxi or rideshare services better options.

TRAIN

Many of the region's major cities have frequent rail connections, making train a useful way to arrive. Amtrak services Washington, DC, Baltimore, Wilmington, Harpers Ferry and Richmond, and local commuter rail provides additional routes.

TAXIS & RIDESHARES

Taxis are easy to find in major cities. Rideshare apps Uber and Lyft are also available, though away from city centers, it can be hard to find drivers. Only use licensed cabs and certified rideshares.

Maryland, p272

Explore Maryland's colonial- and Civil War–era history and discover its urban hubs against a backdrop of tidal marshes and quiet coves.

Delaware, p263

Get acquainted with the nation's second-smallest state, filled with surf and sand, blooming gardens and centuries-old buildings.

Washington, DC, p240

The nation's capital is relatively small, but it's packed with history, art, nature, museums and international culture.

Virginia, p285

Storied pasts come alive and mountain, ocean and historic city landscapes intertwine, with fall mountain foliage a highlight.

Plan Your Time

Split your time between the Capital Region's quiet backroads, its Atlantic coastline and its cosmopolitan urban hubs, with their outstanding array of museums and restaurants.

BARBARA SAUDER/SHUTTERSTOCK

Colonial Williamsburg (p289)

Pressed for Time

Focus on the Capital area, taking in at least some of the museums (the **National Museum of Natural History** (p241) seems to be everyone's favorite), walking the **National Mall** (p248), visiting the **Capitol** (p246) building and heading up to the top of the **Washington Monument** (p244) for views over the mall and the Tidal Basin. Cross the Potomac River into Virginia, spending a few hours strolling around **Old Town Alexandria** (p296), visiting **Mount Vernon** (p297) or stopping at **Arlington National Cemetery** (p295). To finish up, choose between a day in charming **Annapolis** (p275) or time strolling around Baltimore's **Inner Harbour** (p279), calling in at **Fort McHenry** (p282).

Seasonal Highlights

DC and the Capital Region has year-round appeal, with springtime cherry blossoms, summer beach days, brilliant fall foliage, snow-dusted winter forests, and festivals and concerts throughout.

JANUARY

January can be chilly and damp, but it's also an ideal time to visit DC's **Smithsonian museums** crowd-free.

APRIL

Try to catch DC's cherry blossoms in bloom, or drive the greening slopes of the Blue Ridge Parkway (p292).

JUNE

Watch for arts festivals in Delaware and elsewhere in the region, and enjoy the beaches ahead of July's crowds.

One Week to Travel

Spend a week sampling the region's beaches and eastern reaches. Start at tiny **Lewes** (p270), taking in its charms, before continuing south along Rte 1 to **Rehoboth** (p268) and other Delaware beaches. Continue on to Maryland's **Ocean City** (p278), allowing at least a day to detour to **Assateague** (p272) and perhaps also **Chincoteague National Wildlife Refuge** (p239). If you're travelling in the summer, there will be plenty of traffic, but you can try to catch the pony swim at Chincoteague. Finish with a few days exploring Maryland's **Eastern Shore** (p277), spending your final evening in **Annapolis** (p275).

Take a Road Trip

After several days in **Washington, DC** (p240) getting your fill of capital vibes, head northwest towards **Antietam National battlefield** (p282), **Harpers Ferry** (p304) and **Cumberland** (p283), with perhaps some cycling along the **C&O Canal** (p284) or from **Morgantown** (p303) to **Charleston** (p334). It's then just a short hop to the **New River Gorge** (p300) and some rafting. Carry on, then on to **Charlottesville** (p290) and **Virginia wine country** (p290). Continue on to **Colonial Williamsburg** (p290) before finishing up with time at **Virginia Beach** (p293).

JULY
July 4 fireworks blend into summer beach days, heaping plates of Maryland blue crabs and the Chincoteague pony swim.

SEPTEMBER
Check out crab festivals along Maryland's Eastern Shore and the Mothman festival in West Virginia.

OCTOBER
Drive through Virginia and West Virginia to surround yourself with the best of the region's fall foliage.

DECEMBER
Catch the tree-lighting ceremony in DC and hit the slopes at West Virginia's ski resorts.

Washington, DC

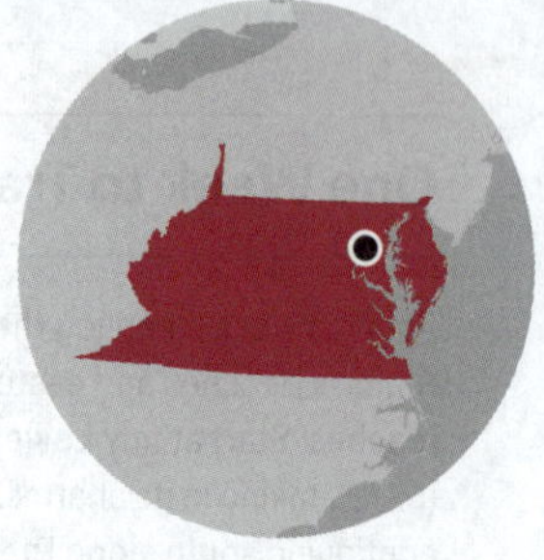

NATION'S CAPITAL | CHERRY BLOSSOMS | MUSEUMS

GETTING AROUND

DC is a walkable city with great public transportation and an expansive **bikeshare program** *(capitalbikeshare.com)*. The best way to explore is to lace up your favorite sneakers and hit the pavement. For longer stretches, the District's famous Metro system is really as good as it sounds, allowing you to get cheaply and easily to nearly anywhere in the city, including both airports, on comfortable, fully ADA-compliant trains.

Washington, DC is a diverse urban center that's easy to navigate, friendly and safe, and has so much to do. It's the United States' capital, and was purpose-built to be so more than 230 years ago on the banks of the Potomac and Anacostia rivers, with Maryland and Virginia donating land to the cause.

The city grew over time, becoming a hub for freed slaves in the mid-1800s and eventually, thanks to immigration and international workers, the culturally diverse and forward-thinking place that it is today.

It's easy to fill your days here with all kinds of activities. You could visit DC just for the museums – the Smithsonian Institution alone has 17 free museums – or simply to explore the history of the nation, its government and its majestic monuments. Then there are all the gorgeous parks, too-cool live-music joints, incredible theater productions and amazing art.

Performing Arts

MAP P241

Discover the Kennedy Center

The **John F Kennedy Center for the Performing Arts** *(kennedy-center.org)*, aka the Kennedy Center, is one of the United States' premier cultural institutions and is home to the National Symphony Orchestra, the National Opera and the National Ballet. The Kennedy Center also hosts symphonies, operas, ballets, theater and live-music shows by national and international artists. There are free daily performances on the smaller Millennium Stage. Don't miss the Reach, a 2019 addition to the center with rehearsal and performance spaces, directly accessible from the Rock Creek Park trail by a stylish pedestrian bridge.

TOP TIP

Keep an eye on DC's social calendars (such as *The Washington Post*'s Weekend section) to make the most out of some of the famous sites, such as the White House and the Kennedy Center.

American Craft

MAP P241

Decorative arts at the Renwick Gallery

The **Renwick Gallery** *(americanart.si.edu/visit/renwick; free)*, located near the White House, is a museum dedicated

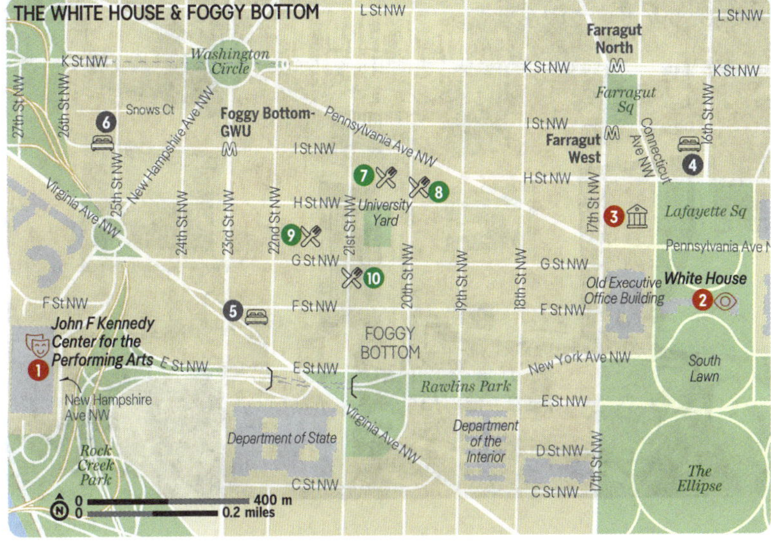

to American crafts and decorative arts from the 19th century to the present. The museum, which is a branch of the Smithsonian American Art Museum, is generally devoted to exhibiting American craft art, though it tends to extend the definitions of craftsmanship and artistic expression, promoting innovative contemporary works that range from the 'Art of Burning Man' to 'Wonder,' a large-scale sculptural exhibit designed to provoke exactly that.

Say Hi to Henry

MAP P244

And the butterflies, too

The free **National Museum of Natural History** *(naturalhistory.si.edu; free)* is one of the most lauded museums in the world and, with so much on offer, it's no wonder. Besides Henry, the giant African elephant greeting you in the Rotunda, museum highlights include the Hope Diamond, the Hall of Fossils (think dinosaurs), the butterfly pavilion filled with living butterflies, and Egyptian mummies – and that's not even a quarter of it all.

From Africa to the World

MAP P244

African American history and culture

Opened in 2016, the **National Museum of African American History and Culture** *(nmaahc.si.edu; free)*, often called the Blacksonian, is one of the country's foremost museums dedicated to African American culture and history. Designed by Ghanaian-British architect David Adjaye, it includes exhibits on slavery and freedom, African American impact on sports, music and film, and the 'Power of Place,' a powerful exhibition about belonging.

HIGHLIGHTS
1 John F Kennedy Center for the Performing Arts
2 White House

SIGHTS
3 Renwick Gallery

SLEEPING
4 Hay-Adams Hotel
5 Hotel Hive
6 River Inn

EATING
7 Captain Cookie & the Milk Man
8 Founding Farmers
9 GW Delicatessen
10 Tonic at Quigley's

ANDREW LEYDEN/SHUTTERSTOCK

Red Room

TOP EXPERIENCE

The White House

A central piece of American identity, 1600 Pennsylvania Avenue NW is both the workplace and residence of the President of the United States of America. You can visit, though due to strict national-security measures, you'll need to do a lot of planning. Getting to walk around this bucket-list site, however, is worth the effort.

DON'T MISS

- Blue Room
- China Room
- Rose Garden
- President's Park
- National Christmas Tree Lighting Ceremony
- White House Garden

The White House Complex

The **White House** was designed by Irish-born architect James Hoban. Its construction took more than eight years, though President John Adams and his wife Abigail moved in in 1801, before it was complete. The North and South Porticoes were added in the 19th century, followed by the 2nd story and the West Wing in the early 1900s. In the 1950s, the entire 55,000-sq-ft building was remodeled to avert structural problems.

PRACTICALITIES

Scan this QR code to learn more about how to arrange a visit.

The White House complex of today is owned by the National Park Service, and includes a six-story Executive Residence, the West Wing (which holds the president's offices), the Eisenhower Executive Office Building (site of the staff offices) and the Blair House guest residence.

House Tours

White House tours take you through all the public rooms in the East Wing, including the Blue Room, Red Room, Green Room, State Dining Room and China Room, and also give you a view of the Rose Garden. While there are no official tour guides, there are Secret Service members posted in every room who can help to answer questions about the house's architecture and history.

To book a tour, US residents must submit a request through their Congress member between 21 and 90 days in advance – tours are subject to availability and security clearance. Foreign visitors should contact their country's embassy in DC. If your tour is confirmed, you'll get a scheduled time between 9:30am and 12:30pm, Tuesday to Saturday. The self-guided tours are free and last about 45 minutes. You'll need an ID card to enter (only valid US-issued ID cards or passports are accepted) and note that there are no restrooms available during the tour, so plan accordingly (especially if you're with kids).

There is a (very long) list of banned items, which can be found online. These include detachable-lens cameras, video cameras and tobacco products. There's no on-site storage, so your best bet is to leave your bag in your hotel before heading out.

Garden Tours & President's Park

Touring the White House Garden is another spectacular, albeit rarer, option. Garden tours only take place twice a year, in October and April, are announced only a week or two in advance and last for just two consecutive days. Free tickets for the timed tours are distributed outside of the White House Visitor Center on the day, starting at 8:30am.

If you don't manage to secure a garden tour, take a walk around the President's Park instead. This is an 18-acre natural setting surrounding the White House that's full of statues, memorials and other important structures. President's Park is open to the public for free.

Holiday Events

The White House hosts two truly special holidays events that are amazing to experience. The first is the Easter Egg Roll, which has been a tradition since 1878 (although it now takes place on the Monday after Easter). The second is the National Christmas Tree Lighting Ceremony, held in December since 1923. Tickets to both events are free, but available by lottery only. Check *recreation.gov* for more info.

BLACK LIVES MATTER PLAZA

In June 2020, during the George Floyd protests, the MuralsDC program painted 16 bright-yellow letters on 16th St NW, just in front of the White House. The 35ft-tall letters spelled out 'Black Lives Matter' and, at the work's unveiling, Mayor Muriel Bowser declared the street would be renamed Black Lives Matter Plaza. In 2025, the letters were painted over due to pressure from the Trump administration.

FUN FACTS

- It takes 570 gallons of white paint to cover the outside surface of the White House.
- The White House became wheelchair accessible in the 1930s, during Franklin D Roosevelt's presidency. There is a movie theater, bowling alley, flower shop and dentist office on the grounds.
- According to lore, Presidents Herbert Hoover and John Quincy Adams both kept pet alligators in the White House.
- The White House Briefing Room used to be a swimming pool.
- Franklin D Roosevelt hosted a toga party at the White House (photos exist).
- The White House has 412 doors, 147 windows, 28 fireplaces, seven staircases and three elevators.

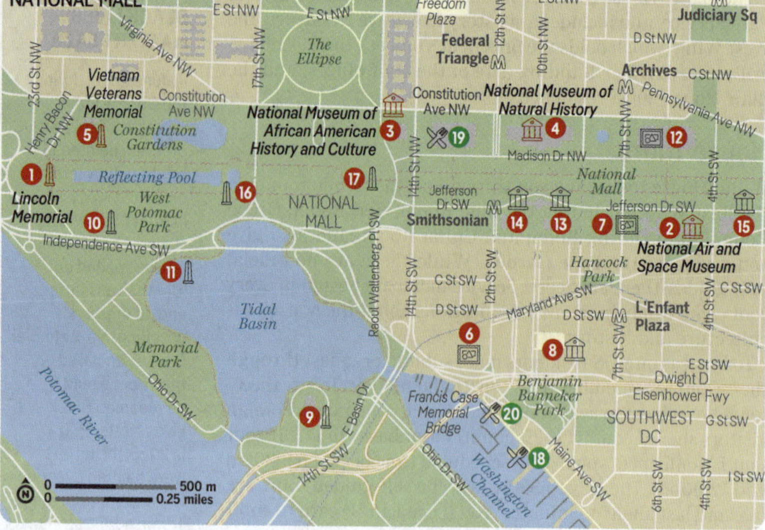

HIGHLIGHTS

1 Lincoln Memorial
2 National Air and Space Museum
3 National Museum of African American History and Culture
4 National Museum of Natural History
5 Vietnam Veterans Memorial

SIGHTS

6 Artechouse
7 Hirshhorn Museum
8 International Spy Museum
9 Jefferson Memorial
10 Korean War Veterans Memorial
11 Martin Luther King Jr Memorial
12 National Gallery of Art
13 National Museum of African Art
14 National Museum of Asian Art
15 National Museum of the American Indian
16 National WWII Memorial
17 Washington Monument

EATING

see 4 Atrium Cafe
18 Camp Wharf at the Firepit
19 Eat at America's Table
see 15 Mitsitam Native Foods Cafe
20 Officina
see 3 Sweet Home Café

Get a Bird's-eye View

MAP P244

Ride 50 stories to the top

One of DC's most iconic structures is a 555ft-tall, Egyptian-style obelisk built to honor the first President of the United States. The **Washington Monument** *(nps.gov/wamo)* is the world's tallest freestanding stone structure and offers amazing views of the National Mall, Capitol building and Lincoln Memorial. Reserve tickets in advance *($1)* or get free same-day tickets

(continues on p248)

EATING ON THE NATIONAL MALL: MUSEUM CAFES

MAP P244

Sweet Home Café: At the Blacksonian, this acclaimed eatery serves soul and Southern food, grilled favorites and on-the-go sandwiches. *11am-3pm Tue-Sun, from noon Mon* **$$**

Mitsitam Native Foods Cafe: In the National Museum of the American Indian, serving dishes inspired by Western Hemisphere Indigenous groups. *11am-4pm* **$$**

Eat at America's Table: Traditional American eatery in the National Museum of American History, serving burgers, hot dogs, barbecue favorites, Tex-Mex and classic salads. *11am-4pm* **$$**

Atrium Cafe: The Natural History Museum's ground-floor cafe is a large, family-friendly affair with craft burgers and seasonal market specials. *11am-3pm* **$$**

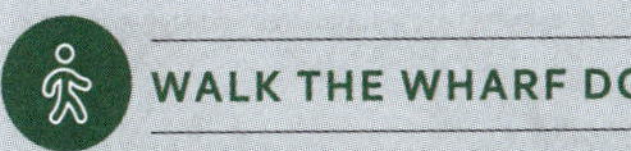

WALK THE WHARF DC

Completed in 2022, the Wharf DC has quickly become the district's waterfront hot spot, where dining, shopping, leisure and live music come together.

START	END	LENGTH
Recreation Pier	High Water Mark	0.5 miles; 1 hour

Start your tour at 1 **Recreation Pier**, where you can rent a kayak or stand-up paddleboard, then head over to 2 **Pearl Street Warehouse**, a live-music haven with a name that is a nod to the largest-known attempted escape from enslavement in America – it took place in 1848 aboard a 65ft schooner called *The Pearl*. (The incident didn't end well for the 77 enslaved people, though it did inspire both Harriet Beecher Stowe and Abraham Lincoln to work towards ending slavery.)

Walk over to 3 **Transit Pier**, a floating dock outside the Anthem theater that's host to outdoor events, shows, markets, the summer Sunset Cinema and the district's only over-water ice-skating rink in winter. Stop by the 4 **Market Docks**, where you can explore DC by water on a City Cruise lunch boat or monument tour, or on a beautifully restored 1950s runabout (retro-fitted with an electric motor) from Retro Boat Rentals DC. Afterwards, refuel with delicious cooked crabs or fresh clam chowder from the 5 **Municipal Fish Market**, the country's oldest continuously running open-air fish market. It's been in operation, without fail, since 1805. While here, take a gander at the 6 **High Water Mark**, a public art installation that takes an honest look at the damage presented by climate change. Colorful buoys are suspended in the air, marking historic and possible future flood levels within DC's floodplain, as predicted by 2020 climate-change models. It's an important reminder of the impact humans are having on the natural world.

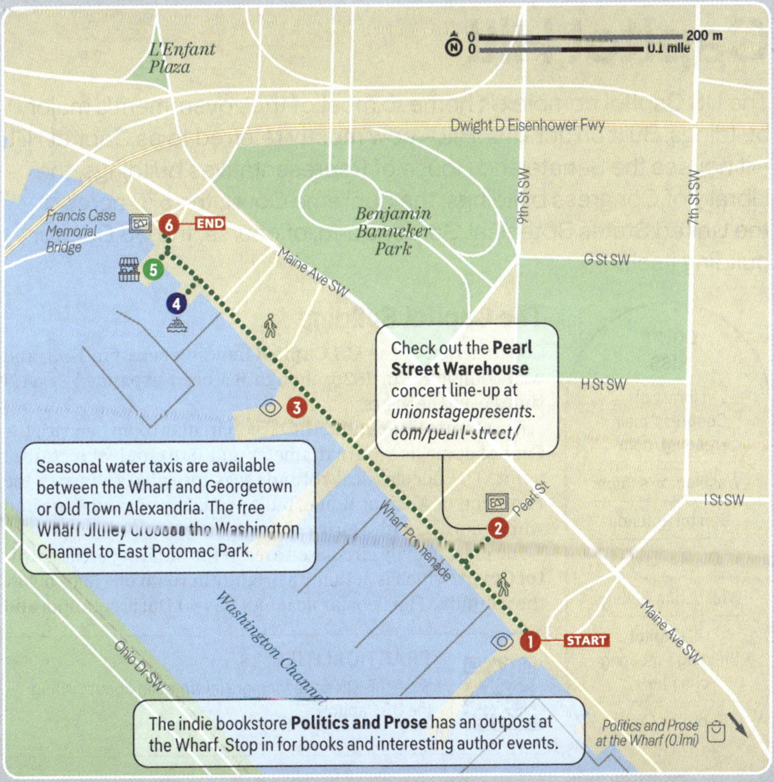

Check out the **Pearl Street Warehouse** concert line-up at *unionstagepresents.com/pearl-street/*

Seasonal water taxis are available between the Wharf and Georgetown or Old Town Alexandria. The free Wharf Jitney crosses the Washington Channel to East Potomac Park.

The indie bookstore **Politics and Prose** has an outpost at the Wharf. Stop in for books and interesting author events.

CLINTON BLACKBURN/500PX

Library of Congress

TOP EXPERIENCE

Capitol Hill

The US Capitol complex is home to most of the government's major buildings. Built on Jenkins' Hill – now mostly referred to as Capitol Hill – it houses the Senate and House of Representatives buildings, the Library of Congress buildings, the Supreme Court, the 570 acres of the United States Botanical Gardens and, of course, the US Capitol building itself.

DON'T MISS

- Library of Congress' main reading room
- Washington's tomb
- Capitol Rotunda
- Capitol Crypt
- Whispering Gallery
- US Capitol Building's meeting chambers
- Supreme Court

The Capitol Building

Construction of the **US Capitol** building began in 1793, and was completed in 1826, though it's been expanded several times over the years.

The **Capitol Rotunda**, the large, circular room beneath the Capitol dome, is 96ft in diameter and 180ft high at its tallest point. The neoclassical rotunda was intended to invoke the Pantheon of Ancient Rome, built primarily of sandstone and white marble, with Doric columns.

The most heavily circulated area of the building is the **Capitol Crypt**, which is actually a brightly lit room one floor below the rotunda. The neoclassical hall has 40 Doric columns and

PRACTICALITIES

Scan this QR code for more information about visiting the US Capitol.

sandstone floors, and is centered on the exact spot where the city's (original) four quadrants meet.

The **National Statuary Hall's** half-dome shape has some unique acoustics that have earned it the name 'Whispering Gallery.' There are some spots in which a person on the other side of the room can be heard more clearly than one next to you, meaning a whispered secret might be unintentionally heard across the room. In the same hall you'll find a collection of 100 statues of renowned citizens from across history – two from each US state (though only 12 are of women). The largest is a 15,000lb statue of Hawaiian King Kamehameha I, standing at 9ft, 10in tall, donated by his island state.

Every visitor to the Capitol building will inevitably pass through **Washington's tomb** – or rather, the tomb that wasn't. The area beneath the crypt was originally reserved for George Washington's remains, though his final wish was to be buried at his home in **Mount Vernon** (p297), so the tomb remains empty.

You can also watch the government in session in the **meeting chambers** from the galleries with a pass procured from your senator or representative or, for noncitizens, from the appointment desks on the upper level. Tours of the Capitol building can also be organized through your congressperson (ideally) or through the **US Capitol Visitor Center** *(visitthecapitol.gov)*. There are often walk-up tours available, though reservations are strongly recommended.

The Library of Congress

The **Library of Congress** *(loc.gov)* is said to be the world's largest library, with approximately 173 million books, maps, photographs, films, recordings and manuscripts on file in more than 470 languages. Established in 1800, the library, which is housed in three separate buildings, functions primarily to research questions presented by Congress members through the Congressional Research Service.

In the Thomas Jefferson Building, you'll find the **main reading room**, a grand research center that's the library's main attraction. See it from above on a self-guided tour (by appointment) or visit the main floor, which is open twice a day (Tuesday to Friday). Credentialed researchers can freely use the space and its resources.

Every Friday in July and August, movies from the National Film Registry are shown on the southeast lawn during the annual **Summer Movies on the Lawn** event.

Supreme Court

The **Supreme Court** *(supremecourt.gov)* building is home to the US's judicial branch of government and is the site where monumental, country-changing decisions are handed down. Download a PDF from the website and take a self-guided tour through the majestic Great Hall, past the ground floor's two self-supporting gold and marble spiral staircases, and into the courtroom, where you can sit in on a case or listen to opinions being handed down (seating is first come, first served).

FROM JUNGLE TO DESERT

In the middle of humid, steamy (or cold, wet) Washington is the **United States Botanic Garden** *(usbg.gov)*, one of the oldest botanical gardens in North America. Although unassuming from the outside, its glass-encased conservatory contains rare and endangered plants from around the world on display in a profusion of greenery and color. Exhibits are thoughtfully divided by species or biome, meaning that in just a few steps you can explore plants from tropical rainforests and then surround yourself with the succulents of the US's arid Southwest, immerse yourself in medicinal plants or take a tour through the orchid collection, where all the orchids are watered by hand.

TOP TIP

- Many of the buildings on Capitol Hill are connected by underground passageways, some of which are open to visitors. Walk through the tunnel that connects the library's Thomas Jefferson Building to the Capitol Hill Visitor Center. There is an underground subway system for Congress members, built in 1909. Some Capitol Hill tours will take you on it, so ask your congressperson if that's possible.

THE NATIONAL MALL

Also known as 'America's Front Yard,' the National Mall has more than 1000 acres of green space running from the Lincoln Memorial in the west to the US Capitol building in the east. The sprawling park is lined by some of the Smithsonian Institution's most popular museums, along with memorials to war veterans and past American leaders. The National Mall is also a hot spot for activist rallies, a space for festivals and events and a place to celebrate some of the nation's biggest holidays, such as July 4. There are few restaurants on the strip, so if the weather is sunny, pack a picnic to enjoy while museum-hopping.

KOSOFF/SHUTTERSTOCK

National Air and Space Museum

(continued from p244)

for the minute-long elevator ride up – expect lines in summer. There's a small museum at the top and, on the two-minute ride down, look for the memorial stones gifted from different states on the monument's inner walls.

Eclectic Art Galleries

MAP P244

From Asia to Africa

For a global art immersion, start at the Smithsonian's **National Museum of Asian Art** *(asia.si.edu; free)*, which is split between two galleries – the Freer Gallery of Art and the Arthur M. Sackler Gallery – situated in two separate but contiguous buildings. This century-old institution was the Smithsonian's first art museum and includes works from China, Korea, Japan, Southeast Asia, South Asia and the Middle East from as far back as the Neolithic period. Head also to the **National Museum of African Art** *(africa.si.edu; free)*, which was originally located in Frederick Douglass' former townhouse before it was acquired by the Smithsonian and moved to a purpose-built building. The collection expanded beyond traditional sub-Saharan art to include modern works, becoming the first museum in the US with a sustained focus on contemporary African art.

Indigenous Stylings

MAP P244

From Indigenous communities to the world

The curvilinear, limestone building of the **National Museum of the American Indian** *(americanindian.si.edu; free)* was designed entirely by Native American architects. It's one of DC's most visually striking structures, and is home to one-third of one of the world's largest collections of objects, archives and photographs of Indigenous populations from the

American continents. The Smithsonian museum covers Indigenous populations across North and South America, and all of its exhibitions, landscaping and structures are designed in collaboration with Indigenous communities.

Let Your Mind Soar

MAP P244

Fly high at the Air and Space Museum

It isn't just one of the most popular museums in the city – year after year, the Smithsonian's **National Air and Space Museum** *(airandspace.si.edu; free)* is one of the most visited museums in the world. Exploring the planet's largest collection of aviation and space artifacts is true immersion into all things airborne. See the Wright Flyer that took the world's first successful flight in 1903, as well as the Spirit of St Louis, the first airplane to fly nonstop from New York to Paris. There are several Mars Rovers on display, and even one of George Lucas' original X-wing fighters (a highlight for *Star Wars* fans).

The Man Who Had a Dream

MAP P244

Monument to MLK

Along the Tidal Basin, at 1964 Independence Ave SW (an address honoring the Civil Rights Act of 1964), is the fourth DC monument built in honor of a non-president, and the first for a person of color. The centerpiece of the **Martin Luther King Jr Memorial** *(nps.gov/mlkm; free)* is a 30ft-high statue of Dr King, carved from the 'Stone of Hope,' which is emerging from two large boulders called the 'Mountain of Despair' – references from King's 'I Have a Dream' speech: 'Out of the mountain of despair, a stone of hope.' There is also a 450ft-long Inscription Wall with quotes from King's speeches and sermons.

See the Cherry Blossoms in Bloom

Favorite spring festival

Visit DC around March or April and you're likely to experience one of the city's star attractions: cherry blossoms. Walk around the Tidal Basin and delight in the light-pink blooms, then check out the events of the **National Cherry Blossom Festival** *(nationalcherryblossomfestival.org)*, such as live-music performances, outdoor markets and a parade. According to the festival's organizers, 'forecasting peak bloom

AN ART GALLERY TOUR

The National Mall's federally owned **National Gallery of Art** *(nga.gov; free)* is home to a classical art collection featuring works by Miró, Mondrian, da Vinci, Monet, Kandinsky and more. The museum and its delightful sculpture garden are free and often host events, such as an outdoor ice-skating rink in winter, or Jazz in the Garden on Friday evenings in summer. Also stop by the Smithsonian's **Hirshhorn Museum** *(hirshhorn.si.edu; free)* inside a 'brutalist donut' (as it's often lovingly called) – a 1960s construction by architect Gordon Bunshaf that's endowed with the contemporary and modern-art collection of Joseph H Hirshhorn, featuring works by Picasso, Matisse, Cassatt, Pollock and Rothko, among other artists.

EATING IN FOGGY BOTTOM: OUR PICKS

MAP P241

Founding Farmers: Farm-to-table eatery cooperatively owned by growers. One of the city's best brunch spots. *7am-10pm Mon-Thu, to 11pm Fri, 8:30am-11pm Sat, to 10pm Sun* **$$**

Tonic at Quigley's: Once a local drugstore and soda fountain, now a favorite for classic American cuisine. *11:30am-10pm Mon-Wed, from 11am Thu-Sun* **$**

GW Delicatessen: Of all GWU's sandwich spots, only this one serves an absurd amount of bacon in your BLT. *6:30am-5pm Mon-Fri, 8am-4pm Sat & Sun* **$**

Captain Cookie & the Milk Man: Former food truck serving the best ice cream, cookies and milkshakes around. *9am-midnight Mon-Thu, to 1am Fri, 11am-1am Sat, to midnight Sun* **$**

THOMAS JEFFERSON

Thomas Jefferson wore many hats. He wrote the Declaration of Independence's first draft and was the US's secretary of state and third president, along with being a scientist, linguist, diplomat, scholar and a farmer. His **memorial** *(nps.gov/thje; free)*, designed by John Russell Pope and constructed between 1939 and 1943, is meant to recall the Pantheon of Rome and has a 19ft-high bronze statue of Jefferson inside (which was installed four years after the monument's inauguration).

The location of Jefferson's Memorial by the Tidal Basin was a controversial move, as it meant removing some cherry trees, which sparked a protest by 50 local women that came to be known as the Cherry Tree Rebellion.

is almost impossible more than 10 days in advance,' and once the buds open, they only last about two weeks. While seeing them is never guaranteed, it's a wonderful surprise when it does happen.

President Lincoln's Memorial

MAP P244

Shrine to America's 16th president

You've seen it on the back of a penny or a $5 bill, but the **Lincoln Memorial** *(nps.gov/linc; free)* is something altogether different when seen in person. The neoclassical, Parthenon-like structure was idealized by architect Henry Bacon, while the 19ft-tall white-marble statue inside was designed by Daniel Chester French and carved by New York's Piccirilli brothers. The memorial is full of symbolism. For example, the 36 supporting columns represent the US states existing when Lincoln died. Inside, you'll find some of Lincoln's words, including the entire 1863 Gettysburg Address, etched into the walls.

Arrive from the east – entering across the Reflecting Pool best illuminates the scene – and, after you've taken it all in, head around back to watch one of the city's best sunsets over the Potomac.

Across the 38th Parallel & Beyond

MAP P244

Remembering America's overseas wars

The **Korean War Veterans Memorial** *(nps.gov/kwvm; free)*, built in 1995, has two long walls that come together like the point of a triangle over the Reflecting Pool of Remembrance. In the middle, you'll find 19 stainless-steel statues from all branches of the armed forces. When they reflect against the shining granite walls, an optical illusion doubles them into 38 statues, the same number as the parallel that divides North and South Korea.

Dedicated in 2004, the **National WWII Memorial** *(nps.gov/wwii; free)* is a circular, open-air construction with a central fountain surrounded by 56 columns (representing each of the states, territories and the District) and two 43ft-tall arches along the perimeter – one for the Atlantic, the other for the Pacific. There are also two hidden 'Kilroy was here' inscriptions, a cartoon-like graffiti used by American troops during WWII to indicate that friendlies were in the area. Try finding them.

EATING IN PENN QUARTER & CHINATOWN: OUR PICKS

MAP P251

Zaytinya: Greek-Turkish joint by renowned chef José Andrés with floor-to-ceiling windows. *11:30am-10pm Mon, to 11pm Tue-Thu, to midnight Fri, 11am-midnight Sat, to 10pm Sun* **$$$**

Immigrant Food: Adorable cafe below Planet Word, serving global dishes and creative cocktails. *11am-9pm Tue-Thu, to 10pm Fri, 11:30am-10pm Sat, to 3pm Sun* **$$**

China Boy: No-frills, cash-only Chinese takeout that has never disappointed anyone, ever. *9:30am-5pm* **$**

Cuba Libre: Cuban cuisine and a rum bar in a Havana-style dining room; salsa nights are the true draw. *4-9pm Mon, Tue & Thu, to 3am Fri, noon-3am Sat, to 9pm Sun* **$$**

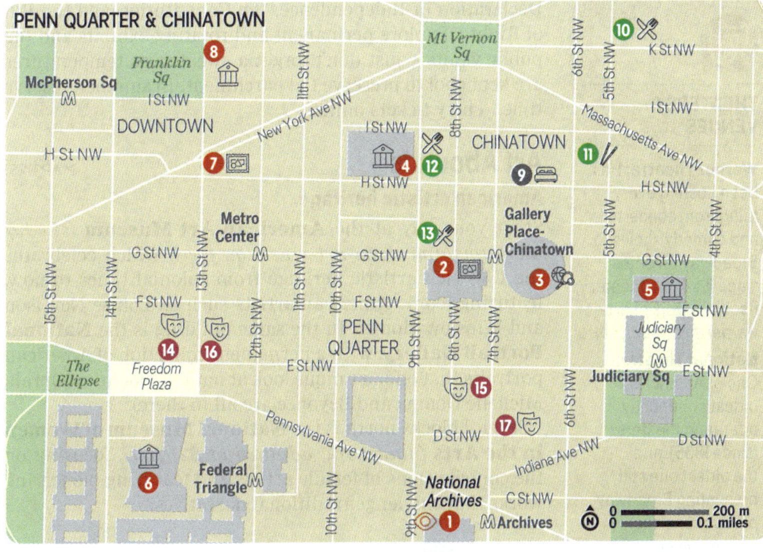

HIGHLIGHTS
1 National Archives

SIGHTS
2 American Art Museum
3 Capital One Arena
4 Museum of Illusions
5 National Building Museum
6 National Children's Museum
7 National Museum of Women in the Arts
8 Planet Word

SLEEPING
9 Motto by Hilton

EATING
10 Busboys & Poets
11 China Boy
12 Cuba Libre
see 8 Immigrant Food
13 Zaytinya

ENTERTAINMENT
14 National Theatre
15 Shakespeare Theatre Company
16 Warner Theatre
17 Woolly Mammoth Theatre Company

The 2-acre **Vietnam Veterans Memorial** *(nps.gov/vive; free)* was less well received in its early days, due to American architect Maya Lin's somber design. The two black granite walls engraved with names of the fallen were called a 'nihilistic slab of stone,' yet, after some adaptations, the design was built and inaugurated in 1982.

Charters of Freedom

MAP P251

We hold these truths

The **National Archives** *(visit.archives.gov; free)* is home to the country's most significant documents – notably the

> **SMITHSONIAN FOLKLIFE FESTIVAL**
>
> The Smithsonian Folklife Festival in July brings together artists, musicians, storytellers and chefs from around the world for a gathering and celebration on the National Mall.

EATING AROUND DC: DISTINCTIVE BITES

MAP P258

Tsehay: This crowd-pleaser is an homage to owner Selam Gossa's late mother's Addis Ababa cafe, with authentic ingredients and hand-ground spices. *4-10pm Mon-Wed, noon-10pm Thu-Sun* **$$**

Camp Wharf at the Firepit: Adorable Airstream trailer serving make-your-own s'mores kits by a wood-burning firepit. *6-10pm Thu, to 11pm Fri, 5-11pm Sat, to 10pm Sun* **$**

All-Purpose Riverfront: Italian-American artisanal pizzas; popular for its egg-topped breakfast pizzas on weekends. *5-9pm Tue-Thu, to 10pm Fri, 11am-10pm Sat, to 9pm Sun* **$**

Officina: Three-story Italian nirvana: cafe, bar, Italian market, 2nd-floor trattoria and rooftop terrace. *11am-9pm Sun & Tue-Thu, to 10pm Fri & Sat* **$$**

THEATERS & VENUES

Warner Theatre: Has been hosting everything from concerts and comedy shows to Broadway favorites since 1924; the theater itself is a work of art. *warnertheatredc.com*

National Theatre: One of America's oldest continually operating theaters (since 1835), and the oldest one still presenting Broadway productions. *thenationaldc.org*

Shakespeare Theatre Company: Has two locations in Penn Quarter – both offer classic and contemporary takes on Will's writings. *shakespearetheatre.org*

Capital One Arena: Hosts everything from high-profile sporting events to headlining concerts, Cirque du Soleil shows, monster-truck rallies and NBA playoff games. *capitalonearena.com*

Woolly Mammoth Theatre Company: Known for its original, thought-provoking productions. *woollymammoth.net*

Declaration of Independence, the Constitution and the Bill of Rights. Explore permanent and rotating exhibits and the public vaults – just don't forget a sweater, as temperatures are kept cool to preserve the parchment. In summer, reserve timed-entry tickets online.

Art Abounds

MAP P251

American artistic heritage

Start your day at the **American Art Museum** *(si.edu/museums/american-art-museum; free)*, which celebrates the US's rich artistic heritage from colonial times to now, featuring iconic American artists such as Louise Nevelson and Winslow Homer. In the same building is the **National Portrait Gallery**, with a permanent collection of American portraits that offer a unique look at national identity (Oprah, Michelle Obama and Beyonce are all in there).

Several blocks north is the **National Museum of Women in the Arts** *(nmwa.org; adult/child $21/free)*, focusing on the contributions of female artists and featuring pioneering works that challenge traditional narratives.

Child's Play

MAP P251

Museums for kids and families

In DC's Penn Quarter, north of Pennsylvania Ave, are some fun museums for kids. **Planet Word** *(planetwordmuseum.org; by donation)* is an interactive language arts museum that compares languages and dialects from around the world, posing interesting questions about why we say things the way we do. The **National Children's Museum** *(nationalchildrensmuseum.org; $19)* is an interactive play space that's intellectually stimulating and great for burning off excess energy. The **National Building Museum** *(nbm.org; adult/child $10/7)* is an underrated gem, with exhibits that range from understandable architecture to LEGO structures. Finally, hit up the **Museum of Illusions** *(moiwashington.com; adult/child $24/19)*, a weird and wild no-holds-barred favorite for kids from three to 73.

Contemporary Culture

MAP P253

Art spaces sprout in SW

Contemporary art has found a home in Southwest DC, thanks to spots such as the **Rubell Museum** *(rubellmuseum.org/dc; adult/child $15/10)*, displaying pieces from one of the world's largest private collections of contemporary art (Keith Haring and Yayoi Kusama are on the list). Entrance is free for DC residents or members; Wednesday to Friday is pay what you wish. The **Culture House DC** *(culturehousedc.org; free, donations appreciated)* is an uber-colorful church turned cultural center, run on the principle that 'art is a catalyst for change.' Stop also at **Artechouse** *(artechouse.com; adult/child $22/16)*, where digital art and technology come together to create truly immersive experiences – think colorful interactive projections,

CAPITOL HILL

HIGHLIGHTS
1 Library of Congress
2 US Capitol

SIGHTS
3 Barracks Row
4 Culture House DC
5 Hill Center
6 Marine Barracks
7 Rubell Museum
8 Supreme Court
9 United States Botanic Garden

SLEEPING
10 Friends Place on Capitol Hill
11 Kimpton George Hotel
12 Phoenix Park Hotel
13 YOTEL Washington DC

EATING
see 13 Art and Soul
14 Belga Cafe
15 Pineapple & Pearls
16 Ted's Bulletin

ENTERTAINMENT
17 Miracle Theatre

SHOPPING
18 Eastern Market

EATING ON CAPITOL HILL: OUR PICKS

MAP P253

Art and Soul: Seasonal, locally sourced Southern comfort food with a view of the Capitol dome. *7:30am-3pm Mon, to 9pm Tue-Fri, 9am-9pm Sat, to 8pm Sun* $$

Pineapple & Pearls: Fine dining with two Michelin stars, four courses, a disco-chic dress code and no disappointments. *6-9pm Wed & Thu, 5-10pm Fri & Sat* $$$

Belga Cafe: Belgian-French brasserie serving savory waffles and stuffed truffle brie. *5-9:30pm Mon, from noon Tue-Thu, noon-10pm Fri, 9:30am-10pm Sat, to 3:30pm Sun* $$

Ted's Bulletin: American eats done right, with homemade pop tarts and boozy milkshakes. *7am-10pm* $

OUT TO A BALL GAME

DC natives are sports fans to the core, and two of the city's biggest teams have their home in the aptly named Stadium District. Baseball fans can root for the home team (the Nationals) at **Nationals Park** *(mlb.com/nationals)*, where you can also take a non-game-day, two-hour tour of the facilities, including the clubhouses, media box, bullpen and dugout. Pregame tours are also available, where you'll learn fun facts and history about the Nationals' stadium and team. Next, hit up **Audi Field** *(dcunited.com)* for a riveting DC United soccer match, or cheer on the women of the Washington Spirit. Audi Field is also home stadium for the DC Defenders UFL team.

ANTARES_NS/SHUTTERSTOCK

International Spy Museum

and installations that take you into someone's imagination. It's as cool for art lovers as it is for techies.

Go Undercover

MAP P244

See what it takes to be a spy

Go undercover at the **International Spy Museum** *(spymuseum.org; adult/child $37/23, advance purchase discounts available)*, a longtime DC favorite that gives visitors an interactive and exciting peek into the world of espionage. Learn the art of code breaking, understand why spies have to dress the part, and find out why we have spies in the first place. The museum even confronts controversial topics such as counterfeiting, torture and secret surveillance in a multi-perspective manner that sparks instant debate. Check out an immense collection of the coolest spy gadgets, or head to the 5th floor, where you'll find fascinating stories of the world's most famous spies.

Historic & Culinary Hot Spots

MAP P253

Visit Eastern Market and Barracks Row

Eastern Market is as much a historic stop as it is a culinary one. Stop by the 19th-century brick building for all your meat, poultry, seafood, baked-good, flower and deli needs, or visit one of the short-order spots for a meal (don't miss the Market Lunch's wildly popular crab cakes). Head also to **Barracks Row**, an olde-times main street full of shops, restaurants and cool sites. Stop by the birthplace of American composer John Philip Sousa, catch a flick at the **Miracle Theatre** and check out the artwork at the **Hill Center**, an art gallery in a renovated Civil War–era hospital before catching the evening parade at the **Marine Barracks** *(barracks.marines.mil)* every Friday from May through August.

Festival Day

Celebrate Adams Morgan Day

DC's longest-running neighborhood festival is a vibrant celebration of community and culture. Adams Morgan Day has been held on 18th St on the second Sunday in September for the past 45 years, showcasing the area's food, music, art and music. You'll find local artists and international cuisine lining the street, and for entertainment, expect everything from drag-queen story time, reggae bands and gospel miming to go-go fitness, flag football clinics and dance collectives. There's also live music, DJ performances and a dedicated kids zone with activities for the little ones.

The festival, organized entirely by volunteers, welcomes residents and visitors alike to meet the neighborhood's businesses and enjoy the local offerings – but mostly to celebrate living in one of DC's most diverse neighborhoods.

Furry Friends

MAP P258

A menagerie at the National Zoo

Established in 1889, the 163-acre **Smithsonian's National Zoo** *(nationalzoo.si.edu; free)*, just north of Adams Morgan in Rock Creek Park, is home to more than 2100 animals from nearly 400 different species – elephants and sea lions to sloths, bison and orangutans.

The lovely meandering pathways take you through regional exhibits, such as the American Trail, where California sea lions, North American beavers and red wolves live; the Great Ape House, where you'll find gorillas and orangutans (a high-wire trail allows them to travel over the heads of visitors to their second home at the 'Think Tank'); and the Africa Trail, where you can spot cheetahs, zebras, warthogs, gazelles, lesser kudu and ostriches.

Tree Spotting

MAP P253

Azaleas, bonsai and Corinthian columns

Established in 1927, the 450-acre **United States National Arboretum** *(usna.usda.gov; free)* is a the perfect DC escape into nature. Wander along the 9 miles of parkland roads, stopping to visit attractions such as the National Bonsai and Penjing

(continues on p259)

STUDIO THEATRE

Studio Theatre *(studiotheatre.org)* is a nonprofit theater company whose 1978 creation was a catalyst for the Logan Circle neighborhood's revitalization. The company, which began in a former warehouse, now has a multimillion-dollar building (renovated in 2021–22) spanning half a city block. Its thought-provoking, contemporary shows feature national and international players, and the troupe also offers apprenticeships, in-house residencies, student-priced matinees and myriad community-engagement programs. It also has some of the most accessible offerings of any DC theater, with wheelchair-accessible areas in all its theaters, as well as free assistive-listening devices and regularly scheduled sign-language-interpreted and audio-described performances.

EATING IN ADAMS MORGAN & THE U STREET CORRIDOR: OUR PICKS MAP P258

Rita Loco: Counter-service burritos, tacos and cocktails, with a popular upstairs patio. *5pm-midnight Tue-Thu, to 1:30am Fri, noon-1:30am Sat, to 6pm Sun* $

Busboys & Poets: Bookshop, coffee shop and world-food cafe, serving as a neighborhood cultural hub. *8am-10pm Mon-Thu, to 11pm Fri, 9am-11pm Sat, to 10pm Sun* $

Compass Rose: Eclectic international restaurant in a brick townhouse with a cool bar. *5pm-midnight Mon-Thu, to 1am Fri & Sat, 11am-10pm Sun* $$

Chercher: In a townhouse just outside of DC's 'Little Ethiopia,' with a mouthwatering menu plus flavorful off-the-menu stews and other dishes. *4-10pm Tue-Thu, from noon Fri-Sat* $$

EQROY/SHUTTERSTOCK

Howard University

TOP EXPERIENCE

Black Broadway

Until NYC's Harlem took over in 1920, DC was the cultural and social capital of Black America, boasting the largest urban Black population in the country. A strong society of Black-owned and -run businesses, newspapers, civic groups and churches sprouted along the U Street Corridor, along with the country's first Black University, transforming DC into a Black cultural and intellectual epicenter.

DON'T MISS

- Howard University
- Howard Theatre
- Lincoln Theatre
- Dunbar High School
- Duke Ellington's Statue
- Ben's Chili Bowl
- Meridian Hill Park

Howard University

The country's first African American research **university** *(howard.edu)* opened in 1867, quickly becoming a magnet for Black intellectuals from around the country. Howard University was an anchor for the community that would become the largest and most prosperous Black middle class of its time.

Howard Theatre

When the **Howard Theatre** *(thehowardtheatre.com)* opened in 1910, it was dubbed the largest colored theater in the world and received all the greats of the era – Louis Armstrong, Billie

PRACTICALITIES

For an in-depth history of Black Broadway, scan this QR code.

Holliday, Ella Fitzgerald, Duke Ellington and Nat King Cole all graced the stage. The theater remained a hot spot for Black American culture until the 1980s, when it was neglected and shuttered, before being reborn in 2012 as the cultural powerhouse it remains today.

Lincoln Theatre

Shortly after it opened more than 100 years ago, the **Lincoln Theatre** *(thelincolndc.com)* became the epicenter of Black Broadway. The theater had a 1600-seat auditorium and movie theater backed by the Lincoln Colonnade, a big-band dance hall that became the place to meet on U St.

Dunbar High School

The first high school for African Americans in the nation, **Dunbar High School**, opened in 1870, and had such an incredible reputation that families from all over the country shipped their children to DC to study. Teachers often had doctorate degrees and were some of the highest-paid African Americans in the country, as the federal government paid Black and white teachers in the District the same wages. High percentages of the student graduates went onto college, an extreme rarity at the time.

Duke Ellington's Statue

Before becoming famous in Harlem, the king of jazz, Edward Kennedy 'Duke' Ellington, was born and raised in Washington, DC, where he quickly became a well-known musician. A statue, entitled *Encore*, sits outside the Howard Theatre in honor of the hometown hero.

Langston Hughes Residence

From 1924 to 1926, poet Langston Hughes lived in a small house on S St while working odd jobs to help support his family. His first book of poems was published after his time at the DC residence (now a private home) and the rest, as they say, is history.

Thurgood Marshall Center

The 12th St YMCA was the first YMCA established in the nation for 'colored men and boys.' The original 1853 structure was designed by William Sidney Pittman, one of the nation's earliest Black architects, and Langston Hughes once had a room here. The building was fully restored and renamed the **Thurgood Marshall Center** *(tmcsh.org)*, a community center with some historical displays inside.

Old Whitelaw Hotel

The **Old Whitelaw Hotel** was a community masterpiece. Funded by Black investors and built by Black entrepreneurs and craftsmen, the gray-brick hotel was named for its builder, John Whitelaw Lewis (and not for the 'white laws' that segregated the city). In its heyday, the Whitelaw attracted Washington's Black elite, though it deteriorated into a drug den in the 1960s and '70s, before being fully restored into apartment buildings in the early '90s, as it remains today.

A BOWL OF CHILI

A late addition to the scene is the area's most important culinary landmark: **Ben's Chili Bowl**. Opened in 1958 by wife-and-husband team Virginia and Ben Ali, Ben's quickly became a watering hole for Washington's Black community and, with the Lincoln Theatre next door, for entertainers as well.

TOP TIPS

- When you're ready for a rest, stop at the corner of 10th and U Sts and contemplate the **African American Civil War Memorial**, a striking monument designed by sculptor Ed Hamilton. Its centerpiece depicts a sailor and a soldier going off to war while loved ones wave them away.
- Read through the Wall of Honor, where you'll find the names of the 209,145 Black men who served in the Civil War.
- Head to **Meridian Hill Park** (aka Malcom X Park), a 12-acre park with cascading waterfalls and a sculpture garden. The park was ground zero during segregation – white DC lay to the west, while Black DC was to the east.

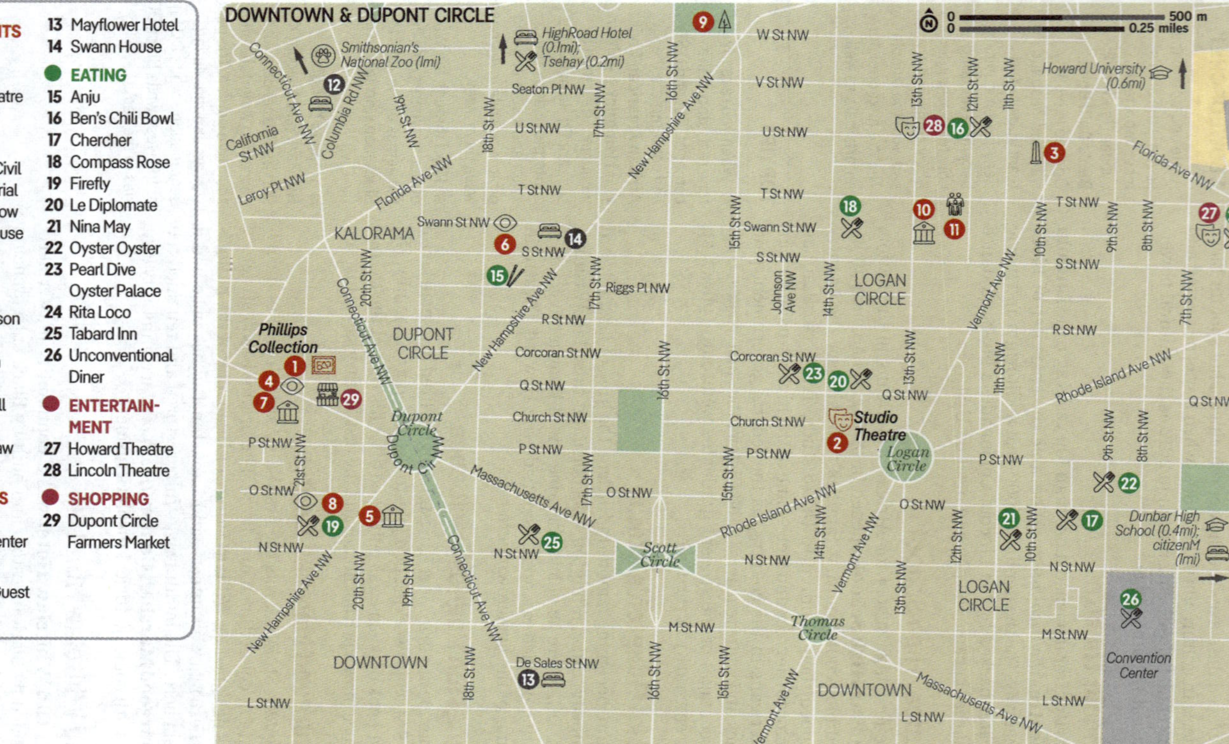

HIGHLIGHTS
1 Phillips Collection
2 Studio Theatre

SIGHTS
3 African American Civil War Memorial
4 Embassy Row
5 Heurich House
6 Langston Hughes Residence
7 Larz Anderson House
8 Mansion on O Street
9 Meridian Hill Park
10 Old Whitelaw Hotel

ACTIVITIES
11 Thurgood Marshall Center

SLEEPING
12 American Guest House
13 Mayflower Hotel
14 Swann House

EATING
15 Anju
16 Ben's Chili Bowl
17 Chercher
18 Compass Rose
19 Firefly
20 Le Diplomate
21 Nina May
22 Oyster Oyster
23 Pearl Dive Oyster Palace
24 Rita Loco
25 Tabard Inn
26 Unconventional Diner

ENTERTAINMENT
27 Howard Theatre
28 Lincoln Theatre

SHOPPING
29 Dupont Circle Farmers Market

(continued from p255)
Museum (a collection of the legendary minute Japanese and Chinese trees), the National Herb Garden, the Gotelli Conifer Collection, the azalea collection and the Flowering Tree Walk.

Then there are the columns – 22 huge Corinthian sandstone columns that somewhat awkwardly supported the US Capitol's frieze from 1828 until 1958, when the building was renovated and the columns were replaced. In the 1980s, the ousted columns were cleverly reassembled in the Ellipse Meadow of the National Arboretum, where they became a favorite (and very Instagram-worthy) tourist attraction.

Modern Art, Storied History

MAP P258

America's first modern-art museum

Founded in 1921 by Duncan Phillips, the **Phillips Collection** *(phillipscollection.org; adult/child $20/free)* is considered to be America's first modern-art museum. It was founded on the pioneering idea of (in Phillips' words) 'a museum where one could encounter the art of the past and the present on equal terms' and features works by artists such as O'Keeffe, Van Gogh and Renoir, in a space where visitors can connect deeply with each piece of art on display. Reserving tickets in advance is encouraged, although walk-ins are welcome.

Market Mornings

MAP P258

Farm-fresh produce with community vibes

Every Sunday from 8:30am to 1:30pm, Dupont Circle transforms into the lively outdoor **Dupont Circle Farmers Market** *(freshfarm.org)*, where colorful stalls offer a diverse selection of farm-fresh produce, locally sourced meats and cheeses, fresh-baked goods and artisanal products. In peak season, more than 50 vendors make up what the *Financial Times* called 'one of the top farmers markets in the country.'

This beloved community gathering began in 1997 and has become a weekend staple for locals and visitors alike, who come not just to shop but also for the community atmosphere. Arrive early to get the best produce, but stay later to try goods such as artisanal bourbon or to get a fresh-made meal on-site.

COOLEST HISTORIC BUILDINGS

Mayflower Hotel: The 1925 'Hotel of Presidents' has been host to countless prominent people and events throughout the last century.

Heurich House: This Gilded Age mansion turned museum was built for German immigrant Christian Heurich, whose brewery was once DC's second-largest employer.

Mansion on O Street: Actually four historic row houses stuck together, the 'mansion' is a black hole of oddities, memorabilia, hidden doorways and funky stuff.

Larz Anderson House: This 1905 beaux-arts Gilded Age mansion, now a museum, takes opulence to a new level.

Embassy Row: Many of Massachusetts Ave NW's chic residences – once known as Millionaires Row – were converted into embassies and social clubs after the Great Depression, giving birth to Embassy Row.

EATING IN DOWNTOWN & DUPONT CIRCLE: BEST RESTAURANTS

MAP P258

Tabard Inn: DC's oldest restaurant, with a Michelin Star–studded chef in a Civil War–era-style dining room. *8am-3pm, plus 5-9pm Sun-Wed, 5-10pm Thu-Sat* **$$$**

Oyster Oyster: Chic, carefully sourced, plant-based cuisine with a sustainability ethos. *5:30-8:30pm Tue-Sat* **$$$**

Le Diplomate: Old-style French cafe with Hemingway-in-Paris vibes and an excellent brunch. *11:30am-3pm & 5-11pm Mon-Thu, to midnight Fri, 9:30am-midnight Sat, to 11pm Sun* **$$$**

Anju: Homey Korean joint with comfy seating and comfort food to match. *5-9pm Mon-Thu, to 10pm Fri, 11am-1:30pm & 5-10pm Sat, to 9pm Sun* **$$**

NIGHTLIFE IN GEORGETOWN

Blues Alley: This landmark jazz supper club has hosted all the greats, from Ella Fitzgerald and Count Basie to Dizzy Gillespie and Tony Bennett. *bluesalley.com*

Sovereign: This Belgian resto-bar has more than 50 beers on tap, with 300 bottles and rare brews to boot. *thesovereigndc.com*

El Centro D.F.: Authentic Mexican fare and mezcal served in a two-story space with a happening back patio. *eatelcentro.com*

Mr. Smith's: Georgetown's favorite karaoke piano bar since 1965, with American-style fare and classic decor. *mrsmiths.com*

Clydes: This well-loved saloon still serves cold beers in the location in where it opened in 1963. *clydes.com*

Spend a Day in Georgetown's Book Hill

MAP P261

Hilltop stop for intellectuals and artists

Start your day at Book Hill's namesake attraction, perusing the shelves of independent booksellers such as **Bridge Street Books** *(bridgestreetbooks.com)*, or the used and rare-edition treasure trove that is the **Lantern Bookshop** *(lanternbookshop.org)*. Next, wander in and out of some of the numerous art galleries lining Wisconsin Ave, such as the **Washington Printmakers Gallery** *(washingtonprintmakers.com)*, **Addison/Ripley Fine Art** *(addisonripleyfineart.com)* and **Gallery Article 15** *(article15gallery.com)* for vibrant Congolese art.

After browsing the shops, it's time to refuel. Grab some noodles at the colorful and quirky **Oki Shoten**, followed by a creamy cone from old-school ice-cream shop **Thomas Sweet**, a mouthwatering pastry from **Boulangerie Christophe**, or a cookie from Oprah's favorite French bakery, **Maman**.

Still feeling stressed? Locals rave about the affordable acupressure and massages at **Meridian Health and Relaxation**, located at the top of Book Hill – think 30-minute massages for less than $30.

Scientific Discovery

MAP P261

Historic laboratory

Nestled among Georgetown's quiet streets is an important scientific site: the **Volta Laboratory and Bureau** *(nps.gov/places/volta-bureau.htm)*, which was Alexander Graham Bell's research center. Built in 1893, after Bell won 50,000 francs from the French government for his invention of the telephone, the Volta Bureau was dedicated to the 'increase and diffusion of knowledge relating to the deaf,' a cause Bell took on for his mother, who was nearly deaf, and his wife, Mabel Gardiner Hubbard, who was deaf. The building is currently closed to the public.

May the Force Be with You

MAP P261

Gargoyle hunting at the National Cathedral

Officially named the Cathedral Church of St Peter and St Paul, the neo-Gothic **Washington National Cathedral** *(cathedral.org)* is just north of Georgetown. From the day the cornerstone was laid in 1907, the cathedral took 83 years to complete, and is the sixth-largest cathedral in the world. It has 215 stained-glass windows – standouts include the Space Window, which

EATING BRUNCH: OUR PICKS

MAP P258

Nina May: Hyper-local farm-to-table American cuisine with outdoor seating and weekend brunch. *5-9:30pm Tue-Thu, to 10:30pm Fri, 10am-10:30pm Sat, to 9:30pm Sun* **$$**

Firefly: American comfort food served around a large indoor tree, boasting one of the area's best brunches. *7-11am & 4-10pm Mon-Fri, 9am-3pm & 5:30-10pm Sat, 9am-3pm Sun* **$$**

Unconventional Diner: Contemporary-chic New American diner with a nod from Michelin, serving brunch until late afternoon. *9am-10pm* **$$**

Pearl Dive Oyster Palace: Southern-inspired oyster house serving lip-licking seafood. *4-10pm Mon, Wed & Thu, 11am-11pm Fri & Sat, to 10pm Sun* **$$**

SIGHTS
1 Volta Laboratory & Bureau

ACTIVITIES
2 Key Bridge Boathouse
3 Meridian Health & Relaxation
4 Thompson Boat Center

SLEEPING
5 Graham Georgetown

EATING
6 Bluefin Sushi
7 Boulangerie Christophe
8 Chaia
9 Good Stuff Eatery
10 Il Canale
11 Maman
12 Oki Shoten
13 Thomas Sweet

DRINKING & NIGHTLIFE
14 Clydes
15 El Centro D.F.
16 Mr. Smith's
17 Sovereign

ENTERTAINMENT
18 Blues Alley

SHOPPING
19 Addison/Ripley Fine Art
20 Bridge Street Books
21 Gallery Article 15
22 Lantern Bookshop
see 3 Washington Printmakers Gallery

PAINTING STORIES

In 2007, DC's Department of Public Works started a Murals Program, aimed to beautify walls in every part of the city. The initiative has resulted in 141 murals across the district, each depicting or supporting important themes from the area, including a handful of murals that memorialize DC's Black history and immigrant stories around DC's U St area. Some favorites include *The Wailin' Mailman: A Portrait of Buck Hill* by Joe Pagac (a masterpiece more than 70ft high) and *The Torch*, in which Aniekan Udofia tells the story of 'the torchbearers who illuminate the way,' including Harriet Tubman, Muhammed Ali and the Obamas (it's located on the alley wall of Ben's Chili Bowl (p257)).

BILL PERRY/SHUTTERSTOCK

Washington National Cathedral (p260)

contains a rock from the moon, and the Rose Window, made of more than 10,500 pieces of glass. The grounds are home to one of the city's few remaining old-growth forests, but the most fun activity at the cathedral is gargoyle spotting. Among the 112 gargoyles on its exterior are an alligator, an American rattlesnake, a raccoon and Darth Vader.

Paddle the Potomac

MAP P261

A wetter way to explore DC

The Potomac River is a renowned rowing and kayaking spot, and if you're keen to join in, the **Thompson Boat Center** *(boatingindc.com)* and the **Key Bridge Boathouse** *(boatingindc.com)* are the two main spots to rent watercraft. Whether you're a master kayaker or looking simply to cruise, either boating center will help you find the best way to get on the water. Both locations provide paddling and safety instructions and gear, and offer introductory classes for those who've never paddled. At Thompson, you can even learn to row a scull, or rent one if you're already a rower.

EATING IN GEORGETOWN: OUR PICKS

MAP P261

Il Canale: Thin-crust, wood-fired pizza done to perfection from a place named one of the US's top 100 pizza spots. *11am-10:30pm Mon-Thu, to 11pm Fri & Sat, to 10pm Sun* **$$**

Bluefin Sushi: Serving high-grade sushi and sashimi in a tiny canal-front dining room for nearly 30 years. *4-9pm Tue, noon-9:30pm Wed-Sat, 1-9pm Sun* **$$**

Good Stuff Eatery: Nothing but burgers, fries and shakes served just right by Spike Mendelsohn of *Top Chef* fame. *11:30am-10pm Mon-Sat, 11am-9pm Sun* **$**

Chaia: The chic vegan and vegetarian tacos of farmers-market fame have found an adorable red-brick-and-mortar location. *11am-9pm* **$**

Delaware

BEACHES | HISTORY | NATURE

In just two hours you can drive from Delaware's southern beaches to its countryside estates in the Brandywine Valley bordering Pennsylvania, passing historic towns and nature reserves en route. Its diminutive size has earned it a few nicknames, including 'small wonder' and the Diamond State. Delaware's precious rivers, bays and ocean attracted European colonists and it played an integral role in shaping US history. It was the first state to ratify the US Constitution in 1787, which had a domino effect on the other 12 states.

Delaware's commitment to preserving its history is evident throughout the state, with numerous museums and walking tours featuring costumed reenactors. Historical attractions also recount the arduous struggle for African American residents. Delaware was an essential conduit for the Underground Railroad, with Harriet Tubman and other abolitionists relying on its safe houses and forests to secure freedom as they escaped north.

Places

Wilmington p265
Dover p268
Milford p268
Rehoboth Beach p268
Sussex County p269

TOP TIPS

Beach lovers should head straight to Delaware's southern end to soak up the joy of being surrounded by surf, sand and saltwater taffy.

GETTING AROUND

Driving is the most efficient way to travel around Delaware, allowing you to explore off-the-beaten-path towns, parks and attractions. **DART** *(dartfirststate.com)*, Delaware's transit system, operates more than 60 bus routes in the state's three counties: New Castle in the north, Kent in the middle (encompassing Dover and Milford) and Sussex in the south, including Rehoboth and Lewes. DART has seasonal routes connecting Dover and Wilmington with the beach and also runs seasonal buses from park-and-ride stops on Coastal Hwy (SR1) to Rehoboth Beach. Wilmington is well connected to other east-coast hubs by Amtrak.

DELAWARE
PENNSYLVANIA
Kennett Square
Camden
Wilmington
Newark
New Castle
Elkton
Pennsville
Mannington Meadow
Salem
Glassboro
NEW JERSEY
Delaware River
Middletown
Vineland
Bridgeton
Millville
Blackbird State Forest
Smyrna
Dover
Delaware Bay
MARYLAND
Killen Pond State Park
Milford
Ellendale State Forest
Redden State Forest
Lewes
Sussex County
Rehoboth Beach
Dewes Beach
Federalsburg
Georgetown
Seaford
Delaware Seashore State Park
Millsboro
Laurel
Dagsboro
Bethany Beach
Trap Pond State Park
Selbyville
Salisbury
0 20 km
0 10 miles

Wilmington

MAP P266

Explore Wilmington's riverfront

Once the site of thriving shipbuilding businesses, Wilmington's Christina River continues to benefit the city today as a prime recreation spot. The **Riverfront Wilmington** *(riverfrontwilm.com)* features an accessible boardwalk with restaurants, museums and parks. You'll find joggers, rowers and cyclists, as well as folks enjoying more leisurely activities such as playing cornhole at the seasonal beer garden or just enjoying the water views.

At the north end, the 1.3-mile stretch begins at the **Du Pont Environmental Education Center**, the elevation of which provides a bird's-eye view of the 212-acre tidal marsh and wildlife refuge below. Abundant trees and cooling breezes make it a good place for respite on warmer days.

Walk south on the riverfront path for an impressive view of the city skyline, passing Minor League Baseball venue **Frawley Stadium**, the **Delaware Children's Museum** *(delawarechildrensmuseum.org; $12)*, and food stalls in a restored warehouse at **Riverfront Market**. Just across Market St lies **Tubman Garrett Riverfront Park**, a popular spot for city festivals, anchored by a moving statue depicting abolitionists Thomas Garrett and Harriet Tubman guiding the enslaved people through the Underground Railroad.

Tour a Swedish ship and church

A mile north of Tubman Garrett Riverfront Park, the **Kalmar Nyckel Shipyard** features a replica of a Dutch tall ship that brought Swedish and Finnish settlers to Wilmington in 1638 and laid the foundation for the city's robust shipbuilding business. The site's **Copeland Maritime Center** *(kalmarnyckel.org; adult/child $10/5)* highlights the area's first European settlement and the city's maritime history with educational videos, artifacts, model ships and a log-cabin replica. Check the schedule for free deck tours and ticketed sailings in Wilmington or New Castle, and step out on the museum balcony for a prime view of the river and boat when it's docked.

Scandinavians buried their dead and worshipped at the church and cemetery at **Old Swedes Historic Site** *(oldswedes.org; free)* down the street. Enter through Hendrickson House, a 1722 stone home owned by a Swedish American family that was moved from its original location in Pennsylvania. Old Swedes is one of the oldest Protestant churches in North America; its sparkle comes from crushed oyster shells

---

MUSIC CITY

Eunice LaFate, local artist and owner of LaFate Gallery. *@lafategallery*

Bob Marley's family is establishing a museum in Wilmington to honor him, his Jamaican heritage and reggae music. He lived here in the 1960s and early '70s. He and I are from the same place in Jamaica – St Ann Parish. There is a park in Wilmington called One Love Park (named after the Marley song) at W 24th and N Tatnall Sts. I have a permanent wall in my gallery for Marley. The annual People's Festival Tribute to Bob Marley features music, storytelling and food. Music fans should also visit during the annual Clifford Brown Jazz Festival in June. Thousands of people come from all over. It's big.

EATING IN WILMINGTON: OUR PICKS

MAP P266

Bardea Food & Drink: Italian James Beard–nominated eatery serving pizza, pasta and seafood, with an adjoining seasonal garden and steakhouse. *5-9pm Mon-Thu, to 11pm Fri & Sat* **$$**

DECO Wilmington: Food hall with vegan comfort food, pizza, chicken and waffles, livened up with art markets, karaoke and trivia. *hours vary by vendor* **$**

Oath 84: Black-owned New American restaurant carrying creative meat and seafood small plates. *4-10pm Tue-Fri* **$$**

Jessop's Tavern: Colonial-era decor, pub fare and Belgian beer in a 350-year-old building in historic New Castle. *11:30am-9pm Mon-Thu, to 10pm Fri & Sat, to 8pm Sun* **$$**

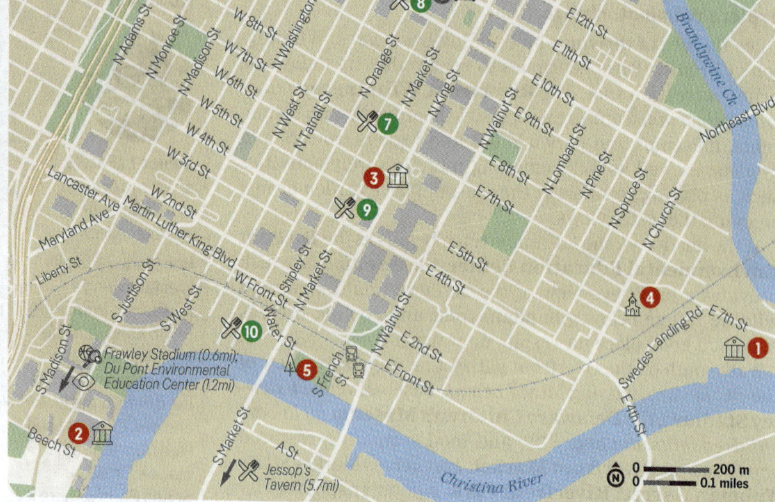

SIGHTS
1 Copeland Maritime Center
2 Delaware Children's Museum
3 Delaware History Museum
4 Old Swedes Historic Site
5 Tubman Garrett Riverfront Park

SLEEPING
6 Hotel du Pont

EATING
7 Bardea Food & Drink
8 DECO Wilmington
9 Oath 84
10 Riverfront Market

from the Christina River that builders added to the mortar. Inside, white pews contrast with colorful stained-glass windows. Visitors get to try their hand at pulling the heavy church bell during tours.

A window to the past

The **Delaware History Museum** *(dehistory.org; adult/child $10/5)* and **Mitchell Center for African American Heritage** chronicle the state's journey over hundreds of years, starting with its earliest residents, the Lenni Lenape Native American tribe, and continuing with the fight for freedom faced by African Americans. Permanent exhibits reside in an art-deco former-Woolworth building connected to the brick-covered Old Town Hall, Delaware's first government building, completed in 1799.

Delaware held enslaved people during the Civil War and was among the last of the states to ratify the 13th Amendment abolishing slavery, so the road to freedom and equality here was an arduous one for African Americans. That struggle is chronicled, from the Underground Railroad's route through the state, to the end of segregation in public schools, to the role of churches.

TOUR THE BRANDYWINE VALLEY'S ESTATES

The French-style sprawling estates in the Brandywine Valley – known as château country – are a testament to the outsized legacy of the industrialists and philanthropists of Delaware's Du Pont family.

START	END	LENGTH
Nemours Estate	Winterthur	13 miles; 1-2 hours

Start at **1 Nemours Estate**, a 15-minute drive north of Wilmington, flanked by towering black-and-gold iron gates, one hailing from Wimbledon Manor and the other with the initials of Catherine the Great. Helpful staff guide visitors through the bedrooms and elaborate reception hall outfitted with 18th- and 19th-century paintings, wall tapestries and du Pont family portraits. There are 25-minute tours of the 200-acre garden filled with statues, a pool and a maze of evergreen trees.

It's a 10-minute drive to the indoor-outdoor **2 Hagley Museum & Library**, which features dozens of stone structures, waterwheels and a coal-fired steam engine that whisks you back to the 19th century gunpowder factory founded by EI du Pont. One highlight is a booming black powder-explosion demonstration.

Drive slowly along narrow winding roads to the **3 Mt Cuba Center**. This botanical garden blooms with various native plants and habitats along newly ADA-accessible, fragrant garden paths. Set out on one of the trails or take a horticultural class.

After this, it's five minutes' drive to **4 Winterthur Museum, Garden & Library**, where tens of thousands of furniture items, porcelain and other decorative objects are spread throughout rooms in the former home of Henry Francis du Pont. One of the two buildings resembles the original mansion and the other is a conventional museum. Signs show what's in bloom each month in the garden, which can be viewed from a tram.

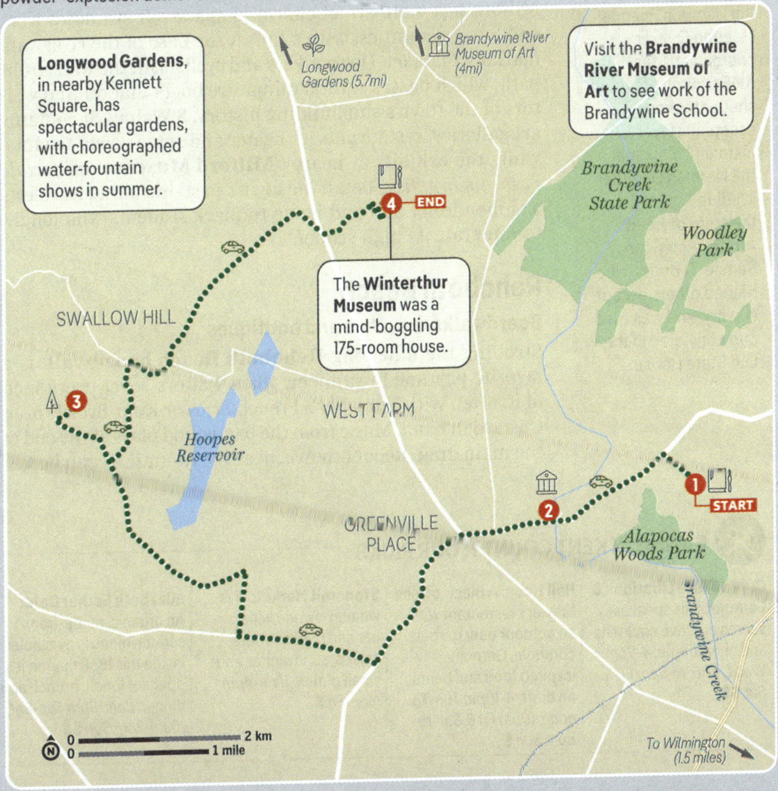

Longwood Gardens, in nearby Kennett Square, has spectacular gardens, with choreographed water-fountain shows in summer.

Longwood Gardens (5.7mi)

Brandywine River Museum of Art (4mi)

Visit the **Brandywine River Museum of Art** to see work of the Brandywine School.

Brandywine Creek State Park

Woodley Park

4 END

The **Winterthur Museum** was a mind-boggling 175-room house.

SWALLOW HILL

3

WEST FARM

Hoopes Reservoir

GREENVILLE PLACE

2

1 START

Alapocas Woods Park

Brandywine Creek

0 2 km
0 1 mile

To Wilmington (1.5 miles)

HARRIET TUBMAN'S LEGACY

Kent County is home to six sites associated with abolitionist Harriet Tubman, whose journeys rescued 70 enslaved individuals. Tubman relied on a network of safe houses, trails and waterways (the Underground Railroad) in Maryland and Delaware to reach the free state of Pennsylvania. The 6000-acre Blackbird State Forest is said to be one of her landmarks during her passages, while the Camden Friends Meeting Quaker church and Star Hill AME Church provided shelter to those escaping slavery. A historical marker at the Norman G Wilder Wildlife Area tells the story of freed African American Samuel D Burris, who helped others escape slavery, and was tried and convicted in the Old State House.

Dover

Relive history in the downtown

Downtown Dover's half-acre, tree-filled lawn surrounded by historic buildings, known as the **Dover Green**, holds most of the town's treasures. It's where suffragettes demanded the right to vote and legislators voted to ratify the US Constitution. **First State Heritage Park** *(destateparks.com)* storytellers dressed in 18th-century garb recount these pivotal moments during walking tours held Wednesday through Saturday.

Visitors can also tour the former and current homes of the **Delaware General Assembly**. Built in 1791, the Georgian-style Old State House features an exhibit on free Black man Samuel D Burris, who was tried and convicted for helping enslaved people escape. Members of the State House and Senate met in the two chambers upstairs until 1933, when the new Legislative Hall was built. Murals depicting scenes from Delaware history, painted by artist John Lewis, were added to the chambers of the **Delaware Legislative Hall** in 1987 to memorialize the 200th anniversary of Delaware signing the US Constitution.

Milford

A charming main street

With several attractive buildings and a scenic riverwalk, Milford has main-street charm in spades. It straddles Kent and Sussex counties, with a line at the base of the riverwalk marking that fact. Dog walkers and cyclists fill the waterfront path, which passes several miniature boats that remind visitors of the town's shipbuilding history. S Walnut St contains art galleries, restaurants, a theater and some newer tenants, while the exhibits at nearby **Milford Museum** *(milforddemuseum.org; free)* detail the town's past, including its role as a shipbuilding hub and home to Black students who fought to integrate its high school.

Rehoboth Beach

Boardwalks, beaches and boutiques

Strolling the mile-long **Rehoboth Beach boardwalk** is a favorite pastime in summer, when visitors cover every inch of it, often with Thrasher's French Fries or Kohr Bros Frozen Custard in hand. Music from the bandstand plays at the end of the main drag, Rehoboth Ave, near the Atlantic Ocean beach.

EATING IN KENT COUNTY: OUR PICKS

Cured Plate Libations & Lounge: This speakeasy serves creative cocktails and charcuterie. *4-9pm Wed & Thu, to 11pm Fri & Sat* $$

Rail Haus: A Black-owned brewery restaurant with an outdoor beer garden, cornhole, German-inspired food and beers on draft. *4-10pm Tue-Thu, noon-10pm Fri & Sat, to 8pm Sun* $

Stonerail Market: This women-owned wine bar and market offers salads, sandwiches and small plates. *11am-4pm Mon-Fri* $

Elizabeth Esther Cafe: An organic, made-from-scratch menu is available inside this 1868 manor; it's open for lunch, brunch and dinner. *11am-8pm Tue-Sat, 10am-2pm Sun* $$

Delaware Legislative Hall

Arrive early to grab a parking spot and plop your umbrella on the beach before sunbathers and swimmers swallow every available space. It's worth venturing past the souvenir shops near the beach to peruse the assortment of independent stores. The long-standing **Browseabout Books** features author signings, while **Buddhas & Beads** sells crystals, jewelry and antiques. Venture down the storybook-like **Penny Lane Mall** to grab a sweet crepe or savory croissant from **Cafe Papillon**.

Sussex County

Explore the Delaware beach towns

While Rehoboth commands the most name recognition, Sussex County contains a cluster of waterside hamlets stretching 24 miles along the Coastal Hwy from Lewes to Fenwick Island, passing through Dewey Beach and Bethany Beach. Explore each for a few hours or days.

Filled with remarkably well-preserved historic homes and blooming gardens, Lewes (p270) looks like it's been plucked from the English countryside. After driving past Rehoboth, the road turns narrow, with the rushing Atlantic Ocean waves on one side and serene bay waters on the other. Party hot spots and live-music venues such as the Starboard, Bottle &

BEST FOR ART & FILM LOVERS

Cinema Art Theater: The Rehoboth Beach Film Society operates this two-screen movie hall showcasing foreign and independent movies from emerging filmmakers.

Rehoboth Art League: With exhibits, lectures and festivals, this nonprofit continuously hosts events for art lovers.

Clear Space Theatre Company: Featuring plays and Broadway musicals, this regional theater company also holds acting classes for all ages.

Milton Theatre: Live bands, musical theater and a Pride festival are just some of the events held at this two-story building, constructed in 1910.

Clayton Theatre: Classic and first-run movies are shown at this single-screen movie theater, with its retro marquee lit at night.

EATING IN SUSSEX COUNTY: UPMARKET MEALS

Henlopen City Oyster House: Arrive early to grab a seat at this popular no-reservations eatery offering a wide fish selection and a raw bar. *noon-9pm Mon-Sat* $$$

Cafe Azafran: Garlic shrimp, ratatouille and other Mediterranean dishes are on offer here, with a sister cafe in Lewes. Check for weekly specials. *5-8:30pm Mon-Sat* $$$

One Coastal: A James Beard–nominated chef sources ingredients from local farms and waters to deliver standout meat and seafood dishes. *5-9pm Tue-Sun* $$$

Blue Hen: A hotel restaurant with a daily-changing menu, weekly specials and good happy-hour specials. *4-8:30pm Mon-Thu, to 9pm Fri & Sat* $$$

NATURE SPOTS BEYOND THE BEACH

Lavender Fields at Warrington Manor: The lavender fields are the main attraction, but don't skip the native-plant gardens and the shop selling lavender products.

Delaware Seashore State Park: With 6 miles of oceanfront and 20 miles of bay shoreline, this is a prime spot for all water activities.

Georgetown–Lewes Trail: This bicycle and pedestrian trail will add its final leg in fall 2025, making it 17 miles to connect the towns of Lewes and Georgetown.

Gordons Pond Trail: The loop traverses its namesake saltwater lagoon and Cape Henlopen State Park, where you'll see sand dunes and remnants of the former WWII military base.

Prime Hook National Wildlife Refuge: At this migratory bird sanctuary you might spot bald eagles, ospreys or waterfowl.

DAVID KAY/SHUTTERSTOCK

Cork and Rusty Rudder overflow with singles in the summer. The 15-minute drive to **Bethany Beach** takes you across the Charles W Cullen Bridge, the slanted pylons of which resemble a ship's sails and are lit up an ocean-blue. Stop in Delaware Seashore State Park, or at the Big Chill Beach Club restaurant, for a prime bridge view.

Collectively called 'the quiet resorts,' Bethany Beach and **Fenwick Island** have a tranquil atmosphere that draws families. The half-mile boardwalk in Bethany contains a couple of arcades, souvenir shops and restaurants with beach views, while mini golf and a water park are the highlights of Fenwick's small boardwalk. The gentle waters of **Assawoman Bay** make an excellent spot for beginners to rent kayaks, paddleboards and sailboats from Coastal Kayak.

Walk through historic Lewes

The picturesque town of **Lewes** packs five centuries of architecture into its historic district, which contains a mishmash of styles from colonial to Federal and Victorian. The Dutch settled here in 1631, earning Lewes the 'first town in the first state' moniker. Its Dutch history is on display at the free **Zwaanendael Museum** *(history.delaware.gov/museums;*

EATING IN SUSSEX COUNTY: OUR PICKS

Fish On: One of a dozen restaurants under local SoDel Concepts' domain, with a happy hour and seafood specials daily. *5-9pm* **$$**

Confucius Chinese Cuisine: Long-standing Chinese spot with shareable Hunan dishes, including salt-and-pepper shrimp and roasted Peking duck. *5-9pm Thu-Mon* **$$**

Raas: Indian cuisine in a 125-year-old Victorian home with traditional and unique fare, including chili olive naan and a dedicated street-fare menu. *noon-9pm Tue-Sun* **$$**

Off the Hook: Standout farm-to-table small plates and seafood dishes with a daily happy hour and weekday specials. *11:30am-9pm* **$$$**

Bethany Beach

free), where the striking red-and-white shutters take after a town hall in the Netherlands.

Park your car or bicycle and explore the town on a **walking tour** *(historiclewes.org)* with Lewes Historical Society. Engaging storytellers in period costumes take you past landmarks such as the **Ryves Holt House** *(historiclewes.org/locations/ryves-holt-house-museum; free)*, Delaware's oldest building. You can also pop into the 18th- and 19th-century buildings at the organization's main Shipcarpenter St campus, including a former school, doctor's office and a tavern that sells cocktails made from colonial-era recipes on the first Friday of each month.

Lewes' main thoroughfare, 2nd St, houses an eclectic assortment of independent stores selling antiques, vintage jewelry and art, women's clothes and books. A leisurely walk toward the water leads to the picturesque **Lewes Canalfront Park** *(lewescanalfrontpark.org)*, where you can tour the last lighthouse boat made for the US Lighthouse Service, the **Lightship Overfalls** *(overfalls.org; adult/child $5/free)*.

En route to or from Lewes, it's worth making the 23-mile detour to the **Delaware Botanic Gardens** *(delawaregardens.org; adult/child $15/free)* at Pepper Creek, where the central 2-acre meadow is filled with native plants that change throughout the year.

WHY I LOVE LEWES

Julekha Dash, Lonely Planet writer

After my husband and I moved from Lewes, I still visit at least every other month. While the highway traffic and businesses have quadrupled in the last 20 years, the heart of Lewes remains unchanged. The calm waters of Savannah Beach appeal to a nervous ocean swimmer like me, and even during high season you can find a stretch of sand to call your own. I've spent many afternoons at Cape Henlopen State Park walking the 3-mile loop past sand dunes, wetlands and the lookout point where the Delaware Bay meets the Atlantic Ocean. I love taking visitors on boat tours from the Lewes Canal to the Delaware Bay to spot dolphins, waterfowl and lighthouses, or on the Cape May–Lewes Ferry.

Maryland

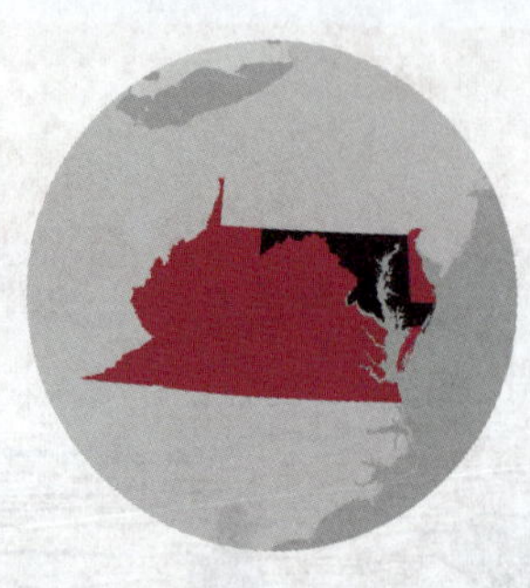

CHESAPEAKE BAY | WILD HORSES | HISTORY

Places

Annapolis p274
St Mary's City p274
Cambridge p276
Ocean City p278
Assateague Island p278
Baltimore p279
Antietam National Battlefield p283
Cumberland p283

TOP TIP

Annapolis and the Eastern Shore make an ideal focus if you only have a day or two in the state. With more time, linger along the coast, discover Baltimore or head west towards Antietam and Cumberland.

Straddling the historical divide between north and south, Maryland mixes southern charm with northern savvy, its attractions rimmed by a long eastern shoreline and rolling western highlands. Wild horses wander the dunes and coastal grasses of Assateague Island. Spring redbuds and fall foliage brighten the slopes of the Allegheny Mountains around Cumberland. Watermen ply their trade amid the coves and waterways of Chesapeake Bay, and 19th-century drum rolls seem to echo across the now-peaceful expanses of Antietam's Civil War battlefields. In Baltimore, the state's commercial hub, creative chefs dish up some of the Mid-Atlantic's most exciting cuisine, while in Annapolis, Maryland's picturesque waterside capital, a fine collection of 18th-century buildings set the backdrop for museums, eateries and international-class boat shows. Wherever you go, you'll find something for every taste and budget, wrapped up in a small enough package that you can sample it all with ease.

GETTING AROUND

Check *visitmaryland.org* for scenic byway routes. Bay Runner Shuttle links Baltimore and BWI Airport with Ocean City, Cambridge and Cumberland. Flixbus connects Washington, DC and Annapolis. **MUST Bus** *(mustbus.org)* has a handful of eastern routes, and Shore Transit links Salisbury (which is served by Greyhound and the Bay Runner Shuttle) with Crisfield, Berlin and Ocean City, but you'll need a car to really explore the Eastern Shore. **Maryland Transit Administration** *(mta.maryland.gov)* has commuter bus info for Baltimore. MARC commuter trains also link Washington, DC with Baltimore, and Amtrak's Capitol Limited runs between Washington, DC and Cumberland. Downtown Annapolis is eminently walkable. In Baltimore, the **Water Taxi** *(baltimorewatertaxi.com)* has free connector service around the Inner Harbor in good weather and a paid route to Fort McHenry. There's also the free Charm City Circulator bus serving downtown neighborhoods.

MARYLAND
PENNSYLVANIA
NEW JERSEY
DELAWARE
VIRGINIA
WEST VIRGINIA
ATLANTIC OCEAN
Delaware Bay
Wilmington
Newark
Pennsville
Salem
Middletown
Bridgeton
Elkton
Dover
Milford
Georgetown
Seaford
Federalsburg
Ocean City
Berlin
Assateague Island
Salisbury
Pokomoke City
Princess Anne
Crisfield
Janes Island State Park
Whitehaven
Crapo
Cambridge
Easton
St Michaels
Chestertown
Havre De Grace
Aberdeen
Bel Air
Joppatowne
Baltimore
Annapolis
Bowie
WASHINGTON, DC
Alexandria
Arlington
Manassas
Woodbridge
Indian Head
Waldorf
La Plata
Hughesville
Huntington
Cedarville State Forest
Gilbert Run Park
Newburg
Lexington Park
St Mary's City
Ridge
St Marys River Watershed Park
Tappahannock
Fredericksburg
Orange
Gordonsville
Charlottesville
Lake Anna
Culpeper
Warrenton
Front Royal
Leesburg
Potomac River
Rockville
Gaithersburg
Patuxent River State Park
Ellicott City
Patapsco Valley State Park
Sykesville
Mount Airy
New Windsor
Westminster
Taneytown
Hanover
Gettysburg
Waynesboro
Hagerstown
Thurmont
Walkersville
Frederick
Harpers Ferry
Charles Town
Shepherdstown
Antietam National Battlefield
Martinsburg
Winchester
Strasburg
Woodstock
Timberville
Broadway
Shenandoah
Elkton
Harrisonburg
Shenandoah National Park
Grottoes
Crozet
Staunton
Waynesboro
Craigsville
Blue Ridge Mountains
Blue Ridge Parkway
Appalachian Mountains
George Washington National Forest
Lost River State Park
Moorefield
South Branch Potomac River
Romney
Paw Paw
Cumberland
Green Ridge State Forest
El Air
Frostburg
Grantsville
New Germany State Park
Savage River State Forest
McHenry
Oakland
Potomac State Forest
Thomas
Davis
Loch Raven Reservoir Park
Gunpowder Falls State Park
0 50 km
0 25 miles

HOW TO EAT A STEAMED MARYLAND BLUE CRAB

To eat Maryland's favorite crab delicacy, take the following steps:

1. Spread newspapers or crab paper on the table.
2. Pull off the crab's apron (the abdominal flap with a point that's narrow on males, and wider and more rounded on females).
3. Remove the top shell, guts, gills and yellowish 'mustard' and break the crab in half.
4. Extract the meat.
5. Finally, the best part: crack the claws with a wooden hammer and enjoy the chunks of meat inside.

If you're in Maryland between mid-May and early September, also watch for softshell crabs – a local delicacy. These are crabs that have been caught just after molting, and are eaten whole.

Annapolis

Sailboats and duck decoys

With its cobbled central area, 18th-century architecture, sailing vibe and waterside setting, Annapolis easily ranks as one of the USA's most charming capitals. It's a wonderfully walkable place, with quaint streets radiating from its **City Dock**, all lined with boutique shops, eateries and historic inns. Wherever you wander, the Chesapeake Bay, with its wind-whipped whitecaps and circling gulls, is never far away. Get a feel for things on a half-day **walking tour** or explore further afield, discovering the bay's 11,000-plus-mile shoreline. Annapolis is an ideal jumping-off point for discovering the bay, with **Schooner Woodwind** *(schoonerwoodwind.com)* and **Watermark** *(watermarkjourney.com)* offering cruises from the City Dock.

At the bay's northernmost end, by the mouth of the Susquehanna River, is the pretty town of **Havre de Grace**. This is the self-proclaimed 'decoy capital of the world,' where the skill of decoy carving has been elevated to an art form. Decoy carving is a traditional technique of hand-carving bird figures used to lure live waterfowl for hunting purposes. The best place to learn about it is at the **Havre de Grace Decoy Museum** *(decoymuseum.com; free)*, which hosts the Decoy & Wildlife Art Festival each May.

St Mary's City

Colonial-era life in southern Maryland

On March 23, 1634, the Yaocomico people living in what is now southern Maryland were surprised by the arrival of an English ship, the *Dove*, which together with its larger sister ship, *Ark*, tied up at St Clement's Island after several months at sea. The Yaocomico welcomed the new arrivals and – in exchange for cloth, tools and other items – gave them permission to settle on land around 15 miles southeast, overlooking the St Mary's River. The settlement, which soon became Maryland's first capital, is commemorated at the **Historic St Mary's City** *(hsmcdigshistory.org; adult/child $10/6)* open-air site, a two-hour drive from Annapolis. You can visit reconstructions of many of the original buildings, including the 1676 State House, and learn about life here during the colony's early days. There's also the Woodland Indian Hamlet, which aims to portray the daily life of the Yaocomico. Anchored in the river below is a life-sized replica of the *Dove*.

EATING & DRINKING IN ANNAPOLIS: OUR PICKS

Chick & Ruth's Delly: This informal eatery is an Annapolis institution, with huge sandwiches and all-day breakfasts. *6:30am-10pm Sun-Thu, to 11pm Fri & Sat* $

Osteria 177: This popular place draws in guests with a convenient Main St location, authentic Italian cuisine and a chilled, welcoming vibe. *5-10pm, plus 11:30am-2pm Fri* $$

Reynold's Tavern: Ambience is key at this mid-18th-century establishment, whether in the cozy 1747 Pub, upper tearoom or outdoor beer garden. *11am-11pm*

Vin 909: An intimate, casual ambience, seasonal neo-American cuisine and pleasant Eastport setting make this a perennial favorite. *hours vary* $$

ANNAPOLIS ON FOOT

The best way to explore Annapolis' cobbled streets and dock area is on foot. You may need a car for attractions away from the centre.

START	END	LENGTH
State House	WWII and Gold Star Families Memorial	6 miles; 3-4 hours

Maryland's late-18th century 1 **State House** (open daily for self-guided tours with photo ID) is the oldest state capitol in continuous legislative use. Atop its dome, an upside-down acorn symbolizes wisdom. Nearby is Church Circle, with 2 **St Anne's Episcopal church** (1692). From here, follow Franklin St to the 3 **Banneker-Douglass-Tubman Museum**, highlighting the achievements of Marylanders of African American ancestry. It's named after orator and abolitionist Frederick Douglass, Harriet Tubman (p276) and Benjamin Banneker, an astronomer and mathematician. Return past Church Circle before turning southeast on 4 **Main St**. At its eastern end is 5 **City Dock** and the 6 **Kunta Kinte–Alex Haley Memorial**, commemorating Kunta Kinte's 1767 arrival at this spot. The surrounding Story Wall has quotes on reconciliation and healing. Just beyond is the boat-turnaround channel known as 7 **Ego Alley**. Bordering this is Compromise St, leading over Spa Creek to Eastport and the 8 **Annapolis Maritime Museum**. Back at City Dock, pass 9 **Market Sq** en route to the 10 **US Naval Academy**, where you can walk or arrange driving tours in one of the academy's electric vehicles. Diagonally opposite is 11 **St John's College**, one of the US's oldest post-secondary institutions. From here, it's about 2 miles (but worth it) across the Severn River bridge to the 12 **WWII and Gold Star Families Memorial**, overlooking the Severn River, with the names of 6000-plus Marylanders who lost their lives during the war.

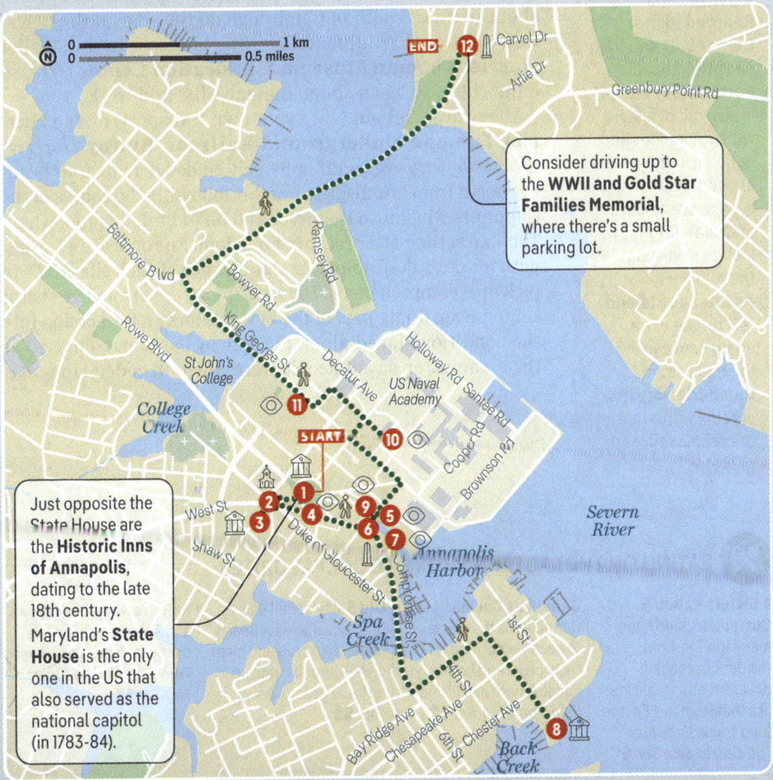

MARYLAND FOR KIDS

Maryland offers so much for kids of all ages. Get to know its waterways on a sightseeing **cruise** *(watermarkjourney.com)* in Annapolis or Baltimore, or watch a boat being constructed at the Chesapeake Bay Maritime Museum in St Michaels. The **Maryland Science Center** (p280) has displays for all ages. History-loving teens will likely find the **Harriet Tubman Underground Railroad Visitor Center** both sobering and inspirational. **Fort McHenry** (p282) is also full of history with its cannons and national anthem story. In good weather, it's easy to spend days at **Ocean City** (p278), including visiting the wild horses at **Assateague Island** (p278). Get extra energy out cycling the trails around **Cumberland** (p283) or relax with a ride on the scenic **railroad** (p284).

About 10 miles south of St Mary's City, where the Potomac River flows into Chesapeake Bay, is **Point Lookout State Park** *(dnr.maryland.gov/publiclands; $7)*, the site of a medical center for wounded Union soldiers during the Civil War and now a quiet area of pines and marshes. Its camping area is currently closed for renovations, but the setting is peaceful and, in season, there's a half-day ferry excursion to and from Smith Island, which lies about two hours southeast of Point Lookout in the bay.

Cambridge

The underground railroad

The underground railroad was a secret network of people and safe houses that offered support and assistance to enslaved people trying to escape bondage by fleeing north or into Canada. During the early to mid-19th century, hundreds of mostly unsung heroes, Black and white, helped what is estimated to be thousands of enslaved people to reach freedom. One of the most famous 'conductors' of the underground railroad was Harriet Tubman (1822–1913), who was born near Cambridge. After managing to escape, she repeatedly travelled back to the Eastern Shore to help family and friends to safety. Her story is movingly portrayed in the excellent **Harriet Tubman Underground Railroad Visitor Center** *(nps.gov/hatu; free)*, about 10 miles south of Cambridge on the edge of the Blackwater National Wildlife Refuge. Start here, or in the smaller **Harriet Tubman Museum & Education Center** *(free)* in Cambridge, to learn about Tubman's life and work.

Afterwards, set out (with your own transport) on the **Harriet Tubman Underground Railroad Byway** *(harriettubmanbyway.org)*, a 125-mile, self-guided driving tour heading north from Cambridge, roughly following the course of the Choptank River into Delaware and on to Philadelphia, where Tubman settled after reaching freedom. En route are 45 stops, with markers describing the significance of each site. You can pick up a comprehensive *Driving Tour Guide* from the visitor center. Even doing part of the byway offers an immersion into the conditions faced along the way by early 'passengers,' as the escaping enslaved people were called in coded language.

EATING ON THE EASTERN SHORE: LOCAL FAVORITES

4 Sisters Kabob & Curry: Maryland has many foreign-born residents, meaning delicious ethnic cuisine like that from this Easton food truck. *11am-8pm Tue-Sat, to 6pm Sun* $

Carmela's Cucina: Carmela's is the place to go in Cambridge for tasty pizza and homestyle ItalianAmerican cuisine. *11am-9pm Mon-Sat* $$

Old Salty's: Pull up by boat or vehicle for hearty, homestyle crab and meat dishes and to catch up on local gossip. *hours vary* $$

RaR Brewing: Craft brews and American pub-style dining in Cambridge. *11am-9pm Sun-Wed, to 10pm Thu-Sat* $$

EASTERN SHORE MEANDERINGS

The pace slows down as soon as you get over the Bay Bridge. Maryland's Eastern Shore is worth as much time as you can give it.

START	END	LENGTH
Annapolis	Assateague Island	187 miles; 2-3 days

From Annapolis, follow Rte 50 to ❶ **Easton** and then Rte 33 to ❷ **St Michaels**, with its shop- and eatery-lined main street and the Chesapeake Bay Maritime Museum. Continue towards tiny ❸ **Bellevue**, catching the seasonal vehicle ferry (dating to 1683) across the Tred Avon River to ❹ **Oxford**, also dating to 1683 and one of Maryland's oldest towns. Continue southeast towards ❺ **Cambridge**, where the historic center has plenty to offer, including the Choptank River lighthouse (a replica of the original 1870s structure). Continue along Rtes 16 and 335 to ❻ **Blackwater National Wildlife Refuge**, which offers a haven for birds migrating along the Atlantic Flyway – one of the USA's four major migratory bird flyways. Neighboring Blackwater is the moving ❼ **Harriet Tubman Underground Railroad Visitor Center**. Rejoin Rte 50 near Vienna, following it to Salisbury and then exiting towards ❽ **Crisfield**, a working watermen's town known for its September crab festivals – the Hard Crab Derby and the Tawes Crab and Clam Bake. Crisfield is the departure point for boats to ❾ **Smith Island**, 7 miles offshore. The ferry can be booked at Captain Tyler Motel near the dock. Smith Island is known for its distinctive old English accent and its traditional way of life. Back on the mainland, finish with time at ❿ **Ocean City** and ⓫ **Assateague Island**, where you can arrange kayaking with Assateague Outfitters *(assateagueoutfitters.com)*.

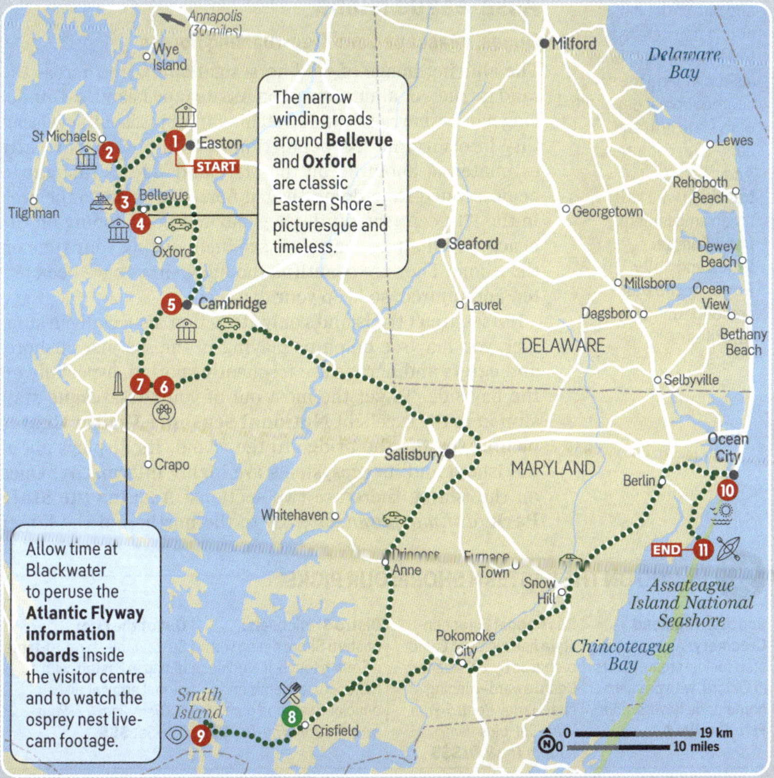

The narrow winding roads around **Bellevue** and **Oxford** are classic Eastern Shore – picturesque and timeless.

Allow time at Blackwater to peruse the **Atlantic Flyway information boards** inside the visitor centre and to watch the osprey nest live-cam footage.

OCEAN CITY ATTRACTIONS

Apart from walking for miles along the beach, there's plenty more to do in Ocean City. Visit the small **Life-Saving Station Museum** for a historical overview and stroll the boardwalk, grabbing an ice cream along the way. Wander past the historic **Henry Hotel** (currently closed, but slated for renovation). Dating to the late 19th century, it's one of Ocean City's oldest buildings and one of the few hotels that catered to African American visitors during the segregationist days of the late 19th and early 20th centuries. And if you're travelling with kids, try an amusement park: **Trimper Rides** and **Jolly Roger at the Pier** are long-standing favorites.

Ocean City

Beach and boardwalk fun

Especially in August, it can seem as if the entire population of the Washington, DC metropolitan area has descended on Ocean City for a holiday, but don't let that dissuade you from a visit. In the low season, you'll have the long, wide beach almost to yourself, and even in season, the sea air, surf and cooler temperatures are a balm. If you're a fan of boardwalks, Ocean City's 2-mile-plus **boardwalk** is one of the region's best, with a smooth, wooden, wheelchair-friendly surface (beach wheelchair rentals are also available), the Giant (Ferris) Wheel, arcades, rides, waterslides and amusements. If this doesn't appeal, the surrounding area offers quieter pursuits. Tiny **Berlin**, about 9 miles inland from Ocean City, has a walkable historic town center with narrow streets lined with boutiques and shops.

Ocean City has ridesharing services (Uber and Lyft) and the Ocean City Beach Bus runs along the Coastal Hwy to 144th St (no winter service), making it easy to get around. In summer season, there's also the Boardwalk Tram and a Park & Ride lot in West Ocean City, with free shuttle service to/from South Division St at the boardwalk's southern end.

Assateague Island

Dunes, seascapes and free-roaming horses

The alluring image of wild horses galloping free across the sand is true – or almost true – on Assateague Island, a 37-mile-long narrow barrier island stretching from just south of Ocean City into Virginia. Its population of wild horses, currently estimated at about 80 on the Maryland side, is thought to be descended from domesticated horses brought to the area in the 17th century. While they may not be galloping on the beach, you'll almost certainly see them during your time on the island. They are beautiful, though visitors have been bitten and injured, so keep your distance.

Horses aren't the island's only attraction. Especially in summer, you may see dolphins playing in the sea just offshore, and egrets and herons are frequently spotted, especially on the bay side. To get the most out of your Assateague stay, stop in at the excellent **National Seashore Visitor Center** before crossing the bridge to the island. Its displays about the island and its ecosystems are highly informative. Once on the island, there are two sections: **Assateague State Park** *(dnr.maryland.gov; $5)* to the north, and the larger

EATING ON THE EASTERN SHORE: OUR PICKS

Scottish Highland Creamery: An essential stop for ice-cream lovers in Oxford, with premium homemade flavors. *noon-9pm Thu-Tue* **$**

Bas Rouge: European-style fine dining in Easton, prepared by 2024 James Beard award-winning chef Harley Peet. *5-9pm Wed-Sat, plus 11am-1:30pm Thu & Fri* **$$$**

Bistro St Michaels: Eastern Shore dining with a French touch, including multicourse menus and a delicious seafood gumbo. *from 4:30pm Thu-Tue* **$$$**

Out of the Fire: Sustainable, farm-to-table dining in Easton, with a global array of dishes. *11:30am-2pm & 5-9pm Tue-Sat* **$$$**

Baltimore's Inner Harbor

Assateague Island National Seashore *(nps.gov/asis; per week per person/vehicle free/$25)* to the south. During the warmer months, you can rent bicycles and kayaks in the park from **Assateague Outfitters** *(assateagueoutfitters.com)*, and hiking is possible year-round. There are campsites on both the bay and ocean sides, including rustic walk-in (or kayak-in) sites. Make bookings up to six months in advance as spots fill quickly, and bring mosquito repellent. Note that backcountry (walk-in) campsites can't be reserved. While winter visits are for the hardy, the island's magic and serenity are easier to feel with fewer visitors around. Summer brings warmth and crowds, while spring and fall are both lovely, with fewer visitors and insects.

Baltimore

MAPS P280, P282

A day around the Inner Harbour

Baltimore's **Inner Harbor** is a destination in itself and a convenient jumping-off point for exploring the city. If it's a clear day, start with a bird's-eye view of the city from the **Top of the World** *(viewbaltimore.org; adult/child $8/5)* observation deck at the Baltimore World Trade Center before choosing between the nearby **National Aquarium** *(aqua.org; adult/child $50/40)* – one of the USA's best – and visits to the Inner Harbor's historic ships. In addition to the *USS Constellation*,

BEST MARYLAND FESTIVALS

Maryland Renaissance Festival: Held near Annapolis on weekends from late August through October. *rennfest.com*

Kunta Kinte Heritage Festival: In Annapolis; commemorates Maryland's African and African American heritage (September). *kuntakinte.org*

Baltimore Pride: Takes place over a week in June. *baltimorepride.org*

Annapolis Boat Show: There are now several, but the October sailboat show remains one of the best. *annapolisboatshows.com*

Deal Island Skipjack Race: Skipjack races, seafood and a parade (September).

Watermen Appreciation Day: At Chesapeake Bay Maritime Museum (August).

Maryland Crab Cake Festival: Sample Maryland's best crab cakes at Carroll County Farm Museum (October).

EATING IN & AROUND OCEAN CITY: OUR PICKS

Berlin Farmers Market: The emphasis is on fresh, homemade and artisanal. *9am-1pm Sun May-Sep* $

Island Creamery: Try flavors such as java jolt and key lime pie, all homemade at the Chincoteague (Virginia) main shop. *11am-9pm Sun-Thu, to 10pm Fri & Sat* $$

Blacksmith Restaurant & Bar: A Berlin favorite, with craft beer, well-prepared farm-to-table dishes and a laid-back vibe. *11:30am-9pm Mon-Sat* $$

Ripieno's Italian Bistro: Probably Ocean City's best (and biggest) pizzas. Also has sandwiches, subs and platters. *10am-9pm Mon-Thu, to 10pm Fri & Sat* $$

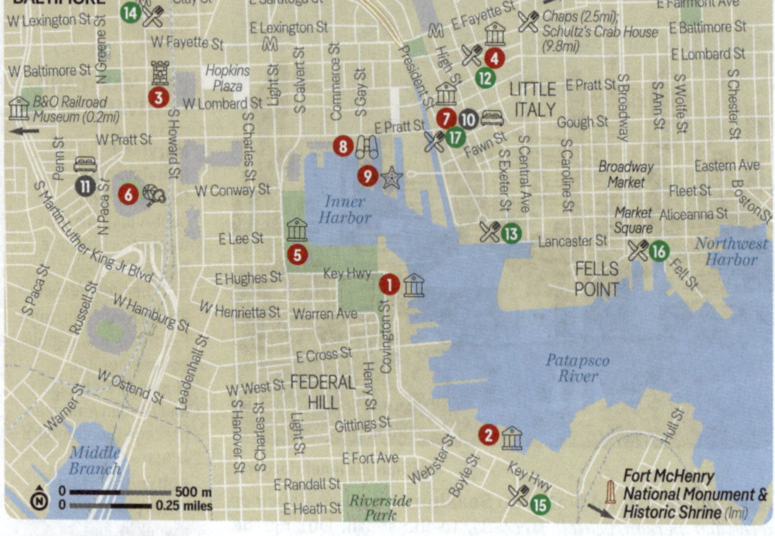

SIGHTS
1 American Visionary Art Museum
2 Baltimore Museum of Industry
3 Bromo Seltzer Tower
4 Jewish Museum of Maryland
5 Maryland Science Center
6 Oriole Park at Camden Yards
7 Reginald F Lewis Museum
see 7 Star-Spangled Banner Flag House
8 Top of the World Observation Deck

ACTIVITIES
9 National Aquarium

SLEEPING
10 BlancNoir
11 Rachael's Dowry B&B

EATING
12 Attman's Deli
13 Charleston
14 Faidley Seafood
see 14 Lexington Market
15 Locust Point Steamers
16 Thames Street Oyster House
17 Vaccaro's Italian Pastry

FREDERICK DOUGLASS

Frederick Douglass, the famed abolitionist, writer, orator and civil-rights activist, was born around 40 miles east of Annapolis on the Eastern Shore, near Tuckahoe Creek, but came to Baltimore for five years as a child to work in the shipyards at Fells Point, and again when he was 18. It was from Baltimore that he escaped by train to Pennsylvania and freedom.

the US Navy's last sail-only warship (notable also for its role in working to halt the foreign slave trade), these include the *USS Torsk* submarine, the lightship *Chesapeake* and US Coast Guard Cutter 37, all of which you can board and tour.

Continuing around the west side of the Inner Harbor, you'll reach the **Maryland Science Center** *(mdsci.org; adult/child $30/22)* and Davis Planetarium, which are particularly good stops if you're traveling with kids. There's also an adventure playground next door. Just beyond is Baltimore's Federal Hill

EATING & DRINKING IN BALTIMORE: A CITY SAMPLER

MAPS P280, P282

La Cuchara: Well-prepared Basque cuisine in an atmospheric setting. *5-9pm Sun-Thu, to 10pm Fri & Sat* **$$**

Thames Street Oyster House: Get your fill of oysters and other seafood at this iconic Fells Point eatery. *hours vary* **$$**

WC Harlan: Vintage, speakeasy-style cocktail bar in Remington neighborhood. *5pm-midnight Mon-Wed, to 1am Thu-Sat*

Charleston: Take advantage of the small-plate approach to maximize your culinary experience. *5:30-9pm Mon-Thu, 5-9:30pm Fri & Sat, to 8:30pm Sun* **$$$**

neighborhood and the community-oriented **American Visionary Art Museum** *(avam.org; adult/child $16/10)*. Featuring the work of self-taught artists, including homemade robots and matchstick models, this place will challenge your ideas of both museums and art. Nearby is the **Baltimore Museum of Industry** *(thebmi.org; adult/child $15/8)*, a fascinating place focused on the city's entrepreneurs and inventors, with live demos and hands-on activities. Once finished, head around to the harbor's east side, past cruise operators and paddle boats, to Fells Point, a former shipbuilding hub known for its multicultural neighborhoods, cobbled streets, restaurants and pubs. In the evenings, Fells Point is as good as it gets around the Inner Harbor. Another option is to catch an Orioles game at nearby **Oriole Park at Camden Yards** *(orioles.com)* stadium.

Museum round-up

Baltimore has enough museums to keep you busy for months. The city's art museums are a highlight, starting with the **Baltimore Museum of Art** *(artbma.org; free)*, known for its collections of Matisse and African art. About 3 miles south of here, in the Mount Vernon neighborhood, is the equally wonderful **Walters Art Museum** *(thewalters.org; free)*, with permanent collections that span continents and millennia, from ancient Egypt to Renaissance Europe, with illustrated Islamic manuscripts and an impressive collection of medieval arms and armor. From here, it's about 1.5 miles southeast to the edge of the Little Italy neighborhood – well worth a stroll, if only to sample a pastry at **Vaccaro's Italian Pastry** – and the **Reginald F Lewis Museum** *(lewismuseum.org; adult/child $12/9)* of African American history and culture. For more on African American history, check out the simple but thought-provoking **National Great Blacks in Wax Museum** *(greatblacksinwax.org; adult/child $18/15)*, spotlighting famous people such as Jackie Robinson as well as lesser-known figures such as Maryland-born explorer Matthew Henson. For more niche interests, try the **B&O Railroad Museum** *(borail.org; adult/child $20/12)* with its old locomotives and roundhouse, or the **Evergreen Museum** *(museums.jhu.edu; adult/child $12/10)*, offering glimpses into upper-class Baltimore life during the 1800s. Surrounding it are expansive, landscaped grounds and the campuses of several universities. The **Jewish Museum of Maryland** *(jewishmuseummd.org; adult/student/child $10/6/4)*, just reopened after extensive renovations, offers tours of two well-preserved synagogues that open doors into the history of Jewish Baltimore.

BALTIMORE INSIDER TIPS

Jon Patrick Leary, a lifelong Baltimorean, recommends the following places for visitors. *facebook.com/jon.p.leary*

Attman's Deli: It's 100-plus years of age and like NYC.

Club Charles: Come for cocktails. Blondie, Johnny Depp, John Waters and Ric Ocasek have been here – you never know who you'll meet.

Bromo Seltzer Tower: Climb behind the big clock face – really neat.

Lexington Market: One of the country's oldest markets.

Schultz's Crab House: An old-school rarity, about 10 miles from Baltimore in Essex.

Koco's Pub: The best crab cakes around.

Baltimore Museum of Industry: A tourist destination, but still well worth a visit.

EATING IN BALTIMORE: BEST FOR LOCAL FLAVOR

MAPS P280, P282

Faidley Seafood: This long-standing place at Lexington Market is famous for its crab cakes and other seafood. *10am-5pm Mon-Thu, to 5:30pm Fri & Sat* **$$**

R House: This sleek food hall in Remington offers an array of cuisines, including Egyptian, Korean and Italian. *8am-10pm Sun-Thu, to 11pm Fri & Sat* **$**

Chaps: The go-to stop for pit beef (grilled, sliced top-round on a kaiser roll with 'tiger sauce' and onion slice). *10:30am-9pm Sun-Thu, to 10pm Fri & Sat* **$**

Locust Point Steamers: A classic Baltimore crab house, with a hometown vibe and tasty seafood. *11am-9pm Sun-Thu, to 9:30pm Fri & Sat* **$$**

CHARLES ST

If you could pick one Baltimore street that encapsulates all the city has to offer, it would likely be Charles St, which runs north from the Inner Harbor for about 5 miles. En route, it takes you through the Bromo and Station North arts districts, historic Mount Vernon with its 178ft Washington Monument (climb to the top for views), several historic churches, including the neoclassical Basilica of the Assumption, the Walters Art Museum and the Baltimore Museum of Art before coming to the Johns Hopkins University campus. Just west of campus is Hampden, known for its hipster-creative working-class vibe and the vintage shops and eateries lining 'The Avenue' (W 36th St).

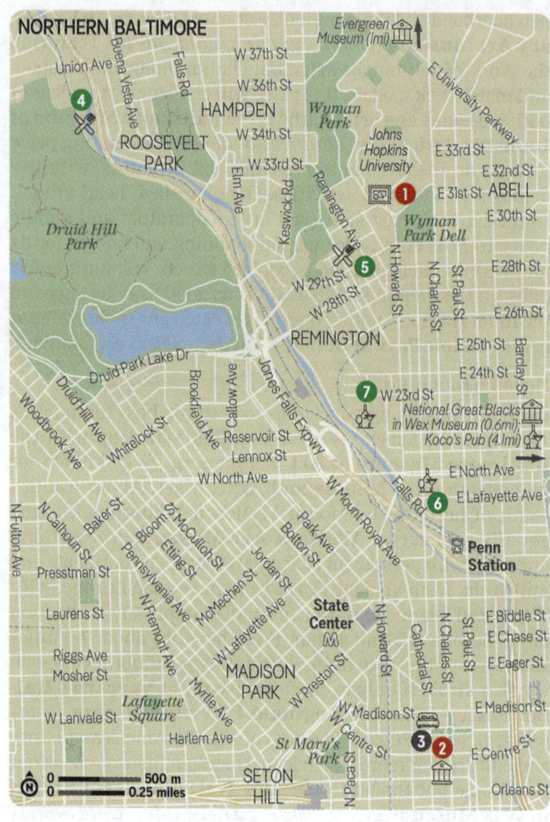

SIGHTS
1 Baltimore Museum of Art
2 Walters Art Museum

SLEEPING
3 Hotel Revival

EATING
4 La Cuchara
5 R House

DRINKING & NIGHTLIFE
6 Club Charles
7 WC Harlan

O say can you see...

On a dark, rainy night in September 1814, American lawyer Francis Scott Key found himself stuck on a ship in the Patapsco River, watching as the British attacked Fort McHenry as part of their efforts to seize control of Baltimore. When dawn finally came, Key's incredulity, pride and gratitude at seeing the giant (30ft by 42ft) American flag still waving over the fort, despite the heavy shelling, prompted him to pen the stanzas of a poem, which he called 'The Defense of Fort M'Henry.' The poem's title was later changed to 'The Star-Spangled Banner' and, in 1931, its words became the US national anthem. The whole series of events is commemorated at the **Fort McHenry National Monument and Historic Shrine** *(nps.gov/fomc; adult/child $15/free)*, starting with a short but moving film that concludes with a stirring rendition of the anthem, followed by time to wander the grounds and take in the views over the harbor. In town, at the **Star-Spangled Banner Flag House** *(flaghouse.org; adult/child $8/6)*, you can visit the place where seamstress Mary Pickersgill made the original Fort McHenry flag, which is now on display in the Smithsonian's National Museum of American History in Washington, DC.

Antietam National Battlefield

Hear the echoes of the Civil War

In the open, rolling farm country on the edge of Sharpsburg, about 25 miles northwest of Frederick, is **Antietam National Battlefield** *(nps.gov/anti; per person/vehicle $10/$20)*, where, in 1862, an estimated 23,000 people were killed or injured in what is considered the bloodiest single-day conflict in US history. The battle marked the end of the southern attack aimed at Maryland and Washington, DC. It was also a significant turning point in the Civil War, and served as a springboard for Abraham Lincoln's Emancipation Proclamation. Today, surrounded by the battlefield's bucolic expanses, it's difficult to imagine the battle's carnage and suffering. To relive some of the history and learn more about Antietam, start at the visitor center, where there is an informative welcome film. It's then easy to explore the battlefield on a self-guided driving tour, taking advantage of informative plaques at each of the designated stops. Alternatively, you can arrange in advance to take a guided tour. However you visit, don't miss the Dunker Church, Burnside Bridge and the Observation Tower, with wide views over the surrounding area. If you want to immerse yourself even more in Civil War history, the smaller **Monocacy National Battlefield** *(nps.gov/mono; free)*, site of a decisive battle for the national capital, is about 25 miles southeast of Antietam on Frederick's southeastern outskirts, and also well worth a stop. It has short walking trails and a similar self-guided-drive setup.

GLEN ECHO CAROUSEL

If you're departing Washington, DC and heading northwest towards Frederick or Antietam, take time for a detour to Maryland's **Glen Echo Park** *(glenechopark.org; free)*. Its historic (and still operational) carousel – at its best on the park's annual Carousel Day in late April – became a focal point for the Civil Rights movement in 1960, when Black and white protesters joined forces and picketed for several months against Glen Echo's segregationist policies, until the park's owners finally announced that the park would open to all visitors. The 2024 documentary film *Ain't No Back to a Merry-Go-Round* tells the story in detail.

Cumberland

Crossroads of America

Tiny Cumberland's historical designation as 'Crossroads of America' might seem an exaggeration, but the more you delve into the area's rich history, the more apt the name becomes. Start at the **Allegany Museum** *(alleganymuseummd.org;*

EATING & DRINKING IN FREDERICK: CREATIVE CUISINE & CRAFT BEER

Carroll Creek Breweries: Get introduced to Frederick's craft-beer culture at this cluster of breweries around Carroll Creek's eastern side. *hours vary*

Ordinary Hen: Enjoy cornbread, squash-and-dumplings and other Appalachian-inspired cuisine, plus live music Fridays at the outdoor Shed. *11am-3pm & 5-9pm Thu-Sat, 4-8pm Sun* $$

Wine Kitchen: Local beef cuts of distinction, plus seafood and vegetarian options and curated wine pairings. *noon-9pm Tue-Thu & Sun, to 10pm Fri & Sat* $$

Bentztown: Southern cuisine goes upmarket at this place, where music is as much a draw as the menu. *11am-10pm Mon, Wed, Thu & Sun, to 1am Fri & Sat* $$

CYCLING THE C&O CANAL

One of the Mid-Atlantic's great cycling trails runs between Washington, DC and Pittsburgh, first following the C&O Canal (184 miles) and then the Great Allegheny Passage (GAP; 149 miles). Cumberland's Canal Pl is the meeting point of the two. The three-season ride can be done in either direction, is mostly flat (with some gradual ascents/descents around Cumberland) and is a great mix of nature and scenery. En route, there's rustic but free trail camping and a mix of public and private campgrounds. Alternatively, you can detour into nearby towns to stay at a hotel. Many cyclists do the trail independently, but if you want to arrange a tour, **Wheelz Up Adventures** in Cumberland can help with bike rentals and tours.

VWPICS/GETTY IMAGES

Curtis' Coney Island Famous Weiners

free) where the Crossroads of America exhibit covers everything from Cumberland's earliest inhabitants to its pivotal transportation position during the French and Indian War to the development of the C&O Canal and the B&O Railroad. From here, make your way over to the **Crossroads of America mural**, which stretches for 200ft along the wall in front of the train station. The plaza just beyond the mural marks the starting point for cycling both the C&O Canal towpath to Washington, DC and the Great Allegheny Passage trail to Pittsburgh, Pennsylvania. Back at the train station, check out the **Cumberland Visitor Center and Museum** before taking the **Western Maryland Scenic Railroad** *(wmsr.com)* – these days, a historic diesel train – to Frostburg (4½ hours return, including about 1½ hours in Frostburg). Finish up back in Cumberland with a walk around the historic central pedestrian area focused around Baltimore and Center Sts. It's lined with late-19th-century buildings and, especially in the summer, serves as Cumberland's town hub, with a farmers market and frequent sidewalk festivities.

EATING IN CUMBERLAND: LOCAL FAVORITES

Caporale's Bakery: Don't miss the pepperoni rolls, ramp rolls and other delicacies at this old-style Cumberland institution. *10am-5pm Mon & Wed-Fri, 9am-3pm Sun* $

Curtis' Coney Island Famous Weiners: Serving hot dogs, burgers and its signature Coney Island sauce to a loyal clientele for over a century. *9am-8pm Mon-Sat* $

Crabby Pig: Crab cakes, cream of crab soup, pulled pork sandwiches and other seafood and meat dishes. *11am-9pm Tue-Sat, to 8pm Sun* $

Ristorante Ottaviani: Enjoy wine tastings and well-prepared Italian-American cuisine in downtown Cumberland. *5-9pm Tue-Thu, to 10pm Fri & Sat, 4-8pm Sun* $$

Virginia

BEACHES | HISTORY | SHENANDOAH MOUNTAINS

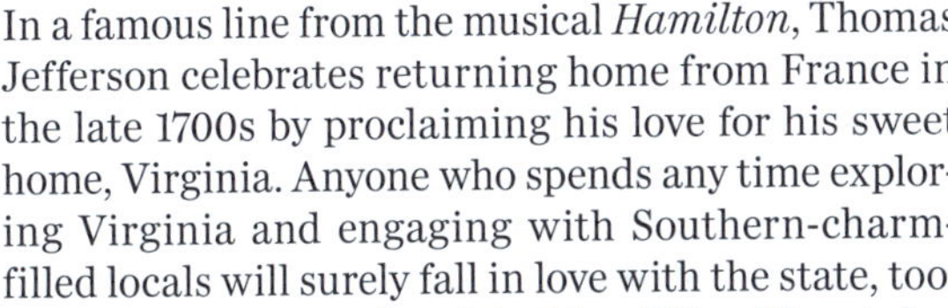

In a famous line from the musical *Hamilton*, Thomas Jefferson celebrates returning home from France in the late 1700s by proclaiming his love for his sweet home, Virginia. Anyone who spends any time exploring Virginia and engaging with Southern-charm-filled locals will surely fall in love with the state, too.

From the misty peaks of the Blue Ridge Mountains to the serene ripples of Chesapeake Bay, the state offers an array of natural beauty. Virginia's past is as varied as its geography: it's where the first English settlement of Jamestown was established, and the site of crucial Civil War battles. Bustling urban epicenters, from the capital of Richmond to the DC-adjacent Arlington, brim with architectural landmarks, while Virginia's coastal towns exude a nautical heritage that's a mix of quaint and captivating.

Whether you're tracing the founding fathers' footsteps, exploring wine country or hiking Appalachian trails, Virginia will enchant with its stories and scenery.

Places

Richmond p287
Williamsburg p289
Charlottesville p290
Blue Ridge Parkway p292
Shenandoah National Park p292
Virginia Beach p293
Norfolk p294
Chincoteague National Wildlife Refuge p294
Arlington p295
Fredericksburg p296
Alexandria p296
Mount Vernon p297

TOP TIP

Plan a few days in each region – the coastal plains and Virginia Beach, the central Piedmont region and Richmond, the Blue Ridge Mountains and points west – to experience Virginia's unique zing.

GETTING AROUND

Renting a car is the easiest way to navigate the state's entirety. Take note, particularly in Northern Virginia and along major highways, of HOV lanes (often requiring two or more passengers per vehicle) and snag an E-Z Pass toll pass to navigate rush-hour traffic. Amtrak connects the entire state, from Roanoke and Danville in the southwest to Norfolk in the southeast and Alexandria in the north. The trains connect with other major Virginia systems, including Virginia Railway Express and Metro.

Richmond and Charlottesville have bikeshare programs and the Greater Richmond Transit Company (GRTC) has free Pulse buses serving most tourist routes.

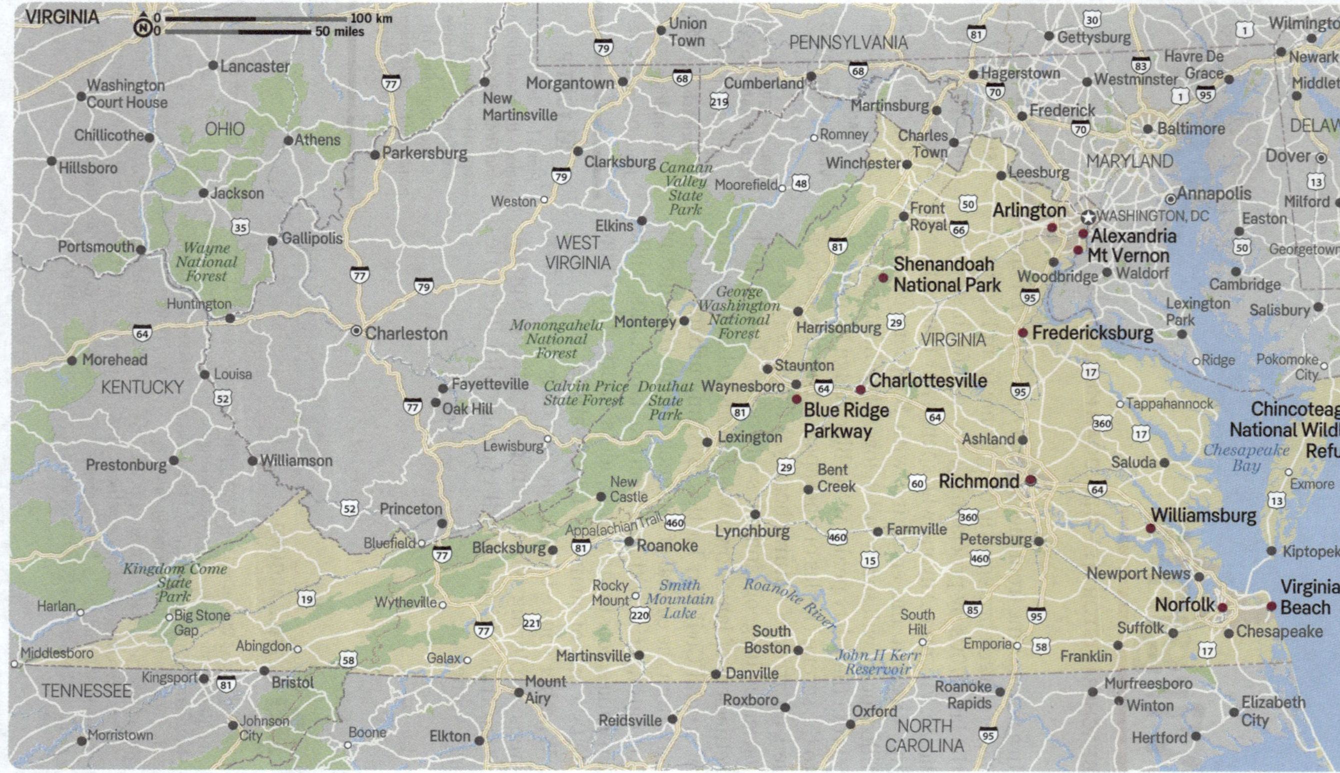
VIRGINIA
0 100 km
0 50 miles
PENNSYLVANIA
MARYLAND
DELAWARE
OHIO
WEST VIRGINIA
VIRGINIA
KENTUCKY
TENNESSEE
NORTH CAROLINA
Union Town
Gettysburg
Wilmington
Newark
Middletown
Havre De Grace
Westminster
Hagerstown
Cumberland
Morgantown
Lancaster
Washington Court House
New Martinsville
Martinsburg
Frederick
Baltimore
Chillicothe
Athens
Parkersburg
Romney
Charles Town
Dover
Hillsboro
Clarksburg
Canaan Valley State Park
Moorefield
Winchester
Leesburg
Annapolis
Milford
Jackson
Weston
Front Royal
Arlington
WASHINGTON, DC
Easton
Portsmouth
Wayne National Forest
Gallipolis
Elkins
Alexandria
Mt Vernon
Georgetown
Shenandoah National Park
Woodbridge
Waldorf
Cambridge
Huntington
George Washington National Forest
Lexington Park
Salisbury
Monongahela National Forest
Monterey
Harrisonburg
Charleston
Fredericksburg
Morehead
Staunton
Ridge
Pokomoke City
Louisa
Fayetteville
Calvin Price State Forest
Douthat State Park
Waynesboro
Charlottesville
Tappahannock
Chincoteague National Wildlife Refuge
Oak Hill
Blue Ridge Parkway
Lexington
Ashland
Chesapeake Bay
Lewisburg
Prestonburg
Williamson
Saluda
Bent Creek
New Castle
Richmond
Exmore
Princeton
Appalachian Trail
Lynchburg
Farmville
Williamsburg
Bluefield
Blacksburg
Roanoke
Petersburg
Kiptopeke
Kingdom Come State Park
Rocky Mount
Smith Mountain Lake
Roanoke River
Newport News
Virginia Beach
Harlan
Big Stone Gap
Wytheville
South Hill
Norfolk
Abingdon
South Boston
Suffolk
Chesapeake
Middlesboro
Emporia
Galax
Martinsville
John H Kerr Reservoir
Franklin
Kingsport
Bristol
Danville
Mount Airy
Roanoke Rapids
Murfreesboro
Roxboro
Winton
Elizabeth City
Johnson City
Reidsville
Oxford
Morristown
Boone
Elkton
Hertford

Richmond

MAP P288

Museum hop in the downtown

Begin at the **Virginia Museum of Fine Arts** *(vmfa.museum; free)*, where a highlight is the permanent 'Fabergé and Russian Decorative Arts' exhibit, with nearly 300 gold and precious-metal-draped objects. Hit also the free Institute for Contemporary Art (ICA) at Virginia Commonwealth University, with its modern sculpture garden.

The **Branch Museum of Architecture and Design** *(branchmuseum.org; suggested $5)*, housed in a stately brick castle of sorts on Monument Ave, has rotating exhibits focusing on a range of topics, including the origins of Richmond's cityscapes and international women's-rights posters. The hands-on **Science Museum of Virginia** *(smv.org; adult/child $18/15)* captivates curious minds of all ages. You can generate tornadoes, or test your reflexes against the speed of light in interactive labs. The **American Civil War Museum** *(acwm.org; adult/child $18/9)* includes personal artifacts and narratives conveying various wartime characters, with its exhibits often focusing on one of three perspectives – the north, the south or African American. The museum is housed in the former Tredegar Iron Works building; cannons made on its grounds fired the first shots at Fort Sumter in South Carolina to kick off the Civil War.

Stroll the cobblestoned Shockoe Bottom

From your first step on Shockoe Bottom's cobblestones, you know the streets have been a setting for the extraordinary through the centuries. This is where George Washington mapped out a national system of transportation canals, laying the groundwork for America's infrastructure. It's where Thomas Jefferson signed the Virginia Statute for Religious Freedom, a cornerstone of American civil liberties. And it's where Abraham Lincoln famously arrived by canoe to witness the historic fall of the Confederacy. Knowing Shockoe Bottom's lore makes it a magical stop.

The neighborhood's hub is **17th Street Market**, which regularly hosts art shows as well as a bimonthly farmers market. A communal favorite is the Richmond Night Market (second Saturday of every month), with an artisan village, live art activations and jam sessions from local bands. The **Tobacco Company** *(www.thetobaccocompany.com)* is a three level, charm-filled restaurant that was once a – you guessed it

LIVE-MUSIC VENUES IN RICHMOND

The National: Has large capacity, an intimate feel, stunning architecture and a state-of-the-art sound system.

The Camel: Catch up-and-coming local talent in a cozy setting, with yummy smashburgers, too.

Canal Club: Industrial chic, adjacent to Canal Walk, with indoor and outdoor performance spaces.

Richmond Music Hall at Capital Ale House: Mid-size venue with a big sound that's attached to a craft-beer haven.

Altria Theater: Historic space with opulent features and arguably the best sight lines and acoustics in town.

EATING IN RICHMOND: OUR PICKS

MAP P288

Stella's: Intimate Greek eatery with authentic flavors evoking a homemade charm in every bite. Reservations recommended. *11:30am-3pm Mon-Fri, plus 4-10pm Mon-Sat* **$$$**

Lunch.SUPPER!: Southern fare featuring locally sourced ingredients. You can't miss the deer-antler chandelier and ornate decorations. *11am-9pm Mon-Fri, from 10am Sat & Sun* **$$**

Pho Tay Do: Vietnamese cuisine in a quirky house setting, with authentic pho and other dishes. Cash only. *10am-6pm Mon, Tue & Thu-Sat, to 5pm Sun* **$$**

Hot for Pizza: A divey den, boasting drink deals and a lineup of pies with ingredients like fennel sausage and oyster mushrooms. *11am-2am Mon-Sat, from noon Sun* **$$**

★ **HIGHLIGHTS**
1 Poe Museum
2 Science Museum of Virginia
3 Virginia Museum of Fine Arts

● **SIGHTS**
4 American Civil War Museum
5 Branch Museum of Architecture and Design

● **SLEEPING**
6 Linden Row Inn

● **EATING**
7 17th Street Market
8 Hot for Pizza
9 Lunch.SUPPER!
10 Stella's
11 Tobacco Company

● **DRINKING & NIGHTLIFE**
12 Capital Ale House

● **ENTERTAINMENT**
13 Altria Theater
14 Canal Club
15 The Camel
16 The National

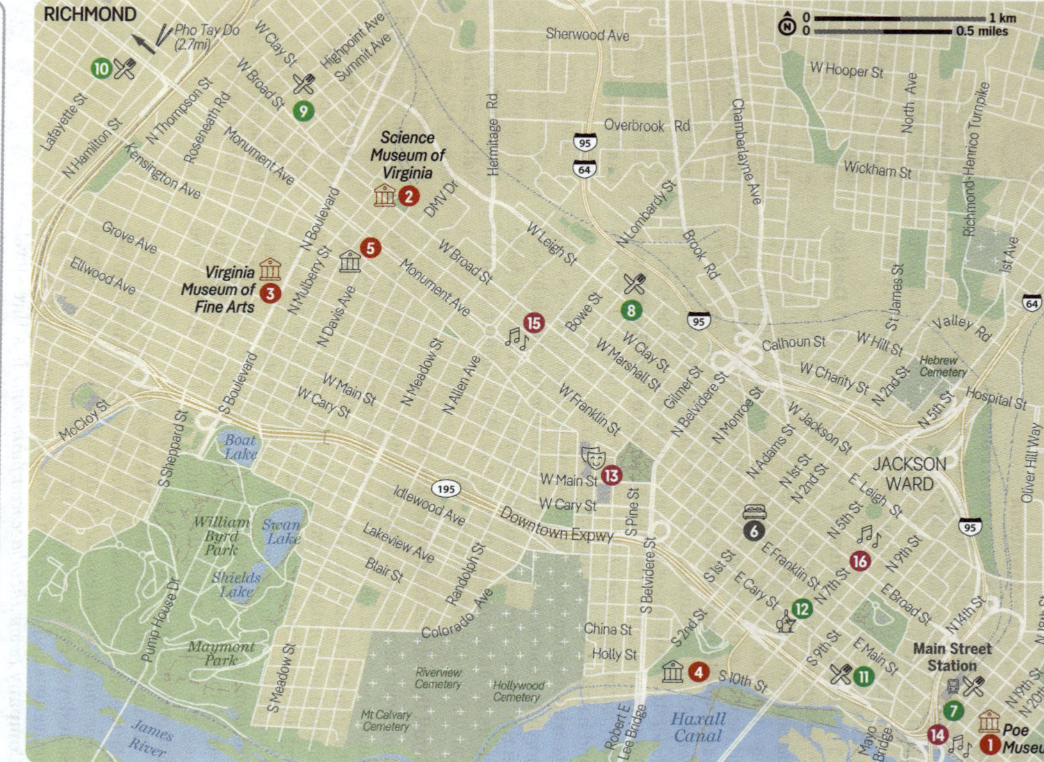

– tobacco warehouse. The pecan-crusted lollipop lamb chops, brass elevator and central walnut staircase dazzle 'round the clock. The **Poe Museum** *(poemuseum.org; adult/child $10/free)* is a living homage to famed Richmond resident, Edgar Allan Poe, offering insights into his enigmatic life and the theories surrounding his demise. The courtyard space – dubbed the Enchanted Garden, which was inspired by Poe's 'To One in Paradise' poem – is a quiet oasis and regularly hosts 'Un-Happy Hours' sponsored by local breweries.

Williamsburg

Hitch a wagon ride in Colonial Williamsburg

Williamsburg was Virginia's capital during the American Revolution and today's **Colonial Williamsburg** *(colonial williamsburg.org; adult/child $32/9)* is a living time capsule that transports locals and visitors alike to the 1700s. Throughout the 300-plus-acre area, historical reenactors with powdered wigs and tricorn hats wander about as horse-drawn carriages roll by. For a carriage ride *(from $10),* head to the Colonial Williamsburg Visitor Center.

By wagon or foot, prioritize a stop at the Governor's Palace. Amid its three-story brick grandeur, note all the pineapple accents – an emblem of hospitality and wealth in the mansion's 1700s heyday and beyond. From the palace, head just west to the Capitol building – this is where the House of Burgesses initially proposed US independence from the British in 1776. A final stop is the Public Gaol, where you can learn about colonial-era crime and punishments. Take note of the historic pillory, a wooden structure with slots for criminals' heads and hands. It was common for passersby to hurl tomatoes and other objects at criminals, so come to this photo op – and the other pillories scattered about Colonial Williamsburg – creatively.

Unexpected historical pizzazz

Don't let Williamsburg's generally refined vibe fool you – there's some quirkiness to explore here. Hit the **Virginia Musical Museum** *(virginiamusicalmuseum.com; free),* which celebrates the state's musical heritage through a collection of rare musical instruments and memorabilia celebrating Virginia-bred icons. Learn all about the likes of country-pop legend Patsy Cline and the 'Queen of Jazz,' Ella Fitzgerald. Among the more unique items is the country's first talking doll and a 1790 Joshua Shudi harpsichord – one of two in existence today. The **College of William & Mary** is the US's second-oldest institution of higher education (Harvard is the oldest). Stop at the Crim Dell Bridge – local lore promises eternal love to those who kiss atop its burgundy-and-gold-railed steps and, if you cross the bridge alone, well, you're doomed to solitude. While at William & Mary, check out the Wren Building, which has survived three major fires since its 1700 inception and is the oldest college building still in use in the country.

When hunger inevitably beckons, **Charly's Airport Restaurant** is a quirky and unexpected find. Situated at Williamsburg Jamestown Airport, it allows you to watch smaller and

WILLIAMSBURG WALKING TOURS

Ultimate Pirate Tour: All-ages tour that delves into the history of pirates and their impact on early colonies.

Murder Tour and Pub Crawl: Learn about the town's seedy, murderous history while sipping on a libation at each pub.

Haunted Williamsburg: Candlelight tour in which you get to enter historic buildings in Colonial Williamsburg.

We Shall Overcome: Hear inspiring stories of African Americans while visiting the Williamsburg landmarks connected to their stories.

Taste of Williamsburg: Williamsburg's best bites and craft drinks are the focus of this tasty tour.

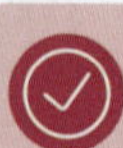

TIPS FOR NAVIGATING WILLIAMSBURG

At approximately 9 sq miles, Williamsburg is compact and largely walkable. Colonial Williamsburg is particularly easy to stroll, with wide, pedestrian-friendly expanses.

Beyond its colonial core, the Williamsburg Area Transit Authority (WATA) serves key tourist attractions such as Jamestown, Busch Gardens and the College of William & Mary. WATA has an all-day pass for $3 and is particularly handy for venturing beyond Colonial Williamsburg. Pay cash for the all-day pass on the bus (credit cards are not accepted).

There's a fee to enter buildings and experience educational programming in Colonial Williamsburg. Odds are that you may want to pair your visit with a Yorktown trek, a Busch Gardens trip or more, and a variety of discounted packages are available at *colonialwilliamsburg.org*.

sometimes vintage aircraft depart and land as you nosh on homestyle plates. Round out a day of the extraordinary at the **Archaearium** *(historicjamestowne.org; adult/child $15/5)*, an archaeology museum dedicated to America's first English colony, Jamestown. The museum has more than 2000 artifacts,including Native American arrowheads and tobacco pipes bearing the names of prominent settlers.

Charlottesville

Exploring past and present

In the foothills of the Blue Ridge Mountains, Charlottesville is as ahhhh-worthy visually as it is historically. It is home to the **University of Virginia**, which was founded by Thomas Jefferson in 1819 and remains a centerpiece of the city's architectural and cultural story. The university's Rotunda and vast lawn are quintessential landmarks, embodying Jefferson's vision of an 'academical village.' President James Monroe's home, **Highland** *(highland.org; adult/child $18/13)*, is notably in Charlottesville as well. Just outside of town is **Monticello** *(monticello.org; adult/child from US$22/8)*, Jefferson's historic home with graceful grounds that you can stroll on your own, capped by the main house, for which you'll need to take a guided tour. Afterwards, spend time exploring Charlottesville's pedestrian-friendly **Downtown Mall**. It's a brick- and column-draped experience with pops of energy coming in the form of buzzing breweries, the facade of the ever-glowing **Paramount Theater** *(theparamount.net)* and more. The mall is a seven-block stretch, with the Ting Pavilion and Omni Charlottesville Hotel as its east and west anchors. Between them, hit **Lone Light Coffee** for a coffee concoction or sweet treats such as bourbon vanilla-infused ice cream.

Uncork Virginia's wine wonderland

Charlottesville wasn't named *Wine Enthusiast*'s Wine Region of the Year in recent times for no reason. The city and surrounding Albemarle County are home to more than 40 wineries, producing everything from the heartiest of merlots to light hybrids. Companies such as **Central Virginia Wine Tours** *(centralvirginiawinetours.com)* offer transportation and winery hops. If you're plotting your own wine adventure, start at **Blenheim Vineyards** *(blenheimvineyards.com)*. The property dates to 1730 and was started as a sustainable winery by world-renowned musician

EATING IN WILLIAMSBURG: HISTORIC TAVERNS

King's Arms Tavern: Authentic colonial dining, blending 18th-century recipes with modern flavors. *11am-2pm daily, plus 4:30-8pm Thu-Mon* **$$$**

Christiana Campbell's Tavern: George Washington's favorite local seafood spot. Come for the crab cakes, stay for the balladeers. *4-8pm Tue-Sat* **$$$**

Chowning's Garden Bar: Relaxed open-air dining with a colonial twist, offering classics such as burgers and hot dogs. *11am-5pm Thu-Sat* **$$**

Raleigh Tavern Bakery: Fresh ginger cake, sandwiches and baked treats from this bakery with wood-fired ovens. *9am-5pm* **$**

DRIVE THROUGH WARTIME & COLONIAL HISTORY

This tour takes you through some of Virginia's most historic sites against a scenic tidewater backdrop.

START	END	LENGTH
Yorktown Battlefield	Historic Jamestowne Island Loop	30 miles; 4-5 hours

Begin at ❶ **Yorktown Battlefield** to soak in Revolutionary War history seeped into the ground. This 1781 battle was a turning point in the war, leading to its end and the USA's independence from Great Britain. Make your way towards ❷ **Nelson House**, one-time residence of Thomas Nelson Jr, a signatory of the Declaration of Independence. Most features in the Georgian home are original. If you visit when enough staff are present, a tour of the interior is possible. Wind your way through the streets of ❸ **Yorktown's historic waterfront**, where restored 18th-century homes line the streets. Water St leads to the ❹ **French Memorial**, a tribute to the French soldiers who lost their lives in battles in and around Yorktown. Hop on the ❺ **Colonial Parkway** from here. This 23-mile scenic drive weaves its way through pine and hardwood forests, tidal estuaries along the James and York rivers and through Williamsburg on its way to Jamestown. Overlooks dot the parkway. Head to Jamestown Island where you'll find the ❻ **Jamestown Settlement**. Exhibits and outdoor re-creations tell the story of America's beginnings, including its Indigenous people and the arrival of English colonists in 1607. Around the corner from the settlement, you'll find ❼ **Jamestown Glasshouse**, where modern glassblowers hold demonstrations while utilizing tools and techniques similar to those used in the 17th century. Just a bit further and you can cruise the ❽ **Historic Jamestowne Island Loop**, discovering the beauty of the island's marshy landscape.

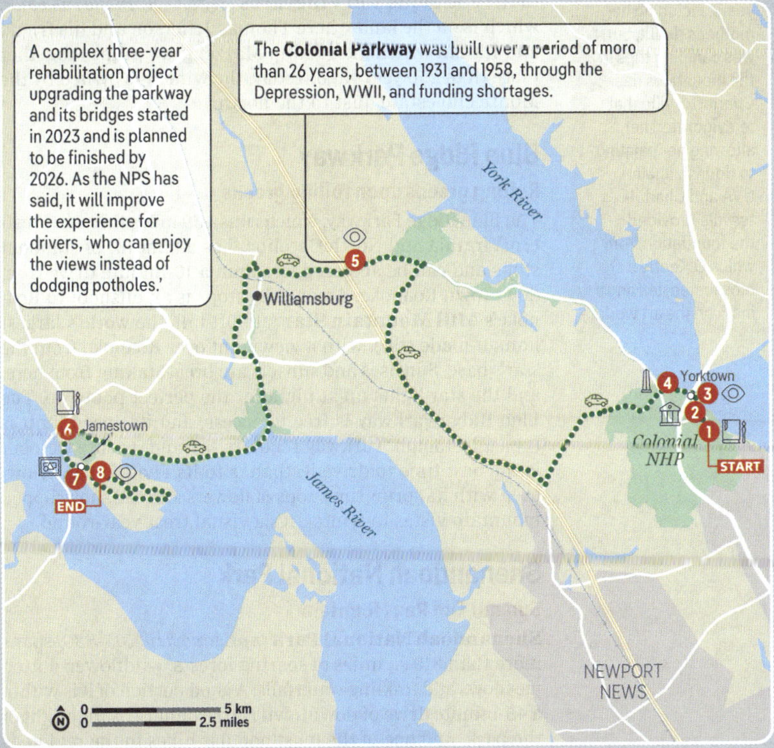

A complex three-year rehabilitation project upgrading the parkway and its bridges started in 2023 and is planned to be finished by 2026. As the NPS has said, it will improve the experience for drivers, 'who can enjoy the views instead of dodging potholes.'

The **Colonial Parkway** was built over a period of more than 26 years, between 1931 and 1958, through the Depression, WWII, and funding shortages.

York River
Williamsburg
Yorktown
Colonial NHP
START
Jamestown
END
James River
NEWPORT NEWS
0 5 km
0 2.5 miles

PROFESSOR O'KEEFFE

We can thank the hallowed halls of the University of Virginia for inspiring Georgia O'Keeffe to be the artist we recognize today. O'Keeffe spent summers at UVA studying art, eventually teaching some courses herself. It was under her teachers' mentorship that she began exploring the abstract, drawing inspiration from the Blue Ridge Mountains and campus life. O'Keeffe endured many trials over those years, including her mother's death, but it was camping trips in the mountains near Charlottesville that reinvigorated her, allowing her painting to flourish again. UVA and Charlottesville provided the foundation from which O'Keeffe's art blossomed, leaving a mark on the art world.

ANDREW GITTIS/SHUTTERSTOCK

and local icon Dave Matthews. Others to take in include **King Family Vineyards**, situated on a former thoroughbred horse farm; **Pippin Hill** *(pippinhillfarm.com)*, which is a rolling-hills staple with farm-to-table dinners and estate tours; and **Jefferson Vineyards** *(jeffersonvineyards.com)*, which is on the land where Thomas Jefferson and his friend and Italian winemaker Philip Mazzei grew grapes together more than 250 years ago. Today, the winery is owned by the Monticello estate, just to the north.

Blue Ridge Parkway

Rolling greens upon rolling greens

The Blue Ridge Parkway, which runs 469 miles through Western Virginia and North Carolina, has a handful of standout stops and can be accessed less than a 10-minute drive from downtown Roanoke. Among the stops is an offshoot to Roanoke's **Mill Mountain Star** (at 90ft tall, the world's largest human-made star), with a viewpoint over Roanoke from the star's base. Sunrises and sunsets are breathtaking from here, and the star lights up at night for the perfect photo op. The Blue Ridge Parkway is free to access, and its speed limit is typically 45mph. Parkway regulars say mid- to late October is the best time to drive it, thanks to its vivid foliage. However, with its springtime pops of flowers and the snowcapped mountain vistas in winter, it's a visual treat year-round.

Shenandoah National Park

Summit Old Rag Mountain

Shenandoah National Park *(nps.gov/shen, $15-$30)* spans more than 310 sq miles of soaring forests, wildflower-dotted meadows and tinkling waterfalls. A good portion of it is within a 45-minute drive of downtown Harrisonburg. A highlight of the park, and one of the most popular hikes in the region, is

Old Rag Mountain

Old Rag Mountain. You'll need to snag a day-use ticket in advance during peak season (March 1 through November 30). Allow seven hours for the hike – there are two different routes you can take, amassing approximately 2500ft in elevation. Along the way, count on some rock scrambles and boulder hiking. On completion, you'll be rewarded with 360-degree views of the valley, which glows yellow and orange during the fall foliage season.

Appreciate views on Skyline Dr

With 105 miles of mountain bliss, this public road through Shenandoah National Park provides awe-inspiring views from the crest of the Blue Ridge Mountains. There is no shortage of opportunities for snapping photos, with 75 overlooks along the way.

Virginia Beach

A non-bored walk

This much is certain: you might be on vacation, but you'll still want to wake early, plop it on the **Virginia Beach Boardwalk** adjacent to white sands and take in a sunrise. Beyond that, there is so much to explore along the boardwalk. Starting in the south at 2nd St and running north to 40th St, it

THE JM IN JMU

James Madison, born in Virginia in 1751 and nicknamed 'Father of the Constitution,' helped write the US Constitution and the Bill of Rights. Madison also cowrote the Federalist Papers, pushing for the Constitution's approval. As the fourth president, he led the nation during the War of 1812 and helped negotiate the Treaty of Ghent. Back home in Virginia, he was involved in founding the University of Virginia and served in the state's House of Delegates and the US House of Representatives. His legacy is closely tied to Virginia's history and politics. Today, Harrisonburg's own James Madison University bears his name as tribute.

EATING IN HARRISONBURG: FARM-TO-TABLE RESTAURANTS

Rocktown Kitchen: Locally sourced, seasonal American cuisine in an elevated yet casual dining venue. *11am-2:30pm & 5-9pm Tue-Sat* $$$

Local Chop & Grill House: Organic ingredients from neighborhood farms in the historic City Produce Exchange building; extensive whiskey selection. *4-11pm Mon-Sat* $$$

Magpie Diner: A 1950s service station turned modern diner, with locally roasted coffee and craft cocktails alongside seasonally inspired classic dishes. *8am-2pm Tue-Fri, from 9am Sat & Sun* $$

Little Grill: Cozy spot offering a menu for vegetarians and those seeking locally sourced organic-meat options. *hours vary* $

SURF'S UP, DUDE

Virginia Beach is home to the world's oldest continuously run surfing competition, the Coastal Edge East Coast Surfing Championship, locally known simply as ECSC. For more than 60 years, competitive surfers have flocked to the area to claim their place on the podium, creating an event that has morphed into so much more. The weeklong festival, typically held in August, delights with showcases in longboard, shortboard and stand-up paddleboarding. Through the years, other beach-favorite activities such as volleyball and street skating, live music, arts-and-crafts vendors and more have been added to the festival lineup, making ECSC an event for more than just wave riders.

spans 3 miles and is nearly 30ft wide in most spots. Among its quirkier highlights: just north of 30th St is Neptune's Park, where you'll find a large statue of the Roman god. At 38th St is the Navy Seal Monument, a life-size statue of a serviceman donning a swimsuit, flippers and weapon. At 25th St is the *Norwegian Lady* statue, commemorating a nearby shipwreck from the 19th century. For bird enthusiasts, the Atlantic Wildfowl Heritage Museum is housed in a small cottage near 12th St and is loaded with waterbird art, relics and exhibits, leaving you to surely say, 'What the...duck!' by the end.

Climb Cape Henry Lighthouse

There are many firsts pertaining to the 90ft-tall, red- and tan-bricked **Cape Henry Lighthouse**. Beyond being near the first landing site of English settlers in the US, the lighthouse also marks the first public-works project of the US government, overseen by Alexander Hamilton. The lighthouse is on the Fort Story military base, so you'll need to provide ID at the base's gate and then shuttles (which run every 15 minutes) take non-military civilians directly to the lighthouse. On arrival, there are 191 steps to climb to enjoy 360-degree coastal views from the cozy lantern room.

Norfolk

Explore naval history

It's only appropriate that Norfolk, about a 20-minute drive from Virginia Beach, has a naval museum on a ship. Part of the **Nauticus** maritime discovery center, the Battleship *Wisconsin* includes interactive spaces that you can stroll through, including an on-ship hospital with a surgery center, barber shop and even a brig where misbehaving sailors were temporarily jailed. There's also a sailing center on-site where you can take a craft for a guided spin on the water, with a unique perspective on downtown Norfolk's skyline. For a more relaxed time on the water, Half Moone Cruise and Victory Rover Naval Base Cruises are next door and offer narrated cruises of the city's coastline.

Chincoteague National Wildlife Refuge

Horsing around on the Eastern Shore

It's an otherworldly scene here, with wild horses roaming, chomping on marsh grasses and slurping up water from ponds, and **Chincoteague National Wildlife Refuge** *(fws.gov; pedestrian & cyclist/vehicle per day free/$10)* is the epicenter

DRINKING IN VIRGINIA BEACH: ORANGE CRUSHES

Waterman's Surfside Grille: The OG – Waterman's vodka, fresh OJ, a splash of Sprite, enjoyed at the beach. *hours vary*

Shack on 8th: Crush on Classic Orange to Honey Habanero among patio vibes with fire pits and yard games. *4pm-late Thu & Fri, from noon Sat & Sun*

Back Deck: Indulge in refreshing crush variations at this laid-back bayside waterfront venue. *11am-10pm*

Chix on the Beach: Beachfront crushes with the personal touch of lime and cranberry. *11am-10pm Sun-Thu, to 2am Fri & Sat*

ANTON_IVANOV/SHUTTERSTOCK

Arlington National Cemetery

of the action. In the refuge, which is located mostly on the Virginia side of Assateague Island (p278), about a two-hour drive from Virginia Beach, nearly 300 ponies wander through the forests and prairies and it's not uncommon to see colorful shorebirds and bald eagles soaring in the sky. **Assateague Explorer** *(assateagueexplorer.com)* has a Pony Express Nature Cruise, which lasts about two hours and coasts safely up to the horses. Perhaps the most unique pony spectacle in the region, held on the last consecutive Wednesday and Thursday in July, is the annual Pony Penning, where the area's ponies are guided to swim across the Assateague Channel to Chincoteague Island, where select foals are auctioned off. This sale helps to humanely control the pony population and proceeds benefit veterinary care for the herd.

Arlington

In solemn tribute

Arlington National Cemetery *(arlingtoncemetery.mil; free)* is a 693-acre military cemetery where over 400,000 people, including more than 300,000 veterans, lie at rest. The country's most famous cemetery isn't just a place to reflect or grieve – it's also a solemn but scenic walk through the nation's military history. Main sites include Arlington House, the former residence of Robert E Lee, and the gravesite of President

NAVIGATING IN & AROUND VIRGINIA BEACH

If you're sticking to the beach, strolls and a periodic rideshare (Uber or Lyft) will do the trick. Hampton Roads Transit operates an Atlantic Ave trolley that runs parallel to the boardwalk. There are plenty of touristy bike shops along the boardwalk area with hourly rentals as well as day packages in the $40 range.

For ventures beyond Virginia Beach, you'll need a car. Norfolk is an east-west straight shot along Interstate 264. The drive to Virginia's Eastern Shore has at its core a 17-plus-mile journey across the Chesapeake Bay Bridge-Tunnel. Within the over-under-water stretch, there are two 1-mile sections of tunnel. There's a $22 fee (round trip) on the Bridge-Tunnel, which is best navigated with an E-Z Pass.

EATING IN CAPE CHARLES: OYSTERS

Oyster Farm Seafood Eatery: Raw and steamed offerings, with a deck overlooking Chesapeake Bay. *4-8pm Wed & Thu, 11:30am-8pm Fri & Sat, to 3pm Sun* $$$

The Shanty: Cottage vibe with local oyster selections, rice bowls and orange miso-glazed calamari. *11:30am-9pm* $$

Hook @ Harvey: Open for dinner, with a bistro setting, rotating fare and ever-fresh seafood catches. *5-9pm Tue-Sat* $$$

Coach House Tavern: Tucked into a golf community, this neighborhood restaurant has fresh oysters served on the half shell. *hours vary* $$

John F Kennedy, with its eternal flame. The most notable site, however, is the Tomb of the Unknown Soldier, a tribute to the unknown fallen soldiers of the US's major wars. The neoclassical white-marble sarcophagus is guarded 24 hours a day.

To find a specific grave or memorial, download the ANC Explorer app, which has maps and photos down to individual tombstones.

WHY I LOVE FREDERICKSBURG

Jesse Scott, Lonely Planet writer

Consider me one of those dudes that's ultra-proud to be where he's from. Hint: it's Fredericksburg. In my 37 years, I've seen this town blossom from a sleepy Civil War town to one with a rockin' culinary scene, a broadminded and artsy vibe and rad public spaces. Rte 3 is now nuts with shopping and there's even a baseball team. Who woulda thought? Hurkamp Park has the giant word LOVE to take photos with – it's painted a different vibe each season. This town is full of love – people say hi to you on the streets, and generations want to tell you how proud they are to be from 'the 'Burg.' I don't blame them.

Fredericksburg

Historic-house hopping between revolutionary residences

The 'midpoint between Washington, DC and Richmond' and George Washington's boyhood home, beautifully preserved, heritage-filled Fredericksburg is home to numerous historic homes, some of which are open to the public and host regular tours.

Chatham Manor *(nps.gov)* looms over the Rappahannock River and dates back to 1771. During the Civil War, it was a hospital and Union headquarters, with famous visitors such as Abraham Lincoln and Walt Whitman. There are free walking tours of the grounds, including a stop with views of Fredericksburg's steeple-filled skyline. **Mary Washington House** *(washingtonheritagemuseums.org)* is a larger, white-paneled downtown home where George Washington's mother lived toward the end of her life (from 1772–1789). Beyond rooms set up to replicate Mary's lifestyle, the lush-yet-quaint gardens offer a lovely and colorful stroll, particularly in springtime.

Kenmore *(kenmore.org)* is another standout residence, constructed in 1775 by Fielding Lewis and his wife, Betty, who was George Washington's sister. At the time of its construction, it was an architectural marvel for its ornate plasterwork and ceilings, which have been tastefully restored through the years. If you plan to visit both Kenmore and Mary Washington House, buy a combo ticket at Kenmore for discounted entry.

Alexandria

A walk fit for a king

Old Town Alexandria is a nationally designated historic district and its core, King St, puts much of its zest on display, particularly between the King St Metro station and the Potomac River waterfront. Among the highlights is **Torpedo Factory Art Center**, a former munitions plant and now an art gallery. Inside, you can weave through the galleries of 70-plus local artists. For Alexandria-themed tchotchkes, the **Old Town Shop** has Americana-inspired ornaments, puzzles and charms. The **Alexandria Visitor Center** has some fun keepsakes, too, including an ever-evolving collection of history-themed candles. Eastward, King St culminates at a waterfront park with views of DC's skyline.

BOB POOL/SHUTTERSTOCK

Mount Vernon

Mount Vernon

Walk in Washington's footsteps

Mount Vernon *(mountvernon.org; adult/child $28/15)* was George Washington's most famous home, built by his dad in 1734. George and his wife, Martha, lived here for 40-plus years, with George dying here in 1799. To enter the grounds, you'll need to purchase a pass, with an additional fee to access the main mansion. There are a number of add-ons available from there – the best are a 45-minute boat excursion on the Potomac River and, for *Hamilton* lovers, a look at how Washington's life correlated with the famed Broadway show's songs.

Highlights in the mansion include Washington's private study and the majestic New Room. You'll also want to check out the farm space, with costumed interpreters depicting how Mount Vernon's workers sheared sheep, harvested crops and more. Mount Vernon was also once home to hundreds of enslaved people and among the more moving moments at the mansion is a small, replica slaves' cabin.

COBBLE, COBBLE

Embracing the historical whimsy of Old Town's cobblestone streets is no challenge. It's like stepping back in time. This style of paving wasn't chosen for its charm – during construction, cobblestones were affordable and readily available as merchant ships used river-rounded rocks as ballast in Alexandria. However, their durability posed challenges. Alignment issues and erosion meant ongoing maintenance, which eventually became unsustainable. Cobblestones eventually became a thing of the past in Alexandria as brick and other sturdier materials became more common. Ongoing preservation efforts, including the repaving of some cobblestones in 1979, have contributed to local conservation.

EATING IN ALEXANDRIA: BEST RIVER VIEWS

Vola's Dockside: Premier riverfront dining, with seafood, tacos, American classics and a mid-century-modern throwback in the Hi-Tide Lounge. *hours vary* **$$$**

Ada's on the River: Seafood and steaks surrounding a custom wood-burning oven with views of the Potomac. *hours vary* **$$$**

BARCA: Mediterranean fare, tapas and a wine bar situated on a pier. *hours vary* **$$**

Jula's on the Potomac: American classics on the 4th floor, with a terrace overlooking the river. *hours vary* **$$$**

West Virginia

WHITE-WATER | APPALACHIA | FORESTED SLOPES

Places

Charleston p299
New River Gorge p300
Hatfield-McCoy Trails p301
Point Pleasant p301
Sutton p302
Morgantown p303
Harpers Ferry p304
Berkeley Springs p305

'The sun doesn't always shine in West Virginia,' President John F Kennedy once said, 'but the people do.'

Kennedy wasn't alone in his affection for the Mountain State. 'Take Me Home, Country Road' is one of John Denver's most enduring ballads, and countless writers have waxed poetic on this wild and wonderful land. Yes, West Virginia has seen plenty of drama over the years, from the Hatfield-and-McCoy blood feud to the complicated legacy of coal mining, but open-minded visitors will find the best of Appalachia in these textured highlands. Nearly 80% of West Virginia is blanketed in forest, and its six national parks are a paradise for temperate wildlife – as well as birders, hikers and anglers. West Virginia's reputation for hospitality is also well earned, and locals tend to wear their hearts on their sleeves. As you fall into its down-home rhythms, you'll likely find yourself shining, too.

GETTING AROUND

With its odd shape and rolling topography, West Virginia is best explored 1 mile at a time. Drives can be long and service stations scattered, so keep an eye on the fuel gauge. While Greyhoud connects most major towns, tickets aren't cheap and the winding routes burn time: Morgantown to Charleston takes almost 10 hours. A car makes things easier and is necessary to really explore southern West Virginia. The tougher your vehicle, the better – while highways are well maintained, secondary roads have their share of potholes, and you don't have to stray too far to hit gravel and severe inclines. Central Charleston and Morgantown are walkable, and there are local buses.

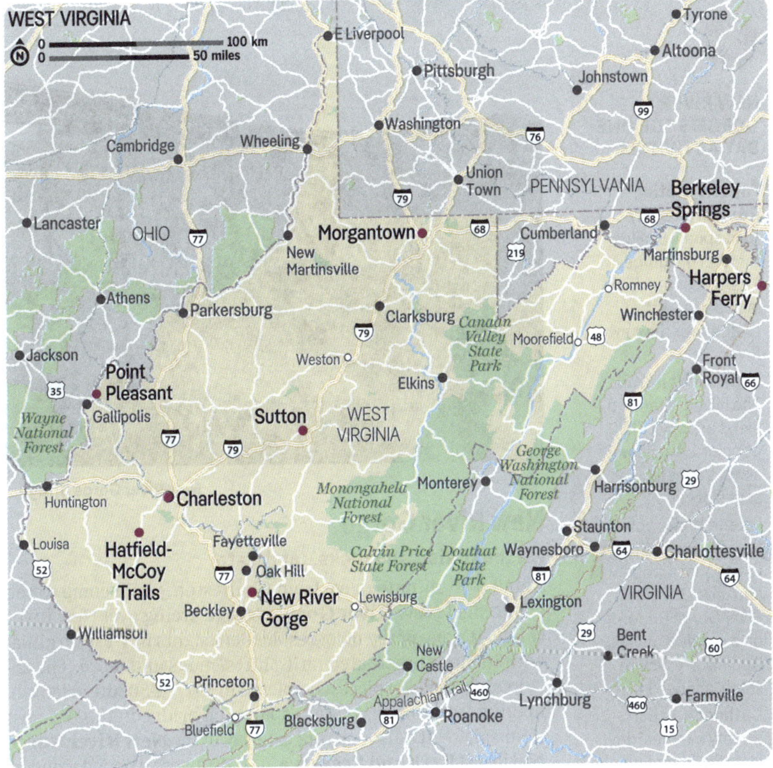

Charleston

A dusty district turned hip

Charleston, West Virginia's low-key capital, stands at the confluence of the Elk and Kanawha rivers and is hours from any major city, yet it packs a lot into its walkable central area. **Capitol St** is a tree-lined commercial strip with vintage storefronts, brick-paved sidewalks, brewpubs and restaurants. You can amble across downtown Charleston in no time, but the neighborhood is rich in historic architecture and commemorative plaques. The most recent addition is **Slack Plaza**, a beautiful pedestrian concourse, playground and splash pad. Two whimsical sculptures of fiddling musicians welcome you to the plaza, and real-life instrumentalists play here in the warmer months. Downtown Charleston is best enjoyed in the summer, when the streets are busy and food trucks are out, but Slack Plaza also has a skating rink in the winter. Just a few blocks away is the **Clay Center for the Arts and Sciences** *(theclaycenter.org; free)*, where you'll find a theater, art museum and planetarium in one facility – perfect for families and kids.

TOP TIP

Driving from Virginia, you can explore West Virginia's history in roughly chronological order – from the colonial getaway of Berkeley Springs (p305), head to Harpers Ferry (p304) for a lesson in abolitionism or Morgantown (p303) for a course on the Industrial Revolution. Then hike in the footsteps of Hatfield and McCoy (p301) before finishing at Charleston.

NEW RIVER GORGE'S TOP ONE-DAY ACTIVITIES

Fayette Station Rd: This one-way road spirals 8 miles through the gorge. The 40-minute drive includes a trestle bridge over the New River.

Endless Wall Trail: The hiking is tame; the views are epic. This popular 2.4-mile walk skirts a spectacular series of cliffs.

Bridge Walk: Join this tour *(bridgewalk.com)* to conquer acrophobia and cross the New River Gorge Bridge on a narrow catwalk. Don't worry; you're safely clipped in.

Cathedral Falls: Twenty minutes' drive from the bridge, this waterfall makes for a spectacular selfie. Park in the lot and you're steps away.

Bridge Day: Mark your calendars: the bridge is closed to motor traffic on the third Saturday of October. Pedestrians, vendors and BASE jumpers rejoice.

ZACHARY HOOVER/SHUTTERSTOCK

New River Gorge Bridge

New River Gorge

Hit the trails...and rocks...and water

About a 70-minute drive from Charleston, you'll come to the iconic steel **New River Gorge Bridge** arcing over New River Gorge. It's one of the most resplendent sights in West Virginia, with its image recreated on T-shirts, mugs and more. The architectural masterpiece, completed in 1977, is 3030ft in length, making it the longest single-span arch bridge in the Western Hemisphere. It's also a fitting gateway to the **New River Gorge National Park and Preserve**, a 70,000-acre wooded wonderland. The park is a magnet for hikers, campers, rock climbers and mountain bikers, especially in summer. Motor activities are also common here, with routes for 4WDs and snowmobiles and, after a good winter storm, snowshoers and cross-country skiers take over the trails. But even in the busiest months, you can find peace and solitude among the corrugated hills. The New River itself extends 53 miles through the protected landscape, with waters that range from calm and glassy to frothing class III rapids. The waterway's length attracts kayakers and white-water rafters from around the world, and the varying conditions appeal to both newbies and veterans. Many tour operators are based in Fayette County, but the largest and most dynamic is **Adventures on the Gorge**

EATING & DRINKING IN CHARLESTON: OUR PICKS

Adelphia Sports Bar: Bustling bar and dining room with a diverse pub menu and lots of TVs. *11am-11pm Mon-Wed, to midnight Thu-Sat, 1-10pm Sun* $$

Black Sheep Burrito & Brews: Upmarket Mexican fusion restaurant with reasonable prices, plus cocktails. *11am-9pm Mon-Thu, to 10pm Fri & Sat, 11am-3pm Sun* $$

Hale House: Refined bistro with a brick dining room and menu of 240 varieties of bourbon. Head downstairs to the Volstead speakeasy. *4-10pm Mon-Sat* $$

Fife Street Brewing: Lively taproom with high ceilings and big windows, on a lively pedestrian walkway. *11am-10pm* *(adventuresonthegorge.com)*, based in Lansing. This outfit can arrange class-V rafting trips, family ziplining and accommodations in its luxury cabins.

Fayetteville, a tiny historic town on the western side of New River Gorge, is just a mile from the bridge and makes a good base. Its Court St is lined with bistros, outfitters and antebellum houses, and visitors typically stop here to grab lunch and get their bearings. The town is ringed with hotels, lodges and campgrounds, and plenty of visitors bed down in Fayetteville while spending daylight hours in the park.

Hatfield-McCoy Trails

Hike through history

It's strange to think that these peaceful paths were once the backdrop for a bitter blood feud, with members of the Hatfield and McCoy clans spending 28 years treading these very routes in their quest for shotgun justice. What started as an argument over land rights in the 1860s ballooned into an interfamilial conflict, and at least 20 lives were lost in West Virginia's woodlands before its ceasefire in 1891. Founded in 2000, the **Hatfield-McCoy Trails** *(trailsheaven.com; permit $50)* extend more than 1000 miles through the southwestern quarter of the state, spanning nine counties.

Such a vast network has plenty of segments and trailheads, but the closest to Charleston is the **Ivy Branch trail system**. An entry point in the town of **Julian** stands about a half-hour drive from the capital, and you'll find a sizable parking lot and welcome center. From here, you can access 60 miles of rugged, wending paths.

Point Pleasant

A living folk hero?

West Virginia has many folk heroes, but none of them excites the imagination like the Mothman. This insect-human hybrid made its debut in *The Mothman Prophecies*, a 1975 memoir by John A Keel, which takes place in the small riverside town of Point Pleasant, about an hour's drive northwest of Charleston. The Mothman has gone on to win worldwide attention among cryptozoologists, and many a local has claimed to spot this winged, 10ft-tall critter in the wild. The legend inspired a 2002 feature film, *The Mothman Prophecies*, starring Richard Gere. A year later, a Mothman statue was unveiled in the middle of Point Pleasant. The statue stands directly in front of

OUTDOOR EXCURSIONS IN NEW RIVER GORGE

Bill Chouinard, pilot, vacation-rental operator and owner of Wild Blue Adventure Co *wildblueadventure company.com*

Fayette County is the epicenter of multisport days in the US. I moved here nearly 30 years ago, dropping out of college with $300 and a one-way ticket to the world-class climbing at New River Gorge.

I've spent almost three decades climbing, kayaking, mountain biking, running, paragliding, BASE jumping and now flying here. This place is more than just our home. It's fuel for daily inspiration, exploration and adventure. The thing that really makes this place stand out is the people – an incredible mix of locals and transplants drawn here by a common interest in the outdoors and everything it offers.

EATING IN FAYETTEVILLE: BEST GRUB

The Stache: Come for the toys and knickknacks; stay for the eclectic ice cream and candy. *11:30am-6pm* $

Wanderlust Creativefoods: Elegant and sophisticated plates in a cozy setting, with decor highlighted with attractive woodwork. *4-9pm Thu-Sun* $$

Southside Junction Tap House: LGBTIQ+-friendly corner bar in an old brick building. Craft beers, burgers and live music. *3-11pm Mon, Tue, Thu & Fri, 2-11pm Sat, to 9pm Sun* $$

Pies & Pints: Funky pizzas and a dizzying range of beers on tap in a polished modernist venue. *11am-9pm Sun-Thu, to 10pm Fri & Sat* $$

YARNS SPUN ABOUT THE HATFIELD-MCCOY FEUD

Blood Feud: The Hatfields & McCoys Novelist Lisa Alther presents an authoritative nonfiction biography of the Hatfields and McCoys and their multigenerational feud.

The Feud: The Hatfields & McCoys Dean King describes the peaceful coexistence between the two families before the Civil War wrenched them apart.

The McCoys Before the Feud: A Western Novel This fictional account by author Thomas A McCoy imagines his ancestors' less-known exploits in the American West.

The Coffin Quilt Ann Rinaldi's young-adult novel illustrates life in 1870s Appalachia through the eyes of young Fanny McCoy.

Hatfields & McCoys Kevin Costner and Bill Paxton star as rival patriarchs in this action-packed History Channel miniseries.

GEORGINA BURROWS/SHUTTERSTOCK

the **World's Only Mothman Museum** *(mothmanmuseum.com; adult/child $5/2)*, a small storefront that houses newspaper clippings, artwork and other ephemera. In the third week of September, the whole thing is commemorated with the annual Mothman Festival.

Sutton

Supernatural sightings and Bigfoot

About an hour's drive northeast of Charleston, in Sutton, is some more food for the imagination. The **Flatwoods Monster Museum** *(braxtonwv.org/the-flatwoods-monster; free)*, a former soda fountain, features the Flatwoods Monster, a 10ft-tall extraterrestrial with a red face and flowing gown that locals claimed to have spotted in 1952. The town embraces this strange episode with a sign that reads 'Home of the Green Monster,' a reference to the creature's green outfit. Just a block away is the **West Virginia Bigfoot Museum** *(wvbigfootmuseum.org; free)*, a roomy exhibition space dedicated to all things Sasquatch. This newest addition opened in 2021 and displays art, artifacts and testimonials from Bigfoot lore.

DRINKING IN CHARLESTON: LOCAL HAUNTS

Red Carpet Lounge: Local favorite, with a sizable patio out back and bargain prices. *11am-midnight Mon-Wed, to 1am Thu, to 2am Fri, noon-2am Sat, 1pm-midnight Sun*

Bar 101: Busy bar with craft beer, pub menu, regular DJs and throbbing dance floor. *11:30am-12:30am Mon-Thu, to 2am Fri, 1pm-2am Sat, to midnight Sun*

ROQ: Atmospheric lounge specializing in cocktails, live music and salsa dancing. Thoughtful menu, including flatbreads. *4pm-late Tue-Fri, from 5pm Sat*

Vino's Bar & Grill: Upstairs is a West Virginia lounge with a Manhattan streak; downstairs is a casual hangout. DJs, pool and pinball. *4pm-2am Tue-Fri, from 8am Sat*

Morgantown Rail Trail, Mon River Trail (p304)

Morgantown

Stroll High St

Most of the culture and nightlife in Morgantown, former coal capital and home of West Virginia University (WVU), is squeezed into High St, a long commercial corridor just east of the Monongahela River. On the north end, WVU campus crowns a hilltop with stately brick buildings, and students trickle down steep walkways to the restaurants, bars and galleries below. Weekends can get rowdy, as WVU has a long-standing party-school rep. One exception is First Friday, a family-friendly showcase of local artists and gourmands. The lynchpin of First Friday is the **Monongalia Arts Center** *(MAC; monartscenter.com)*, an historic gallery and performance venue.

The **Metropolitan Theatre** *(morgantownmet.com)* is an active show space for concerts, plays and comedians. Each year, some 35,000 theatergoers travel from across the tristate area, most to catch touring musicians. The auditorium dates back to 1924, when it served as a vaudeville stage. Nearby stands a statue of TV star Don Knotts, a beloved native son.

THE ORIGINAL MORGAN

Morgantown is named after its tough-as-nails founder, Colonel Zackquill Morgan, who was born in Wales and fought in both the French and Indian War and the American Revolution. Morgan and his wife, Catherine Garretson, weren't just early settlers in the region; they were the first known colonists to build a home on the land that would become West Virginia. In his postwar life, Morgan commissioned a courthouse and public square, and he personally opened the town's first tavern. In 2016, some 221 years after his death, a statue of Morgan was unveiled on Spruce St. It was sculpted by artist Jamie Lester, who also created the Don Knotts monument around the block.

DRINKING IN MORGANTOWN: BEST BARS

Gibbie's Pub & Eatery: Deep hangout with multiple bars, an impressive local beer selection and generous patio. Lots of local regulars. *11am-2:30am*

Apothecary Ale House & Cafe: Hip pub with vintage interior and wide selection of brews on tap. *11am-midnight Mon-Thu, to 1am Fri & Sat, noon-8pm Sun*

Metropolitan Billiard Parlor: Basement pool hall with a small bar and lots of vintage decorations. A local institution since Prohibition. *5-11pm Sun-Wed, to midnight Thu-Sat*

Sports Page: Immensely popular sports bar with TVs, wings baskets and a locally famous iced tea. *7pm-3am Thu, from 5pm Fri, 11am-3am Sat, noon-3am Sun*

OUTDOOR ACTIVITIES AROUND HARPERS FERRY

Maryland Heights Trail: This 6.5-mile trail has some tough climbs, but hikers are rewarded with unparalleled views of the town and valley.

River tubing: The lazy currents are ideal for floating downriver in an inflatable tube. Come summer, make arrangements with **River Riders** *(riverriders.com)*.

Ziplining: Fly along seven ziplines through the canopy, or walk an elevated skybridge, at **Harpers Ferry Adventure Center** *(harpersferryadventurecenter.com)*.

C&O Canal towpath: This segment of rail trail is part of a 333-mile bike route between Pittsburgh and Washington, DC.

Bolivar Heights Battlefield: These peaceful meadows and forest were hotly contested during the Civil War. See the cannons, fences and still-visible trenches.

The river itself – the 'Mon' – has always been the lifeblood of Morgantown, first for industry and now for recreation. Cycle or jog along the **Mon River Trail**, which snakes along the river for 19.5 miles, ending in the town of Reedsville, or rent a kayak or stand-up paddleboard from **Morgantown Adventure Outfitters** *(adventurewv.wvu.edu)* between April to October.

Harpers Ferry

Explore a Blue Ridge paradise

To call Harpers Ferry, about a three-hour drive from Morgantown, a special place is a serious understatement. Here, the beloved Shenandoah River merges with the Potomac on its journey to Chesapeake Bay. Three states – Maryland, Virginia and West Virginia – huddle together, and you can hopscotch across multiple borders without breaking a sweat. This valley has received more than its share of natural and structural beauty, thanks to rolling hills, soaring cliffs and two railroad bridges that span the wide waters. Even its architecture excels: the Historic District's stone houses, federalist brick facades and cobbled streets look virtually unchanged since hoop skirts were in fashion.

Harpers Ferry was also the backdrop for John Brown's final standoff. In 1859, the radical abolitionist attempted to attack the town, raid its armory and free enslaved people across the region. Instead, Brown's men embedded themselves in a local engine house and clashed with the US Army. Brown was tried and executed, but he became a hero of the antislavery movement.

You can see this story in three dimensions at the **John Brown Wax Museum** *(johnbrownwaxmuseum.com)*, which vividly brings this final struggle to life. Check before visiting, as the museum's fate was uncertain at the time of research. The center of the action was **John Brown's Fort** *(nps.gov; free)*, the name given to the little brick firehouse he used as a stronghold. The 'fort' has been moved slightly from its original location, but visitors can still tour the structure, and Harpers Ferry is packed with other monuments from the era. The town was literally designed for walking, but note that some streets are steep and not ideal for wheelchairs.

EATING IN HARPERS FERRY: UNIQUE VENUES

Rabbit Hole Gastropub: Craft cocktails and gourmet dining in a discerning country-charm setting. Beautiful porch and stone walls. *noon-8pm Mon-Thu, 11am-9pm Fri-Sun* **$$**

Kelley Farm Kitchen: West Virginia's first plant-based restaurant, set in a farmhouse. Riffs on traditional entrees and great ramen. *4-8pm Wed, from 11am Thu-Sat, noon-4pm Sun* **$$$**

Barn of Harpers Ferry: Converted barn with regular live concerts and creative libations. Food served Fridays and Saturdays. *4-11pm Wed-Sun* **$$**

Yatai Hibachi Food Trailer: Pan-Asian food truck. Claim a picnic table and watch chef Made Sudira work the hibachi. *11am-8pm Wed-Sat, noon-7pm Sun* **$$**

JON BILOUS/SHUTTERSTOCK

Harpers Ferry

Berkeley Springs

Soak in waters fit for a president

Not only did George Washington sleep here, he also bathed in Berkeley Springs – indeed, he was such a fan of the area, he bought up much of its real estate. Travelers have flocked to the town's 74°F thermal pools since colonial times, and Indigenous people likely enjoyed the mineral-rich waters long before that. Berkeley Springs is a two-hour drive from Morgantown and an hour's drive northwest of Harpers Ferry, but the mineral baths and quaint downtown are well worth the trip.

The town has two full-service retreats: **Atasia Spa** *(atasiaspa.com)* and Renaissance Spa at the **Country Inn** *(thecountryinnwv.com)*. You can also find warm waters in **Berkeley Springs State Park** *(berkeleyspringssp.com)*, home to the Old Roman Bath House. This historic brick structure contains a 750-gallon private mineral bath, where four adults can soak for up to an hour. All facilities offer a complete menu of facials, massages and other wellness services.

The town's main drag is, naturally, named Washington St, and its handful of shops and restaurants should occupy most visitors for an afternoon or two.

TOP SKI RESORTS OF WEST VIRGINIA

Canaan Valley: This state park has a sizable lodge, cabins and tent sites. There are 47 ski trails in the winter, plus an 18-hole golf course in summer. *canaanresort.com*

Snowshoe Mountain Resort: A beloved resort modeled on Alpine villages, boasting 14 lifts and 60 ski trails. Fire-tower visits and mountain biking are popular in summer. *snowshoemtn.com*

Winterplace Ski Resort: An intimate four season resort in southern West Virginia, with 28 trails, nine lifts and 16 lanes of snow tubing. *winterplace.com*

Timberline Mountain: A great place for beginners and crowd-shy skiers. Timberline has 37 easygoing trails and a 20-room boutique hotel. *timberlinemountain.com*

EATING AROUND BERKELEY SPRINGS: BEST BITES

Naked Olive Lounge: This Berkeley Springs olive-oil tasting room triples as a gourmet food market and LGBTIQ+-friendly cocktail lounge. *11am-11pm Fri & Sat, noon-6pm Sun* $$

Cacapon Mountain Brewing: Follow your spa session with a craft beer in an upbeat Berkeley Springs taproom. Kitchen window available for bites. *4-8pm Thu, noon-8pm Fri & Sat, to 6pm Sun* $$

Lot 12 Public House: Savor chef Damien Heath's masterful dishes and thoughtful wine pairings in a converted, century-old Berkeley Springs house. *5-9:30pm Fri & Sat, to 9pm Sun* $$$

Prima Marina: Riverside restaurant in Moundsville serves up hoagies, freshwater-fish platters and beautiful Ohio River sunsets. *11am-8pm Tue-Sat, to 3pm Sun* $$

Places We Love to Stay

$** Budget **$$** Midrange **$$$ Top End

Washington, DC

MAPS P241, P251, P253, P258, P260

Friends Place on Capitol Hill $ This Quaker guesthouse is possibly the friendliest and most affordable hostel in the city.

HighRoad Hotel $ One of the city's better budget options, with clean rooms, dorms and stylish decor in the heart of Adams Morgan.

Hotel Hive $$ Affordable, friendly and convenient (albeit with small rooms), with a bar and rooftop.

River Inn $$ Although not on the river, this quiet hotel near the Kennedy Center offers well-appointed suites and kitchenettes.

Motto by Hilton $$ The Motto offers 245 small, clean rooms in a great location with a rooftop bar.

Phoenix Park Hotel $$ Clean rooms, respectable amenities and solid service close to Union Station and Capitol Hill.

YOTEL Washington DC $$ Four-star contemporary business hotel with a rooftop pool and cool outdoor terrace, steps from Capitol Hill.

citizenM $$ Small but super-high-tech rooms and thoughtfully decorated common areas – perfect for single travelers.

American Guest House $$ Twelve-bedroom B&B in a home-style environment with comfortable rooms, friendly staff and great breakfast.

Swann House $$ Historic B&B with spacious rooms, aesthetically pleasing minimalist decor, impeccable service and a seasonally open outdoor swimming pool.

Mayflower Hotel $$$ Nicknamed the Hotel of Presidents for good reason – expect service worthy of a head of state.

Hay-Adams Hotel $$$ Expect old-school elegance at this luxurious heritage hotel with White House views.

Kimpton George Hotel $$$ Creamy-white rooms adorned with presidential pop art near Union Station. Kid- and pet-friendly.

Graham Georgetown $$$ Modernist boutique hotel in the middle of Georgetown with contemporary decor and rooftop lounge that's perfect for sundowners.

Delaware

MAP P266

Home2 Suites by Hilton (Dover) $$ A suite hotel within walking distance of downtown Dover attractions, with free breakfasts and an indoor pool.

Hilton Garden Inn Dover (Dover) $$ Close to Dover's casino, with an indoor pool and rooms with microwaves and mini fridges.

Causey Mansion Bed & Breakfast (Milford) $$ This landmark 18th-century building, set on a 3-acre property in Milford, is sprinkled with art, fountains and antique period details.

Hotel Rodney $$ (Lewes) In downtown Lewes, this historic hotel has fun furnishings and a British-style gastropub.

Hotel du Pont $$$ (Wilmington) Luxury Wilmington property with a spa, opulent lobby and food court in an Italian Renaissance building that debuted in 1913.

Avenue Inn & Spa $$$ (Rehoboth) One block from the beach in Rehoboth, with a spa and James Beard semi-finalist restaurant, the Blue Hen (p269).

Maryland

MAPS P280, P282

Assateague Island Campground (Assateaugue Island) $ Basic facilities and sometimes-crowded camping, but you'll wake to unobstructed views of the sea or bay.

Days Inn Ocean City Oceanfront (Ocean City) $ A good beachfront location at the northern end of the boardwalk, with helpful staff. The beach-facing rooms are worth the extra money.

King Charles Hotel (Ocean City) $ This aging but functional hotel is near the boardwalk.

Inn on Main (Annapolis) $$ In a central Main St location above Chick & Ruth's Delly (p274), with small, homey rooms. Breakfast included.

Historic Inns of Annapolis (Annapolis) $$ Enjoy Annapolis' 18th-century architectural heritage at three historic inns: Maryland Inn, Governor Calvert House and Robert Johnson House.

Whitehaven Hotel (Whitehaven) $$ This early 19th-century house overlooks the Wicomico River near Blackwater National Wildlife Refuge.

Rachael's Dowry B&B (Baltimore) $$ Spacious rooms in a restored historic house near Camden Yards.

ROB CRANDALL/SHUTTERSTOCK

Hay-Adams Hotel (p241), Washington, DC

BlancNoir (Baltimore) **$$** In Little Italy, easy walking distance from the Inner Harbor, with spotless, comfortable rooms.

Hotel Revival (Baltimore) **$$** Well located in the heart of the trendy Mount Vernon neighborhood, and billing itself as the city's only boutique art hotel.

Inn on Decatur (Cumberland) **$$** This biker-friendly B&B is near the trails in Cumberland. Management also runs the nearby budget- and cyclist-friendly 9 Decatur Guest House.

Virginia

MAP P288

Linden Row Inn (Richmond) **$$** Victorian-style inn with modern comforts. Enjoy the terrace and garden before making your way on foot to bustling Broad St.

Cedars of Williamsburg (Williamsburg) **$$** Georgian architecture, cozy rooms, friendly service and walkable to downtown.

Liberty Trust (Roanoke) **$$** Restored downtown bank incorporating original features such as a tasting room in the original vault.

Hotel Madison (Harrisonburg) **$$** Comfortable accommodations with refined touches close to downtown. Catch views of the city or the mountains and nods to James Madison.

Ironclad Inn (Fredericksburg) **$$** Historic residence turned inn walkable to downtown, with an Ironclad Distillery bourbon tasting room.

Boar's Head Resort (Charlottesville) **$$$** Modern amenities and outdoor activities with a classic appeal, surrounded by the rolling foothills of the Blue Ridge Mountains.

Hilton Virginia Beach Oceanfront (Virginia Beach) **$$$** Private balconies, panoramic ocean views, prime boardwalk location and a rooftop pool and bar.

West Virginia

Outpost (Fayetteville) **$** Cabins, tent platforms and RV hookups – this Outpost is ready for almost any kind of outdoors enthusiast. Regular fireside jams for music fans.

Brass Pineapple Inn (Charleston) **$$** This century-old inn was formerly a private home, and rooms retain an Edwardian homeyness. Some have claw-foot tubs. Room service on silver trays.

Glen Ferris Inn (Glen Ferris) **$$** A lovely way station for travelers for nearly two centuries, just a stone's throw from photogenic Kanawha Falls. Home-style restaurant.

Country Inn (p305; Berkeley Springs) **$$** Built in 1933, this Greek Revival–style estate is Berkeley Springs' keystone. Two restaurants, live music and a firepit.

Hotel Morgan (Morgantown) **$$$** Distinguished flagship hotel in the middle of Morgantown, fully renovated in 2020. Anvil + Ax is a gorgeous cocktail lounge on the 1st floor.

1799 Inn (Harpers Ferry) **$$$** When the Harpers Ferry armory was being built in 1799, workers stayed in this very house. The beautiful rooms thoughtfully blend old and new.

For places to stay in the South, see p424

MICHAEL WARREN/GETTY IMAGES

Above: Vicksburg National Military Park (p395); Right: Sun Studio (p347)

THE MAIN AREAS

NORTH CAROLINA
Enchanting cities, mountains and islands.
p314

SOUTH CAROLINA
Coastal allure and charming Charleston.
p333

TENNESSEE
The epicenter of country and blues.
p345

KENTUCKY
Bourbon distilleries, racehorses, wilderness.
p358

GEORGIA
Urban attractions and seaside beauty.
p366

Written and curated by
Regis St Louis

The South

BIRTHPLACE OF AMERICAN MUSIC AND CIVIL RIGHTS

Explore the nation's most misunderstood region, a dynamo of music, culture and history, set against a backdrop of vibrant towns and cinematic natural beauty.

The South is a land of ancient mountain peaks, alluvial plains and remote islands where wild horses still roam. It was one of the first regions of the US to be considered its own distinct place, not merely for its geography, but its literature, cuisine, lilting accents and above all its history – one that is long and beautiful in places, cruel and harrowing in others.

Jazz, blues, country and even rock and roll were born in the South. Music pilgrims come to visit famous sites like Graceland and Sun Studio to connect with the people and events that shaped history. Meanwhile fans of those distinct American sounds fill the clubs of Clarksdale, Memphis, Atlanta, Nashville and New Orleans to hear the great performers of today.

The human presence in the South dates back thousands of years, evident in the ruins left behind by the ancient mound builders. Native American tribes still retain strong ties to the land (visible in towns like Cherokee), while national park sites preserve the battlefields of the Civil War, as well as pivotal places in the fight for Civil Rights.

Despite all its heartache, the South has always been a hotbed of creativity, which you can explore in rural settlements and urban neighborhoods alike. It's also a place of unbridled outdoor adventure, whether biking the Ozarks, rafting Appalachian mountain rivers or hiking wilderness trails all across the region.

FIIPHOTO/SHUTTERSTOCK

ALABAMA
The heart of the Civil Rights movement.
p380

MISSISSIPPI
Historic sites and the Delta blues.
p389

ARKANSAS
Mountain biking, hiking and kayaking.
p397

NEW ORLEANS
Food-loving city of jazz and joie de vivre.
p407

LOUISIANA
Cajun music amid lush wetlands.
p420

Find Your Way

The South encompasses plains, forests, mountains and coastline, plus small towns and big cities found across the landscape. If time is limited, focus on a state or two rather than trying to see it all.

Arkansas, p397

Visit the Natural State for incredible mountain biking, hiking and canoeing, plus grand art museums, arts-minded communities and progressive college towns.

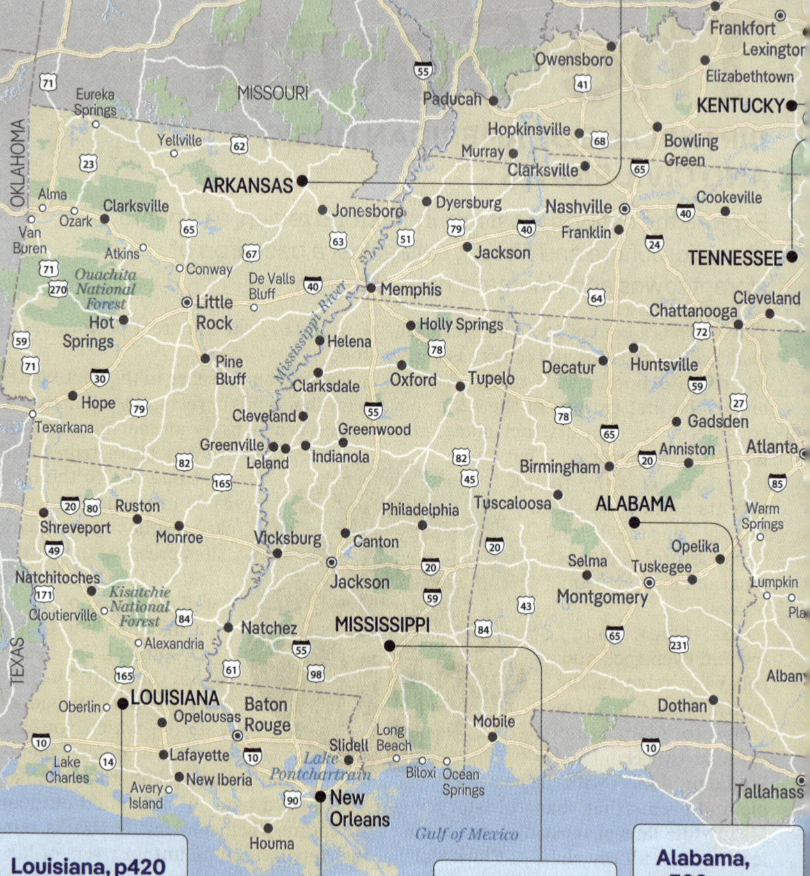

Louisiana, p420

Walk where ancient mound-builders dwelled, work the floorboards at a Cajun dancehall, and spy alligators and ibises on a wildlife-filled swamp tour.

New Orleans, p407

Home to French and Spanish colonial architecture and fiery jazz clubs, NOLA captivates with its decadent cuisine, buzzing nightlife and music-fueled festivals.

Mississippi, p389

The birthplace of the blues has juke joints and heritage museums, Civil War sites and serene towns perched alongside the USA's mightiest waterway.

Alabama, p380

Journey into the past at Civil Rights sites in Birmingham and Montgomery, then launch into the future in Huntsville (aka Rocket City).

Kentucky, p358

See the Derby in Churchill Downs, sip fine bourbons at famed distilleries, and trek the forests and falls of the Red River Gorge.

Tennessee, p345

Nashville's legendary music scene hogs the limelight, though there's also blues in Memphis, hiking in Chattanooga and mountain adventures in the Smokies.

North Carolina, p314

Go island-hopping in the Outer Banks, get active in the Appalachian mountains, and explore the arts in Asheville, Charlotte and Durham.

South Carolina, p333

Wonderful beaches are a big draw, as is charming Charleston. There are also islands, Gullah culture and paddling adventures in Congaree National Park.

Georgia, p366

Explore lively neighborhoods in Atlanta, see the Ocmulgee Mounds, get a taste of Savannah and unwind on picturesque islands like Jekyll and Cumberland.

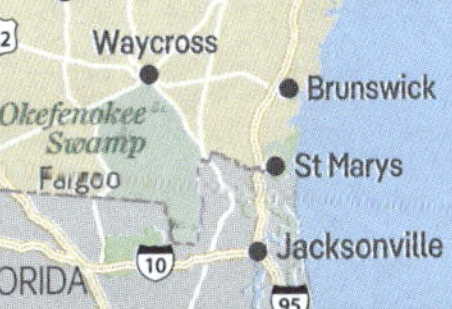

CAR

Getting behind the wheel gives you the freedom to explore beyond city centers. The South is a fine place for a road trip, whether tracing the Mississippi on the Blues Highway or discovering mountain towns across Appalachia.

BUS

Without a car, your best bet for navigating this vast region is Greyhound *(greyhound.com)*, which links major towns across the South. Megabus *(us.megabus.com)* also operates a few routes, mostly in Arkansas, Georgia and the Carolinas.

TRAIN

Various long-haul routes operated by Amtrak pass through the South. While not all that practicable, these train journeys offer outstanding scenery. One route links New Orleans with Memphis, while another connects numerous cities between New Orleans and NYC including Birmingham, Atlanta and Charlotte.

Plan Your Time

Don't try to cram in too much, though with a week or more to spare, you can see a few different regions of the South, including coastline, mountains and music-filled city neighborhoods.

MEUNIERD/SHUTTERSTOCK

Fort Sumter (p339)

24 Hours in the Big Easy

Head straight for **New Orleans** (p407), one of the most fascinating cities in the country. Start with a morning stroll in the **French Quarter** (p410). Get a dose of history at the **Historic New Orleans Collection** (p409) and learn about primitive medical practices at the **New Orleans Pharmacy Museum** (p409). Have lunch at the legendary Creole spot of **Dooky Chase** (p414), then board a vintage streetcar along Canal St to **City Park** (p419). Have beignets and chicory coffee at **Cafe Du Monde** (p419), stroll the Spanish moss-draped live oaks lining the bayou and visit the sculpture garden. In the evening, treat yourself to a meal in the delightful hideaway of **N7** (p415). Later, join the jazz-loving crowds on **Frenchmen Street** (p415).

Seasonal Highlights

The South is a year-round destination, with hiking, biking and aquatic adventures in the warmer months, abundant cultural offerings in the winter, and big celebrations and music fests throughout the year.

FEBRUARY

Head to the South to escape the winter chill. It's the most festive time of the year in New Orleans, which hosts several weeks of revelry (parades, costuming, music, merriment) leading up to **Mardi Gras** (p407).

APRIL

Clarksdale, Mississippi, draws blues fans from far and wide to its fabulous **Juke Joint Festival** (p392). You can catch outdoor concerts at stages around town and keep the party going at old-school music venues by night.

MAY

With spring in full bloom, pull out the pastel hues and head-turning hats for a trip to the Kentucky Derby. The exciting race is preceded by two weeks of celebration during the **Kentucky Derby Festival** (p360).

Seven Days in Georgia & the Carolinas

Start off in photogenic Savannah with a stroll through the **Historic District** (p376) and a tour of the **Owens-Thomas House & Slave Quarters** (p377). Crossing into South Carolina, visit **St Helena Island** (p340) to learn about Gullah culture, then enjoy some beach time at **Hunting Island State Park** (p341). Continue to **Charleston** (p334), one of the South's most beguiling cities. Take a deep dive into the past at the **International African American Museum** (p336) and the **Aiken-Rhett House** (p336), then see where war erupted at **Fort Sumter** (p339). Next up is **Wilmington** (p316), North Carolina, with its vibrant **river district**. Drive to Cedar Island and take the ferry to **Ocracoke** (p319), gateway to beaches and island lore on the Outer Banks.

10-day Road Trip from Appalachia to Mississippi

Begin in **Asheville** (p325), a bohemian town of crafts and breweries in the North Carolina Mountains. Enjoy outdoor adventures near **Brevard** (p327), then learn about the **Cherokee** in the town named for them (p328). It's a short drive into **Great Smoky Mountains National Park** (p329) for hikes amid forests, streams and waterfalls. Dust off your cowboy boots (or buy a pair) in **Nashville** (p351), country music capital, then continue west to **Memphis** (p347) for blues and barbecue. The theme continues south in **Clarksdale** (p391), where you can enjoy a night of Delta blues in juke joints like **Red's** and **Ground Zero** (p392). Head east into Alabama to visit the country's most powerful Civil Rights memorials, including the **Birmingham Civil Rights Institute** (p384) and Montgomery's **Legacy Sites** (p386).

JUNE

Summer days offer unrivaled adventures, especially in the mountains of North Carolina and Tennessee, where there's great mountain biking and hiking, as well as white-water adventures down the **Nantahala** (p328).

SEPTEMBER

With the summer crowds subsiding, it's a good time to head to the coast (but be mindful of hurricanes). You'll still find warm, pleasant temperatures along **Cape Lookout National Seashore** (p317) in North Carolina's Outer Banks.

OCTOBER

The forests in the upper South blaze with red, yellow and orange during the height of autumn. A prime place to experience the beauty is on the trails in the **Great Smoky Mountains National Park** (p329).

NOVEMBER

In the South, college football is practically a religion. Seeing a home game at any Southeastern Conferene stadium is not something you'll forget, especially if you watch the Alabama Crimson Tide take the field in **Tuscaloosa** (p385).

North Carolina

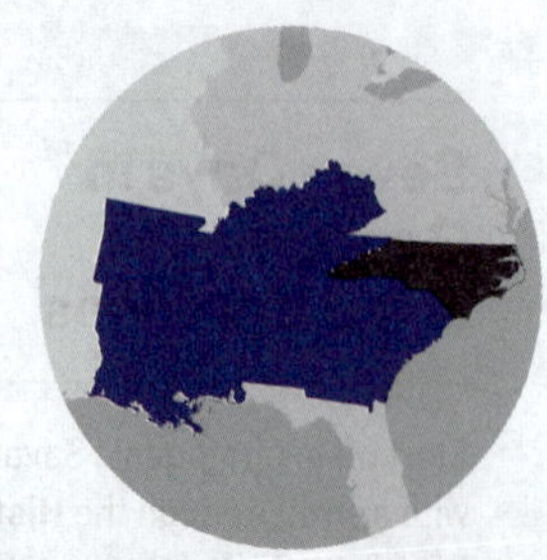

WILD COASTLINE | APPALACHIAN PEAKS | ARTS & CRAFTS

Places

Wilmington p316
Beaufort p316
Cape Lookout National Seashore p317
Outer Banks p318
Charlotte p321
Winston-Salem p323
Greensboro p323
Durham p323
Chapel Hill p323
Carrboro p325
Saxapahaw p325
Asheville p325
Blowing Rock p327
Brevard p327
Cherokee p328
Bryson City p328
Great Smoky Mountains National Park p329

TOP TIPS

On the Outer Banks, many restaurants have limited hours or close from November to March; call ahead to ensure your destination is open.

Blessed with islands and mountains, dynamic cities and arts-loving small towns, North Carolina seems to have it all. The state of 11 million residents also boasts astonishing diversity and a road trip here can take in everything from famous Civil Rights sites (Greensboro) to communities with deep-rooted Native American heritage (Cherokee).

The coast is synonymous with the Outer Banks – affectionately dubbed OBX – the chain of barrier islands that remain largely underdeveloped despite their popularity with summer vacationers. This is the region for visiting landmark lighthouses, seeing herds of wild horses and exploring hundreds of miles of windswept beaches.

Central North Carolina, also known as the Piedmont, is home to buzzing cities and appealing college towns (like Durham and Chapel Hill). West of there, the Appalachian Mountains hold some of the tallest peaks east of the Mississippi, and make a memorable setting for hiking, mountain biking, wildlife watching, rafting and numerous other outdoor adventures.

GETTING AROUND

Charlotte and the Triangle cities (Raleigh, Durham, and Chapel Hill) all have public bus systems, though using them takes some planning as they may be infrequent or limited. There are also intercity buses operated by Greyhound. Amtrak has several rail lines through North Carolina, connecting Raleigh, Durham, Greensboro and Charlotte by train. The North Carolina Ferry System *(ferry.ncdot.gov)* runs the state's ferry routes, including three to Ocracoke Island. Island Express Ferry Service *(islandexpressferryservices.com)* provides additional boats to the islands of the Cape Lookout National Seashore. Once on the islands, getting around by bicycle is an excellent option (especially in summer, when vehicular traffic can be a nightmare).

NORTH CAROLINA
KENTUCKY
VIRGINIA
TENNESSEE
NORTH CAROLINA
SOUTH CAROLINA
GEORGIA
ATLANTIC OCEAN
Lynchburg
Roanoke
Blacksburg
Petersburg
Virginia Beach
Norfolk
Danville
Kerr Lake
Currituck Sound
Kingsport
Mt Airy
Hyco Lake
Roanoke Rapids
Elizabeth City
Corolla
Bodie Island
Henderson
Hertford
Kitty Hawk
Nags Head
Manteo
Grandfather Mountain (5964ft)
Boone
Blowing Rock
Winston-Salem
Greensboro
Carrboro
Durham
Rocky Mount
Roanoke River
Albemarle Sound
Roanoke Island
Williamston
Knoxville
Mt Mitchell (6684ft)
Pisgah National Forest
Hickory
Morganton
Statesville
Saxapahaw
Chapel Hill
Raleigh
Wilson
Greenville
Belhaven
Outer Banks
Cape Hatteras National Seashore
Cherokee
Bryson City
Waynesville
Asheville
Brevard
Southern Nantahala Wilderness
Lake Norman
Mooresville
Concord
High Rock Lake
Asheboro
Uwharrie National Forest
Goldsboro
Washington
Hatteras Island
Avon
Hatteras
Pamlico Sound
Ocracoke
Ocracoke Island
Portsmouth Island
Shelby
Charlotte
Monroe
Southern Pines
Fayetteville
Kinston
New Bern
Croatan National Forest
Morehead City
Beaufort
Cape Lookout National Seashore
Spartanburg
Greenville
Broad River
Great Pee Dee River
Laurinburg
Lumberton
Cape Fear River
South River
Jacksonville
Toccoa
Florence
Whiteville
Wilmington
Carolina Beach
Athens
Atlanta
Columbia
Myrtle Beach
Bald Head Island
Augusta
Savannah River
Georgetown
0 100 km
0 50 miles
81
77
85
95
40
26
95
40

VENUS FLYTRAPS

Anybody who has seen *The Little Shop of Horrors* might be alarmed to learn that carnivorous plants grow wild in the wetlands of North Carolina. But never fear – real Venus flytraps and their brethren feast on insects and arachnids, not human flesh. A 'trap' is located at the end of each leaf; tiny hairs detect movement on the leaf and trigger its 'jaws' to clamp shut on the prey.

The Venus flytrap is cultivated around the world, but this unique plant is native only to the coastal bogs in North and South Carolina (specifically, within a 60-mile radius of Wilmington). See them in late spring and early summer, when the plants are blooming and actively trapping.

Wilmington

Bustling riverside city

Perched at the edge of the Cape Fear River, Wilmington grew prosperous on trade, especially after the arrival of the railroad in the 1840s. Nowadays, the historic downtown area is packed with handsome 18th- and 19th-century houses, plus colorful boutiques, craft-beer bars and classy restaurants, making it perfect for a wander.

Locals and visitors alike flock to the scenic riverfront boardwalk for waterside dining and sunset views. Docked on the west bank of the Cape Fear River, the mighty **Battleship North Carolina** *(battleshipnc.com; adult/child $14/6)* is an impressive sight from your vantage point across the river. Take the Bizzy Bee water taxi across to learn about the history and engineering of this storied WWII vessel.

Among Wilmington's most beloved destinations, **Airlie Gardens** *(airliegardens.org; adult/child $10/3)* is a 67-acre expanse of lawns, flowers and forest, bursting with blooms and dotted with artworks. Walking trails wind through the grounds and around a lagoon, connecting formal gardens and ungroomed forests.

Just 10 miles east of downtown are the sandy shores and crashing surf of **Wrightsville Beach**. Occupying a barrier island, this is a classic beach town, complete with windblown houses, seafood shacks, fishing piers and ice-cream stands, all lined up along the sandy lanes.

Beaufort

Discover the old town

Not to be confused with the similarly named town in South Carolina, Beaufort is one of North Carolina's oldest cities (c 1709), and it has the historic charm to show for it. In the heart of town, the delightful **Beaufort Historic Site** *(beaufort historicsite.org; tours adult/child $15/6)* includes seven 18th- and 19th-century buildings clustered around a shady green. Three historic houses are packed with period furnishings and artifacts, depicting daily life back in the day. There's also a jail, a courthouse and a 19th-century apothecary.

Wilderness of Rachel Carson Reserve

Beaufort overlooks a mosaic of scenic islands, marshlands and waterways that comprise the **Rachel Carson National Wildlife Refuge** *(fws.gov/refuge/rachel-carson)*. Here, ever-shifting

EATING & DRINKING IN WILMINGTON: OUR PICKS

Dixie Grill: Classic retro diner with retro diner fare, especially Southern classics like biscuits and gravy. *8am-3pm Mon-Sat, to 2pm Sun* $

Savorez: Its walls covered with artwork, this classy spot serves creative Southern food with Latin flair. Tops for Sunday brunch. *11:30am-10pm Mon-Sat, 10am-2pm Sun* $$

Fork 'N' Cork: Convivial bar with a dozen decadent burgers on the menu, plus craft cocktails and a daily-changing special mac and cheese. *11am-11pm* $

Flytrap Brewing: Sample American and Belgian-style ales alongside food-truck fare (and weekend live music). *3-10pm Mon-Thu, noon-midnight Fri & Sat, noon-10pm Sun*

Battleship North Carolina

islets and shoals provide refuge for wild horses, river otters and water birds. The best way to experience this blissful place is to rent a kayak or take a tour with **Beaufort Paddle** *(beaufortpaddle.com; half-day rental single/double $60/75, tour adult/child $65/45)*. Pull your kayak up onto the sandy beach at the western end of Town Marsh to explore several different habitats on two 1-mile loop trails. Be sure to bring water, as there are no facilities and little shade in the reserve.

You can also visit the Rachel Carson Reserve in the comfort of a covered boat with **Water Bug Tours** *(waterbugtours.com; adult/child $20/10)*. No paddling required!

Cape Lookout National Seashore

Explore the rugged coastal beauty

The most rewarding day trip from Beaufort, **Cape Lookout National Seashore** *(nps.gov/calo)* is a 56-mile stretch of windswept, wave-beaten barrier islands. The jumping-off point is Harkers Island, which is 17 miles east of Beaufort. There's a visitor center with a few exhibits, but most folks just hop on the Island Express Ferry Service *(islandexpressferryservices.com; adult/child $30/20)* and head out to the islands.

Your first stop is **Shackleford Banks**, a starkly beautiful place strewn with wildflowers and home to wild 'Banker'

BLACKBEARD THE PIRATE

Fierce and fearsome, Blackbeard terrorized ships up and down the East Coast in the early 18th century. In 1718 his fleet blockaded the port of Charleston, SC, demanding food and supplies and holding the city hostage for several weeks. Shortly thereafter, Blackbeard surrendered to the North Carolina governor, promising to change his ways. The reformed pirate settled down with his new wife in Bath.

This period of respite did not last long, however. Blackbeard soon returned to piracy, with the Royal Navy in hot pursuit. On November 22, 1718, Lieutenant Robert Maynard ambushed the pirate at Ocracoke Inlet, arresting or executing his crew. Blackbeard's head was cut off and hung from the bow of Maynard's ship, an ignominious end for a notorious swashbuckler.

EATING & DRINKING IN BEAUFORT: OUR PICKS

Turner Street Market: A quick, central place for fresh sandwiches, salads or hot breakfast. *7am-2pm* $

Black Sheep: A lovely waterfront setting to nosh on crusty pizzas with tasty toppings. Extensive drink menu too. *11am-9pm Wed-Sun* $$

Beaufort Grocery: Cozy, convivial bistro serving homemade soups and sandwiches by day, fancy dinners by night. *11:30am-9:30pm Thu-Sat & Mon, 10am-2pm Sun* $$$

Backstreet Pub: Cool cubbyhole with a breezy courtyard. Weekend live music, midweek 'Hoot Nite' jam sessions. *noon-close Mon-Sat, from 5pm Sun*

BEST ART GALLERIES IN OCRACOKE

Village Craftsmen: Run by the 10th generation of Howards on Ocracoke, this gallery features local arts and crafts and plenty of history.

Down Creek Gallery: This place overlooking Silver Lake offers fine art by Ocracoke and Hatteras artists, including paintings, pottery, glasswork and more.

Bella Fiore: Creative gifts and accessories, including scarves, bags, hats and exquisite handcrafted jewelry.

Over the Moon: Packed with quirky and clever gifts, art from recycled materials and funky arts and crafts.

Art Ocracoke: Island-inspired pieces, especially paintings of lighthouses, beaches and resident creatures.

CHANSAK JOE/SHUTTERSTOCK

Ocracoke Lighthouse

ponies. Trails crisscross the island, but they can be marshy depending on the tide. Pack a picnic and spend a few hours birding, pony-spotting and snapping pics of the supremely picturesque landscape.

From here it's a short ride to **Cape Lookout** with its distinctive diamond-patterned lighthouse. Wide and wild, the beach here is prime for swimming and beachcombing. 'Beach shuttles' take passengers around the abandoned buildings of Cape Lookout Village and down to the Point, the southernmost tip of the cape.

Outer Banks

Shipwrecks and wild beaches

Hatteras and neighboring Ocracoke Islands make up the **Cape Hatteras National Seashore**, a preserve of sand dunes and salt marshes, including 70 miles of glorious, undeveloped beaches. At the southern end of Hatteras, a few laidback beach towns cater to families, fisherfolk and surfers, but it's pretty quiet outside of the summer months.

The seafloor here is strewn with thousands of shipwrecks, earning it the nickname 'Graveyard of the Atlantic.' Every wreck has a story, and many are told at the **Graveyard of the Atlantic Museum** *(graveyardoftheatlantic.com; free)*

EATING ON HATTERAS ISLAND: OUR PICKS

Buxton Munch: Cheerful longtime favorite serving up nosh-worthy fish tacos, avocado wraps and crabby patties. *11am-3pm Tue-Sat* $

Orange Blossom Bakery: Filling breakfast sandwiches and irresistible pastries. A Buxton institution and worth the wait. *6:30-11am* $

Tavern on 12: Wildly popular local spot for elevated pub fare, including crab cakes, po' boys and Hatteras-style clam chowder. *11am-8pm Tue-Sun* $$

Oceanas Bistro: Islanders congregate at this Avon haunt for delectable 'grillers' (open-faced quesadillas), many featuring local seafood. *8am-10pm* $$

in Hatteras. Artifacts, photographs and video footage bring the history to life – not just the disasters but also the heroic lifesaving efforts of local villagers.

The **Hatteras Island Ocean Center** *(hioceancenter.org; free)*, is an indoor-outdoor nature center that's all about life in the marsh. See it up close as you walk along the scenic boardwalk and trail that wind through the salt marsh and maritime forest. Look for birds including herons, egrets, kingfishers, ibises and ospreys, as well as turtles, snakes and skinks. It's particularly lovely in the early morning and late afternoon.

Go carefree (and car-free) on Ocracoke

Take the ferry to Ocracoke Island to frolic on untamed beaches, explore the historic village and immerse yourself in local lore. The island's unofficial historian, Philip Howard, is a descendent of William Howard, the first European owner and settler of Ocracoke. Howard narrates two entertaining walking tours that are available for download at Ocracoke Navigator *(ocracokenavigator.com)*. Follow the tour 'Around Creek' to see the historically important sites northeast of Rte 12, such as the **British Cemetery** and the **Ocracoke Preservation Museum** *(ocracokepreservation.org; free)*. Southwest of Rte 12, the tour 'Down Point' includes the **Ocracoke Lighthouse** and grand **Berkley Manor**, built by inventor, industrialist and local icon Sam Jones. Packed with anecdotes and quirky characters, the tours offer fascinating insights into Ocracoke history, culture and island life. Both tours start at the Village Craftsmen *(villagecraftsmen.com)*.

A well-groomed (but poorly marked) half-mile trail traverses **Springer's Point Preserve** *(coastallandtrust.org)*, a lush and scenic area of maritime forest, salt marsh and sandy beach. Look for the side-by-side graves of the former property owner, the aforementioned Sam Jones, and his beloved horse Ikey D. The route ends at the waterfront, where herons, egrets and ibises nest nearby.

Searching for the Lost Colony

In the 1580s – more than two decades before Jamestown – English settlers came to Roanoke Island to establish the first British colony in the Americas. The first English-American baby, Virginia Dare, was born in 1587. The site of this settlement is part of the **Fort Raleigh National Historic Site** *(nps.gov/fora)*. Unfortunately, the colony struggled from the get-go, and the governor had to return to England for supplies. By the time he made it back, his 116 compatriots had disappeared, almost without a trace. The fate of the 'Lost Colony' remains one of the United State's greatest mysteries.

Exhibits at the visitor center delve into the settlement's backstory and the theories behind its disappearance. Nearby are the remains of the earthen fort that was constructed by colonists in 1585. The next stop in your 'Lost Colony' experience is **Roanoke Island Festival Park** *(roanokeisland.com; adult/child $11/8)*, an indoor-outdoor living history museum on the Manteo waterfront. Back at Fort Raleigh,

FREEDMEN'S COLONY

Mike Anderson is an interpretive park ranger at Fort Raleigh National Historic Site *@fortraleighnps*

While Fort Raleigh National Historic Site is best known for the 16th-century Lost Colony, my favorite piece of the park's history is the 19th-century Freedmen's Colony, which was a safe haven for thousands of freedom-seekers during the Civil War. The goal of the Freedmen's Colony was to help formerly enslaved people claim their rights, by reuniting families, providing education, creating jobs and giving opportunities for property ownership. This story sheds light on the role of Roanoke Island in the struggle for freedom from slavery. Visitors can learn more by participating in a ranger program, exploring the exhibits at the visitor center or walking the Freedom Trail.

BEST HIKES IN THE OUTER BANKS

Nags Head Woods Preserve: Eight trails cross the maritime forest, thick with ancient oaks, hickories and birch.

Kitty Hawk Woods: Nearly 2000 acres of maritime forest, swamp and freshwater wetlands, rich with bird and animal life.

Dogwood Trail: A 5-mile paved path loops around Duck Woods Country Club, alongside a picturesque creek in Southern Shores.

Currituck Banks Maritime Forest Trail: A 1-mile trail snakes through salt marsh and maritime forest, ending at Currituck Sound. Lovely for sunsets.

Freedom Trail: This 1.3-mile route connects Fort Raleigh to Croatan Sound, with signposts detailing the history of the Freedmen's Colony.

the highlight of Manteo's historical experiences is surely the Tony-winning play the **Lost Colony** *(thelostcolony.org; adult/child from $25/12; late May-Aug)*, performed at the outdoor theater. This extravagant musical dramatization features Native American dance, Elizabethan costumes and epic battle scenes.

Flounder and dunes on Nags Head

Many a fisher has been known to while away a summer day (or a summer) waiting for a bite at **Jenette's Pier** *(jennettespier.net; adult/child fishing $14/7, walk-on $2/1, rod rental $12)*. Anglers of all ages and backgrounds line the rails, nurse cold drinks, cast their lines and share stories about big catches and near misses. It's fun to watch and even more fun to join in. All-inclusive 'family fishing' lessons (adult/child $20/10) are available for first-timers.

Five miles north of the pier, **Jockey's Ridge State Park** *(ncparks.gov/jockeys-ridge-state-park)* is a vast, desert-like landscape comprising the tallest dune system on the East Coast. Miles of sandy hills roll all the way to Roanoke Sound. Tracks in the Sand is an out-and-back, 1.2-mile trail that traverses the dunes. For a bit more adventure, rent a sandboard from **Kitty Hawk Kites** *(kittyhawk.com; $25)* and sled down. The steeper the hill, the faster you go. Prepare to get sandy.

Powerful winds mean that kite-flying at Jockey's Ridge is a popular pastime. The summit is also a premier spot to watch the sunset over the sound.

Historic flight from Kitty Hawk

On December 17, 1903, Wilbur and Orville Wright launched the world's first successful airplane flight at Kitty Hawk (now Kill Devil Hills). The 12-second flight is memorialized at the impressive **Wright Brothers National Memorial** *(nps.gov/wrbr; adult/child $10/free)*. The First Flight Boulder marks the takeoff point, with additional markers showing the distances of their four increasingly successful flights that day. The on-site visitor center has a full-size reproduction of the 1903 flyer, as well as excellent exhibits about Wright family life, the brothers' scientific process and their competitors in the race to fly.

Village and equine life in Corolla

The centerpiece of this little village is **Historic Corolla Park** *(visitcurrituck.com)*, a pleasant manicured space dotted with museums and historic buildings, including a

EATING & DRINKING IN THE OUTER BANKS: OUR PICKS

Art's Place: Fab local spot in Kitty Hawk for beers and burgers, plus live music on the outdoor stage. *7am-9pm* **$$**

Kill Devil Grill: In a historic diner car, this casual place serves sophisticated Southern-influenced fare. *11:30am-9pm Tue-Sat* **$$**

Corolla Beer Garden: Tiny wooden shack with a big shady garden and 14 beers on tap, plus occasional live music. *2pm-sunset Apr-Oct*

Blue Moon Beach Grill: Not on the beach but still a fabulous stop in Nags Head for seafood and sandwiches. *11:30am-9pm Wed-Mon* **$$**

ACESHOT1/SHUTTERSTOCK

Whalehead Club

fabulous art-nouveau 'cottage,' dubbed the **Whalehead Club** *(adult/child $7/5)*. A 45-minute audiotour of the house gives insights about the history of the property and shows off its art-nouveau ornamentation. Nearby, the red-brick **Currituck Beach Lighthouse** *(obcinc.org; adult/child $13/free)* still shines its beacon to warn ships away from the barrier islands. You can climb the 220 steps to the top, which offers 360-degree views of sea and sound.

Wild mustangs roam freely on the beaches and dunes north of Corolla. If you don't have a 4WD, **Corolla Outback Adventures** *(corollaoutback.com; $68)* and **Wild Horse Adventure Tours** *(wildhorsetour.com; $65)* offer excursions that bounce you down the beach and over the dunes in the back of an open-air truck in search of the feral creatures.

Charlotte

Museums and galleries galore

North Carolina's largest city, Charlotte has an increasingly big and boisterous arts scene, with once-empty industrial zones now teeming with record stores, galleries, vintage boutiques and concert venues. A single block holds three of the best art spaces, all under the umbrella of the Levine Center for the Arts. The impressive **Mint Museum Uptown** *(mintmuseum.org;*

WILD-HORSE HISTORY

Nobody knows exactly how the wild Spanish mustangs ended up in the Outer Banks, but historians believe they arrived with the first Spanish explorers, as early as 1526. Others theorize that some horses swam ashore from shipwrecks – or were deliberately offloaded as extra weight when ships ran aground on the sandbars. In any case, the so-called Banker horses have flourished on the Outer Banks for hundreds of years, with a peak population of 5000 animals in the early 20th century.

Nowadays, the **Corolla Wild Horse Fund** *(corollawildhorses.com)* manages and protects the herd of about 100 members in Corolla. Visitors can learn more (and meet rescued and rehabilitating horses) at its Betsy Dowdy Equine Center *(10am-2pm Wed Jun-Sep)* in Grandy.

EATING IN CHARLOTTE: OUR PICKS

Mert's Heart & Soul: Homey soul food and Lowcountry cuisine diner. Don't miss the salmon cakes or the shrimp and grits. *11am-8pm* $$

Optimist Hall: Buzzy food hall with global offerings; crispy okra fries at Botiwalla and buns at Bao & Broth are highlights. *7am-9pm* $

Alexander Michael's: In an old blue house, this beloved Uptown tavern has welcoming vibes and comfort food with a twist. *11am-10pm Tue-Sat* $$

Supperland: In a former church, 'Supperland' describes itself as 'Southern steakhouse meets church potluck.' *5-10pm Mon-Thu, to 11pm Fri & Sat, brunch 10:30am-1:30pm Sat & Sun.* $$$

THE GREENSBORO SIT-INS

On February 1, 1960, four Black college students sat down at a whites-only lunch counter at Greensboro's Woolworth's department store. When asked to leave, they refused; they sat until the store closed that night. The next day, more students joined. Soon, hundreds of Black students were participating in what became known as the Greensboro Sit-Ins. These sit-ins quickly spread to other cities in the South, where segregation persisted in stores, restaurants, buses and schools. Sit-ins became boycotts of stores with segregated lunch counters, and owners began losing revenue. By July the Greensboro Woolworth's had taken a major financial hit and agreed to desegregate. Sit-ins as a form of nonviolent protest would continue throughout the Civil Rights movement.

JAY YUAN/SHUTTERSTOCK

Duke University

adult/child $15/free) has galleries surrounding a four-story atrium. Just across the way is the **Bechtler Museum of Modern Art** *(bechtler.org; adult/child $10/5)*, with a small-but-mighty collection of work by mid-20th-century modernists like Giacometti, Miró and Picasso. A block away is the ochre modernist building of the **Harvey B Gantt Center** *(ganttcenter.org; adult/child $9/7)*, with a small permanent collection and rotating exhibitions of contemporary Black works.

Raft the urban environment

Northwest of Charlotte, on the banks of the Catawba River, the **US National Whitewater Center** *(whitewater.org)* is all about outdoor adventure – especially the kind that gets you extremely wet. The main attraction is the artificial river, where visitors run rapids in kayaks or guided rafts *($59)*. But an all-access day pass *(adult/child $79/69)* will also get you climbing, ziplining, stand-up paddleboarding, doing yoga and more. Reserve your rafting time when you buy tickets, ideally for the first trip of the day – these can fill up.

EATING IN DURHAM: OUR PICKS

Guglhupf: Crowds pack the patio of this German-style bakery-cafe for schnitzel and *schnecken* (sweet rolls), washed down with pilsner. *8am-8pm Tue-Sat, to 3pm Sun* **$$**

Little Bull: Creative Mexican-American comfort food like *birria* (stewed meat) dumplings and steak with peanut salsa draw raves. *5-10pm Wed-Sun, plus 11am-2:30pm Sun* **$$$**

King's Sandwich Shop: Order at the window and take your chili dog and milkshake to a picnic table at this 82-year-old institution. *11am-4pm Mon-Sat* **$**

Zweli's: Bright cafe in a renovated tobacco warehouse serving Zimbabwean classics like piri piri chicken and greens in peanut-butter sauce. *5-9pm Tue-Thu, 11am-8pm Sun* **$$**

Winston-Salem

Peer back to the 18th century

Members of a German-speaking Protestant sect called the Moravians settled in what's now Winston-Salem in the late 1700s. Today, **Old Salem** *(oldsalem.org; adult/child $30/16)* is a living history museum extending across several blocks south of downtown. It's free to admire the architecture, shop for crafts or buy cookies at the wonderful, wood-fired Winkler Bakery. But you'll have a much richer experience if you pay for access to the on-site museums, houses and workshops, where costumed guides demonstrate Moravian traditions such as gardening, doctoring and gunsmithing.

Greensboro

Pioneers of the Civil Rights

In the Woolworth's building that was the site of the original Greensboro Sit-Ins, the powerful **International Civil Rights Center & Museum** *(sitinmovement.org; self-guided tour $15)* is dedicated to the history and legacy of the USA's Civil Rights movement. You can take a self-guided tour of the permanent exhibit, with pictures, videos and artifacts including the original Woolworth's lunch counter, but spending the extra $5 for the guided tour is well worth it.

Durham

A Day at Duke

In the town of Durham, **Duke University** is one of the country's most prestigious institutions of higher learning, with a splendiferous Gothic-style campus to match. The main attraction for visitors is **Sarah P Duke Gardens** *(gardens.duke.edu; free)*, an expansive 55 acres of koi ponds, terraced flower gardens and magnolia groves. Descend the original terrace where seasonal flowers are planted in luscious tapestries, wander the graceful bridges and stone paths of the Asiatic Garden, and picnic on the wide lawns.

Durham's coolest attraction has to be the **Duke Lemur Center** *(lemur.duke.edu; adult/child $17/12)*, a research and conservation institute that's home to the largest collection of lemurs outside their native Madagascar. Visits are by guided tour only, and must be reserved weeks if not months in advance.

Chapel Hill

College days

Strolling along a brick path through a shady quad surrounded by antebellum buildings: this is the **University of North Carolina** *(unc.edu)*, the US's oldest public university. You can easily spend half a day walking the historic campus, visiting photo hot spots like the Old Well (drinking from it is said to bring straight As), the flower-filled Coker Arboretum, and the Davie Poplar, which was already a century old when UNC was founded in 1793.

THE TRIANGLE

Raleigh, Durham, Chapel Hill: three points on the isosceles triangle that give the region its name. The three cities are deeply interconnected but also have their own identities. **Raleigh** has all the things you'd expect of a state capital: government workers bustling around downtown on their lunch hour, big museums full of kids on field trips, steak houses serving rib eyes to movers and shakers. **Durham** is diverse and progressive, with a downtown of old brick tobacco warehouses now full of restaurants, bars, bookshops and tech-company offices. College town **Chapel Hill** has long been nicknamed 'The Southern Part of Heaven,' and in the spring when the dogwoods and cherry trees bloom on campus and the sky is Carolina blue, it's easy to see why.

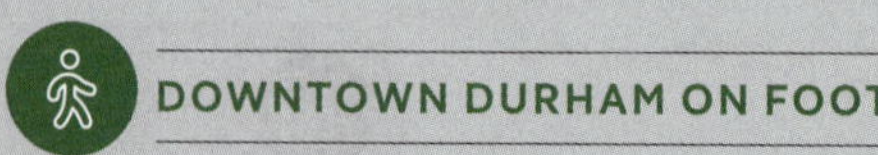

DOWNTOWN DURHAM ON FOOT

Wander among the stylishly renovated warehouses of this tobacco town turned arty hot spot.

START	END	LENGTH
Brightleaf Sq	Durham Bulls Athletic Park	1.2 miles; 2 hours

Begin at ❶ **Brightleaf Square**, where two historic brick tobacco warehouses are home to restaurants, boutiques and a charming antiquarian bookstore.

Walk southeast down Main St, noting the massive 1948 ❷ **Chesterfield Building**, one of the last cigarette factories to be built in Durham.

After 0.5 miles you'll come to ❸ **Five Points**, where Main St meets Chapel Hill St. Continue past the pretty brick and stone storefronts and restaurants on Main until you reach Corcoran St. Here you'll find the ❹ **21c Hotel**, with edgy public art in an old bank tower designed by the architects of the Empire State Building.

Go north on Corcoran to CCB Plaza, where the iconic bronze ❺ **bull statue** (its official name is *Major*) is the subject of thousands of Instagram posts.

Half a block east on Chapel Hill St is the ❻ **Durham Hotel**, in a mid-century modern bank building.

Turn right on charmingly cobblestoned ❼ **Orange St**, then again on ❽ **Parrish St**, once known as 'Black Wall St' for its many Black-owned banks and businesses in the late 1800s and early 1900s.

Two blocks south, at 201 Pettigrew St, is the splendid Italianate ❾ **Old Bull Building**. Finished in 1874, it's downtown's oldest edifice. Continue south to the restaurant- and shop-filled ❿ **American Tobacco Campus**, across from the beloved ⓫ **Durham Bulls Athletic Park**.

The Five Points area has some of Durham's best restaurants, from Italian to tapas to fried chicken and waffles.

The *Life is So Beautiful. Life is So Hard* mural in the Brightleaf Sq parking lot is a quote from author and Duke professor Kate Bowler.

On the American Tobacco Campus, the iconic Lucky Strike water tower has presided over downtown since the 1930s.

START
END
N Gregson St
N Duke St
Fuller St
Liggett St
Morris St
W Peabody St
W Pettigrew St
W Morgan St
W Main St
N Great Jones St
Durham
S Duke St
W Chapel Hill St
E Chapel Hill St
N Mangum St
Ramseur St
W Pettigrew St
E Parrish St
E Main St
Willard St
Blackwell St
Durham Fwy
N Svc Rd W
0 200 m
0 0.1 miles

Carrboro

NC's most charming small town

Chapel Hill's little sister, Carrboro, is a former mill town turned progressive paradise. It's adjacent to Chapel Hill – get there by walking west on Franklin St. Once called West End, it was long the working-class neighbor to the wealthier college town next door. But things have changed. Today the old mill is Carr Mill Mall, whose co-op grocery, the **Weaver Street Market**, is the spiritual center of town, with locals eating and dancing on the lawn all day. Other major attractions of Carrboro include the **farmers market**, which draws crowds on Saturday mornings and Wednesday afternoons, the many coffee shops and bars, and the two-day Carrboro Music Festival, with some 100 bands playing at venues around town in early fall.

Saxapahaw

Explore a mill village

On the Haw River west of Chapel Hill, the village of Saxapahaw was a cotton mill town until the 1990s, when it was largely abandoned. It's been redeveloped now, and is a popular weekend destination for lunch and river activities like stand-up paddleboarding. Draws include the **Haw River Ballroom**, a music venue with a riverside deck in the mill's old dye room; the biscuits at **Saxapahaw General Store**, a laid-back gourmet cafe in an old gas station; and the trails and whale-shaped slide at **Saxapahaw Island Park**.

Asheville

Artists and artisans

The North Carolina Mountains have deep craft-making traditions. See the imagination on full display by heading to the galleries and collectives of Asheville. Occupying a prime position on Pack Sq and Biltmore Ave, the **Asheville Art Museum** *(ashevilleart.org; adult/child $20/10)* has a stellar collection of 20th- and 21st-century American art, with a focus on the Southeast.

Nearby, the **Noir Collective** *(noircollectiveavl.com)* is a pillar of the historic Black business district, and a great place to discover emerging and established artists, artisans and designers from Asheville's Black community. You'll find paintings, graphic T-shirts, jewelry and incense, as well as books.

BEST LIVE MUSIC SPOTS IN ASHEVILLE

Orange Peel: A showcase for big-name indie bands since 2002. Seats a thousand-strong crowd.

Asheville Music Hall: Upstairs is AMH; One Stop is downstairs. Diverse sounds from funk, reggae and jazz to rock tribute bands.

Grey Eagle: All-ages club that's a great place to catch rising and established stars playing bluegrass, rockabilly, folk and blues.

Jack of the Wood Pub: Welcoming tavern with a small stage where you can catch Irish folk and Appalachian music jams.

Highland Brewing Co: A 10-minute drive from downtown, Asheville's largest independent brewery hosts mountain music and other sounds.

EATING & DRINKING IN ASHEVILLE: OUR PICKS

Huli Sue's: Perfect barbecue stars in smokehouse salads and pulled-pork sandwiches. Also blackened-fish tacos, poke bowls and tropical cocktails. hours vary *hours vary* $$

Chai Pani: Like a colorful Bollywood film, with small plates perfect for sharing; try the okra fries or kale *pakoras* (fritters). *11am-3pm & 5-9pm* $$

Cúrate: Convivial hangout celebrating the elegant simplicity of Spanish tapas, with an occasional Southern twist. *4-10:30pm Tue-Thu, from 11am Fri-Sun* $$$

Battery Park Book Exchange & Champagne Bar: Raise a glass in Asheville's most atmospheric drinking den. *hours vary*

BLACK CULTURE IN ASHEVILLE

Alexandria Ravenel, co-founder of Noir Collective (p325), shares insight on the heritage of Black Asheville *@noir collectiveavl*

The YMI Cultural Center has been here for over 130 years, and it sits central to what is now called the historic Black business district. Before my time there were a lot of Black-owned businesses on South Market St and Eagle St. YMI was at the heart of all that activity, and it still plays a vital role in what's sometimes called 'the Block.' It offers extensive programming on workforce development and housing opportunities, with space for youth projects. With a beautiful gallery space and a state-of-the-art ballroom, YMI also does a great job in keeping the culture going strong in Black Asheville, with lecture series, town halls and jazz nights.

Some of the old buildings of downtown now hold galleries. At the **Woolworth Walk**, you can browse works by dozens of creators in a 1938 Woolworth store.

Badly affected by flooding from Hurricane Helene in 2024, the **River Arts District** *(RAD; riverartsdistrict.com)* nevertheless continues to play a vital role in the city's creative community. Start the journey through RAD at the **Odyssey Gallery of Ceramic Arts** *(odysseygalleryofceramicarts.com)*, which features the wide-ranging work of nearly two dozen artists.

Beer City USA

A walk through the South Slope Brewing District is an easy introduction to 'Beer City USA' – an apt nickname for a metropolitan area with more than 50 breweries and cideries catering to a population of just 95,000. The massive **Wicked Weed** *(wickedweedbrewing.com)* mothership, with over two dozen taps, is a stalwart of Biltmore Ave. Never mind the menacing logo at **Burial** *(burialbeer.com)*: this friendly joint whips up some of Asheville's finest and most experimental Belgian-leaning styles. Step inside the multistory **Green Man** *(greenman brewery.com)* for English-style ales. Its original Dirty Jack's taproom has a scruffy, everybody's-welcome appeal; it's also a favorite of soccer fans.

Beyond the city limits you'll find some appealing options. Some 18 miles south of Asheville, **Sierra Nevada** *(sierranevada.com/visit/mills-river)* is a massive brewery from the California-based icon with great food, 23 taps, daily tours, a patio and live music on weekend afternoons from 2pm to 5pm.

America's grandest mansion

The largest privately owned home in the US, Biltmore House was completed in 1895 for shipping and railroad heir George Washington Vanderbilt II, and modeled after a French Renaissance–style chateau. **Biltmore** *(biltmore.com; adult/child from $85/50)* is extraordinarily expensive to visit, but you could spend the better part of a day exploring this 8000-acre estate with its dazzling art-filled house (which you'll see on a self-guided tour), gardens and satellite areas including the farmyard and winery, plus 22 miles of hiking trails. Buy your tickets in advance, and arrive right at opening time to make the most of the experience. You can also eat at the Biltmore: there are numerous options around the estate, from casual cafes and bustling taverns to decadent, multicourse meals at the Dining Room.

EATING & DRINKING IN BREVARD: OUR PICKS

Square Root: Award winner with a creative menu including local mountain trout, cedar plank salmon and wok-fried brussels sprouts. *11am-9pm Tue-Sat* $$$

Oskar Blues: Wide variety of brews (and food-truck burgers) on a spacious covered patio, plus live music weekends. *noon-8pm Sun-Thu, to 9pm Fri & Sat* $

185 King Street: Proudly calls itself 'Brevard's Backyard,' with outdoor seating, craft beers and live music. *4-9pm Tue-Fri, noon-9pm Sat & Sun* $

Wood & Vine: Atmospheric spot for innovative wines, plus oysters, wood-fired pizzas and truffle ravioli. *4:30-8pm Tue-Sat* $$

KONSTANTIN L/SHUTTERSTOCK

Biltmore

READING THE NORTH CAROLINA MOUNTAINS

Cold Mountain: (Charles Frazier; 1997) Adventure, savagery and heartache as a soldier journeys home during the Civil War.

The Caretaker: (Ron Rash; 2023) Friendship, love, betrayal and the legacy of war in 1950s Blowing Rock.

Even As We Breathe: (Annette Saunooke Clapsaddle; 2020) Set in the 1940s and focused on a young Cherokee man on a journey of discovery.

When These Mountains Burn: (David Joy; 2020) Masterfully told tale of addiction and redemption against the devastating fires of 2016.

Big Lies in a Small Town: (Diane Chamberlain; 2020) Mystery and murder in a small NC town; narrated by two women born in different times.

Blowing Rock

Forested beauty

The stately and idyllic mountain village of Blowing Rock makes a scenic base for exploring North Carolina's forests and mountains – among the tallest in the Eastern USA. Just a few minutes' walk from Main St, the **Glen Burney Falls Trail** takes you past a series of waterfalls, where you can admire the silvery streams pouring over slick smooth boulders amid birdsong and rhododendron.

The highest of the Blue Ridge Mountains, **Grandfather Mountain** *(grandfather.com; adult/child from $25/10)* is famous for the Mile High Swinging Bridge (though a mile above sea level, the bridge stretches just 80ft above a chasm). There's also a nature center with rescued wildlife, and plenty of walks. The challenging Grandfather Trail to Calloway Peak (2.4 miles one way) takes you scrambling up ladders and holding on to cables as you ascend steep slopes.

If you're just here to hike, you can head instead to **Grandfather Mountain State Park** *(ncparks.gov; free)*. Access its 13 miles of wilderness trails at Mile 300 on the Blue Ridge Pkwy.

Brevard

Hiking, biking and gallery-hopping

It's easy to fall for Brevard, a charming little mountain town with a downtown full of indie shops, craft breweries, cafes and wine bars. Take in the art scene at the **Lucy Clark Gallery** *(lucyclarkgallery.com)*, with works in fabric, metal, textiles and ceramics by 45 artists.

Serious mountain bikers give high marks to the 86 miles of trails in **DuPont State Forest**, a 10,000-acre reserve located about 11 miles southeast

DRIVING THE BLUE RIDGE

The scenic **Blue Ridge Parkway** (p292) winds its way past overlooks and hiking trails for 469 miles in North Carolina and Virginia. Sections of the NC side were badly damaged by Hurricane Helene in 2024. Check road closures on *nps.gov/blri*.

SEQUOYAH'S SYLLABARY

Although he could neither read nor speak English, Sequoyah (1770–1843) became obsessed with the 'talking leaves' (words on paper) and felt they were somehow key to white settlers' power. After working assiduously for nearly a decade, he invented a writing system for the Cherokee language, which he unveiled in 1821. Consisting of 86 characters, the Cherokee Syllabary became widely adopted by the tribe within a decade. Literacy spread quickly, and five years after the appearance of the syllabary, thousands of Cherokee could read and write – far surpassing the literacy rates of the white settlers around them. Sequoyah became something of a folk hero for the Cherokee, and his achievement is astonishing: it's the only recorded instance of one person single-handedly creating a system of writing.

of Brevard. Rent bikes and enjoy a post-ride craft brew at the **Hub** *(thehubpisgah.com)*.

For more great outdoor experiences, head to **Pisgah National Forest**. Pick up maps at the Pisgah Visitor Center, a 10-minute drive from Brevard, then take a hike. Among many options, the trail to **Looking Glass Rock** is a strenuous, mostly uphill journey (around 6 miles round trip) to a sweeping panorama over the Blue Ridge Mountains. Afterwards, cool off by zipping down **Sliding Rock** *($5)*, a natural 60ft slide of smooth, gently sloping granite into an 8ft deep pool at the bottom.

Cherokee

Vibrant native community

North Carolina's westernmost tip is blanketed in parkland, sprinkled with tiny mountain towns and rich in Native American history. At the **Museum of the Cherokee People** *(motcp.org; adult/child $15/8)*, you can learn about Cherokee history and see works by living Cherokee artists and craft makers. Across the street, **Qualla Arts & Crafts** *(quallaartsandcrafts.org)* sells high-quality baskets, beadwork, wooden carvings, copper jewelry, pottery, finger weavings and paintings. There's also a small gallery displaying the work of legendary makers of the past.

Run by the nonprofit Cherokee Historical Association, the **Oconaluftee Indian Village** *(cherokeehistorical.org/oconaluftee-indian-village; adult/child $25/15)* transports visitors back to the 1700s in a recreated settlement. Cherokee guides will take you through the open-air space, stopping at various stations where you can learn about tribal craft traditions, hunting and weapon-making.

Bryson City

Taking a scenic train ride

The **Great Smoky Mountains Railroad** *(gsmr.com)* chugs from Bryson City out into the wilderness on one of two memorable train trips *(from $65)*, each lasting around four hours. Special seasonal excursions are offered throughout the year, including a holiday-themed Polar Express from early November through December.

Rafting and other adventures

A true crossroads for adventure, the **Nantahala Outdoor Center** *(noc.com)* specializes in wet and wild rafting trips down the Nantahala River. The center's 500-acre main campus also offers ziplining and mountain biking, and it has its own lodging and dining options. The standard, three-hour guided trip **($70)** sweeps eight-person groups on yellow rafts through the dramatic Nantahala Gorge. The scenery is superb, with dense forest lining both banks of the broad, ever-frothing river.

ZACK FRANK/SHUTTERSTOCK

Mountain Farm Museum

TOP EXPERIENCE

Great Smoky Mountains National Park

The Smokies are a magical place to reconnect with nature. Days here are spent hiking past shimmering waterfalls and picnicking beside boulder-filled mountain streams, followed by evenings watching fireflies on the move. Lofty summits offer mesmerizing viewpoints over the rolling mountains, while the dense forests and open valleys create memorable opportunities for spotting elk, black bears and numerous bird species.

DON'T MISS

- Oconaluftee Visitor Center
- Mountain Farm Museum
- Charlies Bunion
- Alum Cave Trail
- Kuwohi
- Roaring Fork Motor Nature Trail
- Rainbow Falls
- Cades Cove Loop

Gateway to the Southern Smokies

Just 2 miles north of Cherokee, NC, the inviting, modern **Oconaluftee Visitor Center** straddles a vast open meadow by the Oconaluftee River. Inside, interpretive displays inform visitors about the area's attractions, and volunteer staff give suggestions about hikes and present talks on wildlife.

Out back, the open-air **Mountain Farm Museum** (*free*) is a recreation of a Great Smokies farmstead, providing a glimpse into the everyday lives of hardworking mountain people in the 19th and early 20th centuries. The field beyond the fence is a prime grazing spot for elk – come early or late in the day to spot them.

PRACTICALITIES

- nps.gov/grsm
- admission (parking pass) $5/15 per day/week
- 24hr

OVERNIGHT HIKES

There are scores of options for overnight hikes in the Smokies, including the granddaddy of backpacking trips, the Appalachian Trail. There are few dedicated loop routes in the Smoky Mountains, though the many intersecting trails allow you to plan a loop without having to end far from your starting point. A backcountry permit and campsite reservation are required for all backcountry stays in the park *(nps.gov/grsm/planyourvisit/backcountry-camping.htm).*

RETURN OF THE ELK

Before European settlement, an estimated 10 million elk ranged across the future United State, including southern Appalachia. By the mid-1800s the region's elk were wiped out by habitat loss and overhunting. In 2001 after years of study and planning, the park reintroduced a small herd of elk to the Smokies. Today the population numbers around 300, and they range throughout the park; look for them in the Oconaluftee Valley.

THERON STRIPLING III/SHUTTERSTOCK

Alum Cave Trail

Horseback Rides & Wagon Trips

Smokemont Riding Stables *(smokemontridingstable.com)* offers two different rides. On the one-hour River Crossing Trail *($50)*, you will indeed get to splash through the water during a scenic 3-mile loop. The 2½-hour Waterfall and Riverside Trail *($125)* visits Chasteen Creek Cascade. Smokemont also offers a 40-minute wagon ride *($30)*. Reserve ahead.

Hiking to Charlies Bunion

For a taste of the US' oldest long-distance trail, make the journey to **Charlies Bunion**, which offers a stunning panorama over a vast swath of the Smokies. From **Newfound Gap**, this 8-mile out-and-back jaunt follows the Appalachian Trail along the North Carolina–Tennessee border before reaching an outcropping with an awe-inspiring overlook.

Ascent to Alum Cave

The 4.6-mile (out-and-back) **Alum Cave Trail** is one of the Smokies' most popular, thanks to its scenic beauty and variety. A few steps off the busy main road you'll find yourself in a gorgeous green forest where canopies of rhododendrons overhang the rushing waters of Walker Camp Prong. The path's wide and flat first mile offers a delightful stroll with minimal exertion. At 1.4 miles the route crosses a log bridge and spirals up through Arch Rock, a photogenic cleft navigated by graceful stone steps. From here a more pronounced climb, punctuated by breathtaking views of the valley below, leads to Alum Cave (2.3 miles), a dramatic overhang of sandy-hued stone that contrasts fetchingly with the surrounding forest and serves as a convenient umbrella during rainstorms. Most people retrace their steps from here, but you can continue

2.7 miles further on the steep trail toward the summit. The views just keep getting better, while strategically placed cables serve as handholds for navigating slippery stretches of rock underfoot. At trail's end (5 miles), turn right on the Rainbow Falls Trail to reach LeConte Lodge, Mt LeConte's summit and a pair of classic viewpoints: Cliff Tops and Myrtle Point.

Overnighting on the Mountain

Spending the night in the **LeConte Lodge** is a bucket-list goal for many in-the-know Smokies visitors. The rustic cabins clustered at 6400ft above sea level offer the national park's only indoor accommodation. While amenities are generally simple – bunk beds, kerosene lamps, front-porch rockers, a washbasin and a shared outhouse – the effort of getting here makes it all the sweeter. The only way in is on foot, tackling one of several steep trails – none less than 5 miles – to reach your accommodation.

Reservations are awarded by lottery. In September the lodge accepts reservation requests (via *lecontelodge.com/reservations*) for the following season (March through November), with winners notified on October 1. Lodging and meals per person costs $190 ($104 for children).

Greet the Dawn at Kuwohi

At 6643ft, **Kuwohi** (formerly known as Clingmans Dome) is the highest point in Great Smoky Mountains National Park. In 1959 the National Park Service added a space-age viewing platform near the summit, which affords 360-degree views of the Smokies' grandeur. A magical time to visit is in the early morning on a clear day, when the sun crests the mountains' eastern slopes and mists hang in the valleys below. You'll also enjoy the experience without the sizable crowds that come

GHOST TOWN IN THE FOREST

From 1910 until the creation of the park in 1934, Elkmont saw the rise of small vacation homes, complete with large porches, bold colors and plenty of natural wood details. Today you can experience a remnant of the whimsical world created a century ago with a visit to **Daisy Town** (aka Elkmont Historic District), a painstakingly restored cluster of structures near the Elkmont Campground. Afterwards, continue uphill and onto the **Jakes Creek Trail** to see more ghostly ruins, including solitary chimneys, moss-covered steps and low stone walls, as well as one restored two-story house you can enter.

SK TANNER PHOTOGRAPHY/SHUTTERSTOCK

Kuwohi

later in the day. Kuwohi is reached from Newfound Gap via a 7-mile spur road. From the parking lot it's a taxing half-mile climb (up a paved trail) to the viewing platform, with an elevation gain of 300ft.

TOP TIPS

- Gatlinburg (Tennessee) and Cherokee (North Carolina) are the closest towns to the park, and good places to arrange last-minute lodging.
- There are no restaurants in the park so be sure to pack a picnic.
- Arrive early in the morning at popular trailheads (like Alum Cave). Parking lots can fill up by 8am, leaving you out of luck. Alternatively, book a ride on a shuttle with **A Walk in the Woods** *(awalkinthewoods.com)* from Gatlinburg.
- The best way to travel the 11-mile Cades Cove loop is by bicycle on vehicle-free Wednesdays (mid-June to September). You can rent bikes on site.

The Climb to Ramsey Cascades

For those with the stamina to tackle it, the beautiful climb to **Ramsey Cascades**, the park's highest waterfall, is one of the Smokies' most rewarding hikes. Ascending 2280ft over 4 miles, the Ramsey Cascades Trail starts in the remote Greenbrier section of the park, 11 miles east of Gatlinburg via the mostly unpaved Greenbrier and Ramsey Prong Rds. Along the way, you'll pass through old-growth forest with some massive tulip trees.

Driving the Roaring Fork Motor Nature Trail

The Roaring Fork area is named for one of the park's biggest and most powerful mountain streams and is well loved for its waterfalls, glimpses of old-growth forest and excellent selection of preserved cabins, gristmills and other historic structures. The one-way 5.5-mile **Roaring Fork Motor Nature Trail** begins and ends a short distance from downtown Gatlinburg.

A worthwhile add-on is the hike to **Rainbow Falls**, one of the park's most dramatic – and one sure to give you a good workout. From the trailhead, it's a 2.8-mile uphill trek with 1600ft of elevation gain. Your reward is one of the Smokies' highest waterfalls, cascading 90ft down a cliff immersed in forest. The fine stone-slab bridge over LeConte Creek makes for a delightful place to soak up the view.

Other fine routes here include the walk to **Grotto Falls**, most easily accessed via a 1.4-mile section of the **Trillium Gap Trail**. Beyond the beauty of the falls themselves, this outing offers two unique features: the chance to walk behind the 25ft cascades (a classic Smokies photo op) and the rare opportunity to cross paths with llamas carrying supplies to and from LeConte Lodge. Llamas travel the Trillium Gap Trail on Monday, Wednesday and Friday.

Time Travel on Cades Cove Loop

Thanks to its history, wildlife and pastoral scenery, the 11-mile **Cades Cove Loop** has become one of the Smokies' most sought-after tourist destinations. Alas, its popularity all too often translates into traffic congestion. To fully appreciate Cades Cove's majesty without the crowds, set off at dawn or in the late afternoon.

The one-way road encircles land used as a hunting ground by the Cherokee before English, Scots-Irish and German settlers arrived in the 1820s. These determined newcomers built cabins and churches while clearing the valley's trees for farmland. Mills, forges and blacksmith shops soon followed, creating a thriving community. Today the creaky cabins, mossy spring houses, weathered barns and tidy cemeteries whisper the stories of the families who made this place their home.

South Carolina

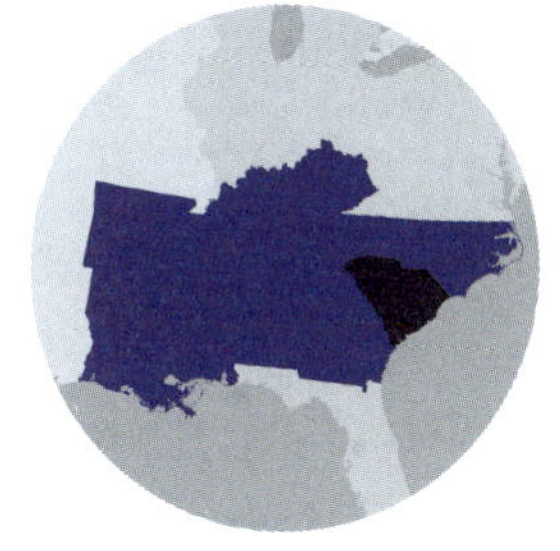

CULTURE & HISTORY | GOLDEN BEACHES | SOUTHERN CHARM

There's a reason South Carolina ranks among the country's fastest-growing states. Yes, affordable housing and the low cost of living are factors, but the state's natural beauty and welcoming vibes surely play a part too. Most travelers begin along the Low-country coast, home to splendid historic cities such as Beaufort and Charleston as well as wide sandy beaches studded with dunes and palms. Along the barrier islands you can immerse yourself in Gullah culture, its language and stories created by the formerly enslaved, who held onto West African traditions through centuries of hardship.

Innovative cities including Greenville and Columbia are hubs of culinary and cultural expression in the state's interior. Museums, plantations and galleries in these destinations and along the coast are re-examining the state's past and sharing more comprehensive accounts. There's also plentiful scope for outdoor adventure amid landscapes ranging from rugged state parks in the mountains to spooky black-water swamps to sun-kissed salt marshes.

Places

Charleston p334

Beaufort p340

St Helena & Hunting Islands p340

Myrtle Beach p341

Columbia p342

Greenville p342

Congaree National Park p344

TOP TIP

Dress up like greenskeeper Carl Spackler and jump into the ocean on January 1 during the Bill Murray Look-a-Like Polar Plunge on Folly Beach. This subzero swim pays homage to Charleston's most distinguished resident, Bill Murray, with participants attempting to resemble him in various roles.

GETTING AROUND

Driving your own vehicle is the best way to explore the state, though if you're just stopping through Charleston, you can explore its compact and pedestrian-friendly downtown on foot.

Amtrak *(amtrak.com)* runs through South Carolina on four routes. The *Silver Meteor* links NYC and Miami, with stops in Florence, Charleston and Savannah, GA. The *Palmetto* connects Charleston with New York City and Savannah. The *Silver Star* stops in Columbia, while the *Crescent* links Greenville and Clemson.

Greyhound *(greyhound.com)* has stations in Charleston, Columbia, Florence, Georgetown, Greenville and Myrtle Beach. Megabus *(us.megabus.com)* stops in Florence and Columbia.

Charleston

MAP P335

Step back in time

Cobblestone streets, hidden alleyways and photogenic homes straight from the 1800s set the stage for rewarding exploring in Charleston, one of the South's most fascinating cities.

The **Charleston Museum** *(charlestonmuseum.org; adult/teen/child $15/12/6)* may be the oldest museum in the country – it opened in 1773 – but it certainly isn't stuffy. Exhibits spotlight various periods of the city's long and storied past. Artifacts include a whale skeleton, tags worn by the enslaved and the 'secession table' used for the signing of the state's secession documents before the Civil War.

EATING IN CHARLESTON: SOUTHERN FARE

MAP P335

Marina Variety Store: A long-standing, down-home kinda place, with harbor views and Southern hospitality as warm as the buttermilk biscuits. *7am-9pm Wed-Sat, to 2pm Sun* **$**

Poogan's Porch: The homemade buttermilk biscuits are out of control and the chicken and waffles are second to none. Boozy brunchers have plenty of options. *9am-3pm & 4:30-9:30pm* **$$**

Slightly North of Broad: Lowcountry comfort dishes reinvented with flair. Try the peach salad with prosciutto, goat cheese and pecans. *11am-2:30pm & 5-10pm* **$$$**

FIG: Foodie favorite known for welcoming staff, efficient but unrushed service and sustainably sourced nouvelle Southern fare. *5-10:30pm Tue-Sat* **$$$**

HIGHLIGHTS

1 Old Slave Mart Museum

SIGHTS

2 Aiken-Rhett House
3 Charleston Museum
4 International African American Museum
5 Marion Square

ACTIVITIES

6 Gateway Walk

SLEEPING

7 Andrew Pinkney Inn

EATING

8 Chez Nous
9 FIG
10 Marina Variety Store
11 Poogan's Porch
12 Slightly North of Broad
13 Ordinary

DRINKING & NIGHTLIFE

14 Bin 152
15 Blind Tiger
16 Citrus Club
17 Fiat Lux
18 Henry's on the Market
19 Palmetto Lobby Bar
20 Pavilion Bar
21 Prohibition
22 Rooftop at the Vendue

SHOPPING

23 Charleston City Market

INFORMATION

24 Fort Sumter Visitor Education Center at Liberty Square

With its grand homes and manicured gardens, Charleston is awash in aesthetic charms. But the city owes much of its beauty and success to an economy that was once driven by enslaved labor. On the grounds of an open-air market that auctioned men, women and children, the simple but powerful **Old Slave Mart Museum** *(oldslavemart.org; $7)* spotlights the day-to-day realities and horrors of the slave trade in the years leading up to the Civil War. It was the largest of 40 or so similar auction houses in the city.

More than 250,000 enslaved Africans entered the United States in Charleston, and many disembarked at Gadsden's

AFRICAN AMERICAN HERITAGE IN CHARLESTON

For a list of Black-owned restaurants and businesses, pick up the free Explore Black History booklets found around town or visit *exploreblack charleston.com.* The website has an interactive map, and it shares itineraries that spotlight destinations with connections to Black history. Located 1 mile north of the International African American Museum, **Hannibal's Kitchen** *(hannibalkitchen .com; 11am-8pm Mon-Sat)* serves soul food, including Gullah-Geechee standards such as shrimp-and-crab rice (its signature dish) and collard greens. Opened by family patriarch Robert 'Hannibal' Huger in 1985, the restaurant is now managed by his granddaughters.

Wharf beside the Cooper River. The wharf is now home to the striking **International African American Museum** *(iaamuseum.org; adult/child $22/10),* which shares the stories of the African American diaspora through interactive exhibits, firsthand recollections, eye-catching artifacts and compelling art. Gullah-Geechee culture is also featured – be sure to step into the recreated Praise House and watch the short film about the uplifting Moving Hall Star Singers, a multigenerational gospel group from Johns Island.

The only surviving urban townhouse complex in the city, the 1820 **Aiken-Rhett House** *(historiccharleston.org; adult/child $15/7)* gives a fascinating glimpse of antebellum life on a 45-minute self-guided audiotour. The Historic Charleston Foundation has conserved but not restored the home, so when you step through the ornate doors of this tangerine-colored mansion, once home to South Carolina governor William Aiken, it feels like time-traveling to 1858. The collection of books, furnishings, art and architectural details, though worn, is largely intact.

Be sure to also take a peek in the **Charleston City Market** *(thecharlestoncitymarket.com),* which stretches four blocks along Meeting St in the French Quarter. It's one of the nation's oldest markets, getting its start in 1804.

Ghosts in the graveyard

If you're a fan of spooky Southern Gothic fiction, welcome to your unhappy place. The **Gateway Walk** is a loose, natural-feeling corridor that ribbons through downtown's hustle and bustle, but the weathered headstones, walled pathways and live oaks are an instant portal to another, quieter time. The silence is occasionally broken by church bells ringing in the distance. Defying the melancholy? Wildflowers deliver bursts of color in spring.

The western entry is on Archdale St at St John's Lutheran Church. If the gate is closed, begin next door at the Unitarian Church. A memorial to the enslaved workers who built the church rises near the entrance. The path winds through the graveyard and its intentionally overgrown foliage and concludes at St Philips Episcopal.

Afterwards, take a breather from the Gothic intensity by heading south to the Battery. A promenade follows along the harbor and offers views of Fort Sumter, while live oaks provide shade for cannons and statues of military heroes in the adjacent garden. Flanked by historic homes and the harbor, the area is a pretty spot to relax.

EATING IN CHARLESTON: OUR PICKS

MAPS P335 & P338

Edmund's Oast: Charleston's highest-brow brewpub serves Southern faves and a long list of cocktails and draft beers. *11am-10pm* **$$**

Leon's Oyster Shop: In a converted old body shop reimagined as an industrial-chic eatery, Leon's is a local favorite for oysters, fried chicken and scalloped potatoes. *11am-10pm* **$$**

Ordinary: Inside a cavernous 1927 bank building, this buzzy seafood hall and oyster bar feels like the best party in town. *5-10:30pm Wed-Mon* **$$**

Chez Nous: A diminutive restaurant with a short menu of dishes and wines from southern France, northern Italy and northern Spain. *11:30am-3pm & 5-10pm* **$$**

STROLLING HISTORIC CHARLESTON

Three centuries of history jostles for attention between Broad St and the Battery, which means wandering off course is entirely expected.

START	END	LENGTH
Old Exchange & Provost Dungeon	Four Corners of Law/ St Michael's Church	1.5 miles; 1 hour

Begin at the 1 **Old Exchange & Provost Dungeon**, where costumed guides lead tours of the dungeon where Stede Bonnet, the Gentleman Pirate, and Revolutionary War prisoners were once held.

Walk south to the pastel beauty of 2 **Rainbow Row**, a block of redone 1730s merchant stores that inspired the birth of the Preservation Society of Charleston in the 1920s.

Follow Tradd St to Church St and turn right. The 3 **Heyward-Washington House**, where the first president slumbered in 1791, is on your left.

Head south to East Battery and the 4 **Edmondston-Alston House**, where tours pass intricate woodwork and family artifacts.

Continue south to approach the 5 **Battery & White Point Garden**, named for the fortifications that lined the seafront and for the mounds of oyster shells once piled over the point.

Cut through the park and walk north along Meeting St to the 6 **Williams Mansion**, formerly known as the Calhoun Mansion. Famed for its opulent decor, this Gilded Age manor is Charleston's largest single-family residence.

Continuing north, the 7 **Nathaniel Russell House** appears on the left. You can see its free-flying spiral staircase on a tour.

At the 8 **Four Corners of Law**, notice St Michael's Church, representing God's law, on the southeastern corner.

Sweetgrass baskets are often for sale along Meeting St near the Four Corners of Law.

In the backyard at Nathaniel Russell House, the 16ft joggling board was used in the 1800s to help with rheumatoid arthritis.

The country's oldest liquor store, the Tavern at Rainbow Row has been selling spirits since 1686! Check its Facebook page for details about special tastings.

DEFINING THE LOWCOUNTRY

Much of South Carolina's southeastern coastline, dubbed the Lowcountry, is a patchwork of barrier islands marked by small inlets and salt marshes as well as stretches of shimmery, oyster-gray sand and wild, moss-shrouded maritime forests. Bridges link to some of these islands, but many can be reached only by boat or ferry. Descendants of West African enslaved have long called the region home. Known as the Gullah-Geechee, these people have maintained strong cultural and culinary traditions over centuries, but their communities continue to shrink as resorts and commercial developments gobble up land.

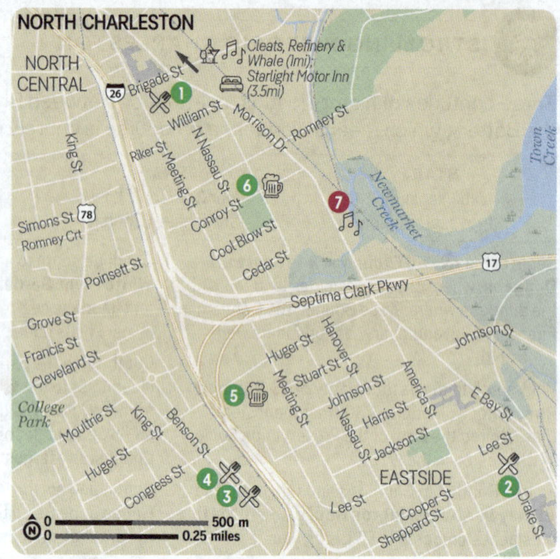

EATING
1 Edmund's Oast
2 Hannibal's Kitchen
3 Leon's Oyster Shop

DRINKING & NIGHTLIFE
4 Little Jack's Tavern
5 Palmetto Brewing Company
6 Revelry Brewery

ENTERTAINMENT
7 Royal American

Panoramic bars and creative hubs

Several great rooftop lounges can be found in the French Quarter. With an infinity pool, illuminated umbrellas and stunning city views, the chic **Pavilion Bar** *(marketpavilion.com)* attracts a well-heeled set, but people sometimes end up barefoot when the staff throws plexiglass over the pool and converts it into a dance floor. **Rooftop at the Vendue** *(rooftopcharleston.com)* also has sweet views of downtown. **Henry's on the Market** *(henrysonthemarket.com)* is not the swankiest of the lot, but it sits atop Henry's, the oldest restaurant in the state, dating to 1932.

Further north, a bright neon orange overlooks the bar at the ever-stylish **Citrus Club** *(thedewberrycharleston.com),* which has impressive views of Holy City Church's steeples, Marion Sq

DRINKING IN CHARLESTON: COCKTAILS & WINE

MAP P335

Palmetto Lobby Bar: Foam-topped cocktails give a kick – the foam is infused with alcohol – at this stylish hotel bar. *4-11pm Mon-Thu, 11am-midnight Fri & Sat, 11am-11pm Sun*

Prohibition: Jazz Age gastropub serving excellent craft cocktails (from $16) that pair well with the lip-smackin' Southern grub. *4pm-2am Mon-Thu, from 11am Fri-Sun*

Ordinary (p336): Yes, there are oysters, but the cocktails shine too inside this former bank building that has an appealing join-the-party vibe. *5-10pm Wed-Mon*

Bin 152: Pair adventurous wine selections with imported cheese, freshly baked bread and charcuterie at this elegant downtown wine bar. *2pm-midnight Mon-Thu, from noon Fri-Sun*

and the Ravenel Bridge from its perch atop the Dewberry. Around the corner, admire the artwork in the Hotel Bennett's lobby before gliding up to **Fiat Lux** *(hotelbennett.com)*, where you'll enjoy views of **Marion Square** with your cocktails.

A few miles further north, the **Refinery** *(therefinerychs.com)* is a special place to watch live music. Check for upcoming shows at this 2000-person outdoor venue beside the railroad tracks in North Charleston. Other tenants in this creativity hub include the **Whale**, a bar with a lengthy craft-beer list, and the sports bar **Cleats**.

An infamous fort

Grab a seat on the upper deck for the boat ride across Charleston Harbor to **Fort Sumter** *(nps.gov/fosu; free)*, where the first shots of the Civil War were fired. Upon arrival you'll disembark the ferry and walk to the fort. Travelers on the first ferry of the day may be asked to help raise the US flag, while those on the last may be asked to lower it. National park rangers and docents are available to answer questions and share information about the history of the site and its role in the Civil War. Buy tickets *(fortsumtertours.com; adult/child $40/26)* ahead of your visit to avoid missing out. Expect to spend about 2¼ hours total on your trip, including the ferry rides. Boats depart from both Liberty Square (in downtown Charleston) and Patriots Point.

Before hopping on the ferry, stop by the **Fort Sumter Visitor Education Center at Liberty Square** *(free)* to see exhibits about the roots of the conflict that led to South Carolina's secession, the Civil War and the war's aftermath.

Reachable by car, **Fort Moultrie** *(nps.gov/fosu; adult/child $10/free)* offers a deeper dive into the region's coastal defense systems, as its exhibits and structures span nearly 200 years. Across the street from the fort, the visitor center has an information desk staffed by park rangers, along with a theater, a museum and a bookstore.

Kayaking the coast

Numerous companies lead tours and boat trips through the marshes and along the coasts of Charleston County's sea islands. **Adventure Harbor Tours** *(adventureharbourtours.com)* runs harbor cruises, sunset excursions and fun trips to uninhabited Morris Island – great for shelling. Trips leave from the marina at Ashley Point in Charleston. Well-established **Coastal Expeditions** *(coastalexpeditions.com; kayak tour*

CHARLESTON'S LIVE-MUSIC VENUES

Liv Brownstein, Charleston musician and College of Charleston student, shares her favorite music venues.

At Folly Beach, **Chico Feo** is a relaxed kind of place. The tacos are really good. On Monday it has an open-mic night where lots of bands or solo people go and play all original music. It's super cute, outdoors and right off the beach.

Every single night there's something happening at **Pour House**. The farmers market on Sunday has live music.

On the way to North Charleston at the top of the peninsula, **Royal American** is an indoor-outdoor venue. It has food and a sit-down area. Lots of different kinds of bands come here and there's a lot of rock music.

DRINKING IN CHARLESTON: BREWERIES & PUBS

MAPS P335 & P338

Palmetto Brewing Company: The city's first microbrewery (since Prohibition, anyway) produces an amber ale, a pilsner and a couple of IPAs. *4-10pm Mon-Thu, noon-10pm Sat, noon-7pm Sun*

Revelry Brewery: Knock back artfully crafted cold ones on the fairy-lit and fire-pit-heated rooftop with Ravenel Bridge views. *noon-10pm Mon-Thu, to 11pm Fri & Sat, to 8pm Sun*

Blind Tiger: This atmospheric bar seduces with stamped-tin ceilings and good pub grub. Enjoy your cocktail in the expansive courtyard. *4-11pm Mon-Thu, 11am-midnight Fri & Sat, 11am-11pm Sun*

Little Jack's Tavern: A classy neighborhood cocktail bar and restaurant, with one helluva hamburger. *noon-10pm*

BEST SEA ISLANDS NEAR CHARLESTON

Isle of Palms: The 7-mile stretch at Isle of Palms is well suited to families, and there's a playground steps from the beach.

Sullivan's Island: A broad commercial-free swath of sand south of Mount Pleasant. Come here to decompress and avoid the crowds.

Folly Beach: A favorite of locals, this festive spot with good surfing feels most like a beach town (particularly around Center St).

Kiawah: A mostly private island, but visitors can enjoy a family-friendly beach day at **Kiawah Beachwater Park**.

Edisto Beach State Park: A gorgeous, uncrowded beach with oak-shaded hiking trails. Stop for gossip and fried seafood baskets at Whaley's Store

adult/child from $48/38) leads kayak tours through the salt marshes at Shem Creek and along the Kiawah River, where full-moon trips are on the schedule. They also rent kayaks.

Sunsets and nature walks in Mount Pleasant

Mount Pleasant, originally a summer retreat for Charlestonians, sits just north of the Cooper River from Charleston. It has a historic downtown, and some great spots for catching the sunset, including along Shem Creek, where folks drink beer on restaurant patios and soak up views of the creek and Charleston Harbor. You can also stretch your legs and scan for dolphins along the dock-lined **Shem Creek Boardwalk**, which overlooks the marsh. For an easygoing vibe after your walk, settle in with a beer on the deck at **Red's Ice House** *(redsicehouse.com)*.

Beaufort

Learn Reconstruction Era history

The southern half of the South Carolina coast is a tangle of islands cut off from the mainland by inlets and tidal marshes. From 1861 to 1900, Beaufort and the surrounding sea islands became a hub for organization, education and self-determination for the formerly enslaved, who comprised 80% of the local population. Established by Congress in 2019, the **Reconstruction Era National Historical Park** *(nps.gov/reer)* covers the history of this era at three separate sites – all free – near Beaufort. Start at the **Old Beaufort Firehouse Visitor Center** downtown where you'll find a few exhibits as well as details about the other locations and scheduled park programs.

The best way to experience this evolving park is by listening to the stories and history shared by rangers. Check the online calendar for program times.

St Helena & Hunting Islands

Gullah culture and history

St Helena Island, east of Beaufort, has the highest concentration of Gullah people in the state and is the best place to learn about their culture. The **Penn Center** *(penncenter.com; tours $15-20)* has a museum that's a great starting point. Exhibits cover Gullah culture and trace the history of the center.

South Carolina's best seaside state park

The lush and inviting **Hunting Island State Park** *(southcarolinaparks.com/hunting-island; adult/child $8/4)* impresses

EATING IN BEAUFORT: OUR PICKS

Lowcountry Produce: A fantastic market for picnic supplies with an equally appealing cafe. Try an Oooey Gooey, a grilled pimento-cheese sandwich with bacon and garlic-pepper jelly. *11am-2:30pm* $

Blacksheep x Sabbatical: This small wine shop and restaurant serves an eclectic selection of toasts, sips and sandwiches downtown. *11am-6pm Tue-Sat* $

Old Bull Tavern: Delicious food and cocktails amid a low-lit, worldly aesthetic. Menu changes daily but always features playful American and European comfort dishes. *5-9pm Tue-Sat* $$

Ribaut Social Club: Celebrate a special occasion inside a refurbished mansion a short walk from downtown. Seafood dishes shine. *5-7:45pm Tue-Sat* $$$

SkyWheel, Myrtle Beach

with its acres of spooky maritime forest and tidal lagoons. The bone-white beach is littered with seashells and the occasional shark tooth. The Vietnam War scenes from *Forrest Gump* were filmed in the marsh, a nature-lover's dream. Climb the lighthouse *($2)* for coastal views.

Myrtle Beach

Sand and boardwalk fun

Stretching for 60 miles along South Carolina's north coast, Myrtle Beach is famously overdeveloped, but there's plenty of fun to be had if you're willing to embrace the kitsch. Get the lay of the land by taking a spin on the **SkyWheel** *(skywheelmb.com; adult/child $20/16)*, which overlooks the 1.2-mile coastal boardwalk. Get your fill of mini-golf, T-shirt shops and arcade games along the **boardwalk**. When you need a break, enjoy a nature fix at **Myrtle Beach State Park** *(southcarolinaparks /myrtle-beach.com; adult/child $8/4)*. Unfurling along an undeveloped mile of coastline 3 miles south of central Myrtle Beach, this park is a pretty destination for walking the two short (half-mile) nature trails through maritime forest. There's also a long pier that's ideal for fishing *(fishing pass for adults/children $8/3)* and rods are available for rental *($25 for the day)*.

A day at Brookgreen Gardens

A true storybook setting, **Brookgreen Gardens** *(brookgreen.org; adult/child $22/12)* in Pawleys Island has the largest collection of American figurative statuary in the United States. Botanical gardens, art galleries, Gullah-Geechee sites and a Lowcountry Zoo are also highlights on the 9100-acre property, founded by Archer and Anna Hyatt Huntington in 1931. Lowcountry classics, including salt marshes, live oaks and longleaf pines, provide the outer-garden backdrop.

FAMILY FUN IN MYRTLE BEACH

Family Kingdom: Old-fashioned amusement-and-water-park combo overlooking the ocean.

Market Common: Vast retail and entertainment hub with disc golf and the wonderful, all-abilities Savannah's Playground for the toddler set.

Broadway at the Beach: Outdoor mall with shops, restaurants, rides, a Ripley's aquarium, a Wonderworks funhouse and a movie theater.

Myrtle Beach Boardwalk & Promenade: Go old school: walk the piers, play arcade games, ride the SkyWheel and eat some ice cream on the 1.2-mile promenade.

Topgolf: Yep, it's a national chain, but this multilevel golf-game outpost offers bays that are cooled or heated year-round.

GULLAH CULTURE

Starting in the 16th century, African people were transported from the so-called Rice Coast (Sierra Leone, Senegal, Gambia and Angola) to a remarkably similar landscape of swampy coastlines and tropical vegetation. These new African Americans were able to retain many of their homeland traditions after the fall of slavery and well into the 20th century. The resulting culture of Gullah (also known as Geechee in Georgia) has its own language, an English-based Creole with many African words and sentence structures, and traditions including storytelling, art, music and crafts. Gullah culture is celebrated during the Original Gullah Festival in Beaufort, while **Gullah-N-Geechie Mahn Tours** *(gullahngeechietours.com)* stop at sites on St Helena Island.

KEVIN RUCK/SHUTTERSTOCK

Columbia

River adventures

The Saluda and Broad Rivers merge just northwest of state capital Columbia, joining forces to create the Congaree River. June through August you can inner tube down the Lower Saluda to the Congaree, floating past Riverbanks Zoo. **Palmetto Outdoor** *(palmettooutdoor.com; tube & shuttle $20)* will rent you a tube and shuttle you upriver from the West Columbia Riverwalk & Amphitheater beside the Gervais Bridge. After your float, which runs about three hours, walk to **Savage Craft Ale Works** for a pint and river views from its rooftop.

Greenville

South Carolina's prettiest town center

In photogenic Greenville, the Reedy River twists through the city center, and its dramatic falls tumble beneath the sleek Liberty Bridge at Falls Park. Downtown Main St rolls past a lively array of indie shops, great restaurants and craft-beer pubs. Public art on Main honors town founders and features a whimsical collection of objects, from suitcases to mice. Good bets for shopping are **Mast General Store** *(mastgeneralstore.com)*, a regional outdoor shop and old-fashioned candy

EATING & DRINKING IN MYRTLE BEACH: OUR PICKS

Earth Cafe: Tuck into the salads, wraps and smoothies at this hip and healthy place. *8:30am-4pm Mon & Tue, to 10pm Wed-Sun* $$

Hook & Barrel: Join the fun at this natty central bar where seafood is the showstopper. *4-9pm Mon-Thu, to 9:30pm Fri & Sat* $$$

New South Brewing: Try the bestselling Dirty Myrtle DIPA at this hyperlocal craft brewery – at it since 1998. *4:30-7pm Mon-Fri, 1-5pm Sat & Sun*

Atlas Tap House: Scruffy but friendly, with numerous craft beers on tap, near the boardwalk. Top-notch happy-hour tacos (from $1). *4pm-2am*

Greenville

emporium, and nearby **Poppington's** *(poppingtons.com)*, known for its imaginatively flavored gourmet popcorn. **M Judson Booksellers** *(mjudsonbooks.com)* is a sunny woman-owned bookshop (with cafe) in the old courthouse, while the patio at **Soby's** *(sobys.com)* is the place to see, be seen and savor Southern favorites like shrimp and grits. The chocolate-chunk cookies are a delicious complement to your latte at **Coffee Underground** *(coffeeunderground.info)*. Main St downtown closes to cars every Saturday morning May through October for the **Saturday Market** *(saturday marketlive.com)*.

Cycle the Swamp Rabbit Trail

You can walk it, jog it or skate it, but the most popular way to experience the fabulous **Swamp Rabbit Trail** – a former railway corridor – is on two wheels. The best section of the paved, tree-shaded greenway stretches 22 miles along the Reedy River, linking downtown Greenville with Furman University and the town of Travelers Rest. Pretty bridges, cafes and breweries dot the path. Expect the round-trip ride to take half a day. You can rent bikes in downtown Greenville from **Reedy Rides** *(reedyrides.com)* or a city bikeshare with **Greenville B Cycle** *(greenville.bcycle.com)*.

SWEETGRASS BASKETS

Sweetgrass baskets are for sale across the Lowcountry. These eye-catching coiled baskets have been made by hand by the Gullah-Geechee since the 18th century, when they were used by the enslaved on the region's rice plantations, and the craft of sweetgrass weaving was passed down through the generations. Today the baskets are often intricately patterned and are considered pieces of decorative art. Designs may vary by family. Learn more about the history behind sweetgrass baskets at the Sweetgrass Basket Pavilion – where they are also for sale – beside the Mount Pleasant Visitor Center and Memorial Waterfront Park. The park also hosts the annual Sweetgrass Festival in late July.

EATING IN GREENVILLE: OUR PICKS

Soby's: Book yourself one of the intimate brick-walled banquettes at this bastion of New Southern cuisine. *5-9pm, plus weekend brunch* $$

Trappe Door: Descend beneath E Washington St for rib-sticking Belgian food and an extensive beer list. *5-10pm Sun-Thu, to 11pm Fri & Sat* $$

Jianna: Savor rustic Italian cuisine and oysters galore in this cheerful 2nd-floor restaurant near Falls Park. *5-9pm Tue-Fri, from 11am Sat & Sun* $$

Anchorage: Local food and booze reign supreme in West Greenville – particularly true at the Anchorage. Look for its bright, enormous mural depicting produce. *5-9:30pm* $$

TOP EXPERIENCE

Congaree National Park

Thick with knobby bald cypress trees, moss-covered tupelos and tangled Spanish moss, the swampy interior of Congaree National Park is a Southern Gothic setting at its most elemental. Home to the largest old-growth forest in the Southeastern USA, the park is on a plain fed by the floodwaters of the Congaree and Wateree Rivers. This eerie wonderland is 20 miles southeast of Columbia.

Boardwalk Trail

TOP TIPS

- Pack a picnic or snacks for your visit. There are no restaurants in the park and few options nearby.
- Some ranger-led tours require a reservation and have limited availability. Check the park website to see what's on.
- Don't forget the bug spray.

PRACTICALITIES

- nps.gov/cong
- park 24hr; visitor center 9am-5pm
- admission free

Boardwalk Trail

The most efficient way to explore the floodplain here is to walk the 2.6-mile **Boardwalk trail**, an elevated walkway that loops through the park's old-growth bottomland forest. This easy route passes beneath loblolly pines, water tupelos and bald cypresses, and it provides up-close views of the dark Dorovan muck, an 8ft-deep mix of clay and dead leaves. The trail also swings past boggy Weston Lake.

Paddling Through a Primeval Landscape

For an even more interactive experience, join a half-day guided paddling trip on the Cedar Creek Canoe Trail. This 15-mile water trail meanders through the park's old-growth forest, which provides thick shade. Look for otters, deer, snakes and even alligators while kayaking or canoeing along the marked path. The soundtrack may be the ratatatat of pileated woodpeckers doing their thing and the spooky calls of barred owls. Guided trips take about three hours and cost around $100 per person. Palmetto Outdoor (p342) among other approved outfitters lead trips. It's a relatively easy excursion, but some paddling experience is helpful and will keep you from holding up the group. Outings depart from the South Cedar Creek Canoe Landing, which is a seven-minute drive from the park visitor center.

Tennessee

BLUES & COUNTRY | FORESTED PEAKS | CAPTIVATING CITIES

Most states have one official state song. Tennessee has 11 – and for good reason: this place has music deep within its soul. Here, you can find the mountain twang of folk music in Appalachia, bluesy rhythms of African American communities in the western Delta, and those polished country chords for which Nashville is famed.

The state's three geographic regions are represented by the three stars on the Tennessee flag. Each has its own unique beauty: the heather-colored peaks of the Great Smoky Mountains; the lush green valleys of the central plateau around Nashville; and the sultry lowlands near Memphis.

Apart from visiting fabled recording studios and hallowed Graceland, the Volunteer State is the place for art and culture, dining and nightlife, from Memphis to Chattanooga. Follow this with some nature time amid forested trails, shimmering waterfalls and rocky overlooks – the perfect complement to big-city rambles.

Places

Memphis p347
Nashville p351
Chattanooga p354
Rainbow Lake Wilderness Area p356
Knoxville p357

TOP TIPS

While traveling through Tennessee, be sure to tune in to its excellent radio stations. The nonprofit, community-run WYXR (91.7 FM) in Memphis plays blues, hip-hop, jazz and indie rock. In Nashville, WNXP (91.1 FM) plays wide-ranging grooves with a focus on Music City's local talent. In Chattanooga check out WUTC (88.1 FM) for live local music.

GETTING AROUND

In Memphis, MATA *(matatransit.com)* operates buses as well as a vintage trolley line that runs up Main St (passing Beale St along the way). In Nashville, WeGo Public Transit *(wegotransit.com)* has decent service for getting around town (Rte 4 is useful for getting from downtown to East Nashville). You can also get around town on Nashville's good bikesharing network *(nashville.bcycle.com)*. Memphis and Nashville both have Uber and Lyft. For city-to-city transport, Greyhound is about your only option, though you can take the scenic train to New Orleans if you're heading south from Memphis.

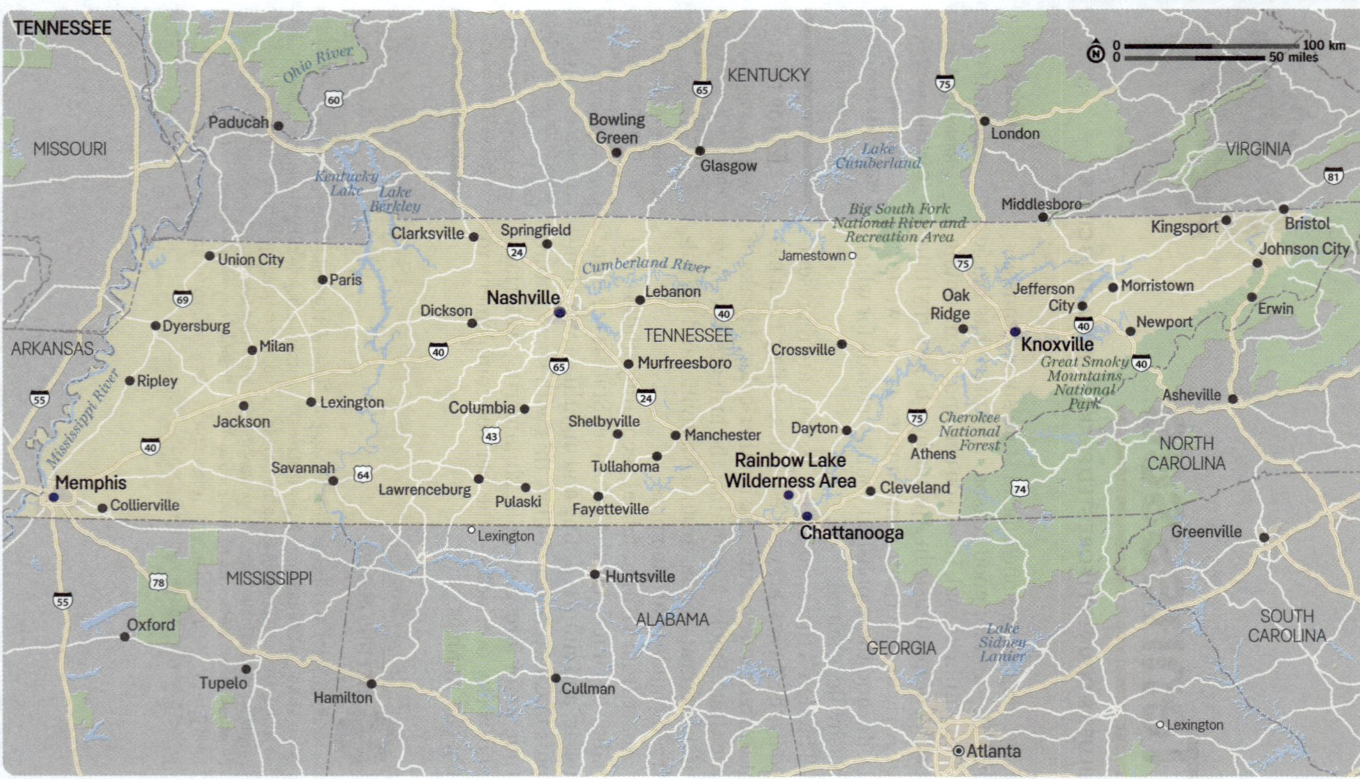
TENNESSEE
0 100 km
0 50 miles
KENTUCKY
MISSOURI
VIRGINIA
ARKANSAS
TENNESSEE
NORTH CAROLINA
MISSISSIPPI
ALABAMA
GEORGIA
SOUTH CAROLINA
Ohio River
Paducah
Bowling Green
Glasgow
London
Lake Cumberland
Kentucky Lake
Lake Berkley
Big South Fork National River and Recreation Area
Middlesboro
Kingsport
Bristol
Johnson City
Clarksville
Springfield
Union City
Paris
Cumberland River
Jamestown
Nashville
Lebanon
Dickson
Oak Ridge
Jefferson City
Morristown
Erwin
Newport
Knoxville
Dyersburg
Milan
Crossville
Murfreesboro
Great Smoky Mountains National Park
Ripley
Mississippi River
Lexington
Jackson
Columbia
Shelbyville
Manchester
Dayton
Cherokee National Forest
Athens
Asheville
Memphis
Collierville
Savannah
Lawrenceburg
Pulaski
Tullahoma
Fayetteville
Rainbow Lake Wilderness Area
Cleveland
Chattanooga
Lexington
Greenville
Huntsville
Oxford
Tupelo
Hamilton
Cullman
Lake Sidney Lanier
Lexington
Atlanta
60
65
75
81
24
69
40
65
24
75
43
64
55
74
78

Memphis

MAP P348

The fight for Civil Rights

Housed partly inside the Lorraine Motel, where Martin Luther King Jr was fatally shot on April 4, 1968, is the gut-wrenching **National Civil Rights Museum** *(civilrightsmuseum.org; adult/child $20/17)*. Its engaging and compelling exhibits chronicle the struggle for African American freedom and equality from the earliest days of slavery in the United States. Both Dr King's cultural contribution and his assassination serve as prisms for looking at the Civil Rights movement, its precursors and its continuing impact on American life. The turquoise exterior of the 1950s motel and two preserved interior rooms, which are on view, remain much as they were at the time of King's death.

Musical pioneers who changed history

Memphis draws music-loving pilgrims who come to pay their respects in a city famed for its connection to rock and roll. A good place to start is the **Memphis Rock 'n' Soul Museum** *(memphisrocknsoul.org; adult/child $14/11)* which takes you through the evolution of the genre, from the rural music of Black Americans singing gospel, field hollers and work songs, through the early days of blues recordings and into the emergence of rock and roll itself. Exhibitions and objects (a sharecropper's wagon piled high; an early vinyl-playing juke box; dazzling costumes worn by performers) bring the past to life, and there are lots of listening stations along the way where you can hear songs by innovators like BB King, the Staple Singers and Carl Perkins.

At **Sun Studio** *(sunstudio.com; adult/child $20/15)*, you can see (and hear) where the magic happened. Starting in the early 1950s, Sun's Sam Phillips recorded blues artists such as Howlin' Wolf, BB King and Ike Turner, followed by the rockabilly dynasty of Jerry Lee Lewis, Johnny Cash and, of course, the King himself (who started here in 1953). Packed 45-minute tours (hourly from 10:30am to 4:30pm) take you into the tiny studio, where you'll hear original tapes of historic recording sessions. Guides are full of great stories, and you can pose for photos on the 'X' where Elvis once stood and touch the microphone used by so many legends. Go early; tours sell out.

Wanna feel the funk? Head to the **Stax Museum of American Soul Music** *(staxmuseum.com; adult/child $20/16)*, aka Soulsville USA, a museum on the site of the old Stax recording

BACKSTAGE PASS

If you want to visit all of Memphis' major music sites, be sure to buy the **Backstage Pass** *($108)*, which is sold at **Rock 'n' Soul** and **Stax**. It gives admission to Graceland, Stax, Sun Studio and the Memphis Rock 'n' Soul Museum (saving you 20% vs buying tickets individually), and you can use it over multiple days. Elvis fans have plenty of other options, including VIP tours with a private guide and access to special collections *($145 to $250)*. You can further the experience by staying at the **Guest House at Graceland**, a 450-room resort featuring lots of Elvis touches (Priscilla Presley had a big hand in the design).

EATING IN MEMPHIS: OUR PICKS

MAP P348

Charlie Vergos' Rendezvous: Tucked along a downtown alley, this place has been serving its famous dry-rub ribs since 1948. *11am-9pm Tue-Sat* **$$**

Blues City Cafe: Buzzing spot on Beale St with a big menu, including turnip greens, skillet shrimp and juicy ribs, plus live music nightly. *11am-1am* **$$**

The Four Way: A 1940s landmark serving the best soul food in Memphis, from fried green tomatoes to catfish filets with yams, greens and cornbread. *11am-5pm Wed-Sun* **$**

Majestic Grille: This classy former 1913 movie palace has a broad menu of flatbreads, steaks and seared tuna, as well as weekend brunch. *11am-9pm* **$$**

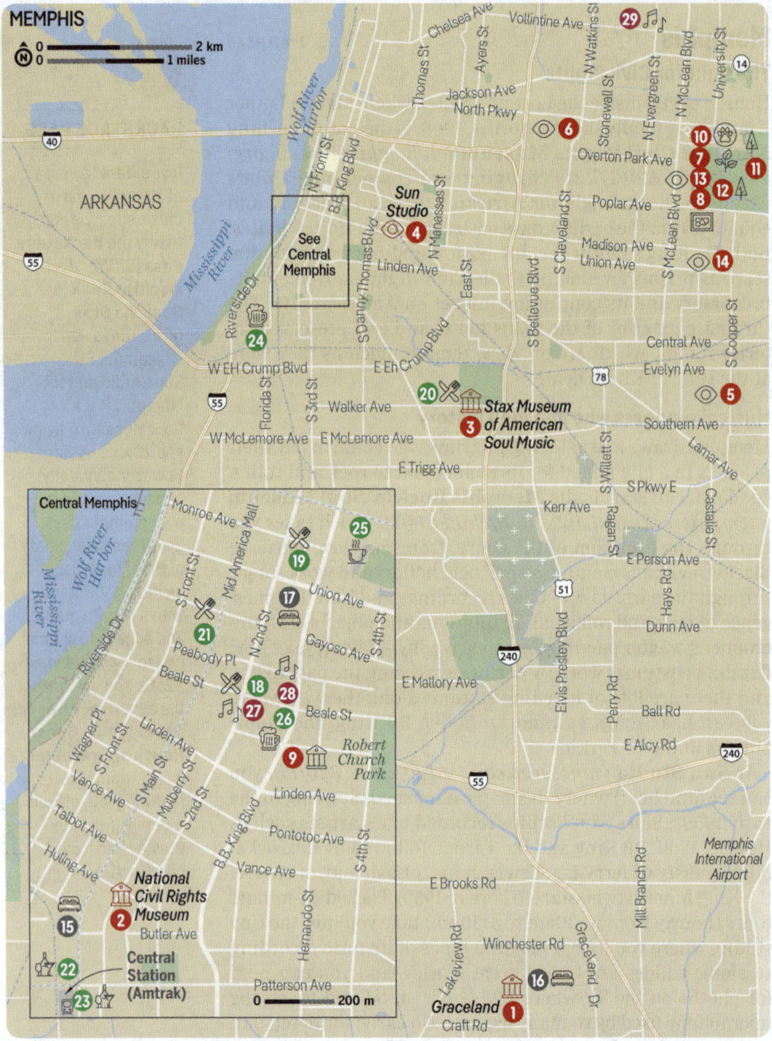

MEMPHIS

HIGHLIGHTS
1 Graceland
2 National Civil Rights Museum
3 Stax Museum of American Soul Music
4 Sun Studio

SIGHTS
5 Cooper-Young
6 Crosstown Concourse
7 Formal Gardens
see 5 Jay Etkin Gallery
8 Memphis Brooks Museum of Art
9 Memphis Rock 'n' Soul Museum
10 Memphis Zoo
11 Old Forest State Natural Area
12 Overton Park
13 Overton Park Shell
14 Overton Square

SLEEPING
15 Arrive
16 Guest House at Graceland
17 Peabody

EATING
18 Blues City Cafe
19 Charlie Vergos' Rendezvous
20 Four Way
see 5 Imagine Vegan Cafe
21 Majestic Grille

DRINKING & NIGHTLIFE
see 5 Bar DKDC
see 5 Celtic Crossing
22 Earnestine & Hazel's
23 Eight & Sand
see 5 Java Cabana
24 Loflin Yard
25 Memphis Chess Club
26 Silky O'Sullivan's
see 5 Young Avenue Deli

ENTERTAINMENT
27 BB King's
28 Blues Hall
see 14 Lafayette's Music Room
see 28 Rum Boogie
29 Wild Bill's

SHOPPING
see 5 901 Comics
see 5 Burke's Book Store
see 5 Goner Records

studio. Dive into soul-music history with photos, displays of '60s and '70s stage clothing, a Soul Train dance floor complete with musical accompaniment and video, and Isaac Hayes' 1972 Superfly Cadillac, outfitted with shag-fur carpeting and 24-karat-gold exterior trim.

The world of Elvis Presley

Some 8 miles south of downtown, **Graceland** *(graceland.com; adult/child $84/48, parking $10)* is hallowed ground for Elvis lovers, who come to visit the King's former home and the sprawling museum complex adjoining it. Though born in Mississippi, Elvis Presley was a true son of Memphis, raised in the Lauderdale Courts public-housing projects, inspired by blues clubs on Beale St, and discovered at Sun Studio. In the spring of 1957, the already-famous 22-year-old spent $100,000 on a colonial-style mansion, named Graceland by its previous owners. A visit here starts with a short film, after which you'll receive a video tablet and headphones, then hop on a shuttle and head to the mansion. The tablet gives audio commentary (by John Stamos) as you make your way through the ostentatiously decorated home, complete with a 15ft couch, numerous TVs and some wildly imagined rooms (like the Jungle Room, which has shag carpet on floor and ceiling alike and a once-functioning artificial waterfall). The self-guided house tour ends near his grave. Next, you'll head to the entertainment complex, which houses Elvis' car museum, an exhibit on his time in the army, and a near-exhaustive lineup of memorabilia including a beautifully displayed collection of his jumpsuits, in all their bedazzled glory. Don't miss Elvis' planes parked nearby.

Exploring Cooper-Young & Overton

Some 5 miles southeast of downtown, **Cooper-Young** *(cooperyoung.com)* is a vibrant district sprinkled with restaurants, shops and drinking spots. Everything is within a few blocks of the intersection of Cooper and Young Sts. You can browse for new and used vinyl at **Goner Records** *(goner-records.com)*, find some fresh or vintage comics and/or action figures at **901 Comics** *(facebook.com/901comics)* and discover new authors around the corner at the famed **Burke's Book Store** *(burkesbooks.com)*, which opened back in 1875. It has a special section on Memphis authors and local history, with used and new titles. You'll find works from artists with a Memphis connection as well as African carvings at **Jay Etkin Gallery** *(jayetkingallery.com)*.

LIVE MUSIC SPOTS

Beale St's music clubs draw mostly tourists, but this is the place for classic blues. Check the Memphis Flyer *(memphisflyer.com)* for shows elsewhere.

BB King's: The original Beale St nightclub from the blues legend brings a fine lineup of talented performers.

Rum Boogie and Blues Hall: Two adjoining spots on Beale St host popular blues nights; one cover *($5)* gets you into both.

Silky O'Sullivan's: Dueling pianos (and requests) make for a kitschy fun time on Beale St.

Lafayette's Music Room: Famous venue for quality performances (and good Southern fare) in an intimate setting near Overton Sq.

Wild Bill's: A gritty hole-in-the-wall juke joint with utterly authentic original blues. It's 4 miles northeast of downtown.

DRINKING IN MEMPHIS: OUR PICKS

MAP P348

Memphis Chess Club: Inviting rainy-day escape with good coffees, snacks and craft beer, plus board games including, of course, chess. *7am-8:30pm Mon-Sat, from 8am Sun*

Earnestine & Hazel's: This brothel turned dive bar has a 2nd floor of claw-foot tubs and tattered furniture. The Soul Burger is legendary. *5pm-late Wed-Sun*

Eight & Sand: DJs spin vinyl beneath a soaring record wall in this lounge-bar in the Central Station Hotel. *4-11pm Sun-Thu, to 1am Fri & Sat*

Loflin Yard: A massive junkyard-aesthetic beer garden with local beers on draft, barrel-aged cocktails, smoked brisket and other temptations. *4-10pm Wed & Thu, 11am-1am Fri & Sat, 11am-10pm Sun*

BEST ATTRACTIONS IN OVERTON PARK

Old Forest State Natural Area: Get a taste of the wilderness on the paved (1.4 mile) and unpaved (4 miles) trails lacing through this verdant old-growth forest.

Overton Park Shell: Spread a picnic blanket on the grass and enjoy free concerts from May through October, with food and drink for sale.

Formal Gardens: See what's in bloom or join a free yoga or tai chi class.

Memphis Brooks Museum of Art: Tennessee's oldest museum has excellent temporary exhibitions, plus live music, film screenings and art workshops (nude drawings, watercolors, printmaking).

Memphis Zoo: Earns high marks for its well-organized layout, fair prices and chance to feed giraffes.

FOTOLUMINATE LLC/SHUTTERSTOCK

Bicentennial Capitol Mall State Park

Stop for coffee at **Java Cabana**, a welcoming gathering place day and night (especially Thursdays at open mic from 7pm to 10pm). Grab a bite in the neighborhood. **Imagine Vegan Cafe** *(imaginevegancafe.com)* serves meat-free versions of Memphis classics, including a decadent barbecue sandwich. There's live music and good pub fare at spots like **Young Avenue Deli** *(youngavenuedeli.com)*, and cocktails and live bands (especially soul) at **Bar DKDC** *(bardkdc.com)*, plus some fine bars with terraces – like **Celtic Crossing** *(celticcrossingirishpub.com)* for nursing cold drinks amid a laid-back crowd.

About a mile north of Cooper-Young, Overton is another restaurant- and bar-filled district, with a dozen spots – many with patios. The epicenter is **Overton Square** *(overtonsquare.com)*, where you can catch free film screenings, food festivals and other periodic events.

Seven blocks north of the neighborhood is **Overton Park** *(overtonpark.org)*, a beloved green space that draws a wide cross section of Memphis to walking trails, sports fields, outdoor concerts, a zoo and more.

Wander a vertical village

One of Memphis' best-loved recent developments, the **Crosstown Concourse** *(crosstownconcourse.com)* transformed a massive (and long abandoned) Sears distribution center (built

EATING IN NASHVILLE: OUR PICKS

MAP P353

Acme Feed & Seed: A multilevel original on Broadway with Southern cooking, live music and rooftop parties (plus Sunday yoga). *4:30-11pm Mon-Thu, 11am-2am Fri-Sun* $$

Puckett's Restaurant: The Nashville original of this small chain boasts a barn-like decor, huge menu (breakfasts, Southern, sandwiches, barbecue) and nightly concerts. *7am-10pm* $$

Peg Leg Porker: Fall-off-the-bone ribs and tender pulled pork at this barbecue icon in the popular Gulch neighborhood. *11am-9pm Mon & Tue, to 10pm Wed-Sat* $

Black Rabbit: Beautifully prepared local rainbow trout, bone-in pork chop, creative cocktails and happy hour specials. Reserve ahead. *4-11pm Mon-Fri, 10am-midnight Sat* $$$

in 1927) into a live-work-entertainment complex with indie restaurants, shops and community organizations. Stop in the Memphis Listening Lab *(memphislisteninglab.org; free)* to hear rare grooves on vinyl; it also hosts music-related listening sessions, artist talks and book signings. On the same level (2nd floor), you can peek in a few galleries, or catch a periodic concert at the intimate Green Room *(crosstownarts .org/music/green-room)*. Next door, you can order cocktails from the small stylish drinking den, the Art Bar *(5pm to midnight)*. Restaurants and snack spots are sprinkled along the 1st floor. Top choices include the beautifully designed Bao Toan *(baotoanmemphis.com)* for elevated Vietnamese fare and creative cocktails, and Global Cafe *(globalcafememphis. com)* with cuisine from far-flung regions of the world. At Crosstown Brewing *(crosstownbeer.com)*, you can linger over microbrews (including their excellent IPA Traffic), munch on pizza and burgers, and catch trivia nights, live music and adult spelling bees.

Nashville

MAP P353

Discovering downtown Nashville

Tennessee's biggest city and capital is packed with intriguing attractions – not all of which revolve around Nashville's dynamic music scene. Before hitting the country-music bars, start your explorations at the **Tennessee State Museum** *(tnmuseum.org; free)*, where you'll find free parking and excellent multimedia exhibits spanning the ages (including well-done short films introducing different periods). You could spend several hours time-traveling through displays on natural history, First Peoples, the Civil War, World Wars and the battle for Civil Rights.

Next door is the **Nashville Farmers Market** *(nashville farmersmarket.org)*, where a large food hall has wood-fired pizza, Korean bowls, crepes, hot chicken, vegan tacos and more. Across the street, you can stroll through **Bicentennial Capitol Mall State Park** with its history-laden plaques and fountains, and make your way (up a steep hill) to the **Tennessee State Capitol** *(capitol.tn.gov; free)*. There you can wander through the lavishly decorated rooms or take a guided tour *(free, departing on the hour)* for more insight into Tennessee history and governance.

A few blocks south of the capitol, head inside the grand **Nashville Public Library** on Church Street *(library.nashville.org;*

TOP MUSIC SITES IN NASHVILLE

Country Music Hall of Fame & Museum: At the great cathedral of country music, you can gaze at Carl Perkins' blue suede shoes, Elvis' gold Cadillac and Taylor Swift's tiered gown from the Eras Tour.

Grand Ole Opry: Hosts the *Grand Ole Opry*, a lavish tribute to classic Nashville country music, every Tuesday, Friday and Saturday night from February through October.

Ryman Auditorium: See a show in the tabled venue where countless legends have performed.

Station Inn: Catch live bluegrass nightly at this long-running venue.

Johnny Cash Museum: Small but comprehensive collection of Johnny Cash artifacts and memorabilia.

Bluebird Cafe: Never mind the strip mall location, some of the best up-and-coming singer-songwriters in country music play here. Reserve ahead.

DRINKING IN NASHVILLE: OUR PICKS

MAP P353

6th & Peabody: Always a lively time at this sprawling indoor-outdoor space with a moonshine distillery, microbrewery and taco shop. *11am-10pm Mon-Wed, to 11pm Thu-Sun*

Close Company: In a redesigned candlelit warehouse in hip Germantown, you can sip inventive elixirs and munch on pastry pockets. *4pm-midnight*

Monday Night Brewing: Another favorite in Germantown, with an industrial-chic interior, huge patio and delicious house-made brews. *noon-10pm Mon-Sat, noon-8pm Sun*

Patterson House: Go early to score a spot at this intimate lounge with a Gatsby-esque vibe serving Nashville's best cocktails. *4pm-2am*

HIGHLIGHTS
1 Country Music Hall of Fame & Museum

SIGHTS
2 Bicentennial Capitol Mall State Parkl
3 Johnny Cash Museum
4 Riverfront Park
5 Tennessee State Capitol
6 Tennessee State Museum

ACTIVITIES
7 Nashville Public Library

SLEEPING
8 Union Station Hotel

EATING
9 Acme Feed & Seed
10 Assembly Food Hall
11 Black Rabbit
12 Peg Leg Porker
13 Puckett's Restaurant

DRINKING & NIGHTLIFE
14 6th & Peabody
15 Patterson House

ENTERTAINMENT
16 Robert's Western World
17 Ryman Auditorium
see 16 Stage on Broadway
18 Station Inn
19 Tootsie's Orchid Lounge

SHOPPING
20 Boot Country
21 Nashville Farmers Market

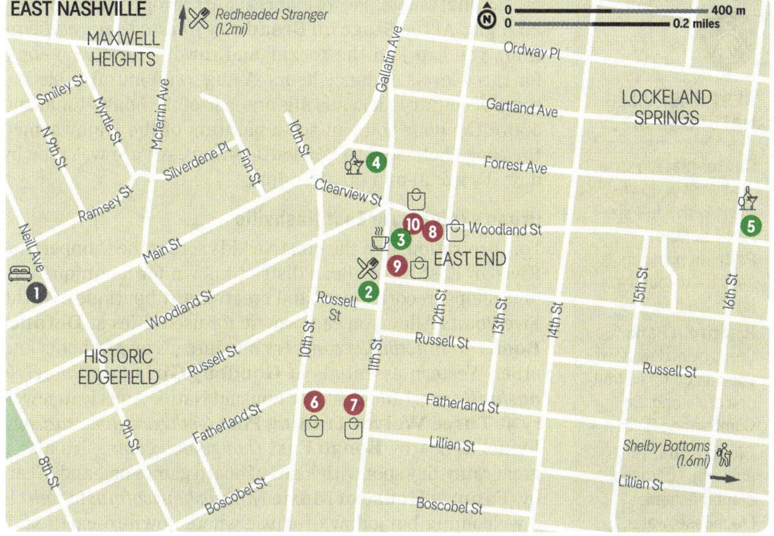

free). Head up to the 2nd floor to check out the Civil Rights Collection, a permanent exhibit with a symbolic lunch counter and various on-demand videos you can watch that spotlight different aspects of the movement.

From there it's an easy walk to Lower Broadway, which is thumping with shops, restaurants and honky-tonks. If you're in the market for Nashville's quintessential footwear, visit **Boot Country** *(twofreeboots.com)*, where it's 'buy one pair, get two pair free.' There are loads of dining options nearby, but for the indecisive, head to **Assembly Food Hall** *(assembly foodhall.com)* with dozens of vendors (and several bars) firing up a wide array of high-quality delicacies.

Hit the honky-tonks

The heart of Nashville's live music scene is Lower Broadway, a four-block stretch of downtown lined with music-filled bars, their bold neon signs lighting the way. The most venerated of the honky-tonks, **Tootsie's Orchid Lounge** *(tootsies.net)*, is a blessed dive oozing boot-stomping, hillbilly, beer-soaked grace with stages on each of its three floors. Nearby, **Robert's Western World** *(robertswesternworld.com)* is a cut above other joints, and a must for folks making a country

SLEEPING
1 Waymore's

EATING
2 Bad Idea

DRINKING & NIGHTLIFE
3 Bongo East
4 Red Door Saloon East
5 Urban Cowboy Public House

SHOPPING
6 Abode Mercantile
7 Daydream Records
8 Defunct Books
see 7 Ellie Monster
9 Fanny's House of Music
10 Goodbuy Girls
see 10 Three Wolves Trading Post

EATING & DRINKING IN EAST NASHVILLE: OUR PICKS

MAP P353

Urban Cowboy Public House: Stylish lounge and inviting patio make a memorable setting for inventive cocktails and wood-fired pizzas. *4-11pm* **$$**

Redheaded Stranger: Nashville's finest tacos, topped with ingredients like brisket, red hatch chilies and poblano peppers. Best enjoyed on the front terrace. *10am-10pm* **$**

Red Door Saloon East: Classic dive in bar-dotted Five Points with indoor and outdoor seating and plenty of love for the (Chicago) Bears. *11am-3am*

Bad Idea: Strange and wonderful mashup of Lao cuisine meets wine bar, set (naturally) in a converted church sanctuary. *5pm-midnight* **$$$**

BEST NASHVILLE NATURE ESCAPES

Centennial Park: Just west of downtown, with a full-size replica of the Parthenon and an easy trail around a lake.

Riverfront Park: Steps from downtown, you can go for a stroll or a run along the Cumberland River.

Cheekwood: The numerous gardens combine themes (Japanese, water, wildflower) with art, and surround a straight-out-of-a-Jane-Austen-novel house, where exhibitions are held regularly.

Shelby Bottoms: Boasts over 10 miles of multi-use trails including a paved trail that winds alongside the scenic Cumberland River.

Warner Parks: Picturesque overlooks, 200-year-old stone walls, old-growth forest and over 60 miles of trails, plus a nature center, play areas for kids, and regular events.

music pilgrimage. Performances start at opening and goes all night. At the **Stage on Broadway** *(thestageonbroadway.com)*, you can join the rockin' and rowdy crowd who come for three levels of dance floors. A huge wall mural depicting some of country's legends fills one side of the honky-tonk, and above the door you can see a painting of the Highwaymen that once belonged to Waylon Jennings. All are welcome by day; it's age 21 and up after 6pm.

Urban exploring in East Nashville

For inspiration, join the creative kids across the Cumberland River in East Nashville, a district known for its unique vintage shops, record stores and creative gift boutiques. At the Five Points Alley, you can browse for used titles at **Defunct Books** *(defunctbooks.com)*, try on vintage cowgirl boots and other Western essentials at **Goodbuy Girls** *(goodbuygirlsnashville.com)* and discover unusual Native American jewelry at **Three Wolves Trading Post** *(@threewolvestrading)*. Refuel at nearby **Bongo East** *(bongojava.com)* – it's also a great rainy-day spot with loads of board games on hand. Nearby, **Fanny's House of Music** *(fannyshouseofmusic.com)* is a welcoming bungalow of music where down-to-earth staff can you help you find your next new or vintage guitar, banjo or ukulele. There's also a small collection of vintage clothing and accessories.

Several blocks south of there the Fatherland District *(fatherlanddistrict.com)* is another indie shopping spot. Pick up western and retro-styled clothing at **Ellie Monster** *(elliemonster.com)*, hunt for old vinyl at **Daydream Records** *(@daydreamrecordshop)* and pick up assorted gifts (fragrances, jewelry, whimsical socks) at **Abode Mercantile** *(abodemercantile.com)*.

Chattanooga

Art and river life in downtown Chattanooga

It's easy to fall for the charms of Chattanooga, a Tennessee River town with a dynamic arts scene and a great love of the outdoors. At the **Bluff View Art District** *(bluffviewartdistrictchattanooga.com)*, you can wander through a sculpture garden overlooking the river. Amid the greenery are over a dozen works, including pieces by Richard Serra and Leonard Baskin. Nearby, the **River Gallery** *(river-gallery.com)* showcases paintings, ceramics, glasswork and jewelry by numerous artists, many with local

EATING & DRINKING IN CHATTANOOGA: OUR PICKS

Niedlov's Cafe & Bakery: Heavenly pastries, outstanding coffees and flavor-rich sandwiches on perfectly baked breads. *7am-6pm Mon-Fri, to 4pm Sat* $

STIR: Artfully designed space in the historic Chattanooga Choo Choo complex, serving oysters, fish tacos, veggie bowls and steak frites. *11am-midnight Mon-Fri, from 10am Sat & Sun* $$

Hi-Fi Clyde's: Play ping pong, catch live music on weekend nights or linger over smoked wings and brisket nachos at this friendly corner bar. *11am-midnight Sun-Thu, to 2am Fri & Sat* $

1885 Grill: Tuck in to shrimp and grits, rainbow trout or fried chicken while relaxing on the tree-shaded patio opposite the Incline Railway station. *11am-9pm* $$

SEAN PAVONE/SHUTTERSTOCK

View from Lookout Mountain

ties to Chattanooga. Take a break at various restaurants in the area, including **Rembrandt's Coffee House** *(@rembrandts coffeehouse)*, with its shaded courtyard.

Anchoring the district is the **Hunter Museum of American Art** *(huntermuseum.org; adult/child $20/free)*, set in a striking building of elegant curving steel (like a mini Bilbao Guggenheim) adjoining an early-20th-century mansion. There's a fine permanent collection of 19th- and 20th-century works, along with Chattanooga's best temporary exhibitions.

It's a short stroll from here, via a pedestrian bridge over the Parkway, to the **Tennessee Aquarium** *(tnaqua.org; adult/child $40/30)*. This impressive destination spotlights the inhabitants and ecology of the Tennessee River as it flows from the Appalachian Mountains to the Mississippi Delta. Exhibits in the Ocean Journey building display saltwater marine life. Crowd-pleasers include river otters, penguins and leaping lemurs.

Next to the aquarium, take the Passage, a lane that leads down to the river. Here, water cascades down the steps and into a small wading pool. It's a great spot for kids to cool off. Just below is **Ross's Landing** *(nps.gov/places/ross-s-landing.htm)*, a stretch of greenery that was the starting point of the Trail of Tears. Artwork memorializes the forced removal of the Cherokee in 1838.

For hands-on adventures in downtown, head to the nearby **High Point Climbing** *(highpointclimbing.com; adult/child $31/29)*, a requisite stop for rock climbers. The large center has bouldering walls and dozens of routes for top-rope climbing as well as auto-belay climbs covering a wide range of levels.

Trails and rails on Lookout Mountain

Some of Chattanooga's oldest and best-loved attractions are 6 miles southwest of downtown at Lookout Mountain, near the Georgia state line. Visitors come to ride the **Incline Railway**

GATEWAYS TO THE SMOKIES

Eastern Tennessee is a popular base for visiting Great Smoky Mountains National Park (p329).

Gatlinburg: At the entrance to the national park. Lures visitors with pancake breakfasts, moonshine distilleries and various odd museums and campy attractions, plus the mountaintop adventure park of Anakeesta.

Pigeon Forge: Some 10 miles north of the park entrance, the buzzing, often congested town of Pigeon Forge is another handy base, with myriad amusements, including the Dolly Parton theme park of Dollywood.

Townsend: A smaller settlement to the park's west; handy for reaching the Cades Cove section, some 16 miles away.

You can also access the park via the scenic North Carolina town of Cherokee (p328).

BEST ADVENTURES IN CHEROKEE NATIONAL FOREST

The 660,000-acre **Cherokee National Forest** in Tennessee's east offers unrivaled adventures.

Cherokee Rafting: Splash through family-friendly rapids on the Ocoee River or go epic on class III and IV rapids of the Olympic section.

Cherohala Skyway: See spectacular mountain scenery on the 43-mile drive from Tellico Plains (TN) to Robbinsville (NC).

Conasauga River Blue Hole: Snorkel the clear waters of the Conasauga River, home to over 39 different fish species.

Raft One: A one-stop shop for rafting trips, ziplines, horseback riding and mountain bikes for hire.

Benton Falls Trail: One of countless hikes in Cherokee, this 3-mile out-and-back route takes in Appalachian forests and a 65ft waterfall.

KEVIN RUCK/SHUTTERSTOCK

Rock City trail

(ridetheincline.com; adult/child $22/10), which chugs up a steep slope to a lofty neighborhood. From the top, you can stroll (head right 0.3 miles) to **Point Park** *(adult/child $10/free)*, a 10-acre site full of monuments and fine views that played a pivotal role in a Civil War battle. It's part of the Chickamauga & Chattanooga National Military Park *(nps.gov/chch)* run by the National Park Service, and you can learn more about the battle at the free visitor center and museum facing the entrance to Point Park. There are also numerous scenic hikes in the area, including the 3-mile out-and-back journey along the Bluff Trail to Sunset Rock. Access the trailhead in Point Park or start at the base of the hill at Cravens House (free parking) – the oldest surviving structure on Lookout Mountain and a major focal point during the battle.

Other attractions on Lookout Mountain include stunning **Ruby Falls** *(rubyfalls.com; adult/child $29/19)*, the world's longest underground waterfall. Next to it is **High Point Zip Adventure** *(rubyfalls.com; $22)* with some 700ft of ziplines and a 40ft climbing tower. Four miles south of there (in Georgia) is **Rock City** *(seerockcity.com; adult/child $43/33)*, a garden marked by dramatic rock formations and a clifftop overlook.

Rainbow Lake Wilderness Area

Waterfalls and lookouts

Near the settlement of Signal Mountain, some 20 minutes' drive north of downtown Chattanooga, the **Rainbow Lake Wilderness Area** *(free)* is home to bouncy suspension bridges, waterfalls, scenic overlooks and many miles of trails lacing through the area. Those out for a short-ish, easy-going excursion to the reserve's highlight can start at the Ohio Ave trailhead and make the 1.5-mile (round-trip) hike to Rainbow Lake. After rains, the water cascades 20ft over the dam, creating a lovely waterfall, and you can swim in the pool below.

For a longer outing, instead of heading straight to the lake, take the Bee Branch Trail, which will take you over an Indiana Jones–style suspension bridge. Turn left right after crossing the bridge and follow it down to Rainbow Lake. Afterwards, continue along the Cumberland Trail. This will take you past the spur trail to Rainbow Falls. For adventurers only, this super steep descent (0.1 miles) along slippery terrain has ropes that you'll need to hold on to to make it safely down and back. The reward: one of the region's most beautiful waterfalls, an 80ft cascade into a shimmering pool that you may have entirely to yourself (don't forget swimwear). Continuing on the Cumberland Trail you'll pass the Julia Falls overlook with its jaw-dropping views over the Tennessee River as it winds past Raccoon Mountain. The trail ends near Signal Point (another parking area/trail access point), where you can complete the loop by walking 0.5 miles on the road (it's a pleasant, little trafficked neighborhood).

Knoxville

Delving into the past in a World's Fair city

Dubbed a 'scruffy little city' by the *Wall Street Journal* before the 1982 World's Fair, Knoxville is these days a polished destination when it comes to the arts and outdoor attractions. The visual centerpiece is the **Sunsphere** *(worldsfairpark.org/sunsphere; adult/child $10/5)*, a golden orb atop a tower built for the Fair. You can take the elevator to the 4th-floor observation deck to see the skyline. Nearby, you'll find green space, fountains and a waterway, along with the **Knoxville Museum of Art** *(knoxart.org; free)*, well worth visiting for its impressive collection of East Tennessee artists. Seek out the turbulent works by the Delaney brothers, as well as spiritually charged mixed-media pieces by Bessie Harvey and the miniaturized wonderland of the Thorne Rooms.

Next, stroll a few blocks east to the **Museum of East Tennessee History** *(easttnhistory.org; adult/child $10/free)*. Interactive displays cover the Civil War (when many in the region sided with the Union against the Confederacy), 'hillbilly' stereotypes and mountain music, and the little-known role East Tennessee played during WWII, when the 'secret city' of Oak Ridge was created to refine uranium for the atomic bomb.

Afterward, walk through the sculpture-filled Charles Krutch Park and up to **Market Square**, where you'll find an assortment of outdoor cafes, restaurants and bars with tables on the plaza.

About 1.5 miles east of Market Sq, the **Beck Cultural Exchange Center** *(beckcenter.net; free)* is a great place to learn about African American history in Knoxville. The converted mansion houses rooms full of historic photos and artifacts, and kindly staff will put on a documentary about the destruction of Black neighborhoods owing to urban renewal. Next door, a museum dedicated to the artist Beauford Delaney is in the works.

MOONSHINE

Eastern Tennessee has deep ties to moonshine – un-aged whiskey, often sourced from corn. Moonshine earned its modern reputation during Prohibition, when alcohol production and consumption was banned in 1920. Enforcement, however, was difficult, and making illegal spirits provided extra income for Appalachian home distillers. To hide the smoke from their stills, the distillers made their corn liquor at night, under the light of the moon, hence the name moonshine. Although Prohibition was repealed in 1933, moonshining was a good way for families to make extra cash during the Depression, which continued across the 1930s. NASCAR racing is a descendant of the wild automobile chases of the era, when federal agents chased the souped-up cars used by the bootleggers to deliver their product.

Kentucky

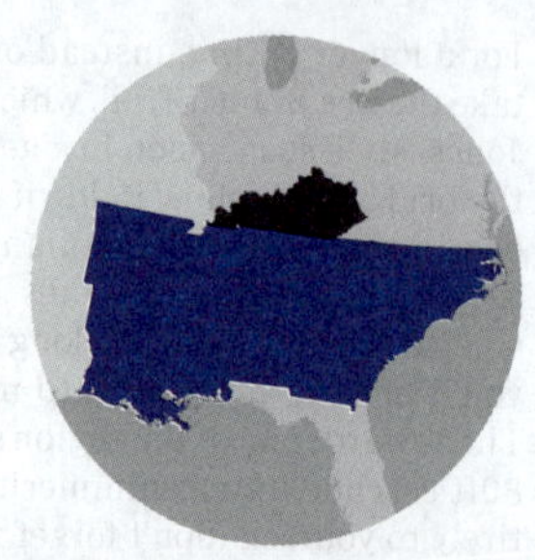

THOROUGHBREDS | BOURBON | RUGGED WILDERNESS

Places

Louisville p360
Bardstown p361
Lexington p361
Frankfort p362
Mammoth Cave National Park p363
Red River Gorge p364
Daniel Boone National Forest p365

TOP TIPS

Kentucky's farmers markets offer great ways to experience the state's bounty. Louisville has two excellent ones: **Bardstown Road** *(bardstownroadfarmersmarket.com; Sat year-round)* and **Douglas Loop** *(douglassloopfarmersmarket.org; Sat Apr-Dec)*. Lexington also has several farmers markets *(lexingtonfarmersmarket.com)* including a **downtown market** *(Sat year-round)*.

Horses thunder around racetracks, bourbon pours from distilleries and banjos twang in Kentucky, a geographical and cultural crossroads that's part North, part South, part genteel and part country cousin. Every corner is easy on the eye, but there are few sights more beautiful than the rolling limestone hills around Lexington, where long-legged steeds nibble under poplar trees on multimillion-dollar farms. Bourbon distilleries also speckle the countryside, prime for scenic road tripping to swirl and sniff a dram at the source. It's like an offbeat version of California's Napa Valley, but with fewer crowds and headier alcohol. Outdoor adventures prevail in the state's unspoiled parks and forests, which offer some dazzling attractions – including the world's largest caverns and thundering waterfalls that glisten with moonbows at certain times of the month. And while big cities like Louisville have farm-to-table restaurants, cocktail bars and a vibrant music scene, most of Kentucky is made up of small towns, including its delightful state capital, Frankfort.

GETTING AROUND

Kentucky is generally a tough place to get around without a car. In Louisville **TARC** *(ridetarc.org)* runs a decent bus network that can get you around town (though not always all that quickly). Downtown is quite walkable, and route numbers 4, 6 and 29 run from there to Churchill Downs (with frequent service during the Kentucky Derby). In Lexington, there's a smaller bus network run by Lextran *(lextran.com)*. During racing season in April, buses connect Lexington's transit center (Vine St) with Keeneland. You'll find decent rideshare service from both Uber and Lyft in Louisville and Lexington.

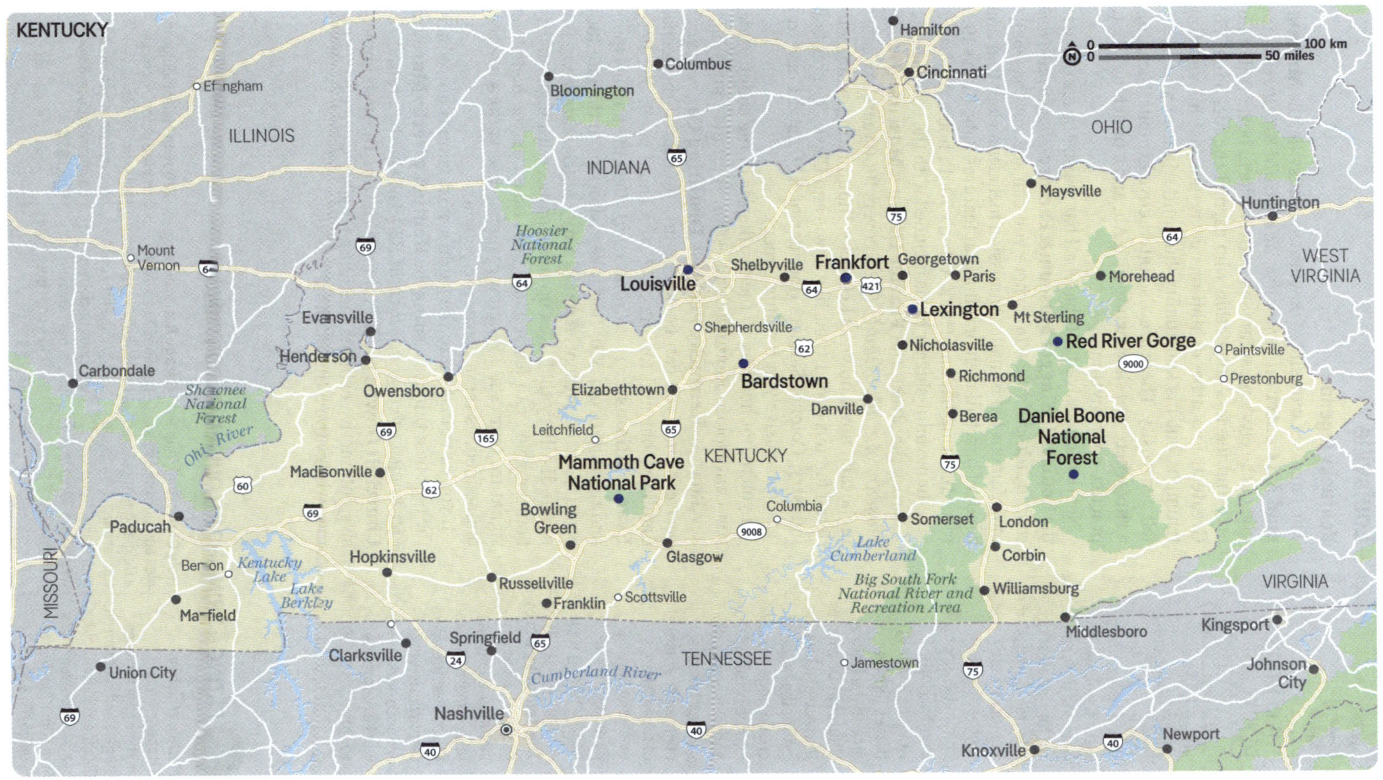
KENTUCKY
0 100 km
0 50 miles
ILLINOIS
INDIANA
OHIO
WEST VIRGINIA
VIRGINIA
TENNESSEE
MISSOURI
KENTUCKY
Hamilton
Columbus
Cincinnati
Bloomington
Maysville
Huntington
Mount Vernon
Hoosier National Forest
Louisville
Shelbyville
Frankfort
Georgetown
Paris
Morehead
Lexington
Mt Sterling
Evansville
Shepherdsville
Nicholasville
Red River Gorge
Paintsville
Henderson
Carbondale
Richmond
Prestonburg
Owensboro
Elizabethtown
Bardstown
Danville
Berea
Daniel Boone National Forest
Leitchfield
Mammoth Cave National Park
Madisonville
Paducah
Bowling Green
Columbia
Somerset
London
Glasgow
Lake Cumberland
Corbin
Hopkinsville
Russellville
Big South Fork National River and Recreation Area
Williamsburg
Franklin
Scottsville
Middlesboro
Kingsport
Springfield
Clarksville
Jamestown
Johnson City
Union City
Cumberland River
Nashville
Knoxville
Newport
75
64
65
69
421
62
9000
165
60
9008
24
40

THE KENTUCKY DERBY

On the first Saturday in May, a who's who of upper-crust USA put on their seersucker suits and most flamboyant hats and descends for the 'greatest two minutes in sports': the Kentucky Derby, the longest-running continuous sporting event in North America, when 20 horses thunder around the track at **Churchill Downs** for the race of a lifetime.

After the race, the crowd sings 'My Old Kentucky Home' and watches as the winning horse is covered in a blanket of roses. Then everyone parties. Actually, they've been partying for a while by this point. The **Kentucky Derby Festival**, which includes a balloon race, a marathon and the largest fireworks display in North America, starts two weeks before the big event.

Louisville

Kentucky legends

The must-see museum of downtown Louisville, the **Muhammad Ali Center** *(alicenter.org; adult/child $20/10)* tells the tale of the city's most famous native: a local boxer full of poetry and fearless conviction who earned the nickname The Greatest. Evocative exhibitions cover not just his sporting triumphs but his spirituality, humanitarianism and heartfelt generosity. There are also interactive exhibits, including a ring where you shadowbox with Ali, and a punching bag to practice your rhythm.

Nearby, a massive 120ft baseball bat marks the entrance to the **Louisville Slugger Museum & Factory** *(sluggermuseum.com; adult/child $24/16)*, where you can see how baseball's most famous bat is made. Admission includes a plant tour and a hall of baseball memorabilia that features Babe Ruth's 1927 record-setting bat and Hank Aaron's 700th home run bat. A take-home mini-slugger bat is included with the entrance fee.

Across the street, the **Frazier History Museum** *(fraziermuseum.org; adult/child $16/10)* covers 1000 years of history in the land now known as Kentucky. Illuminating exhibitions detail famous expeditions like Lewis and Clark, the bourbon industry, Colonel Sanders (founder of KFC) and Corvettes (made exclusively in Bowling Green).

If you're not heading to the distilleries in the countryside, you can explore Kentucky's finest on the mile-long Whiskey Row. At **Kentucky Peerless Distilling Co** *(kentuckypeerless.com)*, you can book a 75-minute behind-the-scenes distillery tour and tasting *($32)* at a small-batch distillery. **Evan Williams** *(evanwilliams.com)* offers memorable tours and tastings (from $20) that take visitors from the late 18th century to the present. **Angel's Envy** *(angelsenvy.com)* is a micro-distillery that lives up to its name, with high-quality bourbons you can learn about (and taste) on the hour-long signature tour ($30). Wherever you go, reservations are recommended, as these places are popular.

If you can't make it to the world's most famous horse race, the next best thing is visiting the **Kentucky Derby Museum** *(derbymuseum.org; adult/child $20/12)*. On the grounds of **Churchill Downs** you'll explore derby lore through immersive, interactive exhibits including a jockey's-eye view of the race while atop a thoroughbred model.

EATING & DRINKING IN LOUISVILLE: OUR PICKS

Merle's Whiskey Kitchen: Buzzing, anytime spot for tacos, burgers and southern hits (like fried chicken), plus live music on weekends. *11am-10pm Tue-Thu, to midnight Fri & Sat* **$**

Holy Grale: Drink Trappist ales and slurp mussels in a Belgian gastropub and former chapel complete with stained-glass windows. *5-10pm Mon-Fri, from 2pm Sat & Sun*

Garage Bar: In buzzing bar-lined NuLu (New Louisville), this former auto garage fires up delicious brick-oven pizzas best enjoyed with an Atrium craft beer. *hours vary* **$$**

Proof on Main: Indulge in charred octopus, chicken Milanese and creative cocktails in an art-filled downtown space. *8am-10pm* **$$$**

JOSEPH HENDRICKSON/SHUTTERSTOCK

Muhammad Ali Center

Bardstown

On the bourbon trail

The elegant streets of Bardstown in Central Kentucky make an excellent base for exploring the nearby bourbon distilleries. Learn about the spirit's history from pre-colonial days through Prohibition and up to today at the **Oscar Getz Museum of Bourbon History** *(facebook.com/whiskeymuseum; free)*, then head to top-notch distilleries in the area like **Willett** *(kentuckybourbonwhiskey.com)*, where you can learn about production methods and family history on a 75-minute tour *($27)*, with samples throughout the experience. On a former tobacco farm, **Preservation Distillery** *(preservation distillery.com)* offers intimate tours *($24)* of its small-batch operations. Plan your visit around the **Kentucky Bourbon Festival** *(kybourbonfestival.com)*, featuring three days of tastings, panel discussions and workshops in early September. If you don't have a designated driver, consider booking a tour with **Mint Julep Experiences** *(mintjuleptours.com; from $200)*, which includes three distillery tours and tastings, lunch and transportation.

Lexington

Horsing around

Kentucky's second largest city is often dubbed the horse capital of the world, owing to the staggering number of thoroughbred farms in the area. Some 10 miles north of downtown Lexington, you can get a deeper understanding of equine culture at the **Kentucky Horse Park** *(kyhorsepark.com; adult/child $28/14)*. Apart from the excellent museum documenting horses and their deep impact on human history (warfare, colonization, farming, transportation), the sprawling complex has shows and activities throughout the day – from horse-drawn trolley rides to draft horse and champion presentations, where you

THE LAND OF BOURBON

Silky, caramel-colored bourbon whiskey was likely first distilled in Bourbon County, north of Lexington, around 1789. Today 95% of the world's bourbon is made in Kentucky, thanks to the state's pure, limestone-filtered water, which contains a high proportion of minerals (like calcium and magnesium) that are optimal for distilling. Bourbon must contain at least 51% corn, and be stored in charred oak barrels for a minimum of two years. The char is essential for imparting those notes of vanilla, caramel and toffee, not to mention the smokiness. While connoisseurs drink it straight or with water, you must try a mint julep, the archetypal Southern drink made with bourbon, simple syrup and crushed mint.

A LEGENDARY FRONTIERSMAN

Lee Muncy, historical interpreter and member of the Sons of the American Revolution *@sar.org*

Before the Revolution, Daniel Boone was an employee of the British-run Transylvania Company, and he helped cut out a trail through the Cumberland Gap of the Appalachian Mountains down in Virginia. He ultimately founded Boonesborough, one of the first settlements in Kentucky. After the Revolutionary War, Boone moved to Missouri, which is where he was living when Lewis and Clark came to see him before their great expedition in 1802. They told him they were going in search of the Pacific Ocean. Boone said he'd already been there. Sure enough, when Lewis and Clark met various Indian tribes, a lot of them talked about that guy from Kentucky.

WANGKUN JIA/SHUTTERSTOCK

Mammoth Cave National Park

can meet the four-legged stars of the park. Check the schedule before heading here to avoid missing out.

Lexington is also home to **Keeneland** *(keeneland.com)*, with exciting thoroughbred races run in April and October, and opportunities to watch morning training sessions *($22)* or take a behind-the-scenes tour *($50)*.

Frankfort

Small-town charm

One of the south's most appealing little towns, Frankfort lies along the banks of the idyllic Kentucky River and its brick streets are dotted with indie shops, cafes and local restaurants. The diminutive capital of Kentucky also has a handful of museums where you can explore the past. Start off at the **Kentucky Historical Society** *(history.ky.gov; adult/child $8/6)*, where you can spend an hour or more learning about the lives of its former inhabitants, including Native Americans, pioneers, enslaved people, Civil War soldiers and moonshiners. There are lots of curious items here, like the pocket watch President Abraham Lincoln carried in 1860. Your admission ticket gives you access to two other nearby sites: the **Old State Capitol**, which was the seat of power from 1830 to 1910, and the **Kentucky Military History Museum** – the best place to find out about the state's involvement in wars dating back to the 1800s.

It's also worth visiting the **Capital City Museum** *(capitalcitymuseum.org; free)* for its displays on surprising events, like the assassination of Senator William Goebel, with accurately detailed mannequins gathered around the supine figure, who died in this building back in 1900.

When you need a break, take a stroll along West Broadway and intersecting St Clair Street. You can browse for regionally made crafts and artwork at **Completely Kentucky** (*completelykentucky.com*), pick up new (and secondhand) reading material at **Poor Richard's Books** (*poorrichardsbooksky.indielite.org*) and purchase new and used records – as well as guitars – at **Musket's Music Station** (*musketsmusicstation.com*). Enjoy coffee, snacks and yet more books at the **Kentucky Coffeetree Cafe** (*kentuckycoffeetree.com*) or head 1½ blocks southwest of there to **Engine House** (*enginehouse1868.com*), a former fire station that today serves Frankfort's best lattes and cold brews.

Frankfort also has some distilleries near town. The legendary **Buffalo Trace** (*buffalotracedistillery.com*), the nation's oldest distillery, has lovely grounds you can wander, in addition to free tastings. **Castle & Key** (*castleandkey.com; tour $30*) is among the most photogenic distilleries with its medieval-looking buildings.

Mammoth Cave National Park

Caving, hiking, horseback riding and canoeing

Home to the longest cave system on earth, **Mammoth Cave National Park** (*nps.gov/maca*) has more than 400 miles of surveyed passageways. It's at least three times longer than any other known cave, with vast interior cathedrals, bottomless pits and strange, undulating rock formations.

Excellent ranger-guided tours (*adult/child from $23/19*) explore the subterranean expanse. Book ahead if possible (*at recreation.gov*) as they do sell out, especially in summer and on weekends, and some tours are offered only at specific times on certain days of the week.

Jaunts range from hour-long strolls to strenuous, day-long spelunking adventures (*adults only*). The **Frozen Niagara Tour** is the easiest of the bunch. There are several options that take place by lantern light, including **Star Chamber**, **Great Onyx** and **Violet City** – a nostalgic way of experiencing these caverns.

If you're short on time, opt for the self-guided **Discovery Tour** (*adult/child $12/9*), where you can explore at your own pace through large open passageways dotted with artifacts from the cave's early days. There's also one accessible tour, where you can visit (via elevator) several impressive formation-filled rooms with no stairs involved.

In addition to the caves, the park contains 85 miles of trails. You can head off on memorable hikes, like the moderate 2.5-mile loop along the **Green River Bluffs** and **Heritage Loop** trails, where you'll enjoy some wonderful views over the dense forests. You can also experience the woodlands by horseback: family-owned **Double J Stables** (*doublejstables.com; rides $40-75*) offers scenic one- and two-hour trail rides.

Some 30 miles of the Green and Nolin Rivers wind through the national park. Several outfitters rent out kayaks and canoes, including **Adventures of Mammoth Cave** (*adventuresofmammothcave.com; canoe or kayak $65*). They'll provide shuttle transport to the launch, where you can leisurely paddle your way along a 7.5-mile stretch of forest-lined riverside. Allow three to four hours to complete the journey.

RED RIVER GORGE ESSENTIALS

Info & Dining: Tiny Slade has a handy visitor center (*gopoco.org/visitor-center*) with maps and trail recommendations. Fill up at **Miguel's** (*7am-9:45pm*) on breakfasts, pizza and sandwiches, or cabin-like **Sky Bridge Station** (*noon-9pm Mon-Sat, to 6pm Sun*) for burgers and craft beer.

Roads: Many trailheads are reached off Hwy 77 and Hwy 715, which form a 33-mile loop near Slade.

Trails:

Rock Bridge Arch A 1.5-mile loop passing a small waterfall and shallow pool, where kids (and dogs) love to splash about.

Chimney Top This easy 0.7-mile trail is a scenic outing for all levels, as is the neighboring Princess Arch Trail.

Auxier Ridge A 4.5-mile out-and-back hike with great views. Many nearby trails too. Access it via Tunnel Ridge Rd.

THE MOONBOW

Cumberland Falls is one of the few places in the world to see a moonbow. Also called a lunar rainbow, this brilliant display forms in the water's mist when conditions are right. It can only happen during a full moon and on the two days before and after the full moon. There must also be clear skies and abundant mist (with decent wind). None of this would be possible without the atypical location of the falls – they face north with water cascading in a northward direction. Plan your visit sometime between dusk and midnight when the moon hangs low in the sky. The park website has dates for when the phenomenon occurs each month and it can happen throughout the year.

SEAN PAVONE/SHUTTERSTOCK

Red River Gorge

Hikes and cave paddles

A vast tract of cliffs, trickling streams and natural arches set amid dense forests, the **Red River Gorge** *(redrivergorge.com)* is Kentucky's top spot for outdoor activities. Hikers will find numerous trails traversing the forest of hemlock and white pine, past wild rock formations and thickets of rhododendron. Bordering the gorge area is the **Natural Bridge State Resort Park** *(naturalbridgestatepark.com; free)*, where you can hike a 1-mile trail up to the 65ft high, 78ft wide sandstone bridge. Take the narrow stairs up to the top and keep going (along the Laurel Ridge Trail) to reach a sweeping overlook across the forested landscape. From here, you can complete the loop via the Battleship Rock Trail, which will take you past high cliffs and fern-covered rock shelters. Alternatively, you can ride the **Sky Lift** *(naturalbridgeskyliftandgiftshop.com; adult/child $17/14)* up to a viewpoint near the natural bridge.

For a different perspective on this unusual geological region, book an excursion with **Gorge Underground** *(gorgeunderground.com; tour $55)*. You'll take a one-hour guided kayaking visit through a century-old, now-flooded limestone mine where you might see bats winging past and massive trout swimming below. Helmet and headlamp included, but dress warmly (thick socks) for the chilly subterranean temperatures.

Cumberland Falls

Daniel Boone National Forest

Natural wonders in Cumberland Falls

Part of the vast Daniel Boone National Forest in eastern Kentucky, **Cumberland Falls State Resort Park** *(cumberlandfallsstatepark.com; free)* is a verdant expanse of densely forested ridges on either side of the meandering Cumberland River. The star of the show is the thundering **Cumberland Falls**, a 69ft tall, 125ft wide cascade that's sometimes dubbed 'the Niagara of the South.' Viewing platforms run along the east side of the falls, and some 17 miles of trails wind through the pristine forests surrounding them. One of the best short hikes is the 1.5-mile (round trip) out-and-back hike to **Eagles Falls**, a hidden cascade on the west side of the river. You can also tack on another half mile by following signs for the loop trail. A short drive (or walk) from the falls (and also part of Cumberland Falls State Resort Park), you'll find camping, cabins and lodge rooms as well as a simple old-fashioned restaurant. Just up the road, **Sheltowee Trace Adventure Resort** *(ky-rafting.com)* offers many activities: rafting, kayaking and ziplines. Also in the area, **Cumberland Falls Horse Stables** lead 45-minute rides *($25 per person)* through the forests. These depart hourly from 10am to 6pm.

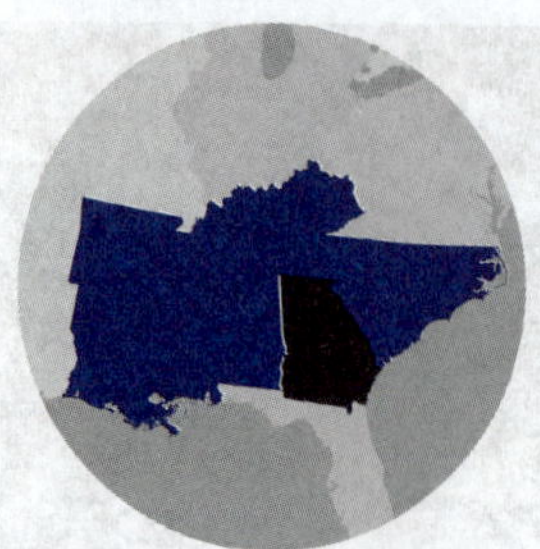

Georgia

ARTS & CULTURE | CAPTIVATING NEIGHBORHOODS | ISLAND ESCAPES

Places

Atlanta p367
Athens p374
Macon p374
Okefenokee National Wildlife Refuge p375
Savannah p376
Georgian Coast p376

When it comes to the Peach State, Atlanta hogs headlines (a film industry upstart, Fortune 500 epicenter and sporting powerhouse) while everything else seems to fly bewilderingly under the radar (Georgia has beaches?). That's just fine by natives, who'd love nothing more than to keep Georgia's other gems, including the northern mountains – and their surrounding foothills and upcountry – to themselves. Other lesser-known attractions pockmark the hinterlands, including the wildlife-rich landscape of the Okefenokee Swamp and the astonishing Native American legacy of Ocmulgeee Mounds.

Along the coast, Savannah has long captivated out-of-towners with its mix of history, creativity and culinary prowess, not to mention a heavy dollop of Southern charm. Nightlife thrives year-round and there are bustling watering holes aplenty. Savannah is also the gateway to picturesque sea islands lapped by salt tides and peppered with marshes, estuaries and beaches. These islands have a lost-in-time, almost Gothic, beauty; every corner seems to drip with sweat and Spanish moss.

TOP TIP

A good Southern meal needs to be washed down with iced tea, and the default here is always sweet (ask for unsweetened if you have a lower sugar tolerance). Most soul food spots will likely send you home with another one to go.

GETTING AROUND

In Atlanta the four-line **MARTA** train system is generally a plus-sign shape, with two north-south lines (red and gold) and two east-west ones (blue and green). The Atlanta Streetcar line circles between Centennial Olympic Park and King Historic District, and there's an extensive bus system. You can explore Savannah's historic core by foot or the free DOT shuttle. A car is also your best bet for getting around coastline. Bus service is fairly limited though Greyhound and Megabus connect Atlanta to both Athens and Savannah, among other places.

Atlanta

MAPS P368, P370, P371

Exploring downtown

Some of Atlanta's biggest attractions all fall within a peach's throw of each other in the downtown area.

The city was a key focal point during th Civil Rights movement, and the **National Center for Civil & Human Rights** *(civilandhumanrights.org; adult/child $20/16)* shines a light on the past. One of the most powerful (and popular) installations is the interactive Lunch Counter Sit-In Simulation, inviting visitors to sit and gain an idea of the patience necessary to be part of nonviolent protests.

EATING IN DOWNTOWN ATLANTA: OUR PICKS

MAP P368

Food Shoppe: Creole specialties like shrimp and grits in easy-to-transport Walk & Eat bowls. Try Angie's bread pudding. *8:30am-8pm* $

Aviva by Kameel Downtown: Organic Mediterranean dishes in a corner of the Hub at Peachtree Center. *11am-3pm Mon-Fri* $$

Alma Cocina: Modern Mexican cuisine; guacamole and salsa samplers, and street tacos including chicken tinga. *11:30am-3pm & 5-10pm Mon-Fri, 5-10pm Sat, to 9pm Sun* $$$

Kwan's Deli & Korean Kitchen: Bustling deli with everything from bibimbap and katsu to Italian sandwiches and chicken wings. *10:30am-3pm Mon-Thu, to 8pm Fri & Sat* $

ATLANTA'S FOOD TRUCKS

Chase Davis, an Atlanta chef who launched King Kabob in 2015, shares his insight on the city's food trucks *@thekingkabob*

The Atlanta food-truck scene is special for its rich diversity, offering cuisines from around the world, often fused with Southern flavors reflecting the city's cultural melting pot. It thrives in vibrant, community-centered spaces like food-truck parks and festivals, creating a lively social atmosphere. Apart from **King Kabob**, one must-visit food truck is the **Kitchen**, which serves Asian-soul fusion delights such as Korean barbecue tacos. For dessert, don't miss the **Experience**, offering decadent Southern-style sweets including peach-cobbler milkshakes.

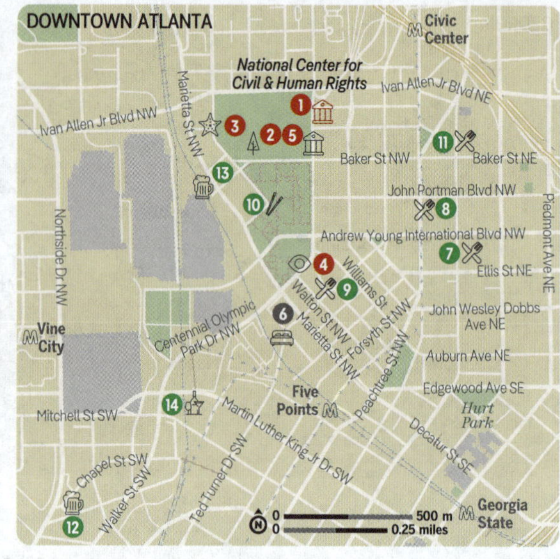

HIGHLIGHTS
1 National Center for Civil & Human Rights

SIGHTS
2 Centennial Olympic Park
3 Georgia Aquarium
4 SkyView
5 World of Coca-Cola

SLEEPING
6 Glenn Hotel

EATING
7 Alma Cocina
8 Aviva by Kameel Downtown
9 Food Shoppe
10 Kwan's Deli & Korean Kitchen
11 Sun Dial Restaurant & View

DRINKING & NIGHTLIFE
12 Atlantucky Brewing
13 Der Biergarten
14 RT60
see 6 SkyLounge

Next door, the **World of Coca-Cola** *(worldofcoca-cola.com; adult/child from $23/19)* is an ode to the beloved beverage – some 1.9 billion servings are enjoyed across 200-plus nations daily. Start by entering The Loft, packed with more than 200 relics of the brand's history, before watching a six-minute film about its global impact, and then entering the museum for exhibits on its formula, history and pop culture impact.

Nearby, the **Georgia Aquarium** *(georgiaaquarium.org; from $43)* is packed with wonders from the sea, including one of the world's largest single aquatic exhibits (a tank holding

DRINKING IN DOWNTOWN ATLANTA: OUR PICKS

MAP P368

Atlantucky Brewing: Craft-brew bar in Castleberry Hill opened by rapper Nappy Roots; affordable beers on tap in a beer hall–like space. *3-10pm Wed-Sun*

SkyLounge: Covered rooftop in the Glenn Hotel; cocktails on weeknights and small plates on weekends. *4-9pm Mon-Thu, 6pm-midnight Fri & Sat*

RT60: Hard Rock Hotel's 34th-floor bar rocks, well, hard. DJs and drinks including a mini martini flight and sangria tower. *4pm-midnight Mon-Wed, to 2am Thu-Sat, to 11pm Sun*

Der Biergarten: Ascending the staircase feels like walking into Germany: lagers, wine and cocktails alongside Wiener schnitzel and wurst. *4-9pm Wed-Fri, from noon Sat & Sun*

TOP EXPERIENCE

Martin Luther King Jr National Historical Park

America's Civil Rights movement was powered by the fearless leadership of Martin Luther King Jr, who believed in peaceful protest as a means to action. Long before he gave his most famous 'I Have a Dream' speech in Washington, DC, he was a boy spending his formative years in the neighborhood along Atlanta's Auburn Ave that is now the Martin Luther King Jr National Historical Park preserved as a time capsule to his legacy.

Ebenezer Baptist Church

Understand the Context of King's Life

Since the park site is spread out over a few blocks, make the **visitor center** your starting point to get oriented. The information desk will also provide the times for that day's programs, including must-hear talks inside the Ebenezer Baptist Church. The main exhibit, 'Courage to Lead,' outlines King's life and the growth of the Civil Rights movement, culminating in a life-size rendition of the Freedom Road walkway with marchers of every age.

Walk in King's Footsteps

On the next block, at 501 Auburn Ave, is a brown-and-beige **Queen Anne Victorian house** built in 1895. This is where King's mother grew up and where King himself was born. Birth Home tours are available on a first-come, first-served basis on the day of the tour. On the corner, peek in at Fire Station No 6, which served the segregated neighborhood.

One of the most moving experiences at the historical park is sitting in the pews of the **Ebenezer Baptist Church**, where King was baptized and also where he was ordained as a minister when he was 19, eventually becoming co-pastor with his father.

TOP TIPS

- On the way to the visitor center, stop and smell the roses. They're one of five major World Peace Rose Gardens in the world.
- Find the side-by-side tombs of Dr and Mrs King amid the fountains at the King Center for Nonviolent Social Change.

PRACTICALITIES

- nps.gov/malu
- 9am-5pm
- free

TINY DOORS ATL

Atlanta has its own brand of geocaching in the form of **Tiny Doors ATL** *(tinydoorsatl.com)*. Launched by artist Karen Singer in 2014, the project consists of more than 30 colorful little art pieces in the shape of doors hidden throughout the city. Her three main criteria are to make them all accessible, public and free. For instance, a trio of doors is hidden in one art piece in Centennial Olympic Park. (Hint: search for colorful scenery and don't forget to look up.) Also keep your eyes open at the Krog Street Tunnel, the Trap Music Museum and State Farm Arena.

HIGHLIGHTS
1 High Museum of Art

SIGHTS
2 Atlanta Botanical Garden
3 Piedmont Park

EATING
4 Delilah's Everyday Soul
5 Holeman & Finch
6 Pretty Little Tacos
7 Rumi's Kitchen

SHOPPING
8 Colony Square

6.3 million gallons of water). Highlights include standing in the shadows of the beluga whales in Cold Water Quest, eyeballing great hammerhead sharks in Sharks! Predators of the Deep and climbing through a tunnel to come face-to-face with African penguins.

Anchoring these attractions is 22-acre **Centennial Olympic Park** *(gwcca.org/centennial-olympic-park)*, which commemorates the 1996 Games and serves as the city's central plaza.

On the southeast corner of the park, you can enjoy dazzling views over the city by taking a spin on the **SkyView Ferris wheel** *(skyviewatlanta.com; adult/child $19.50/14.45)*. It rises 20 stories high in 42 sealed, climate-controlled gondolas with floor-to-ceiling windows.

For dining (or not) with a view, there's the Westin Peachtree Plaza, home to the upscale **Sun Dial Restaurant & View**

EATING IN MIDTOWN ATLANTA: BEST COLONY SQUARE EATS

MAP P370

Pretty Little Tacos: Started as a food truck and quickly known for juicy birria tacos. *11am-9:30pm Mon-Thu, to 10:30pm Fri & Sat, to 8:30pm Sun* $

Delilah's Everyday Soul: Oprah Winfrey called the mac 'n' cheese here the best in the country. *11am-10pm Mon-Thu, to 11pm Fri & Sat, to 9pm Sun* $$

Rumi's Kitchen: Bustling Persian favorite; kebabs and labne are among popular picks. *11:30am-10pm Mon-Thu, to 11pm Fri, 11am-11pm Sat, to 10pm Sun* $$$

Holeman & Finch: Cozy lounge with elevated pub food, in chic digs with a dress code. *11am-10pm Sun-Wed, to midnight Thu-Sat* $$

HIGHLIGHTS
1 Martin Luther King Jr National Historic Park

SIGHTS
2 Historic Fourth Ward Park
3 Jimmy Carter Presidential Library & Museum
4 Krog Street Tunnel

EATING
5 Krog Street Market
6 Ponce City Market
7 Vortex

DRINKING & NIGHTLIFE
8 Euclid Avenue Yacht Club
9 Nine Mile Station
10 Porter
11 Star Community Bar
12 Village Coffee House

ENTERTAINMENT
13 Skyline Park

SHOPPING
14 Little Five Points

(sundialrestaurant.com; adult/child $10/5), which rotates on the 72nd floor. Between 11am and 9pm daily, visitors can take in the panorama.

Art and greenery in Midtown

Hailed as the Southeast's most renowned art destination, the **High Museum of Art** *(high.org; $23.50)* boasts a vast collection ranging from classic European paintings to contemporary works, with an emphasis on artists of the South. Of particular note is the folk and self-taught gallery, as well as its many rotating exhibitions showcasing the work of Black artists. For a personalized (and fun) experience, the museum's site *heartmatch.org* lets you swipe on art you like (much like a dating site) and generates a custom map.

A short walk south of the museum, **Colony Square** *(colony square.com)* feels like Midtown's living room, with its beauty spas, yoga, Pilates and a robust calendar of events. Step into the buzzy 20,000-sq-ft Politan Row food hall, where each of the dozen or so options is chef-driven with a local twist. There are also lively sit-down restaurants and bars. Top off the day by catching a flick at IPIC Theaters, which serves food and cocktails at your seat.

HIPPIE HAVEN

Bart Pond is a musician and a Little Five Points resident since 2010.

Little Five is Haight-Ashbury with Southern charm and hospitality. The murals here are constantly changing. This isn't graffiti; it's art. You learn who the artists are through their tags – this one is the Junkyard Chef and this is Paul Athol. Even the sidewalks have them. I can't give away all my secrets, but they have messages and if you follow them they'll lead you to two secret venues. There's other kinds of art too, like this sticker on the back of the street sign. A guy just puts free stories up. This one starts, 'My child was possessed by a demon who injured him through his rotting baby teeth....'

A few blocks east of there, the nearly 200-acre **Piedmont Park** *(piedmontpark.org)* has woods, wetlands and walking paths, plus a race track and the 11.5-acre Lake Clara Meer. Along the park's northwestern side is the 30-acre **Atlanta Botanical Garden** *(atlantabg.org; adult/child $29/26)*. There, the Cascades Garden is anchored by a topiary goddess sculpture, while the Kendeda Canopy Walk allows visitors to walk 40ft up among the trees. Piedmont Park is a popular site for events such as the Atlanta Dogwood Festival *(dogwood.org)* in April.

Experience the cutting edge at Little Five Points

At **Little Five Points**, a skeleton head with psychedelic eyes welcomes customers into the **Vortex** *(thevortexatl.com)* bar and grill, while the **Village Coffee House** *(instagram.com/villagecoffeehouselittle5)* has a retro photo booth outside and a rack of vintage clothes for sale inside. Tattoo parlors and smoke shops are interspersed among a metaphysical crystal store and a record shop, while in between there are vintage boutiques for every kind of shopper, imaginative bars and some dazzling street art.

DRINKING IN ATLANTA'S LITTLE FIVE POINTS: OUR PICKS

MAP P371

Euclid Avenue Yacht Club: Standard dive-bar fare in an eclectic environment. *noon-3am Mon-Sat, to midnight Sun*

Star Community Bar: All about its characters, with events from honky-tonk dance lessons to drag competitions. *5pm-2:30am Mon-Thu, 1pm-2:30am Fri & Sat, to midnight Sun*

Vortex: Entered through a skeleton's mouth, this bar delivers on memorable clientele. *11am-midnight Sun-Thu, to 2am Fri & Sat*

Porter: Relatively clean-cut Porter has 60 craft brews on draft and a massive beer cellar. *5pm-midnight Wed-Fri, from 11am Sat & Sun*

NICHOLAS LAMONTANARO/SHUTTERSTOCK

Skyline Park mini golf

Explore Atlanta BeltLine's Eastside Trail

Any time of day along the **Atlanta BeltLine's Eastside Trail** *(beltline.org)* there will be folks running, biking, walking their dogs and riding scooters. In essence, this 3-mile section of what will eventually be part of a 22-mile loop around the entire city is proof of what all of Atlanta could soon become. A colorful starting point is the mural-covered **Krog Street Tunnel** connecting Cabbagetown and Inman Park. Heading north, just to the left the paved trail soon comes into view. You'll walk past **Krog Street Market** *(thekrogdistrict.com)*, an enticing food hall in an 1889 building. Let your instincts guide you, whether it's stopping off at a brewery for a pint or taking a break to watch the daredevils in the skatepark. You'll soon arrive near **Historic Fourth Ward Park** *(h4wpc.org)* and the vast **Ponce City Market** *(poncecitymarket.com)*, one of the biggest and best food halls in the South. Don't miss the rooftop, where you'll find **Skyline Park** *(poncecityroof.com/skyline-park; from $7)*, with boardwalk games, mini golf, a three-story slide and Heege Tower for even higher views. Also up top is the **Nine Mile Station** *(9milestation.com)* beer garden, which has private igloos in the cooler months.

The city's past through living history

Set on 33 acres, the **Atlanta History Center** *(atlantahistorycenter.com; adult/child $27/15)* is unlike other city historical society museums. With a rare in-the-round painting, a mansion made famous by a movie franchise, blooming gardens, sunken woods, historic buildings and a farm – with sheep and goats. – this Buckhead neighborhood museum is creating its own history as much as it's preserving the city's. Follow the events that shaped Atlanta through exhibits on how railroads set the city's foundation (even climb aboard a restored Texas

THE BEER BUS

Hopping from brewery to brewery is a great way to get to know the city, with each brewery offering its own unique atmosphere. The Upper Westside has emerged as the newest favorite concentration for breweries in the city. A cluster of them have established an Ale Trail and offer rides on the **Atlanta Beer Bus** *(atlantabeerbus.com; free)*, which runs alternating routes on Sunday. From 1pm to 7pm riders can start from any one of the area breweries and pick up a passport and get a beer at each spot. The stops include **Fire Maker Brewing Company** *(firemakerbeer.com)*, **Bold Monk Brewing Co** *(boldmonkbrewingco.com)* and **Monday Night Brewing** *(mondaynightbrewing.com)*.

BEST OUTDOOR FUN IN NORTHERN GEORGIA

Tallulah Gorge State Park: Both easygoing and challenging hikes amid forests and waterfalls, plus a dramatic suspension bridge.

Unicoi State Park & Lodge: See sublime cascades, including Anna Ruby Falls in the Chattahoochee-Oconee National Forest.

Brasstown Bald: Ascend Georgia's highest point (elevation 4784ft); it's a paved, 0.6-mile hike uphill walk from the parking lot.

Blood Mountain: Get a taste of the Appalachian Trail on this iconic, moderately difficult 4.4-mile (round-trip) day hike from Neel Gap to the 4452ft mountaintop.

Vogel State Park: One of Georgia's oldest parks sits at the base of Blood Mountain and has many trails, including an easy 1-mile (round-trip) walk to Trahlyta Waterfall.

locomotive) and another on Atlanta 1996 (meet the fuzzy blue Olympic mascot, Izzy).

Explore the Jimmy Carter Presidential Library

Set in the midst of 30 acres of landscaped greenery between a pair of lakes, the **Jimmy Carter Presidential Library & Museum** *(jimmycarterlibrary.gov; adult/child $12/free)* feels like a peaceful sanctuary in the center of Atlanta. Inside, interactive exhibits trace Carter's path from his modest roots to the Oval Office, including a replica of the White House space as it was during his tenure. Also fascinating is the exhibit on the Camp David meetings: the secret negotiations between Israel and Egypt. Don't miss the chance to pose behind the presidential podium on the way out.

Athens

Visit Georgia's finest college town

One of the USA's quintessential college towns, beery, artsy and laid-back Athens is home to the **University of Georgia** and its fiercely followed football team. If you don't manage a ticket for a game at **Dooley Field at Sanford Stadium** (look on *seatgeek.com*), head downtown and pick a bar – they'll all be packed. You can freely wander the 760-acre campus. The **Athens Welcome Center** *(athenswelcomecenter.com)* produces a self-guided walking tour.

For a different take on the Athens' experience, head to the excellent **Georgia Museum of Art** *(georgiamuseum.org; free)*. Here you can gawk at modern sculpture in the courtyard garden as well as the tremendous collection from American realists of the 1930s.

At the 323-acre **State Botanical Garden of Georgia** *(botgarden.uga.edu; free)* at the University of Georgia, 3 miles south of town, gorgeous winding outdoor paths lead to an amazing collection of plants, including rare and threatened species, across eight specialty gardens. There are nearly 5 miles of top-notch woodland walking trails, too. If you're toting little ones, the interactive children's garden features a treehouse, a fossil wall, a granite map of Georgia and more.

Macon

Walking the Ocmulgee Mounds

Poised to become the country's newest national park, **Ocmulgee Mounds** *(nps.gov/ocmu; free)* has Indigenous ceremonial

EATING & DRINKING IN & AROUND ATHENS: OUR PICKS

Mama's Boy: Fluffy, buttery biscuit sandwiches are the calling card of this detour-worthy Southern breakfast bastion off the North Oconee Greenway. *7am-2.30pm* $

Last Resort Grill: Southwestern-inspired plates satiating Athens for 30 years. Fantastic patio. *hours vary* $$$

Hendershots: Quintessential Athens coffeehouse; also a great bar and live-music venue. *hours vary*

Creature Comforts Brewing Co: In a former tire shop, the three-bar, 54-tap brewery is the epitome of everything great about Athens. *hours vary*

Okefenokee National Wildlife Refuge

JOANNE DALE/SHUTTERSTOCK

mounds dating back thousands of years with special ties to the Muscogee (Creek) people who lived here before their removal on the Trail of Tears. The park has a museum with artifacts recovered from a 1930s archaeological dig that was the largest in US history. You can also climb the stairs to the top of the Great Temple Mound Complex, which offers views of the Ocmulgee River and beyond. Try to time your visit to catch a ranger-led tour, held on alternating weekends throughout the year. Better yet, plan your trip around Ocmulgee's cornerstone annual events, such as the **Lantern Light tours** (March) and the **Ocmulgee Indigenous Celebration** (September).

Okefenokee National Wildlife Refuge

Primeval wetlands

The **Okefenokee National Wildlife Refuge** *(fws.gov/refuge/okefenokee; $5)* is the nation's largest blackwater swamp – 'blackwater' refers to the tea-like hue created by the ancient peat at the bottom. Spanning 354,000 acres of rivers, lakes and islands, the swamp's name comes from the Indigenous word for 'land of the trembling earth.' Several creatures call the area home, including thousands of alligators and more than 200 species of bird, plus endangered indigo snakes and wood storks. There are a few short trails here (all less than a mile), but the best way to experience this watery landscape is by boat. Guided 90-minute boat tours are operated by **Okefenokee Adventures** *(okeswamp.org; adult/child $35/30)* and you can also rent canoes *($50)* and kayaks *($30 to $50)*.

For a driving tour, pick up a brochure at the **Bolt Visitor Center** to make the scenic 7-mile Swamp Island Drive by car or bicycle. Along the way, signs indicate several trails including the 1.5-mile (round-trip) boardwalk to the old Chesser Island Homestead. There are also markers pointing out the habitats of alligators, black bears and woodpeckers.

MOTHER OF THE BLUES

If there's one artist to add to your Georgia soundtrack, it's **Gertrude 'Ma' Rainey**, who was born in Columbus in 1886. She started singing at a young age, following in the footsteps of her parents, performing at a talent show at the famed Springer Opera House at age 14. She joined the touring circuit, performing around the country in her unique style, a mix of jazz and blues with her signature raspy voice. Rainey returned to her hometown in 1933, where she retired and is now buried. Her former home still stands, and tours *(parks.columbusga.gov/parks/ma-rainey-home)* are offered on an appointment basis. Don't miss the award-winning 2020 film *Ma Rainey's Black Bottom*, set in 1920s Chicago.

BEST HISTORIC HOUSE TOURS

Mercer-Williams House: Tour the 1st floor of Savannah's most notorious house.

Flannery O'Connor Childhood Home: This stone row house on Lafayette Sq is where the literary great was born in 1925 and lived until she was 13.

Juliette Gordon Low Birthplace Museum: Childhood home of the founder of the Girl Scouts of the USA, which runs the museum.

Sorrel Weed House: Fans of the paranormal can get their thrills at one of Savannah's spookiest mansions.

Owens-Thomas House & Slave Quarters: Completed in 1819 by British architect William Jay, this gorgeous villa exemplifies English Regency-style architecture, known for its symmetry.

Savannah

Step back in time in the Historic District

Savannah's Historic District is home to 18th- and 19th-century homes, fascinating museums and monuments, and world-class restaurants, all enveloped by a canopy of Spanish-moss-laden live oaks. After taking a stroll around the neighborhood, head to the **Telfair Academy** *(telfair.org; adult/child $30/10)*, considered Savannah's top art museum. Ensconced in the historic and captivating Telfair family mansion, the gallery is filled with 19th-century American works and a smattering of European pieces. Admission includes unlimited entries to the **Jepson Center** (which focuses on 20th- and 21st-century art) and the early-19th-century **Owens-Thomas House** for a week.

Visit the Plant Riverside District

Stepping into the generator hall at this former power station (now a JW Marriott hotel) in the **Plant Riverside District** *(plantriverside.com)* is a big 'Whoa!,' especially if you're walking in from the riverfront or the leafy Historic District. Throngs of people flow past as they explore the vast space, and there's an enormous chrome-dipped dinosaur hanging overhead. Glittering geodes and minerals beckon in every direction.

Galleries, boutiques and exuberant works of art fill the cavernous lobby, which exudes steampunk cool with its mix of modern amenities and original power-plant fixtures. After checking out whimsical creations at art-minded shops like **18Loves Art** *(18loves.com)*, head skyward to the **Myrtle & Rose Rooftop Bar** or the nearby **Electric Moon Skytop Lounge** for drinks overlooking the river. For something more structured, check out the indoor music venue here, **District Live**, which hosts touring acts with regional and national followings.

Georgian Coast

Beachcombing on Tybee Island

Savannah's favorite getaway is **Tybee Island**, with its eclectic art shops, laid-back cafes and pretty beaches. For sheer beauty, set your sights on **North Beach**, a beautiful swath of white sand. With fewer services and a vibe that feels more remote, this stretch of shoreline is a great place to relax – though you can also get active, climbing the 178-step staircase that corkscrews to the top of the **Tybee Island Light Station**

EATING IN SAVANNAH: OUR PICKS

Treylor Park: Amid a retro-chic aesthetic, enjoy fried chicken on a biscuit paired with an excellent cocktail. *11am-1am Mon-Fri, from 10am Sat & Sun* $

Mrs Wilkes Dining Room: Once you're seated family-style, the kitchen unloads the likes of fried chicken, beef stew and black-eyed peas. *11am-2pm Mon-Fri* $$

Grey: A wonderfully retro makeover of a 1930s Greyhound bus terminal, serving up deliciously inventive 'Port City Southern' cuisine. *5-9pm Tue-Sun, also 11am-3pm Sun* $$$

Starland Yard: For alfresco dining and drinking, stop in this lively food-truck park, which offers plenty of variety, plus events (live music, line dancing). *5-10pm Mon-Wed, noon-9pm Thu-Sun* $

WALKING SAVANNAH'S SQUARES

One of the joys of visiting Savannah is walking around the Historic District amid some of the most beautiful residential architecture in the country.

START	END	LENGTH
Forsyth Park	Johnson Square	1¾ miles; 2 hours

Begin at the iconic fountain in **1 Forsyth Park**. Continue north on Bull St toward the intersection with Wayne St, where a statue of General Casimir Pulaski soars above **2 Monterey Square**. Walk north and turn right on cobblestoned Jones St, flanked by Greek Revival homes and live oaks. Turn left on Abercorn to see the spectacular **3 Cathedral Basilica of St John the Baptist**. Head north to Colonial Park Cemetery. Wander past Gothic tombs and monuments, then turn west on E Perry St. A bronze statue of Savannah founder James Oglethorpe oversees the action from **4 Chippewa Square**. The park-bench scenes in *Forrest Gump* (1994) were shot on the north side along Hull St (the actual bench was a prop). Keep truckin' north on Bull St to **5 Wright Square**, burial site of Tomochichi, the Yamacraw tribe leader who befriended Oglethorpe and helped him establish the colony. Head west to **6 Telfair Square**, where the Telfair Academy and the Jepson Center border Barnard St. Continue north, cross busy Broughton St and continue to **7 Ellis Square**, a hub of commerce from the 1730s through the 1950s. In the 1850s it housed a market for the sale of enslaved human beings. Head east down St Julian St toward Bull St and end at **8 Johnson Square**, Savannah's first and largest square.

Thanks to the work of the Colonial Dames of Georgia, a boulder made of granite from Stone Mountain honors Tomochichi in **Wright Square**.

Running east-west, **Jones Street** is famed for its cobblestones and high-stooped Greek Revival homes tucked under a canopy of live oaks.

The remains of Revolutionary War hero General Nathanel Greene were exhumed in 1902 from **Colonial Park Cemetery** and reinterred in Johnson Square.

BEST ANNUAL EVENTS ON TYBEE ISLAND

SCAD Sand Arts Festival: Students from the Savannah College of Arts & Design create magical sand sculptures on South Beach in August.

Tybee Island Beach Bum Parade: Come prepared with a water gun – no one's safe at this giant traveling water fight – which is oh so welcome on hot days. Held mid-May.

Tybee Turtle Trot: Coinciding with sea-turtle nesting season in late April, this 5km beach run is a fundraiser for turtle-preservation efforts.

Fourth of July: Catch the spectacular fireworks show, with views anywhere along the eastern beaches.

Pirate Fest: Dress up like your favorite buccaneer and party like it's 1699 at this four-day fest in mid-October.

DENNIS MACDONALD/SHUTTERSTOCK

(tybeelighthouse.org; adult/child $12/10; closed Tue), where even more glorious views await. Tickets include admission to the adjacent lighthouse keeper's cottage and museum.

Exploring Wormsloe & Gullah-Geechee culture

Just south of Savannah, the **Wormsloe State Historic Site** *(gastateparks.org/Wormsloe; adult/child $12/6)* spotlights the state's earliest history. On a visit here, you can learn all about this colonial estate, founded in the 1730s. Stop by the visitor center to buy admission tickets and pick up a property map. You'll also board the tram that shuttles between the visitor center and the park museum via Live Oak Ave, which was originally flanked by more than 400 moss-draped oaks. Property highlights include the ruins of the original tabby house (tabby is a crude concrete composed of oyster shells and lime mortar), the Colonial Life Area, where interpreters in period costumes may be on hand to demonstrate Colonial-era crafting and tool work, and an observation deck overlooking a pretty stretch of marsh.

Nearby, the **Pin Point Heritage Museum** *(chsgeorgia.org/pin-point-heritage-museum; adult/child $15/7)* spotlights the culture of the Gullah-Geechee people in the secluded village of Pin Point. The community, which was established by first-generation formerly enslaved, thrived for nearly 100 years.

DRINKING IN SAVANNAH: OUR PICKS

Two Tides Brewing Co: A small quirky brewery and cafe with an adventurous beer list and good coffees, plus a cocktail bar downstairs. *7am-10pm Sun-Thu, to midnight Fri & Sat*

Savannah Smiles Dueling Pianos: It's a deliciously kitschy good time at this sing-along nightspot, where patrons decide what's played on stage. *7pm-2am Thu-Sat*

Artillery: Mixologists craft novel, quality cocktails in this opulent space where 19th-century eclecticism meets modern design. *4-11pm Mon-Thu, to midnight Fri & Sat*

El-Rocko Lounge: You'll feel the '70s-inspired swank but then realize that the vibe is absolutely chill. DJs keep the energy high. *5pm-midnight Mon-Wed, to 3am Thu-Sat*

Wormsloe State Historic Site

Vibrant arts-loving Brunswick

Some 80 miles south of Savannah, the town of Brunswick dates from 1771, and has a multicultural vibe with West Indian flavors and a rich local art scene. Check out the new restaurants, bars and tasting rooms that have opened on the main drag, Newcastle St, and if you're sticking around for the night, catch a performance at the **Historic Ritz Theatre** *(goldenislesarts.org),* which hosts plays, concerts and films.

Captivating Jekyll Island

An easy 20-minute drive from Brunswick, Jekyll Island has miles of beaches, wilderness and historic buildings. Get the lay of the land at **Mosaic Jekyll Island Museum** *(jekyllisland.com; $10),* which shares the history of the island across a half dozen or so historic time periods, with evocative exhibits – sweetgrass baskets, a miniature portrait and a Red Bug flyer – highlighting the varied stories. Trolley and historic tours *(from adult/child $20/15)* depart the museum throughout the day, including the new Millionaire Motorcar Tour *(up to four people $125)* in a 1930s Model T replica.

Beaches & wild horses of Cumberland Island

More remote, Cumberland Island is the southernmost barrier island in Georgia, and was once an exclusive playground for the elite. Visitors can access it via daily ferries *(cumberlandislandferry.com; adult/child round trip $40/30)* from tiny St Marys and explore the ancient 17-mile-long stretch of moss-covered oak forests, salt marshes and untouched beach. Wild horses roam, sea turtles hatch, and the ruins of a once-grand mansion still stand, begging to be discovered. Reserve well ahead for the ferry.

JEKYLL ISLAND: NEED TO KNOW

An exclusive refuge for millionaires in the late 19th and early 20th centuries, Jekyll Island is a 4000-year-old barrier island with 10 miles of beaches. These include photo darling Driftwood Beach, famed for its fallen skeleton trees. Today the island is an unusual clash of wilderness, preserved historic buildings, modern hotels and a massive campground. And, oddly, it's all part of **Jekyll Island State Park** *(jekyllisland.com),* complete with a $10 per day parking fee payable upon entry. It's also an easily navigable place – you can get around by car, horse or bicycle.

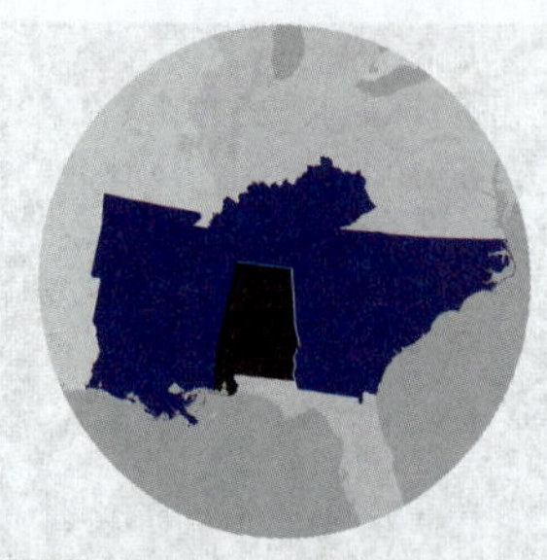

Alabama

CIVIL RIGHTS | OUTER SPACE | OFFBEAT ADVENTURES

Places

Huntsville p380
The Shoals p382
Birmingham p384
Montgomery p385
Moundville Archaeological Park p387
Mobile p387
Fairhope p388

TOP TIP
Several regions in Alabama (including Muscle Shoals, Huntsville, Montgomery and Birmingham) offer an All-in-One Ticket, allowing you to visit multiple attractions over a set time period at a substantial saving. Purchase it online *(alabama.travel/attraction-tickets)*.

The land of red soil and lilting accents, Alabama is a complicated and oft misunderstood place. Follow a meandering road trip across the state and you'll see cotton fields and vast forests, peaceful riverside towns and booming cities (Huntsville) fueled by burgeoning aerospace and tech industries. And Alabama's nature reserves encompass both sandy Gulf beaches and wooded canyons dotted with waterfalls.

As elsewhere in the South, locals' love for the state runs deep – and not just when it comes to college football. Alabamans take pride as being the birthplace of the Civil Rights movement, where pioneers like Martin Luther King, Rosa Parks and John Lewis inspired people around the globe to fight for a more just and inclusive society. The state is also home to an incredible musical heritage (visit Muscle Shoals for the inside scoop), and the oldest Mardi Gras celebrations in the country – with colorful parades rolling through the Franco-Caribbean streetscape of Mobile.

Huntsville

Culture and green spaces downtown

The birthplace of Huntsville was the gushing **Big Spring**, which produces some 7 million gallons of fresh water each day. A scenic **park** surrounds the meandering waterway, which also anchors downtown Huntsville. You can go for a pleasant stroll here, or feed the ducks, geese and koi fish (strategically placed dispensers dole out pellets for 25 cents).

GETTING AROUND

Decent intercity transportation is lacking across Alabama, though it is possible to reach some urban areas (including Birmingham, Mobile and Montgomery) by slow Greyhound bus. You'll find walkable centers in some cities, though you'll need a car to reach many sites. Huntsville and Montgomery also have a bikeshare network, Blue Bikes (find details on *tandem-mobility.com*). In 2025, Amtrak re-established train service between Mobile and New Orleans, with two daily departures (morning and evening) in each direction.

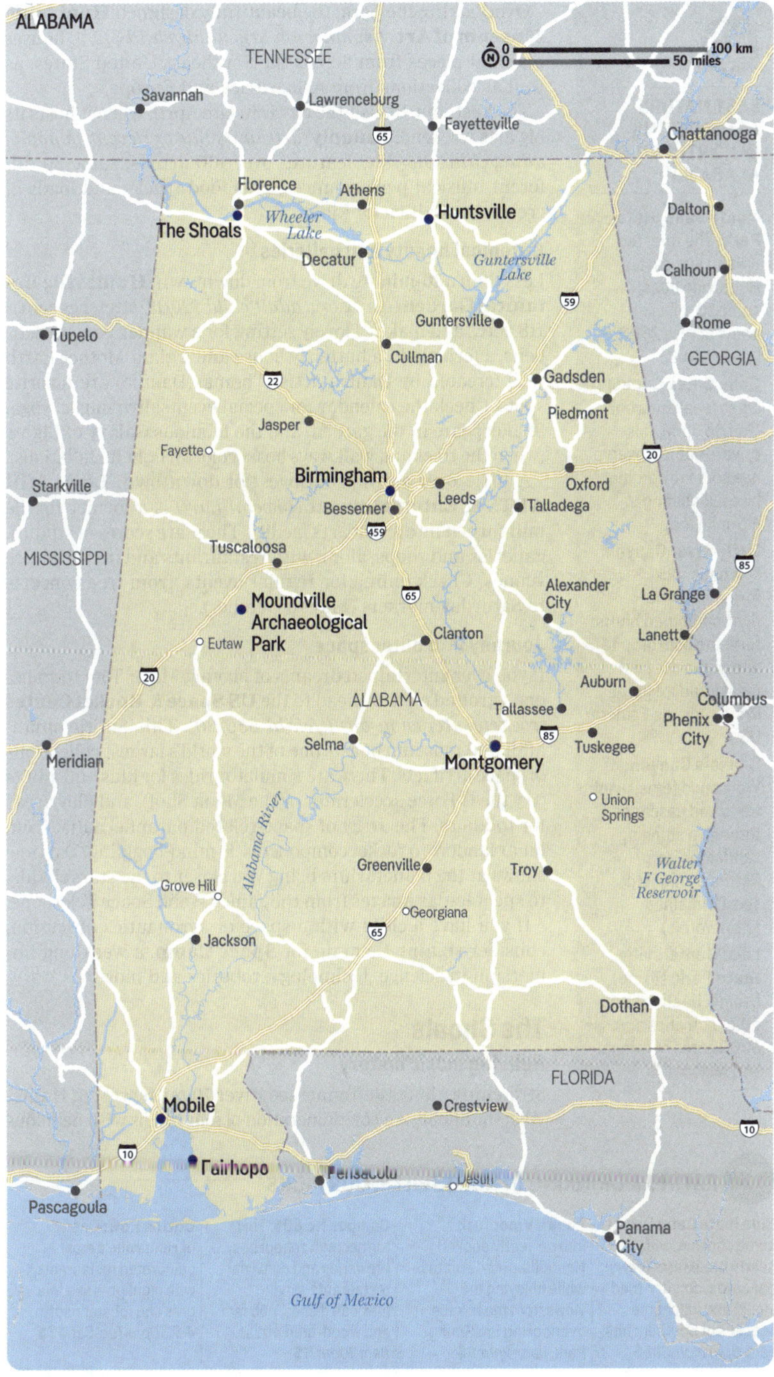
ALABAMA
TENNESSEE
100 km
50 miles
Savannah
Lawrenceburg
Fayetteville
Chattanooga
Florence
Athens
The Shoals
Wheeler Lake
Huntsville
Dalton
Decatur
Guntersville Lake
Calhoun
Guntersville
Rome
Tupelo
Cullman
GEORGIA
Gadsden
Piedmont
Jasper
Fayette
Birmingham
Oxford
Leeds
Starkville
Bessemer
Talladega
Tuscaloosa
MISSISSIPPI
Alexander City
La Grange
Moundville Archaeological Park
Eutaw
Clanton
Lanett
Auburn
ALABAMA
Columbus
Tallassee
Phenix City
Selma
Tuskegee
Meridian
Montgomery
Union Springs
Alabama River
Walter F George Reservoir
Greenville
Troy
Grove Hill
Georgiana
Jackson
Dothan
FLORIDA
Mobile
Crestview
Fairhopo
Pensacola
Destin
Pascagoula
Panama City
Gulf of Mexico

BEST NATURE ATTRACTIONS IN NORTHERN ALABAMA

Monte Sano State Park: The forested upland just east of Huntsville boasts some 20 miles of paths across 2000 lovely acres.

Cane Creek Canyon: Open weekends only (7am to 5pm), this private nature reserve has some rewarding hikes, including a 6.5-mile loop.

Little River Canyon: Dramatic rock formations and river-smoothed bluffs form the backdrop to one of the deepest, most intricate gorge systems in the Eastern USA.

Dismals Canyon: Walk amid ferns, giant trees and cascades through a stunning sandstone gorge. Return by night to see 'Dismalites' (glowworms).

Lake Guntersville State Park: Hiking, fishing, boating and other activities across 6000 acres of forests and waterways.

Overlooking the park, the beautifully designed **Huntsville Museum of Art** *(hsvmuseum.org; adult/child $12/5)* houses regional pieces from across the Southeast United States, as well as collections from Asia, Africa and Europe.

The best time to visit the city is in late April, when it hosts its big arts weekend. **Panoply** *(artshuntsville.org/event/panoply; adult/child $15/free)* features over 100 artists, some 30 different musical performances, plus food trucks and loads of creative activities for kids.

Botanical beauty and galleries

Less than a 10-minute drive from downtown, **Huntsville Botanical Garden** *(hsvbg.org; adult/child $20/13)* stretches across 118 acres and makes a lovely setting for a wander. Aquatic gardens, a fern glade, a butterfly house and a giant Mother Earth troll (created by Danish artist Thomas Dambo) are favorite spots. Check the calendar for special events: live music, yoga, Shakespeare in the garden, and the fabulous Galaxy of Lights (when the trees and walkways boast colorful light installations).

A little over a mile southwest of downtown, **Lowe Mill ARTS & Entertainment** *(lowemill.art)* is a former textile mill turned into a vast arts facility. There are scores of studios, galleries and shops, along with restaurants and performance venues. Check online for regular events, from free concerts to Saturday markets (May to October).

Journey into outer space

If you ever entertained dreams of playing Major Tom to someone's ground control, head to the **US Space & Rocket Center** *(rocketcenter.com; adult/child $30/20)*. This Smithsonian-affiliated museum boasts one of the world's largest collections of space artifacts. There are simulator rides for kids and adults (try the G Force accelerator or the Moon Shot), and play areas for toddlers. The array of space-related paraphernalia, from lunar landers to rocket components, is mind-boggling. Daytime shows at the planetarium bring you closer to the stars thanks to spectacular images from the James Webb Space Telescope.

If you have a child with a space or aeronautics obsession, consider signing them up for **Space Camp**, a weeklong immersion in science, technology, robotics and more.

The Shoals

Reliving music history

Stretching along the Tennessee River 70 miles west of Huntsville, the Shoals is a conglomeration of four towns with nebulous

EATING & DRINKING IN HUNTSVILLE: OUR PICKS

Blue Plate Cafe: Down-home cooking, with hearty breakfasts (berry pancakes, country-fried steak) and lunchtime specials of Southern hits. *6am-8pm Mon-Sat* $

Pane e Vino: Tuck into perfectly cooked Neapolitan-style pizzas, while enjoying the views from the terrace overlooking Big Spring Park. *11am-9pm* $$

Campus No 805: This former high school has breweries and convivial restaurants serving Mexican dishes, pub fare and wood-fired pizzas. *11am-10pm* $$

Cotton Row: One of Huntsville's most celebrated restaurants, with highlights like foie gras and lobster risotto. *4-9:30pm Tue-Sat* $$$

DANITA DELIMONT/SHUTTERSTOCK

US Space & Rocket Center

boundaries and little-known but captivating attractions. Beginning in the 1960s, this lightly populated region became ground zero for some of the most important music production of an era. At **Muscle Shoals Sound Studios** *(muscleshoals soundstudio.org)*, you can learn all about the legends that recorded here, including the Rolling Stones, Bobby Womack, Paul Simon and countless others. On a small, intimate guided tour *(adult/child $25/12)*, you'll hear some wild stories from the recording days and listen to iconic songs made right in the studio. Hour-long tours typically run throughout the day, Tuesday through Saturday.

A couple miles south, you can take a similar guided tour through **Fame Studios** *(famestudios.com; adult/child $20/15)*, where Wilson Pickett recorded 'Mustang Sally' and Aretha Franklin cut 'Do Right Woman' – among many, many other tracks.

Complete the musical journey with a visit to the **Alabama Music Hall of Fame** *(alamhof.org; adult/child $15/8)*, which has instruments, attire and even an over-the-top golden convertible belonging to some of the musical stars that emerged from the state.

Learn about a sightless pioneer

Helen Keller – to this day perhaps the most beloved native of Alabama – was blind and deaf from the age of 19 months. With the aid of companion Anne Sullivan, Keller would go on to attend Radcliffe College, earn a degree and become a noted writer, lecturer and activist for pacifist and socialist causes. The **Helen Keller Birthplace** *(helenkellerbirthplace.org; adult/child $10/5)*, her childhood home, is maintained with personal mementos, and guides on hand are happy to share pivotal episodes from Helen's life. *The Miracle Worker*, a play based on Keller's autobiography, is performed here at select dates in June and July.

THE MUSCLE SHOALS SOUND

Chase Brandon, sound engineer at Muscle Shoals Sound Studio, describes the versatile musicians that everyone wanted to record with back in the '60s and '70s *@muscleshoals soundstudio*

The Swampers have been described as very soulful musicians. They confused a lot of people because they looked kind of nerdy. You might see them and think country music, but they were totally into soul and R&B. In the '60s they worked almost exclusively with Black artists doing R&B records: Aretha Franklin, Wilson Pickett, Percy Sledge, the Staple Singers. In the '70s, the Swampers evolved from this one-genre rhythm section, and they recorded with a huge variety of artists: Boz Scaggs, Lulu, Duane Allman, Bob Seger and Paul Simon among many others.

BIRMINGHAM'S BEST OUTDOOR ATTRACTIONS

Sloss: Wander past soaring, iron-producing blast furnaces that powered Birmingham's economy from 1882 to 1971.

Vulcan: On a hill above Birmingham, a cast-iron statue of the Roman god of metal-working celebrates the city's industrial past. Head up the observation tower for wide views.

Railroad Park: A much-loved downtown green space where all are welcome to regular events (zumba, yoga, line dancing, outdoor concerts).

Red Mountain Park: Some 16 miles of trails including overlooks along forested ridge lines, 8 miles southwest of downtown.

Oak Mountain State Park: Hiking and mountain-biking on over 100 miles of trails in Alabama's largest state park *(adult/child $5/2)*. It's 18 miles south of downtown.

Birmingham

MAP P385

Civil Rights history

One sight not to miss in Alabama is the **Birmingham Civil Rights Institute** *(bcri.org; adult/child $15/13)*, which takes you on a journey through one of the country's most tumultuous periods. A maze of moving audio, video and photography exhibits tells the story of racial segregation and the Civil Rights movement, with a focus on the activities in and around Birmingham.

Nearby, you can learn about the horrifying bombing of the **16th Street Baptist Church** *(16thstreetbaptist.org; adult/child $10/5)*, when four Black children were killed in 1963. Visits are by hourly tour (10am to 3pm Tuesday to Saturday). Today the rebuilt church is a memorial and house of worship (services 11am Sunday).

Across the street, in **Kelly Ingram Park**, walk in the footsteps of those who risked it all to bring an end to segregation. Various sculptures and monuments depict a moment in the Civil Rights struggle. In one space, the path becomes a gauntlet of snarling police dogs, while further along, a water cannon is aimed at visitors.

Around the corner from the park, the **AG Gaston Motel** was where Civil Rights leaders, including Martin Luther King Jr, stayed while in town. It's now run by the National Park Service, with exhibits about the dynamic entrepreneur AG Gaston, a pillar of the Black community.

Showtime!

Going strong since 1927, the **Alabama Theatre** *(alabamatheatre.com)* is one of the anchors of cultural life in downtown Birmingham. Built as a 2000-seat movie palace, the architectural landmark hosts plays, concerts, big-name comedians and classic films – often followed by audience sing-alongs with the Mighty Wurlitzer (a red-and-gold pipe organ). Across the street, the **Lyric** *(lyricbham.com)* is a former vaudeville theater that offers a similar line-up of concerts, comedy and dance.

Up the road, the **Sidewalk Film Center** *(sidewalkfest.com)* is an artfully designed space set beneath the Pizitz Building. Its two theaters screen independent films, and you can while away the evening in the bar and comfy lounge areas before or after catching a film.

Two miles east of downtown, **Saturn** *(saturnbirmingham.com)* is a sleek live-music venue with a '70s-meets-outer-space aesthetic. There's a fine roster of talent featuring up-and-coming indie rock stars (shows are ages 18 and up). Music aside, there are pinball machines, video consoles and board

EATING & DRINKING IN BIRMINGHAM: OUR PICKS

MAP P385

Fish Market: Casual spot for fresh-off-the-boat seafood, including crab legs and red snapper. *11am-8:30pm Mon-Sat* $$

Essential: Trendy spot with a creative menu and popular weekend brunches. *11am-9pm Mon-Fri, 9am-2pm & 5-9pm Sat & Sun* $$

Collins Bar: A beautiful space for sipping handmade cocktails under a Birmingham-centric periodic table of the elements. *4pm-midnight Mon-Sat*

House of Found Objects: Bubble machines, a video booth, costumes (ask about cookie monster) and a backroom, entered via a birth canal. *4pm-midnight Tue-Sat*

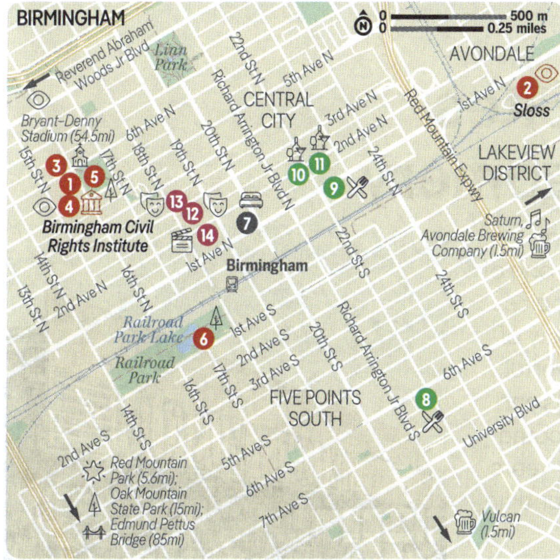

HIGHLIGHTS
1 Birmingham Civil Rights Institute
2 Sloss

SIGHTS
3 16th Street Baptist Church
4 AG Gaston Motel
5 Kelly Ingram Park
6 Railroad Park

SLEEPING
7 Elyton Hotel

EATING
8 Fish Market
9 The Essential

DRINKING & NIGHTLIFE
10 Collins Bar
11 House of Found Objects

ENTERTAINMENT
12 Alabama Theatre
13 Lyric
14 Sidewalk Film Center

games. You can even stop in early (from 8am) if you're after coffee and warm pastries.

Across the road from Saturn, **Avondale Brewing Company** *(avondalebrewing.com)* pours out the good times courtesy of hazy IPAs, farmhouse ales and easy-drinking lagers. It also has a large outdoor concert venue, where all ages can catch rock, indie and country bands.

Montgomery

In the footsteps of Martin Luther King and Rosa Parks

Martin Luther King Jr had other job offers, but he and his wife Coretta Scott were drawn to Montgomery, and he served as pastor to a dynamic church – with a long history of progressivism – from 1954 to 1960. Now known as the **Dexter Avenue King Memorial Church** *(dexterkingmemorial.org)*, this beautifully designed house of worship draws visitors who want to feel close to an inspiring man – and a congregation – that changed history. Call ahead for a guided tour *($10)*, which touches on King's leadership during the Civil Rights movement. All are welcome at Sunday services, which begin at 10:30am.

ROLL TIDE!

In the fall, the battle cry of 'Roll Tide' is ubiquitous across Alabama. The 'Tide,' in this case, is the Alabama Crimson Tide, the name of the University of Alabama's football team in Tuscaloosa (an hour's drive from Birmingham), which supposedly derives from a celebrated game of yesteryear. During the 1907 Iron Bowl against Auburn University (still one of the most fiercely contested college-sports rivalries in the country), the Alabama players, dressed in white jerseys, held off their much-favored opponents to a tie while playing in a slurry of red mud.

Seeing Alabama take the field in 100,000-seat **Bryant-Denny Stadium** is a near spiritual experience for avid football fans. Games usually sell out, but you can find resale tickets on StubHub and other sites.

TOP EXPERIENCE

Legacy Sites of Montgomery

Three different sites in Montgomery explore one of the most important topics in US history: the legacy of slavery. Through powerful exhibitions, memorials and monuments, visitors come face to face with 400 years of racial injustice, extending from the first people kidnapped in Africa, through the Jim Crow laws of the post–Civil War era to the rise of mass incarceration today.

JNIX/SHUTTERSTOCK

The Legacy Museum

TOP TIPS

- You needn't visit all three sites on one day. Your ticket grants admission on subsequent days.
- Free shuttles connect the three sites and the boat launch. A good plan is to park at the Legacy Museum and take the shuttle from there.

The Legacy Museum

Allow at least two hours to wander amid evocative **exhibitions** that bring the horrors of enslavement to life: a wall of waves crashing over the heads of the captured and drowned, jars containing dirt gathered at sites where innocents were lynched, and dramatizations of families being split apart. There are film clips, sound recordings, screenings in small theaters and lots of interactivity – including simulated one-on-one encounters with incarcerated people.

National Memorial for Peace & Justice

On a 6-acre site, a grassy courtyard frames 800 steel **monuments**, each suspended from a metal pole and bearing the names of lynching victims from a particular county. In all, these sculptures memorialize 4400 Black people violently killed across the south and beyond between 1877 and 1950.

Freedom Monument Sculpture Park

Though you can drive there, it's more memorable to take the boat ride (included with admission) to reach the **Freedom Monument Sculpture Park**. The journey alludes to the (involuntary) voyage taken by over 12 million enslaved Africans, nearly two million of whom would die along the way. Once at the park, a path winds past brilliantly conceived sculptures that touch on the traumas of everyday life for those without freedom.

PRACTICALITIES

- legacysites.eji.org
- $5
- 9am-6pm Wed-Sun

For deeper insight into Martin Luther King's life in Montgomery, visit the **Dexter Parsonage Museum** *($10)*, open Friday and Saturday from 10am to 4pm. You'll watch a short introductory film, then take a docent-led tour through the house where King and his family lived. There's an intimacy to the well-preserved 1950s-era spaces, and it's hard not to feel the great man's presence in rooms like his office, with some of his books on theology, philosophy and activism.

King would make history thanks in large part to Rosa Parks. In 1955, activist Parks refused to give up her seat in the whites-only section of a public bus. The **Rosa Parks Museum** *(facebook.com/TroyUniversityRosaParksMuseum; adult/child $7.50/5.50)*, set in front of the bus stop where Parks took her stand, delves into the story behind her courageous stand. Parks, along with Martin Luther King, helped launch the Montgomery bus boycott, which inspired countless communities across the South to stand up to injustice during the Civil Rights movement.

Moundville Archaeological Park

Traces of an ancient civilization

One of the largest and best-preserved sites of the pre-Columbian Mississippian civilization, the 326-acre **Moundville Archaeological Park** *(moundville.museums.ua.edu; adult/child $8/6)* preserves the grassy remains of a mound city. Within the complex you find 29 mounds of varying sizes, arranged in a manner that suggests a highly stratified social structure. The excellent on-site museum is filled with pre-Columbian art, including pottery and disks inscribed with underwater panthers, feathered serpents and skulls. The site is about an hour's drive southwest of Birmingham.

Mobile

Exploring downtown Mobile and the waterfront

The only sizable coastal city in Alabama, Mobile (moh-*beel*) was founded in 1702 – 16 years before New Orleans – and its walkable downtown is awash in history. Speaking of New Orleans, Mobile throws some impressive Mardi Gras parades itself, with bead-tossing, marching bands and abundant merrymaking over several weekends leading up to the big day in February (or early March).

Get your bearings by taking a stroll through the old streets. Conti and Dauphin are dotted with restaurants and pubs, with live music spilling out of doors come sundown. Along the way, stop in scenic green spaces like Bienville Sq and Cathedral Sq, and take in the grandeur of the

REMEMBERING MARTIN LUTHER KING

Nikki Tucker Davis, Deacon at Dexter Avenue King Memorial Baptist Church *dexterkingmemorial.org*

For our church in those days, Dr King was just our pastor. He was very approachable. The kids loved him, the members loved him. When he announced that he was resigning in order to go do more work, he was tearful and emotional, just as our membership was tearful and emotional. He was a funny, caring, charismatic man, who brought forth these big ideas. My uncle, who is 101 years old, was at that first meeting when Mrs Rosa Parks was arrested. He talked about how dynamic Dr King was when he spoke. He moved a whole community, and that spread. That inspiration went throughout this state, and then it spread throughout the world.

EATING & DRINKING IN MONTGOMERY: OUR PICKS

Martin's Restaurant: Casual spot in a strip mall that's famed for its fried chicken. *11am-7pm Mon-Fri, 10:45am-2:30pm Sun* $

Central: Fine dining on wood-fired dishes with international accents, served in an atmospheric 19th-century setting. *5:30-9pm Tue-Sat* $$$

Red Bluff Bar: Family-friendly outdoor spot with pub fare, live music and sweeping river views. *4-10pm Tue-Fri, from 1pm Sat & Sun* $

Tower Taproom: Lively spot downtown with pour-your-own craft beers, juicy burgers, wings and salads. *11am-9pm Mon-Fri, 2-10pm Sat* $

BEST OUTDOOR SITES ON THE GULF COAST

Audubon Bird Sanctuary: On Dauphin Island, a 3-mile trail wends through maritime forest, sand dunes and wetlands – a prime bird habitat.

Gulf State Park: A lovely spot to enjoy the seaside, with beaches, a small nature center (open weekdays) and 28 miles of hiking and cycling trails.

Fort Morgan State Historic Site: Explore this fascinating relic from the past – built during the War of 1812 to protect against potential British invasion of Mobile Bay.

Bon Secour National Wildlife Refuge: Ospreys, alligators and sea turtles can all be found here, along with four trails and a lovely beachfront.

Graham Creek Nature Preserve: Some 10 miles of trails (including accessible boardwalks), plus kayaks for rent.

Cathedral Basilica of the Immaculate Conception *(mobilecathedral.org)*.

A good place to learn about the city is the **History Museum of Mobile** *(historymuseumofmobile.com; adult/child $14/11)*, with interactive exhibits covering Indigenous people, colonial times, slavery, Civil War days, shipbuilding during WWII and the Civil Rights era. Admission also gives you access to the nearby colonial **Fort Condé**, with both reconstructed and original rooms dating back to the early 18th century.

Nearby, the **National Maritime Museum of the Gulf** *(nmmog.org; adult/child $14/11)* has interactive exhibits on nautical topics like sailing, piloting big vessels, shipwreck exploration and navigation skills. It's a hit with kids.

Three miles east of downtown, the **USS Alabama** *(ussalabama.com; adult/child $18/6)* is a 690ft behemoth famous for escaping nine major WWII battles unscathed. It's worth taking the self-guided tour just to experience the awesome size and might of the 'Lucky A.'

Fairhope

Small-town charm

On the eastern shore of Mobile Bay, the small town of Fairhope has a quaint and pedestrian-friendly center where the order of the day is browsing independent shops, gallery-hopping and enjoying a fine array of food and drinks. You can park at the (free) lot on Oak Ave, then head into the **Eastern Shore Art Center** *(esartcenter.org; free)* for a look at painting, photography and sculpture by local and regional artists. From there, it's a five-minute walk south to the **Fairhope Museum of History** *(free)*, where you can peer at a vintage 1935 fire engine, learn about the founders' utopian ideals and see photos of important figures from the Civil Rights era.

Half a block further along, you'll reach the heart of Fairhope (Section St and Fairhope Ave). There's prime shopping within one block in any direction. Staff at the beloved bookstore **Page & Palette** *(pageandpalette.com)* can help you find some new reading material, or head to the back for coffee, cocktails or (later in the day) live music. Music fans should stop in **Dr Music Records** *(drmusic123.com)*, which is packed with new and used vinyl. If you have kids in mind, **Fantasy Island Toys** *(fantasyislandtoys.com)* stocks puzzles, board games, dolls and lots of other eye-catching items for children of all ages.

The big event of the month is the **First Friday Art Walk**, when you can catch art openings, live music and special store events (6pm to 8pm).

EATING IN MOBILE & FAIRHOPE: OUR PICKS

Wintzell's: A Mobile classic since 1938, there's no better spot for fresh or grilled oysters and other Gulf seafood. *11am-9pm Tue-Sun* **$$**

Loda Bier Garten: Landmark on Mobile's lively Dauphin St, with comfort food, outdoor tables and over 100 draft beer choices. *11am-midnight* **$**

Panini Pete's: Follow the brick walkway under Fairhope's 'French Quarter' sign to this charming back courtyard, with fabulous beignets and panini. *8am-2:30pm* **$**

Tamara's: Fairhope's favorite restaurant boasts a wide-ranging menu for brunch, lunch and dinner, and unrivaled happy hour deals (3pm to 5:15pm). *10am-9pm Wed-Mon* **$$**

Mississippi

THE BLUES | SOUL FOOD | HISTORY

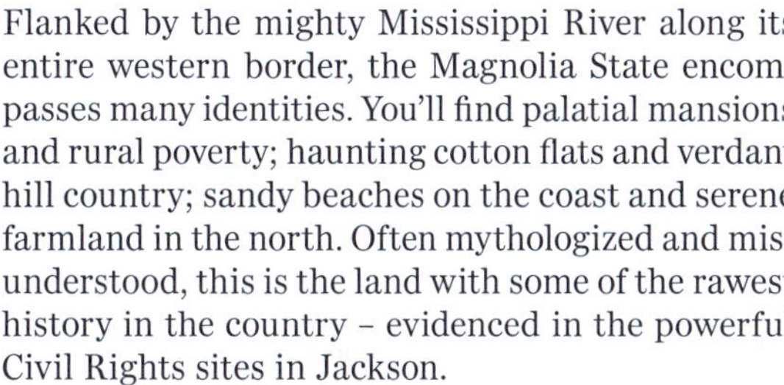

Flanked by the mighty Mississippi River along its entire western border, the Magnolia State encompasses many identities. You'll find palatial mansions and rural poverty; haunting cotton flats and verdant hill country; sandy beaches on the coast and serene farmland in the north. Often mythologized and misunderstood, this is the land with some of the rawest history in the country – evidenced in the powerful Civil Rights sites in Jackson.

Mississippi is also a place of exceptional artistry. You can see it for yourself in the one-room juke joints of the Delta (especially Clarksdale), where blues players sing heartfelt ballads of love and sorrow that echo the creative spirit that reaches back to the earliest forms of American music. There's folk art on display in shops and galleries across the state, and a rich literary heritage. Richard Wright, Tennessee Williams and Eudora Welty were all born in Mississippi, as was William Faulkner, whose grand house in Oxford draws literary pilgrims from across the globe.

Places

Mississippi Delta p391
Oxford p392
Jackson p393
Vicksburg p394
Natchez p395

TOP TIP

Clarksdale is the big draw for live music, with lots happening on Friday and Saturday nights (it's quieter other days). Check the Cathead store's website *(cathead.biz/music-calendar)* for blues performances in Clarksdale. Find out what's happening elsewhere in Mississippi at *visitmississippi.org/events*.

GETTING AROUND

Most visitors explore the state by car, but there is an Amtrak train (the *City of New Orleans* line) that passes through Mississippi on its run from the Big Easy to Memphis on to Chicago. The train stops in downtown Jackson, and as well as Marks, which is 18 miles east of Clarksdale – reach out to **CDRY Touring and Cab Services** *(facebook.com/cdrytouringandcabservice)* for a ride. Drivers who want to get off the beaten path can plan their route around scenic byways like Hwy 61 (aka the Blues Highway) or the Natchez Trace Pkwy.

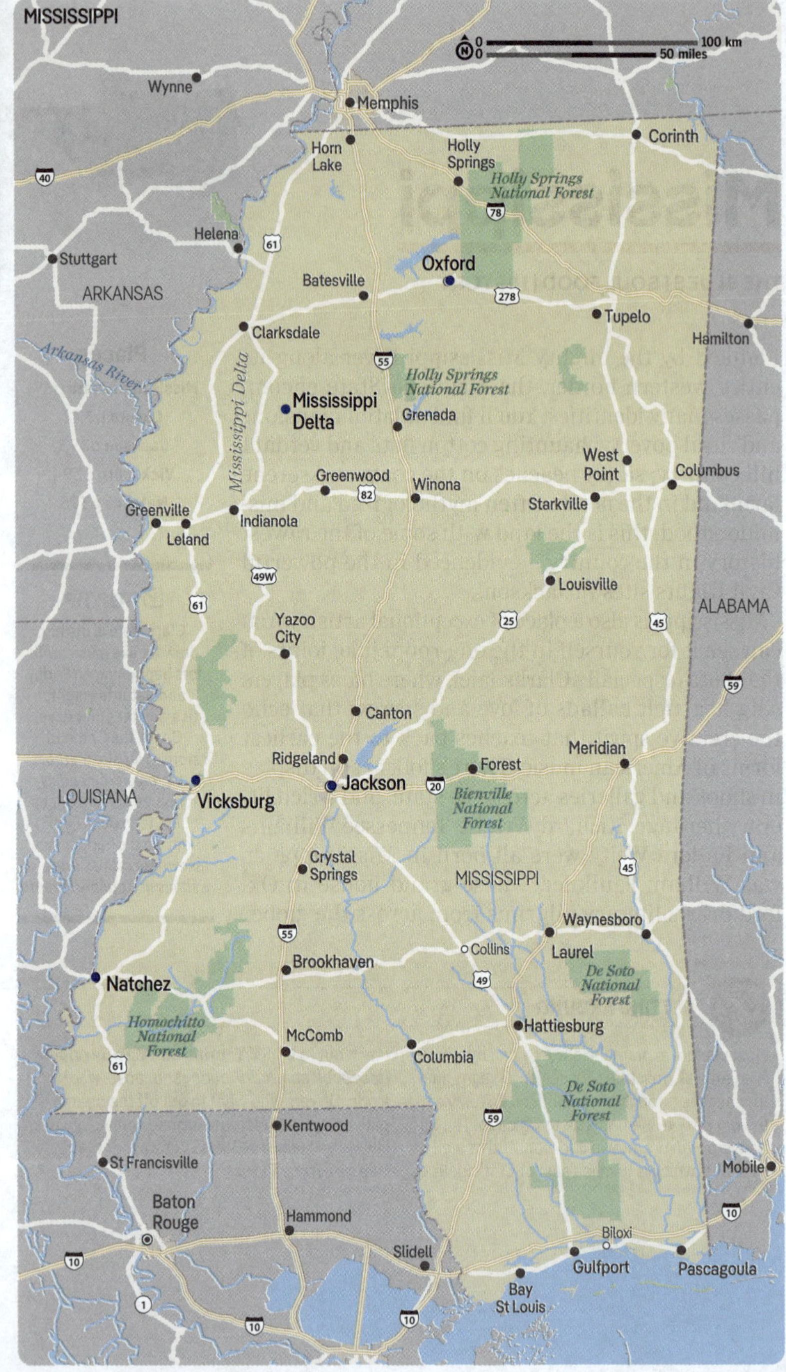
MISSISSIPPI
0 100 km
0 50 miles
Wynne
Memphis
Horn Lake
Holly Springs
Holly Springs National Forest
Corinth
40
78
Helena
61
Stuttgart
ARKANSAS
Oxford
Batesville
278
Tupelo
Hamilton
Clarksdale
Arkansas River
Mississippi Delta
55
Holly Springs National Forest
Mississippi Delta
Grenada
West Point
Columbus
Greenwood
82
Winona
Starkville
Greenville
Leland
Indianola
49W
Louisville
61
Yazoo City
25
45
ALABAMA
59
Canton
Ridgeland
Meridian
Forest
Jackson
20
LOUISIANA
Vicksburg
Bienville National Forest
Crystal Springs
MISSISSIPPI
45
Waynesboro
55
Collins
Laurel
Brookhaven
49
De Soto National Forest
Natchez
Homochitto National Forest
Hattiesburg
McComb
Columbia
61
De Soto National Forest
59
Kentwood
St Francisville
Mobile
Baton Rouge
Hammond
10
Biloxi
10
Slidell
Gulfport
Pascagoula
Bay St Louis
1
10
10

Mississippi Delta

Tracing the Blues Highway

Hwy 61, which follows along the course of the Mississippi River, is often called the Blues Highway for its connection to the USA's rich musical heritage. If you're driving down from Memphis, the **Gateway to the Blues Museum** *(tunicatravel.com; admission $10)* provides a fine introduction to the Delta. Stepping inside the weathered building (modeled after an old-fashioned juke joint), you'll find musical instruments and artwork that reference Muddy Waters, WC Handy and other blues greats. There's also a mini recording studio, where you can record your own song.

Leave ample time for Clarksdale, then continue the journey south to Leland. Take a stroll through the tiny downtown, checking out the various trail markers describing some of the talent (Johnny Winter, James 'Son' Thomas, Charley Booker) connected to the town. Afterwards, visit the **Highway 61 Blues Museum** *(adult/child $7/free)*, which has a collection of photos, memorabilia and folk art affiliated with Delta blues singers. The folks who run the place are usually willing to regale you with local stories and blues lore.

Before leaving Leland, check out the **Birthplace of Kermit the Frog** *(free)*. Local luminary Jim Henson, the creator of the Muppets, spent the first 12 years of his life in Leland, and his creative work is celebrated at this small exhibit on the bank of Deer Creek. Head onto the deck overlooking the slow waters and bottomland forest, and it's easy to imagine the inspiration for a certain green felt frog.

Take a 15-mile detour east off Hwy 61 to reach Indianola, another sleepy town with deep blues roots. Music fans come here to visit the **BB King Museum** *(bbkingmuseum.org; adult/child $15/10)*, which charts the life of the pioneering musician through photographs, film footage, interviews and, of course, music. There are lots of guitars to gawk at (he even gave one to the pope) as well as vehicles (a Rolls Royce, El Camino, and his sleek touring bus). On the grounds attached to the museum, you can see King's final resting place, surrounded by the lyrics of his songs.

Catching live blues in Clarksdale

The scrappy epicenter of the Delta blues scene, Clarksdale is also the region's most useful base. You'll want to spend the night so you can hit the music scene (cover charges range from $10 to $20). Get an overview at the **Delta Blues Museum** *(deltabluesmuseum.org; adult/child $15/10)*, which has a small but

SONGS OF THE DELTA

Wilsherie Hopson is a pianist, singer and author of *Recluse: Neglect, Survival, Recovery* *@starjukezeta2k1112*

Gospel and blues intertwine in Clarksdale. Most blues singers start off in the church. People begin at a young age – often in the choir. It's the foundation for the music scene in Clarksdale, which then becomes our own expression of life, celebration and heartache. The blues are a form of storytelling. There are a lot of great artists here – people like Edna Nicole. We call her 'the sweetheart of the Delta.' Her recent single 'Delta Dirt' basically describes the Delta in one song. You've got to listen to it.

EATING IN CLARKSDALE: OUR PICKS

Our Grandma's House of Pancakes: Start your day off with a hearty breakfast made with care at this old-fashioned charmer. *7am-1pm* $

Hooker Grocer & Eatery: Named after bluesman John Lee Hooker, this inviting place serves up brisket sliders, catfish platters and other comfort classics. *5-9pm Wed-Sun* $$

Abe's Bar-B-Q: Facing the crossroads, Abe's fires up Clarksdale's best pulled pork, plus nicely spiced tamales. *10am-8pm Mon-Sat, 11am-1:30pm Sun* $$

Meraki: The convivial community coffeehouse makes a fine place to recharge over cappuccinos, breakfast sandwiches and occasional live music. *7am-2pm Sun-Thu, to 8pm Fri & Sat* $

BIRTHPLACE OF THE BLUES

The alluvial plains that stretch across the low-lying stretch of Mississippi are a patchwork of cotton fields, lush bayous and lonely roads. American music took root in this place, evolving from the simple but soul-stirring songs developed by Black sharecroppers on cotton fields in the early 1900s. Musician and promoter WC Handy, dubbed the 'Father of the Blues,' helped popularize the 12-bar sound after hearing a sharecropper pluck his guitar with a knife and sing a repetitive tune while the two waited for a train in 1903. Across the Delta today, blues pilgrims can dig deep into the music's genesis and development. Historic interpretive markers pepper the region, noting key sites on the Mississippi Blues Trail *(msbluestrail.org).*

JAMES KIRKIKIS/SHUTTERSTOCK

Square Books

well-presented collection of memorabilia (including guitars from John Lee Hooker and BB King). The shrine to Delta legend Muddy Waters includes the actual cabin where he grew up.

Clarksdale is home to half a dozen atmospheric places to catch live blues. Co-owned by actor Morgan Freeman, **Ground Zero** *(groundzerobluesclub.com)* is a huge and friendly hall with a dance floor surrounded by tables. Bands take to the stage Wednesday to Saturday, and there's good food available. Going strong since the 1980s, the famous **Red's** *(facebook.com/RedsBluesLounge)* has neon-red lighting, which makes a moody backdrop for watching the blues players howl. Another battered juke joint not to miss is **Bad Apple Blues Club** *(facebook.com/badappleblues club),* with memorable afternoon sessions (3pm to 6pm Wednesday to Saturday).

Another requisite stop in Clarksdale is **Cat Head** *(cat head.biz),* a colorful, all-purpose, blues emporium. Shelves are jammed with books, face jugs, local folk art and blues records. Owner Roger Stolle seems to be connected to everyone in the Delta, and knows when and where the bands will play. Stop here for his weekly 'Sounds Around Town!' music calendar, also posted on the website.

In mid-April, the **Juke Joint Festival** *(jukejointfestival.com)* draws blues lovers to four days of live music from an array of talented musicians. Saturday is the big day, with some 17 outdoor stages scattered around an eight-block stretch of Clarksdale. Daytime events are free, but it's worth buying a wristband *($60)* to get access to nighttime performances at over two dozen venues.

Oxford

Faulkner and Ole Miss

Mississippi's most famous college town has a attractive town center, with restaurants, bars and shops encircling the main square (aka **Courthouse Square**). Start the day with a cafe latte among the collegiate at **Heartbreak Coffee Roasters** (two blocks north of the square), then pick up some new reading material at the excellent **Square Books** *(squarebooks.com)*, one of several booksellers facing the old courthouse.

From here, you can drive or stroll into the campus of the University of Mississippi, better known as Ole Miss. It's about a half mile from Courthouse Sq to the **University of Mississippi Museum** *(museum.olemiss.edu; free)*, where you'll find an intriguing collection of Southern folk art, American luminaries (like Georgia O'Keeffe) and some surprising ancient Greek and Roman works. It's another half mile from here to the Grove, the park-like epicenter of the pretty campus. Alternatively, the museum is also the starting point for a pretty 0.6-mile walk along the easy-going **Bailey Woods Trail**. The path ends at the edge of **Rowan Oak** *(rowanoak.com; adult/child $5/free)*, the grand manor home of William Faulkner, one of America's most lauded 20th-century writers. On a self-guided tour, you can peer in beautifully preserved rooms (some with original furnishings) and learn curious episodes from the author's life – like angrily writing drafts for *A Fable* on the walls of his office after the fan kept blowing his pages around.

Jackson

History and the fight for Civil Rights

You could easily spend half a day exploring the powerful **Mississippi Civil Rights Museum** *(mcrm.mdah.ms.gov; adult/child $15/8, Sun free)* located just a few blocks from the old domed capitol building. Whether it's a voice from overhead yelling at you to 'keep on moving,' graphic photos of lynchings hitting you with a gut punch, or the towering wall of mugshots of Freedom Riders stopping you in your tracks, the exhibits at this compelling museum keep you on high alert. The national Civil Rights movement is explored through the lens of the fight for racial equality in Mississippi, with eight exhibit halls tackling the key eras through photos, film footage, news clippings and interactive screens.

Your ticket also gives you admission to the adjoining **Museum of Mississippi History** *(mmh.mdah.ms.gov)*. For a broader context on the state's history, start here – watch the 10-minute film narrated by Mississippi's favorite native son Morgan Freeman, then wander through the thoughtfully presented galleries. Noteworthy displays, which are often supplemented by informative videos, cover prehistoric mound builders, the Chickasaw and Choctaw tribes and their legends,

BEST MISSISSIPPI MUSIC FESTS

Bentonia Blues Festival: Going strong for over 50 years, this admission-free fest draws blues fans to Bentonia (34 miles north of Jackson) over three days in late June.

Juke Joint Festival: Clarksdale's big mid-April gathering features dozens of bands playing at outdoor stages by day, and packing into the clubs by night.

King Biscuit Blues Festival: The huge October jam happens across the river in Helena, Arkansas, though everyone stays in nearby Clarksdale, and top blues performers play here afterwards.

Bright Lights: In September, several venues in Jackson's Belhaven district host this music and arts fest, featuring jazz, soul, indie-rock and blues.

Double Decker Arts Festival: Catch over a dozen bands playing over one fun weekend in Oxford in late April.

EATING & DRINKING IN JACKSON: OUR PICKS

Brent's Drugs: By day, enjoy burgers and milkshakes at a '50s-style diner. By night visit the hidden bar (Apothecary) for well-made cocktails. *hours vary* $

Elvie's: In a restaurant-packed corner of upscale Belhaven, this stylish gastropub showcases imaginative cooking from Gulf and pasture. *8am-2pm & 4:30-9pm Tue-Sat* $$$

Saltine: A spacious indoor-outdoor spot for seafood, especially oysters, which you can enjoy raw or wood-fired with creative toppings. *11am-10pm* $$

Bean: A delightful coffeeshop with breakfast bowls, avocado toast and sweet pastries, plus a bigger Saturday brunch menu. *7am-6pm* $

THE SIEGE OF VICKSBURG

In 1863 General Grant set his sights on Vicksburg, a city deemed vital to the Civil War's success. The challenge: Vicksburg sat high on bluffs over the Mississippi and was heavily fortified by the Confederates. After several unsuccessful attacks, the Union army laid siege, aiming to starve the city into submission. Under constant shelling, civilians dug shelters underground, making Vicksburg – as one resident described it, 'so honeycombed with caves that the streets look like avenues in a cemetery.' With provisions scarce, mules were eaten, dogs and cats went missing, and even rats were skinned and sold at the market. After 47 days, the Confederates surrendered, and the Union army took control of Vicksburg, which proved a turning point in the war.

the cotton industry, the barbaric practice of slavery, the Civil War and Mississippi's rich cultural heritage.

About a mile west of Mississippi Civil Rights Museum, the **Smith Robertson Museum** *(jacksonms.gov/smith-robertson-museum adult/child $7/4)* is housed in the state's first public school for African American children. The alma mater of the famed novelist Richard Wright, the former school offers insight and explanation into the pain and perseverance of the African American legacy in Mississippi.

Around 3½ miles northwest of there, the **Medgar and Myrlie Evers Home** *(nps.gov/memy; free)* is the ranch-style house where Civil Rights activist Medgar Evers lived with his young family from 1956 until 1963. You can freely wander through the home (don't forget to peek in the fridge), and learn about one of the rising stars in the fight for Civil Rights who was murdered here – shot in the back by a sniper while standing in the carport in 1963. It's run by the National Park Service, with tours hourly from 9am to 4pm (except noon).

Vicksburg

Strolling Mississippi's prettiest town center

Washington St (aka Hwy 61) between Clay and Main Sts is lined with historic buildings that today house galleries, cafes and tiny museums – the fine backdrop to a few hours of exploring. Parking is free on the street.

Get a dose of history at the **Vicksburg Civil War Museum** *(vicksburgcivilwarmuseum.org; adult/child $10/3.50)*. One of the region's only African American–owned Civil War museums gives insight into the conflict, with a special focus on Black soldiers, freedmen and abolitionists.

Just up on the right, **Lorelei Books** *(loreleibooks.com)* is an atmospheric little shop, where you can discover new titles – and there's a good selection from regional authors. Next door, **Highway 61 Coffeehouse** (open 7am to noon) is a cozy spot to curl up with your new book. Upstairs, you'll find one of the best folk art galleries in the state. The **Attic Gallery** *(atticgalleryvicksburg.com)* is packed from floor to ceiling with extraordinary works (paintings, sculptures, mixed media) created by self-taught artists.

One block up, the **Lower Mississippi River Museum** *(free)* explores the region's deep ties to the famous waterway, from the ancient peoples that hunted and fished here to the devastating floods of the 20th century. Head through the galleries to reach the MV *Mississippi IV*, a dry-docked research vessel that you can wander through (a favorite of young visitors).

EATING & DRINKING IN VICKSBURG: OUR PICKS

Walnut Hills: Savor rib-sticking, down-home Southern food, served family-style (solo diners enjoy the round table). *11am-9pm Mon & Wed-Sat, to 2pm Sun* $$

10 South: Take in the views while munching salads, shrimp and grits or hearty sandwiches from this rooftop spot. *5-9pm Tue-Sun, plus 11am-2pm Sat* $$

Key City Brewery: Satisfying house-brewed beers, plus creatively topped pizzas, swordfish and perfectly crispy fries. *4-10pm Mon-Thu, from 11am Fri-Sun* $$

Sun Izakaya: Buzzing new addition, with good sushi, soba and Japanese snacks like *takoyaki* (fried octopus balls). *11am-2:30pm & 4-9:30pm Mon-Sat* $$

USS Cairo Museum

Across the street, visit the small **Catfish Row Museum** *(catfishrowmuseum.org; free)*, which touches on Vicksburg history – including the fight for Civil Rights. Don't miss the drumset of the Red Tops, a group symbolizing the unifying force of the era. More recent is the evocative *Faces* mural painted by Vicksburg artist Kennith Humphrey.

Speaking of murals, it's well worth heading downhill to Levee St, for a look at the **Vicksburg Riverfront Murals** *(riverfront murals.com)*. Created to beautify the city's flood wall in the early 2000s, the 32 works spotlight key people and events in Vicksburg's past: Civil War, natural disasters (like the tornado of 1953) and cultural luminaries (famed Bluesman Willie Dixon).

Driving into the past

Vicksburg controlled access to the Mississippi River, and its seizure was one of the turning points of the Civil War. At the **Vicksburg National Military Park** *(nps.gov/vick; car $20)*, you can follow a 16-mile driving tour that passes artfully carved memorials and historic markers explaining battle scenarios and key events from the city's long siege. Get an overview at the visitor center, where you can watch a 20 minute film and peruse displays about the siege. Afterwards, follow the road to some 15 numbered stops. Don't miss the **USS Cairo Museum**, which covers the ironclad gunboats used by Union forces, including the salvaged USS *Cairo*. For audio commentary along the way, download the free NPS app and follow the Vicksburg self-guided park tour.

NATCHEZ' COMPLICATED PAST

Before the Civil War, the cotton plantations on the eastern banks of the Mississippi River produced the most millionaires in the US – all on the backs of enslaved Africans. In Natchez, plantation owners built over-the-top estates. By the time the Civil War came to Natchez, the town surrendered to Union forces without a fight (interestingly, locals voted against secession in 1861). Abolition stripped plantation owners of their income, but their estates remain frozen in time. Some plantations have been transformed into B&Bs, although it's far more enlightening to visit the federally managed sites (including Melrose) that are part of the Natchez National Historical Park *(nps .gov/natc)*.

Natchez

Centuries of history in a riverside city

Sprawled across a bluff overlooking the Mississippi, the old city of Natchez (settled in 1716) is packed tight with historic buildings – some transformed into museums, restaurants and shops.

THE NATCHEZ TRACE

If you're driving through Mississippi, it's worth planning at least part of your trip around one of the oldest roads in North America: the **Natchez Trace Parkway** *(nps.gov/natr)*. This 444-mile road, today administered by the National Park Service, traces a route once used by Native American tribes and runs from the edge of Natchez, Mississippi, to just outside of Nashville, Tennessee. It's a lovely, scenic drive that traverses a wide array of Southern landscapes: thick forests, soggy wetlands, gentle hill country and long swaths of farmland. There are more than 50 access points to the parkway and a helpful visitor center outside Tupelo. There are no stoplights or stop signs to ruin your ride.

DENNIS MACDONALD/SHUTTERSTOCK

Swamp along the Natchez Trace Parkway

Before delving into the town center, stop at the **Grand Village of the Natchez Indians** *(mdah.ms.gov; free)*. A visitor center displays pottery, tools and fragments of baskets while shedding light on the Mississippian people that lived here for over a thousand years (roughly CE 700 to 1730). Afterwards, take a stroll across the grassy expanse (once a plaza) to see the bare mounds that were previously topped with a temple and a chief's residence.

Fast forward through the years to the 19th century, with a visit to the **Melrose Estate** *(nps.gov/places/melrose.htm; free)*, a sprawling Greek Revival mansion and former plantation. You can freely wander the grounds, but to see inside the house, you'll need to book a guided tour *(recreation.gov; adult/child $11/1)*. Rangers do a decent job describing life for both the plantation-owning McCurran family as well as the enslaved.

Next head into central Natchez and continue your visit on foot. The **Natchez Museum of African American Culture and History** *(visitnapac.net; free)* highlights Black Mississippians who helped shape the state's history, including the writer Richard Wright and musician Clarence 'Bud' Scott. There are also exhibits on slavery, the cotton industry and Civil Rights.

A few blocks away, the displays inside the **William Johnson House** *(free)* show what life was like for free African Americans in the pre–Civil War South. When you need a break from the heavy weight of the past, head down to the river and admire the views along the half-mile **Natchez Bluff River Trail**.

EATING & DRINKING IN NATCHEZ: OUR PICKS

Camp Restaurant: Fun atmosphere, good pub grub (pork belly tacos, catfish) and craft beer on tap with Mississippi River views. *11am-8pm* $$

Frankie's on Main: Tuck in to high-end southern cooking inside a grand Greek Revival dining room (and former 1826 bank). *11am-10pm Tue-Sat* $$$

Pig Out Inn: Barbecue fans can't leave Natchez without trying smoky pork or brisket at this casual spot. *11am-9pm Mon-Sat, to 7pm Sun* $

Smoot's Grocery: Listen to blues while sipping tall bloody Marys at this river-facing bar. *6-10pm Thu & Fri, 1pm-late Sat, noon-6pm Sun*

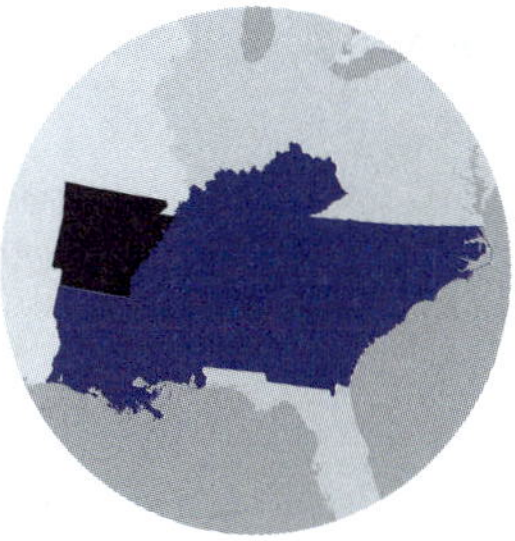

Arkansas

MOUNTAIN BIKING | HIKING | ARTS & CULTURE

Bridging the Midwest and the Deep South, 'the Natural State' exemplifies its nickname with swift-rushing rivers, dark leafy hollows and the crenelated granite outcrops of the age-old Ozark Mountains. The most impressive scenery lies in Arkansas' upper half, but the entire state is blessed with exceptionally well-presented (and generally admission free) state parks and tiny, empty roads crisscrossing dense woodlands and rolling farm fields.

Adventure comes in many forms, from paddling the Buffalo River on day-long or multiday excursions to mountain biking the rugged woodland trails in Bentonville. There are caves to explore and forested paths that lead to towering waterfalls and dramatic overlooks. You can even dig diamonds in one of the state parks – or take it easy with a bit of hydrotherapy in the rejuvenating waters of Hot Springs. Nature aside, Arkansas' towns and small cities are a delight to explore, especially Little Rock, Fayetteville, Bentonville and Eureka Springs.

Places

Little Rock p397
Hot Springs National Park p400
Tri-Peaks Region p401
Crater of Diamonds State Park p402
Fayetteville p402
Eureka Springs p404
Bentonville p405
Ozark Mountains p406

TOP TIP

Be sure to visit at least one Arkansas state park *(arkansasstateparks.com)* while you're here. The state's 52 parks (most admission free) have an outstanding reputation, and many offer camping and good-value cabin accommodations. Some also have restaurants – like Petit Jean, with its fireplace and sweeping views.

Little Rock

MAP P399

See Clinton's legacy

Former President Bill Clinton served nearly 12 years as governor of Arkansas, so it's fitting that Little Rock houses the

GETTING AROUND

Amtrak's *Texas Eagle* train, which runs from Chicago to Los Angeles, makes stops in Arkansas, including in Little Rock (the station is about 1.4 miles west of the River Market District). Greyhound buses also connect a few cities, but having a car is essential if you plan to explore beyond town centers. Arkansas' roads are generally in good shape, though take things slowly when traveling the narrow mountainous thoroughfares in the north of the state. Parking is free in most places, with the exception of downtown Little Rock and Fayetteville, as well as the streets near Hot Springs National Park.

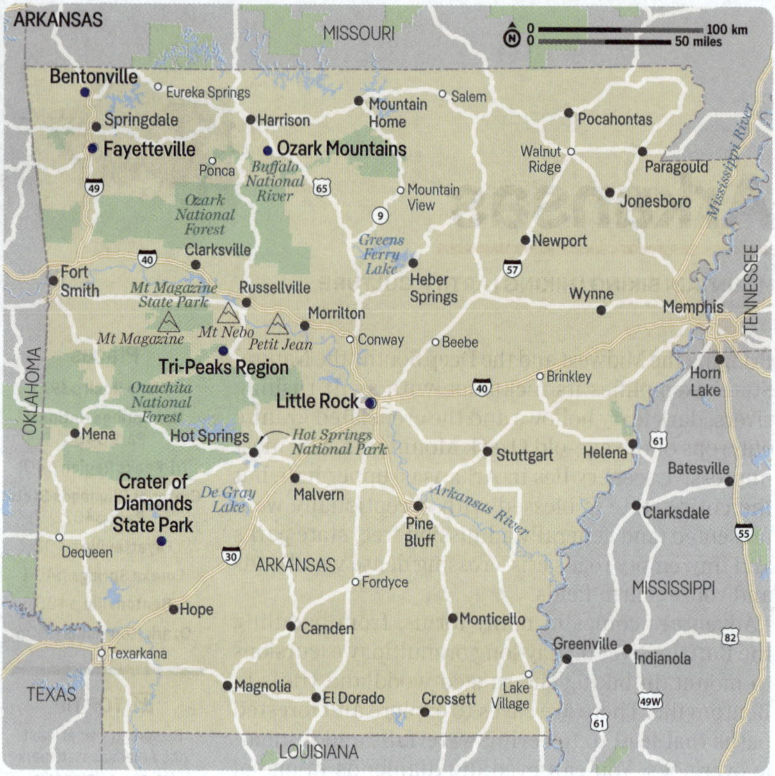

Clinton Presidential Center *(clintonlibrary.gov; adult/child $12/7)*. The excellent museum serves as a time capsule of the 1990s when the boy from Hope (Arkansas) was in the White House. Start off with a video about Clinton (narrated by the man himself), then check out the displays of photos and videos highlighting different aspects of his presidency, from his successes bringing down the national debt to his relationships with world leaders (including Nelson Mandela). Speaking of relationships, there's scant attention paid to a certain affair with a White House intern, though his impeachment is mentioned in passing. You can also wander through full-scale replicas of the White House Cabinet Room and the Oval Office, and see gifts from visiting dignitaries

EATING & DRINKING IN LITTLE ROCK: OUR PICKS

MAP P399

Community Bakery: A well-loved gathering space for coffees, flaky bakery items and soups, sandwiches, quiches and daily specials. *7am-8pm* **$**

Flying Fish: Feast on catfish, barbecue shrimp and fried oyster po'boys at this Cajun-style seafood joint with a vintage diner interior. *11am-9pm* **$$**

Brood & Barley: Atmospheric gastropub in North Little Rock serving bistro fare (steamed mussels, sliders) along with creative cocktails. *11am-11pm Mon-Sat* **$$**

Lost Forty Brewing: Little Rock's top craft brewer has a rotating array of IPAs, seasonal brews and Belgian-style ales, plus good pub grub. *11am-9pm* **$$**

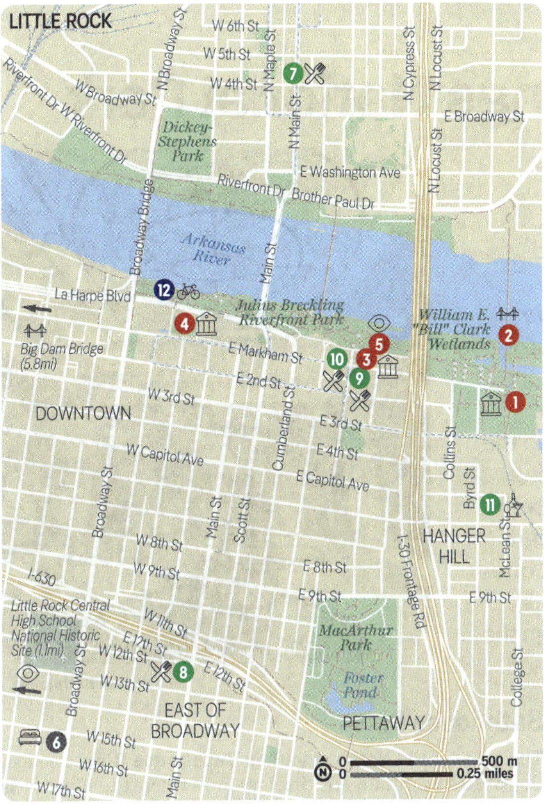

SIGHTS
1 Clinton Presidential Center
2 Clinton Presidential Park Bridge
3 Museum of Discovery
4 Old State House Museum
5 Witt Stephens Jr Nature Center

SLEEPING
6 Rosemont Cottages

EATING
7 Brood & Barley
8 Community Bakery
9 Flying Fish
10 Ottenheimer Market Hall

DRINKING & NIGHTLIFE
11 Lost Forty Brewing

TRANSPORT
12 Arkansas River Trail

NEIGHBORHOODS OF LITTLE ROCK

River Market District: Waterfront trails, playgrounds and nearby attractions (a theater, restaurants, cafes) on President Clinton Av.

Main Street Corridor: Running south of the waterfront, this stretch of Main St has restaurants and a pocket park that hosts occasional events.

North Little Rock: Just across the Arkansas River from the Riverfront District. Stroll across the pedestrian-only Junction Bridge and head over to Main St, which is filled with shops and eateries (between West Broadway and East 6th Sts).

SoMa: Short for South Main, SoMa is a vibrant neighborhood of galleries, indie shops, restaurants and even a distillery; it's best between West 12th and West 16th Sts.

(and also look at menus from state dinners). Don't miss those metal binders – you can peruse Clinton's schedule for every day he was in office.

Explore the riverfront

Stretching along the south bank of the Arkansas River, Little Rock's **River Market District** contains sculpture gardens, playgrounds and even a small wetlands sanctuary. Pedestrian paths wind along the riverfront, providing fine views for the strollers and cyclists passing through. Various bridges cross the river, including the **Clinton Presidential Park Bridge**, a scenic car-free path located near the Clinton Presidential Center.

TOP EXPERIENCE

Hot Springs National Park

Famed for its warm geothermal waters, Hot Springs is both a tiny national park and a charmingly low-key mountain town. Native Americans called this region the Valley of the Vapors, while Euro-American settlers were drawn to the springs' alleged healing powers. Today, restored bathhouses offer insight into the past (several offer old-school treatments), and trails lace through the surrounding woodlands.

EWY MEDIA/SHUTTERSTOCK

Fordyce Bathhouse

TOP TIPS

- Free ranger-led tours from Fordyce Bathhouse happen Thursdays to Mondays (typically 10am and 2pm).
- Behind Bathhouse Row, the **Grand Promenade** passes flowing springs (and a hot-water fountain off Reserve St).
- Near Bathhouse Row, **Maxine's** *(maxineslive.com)* has deep dish pizzas, burlesque shows and live music.

PRACTICALITIES

- nps.gov/hosp
- Fordyce Bathhouse Visitor Center 9am-5pm Thu-Mon
- free

Bathhouse Row

The heart of the National Park is **Bathhouse Row**, a collection of architecturally striking buildings where the upper class once came for several weeks of treatments. Get the lowdown at the 1915 **Fordyce Bathhouse**, which serves as the NPS visitor center and a museum. The well-preserved building has stained-glass, Greek statues and a vintage gymnasium. To experience it for yourself, book an old-fashioned hydrotherapy treatment a few doors down at the **Buckstaff Bathhouse** *(buckstaffbaths.com; from $45)*; reserve well ahead.

Hiking Trails

The park has 26 miles of trails, many of them are short and scenic, and they link up to form a network across the town's mountains. For a pleasant outing, you can hike up from Bathhouse Row via the Peak Trail (0.6 miles) to **Hot Springs Mountain Tower** *(hotspringstower.com; adult/child $14/11)*; there an elevator goes up to a 216ft observation deck. Or skip the expense and continue along the Hot Springs Mountain Trail, the Gulpha Gorge Tail, the Goat Rock Trail and the Upper Dogwood Trail, before completing the loop on the Hot Springs Mountain Trail – all in, a 5-mile (2½-hour) loop.

Cyclists and runners can put in some mileage along the **Arkansas River Trail**, which hugs both sides of the river for 15.6 miles (the **Big Dam Bridge** to the west and the Clinton Presidential Park Bridge to the east are key anchors).

A prime spot for learning about Arkansas' natural world is the **Witt Stephens Jr Nature Center** *(agfc.com/things-to-do/nature-centers/little-rock; free)*. Exhibits explore all of the state's ecological zones, and include small aquariums with fish and even an alligator.

Young travelers will also enjoy the nearby **Museum of Discovery** *(museumofdiscovery.org; adult/child $14/12)*. The fun science-and-natural-history center is perfect for families. Inside hands-on galleries, you can lie on a bed of nails, meander through a kaleidoscope tunnel, climb amid netting and tunnels in a tower, and feel the rumble and roar of a tornado.

For a dose of Arkansas history, visit the **Old State House Museum** *(arkansasheritage.com/old-state-house-museum; free)*, which covers key events of the past since the 1830s. There's a special collection on dresses worn by first ladies, and several galleries devoted to Arkansas governors, including Sarah Huckabee Sanders, who spent time in the governor's mansion as both a teenager (as daughter of Governor Mike Huckabee) and in more recent years as the state's first female governor.

When hunger strikes, stop in the **Ottenheimer Market Hall** *(10am to 2pm Monday to Saturday)*. The spacious food hall has some tempting good-value lunch options, including sushi, Thai cuisine, Middle Eastern cooking, barbecue and fish and chips.

Tri-Peaks Region

Trails, waterfalls and scenic drives

Stretching between the Ouchita and Ozark mountain ranges in the verdant Arkansas River Valley, the Tri-Peaks region is home to three impressive mountains, each protected by its own state park – there's no admission fee at any of them, though you'll have to pay extra for camping or overnighting in a rustic cabin.

The easternmost is **Petit Jean**, which is Arkansas' oldest state park (founded 1923). This is a great place for a hike, followed by a meal with a panoramic view in the old lodge (you can also overnight in a cabin). Some 20 miles of trails wind through this 2658-acre park. The most famous is the moderately challenging Cedar Falls Trail, a 2-mile out-and-back excursion leading to an impressive 90ft waterfall. To see the falls from overhead, you can drive to the Cedar Falls Overlook. Speaking of drives, don't miss the short ride along Red Bluff Dr, which has several fine viewpoints including the Mary Ann Overlook offering glimpses of Mt Nebo and Mt Magazine.

A twisting 25 miles northwest of Petit Jean, **Mt Nebo** may lack vertical glory (topping out at 1350ft) but the valley views are still outstanding from this leafy state park. There are some 32 miles of hiking and biking routes here. On foot, the moderate Rim Trail (a 3.5-mile loop) offers grand views that stretch nearly 100 miles on clear days. The mountain biking is excellent (though you'll need to BYO bike since there's no rental nearby);

TOP FESTIVALS IN ARKANSAS

Ozark Folk Festival: Eureka Springs' big jam fest features flat-picking, mandolin playing and jig dancing over three days in early September.

Hot Springs Documentary Film Festival: Nine days of innovative films in October, plus discussions, parties and even wellness events like hiking and meditation.

Bentonville Bike Fest: Held in May, this major cycling event features competitions, skill workshops, demonstrations, kid activities and group rides.

Bentonville Film Festival: In June, this is a week-long showcase of under-represented voices in cinema. Don't miss outdoor screenings at The Momentary.

Bean Fest & Championship Outhouse Races: Live music, bean feasting and people-powered potty races happen in Mountain View one weekend in October.

THE LITTLE ROCK NINE

In 1954, the US Supreme Court issued a landmark decision that outlawed segregation in public schools. Despite the ruling, many cities, including Little Rock, bucked the law and kept African Americans out of all-white schools. Change came when nine brave Black students – later known as the Little Rock Nine – enrolled at Central High School in 1957. The backlash was severe. Arkansas governor Orval Faubus sent the state's National Guard to block their entrance. They also faced an angry mob. President Dwight Eisenhower eventually got involved and sent the US Army to guard the students. Learn more about those tumultuous times by visiting the small **Little Rock Central High School National Historic Site** *(nps.gov/chsc; free)* near the still-functioning high school.

RCHAT/SHUTTERSTOCK

you'll find everything from the beginner friendly Miller's Goat Trail (5.3 miles) to the experts-only Lizard Tail (1.9 miles), not to mention the rewarding intermediate-level Chickalah Loop Trail (4.8 miles), among the best in the park.

Another 35 miles west of Mt Nebo, you'll reach **Mt Magazine**. Home to Arkansas' highest point (at 2753ft), this state park is a draw for hikers seeking bragging rights. The climb up Signal Hill takes you there, and it's a fairly easy 1.8-mile loop, with just over 250ft of elevation along the way. If you don't have time for a walk, the **Mt Magazine Scenic Byway** traverses the park and includes some memorable vistas of forests, lakes and valleys along the way as it connects Havana with Webb City along Hwy 309.

Crater of Diamonds State Park

Dig for diamonds

Some 60 miles southwest of Hot Springs, the **Crater of Diamonds State Park** *(adult/child $15/7)* is a one-of-a-kind place where you can dig through a 37-acre field (a former volcanic crater) in search of rocks, minerals and gemstones. Some 35,000 diamonds have been unearthed here, including an 8.5 karat one in 2015 worth a cool $1 million. On the downside, you'll be digging in the dirt on an exposed field in often scorching temperatures. You can bring your own gear, or rent tools from the park (shovel, box screen, bucket).

Fayetteville

Arts and culture

Nestled in the woodsy hills of the Ozarks, Fayetteville is the state's third largest town, fueled by the youthful energy of the **University of Arkansas**. On Fayetteville's west side, the leafy campus has wide-ranging cultural offerings, from classic and cutting-edge plays at the **University Theater**

Crater of Diamonds State Park

(theatre.uark.edu/productions) to concerts at the **Faulkner Performing Arts Center** *(faulkner.uark.edu)*.

The town's love of the arts isn't limited to the university. In the center, the **Walton Arts Center** *(waltonartscenter.org)* stages Broadway musicals, comedy shows, rock concerts and even puppet theater. Nearby, **TheaterSquared** *(theatre2.org)* stages more avant-garde shows, with a packed calendar of more than 350 performances and events each year.

Walkng around downtown Fayetteville

Fayetteville's attractive downtown is has plenty of indie shops, restaurants and cafes. A good place to begin the exploration is at **Fayetteville Historic Square** – especially lively on Saturday mornings during the weekly **farmers market** *(fayettevillefarmersmarket.org; 7am-2pm)*. Nearby, you can browse for quality home items, outdoor gear and gourmet provisions at **City Supply** *(citysupplyfayetteville.com)*. You can also pick up some vinyl at **Block Street Records** *(facebook.com/blockstreetrecords)*, and recharge over lattes and bakery items at **Little Bread Company** *(littlebread.com)*.

Later in the day you can enter a hallowed electric realm at **Pinpoint** *(pinpointfayetteville.com)*, a bar full of pinball machines, or drink quality bourbon cocktails at **Vault** *(vault.bar*; the mint juleps are ideal warm-weather refreshment).

PRIME MOUNTAIN BIKING SPOTS

Dave Neal, owner of Mojo Cycling, shares his favorite rides for first-time visitors to the Bentonville area *@mojocycling.com*

A good starting point is Bella Vista, just north of Bentonville. In the Back 40, there's a little entry park called Blowing Springs. It has numerous short trails that vary in technicality. There are beginner trails, where I taught my kids to ride, and more robust and tough trails too. There's also camping in the middle of it. So you can stay there and roll right out of your tent and on to a trail. Another great spot is called the Castle, found in Slaughter Pen. There are trails for all different levels here, and also a skills park where you can really progress as a rider.

EATING & DRINKING IN FAYETTEVILLE: OUR PICKS

Hammontree's Grilled Cheese: Inviting spot for elevated comfort food: panko-fried artichoke hearts, French onion soup and decadent sandwiches. *11am-9:30pm Mon-Sat* $

Cheers at the OPO: Upscale Southern comfort fare (fried green tomatoes, wood-fired meats) inside a grand building that was a former post office. *11am-10pm Wed-Sun* $$

Farmer's Table: An old house turned restaurant with outstanding locally sourced dishes. Best choice for breakfast. *7am-3pm Tue-Sun, plus 5-9pm Fri & Sat* $$

Maxine's Tap Room: An atmospherically lit drinking den with well-crafted cocktails and regional microbrews. *4pm-2am Mon-Sat, from 6pm Sun*

STROLLING EUREKA SPRINGS

One of the Ozarks' most photogenic towns, Eureka Springs is a hilly enclave of winding streets, Victorian architecture and eye-catching shops.

START	END	LENGTH
Crescent Hotel	Eureka Springs Historical Museum	1 mile; 1½ hours

Park just above the town at the ❶ **Crescent Hotel**. Step inside this still-functioning 1886 grande dame, which is full of vintage character. Head to the top-floor Skybar for a bite or drinks on the terrace. Walk out the back through the hotel grounds and cross the street to ❷ **St Elizabeth**, a striking limestone church built in 1909. Turn left out of the church, and find the ❸ **Magnolia Path**. Descend through the trees and keep going downhill (at times on a wooden sidewalk). You'll eventually end up on Spring St, which takes you past vine-draped ❹ **Harding Spring**, one of many picturesque springs for which the town is famed. Further along, you can pick up handmade watercolors and other creative supplies at ❺ **Adventure Art**. Across the road, ❻ **MoJo's Records** stocks quality vinyl, and there's a cafe attached.

Keep following Spring St as it winds and curves down the hillside, and you'll soon be in the heart of town, with colorful shops and galleries, cafes and restaurants. Finish at the ❼ **Eureka Springs Historical Museum**, where you can learn about local history. If you don't want to walk back up the hill, hop on the trolley (red line; $4), which will take you back to your starting point.

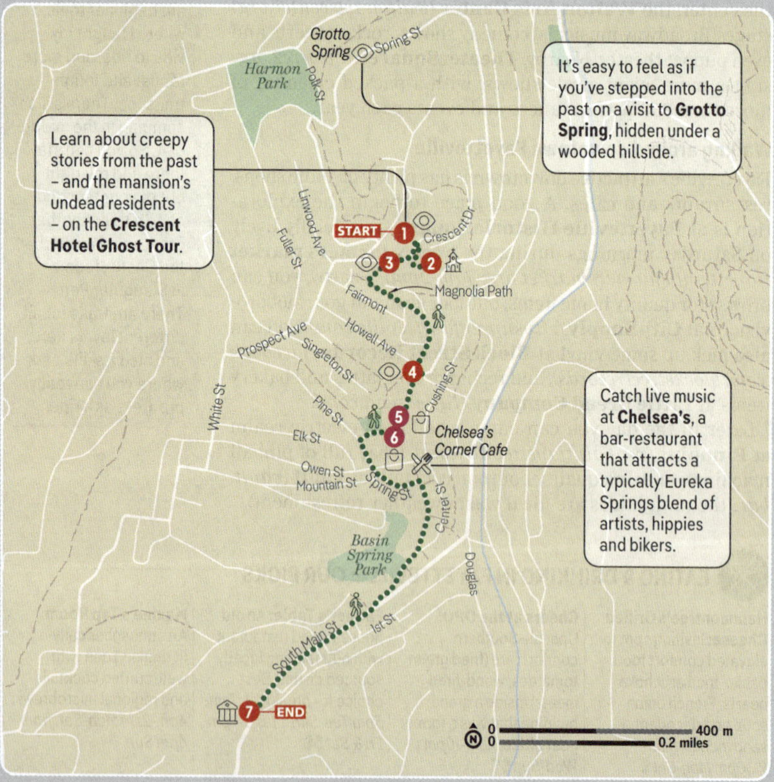

It's easy to feel as if you've stepped into the past on a visit to **Grotto Spring**, hidden under a wooded hillside.

Learn about creepy stories from the past – and the mansion's undead residents – on the **Crescent Hotel Ghost Tour**.

Catch live music at **Chelsea's**, a bar-restaurant that attracts a typically Eureka Springs blend of artists, hippies and bikers.

Grotto Spring
Spring St
Harmon Park
Polk St
Linwood Ave
Fuller St
START
Crescent Dr
Magnolia Path
Fairmont
Howell Ave
Prospect Ave
Singleton St
Cushing St
White St
Pine St
Elk St
Chelsea's Corner Cafe
Owen St
Mountain St
Spring St
Center St
Basin Spring Park
Douglas
South Main St
1st St
END
0 400 m
0 0.2 miles

For the unadulterated student-life experience, head a few blocks northwest to **Dickson Street**. Between University and Thompson Aves, you'll find live music spots (**George's Majestic Lounge**, the **Piano Bar**), buzzing little cafes and inviting stores – like the excellent **Dickson St Bookshop** *(dicksonstreetbooks.com)*.

Bentonville

Ride the fabled trails

One of the best places for mountain biking in the US east of the Rockies, the Bentonville area has over 160 miles of pathways and bikeways, streetside bicycle paths and looped trails. You could spend many days happily exploring this system with its free well-marked trails, each rated beginner (green), intermediate (blue) or expert (black diamond).

With limited time focus your attention on **Slaughter Pen**, with its 40-plus miles of single track of all levels. Between berms, big rocks and forests, you'll get a great taste of local nature. You can access the Pen via the All American Trail, a mountain-biking route that connects to the Crystal Bridges Museum. Another highlight is **Coler Mountain**, with its 17 miles of varied trails (best accessed via NW 3rd St, about 1.8 miles west of Bentonville City Sq).

Pick up a free map of the entire network at the visitor center or at outfitters like **Mojo**, which rents high-quality mountain bikes *(mojocycling.com; 4hr rental $40-100)*.

Be sure to also check out the **Ledger**, a rare bikeable building (follow the jewel-carrying insect mosaics up six stories of ramps). Stop for a pick-me-up on the ground floor at **Airship Coffee**.

See cutting-edge art in the Crystal Bridges Museum

Sprawling across a series of creek ponds fed by mountain streams, the enormous **Crystal Bridges Museum** *(crystalbridges.org; free; closed Tue)* is an unexpected find, to say the least. The curved pavilions, designed by acclaimed architect Mosh Safdie, house extensive collections that are connected by glass-encased tunnels, and the experience consistently filters sunlight through and across the grounds. The permanent collection focuses on artists active in the USA – everyone from Harlem Renaissance painter Jacob Lawrence to Osage photographer Ryan RedCorn. Special exhibitions (with admission prices) roam the globe, with recent retrospectives devoted to Yayoi Kusama, KAWS and Diego Rivera. Surrounding the museum, sculptures by renowned artists punctuate several leafy trails, including the **Art Trail**.

BENTONVILLE'S BEST ART & CULTURE EXPERIENCES

Skyspace: James Turrell's sky-centric circular chamber features a mesmerizing light installation beginning 45 minutes before sunrise and 10 minutes before sunset.

Bachman-Wilson House: Wander through this small, ingeniously designed home, dreamed up by the great Frank Lloyd Wright. Reserve a free ticket through *crystalbridges.org/calendar/frank-lloyd-wright-tours*.

Museum of Native American History: Impressive collection of artifacts made by cultures across the Americas.

Amazeum: A huge kids' museum with loads of fun, hands-on activities.

Walmart Museum: Learn the story behind Walmart.

Momentary: The factory-turned-creative hub has art exhibitions, live music and a top-floor cafe-bar.

EATING & DRINKING IN BENTONVILLE: OUR PICKS

Meteor Cafe: Sunny, anytime spot with well-pulled espressos and tasty breakfast tacos, plus pizzas and margaritas later on. *7am-10pm* $

Wright's Barbecue: The famed destination for brisket, pulled pork, fall-off-the-bone ribs and other smoky decadence. *10:30am-8pm Tue-Sat* $$

Hub: A favorite post-ride gathering spot for Tex-Mex, craft beers and events (live music Fridays, trivia night Wednesdays). *11am-10pm Tue-Sun* $$

Table Mesa Bistro: One of many appealing spots overlooking Bentonville's photogenic main square, serving creative bowls, Mexican fare and burgers. *8am-9pm Mon-Sat, 9am-8pm Sun* $$

TOP HIKES IN THE OZARKS

Go after the rains to see waterfalls in all their flowing majesty.

Hemmed-in Hollow Falls: From the Compton Trailhead, make the 2.5-mile descent to this stunning 209ft waterfall. It's a challenging return (over 1300ft elevation gain).

Big Bluff & the Goat Trail: Start at the Centerpoint Trail to eventually reach (via exposed ledges in places) a fantastic view over the Buffalo River (6 miles return, with 1000ft elevation gain).

Hawksbill Crag: A moderate 2.7-mile out-and-back hike to cinematic Hawksbill Crag (aka Whitaker Point).

Glory Hole Falls: This moderate 2-mile return hike takes you to an unusual waterfall that pours through a hole in a rockface.

Alum Cove: Make the fairly easy 1.2-mile loop to see a natural rock bridge spanning over 130ft.

DAMON SHAW/SHUTTERSTOCK

Buffalo National River

Ozark Mountains

On the trail in Devil's Den

Tucked in the lush Lee Creek Valley, some 25 miles south of Fayetteville, the **Devil's Den State Park** *(free)* is a favorite getaway for hiking, trail running, mountain biking and camping. The route not to miss is the relatively straightforward 1.5-mile Devil's Den Trail, which courses past waterfalls (flowing after the rains), dense greenery and the eerie rock formations that give the state park its name.

Paddle the Scenic Buffalo National River

Designated the nation's first national river, the **Buffalo** rolls west to east for 135 glorious miles through the heart of northern Arkansas. Along the way, the rushing waters pass by ochre cliffs and granite outcroppings, while lapping at small sandy beaches that fringe deep tracts of Ozark forest. For a memorable DIY adventure, rent a kayak or canoe for the day *($72 to $102)* from **Buffalo Outdoor Center** *(buffaloriver.com)* in Ponca and make the 10-mile paddle to **Kyle's Landing**. They also offer shuttle service *(from $46),* which means they'll drive your car to your arrival point, so you can head off when you finish the day's paddle. This wild river is also a great spot for multiday trips, and you can camp at designated campsites along the way. Check the National Park site *(nps.gov/buff)* for more details.

Into the Underworld at Blanchard Springs Caverns

The spectacular **Blanchard Springs Caverns** *(blanchardsprings.org),* 15 miles northwest of Mountain View, were carved by an underground river. It's a little-known, mind-blowing spot in Arkansas. Guided tours *(adult/child $15/10)* like the accessible one-hour Dripstone Trail and the 1½-hour Discovery Trail (more challenging, with its 700 steps) are offered regularly. Reserve ahead through *recreation.gov.*

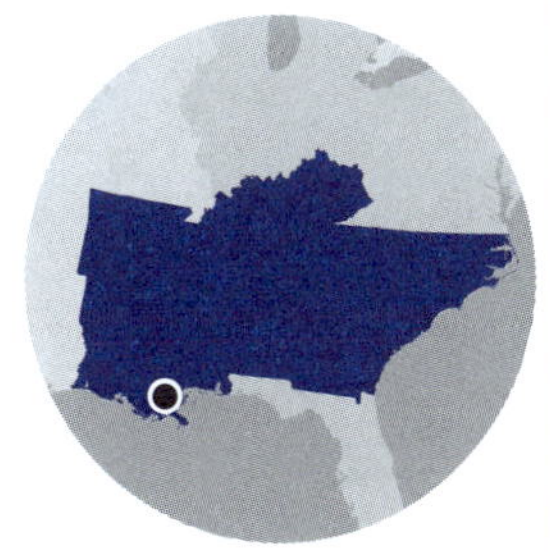

New Orleans

CREOLE COOKING | FIERY JAZZ | EUROPEAN ARCHITECTURE

No matter how many cities on this planet you visit, you'll never find one quite like New Orleans. When it comes to food, live music and celebration, New Orleanians have perfected the art of living large. Creole chefs have honed recipes for gumbo, jambalaya, char-grilled oysters, crawfish and decadent seafood combinations from the bountiful Gulf Coast. The city is famed for Mardi Gras and its weeks of parades, bands and costuming, but there's revelry throughout the year – from the myriad performances at Jazz Fest to the merriment of Halloween. The birthplace of jazz is also a great place to enjoy the vibrant, ever-evolving soundtrack that defines the Big Easy.

The starting point for the New Orleans experience is undoubtedly the French Quarter, with its centuries-old architecture, historic restaurants and cobblestone streets both elegant (Royal) and louche (Bourbon). Outside the Quarter, you'll find fascinating, largely local-centric neighborhoods, including the bohemian-loving Bywater, the grand Garden District and the Marigny – the epicenter of NOLA's live music scene.

GETTING AROUND

New Orleans has a flat, fairly compact center. Streetcars, buses, bikeshares and rideshares connect different parts of the city. Within neighborhoods, walking is one of the best ways to get around. Riding one of New Orleans' historic streetcar lines is a must. The most scenic is the St Charles Ave line, which runs from the the edge of the French Quarter, passing through the Garden District, Uptown and lovely Audubon Park. Two slightly different lines follow Canal St to Mid-City, including the City Park line, which takes you to the entrance of New Orleans' biggest green space.

Celebrating New Orleans' Style

Fun times during Mardi Gras and Jazz Fest

Mardi Gras *(mardigrasneworleans.com)* is about many things: massive floats rolling through packed streets, hilariously costumed krewes shimmying in unison to vintage disco and vast marching bands blasting out heart-pounding rhythms. There are also walking parades open to all (with a costume), and joining in is the best way to experience New Orleans' biggest celebration.

The parade season is a 12-day period beginning two Fridays before Fat Tuesday (in February). Early parades are charming, neighborly processions that whet your appetite for later events, which increase in size and grandeur until the spectacles of the

HIGHLIGHTS
1 Cabildo
2 Presbytère
3 Royal Street
4 St Louis Cemetery No 1

SIGHTS
5 Bourbon Street
6 Congo Square
7 Gallier House Museum
8 Historic New Orleans Collection
9 Louis Armstrong Park

ACTIVITIES & TOURS
10 Cemetery Tours NOLA
11 New Orleans Pharmacy Museum
12 Steamboat Natchez

SLEEPING
13 Olivier House

EATING
14 Bayona
15 Brennan's
16 Central Grocery
17 Deanie's Seafood Restaurant
18 Jewel of the South
19 Namaste Nola
20 Napoleon House
21 Sylvain
22 Tableau

DRINKING & NIGHTLIFE
23 Bar Tonique
24 Carousel Bar
25 Fritzel's European Jazz Pub
26 Latitude 29

ENTERTAINMENT
27 21st Amendment Bar
28 Balcony Music Club
29 Davenport Lounge
30 House of Blues
31 Mahogany Jazz Hall
32 Preservation Hall

TRANSPORT
33 Canal Streetcar

superkrewes emerge during the final weekend. Download the WDSU Parade Tracker app to see what's on when.

Held in late April and early May, the New Orleans **Jazz & Heritage Festival** *(nojazzfest.com)* features a fabled lineup of bands and soloists from a wide range of genres. Local talent adds to the national and international superstars, and there's also outstanding food, a folklife village and kids' activities. In January, the musical acts are announced and tickets go on sale. Get info and buy tickets on the website. It all happens in Mid-City at the Fair Grounds Race Course.

Delve into New Orleans' History & Culture

MAP P408

A quartet of thought-provoking museums

A combination of preserved buildings, museums and research centers all rolled into one, the **Historic New Orleans Collection** *(hnoc.org; free)* presents a series of regularly rotating exhibits – among the most insightful in the city. Don't miss the French Quarter Galleries, with multimedia displays ranging from Native American settlement to 18th-century French colony to buzzing modern cultural hub.

The former seat of power in colonial Louisiana, the **Cabildo** *(louisianastatemuseum.org; adult/child $11/9)* gives a fine overview of the past with its collection that covers everything from Native American tools (1st floor) to 'Wanted' posters for escaped enslaved people (3rd floor).

Next door to the Cabildo, the 1791 **Presbytère** *(louisiana statemuseum.org; adult/child $11/9)* focuses on both the positive and negative aspects of life in New Orleans, namely Mardi Gras revelry and devastating hurricanes – in particular Hurricane Katrina.

Set in one of the country's oldest apothecaries, the **New Orleans Pharmacy Museum** *(pharmacymuseum.org; adult/child $10/7)* has cabinets full of assorted elixirs once thought to be therapeutic, along with frightening-looking hypodermic needles and bone saws. Book ahead for 45-minute guided tours *(adult/child $20/17)* that shed light on the epidemics, nefarious 'cure-alls' and primitive medical treatments (opium, leeches, mercury injections) of centuries past.

THE CARIBBEAN CONNECTION

Following a 1791 revolt led by enslaved people, thousands of slaveholders fled St Domingue (now Haiti) with their 'property' (enslaved human beings) to Louisiana, which bolstered French-speaking Creole traditions. At the same time, thousands of the formerly enslaved also relocated from St Domingue to New Orleans as free people of color. By 1810, some 10,000 of these islanders had come to the city, doubling the total population and tripling the population for the free people of color. This influx from St Domingue also injected an indelible trace of Caribbean culture that remains in evidence to this day. Their most obvious contribution was the practice of voodoo, which became popular in New Orleans during the 19th century.

EATING IN THE QUARTER: CASUAL DINING

MAP P408

Napoleon House: A 1797 building packed with history; its atmospheric courtyard is a magical spot for classic Creole cooking. *11am-10pm* $$

Sylvain: In a stylish carriage house, Sylvain is a convivial spot for well-executed comfort fare. *10:30am-3pm Fri-Sun, plus 4-11pm daily* $$

Central Grocery: Famed for its muffuletta, a massive sandwich stuffed with meat, cheese and olive salad. Get it to go and eat by the river. *9am-5pm* $

Deanie's Seafood Restaurant: Temptations run from BBQ shrimp to charbroiled oysters. *11am-9:30pm Thu-Mon, from 4pm Tue & Wed* $$

A PROMENADE IN THE FRENCH QUARTER

Explore the historic heart of New Orleans, taking in eclectic architecture, iconic monuments and a grand sweep of riverside.

START	END	LENGTH
Jackson Square	Riverfront	1 mile; 1½ hours

Start on Chartres St on the edge of 1 **Jackson Square**, which is quiet in the morning but later in the day bubbles with activity (buskers, tarot readers, tour groups). From here, you can take in some of the Quarter's grand architecture, including 2 **St Louis Cathedral**. Though the current building dates from the 1850s, previous iterations of the church date as far back as 1718.

At 3 **632 1/2 St Peter Street**, you can peer up at the 2nd-floor balcony of the house, where Tennessee Williams lived in 1946 and 1947. It was here that he wrote his famed *A Streetcar Named Desire*. Head around the corner and continue along elegant 4 **Royal St**, which has plenty of architectural eye candy, before making your way to the 5 **French Market**, which has numerous food and craft stalls. A trading post for centuries, the present 19th-century structure was designed by Joseph Abeilard, one of the USA's first African American architects.

New Orleanians have an abiding affection for Joan of Arc, manifest in the gilded 14ft, 2700-pound 6 **statue** that was gifted to the city by the people of France in 1964. Cross Decatur and head up to the 7 **riverfront**. From here you can amble along the muddy Mississippi enjoying fine views across the water.

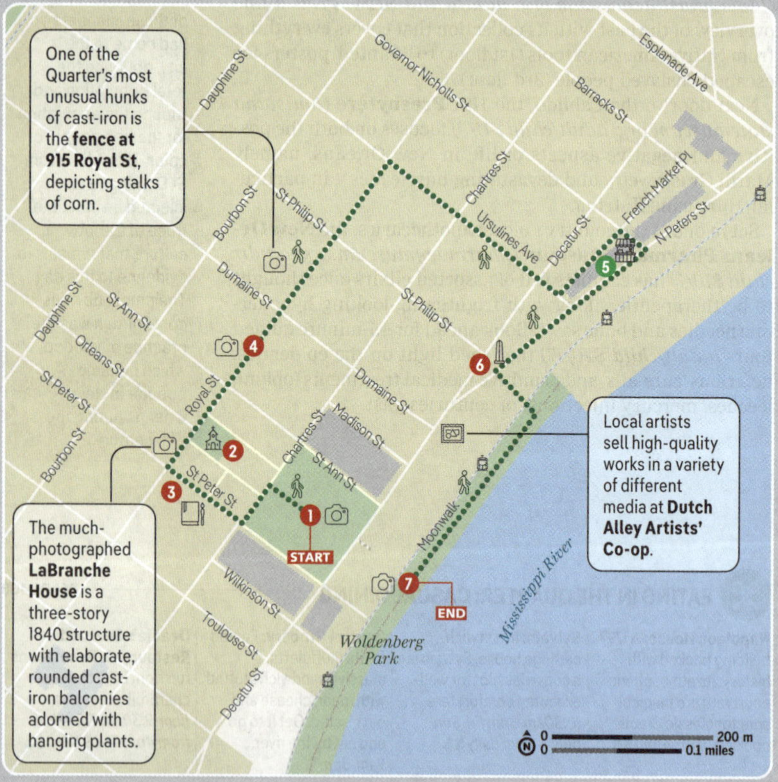

One of the Quarter's most unusual hunks of cast-iron is the **fence at 915 Royal St**, depicting stalks of corn.

Local artists sell high-quality works in a variety of different media at **Dutch Alley Artists' Co-op**.

The much-photographed **LaBranche House** is a three-story 1840 structure with elaborate, rounded cast-iron balconies adorned with hanging plants.

Strolling Royal Street

MAP P408

Architecture and eye-catching shops

Royal Street, with its handsome storefronts stretching beneath cast-iron balconies, is one of the Quarter's prettiest thoroughfares. Several blocks of the strip are dedicated to antiques stores and art galleries, making Royal a sort of elegant 19th-century outdoor shopping arcade. The stretch between Bienville and Orleans closes to traffic between 11am and 4pm (until 7pm weekends), when musicians, performers and other buskers set up shop (don't forget to tip).

Cruising the Mississippi

MAP P408

Fun times on a paddlewheeler riverboat

For an old-fashioned dose of slow travel, book a trip along the Mississippi in an old paddle wheeler. Two main boat companies offer similarly themed cruises, including history-themed tours *(adult/child $42/17)*, jazz brunches *(adult/child $69/35)* and dinner excursions with live music (adult/child $95/40). The **Steamboat Natchez** *(steamboatnatchez.com)* departs from a pier near the base of Toulouse St, while the **Creole Queen** *(creolequeen.com)* sails from the river end of Poydras St, behind the Four Seasons Hotel.

Portal into the Past

MAP P408

Take a historic house tour

Get a deeper understanding of New Orleans by taking a guided tour through one of its house museums (reserve these ahead). The **Gallier House Museum** *(hgghh.org; adult/child $17/14)* exemplifies a style unique to the French Quarter thanks to the innovations of famed architect James Gallier Jr, who designed the house in 1860. Guides point out unique features like double skylights and indoor plumbing with hot and cold running water – cutting-edge technology at the time. You'll also learn about the residents, including the four enslaved people – Laurette, Rose, Julienne and Francois – who occupied the quarters out back.

The Legendary Jazz Spot

MAP P408

An evening at Preservation Hall

Housed in a former art gallery dating from 1803, **Preservation Hall** *(preservationhall.com; $25)* is one of New Orleans' most storied live-music venues, but it's unlike other places in town. You must purchase tickets online before coming, shows

TOP LIVE MUSIC SPOTS IN THE QUARTER

21st Amendment Bar: A great jazz bar that rarely has a cover charge (one drink minimum) on Iberville.

House of Blues: Home to several different live music venues, this national chain stages some excellent bands – not just blues.

Davenport Lounge: The Davenport is inside the Ritz Carlton and offers quality jazz to a well-dressed crowd.

Balcony Music Club: This buzzing spot on Decatur St has live music daily with a wide range of acts – jazz, blues, rock and funk.

Mahogany Jazz Hall: This somewhat newish space has vintage vibes and outstanding performances from the likes of trumpeter Leroy Jones.

EATING IN THE QUARTER: FINE DINING

MAP P408

Jewel of the South: Tucked behind a cottage, the courtyardhere is as enchanting as the cuisine. *5-11pm Wed-Mon, from 11:30am Fri & Sat* $$$

Bayona: A slow-food pioneer, Bayona is classy but unpretentious. *6-8:30pm Tue-Sat, plus 11:30am-1:30pm Thu-Sat* $$$

Brennan's: One of the grandes dames of Creole dining, Brennan's has famous dishes (Gulf fish amandine) and decadent breakfasts. *9am-9pm* $$$

Tableau: Book a table on the balcony for memorable views while indulging in haute-Creole cuisine and crème brûlée. *11am-9pm Wed-Sun* $$$

THE BOURBON-POWERED ECONOMY

Locals love to hate on **Bourbon St** – which can indeed be crass and malodorous – and yet it plays a vital role in the city's economy. Each year New Orleans welcomes over 18 million visitors, who spend some $9 billion during their stay. An estimated 80% of those visitors come to Bourbon St, pumping tens of millions of dollars into the local economy. It also supports over 7000 jobs compressed into 20 square blocks straddling both sides of the street – a job density that is nearly 100 times more productive than the rest of New Orleans. The real estate value of the street is also no small matter, with estimates hovering around $500 million.

run just 45 minutes and happen several times nightly, and all ages are welcome.

Behaving Badly on Bourbon Street

MAP P408

Neon-lit debauchery

Like Vegas and Cancún, the main stretch of **Bourbon Street** is where the great id of the repressed American psyche is let loose into a seething mass of karaoke, strip clubs and bachelorette parties. It's one of the tackiest experiences in the world, but there's never a dull moment here, and you can't come to New Orleans and not visit the place.

At St Philip St, Bourbon shifts from a Dante's Inferno–style circle of neon-lit hell into an altogether more agreeable stretch of historical houses, diners and bars, many of which cater to the LGBTIQ+ community. Great spots here include Lafitte's, the oldest continuously operating gay bar in the country.

Tour St Louis Cemetery No 1

MAP P408

City of the dead

New Orleans is famed for large above-ground necropolises. The most impressive is **St Louis Cemetery No 1**, with its artfully designed tombs and burial sites of famed residents (like Voodoo practitioner Marie Laveau). Access is by guided tour only. Book with **Cemetery Tours NOLA** *(cemeterytour neworleans.com; adult/child $25/18)*. The 45-minute tour departs from across the street at Basin St Station *(basinststation.com)*, which also has exhibits on city history.

The Heart of the Backstreet

MAP P413

Explore the culture of the Tremé

The Tremé sits at the heart of New Orleans Black culture, and is a great place to learn about the city's deep-rooted traditions. Start your visit at the small **Backstreet Cultural Museum** *(backstreetmuseum.org; adult/child $25/10)* on St Philip St. Mardi Gras Indian suits grab the spotlight with dazzling flair – and finely crafted detail – in this informative space, which examines many of the distinctive elements of African American culture in New Orleans.

Everyone Is a Star

MAP P413

A DIY music experience

Created by a group of local artists and tinkerers, **Music Box Village** *(musicboxvillage.com, adult/child$15/7)* is not just

DRINKING IN THE QUARTER: OUR PICKS

MAP P408

Carousel Bar: Go early to snag a seat at the spinning carousel, a 1949 landmark inside the Hotel Monteleone. *11am-midnight*

Fritzel's European Jazz Pub: A Bourbon St original, this atmospheric spot often has live music. *4pm-midnight Mon, noon-2am Tue-Sun*

Bar Tonique: Walking a fine line between lounge and dive bar, this place shakes excellent cocktails in a low-lit setting. *noon-2am*

Latitude 29: Hallowed ground for Tiki lovers, Latitude 29 serves delicious rum cocktails. *3-9pm Sun-Thu, noon-11pm Fri & Sat*

THE MARIGNY, BYWATER & THE TREMÉ

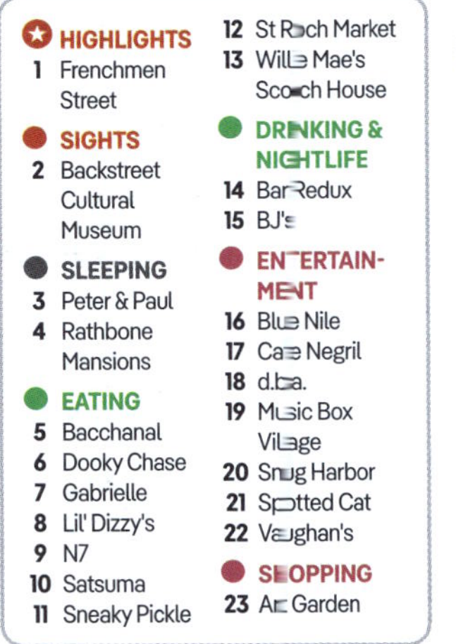

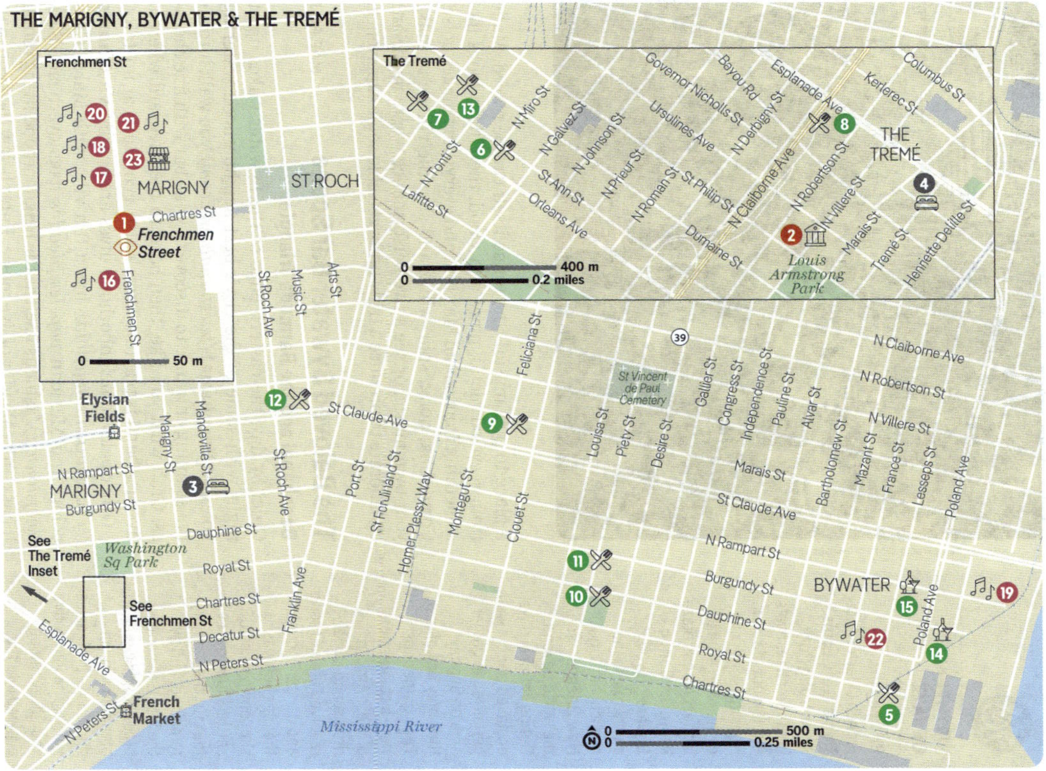

HIGHLIGHTS

1 Frenchmen Street

SIGHTS

2 Backstreet Cultural Museum

SLEEPING

3 Peter & Paul
4 Rathbone Mansions

EATING

5 Bacchanal
6 Dooky Chase
7 Gabrielle
8 Lil' Dizzy's
9 N7
10 Satsuma
11 Sneaky Pickle
12 St Roch Market
13 Willie Mae's Scotch House

DRINKING & NIGHTLIFE

14 Bar Redux
15 BJ's

ENTERTAINMENT

16 Blue Nile
17 Cafe Negril
18 d.b.a.
19 Music Box Village
20 Snug Harbor
21 Spotted Cat
22 Vaughan's

SHOPPING

23 Art Garden

TOP TIPS

From March through early May, you can catch free concerts in Lafayette Sq in downtown. These happen Wednesdays from 5pm to 8pm (*ylcwats.com*). Bring an appetite – food vendors serve up all sorts of decadence.

BIRTHPLACE OF JAZZ

Bridging the French Quarter and Tremé, leafy **Louis Armstrong Park** hosts small festivals throughout the year. Near the south end of the park, a small inconspicuous plaza known as **Congo Square** played a vital role in the musical heritage of New Orleans – and the world beyond. During colonial days, enslaved people were permitted to gather here on Sundays, their only day of rest. Their gatherings were a celebration of West African rituals, and largely revolved around song and dance. Though the practice was shut down when US settlers took over the city, the memory remained, and by the late 19th century, brass bands were blending African rhythms with classical music. The innovative sounds eventually evolved into the well-known music of jazz.

MICHAEL SERNA/500PX/GETTY IMAGES

a place to play music – the venue itself can be played. Made from recycled metal, pipes and wood, the village looks like something from a Mad Max film and everything makes noise. Come ding, dong, spin, whizz and slap the village to make your own music, or see a live performance where musicians collaborate to produce a truly unforgettable sonic experience.

The Beloved Bywater Bar Scene

MAP P413

Bacchanal and the Barmuda Triangle

Quiet by day, the eastern edge of the Bywater wakes up at night with some of the city's best neighborhood watering holes. At **Bacchanal** *(bacchanalwine.com)*, you walk into an unassuming entrance to discover a wine bar with fine cheeses. Grab what you like, then head to the backyard where a live jazz band is playing. There's also a cocktail bar upstairs.

Other beloved neighborhood dives are nearby. **Vaughan's** *(@vaughansloungenola)*, has a fun vibe with Mardi Gras colors and Mexican *papeles picados* flags overhead. **BJ's** *(@bjslounge)* fashions itself as the neighborhood living room; it has a full calendar of live music. Enter below the neon 'Bar' sign to **Bar Redux** *(@barreduxnola)*, another dive bar with performers in the garden along with finger-lickin-good Creole fried wings and gumbo.

EATING IN TREMÉ: OUR PICKS

MAP P413

Gabrielle: This little cottage doles out rich Cajun plates of braised rabbit, slow-roasted duck and other favorites. *5-10pm Wed-Sat* $$$

Lil' Dizzy's: Join the crowds at this legendary lunchtime Creole buffet on the corner of Claiborne. *11am-3pm Mon-Sat* $

Willie Mae's Scotch House: Serves up signature fried chicken – among the world's best! *hours vary* $

Dooky Chase: New Orleans' most famous destination for Creole cooking has been dazzling diners (President Obama included) since 1941. *11am-3pm Tue-Fri, plus 5:30-9pm Fri & Sat* $$

Frenchmen Street

Go Bar-hopping on Frenchmen Street MAP P413

Join the jazz-fueled street party

Lined with music venues, street jazz and perhaps a piano on wheels, **Frenchmen Street** is a chaotic cacophony and loads of fun. A who's who of legendary jazz musicians frequently play here, including Kermit Ruffins and John Boutté. Top events are usually held at **Snug Harbor** *(snugjazz.com)*, **d.b.a.** *(dbaneworleans.com)*, the **Spotted Cat** *(spottedcatmusic club.com)*, **Blue Nile** *(bluenilelive.com)* and **Cafe Negril** *(cafenegrilnola.com)*.

Take a break from the music to browse the arts and crafts for sale at the **Art Garden** night market *(artgardennola.com; 7pm-midnight Thu-Sun)*.

Art Gazing Downtown MAP P416

A top museum and gallery district

The **Ogden Museum of Southern Art** *(ogdenmuseum.org; adult/child $11/6)* illuminates unique facets of the South in all its complexity. Rotating exhibitions showcase lots of intriguing subjects, from photography on the streets of New Orleans to the overlooked communities of Appalachia. The permanent collection (3rd floor) has 18th-century portraits

SECOND LINES!

Second Line refers to New Orleans' neighborhood parades, especially those put on by the city's African American Social Aid and Pleasure (S&P) clubs. The S&P members deck themselves out in flash suits, hats and shoes, and carry decorated umbrellas and fans. This snazzy crowd, accompanied by a hired band, dances through the city. This is the First Line. Marching behind it is the Second Line: the crowds that gather to celebrate the music. Hundreds, sometimes thousands, of people dance in the Second Line, stopping for drinks and food along the parade route. All are welcome to join. Second Lines occur every Sunday from September through May. To find the parade route, check out WWOZ's Takin' It to the Streets section *(wwoz.org)*.

EATING IN THE MARIGNY & BYWATER: OUR PICKS MAP P413

Sneaky Pickle: Mostly vegan pub with excellent mac 'n' cheese, smoked tempeh Reubens and carrot juice Micheladas. *11am-9:30pm Wed-Mon* **$$**

St Roch Market: Food court in an 1875 market with cuisine from Cuba, Italy, Malaysia and elsewhere. *7am-9pm Sun-Thu, to 10pm Fri & Sat* **$$**

Satsuma: Bohemian, exposed-brick cafe with a shaded garden and sandwiches for breakfast and lunch. *8am-2pm* **$**

N7: Memorable French, Japanese and fish tapas served in a romantic, twinkly-lit garden. *5-9pm Mon-Thu, 11:30am-2:30pm & 5-10pm Fri-Sun* **$$$**

GARDEN DISTRICT, LOWER GARDEN & CENTRAL CITY

Among the most photogenic corners of the city, the **Garden District** exudes Old Southern excess with its historic mansions, lush greenery, chichi bistros and upscale boutiques (namely along Magazine St). Between the Central Business District (CBD) and the Garden District, the **Lower Garden District** is somewhat like its upriver neighbor but not quite as posh. There's a slightly more bohemian vibe, and plenty of bars and restaurants. Up above St Charles Ave, **Central City** is very much in transition. While there are large stretches of urban blight, there is also a dynamic concentration of community activist organizations rebuilding what was once one of the city's most important African American neighborhoods (Oretha Castle Haley is the main thoroughfare).

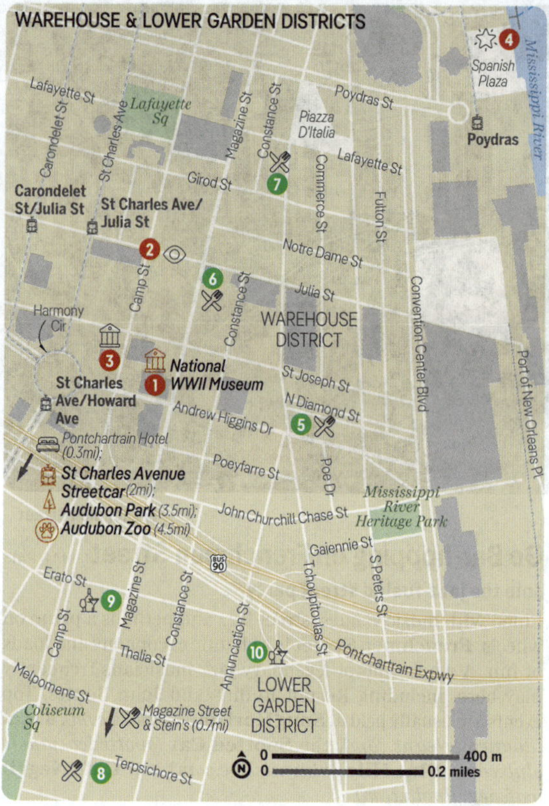

WAREHOUSE & LOWER GARDEN DISTRICTS

HIGHLIGHTS
1 National WWII Museum

SIGHTS
2 Julia Street
3 Ogden Museum of Southern Art

ACTIVITES
4 Creole Queen

EATING
5 Cochon
6 Pêche
7 St James Cheese Company
8 Surrey's Cafe & Juice Bar

DRINKING & NIGHTLIFE
9 Barrel Proof
10 Tell Me Bar

by French artists, lush Louisiana landscapes of the 1800s and socialist-realist artists of the 1930s.

Sometimes referred to as Gallery Row, **Julia Street** (between St Charles and Tchoupitoulas) is the heart of the Warehouse Arts District *(artsdistrictneworleans.com)*, with a smattering of galleries dotting the old buildings along this one-way thoroughfare. Things are liveliest on the first Saturday of the month *(6pm to 9pm)*, when there are special exhibitions and free wine.

See WWII in all its complexity

MAP P416

A sprawling, immersive museum

The **National WWII Museum** *(nationalww2museum.org; adult/child $36/26)* drops you straight into the action. Wall-sized photographs capture the confusion of D-Day. Riveting oral histories tell remarkable stories of survival. A walk through the snowy woods feels eerily cold. Exhibits like these make this grand facility engaging; artifacts, battles and war strategies are humanized through personal recollections and heat-of-the-moment displays. You could easily spend a full day (or more) here, so plan your visit carefully.

The must-see film of the museum is *Beyond All Boundaries*, which takes a 4D look at the USA's involvement in the war on a panoramic 120ft-wide screen. Get ready for rumbling seats and a dusting of snowflakes. Oscar-winning actor Tom Hanks narrates this evocative 48-minute experience, which runs on the hour from 10am to 4pm daily.

HIGHLIGHTS
1 City Park

SIGHTS
2 Botanical Gardens
3 New Orleans Museum of Art
4 Sydney & Walda Besthoff Sculpture Garden

ACTIVITIES
5 City Putt
6 Louisiana Children's Museum

DRINKING & NIGHTLIFE
7 Cafe du Monde

ENTERTAINMENT
8 Carousel Gardens
9 Jazz & Heritage Festival
10 Storyland

EATING IN THE CBD & WAREHOUSE DISTRICT: OUR PICKS

MAPS P408, P416

Namaste Nola: Despite the hotel setting, this place fires up beautiful Indian fare, including a rich paneer tikka masala. *11am-3pm & 5-10pm Thu-Tue* $$

Cochon: Donald Link pays homage to his Cajun culinary roots, serving meats smoked and wood-fired to perfection. *11am-10pm* $$

Pêche: One of New Orleans' best seafood restaurants lets the high-quality ingredients speak for themselves. *11am-10pm* $$$

St James Cheese Company: Heavenly cheesy sandwiches like Gruyère with caramelized onions. *11am-6pm Mon-Sat, to 4pm Sun* $

BEST KID-FRIENDLY SPOTS IN CITY PARK

Louisiana Children's Museum: Interactive exhibits, huge grounds and an enormous outdoor play area. Take your kids here on a hot day.

Storyland: Chase small children past life-size replicas of storybook characters at what might be the gentlest tourist attraction around.

City Putt: Home to two separate courses, this 36-hole putt-putt is the only minigolf attraction in the city.

Couturie Forest: A spaghetti tangle of pleasant trails wind past waterways and the 'highest point in New Orleans.'

Carousel Gardens: There are rides, a merry-go-round, a mini-roller coaster and plenty of fun to be had.

JTUCKER/SHUTTERSTOCK

St Charles Avenue Streetcar

Strolling & Shopping on Magazine

MAP P416

Indie boutiques, cafes and restaurants

Magazine Street is by far Orleans' best shopping strip. As a center for commercial activity it begins in the Lower Garden District, near the intersection with Felicity St. From here, you can follow Magazine west all the way to Audubon Park and shop or window browse in antiques stores and boutiques almost the entire way. The densest concentration of shops and restaurants lies around these intersections: Jackson, Washington, Louisiana and Napoleon.

Ride the St Charles Avenue Streetcar

MAP P416

Vintage DIY adventure

Some of the grandest homes in the US line St Charles Ave, shaded by enormous oak trees. Clanging through this bucolic corridor comes the iconic **St Charles Avenue Streetcar**, running since 1835. It's a delightfully nostalgic way to get across town. Hop on at Canal – or anywhere along the line (there are stops every few blocks) and ride it to Audubon Park. Pay the $1.25 fare in cash ($3 for an all-day pass), or via the city's Le Pass app.

EATING & DRINKING IN THE GARDEN DISTRICT: OUR PICKS

MAP P416

Surrey's Cafe & Juice Bar: Colorful neighborhood charmer offering outstanding breakfasts like shrimp and grits. *8am-3pm Thu-Mon* $

Stein's: The famed deli is an unrivaled spot for bacon, egg and cheese bagels and pastrami on rye. *8am-5pm Tue-Fri, from 9am Sat & Sun* $

Barrel Proof: A festive bourbon-centric option with corrugated iron walls, a long dark wood bar and fine cocktails with a creative edge. *4pm-1am*

Tell Me Bar: This well-hidden natural wine bar has a beautiful indoor and outdoor design and unusual wines from around the globe. *4-11pm*

Walk Amid Leafy Audubon Park

MAP P416

Verdant oasis and zoo

Audubon Park is a grand green space, run through with live oak trees, walking and cycling paths and a picturesque little lake, all framed by some lovely houses. Students lounge on the grass under Spanish moss while joggers lope by, dog owners play with their pets, golfers tee off and friends share an outdoor sundowner.

Appropriately enough, the **Audubon Zoo** *(audubonnature institute.org; adult/child $30/25)* is inside Audubon Park. It's a large place with sections including African, Asian and South American landscapes and fauna, and kids will find some of the world's most popular animals here, from elephants to giraffes. During the summer months, part of the zoo becomes a dedicated water park for youngsters. Don't miss the Louisiana Swamp section: a wet wonderland of bald cypresses and Spanish moss, carefully landscaped to reflect the natural wonders of southern Louisiana bayou country.

A Day at City Park

MAP P417

Art, sculpture and hands-on hijinks

City Park is so big that it includes two of the city's most wonderful museums, plus a sculpture garden, botanical garden and lots of walking paths. You can get there on the streetcar – take the **Canal Street line** (board the No 48 'City Park/ Muse' route).

A good place to begin at **Cafe Du Monde** *(shop.cafe dumonde.com)*. Order beignets and coffee with chicory, while listening to birdsong. Afterwards, take a stroll along the narrow bayou, which is lined with huge centuries-old live oak trees.

A short hop from there, the elegant **New Orleans Museum of Art** *(NOMA; noma.org; adult/child $20/free)* was opened in 1911 and is well worth a visit for its special exhibitions, gorgeous marble atrium and galleries of African, Asian, Flemish, Italian and American Southern art.

The **Sydney & Walda Besthoff Sculpture Garden** *(free)* is just outside NOMA, amid a wooded quilt of streams, pathways, lovers' benches and, of course, sculpture – mainly of the contemporary sort. For even more greenery – and countless flower species – head to the **Botanical Garden** *(adult/child $12/6)*.

LEGENDARY GUMBO

Candi Vanardo, sous-chef at Deelightful Roux School of Cooking, gives insight into New Orleans' quintessential dish. *chefdeelavigne.com*

The secret to gumbo is your roux and filé. If there is no filé – ground sassafras leaves – then it is not gumbo. The filé gives it a certain taste, texture and color. They say gumbo should look like the Mississippi River, and file has that ability that makes it kind of dredgy. What you put in it depends on where you grew up. People put different things in their gumbo. For me, there's going to be filé, seafood, smoked sausage, hot sausage – this is a 9th Ward gumbo we're talking about. For seafood, I use shrimp, blue crab or even snow crab.

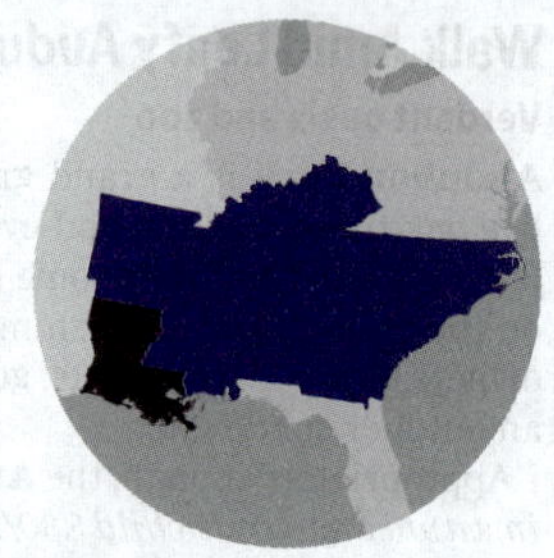

Louisiana

BLACK HISTORY | CAJUN CULTURE | WETLANDS & WILDLIFE

Places

Plantation Country p421
Lafayette p422
Tabasco p423
Poverty Point p423

French and Spanish explorers alike were drawn to the magnificent Mississippi River, and both countries would lay claim to the region, which was ultimately named after French king Louis XIV in the 17th century. Even after Louisiana was purchased from France by the fledgling United States in 1803, it retained its francophone roots thanks to the generations of Europeans living here, along with the influx of French-speaking Acadians (later known as Cajuns) and Haitians in the years following the St Domingue Revolution.

Not surprisingly, Louisiana feels completely different from other parts of the country. Cajun and Creole music still spills out of dance halls along the bayou, and you may feel like you're entering another realm while boating through fertile wetlands of alligators, birdsong and soaring bald cypress trees. There are also ample opportunities to explore the past, whether visiting a Native American mound-building settlement (and present-day World Heritage Site) or learning about the enslaved people who helped build this nation.

TOP TIP

The best time to visit Lafayette is during **Festival International de Louisiane** *(festivalinternational.org)*. Held on the last weekend in April, the free music event (simply called 'Festival' in these parts) brings incredible talent from far-flung corners of the world to the multiple stages set up around town.

GETTING AROUND

Most travelers explore Louisiana by car as it's quite difficult to get around without your own wheels. If you're flying in, New Orleans is the best place to arrange affordable rentals. If you don't plan on doing much traveling within the state, rail fans can take one of three weekly departures aboard Amtrak's *Sunset Limited*, which connects New Orleans with Los Angeles. The train makes several stops in Louisiana, including in New Iberia and Lafayette, though once there you'll still need a vehicle to get around (Uber and Lyft both operate in Lafayette, however).

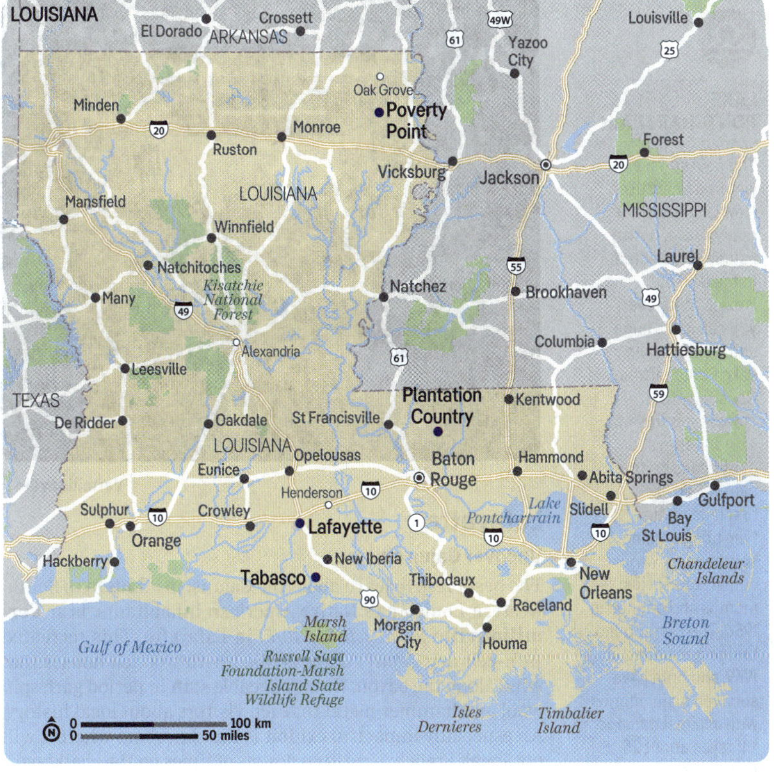

Plantation Country

See the other side of plantation life

The excellent **Whitney Plantation** *(whitneyplantation.org; adult/child guided tour $32/18, self-guided tour $25/11)* rewrites the script with 1½- to two-hour guided tours that focus on the lives of the enslaved. It isn't easy history to hear, but the guides do a wonderful job – many of them locals whose ancestors may have worked on the plantation. Guided tours are offered Wednesday to Monday at 10:45am, 12:45pm and 2:15pm. Self-guided tours with an audio device or app are available from 9:30am to 3pm.

Another 10-minutes' drive up the road, the **Laura Plantation** *(lauraplantation.com; adult/teen/child $28/20/15)* also does a remarkable job of contextualizing the life of both the free and enslaved on the Duparc Sugar Plantation. Guides rely on historical records and the first-hand accounts of Laura Locoul, a Creole woman who grew up here. Guided tours, available in English and French, last about 75 minutes and run every 20 to 40 minutes from 10am to 3:20pm.

LAKE PONTCHARTRAIN

The 630-sq-mile waterbody north of New Orleans is not really a lake, but an estuary connected to the Gulf of Mexico. Whatever you call it, it's huge, and the 23.8-mile Lake Pontchartrain Causeway that crosses it is the world's longest continuous bridge over water. The first lane of the twin bridge, going southbound, was constructed in just 14 months and opened in 1956. The northbound bridge was added in 1969, and both have survived major storms with minimal damage.

It takes about 25 minutes to drive across the bridge. Unsurprisingly, you won't see land for most of the journey. Driving northbound is free, but you'll have to pay a $6 toll on the drive back.

PHILIP GOULD/GETTY IMAGES

Vermilionville

Lafayette

Uncover Cajun culture

The best place to learn about the Cajuns, in addition to Southwestern Louisiana's Native American inhabitants, is at **Vermilionville** *(adult/child $10/6)* in Lafayette. This recreated 19th-century Cajun village is filled with wooden houses that wind along the bayou. Knowledgeable staff in period garb spin wool and hammer metal to teach visitors about local history. An especially impactful exhibit is the classroom where 'I will not speak French' is written dozens of times on the chalkboard – for decades, French was banned in public schools. There's plenty to read and an excellent restaurant if you're hungry. Check the calendar for live music on weekends.

Dance to Cajun & Creole rhythms

If you overnight in Lafayette, be sure to check out the town's renowned music scene. At the **Blue Moon Saloon** *(bluemoon presents.com)*, you can catch one of the best backyard jam sessions in town (it's also a guesthouse). For something a little different, head to **Pat's Fisherman's Wharf** *(patsfishermans wharf.com)* in Henderson (a 25-minute drive east of Lafayette), where Cajun bands draw dance-loving crowds on Saturdays *(8:30pm)* and Sundays *(4:30pm)* at the **Atchafalaya Club**.

Some 10 miles east of Lafayette, tiny Breaux Bridge is famous for its Saturday morning zydeco breakfasts at **Buck & Johnny's** *(buckandjohnnys.com; $10)*. The Cajun-meets-Italian restaurant has a dining hall that vibrates with zippy zydeco (a genre that blends Creole, R&B and blues) from 8:30am to 11:30am. It's an uproarious time as young and old bob and spin on the dance floor – the $20 for bottomless mimosas certainly helps. If you can't make it on Saturday, Buck & Johnny's also has live music from around 6pm to 9pm on Thursdays, Fridays and Saturdays.

Go boating in the swamp

Touring the swamps and bayous ('streams' in the Choctaw language), on the lookout for alligators and bald eagles, is a bucket-list experience. Recommended outfitters such as **Cajun Country Swamp Tours** *(cajuncountryswamptours.com; $25)* will take you on a two-hour boat excursion to see alligators, yellow-crowned herons and other wetland wildlife on Lake Martin, some 15 miles east of Lafayette. If you prefer to get a bit of a workout while you sightsee, **Champagne's Swamp Tours** *(champagnesswamptours.com)* rents kayaks *($20 per person per hour)*. You can paddle your way across mirror-like waters and stop in secluded spots where you'll hear nothing but the sound of the birds.

Tabasco

Birds & Hot Sauce

Near the town of New Iberia, you can visit Avery Island, home to one of the country's most famous hot sauces, **Tabasco** *(tabasco.com; adult/child $16/13)*. Avery is not really an island but rather a salt dome that extends 8 miles below the surface. The salt mined here goes into Tabasco sauce, as do locally grown peppers. You'll learn all this on a self-guided tour that takes you from seed to sauce, with tastings at the end. Afterwards, you can walk or drive through **Jungle Gardens** (included with Tabasco admission), with its 250 acres of moss-covered live oaks and subtropical jungle flora. There's an amazing array of waterbirds (especially snowy egrets, which nest here in astounding numbers) as well as turtles and alligators.

Poverty Point

Engineers of the ancient world

Louisiana has just one UNESCO World Heritage Site, and it remains little known, even to many state residents. Near the Mississippi border, some four hours north of New Orleans (and just an hour northwest of Vicksburg, p394), **Poverty Point** *(povertypoint.us; admission $4)* preserves the monumental earthworks built by a highly organized society some 3400 years ago. In the visitor center, you can browse exhibits and pick up a map for a self guided tour of the site. A 2.6-mile walking trail takes you past 20 points of interest and through various landscapes (including a stretch of forest and a view over the Bayou Macon), and up a 72ft mound built by hand from some 15 million bushels of earth brought from elsewhere. If you're not up for the walk, you can instead do a more condensed 2-mile driving tour of the site passing 11 points of interest – ask rangers for this separate driving tour guide.

CAJUNS & CREOLES

You may be excused if you're confused by the terms Cajun and Creole – they are confusing indeed. The initial definition of a Creole was someone born in the European colonies who spoke a Romance language and practiced Catholicism, though it later became associated with people of mixed European, African and Native American ancestry. Cajun derives from Acadian, the French-speaking people who settled in Louisiana after the British exiled them from what's now eastern Canada in Le Grand Dérangement (The Great Displacement; 1755–64). In the present day, most people identifying as Cajuns are white, while Creoles are Black or of mixed race, though the two cultures have historical and genealogical connections that are often overlooked.

Places We Love to Stay

$ Budget $$ Midrange $$$ Top End

North Carolina

Crews Inn (Ocracoke) **$** An authentic old island home, with five lovely light-filled rooms named for its original inhabitants, plus the delightful innkeeper's cottage out back.

Dunhill Hotel (Charlotte) **$** Small, historic Uptown hotel with a quiet lobby and rooms that nod to the 1920s.

Arrive (Wilmington) **$$** This stylish boutique operation has modern, bright rooms, a creative restaurant and an inviting courtyard, complete with lawn games.

Atlantic Inn (Hatteras Island) **$$** A century-old property in Hatteras that's been revamped and reopened as a classy, comfortable lodging with a vintage vibe.

Princess Anne Boutique Hotel (Asheville) **$$** Offers handsomely furnished rooms and spacious suites in a quiet, leafy neighborhood.

South Carolina

MAPS P335, P338

Starlight Motor Inn (Charleston) **$** Spare but snazzy, this revamped motor court in North Charleston has a pool and an on-site pub.

Andrew Pinkney Inn (Charleston) **$$** Two restored historic buildings hold bright, comfy rooms. Complimentary wine social and breakfast in upper-level atrium. Great value.

Old Village Post House (Mt Pleasant) **$$** This pale-yellow-and-blue clapboard house is a down-home, relaxing option tucked into a historic fishing community.

Swamp Rabbit Inn (Greenville) **$$** Fun six-room inn in a '50s-era former boarding house downtown. Feels like a hostel but features colorfully decked-out private rooms.

Tennessee

MAPS P348, P352, P353

Crash Pad (Chattanooga) **$** Nicely run hostel with dorms and private rooms, guest kitchen-lounge and a courtyard in a great Southside location near restaurants and bars.

Arrive (Memphis) **$$** Beautiful redesign of an industrial building just steps from the train station. Great ground-floor cafe and bar.

Peabody (Memphis) **$$** A 464-room downtown property with classically furnished rooms and a lobby where ducks are marched in daily to swim about in the fountain.

Waymore's (Nashville) **$$** In uber-hip East Nashville, this 93-room hotel hits all the right notes, with artfully minimalist rooms and a rooftop bar with skyline views.

Hotel Chalet (Chattanooga) **$$** On the grounds of the historic train station, this revamped classic has stylish rooms set in Victorian railcars.

Union Station Hotel (Nashville) **$$$** This soaring Romanesque gray-stone castle (and former train station) boasts grand common areas and contemporary rooms with playful accents.

Kentucky

DuPont Lodge (Daniel Boone National Forest) **$** Near Cumberland Falls, this forest-fringed lodge has pleasant rooms, and you can also bunk in a rustic cottage with a fireplace.

Jailer's Inn (Bardstown) **$$** In a former jail from 1819, you'll find a B&B kitted out with wallpaper-covered rooms with antique furnishings. Good cooked breakfasts.

21c Museum Hotel (Louisville) **$$$** Art-focused option featuring edgy design details and changing exhibitions in common areas, plus inviting rooms with ample natural light.

Georgia

MAP P368

Thunderbird Inn (Savannah) **$** A vintage-chic 1964 motel offering complimentary popcorn and frosted breakfast donuts in the lobby, and RC Colas and Moon Pies in every room.

Glenn Hotel (Atlanta) **$$** This 1920s neoclassical revival building boasts a cozy boutique feel and one of Downtown's best rooftop bars, SkyLounge.

River Street Inn (Savannah) **$$** Historical-chic rooms with hardwood floors and four-poster beds – the best ones have balconies. The building dates to 1817.

Rivet House (Athens) **$$$** In the repurposed Mill District, this 50-room newcomer turned a former denim factory into Athens' hippest hotel. Great Italian restaurant, cool bar, no breakfast.

Alabama

P380 & MAP P385

106 Jefferson (Huntsville) **$$** Stylish, newish boutique hotel in a great downtown location, with mid-century modern-style rooms and a rooftop bar.

Elyton Hotel (Birmingham) **$$** In a grand 1909 building, this boutique beauty has crisp white rooms with pops of color and contemporary art. Great downtown location.

SpringHill Suites (Montgomery) **$$** Though part of the Marriott chain, this historic property is no cookie-cutter, with industrial chic style in a walkable downtown setting.

Malaga Inn (Mobile) **$$** Tastefully designed rooms with a Victorian-era vibe are set in two converted townhouses from the 1860s. Lovely courtyard and a central location.

Mississippi

Auberge Clarksdale Hostel (Clarksdale) **$** Perfect downtown setting and a convivial traveler vibe (the lounge has a turntable and guitars) with simple dorms and private rooms.

Shack Up Inn (Clarksdale) **$** Stay outside of town in refurbished sharecropper cabins or the creatively renovated cotton gin. There are loaner guitars and a barnlike bar.

Natchez Grand Hotel (Natchez) **$** Contemporary design with 119 rooms in a great central location. Book a room with views of the Mississippi River.

Corners Mansion Inn (Vicksburg) **$$** Delightful B&B with a welcoming host, atmospheric rooms, homemade breakfasts and river views from the front porch swing.

Arkansas

MAP P399

Gold-Inn (Hot Springs) **$** A delightfully renovated vintage hotel with colorful rooms and a swimming pool less than a mile from Bathhouse Row.

Bike Inn (Bentonville) **$** A welcoming base for mountain bikers, with suites and simple cabins with shared bathrooms, and there's a sauna and gear for hire.

Rosemont Cottages (Little Rock) **$$** In the vibrant Soma district, you can stay in attractive, uniquely designed cottages and suites that ooze southern charm.

Treehouse Cottages (Eureka Springs) **$$$** Amid pine forest, these delightful stilted wooden cottages make a charming hideaway. Some boast Jacuzzi tubs and wrap-around decks.

New Orleans

MAPS P408, P413, P416

Rathbone Mansions (Tremé) **$** These pre–Civil War mansions have hardwood floors, four-poster beds and an art-deco-meets-the-19th-century vibe at a very forgiving price point.

Olivier House (French Quarter) **$$** 1838 gem offering wide-ranging options, from the economical to the elaborate, with balconies, exposed brick and antique furnishings.

Peter & Paul (Marigny) **$$** Like a page from an architecture magazine, with 71 antique-filled rooms spread across several buildings: a 19th-century Catholic schoolhouse, rectory, convent and church.

Pontchartrain Hotel (Garden District) **$$** On St Charles, this grande dame has handsomely furnished rooms with old-fashioned charm. There's great dining, live music and a rooftop bar.

Louisiana

Blue Moon Saloon (p422) (Lafayette) **$** A draw for music lovers with fun (but loud) backyard jam sessions; boasts a friendly backpacker vibe, with dorms and private rooms.

Bayou Cabins (Breaux Bridge) **$** Quintessential Cajun spot on a bayou with 14 historic cabins boasting retro furnishings (ranging from 1949 wallpaper to century-old cypress flooring).

Maison Mouton (Lafayette) **$$** An oasis amid flower-filled gardens and live oaks with 12 rooms spread over historic cottages dating back to 1820.

RANDY DUCHAINE/ALAMY

Union Station Hotel (p352), Nashville

Written and curated by
Jesse Scott

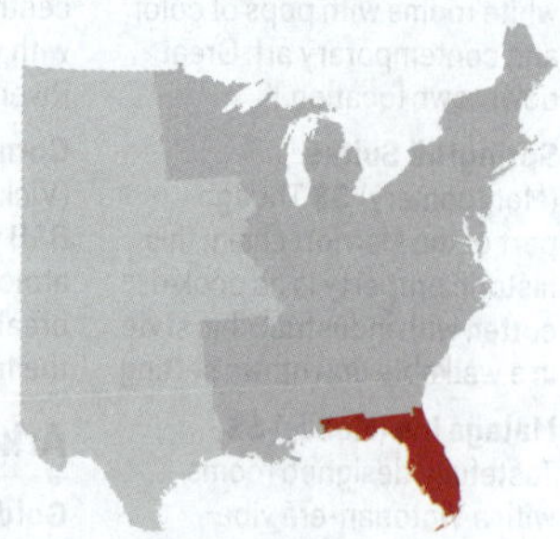

Florida

BEACHES, CULTURE AND SUN-SOAKED TROPICS

Shoreline rhythms, lively cities and wild backwaters shape a state of contrasts – electric, eccentric and steeped in stories old and new.

Florida refuses to be just one thing. At first glance, it's all sunshine and shoreline – a long, lanky canvas brushed with pastel lifeguard towers, sea oats swaying in Atlantic winds, and sunsets that melt into the Gulf. But scratch below the sunburn and you'll find a land of contrasts: cosmopolitan and kitschy, wild and refined, proudly weird and endlessly welcoming.

Start in Miami, where art-deco façades glitter against Latin beats, Wynwood murals blaze bold, and Cuban cafes fuel locals and night owls alike. Glide south into the Everglades, where the modern world disappears in a sweep of sawgrass, cypress domes and prehistoric silence pierced by the bellow of a gator. Keep going and you hit the Keys – a coral-capped chain where time slows, the water glows and sundowners are a ritual.

In Southeast Florida, high-rises kiss the sea while retirees, creatives and snowbirds mingle in brunch lines. Central Florida is another universe altogether – especially in Orlando, where theme parks aren't just attractions, but their own gravity. Along the Space Coast, rockets streak skyward, reviving dreams of the cosmos. Tampa blends Gulf Coast breezes with cigar-rolling heritage, and in the northeast, moss-draped oaks line brick streets in cities like St Augustine and Jacksonville, where history lingers in the humid air. Florida dazzles, defies and demands a closer look.

DENNIS W DONOHUE/SHUTTERSTOCK

THE MAIN AREAS

MIAMI
Swagger, style and cityscape sizzle.
p432

EVERGLADES & BISCAYNE NATIONAL PARK
Wild silence reigns in the grasslands.
p444

FLORIDA KEYS & KEY WEST
Island breezes, sunsets and conch-fried freedom.
p450

SOUTHEAST FLORIDA
Coastal luxury and ever-evolving charm.
p456

For places to stay in Florida, see p488

FOKKEBOK/GETTY IMAGES

Left: Alligator in Everglades National Park (p444); Above: South Beach (p[illegible]), Miami

ORLANDO & WALT DISNEY WORLD®
Imagination, fantasy and thrills beyond rides.
p464

SPACE COAST
Launchpads, surf towns and stars align.
p471

NORTHEAST FLORIDA
Colonial echoes, oak canopies, golden shores.
p476

TAMPA BAY & SOUTHWEST
Sun-drenched cities, art and calm waters.
p482

Find Your Way

Stretching more than 500 miles from the Gulf Panhandle to the Keys, Florida fans out into beaches, swamps and cities – with distinct regions spanning coasts, wetlands, islands and inland theme-park country.

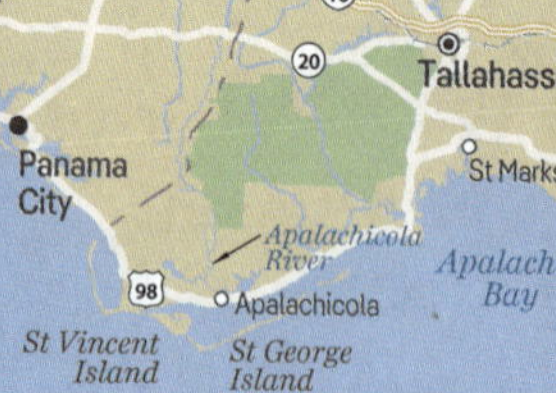

Orlando & Walt Disney World®, p464

Theme parks reign, but Orlando surprises with a vibrant LGBTIQ+ scene, cultural events and international flair beyond the thrill rides.

Tampa Bay & Southwest, p482

Tampa buzzes with nightlife, while St. Pete shines with arts, beaches, and offshore islands for a laid-back Gulf escape.

Everglades & Biscayne National Park, p444

These wild wetlands teem with gators, birds and beauty. A rare pocket of primordial nature tucked between Florida's cities and suburbs.

Gulf of Mexico

BUSES

Although cars are recommended for getting around Florida, **Greyhound** (*greyhound.com*) runs intercity buses between 40 cities. They might move at the pace of a sea turtle, but they're more economical and eco-friendly. **Megabus** (*megabus.com*) also serves Miami, Orlando and Jacksonville.

TRAINS

Amtrak offers limited service within Florida, but other rail services pick up the slack. **Tri-Rail** (*tri-rail.com*) connects cities in the south, while **SunRail** (*sunrail.com*) serves 16 stops in Central Florida. **Brightline** (*gobrightline.com*) offers economical high-speed service connecting Miami and Orlando.

PLANES

Florida has many international and regional airports, so there's always a fast way to get around. **Southwest Airlines** (*southwest.com*) is a popular go-to for quick city hops. Otherwise, save the airport hassle and drive or use commuter rail services instead.

Northeast Florida, p476

St. Augustine oozes charm. Jacksonville brings barbecue and beach vibes. Amelia Island blends historic grace and Southern serenity on the Atlantic.

Space Coast, p471

Rockets roar over quiet shores. The Space Coast mixes NASA wonder with surfing, kayaking and beaches perfect for space buffs and nature lovers alike.

Southeast Florida, p456

Fort Lauderdale and beyond blend yacht culture, mansions, malls and beach-town cool. Expect surf, sun and anything-goes energy with a luxe twist.

Miami, p432

Latin-meets-Caribbean spirit with glitz to match. Miami pulses with glamour, global flavor, neighborhood pride and vibrant culture from Little Havana to Wynwood.

Florida Keys & Key West, p450

A quirky island chain brimming with bars, fishing and charm, Key West dazzles with creativity, character and come-as-you-are energy.

Plan Your Time

With everything from untamed wilderness to world-renowned theme parks, planning a Florida trip means first choosing your vibe – beachy, wild, cultural, whimsical or a little of it all – and letting the Sunshine State do the rest.

CONNECT IMAGES/GETTY IMAGES

Christ of the Abyss (p452), John Pennekamp Coral Reef State Park

Iconic South Florida

Start in **Fort Lauderdale** (p456) and cruise its scenic waterways via water taxi, stopping at Bonnet House or the Riverwalk for breezy bites and people-watching. Next, dive into Miami's color-splashed culture: admire the murals of **Wynwood Walls** (p437), dig into Cuban flavors in **Little Havana** (p440), and dance the night away in **South Beach** (p432). Then head west for a day with the gators in **Everglades National Park** (p444) – get on the water in a canoe or kayak to view wildlife. Finally, cruise the Overseas Highway to the Florida Keys. Start in **Key Largo** (p450) for snorkeling or a slice of key lime pie, then roll south to **Islamorada** (p454) or funky **Key West** (p451), where sunsets, street performers and rum punches make for a perfect finale.

Seasonal Highlights

Florida's subtropical climate means year-round adventures – from turtle hatchings and rocket launches to food fests and art fairs.

JANUARY

Art Deco Weekend transforms Miami's Ocean Dr, manatees gather near Tampa, and dry weather is ideal for Everglades hikes and stone crab feasts.

FEBRUARY

Dry, crisp days for patio dining on Gulf oysters or spotting roseate spoonbills and nesting bald eagles in wetlands.

MARCH

Spring break fills beaches, citrus is at its peak – sip fresh OJ or try key lime pie.

Gulf Coast Swing

Start in **Tampa** (p484) with riverfront walks, Cuban sandwiches in **Ybor City** (p484) and a nightcap at a rooftop bar. Then hop to **St Petersburg** (p486) to admire Dalí's surreal genius, hunt murals downtown and sip small-batch beers at breweries aplenty. Afterward, it's off to the sands: unwind on the family-friendly beaches of **St Pete Beach** (p487). From here, you're at the epicenter of some of the Gulf's most prized beaches – head south to **Pass-a-Grille Beach** (p487) and take a ferry out to the unspoiled Shell Key. Make sure to spend an evening at nearby **Clearwater Beach** (p487), where its Pier 60 nightly sunset celebrations – with entertainers galore – rival those in Key West.

Theme Park Parade

Kick things off with two days at **Walt Disney World®** (p467), diving into the world's most beloved theme-park empire. Zoom through space, soar on banshees and sing along with animatronic dolls (you know the ones). Next, give the grown-ups their due: take in downtown Orlando's **Leu Gardens** (p468) or cool off at **Wekiwa Springs State Park** (p466). **Universal Orlando Resort** (p469) is next – where Diagon Alley, Marvel heroes and Jurassic coasters collide. Cap things off with a day at **SeaWorld Orlando** (p470) or **LEGOLAND Florida** (p468) in Winter Haven – ideal for kids and anyone still clinging to their inner child. End your trip with a breezy evening at **Disney Springs** (p467), where souvenirs and chef-driven fare await.

MAY

Sunrise beach walks are magical, mangoes ripen in South Florida and rising heat calls for mid day breaks indoors or by water.

JULY

Fireworks light up St Augustine's bayfront and Tampa's **Riverwalk**. Expect daily afternoon thunderstorms and steamy heat.

OCTOBER

Universal's haunted houses and costumed crowds fill Orlando for Halloween, while migrating butterflies flutter over wildflower patches and coastal dunes statewide.

DECEMBER

Boat parades in the Keys, Miami's **Art Basel** draws global crowds, and cool, dry weather is ideal for beach strolls and spiny lobster dinners.

Miami

FIRE, FLAIR, FLAVOR – MORE THAN BEACHES

GETTING AROUND

South Beach is best explored on foot – it's compact, vibrant and packed with visual treats. The free Miami Beach Trolley is a breezy option for hopping between SoBe, Mid-Beach and North Beach. To explore the broader city, rideshares, the Metrorail and the free Metromover in downtown Miami make it easy to zip between neighborhoods.

Miami is a city of many moods – a place where Caribbean heat, Latin flair and coastal cool collide. Yes, Miami Beach still shines with its signature art-deco glow, oceanfront energy and ever-buzzing nightlife. But cross the causeways and you'll find a wider city with just as much pulse. Wynwood's street art and indie galleries rival any major art capital, Little Havana hums with café cubano culture and domino games, and Coconut Grove offers breezy bayside calm beneath lush tropical canopies. Whether it's sunrise yoga in South Beach, a foodie crawl through Calle Ocho or sunset cocktails in Brickell's glassy high-rises, the typical Miami experience isn't one-size-fits-all. It really is a choose-your-own-adventure city, where beach mornings, museum afternoons and all-night dance floors coexist with jungle gardens, historic districts and family-run bakeries. Don't just stay put in Miami – explore. Miami rewards the curious with culture, rhythm and sunshine around every colorful corner.

TOP TIP

From college reunions and spring break to foodie, music and art festivals, Miami is ground zero for large-scale gatherings in every season. Check the calendar before you arrive – the vibe is often dictated by the theme of whatever event is on, and Miami tends to go all-in on whatever it's celebrating.

Lay of the Sandy Land

MAP P433

Beaches beyond South Beach

When it comes to sun, sand and surf, Miami Beach covers all the bases – and with a different vibe to look forward to depending on the stretch where you choose to unfurl your beach towel.

South Beach is without a doubt the section of sand most people think of when they hear the words 'Miami Beach,' but there's far more coast to saunter along out here. Unless otherwise noted, the numbered streets here all extend off Collins Ave (A1A), which runs north and south parallel to the beach itself.

Mid-Beach spans the sands from 23rd to 63rd Sts. It's not like the crowds out here stop preening and showing off – this is still model/influencer territory – but many have shifted from posting TikToks of their nights at the club to boosting reels of their growing families. The Mid-Beach area is attached to

(continues on p435)

MIAMI BEACH

HIGHLIGHTS
1 Faena Hotel Miami Beach
2 Fontainebleau
3 Freehand Miami
4 Miami Beach Boardwalk
5 South Beach

SIGHTS
6 Art Deco Museum and Welcome Center
7 Bass Museum
8 Jewish Museum of Florida-FIU
9 Mid-Beach
10 Romero Britto Fine Art Gallery
11 Wolfsonian-FIU

SLEEPING
12 Kimpton Surfcomber

EATING
13 Abbalé Telavivian Kitchen
14 Baires Grill
15 Forte dei Marmi
16 Lilikoi
17 Macchialina
18 MILA
19 RAO's
20 Stubborn Seed

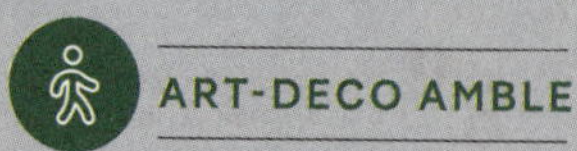

ART-DECO AMBLE

Spend a morning walking around South Beach to admire the world's largest collection of 1920s and 1930s art-deco buildings.

START	END	LENGTH
Art Deco Museum	Wolfsonian-FIU	1 mile; 1 hour

Some 800 art-deco buildings here are listed on the National Register of Historic Places, and you'll encounter many of them whether you set out on a purposeful stroll past bold facades and whimsical tropical motifs or not.

Start at the 1 **Art Deco Museum** for background and exhibits on art-deco style. Stroll north along Ocean Dr between 12th and 14th Sts to spot some of the area's most famous art-deco hotels. 2 **The Leslie** is known for its boxy shape and 'eyebrows' (cantilevered sunshades) that wrap around the building; 3 **The Carlyle** has modernist styling; and the graceful 4 **Cardozo South Beach**, built by Henry Hohauser and now owned by Gloria and Emilio Estefan, is recognized for its sleek, rounded edges.

When you arrive at 14th St, peek inside the 5 **Winter Haven Hotel** to admire its fabulous terrazzo floors, made of stone chips set in mortar and polished to a shine. Then turn left down 14th St to Washington Ave and the 6 **US Post Office**, located at 13th St, known for its curvy block of white art-deco and stripped classical style.

Finish your amble nearby at the 7 **Wolfsonian-FIU**, an excellent design museum in the former Washington Storage Company, where wealthy snowbirds of the '30s stashed their pricey belongings before heading back north.

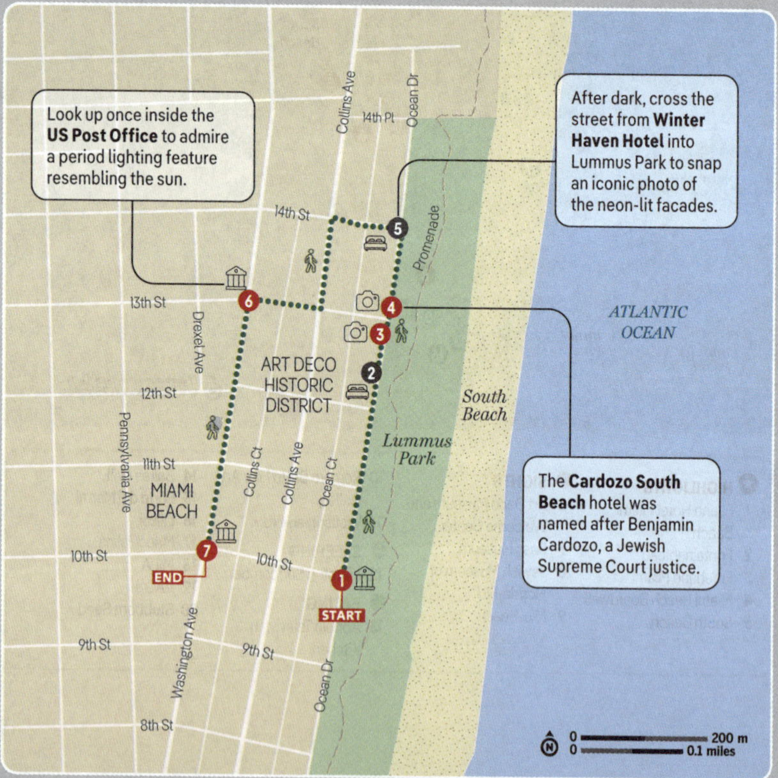

Look up once inside the **US Post Office** to admire a period lighting feature resembling the sun.

After dark, cross the street from **Winter Haven Hotel** into Lummus Park to snap an iconic photo of the neon-lit facades.

The **Cardozo South Beach** hotel was named after Benjamin Cardozo, a Jewish Supreme Court justice.

(continued from p432)
a lot of the area's big luxury hotels, such as the **Fontainebleau** and **Faena Hotel Miami Beach**. On the bay side of the beach is North Bay Rd, where you can see (well, glimpse over the walls) some of the area's largest mansions. This area includes the official **Miami Beach Boardwalk** *(miami beachboardwalk.com; free)*. It runs between 21st and 46th Sts, where Orthodox Jews often mix with social media mavens.

North Beach extends from 63rd St to 87th Tce. The beaches here are smaller and more family-friendly, although this is also where you'll find **Haulover Beach** (4.5 miles north of 71st St); the northern section of this beach park is clothing-optional and has been popular with naturists since the 1990s.

Free Downtown Tour up High

MAP P436

Metromover groovin'

What's that train whirring overhead through some of Miami's densest real estate? The answer is the **Metromover** *(miamidade.gov/global/transportation/metromover.page; free)*, an elevated, electric monorail meant to alleviate the traffic woes of Downtown and Brickell. The Metromover did not succeed in doing this, as anyone who has driven in South Florida can attest. But it's a beloved, complete rail line that moves thousands of passengers each month – for free! It also happens to be a pretty cool way to see central Miami from above, which is a nice thing, given the city's 'skyscraper canyon' landscape.

The Metromover opened in 1986 and sports that distinctive, so-modern-it-looks-dated appearance of public works from that period. Its three lines – the Omni Loop, Inner Loop and Brickell Loop – span 4.4 miles and connect major Downtown spots like **Bayfront Park**, the **Kaseya Center** (where the Miami Heat play) and the **Adrienne Arsht Center for the Performing Arts**, among others. The mover is a particularly good way of seeing the full architectural span and beauty of the **Freedom Tower** (p438), modeled after the Giralda bell tower in Seville.

MIAMI BEACH'S BEST MUSEUMS & GALLERIES

The Bass: Founded in 1964, this contemporary art museum sits in a 1930s art-deco building *(thebass.org)*.

Jewish Museum of Florida-FIU: Florida Jewish history is celebrated within two art-deco buildings, one a former synagogue *(jmof.fiu.edu)*.

Wolfsonian-FIU: A museum, library and research center devoted to art and design *(wolfsonian.org)*.

Romero Britto Fine Art Gallery: This gallery of the eponymous visual artist from Brazil bursts with color, inside and out *(shopbritto.com)*.

Art Deco Museum: Dive into the major design styles that influenced Miami Beach: Mediterranean revival, art-deco and Miami Modern *(mdpl.org)*.

EATING IN MIAMI: MIAMI BEACH

MAP P433

Lilikoi: Laid-back, indoor-outdoor spot for healthy, mostly organic, veg-friendly dishes. *8am-3pm* **$$**

Macchialina: Rustic-chic Italian trattoria with all the ingredients for a terrific night out. *6-11pm Mon-Thu, from 5pm Fri-Sun* **$$**

Abbalé Telavivian Kitchen: Mediterranean-inspired weekend brunch and shared mezze plates. *11am-10pm Mon-Thu, to 11pm Fri, 10am-11pm Sat, to 10pm Sun* **$$**

Baires Grill: Argentinean *parrillada* (barbecue) alongside *milanesas* just like in Buenos Aires. *noon-11pm Sun-Thu, to 11:30pm Fri & Sat* **$$**

MILA: Omakase-style rooftop bar, this swanky restaurant takes guests on a culinary odyssey. *hours vary* **$$$**

Stubborn Seed: Michelin starred and James Beard awarded for its adventurous haute-American cuisine. Reserve. *6-10pm Sun-Thu, to 11pm Fri & Sat* **$$$**

RAO's: Italian restaurant in Loews Miami Beach Hotel. Raw bar, antipasti and southern Neapolitan cuisine. *5:30-10pm Sun-Thu, to 11pm Fri & Sat* **$$$**

Forte dei Marmi: Led by a two-Michelin-starred chef, this coastal Italian spot evokes a Tuscan villa in a Mediterranean revival building. *hours vary* **$$$**

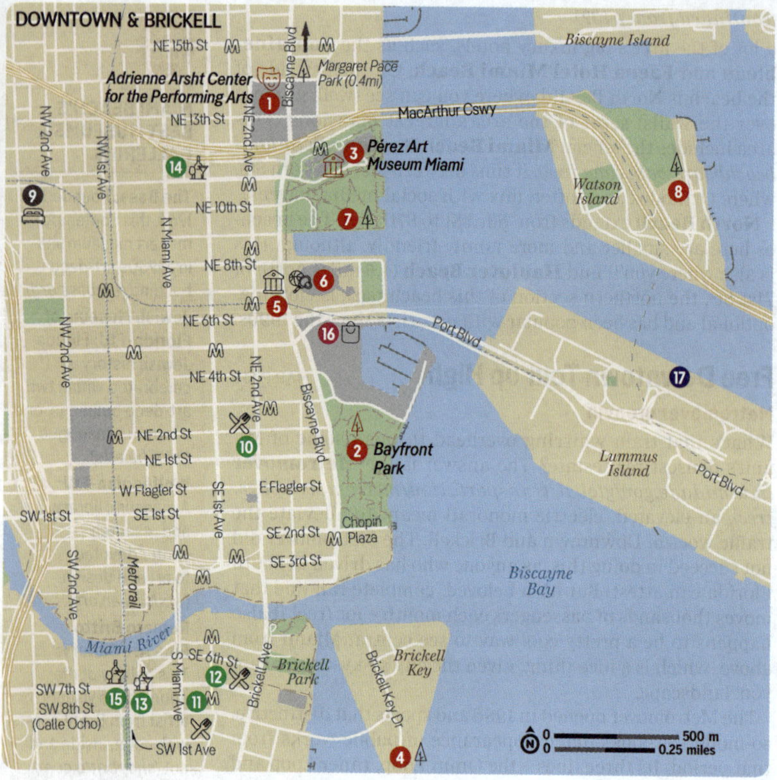

DOWNTOWN & BRICKELL

HIGHLIGHTS
1 Adrienne Arsht Center for the Performing Arts
2 Bayfront Park
3 Pérez Art Museum Miami

SIGHTS
4 Brickell Key Park
5 Freedom Tower
6 Kaseya Center
7 Maurice A. Ferré Park
see 5 Museum of Art & Design
8 Watson Island Park

SLEEPING
9 Dunns Josephine

EATING
10 NIU Kitchen
11 Quinto
12 River Oyster Bar
see 3 Verde

DRINKING & NIGHTLIFE
13 Blackbird Ordinary
14 Elleven Miami
15 Rosa Sky
see 11 Sugar

SHOPPING
16 Bayside Marketplace

TRANSPORT
17 Port of Miami

EATING IN MIAMI: DOWNTOWN

MAP P436

Quinto: Sexy rooftop in the EAST Miami hotel with tropical greenery, incredible cocktails and fusion fare. *hours vary* **$$**

Niu Kitchen: Stylish, living room-sized restaurant serving Catalan cuisine and a killer wine list. *6-10pm Tue-Thu & Sun, to 10:30pm Fri & Sat* **$$**

Verde: Inside the Pérez Art Museum Miami is a local favorite for tasty market-fresh dishes in an atmospheric setting. *11am-4pm Fri-Mon, to 8pm Thu* **$$**

River Oyster Bar: A few paces from the Miami River, this buzzing little spot whips up excellent plates of seafood. *noon-10:30pm* **$$**

The high-rises of Brickell make for a shiny sight from the Metromover, and the Omni Loop offers great views of Biscayne Bay, the Miami River and the **Pérez Art Museum Miami**. Trains run from 5am to midnight every day, arriving roughly every three minutes (more frequently during rush hour).

The Metromover isn't the only elevated rail line in town. Miami's **Metrorail** links Downtown with residential neighborhoods like Coral Gables and Coconut Grove. Beneath it runs the **Underline** – a planned $146 million, 10-mile-long linear park to be completed in 2026. The section from Brickell to Vizcaya Station was unveiled in 2024. You'll find weekly community yoga classes staged on the Underline, an outdoor gym, a meditation garden, and a walking and biking path to explore.

Get out on the Water

MAP P436

Cruise on Biscayne Bay

The Atlantic Ocean might be a causeway away from Downtown Miami, but you can still get out on the area's sparkling waterways from Downtown's shoreline when you head out on a boat tour with one of the companies operating from **Bayside Marketplace**.

For a serious rush, **Thriller Miami Speedboat Adventures** *(thrillermiami.com; $45)* offers 45-minute 'Miami Vice–style' tours (Don Johnson sightings not guaranteed) aboard its fleet of three catamarans that take you across Biscayne Bay and past the mansions of Fisher Island and Star Island.

Island Queen Cruises *(islandqueencruises.com; $35, child 4-12 $25, child under 4 $5)* offers a slower-paced, 90-minute sightseeing jaunt on a private ship with an open upper deck and air-conditioned salon during which you'll cruise pass sites like **Millionaire's Row**, Miami Beach and the **Port of Miami**.

On both tours, it's impressive to catch sight of Downtown Miami's shoreline and skyscrapers from the turquoise waters, showcasing just how truly tropical the city is.

Color Pop & Shop

MAP P438

Walk the Wynwood Walls

One of the most photographed locations in Miami (if social media hashtags are anything to go by), **Wynwood Walls** *(thewynwoodwalls.com; adult/child $12/5)* is a collection of murals and paintings laid out over an open courtyard that bowls people over with its exuberant colors and commanding

DOWNTOWN MIAMI'S BEST PARKS

Bayfront Park (p435): Downtown Miami's green heart spans 32 acres fronting Biscayne Bay. It has two performance venues, playgrounds and picnic areas.

Watson Island Park: Follow the MacArthur Causeway to this small park with grand views of Downtown Miami's spectacular skyline.

Brickell Key Park: Beautifully landscaped, waterfront park with picnic areas, palms and walking trails.

Maurice A Ferré Park: A 21-acre urban park featuring the longest waterfront bay walk in Miami, a jogging and strolling favorite.

Margaret Pace Park: Waterfront park on Biscayne Bay with basketball courts, picnic tables, outdoor gym equipment, playground and walking trails.

DRINKING IN MIAMI: PARTYING PICKS

MAP P436

Rosa Sky: Rooftop cocktail bar in Brickell with jaw-dropping views of the Downtown Miami skyline. *4:30pm-2am Tue-Sat, 2pm-1am Sun*

Blackbird Ordinary: Late-night drinking spot in Brickell with excellent cocktails that draw a neighborhood crowd. *3pm-5am*

E11even: Multi-level club and social playground spread over 20,000 sq ft. Great cocktails and huge party vibes. *hours vary*

Sugar: Come for creative cocktails and Biscayne Bay views on the tropical rooftop deck of the EAST Miami hotel. *hours vary*

IMMIGRATION ICON AMID SKYSCRAPERS

Impossible to miss along Biscayne Blvd, the richly ornamented **Freedom Tower**, completed in 2025, is one of two surviving towers modeled after the Giralda bell tower in Spain's Cathedral of Seville. As the 'Ellis Island of the South,' it served as an immigration processing center for almost half a million Cuban refugees in the 1960s. Placed on the National Register of Historic Places in 1979, the tower houses the **Miami Museum of Art & Design** *(MOAD; moadmdc.org)*, with exhibits ranging from contemporary sculpture to historical photography. The tower and MOAD are scheduled to reopen to the public in late 2025 with a re-imagined visitor experience celebrating the tower's 100th anniversary.

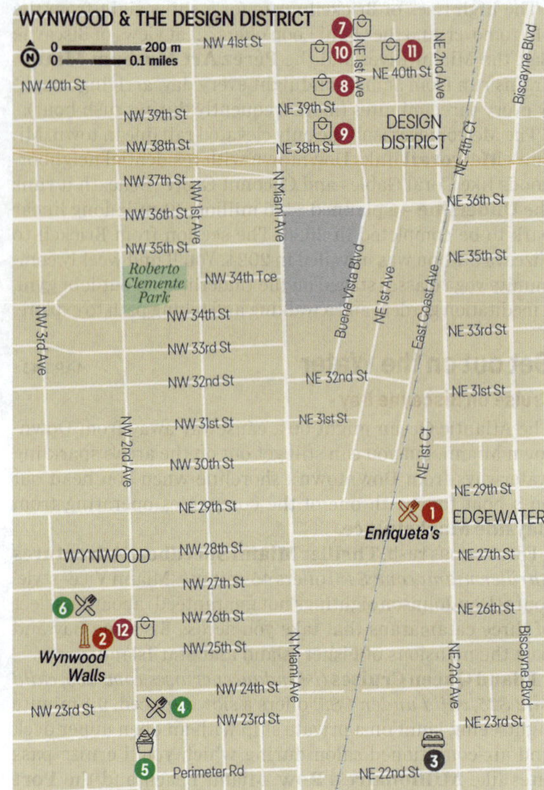

HIGHLIGHTS
1 Enriqueta's
2 Wynwood Walls

SLEEPING
3 Arlo

EATING
4 1-800-Lucky
5 Dasher & Crank
6 Zak the Baker

SHOPPING
7 Acne Studios
8 Alice + Olivia
9 GANNI
10 Golden Goose
11 Maison Francis Kurkdjian
12 Wynwood Walls Shop

EATING IN MIAMI: WYNWOOD

MAP P438

Enriqueta's: No-frills Cuban diner with daily specials, great Cuban sandwiches and coffee. *7am-3pm Mon-Fri, to 2pm Sat* $

1800 Lucky: Miami's take on an Asian hawker market, with tons of street food and Wynwood neon to boot. *noon-1am Mon-Thu, to 3am Fri-Sun* $

Zak the Baker: Artisan and kosher bakery helmed by a Miami native, known for its pastries and BLTs on croissants. *7am-5pm Sun-Fri* $

Dasher & Crank: Quite literally churns out ice cream, ranging from passion fruit sorbet to (of course) mojito. *noon-11pm Mon-Thu, to midnight Fri-Sun* $

presence. What's on offer tends to change with the coming and going of major arts events, such as Art Basel, but it's always eye-catching, interesting stuff, and the energy that congregates around the Walls is buzzy and exciting. Depending on your worldview, the Walls are either a triumph of Wynwood's unwritten mission of bringing street-generated contemporary art to the masses...or a triumph of the commercial forces that have taken the creative energy of the street and repackaged it for conspicuous consumption. Are we thinking too hard about it? Maybe, but that's the point of art, right? In any case, if you want to take a little piece of the Walls home, pop into the on-site shop. You can also learn the spray paint basics and create your own piece of graffiti here with the **Wynwood Graffiti Experience** (*wynwoodartwalk.com; adult/child $42/34*).

The Soundtrack Goes Clickety-Clack MAP P440

Doing Domino Park

Perhaps Little Havana's most evocative reminder of street life from Cuba is **Máximo Gómez Park** (*miami.gov; free*). More commonly called Domino Park, it's a tree-shaded, gated oasis on Calle Ocho. The big iron gates are open between 9am and 6pm daily. Regulars file in from around the neighborhood and across Miami, and the competitive banter and strategizing get going as cups of Cuban coffee are sipped. The sound of seasoned players trash talking over games of dominoes is harmonized with the quick clack-clack of slapping tiles – though photo-taking tourists do give an odd spin to the experience, not that the players pay them any heed. In fact, they don't seem to mind people watching them at all – if anything, they feed off the crowd's energy.

The heavy cigar smell and a sunrise-bright mural of the 1994 **Summit of the Americas** add to the atmosphere. You might spend a few minutes here passing through or get sucked into watching a game for longer. The walkways around the park are decorated with domino-inspired tiles and there are benches where you can sit for a spell to soak up the ambience of it all in the shade. The neighborhood's cult ice creamery, **Azucar** (*azucaricecream.com*), is right across the street if all the spectating makes you peckish.

THE DESIGN DISTRICT'S BEST SHOPS

Acne: Italian leather and Japanese denim are among the elite raw ingredients in this cult Swedish atelier's stable.

Alice+Olivia: Women's clothing boutique known for designer denim and beautiful print dresses.

Golden Goose: There are sneakers, and then there is this beloved high-fashion Italian brand known for its emblematic star.

Maison Francis Kurkdjian: Pop in for a signature scent from this luxury French perfumery. Candles and scented body lotions round out the offerings.

GANNI: If it's cool enough for Copenhagen's cool girls, you'll find the Scandinavian fashion favorite here.

EATING IN MIAMI: LITTLE HAVANA MAP P440

Sanguich de Miami: Gourmet takes on Cuban sandwiches have 'em lining up at this cult neighborhood spot owned by first-gen Cuban Americans. *10am-6pm* $

Old's Havana Cuban Bar & Cocina: Snag a table in the tropical garden of this Calle Ocho *cocina* to feast on *picadillo, ropa vieja* and *vaca frita. 11am-11pm Sun-Thu, to midnight Fri & Sat* $$

Sala'o Cuban Restaurant & Bar: With live music every night, this Calle Ocho eatery does specialties like *rabo encendido* (oxtail). *noon-midnight Sun-Wed, to 2am Thu, to 3am Fri & Sat* $$

Versailles: Miami's not-to-miss Cuban restaurant on Calle Ocho, famed for sit-down feasts and walk-up window *cafecitos. hours vary* $$

VIERNES CULTURALES

Every third Friday of the month, from noon until late, **Viernes Culturales** (Cultural Fridays) turns Little Havana into a street festival celebrating art, music and culture. Expect live music on stage, and galleries open until 11pm to celebrate the neighborhood's creativity and *joie de vivre*. The action plays out in the **Little Havana Historic District** along Calle Ocho, between SW 15th and 17th Aves, and features cigar rollers, local arts and crafts for sale, *mucho* music and dancing under the stars. The event draws thousands of revelers – come ready for a good time, and you'll fit right in the mix.

HIGHLIGHTS
1 Máximo Gómez Park

EATING
2 Azucar Ice Cream
3 Old's Havana Cuban Bar & Cocina
4 Sala'o Cuban Restaurant & Bar
5 Sanguich de Miami

ENTERTAINMENT
6 Viernes Culturales

SHOPPING
7 Little Havana Visitors Center

Beauty at the Biltmore

MAP P441

Take a free tour of a grande dame

In the most opulent neighborhood of one of the showiest cities in the world, Coral Gables' **Biltmore Hotel** *(biltmorehotel.com)* has a classic beauty that seems impervious to the passage of time. Sure, you could book a room to fully bask in its beauty – or save some pennies and reserve a spot on one of the free tours of this National Landmark Hotel. Led by guides from the **Dade Heritage Trust** *(dadeheritagetrust.org; free)*, tours take place every Sunday at 2pm.

This elaborate hotel spans 150 acres, encompassing tropical grounds, tennis courts, a massive swimming pool, and a restored 18-hole golf course. Inside, you could spend a few days occupied by the many activities on offer. One example:

EATING IN MIAMI: CORAL GABLES & COCONUT GROVE

MAP P441

Coral Bagels: They are bagels, and they are cheap, and they are also very, very good at this family-owned shop. *7am-3pm* $

PLANTA Queen: This bright, beautiful queen is a vegan's dream, serving plant-based Asian-inspired fare. *hours vary* $$

Matsuri: Miami doesn't want for trendy sushi spots, but this strip-mall hideaway trades in the real deal. *hours vary* $$

Threefold Cafe: Cheerful cafe with Down Under vibes, espresso drinks, divine eggs Benedict and a memorable salmon salad. *7:30am-3pm Mon-Thu, to 4pm Fri-Sun* $$

CORAL GABLES & COCONUT GROVE

HIGHLIGHTS
1 Biltmore Hotel

SIGHTS
2 Alhambra Entrance
3 Alhambra Water Tower
4 Coral Way Entrance
5 Country Club Prado
6 Granada Entrance

SLEEPING
7 Mr C

EATING
8 Coral Bagels
9 PLANTA Queen
10 Threefold Cafe

DRINKING & NIGHTLIFE
11 Copper 29
12 Happy Wine in the Grove
13 The Bar
14 The Globe

ENTERTAINMENT
15 GableStage

GATES TO THE CITY BEAUTIFUL

Designer George Merrick planned a series of elaborate entry gates to Coral Gables, but a real-estate bust left many unfinished. It's a shame, as the gorgeous Gables deserve over-the-top entrances. Then again, the unfinished nature adds a timeless atmosphere... or maybe speaks to humanity's hubris? Either way, they look cool.

Among the completed gates worth seeing – many resembling and named after entrance pavilions to grand Andalusian estates – are the **Country Club Prado**, the **Alhambra Entrance**, the **Granada Entrance** and the **Coral Way Entrance**. Also notable is the **Alhambra Water Tower**, where Greenway Ct and Ferdinand St meet Alhambra Circle, which resembles a Moorish lighthouse.

FELIX MIZIOZNIKOV/SHUTTERSTOCK

GableStage *(gablestage.org)*, a local theater company, puts on thought-provoking contemporary works in an intimate venue at one end of the Biltmore – there's not a bad seat in the house.

Design-wise, there's nothing subtle about the grande dame's soaring central tower, modeled after Seville's 12th-century La Giralda. The showy grandeur continues inside, starting in the colonnaded lobby with its hand-painted ceiling, antique chandeliers, and Corinthian columns, and flowing into the landscaped courtyard set around a central fountain. Back in the day, gondolas transported celebrity guests like Judy Garland and the Vanderbilts around via a private canal system. Though the waterways are gone, the lavish pool remains.

Are there ghosts? The mobster Thomas 'Fatty' Walsh was gunned down by another gangster on the 13th floor, and some say his spirit still roams the hallways.

DRINKING IN MIAMI: CORAL GABLES & COCONUT GROVE

MAP P441

The Bar: Count on this spot to be divey, laid-back and big on cold brews and burgers. Very affordable, too. *3pm-3am*

Copper 29: Retro gastropub on the Miracle Mile with DJs, craft cocktails and bottle service for those who wouldn't have it any other way. *hours vary*

The Globe: A lively bar, Euro cafe undertones and Saturday-night live jazz make it a perennial pick. *hours vary*

Happy Wine in the Grove: Happy-hour tapas at this neighborhood spot go down even better when you have hundreds of wine labels on offer. *hours vary*

Biltmore Hotel (p440)

The Magic City's Magic Mansion

MAP P441

Go full golden age at Vizcaya

Back in 1916, industrialist James Deering started a Miami tradition of making a ton of money and building ridiculously grandiose digs. He employed 1000 people (then 10% of the local population) and stuffed his home with Renaissance furniture, tapestries, paintings and decorative arts.

You'll want a few hours to see all there is to see at **Vizcaya Museum & Gardens** (*vizcaya.org; adult/child $25/10*). The Coconut Grove mansion fronts Biscayne Bay and is a classic of Miami's Mediterranean-revival style. The largest room is the informal living room, sometimes dubbed 'Renaissance Hall' for its works dating from the 14th to 17th centuries. The music room is intriguing for its beautiful wall canvases from northern Italy, while the banquet hall's regal furnishings evoke the grandeur of European imperial dining rooms. On the south side of the house, a series of gardens, modeled after the formal Italian gardens of the 17th and 18th centuries, form a counterpoint to the wild mangroves beyond. Sculptures, fountains and vine-draped surfaces give an antiquarian look to the grounds, and an elevated **Garden Mound** terrace provides a fine vantage point over the greenery. You can access a free, informative audio tour by downloading the Vizcaya app.

A CHURCH WITH TIES TO THE ISLA

The Catholic diocese purchased some bayfront land from Deering's Villa Vizcaya estate and built a shrine here for its displaced Cuban parishioners. Built in 1967, **Ermita de la Caridad** is a beacon, facing the homeland, 290 miles due south, as well as a lighthouse for those Miamians who long for a land they may never have visited. This isn't the only way this church, Santuario Nacional de Nuestra Señora de la Caridad, engages with Cuba. A mural depicts the island's history, and a Spanish-language presence is the norm for the congregation. Outside the church is a grassy stretch of waterfront that makes a fine picnic spot.

Everglades & Biscayne National Park

WILD WETLANDS | GATORS GALORE | WATER ADVENTURES

GETTING AROUND

A car is essential for exploring Everglades National Park, with its far-flung entrances and sprawling terrain. From Shark Valley to Flamingo, most sites require driving, but once inside, you can explore by tram, bike, foot, canoe, or kayak – with rentals through park-approved vendors. Over at Biscayne National Park, it's all about the water – you'll need to book a guided boat tour to truly experience it. Most departures leave from the Dante Fascell Visitor Center, located near Homestead.

Stretching across South Florida, Everglades National Park is a vast, otherworldly wilderness of marshes, mangroves and slow-moving sawgrass sloughs. Whether by tram, bike, kayak or on foot, there's no wrong way to explore it. Shark Valley, about 40 miles west of Miami, offers a 15-mile paved loop perfect for tram rides, cycling and wildlife-watching. The Gulf Coast Visitor Center in Everglades City launches boat tours through the bird-rich Ten Thousand Islands. Near Homestead, Royal Palm provides easy-access trails and alligator sightings, while Flamingo, farther south, is a launchpad for paddling Florida Bay and camping under the stars. Just east of Homestead lies another natural marvel: Biscayne National Park. Though 95% underwater, it's a snorkeler and paddler's paradise, with coral reefs, shipwrecks and uninhabited keys offering a watery contrast to the Everglades' swampy sprawl. Together, these two parks show off South Florida's wild side – above the waterline and below.

Primordial Wilderness Vistas

Cycle or tram Shark Valley

A major destination for many visitors to the Everglades, **Shark Valley** *(nps.gov; pedestrian/motorcycle/car $20/30/35)* is named not for its marine life but rather its location at the headwaters of the little-known Shark River, which drains into the Gulf of Mexico. The big draw is the 15-mile paved loop trail that leads into Shark River Slough. You'll pass small creeks, tropical forest and 'borrow pits' (human-made holes now used as basking spots for gators, turtles and birdlife). Herons stalk prey along the water, and clouds shimmer like mirror images on the vast expanse of the River of Grass.

Closed to cars, the pancake-flat trail is perfect for bicycles. The halfway point is the spiraling 45-ft-high **Shark Valley Observation Tower**, a brutalist concrete structure with dramatic 360-degree views of the landscape. If you don't feel

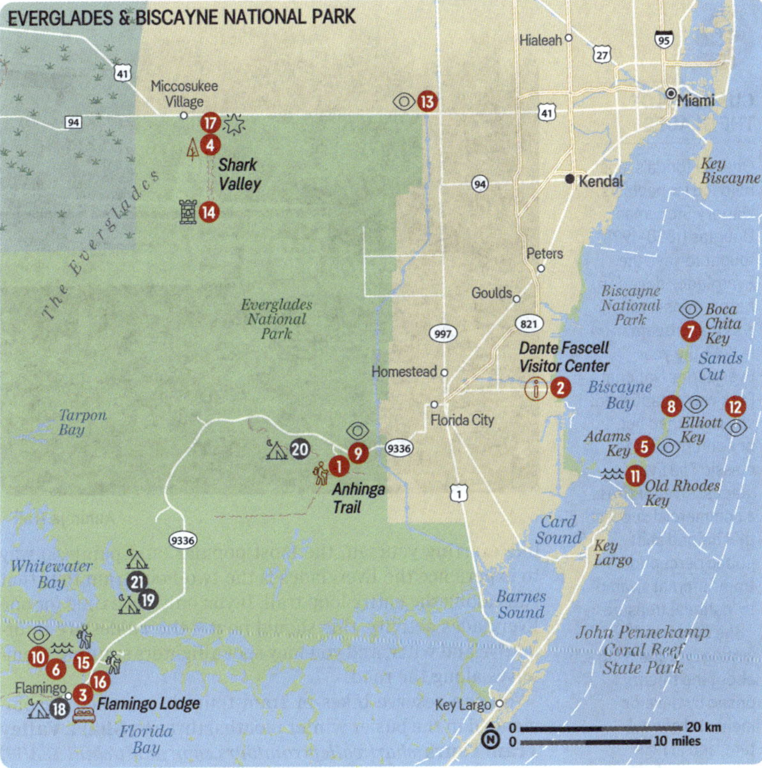

HIGHLIGHTS
1 Anhinga Trail
2 Dante Fascell Visitor Center
3 Flamingo Lodge
4 Shark Valley

SIGHTS
5 Adams Key
6 Bear Lake
7 Boca Chita Key
8 Elliott Key
9 Ernest F Coe Visitor Center
10 Homestead Canal
11 Jones Lagoon
12 Mandalay Shipwreck
13 Miccosukee Casino & Resort
14 Shark Valley Observation Tower

ACTIVITIES
15 Bear Lake Trail
16 Christian Point Trail
see 1 Gumbo Limbo Trail
17 Shark Valley Tram Tours

SLEEPING
see 7 Boca Chita Key Campground
see 8 Elliott Key Campground
18 Flamingo Campground
19 Lard Can Campsite
20 Long Pine Key Campground
21 Pearl Bay Chickee

INFORMATION
see 3 Flamingo Visitor Center
see 1 Royal Palm Visitor Center

TOP TIP

The culinary landscape is sparse in Everglades National Park. Snacks and drinks are available at visitor centers, but the restaurant at the Flamingo Lodge (p488) is the sole sit-down option. Your best bet is to stock up and pack a cooler in nearby Homestead, Florida City, Miami or near the Miccosukee Casino & Resort.

GUARDIAN OF THE GLADES

One of Florida's most beloved iconoclasts, Marjory Stoneman Douglas (1890–1998), fought to save the Everglades decades before conservation was mainstream. In 1947, the year Everglades National Park was established, she published her beautifully written classic *The Everglades: River of Grass*, a commercial success that helped shift public perception from 'infernal swamp' to 'national treasure.'

She continued writing and speaking about the threats posed by development and agriculture, and in 1969 (at the age of 79), founded Friends of the Everglades – a nonprofit that still plays a pivotal role in garnering political and financial support for restoration.

BLUEBARRONPHOTO/SHUTTERSTOCK

Anhinga Trail

like exerting yourself, the most popular (and painless) way to experience the Everglades is the two-hour tram tour that runs along the entire loop trail. If you only have time for one Everglades activity, this should be it – the guides are informative and witty, and you may spot alligators sunning themselves along the road.

You can reserve bikes or tram tours in advance (recommended in the busier winter months) through **Shark Valley Tram Tours** *(sharkvalleytramtours.com; adult/child $33/18)* at the visitor center. Plan to go early in the day to beat both the heat and the crowds.

An Overnight Serenade

Camp on an above-water chickee

Everglades National Park has two drive-in campgrounds, accessible via the Homestead entrance: the 274-site **Flamingo Campground** *(flamingoeverglades.com/campgrounds; per night $33-60)* and the 108-site **Long Pine Key Campground** *(flamingoeverglades.com/campgrounds; per night $33-60).*

And then there are chickees. What's a chickee, you ask? In Everglades-speak, it's a wooden platform built above the water where you can set up a tent. It's like having your own little island with seemingly endless horizon – sunrises and sunsets are unobstructed, and depending on the day, you may see gators coasting by, wading birds galore and frogs crooning you to sleep.

Most chickee sites are found near the **Flamingo Visitor Center** *(nps.gov/ever/planyourvisit/gbvc; per night $20-35).* You'll need a few things in addition to your camping gear: a backcountry camping permit (available at any park visitor center), bug repellent for the inevitable mosquitoes, and a canoe, since the platforms are only reachable by water. Canoes and kayaks can be rented from several spots around the park. Off the Hell's Bay Trail, a handful of chickee sites sit within a 5-mile paddle, including **Lard Can** and **Pearl Bay Chickee** *(nps.gov; $21, plus per person per night $2)*.

Beaches, Boardwalks & Prairies

Check off quick hikes aplenty

You'll find fewer than three dozen trails in the entirety of Everglades National Park, many of which are short interpretive trails less than a mile long. Yet the trails you'll find are ones you won't soon forget. Regardless of where your Everglades hiking adventure takes you, you can be sure the route will be flat. Just make sure to pack sun-protective clothing, sunscreen and bug repellent for any Everglades hike to mitigate sun- or mosquito-related headaches.

For a moderate hike with a little history, **Bear Lake Trail**, located 2 miles north of the Flamingo Visitor Center in Homestead, is the top choice. Trickling alongside the trail, you'll see the **Homestead Canal**, which was constructed in 1922 to funnel freshwater from the marshland out to sea. The project's (dubious) goal? To create a drier piece of land for future development. The result? Just the opposite, as saltwater entered what had been a freshwater ecosystem, forever making a hybrid habitat in that portion of the park. The 3.3-mile trail features more than 50 different tree species, with hardwood hammocks towering above, culminating in a sweeping vista of **Bear Lake**, dotted with mangrove islands. Wear sturdy hiking shoes to navigate the thick grass patches and downed branches.

Christian Point Trail is for experienced hikers with its multifaceted terrain and takes upwards of three hours for the 3.2-mile experience. You'll find the trailhead 1 mile north of the Flamingo Visitor Center – and once you set out, you'll discover that the trail's difficulty stems from its jagged terrain, including thick mangrove patches and sporadic debris from hurricanes of yesteryear. A stretch of open prairie offers a welcome respite on dry days. If rain is in the forecast or the area has seen recent downpours, prepare for a muddy experience. Even the flattest prairies are a slushy mudfest, so bring the right pants and boots.

For families and a gentle saunter, the **Anhinga Trail** is 0.8 miles. This pristinely paved trail, with portions of well-kept and railed wooden boardwalks hovering over the marshland, is perhaps your easiest and best chance to see turtles and a hearty selection of the Everglades' bird species. To access the Anhinga Trail trailhead, venture to the **Ernest F Coe Visitor Center** *(nps.gov/ever/planyourvisit/coedirections)* in Homestead and head approximately 4 miles south to the **Royal Palm Visitor Center** *(nps.gov/ever/planyourvisit/royal-palm)*. The trailhead is about 50ft behind the building. If you're itching for a bonus hike, the 0.4-mile **Gumbo Limbo Trail**, draped in massive hammock trees, is a stone's throw from the visitor center.

ALLIGATORS & CROCS COEXISTING

While Florida and the Everglades receive a lot of hype around the number of American alligators lurking below the surface of freshwater ecosystems, it's not so well known that American crocodiles are also native to the Sunshine State. In fact, this is the only place in the world where alligators and crocodiles coexist. Though it's less common to spot a crocodile due to their lower population and elusive habits, the lucky few who do differentiate the two by their color and snout. Alligators tend to be darker with broad snouts and only live in freshwater, while crocodiles are lighter with narrow snouts and can thrive in both fresh and saltwater environments.

LORE AMID THE LUSHNESS

There's no shortage of lore surrounding Everglades National Park. Its history and remoteness are the perfect backdrop to stories of mystery and paranormal activity. Al Capone was rumored to have made moonshine in the desolate Lost City. Hauntings have been reported on aircraft built with scraps from the Eastern Airlines Flight 401 crash. Several murders were allegedly committed by Ed Watson, an Everglades farmer, and townsfolk took justice into their own hands and killed him – his farm is said to be haunted. Today, you can backcountry camp at Watson Place, view memorials for plane crashes, and visit the now-abandoned, hard-to-find Lost City.

FRANCISCO BLANCO/SHUTTERSTOCK

Gliding Above & Below the Surface

Boating, kayaking and making a splash

Most travelers come for a day's adventure in **Biscayne National Park**, which could entail kayaking, snorkeling or island exploring. The Biscayne National Park Institute, located at the **Dante Fascell Visitor Center** *(nps.gov/bisc)*, offers a variety of excursions, all of which are best reserved in advance. Wherever you go in Biscayne, you're likely to see plenty of seabirds, from cormorants perched on mooring posts and flocks of brown pelicans flying in formation to steely-eyed osprey gliding just above the water. Pods of bottlenose dolphins zip across the horizon, while crabs and lizards scuttle among the roots of red mangroves along the water's edge.

The **Heritage of Biscayne cruise** *(biscaynenationalpark institute.org; adult/child $83/49)* takes you across the bay and past **Adams**, **Elliott** and **Boca Chita Keys**. Aboard this half-day tour, guides bring the islands' past to life, sharing stories of some of the people who lived here over the years. There was Israel Jones, an African American man who settled on Porgy Key in the 1850s and transformed it into one of South Florida's most prosperous key-lime and pineapple farms. His descendants were instrumental in helping preserve the islands for future generations (instead of taking a hefty payout from developers).

Industrialist Mark Honeywell, on the other hand, left his mark on Boca Chita Key. After founding his eponymous

Kayaking through mangroves

thermostat and home-heating company, he purchased the key as a holiday retreat, constructing an ornamental lighthouse and a chapel, and polishing up old Spanish cannons that were fired to welcome guests to the lavish parties he loved to host. The cruise typically stops at Boca Chita, where you can admire the views from atop the lighthouse, walk a short nature trail amid the mangroves and relax on the island's tiny beach.

For a closer look at the park's natural beauty, you can sign up for one of several **paddling tours** *(1½hr $39)*. Hidden between Totten Key and Old Rhodes Key, **Jones Lagoon** has calm, clear waters fringed by mangroves. After a 30-minute motorboat ride from the mainland, you'll hop onto a stand-up paddleboard (which offers better visibility of marine life than a kayak) and look for great blue herons, great egrets and roseate spoonbills as you glide silently along. In the aquamarine waters below, you might spy sea turtles, baby sharks, rays, upside-down jellyfish or sea stars.

Snorkeling trips *(3½hr $115)* offer you immersion in Biscayne's most biologically diverse ecosystem. On a half-day trip, you'll visit two different sites, exploring coral reefs, a shipwreck or a bayside mangrove, where you can see soft coral and sea sponges. Scuba-certified divers can opt for a six-hour trip with two **dives** *($298)*. There's also the option to explore half a dozen sunken ships on the park's Maritime Heritage Trail. Three of the vessels are suited for scuba divers, while the others, especially the **Mandalay**, a two-masted schooner that sank in 1966, can be accessed by snorkelers.

A PARTY ON STILTS

Stiltsville's history is shrouded in mystery, but it was once a hot spot for parties and socializing. The collection of wooden shacks on stilts, only accessible by boat, hovers above the water of Biscayne Bay. Stiltsville began when its original core shack was built in the 1930s, and in its heyday, it was home to as many as 27 buildings. Some were social clubs or fisheries, others weekend getaways. Only a handful remain due to the exposed location and havoc-wreaking storms. In 1985, the area became a part of Biscayne National Park. Use of the houses is by permit only, but the structures are preserved to highlight the park's marine resources and remain a reminder of the area's history.

Florida Keys & Key West

ISLAND-HOPPING | SUNSET CELEBRATIONS | QUIRKY CHARM

GETTING AROUND

Getting around the Florida Keys is best done by car, especially if you're exploring the full stretch from Key Largo to Key West. From Miami, Miami-Dade Transit's bus 301 reaches Key Largo in about 90 minutes, but beyond that, public transport options thin out. Most towns are compact and walkable, but a car or bike is best for reaching beaches, state parks and waterfront eateries. Rideshare services like Uber and Lyft operate throughout the Keys, though availability can dip late at night or during low season. Boat rentals and charters are also widely available.

☑ TOP TIP

For a quieter sunset than Mallory Square, head to the pier at Fort Zachary Taylor Historic State Park. Bring a blanket and snacks to watch the sun dip into the Gulf with fewer crowds.

The Florida Keys stretch like a lazy smile across the southern tip of Florida, offering an island-hopping escape packed with natural wonders, fresh seafood and offbeat charm. While Key Largo greets you with mangroves and the coral treasures of John Pennekamp Coral Reef State Park, the journey only entices further as you follow the Overseas Highway south. Islamorada reels in anglers with world-class sportfishing and breezy waterfront bars, while Marathon has family-friendly beaches and dolphin encounters. Big Pine Key slows the pace with quiet nature trails and glimpses of the elusive Key deer. Then there's Key West – the irreverent, free-spirited finale where pastel streets, live music and historic homes channel tropical nostalgia and sunset celebration. Just 70 miles farther west, accessible only by boat or seaplane, lies Dry Tortugas National Park, home to 19th-century Fort Jefferson and pristine snorkeling waters. Together, the Keys deliver a sun-soaked, sea-sprayed adventure unlike anywhere else in the US.

Soaking up Scenery & Sun

Diving into the John Pennekamp Coral Reef State Park

John Pennekamp *(floridastateparks.org; vehicle $8, plus per person 50¢)* holds the distinction of being the USA's first underwater park. It includes 170 acres of dry parkland here and more than 48,000 acres (75 sq miles) of water – the vast majority of the protected area is ocean. Before heading out onto or into the water, be sure to enjoy the pleasant beaches and stroll the park's nature trails.

Three trails are short, flat and more educational than strenuous. The **Mangrove Trail** is a good boardwalk introduction to this ecologically awesome species (the trees, often submerged in water, breathe via long roots that act as snorkels). At a whopping 0.6 miles long, the **Grove Trail** is the longest and winds through tropical fruit groves that occasionally attract butterflies. If you're curious about the trees of the Keys, have

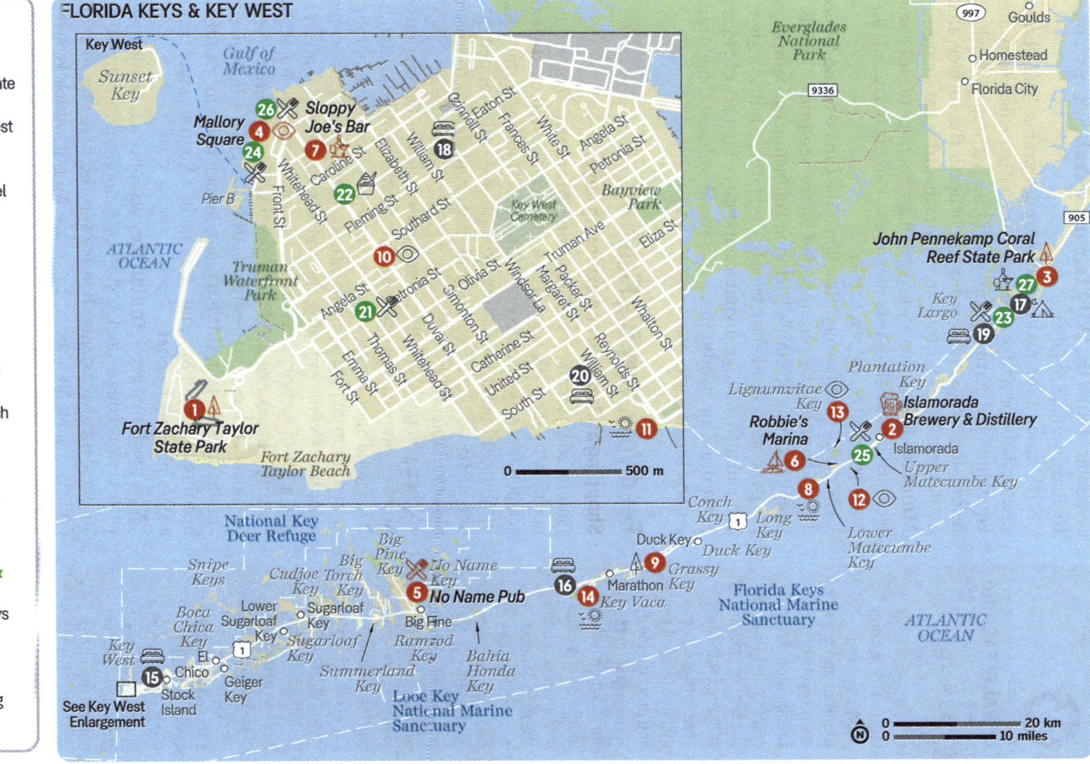

HIGHLIGHTS
1 Fort Zachary Taylor State Park
2 Islamorada Brewery & Distillery
3 John Pennekamp Coral Reef State Park
4 Mallory Square
5 No Name Pub
6 Robbie's Marina
7 Sloppy Joe's Bar

SIGHTS
8 Anne's Beach
9 Curry Hammock State Park
10 Duval Street
11 Higgs Beach
12 Indian Key Historic State Park
13 Lignumvitae Key Botanical State Park
see 13 Matheson House
14 Sombrero Beach

SLEEPING
15 Havana Cabana
16 Isla Bella
17 John Pennekamp Coral Reef State Park
18 NYAH Key West
19 Playa Largo Resort & Spa
20 Seashell Motel & Key West Hostel

EATING
21 Blue Heaven
22 Kermit's Key Lime Shoppe
23 Key Largo Conch House
24 Key West Original Conch Fritters
25 Lazy Days
see 2 Lorelei
see 19 Sol by the Sea
26 Sunset Pier

DRINKING & NIGHTLIFE
see 2 Florida Keys Brewing Company
27 Jimmy Johnson's Big Chill

CORAL BLEACHING

Coral reefs develop over thousands of years, with tiny reef-building coral polyps coming together and growing many layers of hard exoskeleton. Their color comes from the symbiotic relationship with zooxanthellae, a microscopic algae that live in coral tissue and produce food and oxygen for the coral. When water temperatures become too hot or coral gets stressed, it loses its zooxanthellae and appears white or bleached. If the coral goes too long without its main energy source, they can starve and die. Coral bleaching leads to larger issues, like loss of biodiversity and increased risks of coastal flooding. Widespread restoration efforts in the Keys continue to focus on preventing and repairing one of Florida's important natural resources.

a saunter around the **Wild Tamarind Trail,** where many of the hardwoods are labeled.

Stick around for nightly campfire programs. The **visitor center** is informative and well run, with a small saltwater aquarium and nature films providing a glimpse of what's below those waters. To really get beneath the surface, take a 2.5-hour, glass-bottom-boat tour aboard a catamaran to **Molasses Reef**, where you'll see filigreed flaps of soft coral, technicolor schools of fish, dangerous-looking barracuda and massive yet graceful sea turtles.

The park's most famous attraction is the **Christ of the Abyss**, a coral-fringed, 8.5ft, 4000-pound bronze sculpture of Jesus – a replica of one off Italy's Portofino Peninsula. On calm days, the park offers snorkeling trips to the statue, 6 miles offshore. You can also arrange diving excursions, which are obviously a big draw, or paddle through several miles of 'blue' trails among the mangroves.

Feed Very, Very Big Fish

Shopping at Robbie's and exploring beyond

Islamorada's scruffy jewel, **Robbie's Marina** *(robbies.com)*, covers all bases: it's a local flea market, tacky tourist shop, sea pen for tarpons (massive fish), waterfront restaurant and jumping-off point for fishing expeditions – all wrapped into one driftwood-laced compound. Boat rentals and tours are also available.

When you park, you'll first encounter the market section of Robbie's, showcasing crafts and art from around the islands. It's a good spot for picking up a unique piece of memorabilia. If folks aren't perusing paintings, they might be knocking back beers while enjoying the waterfront view. If it all feels like a bit of sensory overload, you can escape the bustle by renting a kayak *(kayakthefloridakeys.com; per day $50-60)* for a peaceful paddle through nearby mangroves, hammocks and lagoons. In fact, this is a major launch point for paddlers heading to Indian Key and Lignumvitae Key, two state parks accessible only by boat.

Now lonely and eerie, **Indian Key** was once a thriving town with a warehouse, docks, streets, a hotel and about 40 to 50 permanent residents. It was even the first seat of Dade County – now dominated by metro Miami, which is just a wee bit larger on the population scale. **Lignumvitae Key Botanical State Park** is a 280-acre island of virgin tropical forest ringed by alluring waters. The official attraction is the

EATING IN THE KEYS: OUR PICKS

Key Largo Conch House: Fresh seafood abounds at this waterfront restaurant. For an authentic Keys taste, start with conch fritters. *8am-9pm* **$$$**

Sol by the Sea: Opt for the 'water table' experience for sunset dining around a table in the water. *11am-10pm Mon-Fri, from 10am Sat & Sun* **$$$**

Lorelei: Relax and enjoy drinks, bites and live music on the Islamorada waterfront. Try the key lime peppercorn snapper. *7am-10pm* **$$**

Lazy Days: Take your pick of award-winning seafood and ocean-view dining: tables in the Islamorada sand, on the patio or indoors. *11am-10pm* **$$$**

HERITAGE TRAIL ROAD TRIP

Cruise the Upper Keys on the Overseas Highway. Pull off the road for biker bars, seafood grills and blissful beaches along the way.

START	END	LENGTH
Dagny Johnson Key Largo Hammock Botanical State Park	Long Key State Park	45 miles; 8 hours

How many of the 84 protected species of plants and animals – including the elusive American crocodile – can you count at 1 **Dagny Johnson Key Largo Hammock Botanical State Park**? Drive south next along the Overseas Highway to 2 **John Pennekamp Coral Reef State Park**. Stroll along the Mangrove Trail, a short loop adjacent to the park's paddling trail. After, whet your whistle at the 3 **Caribbean Club**, the oldest bar in the Upper Keys, just a six-minute drive from the state park.

As you make your way further south, satisfy your sweet tooth with a slice of authentic key lime pie at 4 **Blond Giraffe Key Lime Pie Factory**.

Down the road in Islamorada, pause to snap a photo with the 30-ft-high sculpture of Betsy the Lobster at 5 **Rain Barrell Village** and explore art by local artisans.

Following the highway further south brings you to the 6 **History of Diving Museum** where you can nerd out on the history of underwater exploration. After working up an appetite learning about diving, fuel up with craft bites and brews at 7 **Islamorada Brewery**. Keep it classic with a draft of the subtly citrus Sandbar Sunday or taste the Keys with the key lime and coconut-y No Wake Zone. Wrap up your road trip at 8 **Long Key State Park** with a geocaching session.

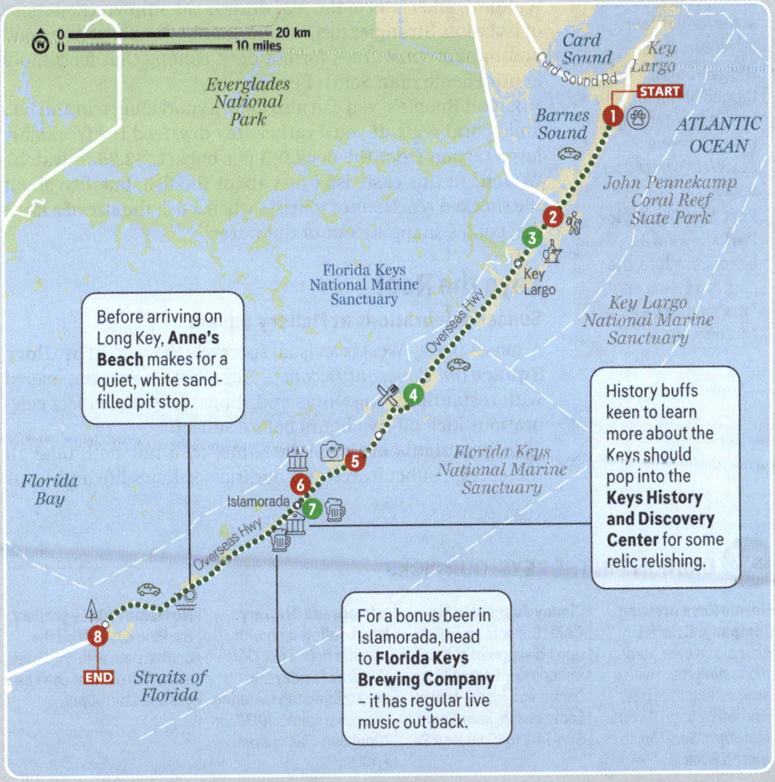

Before arriving on Long Key, **Anne's Beach** makes for a quiet, white sand-filled pit stop.

History buffs keen to learn more about the Keys should pop into the **Keys History and Discovery Center** for some relic relishing.

For a bonus beer in Islamorada, head to **Florida Keys Brewing Company** – it has regular live music out back.

BEST BEACHES IN THE KEYS

Anne's Beach: Family-friendly Islamorada beach with calm shallow waters, pavilions, a boardwalk and restrooms.

Sombrero Beach: This tranquil Marathon beach has shaded picnic spots, barbecue pits, a playground, volleyball courts and plenty of space to unwind.

Curry Hammock: Between Duck Key and Marathon, this park sports 1000 lush acres for outdoor adventures.

Higgs Beach: If Fido tagged along for your Keys adventure, this beach has one of Key West's best dog parks.

Fort Zachary Taylor Park: Beyond its historical allure, the park is a stellar spot for a swim in shallow, serene waters.

ERIKA CRISTINA MANNO/SHUTTERSTOCK

1919 **Matheson House** *(floridastateparks.org; $2.50)*, with a windmill and cistern; the real draw is the shipwrecked sense of isolation. Strangler figs, mastic, gumbo-limbo, poisonwood and lignum vitae trees form a dark canopy that feels more South Pacific than South Florida.

Back at Robbie's, you can also book a snorkeling trip and bob amid coral reefs. If you'd rather stay dry, feed the freakishly large tarpon from the dock ($3 per bucket, $2.25 to watch). 'Watch,' in this case, isn't just about the fish, but also about the shocked reactions of tourists when a fish the size of a large dog comes snapping out of the water.

Rays the Roof

Sunset celebrations at Mallory Square

A sunset in Key West is a visual spectacle in itself. At **Mallory Square** *(mallorysquare.com)* – Key West's epicenter, loaded with restaurants, museums and shops – nightly sunset celebrations kick off two hours before sunset.

No two nights are ever the same. In a nutshell, take all the energy, subcultures and oddities of Key's life and focus

DRINKING IN THE KEYS: OUR PICKS

Florida Keys Brewing Company: Colorful Islamorada beer garden and tasting room with a large selection of beer inspired by local flavors. *11am-10pm Sun-Thu, to 11pm Fri & Sat*

Jimmy Johnson's Big Chill: Sunsets and drinks don't disappoint at this famous Key Largo tiki bar named for the Hall of Fame coach. *11am-9pm Sun-Thu, to 10pm Fri & Sat*

Islamorada Brewery: Neon-yellow icon with popular brews like OG Sandbar Sunday and cocktails on tap featuring their own spirits. *10:30am-10pm Sun-Thu, to 11pm Fri & Sat*

No Name Pub: Legendary Big Pine Key pub off the beaten path with cold beer and a fish dip that can't be missed. *11am-10pm*

Mallory Square

them into one torchlit, family-friendly (but playfully edgy), sunset-infused street party. The result of all these raucous forces is cinematic and a bit tourist-clogged. The waterfront setting is magnificent, and food vendors often gather here. Among the oft-kitschy activities, you can watch a dog walk a tightrope, a man swallow fire, and British acrobats tumble and sass each other. The showmanship and camaraderie of the performers are matched by the crowd's energy and the fading light of day.

Then – lucky you – you'll find yourself right at the top of **Duval Street**, ready for the **Duval Crawl**. Duval is Old Town Key West's main drag, a conglomeration of neon and historic buildings. Its upper reaches are packed with bars and restaurants, while the southern end has more galleries and gift shops – though it certainly doesn't lack for bars and restaurants either. From Mallory Square, you'll want to pace yourself as two of Duval's biggest dive bars, **Hog's Breath Saloon** *(hogsbreath.com)* and **Sloppy Joe's Bar** *(sloppyjoes.com)*, are right there.

WHY I LOVE THE FLORIDA KEYS

Jesse Scott, Lonely Planet writer

I've called Fort Lauderdale home for nearly a decade. We have pristine beaches and stretches of world-class resorts. Honestly, a beach is the last place I want to vacation. But the Keys hit differently. Key West has a bohemian-historic vibe that is seldom found in South Florida and worth the jaunt. Talking to the story-filled locals fuels my soul. As do the ever-orange sunsets – a memorable one being a recent dinner with my wife at the Playa Largo resort. We sat at a 'water table' – literally a table anchored in shallow waters, noshing fresh ceviche and watching kids frolic on floating cabanas nearby. The Keys are a true escape, even if you're a local.

EATING IN KEY WEST: ICONIC SPOTS

Sunset Pier: The views from this spot, poised for best sunset dining, are undeniable. *11:30am-8:30pm* $$$

Key West Original Conch Fritters: Skip the sit-down meal and snag a classic Key West snack from this stand at the heart of Mallory Square. *10:30am-6pm* $

Kermit's Key Lime Shoppe: A popular place to relish all things key-lime flavored. The frozen, chocolate-dipped key-lime-pie bar is a hit. *10am-9:30pm* $

Blue Heaven: Customers (and free-ranging fowl) flock to dine on Caribbean fare in a ramshackle tropical garden. *8am-2:30pm & 5-10pm* $$

Southeast Florida

SUNNY BEACHES | LGBTIQ+ HOT SPOTS | WATER EXCURSIONS

GETTING AROUND

Getting around Southeast Florida is easiest by car, but alternatives abound – especially in urban areas. In Fort Lauderdale, skip pricey parking and hop on LauderGO! shuttles or the free electric Micro Mover to reach spots like Las Olas, downtown and the beach. In West Palm Beach, the free downtown trolley connects the waterfront with key districts. Brightline, a sleek high-speed rail, links Fort Lauderdale, West Palm Beach and beyond, making coastal travel a breeze. In Vero Beach, consider biking waterfront trails or strolling its walkable downtown.

Southeast Florida, stretching from Vero Beach to Fort Lauderdale, blends laid-back beach towns, vibrant cultural hubs and sun-soaked luxury into a scenic coastal corridor like few others. Once known as the raucous spring-break capital, Fort Lauderdale has gracefully outgrown its party-hard past. Today, it's a polished, palm-fringed city of yachts, waterfront dining and stylish hotels lining the A1A and well inland. With 300 miles of inland waterways and more than 50,000 registered yachts, it's earned nicknames like the 'Yachting Capital of the World' and the 'Venice of America.' But Southeast Florida doesn't stop here. Head north and you'll find West Palm Beach, where historic charm meets a buzzing arts and dining scene, particularly along Clematis St and in the Warehouse District. Further up, Vero Beach offers a quieter coastal retreat with white-sand beaches, elegant resorts and a small-town vibe that's long attracted artists and snowbirds alike. From glossy marinas to turtle-tracked shores, Southeast Florida delivers sun, style and evolving appeal.

Catch Some Rays

MAP P457

Enjoy the largest beach in Lauderdale

Fort Lauderdale's sandy shoreline, stretching for miles along the Atlantic, is conveniently sectioned into smaller portions, each radiating its own unique personality and flavor. The largest and most popular of the bunch is **Fort Lauderdale Beach**. It's swank and chic, targeted by Instagrammers. At its heart is **Fort Lauderdale Beach Park**, sporting volleyball and basketball courts, a playground, restrooms and showers. The promenade's always hopping with rollerbladers and joggers, while yoga groups stretch on the beach. Luxury hotels, surf-inspired stores and oceanfront restaurants abound, with plenty of parking *($6/hr)* nearby.

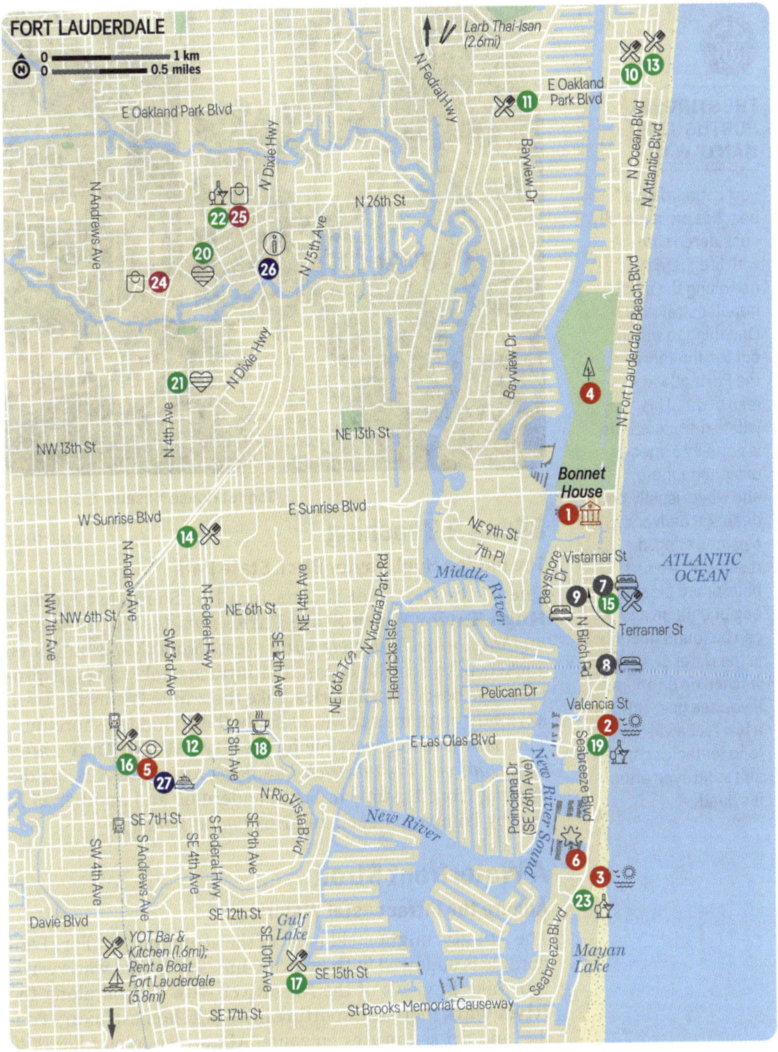

FORT LAUDERDALE

0 — 1 km
0 — 0.5 miles

HIGHLIGHTS
1 Bonnet House

SIGHTS
2 Fort Lauderdale Beach & Promenade
3 Fort Lauderdale Beach Park
4 Hugh Taylor Birch State Park
5 Riverwalk

ACTIVITIES
6 Jungle Queen Riverboat

SLEEPING
7 Conrad Fort Lauderdale Beach
8 Snooze Hotel
9 The Grand Resort & Spa

EATING
10 Bohemian Latin Grill
11 Café Seville
see 8 Casablanca Cafe
12 Coyo Taco
13 Greek Islands Taverna
14 Heritage
15 MAASS
16 Mykonos
17 Southport Raw Bar
see 7 Takato
see 7 Vitolo

DRINKING & NIGHTLIFE
see 10 4:30 Boardroom Bar
18 Ann's Florist & Coffee Bar
19 Elbo Room
20 Georgie's Alibi Monkey Bar
21 Ramrod
see 16 Swizzle Rum Bar
22 The Manor
23 Wreck Bar

SHOPPING
24 Out of the Closet
25 Pride Factory

INFORMATION
26 Pride Center

TRANSPORT
27 LauderGO! Water Trolley

THE STINGING PORTUGUESE MAN O' WAR

Fort Lauderdale's beaches are generally considered safe, with lifeguards patrolling the most popular stretches. One thing to watch out for, though, is the Portuguese man o' war. This jellyfish-like creature is actually a species of siphonophore, and while usually not deadly, it delivers a painful sting. It resembles a small, blue-tinted plastic bag or balloon and can be found floating in the water or washed up on shore. If you see one, stay a few feet away: its long tentacles can still sting even after it's dead.

BRIAN LOGAN PHOTOGRAPHY/SHUTTERSTOCK

Bonnet House Museum & Gardens

Biking & Beaching

MAP P457

The hidden Hugh Taylor Birch State Park

One of the best-kept secrets in all of Southeast Florida, **Hugh Taylor Birch State Park** *(floridastateparks.org/hughtaylorbirch; vehicle $6)* is great for all things outdoors. Tucked between the ocean and intracoastal waters, it provides the best of both worlds. Bike the 2-mile Perimeter Trail, kayak through mangroves or sunbathe on hidden shorelines. The park is also accessible by the city's **Water Taxi** *(watertaxi.com; per day adult/child $38/18, after 5pm $25/18)*, departing from 11 stops in Fort Lauderdale and another 15 in nearby Pompano Beach and Hollywood Beach.

A Waterfront Stroll

Admire the Intracoastal Waterway

The Atlantic might steal most of the attention, but Fort Lauderdale is endowed with over 300 miles of inland waterways, too. Take in views of the New River with a stroll along the **Riverwalk** footpath, spotting historical homes, luxury condos and art sculptures en route. Allow a couple of hours to stroll the circular route or, if you succumb to the heat, hop aboard the free **LauderGO! Water Trolley**, which makes

EATING IN SOUTHEAST FLORIDA: FORT LAUDERDALE BEACH

MAP P457

MAASS: Fort Lauderdale's first Michelin-starred restaurant wows with contemporary American fare. *5-10pm Mon-Thu, from 11:30am Fri-Sun* $$$

Takato: Ocean views and pan-Asian dishes at Conrad Fort Lauderdale Beach. Pair duck bao buns with a lychee martini. *8-10:30am & noon-10pm Sun-Thu, to 11pm Fri & Sat* $$$

Vitolo: This high-end Italian restaurant has all of the classics. Don't miss 4pm to 6pm happy hour. *noon-10pm Sun-Thu, to 11pm Fri & Sat* $$$

Casablanca Cafe: Perfect date-night spot where the architecture and ocean views are as charming as the Mediterranean food is delicious. *hours vary* $$$

eight stops. Bicycle and Segway rentals are also available, but narrow paths and sharp turns present a challenge when it's crowded.

Water Taxis to Luxury Boats

MAP P457

Cruise the waterfront

Swap your walk for a cruise along Fort Lauderdale's inland waterways. The **Jungle Queen Riverboat** *(junglequeen.com; adult/child $31.50/21, parking $13)* offers 90-minute, fully narrated cruises showcasing homes of the rich and famous – an area dubbed 'Millionaire's Row.' For something more intimate, the locally owned **Rent a Boat Fort Lauderdale** *(rentaboat fortlauderdale.com; 4hr for up to 10 people from $400)* offers private deck boat and pontoon rentals, with or without a captain. The most affordable option is the **Water Taxi** *(watertaxi.com; per day adult/child $38/18, after 5pm $25/18),* which provides lighthearted, narrated cruises around town between 10am and 10pm. Hop on and off at 10 different stops.

History & Nature Unite

MAP P457

An orchid oasis at Bonnet House

Bonnet House Museum & Gardens *(bonnethouse.org; adult/child $25/8)* is a plantation-style, oceanfront homestead. Its 35 acres of subtropical gardens feature one of America's most esteemed orchid collections. The buildings were designed by professional artist and self-taught architect Frederic Bartlett in the early 1920s. Frederic's second wife, Evelyn, deeded the property to a historical trust before her death in 1997 to secure it against greedy developers. Thanks to her, you can enjoy nature trails winding through five distinct ecosystems on the area's last bastion of undeveloped shoreland. (Watch for spider monkeys in the treetop canopies.)

LGBTIQ+ Hot Spot

MAP P457

Explore Wilton Drive

Wilton Drive (sometimes called 'The Drive') is abundant with queer-friendly restaurants, shops and watering holes. LGBTIQ+ nightclub **Georgie's Alibi Monkey Bar** *(alibiwiltonmanors.com)* is perpetually packed, while **The Manor** *(themanor complex.com)* is a glamorous club featuring flashy chandeliers and more bars than you can shake a stick at. Younger crowds often spill onto its second level.

If leather's your thing, you'll enjoy the raunchy cowboy vibe at **Ramrod** *(ramrodbar.com),* a popular hangout since 1994, where patrons rock to edgy tunes in a medieval dungeon-style setting.

Eager to shop? Neighborhood thrift shop **Out of the Closet** *(outofthecloset.org)* sells size 12 stilettos and offers free HIV testing while you browse. You'll also find quite a selection of gay clientele-geared clothing around the corner at **Pride Factory** *(pridefactory.com).*

CELEBRATE FLORIDA'S LGBTIQ+ CAPITAL

Despite the state government's push for anti-LGBTIQ+ legislation in 2023 and 2024, Fort Lauderdale remains a thriving LGBTIQ+ community and a popular queer holiday destination. LGBTIQ+ retirees and remote workers flock to Wilton Manors and neighboring Victoria Park, cementing its status as the hub for LGBTIQ+ nightclubs, bars, restaurants and social clubs. A rainbow-painted 'Love Wins' bridge welcomes visitors to Wilton Manors, where street lamps glow with artistic wire sculptures. The local **Pride Center** *(pridecenterflorida.org)* distributes information on area highlights.

But the LGBTIQ+ pride really comes to life during the **Greater Florida Pride Parade and Festival** *(pridefort lauderdale.org),* with floats, costumes and a celebration of diversity and love.

GREAT LOCAL HANGOUTS

Captain Danny Grant, owner of Floridian Coastal Charters *(floridiancoastal charters.com)*, shares his favorite spots to eat and drink.

4:30 Boardroom Bar: Awesome saloon in the north entertainment district with strong drinks and a surf-skate-hot-rod-inspired setting. Free vintage car show Saturdays.

Bohemian Latin Grill: A friendly couple serving up the tastiest Latin food in town. They'll even deliver to your bar stool next door at the Boardroom Bar.

Southport Raw Bar: Locals love grabbing fresh oysters and a pitcher at this casual waterfront restaurant with tasty seafood.

Café Seville: Every dish is a winner, with traditional Spanish cuisine and great wine. Start with *gambas as ajillo* (garlic seafood dish) and *ensalada maite* (palm hearts). Reserve.

IAN G DAGNALL/ALAMY

A Fort Lauderdale Tradition

MAP P457

Elbo Room

Hopping since 1938, this famed two-level beach bar is the ultimate throwback. Immortalized in the 1960 film *Where the Boys Are,* it became a magnet for spring breakers and a rite of passage for an entire generation of college students. Today, the legendary **Elbo Room** *(elboroom.com)* – often called the world's best beach bar – might feel lonely and forgotten by day, but by night, it morphs into a loud, brash party zone. The crowds pack so tightly it's nearly impossible to reach the bar (cash only). Elbo Room may be showing some wrinkles, but it's unlikely this old-school favorite will ride into the sunset anytime soon.

Brunch with Swimming Mermaids

MAP P457

Showtime at the Wreck Bar

Frank Sinatra strutted the hallways at the historic **Wreck Bar** *(boceanresort.com/dining/the-wreck-bar)* when it opened in the 1950s at B Ocean Resort. The bar's nautical theme,

EATING & DRINKING: DOWNTOWN FORT LAUDERDALE

MAP P457

Mykonos: A Greek island-inspired riverwalk spot serving seafood and small plates. *5-10pm Sun-Thu, to 11pm Sat & Sun* **$$$**

Coyo Taco: Enjoy 50% off select tacos on Taco Tuesdays! Don't miss the incredible smoky cauliflower tacos. *11am-9pm Sun-Thu, to 11pm Fri & Sat* **$**

Swizzle Rum Bar: Feel the speakeasy vibes when you cozy up in a booth with the best craft cocktails in town. *6pm-2am Mon-Thu, to 3am Sat & Sun*

Ann's Florist & Coffee Bar: Grab lunch and flowers, plus floral-inspired drinks and snacks from the back bar. *8am-11pm Mon-Sat, 9am-9pm Sun* **$$**

Clematis Street

with its chiseled wood bar and briny decor, suggests you're in a 1600s Spanish galleon. But it's the aquarium portholes behind the bar that reveal some extraordinary sights: on Saturday and Sunday mornings, mermaids and mermen put on a magical, family-friendly show ($15 excluding food and drinks). Enjoy standard American brunch fare as they swim past. The mermaids also make brief appearances during Thursday and Friday dinners. For an adults-only (ages 21+) mermaid show, reserve a Saturday dinner show ($40 excluding food and drinks).

> **TOP TIP**
>
> Avoid extra driving and parking fees by selecting accommodations based on what matters most. For beach access, stay at a hotel along A1A. For restaurants, nightlife and shopping, opt for a place near main corridors like Las Olas Blvd in Fort Lauderdale.

The Heart of West Palm Beach

MAP P462

A night out on Clematis Street

Stroll over to **Clematis Street** *(clematisstreet.org)*, a vibrant entertainment strip dripping in history. Henry Flagler, the founder of West Palm Beach, was florally obsessed, naming downtown streets after plants and flowers – in this case, a bright purple buttercup. During the day, the street isn't all that busy, with shops and midday restaurants being the primary draw. But when night falls, things turn up a notch.

EATING IN SOUTHEAST FLORIDA: GREATER FORT LAUDERDALE

MAP P457

Heritage: Innovative takes on Italian favorites: think sweet-and-sour calamari and short rib masala pizza. *11:30am-3pm & 5-11pm Wed-Sun* $$

YOT Bar & Kitchen: Watch yachts sail by as you enjoy cinnamon buns and lobster rolls at this riverfront brunch hot spot. *hours vary* $$

Larb Thai-Isan: This casual Thai restaurant between Fort Lauderdale and Pompano Beach is beloved by visitors and locals alike. *11:30am-10pm Wed-Mon* $

Greek Islands Taverna: You can't go wrong at this family-owned restaurant, which offers perhaps the best Greek food in town. *11am-10pm Mon-Sat, from noon Sun* $$

MEET THE JAEGA PEOPLE

Prior to colonization, the Native American tribe known as the Jaega called West Palm Beach – and the rest of modern-day Palm Beach County – their home. They were hunter-gatherers who relied heavily on marine resources such as fish, shellfish and sea turtles, as well as skilled canoeists and traders.

Unfortunately, the Jaega people were decimated by European diseases and warfare in the 18th century, and there are no known descendants of the Jaega people today. However, their legacy lives on via the archaeological sites and artifacts found in Palm Beach County.

HIGHLIGHTS
1 Blind Monk

SIGHTS
2 Centennial Square
3 Clematis Street

SLEEPING
4 Hilton West Palm Beach

5 The Ben

EATING
6 Galley
7 Hullabaloo
8 Kapow Noodle Bar
9 Proper Grit
10 Spruzzo

DRINKING & NIGHTLIFE
11 Clematis Social
12 Juicy
13 Spazio

ENTERTAINMENT
14 Respectable Street

Clematis' trendy dining and drinking options have exploded, stealing attention from their flashy nightclub neighbors. The manga-themed **Kapow Noodle Bar** *(kapownoodlebar.com)* pairs artfully crafted drinks with contemporary pan-Asian bites. Next door at **Hullabaloo** *(sub-culture.org/locations/hullabaloo)*, musician-inspired cocktails are always a blast. Nearby, **Juicy** *(juicywpb.com)* is a popular spot known for using the highest-quality ingredients in its internationally inspired drinks, while rooftop bar **Spruzzo** *(spruzzowestpalm.com)* offers panoramic views to go with its top-notch drinks and Mediterranean plates.

EATING IN SOUTHEAST FLORIDA: WEST PALM BEACH

MAP P462

Blind Monk: A classy, romantically lit tapas and wine bar. Pop in during happy hour for a chill and affordable night out. *5-10pm Mon-Sat* $$

Okeechobee Steakhouse: Florida's oldest steakhouse perfects Kansas City strip steak and key lime pie. *11:30am-10pm Mon-Fri, 4-10pm Sat, to 9pm Sun* $$$

Galley: Enjoy trendy bistro fare on an outdoor patio with an aromatic fire pit. Best smoky Old Fashioned cocktails around. *5-10pm* $$$

Proper Grit: Cozy and intimate. Try the hanging bacon and sticky citrus boar rib appetizers before your pick of flavor-bomb mains. *7am-10pm* $$$

Looking for live music? **Clematis Social** *(clematissocialwpb.com)* has long been the go-to spot, with its Billboard Hot 100 songs and large dance floor. Then, there's **Respectable Street** *(sub-culture.org/locations/respectable-street)*, known for its punk rock vibes, and **Spazio** *(lynoras.com/spazio)*, where EDM fans find their home. Last but not least, the free live-concert series **Clematis by Night** takes the stage at **Centennial Square** on Thursday evenings from 6pm to 9pm.

Spot Gentle Giants

MAP P462

Learn about magical manatees

After discovering that warm-water outflows from their Riviera Beach generating station attracted manatees in winter, Florida Power & Light opened an eco-discovery center to honor these gentle giants. **Manatee Lagoon** *(visitmanateelagoon.com; free)* provides educational exhibits and two levels of observation decks for visitors to view these docile sea cows – along with nurse sharks, sea turtles and other colorful marine life – as they swim freely through the Intracoastal Waterway. The best viewing is from November to March.

Stroll Through the First US National Wildlife Refuge

MAP P462

Explore the Pelican Island National Wildlife Refuge

Established in 1903 in Vero Beach to protect pelicans from feather hunters, **Pelican Island National Wildlife Refuge** *(fws.gov/refuge/pelican-island; free)* encompasses 5445 acres of protected water and land. With more than 218 species of birds, the area's a huge hit with bird-watchers. Almost 8 miles of nature trails lead walkers through multiple habitats packed with greenery and wildlife. Even better, the Centennial Trail is ADA-accessible, ending at an observation tower.

All of that said, bird-spotting can be difficult for newbie ornithologists, so consider a free guided tour. Taking place each Wednesday from January to April, these tram tours come with an expert local guide and a pair of binoculars. Call 772-581-5557 to reserve.

FLORIDA CITRUS PRODUCTION

It is widely believed that Spanish explorer Ponce de Léon introduced orange trees to Florida near St Augustine in the mid-16th century. It wasn't until 1763, however, that a man named Jesse Fish started the first commercial orange grove in the same area. For about 100 years, this grove – and many more – continued to thrive in the warm north Florida sun. But in the late 1800s, northern Florida was hit with devastating freezes, decimating most of the state's citrus crops. Some farmers left, while others migrated further south to the warm and soil-rich Indian River, where many of the world's best oranges are grown today.

EATING IN SOUTHEAST FLORIDA: VERO BEACH

Tres Hermanos: Hole-in-the-wall eatery in the back of a Mexican grocery store with incredible, authentic tacos. *7am-7pm Mon-Sat* **$**

Citron Bistro: Innovative American fare with a breezy patio and can't-miss weekend brunch. *11am-3pm & 5-8pm Mon-Sat, from 9am Sun* **$$**

Mama Hue: Unassuming strip-mall spot serving pan-Asian food. Must-try pad thai and tapioca dumplings. *10am-8pm Mon-Wed & Fri, from noon Sat & Sun* **$$**

Pepper & Salt BBQ: Under-the-radar BBQ restaurant known for tender, flavorful brisket – with a side of creamy mac and cheese, of course. *10:30am-3pm Wed-Sat* **$$**

Orlando & Walt Disney World®

STUNNING GARDENS | IMMERSIVE MUSEUMS | THEME PARK UTOPIA

GETTING AROUND

For the most part, you'll need a car to get around Orlando. There are some exceptions to the rule, like the adorable I-Ride Trolley on International Dr and the LYMMO bus in downtown Orlando. Rideshares are widely available in Greater Orlando and can be more economical. For a more sustainable option, Orlando has electric bikes and scooters (from $1 per ride) through Lime, Bird and Veo.

TOP TIP

Prepare for Orlando's heat, humidity and daily summer thunderstorms. Dress is typically casual in this Theme Park Capital of the World, so pack lightweight, breathable clothing, comfortable shoes, a rain poncho and a wide-brimmed hat to keep the sun off your face.

Most visitors to Orlando rarely venture beyond the fabricated worlds of Disney and Universal Orlando. Yet beyond the theme park thrills, the city of Orlando is home to several fantastic gardens and nature preserves, plus a delightfully slower pace.

Prior to 1965, when Walt Disney announced plans to build Walt Disney World®, Orlando had been a sleepy city. Its historic core, Old Orlando, is located along Church St between Orange and Garland Aves. Wetlands make up much of Greater Orlando, its landscape dotted with lakes, including the largest, Lake Apopka. The rainy season lasts from May to late October, and northern sunseekers flock during its delightful warm and dry season, from November through April. While the average visitor to Orlando spends their vacation indulging in themepark food, locals know that just a few miles outside of these tourist attractions is a gateway to true Central Florida charm.

Black History & Culture

African American heritage at Wells'Built Museum

In the center of Orlando's historic Parramore district, the small **Wells'Built Museum** *(wellsbuilt.org; $5)* is dedicated to the city's African American history and culture. It's housed in the former Wells'Built Hotel, opened in 1926 by Dr William Monroe Wells to host African American performers forbidden from staying in the city's segregated accommodations. Count Basie, Cab Calloway, Billie Holliday, Ella Fitzgerald and Duke Ellington all spent a night under its roof. On the top floor, a hotel room remains frozen in time, complete with furniture and decor that would have greeted guests in the 1930s.

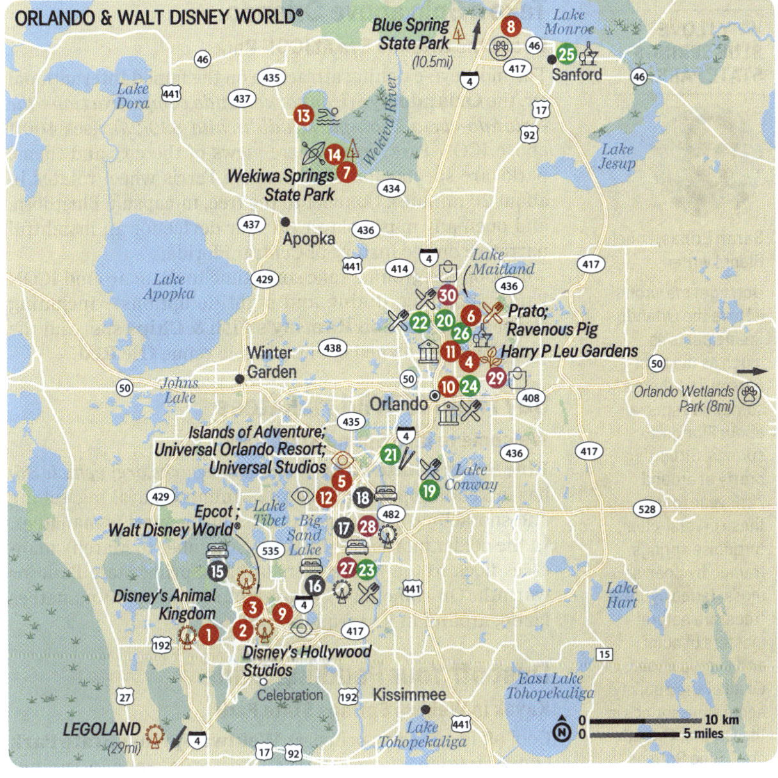

HIGHLIGHTS
1 Disney's Animal Kingdom
2 Disney's Hollywood Studios
3 Epcot
4 Harry P Leu Gardens
5 Islands of Adventure
6 Prato
see 6 Ravenous Pig
see 5 Universal Orlando Resort
see 5 Universal Studios
see 3 Walt Disney World®
7 Wekiwa Springs State Park

SIGHTS
8 Central Florida Zoo & Botanic Gardens
9 Disney Springs
10 Orange County Regional History Center
11 Orlando Science Center
see 5 Universal CityWalk
12 Volcano Bay
see 10 Wells' Built Museum

ACTIVITIES
13 Kelly Park
14 Nature Adventures

SLEEPING
see 6 Alfond Inn
see 12 Cabana Bay Beach Resort
15 Disney's Polynesian Village Resort
see 10 Grand Bohemian Hotel
16 Hilton Garden Inn Lake Buena Vista
17 Rosen Inn at Pointe Orlando
18 Villatel Orlando Resort

EATING
19 Bombay Street Kitchen
see 17 Gordon Ramsay Fish & Chips
20 Hunger Street Tacos
21 Isan Zaap
22 Mediterranean Deli
see 17 Ole Red
23 Selam Ethiopian & Eritrean Cuisine
24 Swine & Sons

DRINKING & NIGHTLIFE
see 17 Icebar
see 24 Otto's High Dive
25 Suffering Bastard
26 The Courtesy

ENTERTAINMENT
see 15 Magic Kingdom
27 SeaWorld
see 17 Orlando Eye
28 Universal Epic Universe

SHOPPING
29 Atomic Horror
30 Bossa N' Roll Records
see 6 Frank
see 6 Gasp
see 6 Winter Park Farmers' Market

WHY I LOVE BLUE SPRINGS STATE PARK

Sarah Etinas, Lonely Planet writer

Don't get me wrong – I love the Orlando theme parks as much as the next person, but there's something special about Florida's springs. Sitting pretty at around 72°F year-round, these crystal-clear, turquoise springs, framed by Spanish moss–laden cypress trees, are natural masters of color and composition. Of all of the publicly accessible springs in the Greater Orlando area, Blue Springs State Park is my personal favorite. Each winter, it's easy enough to check the park's Facebook page for an update on the daily manatee count – the number occasionally reaches 400 – and drive on over for an afternoon watching the manatees float on by.

Take a Spin above Orlando

Board the Orlando Eye at ICON Park

The most eye-catching attraction on the famed International Dr, the **Orlando Eye** *(iconparkorlando.com/attractions/the-orlando-eye-at-icon-park; adult/child $30/25)* rises 400ft above ICON Park, from where views of the city and theme parks are spectacular. The massive Ferris wheel rotates in about 20 minutes. Connect to the free, in-capsule Bluetooth, and open any music player on your device for an insightful narrative on the history of Central Florida.

Back on the ground, take some time to roam around ICON Park's shopping, dining and nightlife options – including famous chef **Gordon Ramsay's Fish & Chips** spot and the Blake Shelton–owned country-music venue **Ole Red**.

Say Hello to Wild Manatees

Welcome to Blue Spring State Park

Blue Spring State Park *(floridastateparks.org; vehicle $6)* has incredible opportunities for swimming, kayaking, tubing and snorkeling. But what sets this spring apart is manatees. In the colder months of the year (November to March), manatees flock to the 72°F waters of Blue Spring State Park for warmth. On some days, you might see over 500 manatees lazing around in its turquoise waters.

Dust off Your Paddling Skills

Kayak in Wekiwa Springs State Park

Cool off in emerald springs at **Wekiwa Springs State Park** *(floridastateparks.org/parks-and-trails/wekiwa-springs-state-park; vehicle $6)*, about 20 miles northwest of downtown Orlando in Apopka. Spot some of the 190 species of birds recorded here while hiking miles of trails meandering through woods, swamplands and along the banks of the Wekiva River.

You can rent a kayak or canoe from **Wekiwa Springs Adventures** *(wekiwaspringsadventures.com; 2hr from $40)* to paddle the scenic, still waters. It's actually possible to kayak 8.5 miles from the state park, through neighboring **Rock Springs Run State Reserve** *(floridastateparks.org; vehicle $3)*, into **Kelly Park** *(ocfl.net; vehicle $3)*. Along the way, enjoy the beauty of the turquoise waters and the fairytale-like, Spanish moss–laden trees, all while keeping an eye out for birds, fish, turtles, and the occasional alligator. Be sure to arrive early, as parking regularly reaches maximum capacity.

EATING IN ORLANDO: CHEAP EATS

Bombay Street Kitchen: Casual Indian spot known for great food and value. Don't miss the kale chaat and street special dosa. *11:30am-3pm & 5-10pm* $

Swine & Sons: Fill up on Southern comfort classics like breakfast biscuits, fried pickles and spicy fried chicken sandwiches in Winter Park. *hours vary* $

Mediterranean Deli: Greek sandwiches here are affordable and flavor-packed. *10:30am-5:30pm Mon-Sat* $

Isan Zaap: Delicious northeastern Thai cuisine, with dishes like *som tum* (Thai papaya salad) and *laab* (minced pork). *11:30am-10pm* $$

TOP EXPERIENCE

Walt Disney World®

Where else can you dine in a castle, race through space and shake hands with a mouse in one day? Walt Disney World® is a storytelling spectacle with four theme parks, two water parks and a slew of hotels, restaurants and entertainment all working to make magic. From nostalgic rides to cutting-edge attractions, it's a choose-your-own-adventure playground for kids, grown-ups and superfans.

Fireworks at Disney's Magic Kingdom

Themed Lands, Legendary Rides

Start with Cinderella Castle at **Disney's Magic Kingdom®**, where fairy tales come to life and fireworks dazzle nightly. Over at **EPCOT®**, it's a race through the cosmos on *Guardians of the Galaxy: Cosmic Rewind* or a stroll through 11 countries in World Showcase. **Disney's Hollywood Studios®** delivers *Star Wars* drama and *Toy Story* whimsy, while **Disney's Animal Kingdom®** pairs thrills with wildlife encounters, from Everest coasters to jungle safaris.

Getting Around

Spanning 47 sq miles, Walt Disney World Resort is a city unto itself. Hop between parks by Monorail, Disney Skyliner, water taxi or bus. Rideshares and Minnie Vans offer extra convenience, but driving remains popular – just factor in time to transfer from parking areas to park gates.

Beyond the Parks

Shopping and dining districts like **Disney Springs®** tempt with Cirque du Soleil shows, chef-driven restaurants and one-of-a-kind shops. At resort hotels, you'll find everything from African savannas with roaming giraffes to poolside Polynesian luaus.

TOP TIPS

- Arrive early or stay late to enjoy cooler temps and lighter crowds.
- Lightning Lane passes save major time on high-demand rides.
- For the best castle fireworks view, claim a Main Street spot at least 30 minutes early.

PRACTICALITIES

- disneyworld.disney.go.com
- 9am-10pm
- prices vary

BEST BOUTIQUES & SHOPPING IN ORLANDO

Winter Park Farmers' Market: Shop for local goods like cheeses, flowers, baked goods and produce at this Saturday morning market.

Gasp: Winter Park boutique selling stationery, accessories and home decor from artists and creators. Girly-pop core at its finest.

Frank: Gift shop in Winter Park showcasing curated goods like precious-stone jewelry and coconut wax candles.

Bossa N' Roll Records: Leaning into old-school Orlando, this Maitland store boasts a well-curated vinyl selection.

Atomic Horror: A haven for horror enthusiasts in Baldwin Park with memorabilia and merch from horror film franchises.

Stroll a Flora-Filled Oasis

Take in Harry P Leu Gardens

Stroll the 50-acre **Harry P Leu Gardens** *(leugardens.org; adult/child $15/10),* an impressive botanical oasis just minutes from downtown Orlando. The plant collection includes primitive cycads, bright red hibiscus and almost 400 species of palm trees. The citrus grove's 50 different kinds of citrus trees highlight Florida's agricultural bounty, while a native wetland garden attracts wading birds and other wildlife. Tours of the 18th-century **Leu House** run every 30 minutes: former owner Mary Jane Leu loved roses, and her collection of old garden roses (those existing before 1867) forms the most extensive formal rose garden in Florida. Bring provisions for a lakeside picnic.

Say Hello to Wildlife in the Wild

Birding in the Orlando Wetlands

The artificial **Orlando Wetlands Park** in Christmas, about 30 miles east of downtown Orlando, was designed to provide advanced treatment for reclaimed water. An education center houses seasonal exhibits that include live animals and interactive displays. From the center, set off on the 2-mile **Birding Loop**, one of many trails that wind through the park. Not all trails are open to cyclists, but many are accessible for horseback riders. Be cautious of alligators on the trails – they're especially attracted to the sun-warmed, lime-rock surfaces that line many trails.

A Colorful World Built with Iconic Bricks

LEGO's relaxed theme-park experience

Manageable crowds and lines, interactive and educational exhibits, a fun, colorful backdrop and a water park make **LEGOLAND** *(legoland.com/florida; adult/child under 2 from $74/free)* a fantastic destination for families looking for a more stress-free vacation.

Located in Winter Haven, about 50 miles southwest of downtown Orlando, LEGOLAND has attractions geared toward children aged two to 12. At **Ford Driving School**, kids can drive cars through a pretend town, while **Miniland** is a grand LEGO-made model of iconic American landmarks and cities. Don't miss the **Imagination Zone**, an interactive learning

DRINKING IN ORLANDO: OUR PICKS

The Courtesy: Speakeasy vibes and crafted drinks at Greater Orlando's first cocktail bar. *4pm-midnight Tue-Thu, to 1am Fri & Sat, to 10pm Sun*

Suffering Bastard: Savor tropical cocktails at this tiki bar in the Sanford suburb. *5-10pm Wed, Thu & Sun, to midnight Fri & Sat*

Otto's High Dive: Known more for its rum than cuisine, the guava pastelito and coquito cocktails are incredible. *4pm-midnight Tue-Sat, 11am-10pm Sun*

Icebar: Sit on an ice-cold seat and sip icy drinks at this out-of-the-ordinary ice bar. *5pm-midnight Mon-Thu, to 2am Fri & Sat, to 1am Sun*

TOP EXPERIENCE

Universal Orlando Resort™

Welcome to the ultimate movie-lovers' playground, where rides, lands and shows bring blockbusters to life. Universal Orlando Resort features three epic theme parks – Universal Studios Florida™, Islands of Adventure™ and Epic Universe™ – plus splash-filled Volcano Bay™ and Universal CityWalk™. From dodging dinosaurs to casting spells or racing Mario, it's nonstop action and storytelling at every turn.

How to Train Your Dragon, Isle of Berk

Movie Magic in Every Direction

Universal Studios is where the silver screen springs to life. Race alongside Harry Potter through Gringotts, laugh with the Minions and blast aliens with Men in Black. Grab a Butterbeer in Diagon Alley or spot the fire-breathing dragon atop the wizarding bank. Over at Islands of Adventure, ride the Jurassic World VelociCoaster, soar with Spider-Man or brave Hagrid's Magical Creatures Motorbike Adventure. Don't skip E.T. Adventure – a charming classic still loved today.

Brand-New Worlds Await

The 2025 debut of Epic Universe introduced five new lands. Highlights include Super Nintendo World, complete with Mario Kart races, and Dark Universe, a moody realm of reimagined monsters. The Isle of Berk invites *How to Train Your Dragon* fans to soar through the sky, while the Wizarding World's Ministry of Magic blends 1920s Paris with wizard-filled London. Celestial Park, the park's radiant hub, offers intergalactic rides and a futuristic promenade.

Soak, Stroll & Snack

Cool down at Volcano Bay, a tropical water park with slides, splash pads and the Krakatau Aqua Coaster – all accessed with wristbands that hold your place in line. Come evening, unwind at CityWalk with mini golf, global eats, cocktails and entertainment. It's also the easiest way to walk between parks.

TOP TIPS

- Stay at a Universal Premier Hotel to receive complimentary Express Passes (a serious time-saver).
- Catch the Hogwarts Express between parks – it's different each way, and you'll need a park-to-park ticket.
- Arrive 30 minutes before park opening and head straight to Hagrid's or Mario Kart.

PRACTICALITIES

- universalorlando.com
- tickets from $119
- generally 9am–9pm

ORLANDO FAMILY ATTRACTIONS

Jeff Stanford, Orlando local and VP of Marketing at Orlando Science Center (*osc.org*), shares his favorite family attractions.

Orlando Science Center: There's something for kids of all ages...exhibits for infants and toddlers, dinosaurs and live animals for young kids, a Maker's Space and a giant-screen theater for teens.

Central Florida Zoo & Botanic Gardens: Besides animals, they've got a train, ziplines and merry-go-rounds. It's big enough to spend the day, but small enough to feel like an intimate experience.

Orange County Regional History Center: There's more to Orlando than theme parks. The OCRHC is a nice spot to learn about Orlando's history.

DOUBLE2A/SHUTTERSTOCK

LEGOLAND (p468)

center where skilled LEGO builders are on hand to help children of all ages build their next block masterpiece.

An Emphasis on Conservation & Sustainability

Consider the new SeaWorld Orlando

SeaWorld *(seaworld.com/orlando; adult/child under 2 from $143/free)* is one of the largest theme-park franchises in Orlando. When the 2013 documentary *Blackfish* was released, alleging SeaWorld's mistreatment of its captive orcas, things took a turn, both in visitor numbers and in SeaWorld's practices. Today, SeaWorld Orlando works hard on education and conservation, rehabilitating hundreds of marine animals and implementing sustainable practices across its Orlando parks.

Oddly enough, SeaWorld Orlando is also making a name for itself in the thrill-ride world with ocean-themed roller coasters like Mako and Pipeline. SeaWorld Orlando's water park **Aquatica** *(2-day combined ticket with SeaWorld adult/child under 2 $215/free)* holds its own, too.

EATING IN ORLANDO: OUR PICKS

Hunger Street Tacos: This spot is a contender for Greater Orlando's best tacos. The brisket or fried avocado tacos are top-notch. *11:30am-8pm Mon-Sat* $$

Selam Ethiopian & Eritrean Cuisine: From lentil samosa starters to the concluding coffee ceremony, Selam is a treat. *noon-9pm Mon, Wed & Thu, to 10pm Fri-Sun* $$

Ravenous Pig: Innovative takes on locally sourced American gastropub fare. The restaurant is a long-time local favorite. *hours vary* $$

Prato: Modern takes on Italian classics, celebrating local and sustainable ingredients. Don't miss the meatball appetizer. *hours vary* $$$

Space Coast

ASTRONAUTS | BEACHES | UNTAMED REFUGE

Florida's Space Coast is where cosmic dreams and coastal charm reign. Titusville and Kennedy Space Center form the epicenter of interstellar intrigue, a place where you don't just watch rockets launch, you feel them shake the earth. Since NASA planted its flag here in 1958, this stretch of Merritt Island has been launching missions, telescopes and imaginations skyward. But there's more to the region than space-age feats. Cape Canaveral is home to active launchpads, pristine beaches and the scenic Canaveral National Seashore. Just south, Cocoa Village adds a dose of vintage Florida with walkable streets, galleries, waterfront dining and a healthy dose of small-town soul. Nature and technology coexist here: one minute you're kayaking among manatees in the Indian River Lagoon, the next you're walking beneath a Saturn V rocket. Whether you're here for liftoffs, lattes or lagoons, the Space Coast delivers a down-to-earth adventure with out-of-this-world appeal (literally).

GETTING AROUND

There's considerable distance between the space attractions and the surrounding wildlife refuge and national seashore, so you'll definitely want your own car to explore. If you're coming over from Orlando for the day, **Gray Line Orlando** *(graylineorlando.com)* offers round-trip sightseeing excursions from Disney, Kissimmee and Orlando to Kennedy Space Center Visitor Complex aboard comfortable buses.

Secrets of Space Travel

Stratospheric fun at Kennedy Space Center

No visit to the Space Coast is complete without spending several hours – or a couple of days – at ground zero for America's space program, **Kennedy Space Center Visitor Complex** *(kennedyspacecenter.com; adult/child $75/65)*, where decades of interstellar history has been made. Part of a working launch facility, this popular attraction offers something for anyone who's ever stared at the sky and wondered.

Embark on the 90-minute bus tour (included with admission) for close-as-you-can-get views of launch facilities (unless you're an astronaut) and the massive Vehicle Assembly Building (the world's largest one-story building, its 465ft-high doors also the largest in the world). Tours stop at the Apollo/Saturn V Center, where you'll see the largest rocket ever flown (one of just three remaining), which transported astronauts to the moon, and many other Apollo mission artifacts.

TOP TIP

Looking for an epic spot to watch space launches? Head to **Scobie Park** in Titusville, a postage-stamp-sized park across from NASA's launching pads. Two Hi-Spy viewing machines are at your disposal for even closer views – free of charge! Download the Next Spaceflight *(nextspaceflight.com)* app for up-to-date launch schedules.

SPACE COAST

HIGHLIGHTS
1 Crydermans Barbecue
2 Dixie Crossroads
3 Fat Snook
4 Kennedy Space Center
5 Merritt Island National Wildlife Refuge
6 Pompano Grill

SIGHTS
7 Cocoa Riverfront Park
8 Jetty Park
9 Scobie Park

ACTIVITIES
10 Island Watercraft Beach Rentals

SLEEPING
11 Beachside Hotel & Suites
12 Courtyard Titusville Kennedy Space Center
see 12 Hyatt Place Titusville/Kennedy Space Center
see 8 Jetty Park Campground

EATING
13 Café Margaux
14 Fishlips Waterfront Bar & Grill
15 Flavour Kitchen & Wine Bar
16 Milpa Tacos y Tortillas
17 Orleans Bistro & Bar
18 Pier 220 Seafood & Grill
see 9 Tree of Life Cuban Bakery

DRINKING & NIGHTLIFE
19 Coconuts on the Beach
20 Ellie Mae's Tiki Bar
21 Rikki Tiki Tavern
22 Village Bier Garten
23 Wine Lady

SHOPPING
24 Antilles Trading Company
25 Antiques & Collectibles Too
26 Carolyn Seiler Studios

TRANSPORT
27 Port Canaveral

Or perhaps taking in a movie at the IMAX Theater and catching some thrills aboard one of four immersive rides at Gateway: The Deep Space Launch Complex – starring the awesome Red Planet ride that takes you to Mars – is more your speed.

Immerse yourself in deeply cerebral experiences, from the US Astronaut Hall of Fame's films and multimedia exhibits to touring the actual Space Shuttle Atlantis that's on display. For goosebumps and an adrenaline rush, board the immersive Shuttle Launch Experience or Spaceport KSC flight simulators. Kids (ages two to 12) enjoy space-themed activities at Planet Play, while exhausted parents enjoy a drink at its bar lounge. You can even meet NASA astronauts, hearing all about their training and experiences during daily scheduled Astronaut Encounters – just be sure to check the center's event calendar in advance if you've got your heart set on meeting a certain someone. Pet kennels are available on-site (with proof of vaccinations).

A Perfect Beach Day

Great surf and pristine sands in Jetty Park

More than your average park, fabulous **Jetty Park** *(shop.portcanaveral.com; day pass $15)* is a 35-acre oasis located on the water's edge right in **Port Canaveral**. While it's perfect for enjoying a beautiful day at the beach, watching cruise ships pass by, some extend their visit by camping in a tent or RV under star-filled skies at its excellent on-site campground.

Day passes must be bought online in advance, as no payment is accepted at the gate. Pets are only permitted with registered campers.

When there's a launch scheduled from Cape Canaveral – which happens regularly these days – views from the park's golden strip of beach and 1200ft-long fishing pier are as good as they get for watching rockets blast off over the Atlantic.

The sloping sandbar just offshore makes Jetty Park a popular surf break for consistent wave action, and you'll usually find a gaggle of surfers scanning the horizon, waiting for a behemoth to roll in. If you're tempted to paddle out, you can rent boards from **Island Watercraft Beach Rentals** *(islandwatercraftbeachrentals.com)*, which also offers umbrellas, chairs, kayaks and other beach-day essentials.

When the fishing pier isn't closed due to hurricane damage and refurbishments, you'll find throngs of anglers trying to hook red fish, jack, Spanish mackerel and more.

WHERE TO WATCH A LAUNCH

Chris Eckles, who works in the commercial space industry on Cape Canaveral, shares locations he loves for catching a launch.

Westgate Cocoa Beach Pier: It's hard to beat a perch over the ocean at the tiki bar at the end of the pier, something frosty in hand, while scoping the horizon.

Port St John Boat Ramp: Right on the Indian River in Port St John, the boat ramp at the end of Fay Blvd has great views across to the launch pads.

Harbor Heights Beach: Grab a spot on the sand at this Cape Canaveral beach or head out for a surf and look north to see the streak in the sky at launch time.

EATING IN THE SPACE COAST: TITUSVILLE

Dixie Crossroads: A local favorite for wild ocean-caught seafood and steaks. Don't miss their buttery, broiled rock shrimp. *11am-9pm* $$

Pier 220 Seafood & Grill: Historic spot on the Indian River Lagoon. Tasty grouper tacos and peel-and-eat shrimp. *10:30am-9pm Sun-Thu, to 10pm Fri & Sat* $$

Orleans Bistro & Bar: Shrimp and crawfish get the Cajun treatment at this fashionable New Orleans–style spot. Try the Nola Boil. *11am-midnight Sun-Thu, to 1am Fri & Sat* $$

Tree of Life Cuban Bakery: Enjoy authentic Cuban sandwiches, coffees and other treats in the spirit of Old Havana. *hours vary* $$

SPACE COAST STATE PARKS & REFUGES

Sebastian Inlet State Park: Pristine beaches, great waves, one of Florida's best fishing piers and a secluded snorkeling cove.

Archie Carr National Wildlife Refuge: Stretching more than 20 miles along the coast, an important habitat for nesting loggerhead sea turtles.

Merritt Island National Wildlife Refuge: Originally acquired for NASA's Space Program, 218 sq miles of hiking trails and a self-guided wildlife drive.

Indian River Lagoon State Park: Featuring lots of native plants, birds and sea life, it's popular with kayakers, boaters and water waders.

WIRESTOCK/GETTY IMAGES

Something particularly fun to do here is bidding adieu to skyscraping cruise ships bound for the Bahamas and other ports of call as they pass along the shoreline on their way out of Canaveral Barge Canal into the wide-open Atlantic.

Antiquing & Cafe-Hopping

Explore historic Cocoa Village

Lest you think the Space Coast is all rockets, surfers and wildlife, you can also find one of Florida's most atmospheric downtowns for cafe-hopping, boutique shopping and antiquing here. Drive roughly 8 miles inland (west) from Cocoa Beach – crossing the sparkling waters of the Banana River and Indian River Lagoon – to reach Cocoa Village, a former riverfront trading post turned eclectic, artsy town.

A leafy urban oasis by the lagoon's edge, it's lined with historic buildings housing independent restaurants and cafes, wine bars and shops. Start your explorations at **Cocoa Riverfront Park**, where an amphitheater overlooking the Indian River often hosts concerts and festivals. The surrounding park affords a scenic view of the river and is a nice spot to sit for a spell atop benches painted with images of flamingoes and octopuses by local artists, watching boats sail by.

DRINKING IN THE SPACE COAST: BEST TIKI BARS

Rikki Tiki Tavern: Cocktails in a colorful setting above rolling surf at the end of Westgate Cocoa Beach Pier. *11am-9pm Sun-Thu, to 10pm Fri & Sat*

Ellie Mae's Tiki Bar: Friendly neighborhood place in Cape Canaveral with tiki cocktail specials and smoked fish dip. *hours vary*

Coconuts on the Beach: Classic, lively oceanfront tiki bar, steps from the sand in Cocoa Beach. Killer piña coladas! *11am-10pm*

Fishlips Waterfront Bar & Grill: Watch passing cruise ships from this nautical rooftop tiki bar in Port Canaveral. Frosty drinks, pub grub. *hours vary*

Cocoa Riverfront Park

Then venture a few blocks inland to explore the village's cute shops and eateries.

Carolyn Seiler Studios *(carolynseiler.com)* is a wonderful artist co-op housed inside a colorful cottage where you can shop for things like glass jewelry, coasters, wind chimes and paintings created by more than 30 local artisans. **Antiques & Collectibles Too** *(facebook.com/actcocoavillage)* has a maze of rooms filled with things like estate jewelry, decades-old Disney snow globes, rare chess sets and vintage NASA mission patches. And don't miss **Antilles Trading Company** *(antillestradingcompany.com)*, a pirate oddities store featuring an adjoining museum with timeless artifacts and pirate-related interactive exhibits.

Favorite spots for a drink or meal include German-themed **Village Bier Garten** *(villagebier.com)*, **Milpa Tacos y Tortillas** *(milpataco.com)* for Oaxacan and Baja-style fare, and boutique wine store and tasting bar **Wine Lady** *(thewineladycocoa.com)*. If you love barbecue, don't miss **Crydermans** *(crydermansbarbecue.com)* for succulent meat that pairs wonderfully with local craft beers and ciders. Just look for the gigantic cow mural – sporting sunglasses, of course.

HOMETOWN SURFING LEGEND

Look for a statue of the Space Coast's most famous surfer on the median strip approaching downtown Cocoa Beach on the AIA heading south. It pays homage to Kelly Slater, who was born in Cocoa Beach and surfed the area's beach breaks from the age of five. In fact, the area's consistently imperfect-shaped waves are often attributed with Slater's prowess – as they were more challenging beasts to master than perfect ones! A Cocoa Beach legend, this record-holding, 11-time World Surfing League champion still occasionally visits the Space Coast, so you never know when or where you might spot him along a casual paddle out (especially if surf's up at Sebastian Inlet).

EATING IN SPACE COAST: COCOA BEACH

Pompano Grill: A tiny, sweet hideaway for steak, seafood and crème brûlée. Family-run and welcoming. *5:30-8:30pm Tue-Thu, 5-9pm Fri & Sat* **$$**

Flavour Kitchen & Wine Bar: Exquisite dishes by affable Chef Jason. The seafood paella rocks, but so does everything else! *hours vary* **$$**

Fat Snook: Gourmet seafood restaurant in south Cocoa Beach, with a scratch kitchen and Caribbean-inspired dishes. *4-9pm Tue-Sun* **$$$**

Café Margaux: Casual elegance in Cocoa Village, serving French and European-inspired cuisine with fab wine pairings. *11:30am-9pm Mon-Sat* **$$$**

Northeast Florida

STORIED STREETS | BEACH BREAKS | RIVERFRONT BUZZ

GETTING AROUND

You'll need a car to visit many of Jacksonville's attractions and beaches – rent wheels or get a taxi, Uber or Lyft. Local buses *(jtafla.com)* are reliable, but don't cover all areas. There's a free elevated monorail downtown with a few stops, and the St Johns River Taxi takes you to some riverfront parks, docks, hotels and the TIAA Bank Field. Historic neighborhoods like Riverside, San Marco and Avondale are great places to wander on foot, as is the entirety of St Augustine.

Northeast Florida blends historic intrigue, beachside energy, and just the right dose of Southern hospitality. Jacksonville, the state's most populous city, sprawls with surprising ease – a mix of towering downtown, walkable historic districts and vast stretches of sand. Despite its size, Jax still feels like a tight-knit town, where tailgating is a ritual, fishing poles are standard gear and beach days come with live music and cold drinks. Just 40 miles south lies St Augustine, the oldest continuously occupied city in the US, where cobblestone streets, centuries-old forts and Spanish colonial architecture set a storybook scene. You can stroll the Castillo de San Marcos, sip from the legendary Fountain of Youth or simply wander among boutiques and wine bars. From Atlantic Beach's relaxed surf scene to St Augustine's old-world allure, Northeast Florida is a region where the past meets the present and every day ends with an ocean breeze.

Beach-hopping

MAP P477

Pick your Jacksonville beach experience

Jacksonville has lots of entertainment, dining and shopping opportunities, but when residents want to relax, they head to beaches 20 miles east. Smaller towns dot the white sandy shoreline, each offering different coastal vibes.

Jacksonville Beach is a popular weekend getaway for Jacksonvillians, with its wide range of indoor and outdoor activities. Kids love **Adventure Landing Jacksonville Beach** *(jacksonville-beach.adventurelanding.com)* with its Shipwreck Island Waterpark, go-karts, mini golf and arcade. Popular **South Beach Park** *(jacksonvillebeach.org)* boasts Sunshine Playground, a skate park, grills, volleyball courts, walking trails and a seasonal splash pad.

People in their 20s and 30s flock to Jacksonville Beach to dance, hit a bar or soak up live entertainment. All ages enjoy sunbathing, swimming and surfing. Colorful surfboards, boats and pelicans usually dot the Atlantic's blue-gray waves. Enjoy

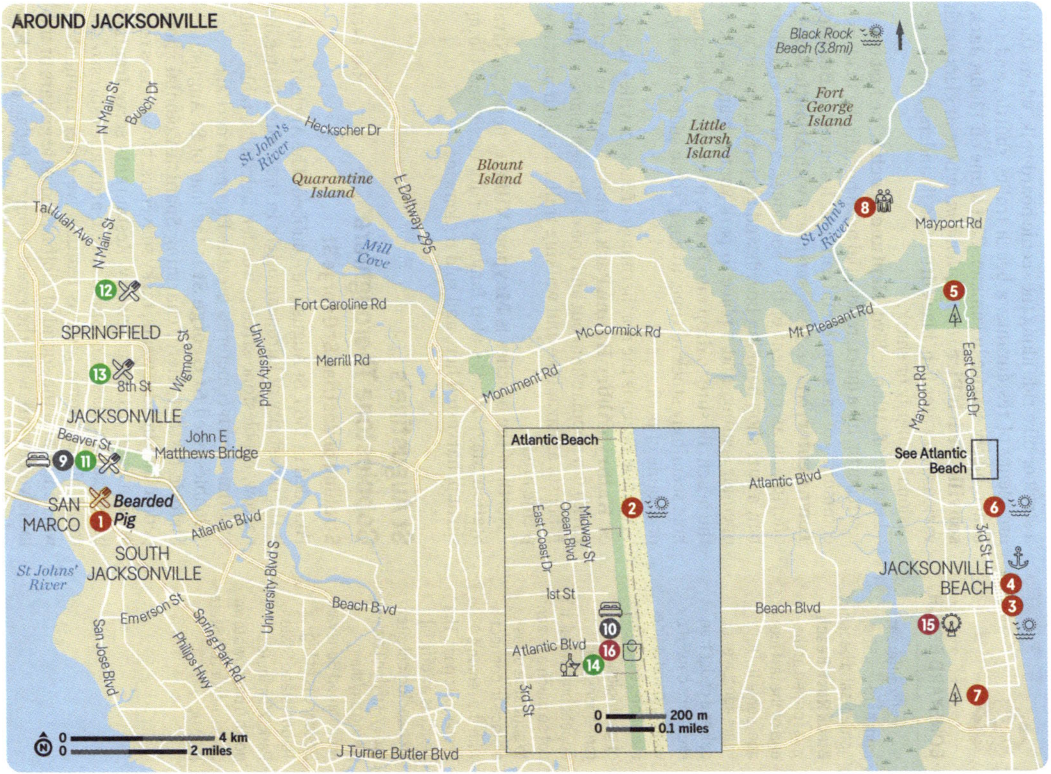

AROUND JACKSONVILLE

TOP TIP

Avoid interstates and major roads during weekday rush hours (7am to 9am and 4pm to 6pm), when accidents happen and delays can triple travel times. Jacksonville trouble spots include I-95 downtown; east–west routes like Butler, Southside and Blanding Blvds; and the Main St, Buckman and Acosta bridges.

BONEYARD BEACH

Radically different from hard-packed, golden-sand beaches, **Black Rock Beach** was formed at the end of the last ice age, some 10,000 years ago. Live oak and cedar tree skeletons carved by wind and water line the shore, comprised of geological soil formations that appear primordial. It's not so much a beach to sunbathe on as a place to connect with the region's prehistoric past. The beach is an official archaeological site today, so don't try taking anything. Nicknamed Boneyard Beach, it is at Big Talbot Island State Park, 20 minutes north from downtown Jacksonville, off State Rd A1A.

a stroll or bike ride along the scenic boardwalk, where there are plenty of restaurants, a beach-trolley shuttle, and free beach-buggy service in summer. Cast a line off 1300ft **Jacksonville Beach Pier** *(thejaxpier.com)* where anglers catch various saltwater fish, black drums to flounders, and the occasional stingray or shark.

Located off Atlantic Blvd, **Neptune Beach** is the first beach town north. It's a quiet, residential town born in the 1930s as a community of vacation rental cottages. It shares the **Beaches Town Center** *(beachestowncenter.com)* with **Atlantic Beach**, offering an assortment of tiny boutiques, a wine and cigar bar, a surf shop hawking boards and gear, restaurants with open-air seating, and a place to park your car and walk to the beach. Be sure to drop into **Pete's**, a legendary watering hole seemingly stuck in time, to enjoy some suds and wings or a game of pool.

Atlantic Beach is the northernmost of Jacksonville's beaches. **Kathryn Abbey Hanna Park** (known locally as 'Hanna Park') is a popular hangout and one of the best places to surf. It boasts a plaza, bike and walking trails, a splash park and picnic areas.

North of the beaches is **Mayport Village**, home to Naval Station Mayport. It's also famous for its fresh and plump shrimp, harvested here and sold regionwide.

St Augustine's Cobblestone Thoroughfare

MAP P480

Strolling pedestrian St George St

Founded in 1565, St Augustine – dubbed 'The Ancient City' – is the oldest city of European origin in the United States. Its narrow, cobblestone streets, wooden balconies, tabby walls and time-worn cemeteries breathe European heritage.

Cobblestoned **St George St** is the hub of St Augustine's historic district. Here, charming Spanish-Colonial shops peddle handmade sweets, tacky souvenirs, blown-glass confections and artisanal jewelry. Restaurants serve fragrant baked goods, glasses of Spanish red, aromatic espresso and tapas plates. Some taverns feature live entertainment on weekends, and the sound of violins, acoustic guitars or melodic voices mix with the sweet aroma of fudge from **Kilwins** *(kilwins.com)*. Stop for a vintage-style soft pretzel from **Ben's Soft Pretzels** *(order.benspretzels.com)* and devour it at a bistro table in the tranquil gardens hidden out back. If

EATING IN NORTHEAST FLORIDA: JACKSONVILLE

MAP P477

Bearded Pig: Casual local spot after sports games, serving smoked ribs, wings, pulled pork and tasty sides. *11am-9pm Tue-Sun* $$

J Lemon Pepper Fish & Chicken: Three locations cooking up ginormous portions at good-value prices. *hours vary* $$

Tunis Seafood, Wings & Subs: A Jax fave, serving the best fried shrimp in town – or try the lamb gyro or delish Cajun Ranch wings. *10am-10pm* $$

Cowford Chophouse: Timelessly romantic, this stylish downtown steakhouse boasts a rooftop lounge with views of the city's skyline. *4-10pm Tue-Sat* $$$

ANDRIY BLOKHIN/SHUTTERSTOCK

St George St

you're ready to imbibe, tip one back at **Prohibition Kitchen** *(pkstaug.com)*, a gastropub with rockin' live music and the longest bar in town.

Dating to the 1700s, you'll also find the **Oldest Wooden School House Museum & Gardens** *(oldestwoodenschoolhouse.com; adult/child $8/7)* here, steps from the **Colonial Quarter**. The street is only open to pedestrians. Cabs and trolleys stop at either end, bookended by city gates and the historic **Cathedral Basilica of St Augustine**. Built in 1797, the cathedral was remodelled under the guidance of renowned architect James Renwick Jr after a ravaging fire spared its coquina foundation in 1887.

A short walk from the southern end is **Plaza de la Constitución**, with giant oak-shaded eateries and galleries, and the small, open-air covered **Slave Market**, named for one of its unfortunate historical purposes. There's a ton of history here – each block packed with so many stories that it would take a weekend to stop and read all the memorial plaques.

Consider strolling across the majestic **Bridge of Lions**. Built in 1927 and restored in 2010, two marble lion statues still guard its crossing. The far side of the bridge affords a fantastic view of downtown, red Spanish tile roofs and quaint B&Bs lining the bayfront.

TROLLEY TOURS

Hands down, the easiest – and most fun – way to navigate the nation's oldest city, and score a lay of the land, is by old-fashioned trolley. Along the route, riders are regaled with interesting anecdotes and amusing tales about the businesses and historic sites they're passing.

The **Old Town Trolley** *(trolleytours.com/st-augustine; adult/child $37/18)* has 22 stops and offers 90-minute tours, as well as ghost tours. Tours include hop-on and-off privileges, so passengers can stop to enjoy food and attractions along the way. **Ripley's Red Train Tours** *(ripleys.com/attractions/ripleys-red-train-tours-st-augustine; adult/child $24/13)* offers similar excursions, with 20 stops and an opportunity to visit Ripley's Believe-It-Or-Not Odditorium.

EATING IN NORTHEAST FLORIDA: ST AUGUSTINE

MAP P480

Floridian: Old Florida hipster vibes with courtyard dining, a cozy bar and an eclectic menu with gluten-free and vegan/veg options. *11am-late Wed-Mon* $$

St Augustine Fish Camp: Seafood so scrumptious there's usually a line, but it's worth the wait. Your taste buds will agree. *hours vary* $$

Lotus Noodle Bar: This Japanese-French styled hideaway is a foodie's paradise. Intimate dining. Reservations required. *5-9pm Tue-Thu, to 10pm Fri & Sat* $$

Chez L'Amour: Dimly lit restaurant/bar with live jazz, speakeasy charm, mouthwatering tapas-style cuisine and delectable desserts. *hours vary* $$$

ST AUGUSTINE

HIGHLIGHTS
1 Castillo de San Marcos National Monument
2 St Augustine Eco Tours

SIGHTS
3 Bridge of Lions
4 Cathedral Basilica of St Augustine
5 Colonial Quarter
6 Fountain of Youth
7 Mission Nombre de Dios
8 Oldest Wooden School House
9 Plaza de la Constitución
10 St George St

ACTIVITIES
11 Old Town Trolley Tours
12 Red Train Tours
13 St Augustine Distillery

SLEEPING
14 St George Inn
15 Villa 1565

EATING
16 Ben's Soft Pretzels
17 Chez L'Amour
18 Floridian
19 Kilwins
20 Lotus Noodle Bar
21 St Augustine Fish Camp

DRINKING & NIGHTLIFE
22 Auggie's Draft Room
23 Dog Rose Brewing
24 Prohibition Kitchen
25 Rendezvous

Old Fort, Older Mission: Fountain of Youth?

MAP P480

Exploring 'The Ancient City's' rich history

Meander sacred grounds at **Mission Nombre de Dios** *(missionandshrine.org; free)*, once thought to be the original landing site of Ponce de Léon, the Spanish explorer who discovered 'La Florida.' Although that's been rebuked, there's no disputing the site's historical significance: it was here that Pedro Menéndez de Avilés founded St Augustine in 1565, 55 years before the Pilgrims arrived. The first parish mass was held upon their arrival, with a thanksgiving dinner attended by Indigenous Timucuans.

Nowadays, a **Great Cross**, erected to commemorate the mission's 400th anniversary, towers 208ft above trails, foot bridges and saltwater marshes. Perfect for peaceful reflection, the serene **Memorial Pathway** passes archaeological excavations, a bell tower, crumbling tombstones, rustic buildings, statues and cascading fountains.

Nearby, the dog-friendly **Fountain of Youth Archaeological Park** *(fountainofyouthflorida.com; adult/child $23/10)* attracts visitors curious about its mythical springs. Sadly, it's all historical folklore, but indulge in a free cup o'youth nevertheless. Navigate your way through free-roaming peacocks, exploring a recreated Native Timucua village, and catching reenactors firing cannons and muskets.

Plagued by pirate attacks, military onslaughts, disease, pillaging, raiding and burning, St Augustine has flown five flags during its existence. One British invasion in 1702 saw every building torched to the ground except the formidable **Castillo de San Marcos** *(nps.gov/casa; adult/child $15/free)*, known locally as 'the fort,' which once contained defensive moats.

Built between 1672 and 1695, the imposing fort is the only extant 17th-century military construction in the country. It's also one of two fortresses in the world to be built in coquina, a locally quarried porous rock composed of tiny seashells compressed into limestone and capable of withstanding cannon fire (the other fortress is nearby **Fort Matanzas**). While the fort has changed hands a few times, it's never fallen, even while housing upwards of 1500 people during the English siege.

Allow at least two hours to visit the mostly accessible grounds on a self-guided tour. Parking costs $2.50 per hour.

BOTTLENOSE DOLPHINS

Spotted year-round, those fins slicing through the surface of the Matanzas River likely aren't sharks but, rather, common bottlenose dolphins – popular residents of St Augustine's inshore waters. Highly social, these intelligent, naturally acrobatic and playful sea creatures can live into their fifties, reach 6-12ft and weigh up to 400lb. Living in groups known as pods, they emit clicking noises to navigate, source food and avoid predators. To see and 'hear' these fascinating ocean-dwellers within their natural habitat, join marine naturalists at **St Augustine ECO Tours** *(staugustineecotours.com; prices vary)* on a scenic tour aboard vessels equipped with underwater microphones.

DRINKING IN NORTHEAST FLORIDA: ST AUGUSTINE TAPROOMS

MAP P480

Dog Rose Brewing Co: Fun gathering spot with a huge selection of handcrafted ales. Live music too. *noon-10pm Sun-Thu, to midnight Fri & Sat*

Rendezvous: Globetrot your way around 350 international beers at the city's 'original beer pub.' Family-friendly. *hours vary*

Auggie's Draft Room: Sample and sip at your own pace with 24 self-serve taps to choose from. *11am-8pm Sun-Thu, to 11pm Fri & Sat*

St Augustine Distillery: If you're a fan of premium bourbons, gins, vodkas and wines, you'll love this tour with generous samplings. *10am-6pm*

Tampa Bay & Southwest

WATERFRONT PATHWAYS | GULF HISTORY | GLOBAL MUSEUMS

GETTING AROUND

The TECO Streetcar has downtown routes, including to Ybor City, it's free and runs daily. Rent electric scooters or e-bikes through the Lime and Spin apps downtown. The Hillsborough Area Regional Transit Authority (HART) has bus routes throughout downtown and surrounds, including to Tampa International Airport. Downtown's Marion Transit Center is a hub for services to the zoo, Busch Gardens and the Henry B Plant Museum.

Few places in Florida fuse historic grit, artistic verve and breezy beach life quite like the Tampa Bay region. Tampa, with its brick-paved Ybor City and cigar-chomping past, pulses with a blend of Latin flavor and modern swagger. Its Riverwalk winds past concert halls, museums and sleek towers, while old neighborhoods like Seminole Heights trade in mid-century bungalows and craft beer. Across the bay, St Petersburg feels sun-splashed and soul-fed – a city where glass art, indie cafes and massive Salvador Dalí paintings live steps from marinas and banyan trees. Then there's St Pete Beach, a stretch of pure, powdery bliss where vintage motels and tiki bars keep things delightfully unpolished. This is where Florida loosens its collar a bit, ditches pretense and shows off its depth. It's a region shaped by salt air, immigrant legacies and rebellious creativity. It's where the Gulf isn't just scenery, it's a region's lifeblood.

River Views & Parks Aplenty

MAP P483

All along the Tampa Riverwalk

Stretching along the Hillsborough River, Tampa's best-loved green space takes you past palm-fringed parks and shimmering skyscrapers, always within view of the waterway where dolphins and manatees can be seen frolicking in the shadow of high-rises. For the full experience, you can join the runners, cyclists and skateboarders who traverse the full 2.5 miles, starting in either **Water Works Park** *(tampa.gov; free)* in

DRINKING IN TAMPA & SOUTHWEST: YBOR CITY

MAP P483

Gaspar's Grotto: Pirate-themed bar in the heart of the historic district with live entertainment and outdoor dining. *7am-2am Mon-Sat, from 11am Sun*

Ybor City Tap House: Live music and TVs tuned to whatever game is on draw sports fans, with 65 craft brews on tap. *hours vary*

Dirty Shame: Classic dive bar with darts, billiards and a loyal local crowd. A huge range of beers on tap, plus bottles and cans. *hours vary*

Castle: Ybor City's most famous nightclub has multiple floors and DJs, and crowds from goth to fetish and everything in between. *10:30pm-3am, Fri & Sat*

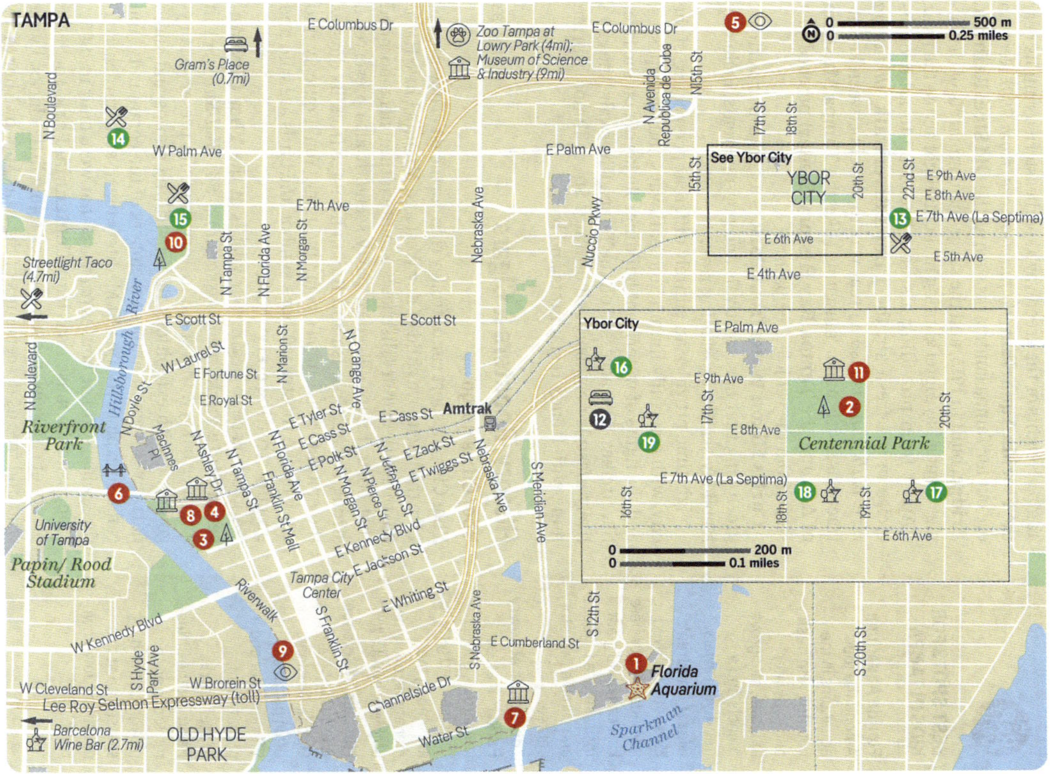

HIGHLIGHTS
1 Florida Aquarium

SIGHTS
2 Centennial Park
3 Curtis Hixon Waterfront Park
4 Glazer Children's Museum
5 JC Newman
6 Old Steel Railroad Bridge
7 Tampa Bay History Center
8 Tampa Museum of Art
9 Tampa Riverwalk
10 Water Works Park
11 Ybor City Museum State Park

SLEEPING
12 Hotel Haya

EATING
13 Columbia Restaurant
14 Rocca
15 Ulele

DRINKING & NIGHTLIFE
16 Castle
17 Dirty Shame
18 Gaspar's Grotto
19 Ybor City Tap House

TAMPA

BEST SPOTS FOR KIDS IN TAMPA

Florida Aquarium: Among the top aquariums in the country, with fresh and saltwater habitats, mangrove tunnels and a free-flying aviary.

Glazer Children's Museum: Beloved rainy-day spot where kids can build giant forts, steer a tugboat and climb a two-story course.

Zoo Tampa at Lowry Park: Manatees, kangaroos, giant tortoises and giraffes are among the menagerie of animals at this nonprofit zoo.

Museum of Science & Industry: Optical illusions, brain puzzles, a VR simulator and a planetarium.

Water Works Park: Let the littles run loose on the playground and splash pad at this riverfront downtown park.

Tampa Heights or the greenway's southeastern terminus near the **Florida Aquarium** *(flaquarium.org; from $30)*. Keep an eye out for Tampa landmarks such as the **Old Steel Railroad Bridge**, built in 1915, and the silver-hued minarets of the former Tampa Bay Hotel glinting in the sunlight across the river.

Apart from providing a scenic backdrop to a bit of exercise in the fresh air, the **Tampa Riverwalk** *(thetampariverwalk.com)* is also a great way to travel between key attractions, with major museums (like the **Tampa Museum of Art** and the **Tampa Bay History Center**) perched just steps from the vehicle-free path.

Curtis Hixon Waterfront Park is a gorgeous riverfront green lung that hosts festivals and pop-up events, including a holiday-season ice-skating rink.

Nighttime provides an entirely different perspective of the city, with colorfully illuminated pathways and underpasses, and the lights of waterfront buildings flickering on the river like fireflies. Also accessed off the Tampa Riverwalk, the city's lively lifestyle neighborhood of Water Street Tampa is brimming with trendy restaurants and bars.

History, Roosters & Cigars

MAP P483

Ybor City a go-go

Ybor City is a short car or trolley ride northeast of downtown. Like the illicit love child of Key West and Miami's Little Havana, this 19th-century district is a multicultural neighborhood that hosts Tampa's liveliest party scene. It also preserves a strong Cuban, Spanish and Italian heritage from its days as the epicenter of Tampa's cigar industry. You'll quickly find out why the rooster is Ybor's symbol: the birds are wild and proudly strutting everywhere.

A good place to begin your visit is at the **Ybor City Museum State Park** *(ybormuseum.org; $4; Wed-Sun)*. Set in a former bakery, this small history museum preserves a bygone era, with exhibitions full of striking photos and audio narratives from prominent members of the community. You can also explore the quaint Mediterranean-style gardens and three cigar-worker houses *(casitas)* that were built in 1895.

Opposite the museum is leafy **Centennial Park**. You'll see plenty of chickens, roosters and possibly little chicks, living wild and free as descendants of the hens kept by Ybor City's working-class residents over a century ago.

Cigar making is mostly a thing of the past, though **JC Newman** *(jcnewman.com; free)* keeps the old traditions alive at

EATING IN TAMPA BAY & SOUTHWEST: TAMPA

MAP P483

Streetlight Taco: Passionfruit margaritas and fabulous carnitas and brisket tacos in South Tampa. *11:30am-9pm Sun-Thu, to 10pm Fri & Sat* $

Rocca: Known for its tableside mozzarella cart, this Michelin-starred Italian in Tampa Heights is perfect for date night. *5-9pm Tue-Thu & Sun, to 10pm Fri & Sat* $$$

Barcelona Wine Bar: Lively spot with a great weekend brunch, a huge range of Spanish tapas and sangria in the south of the city. *hours vary* $$

Ulele: This native Florida-inspired restaurant serves gator tail, Gulf Coast oysters and locally caught grouper. *11am-10pm Sun-Thu, to 11pm Fri & Sat* $$

St Pete Pier

its recently restored El Reloj building. You can peruse the museum or book a guided factory tour *(adult/child $15/12)* and see the art of hand-rolling cigars in action.

End your day with a meal at **Columbia Restaurant** *(columbia restaurant.com)*, a striking Spanish-Cuban restaurant that's been going strong since 1905. The Cuban sandwich is legendary.

Stroll, Eat & Splash

MAP P486

Chill out on St Pete Pier

Before it reopened during the summer of 2020 after being completely renovated, the **St Pete Pier** *(stpetepier.org)* was a beloved but eyesore-inducing landmark on downtown's horizon. The new version of the pier, however, is nothing short of spectacular – all Scandinavian-inspired clean and contemporary lines interjected with beautiful public spaces that include a splash pad, marine-themed playground, **Tampa Bay Watch Discovery Center** *(tbwdiscoverycenter.org; adult/child $8/3)* with interactive conservation exhibits, and a sandy beach with plenty of spots for lounging on Tampa Bay.

You can easily while away a half-day or longer here, pausing for lunch or at least a tiki-themed cocktail with views of the city at **Pier Teaki** *(teakstpete.com/pier-teaki)* rooftop restaurant, or tossing out a fishing line from a dedicated platform on the pier. It's free to stroll the pier, which sprawls across a 26-acre district that hosts things like pop-up pickleball clinics and roller-skating rinks throughout the year.

TOP TIP

Visitors are often surprised to learn that Tampa itself is not on the beach. Clearwater Beach, one of the closest Gulf of Mexico beaches to Tampa, lies roughly 25 miles due west, with more options to the north and south.

SPARRING OVER A SANDWICH

Miami and Tampa both claim to have invented the American version of the Cuban sandwich – and the 'right' way to make the meaty wonder. If you've sunk your teeth into one in each city, you might have noticed the differences. Tampa lore credits the sandwich's origins to Ybor City, where it was made to feed Cuban cigar factory workers. And Tampa's version uses crispier bread on the outside while still fluffy inside and also adds Genoa salami to the usual mix of roasted pork, ham, Swiss cheese, dill pickles and mustard (the salami is said to be a nod to Ybor City's Italian immigrants).

EATING IN SOUTHWEST: ST PETERSBURG

MAP P486

Hangar: Casual spot for burgers and wings with direct views over the bayfront runway of Albert Whitted Airport. *8am-9pm* $

Juno & the Peacock: Sceney corner spot near the Vinoy resort with an incredible raw bar and cocktails. *11am-10pm Mon-Fri, from 10am Sat & Sun* $$$

El Cap: St Pete's most iconic spot for a burger or hot dog has been grilling them up since 1964. *11am-9pm Sun-Thu, to 10pm Fri & Sat* $

Mullet's Fish Camp: Choose from 15 types of fish served with house-made sauces at this South St Pete go-to. *hours vary* $$

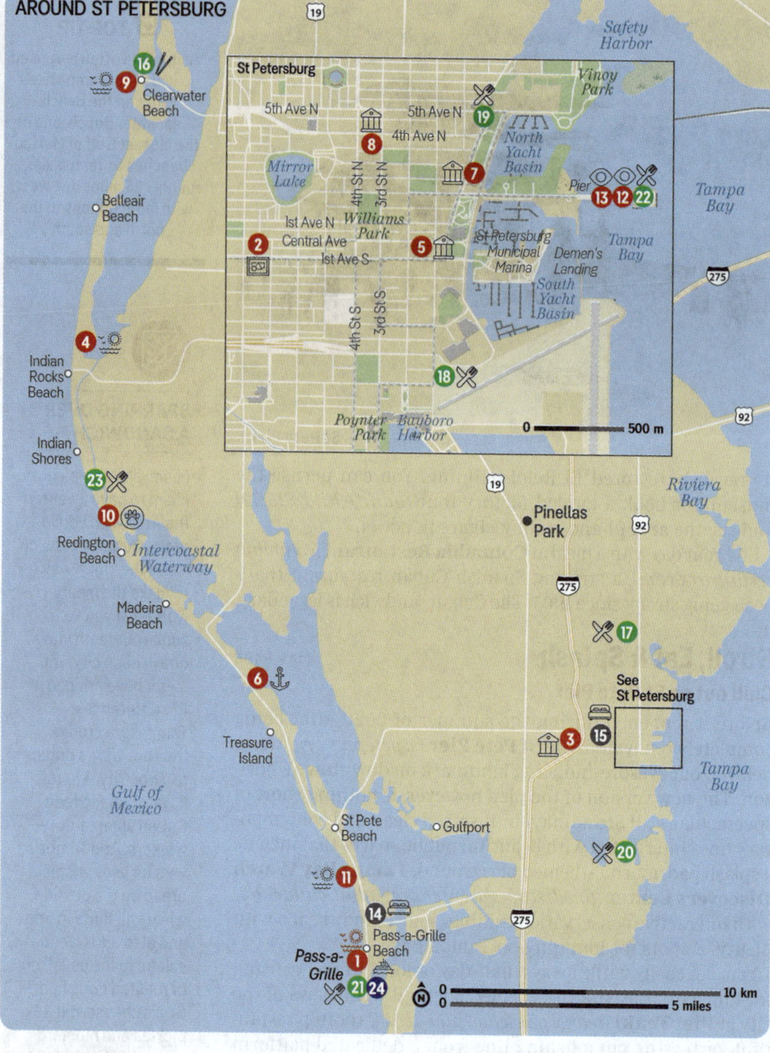

★ **HIGHLIGHTS**
1 Pass-a-Grille

SIGHTS
2 Chihuly Collection
3 Imagine Museum
4 Indian Rocks Beach Nature Preserve
5 James Museum of Western & Wildlife Art
6 John's Pass Village
7 Museum of Fine Arts
8 Museum of the American Arts & Crafts Movement
9 Pier 60
10 Seaside Seabird Sanctuary
11 St Pete Beach
12 St Pete Pier
13 Tampa Bay Watch Discovery Center

SLEEPING
14 Don CeSar
15 Moxy St Petersburg Downtown

EATING
16 Carreta on the Gulf
17 El Cap
see 16 Frenchy's Original Cafe
18 Hangar
19 Juno & the Peacock
20 Mullet's Fish Camp
21 Paradise Grille
22 Pier Teaki
23 Salt Rock Grill

TRANSPORT
24 Shell Key Shuttle

The Downtown Looper and Central Avenue Trolley make stops along the pier's length, in case you just want to view it as a drive-by.

White-Sand Beach Bliss

MAP P486

Clear waters and...Clearwater Beach, too

The closest Gulf of Mexico beachfront to the city is **St Pete Beach**, a mere 15-minute drive (on a good day) from bustling Central Ave in St Petersburg. The shoreline's key landmark is the towering Moorish Mediterranean **Don CeSar** hotel, a historic confection built in 1928 that's known to locals as the 'pink palace.'

The extra-wide beach itself ranks high for its natural beauty, and draws plenty of sunseekers who come for lounging by the waterside, long walks by the crashing waves and fiery sunsets. Proximity to the city has made this the most developed of the barrier-island beaches, with resorts, motels and restaurants just a few steps from the dune-backed sands.

Heading south from St Pete Beach, **Pass-a-Grille** anchors the southern end of Long Key. Here you'll find the most idyllic barrier-island beach, a narrow stretch of sand backed only by beach houses and metered public parking. You can watch boats coming through Pass-a-Grille Channel, hop aboard the **Shell Key Shuttle** *(shellkeyshuttle.com; round trip adult/child $30/15)*, which departs at 10am, noon and 2pm (2pm departure weekdays only) to unspoiled Shell Key, and retire for food and ice cream in the laid-back village center (essentially 8th Ave).

Slender barrier islands continue north of St Pete, harboring a handful of communities, from the tourist traps of **John's Pass Village** to the quieter, family-oriented Indian Rocks Beach. This is where you'll find the **Indian Rocks Beach Nature Preserve** *(indian-rocks-beach.com)*, which has a short boardwalk trail winding through mangroves out to a viewpoint of Boca Ciega Bay.

About a 15-minute drive north from there brings you to **Clearwater Beach**. It's hugely popular with tourists, particularly around **Pier 60** *(sunsetsatpier60.com)*, and hosts a nightly sunset celebration complete with buskers, and arts and crafts for sale.

Apart from beaches, the barrier-island chain is home to the largest wild-bird hospital in North America, the **Seaside Seabird Sanctuary** *(seasideseabirdsanctuary.org; free)*, which is home to over 100 sea and land birds for public viewing. You'll see a resident population of injured pelicans, owls, gulls, parrots and birds of prey, including a bald eagle. Several thousand birds are treated and released back to the wild annually. For a fine view over the beach, climb up the observation tower nestled in the back of the property.

BEST MUSEUMS & GALLERIES IN ST PETERSBURG

Museum of the American Arts & Crafts Movement: A local philanthropist founded the world's only museum that is dedicated to this historic movement.

James Museum of Western & Wildlife Art: Works by primarily living artists evoke the spirit of the West. The museum's façade is designed to resemble a sandstone mesa.

Museum of Fine Arts: Art representing ancient civilizations and modern masters makes up a world-class collection.

Chihuly Collection: Permanent collection of 18 installations by celebrated glass artist Dale Chihuly.

Imagine Museum: One-of-a-kind glass-art museum featuring works by American and international artists.

EATING IN SOUTHWEST: ST PETE BEACH

MAP P486

Paradise Grille: Casual walk-up spot on Pass-a-Grille Beach with tasty seafood, cold drinks and picnic tables overlooking the sand. *7am-8:30pm* $

Salt Rock Grill: Classy Indian Shores dinnertime spot renowned for local seafood and steaks. *4-10pm Mon-Fri, from noon Sat & Sun* $$$

Frenchy's Original Cafe: Famous grouper-sandwich spot at Clearwater Beach and other locations. *11am-10pm* $$

Carreta on the Gulf: Sandpearl Resort's signature restaurant serves divine sushi and seafood. *7am-midnight Sun-Thu, to 1am Fri & Sat* $$$

Places We Love to Stay

$ Budget $$ Midrange $$$ Top End

Miami

MAPS P433, P436, P438, P441

Freehand Miami $ Dorms and private rooms, two craft cocktail bars and an outdoor pool, about a mile north of the South Beach nightlife.

Kimpton Surfcomber $$ With a recently renovated pool, happening beach bar and poolside cabanas in Miami Beach.

Dunns Josephine $$ In historic Overtown, themed rooms celebrate the lives of notable Black figures like Ella Fitzgerland and Langston Hughes.

Arlo $$ With gorgeous murals inside and out, this high-rise hotel in Wynwood has beautiful common spaces that draw the neighborhood in.

Faena Hotel Miami Beach (p435) $$$ Scenic, super-luxurious beachfront and art-centric hotel with restaurants, nightlife and entertainment on-site.

Mr C $$$ Rooms with European glamour wow at this Coconut Grove property. Its rooftop pool gazes out on Biscayne Bay.

Everglades & Biscayne National Park

MAP P445

Flamingo Campground (p446) $ Drive-in campground in Everglades National Park with heated showers, grills, and access to fishing and hiking.

Elliott Key Campground $ A hiking trail and fishing on the island in Biscayne National Park. Restrooms and cold showers available. Access by boat only.

Boca Chita Key Campground $ Waterfront views, picnic tables, grills and toilets on-site in Biscayne. Access by boat only.

Flamingo Lodge $$ Comfortable accommodations deep in the Everglades. Waterfront rooms, dining on-site, rentals, glamping tents, and tours available.

Florida Keys & Key West

MAP P451

John Pennekamp Coral Reef State Park $ The park has campsites that can accommodate both tents and RVs. Restrooms, hot showers and coin laundry on-site.

Seashell Motel & Key West Hostel $ Basic dorm-style housing conveniently located near Old Town Key West.

NYAH Key West $$ Adult-only, elevated, dorm-esque lodging, plus a continental breakfast. Private rooms available.

Playa Largo $$$ This Key Largo oceanfront resort is the classic combination of luxury and seclusion.

Isla Bella $$$ Comfortable oasis where every room overlooks the water in Marathon. Relax with waterfront amenities or dabble in water sports at the marina.

Havana Cabana $$$ Adults-only hotel with vibrant influences of the art and culture of Cuba, plus Key West's largest pool.

Southeast Florida

MAPS P457, P462

Snooze Hotel $ Fort Lauderdale beachfront accommodation complete with a rooftop deck and complimentary beach gear.

Grand Resort & Spa $$ An LGBTIQ+-friendly resort, just steps from Fort Lauderdale Beach.

Historic Driftwood Resort $$ A fun, unique and nostalgic beachfront hotel in Vero, built in the 1920s using locally sourced driftwood.

Conrad Fort Lauderdale Beach $$$ Every room in this luxe, all-suite beach-front resort comes with an Italian marble bathroom, deep-soaking tub, and private balcony or terrace.

The Ben $$$ This luxury boutique hotel in West Palm Beach is part of the Marriott Autograph Collection. A block from Clematis St, many balconies overlook Palm Harbor Marina and the Intracoastal Waterway.

Hilton West Palm Beach $$$ This luxury property exudes style and grace: modern suites, resort-style pool, superb restaurants, full-service spa and complimentary valet parking.

Orlando & Walt Disney World®

MAP P465

Rosen Inn at Pointe Orlando $ A basic, affordable accommodation right in the middle of the action of I-Drive.

Hilton Garden Inn Lake Buena Vista $ An affordable resort, a 1-mile walk from Disney Springs® and the rest of the Walt Disney World® action.

Alfond Inn $$ Charming shops and restaurants

Faena Hotel Miami Beach (p435)

surround this artsy Winter Park boutique hotel.

Universal's Cabana Bay Beach Resort $$ An affordable Universal Orlando Resort hotel with retro-style single rooms and family suites.

Grand Bohemian Hotel $$$ In the heart of downtown Orlando, this AAA Four Diamond Resort combines luxury and a great location.

Disney's Polynesian Village Resort $$$ A volcano-inspired pool and lush grounds at this village resort transport guests to Fiji. Two monorail stops from the Magic Kingdom.

Villatel Orlando Resort $$$ Less hotel, more playful neighborhood, centrally located on I-Drive. Boredom never hits with amenities like water slides, pickleball courts golf simulators and basketball.

Space Coast MAP P471

Jetty Park Campground $ Tent and full-service RV campsites at Port Canaveral with shuffleboard, playground and pier. Watch cruise ships passing by.

Hyatt Place Titusville/ Kennedy Space Center $$ Three-star hotel with a free daily breakfast buffet and outdoor pool.

Beachside Hotel & Suites $$ Retro surf vibes, balconies with ocean views in Cocoa Beach, and a water park with deck-side bar – oodles of family fun! On-site laundry; breakfast included.

Courtyard Titusville Kennedy Space Center $$$ Riverfront hotel with an outdoor pool and rooftop deck with launchpad views.

Northeast Florida MAPS P477, P480

Villa 1565 $ Classic Spanish architecture meets modern hospitality. Clean rooms surround a courtyard, home to a 650-year-old oak tree that pre-dates St Augustine.

Marriott Jacksonville Downtown $$ A four-star Water St hotel that's upscale and has a bar, bistro, pool and fitness area.

St George Inn $$ Centrally located, bodacious boutique inn offering apartment-style kitchenette suites with balconies overlooking St George St and the fort.

One Ocean Resort & Spa $$$ Atlantic Beach resort with oceanfront spa, swimming pool, pool bar and restaurant.

Tampa Bay & Southwest MAPS P483, P486

Gram's Place $ This small, welcoming hostel in Seminole Heights is for travelers who prefer personality over perfect linens.

Moxy St Petersburg Downtown $$ Right on Central Ave with a lively rooftop restaurant and bar, plus a podcast studio guests can use on the ground floor.

Hotel Haya $$$ Boutique hotel in Ybor City, offering art-filled rooms, a pool, and a great restaurant and cafe.

Don CeSar (p487) $$$ Iconic 'pink palace' resort on St Pete Beach with a Gulf-front pool and bar.

For places to stay in Great Lakes, see p578

BO SHEN/GETTY IMAGES

Above: Pictured Rocks National Lakeshore (p550); Right: Chicago (p496)

THE MAIN AREAS

CHICAGO
Art, architecture and chowhounds' playground.
p496

ILLINOIS
Land of Lincoln, Wright and Route 66.
p509

INDIANA
Race cars and towering sands.
p516

OHIO
From big cities to Amish villages.
p525

Written and curated by
Karla Zimmerman and Ann Babe

Great Lakes

OVERLOOKED BEAUTY IN THE USA'S HEARTLAND

Unspoiled, uncrowded national parks mix it up with cool cultured cities and pie-baking small towns.

Here we are: the middle of the country. No mountains. No oceans. Flyover territory, right?

Don't be fooled by all the corn. Behind it lurks surfing beaches and Tibetan temples, car-free islands and the green-draped night lights of the aurora borealis. The Great Lakes takes its knocks for being middle-of-nowhere boring, so consider the moose-filled wilderness areas and Hemingway, Dylan and Vonnegut sites to be its little secret.

Roll call for the region's cities starts with Chicago, which unfurls what is arguably the country's mightiest skyline. Milwaukee keeps the beer-and-Harley flame burning, while Minneapolis shines a hip beacon out over the fields. And Detroit rocks, plain and simple.

DMITRY ZINOVYEV/SHUTTERSTOCK

The Great Lakes themselves are huge, like inland seas, with beaches, dunes, resort towns and lighthouse-dotted scenery. Dairy farms and fruit orchards blanket the region, meaning fresh pie and ice cream aplenty. And when the scenery does flatten out? There's always a goofball roadside attraction, such as the Spam Museum or the world's biggest ball of twine, to revive imaginations.

Most visitors come in summer when the weather is fine for hiking, biking, canoeing and kayaking in the local lakes and forests. Snowmobiling and cross-country skiing take over in the butt-freezing winter (as do eating and drinking in warm taverns). Whatever the season, a true slice of America awaits in the heartland.

MICHIGAN
Beaches, vineyards and forested islands.
p536

WISCONSIN
Pretty landscapes and lots of cheese.
p552

MINNESOTA
Lakes and wilderness aplenty.
p564

Minnesota, p564

Hiking, paddling and other outdoor adventures abound, from the moose-teeming northern wilderness to urban areas like Minneapolis and Duluth.

Wisconsin, p552

Beyond the beery cities lies a vast expanse of shimmering islands, lakefront beaches, forested trails and good-time bashes to help celebrate it all.

Illinois, p509

An ancient city, moss-draped swamp and architecture hotbed emerge from the farmland, along with presidential sites and Route 66 corn dogs and kitsch.

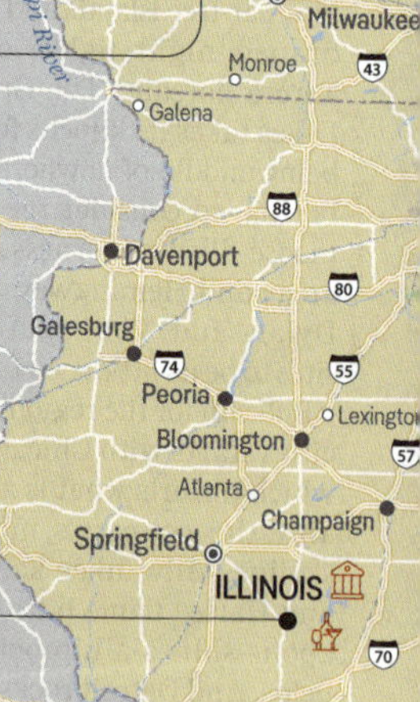

CAR

You'll need your own wheels to travel with ease. There's no other way to get to smaller towns and far-flung parks. Even between major cities, trains and buses are scant. And within cities (except Chicago) public transportation is patchy.

TRAIN

Amtrak trains run in the region, but with fairly limited service. Chicago is the hub. Trains go to Milwaukee (seven daily), Minneapolis (two daily), Detroit (three daily), Cleveland (one daily) and Indianapolis (three per week).

FERRY

Two car ferries can save time when driving around Lake Michigan. The *Lake Express* goes between Milwaukee, WI, and Muskegon, MI, in 2½ hours. The SS *Badger* goes between Manitowoc, WI, and Ludington, MI, in four hours.

Find Your Way

The region is vast, around 1000 miles across from east to west. We've picked the places that capture the Great Lakes' down-to-earth culture and quietly sublime landscapes and presented them here state by state.

Michigan, p536
With four of the five Great Lakes kissing its shores, Michigan has beaches and sand dunes galore, plus the history-rich city of Detroit.

Chicago, p496
The heart of the Great Lakes beats in this cloud-scraping metropolis, a cultural stew of art, nightlife and star restaurants with laid-back style.

Ohio, p525
Vibrant cities mix it up with horse-and-buggy Amish communities, moonshine-making hill towns, party islands and a mist-threaded national park.

Indiana, p516
A trek over sand dunes and a hike through the 'Little Smoky Mountains' are among the unexpected pleasures in this state known for car culture.

Plan Your Time

Factor long distances into your planning. For instance, driving from Cleveland to Minneapolis (east to west across the region) is an 11-hour journey on the Interstate. Rural highways add even more to travel times.

ANTHONY GEORGE VISUALS/SHUTTERSTOCK

Garden of the Gods (p515)

Great Lakes Weekend

You can swoop in for a few days and explore one of the cool Great Lakes cities. Chicago is the obvious choice to walk around (and ride the clackety L trains) and take in the **art** (p497), **architecture** (p499), **blues clubs** (p503) and very large **pizza** (p496). Tack on trips to **Wrigley Field** (p503) and an **improv comedy club** (p503), too. Detroit is another great candidate, where you can check out the **public art** (p537), art-deco **architecture** (p540), jazz and **Motown sounds** (p539) and **car-making history** (p541) with a foray to nearby Dearborn. Minneapolis also gives a solid feel for the region. Spend a couple of days enjoying its **rock clubs** (p569), **art museums** (p565) and **lake fun** (p569), along with jaunts to historic Twin City, **St Paul** (p570) and **Prince's pad** (p570) in the suburbs.

Seasonal Highlights

Whenever you visit, the Great Lakes region is having a party somewhere. Music festivals, food fairs, cultural bashes and snow carnivals fill the calendar.

JANUARY

It's cold and snowy, but that doesn't stop locals from donning parkas and heading out to snowmobile, cross-country ski, curl and party at outdoor events, such as the **St Paul Winter Carnival** (p569).

MARCH

St Patrick's Day celebrations make merry in Cleveland, Detroit, Milwaukee and especially Chicago (p496), which famously dyes its river green. Bundle up, because it's usually still cold outside for these shenanigans.

MAY

As the weather warms, wildflowers start to bloom. Indiana Dunes bursts with lupines, mayapples and many more, while Holland explodes in color at its **Tulip Time** (p546) festival.

Four Days to Travel Around

With four days, you can add some outdoor action. Chicago is close to beachy, bird-filled **Indiana Dunes National Park** (p521) and to the **Lake Michigan Shore Wine Trail** (p547) vineyards in southwestern Michigan. Detroit is within range of the soaring sands and blue waters at **Sleeping Bear Dunes National Lakeshore** (p545). Minneapolis is not too far from the wolf-howling wilderness of the **Boundary Waters** (p575) and to the waterfall-laden parks along **Hwy 61** (p573). Cleveland is a stone's throw from time-warped communities in Ohio's **Amish Country** (p533), where horse-drawn buggies rule the roads, and from the misty woods of **Cuyahoga Valley National Park** (p528).

A Weeklong Stay

A week lets you dig deeper into the area. You can combine a couple of cities and their surrounding sights, or strike out for further-flung regions. Michigan's Upper Peninsula takes you into the sparsely populated northern forest where mountain bikers hang out in **Marquette** (p551), and kayakers paddle at **Pictured Rocks National Lakeshore** (p550). A trip in the south along the Ohio River can include **Cincinnati's Brewing Heritage Trail** (p529), southern Indiana's caves and **scenic river towns** (p523) and southern Illinois' rugged **Shawnee Hills** (p515). To really get away from it all, remote **Voyageurs National Park** (p576) and **Isle Royale National Park** (p549) are among the least-visited wilderness areas in the country, where stars, moose, peace and quiet thrive.

JUNE
By mid-month the region is in full swing. It's finally warm, beer gardens hop, beaches splash, and parties such **Summerfest** (p555) rock most weekends.

JULY
The Great Lakes slowly get warm enough to swim in without teeth chattering. Blueberries and peaches are ready to pick, while the **National Cherry Festival** (p546) celebrates Michigan's favorite fruit.

SEPTEMBER
Peak season winds down in the region. But the coolness in the air also means Oktoberfest celebrations are on tap in cities like Columbus and Milwaukee. Cincinnati's **Oktoberfest** (p530) is the nation's biggest.

OCTOBER
Road trips to see fall colors are a big to-do. Hot spots include Door County, Hwy 61, Brown County and the Shawnee Hills. Bountiful harvests mean fresh apples, pumpkins and corn at markets.

Chicago

VISIONARY ARCHITECTURE | LAKEFRONT ALLURE | MUSIC SCENE

GETTING AROUND

The L (a system of elevated and subway trains) is the best way to travel around Chicago. Its eight color-coded lines are easy to use and get you to most sights and neighborhoods. An unlimited-ride day pass costs $5. Buy it at any L station or via the Ventra app *(ventrachicago.com)*, which also is useful for showing train times. Driving can be tough due to heavy traffic and scarce (and expensive) parking.

TOP TIP

Advance bookings are wise, especially during weekends. Most restaurants take reservations via their websites using Tock, OpenTable or Resy. For museums, buying tickets online in advance can often provide cost savings over same-day purchases.

Chicago is the star of the Great Lakes, a big, teeming, tall-skyscraper buzz of energy. While it is the USA's third-largest city, home to 2.7 million people, its low-key cultured awesomeness tends to fly under the radar. It doesn't brag about its star art collections or reasonably priced food scene that rivals the coasts in Michelin stars. It doesn't gloat over its trendsetting architecture and blow-the-roof-off bands on stages nightly. Its sand-and-surf beaches pop up with typical Midwestern modesty. Which is why so many visitors find the city a surprise – an urbane, multicultural metropolis for all.

The top sights are downtown, around the area known as the Loop. But you'll want to head out into further-flung neighborhoods for the best eating and drinking. Great districts to scope include Wicker Park, Pilsen, Logan Square and Andersonville – all jam-packed with inventive storefront restaurants – and the West Loop, where the buzziest dining venues huddle.

Get a Hefty Slice

MAP P502

Try deep-dish pizza

Chicago's foremost food is deep-dish pizza, a hulking mass of crust that rises two inches above the plate and cradles a molten pile of toppings. Try it at **Lou Malnati's** *(loumalnatis.com)*, which lays claim to inventing the cheesy behemoth. **Giordano's** *(giordanos.com)* makes 'stuffed' pizza: a bigger, doughier version of deep dish. A third version is pan pizza, similar to deep dish, but the crust is baked differently and has a ring of crisp, caramelized cheese. **Pequod's Pizza** *(pequodspizza.com)* makes a mighty one.

One piece is practically a meal wherever you go. Expect to wait 40 minutes or so for the hefty pies to cook.

HIGHLIGHTS
1 Art Institute of Chicago
2 Millennium Park

SIGHTS
3 American Writers Museum
4 Chicago Architecture Center
5 Chicago Cultural Center
6 Cloud Gate
7 Crown Fountain
8 Grant Park
9 Lurie Garden
10 Maggie Daley Park
11 Museum of Contemporary Photography
12 Museum of Illusions
13 Nichols Bridgeway
14 Pritzker Pavilion
15 Riverwalk
16 Rookery
17 St Regis Chicago
18 Willis Tower

ACTIVITIES
19 Chicago Architecture Center First Lady River Cruise

SLEEPING
20 Hampton Inn Chicago Downtown/N Loop
21 HI-Chicago

EATING
22 Native Foods

DRINKING & NIGHTLIFE
23 Cindy's

ENTERTAINMENT
24 Buddy Guy's Legends
25 Chicago Theatre
26 Goodman Theatre

Explore the Art Institute's Masterpieces MAP P497

Impressionist paintings star

Allocate at least a few hours to wander through the **Art Institute of Chicago** (*artic.edu; adult/child $32/free*), the USA's second-largest art museum. The main action happens on the 2nd floor. Stand in awe like Ferris Bueller in front of Georges Seurat's *A Sunday Afternoon on the Island of La Grande Jatte* (Gallery 240). In the adjoining rooms see color-swirled

BEST FAR-FLUNG & OVERLOOKED MUSEUMS

Griffin Museum of Science & Industry: Check out the submarine, coal mine and other mind-blowers at the Western Hemisphere's largest science museum.

Museum of Contemporary Art: The Art Institute's brash, rebellious challenger has a collection that always pushes boundaries.

Museum of Illusions: See your head on a platter and walk on walls at this kid-friendly, date-night favorite.

American Writers Museum: Bibliophiles will have a grand time at the word waterfall, typewriters, book lounge and other hands-on exhibits.

Insect Asylum: Wonderfully offbeat collection of vintage taxidermy and insect aquariums, plus yoga classes surrounded by snakes.

THOMAS BARRAT/SHUTTERSTOCK

canvases by Monet, Renoir and Van Gogh. It takes a while to get through the impressionist and postimpressionist paintings – there are more here than anywhere outside of France. Nearby, Edward Hopper's lonely, neon-lit diner in *Nighthawks* (Gallery 262) and Grant Wood's stern-faced couple in *American Gothic* (Gallery 263) hang in side-by-side galleries.

To take a break from crowds, stroll downstairs to the Thorne Miniature Rooms (Lower Level, Gallery 11) to peer into 68 teeny-tiny, dollhouse-like interiors.

Then head to the light-drenched Modern Wing and up to the 3rd floor to gape at the blue, elongated figure of Pablo Picasso's *The Old Guitarist* (Gallery 391). From here the pedestrian-only **Nichols Bridgeway** arches over into Millennium Park, a fine add-on experience before or after your Art Institute jaunt.

Art by Day, Music by Night

MAP P497

Play in Millennium Park

Located downtown next to the Art Institute, **Millennium Park** *(millenniumpark.org; admission free)* has abundant free and arty sights. The mega draw is **Cloud Gate** – aka the Bean – Anish Kapoor's 110-ton, mirror-smooth sculpture. Go ahead: walk right up to it, feel it, ponder the skyline

EATING IN CHICAGO: LEGENDARY BITES

MAPS P500, P502

Mr Beef: No-frills spot that cooks the spicy, drippy Italian beef sandwich made famous in the TV show *The Bear*. *10am-4pm Mon-Sat* $

Al's #1 Italian Beef: Another longstanding Italian beef purveyor, where queues can be shorter than Mr Beef. *10:30am-midnight Mon-Sat, to 8pm Sun* $

Wieners Circle: Chicago-style hot dogs (with onions, tomatoes, pickle, relish) in a raucous late-night ambience. *11am-2am Sun-Thu, to 4am Fri & Sat* $

Billy Goat Tavern: Mythic subterranean joint for 'cheezborgers,' immortalized in a *Saturday Night Live* skit. *hours vary* $

Lurie Garden

reflection and snap a picture. Then mosey onward to Jaume Plensa's **Crown Fountain**. Its two glass-block towers have video images of Chicagoans spouting water, gargoyle-style. On hot days, it's like a water park when everyone jumps in to cool down. Kids, especially, love it.

For a peaceful patch away from the crowd, seek out the **Lurie Garden**, abloom with prairie flowers. A little river runs through it, where folks kick off their shoes and dangle their feet.

Stay until evening and you might see a Nigerian juju band or a dream pop trio at **Pritzker Pavilion**, the swooping silver band shell designed by architect Frank Gehry. Free concerts take place most nights in summer. For all shows, but especially those by the Grant Park Orchestra, folks bring blankets, food, wine and beer. It's a summer ritual, as the sun dips, corks pop and gorgeous music fills the twilight air. Allow extra time to get in for evening events, as all visitors must go through a security/bag check.

MORE GREAT PARKS

Lincoln Park: Join locals on the running paths, athletic fields and beaches in Chicago's largest green space.

Grant Park: Grassy downtown sprawl dotted by spectacular Buckingham Fountain, which performs an hourly water show.

Northerly Island: Stroll or cycle around this prairie-like refuge, with great skyline views, floating alongside the Museum Campus.

Alfred Caldwell Lily Pool: Enchanting oasis of water lilies and dragonflies that feels like you've stumbled into Monet's Giverny garden.

Montrose Point Bird Sanctuary: Beachside woods known as the Magic Hedge for the 300 bird species that fly through here.

Soak up Chicago's Architecture

MAP P497

Hop on a boat tour, then roam the Riverwalk

Follow the crowds to the docks beneath Michigan Ave, at the north end of the Loop, and climb aboard the **Chicago Architecture Center's First Lady** *(architecture.org; from $56)*. Yes, it's touristy, but it's also marvelous. Grab a seat on deck and look up as you glide under stunning skyscrapers. Docents' design lessons carry on the breeze, so you'll know your beaux arts from international style by journey's end. The boat cruises along the Chicago River for 90 minutes.

Afterward, building buffs can add to their knowledge by ascending to street level and browsing inside the **Chicago Architecture Center**, where

GET YOUR KICKS ON ROUTE 66

A sign across the street from the Art Institute announces the beginning of **Route 66** (p514), which makes a fun road trip through Illinois.

LINCOLN PARK & OLD TOWN

SIGHTS
1 Alfred Caldwell Lily Pool
2 Lincoln Park
3 Lincoln Park Zoo
4 North Avenue Beach
5 Peggy Notebaert Nature Museum

EATING
6 Galit
7 Wieners Circle

DRINKING & NIGHTLIFE
8 Old Town Ale House

ENTERTAINMENT
9 iO Theater
10 Kingston Mines
11 Second City
12 Steppenwolf Theatre

EATING IN CHICAGO: OUR PICKS

MAPS P497, P504, P507

mfk: Spanish dishes and sunny cocktails in a teeny, romantic space that feels like the seaside in Spain. *5-9:30pm Mon-Sat, 4-8:30pm Sun* **$$$**

Tortello: Bowls of supreme comfort at this cute storefront: fresh pasta made before your eyes. *4:30-9pm Mon, from 11:30am Tue-Thu, from 8am Fri-Sun* **$$**

Duck Duck Goat: Chinese-inspired dim sum, mains and cocktails from star chef Stephanie Izard. *4:30-10pm Mon-Thu, to 11pm Fri & Sat, 11am-3pm Sat & Sun* **$$**

Loaf Lounge: Small, sunny bakery-cafe where locals clamor for breakfast sandwiches and the choc cake made famous in *The Bear*. *8am-4pm Wed-Mon* **$**

exhibits provide a quick primer on local structures and visionaries. Excellent walking tours that explore by theme (art deco, women architects) also depart from here.

Or stay by the water and amble along the 1.25-mile long **Riverwalk** *(chicagoriverwalk.us)*, chock-full of alfresco bars and restaurants from which you can gaze out and admire Chicago's built environment.

Get High in the Sky

MAP P497

Views from the top observatories

For superlative-seekers, **Willis Tower** *(theskydeck.com; adult/child from $32/24)* is it: Chicago's tallest (and the USA's second-tallest) skyscraper, rising 1450ft into the heavens. On the 103rd-floor Skydeck, glass-floored ledges jut out in midair, giving a knee-buckling perspective straight down. Before ascending, you'll make your way through fun interactive exhibits about Chicago, so snap a photo with the giant deep-dish pizza and stand on the replica Second City stage. Timed tickets are available online.

You'll find **360 Chicago** *(360chicago.com; adult/child from $30/20)* on the 94th floor of 875 N Michigan Ave (formerly known as the John Hancock Center). Set next to Lake Michigan, it provides unfettered panoramic vistas. The hair-raiser here is TILT *($9)*, a set of floor-to-ceiling windows that you stand in as they move and tip out over the ground. Nighttime views are particularly impressive, especially during the fireworks shows at nearby Navy Pier.

Navy Pier's Crowd-Pleasers

MAP P502

Ferris wheel, fireworks and views

Amble out on half-mile-long **Navy Pier** *(navypier.org; free)* and a carnival's worth of amusements vie for your attention, from the cloud-brushing **Centennial Wheel** *(adult/child $20/18)* to the horse-bobbing carousel *($6)*, ice-cream shops and margarita-slinging beer gardens. Then again, you can always just promenade along the dock's perimeter and enjoy the cool breezes and stellar skyline views. Crowds amass in summer for the fireworks show on Wednesday and Saturday nights.

Polk Bros Park, by the pier's entrance, has performance lawns for free concerts and movies. Competing tour boats depart from the pier's southern side. Set sail on **Windy** *(lakeshoresail.com; adult/child $49/34)*, a tall-masted

BEST ARCHITECTURE ICONS

Marina City: The twin corncob towers were completed in 1968 and look like something from a space-age *Jetsons* cartoon.

Tribune Tower: The neo-Gothic cloud-poker is inlaid with stones from the Taj Mahal, Great Pyramid, Parthenon and more.

Wrigley Building: Its shimmering white terracotta, French Renaissance details and famous clockface are the stuff of postcards.

St Regis Chicago: Look up at the city's third-tallest tower to see the 'blow-through floor' that reduces sway in the blue-glass skyscraper.

Rookery: Looks hulking and fortresslike outside, but it's light and airy inside, thanks to Frank Lloyd Wright's atrium overhaul.

DRINKING IN CHICAGO: OUR PICKS

MAPS P497, P500, P507

Old Town Ale House: Unpretentious neighborhood favorite for jovial late nights near the Second City comedy club. *3pm-4am*

Cindy's: Best rooftop in town. Set on the 13th floor of the Chicago Athletic Association Hotel, it unfurls awesome park and lake vistas. *hours vary*

Goose Island Taproom: Chicago's first craft brewer (now Anheuser-Busch owned) retains its indie spirit here. *noon-8pm Wed, Thu & Sun, to 10pm Fri & Sat*

CH Distillery: Polished facility that makes vodka, aquavit, amaro and Malört (Chicago's local liquor that's famous for tasting awful). *hours vary*

● **SIGHTS**
1 360 Chicago
2 Centennial Wheel
3 Chicago Children's Museum
4 Marina City
5 Museum of Contemporary Art
6 Navy Pier
7 Oak Street Beach
8 Polk Bros Park
9 theMart
10 Tribune Tower
11 Wrigley Building

● **ACTIVITIES**
12 Windy

● **SLEEPING**
13 Acme Hotel

● **EATING**
14 Al's #1 Italian Beef
15 Billy Goat Tavern
16 Giordano's
17 Lou Malnati's
18 Mr Beef

● **DRINKING & NIGHTLIFE**
19 Library at Gilt Bar
20 Three Dots & A Dash

● **SHOPPING**
21 Harry Potter Shop

● **TRANSPORT**
22 Shoreline Water Taxi to Museum Campus

schooner, or hop on the **Shoreline Water Taxi** *(shoreline sightseeing.com; adult/child $16/10)* to the Museum Campus.

Feel the Blues

MAPS P497, P500

Drop by an authentic club

The electric blues is Chicago's claim to music fame. When Muddy Waters and friends plugged their guitars into amplifiers here in the 1940s, sound reached new decibel levels. Chicago became the hub for the groundbreaking genre.

EATING IN CHICAGO: MICHELIN-STARRED

MAPS P497, P500, P507, P508

Smyth: Homey spot with three well-earned stars for creative, perfectly executed seafood, seasonal produce and sweets. *5-9pm Tue-Sat* **$$$**

Galit: Lively Middle Eastern restaurant winning raves for its cocktails and tasting menu made for sharing. *5-9pm Tue-Thu, to 9:30pm Fri & Sat* **$$$**

Moody Tongue: Brewery with beers such as Shaved Black Truffle Lager that pair perfectly with New American plates. *5-10pm Wed-Sat* **$$**

Kasama: Walk-in Filipino bakery by day; 13-course, modern Filipino tasting menu by night. *bakery 9am-3pm Wed-Sun, dinner Thu-Sun* **$$$**

The nation's best players trade licks at **Buddy Guy's Legends** *(buddyguy.com; $15-25),* just south of downtown. The memorabilia-filled room is relatively small, putting you close to the string-benders on stage. Free, all-ages acoustic shows take place at dinner time.

In Lincoln Park, **Kingston Mines** *(kingstonmines.com)* is similarly priced and a bit larger, with two stages where blues bands wail into the wee hours. More crackling grooves fill the air at **Rosa's Lounge** *(rosaslounge.com),* a real-deal little club with top local players and serious fans who dance the night away. It's further flung in Logan Square.

Improv Night Out

MAPS P500, P507

Laugh-out-loud comedy

Improv comedy began in Chicago, and the city remains a hub for the genre. Seeing a show is raucous fun, as performers create sketches based on suggestions (often alcohol fueled) that the audience shouts out. Polished ensembles riff on politics and pop culture nightly at **Second City** *(secondcity.com; from $41),* the most famous venue. **iO Theater** *(ioimprov.com; from $30)* is another established spot, where the Improvised Shakespeare Company ad-libs wacky plays in Elizabethan verse. **Den Theatre** *(thedentheatre.com; tickets from $20)* is a relative newcomer, with fringy, offbeat shows. iO and Den typically have more availability. Book all tickets in advance.

Catch a Game at Wrigley Field

MAP P504

The Cubs' historic ballpark

About 5 miles north of downtown, **Wrigley Field** *(cubs.com; around $60)* pops up smack in the middle of a residential neighborhood - aka Wrigleyville - surrounded on all sides by houses, rollicking bars and even a fire station. The ballpark charms with its lived-in environs, as well as its 1914 old-school features, like the hand-turned scoreboard, ivy-covered outfield walls and distinctive neon entrance sign. Seeing a game here, amid diehard Cubs fans, is a blast.

Gates open 1½ hours before the game's start time. It's good to arrive an hour or so early to browse around inside. Check out the Walk of Fame behind the bleachers in right field to learn about Cubs greats through the ages. Watch players take batting practice. Grab a hot dog and Old Style beer: the quintessential Wrigley foods.

Outside, the grassy plaza just north of the main entrance is **Gallagher Way**. On nongame days it's open to the public

BEST EXPERIENCES FOR KIDS

Lincoln Park Zoo: Watch chimpanzees swing, lions roar and penguins waddle, then feed chickens at the on-site farm, all for free.

Peggy Notebaert Nature Museum: Underrated spot to immerse in gentle thrills, such as the butterfly haven, frog marsh and wilderness walk.

Harry Potter Shop: Buy a wand or belly up to the Butterbeer Bar in this theatrical store that steeps you in the wizard's world.

Chicago Children's Museum: Excavate dinosaur bones, climb a ropey schooner and make art, then enjoy the carnival rides on surrounding Navy Pier.

Maggie Daley Park: Take your pick among the free playgrounds, including an enchanted forest to wander through, and a ship to pretend-sail.

DRINKING IN CHICAGO: BEST COCKTAILS

MAPS P502, P505

Three Dots & a Dash: Fun tiki bar with rum flights and its own speakeasy, the Bamboo Room. *4pm-midnight Sun-Wed, to 1am Thu & Fri, 2pm-1am Sat*

Matchbox: Teeny corner bar in West Town pouring martinis, gimlets, pisco sours and other classic drinks since 1945. *3pm-2am*

Library at Gilt Bar: World-class libations with velvet booths, vintage art and speakeasy vibes. *4-10:30pm Sun-Thu, to 11pm Fri & Sat*

Nobody's Darling: Inclusive, off-the-beaten-path bar stirring cocktails so delicious they were named Beard Award finalists. *hours vary*

BEST ROCK & JAZZ CLUBS

Green Mill: Timeless jazz institution with velvet-cushioned booths where gangster Al Capone used to hang out.

Metro: Chicago's premier loud-rock club and a tastemaker for more than 40 years. Bands on the way up thrash first.

Salt Shed: Cool indoor/outdoor venue carved from the old Morton Salt factory, where edgy, genre-spanning artists play.

Hideout: Feels like a retro basement, but with alt-country and indie-pop bands twanging on the small stage under twinkling lights.

Empty Bottle: Scruffy standby that reigns supreme for nightly shows, ranging from indie rock to punk to psych-pop. Cheap beer!

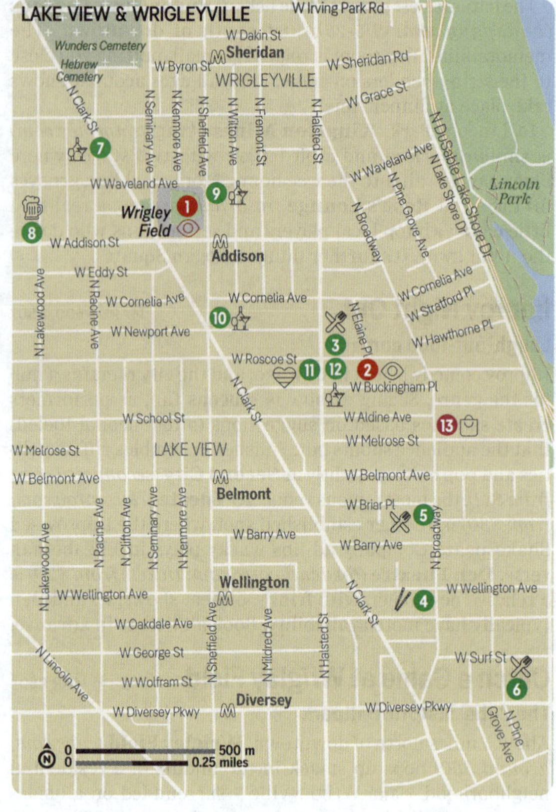

HIGHLIGHTS
1 Wrigley Field

SIGHTS
2 Northalsted

EATING
3 Chicago Diner
4 Crisp
5 Fancy Plants Cafe
6 mfk

DRINKING & NIGHTLIFE
7 GMan Tavern
8 Guthrie's Tavern
9 Murphy's Bleachers
10 Nisei Lounge
11 Roscoe's Tavern
12 Sidetrack

ENTERTAINMENT
see 7 Metro

SHOPPING
13 Unabridged Bookstore

DRINKING IN CHICAGO: TOP WRIGLEYVILLE WATERING HOLES

MAP P504

Nisei Lounge: Festive dive bar to try the Chicago Handshake (an Old Style beer and shot of Malört). *5pm-1:30am Mon-Thu, from 11:30am Fri-Sun*

Guthrie's Tavern: Neighborhood hangout with a glassed-in back porch, patio chairs and board games. *3pm-2am Mon-Fri, from 11am Sat & Sun*

Murphy's Bleachers: Lively, classic saloon steps from the entrance to Wrigley Field's bleacher seats. *11am-2am Mon-Thu, from 9:30am Fri-Sun*

GMan Tavern: Features cool vinyl tunes, eclectic beer and live music beloved by the rock-and-roll crowd. *3pm-2am Mon-Fri, from noon Sat & Sun*

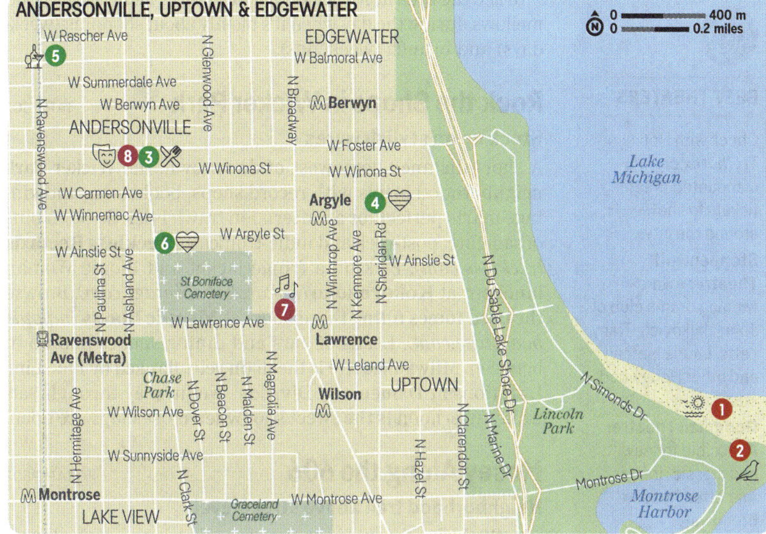

and hosts free movie nights and concerts. On game days it's a beer garden for ticket holders, and kids can run around or cool off in the splash pad.

Buy tickets at the Cubs' website or from online ticket broker StubHub *(stubhub.com)*. Upper Reserved Infield seats are usually pretty cheap. The bleachers are fun. Ninety-minute stadium tours *($30)* are also available most days in season.

SIGHTS
1 Montrose Beach
2 Montrose Point Bird Sanctuary

EATING
3 Hopleaf

DRINKING & NIGHTLIFE
4 Big Chicks
5 Nobody's Darling
6 SoFo Tap

ENTERTAINMENT
7 Green Mill
8 Neo-Futurist Theater

Northalsted Pride

MAP P504

Hot spots in Chicago's LGBTIQ+ hub

Northalsted – sometimes referred to as Boystown, its original name – lies along several blocks of N Halsted and Broadway streets, a short distance east of Wrigley Field. Rainbow crosswalks stripe the intersections, and rainbow pylons rise from the sidewalks. The pylons are part of the Legacy Walk, a mile-long outdoor museum that tells the stories of global LGBTIQ+ icons.

Halsted St holds several thumping bars, as well as thrift and fetish shops to add sass to one's wardrobe. On Broadway, **Unabridged Bookstore** *(unabridgedbookstore.com)* is a community linchpin that stocks everything from gay parenting to queer spirituality titles.

DRINKING IN CHICAGO: BEST LGBTIQ+ BARS

MAPS P504, P505

Sidetrack: Community stalwart with thumping dance music for gay and straight crowds alike. *3pm-2am Mon-Fri, 1pm-3am Sat, noon-2am Sun*

Roscoe's Tavern: Casual bar in front, dance club in back and sun-splashed patio outdoors. *4pm-2am Sun-Thu, from noon Sat & Sun*

Big Chicks: Weekend DJs, a fun dance floor and art displays draw both men and women; cash only. *4pm-2am Mon-Fri, from 9am Sat & Sun*

SoFo Tap: Known for its dog-friendly patio, dartboards, karaoke and bear nights. *5pm-2am Mon-Thu, from 3pm Fri, from noon Sat & Sun*

BEST THEATERS

Check with Hot Tix *(hottix.org)* for discounted theater tickets to shows around the city.

Steppenwolf Theatre: Award-winning drama club of John Malkovich, Tracy Letts, Laurie Metcalf and other Hollywood stars.

Goodman Theatre: A crucible for new and classic dramas that often head to Broadway.

Chicago Theatre: Century-old stunner with an enormous glittering marquee that's an official city landmark and great for photos.

Chopin Theatre: This 1918 venue is full of vintage charm, hosting oddball, thought-provoking plays, concerts and literary events.

Neo-Futurist Theater: The hyper troupe makes a manic attempt to perform 30 original plays in 60 minutes.

To see the area at its peak, visit at night. The neighborhood mellows during the day when it's mostly about shopping (weekdays) and brunch (weekends).

Rock the Shops in Wicker Park

MAP P507

Stock up on stylish wares

A short distance northwest of downtown, the Wicker Park neighborhood brims with record shops, bookstores and vintage marts perfect for an afternoon trawl. Flick through bins of sad-core, post-rock and indie-tronica at **Reckless Records** *(reckless.com)*. Pick up a fringe jacket and Bionic Woman lunchbox at **Kokorokoko** *(kokorokokovintage.com)*. Browse the used tomes filling three floors at **Myopic Books** *(myopicbookstore.com)*. Loads of bars and dining venues pop up in between. Milwaukee Ave is the main vein, flanked by Blue Line L stations at Damen and Division. Wednesday through Saturday afternoon is the sweet spot when most shops are open.

Mosey Along the 606

MAP P507

Neighborhood trail above street level

The **606** *(the606.org)* is an urban-cool elevated path along a repurposed train track now dotted with trees, benches and artworks. Bike or stroll past factories, clattering L trains and locals' backyard affairs. It's great for a morning or afternoon escape.

The trail unfurls for 2.7 miles parallel to Bloomingdale Ave, with its eastern end on Ashland Ave (in Wicker Park), and its western end on Ridgeway Ave (in Humboldt Park). Access points pop up every quarter mile, so it's easy to get on or off the path. Bars and restaurants beckon at ground level.

Blue Line L stations at Western and Damen are within a quick walk. For those wanting to cycle, Divvy bikeshare stations are on Ashland Ave by the trail's eastern end and Milwaukee Ave near **Small Cheval** *(smallcheval.com)*, a festive little shack serving up burgers, fries, milkshakes and beers.

Museum Campus Marvels

MAP P508

Dinosaurs, sharks and asteroids await

Three top-draw museums line up in a row on a lakefront stretch just south of downtown. The mammoth **Field Museum** *(fieldmuseum.org; adult/child $30/23)* houses everything but the kitchen sink. The collection's rock star is Sue, the largest Tyrannosaurus rex yet discovered, who menaces

EATING IN CHICAGO: VEGETARIAN & VEGAN

MAPS P497, P504, P507

Native Foods: Cheery venue for vegan burgers, tacos, hot chicken and meatball sandwiches. *10:30am-8pm Mon-Sat, 11am-7pm Sun* $

Fancy Plants Cafe: Cute vegan spot for a carrot lox bagel, seitan sausage sandwich or smoked lentil lasagna. *8am-4pm* $

Handlebar: Bike-messenger hangout with veg and fish dishes, plus a great back patio for beers. *10am-midnight Mon-Fri, from 9am Sat & Sun* $$

Chicago Diner: Vegetarian comfort food stalwart with vintage red tables and booths. *11am-10pm Mon-Fri, from 10am Sat & Sun* $$

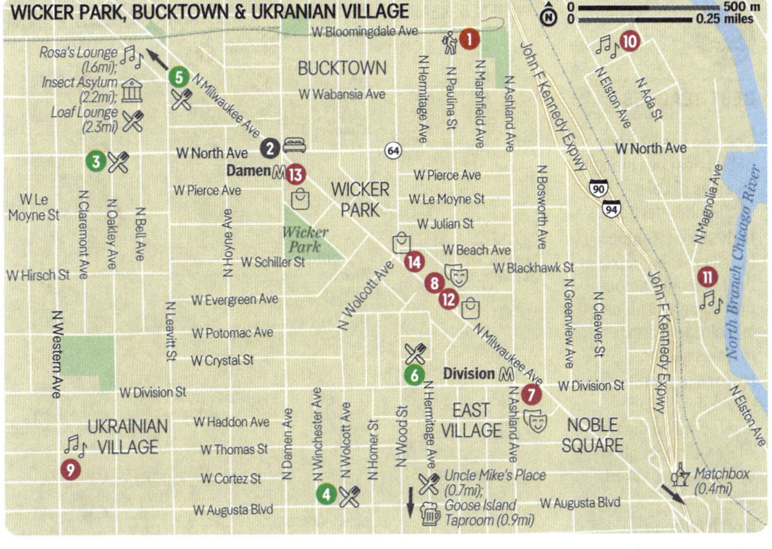

ACTIVITIES
1 The 606

SLEEPING
2 Robey

EATING
3 Handlebar
4 Kasama
5 Small Cheval
6 Tortello

ENTERTAINMENT
7 Chopin Theatre
8 Den Theatre
9 Empty Bottle
10 Hideout
11 Salt Shed

SHOPPING
12 Kokorokoko
13 Myopic Books
14 Reckless Records

the 2nd floor with her toothy companions. Mummies, gemstones and taxidermy lions are also among the stash of 40 million artifacts.

Next door, the **Shedd Aquarium** *(sheddaquarium.org; adult/child from $39/29)* packs in families that come to gawp at the 32,000 aquatic creatures that live here, including sharks – separated from you by just 5in of Plexiglas – stingrays and rescued sea otters. Building renovations through to 2027 mean some galleries might be closed when you visit.

Space enthusiasts will get a big bang out of the **Adler Planetarium** *(adlerplanetarium.org; adult/child $25/13)* with its collection of sundials and the *Gemini 12* space capsule. To see all three museums in a day, start with Shedd, followed by Field and then Adler.

Cycle the Lakefront

Wind-in-your-hair ride

Lake Michigan edges the city from north to south. It's huge, a freshwater 'sea'; its frothy waves rippling over the horizon with no end in sight. The 18-mile Lakefront Trail is a beautiful route along the water, rolling by beaches, parks and harbors. It's split into separate lanes for walkers and cyclists. Pedaling the path is a blast, a great way to blend into the local scene.

BEST FREEBIES

Chicago Cultural Center: Pop in to see terrific art exhibitions, foreign films and the world's largest Tiffany glass dome.

Chicago Greeter: Have a local take you on a two- to four-hour walking tour; book at least two weeks in advance. *chicagogreeter.com*

Art on the Mart: An ever-changing light show projected on a huge building by the Riverwalk each night.

Museum of Contemporary Photography: Small but top-tier venue for works by Henri Cartier-Bresson, Sally Mann, Ai Weiwei and others.

National Museum of Mexican Art: Politically charged paintings and folk art in Pilsen.

BEST BEACHES

Chicago has 22 free public beaches along 26 miles of Lake Michigan waterfront.

12th Street Beach: Small crescent next to the Museum Campus that somehow hides in plain sight and remains serene.

Montrose Beach: Kayak, bird-watch and lounge at the bar while sailboats glide by the dune-backed shore.

North Avenue Beach: Chicago's favorite party beach, with a bar, cafe, volleyball courts, and bicycle and kayak rentals.

Oak Street Beach: Sandy beach downtown for swimming and sunbathing in the shadow of skyscrapers.

Margaret T Burroughs Beach: Play all day at this fab strand with a boat harbor, fishing dock and watercraft rentals.

SIGHTS
1 12th Street Beach
2 Adler Planetarium
3 Field Museum
4 Margaret T Burroughs Beach
5 National Museum of Mexican Art
6 Northerly Island

ACTIVITIES
7 Shedd Aquarium

EATING
8 5 Rabanitos

DRINKING & NIGHTLIFE
9 Moody Tongue

Get a bike from Divvy (*divvybikes.com; day pass $18*). Be prepared for crowds on summer weekends, especially heading north, where there are more beaches.

EATING IN CHICAGO: AROUND THE WORLD

MAPS P504, P505, P507, P508

Crisp: Loud music, bright colors and picnic-style tables set the scene for Korean fried chicken and mixed vegetable bowls. *11:30am-9pm Tue-Sun* $

Uncle Mike's Place: Join construction workers, artsy youth and senior citizens chowing rice porridge and Spam at this fab Filipino breakfast diner. *6am-2pm* $$

5 Rabanitos: Unusual spice combinations and addictive salsa and mole make the dishes shine. *11am-9pm Mon-Fri, 9am-10pm Sat, 9am-9pm Sun* $$

Hopleaf: Cozy tavern for Belgian-style mussels, *frites* (fries) and beers from the 68 taps. *noon-11pm Sun-Thu, to midnight Fri & Sat* $$

Illinois

HISTORIC SITES | RURAL LANDSCAPES | WRIGHT DESIGNS

Outside of mighty Chicago, urbanity falls away fast and Illinois opens into a wide horizon of corn and soybean fields. Flat farmland covers three-quarters of the state, with the only real exception coming in the hilly northwest and knobby, bluff-strewn far south.

Road-tripping in Illinois turns up scattered shrines to local hero Abe Lincoln. Then there's Oak Park, the town with the most Frank Lloyd Wright–designed buildings of anywhere in the world. Historic Route 66 slices across the state, leaving a trail of corn dogs, pies and roadside oddities in its wake. Galena in the northwestern region delights with rolling hills and grazing horses near the Mississippi River (which forms most of Illinois' western boundary). Southern Illinois changes up the scene completely, with thick forests, wild rock formations and a cypress swamp for outdoor adventures.

Places

Oak Park p509
Springfield p511
Galena p513
Cahokia Mounds p515
Shawnee Hills p515

TOP TIP

People tend to forget that Illinois is an agricultural powerhouse. Farm stands are common along the roads in rural areas. Keep an eye out for peaches and apples in southern Illinois, apples in western Illinois, and pumpkins and sweet corn in northern and central Illinois.

Oak Park

See Wright buildings galore

The western Chicago suburb of Oak Park is a repository of famed architect Frank Lloyd Wright's early solo work. Wright lived here for two decades, from 1889 to 1909, and was only 22 years old when he built his Oak Park home, the first house he ever designed. Soon he was drawing up plans for several neighbors. Twenty-five Wright-devised buildings

GETTING AROUND

The main Interstates are I-90 and I-94 that head north to Wisconsin (tolls), I-55 that links Chicago to St Louis following historic Route 66 (no tolls), I-80 that goes east-west passing Chicago to the south (some tolls), and I-57 that runs from Chicago to southern Illinois (no tolls). Amtrak runs a handy train between downtown Chicago and downtown Springfield five times a day. Those trains roll onward to St Louis.

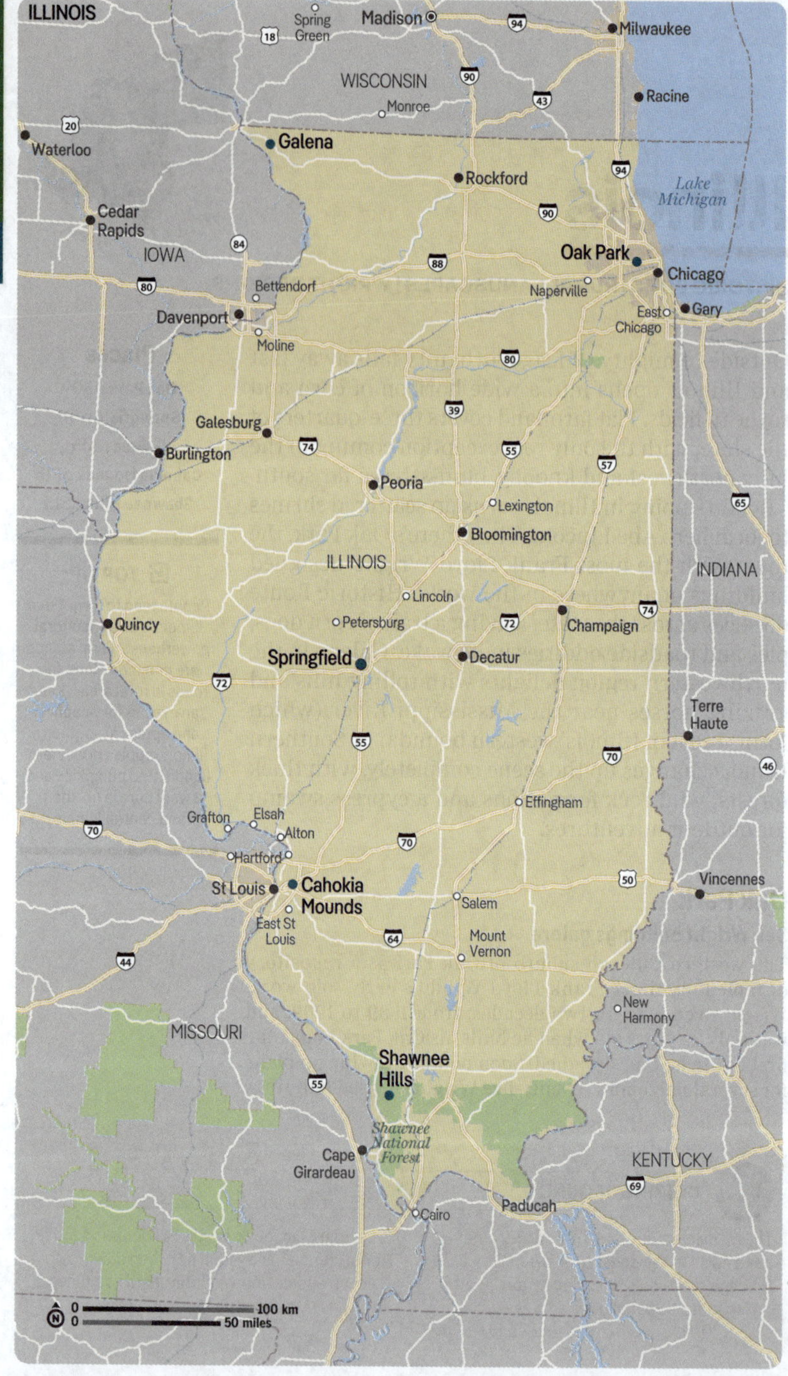
ILLINOIS
Spring Green
Madison
Milwaukee
WISCONSIN
Monroe
Racine
Waterloo
Galena
Rockford
Lake Michigan
Cedar Rapids
IOWA
Oak Park
Chicago
Bettendorf
Naperville
Davenport
East Chicago
Gary
Moline
Galesburg
Burlington
Peoria
Lexington
Bloomington
ILLINOIS
INDIANA
Lincoln
Quincy
Petersburg
Champaign
Springfield
Decatur
Terre Haute
Effingham
Grafton
Elsah
Alton
Hartford
St Louis
Cahokia Mounds
Vincennes
Salem
East St Louis
Mount Vernon
New Harmony
MISSOURI
Shawnee Hills
Shawnee National Forest
Cape Girardeau
KENTUCKY
Paducah
Cairo
0 100 km
0 50 miles

eventually popped up here, the largest concentration anywhere in the world.

The **Frank Lloyd Wright Home & Studio** *(flwright.org/tour/home-and-studio; tours $24)* is the main sight, accessible by guided tour only. It's best to book tickets online in advance. While walk-ups are welcome, slots tend to fill up. The hour-long walk-through reveals a fascinating place filled with original Wright-designed furniture and geometric details that made his Prairie-style architecture distinctive. Look for personal additions, such as the fireplace carved with his family motto: 'Truth is life.'

A half-mile away, Wright's 1908 **Unity Temple** *(flwright.org/explore/unity-temple; tours $18-20)* defies traditional ecclesiastical architecture. Like many of his buildings, the church's entrance is slightly hidden, leading visitors on what he called a 'path of discovery.' Inside, the sanctuary feels much warmer, splashed with sunshine-yellow walls and actual rays streaming in through the skylights.

Monday through Saturday mornings are the best time to visit and take in both sights. If driving, street parking is easy to find. Metra and L trains also have stations nearby.

Where Hemingway grew up

Frank Lloyd Wright wasn't the only influential artist in Oak Park at the turn of the century. Writer Ernest Hemingway grew up in the suburb. He was born in the 2nd-floor bedroom of a sprawling Queen Anne home on Oak Park Ave – a few blocks away from Wright's studio – in 1899. The house has been restored to look as it did then, with old family photos and frilly Victorian decor. Visits to the **Hemingway Birthplace** *(hemingwaybirthplace.com; adult/child $20/free)* are by hour-long guided tour only, offered Thursday through Saturday afternoons, as well as Saturday mornings.

In 1906, the family moved nearby to 600 N Kenilworth Ave. **Hemingway's Boyhood Home** is still a private residence, so you can't go inside, but a plaque marks the location.

Springfield

Follow in Abe Lincoln's footsteps

Illinois' small state capital has a serious obsession with Abraham Lincoln, who spent 24 years here as a young lawyer. A four-block neighborhood of old homes, gravel streets and wooden boardwalks near downtown has been preserved as the **Lincoln Home National Historic Site** *(nps.gov/liho;*

BEST ILLINOIS STATE PARKS

Starved Rock: Hike among 18 waterfall-filled canyons, each slicing through tree-covered, sandstone bluffs (north-central Illinois).

Mississippi Palisades: Hikers and rock-climbers love it, thanks to its Mississippi River-front real estate and dramatic limestone cliffs (northwest Illinois).

Matthiessen: Smaller and less crowded than nearby Starved Rock, but with similar scenery and sunflower fields (north-central Illinois).

White Pines Forest: Getaway to smell the pines, count the stars and stay in rustic log cabins (north-central Illinois).

Giant City: Popular for hiking and climbing amid the striking rock formations and towering trees (southern Illinois).

EATING & DRINKING IN OAK PARK: OUR PICKS

Spilt Milk: Excellent bakery for picking up a quiche, sandwich, scone or slice of creamy, flaky-crust pie. *8am-5pm Mon-Sat, to 2pm Sun* $

Hemmingway's Bistro: A few buildings south of Ernest's birthplace, this elegant spot serves French favorites. *11am-8:30pm* $$$

Citrine Cafe: Devour Mediterranean-influenced pastas, pizzas and seafood dishes, dreamed up by the Serbia-born owner. *hours vary* $$$

Kinslahger Brewing Company: Gorgeous taproom in a retro 1920s building where crisp lagers rule the taps. *4-10pm Wed-Fri, from 2pm Sat & Sun*

WRIGHT SIGHTS WALKABOUT

Gape at some of the 25 buildings Frank Lloyd Wright designed early in his career while living in Oak Park.

START	END	LENGTH
Frank Lloyd Wright Home & Studio	Unity Temple	0.75 miles; 45 minutes

Start at ① **Frank Lloyd Wright Home & Studio** (p511), the only house you can go inside. (The others are privately owned and not accessible.) Head south on Forest Ave, where Wright-designed residences line both sides of the street. One of the most unusual is ② **Nathan G Moore House** at 333 Forest Ave. In 1895, attorney Nathan Moore requested a home in Tudor Revival style, which Wright begrudgingly accepted as his first independent commission because he needed the money. Across the street at 318 Forest Ave, the 1902 ③ **Arthur Heurtley House** looks much more classically Wright: a low roof, long horizontal lines and leaded glass windows.

Turn east on Elizabeth Ct to find ④ **Laura Gale House** (6 Elizabeth Ct) tucked away among mature trees. It seems modest, but Wright said the residence's cantilevered balconies were the 'progenitor of Fallingwater' in Pennsylvania, perhaps his most famous construction.

Backtrack to Forest Ave. Wright considered ⑤ **Frank W Thomas House** at 210 Forest Ave the first of his Prairie-style homes. Outside the gate of ⑥ **Austin Gardens**, a bust of Wright is carved from a boulder.

Continue south on Forest Ave until the intersection with Lake St and turn east. At the corner of Lake and Kenilworth is the hulking concrete block of Wright's ⑦ **Unity Temple** (p511).

Chicago Ave
Superior St
Elizabeth Ct
Erie St
Ontario St
Lake St
North Blvd
South Blvd
Forest Ave
Marion Ct
N Marion St
N Kenilworth Ave
Scoville Park
Oak Park
1 START
7 END

After a fire in 1922, Wright completely redesigned the Moore House, but kept the English manor influence.

Wright designed his Home & Studio to fit around the ginkgo tree already growing in the east courtyard. It's still there.

Wright used concrete for Unity Temple to save money. Lightning struck the prior church, and funds to rebuild were limited.

0 200 m
0 0.1 miles

free). Begin at the park visitor center to get a ticket to enter Lincoln's 12-room abode on a 30-minute ranger-led tour. The house is the only one Lincoln ever owned, and 80% is original, looking as it did when Abe and wife Mary lived here from 1844 until they moved to the White House in 1861.

The modern **Abraham Lincoln Presidential Library & Museum** *(presidentlincoln.illinois.gov; adult/child $15/6)* contains the most complete Lincoln collection in the world. Real-deal artifacts, such as Abe's shaving mirror and presidential seal join whizbang exhibits and Disneyesque holograms that keep the kids agog.

Lincoln's immortal line 'A house divided against itself cannot stand…' was delivered in the **Old State Capitol** *(dnrhistoric.illinois.gov; free)* in the days before the Civil War. Detailed tours outline his early political life, including the dramatic Lincoln–Douglas debates in 1858.

After his assassination, Lincoln's body was returned to Springfield, where it lies today. **Lincoln's Tomb** *(dnrhistoric.illinois.gov; free)* sits in Oak Ridge Cemetery, 2 miles north of downtown. Mary and three of their four sons are buried here, too.

The sites – except the tomb – are in Springfield's center, so park once and walk. All are open daily, except the old capitol (closed Sunday and Monday).

WHAT IS A HORSESHOE SANDWICH?

It's on restaurant menus across Springfield but rarely seen anywhere else: the horseshoe sandwich. Loosen your belt before devouring this calorific concoction: an open-faced stack that consists of thickly sliced toasted bread topped with meat, French fries and a Welsh rarebit cheese sauce. It was first served at Springfield's Leland Hotel in 1928.

Hamburger is now the most common meat option for a horseshoe, but originally it was bone-in ham. Some places offer multiple meat options, including Angus beef, chicken breast, corned beef, buffalo chicken, ground lamb, pulled pork, brisket and even a veggie burger. Fortunately, many menus also offer it as a 'ponyshoe' (a smaller size).

Galena

Evocative mid-1800s boomtown

Tucked in Illinois' northwest corner near the Mississippi River, tiny Galena spreads across wooded hillsides amid rolling, barn-dotted farmland. The town was named after the lead sulfide found here, and was the location of the first mineral rush in the US in the 1820s. At its peak, Galena was the lead-mining capital of the world and had nearly as many residents as Chicago. It was the wealthiest city in Illinois, still reflected in the redbrick mansions in Greek Revival, Gothic Revival and Queen Anne styles that line the streets.

Galena was also home for a short time to Ulysses S Grant, the 18th US president and commanding general of the Union Army during the Civil War. Grant moved to Galena in 1860 to work in his father's leather goods store. When he came back to town following the Civil War, Galena residents gifted him with a two-story brick Italianate-style **home** *(granthome.org; adult/child $5/3),* fully furnished. However, he left for Washington, DC, shortly after and rarely returned. Today, the

EATING & DRINKING IN SPRINGFIELD: OUR PICKS

Luminary Kitchen & Provisions: Its weekly-changing, seasonal menus of New American plates are a treat. *4-9pm Wed-Sat, 10am-2pm Sun* **$$$**

D'Arcy's Pint: Many say this Irish pub makes the best horseshoe sandwich, along with burgers and shepherd's pie. *11am-9pm Tue-Sat* **$$**

Obed & Isaac's: Set in a 150-year-old mansion, this brewery offers sunny rooms for drinking and is also known for its horseshoes. *11am-10pm*

Wakery: Welcoming, artsy space that pours coffee by day and nonalcoholic cocktails, beers and wines by night. *7-11am & 4-10pm Mon-Fri*

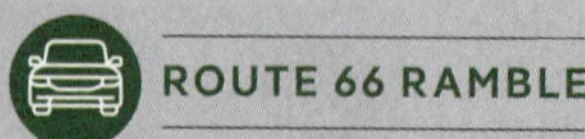

ROUTE 66 RAMBLE

Take a drive into yesteryear on the Mother Road past neon-lit diners and oddball roadside attractions.

START	END	LENGTH
Begin Historic Route 66 sign (Chicago)	Cozy Dog Drive In (Springfield)	220 miles; 6 hours

The nostalgic highway rolls for 2400 miles from Chicago to Los Angeles. No time for it? Drive the section between Chicago and Springfield to sample it in a day.

Snap a photo with the ❶ **Begin Historic Route 66 Sign** at the northwestern corner of Adams St and Michigan Ave in downtown Chicago. Head a mile southwest and fuel up for the journey at ❷ **Lou Mitchell's**, a classic diner.

Motor west to Ogden Ave (aka Old Route 66) and onward through Chicago's western suburbs. Much of Route 66 has been superseded by I-55, so you'll get funneled onto the Interstate eventually. In Bolingbrook take Joilet Rd/IL-53, which parallels I-55. Now you're back on Old Route 66 to mosey into Wilmington to see the ❸ **Gemini Giant** – a 28ft fiberglass astronaut that stands guard along the road.

Continue to Pontiac to check out the free, tchotchke-filled museum at the ❹ **Route 66 Association of Illinois**. Proceed on the Interstate or Old Route 66 beside it until tiny Atlanta, where ❺ **Tall Paul** – a sky-high statue of lumberjack Paul Bunyan – clutches a hot dog. The town's ❻ **American Giants Museum** has even more hulking fiberglass creations. Stay the course to Springfield and finish at ❼ **Cozy Dog Drive In**, where the corn dog was born.

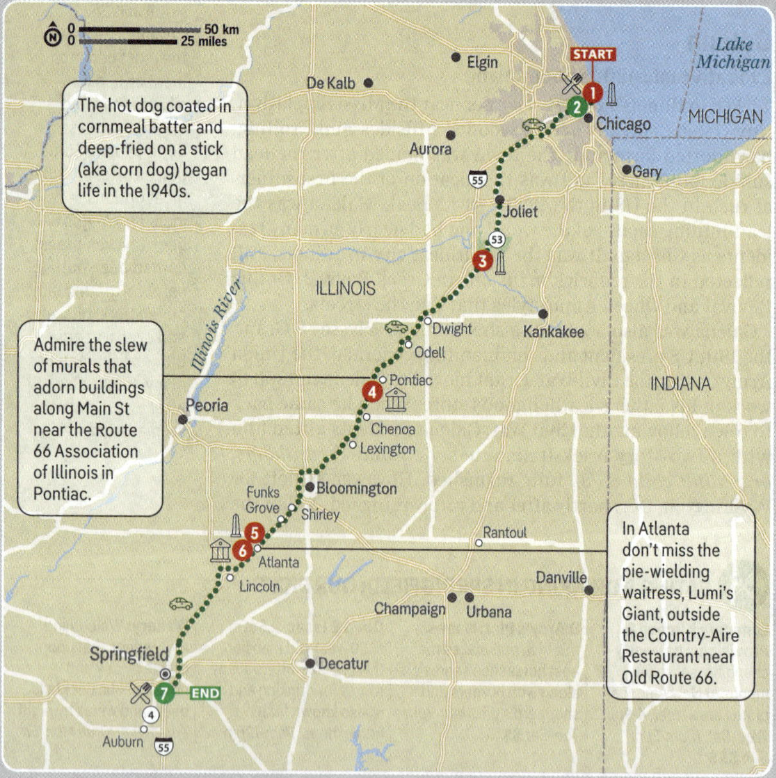

The hot dog coated in cornmeal batter and deep-fried on a stick (aka corn dog) began life in the 1940s.

Admire the slew of murals that adorn buildings along Main St near the Route 66 Association of Illinois in Pontiac.

In Atlanta don't miss the pie-wielding waitress, Lumi's Giant, outside the Country-Aire Restaurant near Old Route 66.

house retains about 90% of its original furnishings, including Grant's favorite green chair, which made it to the White House and back, and Julia Grant's 15lb Bible dating from 1865.

Cahokia Mounds

Ancient city near the Mississippi River

A stone's throw from St Louis, MO, **Cahokia Mounds State Historic Site** *(cahokiamounds.org; free)* is where the largest ancient city in North America once stood. At its peak, c 1100, some 20,000 people lived here – more than London during the same era. It's worth an hour or two of self-guided rambles around the lonely grounds.

About 70 earthen mounds survive, including the massive, 100ft-tall Monk's Mound, which you can climb and see the Gateway Arch and St Louis skyline on a clear day. 'Woodhenge,' a circle of poles used for highly accurate solar observations and date keeping, also impresses.

Shawnee Hills

Where eerie swamp meets vineyards

In the southern part of Illinois, near the border with Kentucky, the forested Shawnee Hills juts up, looking a lot like mini mountains. The rugged area makes for a great weekend break for nature lovers, especially in fall when the trees explode in color.

Start in **Shawnee National Forest** *(fs.usda.gov/shawnee; free)* and its dramatic sandstone rock formations known as **Garden of the Gods** for short trails to big views. About 65 miles southwest, the scenery shifts unexpectedly to Southern-style swampland, complete with moss-draped trees and croaking bullfrogs at **Cypress Creek National Wildlife Refuge** *(fws.gov/refuge/cypress-creek; free)*. **Cache Bayou Outfitters** *(cachebayououtfitters.com; tours adult/child $45/18)* takes you into it by canoe or kayak.

Another surprise in the area: multiple wineries. Sample the wares on the 40-mile **Shawnee Hills Wine Trail** *(shawnee winetrail.com)*. **Blue Sky Vineyard** *(blueskyvineyard.com)* is a sweet stop for a cabernet-style red while listening to live music on the patio.

Finally, if beer is your thing, **Scratch Brewing** *(scratchbeer.com)* hides amid horse-grazing pastures at Shawnee forest's western edge. Bark, berries and herbs foraged from the farm are thrown into the wild ales and sours. The bohemian microbrewery is open Friday through Sunday only.

STAGECOACH TRAIL

For a scenic detour, hop on the 26-mile Stagecoach Trail as an alternative to US 20 for the stretch of the route between Lena and Galena. The twisty road runs through the small communities of Nora, Warren, Apple River and Scales Mound, tempting a longer trip with vineyards and farm-fresh cheese along the way.

The Stagecoach Trail has been a road since the 1830s, and a stagecoach company once operated two daily services that carried passengers, post and parcels between Chicago and Galena. The railroads made the Stagecoach Trail obsolete within two decades. Cars later made the train line obsolete – passenger service ended in 1981. Today the former train station is the **Galena Country Visitor Center**, which has a free parking lot.

EATING & DRINKING IN GALENA: OUR PICKS

Fritz & Frites: This romantic little bistro serves a compact menu of German and French classics. *4-8pm Sun, Wed & Thu, to 9pm Fri & Sat* **$$**

Otto's Place: Breakfast classics and lunchtime sandwiches served in a historic building with pressed-tin ceilings. *8am-2pm Fri-Sun, to 1pm Mon & Thu* **$**

Fried Green Tomatoes: Try the lasagna or the espresso-encrusted steak in the building once owned by Grant's father. *hours vary* **$$$**

Galena Taphouse: Pours beers made within 200 miles of Galena and serves Asian-influenced dishes. *11:30am-10pm Sun-Thu, to midnight Fri & Sat*

Indiana

RACING SPECTACLE | RIVER RIDES | SOARING SANDS

Places

Indianapolis p518
Auburn p520
South Bend p520
Indiana Dunes National Park p521
Fairmount p522
Brown County p523
Ohio River Scenic Byway p523

TOP TIP

Go stargazing at Kemil Park at the Indiana Dunes! It's the one part of the park that's open 24 hours, and it's designated an International Dark Sky Community and outfitted with telescopes.

The state revs up around the Indy 500 race, and cars are cherished in Auburn and South Bend. Otherwise, it's often about the slower-paced pleasures in corn-stubbled Indiana: cycling through its center, pie-eating in Amish Country, meditating in Bloomington's Tibetan temples and admiring big architecture in small Columbus. The northwest has moody sand dunes to climb, while the south has caves to explore and rivers to canoe. A quirky labyrinth, bluegrass music shrine and famed, lipstick-kissed gravestone also make appearances across the state.

For the record, folks have called Indianans 'Hoosiers' since the 1830s, but the word's origin is unknown. One theory is that early settlers knocking on a door were met with 'Who's here?' which soon became 'Hoosier.' It's certainly something to discuss with locals, perhaps at a local cafeteria.

Fun fact: Indiana is called 'the mother of vice presidents' for the six veeps it has spawned.

GETTING AROUND

Indianapolis International Airport is the state's largest airport by far, though, depending on where you're going, Louisville, KY, is also an option. There are a couple of smaller airports, including in South Bend. Amtrak stops in Indianapolis en route to Chicago and New York City. Going by Megabus or Greyhound is faster. Driving is fastest; Hwy 46 connects Bloomington, Nashville and Columbus. I-65 and I-69 are the main regional interstates. Within Indianapolis, **IndyGo** *(indygo.net)* runs the local buses – with two BRT lines so far: Red from Broad Ripple to University of Indianapolis, and Purple from downtown to Lawrence – and **Pacers Bikeshare** *(pacersbikeshare.org)* has bike stations along the Cultural Trail downtown.

INDIANA
Waukegan
94
Lake Michigan
94
Marshall
MICHIGAN
69
Elgin
31
Chicago
Aurora
90
Gary
Indiana Dunes National Lakeshore
South Bend
20
90
Joliet
Auburn
Kankakee
Fort Wayne
57
69
65
Fairmount
OHIO
ILLINOIS
Lafayette
INDIANA
Muncie
Danville
74
Champaign
Indianapolis
70
Richmond
Terre Haute
9
70
46
Brown County
74
Columbus
Bloomington
Charles C. Deam Wilderness
Covington
65
Madison
Ohio River
50
Scottsburg
Vincennes
56
Hoosier National Forest
Milltown
Huntingburg
Ohio River
Louisville
Frankfort
64
Dale
64
Evansville
Ohio River Scenic Byway
KENTUCKY
Henderson
Owensboro
Elizabethtown
0
100 km
0
50 miles

INDIANA'S BEST FESTIVALS

Parke County Covered Bridge Festival: Known for its 31 covered bridges, which are celebrated for 10 days each year starting the second Friday of October.

Bill Monroe's Bluegrass Festival: In Morgantown, a bluegrass festival every June named after the finger-picking hero.

Abbey Road on the River: Over Memorial Day weekend at Jefferson's Big Four Pedestrian & Cycling Bridge, the world's largest Beatles and '60s music festival.

Little 500: Bloomington biking bonanza in April, where cyclists ride one-speeds for 200 laps around a quarter-mile track.

Johnny Appleseed Festival: In honor of the pioneering nurseryman, an apple-themed festival in September in Fort Wayne.

BRUCE ALAN BENNETT/SHUTTERSTOCK

Indianapolis Motor Speedway Museum

Indianapolis

The greatest spectacle in racing

Indy's super-sight is the **Indianapolis Motor Speedway** *(indianapolismotorspeedway.com)*, about 6 miles northwest of downtown and home of the 'Greatest Spectacle in Racing,' the Indy 500. Stop in at the **Indianapolis Motor Speedway Museum** *(imsmuseum.org; adult/youth/child $25/18/free)*, which features some 75 racing cars (including former winners) and championship trophies. Limited availability golf-cart tours *(adult/youth $55/35)* of the grounds and track are available from April to October (OK, you're not exactly burning rubber in a golf cart, but it's still fun to pretend while you take a lap!). A short walk from the Speedway, the **Dallara Experience Hub** *(dallara experiencehub.com; $15-30)* is where you can peek at how the speedsters are made, and try a 10-minute driving simulator.

The big race itself is held on the Sunday of Memorial Day weekend and attended by 350,000 crazed fans. If you'll be in town, Grandstand tickets can be hard to come by, so plan ahead. Try general admission, or the prerace trials and practices, for easier access and cheaper prices.

The nation's premier kids' museum

If you're traveling with kiddos, the **Children's Museum of Indianapolis** *(childrensmuseum.org; adult/youth $32/27)* is

EATING IN INDY: OUR PICKS

Milktooth: Breakfast lovers of the world unite for dishes like sweet sourdough waffles and savory Dutch baby pancakes. *10am-3pm Fri-Mon* $$

St Elmo's: Indy's oldest (1902), best steakhouse. Legendary shrimp cocktail, perfectly grilled beef. *4-10pm Mon-Thu, to 11pm Fri, 3-11pm Sat, 4-9pm Sun* $$$

Tinker Street: Fork into seasonal dishes at this New American favorite. Vegetarian and gluten-free options are plentiful. *5-9pm Mon-Thu, to 10pm Fri & Sat, to 8pm Sun* $$$

Bluebeard: Named after the Kurt Vonnegut book, James Beard–nominated fine-dining spot with daily changing menu. *11am-10pm Mon-Thu, to 11pm Fri & Sat, 5-10pm Sun* $$$

a must. It's the world's largest kids' museum, sprawled over five floors holding incredible exhibitions on dinosaurs, space stations and so much more. Indoors, it's centered around a stunning 43ft sculpture by Dale Chihuly that teaches tykes to blow glass (virtually!); and outdoors, the 7.5-acre Sports Legends Experience is the playground of your dreams.

An outing to Newfields

The 152-acre **Newfields** campus houses the **Indianapolis Museum of Art** *(discovernewfields.org; adult/youth/child $20/13/free)*, home to a terrific collection of European art (especially Turner and postimpressionists), African tribal art, South Pacific art, Chinese works, Robert Indiana's original pop-art *Love* sculpture and the largest gallery dedicated to contemporary and modern design in the US.

The campus also includes the **Virginia B Fairbanks Art & Nature Park**, with striking modern sculptures set amid 100 acres of woodlands. The park has its own entrance and is free, and open daily from sunrise to sunset – perfect for an art fix without the admission price. Adjacent to the Madeline F Elder Greenhouse, a seasonal **beer garden** offers a rotating tap list, including an exclusively brewed saison from Sun King Brewery.

Cycle from the Monon Trail to the Indy Cultural Trail

A 26-mile former rail track turned walking and cycling path, the **Monon Trail** *(bikethemonon.com)* plies through some of Indianapolis' coolest districts, stretching from Sheridan in central Indiana, through the North Indy suburb of Carmel, to hip Broad Ripple and eventually to downtown. Rent a set of wheels (outfitters listed on the Monon Trail site), then head to an access point – major ones with parking, restrooms and other infrastructure are located at, among others, 75th St, 96th St and Carmel Central Park (11th St).

At 10th and Lewis Sts, link up with the **Cultural Trail**, an 8-mile urban bike trail that goes through six downtown cultural districts, including Mass Ave, Mile Square and several public art projects. Along the route, several museums are worth a stop. The **Indiana War Memorial** *(indianawarmemorials.org; free)* is a 210ft-tall mausoleum-evoking limestone tribute honoring Hoosier veterans of WWI, while the **Eiteljorg Museum** *(eiteljorg.org; adult/youth $20/12)* features Native American basketry, pots and masks, as well as a Western painting collection with works by Frederic Remington and Georgia O'Keeffe. Eiteljorg is located within the

INDIANA'S CAFETERIA SCENE

Cafeterias are an Indiana tradition, where diners grab a tray, slide it along a metal railing, and load it up with plates of hot and cold dishes. Fried chicken, meatloaf, mac 'n' cheese, freshly baked rolls and sugar cream pie are all beloved staples. One of Indiana's first cafeterias opened in 1900, with many more arriving on the scene in the decades that followed, like Gray Brothers Cafeteria in 1944 and MCL Cafeteria in 1950. Since then, many of Indiana's time-honored neighborhood cafeterias have disappeared – but Gray Brothers and MCL still remain.

DRINKING IN INDY: OUR PICKS

Sun King Brewery: Indy's young and hip swill pints, flights and growlers, and spill onto the patio in summer. *11am-9pm Mon & Tue, to 10pm Wed-Sat, to 8pm Sun*

Slippery Noodle Inn: Indiana's oldest bar (1850), with stints as various venues; now a blues club. *11am-1am Mon-Fri, noon-2am Sat, 4pm-midnight Sun*

Centerpoint Brewing Company: True-to-style beers in a former race-car-engine factory and mail-sorting facility. *3-9pm Mon-Wed, to 10pm Thu, noon-10pm Fri & Sat, noon-8pm Sun*

Metazoa Brewing Co: Pet-friendliest brewery: on-site dog park, donates 5% of profits to animal/wildlife organizations. *1-10pm Mon-Wed, from 11am Thu-Sat, 11am-9pm Sun*

MORE OF INDIANA'S TOP STATE PARKS & FORESTS

Falls of the Ohio State Park: This park has only rapids, no falls, but is of interest for its 390-million-year-old fossil beds.

Clifty Falls State Park: Large, wooded space in Madison with excellent hiking, waterfall views, creeks, canyons and campgrounds.

Turkey Run State Park: Known for its hiking, particularly the ladders of Trail 3, along with horseback riding, swimming and camping.

Mounds State Park: Featuring 10 prehistoric earthworks, largest is the Great Mound, built around 160 BCE by the Adena and Hopewell peoples.

Clark State Forest: Indiana's oldest state forest, which includes part of Indiana's longest hiking trail, the Knobstone Trail.

White River State Park *(whiteriverstatepark.org)*, the urban green space that encompasses seven city attractions, including the Indianapolis Zoo, Indiana State Museum and NCAA Hall of Champions.

Finally, the **Kurt Vonnegut Museum & Library** *(kurtvonnegutlibrary.org; $12/8)* pays homage to the famous author born and raised in Indy, who was an anti-censorship and peace activist. The museum, free the first Monday of the month, exhibits artifacts from his life.

Auburn

Check out classic cars

Classic-car connoisseurs should stop in Auburn, about 50 miles southeast of Amish Country, where the Cord Company produced the USA's favorite autos in the 1920s and '30s. Two remarkable car museums, the **Auburn Cord Duesenberg Automobile Museum** *(automobilemuseum.org; adult/student $15/10)* and the **National Auto & Truck Museum** *(natmus.org; adult/child $12/7)*, are conveniently lined up next door to one another for your car-viewing pleasure. The former has a 120-strong inventory of early roadsters – including Babe Ruth's Auburn 8-88 Roadster and Frank Lloyd Wright's orange Cord L-29 – in a beautiful art-deco setting that was once part of the original Auburn Automotive Company. The latter has a bit of everything, from toy cars to gas pumps to vintage rigs. You can also purchase a 'campus pass' for combined admission *($25/15)*.

South Bend

From horse-drawn carriages to motor vehicles

South Bend's automotive legacy stems from its homegrown carmaker Studebaker (later the Studebaker-Packard Corporation), which started off by manufacturing horse-drawn wagons and carriages in the 1850s, before transitioning to motor vehicles to put out its first electric car in 1902 and first gas-powered car in 1904. The **Studebaker National Museum** *(studebakermuseum.org; adult/student/child $11/7/free)* is where you can get a sense of the industry's evolution through the ages, as you meander through three floors of shiny vehicles that range from vintage carriages to a gorgeous 1956 Packard.

EATING IN NORTHERN INDIANA: OUR PICKS

Rise'n Roll: Now a northern Indiana chain, it started here in Middlebury; all because of the sought-after cinnamon-caramel donuts. *7am-4pm Mon-Sat* $

Village Inn Restaurant: Sublime pies in Amish Country, baked in the wee hours of the morning. Burgers, meat loaf and other mains. *5am-8pm Mon-Fri, to 11am Sat* $

Octave Grill: In Chesterton, burgers made with grass-fed beef, paired with a wonderful selection of rotating craft beers. *3-9pm Mon & Thu-Sat, to 8pm Sun* $

Rocco's: A South Bend institution, ladling marinara sauce since 1951. After football games, lines of Notre Dame alums run out the door. *4:30-10:30pm Tue-Sat* $

TOP EXPERIENCE

Indiana Dunes National Park

In addition to being the state's most visited site, attracting 3.5 million visitors per year, sunny beaches, rustling grasses and woodsy campgrounds are the Indiana Dunes' claim to fame. The area is hugely popular on summer days with sunbathers from Chicago and towns throughout Northern Indiana. Beyond its beaches, the area is noted for sweet hiking trails that meander up the dunes and through the woodlands.

JON LAURIAT/SHUTTERSTOCK

National Park Trails

The Dunes, which became the USA's 61st national park in 2019, stretch along 15 miles of Lake Michigan shoreline (swimming allowed). A short walk away from the beaches are several hiking paths; the best are the Bailly-Chellberg Trail (2.5 miles) that winds by a still-operating 1870s farm; and the Heron Rookery Trail (2 miles), where blue herons flock (though there's no actual rookery).

Plants & Wildlife

Oddly, all this natural bounty lies smack-dab next to smoke-belching factories, yet it still boasts remarkable features: it has 1100 native species of plants; dunes formed after melted glaciers, which top out at 192ft; and 370 species of birds. Birding and fishing are popular, as is beachcombing (beach glass collecting allowed, fossil and pebble collecting prohibited).

State Park & Three Dune Challenge

The **state park** is a 2100-acre, shoreside pocket within the national park; it's located at the end of Hwy 49, near Chesterton. Don't miss the **3 Dune Challenge**, a 1.5-mile, 552ft vertical climb to the park's three highest dunes: Mt Jackson (176ft), Mt Holden (184ft) and Mt Tom (192ft). It starts on Trail 8, by the **Indiana Dunes State Park Nature Center**.

TOP TIPS

- America the Beautiful Pass holders are covered to enter the national park area, but not the state park area, of the Indiana Dunes.
- For the state park, entrance is free on weekdays, November to mid-April.
- Kemil Beach is one section of the park that's open 24 hours, for stargazing.

PRACTICALITIES

- indianadunes.com
- national park 6am-11pm, state park 7am-11pm
- 7-day pass per car $12-25

TIBETAN CULTURE IN BLOOMINGTON

The 14th Dalai Lama's brother Thubten Jigme Norbu came here from Eastern Tibet, teaching at Indiana University in the 1960s; Tibetan temples, monasteries and culture followed in his footsteps. In 1979, Thubten Jigme Norbu founded the colorful, prayer-flag-covered Tibetan Mongolian Buddhist Cultural Center to introduce the people of Indiana to Tibetan culture and to support Tibetan exile communities. The center, in southern Bloomington, is a draw for its traditional stupas, gift shop, open meditation sessions and various workshops and retreats. Across the city, in northern Bloomington, the Gaden Khachoe Shing Monastery is another place of peace. And downtown, Tibetan fare features at restaurants like Little Tibet.

Tour the University of Notre Dame

Founded in 1842, the **University of Notre Dame** *(nd.edu)* is often touted as one of the USA's prettiest higher education campuses. To get a good look at it, a free walking tour is recommended (it departs from the **Eck Visitors Center**; times vary and tours are limited to the first 25 people who sign up in person). But if you're short on time, at least pop into the stunning Basilica of the Sacred Heart (a neo-Gothic cathedral awash in stained-glass windows and murals painted by Vatican artist Luigi Gregori); the Golden Dome (the university's main admin building – often considered the nation's leading collegiate landmark – with a gorgeous rotunda topped with a 4400lb statue of Mary); and the Grotto of Our Lady of Lourdes (a recreation of the original in France). All three are next to each other on the north side of God Quad.

Fairmount

Hunt down James Dean's hometown

Pocket-sized Fairmount is but a few streets surrounded by farmland, but it's on the international map as the hometown of 1950s actor James Dean, one of the original icons of cool (he was born 10.5 miles north in Marion but raised by his relatives in Fairmount). Fans can follow Dean's footsteps, from birth to death.

Start at the **James Dean Museum** *(thejamesdeanmuseum.com; adult/child $10/free),* where you can see the world's largest collection of his personal belongings, ranging from his baby crib and high-school car, to his 1955 Triumph TR5 Trophy 500cc and 1947 Czech 125cc motorcycles, and more. (You'll also notice tributes to Garfield creator Jim Davis, Fairmount's other famous figure.) Other spots include the **James Dean Birth Site Memorial**, a 6ft-tall black granite monument erected in 2015 to honor the spot where the House of Seven Gables once stood; the farmhouse where Jimmy grew up; and his often lipstick-kissed **gravestone** in Park Cemetery. There's also a privately owned **James Dean Gallery** *(jamesdeangallery.com; free)* with several rooms of memorabilia in an old Victorian home downtown. Every September, Fairmount celebrates the **James Dean Festival** – thousands of fans pour in for three days of music, classic cars, a James Dean lookalike contest and other events honoring the Hollywood legend.

DRINKING IN NORTHERN INDIANA: OUR PICKS

3 Floyds Brewing: In Munster, Zombie Dust, a flowery pale ale; and Dark Lord, a legendary Russian imperial stout, have a cult following. *noon-7pm Tue-Sat*

18th Street Brewery: Warehouse in Hammond for saisons, sours and IPAs. Also in Gary. *noon-9pm Mon-Thu, 11am-10pm Fri & Sat, 11am-6pm Sun*

Mad Anthony's Auburn Tap Room: Taproom in a historic downtown building with big windows and exposed-brick walls. *11am-10pm, to 11pm Fri & Sat*

Crooked Ewe Brewery: Find a wealth of hops-heavy IPAs at this riverside brewpub in South Bend. Elevated bar fare, including vegan options. *noon-9pm, to 10pm Fri & Sat*

WILDNERDPIX/SHUTTERSTOCK

Brown County State Park

ARCHITECTURAL HERITAGE IN COLUMBUS

When you think of the USA's great architectural cities – Chicago, New York, Washington, DC – Columbus, IN, doesn't quite leap to mind, but it's a remarkable gallery of design. Since the 1940s, Columbus and its leading corporation, Fortune 500 engineering company Cummins, have commissioned some of the world's best architects, including Eero Saarinen, Richard Meier and IM Pei, to create both public and private buildings. More than 70 notable structures and public art pieces span a wide area. Some of the most famous are **First Christian Church**, a brick-and-limestone Modernist masterpiece; and **Miller House & Garden**, the mid-century-modern residence of Cummins president J Irwin Miller – both designed by Saarinen.

Brown County

Indiana's largest state park

A few miles southeast of Nashville, **Brown County State Park** *(browncountystatepark.net; $9/day)* is Indiana's largest state park, known as the Little Smoky Mountains for its steep wooded hills and fog-cloaked ravines. Trails stripe the 15,700-acre stand of oak, hickory and birch trees, and give hikers, mountain bikers and horseback riders access to the area's green hill country. The mile-long **Ogle Hollow Nature Preserve Trail** is a good place to see the rare yellowwood tree and its fragrant blossoms. And **Bean Blossom Overlook** is one of the best spots to take in the color-shifting treetops across Brown County.

Ohio River Scenic Byway

A river town, a cave and Lincoln's boyhood home

The Ohio River marks the state's southern border – and Ohio's and Indiana's, too – with the Ohio River Scenic Byway winding its way through nearly 1000 miles of lush and hilly landscape along the churning waterway. Indiana's 303-mile portion *(ohio riverbyway.com)* of the 943-mile route comprises Hwys 56,

EATING & DRINKING IN SOUTHERN INDIANA: OUR PICKS

Samira: Tasty Afghan food in downtown Bloomington: excellent kebabs, vegetarian dishes and lunch buffet. *5-9pm Mon-Sat, plus 11am-2pm Thu & Fri* **$$**

Henry Social Club: New American fine dining and the best bar in Columbus for a boutique cocktail, set in an open-concept kitchen. *5-9pm Tue-Sat* **$$$**

Exchange Pub + Kitchen: In New Albany, upmarket pub with an industrial-chic ambience. Burgers do not disappoint. *11am-10pm, to 11pm Fri & Sat, to 9pm Sun* **$$$**

Wood Shop: In Bloomington, this is the experimental sister site of more mainstream Upland Brewing Co next door – it's the all-sours brewery where funk flows. *5-9pm Fri & Sat*

INDIANA'S HARMONIST & UTOPIAN HISTORY

In southwest Indiana, the Wabash River forms the border with Illinois. Beside it, south of I-64, captivating New Harmony is the site of two early communal-living experiments. In the 1814, the Harmony Society, a German Christian sect led by George Rapp, developed a sophisticated, self-sufficient, model community here while awaiting the Second Coming. In 1825, the Welsh utopian Robert Owen acquired the town, renaming it New Harmony. By 1827, it had failed and dissolved. Today, New Harmony retains an air of contemplation, if not otherworldliness, which can be felt at the town's information center, the Atheneum; the Roofless Church; and the Labyrinth, a recreation of the Harmonists' original hedge-maze design.

ZACK FRANK/SHUTTERSTOCK

Lincoln Boyhood National Memorial

156, 62 and 66, and makes for a scenic drive, with stops at a beautifully preserved mid-19th-century river town, a cave with astonishing underground formations and Abraham Lincoln's boyhood home.

Of all the charms along this stretch, few outdo the convivial and cozy vibe of small town **Madison** *(visitmadison.org)*. Home to the largest contiguous National Historic Landmark District in the US, Madison is a hub of Federal, Greek Revival and Italianate-style architecture along its postcard-perfect Main St. Grab a burger at **Hinkle's** *(hinkleburger.com)*, an old-school diner in action since 1933; and a beer at **Mad Paddle Brewstillery** *(madpaddle.com)*, a couple of blocks south.

Heading west, **Milltown** is where you can access the beautiful **Blue River**, a tributary of the Ohio River that's perfect for a paddle. **Cave Country Canoes** *(cavecountrycanoes.com)* puts on half-, full- or two-day trips (prices vary depending on the group size). About 4 miles west, a plunge into **Marengo Cave** *(marengocave.com; adult/child 40min tour $23/14, 60min tour $26/16, combination tour $32/2)* is highly recommended. The privately owned landmark offers tours walking past stalagmites and other ancient formations.

Then, off I-64 and 4 miles south of **Dale**, the **Lincoln Boyhood National Memorial** *(nps.gov/libo; free)* is where young Abe, who grew up to become the 16th US president, lived from age seven to 21. The memorial also includes admission to a working pioneer farm, open in the summer, that's modeled after the Lincoln farm but is not the original. A 1-mile trail loop from the memorial takes in the highlights.

Ohio

CITY CHARM | ERIE ISLANDS | AMISH COUNTRY

The nation's seventh most populous state has big cities Cleveland, Cincinnati and Columbus that lead its urban charge, rolling out a spread of kicky dining options, IPA-loving breweries and one-of-a-kind museums. Northern Cleveland exudes a feisty, rock-and-roll vibe, while southern Cincinnati feels more languorous and European. Columbus – the largest of the three, with a population of over 900,000 – is the polished tech and art hub that rises up in the middle, home to Ohio State University. Meanwhile, Ohio's rural side is way off the grid, from the horse-and-buggy-filled roads of its enormous Amish community to the moonshine makers in its southeastern hills. It makes for an intriguing mash-up, with just a short drive between wildly different lifestyles. In between, the roadways lead to the world's fastest roller coasters, rocking party islands, beatnik towns, pie shops and a mist-draped national park.

Places

Cleveland p526
Cuyahoga Valley National Park p528
Cincinnati p529
Columbus p530
Sandusky p531
Kelleys Island p532
Ohio Amish Country p533
Logan p534
Dayton p534

TOP TIP

Camp overnight in Hocking Hills State Park! It's Ohio's favorite park for good reason, and there are abundant campsites available, with spectacular scenery all around.

GETTING AROUND

Cleveland Hopkins International Airport is Ohio's busiest airport – linked to downtown by the Red Line train – followed by Columbus, Cincinnati and Dayton. John Glenn Columbus International Airport is 10 miles east of downtown, while Cincinnati/Northern Kentucky International Airport is in Kentucky. Cleveland, Cincinnati and Sandusky are on Amtrak train routes; Columbus is not. Regardless, Megabus and Greyhound are cheaper and faster. Driving is best. For Cuyahoga Valley, the national park is just off I-77. Amish Country lies between Cleveland (80 miles north) and Columbus (100 miles southwest), with I-71 and I-77 flanking the area. US 33 leads to Logan, and US 23 to Chillicothe and the Hopewell mounds.

Within Cleveland, the **RTA** *(riderta.com)* runs buses and trains. Within Cincinnati, there are **Metro** *(go-metro.com)* buses, a **streetcar** *(cincinnatibellconnector.com)* and **Red Bike** *(cincyredbike.org)* stations.

Cleveland

From the Beatles to the Rolling Stones

Cleveland's top attraction, the **Rock and Roll Hall of Fame & Museum** *(rockhall.com; adult/youth/child $39.50/29.50/free)*, is like an overstuffed attic bursting with groovy finds: Jimi Hendrix's Stratocaster, Prince's Cloud #2 Blue Angel Guitar, Keith Moon's platform shoes, John Lennon's Sgt Pepper suit and a 1966 piece of hate mail to the Rolling Stones from a cursive-writing Fijian. It's more than memorabilia, though. Multimedia exhibits trace the history and social context of rock music and the performers who created it.

EATING IN CLEVELAND: OUR PICKS

Citizen Pie: Wood-fired Neapolitan-style pizzas, with a mighty smoked pepperoni. Second location in Ohio City. *noon-9pm Tue-Sat, to 8pm Sun* **$**

Mitchell's Ice Cream: Mitchell's revamped an old movie theater. Watch through big glass windows as staff blend the rich flavors. One of 10 locales. *11am-10:30pm* **$**

Abundance Culinary: Four types of dumplings, along with rice, noodles and mains, plus Sichuan-inspired cocktails. *8am-10pm Tue-Thu, to 11pm Fri & Sat* **$$**

Zhug: Upmarket Mediterranean mezze (braised lamb, smoked calamari and roasted vegetables) in casual environs. *4-10pm Mon-Thu, to 11pm Fri & Sat* **$$$**

Why is the museum in Cleveland? Because this is the hometown of Alan Freed, the disc jockey who popularized the term 'rock and roll' in the early 1950s, and because the city lobbied hard and paid big. Be prepared for crowds.

Explore the arts and entertainment

Cleveland's fine and performing arts are sure to keep you entertained day and night. Begin at the **Cleveland Museum of Art** *(clevelandart.org; free; closed Mondays)*, a mammoth collection of European paintings; African, Asian and American art; and special paid exhibitions – all set around a dazzling, light-drenched atrium. Head to the 2nd floor for works from Impressionists, Picasso and surrealists. Interactive touchscreens are stationed throughout, providing fun ways to learn more; download the free ArtLens app for additional content. Free guided tours depart at 1pm and 1:30pm each day; they're limited to 15 participants, so advance tickets are recommended.

Nighttime is show time at the city's **Playhouse Square** *(playhousesquare.org)*, the nation's second-largest theater district. Several stages comprise the elegant performing arts center, which hosts theater, opera, ballet and beyond. Take note of the massive sparkler dangling above: that's North America's largest outdoor chandelier, 44ft tall and shining with 4200 faux crystals.

A walk on the West Side

The West Side is home to some of Cleveland's hippest neighborhoods. Start your day at the **West Side Market** *(westsidemarket.org)*, a European-style market overflowing with greengrocers and their produce, as well as purveyors of Hungarian sausage, Italian cannoli and Polish pierogi. The surrounding **Ohio City** is an ultra walkable little enclave known for its historic buildings, vibrant street art, cute boutique shops, delicious dining scene and several breweries, including the tried-and-true **Great Lakes Brewing Company** *(greatlakesbrewing.com)*, cozy **Bookhouse Brewing** *(bookhouse.beer)* and Eastern European newcomer **Hansa Brewery** *(hansabrewery.com)*. Also here, in a pocket called Hingetown, is **Transformer Station** *(clevelandart.org; free; open Thursday to Sunday)*, a Cleveland Museum of Art–affiliated gallery that showcases emerging artists, new media and live music at a repurposed industrial substation.

Nearby, the west bank of the Flats is home to the **Greater Cleveland Aquarium** *(greaterclevelandaquarium.com;*

LAY OF 'THE LAND'

Nicknamed 'The Land,' Cleveland is bisected by the Cuyahoga River, which divides the West and East sides. The city's center is at **Public Square**, with most major attractions downtown on the lakefront. Nearby, the Warehouse District and the Flats are abuzz with a youthful vibe. Eastward are Asiatown, University Circle, Little Italy, Coventry Village and Collinwood. Westward are hip Ohio City and Tremont, straddling I-90; the western bank of the Flats; and Gordon Square Arts District, a fun pocket along Detroit Ave between W 56th and W 69th Sts. Cleveland's public transit system, the RTA, is a handy network of buses, a three-line train service and a trolley that runs between Public Square and the Wolstein Center.

DRINKING IN CLEVELAND: OUR PICKS

Noble Beast Brewing Co: A homey place for German-style ales and pub fare. *11:30am-11pm Tue-Thu, to midnight Fri & Sat to 10pm Sun*

Millard Fillmore Presidential Library: Tell your pals you're going to a presidential library. It's actually a dive bar in Collinwood. *4pm-2:30am Mon-Fri, from noon Sat & Sun*

Jerman's Cafe: One of Cleveland's oldest bars, opened in 1908 by a Slovenian immigrant. Just a few beers on tap. *noon-1am Mon & Tue, to 2am Wed-Sat, 1pm-midnight Sun*

Great Lakes Brewing Company: Second-biggest craft-beer maker in the state wins prizes for its brewed suds. *11:30am-10pm Mon-Thu, to 11pm Fri & Sat, 11am-5pm Sun*

TOP EXPERIENCE

Cuyahoga Valley National Park

The Cuyahoga River worms over a forested valley, earning its Native American name of 'crooked river' (or possibly 'place of the jawbone'). Either name is evocative, and hints at the mystical beauty that Ohio's only national park engenders on a cool morning, when the mists thread the woods and all you hear is the honk of Canadian geese and the fwup-fwup-whoosh of a great blue heron flapping over its hunting grounds.

Brandywine Falls

KARENFOLEYPHOTOGRAPHY/SHUTTERSTOCK

TOP TIPS

- Parking lots at the Ledges and Brandywine Falls fill up quickly. Opt for mornings, evenings and weekdays.
- The Boston Mills Visitor Center is a good starting point.
- If you cycle, hike or run along the towpath trail in one direction, ride the train back for just $5.

The Ledges

This overlook is probably the most photographed place in the park, with an unobstructed vista looking west over the valley to eternity. There's a loop trail nearby, a little over 2 miles in length, that's a nice leg stretcher.

Brandywine Falls

Long considered one of the park's best attractions, this pretty spill of ice-cold water sits in a wooden idyll, and is accessed via a 1.5-mile round-trip hike that features some light elevation gain (160ft).

Ohio & Erie Canal Towpath Trail

The park's main trail follows the old Ohio & Erie Canal, which once served as one of the primary historical arteries into the American west. Boats pulled by mules ran adjacent to this path, now an ideal thoroughfare for hikers and cyclists, intersecting with many of the park's other trails.

Cuyahoga Valley Scenic Railroad

An old-school iron carriage *(cvsr.org; adult/child from $25/20)* chugs along a pleasant course from Akron to Independence, going through the heart of the park, with a depot midway at Peninsula. The most expensive seats have glass-topped domes, and special themed rides are offered, too. A full round trip takes around 3½ hours.

PRACTICALITIES

- nps.gov/cuva
- 24hr
- free

adult/child $20/14), a fun and interactive experience for the littles in tow, while **Tremont** and its bevy of trendy bars are a treat for the bigs. In summer, white-sand **Edgewater Park Beach** comes alive with sunbathers, swimmers and concession stands. Finish at nearby **Gordon Square Arts District** *(gordonsquare.org)* for dinner at **Blue Habanero** *(bluehabanerocleveland.com)*, a show at the **Cleveland Public Theatre** *(cptonline.org)* or live music (and a loaded hot dog!) at **Happy Dog** *(happydogcleveland.com)*.

Cincinnati

Get acquainted with Over-the-Rhine

At downtown's northern edge, the historic **Over-the-Rhine** (OTR) neighborhood is home to an impressive collection of 19th-century Italianate and Queen Anne buildings that have morphed into trendy dining venues, bars and shops. Begin at **Findlay Market** *(findlaymarket.org)*, the wrought-iron-framed structure in continuous operation since the 1850s; and mosey around the more than 50 stalls, where you can find meat, cheese, pastries, produce, flowers and more. For a truly local experience, cross the street to **Eckerlin Meats** *(eckerlinmeats.com)* and try some homemade *guetta*, a pan-fried patty made of ground meat and steel-cut oats, often served for breakfast in a sandwich or omelet. It's a unique food you won't find anywhere else besides Cincinnati and Northern Kentucky.

From there, it's on to **Cincinnati's Brewing Heritage Trail** *(brewingheritagetrail.org)*. Findlay marks one of two trailheads – the other being at Grant Park – for this fun three-quarter-mile route that takes you past classic brewhouses and historic saloons in the neighborhood. Markers along the way tell how Cincy was one of the nation's leading beer producers in the late 1800s. Download the free app for a self-guided tour or book a guided tour.

Go museum-hopping

Cincinnati has several museums of note close to downtown, not far from the riverfront, that make for a full day of history and arts. Starting in the West End, begin at the **Cincinnati Museum Center** *(cincymuseum.org; adult/child $19.50/12.50)*, a complex that includes the **Museum of Natural History & Science** (with a cave inside!), a children's museum and a history museum. The complex occupies the 1933 Union Terminal, an art-deco jewel still used by Amtrak; its interior features fantastic murals made of local Rookwood tiles.

OHIO'S QUIRKY SIGHTS

World's Largest Rubber Stamp (Cleveland): At Willard Park, Claes Oldenburg's 70,000lb 'Free' stamp sculpture is a photo-op favorite.

American Sign Museum (Cincinnati): An awesome cache of flashing, lightbulb-studded beacons in an old parachute factory.

World's Largest Cuckoo Clock (Sugarcreek): A 23ft-tall clock lets loose every half-hour, when a mechanical Bavarian couple dances a polka.

Christmas Story House (Cleveland): The original house of the 1983 film *A Christmas Story* sits in Tremont, complete with a leg lamp.

Paul A Johnson Pencil Sharpener Museum (Logan): One man's trove of 3400 pencil sharpeners, reportedly the USA's largest.

EATING IN CINCINNATI: OUR PICKS

Eagle OTR: Serving modern soul food, including fried chicken with spicy honey, white cheddar grits and spoon bread. *11am-10pm Sun, to 11pm Mon-Thu, to midnight Fri & Sat* $

Bee's Barbecue OTR: Tasty brisket, ribs, pulled pork and other offerings in casual environs with welcoming staff. *11am-11pm Tue-Thu, to midnight Fri & Sat, to 9pm Sun* $$

Bridges: Build your own Nepali rice bowl with meat/vegan toppings at this homey spot in Northside. Other locations: downtown, Elmwood. *11am-9pm Mon-Thu, to 10pm Fri & Sat* $$

Sotto: Italian fine dining tucked in a downtown basement. Reservations are a must. *11am-2pm & 4-10pm Mon-Thu, to 11pm Fri, 4-11pm Sat, 4-9pm Sun* $$$

OHIO'S BEST FESTIVALS

Cleveland Kurentovanje: The city's large Slovenian population gathers at this multiday spring festival, where a parade is led by Kurenti, the mythical monsters who chase away winter.

Bockfest Cincinnati: Each March, traditional Bock beers flow at venues across Over-the-Rhine.

Oktoberfest Zinzinnati: Beer, bratwursts and mania. It's the US' largest Oktoberfest celebration, with well over half a million revelers convening at Sawyer Point.

IngenuityFest: In Cleveland, a three-day fall festival full of art, technology and creative experiences.

Blink: Large-scale light projections and interactive art feature at this four-day event in Cincinnati in the fall.

Over in downtown Cincy, the **National Underground Railroad Freedom Center** *(freedomcenter.org; $16.50/11.50)* details the city's history as a prominent stop on the Underground Railroad and a hub for abolitionist activities. The center displays artifacts along the historical road from slavery to freedom, and also covers modern struggles for civil rights. A few blocks north is the **Contemporary Arts Center** *(contemporaryartscenter.org; adult/child $12/free)*, displaying modern art in an avant-garde building designed by Zaha Hadid.

Eastward, round out the day at the **Cincinnati Art Museum** *(cincinnatiartmuseum.org; free)*, where its impressive collection spans 6000 years, with an emphasis on ancient Middle Eastern and European art.

Cross the Ohio River by foot

The mighty Ohio River is the border between Ohio and Kentucky, with a couple of notable bridges connecting Cincinnati to its southern neighbors. For those interested in a little jaunt into Kentucky, it's simple and straightforward to go via one bridge, then return via the other, while also enjoying the lovely green space that flanks the river on each side. Begin by walking around the well-tended **Smale Riverfront Park**, then take the **John A Roebling Suspension Bridge** *(roeblingbridge.org)* across to Covington, KY. A forerunner of John Roebling's famous Brooklyn Bridge in New York, the elegant 1867 spanner features Romanesque arches and draped cables that are highly photogenic. From Covington, it's an easy 30-minute walk through General James Taylor Park to Newport, where you can take the pedestrian-only **Purple People Bridge** *(purplepeoplebridge.com)* back to Cincy. You'll be deposited at **Sawyer Point**, a nifty park dotted by whimsical monuments and flying pigs.

Columbus

Stroll through a German village

Wandering through this remarkably large, restored all-brick **German Village** *(germanvillage.com)*, a half-mile south of downtown, feels like you've entered the 19th century. The historic village, first platted in 1814, is complete with cobbled streets, beer halls, cute boutique shops, arts-filled parks, and Italianate and Queen Anne architecture. The **German Village Society** has archives and maps.

Bibliophiles should stop in at the **Book Loft** *(bookloft.com)*, a sprawling bookshop occupying a block of pre–Civil War

DRINKING IN CINCINNATI: OUR PICKS

Uncle Leo's: Friendly bartenders will serve you a 'spaghett' – Miller High Life with, usually, Aperol. *4-11pm Mon-Wed, to 1am Thu, to 2am Fri, noon-2am Sat, noon-11pm Sun*

Rhinegeist Brewery: One of Ohio's biggest breweries. Try Truth IPA or 20 other brews on tap. Picnic tables and a rooftop. *3-10pm Mon-Thu, noon-1am Fri & Sat, noon-9pm Sun*

Longfellow: Cozy and candlelit cocktail bar in a vintage building with creaking hardwood floors and exposed brick walls. *4pm-2am Wed-Fri, from 2pm Sat & Sun*

Low Spark: Easygoing spot; cocktails served at a bar set around an illuminated fish tank. *4pm-midnight Mon-Wed, to 2:30am Thu & Fri, noon-2:30am Sat, noon-10pm Sun*

CHRISTIAN HINKLE/SHUTTERSTOCK

John A Roebling Suspension Bridge

buildings, where you're guaranteed to get lost in the labyrinth of 32 rooms stacked to the rafters with bestsellers, children's books, manga, memoirs and more. After, head over to **Schmidt's** *(schmidthaus.com)* to shovel in Old Country staples like sausage and schnitzel, but save room for the whopping half-pound cream puffs.

Peep at Ohio's biggest planetarium

COSI *(cosi.org, adult/child from $30/25),* an acronym for the Center of Science and Industry, ranks high in the pantheon of children's museums around the country, with 300-plus hands-on exhibits that include a dinosaur gallery (with a mechanical T. rex), space gallery (with a replica space station to explore) and high-wire unicycle ride. Ohio's largest planetarium, a native prairie, live science shows and a 3D theater round out the whopping spread. Check the calendar for special events, too, like COSI Farm Days and COSI After Dark.

TOP ART SPOTS IN COLUMBUS

Otherworld: Futuristic, fantastical art museum: 32,000 sq ft of immersive mixed-reality installations.

Short North Arts District: Hosts a gallery hop the first Saturday of each month, featuring exhibitions, live performances and vendors.

Columbus Museum of Art: Highlights include Edward Hopper's *Morning Sun* and several works by Henri Matisse and Pablo Picasso.

Franklinton Fridays: Area galleries, studios and bars put on an art crawl on the second Friday of each month, with food and entertainment.

Wexner Center for the Arts: Ohio State University's contemporary arts center has cutting-edge art exhibits, films and performances.

Sandusky

Get topsy turvy and go round and round

In summer the good-time resort region of Erie Lakeshore is one of the busiest places in Ohio. Boaters come to party, daredevils come to ride roller coasters, and outdoorsy types

EATING & DRINKING IN COLUMBUS: OUR PICKS

DK Diner: Classic diner experience in Grandview: omelets, corned beef hash, and biscuits and gravy. *6am-3pm Mon & Tue, to 9pm Wed-Fri, 7am-9pm Sat, 7am-3pm Sun* $

Hoyo's Kitchen: *Hoyo* is 'mother' in Somali, and the siblings running this venue use Mom's recipes. It's in North Market Downtown. *11am-7pm Tue-Sat, to 5pm Sun* $$

Service Bar: It's in Middle West Spirits Distillery, so signature cocktails are made with bourbon fresh from the tanks. Also serves food. *5-10pm Wed & Thu, from 4pm Fri & Sat*

Land-Grant Brewing Co: Couple of dozen taps, and flights. Rotating food-truck line up. *3-10pm Mon-Wed, 11am-10pm Thu, 11am-midnight Fri & Sat, 11am-8pm Sun*

CANTON: BIRTHPLACE OF THE NFL

You may be wondering why the **Pro Football Hall of Fame** is located in Canton, Ohio. It's because Canton is where the American Professional Football Association, which later became the National Football League (NFL), was founded on September 17, 1920. Back then, Canton had its own team, the very successful Canton Bulldogs, who played in the Ohio League, winning titles in 1916, 1917 and 1919, before joining the national league and becoming a 1922 and 1923 champion there too – the NFL's first two-time champion. The Bulldogs' players included the legendary Jim Thorpe. All that and the people of Canton campaigned mightily for it.

DAVID MCGILL 71/SHUTTERSTOCK

Cedar Point

come to cycle and kayak. The season lasts from mid-May to mid-September – and then just about everything shuts down.

For kids (and adults) who love a thrill, a stop at **Cedar Point** *(cedarpoint.com; from $70)* is a must. As one of the world's top amusement parks, it's known for its 18 adrenaline-pumping roller coasters, with such stomach-droppers as Steel Vengeance, which provides 27 seconds of weightlessness, the most 'airtime' of any coaster on the planet.

Nearby, the whimsical **Merry-Go-Round Museum** *(merrygoroundmuseum.org; adult/youth/child $10/6/free)* features a fully refurbished, vintage Allan Herschell carousel headlined by lead horse, the c 1915 Stargazer. Children will delight in taking a spin atop antique ponies, or maybe a lion, an elephant, a pig or an ostrich – and even a less traditional sea monster. In addition to enjoying the museum's centerpiece, you can also go on a tour to learn about merry-go-round history and culture, and watch artisans at work as they restore period pieces.

Kelleys Island

Gargantuan glacial grooves

For a tamer experience, Kelleys Island offers pretty 19th-century buildings, pleasant beaches and scenic landscapes.

EATING & DRINKING ON THE ERIE LAKESHORE: OUR PICKS

Topsy Turvey's Bar & Grill: Wharf-side venue with Lake Erie perch, homemade chili, and Cuban and other sandwiches. *11am-8pm Mon-Fri, from 9am Sat & Sun* $$

Village Pump: Old-school Kelleys Island tavern. Tuck into fried perch, walleye bites and lobster chowder. Brandy Alexander is the house cocktail. *11am-9pm* $$

Forge: In an old blacksmith shop in Put-In-Bay. Stoke your taste buds with crepes and more. *9am-10pm Mon, Thu & Fri, from 8am Sat & Sun, 5-10pm Wed* $$

Beer Barrel Saloon: A Put-In-Bay pub with plenty of space for imbibing – its bar is 406ft long, billed as the world's longest. *noon-11pm*

Get there by ferry *(kelleysislandferry.com; round-trip adult/youth/child $24/16/free)*, which departs from Marblehead (about 30 minutes one way). Once deposited on the island's south shore, take a moment to appreciate the petroglyphs of **Inscription Rock**, not far from the ferry terminal. Native Americans who used the island as a hunting ground carved symbols into this boulder sometime between 1200 and 1600. It's not known exactly who made them, but historians believe they're the work of either the Late Prehistoric Period Sandusky culture, or the Erie, Cat, Neutral or other Indigenous peoples living in the region when Europeans arrived.

On the island's north shore, another wonder awaits: glacial grooves raked through the limestone. Created some 18,000 years ago, they're the largest and most easily accessible glacial grooves in the world, with gouges some 400ft long, 35ft wide and up to 10ft deep. If you're looking to camp overnight, **Kelleys Island State Park** features a popular ground with over 100 tent and RV sites, 6 miles of hiking trails with birds flitting by and a secluded, sandy beach.

Ohio Amish Country

Spend time in the USA's second-largest Amish community

A sojourn in the region provides pleasures of a slow kind. **Kidron**, on Rte 52, makes a good starting point, and if it's a Thursday, there's no better place than **Kidron Auction** *(kidronauction.com)*. Follow the buggy lineup down the road to the livestock barn. Hay and straw get auctioned at 10:15am, followed by cows at noon, pigs at 1pm, and sheep and goats after that. Next up is **Lehman's** *(lehmans.com)*, the Amish community's main purveyor of modern-looking products that use no electricity, housed in a 32,000-sq-ft barn.

About 25 minutes south, at **Yoder's Amish Home** *(yodersamishhome.com; adult/child $15/10)*, tour a local home, one-room schoolhouse and barn, before taking a buggy ride through a field. Over near Berlin, stop in at **Heini's Cheese Chalet** *(bunkerhillcheese.com)* to grab abundant samples of its 100% natural, unpasteurized cheeses, then stock up on all the Gouda, bleu, cheddar and other varieties you could want. Across the street, **Kauffman's Country Bakery** *(kauffmanscountrybakery.com)* has the fresh bread to pair with it. Pick up a couple of loaves, and maybe a cinnamon pretzel doughnut or mint fudge brownie while you're at it.

Further southwest at **Hershberger's Farm & Bakery**, gorge on dozens of kinds of pie, homemade ice-cream cones and

MORE ABOUT THE AMISH

Rural Wayne and Holmes counties are home to the USA's second-largest Amish community. Visiting here is like entering a preindustrial time warp. Descendants of conservative Dutch-Swiss religious factions who migrated to the USA during the 18th century, the Amish continue to follow the Ordnung (way of life), in varying degrees. Many adhere to rules prohibiting the use of electricity, telephones and motorized vehicles. They wear traditional clothing, farm the land with plow and mule, and go to church in horse-drawn buggies. Others are not so strict. Keep in mind the Amish typically view photographs as taboo, so don't take photos of people without permission.

EATING & DRINKING IN AMISH COUNTRY: OUR PICKS

Mrs Yoder's Kitchen: In Mt Hope, enjoy homey Amish fare in simple environs. Order mains à la carte, or fill up a plate at the buffet. *11am-7pm Mon-Sat* $

Boyd & Wurthmann Restaurant: In Berlin, sample pancakes, pies and Amish specialties such as country-fried steak. Cash only. *5:30am-3:30pm Mon-Thu, to 7:30pm Fri & Sat* $

Park Street Pizza: It seems all of Sugarcreek is here at night. Wood-fired pies with farm-grown ingredients. *3-9pm Tue-Thu, from 11am Fri & Sat, 11am-8pm Sun* $

Wooly Pig Farm Brewery: Part of a 90-acre Fresno farm. Sit outside or in the tasting room for German-style beers. *1-9pm Wed & Thu, to 10pm Fri, noon-10pm Sat, noon-7pm Sun*

seasonal produce from the market inside. Pet the farmyard animals *($8)* and take pony rides *($5)* and draft horse rides *($6)* outside.

Logan

Ohio's most beloved park

Twelve miles southwest of Logan is Ohio's most popular park, **Hocking Hills** *(ohiodnr.gov; free)*. Splendid to explore in any season, it's especially lovely in autumn. Thirty miles of hiking trails meander through the forest past waterfalls and gorges. Two of the park's most famed spots are **Ash Cave** and **Old Man's Cave**, where several short paths (less than a half-mile) deliver scenic payoffs beset with cascades. Nearby **Cedar Falls** has a half-mile trail edged by steep rock walls that leads to a peaceful waterfall and pool. You can also rent a boat and paddle the Hocking River. The visitor center has maps and exhibits of the area's unique geology. There are also cabins and campsites for spending the night.

Also inside Hocking Hills is the **John Glenn Astronomy Park** *(jgap.info; free)*, where visitors have the awe-inspiring opportunity to gaze up at some of the country's darkest skies. The park features 12 telescopes – including one of Ohio's largest – that allow earthlings obsessed with the universe to peer at stars, planets, the moon, nebulae, galaxies and comets, with astronomers and other star experts nearby to interpret what you're seeing. Programs, which are free but should be reserved in advance, take place on Friday and Saturday nights, weather permitting, from March through November. Check the park's Facebook page for the most up-to-date information.

In addition to the small, retractable-roof observatory, there is the adjacent Solar Plaza that has been designed to capture the sun's rays during solstices and equinoxes – a tradition practiced at Stonehenge, England; Chaco Canyon, New Mexico; and elsewhere for centuries.

Dayton

On the aviation trail

Dayton leans hard on its 'Birthplace of Aviation' tagline, and the Wright sights definitely deliver. Begin your day of aircraft admiration on the West Side at the **Dayton Aviation Heritage National Historical Park** *(nps.gov/daav; free)*, where the visitor center, **Wright Cycle Company shop** and

MORE OF OHIO'S TOP STATE PARKS & FORESTS

Malabar Farm State Park: This park in Lucas has a lot going on: hiking and horse trails, tractor-drawn farm tours and more.

John Bryan State Park: The highlight at this Yellow Springs park is Clifton Gorge, cut by the pretty Little Miami River.

Hueston Woods State Park: In College corner, golfing, horseback riding, fishing, camping, a nature center and a covered bridge.

Mohican-Memorial State Forest: Between Cleveland and Columbus, more than 4000 acres of forest with over 50 miles of hiking and cycling trails.

South Bass Island State Park: Set atop white cliffs on the island's southwest side, featuring a fishing pier, small rocky beach and watercraft rentals.

EATING & DRINKING IN SOUTHEASTERN OHIO: OUR PICKS

Union Street Diner: Fueling Athenians for decades; everything from omelets and hash browns to chicken-fried steak, pies and milkshakes. *8am-2pm* $

Little Fish Brewing Co: Taproom and beer garden in Athens. Saisons and sours are the specialty. *noon-10pm Tue-Thu, to 11pm Fri, 11am-11pm Sat, 11am-10pm Mon*

Brewery 33: In Logan, sip craft beer, agave cocktails, cider or mead. Dogs bring their humans for the outdoor seating. *noon-9pm Mon-Thu, to 10pm Fri & Sat, to 8pm Sun*

Hocking Hills Moonshine: A stop at this Logan distillery won't disappoint. Friendly staff will give you a tour with very affordable samples, too. *11am-8pm Mon-Sat*

ARTHURGPHOTOGRAPHY/SHUTTERSTOCK

Ash Cave, Hocking Hills

original site of the Wright Brothers' home are all within a one-block radius, between W 3rd and 4th Sts, and S Williams and Shannon Sts. The visitor center screens a film about the Wright Brothers in the original location of their second print shop, while the cycle company presents exhibits in the original building of their fourth bike shop – yes, Orville and Wilbur were busy men.

A couple of miles south in **Carillon Historical Park**, the **Wright Brothers National Museum** is where you'll see the 1905 Wright Flyer III biplane and a replica of the Wright workshop. And about 10 miles northeast is the **Huffman Prairie Flying Field**, looking much as it did in 1904. Walk the 1-mile trail that loops around, pausing at the history-explaining placards. Indoors to out, it's a surprisingly moving experience to see the cluttered workshop where Orville and Wilbur conjured their ideas and the lonely field where they tested their plane.

Then there's the **National Museum of the US Air Force** *(nationalmuseum.af.mil; free)*, a mind-blowing expanse with miles of planes, rockets and more. Located at Wright-Patterson Air Force Base, the staggering complex of hangars holds just about every aircraft you can think of from through the ages – from a Wright Brothers 1909 Flyer to a Sopwith Camel (WWI biplane). Be sure to visit Building 4 for spacecraft and presidential planes (including the first Air Force One).

The aircraft-themed attractions don't stop there. Finish off your day with a cold one at **Warped Wing Brewing Company** *(warpedwing.com)*, which takes its name from the Wright brothers' breakthrough concept of wing-warping.

OHIO'S ADENA & HOPEWELL HERITAGE

Long before the Europeans came, the Ohio River Valley was the Native home in the Early and Middle Woodland periods (200 BCE to 500 CE) of the, respectively, Adena and Hopewell peoples, whose legacies can still be seen in the huge geometric earthworks and burial mounds they left behind.

Of all the mounds that dot Southeastern Ohio, Serpent Mound in Peebles, 50 miles southwest of Chillicothe, is perhaps the most captivating. The giant, uncoiling snake stretches over a quarter of a mile and is the largest effigy mound in the world.

South of Columbus, about 3 miles north of Chillicothe, variously shaped ceremonial mounds spread over 13-acre Mound City, a mysterious town of the dead. It's part of the **Hopewell Culture National Historical Park**.

Michigan

BEACH TOWNS | WINE COUNTRY | DYNAMIC DETROIT

Places

Detroit p537
Dearborn p541
Kalamazoo p542
Lansing p542
Ann Arbor p543
Grand Rapids p543
Charlevoix & Petoskey p544
Sleeping Bear Dunes National Lakeshore p545
Michigan's Wine Country p547
The M-22 p547
Mackinac Island p548
Isle Royale National Park p549
Pictured Rocks National Lakeshore p550
Marquette p551
Porcupine Mountains p551

More, more, more – Michigan is the Midwest state that cranks it up. It sports more beaches than the Atlantic seaboard. More than half the state is covered by forests. And more cherries and berries get shoveled into pies here than anywhere else in the USA. Plus Detroit is one of the Midwest's most exciting cities, reinventing itself daily with street art and fresh architecture.

Michigan occupies prime real estate, surrounded by four of the five Great Lakes – Superior, Michigan, Huron and Erie. Islands – Mackinac, Manitou and Isle Royale – freckle its coast and make top touring destinations. Surf beaches, colored sandstone cliffs and trekkable sand dunes also woo visitors.

The state consists of two parts split by water: the larger Lower Peninsula (LP), shaped like a mitten; and the smaller, lightly populated Upper Peninsula (UP), shaped like a slipper. They are linked by the gasp-worthy Mackinac Bridge, which spans the Straits of Mackinac.

GETTING AROUND

Detroit has an enormously busy airport that serves as a Midwest hub. Within Detroit, the **QLine streetcar** *(qlinedetroit.com)* and the **People Mover** *(thepeoplemover.com)* provide some handy transport. Grand Rapids, Lansing and Traverse City have smaller air facilities. Amtrak stops throughout the Lower Peninsula's southern half, including in Detroit, Grand Rapids, Ann Arbor, New Buffalo and Holland. Megabus and Greyhound are faster and more widespread. Per usual, driving is fastest. I-75 is the only Interstate that enters the Upper Peninsula. Ferries to Isle Royale National Park sail from Houghton and Copper Harbor. On the west, the ferries that sail across Lake Michigan to/from Wisconsin dock in Muskegon and Ludington. On the region's eastern edge, Michigan has four border crossings to Canada, with the busiest at Detroit.

Detroit

MAP P538

Admire Rivera, Picasso and local artists

From fine art to street art, Detroit is a creative wonderland. First, **Detroit Institute of Arts** *(dia.org; adult/child $20/8)* holds one of the world's premier art collections, and its centerpiece is Diego Rivera's mural *Detroit Industry*, which fills an entire room and reflects the city's blue-collar labor history. Beyond it are Picassos, Caravaggios, suits of armor, modern African American paintings, puppets and troves more spread through 100-plus galleries. A 10-minute walk south, the **Museum of Contemporary Art Detroit** *(mocadetroit.org; adult/child $12/free)* is set in an abandoned, graffiti-slathered auto dealership. Heat lamps hang from the ceiling over peculiar exhibits that change every few months. Music and literary events take place regularly. The on-site cafe–cocktail bar is popular.

For street art, head to the **Lincoln Street Art Park**, an industrial site abutting a recycling facility where you'll see vivid graffiti, murals and sculptures made from found objects. It's a quintessential slice of urban-cool, DIY Detroit that's always changing, as local artists continue to add to it. DJ-fueled dance parties take place on occasion; keep an eye on its Facebook page.

TOP TIP

Don't leave Michigan without trying a pasty! Driving around the Upper Peninsula, you'll see plenty of shops selling the local meat-and-vegetable pot pies brought over by Cornish miners 160 years ago.

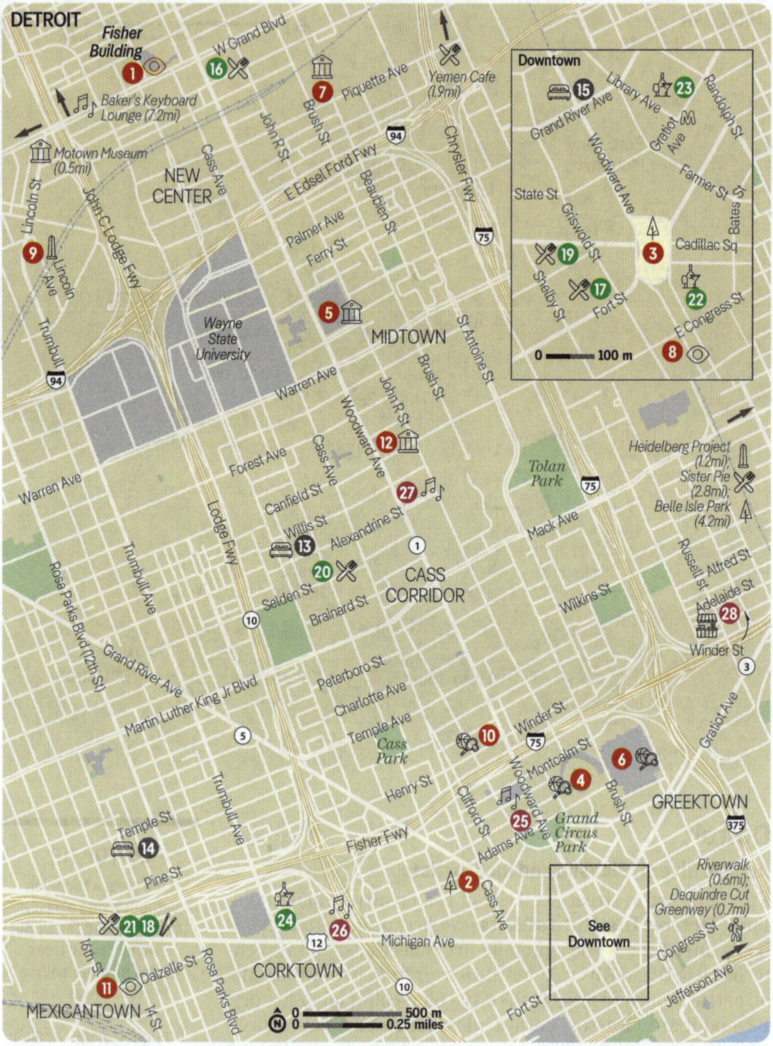

DETROIT

HIGHLIGHTS

1 Fisher Building

SIGHTS

2 Beacon Park
3 Campus Martius Park
4 Comerica Park
5 Detroit Institute of Arts
6 Ford Field
7 Ford Piquette Avenue Plant
8 Guardian Building
9 Lincoln Street Art Park
10 Little Caesars Arena
11 Michigan Central Station
12 Museum of Contemporary Art Detroit

SLEEPING

13 El Moore Lodge
14 Hostel Detroit
15 Shinola Hotel

EATING

16 Baobab Fare
17 Dime Store
18 Ima
19 Lafayette Coney Island
20 Selden Standard
21 Slows Bar BQ

DRINKING & NIGHTLIFE

22 Grand Trunk Pub
23 Standby
24 UFO Bar

ENTERTAINMENT

25 Cliff Bell's
26 Lager House
27 Magic Stick

SHOPPING

28 Eastern Market

And then there's the **Heidelberg Project**: polka-dotted streets, houses covered in Technicolor paint blobs, strange doll sculptures in yards – this is no acid trip, but rather a block-spanning art installation. It's the brainchild of artist Tyree Guyton, who wanted to beautify his rundown community and has been at it for nearly 40 years. It's an ever-evolving work in progress, and now it's undergoing a transformation from a founder-driven project to a community-focused one, celebrating emerging artists.

Eat your heart out at the Eastern Market

The sprawling, multi-shed **Eastern Market** *(easternmarket.org)* bills itself as the largest historic market district in the US, with more than 200 vendors. Whether it's produce, cheese, spices, flowers or beyond, you're sure to find nearly anything your heart desires. Saturday is the main market day, open 6am to 4pm year-round, but you can also turn up Monday through Friday to browse the specialty shops and cafes that flank the halls on Russell and Market Sts. In addition, from June through September, and in November and December, there are scaled-down markets on Tuesdays and craft markets on Sundays. Stop in at the Welcome Center for maps, directories, recipes and more information.

The sounds of jazz, Motown and beyond

Go on a musical tour of Detroit. By day, hit the **Motown Museum** *(motownmuseum.org; adult/youth/child $20/17/free; closed Mon)*, where you can take a tour of the row of modest houses where Berry Gordy launched Motown Records – and the careers of Stevie Wonder, Diana Ross, Marvin Gaye and Michael Jackson – with an $800 loan in 1959. Gordy and Motown split for Los Angeles in 1972, but you can still step into humble Studio A and see where the famed names recorded their first hits. Then by night, bask in the smooth sounds of two of Detroit's most historic jazz clubs, the legendary **Baker's Keyboard Lounge** *(bakerskeyboardloungedet.com)* and **Cliff Bell's** *(cliffbells.com)*. Continuously operating since 1934, Baker's is the world's oldest jazz club, a character-filled time capsule of a space with a small stage and curving art-deco bar, styled as piano keys. Cliff Bell's, meanwhile, is an elegant, candlelit space decked out in mahogany and brass, that started in 1935, before shuttering for a spell between 1985 and 2006. And if rap, rock and indie are more your jam, then **Magic Stick** *(majesticdetroit.com)* is the place for you.

MOTOR CAPITAL OF THE WORLD

French explorer Antoine de La Mothe Cadillac founded Detroit in 1701. Sweet fortune arrived in the 1920s, when Henry Ford began churning out cars. He didn't invent the automobile, as is sometimes mistakenly believed, but he did perfect assembly-line manufacturing and mass-production techniques. The result was the Model T, the first car the USA's middle class could afford to own. Detroit quickly became the motor capital of the world. General Motors (GM), Chrysler and Ford were all headquartered in or near Detroit (and still are). But Japanese competitors shook the industry in the 1970s. Detroit entered an era of deep decline, losing about two-thirds of its population.

EATING IN DETROIT: OUR PICKS

MAP P538

Sister Pie: Owner Lisa Ludwinski (a 2019 James Beard Award finalist) and her female bakers create amazing treats at this corner storefront. *10am-3pm Sat & Sun* $

Dime Store: A cozy, diner-esque venue with sandwiches, truffle mayo-dipped fries and eggy brunch dishes on the menu. *8am-3pm Mon-Tue & Thu-Sun* $

Slows Bar BQ: Southern-style barbecue in Corktown, with three-meat combo plates. Vegetarians have a couple of options, too. *11am-9pm, to 10pm Fri & Sat* $$

Selden Standard: Farm-to-table restaurant serving small plates, including fresh-caught fish, roasted vegetables and house-made bread and butter. *5-10pm* $$$

FROM MOTOWN TO ROCK CITY

Motown Records and soul music put Detroit on the map in the 1960s, while the thrashing punk rock of the Stooges and MC5 was the 1970s' response to that smooth sound. By 1976, Detroit was dubbed 'Rock City' by a Kiss song. In the early 2000s hard-edged garage rock pushed the city to the music-scene forefront, thanks to homegrown stars such as the White Stripes, Von Bondies and Dirtbombs, while Eminem gave Detroit its rap bona fides. And then there's techno, the electronic dance music that DJs in the city created in the mid-1980s; heavy on synthesizer melodies and complex machine rhythms, it became a global sensation. One of the world's largest electronic music festivals still takes place in the city annually in honor of the style.

Support the home team

Detroit is the only US city to host all its major league men's sports teams in the heart of downtown. What's more, they're all in the same neighborhood. If you're in Detroit for a game, spectating can be an affordable and fun way to experience the local sports fandom. Head to **Ford Field** to cheer on Detroit's National Football League (NFL) team, the Lions; **Comerica Park** for its Major League Baseball (MLB) team, the Tigers; and **Little Caesars Arena**, which hosts both the Pistons (National Basketball Association; NBA) and Red Wings (National Hockey League; NHL).

Appreciate architectural grandeur

From Michigan Central Station (the beaux-arts rail terminal designed by the architect of New York's Grand Central) to art-deco beauties like the Fisher and Guardian buildings, Detroit is full of architectural grandeur that harken back to its heyday.

In Corktown, take in the transformation of **Michigan Central Station** *(michigancentral.com; free)*, which after closing in 1988, was left to fall into decline, becoming a symbol of the city's shattered economy. In 2018, Ford Motor Company bought it, and in 2024, it reopened as a new innovation campus. The Station is the focal point of the broader Michigan Central, a 30-acre tech and culture hub with workspace, commercial space, restaurants, parks and plazas. Visitors can book a 90-minute tour journeying through the Station's restoration.

Downtown, the **Guardian Building** *(guardianbuilding.com)* was originally commissioned as a 'cathedral of finance.' Indeed, this distinctive, 40-story, redbrick building with green and white accents was the world's tallest masonry structure when it opened in 1929. The interior is a colorful explosion of marble, mosaic and murals that draw from Aztec, art deco and local influences. For a behind-the-scenes peek of the building's history, arrange a tour through **City Tour Detroit** *(citytourdetroit.com; adult/child $12/6)*.

North, in New Center, the **Fisher Building** *(fisherbuilding.city)* is a 1928 masterpiece from the man who built Detroit, Albert Kahn. Its imposing art-deco exterior is made from Minnesota granite and Maryland marble, while its interior rivals any Italian cathedral – from the soaring vaulted ceilings, featuring an array of intricate, hand-painted patterns, to the sparkling mosaics by Hungarian artist Géza Maróti and gleaming marble on the walls. **Pure Detroit** runs tours *(puredetroit.com; $15)*.

DRINKING IN DETROIT: OUR PICKS

MAP P538

Standby: Hiding in the Belt alleyway, an innovative resto-bar presenting creative cocktails. *5pm-1am Sun, Wed & Thu, to 2am Fri & Sat*

Lager House: Corktown staple: live music, extensive beer list, tasty New Orleans–style grub. *1pm-midnight Mon-Thu, to 2am Fri, 9am-2am Sat, 9am-midnight Sun*

Grand Trunk Pub: Once the Grand Trunk Railroad ticket hall. Vast food and drink menu. *11am-10pm Mon-Wed, to midnight Thu, to 1am Fri & Sat, 10am-10pm Sun*

UFO Bar: A hip hangout featuring cheap beer, grilled cheese sandwiches, indie music and retro vibes. *4pm-2am Tue-Sun*

EQROY/SHUTTERSTOCK

Guardian Building

DETROIT'S BEST PARKS, PLAZAS & PEDESTRIAN WAYS

Belle Isle Park: Floating in the Detroit River, parkland with trails, kayaking, a glass-domed conservatory, beach, aquarium and maritime museum.

Riverwalk: From Hart Plaza to Mt Elliott St, this 3-mile riverfront path passes several parks and outdoor theaters.

Beacon Park: Gathering place featuring food trucks, local vendors, and free concerts and yoga.

Campus Martius Park: In the heart of downtown, a plaza with a fountain, stage, restaurant and bar, plus an ice rink in winter and sandy beach in summer.

Dequindre Cut Greenway: Halfway along the Riverwalk, near Orleans St, a 1.5-mile path juts north, offering a pleasant passageway to Eastern Market.

The first Ford Model T

More than sand dunes, beaches and Mackinac Island fudge, Michigan is synonymous with cars. To trace the state's automotive history, begin in Detroit with a look at the **Ford Piquette Avenue Plant** *(fordpiquetteplant.org; adult/youth/child $20/10/free)*, the landmark factory where Henry Ford cranked out the first Model T. Admission includes a detailed tour by enthusiastic docents, plus loads of shiny vehicles from 1904 onward.

You can see other iconic vehicles in Dearborn, Kalamazoo (p542) and Lansing (p542).

Dearborn

Historical tour of vintage cars

In Dearborn, the quintessential **Henry Ford Museum of American Innovation** *(thehenryford.org; adult/youth/child $38/28.50/free, parking extra, discounted for paying online)* is loaded with vintage cars, including the first one Ford ever built, the 1896 gas-powered Quadricycle. The museum also contains a fascinating wealth of American culture, such as the chair Lincoln was sitting in when he was assassinated, the presidential limo in which Kennedy was killed, the hot-dog-shaped Oscar Mayer Wienermobile and the bus on which Rosa

EATING IN DETROIT: OUR PICKS

MAP P538

Lafayette Coney Island: A 'coney' is a hot dog smothered with chili and onions. It's a Detroit specialty. *9am-midnight, to 2am Fri & Sat* $

Yemen Cafe: Hamtramck favorite serving amazing Arabic food like slow-cooked lamb *haneeth*, *fahsah* (stew) and hummus. *8am-1am* $$

Baobab Fare: Mouthwatering Burundian restaurant. Signature dish is *nyumbani*: a slow-simmered beef and tomato sauce. *11am-9pm Tue-Sun* $$

Ima: Modern *izakaya* experience: outstanding ramen, udon, gyoza, sushi and more. Sake and beer as well. *11am-10pm Mon-Thu, to 11pm Fri, from noon Sat & Sun* $$

DETROIT'S BLACK ROLLER-SKATING CULTURE

Roller-skating remains a beloved pastime in Detroit, and the Black skating community has long been at the center of the city's unique and innovative skating style. In a time when skating rinks barred/limited Black skaters, one family broke barriers when they opened the first Black-owned skating rink, RollerCade, in 1955. In the late 1950s through early 1970s, Black skating culture grew hand in hand with Motown; Detroit-style skating characterized by synchronized movements that follow the beat. RollerCade is still in operation, and many other roller rinks, communities and events have popped up on the scene, like Motown Roller Club and Soul Skate Detroit. The biannual festival draws the world's best skaters and is next slated for May 2026.

PETERSPIRO/GETTY IMAGES

University of Michigan Union building

Parks refused to give up her seat. At the adjacent **Ford Rouge Factory Tour** *(adult/youth/child $26/19.50/free ; closed Sun)*, you can watch F-150 trucks roll off the assembly line; while in **Greenfield Village** *(adult/youth/child $41/30.75/free)*, you can ride in a Model T from 1923. Combination tickets are available. Across the parking lot, the separate interactive **Automotive Hall of Fame** *(automotivehalloffame.org; adult/youth/child $10/4/free; Thu-Sun)* focuses on the people behind notable cars, such as Mr Ferdinand Porsche and Mr Soichiro Honda.

Kalamazoo

Diner and drives

If you're on the car trail and you've got the time, head north of Kalamazoo along Hwy 43 to Hickory Corners and stop at the **Gilmore Car Museum** *(gilmorecarmuseum.org; adult/youth/child $20/12/free)*. Comprising some 20 buildings, this massive museum is filled with nearly 400 vintage autos, including 15 Rolls-Royces dating back to a 1910 Silver Ghost. Take a ride in a classic car, have a hot dog at the Blue Moon Diner and even stay overnight at a rented campsite. Check the calendar in advance, as there are lots of special car shows, seasonal festivals and live music events happening year-round.

Lansing

A riverside route through Michigan's capital

Tour Michigan's capital city by following the **Lansing River Trail** *(lansingrivertrail.org)*, a 16-mile route of paved paths and bridges that run alongside the Grand and Red Cedar rivers. Linking several parks, museums, a farmers market and a zoo, the trail system makes for a convenient way to explore some of the city's top attractions, either by bike or on foot.

Start at **Turner Dodge Park** and head south through **Old Town**, Lansing's arts and entertainment district, and stop at **Brenke Fish Ladder**, a peaceful sculpture-dotted park that's great for picnicking. Keep going and you'll reach the city's indoor farmers market, a science center and the **RE Olds Transportation Museum** *(reoldsmuseum.org; adult/youth/child $10/7/free)*. Featuring a whopping garage full of shiny vintage cars that date back nearly 140 years, the museum, closed Mondays, leads guided 45-minute tours every Friday and Saturday at 1pm *(free with admission)* and hosts the Car Capital Auto Show each summer.

Further south, where the Grand and Red Cedar rivers converge, head east to **Potter Park Zoo**. From there, continue to follow the Red Cedar River eastward toward **Michigan State University**, or opt to veer south and link up with Sycamore Creek. This is the most naturally scenic part of the trail network, with acres of wetlands, wildflower-blanketed meadows and woodlands. (**Fenner Nature Center** makes for a good place to take it all in.) And for those who can't get enough of RE Olds, his tombstone is nearby too, tucked within **Mount Hope Cemetery**.

Ann Arbor

Michigan's most popular college town

Spend some time in the liberal and bookish little city that's home to the **University of Michigan**. Ann Arbor's walkable downtown is loaded with free-trade coffee shops, bookstores and brewpubs. If it's Saturday, peruse the **Farmers Market**: a bounty of goods from the surrounding farms and orchards, offering up everything from spicy pickles to cider to mushroom-growing kits. Make a stop at **Zingerman's Delicatessen** for one of the best Reuben sandwiches you'll ever have. From there, head south toward campus, where you can check out, all for free, the **University of Michigan Museum of Art** – there's a nice collection of Asian ceramics, Tiffany glass and modern abstract works – and the **University of Michigan Museum of Natural History**. Finish with a stroll through **Nichols Arboretum**, a 123-acre oasis of greenery that features a restored prairie landscape and North America's largest peony garden.

Grand Rapids

Tour one of the USA's best beer cities

Once voted the USA's best beer city, Grand Rapids now has 40 craft breweries in and within a half-hour drive of town.

MORE OF MICHIGAN'S BEST MUSEUMS

Great Lakes Shipwreck Museum: Displaying the vestiges of the vessels that have sunk on 'Shipwreck Coast,' the UP stretch from Munising to Whitefish Point.

Broad Art Museum: A parallelogram of stainless steel and glass, designed by Zaha Hadid in East Lansing.

Arab American National Museum: In Dearborn, home to one of the largest Arab American communities, showcasing the artifacts of well-known Arab Americans.

Grand Rapids African American Museum & Archives: Commemorating the contributions of local African Americans to history and culture.

Grand Rapids Public Museum: Established in 1854, Michigan's oldest museum features history, science and a 1928 carousel.

EATING & DRINKING IN CENTRAL MICHIGAN: OUR PICKS

Downtown Market Grand Rapids: Stylish food hall. Standouts are Fish Lads and Love's Ice Cream. *11am-7pm Mon-Thu, to 8pm Fri, 10am-8pm Sat, 10am-7pm Sun* $

Chez Olga: A taste of the Caribbean in Grand Rapids; try curried goat, jerk chicken and creole tofu and more. Looks like a hobbit house! *5-9pm Mon, from 11am Tue-Sat* $$

Stella's Lounge: Grand Rapids restaurant. Award-winning stuffed burgers and other bar fare, including vegan options. *4pm-midnight Mon & Tue, from noon Wed-Sun, to 1am Fri & Sat* $

Naing Myanmar Family Restaurant: Lansing takeout spot. Traditional dishes from Burma, Malaysia and Thailand. Small grocery attached. *11am-8pm Tue-Sat* $

MORE DUNES IN MICHIGAN

They don't call Michigan's 300-mile western shoreline the Gold Coast for nothing.

Warren Dunes: Three miles of beachfront, with climbable dunes 260ft high.

Nordhouse Dunes: Within the Huron-Manistee National Forest, one of Lake Michigan's wildest stretches of shoreline.

Rosy Mound Natural Area: Boardwalk over wooded dunes to the lakeshore; interpretive signs along the way.

Silver Lake Dunes: Only dunes in Michigan where you're allowed to drive your own off-road vehicle.

Arcadia Dunes: Equipped with a universally accessible trail. The Baldy trailhead is here.

Saugatuck Dunes State Park: Dunes over 200ft tall, where visitors can book Saugatuck Dune Rides.

The **Beer City Brewsader app** *(experiencegr.com)* shows you where they are, and allows you to check in at each brewery you visit – when you reach eight, a free Brewsader T-shirt comes your way.

Top picks in Grand Rapids include **Vivant Brewery** for Belgian-style beers in an old chapel, the huge rock-and-roll-style **Founders Brewing Co**, **Mitten Brewing Company** and its wide-ranging brews in a cool old firehouse, and inventive neighborhood gem **Harmony Brewing Company**.

If you prefer a guided experience, book a tour through the popular **Grand Rapids Beer Tours** *(grbeertours.com; incl samples from $70)*. These van tours stop at three or four breweries, where a guide leads you through production facilities and tastings.

Charlevoix & Petoskey

Visit Hemingway's haunts

A number of writers have ties to northwest Michigan, but none are as famous as Ernest Hemingway, who spent the summers of his youth at his family's cottage on Walloon Lake. Go on a self-guided tour of the area to view the places that made their way into his writing. The **Michigan Hemingway Society** *(michiganhemingwaysociety.org)* has all the info you need. In Petoskey, stop at the **Little Traverse History Museum** *(petoskeymuseum.org; adult/child $5/free)* to see a collection that includes rare 1st-edition books the author autographed for a friend when he visited in 1947. Then head over to the nearby **City Park Grill** *(cityparkgrill.com)* to toss back a drink and enjoy some fresh-caught fish at the bar where Hemingway was reportedly a regular.

In Boyne City, there is the **Horton Bay General Store** *(hortonbaygeneralstore.com)*, which readers will recognize for its 'high false front' from Hemingway's short story *Up in Michigan*. The old-time shop now sells sandwiches, charcuterie, ice cream, spirits and wine on the 1st floor, and runs an inn on the 2nd floor. Next door, the **Red Fox Inn**, now listed on the National Register of Historic Places, is where Hemingway would stay with his fishing buddy Vollie Fox. It now operates a shop, with erratic hours, offering Hemingway books and memorabilia.

EATING ON THE GOLD COAST: OUR PICKS

Morning Star Café: Cooking up the best breakfast in Grand Haven. The Michigan blueberry pancakes are a winner. *6:30am-2:30pm* $

Spanglish: Mexican recipes made with Michigan ingredients in Traverse City, with lots of vegetarian and vegan options. *11am-6pm Tue-Sat* $

Paisley Grille: Fried chicken, burgers, fish and chips, and other fantastic gastropub fare at a Grand Haven favorite. *11am-9pm, to 10pm Fri & Sat* $$$

Chandler's: In Petoskey, upmarket fare – from sushi rolls to steak. Extensive wine list. Wine cellar seating available. *11am-9pm Mon-Thu, to 11pm Fri, 9am-9pm Sat & Sun* $$$

TOP EXPERIENCE

Sleeping Bear Dunes National Lakeshore

Extraordinary lake views from atop colossal sand dunes? Water blue enough to be in the Caribbean? Miles of unspoiled beaches? Secluded islands with mystical trees? All here at Sleeping Bear Dunes, along with lush forests, terrific day hikes and glass-clear waterways for paddling. The national park stretches from north of Frankfort to just before Leland, on the Leelanau Peninsula. Several cute towns fringe the area.

Empire Bluff Trail

Manitou Islands

The forest-cloaked **Manitou Islands** provide an off-the-beaten-path adventure. North Manitou is known for star-speckled backcountry camping, while South Manitou is terrific for wilderness-rich day trips. Kayaking and hiking are the big to-dos, especially the 7-mile trek to the Valley of the Giants, an otherworldly stand of cedar trees on South Manitou.

Dune Climb

The park's most popular attraction, this **climb** is up a 200ft-high dune to then run or roll down. Gluttons for punishment can keep slogging all the way to Lake Michigan, a strenuous 1½-hour trek one way.

Trails

The 22-mile paved **Sleeping Bear Heritage Trail** goes from Empire to Bohemian Rd (aka County Rd 669), and makes for a mostly gentle walk/bike ride – though there are some larger hills at the southern end. Trailheads with parking lots are located roughly every 3 miles; the one at Bar Lake Rd, near Empire, is a good place to embark.

The 1.5-mile round-trip **Empire Bluff Trail** rambles through peaceful beech-maple forest and eventually reaches a high bluff with grand views over Lake Michigan. Sunsets are awesome. It's moderately difficult, with a couple of sets of stairs to go up and down.

TOP TIPS

- If you're an America the Beautiful Pass holder, your entrance is already covered.
- This national lakeshore is cashless.
- Planning to camp in summer? Don't rely on first-come, first-served, as sites are likely to be sold out. Reserve online up to six months in advance.

PRACTICALITIES

- nps.gov/slbe
- 24hr
- 7-day pass per car $25

MICHIGAN'S BEST FESTIVALS

National Cherry Festival: A Traverse City tradition since 1931. Nearly 500,000 visitors watch parades, taste cherry pies and crown the National Cherry Queen each first week of July.

Movement: One of the world's largest electronic music festivals is held in Detroit over Memorial Day weekend.

Great Lakes Surf Festival: At Muskegon's Pere Marquette Beach in August, a day of surf lessons, yoga, art, music and more.

ArtPrize: Global artists display pieces throughout Grand Rapids over an annual 16-day period to win juried and popular-vote prizes.

Tulip Time: Holland blooms with millions of tulips – celebrated for nine days in early May, with Dutch food and cultural events at venues around town.

JOHN MCCORMICK/SHUTTERSTOCK

Holland

Tulips, windmills and more

You don't have to cross the ocean for tulips, windmills and clogs. Michigan's Holland has the whole kitschy package, plus a beautiful beach and a destination brewery. In early May, it's **Tulip Time** – the name of Holland's popular nine-day festival that takes over the town with parades, traditional clog dancing, a marketplace with Dutch foods and crafts, and other cultural events. If you haven't timed your trip with the festival, but the tulips are still in bloom, you can see them at **Veldheer Tulip Gardens** *(veldheer.com; adult/child $14/free)*. Outside of tulip season, it's free to check out the wooden-shoe factory, traditional blue-and-white pottery workshop and – somewhat oddly amid the Dutch items – a small buffalo herd.

From there, stop at **Windmill Island Garden** *(holland.org; adult/child $13/6)* to see an original working Dutch windmill, before enjoying lunch at the family-run **DeBoer's Bakkerij and Restaurant** *(deboerbakery.com)*, where the dishes are more Dutch-influenced than true Dutch, but nonetheless tasty. Klompen cakes (like pancakes with caramelized apple or other fruit added), eggs Benedict and croquettes star on the menu. It's touristy, but lots of locals eat here too. Finish with

DRINKING ON THE GOLD COAST: OUR PICKS

Pigeon Hill Brewing Company: In Muskegon, pale ales, IPAs and nitro stouts bubble from the taps. *11am-10pm Mon-Thu, to 11pm Fri & Sat, noon-9pm Sun*

Beards Brewery: A couple of home brewers opened Beards in Petoskey, and they know their stuff. Outside patio overlooking the bay. *11:30am-10pm Tue-Sun*

Odd Side Ales: Experimental suds in Grand Haven, like Tiramisu Bean Flicker and Imperial Mayan Mocha Stout. *11:30am-10pm Mon-Thu, to midnight Fri & Sat, to 9pm Sun*

Beer Church: In a former Methodist church in New Buffalo, signature brews include Pontius Pilate IPA and Crooked Cross cream ale. Wine and cocktails, too. *8am-midnight*

Holland tulip field

a pint at **New Holland Brewing Pub on 8th** *(newhollandbrew.com)*, known for its robust beers, such as Tangerine Space Machine and Dragon's Milk stout.

Michigan's Wine Country

Viticulture along the shore

Michigan has five main wine regions, aka American Viticulture Areas (AVAs) – Fennville, Lake Michigan Shore, Leelanau Peninsula, Old Mission Peninsula and Top of the Mitt – and four of them produce 95% of the state's wines. Those are Lake Michigan Shore, which actually encompasses Fennville; and Leelanau and the next door Old Mission peninsulas, near Traverse City. With so much great wine around, where to go? If you love a bold red, stick down south; if riesling is your thing, head up north; or, of course, there's nothing wrong with doing both.

Hop on the **Lake Michigan Shore Wine Trail** *(miwinetrail.com)*, the stretch of I-94 and I-196 between New Buffalo and Saugatuck (and east to Kalamazoo) where about 15 member wineries are clustered.

Up in the Leelanau Peninsula AVA, there's the **Leelanau Peninsula Wine Trail** *(lpwines.com)* connecting 21 member wineries – go on a guided or self-guided bike tour with **Grand Traverse Bike Tours** *(grandtraversebiketours.com)*. Nearby, north of downtown Traverse City, the **Old Mission Peninsula Wine Trail** *(ompwinetrail.com)* links together 10 more. Tasting prices vary by winery, but range from $5 to $15 for four to six tastes.

The M-22

One of Michigan's most scenic drives

Take a ride along the M-22, arguably Michigan's most scenic drive, with dramatic vistas over Lake Michigan. The pretty

MICHIGAN'S TOP SPOTS FOR WINTER ACTIVITIES

Eben Ice Caves: Fantastical caves form when snow melts and freezes over a cliff's edge, glowing green-yellow from the tannins.

Muskegon Luge Adventure Sports Park: One of the nation's only public luge tracks, with cross-country ski and snowshoe trails, too. Clinics and rentals available.

Boyne Mountain Resort: More than 400 acres of skiing in Boyne Falls, including 63 downhill trails and 11 lifts.

Porkies Winter Sports Complex: Downhill skiing with a 787ft vertical drop, plus 26 miles of cross-country trails. Beginner-friendly.

Munising Snowmobile Trail System: Billed as the 'Snowmobile Capital of the Midwest,' this city has 10 trails that cover 300 miles.

NEED TO KNOW: THE UPPER PENINSULA

Residents of the UP, aka 'Yoopers,' consider themselves distinct from the rest of the state – they've even threatened to secede in the past. Rugged and isolated, with hardwood forests blanketing 90% of its land, the UP is edged by Lakes Huron, Michigan and Superior. Only 45 miles of Interstate highway slice through the trees, punctuated by a handful of cities, of which Marquette is the largest. The Keweenaw Peninsula is the UP's northernmost bit; its largest town Houghton is the jump-off to Isle Royale National Park, with ferries and seaplanes departing in summer. Further ahead on Hwy 26 is the turnoff for the Brockway Mountain Dr, which goes along the spine of the eponymous crag to reach the Copper Harbor, where another ferry sails for Isle Royale.

route goes from Manistee to Traverse City, hugging more than 100 miles of coastline, passing Sleeping Bear Dunes National Lakeshore (p545) and plenty of fun diversions along the way. Don't miss **Fishtown** *(lelandmi.org)*, a tiny commercial fishing village in **Leland** from the early 1900s and one of the few to be preserved on the Great Lakes shore. Wander among the shanties and see fish being cleaned and smoked, then pick up some to try at **Carlson's Fishery** *(carlsonsfishery.com)*.

Stop off for some grub in **Northport** – you can't go wrong at **Fischer's Happy Hour Tavern** *(fischershappyhour.com)*, a vintage tavern tucked in the woods, where the broasted (it combines broiling and roasting) chicken and fish are excellent – before stopping off for some suds in **Suttons Bay**. For beer, head to the outdoor beer garden at the **Hop Lot Brewing Company** *(hoplotbrewing.com)*; for cider, **Tandem Ciders** *(tandemciders.com)*.

At M-22's end in **Traverse City**, aka Michigan's 'cherry capital,' treat yourself to a slice of **Grand Traverse Pie Company's** top-selling cherry crumb pie (or one of its other seven or so pies with cherries). There are also guided kayak pub crawls via outfitters like **Paddle for Pints** *(paddleforpints.com; from $99)* or **Paddle TC** *(paddletc.com; from $69)*. Prices don't include the alcohol.

Mackinac Island

Ditch your car for two wheels

Mackinac's location in the straits between Lake Michigan and Lake Huron made this 3.8-sq-mile island a prized port in the North American fur trade, and a site the British and Americans battled over many times. To get here, catch the ferry from either Mackinaw City or St Ignace.

In 1898, cars were banned to encourage tourism, and 80% of the island is state parkland. Edging the island's shoreline is Hwy 185 (aka Lake Shore Rd), the only Michigan highway that doesn't permit cars. The best way to view the incredible scenery along this 8-mile road is by bicycle; bring your own or rent one at one of the many businesses. You can loop around the flat road in an hour. Along the way, you'll see the huge limestone **Arch Rock** *(mackinacparks.com)*, curving 150ft above Lake Huron and providing dramatic photo opportunities; and **Fort Mackinac** *(adult/child $17/10.25)*, built in 1780 by the British and one of the best preserved military forts in the country. Costumed interpreters, and cannon and rifle firings entertain the kids. Stop at the tearoom for a bite and

(continues on p551)

EATING IN THE UP: OUR PICKS

Syl's Cafe: In Ontonagon, breakfast is Syl's glory. Lunch and dinner don't disappoint either. The UP specialty (pasties) is available anytime. *7:30am-9pm* $

Falling Rock Cafe & Bookstore: New/used books, live music and wi-fi with your sandwich and coffee in downtown Munising. *8am-4pm, to 6pm Thu, to 8pm Fri & Sat* $

Jampot: In Eagle Harbor, bearded, black-robed monks from a nearby monastery sell homemade jams, coffee and pastries. *noon-4pm Tue-Thu, 10am-5pm Fri & Sat* $

Lake Superior Brewing Company: Whitefish and pizzas with house-made brews at this pub in Grand Marais. Also called the Dunes Saloon. *noon-midnight* $$

TOP EXPERIENCE

Isle Royale National Park

Totally free of vehicles and roads, Isle Royale National Park – a 210-sq-mile island in Lake Superior with 2000 moose roaming through the forest – is certainly the place to go for peace and quiet. It gets fewer visitors in a year than Yellowstone National Park gets in a day. The island is laced with 165 miles of hiking trails that connect dozens of campgrounds along Superior and inland lakes.

Greenstone Ridge Trail

At 42 miles, Greenstone Ridge Trail is the longest on Isle Royale, a grand backpacking adventure that spans the entire length of the island from Rock Harbor in the east to Windigo in the west. You can hike it in either direction, but most people start in Rock Harbor and take five to seven days to complete the epic wilderness trek.

The moderately difficult route pays off big time with forest solitude, fab lookouts over the wave-based coast and abundant moose and red fox sightings. The only accommodations along the way are basic campgrounds with pit toilets, so you have to carry all food and gear. Whether you finish in Windigo or Rock Harbor, it's easy to arrange boat transportation back to your starting point.

Stoll Trail

This easy 1.4-mile loop begins at Rock Harbor Lodge (p579) and meanders through old-growth forest and along shoreline bluffs to Scoville Point, an outcrop that unfurls dramatic views of Lake Superior and the craggy landscape. Keep an eye out for moose and osprey.

TOP TIPS

- It may be more cost efficient for groups to purchase a season pass *($60)*, which covers the pass holder, plus three more adults.
- If you're an America the Beautiful Pass holder, you're already covered to enter Isle Royale.
- Pay entrance fees online in advance; otherwise, it's credit card only on-site.

PRACTICALITIES

- nps.gov/isro
- 24hr mid-Apr to Oct
- daily adult/child $7/free

TOP EXPERIENCE

Pictured Rocks National Lakeshore

Stretching along Lake Superior, Pictured Rocks National Lakeshore is a series of wild cliffs and caves, where blue and green minerals have streaked the red and yellow sandstone into a kaleidoscope of color. In between Grand Marais in the east to Munising in the west, you'll find lakeside hikes, kayak trips and boat tours that feature brilliant ways to take in the area's shipwrecks, waterfalls and artist's-palette geology.

Au Sable Point Light Station

TOP TIPS

- If you are an America the Beautiful Pass holder, you're already covered to enter Pictured Rocks.
- This national lakeshore is cashless.
- Cell service is spotty here, so be sure to download maps ahead of time.

Sights

Top sights (from east to west) include the c 1874 **Au Sable Point Light Station** and its surrounding shipwrecks; agate-strewn **Twelvemile Beach**, accessed via the campground; hike-rich **Chapel Falls**, **Chapel Rock** and **Chapel Beach**; and view-worthy **Miners Castle**, one of the lakeshore's most distinctive rock formations.

Cruises

Boats with both deck and enclosed seating glide along the shore for 40 miles, passing many of Pictured Rocks' most popular sights. Rides last between two and three hours – the sunset option is particularly lovely – and depart from Munising's city dock. Book through **Pictured Rock Cruises** *(picturedrocks.com)*; reserving ahead is wise.

Kayaking

Kayaking is popular in Pictured Rocks and no wonder, given that you paddle beneath sheer, color-stained bluffs with names like Lovers Leap, Flower Vase and Caves of the Bloody Chiefs. The duck's-eye view of the geologic features is awesome. Experienced paddlers can go it alone, but conditions are often wavy and windy. Newbies should go with a guide. Several operate out of Munising, with trips from just a few hours to all day. **Pictured Rocks Kayaking** *(picturedrockskayaking.com)* has good ones for beginners.

PRACTICALITIES

- nps.gov/piro
- 24hr
- 7-day pass per car $25

(continued from p548)
a million-dollar view of downtown and the Straits of Mackinac from the outdoor tables. The fort admission price also allows you entry to five other museums in town along Market St, including the **Mackinac Art Museum**, which houses Native American arts, historic maps and island photography.

Marquette

Outdoor adventures in nature's playground

The Upper Peninsula's largest (and snowiest) town, lakeside Marquette draws the outdoor enthusiasts. Forests, beaches and cliffs provide a playground spitting distance from downtown for skiing, hiking, biking, boating and beyond.

The easy **Sugarloaf Mountain Trail** and the harder, wilderness-like **Hogsback Mountain Trail** both have panoramic views, while the **Noquemanon Trail Network** *(noquetrails.org)* is highly recommended for mountain biking and cross-country skiing.

For water-sports enthusiasts, **Down Wind Sports** *(shopdownwindsports.com)* rents all kinds of gear and has the lowdown on kayaking, fly-fishing, surfing, ice climbing and other adventures.

In the city, on a peninsula jutting out into Lake Superior, the high bluffs of **Presque Isle Park** make a great place to catch the sunset.

Porcupine Mountains

Roam Michigan's largest state park

Michigan's largest state park, **Porcupine Mountains** *(michigandnr.com; per day $11)*, with 90 miles of trails, is a wilderness winner. 'The Porkies,' as they're called, are so rugged that loggers bypassed most of the range in the early 19th century, leaving the park with the largest tract of old-growth forest between the Rocky Mountains and Adirondacks. Along with 300-year-old hemlock trees, the Porkies are known for waterfalls, 20 miles of undeveloped Lake Superior shoreline, black bears lumbering about, and the view of the park's stunning Lake of the Clouds, the area's most photographed sight. After stopping at the **visitor center** to pay the park entrance fee, continue to the end of Hwy 107 and climb 300ft via a short path for the stunning view of the shimmering water. Lengthier trails depart from the parking lot.

MORE OF MICHIGAN'S TOP STATE PARKS

Tahquamenon Falls State Park: The Upper Falls' 50ft drop flows with hemlock-tinted waters, while the Lower Falls' series of small cascades swirl around an island.

Petoskey State Park: Beautiful beach featuring indigenous Petoskey stones (honeycomb-patterned fragments of ancient coral).

Grand Haven State Park: A 48-acre urban park that's all beach: popular in summer for swimming, a boardwalk and a tall red lighthouse.

Holland State Park: Has a Lake Michigan beach for sunset gaping, along with an inland Lake Macatawa beach where watercraft can be rented.

Ludington State Park: Once inside, simply pull over on the roadside and make a break for the beautiful beach. Trail system and lighthouse, too.

DRINKING IN THE UP: OUR PICKS

Keweenaw Brewing Company: In Houghton, quality pints, including Widow Maker black ale and Pick Axe blonde ale. *3-10pm Mon-Wed, 11am-midnight Thu-Sat, noon-8pm Sun*

Blackrocks Brewery: Set in a cool refurbished house in Marquette, making deliciously hoppy beers, heavy on American IPAs. *4-11pm Mon, from noon Tue-Sun*

Ore Dock Brewing Co: Across from the docks in downtown Marquette, with laid-back bar, sidewalk seating, often food trucks out front. *noon-11pm, to midnight Fri & Sat*

Drifa Brewing Company: South of downtown Marquette, a dog-friendly brewery with tasty pours, ample outdoor seating area, and food truck. *noon-10pm, to 11pm Thu-Sat*

Wisconsin

FUN TRADITIONS | BEER BONANZA | WATER ADVENTURES

Places

Milwaukee p552
Racine p556
Madison p556
Wisconsin Dells p558
Spring Green p558
Door County p560
Green Bay p561
Apostle Islands p562

TOP TIP

Buy a Wisconsin state park annual pass. It costs $38 per vehicle, whereas a day pass costs $16 per vehcle, so if you're visiting for more than two days it pays off quickly. Buy it online or at any of the parks.

Wisconsin is cheesy and proud of it. Its cow-speckled farmland pumps out more cheddar, Gouda and other pungent wedges than any other US state, and local license plates read 'America's Dairyland' with udder dignity.

So embrace the cheese thing, because there's a good chance you'll be here for a while. Wisconsin has a ton to offer: exploring the rocky coastline and lighthouses of Door County, kayaking through sea caves at Apostle Islands National Lakeshore, touring Green Bay's football shrine of Lambeau Field and driving along the bluff-framed Great River Rd. Families soak up the Wisconsin Dells' kitschy water parks, while architecture buffs marvel at Frank Lloyd Wright's forever home. The state's two largest cities, Milwaukee and Madison, welcome by offering bountiful beer, markets and locavore eats. At week's end, the whole state throws a party known as the Friday night fish fry, a quintessential Wisconsin experience.

Milwaukee

MAP P554

Brewery tours in Brew City

Milwaukee's enduring relationship with beer is no accident. The city was settled by Germans in the 1840s, and many started breweries. A few decades later, the introduction of bulk-brewing technology turned beer production into a major industry here, with Pabst, Schlitz, Blatz and Miller leading the way.

GETTING AROUND

The main Interstates are I-94 (runs east-west, connecting Milwaukee to Chicago and Minneapolis), I-90 (runs east-west near Madison) and I-43 (runs north-south, connecting Milwaukee to Green Bay). Wisconsin has no toll roads. Note that roads into Door County and the Wisconsin Dells often get jammed on summer weekends.

Amtrak runs a popular train between downtown Milwaukee and Chicago seven times per day; the trip takes 1½ hours and is often faster than driving.

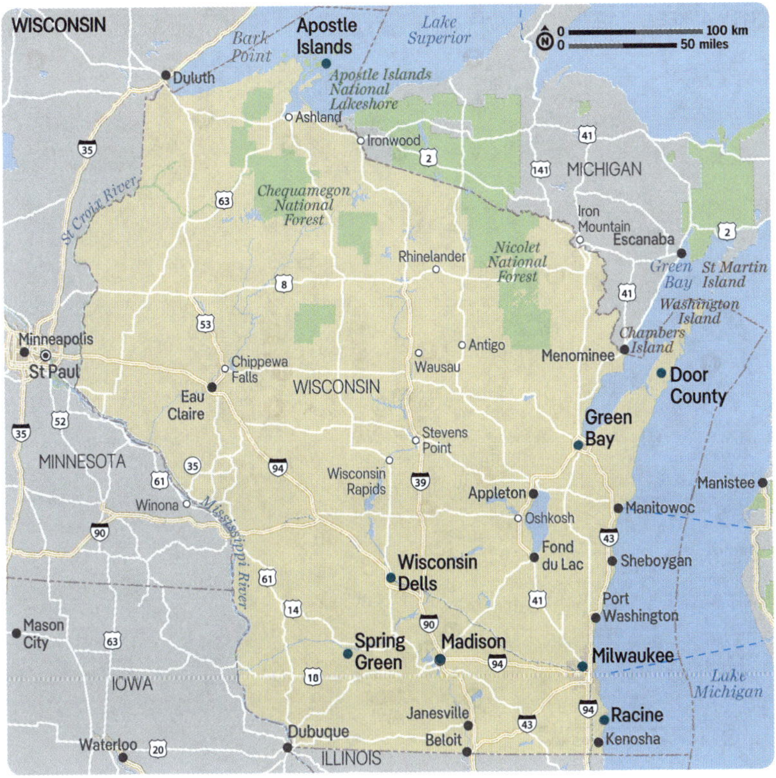

Going on a brewery tour is a beloved Milwaukee activity, and visits typically include several samples. Make all bookings in advance.

Historic **Miller Brewing Company** *(millerbrewerytour.com; tours $20)* is the granddaddy of the scene. Though the mass-produced beer may not be your favorite, the factory impresses with its sheer scale: you'll visit the packaging plant where thousands of cans are filled each minute and the warehouse where half a million cases await shipment. It's closed Tuesday and Wednesday.

Much-loved **Lakefront Brewery** *(lakefrontbrewery.com; tours $13-16)* puts on 50-minute tours daily. Guides have a

EATING IN MILWAUKEE: OUR PICKS

MAP P554

Pitch's Lounge & Restaurant: Retro spot that's been family-run since 1942. Don't miss the baby back ribs. *5-9pm Wed, Thu & Sun, to 10pm Fri & Sat* **$$**

Uncle Wolfie's Breakfast Tavern: The brunch crowd lines up for biscuits and gravy, French toast and Bloody Marys. *8am-2pm Tue-Thu, to 3pm Fri-Mon* **$$**

Comet Cafe: Locals of all types pile in for meatloaf smothered in beer gravy and some of Milwaukee's best mac and cheese. *9am-9pm* **$$**

Odd Duck: Boisterous room for inventive, locally sourced small plates and cocktails; lots of vegetarian options. Reserve ahead. *3pm-midnight Tue-Sat* **$$$**

HIGHLIGHTS
1 Milwaukee Art Museum

SIGHTS
2 America's Black Holocaust Museum
3 Bobblehead Hall of Fame and Museum
4 Bradford Beach
5 Bronze Fonz
6 Discovery World at Pier Wisconsin
7 Harley-Davidson Museum
8 Pabst Mansion

SLEEPING
9 Ambassador
10 Brewhouse Inn & Suites
11 County Clare Irish Inn

EATING
12 Comet Cafe
13 Milwaukee Public Market
14 Odd Duck
15 Pitch's Lounge & Restaurant
16 Swingin' Door Exchange
17 Uncle Wolfie's Breakfast Tavern

DRINKING & NIGHTLIFE
18 Best Place
19 Bryant's Cocktail Lounge
20 Central Standard Craft Distillery
21 Don's TV & Repair
22 Lakefront Brewery
23 Third Space Brewing

ENTERTAINMENT
24 German Fest
see 24 Irish Fest
see 24 Polish Fest
see 24 PrideFest
see 24 Summerfest

great sense of humor, and they take you right up to the bottling line. It's super-fun.

Pabst doesn't brew in Milwaukee anymore, but you can head to **Best Place** *(bestplacemilwaukee.com; tours $14-25)*, a dark-wood tavern in the former brewery headquarters, to tour the company's historic premises.

Chow down at a fish fry

Friday is the hallowed day of the 'fish fry' all over Wisconsin. This communal meal of beer-battered cod, French fries and coleslaw came about years ago, providing locals with a cheap meal to socialize around and celebrate the end of the working week. Milwaukee is a terrific place to take part in the convention, as it's still going strong at many local bars and restaurants.

Lakefront Brewery (p553) hosts a popular fish fry in its beer hall that includes a polka band letting loose. **Swingin' Door Exchange** *(swingindoorexchange.com)* goes beyond the norm with its throwback, dark-wood ambience and elevated side dishes like spicy vermouth carrots. At **South Shore Terrace** *(southshoreterrace.com)*, you'll eat your fish in a sprawling lakefront beer garden.

Renegade bikes at the Harley Museum

Celebrate more than a century of motorcycles at the **Harley-Davidson Museum** *(harley-davidson.com/museum; adult/child $25/11)*. The company was founded in Milwaukee in 1903 when schoolmates William Harley and Arthur Davidson built and sold their first motorcycle. This museum has hundreds of motorcycles that show the styles through the decades, including the flashy rides of Elvis and Evel Knievel and 'Serial Number One,' the oldest known Harley in existence. Even nonbikers will enjoy the interactive exhibits and leather-clad crowds.

Art inside and out

On the shore of Lake Michigan, the **Milwaukee Art Museum** *(mam.org; adult/child $27/free)* showcases more than 32,000 works, including fabulous folk and outsider art and a sizeable collection of paintings by Wisconsin native Georgia O'Keeffe.

The museum building is a work of art itself and features a stunning winglike addition by Spanish architect Santiago Calatrava. Called the Burke Brise Soleil, the moveable shade is made of 72 steel fins spanning 217ft, slightly larger than a Boeing 747's wings. They spread wide with the museum opening at 10am, flap at noon and close at 5pm (8pm on Thursdays). Head to the suspension bridge outside for the best view of the action.

Sights along the RiverWalk

Edged by Lake Michigan and crisscrossed by three rivers, Milwaukee was made for waterfront wandering. The RiverWalk path cuts through downtown along both sides of the Milwaukee River. Don't miss the **Bronze Fonz** on the RiverWalk's east side, just south of Wells St. The Fonz, aka Arthur Fonzarelli, was a character from the 1970s TV show *Happy Days*, which was set in Milwaukee. It's a quintessential photo op.

MILWAUKEE'S BEST FESTS

Summerfest: The 'world's largest music festival' brings 600 rock, blues, country and alternative bands over nine days in June and July.

German Fest: Get ready for the dachshund derby, oompah bands, lots of beer drinking and shouts of 'Prost!' in late July.

Irish Fest: In mid-August, crowds amass for corned beef and cabbage, fiddle music, step dancing and beer guzzling.

Polish Fest: Get your fill of vodka tastings, polka dancing and cooking classes over three days in mid-June.

PrideFest: Beer drinking, live music, a dance pavilion and a family stage are all part of the June festivities.

DRINKING IN MILWAUKEE: OUR PICKS

MAP P551

Bryant's Cocktail Lounge: Opened in 1938, Milwaukee's oldest cocktail bar has no menu, just knowledgeable bar staff who mix up magic. *hours vary*

Don's TV & Repair: Swig boozy shakes named after old gaming consoles, mimosas served in a cute little bathtub and huge old fashioneds. *hours vary*

Central Standard Craft Distillery: Creates its own vodka, brandy, bourbon and whiskey, best enjoyed on the 5th-floor rooftop. *hours vary*

Third Space Brewing: The huge beer garden is an excellent choice for summertime sips, often accompanied by live music. *hours vary*

MORE MILWAUKEE TO-DO'S

America's Black Holocaust Museum: Founded by a lynching survivor, the museum presents a moving story of Black resilience despite centuries of oppression.

Bobblehead Hall of Fame and Museum: You know the bouncy-noggin dolls that look like celebrities? More than 10,000 of them bob here.

Pabst Mansion: Tour the Gilded Age grandiosity of beer baron Captain Frederick Pabst.

Discovery World at Pier Wisconsin: The lakefront science and technology museum features aquariums and a cool Les Paul electric guitar exhibit.

Bradford Beach: Legions of locals swim, play volleyball and lick frozen custard at this sandy strand a few miles north of downtown.

Onward as you head south is the **Milwaukee Public Market** *(milwaukeepublicmarket.org)*, packed with local vendors selling cheese, sandwiches, beer and frozen custard each day.

Continue south along the path and you'll be in the heart of the **Third Ward**, an old warehouse district that's now a hub of galleries, boutiques and cool-cat dining venues powered by area farms, orchards and creameries. Pick a waterside bar or cafe to while away an afternoon or evening.

Racine

Unexpected architecture stop

By most accounts, the southeastern city of Racine is an unremarkable industrial town, but it has two key Frank Lloyd Wright sights. Start at the **SC Johnson Administration Building & Research Tower** *(reservations.scjohnson.com; tours free)*, where Wright designed several striking buildings. Ninety-minute tours cover the 1939 Admin Building, with tall, flared columns in its vast Great Workroom and 43 miles of Pyrex glass-tube windows letting in soft, natural light. You'll also see the 1950 Research Tower – where Raid, Off and other famous products were developed – which features 15 floors of curved brick bands and more Pyrex windows.

About 5 miles north, **Wingspread** *(reservations.scjohnson.com; tours free)* is the house Wright designed for HF Johnson Jr, one of the company's leaders. It's the last and largest of Wright's Prairie-style abodes, completed in 1939, with 500 windows and a 30ft-high chimney. Tours for both sights run Wednesday through Sunday (reduced in winter) and must be booked in advance.

Racine makes a great stop between Milwaukee and Chicago.

Bite into a mega pastry

Racine is a prime place to sample the tire-sized state pastry known as the 'kringle.' The oval-shaped confection consists of 32 or more layers of flaky dough filled with fruits and nuts and baked until golden brown. Racine became a hub for the treat in the late 1800s, when the recipe came over with the many Danish immigrants who settled in the city. The kringles at family-owned **O&H Danish Bakery** (*ohdanishbakery.com*) are addictive wonders in flavors such as cranberry cream cheese, chocolate pecan and almond.

Madison

Wander the college district for art, beer and books

Madison is a pretty combination of small, grassy state capital and liberal, bookish college town. But it's that college – the University of Wisconsin and its 50,000 students – that dominates the scene and invites an afternoon hangout (which may well lead to an evening hangout).

The **Memorial Union** *(union.wisc.edu)* is the gathering spot. The sun-splashed terrace, set on Lake Mendota, could not be more perfect for a pitcher of beer and brat (local parlance for bratwurst). You can rent kayaks and paddleboards,

YOUNGRYAND/SHUTTERSTOCK

State Street, Madison

or walk the trail around the lake. In winter the action moves indoors to the fireplace-warmed beer hall.

Nearby, the **Chazen Museum of Art** *(chazen.wisc.edu; free)* goes way beyond the norm for a university collection. The 3rd floor holds most of the genre-spanning trove: everything from the Old Dutch Masters to Picasso sculptures and Andy Warhol pop art.

State St links the campus to the Capitol. The mile-long, pedestrian-only road is lined with poets' cafes, parked bicycles and stores selling Free Tibet stickers through clouds of jasmine incense. Several locavore and international restaurants also fold in to the scene.

Graze through the Farmers Market

On Saturdays mornings from mid-April to early November, a food bazaar takes over Madison's Capitol Square. The **Dane County Farmers Market** *(dcfm.org; free)* is one of the nation's most expansive markets, famed for its artisan cheeses and breads. Keep your eyes peeled for Bleu Mont Dairy, which makes fantastic cheeses in a climate-controlled cave; and Stella's Bakery, which makes warm, pliable cheese bread. Street musicians and arts-and-crafts vendors add to the bohemian festival atmosphere. It gets crowded, but you can always find a tree-shaded grassy spot for respite.

WISCONSIN'S BEST TRAILS

Ice Age Trail: Zigzags 1200 miles up and down the state, revealing icy springs, pine woods and bluff-top views. *iceagetrail.org*

400 State Trail: Gentle 22-mile cycling path between Elroy and Reedsburg that rolls through a farm-studded river valley.

Elroy-Sparta State Bike Trail: This 33-mile rail-trail meanders up hills, through old tunnels and alongside pastures; connects to the 400 State Trail.

Oak Leaf Trail: a 135-mile paved path that takes in parks, forests and lakefront vistas around Milwaukee.

CAMBA Trail System: The Chequamegon Area Mountain Bike Association has 250 miles of northern Wisconsin trails for beginners and experts.

EATING IN MADISON: OUR PICKS

Mickie's Dairy Bar: Diner near campus that's been slinging breakfast for generations. Try the cinnamon roll French toast. *7am-2pm Wed-Sun* $

Tipsy Cow: Popular spot near Capitol Square for hobnobbing over burgers and beers from small-batch producers. *11am-10pm Mon-Sat* $

Lucille: Concocts inventive pizzas and cocktails across three stylish floors. *3-11pm Mon-Wed, 11am-11pm Thu & Sun, 11am-1am Fri & Sat* $$

Old Fashioned: Woodsy, retro spot for eating walleye, cheese soup and other Wisconsin specialties. *11am-9pm Mon-Thu, to 10pm Fri & Sat* $$

BEST WEIRD WISCONSIN SIGHTS

House on the Rock: Abode stuffed to mind-blowing proportions with wonderments, like whirring music machines, an enormous carousel and glass-walled 'infinity room.'

National Mustard Museum: Born of one man's ridiculously intense passion, it houses around 6000 mustards and kooky condiment memorabilia.

Dr Evermor's Sculpture Park: Found objects welded into a hallucinatory world of futuristic birds, dragons and other bizarre structures.

Cow Chip Throw: In September in Prairie du Sac, 800 competitors fling dried manure patties.

Concrete Park: A lumberjack's extraordinary folk art, featuring 200-plus whimsical, life-size sculptures.

If you're in town on a nonmarket day, get your fix at **Fromagination** *(fromagination.com)*, a shop that carries loads of hard-to-find local cheeses.

Wisconsin Dells

Water parks, both constructed and natural

About an hour's drive north of Madison, the **Wisconsin Dells** *(wisdells.com)* is an epicenter of kitschy diversions, including more than 20 water parks, water-skiing thrill shows, epic mini-golf courses and Ripley's Believe It or Not oddities. Practically every Midwestern family has splashed through a weekend here.

But beyond the carnival-like attractions, the Dells offers a nature fix amid limestone gorges and rushing rivers. **Dells Boat Tours** *(dellsboats.com; adult/child $40/20)* glide into the scenery; the Upper Dells trip is particularly lovely. Or head to nearby **Mirror Lake State Park** *(dnr.wisconsin.gov; vehicle day pass $16)* to hike amid sandstone bluffs that surround a glassy lake where you also can rent kayaks and pontoon boats. In winter, cross-country skiers glide over 18 miles of groomed trails, and ice fisherfolk set up on the lake. Even architecture buffs get a thrill here: Frank Loyd Wright's Seth Peterson Cottage is tucked in the woods, and visitors can rent it if they get on the waiting list two years in advance.

Spring Green

Explore Frank Lloyd Wright's Taliesin

Renowned architect Frank Lloyd Wright chose the rolling green hills and valleys of southwestern Wisconsin for his dream home. He built **Taliesin** *(taliesinpreservation.org; tours from $35)* in 1911 in his signature Prairie style using low horizontal lines and local materials like limestone and river sand. Tours take you inside the house (actually the third Taliesin incarnation, after fires burned the first two), resplendent with warm, natural light and his clever custom-built decor. Longer jaunts go to other parts of the 800-acre estate, such as the Hillside Studio where he taught his apprentices. Wright lived at Taliesin on and off for almost 50 years.

Buy tickets in advance. Park at the visitor center. A shuttle bus takes you to the house. Even if you're not going on a tour, you can park and walk on the public trails that depart from the visitor center. Taliesin is an hour's drive east of Madison.

See a play in the woods

So you're in Spring Green to see Frank Lloyd Wright's mega sight. Why not stay into the evening for a magical show at **American Players Theatre** *(americanplayers.org; tickets from $66)*? The critically acclaimed troupe stages classical productions at an outdoor amphitheater in the woods. There's nothing like seeing *A Midsummer Night's Dream* under a silvery moon. Bring a picnic – it's tradition to hang out and nibble before the show. **Wander Provisions** *(wanderprovisions.com)* is a good place to stock up.

ROLLING ON THE GREAT RIVER ROAD

The Mississippi River forms Wisconsin's southwestern border, and alongside it runs the timeless, cheese-and-pie-laden Great River Rd.

START	END	LENGTH
Ellsworth Cooperative Creamery	La Crosse	105 miles; 5 hours

The Great River Rd follows Old Man River throughout its 2300-mile flow from Minnesota to Louisiana. Wisconsin's sections are among the prettiest. Start inland at ❶ **Ellsworth Cooperative Creamery**, the state's largest cheese-curd producer. Bite a curd, and hear it squeak: a Wisconsin rite of passage.

Head south 15 miles to WI-35. Now you're on the River Rd, curving past bluffs until you reach ❷ **Stockholm Pie & General Store**. Study the blackboard: double lemon, triple chocolate pecan, butterscotch cream? The slice will fuel you 6 miles to Pepin, where *Little House on the Prairie* fans can stop at the ❸ **Laura Ingalls Wilder Museum**, and foodies at renowned, book-stuffed ❹ **Harbor View Cafe**.

Stay on WI-35 a short distance to the ❺ **Nelson Cheese Factory**. The shop carries a stash of Wisconsin cheese and rich ice cream. Take the bridge across the river to Wabasha, MN, where the ❻ **National Eagle Center** gives the lowdown on the mighty birds, about 100 of which flock here each winter.

From Wabasha, stay on Hwy 61 on the Minnesota side for 60 miles, passing bucolic farms and green hills. Cross the bridge to La Crosse, WI. Get your camera ready for the ❼ **World's Largest Six-Pack**, then explore the bars and shops of La Crosse's historic downtown.

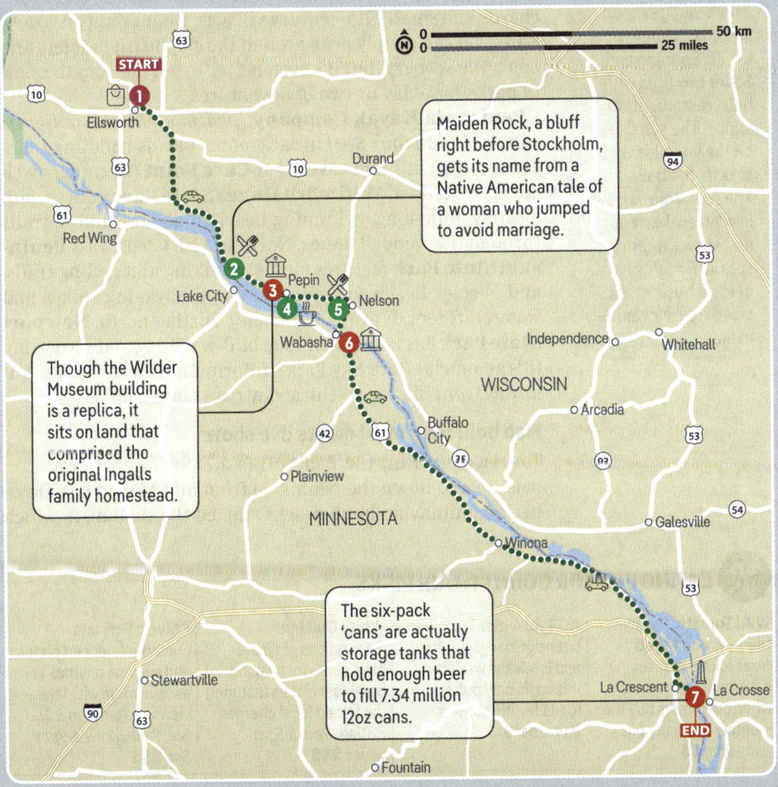

Maiden Rock, a bluff right before Stockholm, gets its name from a Native American tale of a woman who jumped to avoid marriage.

Though the Wilder Museum building is a replica, it sits on land that comprised the original Ingalls family homestead.

The six-pack 'cans' are actually storage tanks that hold enough beer to fill 7.34 million 12oz cans.

DOOR COUNTY ORIENTATION

Door County spreads across a narrow peninsula jutting 75 miles into Lake Michigan. Sturgeon Bay, at the southern end, is the county seat and its only real city. Going north, the side of the peninsula that borders Lake Michigan is the more scenic 'quiet side,' and home to the communities of Jacksonport and Baileys Harbor. The side that borders Green Bay is busier, where villages such as Egg Harbor, Fish Creek, Ephraim and Sister Bay brim with bars, restaurants and shops. The sun rises on the lake side and sets on the bay side. The scene slows down in winter, when cold and snowy weather sets in. Roughly half of local businesses close from November to May.

RANDY KOSTICHKA/SHUTTERSTOCK

Lambeau Field, Green Bay

Door County

Hike, bike and paddle the parks

With its rocky coastline, picturesque lighthouses, cherry orchards and small 19th-century villages, Door County is lovely. Sure, you can simply poke around the clapboard hamlets and enjoy the scenery. But it's even better to get out into the slew of parks for a day or two of adventures.

Peninsula Kayak Company *(peninsulakayakcompany.com; half-day tour $65)* in Jacksonport leads paddling tours around the cliffs and caverns at **Cave Point** (beginners welcome). Next door, **Whitefish Dunes State Park** entices with a sandy, mile-long swimming beach and short hiking trails through the wooded dunes. North in Fish Creek, vast **Peninsula State Park** features bluff-side hiking and cycling trails, and Nicolet Beach for swimming and kayaking (bikes and watercraft rentals available on-site). Further north, **Newport State Park** has tranquil hiking, bird-watching and stargazing (it's an official Dark Sky Park). Information for the parks is at *dnr.wisconsin.gov*; a vehicle day pass costs $16.

Fish boil: fiery meal meets live show

Touristy but fun, the fish boil is a Door County tradition held up and down the peninsula from mid May to late October. Scandinavian lumberjacks started the custom, in which

EATING IN DOOR COUNTY: OUR PICKS

Wild Tomato: Family-friendly, wood-fired pizza joint that gives back to the community when customers buy the monthly specialty pie. *11am-8pm* **$$**

AC Tap: A glowing Pabst beer sign hangs out front and leads the way into this cash-only pub known for its terrific burgers. *11am-2am* **$**

White Gull Inn: Generations of diners have come for heaping breakfast dishes featuring the famed local cherries. *7:30am-2pm & 5pm-varies* **$$$**

Chives: Fork into French-influenced plates and sublime pastries in a rustic room with lake views. *4-9pm Mon & Thu-Sat, 9am-2pm & 4-9pm Sun* **$$$**

whitefish, potatoes and onions are cooked in a cauldron over an open flame outdoors. Stand around the firepit while the 'boil master' prepares the ingredients and shares local lore. Then they douse the flames with kerosene, and whoosh! A fireball creates the requisite 'boil over' (which gets rid of the fish oil), signaling dinner is ready. Several restaurants host dinnertime fish boils. The **Old Post Office Restaurant** *(oldpostoffice-doorcounty.com; adult/child $28.50/18)* in Ephraim puts on a lively one, with a bonus of great sunset views.

Sail to Washington and Rock islands

If Door County starts to feel crowded, steer to its tip for your getaway. Hop aboard the **Washington Island Ferry** *(wisferry.com; adult/child/car $15/8/30)* at Northport Pier for the 30-minute crossing. The time-warped little isle, settled by Icelandic villagers in the 1800s, beckons with some 700 residents, lavender fields, rugged beaches and small resorts. You'll need a car (or bicycle) to get around. The ferry sails year-round. While the crossing is generally smooth, it does go through the strait known as 'Death's Door,' so named by Native Americans and early French explorers due to the treacherous currents that sank many a ship in past centuries. That's where Door County gets its moniker. Modern navigation aids have rendered the strait far less threatening today.

More remote is teeny Rock Island, which has no roads or facilities. It's a true escape for forest hiking and bird-watching. You also can explore the 1858 lighthouse, where volunteers offer free tours daily. The **Rock Island Ferry** *(wisferry.com; adult/child $15/6)* makes the trip from Washington Island's Jackson Harbor in 15 minutes, sailing from late May to mid-October. Leave your car in the parking lot by the dock. It's possible to visit both islands in one long day trip. Bring cash for small purchases like snacks or souvenirs.

STELLAR SUNSETS

Betsy Riley, co-owner of Square Rigger Lodge (p579) in Jacksonport, shares top spots to see Door County's famous sunsets.

Stabbur Beer Garden at **Al Johnson's** Swedish restaurant is a fun place to watch the sky ignite. Or walk across the street to the waterfront park for a closer view. My grandparents would go there often in the evening. They'd plan their day around the sunset.

Shipwrecked Brew Pub has an outdoor patio and sits above the water, so you have a great lookout over Green Bay and boats in the marina.

Ellison Bluff County Park feels off the beaten path – there are never many people there – but it's near the highway. With no buildings around, it's a gorgeous wide-open place to see the sun drop.

Green Bay

Tour fabled Lambeau Field

The Green Bay Packers are legendary as the National Football League's smallest-market team but one of its most successful, winning 13 league championships and four Super Bowls (so far). The franchise is unique as the only community-owned nonprofit team in the NFL; perhaps pride in ownership is what makes the fans so die-hard.

The Packers' storied history makes a half-day visit to Lambeau Field worthwhile even if you aren't a hard-core supporter.

DRINKING IN DOOR COUNTY: OUR PICKS

Pearl Wine Cottage: Cute-as-a-button white bungalow serving European wines alongside cheeses and charcuterie. *4-9pm Thu-Sun mid-May-Oct*

Mink River Basin: Tucked-away bar that's been around for ages with fun games (Pac-Man!) and good beers, whiskies and food. *noon-2am*

Peach Barn Farmhouse & Brewery: Sprawling outdoor space to play lawn games and hear live music while sipping sours and lagers. *11am-8pm*

Bayside Tavern: Locals and visitors mix it up over burgers and beers in this festive, time-honored pub with a lively patio. *11am-2pm*

WHY SO CHEESY?

Wisconsin produces 3.5 billion pounds of cheese per year – a quarter of America's hunks. That's thanks to 5000 state dairy farms and their 1.3 million cows, according to the Department of Agriculture.

Most farming and cheesemaking happens in Wisconsin's hilly southwest. Here, in what's known as the Driftless Region, glaciers did not flatten the landscape as elsewhere in the state, but left hills, valleys and limestone-rich soil – poor for crop farming but perfect for roaming dairy herds that produce distinctive sweet milk.

Immigrants from Germany, Switzerland and Scandinavia who settled in Wisconsin in the 1800s put their old-country cheese-making skills to work. The state has been America's Dairyland ever since.

DANITA DELIMONT/GETTY IMAGES

The hour-long 'classic' **stadium tour** *(lambeaufield.com; adult/child $23/14)* takes in the luxury boxes and lets you walk through the tunnel out onto the field. Guides provide great stories of Packers lore. Tours happen daily year-round (except on game days). Afterward mosey around the Titletown district adjacent to Lambeau, which has live music, markets and other free events open to the public.

Apostle Islands

Kayaking and sea-cave adventures

Forested and windblown, trimmed with cliffs and caves, **Apostle Islands National Lakeshore** *(nps.gov/apis; free)* floats off Wisconsin's northern tip in Lake Superior. Kayaking around the 21-isle archipelago is very popular, paying off with stacks of red-rock arches and pillars rising from the water. Sea caves along the mainland near Meyers Beach and the craggy shores of Devils and Sand islands are the showstoppers. Conditions get rough and winds strong, so it's wise to go with a guide. Reputable companies offering half- and full-day outings include **Lost Creek Adventures** *(lostcreek adventures.org; tours from $80)* and **Trek & Trail** *(trek-trail.com; tours from $75)*.

The resort town of Bayfield has everything you need. The **National Lakeshore Visitors Center** *(nps.gov/apis)* downtown can help with camping permits. The islands themselves have no facilities. June through September is prime time to paddle.

Take a boat tour or hike

You don't have to be in a kayak to enjoy the Apostle Islands. Hop on a sightseeing boat with **Apostle Islands Cruises** *(apostleisland.com; tours adult/child $55/34)* instead. The

Devils Island, Apostle Islands National Lakeshore

three-hour 'grand tour' sails to sea caves and lighthouses, and you can bring your own wine and snacks on-board.

Or hike the first 2 miles of the Lakeshore Trail near **Meyers Beach**, which has terrific sea-cave views from land. Brave souls also can swim at Meyers Beach, but the water is breathtakingly cold. It's near Cornucopia, west of Bayfield, along Hwy 13.

Day trip to Madeline Island

The **Madeline Island Ferry** *(madferry.com; return adult/child/car $21/10/38)* makes the 25-minute trip multiple times per day from downtown Bayfield to bohemian **Madeline Island** and its walkable village of La Pointe. To go beyond, bring your car or rent a bicycle from **Motion to Go** *(motion-to-go.com; per hr $12)* by the dock. Pedaling around the island is pure joy.

Big Bay State Park *(dnr.wisconsin.gov; vehicle day pass $16)* beckons with a pretty beach, cliff-view hiking trails and stargazing. Or walk and forage for mushrooms in lovely **Madeline Island Wilderness Preserve** *(miwp.org; free)*.

SUPPER CLUBS

Supper clubs are a type of time-warped restaurant, common in the upper Midwest. They took off in the 1930s, after Prohibition ended and people once again sought places to socialize over a drink. Most supper clubs today retain a retro vibe. Hallmarks include a woodsy location, mounted fish on the walls, a radish-and-carrot-laden relish tray on the table, a surf-and-turf menu and a mile-long, unironic cocktail list topped by the brandy old-fashioned (brandy, bitters, sugar, soda water, orange slice and cherry). Wisconsin has the most supper clubs by far, though Minnesota and Michigan also uphold the tradition. See *wisconsinsupperclubs.com* for locations around the state.

EATING & DRINKING IN BAYFIELD: OUR PICKS

Hoop's Fish & Chips Dockside: Fresh fish, beer and wine served alfresco, plus live music on weekends. *11am-7pm Mon-Sat, to 6pm Sun* $

Manypenny Bistro: Diner-esque venue for breakfast sandwiches, burgers, lake fish, wood-fired pizzas and Turkish kebabs. *7am-9pm* $$

Fat Radish: Farm-to-table meat, fish and veg dishes in a log cabin in Washburn, just south of Bayfield. *11am-8pm Wed & Thu, to 9pm Fri & Sat* $$$

Copper Crow Distillery: Tasting room on Native land for cocktails with house-made vodka and rum. *3-7pm Thu & Fri, 1-7pm Sat, noon-4pm Sun*

Minnesota

WILDERNESS TRAILS | LAKES | ROCK STARS

Places

Minneapolis p564
Chanhassen p570
St Paul p570
Duluth p572
North Shore p573
Hibbing p575
Boundary Waters p575
Voyageurs National Park p576

TOP TIP

The state is nicknamed 'Minnesnowta' for a reason. It's not uncommon for it to snow in late April or even early May. Then again, it can swing the other way and boil in summer. Moral of the story: bring layered clothing options.

Minnesota really is the land of 10,000 lakes (and then some). All that water is a boon for travelers. Adventurous types can wet their paddles in the Boundary Waters, where nighttime brings a blanket of stars and the lullaby of wolf howls. Voyageurs National Park unfurls another remote landscape, where roads vanish and the boreal backcountry is accessible only by boat. Hwy 61 slices into the cliffy, falls-filled North Shore. For a state with such vast tracts of unspoiled wilderness, Minnesota flies under the radar as an outdoor adventure hub. But that it is.

Urban explorers get the prize of Minneapolis, the biggest, coolest town on the prairie, with swanky art museums, rowdy rock clubs, progressive dining establishments and edgy theaters. It's always happenin,' even in winter. And for those looking for middle ground – a cross between the big city and big woods – the dramatic, ship-laden port of Duluth beckons.

Minneapolis

MAPS P566, P568

Follow Prince's purple path

Minneapolis' most famous former resident is the music star Prince. Even before his death in 2016, visitors flocked to town to follow his trail.

Hot spots include First Avenue (p569), the downtown music club that featured in the film *Purple Rain*. Nearby, a 100ft-tall

GETTING AROUND

The main Interstates are I-94 (runs east–west, connecting Minneapolis to Milwaukee and Chicago), I-90 (runs east–west through southern Minnesota) and I-35 (runs north–south, linking the Twin Cities and Duluth). Minnesota does not have toll roads, though express lanes on Twin Cities highways charge a fee for use. Hwy 61, the scenic road along Lake Superior north of Duluth, gets jammed on summer weekends. Amtrak trains go twice daily to Chicago and Milwaukee.

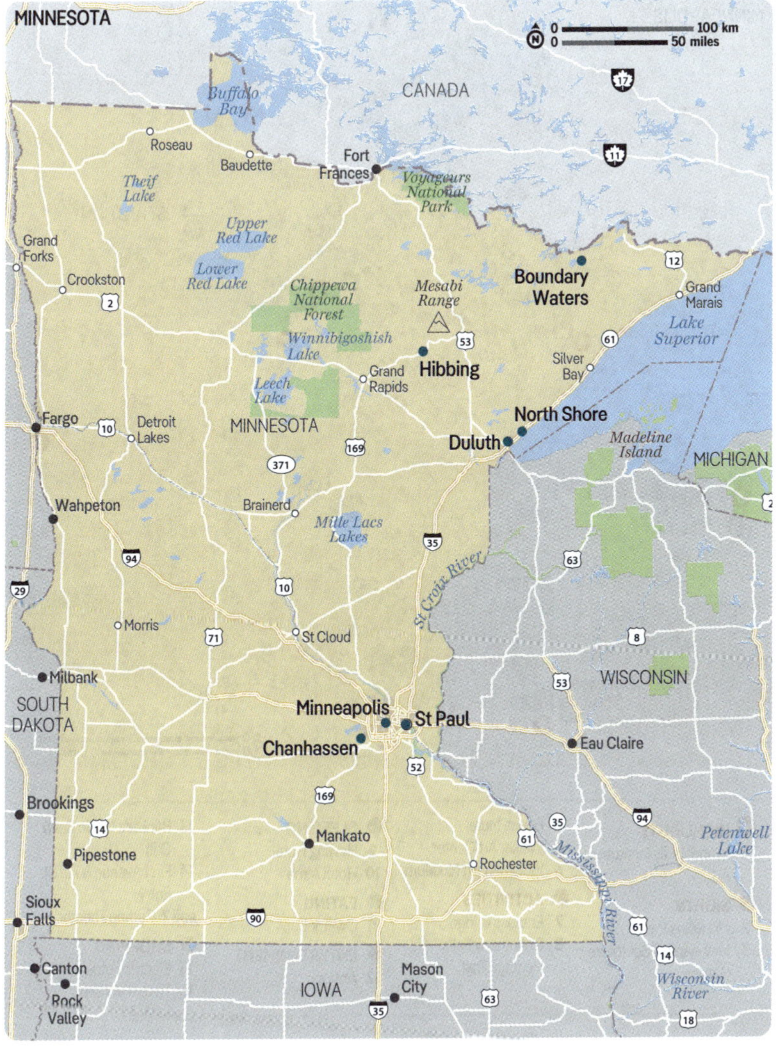

mural of Prince rises on the wall of a parking ramp. Hardcore fans can also seek out Prince's childhood home and more using the city's 'purple path' map *(minneapolis.org/princes-minneapolis).*

The mega sight for fans is Paisley Park (p570), Prince's mansion in Chanhassen, 20 miles southwest of Minneapolis, complete with the Prince Tribute Tunnel.

Go on an art bender

Minneapolis takes its art seriously. Near downtown, the **Walker Art Center** *(walkerart.org; adult/child $18/free)* is one of

HIGHLIGHTS
1 Minneapolis Institute of Art

SIGHTS
2 Mill Ruins Park
3 Minneapolis Sculpture Garden
4 Prince Mural
5 Walker Art Center
6 Weisman Art Museum

ACTIVITIES
7 Endless Bridge
8 St Anthony Falls Heritage Trail

SLEEPING
9 Hewing Hotel
10 Hotel Alma

EATING
11 Owamni

ENTERTAINMENT
12 Armory
13 Bunker's Music Bar & Grill
14 First Avenue & 7th St Entry
see 7 Guthrie Theater

SHOPPING
15 Electric Fetus
16 Twelve Vultures

EATING IN MINNEAPOLIS: CIVIC-MINDED RESTAURANTS

MAPS P566, P568

Owamni: Sun-splashed venue that only uses indigenous ingredients like corn, beans, wild game and native plants. *11am-9pm Tue-Fri, from 10am Sat & Sun* **$$$**

Mama Safia's Kitchen: Somali restaurant serving chicken, goat and spiced rice; it was rebuilt by the community after 2020's civil unrest. *7am-10pm* **$$**

Trio Plant-Based: Breezy vegan soul-food place decorated with photos of civil-rights heroes. *noon-6:45pm Tue-Thu, to 7:15pm Fri & Sat* **$$**

All Square: It's all about grilled cheese sandwiches at this little spot that helps recently incarcerated people get back on their feet. *11am-8pm Tue-Sat* **$**

the nation's top five for modern works. Most of the permanent collection is post-1960, heavy on Andy Warhol soup-can prints and Jasper Johns flag images. It's free on Thursday evenings. The **Minneapolis Sculpture Garden** *(walkerart.org; free)* sits next door, where Claes Oldenburg's beloved *Spoonbridge & Cherry* presides over the 11-acre grounds alongside a whimsical blue rooster and the Robert Indiana *Love* monument. It's delightful to meander.

South of downtown, the **Minneapolis Institute of Art** *(new.artsmia.org; free)* spans centuries and continents, with everything from Tibetan tangkas to Rembrandt paintings to 2000-year-old Mexican jade masks in its warren of galleries. You could spend the entire day here. The **Weisman Art Museum** *(wam.umn.edu; free)* on the University of Minnesota campus is smaller but equally impressive, thanks to its gleaming, Frank Gehry–designed building. It holds a quick-browse mash-up of ceramics, Korean furniture and 20th-century American art. Note: most museums are closed on Monday and Tuesday.

For the local art scene, check out the **Northeast Minneapolis Arts District** *(northeastminneapolisartsdistrict.org)*. Located north of downtown, the area teems with artist lofts and open-house events.

George Floyd Square: site of history and healing

George Floyd was killed by police in May 2020 outside a convenience store at the corner of E 38th and Chicago Aves in south Minneapolis. His death, which became a symbol for racial injustice and police brutality, sparked worldwide protests. Since then, the site – now known as **George Floyd Square** – has become a place to reflect and pay respects to Mr Floyd. People bring rocks, paintings, dolls, candles, beads, flowers and poems as offerings to the ever-changing memorial that has taken over the intersection. Murals, raised fist sculptures and raw art installations in locals' lawns extend for a block in each direction and add to the sobering feel. The square itself is a pedestrian-only zone.

Say Their Names Cemetery, another community-built memorial, lies a few blocks northwest, near where E 37th St and Columbus Ave meet. White cardboard headstones rise up in an empty lot and pay homage to everyone from Floyd to Emmett Till, Breonna Taylor and more than 100 other Black Americans killed by police.

Late morning or afternoon are good times to visit, though the sights are always open.

MINNEAPOLIS: GET YOUR BEARINGS

Minneapolis is relatively spread out. Neighborhoods include the North Loop (stylish warehouse district abutting downtown), Uptown (lively area south of downtown near Bde Maka Ska and other popular lakes), Northeast (art studios, breweries and dive bars northeast of downtown), East and West Banks (home to University of Minnesota's 50,000-plus students near downtown) and Powderhorn (where Floyd Square is in south Minneapolis). St Paul lies 10 miles east of Minneapolis, while the airport and Mall of America lie 10 miles south.

Handy Blue Line trains connect the mall, airport and downtown Minneapolis. Green Line trains connect Minneapolis to St Paul. A Metro Transit *(metrotransit.org)* day pass costs $4.

EATING IN MINNEAPOLIS: OUR PICKS

MAP P566, P568

Hola Arepa: Margaritas and Venezuelan-style arepas. Colorful, festive ambience. *4-10pm Tue-Thu, to 11pm Fri, 10am-11pm Sat, to 10pm Sun* **$$**

Heather's: Bright cafe whipping up from-scratch French toast, burgers, vegan tofu bowls and more. *9am-9pm Mon-Sat, to 8pm Sun* **$$**

Young Joni: Hip industrial space that fuses two seemingly unrelated types: pizza and Korean food. There's a hidden bar in back. *hours vary* **$$**

Creekside Supper Club: Retro knotty pine walls, vintage signs and classic fare like prime rib and martinis. *4-9pm Tue-Fri, 10am-2pm & 4-9pm Sat & Sun* **$$$**

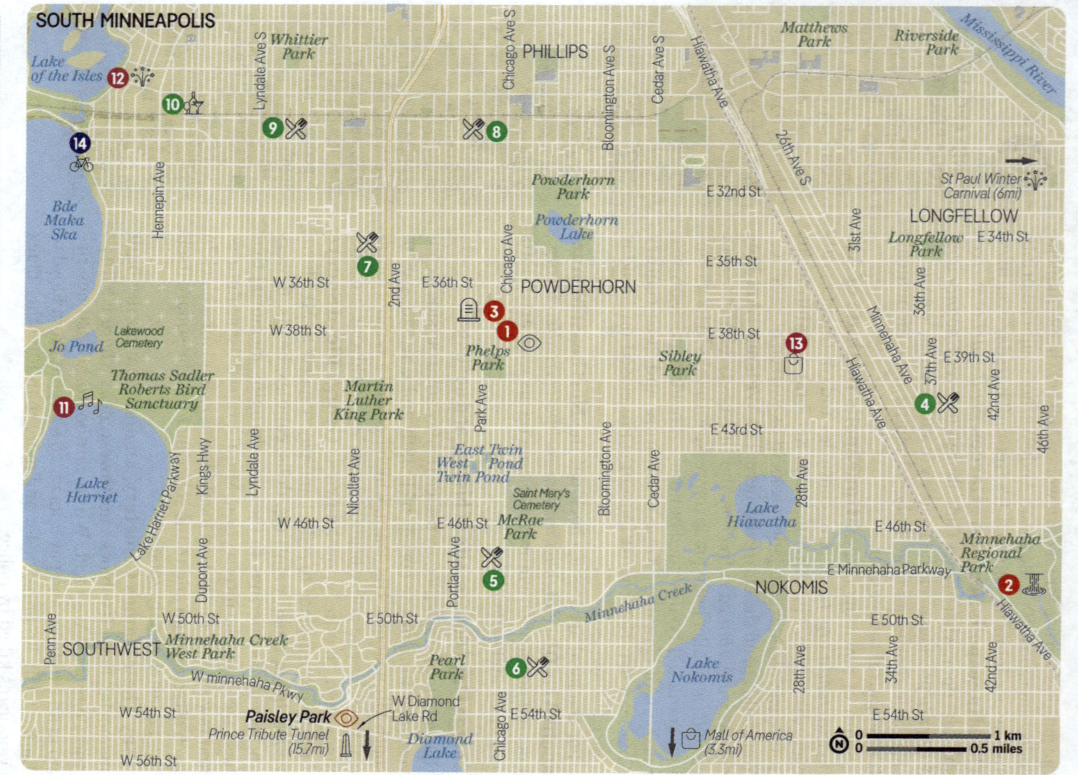

SIGHTS
1 George Floyd Square
2 Minnehaha Falls
3 Say Their Names Cemetery

EATING
4 All Square
5 Creekside Supper Club
6 Heather's
7 Hola Arepa
8 Mama Safia's Kitchen
see 2 Sea Salt Eatery
9 Trio Plant-Based

DRINKING & NIGHTLIFE
see 5 Sidecar at the Tap
10 Troubadour Wine Bar

ENTERTAINMENT
see 9 Jungle Theater
11 Lake Harriet Band Shell
12 Luminary Loppet

SHOPPING
13 Tropes & Trifles

TRANSPORT
14 Wheel Fun Rentals

Riverfront views: mill ruins, a waterfall and more

The Mississippi River slices through downtown Minneapolis, flanked by parkland and a waterside trail. Join the many locals who are out for a stroll.

The cobalt-blue **Guthrie Theater** *(guthrietheater.org)* is a striking place to start. Check to see if the building is open (closed Mondays and most mornings) and then make your way up the escalator to the **Endless Bridge**. The cantilevered walkway juts out over the river and offers a knockout view. Onward along the water is brooding **Mill Ruins Park**, steeped in history from when Minneapolis led the world in flour milling. From here, pick up the **St Anthony Falls Heritage Trail**, a 1.8-mile path that crosses the car-free Stone Arch Bridge, providing a terrific view of cascading St Anthony Falls.

Jump in a lake

Minnesota is dubbed the land of 10,000 lakes, and Minneapolis claims over 22 of them. **Bde Maka Ska** (a Dakotan name) and **Lake Harriet** are among the most popular, where everyone flocks to revel in the summer sunshine. Both have beaches, cafes, walking and cycling paths, and kayaks and stand-up paddleboards from **Wheel Fun Rentals** *(wheelfunrentals.com; per hr $15-25)*. The castle-like **Lake Harriet Band Shell** is always abuzz with free concerts and films. Both lakes are conveniently located a short distance southwest of downtown.

Further north **Lake of the Isles** and **Cedar Lake** are two quieter neighborhood lakes, surrounded by grand historic homes that make for some astonishing scenery.

Summer is the busiest time, but locals are out in all seasons. Autumnal walks around the lakes are particularly marvelous.

Catch a show

The city buzzes with creative energy that spills over into an active nightlife. Downtown's **First Avenue & 7th St Entry** *(first-avenue.com)* – where native son Prince grooved in *Purple Rain* – is the epicenter of the music scene. It's two venues in one: First Avenue is the main room featuring national acts; smaller 7th St Entry is for up-and-comers who play a stage-dive away from the crowd. Stars painted on the building's exterior show the famed names who've rocked here over the years.

The historic **Armory** *(armorymn.com)* pops on the weekends with punk, metal and alt-rock bands downtown. Nearby in the North Loop, **Bunker's Music Bar & Grill** *(bunkersmusic.com)* is a scruffy winner that puts funk, blues or reggae bands on stage six nights a week (closed Mondays).

Theater buffs should see what's on at the **Guthrie Theater** *(guthrietheater.org)*, where Minneapolis' top-gun troupe mounts bold-themed classic and new works downtown. **Jungle Theater** *(jungletheater.org)* offers a more intimate experience, staging high-quality productions in Uptown.

Urban escape to Minnehaha Falls

It's hard to believe a 53ft-tall waterfall crashes down into a limestone gorge just 15 minutes from downtown Minneapolis. But **Minnehaha Falls** *(minneapolisparks.org; free)*

WINTER FESTS

Krista Westendorp, writer, outdoor enthusiast and 40-year Twin Cities resident, shares her favorite winter events.

St Paul Winter Carnival: Cold and snow don't stop locals from being outside. The St Paul carnival has been going for 140 years. It starts in late January, with ice-carving competitions, snow sculptures, parades, winter biking and more over 10 days. It's an annual highlight.

Luminary Loppet: This enchanted evening walk (held every February) goes around Lake of the Isles, lit by 1200 candle luminaries, past intricate ice sculptures. Hot cocoa and s'mores are served along the trail, and the walk ends at a party with food trucks, music and beer. Other parks also host candlelit trail events throughout winter with bonfires and refreshments.

BEST TWIN CITIES SHOPPING

Mall of America: The USA's largest shopping center goes beyond stores with a zipline, mini-golf course and amusement park inside.

Electric Fetus: Prince used to browse at this indie record store, with a great selection of local music and cool gifts.

Twelve Vultures: Theatrical curiosity shop where shelves hold taxidermy foxes, moose antlers, antique-framed insect specimens and more.

Birchbark Books: Native-owned indie bookstore that's a cozy community hub, with creaking wood floors and handwritten staff recommendations.

Tropes & Trifles: Dedicated to romance novels; lots of cheeky gifts supplement the spicy book selection.

does exactly that. Gawp over the ledge from the top or take the stairs down to the bottom and explore the cascade from a different angle. It's particularly stunning in winter when it freezes over and you can walk right around it.

The sublime waterfall sits in the middle of a park with 193 acres of woodlands, bluffs and riverside trails to roam around. Afterward, angle for a seat at **Sea Salt Eatery** *(seasalt mpls.com)*, an open-air seafood spot right by the falls that's open daily April through October. Fish tacos, raw oysters, crab-cake sandwiches and pitchers of beer are available to help you replenish.

Chanhassen

Pay tribute to Prince at Paisley Park

Paisley Park *(paisleypark.com; tours from $75)*, Prince's mansion in Chanhassen, is a stark white building at the highway's edge, and looks like an unsexy office building outside, but inside is a different story. Ninety-minute tours take in the recording studio, soundstage and music club where he hosted his famous late-night bashes.

Outside the building, the **Prince Tribute Tunnel** is an underpass beneath the highway that leads directly toward Paisley Park, which is behind a wire fence. Along the fence, fans have affixed purple love locks, purple guitars, purple flowers, poems and other offerings. The underpass itself is covered in purple drawings and graffiti. It's all quite moving. To reach the tunnel, it's easiest to park at Lake Ann Park and follow the pedestrian path under the road, which heads to Riley Creek Tunnel (its official name).

St Paul

F Scott Fitzgerald's early haunts

St Paul, Minnesota's capital city, is smaller and quieter than its twin to the west, Minneapolis. Strolling through its historic neighborhoods is a delightful way to spend a morning or afternoon.

St Paul's most celebrated literary son is *The Great Gatsby* author F Scott Fitzgerald (1896–1940). The genteel area around Cathedral Hill – named for the colossal church that marks the spot – is his old stomping ground. The **Fitzgerald birthplace**, a Pullman-style apartment, is on Laurel Ave. Nearby, the brownstone at **599 Summit Ave** is where he lived when he

DRINKING IN MINNEAPOLIS: OUR PICKS

MAP P566, P568

Surly Brewing: Family-friendly beer hall with outdoor, dog-friendly beer garden. *3-10pm Mon-Thu, to midnight Fri, 11am-midnight Sat, 11am-11pm Sun*

Troubadour Wine Bar: Low-lit charmer for globally sourced reds and whites amid soulful live music. *5-10pm Mon-Thu, to midnight Fri & Sat*

Dogwood Coffee: Neon-clad industrial space to fuel your day with an espresso and game of ping-pong. *7am-7pm Mon-Fri, 8am-6pm Sat & Sun*

Sidecar at the Tap: Casually chic room for cocktails made with attention to detail. *4-11pm Tue & Wed, to midnight Thu-Sat, to 10pm Sun*

STEVE SKJOLD/SHUTTERSTOCK

Paisley Park

published *This Side of Paradise*. Both are private residences, so you can't go inside. Plaques mark the sites.

From here, continue along Summit Ave toward the cathedral to gape at the Victorian homes rising from the tree-lined street. Gilded Age vibes abound. Walk another half-mile or so toward the Mississippi River for more in the Irvine Park district, which is replete with fountains, gardens and turreted manors. It's next to W 7th St, an eating and drinking hub.

Learn to curl

For those uninitiated in northern ways, curling is a winter sport that involves sliding a 42lb granite stone (sort of like a jumbo hockey puck) down the ice toward a bull's-eye. It's popular in Minnesota, and there are rinks all over the state. The friendly folks at the **St Paul Curling Club** *(stpaulcurling club.org)* don't mind if you stop in to watch the action. Heck, they'll probably invite you to share a microbrew in the upstairs bar. It's the USA's largest club, and open daily in the evening from mid-October to late May.

CULINARY SPECIALTIES

Hearty comfort foods hit the tables in Minnesota. Keep an eye on local menus for walleye, Minnesota's state fish, which offers a mild, white meat. Nutty-tasting, native wild rice often turns up in breads and soups. The Jucy Lucy appears in pubs around the Twin Cities. It's a burger stuffed with a molten core of American cheese, made by pinching two patties around the yellow slices and grilling to greasy perfection. A 'hot dish' (aka casserole) typically includes ground beef, potatoes or pasta, green beans or corn, and a canned cream soup. Tater tots commonly top it. Lutefisk, dried cod that's rehydrated with lye and then cooked, is popular during the winter holidays. The gelatinous dish is an acquired taste.

EATING & DRINKING IN ST PAUL: OUR PICKS

Cecil's Deli: Kosher, family-run classic where locals devour huge sandwiches and matzo-ball soup at close-packed tables. *9am-8pm* **$$**

Hyacinth: Intimate, date-night restaurant serving modern takes on pasta, risotto and other buttery Italian dishes alongside cocktails. *5-9pm Tue-Sun* **$$$**

Nina's Coffee Cafe: In a rambling historic building full of nooks and crannies beloved by writers and cardamom-infused-latte fans. *6:30am-5pm*

Emerald Lounge: Sip creative cocktails (including alcohol-free ones) in plush seats amid vintage, green-toned decor. *4-10pm Tue-Thu, to 11pm Fri & Sat*

BEST QUIRKY MINNESOTA SIGHTS

Spam Museum: Learn all about the peculiar blue-tinned meat that has fed armies and inspired legions of haiku writers.

Darwin Twine Ball: The 'World's Largest Built by One Person': Francis A Johnson wrapped the 17,400lb whopper over 29 years.

Paul Bunyan Statue: The lofty lumberjack and his blue ox, Babe, tower over Bemidji's visitor center, which displays Paul's giant toothbrush inside.

Greyhound Bus Museum: See buses from yesteryear in an art deco–style terminal in Hibbing, where Greyhound Lines originated.

Mary Tyler Moore Statue: Photo op with the beloved 1970s TV character who put Minneapolis on the pop-culture map.

TAMMI MILD/GETTY IMAGES

Duluth

Freighter-filled, eclectic port town

Duluth is a brawny shot-and-a-beer port town that immerses visitors in its storied history as a major shipping center. Start downtown at the **Aerial Lift Bridge**, Duluth's landmark that raises its mighty arm to let horn-bellowing freighters into the harbor. About 900 vessels per year glide through. Pop in to the **Maritime Visitor Center** *(lsmma.com; free)*, next to the bridge, where computer screens tell what time the big ships come and go. Cool model boats and exhibits on Great Lakes shipwrecks also make it a top stop. From here you're a block from **Vikre Distillery** *(vikredistillery.com)*, which makes gin with Northwoods-foraged botanicals. Free tours take place on Monday and Friday (reserve ahead), while the festive tasting room is open every afternoon. Or hop on the Lakewalk outside the maritime center and amble along the paved path that edges Lake Superior. It's part of the long-distance Superior Hiking Trail (p574).

For a hip scene of indie breweries, cider makers and restaurants, ramble through the Lincoln Park Craft District, west of downtown.

EATING & DRINKING IN DULUTH: OUR PICKS

OMC Smokehouse: Buzzing industrial space for revered, slow-cooked meats and local craft brews; try the pulled pork. *11am-9pm Sun-Thu, to 10pm Fri & Sat* **$$**

New Scenic Cafe: Fork into refined meat and fish dishes in a cozy wood-paneled room with partial lake views. *11am-9pm Wed-Sun* **$$$**

Ursa Minor Brewing: Lively indoor-outdoor taproom serving pilsners, hazy IPAs, fruited sour ales and pizzas. *11am-10pm Sun-Thu, to 11pm Fri & Sat*

Duluth Cider: Choose among 14 hard ciders in this cool taproom carved from an old livery. *noon-10pm Mon-Thu, to 11pm Fri & Sat, 11am-8pm Sun*

Gooseberry Falls State Park

North Shore

Highway 61: nature at Lake Superior's rugged edge

Hwy 61 traces Lake Superior's shoreline, winding through red-tinged cliffs and towering firs from Duluth to Canada's edge. Several state parks dot the way, offering spectacular gorges, waterfalls and pine-scented hiking trails, much of it easily accessible from roadside parking lots. The route is 150 miles, drivable in three hours, but most folks make a weekend out of it, overnighting in little towns that speckle the landscape. Crowds amass on summer weekends.

After Duluth and Two Harbors, Hwy 61 ramps up its riches. First, there's pie at **Rustic Inn Cafe**, which wafts berry crumb, lemon meringue and a dozen other flaky-crust flavors from its log cabin at road's edge. **Gooseberry Falls State Park** appears a few miles onward. It's always busy, thanks to its five cascades, scenic gorge and easy trails, including the 2-mile Gooseberry River Loop. Another gorgeous landscape arrives 41 miles later at **Temperance River State Park**, where the waterway roars through a twisting gorge a short hike from the road.

Grand Marais (p574) has good eats, drinks and a lighthouse before hitting **Judge CR Magney State Park**. Here you can view Devil's Kettle, the famous falls where the Brule River splits around a huge rock. Half of the flow drops 50ft in a typically gorgeous North Shore gush, but the other half disappears down a hole and flows underground. Where it goes is a mystery – scientists have never been able to determine the water's outlet. It's a moderately breath-sapping 1.1-mile walk each way.

The road nears its end at **Grand Portage National Monument** *(nps.gov/grpo; free)*, a reconstructed 1788 trading post

TALL TALES

While the legend of Paul Bunyan is heard throughout the northern USA, it's particularly prevalent in Minnesota. Stories of the giant lumberjack with superhuman strength were told in logging camps in the late 1800s and gained widespread popularity in the early 20th century when companies began using the character in ads. Famous feats by Paul and his trusty blue ox, Babe, are myriad. For instance, Paul scooped out the Great Lakes when Babe was thirsty and needed water. And Babe created the Mississippi River when his tank wagon leaked while paving icy logging roads, with the trickle forming the Mississippi. Minnesota leads the USA in Bunyan statues with 11, including the 2.5-ton colossus in Bemidji.

MINNESOTA'S UNOFFICIAL STATE BIRD

Look in any souvenir shop up north, and you'll see a postcard or T-shirt that says 'Minnesota State Bird' with an image of a big, nasty mosquito underneath. These bloodsuckers are relentless in summer. They're drawn to carbon dioxide and body heat, which is why they feast on hikers and paddlers. But mosquitos aren't the only biters in action: black flies sink their teeth into your skin with a sharp pinch. No amount of swatting keeps them away. They annoy mostly in May and June, a bit earlier in the season than mosquitos. Both pests buzz throughout Minnesota, but they're most brutal in the north, where forests and wetlands provide ideal breeding grounds. Use repellent and a net hat to deter them.

CRAIG HINTON/SHUTTERSTOCK

Grand Marais Lighthouse

and Ojibwe village. The site is impressively lonely and windblown, open in summer only. **Isle Royale Ferries** *(isleroyale boats.com; adult/child $100.50/90.50)* also depart from Grand Portage for the 90-minute ride to Isle Royale National Park.

Information for the state parks is at *dnr.state.mn.us*. A vehicle day pass costs $7. An annual pass costs $35. Much of the hiking in the parks is along the Superior Hiking Trail.

Superior Hiking Trail adventure

The 300-mile **Superior Hiking Trail** *(shta.org)* follows the lake-hugging ridge line between Duluth and the Canadian border. Along the way it passes dramatic red-rock overlooks and the occasional moose and black bear. Trailheads with parking lots pop up every 5 to 10 miles, making it ideal for day hikes. The **Superior Shuttle** *(superiorhikingshuttle.com)* makes life even easier, picking up trekkers anywhere along the route as needed (reserve ahead). Overnight hikers will find 94 backcountry campsites and several lodges to cushion the body come nightfall; the trail website has details. The whole footpath is free, with no reservations or permits required. It's easiest to start in the south, where the terrain is more gentle. Thru-hikes take two to four weeks.

GETTING TO ISLE ROYALE

While you can get to **Isle Royale National Park** (p549) from Minnesota, there is greater access from Michigan, which is the state that Isle Royale is officially part of.

Artsy getaway to Grand Marais

Pretty little Grand Marais beckons toward the northern end of Hwy 61 (p573). It makes an excellent base for exploring the parks and trails along Lake Superior, as well as for venturing into the Boundary Waters. Several bars, restaurants, art galleries and antique shops in the tidy downtown give it a 'big city' feel.

Grand Marais' artistic pretensions are genuine. The **Grand Marais Art Colony** *(grandmaraisartcolony.org)* started in 1947 and exists to this day, luring painters, potters and print makers. Do-it-yourself enthusiasts can learn to build boats, sail a schooner and forage for mushrooms at the **North House Folk School** *(northhouse.org)*. If nothing else, make time for the 20-minute walk along the breakwater to **Grand Marais Lighthouse**. The path departs adjacent to **Artist's Point**, a dramatic-looking flat-rock area that is especially luminous as the sun sets.

Gunflint Trail scenic drive

The **Gunflint Trail** *(gunflinttrail.com)*, aka County Rd 12, slices inland through the pines from Grand Marais to Saganaga Lake. The paved, 57-mile-long byway dips into the Boundary Waters area and presents excellent hiking, picnicking and moose-viewing opportunities. It takes 1½ hours to drive one way, but you'll want longer to make stops at roadside pull-offs like the **Moose Viewing Trail**, a 0.3-mile walk to a lake where antlered pals sometimes gather. There aren't any towns along the route, but there are several lodges tucked in woods if you want to grab a meal or snack.

BOB DYLAN'S MINNESOTA ROOTS

Robert Zimmerman was born in Duluth in 1941. His family moved to Hibbing when he was still quite young. As a teenager he listened to radio stations from Chicago and Little Rock, which played the kind of music that few people in Hibbing knew. His first group, the Golden Chords, won a mere second prize at the local talent show. Bobby made frequent trips to big-city Minneapolis, where he hung around the university area, going to jazz joints and coffeehouses. He enrolled at the University of Minnesota for a year, but dropped out and headed to New York City's folk scene. By 1962 he had legally changed his name to Bob Dylan and never looked back.

Hibbing

Explore the Iron Range

An area of red-tinged scrubby hills rather than mountains, the ore-rich Iron Range stretches across northeastern Minnesota. Hibbing is the largest town in the region with a couple of claims to fame. For one, Bob Dylan grew up here. See the papier-mâché Bob and small collection of memorabilia at the **Hibbing Public Library** *(hibbingmn.gov)*. It also provides a free walking tour map to find sites like his **Boyhood Home**, where he lived from 1948 to 1959, when he left for Minneapolis. It's privately owned, but good for a discreet photo.

The **Hull Rust Mine Viewpoint** *(hibbingmineview.org)* is the other must-see. Follow the signs that lead a few miles north of town, and behold the enormous, 3.5-mile-wide, open-pit mine spread below. The mind-blowingly huge display trucks give a sense of scale; go ahead and climb up. It's one of the largest iron-ore mines in the world.

Boundary Waters

Canoeing unspoiled wilderness to sleep under the stars

Legendarily remote and pristine, the Boundary Waters Canoe Area Wilderness is one of the world's premier paddling regions.

EATING & DRINKING IN GRAND MARAIS: OUR PICKS

Fisherman's Daughter at Dockside Fish Market: The morning boat's fresh haul is your fish and chips by lunchtime. *11am-8pm* **$$**

My Sister's Place: Tuck into sandwiches, burgers and fish dishes in this woodsy spot with an old-time saloon atmosphere. *11am-8pm* **$$**

World's Best Donuts: Staff nobly arrive at 3am to fry and glaze; join the queue for the chocolatey, cream-filled results. *7am-3pm Thu-Mon* **$**

Voyageur Brewing Co: Brewpub with a lake-view deck for knocking back sturdy stouts and ales. *11:30am-9pm Sun-Wed, to 10pm Thu-Sat*

TOP EXPERIENCE

Voyageurs National Park

Northern Voyageurs National Park, which marks the border between the USA and Canada, is a mosaic of land and water. Get ready for boating in summer, snowmobiling in winter and starry dark skies year-round. You'll have much of the landscape to yourself, as this is one of the USA's least-visited parks.

PER BREIEHAGEN/GETTY IMAGES

TOP TIPS

- Visit late July to mid-August for warmest lake temperatures and fewest biting insects.
- Boat tours operate mid-June to September; reserve at *recreation.gov*.
- Evening boat tours are often timed to coincide with stargazing tours; check *nps.gov/voya*.

PRACTICALITIES

- nps.gov/voya
- open year-round
- free

Summer Action

During the late May to September peak season, people come to Voyageurs to boat, fish, swim and spot wildlife. Moose, wolves and black bears prowl the forest. Visitor centers at Rainy Lake (open year-round), Kabetogama Lake, Crane Lake and Ash River (all open seasonally) have the lowdown on programs and boat tours. The 2½-hour **Rainy Lake Grand Tour** *(adult/child $50/25)* gives a feel for the scene, as does the **North Canoe Voyage** *(adult/child $15/7.50)* aboard a 26ft birchbark vessel like 17th-century fur traders (aka voyageurs) once paddled. For a true park experience, many visitors rent a houseboat from **Ebel's Voyageur Houseboats** *(ebels.com)* or **Voyagaire Houseboats** *(voyagaire.com)*.

Dark Skies & Winter Fun

Voyageurs is an International Dark Sky Park. The upper parking lot at **Rainy Lake Visitor Center** is an excellent place to stargaze. You might even glimpse the green-draped northern lights (more common in winter). Also prevalent in winter: snowmobiling. Voyageurs is a hot spot for the sport, with 110 miles of staked and groomed trails slicing through the pines. Snowshoeing and cross-country skiing on the trails also are popular.

More than 1000 lakes and streams speckle the piney, 1.1-million-acre expanse, rich in wildlife and sweeping solitude. If you're willing to dig in and canoe for a while, it'll just be you and the moose, bears, wolves and loons that roam the landscape.

The area draws hard-core outdoor adventurers, with most coming for at least four or five days to get away from it all. But it's possible to glide in for a day, too.

However long you plan to stay, know that this is real-deal backcountry and you need to be prepared. Outfitters can help. Ely (pronounced *ee*-lee), the main gateway into the Boundary Waters, has scores of them. The super-knowledgeable folks at **Piragis Northwoods Company** *(piragis.com)* have been around for decades and can set you up with canoes and gear for day trips, overnight stays, guided trips and more. **Ely Outfitting Company** *(elyoutfittingcompany.com)* is another good one.

Entry into the Boundary Waters requires a permit. Day-trip permits are free and can be obtained from the kiosk wherever you enter, no advance booking needed. Overnight permits *(recreation.gov; per trip adult/child $16/8, plus reservation fee $6)* are issued by the US Forest Service and best obtained in advance online. They're limited, and paddlers start snapping them up in January when they are released for the year. It gets a bit complex, as permits are for a specific entry location, of which there are many throughout the vast expanse, some of which require advanced paddling skills. Check *friends-bwca.org* for info. Outfitters are a good resource to help with this, too.

Late May through September is the paddling season, with July and August the peak times. Besides Ely, you can also access the Boundary Waters from Grand Marais by following the Gunflint Trail.

Meet a Boundary Waters rebel

Dorothy Molter lived for 56 years in a cabin in the Boundary Waters' midst, 18 miles from the nearest road. When the Forest Service tried to obtain her land, she refused to move, sparking a long legal battle. Dorothy won and remained in her cabin, paddling, hiking and fishing for whatever she needed. She became famous for providing medical assistance (she was trained as a nurse) and homemade root beer to anyone who dropped by. She died at age 79 (while hauling firewood!) and her friends brought her homestead by dogsled to Ely. It's now a root-beer-selling **museum** *(rootbeerlady.com; adult/child $7/4.50)* that lets you look around her badass abode.

WILDLIFE SPOTTING

Minnesota's northern region, including the Boundary Waters and Voyageurs National Park, holds the star wildlife. Between 13,000 and 18,000 black bears roam the local forests, according to the Department of Natural Resources (DNR). They're relatively common to spot, especially in the fall. Moose are more elusive. The DNR estimates around 4000 rustle through the north woods. Early morning or evening is the best time to see them. Minnesota has the largest population of wolves in the lower 48 states, with some 2900 prowling the area. They're rare to see, but you might hear their eerie howl at night. The loon, Minnesota's state bird, hangs out in the multitude of lakes in summer. Their haunting wail often is heard at night.

Places We Love to Stay

$ Budget $$ Midrange $$$ Top End

Chicago MAPS P497, P502, P507

HI-Chicago $ Chicago's most stalwart hostel is immaculate and adds a staffed information desk, lounge and stocked kitchen to the mix.

Hampton Inn Chicago Downtown/N Loop $$ Features the chain's much-loved amenities in retro environs.

Publishing House Bed & Breakfast $$ Vintage West Loop building with 11 mid-century modern rooms named after Chicago writers.

Robey $$ Sunny rooms stack a 12-story, art-deco tower in Wicker Park, complete with rooftop swimming pool.

Acme Hotel $$ Industrial-chic fills this energetic, 130-room Near North hotel.

Illinois

Inn at 835 (Springfield) **$$** Rooms of the four-poster bed, claw-foot bathtub variety occupy a 1908 arts-and-crafts-style luxury apartment building.

Shawnee Forest Cabins (Herod) **$$** Settle into a cozy log cottage, with hot tub and firepit, in the peaceful woods.

Indiana

Pepin Mansion (New Albany) **$** Standing supremely along New Albany's historical Mansion Row, this 1851 Italianate abode features ornate hand-painted ceilings, original hardwood flooring and gas chandeliers.

Riverboat Inn & Suites (Madison) **$** Parts of this historic inn on the river date back to 1929 (it was a former button factory). Riverfront patio bar and free breakfast.

Hotel Broad Ripple (Indianapolis) **$$** This Scandinavian-accented boutique hotel is a cozy getaway in hip Broad Ripple, offering spacious rooms right along the Monon Trail.

Story Inn (Nashville) **$$** This former general store dating to 1851 (tin roof and metal facade still intact!) drips with countrified rustic charm, offering rooms, cottages and a farm-to-table restaurant.

Riley's Railhouse (Chesterton) **$$** Occupying a decommissioned 1914 freight station, this is a railway-themed boutique B&B with rooms inside a renovated depot and railcars. Train enthusiasts will love it – 86 pass per day!

Oliver Inn (South Bend) **$$** Elegant nine-room B&B in a Queen Anne–style home dating to 1886. Corner turrets, curved-glass bay windows, claw-foot tubs, and spindles and balustrades abound.

Ironworks Hotel (Indianapolis) **$$$** With design touches forged from industrial parts from an abandoned Wisconsin iron foundry, this hotel has several restaurants, a gym and 120 fantastic rooms.

Ohio

Symphony Hotel (Cincinnati) **$** Nine rooms in a traditional Italianate building, each named after a classical composer, and each chock-full of period antique decor. Breakfast included.

Clifford House B&B (Cleveland) **$$** If you don't like animals, this beautiful Ohio City B&B isn't for you. If you do, Henry the dog and Connie the cat are ready for you! Jim the human cooks up a scrumptious breakfast and is great fun to chat with. Free parking.

Inn at Brandywine Falls (Cuyahoga Valley) **$$** An 1848 Greek Revival country home situated in a gentle sweep of pastoral prettiness. Six rooms, of which the Granary suite is particularly lovely. Breakfasts are delicious.

Inn at Honey Run (Millersburg) **$$$** In Amish Country, 25 rooms occupy the lodge-like main building, while 12 'honeycomb' rooms are built right into the hillside Frank Lloyd Wright–style. Adults only.

Metropolitan at the 9 (Cleveland) **$$$** Upscale Marriott-branded property with 156 good-sized rooms, a rooftop bar and a subterranean cocktail lounge set in the building's old bank vaults.

Hotel Kilbourne (Sandusky) **$$$** Near the ferry dock, a boutique hotel complete with rooftop bar, a Mexican restaurant and a gift shop, all on-site.

Michigan MAP P538

Hostel Detroit (Detroit) **$** An old building rehabbed using recycled materials and painted in vivid colors inside and out. Dormitories, private rooms and shared bathrooms and kitchens.

Landmark Inn (Marquette) **$$** This elegant, six-story hotel fills a historic lakefront building and has a couple of resident ghosts.

El Moore Lodge (Detroit) **$$** A unique option in Midtown with a friendly vibe, its 11 rooms occupy a turreted 1898 building that's been renovated;

reclaimed wood and tiles feature in the interior.

Shinola Hotel (Detroit) **$$$** Detroit's homegrown brand known for luxury watches extends to this stylish hotel downtown. The 129 rooms have mid-century modern decor, big windows and Bluetooth speaker systems.

Perry Hotel (Petoskey) **$$$** Grand historic place where Hemingway once stayed (in 1916 after a hiking trip in the region). Count on comfy beds, vintage furniture and a cozy on-site pub.

Grey Hare Inn (Traverse City) **$$$** An intimate, three-room B&B on a working vineyard, with French-style decor and bay views. Free wine tastings.

Glen Arbor B&B (Sleeping Bear Dunes) **$$$** The owners renovated this century-old farmhouse into a sunny, French country inn with eight themed rooms.

Burnt Toast Inn (Ann Arbor) **$$$** Colorful house with a lovely garden, big porch and five rooms that mix sturdy antiques with edgy art. On a leafy street walkable to downtown. Free parking and breakfast.

Rock Harbor Lodge (Isle Royale) **$$$** The island's sole lodge, offering 60 rooms with lake views in the main building, as well as 20 cabins with kitchenettes.

Wisconsin

MAP P554

Julie's Park Cafe and Motel (Door County) **$** Long-standing, crowd-pleasing budget option in Fish Creek right next door to Peninsula State Park.

Ambassador (Milwaukee) **$$** Renovated art-deco gem near Marquette University, chock-full of polished marbled floors, bronze elevator doors and more period details.

County Clare Irish Inn (Milwaukee) **$$** Rooms have a snug cottage feel, with four-poster beds, white wainscot walls and whirlpool baths; there's an on-site pub.

Hotel Ruby Marie (Madison) **$$** A 19th-century railroad hotel retrofitted with modern conveniences while retaining vintage charm; free breakfast and happy-hour drinks.

Graduate Madison (Madison) **$$** Near State St's action, this 72-room hotel wafts a hip academic vibe with its mod-meets-plaid decor and book-themed artwork.

Square Rigger Lodge (Door County) **$$** Guests return year after year to this Jacksonport motel winner that features a private sand beach.

Beachfront Inn (Door County) **$$** Cute Bailey's Harbor lakefront motel that earns extra points for its pool, nighttime beach bonfires and nearby pubs.

Charmant Hotel (La Crosse) **$$** Sweet renovation of a 1898 candy factory into 67 rooms with exposed brick walls, wood floors and industrial-cool charm.

Brewhouse Inn & Suites (Milwaukee) **$$$** A 90-room hotel set in the old Pabst Brewery complex. The large chambers have steampunk-type decor.

Old Rittenhouse Inn (Bayfield) **$$$** Looking for lace, creaky floorboards and a romantic escape? This inn fills two Victorian homes atop a hill with lake views.

Minnesota

MAP P566

Mountain Inn (Lutsen) **$** Well-run motel with spacious rooms that are nothing fancy, but they're great value for the Lake Superior area.

Adventure Inn (Ely) **$** A blue ribbon to the cute tidy motel rooms, which are walkable to eats and drinks in downtown Ely.

Canopy Mill District (Minneapolis) **$$** Ornamental historic building downtown, where contemporary rooms have high, timbered ceilings and exposed brick.

Hewing Hotel (Minneapolis) **$$** Rustic-vibe chambers feature wood-beam ceilings, deer-print wallpaper and plaid wool blankets; near downtown's action.

Celeste of St Paul (St Paul) **$$** Located downtown, this lovingly restored former convent offers 72 smart, lofty rooms and a bouncy bar.

Hungry Hippie Farm & Hostel (Grand Marais) **$$** Pretty farmhouse 8 miles east of Grand Marais, with six rustic-chic private rooms that share bathrooms.

Northern Rail Traincar Inn (Two Harbors) **$$** It doesn't get much cooler than 14 rooms built into renovated train boxcars.

Ash Trail Lodge (Orr) **$$** Family-owned business that offers little cabins and great home cooking right next to Voyageurs National Park.

Hotel Alma (Minneapolis) **$$$** Seven light-wood, Nordic-style rooms set above Alma (the Beard Award–winning restaurant-cafe); delicious breakfast pastries provided.

109
109
brightline
brightline

TOOLKIT

The chapters in this section cover the most important topics you'll need to know about in Eastern USA. They're full of nuts-and-bolts information and valuable insights to help you understand and navigate Eastern USA and get the most out of your trip.

Arriving p582

Getting Around p583

Travel by Train p584

Money p585

Accommodations p586

Family Travel p587

Food, Drink & Nightlife p588

Responsible Travel p590

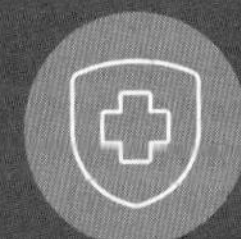

Health & Safe Travel p592

LGBTIQ+ Travelers p593

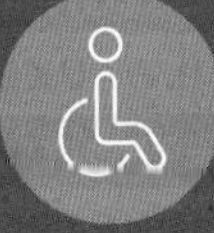

Accessible Travel p594

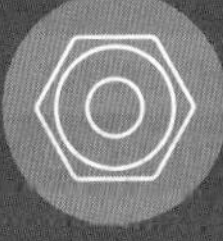

Nuts & Bolts p595

Brightline inter-city rail, Florida (p456)

MARKUS MAINKA/SHUTTERSTOCK

Arriving

The Eastern USA is packed with major airports that serve as both international and domestic gateways. You'll find the largest number of connections (and generally the most competitive prices) at the following major hubs: Atlanta (ATL), Boston (BOS), Charlotte (CLT), Chicago (ORD), Detroit (DTW), Miami (MIA), New York (JFK), Newark (EWR), Orlando (MCO) and Washington, DC (IAD).

Visas

Citizens of many countries are eligible for the Visa Waiver Program, which requires prior approval via Electronic System for Travel Authorization (ESTA). Fill out the online form at least 72 hours prior to departure.

ATMs

Choose wisely when selecting an ATM at the airport. It's better to go with machines linked to a bank rather than currency-exchange ATMs, which tend to charge higher fees.

Wi-fi

All major airports offer free wi-fi. You can also find free wi-fi at hotels, along with at many restaurants, cafe and public libraries. Some cities and towns have free public wi-fi hotspots.

Border Crossings

There are numerous border crossings with Canada. Make sure your documents are in order, and plan your arrival carefully – avoid peak times like weekends and holidays if possible.

Travel to City Center

FROM		TO	DURATION
NYC	>	PHILADELPHIA	1½HRS
NYC	>	WASHINGTON, DC	3½HRS
NYC	>	BOSTON	4½HRS
CHICAGO	>	MILWAUKEE	4½HRS
CHICAGO	>	DETROIT	7HRS
CHICAGO	>	MINNEAPOLIS	9HRS
ATLANTA	>	NASHVILLE	3½HRS
ATLANTA	>	CHARLESTON	7½HRS
ATLANTA	>	ORLANDO	7½HRS
NASHVILLE	>	ORLANDO	6HRS
MIAMI	>	ORLANDO	4HRS

BRINGING ITEMS INTO THE US

The US has fairly strict rules regarding what you can bring into the country, so pack your bag carefully. In general, you're not allowed to bring any agricultural products into the country (food, vegetables, plants etc). Bakery items and prepared foods are permitted (coffee, tea, honey). You can bring in 1L of alcohol for personal use – but not if you're under 21. Although recreational or medical marijuana is legal in some states, it is illegal to bring marijuana and cannabis-infused products into the US. The exception is CBD oil with less than 0.3% THC on a dry weight basis.

CLOCKWISE FROM TOP LEFT: FUSE/GETTY IMAGES, GOGLIK83/GETTY IMAGES

Getting Around

Transportation options vary by location. Urban areas are great for walking, cycling and public transit. Rural areas require a car. Flights are the fastest way to travel long distances.

TRAVEL COSTS

Bus/subway ride **$2-3.50**

Bikeshare rental **from $8/day**

Gasoline **$3-5 per gallon**

Car rental From $50/day

Public Transportation

Public transit networks in large cities may include buses, subways, streetcars and even ferries. Most have dedicated apps for ticketing and trip planning – including MTA (NYC), Ventra (Chicago), MBTA mTicket (Boston), and SmarTrip (DC). See the spectrum of transit possibilities by using the Citymapper app, available in over a dozen Eastern USA cities, showcasing routes and travel time for everything from trains and buses to bikeshares and e-scooters.

Ferry Fun

Various boat services provide efficient links to Atlantic islands and hard-to-reach peninsulas. In New England, avoid Cape Cod traffic by ferrying from Boston to Provincetown *(baystatecruise company.com)* and hop on boats to reach Block Island *(blockislandferry.com)*, Martha's Vineyard and Nantucket *(steamship authority.com)*. Seastreak *(seastreak.com)* sails from NYC to the Jersey Shore, Martha's Vineyard and beyond. The North Carolina Ferry System *(ferry.ncdot.gov)* connects the mainland to the Outer Banks.

TIP

Intercity rail networks such as Metro North (NY), NJ Transit (NJ), Brightline (FL) and national rail company Amtrak (p584) make it possible to travel throughout the US sans car.

DRIVING ESSENTIALS

Drive on the right-hand side of the road.

Speed limits vary: the max speed on interstate is often 65-70mph, 55mph in urban areas and 15-45mph in rural and residential areas.

.08

Blood alcohol limit is 0.08%

Fast Flights

When time is tight, book a flight. The domestic air network is extensive and reliable, with dozens of competing airlines and hundreds of airports – including small, easy-to-navigate hubs everywhere from Savannah, GA, to Burlington, VT. Flying is often more expensive than a bus, train or car.

Cities for Cycling

Cycling is thriving in major cities thanks to the ubiquity of bike-share programs and a steady increase in protected bike lanes. Some of the most successful programs include Bluebikes (Boston), Capital Bikeshare (DC), Citi Bike (NYC), Divvy (Chicago), Indego (Philadelphia) and Lime (Minneapolis).

Budget Bus Rides

Save money by riding a bus – they're often cheaper than planes and trains. Greyhound *(greyhound.com)* is the major long-distance company, with an extensive nationwide network. Other major bus companies include Trailways *(trailways.com)*, Megabus *(megabus.com)* and FlixBus *(flixbus.com)*.

Travel by Train

Once the engine of 19th-century progress, US rail travel was eventually eclipsed by cars – but 21st-century travelers are heading back to the tracks. Amtrak leads the charge, with onboard cafes, spacious seats and sleeper compartments where passengers can admire the shifting landscape through panoramic picture windows. All aboard.

Epic Amtrak Trips

Amtrak's *(amtrak.com)* long-distance routes stitch the Eastern USA together on overnight and multiday journeys, ideal for travelers who enjoy scenic excursions and have time to burn. Delays are common.

The **Adirondack** chugs between New York and Montréal on a 10-hour jaunt, leaving NYC's bustle for the bucolic Hudson Valley and beyond, a leaf-peeper's autumn delight. The **Silver Meteor** cruises south of NYC to Miami in over 28 hours, linking major East Coast cities. **Lake Shore Limited** zooms from Chicago to Boston and on to NYC in 19 hours, connecting the Midwest to the Northeast. Stops in Cleveland (Ohio) and Buffalo (New York) offer chances to explore America's Rust Belt renaissance. The **Crescent** trades the Big Apple (NYC) for the Big Easy (New Orleans) in 30 hours, zipping from the East Coast to the Gulf Coast. More lines criss-cross the region: explore Amtrak's website for additional routes.

Long-Distance Planning

When overnighting on Amtrak, book a private room for maximum comfort. Choose between a roomette (two chairs that form a bed, plus a pull-down bunk bed), bedroom (larger room with a sofa and in-room sink, toilet and shower), bedroom suite (two bedrooms put together), family room (two lower bunks and two upper bunks – no in-unit bathroom) or a wheelchair-accessible room.

All routes stop in multiple cities, but if you want to hop off and explore, you'll have to purchase separate tickets for each segment. To make the most of a multi-stop adventure, consider purchasing a USA Rail Pass *($499)*. Passes are valid for 10 segments, which must be completed within 30 days of the first trip. All passes must be used within 120 days of purchase. Note: these passes are only valid for coach seats – not business class or sleeper cabins.

Great Regional Rails

For short city-to-city trips, regional train routes offer speed and convenience. Amtrak's **Acela** (the nation's fastest rail line) provides service between Boston, NYC, Philadelphia and DC – cities with extensive public transit networks, all navigable sans car. The **Hiawatha** line connects Chicago and Milwaukee in 90 minutes; private company **Brightline** *(gobrightline.com)* hustles from Miami to Orlando in 3½ hours.

PURCHASING AMTRAK TICKETS

The easiest way to secure tickets is online, through the Amtrak app or via phone (1-800-872-7245). You can also make reservations at Amtrak station kiosks or with ticket agents at staffed departure points. Avoid buying tickets onboard: fares are highest and you may be denied seats on packed trains.

Money

CURRENCY: US DOLLAR ($)

Cash or Credit?

Credit cards are widely accepted – and required to make reservations for hotels and car rentals. Still, it's wise to carry cash. Some businesses, usually mom-and-pop restaurants, don't take cards. ATMs are available at banks, gas stations and grocery stores; expect service fees. Carry $20s – some establishments won't accept large bills.

Tax Territories

Sales taxes vary by city and state. Chicago tops the charts with a 10.25% tax rate. The state of Louisiana is close behind: the combined state and local tax can reach over 10%. Save that big shopping spree for Delaware or New Hampshire, where the sales tax is 0%.

Saving Money

The US economy has been a roller coaster since 2020, with rising costs driven by supply-chain hiccups, labor shortages, fuel hikes and tariff wars. Cut expenses by picking up food at farmers markets (no tipping required) and venturing a few blocks from tourist hotspots, where you'll likely find lower-price restaurants and shops.

HOW MUCH FOR A...

National park entry
free-$35

Museum entry
$5-35

Movie ticket
$12-24

City parking garage
$15-60

HOW TO... Tip

Tips aren't appreciated – they're expected. Although it isn't mandatory, gratuity is factored into the wages of service-industry professionals. Receiving tips from customers is an essential part of their income. For restaurants, tip 18% to 20% – unless service is terrible. At bars, start with $1 to $2 a drink, more for speciality cocktails, or 15% to 20% overall. Give taxi drivers a 10% to 20% tip and put aside $2 to $5/day for hotel house-keepers.

MORE MUSEUMS FOR LESS

Many cities have designated days when entrance to museums is free or reduced for visitors, potentially saving culture vultures hundreds of dollars. In NYC, for example, you'll find free or pay-what-you-wish admission days at top museums including the Guggenheim, MoMA and Whitney. Check museum schedules before planning your visit. **CityPASS** *(citypass.com)* offers discounts to museums in Atlanta, Boston, Chicago, NYC, Orlando and Philadelphia. Buy admission to three to five major tourist attractions and save around 40% on prices – just ensure you want to see what's offered.

MOBILE PAYMENTS

No card? No problem. Many shops, cafes and restaurants – and some transit systems – accept mobile payments such as Apple Pay and Google Pay, so you can pay by tapping your phone.

CLOCKWISE FROM BOTTOM LEFT: AUDLEY C BULLOCK/SHUTTERSTOCK, JIANGDI/SHUTTERSTOCK, NEW AFRICA/SHUTTERSTOCK

Accommodations

Get Cozy at B&Bs

It's difficult finding B&Bs in big cities, but these privately owned affairs delight around rural villages and their outskirts. Accommodations range from cozy rooms with shared bathrooms to swanky settings akin to boutique hotels. Anticipate cheery customer service and chatty guests: you'll likely share a table over breakfast. It's common to require two-night minimums in high season.

Camp under Stars

Pitching tents around public parks and private grounds is a beloved summer pastime. Campsites range from remote DIY plots with little more than an outhouse to communal settings with bathrooms and pools. Many sites take reservations on *recreation.gov*. Glamping is increasingly common, with rustic resorts featuring snug cabins and safari-style tents with comfy beds – all creature comforts included.

Relax at Boutique Hotels & Resorts

Boutique hotels tend to be smaller than the big-name chains, with intimate rooms and personalized touches. Resorts ply visitors with on-site activities such as hiking trails, water sports, nightly bonfires and on-site restaurants. Travelers can often score discounts in the low season.

Park It at Motels

'Motor hotels' – modest roadside accommodations with mid-century-modern appeal – surged in popularity after 2020. A lynchpin of 1960s American road-trip travel, these often affordable digs are getting rediscovered by a new generation interested in pulling their front bumper up to their front door. Expect everything from dreary highway hovels to recently renovated hotspots aimed at stylish sightseers seeking retro kitsch.

HOW MUCH FOR A NIGHT IN...

Bare-bones campsite
$25-60

Rural B&B
$100-300

High-end hotel
From $350

Save Big at Hostels

Hostel culture isn't deeply ingrained in the US, but dorm-style, budget-friendly accommodations still exist in cities like New York City, Philadelphia, Chicago, Miami and New Orleans. Try chains like Hostelling International USA's bare-bones bunk beds and Freehand's slightly more sophisticated 'poshtels'. Many hostels organize social events, such as group dinners and walking tours – ideal for meeting fellow penny-pinching travelers.

THE AIRBNB EFFECT

Short-term rentals on Airbnb and Vrbo can be fantastic housing alternatives, with stays on sprawling properties, at reasonable prices and in private locations far from hotels. But not everyone is thrilled with their ever-growing expansion – especially in NYC. In 2023, city officials implemented a law prohibiting rentals under 30 days when a host isn't present on the property. Roughly 80% of NYC's Airbnb units immediately vanished. NYC's arguments mirror those in many destinations: homestays contribute to the city's housing crisis by driving up rents, displacing locals and upending communities.

CLOCKWISE FROM TOP LEFT: ALEXANDIOR/SHUTTERSTOCK, NELEA33/SHUTTERSTOCK, ALESIAKAN/SHUTTERSTOCK

Family Travel

The Eastern USA has activities for all ages. Soon-to-be city slickers, mountaineers-in-the-making, budding academics and roller-coaster tycoons will appreciate the variety of family-friendly entertainment, interactive museums and wild parks. Cities are fantastic for endless options, while rural areas provide space for kids to explore their inner animal. No matter the destination, no one's getting bored.

Be a Park Ranger

Earn brag-worthy badges through the Junior Ranger Program, available at state and national parks from the Everglades to Acadia. To earn the badge, kids must complete a game-centric workbook, occasionally accompanied by an activity such as hiking. Best for kids ages five to 12 – though adults can enjoy it, too; everyone will likely gain a deeper understanding of the surrounding environment.

Plane & Train Travel

Children aged two to 12 can ride most Amtrak trains at 50% of the adult fare; infants under two ride for free, provided they're on an adult's lap. Most public transit in cities allows children under a certain height or age to ride for free with a fare-paying guardian. All infants two and under can ride domestic US flights for free.

BEST ATTRACTIONS FOR FAMILIES

American Museum of Natural History, NYC (p90)
Inspect dinosaur bones, butterfly wings and galaxies far, far away.

Orlando Theme Parks, Florida (p464)
Disney, Universal, SeaWorld, LEGOLAND: the magic only pauses for naptime.

Shedd Aquarium, Chicago (p507)
Greet sea lions and penguins or feed stingrays in summer.

Cedar Point, Ohio (p532)
Ride some of the planet's wildest roller coasters.

National Air and Space Museum, DC (p249)
Inspire budding aviators with rockets, spacecrafts and ride simulators.

Discounts for Kids

From DC's kid-friendly museums to Orlando's theme parks, the options for kid-centric activities can seem endless – and expensive. Many establishments offer 'child tickets' – and while definitions vary, it generally applies to children under 12 years old.

Car Seat Laws

Laws vary by state, but most require rear-facing car seats until at least age two, then forward-facing harness seats through age four or five. Booster seats are usually required until age eight. Children under 13 should ride in the back seat.

DINING WITH KIDS

Many US restaurants cater to families. Greasy-spoon diners and chains offer children's menus with smaller portions and lower prices, and if you need a high chair or booster seat, there's likely one available. Establishments without children's menus don't necessarily discourage kids, though you should think twice before bringing a picky palate to a Michelin-starred hotspot. Luckily, the East Coast excels at cooking up what kids crave: cheesy pizzas, buttered bagels, mayonnaise-glazed lobster rolls and ketchup-drenched hot dogs. If you'd rather dine outdoors with messy eaters, stop by a farmers market, pick out fruits, cheeses and sweets, and voilà – a DIY picnic.

Food, Drink & Nightlife

When to Eat

Breakfast (7am to 11am) Ranges from on-the-go grub like bagels to pancakes and eggs at a diner.

Brunch (11am to 2pm) Usually replaces breakfast on weekends with slightly fancier fare.

Lunch (noon to 2pm) Everything from sandwiches to three-course meals.

Happy hour (5pm to 7pm) Some places serve reduced-price snacks and drinks.

Dinner (5pm to 9pm) Two to three courses: appetizer, main, dessert.

MENU DECODER

À la carte Order individual menu items; sides are usually ordered separately from main dishes.

Antipasti 'Appetizers' – commonly seen on Italian restaurant menus.

Entree The main course in the US.

Omakase Japanese for 'I'll leave it up to you' – a fitting description for this chef-curated experience at sushi-forward restaurants.

BYOB The acronym for 'Bring Your Own Bottle', which means restaurant customers can bring their own alcohol, usually a bottle of wine. Expect a corking fee.

Gratuity included The tip has already been added to the bill, often for parties of six or more. No need to add extra.

Tasting menu A multi-course meal with small portions highlighting the chef's culinary artistry.

Prix fixe A multi-course meal for a 'fixed price', sometimes with limited choices per course.

Where to Eat

Cafes and bakeries Coffee, pastries and light meals served until afternoon.

Crab, clam or lobster shacks Informal coastal eateries serving seafood.

Diners Casual greasy-spoon haunts specializing in breakfast fare and sandwiches.

Food halls Groups of indoor food counters plating a variety of cuisines, usually at reasonable prices.

Food trucks Carts or trucks serving handheld street fare to urban eaters: tacos, dosas, hot dogs and more.

Pubs Drinking establishments that may serve basic bar food; gastropubs plate more innovative dishes.

HOW TO...

Order Barbecue

Ordering at a BBQ counter is fairly straightforward, but first-time visitors may get overwhelmed by the number of choices. Popular restaurants typically post a menu with notes on what's offered or sold out.

Take your pick among the variety of meats on display, often brisket (flavorful beef, smoked or braised), pulled pork (shredded, slow-cooked pork shoulder) and ribs (pork or beef, served with sauces). They're sometimes priced by weight; most adults eating solo will want a third- to half-pound.

Next come the side dishes, often showcased buffet-style, making it easy to point and choose whatever looks most promising. They're normally served in a range of sizes: individual, pint and quart. Vegans and vegetarians – inquire how sides like collard greens are prepared. They may contain animal fats.

After paying, pick a seat. Many restaurants use shared tables. Don't be afraid to plop down next to a stranger if necessary. They won't bite.

CLOCKWISE FROM BOTTOM LEFT: FOODANDPHOTO/SHUTTERSTOCK, ALEXANDER RATHS/SHUTTERSTOCK

HOW MUCH FOR A...

Bagel
$1.75-5

Plain pizza slice
$3-6

Coffee
$2-5

Pint of beer
$4-12

Lobster roll
From $28

Craft cocktail
$12-22

Breakfast at a diner
From $12

Barbecue meal
$15-35

HOW TO... Eat Lobster

Lobster, New England's beloved red-shelled sea treat, plays a starring role on menus everywhere from Boston's award-winning restaurants to Maine's seafood shacks. It's traditionally prepared by boiling it and serving it whole, often with a side of clarified butter for dipping the meat. Eating the mighty crustacean might seem daunting, but if you want to venture beyond lobster rolls and lobster bisque, it's fairly straightforward once you know the basics.

First, make sure the restaurants give you all the necessary equipment: a claw cracker and a tiny fork for extracting difficult-to-reach meat. If you've received a bib, put it on. You're about to get messy.

Start by breaking off the lobster's tail, then use a knife to cut lengthwise down the tail's underside. When removing the meat, you may see a soft green substance emerge: this is the tomalley (liver). Some people love its creamy texture; others discard it. (The tomalley may pick up contaminants from the lobster's environment.) The tail is one of the lobster's prized pieces. Dunk it in butter to indulge.

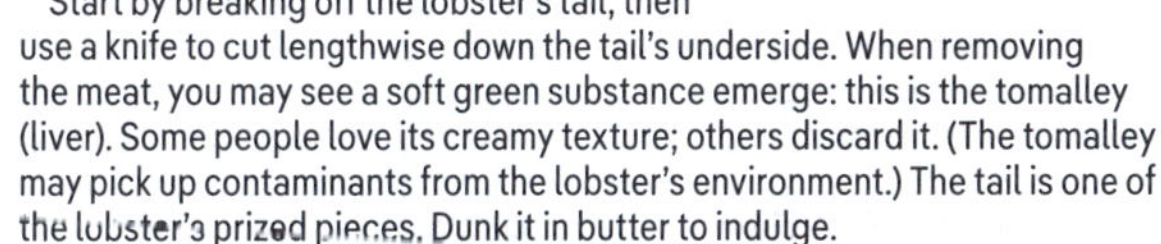

Move on to the claws next. Use your cracker to break the shell, then pull out the meat with a fork. You can also crack open the legs and suck out the briny insides, though there isn't much meat to find. Don't forget the leg-connected knuckles. These tiny rounds of meat are some of the lobster's sweetest.

Lobsters 101

Fishermen in the US harvest around 120 million pounds of lobster each year, with a dockside value exceeding $600 million. It takes about five 1lb lobsters to yield a single pound of meat.

TIME TO PARTY

A night out in the Eastern USA is defined by the destination. In cities, you might see a live performance at 7pm or 8pm, sip cocktails until midnight and step-touch until dawn. In rural areas, you might try beer flights at local brew houses around 5pm and spend the rest of your evening stargazing beside a bonfire.

When it comes to small towns, don't expect late-night shenanigans. On weekdays, you'll be hard-pressed to find restaurants open past 8:30pm, and most bars close by 10pm. Most breweries close shortly after sundown, so if you want to sample local suds, plan an excursion in the late afternoon or early evening. Weekends tend to get rowdier, with the occasional dive bar blaring jukebox tunes until 1am.

If you're looking for a rager, stick to cities. On weekends in NYC, 10pm is too early to hit the dance floor and 2am is too late (bars close at 4am). Try to hit the sweet spot: 11pm means shorter lines; 1am means rowdier crowds.

Urban dance clubs and music venues often require covers at the door (bring cash), and in cities like Miami and Chicago, it's wise to pre-purchase tickets. Events with well-known DJs regularly sell out. If you can't snag a ticket, try queuing early to get in.

If you like electronic music, check out the Resident Advisor app, which allows users to find events and buy tickets in various regions. You can also use the Dice app to search for upcoming parties and live events in half a dozen cities.

Responsible Travel

Climate Change & Travel

It's impossible to ignore the impact we have when traveling; Lonely Planet urges all travellers to engage with their travel carbon footprint, which will mainly come from air travel. While there often isn't an alternative, travelers can look to minimise the number of flights they take, opt for newer aircrafts and use cleaner ground transport, such as trains. One proposed solution - purchasing carbon offsets - unfortunately does not cancel out the impact of individual flights. While most destinations will depend on air travel for the foreseeable future, for now, pursuing ground-based travel where possible is the best course of action.

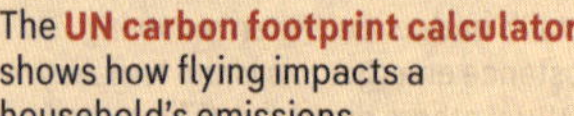

The **UN carbon footprint calculator** shows how flying impacts a household's emissions

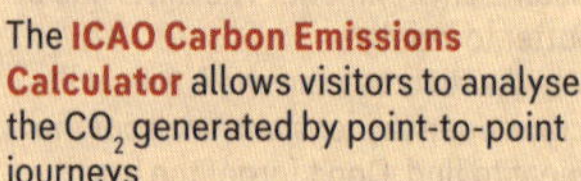

The **ICAO Carbon Emissions Calculator** allows visitors to analyse the CO_2 generated by point-to-point journeys

Choose the Train

Reduce fuel usage by zipping between cities on Amtrak trains or taking regional rails to villages and towns. It's possible to chug between popular cities like Boston, NYC and beyond without pressing a gas pedal.

Take Public Transit

Soak up the cityscape while someone else takes the wheel. Nearly all major metropoles have extensive transit networks; you'll even find reliable options in small cities such as Burlington, VT, and Beacon, NY.

Set Sail Sustainably

Forget gas-powered boats. Instead of hopping on motorboats or airboats for wetland tours and river cruises, try kayaking or canoeing. The experience is often more immersive, less disruptive to the environment and better for spotting wildlife.

Stay at least 50yd away from all wildlife in national parks. Never approach an animal, and if an animal's behavior changes because of your presence, you're too close. Feeding wildlife is prohibited.

The original stewards of America's landscape hold the keys to protecting its ecology. Celebrate Indigenous communities by learning about native ancestors at the **National Museum of the American Indian** in DC (p248) and NYC (p62).

CYCLE THE SIGHTS

Join the zero-emission pedal party by renting a bike or signing up for a bikeshare program. Most cities have decent cycling lanes and some towns connect to nature trails on former railroad tracks *(railstotrails.org)*.

SEEK SUSTAINABLE SEAFOOD

Find out which fish are sustainably sourced with guides from long-running nonprofit Seafood Watch *(seafoodwatch.org)*. Search by region, download the right guide, then choose between the bass and the branzino with confidence.

Pitch a Tent

Go green on an electricity-free camping trip by falling asleep to starlight and waking up with the sun. If you prefer modern conveniences, try glamping. It can be equally sustainable and exponentially more comfortable.

Upcycle Your Wardrobe

Skip fast fashion. Turn sustainability into your aesthetic by buying lightly used goods at thrift shops and vintage stores. On top of reducing waste, you'll score a sartorial snapshot of wherever you're visiting.

High Five a Farmer

Head to farmers markets in every state for juicy berries, local honey and all sorts of artisanal treats made by bakers, cheesemongers and wine makers. Most markets are held on Saturday or Sunday morning.

Eat Meat-Free Meals

Meat production in the US is a significant contributor to greenhouse gas emissions, accelerating climate change. Order plant-based dishes at vegan restaurants to reduce your carbon footprint; search for tasty spots on *happycow.net*.

Tap water is safe to drink, unless explicitly stated otherwise: ditch plastic for reusable water bottles.

Seek out hotels with sustainability policies certified by a credible organization like LEED or EarthCheck.

Flooded Future

The East Coast is on the front lines of human-caused climate change, with rising sea levels and eroding beaches threatening beloved destinations. Scientists predict 60% of Florida's Miami-Dade County will be underwater by 2060 if current trends continue.

RESOURCES

lnt.org
Follow Leave No Trace's outdoor guidelines.

environmentamerica.org
A citizen-based environmental advocacy organization.

thedyrt.com
Find free and affordable campsites; read user reviews.

CLOCKWISE FROM BOTTOM LEFT: PIXEL-SHOT/SHUTTERSTOCK, HYLE/SHUTTERSTOCK

Health & Safe Travel

INSURANCE & MEDICATIONS

International visitors should consider buying travel insurance. Medical care and prescription drugs can be shockingly expensive – and emergency room visits without insurance can cost thousands of dollars. Travel insurance policies may also cover theft-related expenses, lost luggage or delayed travel. Read the fine print to ensure you understand what's covered. For over-the-counter medications, head to pharmacies like CVS or Walgreens.

Coastal Hurricanes

Hurricane season runs from June to October, with peak storms usually hitting the coast in August and September. Powerful winds and heavy rains can cause devastation all along the Eastern Seaboard, though Florida, Louisiana and the Carolinas usually bear the brunt of tropical tempests. It's imperative to follow official directives during storm emergencies to ensure your safety.

Tornadoes & Snow Storms

Tornadoes – violently rotating air columns formed by thunderstorms – can occur in Gulf-adjacent states during winter, but they're most common in the Midwest throughout spring and early summer. Storms strike with little warning – monitor alerts closely and seek shelter in a basement or interior room. Snow storms hit northern states hardest between January and February. Keep abreast of weather reports; avoid driving in whiteout conditions.

MARIJUANA

'Weed' is legal for adults 21+ in some states but criminal in others. Check local laws before buying, carrying or using.

WARNING FLAGS ON THE BEACH

Green flag
Calm conditions; safe to swim

Yellow flag
Waters may be rough: use extreme caution

Red flag
Hazardous conditions: high surf or strong current

Purple/blue flag
Dangerous marine life (jellyfish, sharks) spotted

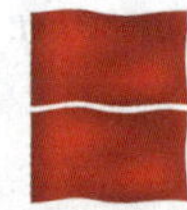

Double red flag
Extreme danger; do not enter water

Temperature Extremes

Prepare for summer heat in the south, where midday temperatures can soar above 100°F: carry water to avoid dehydration, wear a wide-brimmed hat and use sunscreen. Dress for the winter cold in northern states from Minnesota to Maine, where temperatures dip below 0°F: layer your clothing, wear a hat and gloves and bring sturdy boots with solid traction. Limit outdoor exposure.

TICK WATCH

If you go hiking – or frequent wooded, grassy regions where animals roam – look out for ticks. These little bloodsuckers are most active in warm months but live everywhere from the south to northeast year-round – and some carry Lyme disease, particularly in northern states. To protect yourself, wear closed-toed shoes, long socks, long pants and tick repellent. Always do a full-body tick check after spending time outside.

LGBTIQ+ Travelers

The Eastern USA presents a curious paradox for LGBTIQ+ travelers. NYC gave birth to Pride at Stonewall, while Florida's 2022 'Don't Say Gay' bill prohibits instruction of sexual orientation and gender identity in schools. It only takes a few hours to travel from the world's most welcoming queer enclaves to conservative towns. Knowing where to go makes all the difference.

MIDWEST HOTSPOTS

Chicago is home to the nation's first official gayborhood, Northalsted (formerly Boystown, p505), still the go-to for finding LGBTIQ+ community. Lesbians congregate around Andersonville; leather lovers get their kink on in Rogers Park. Visit during August's Market Days *(northalsted.com)* – a queer-themed street fest. Minneapolis has a sizable queer scene, largely centered around downtown's Loring Pl. In Columbus, OH, gay bars congregate around the Short North Arts District.

Out in NYC

NYC's historic LGBTIQ+ heart is the West Village – famous for the 1969 **Stonewall Uprising** (p76) and brimming with queer life since poet Walt Whitman imbibed here in the 19th century. The metro area boasts the nation's largest LGBTIQ+ population, with multiple gayborhoods spread across the city. Other rainbow magnets in Manhattan include Chelsea (den of daddies), Hell's Kitchen (pretty-boy posturing) and the East Village (alternative edge). Numerous LGBTIQ+ bars populate trendy Brooklyn's Williamsburg and Bushwick. Pride events run for the entire month of June, culminating in the world's largest **LGBTIQ+ march** *(nycpride.org)*.

SUMMER HAVENS

May to September is all about the beach. The most popular: Provincetown (on Cape Cod's tip, p179) and Fire Island (a Long Island sand bar, p103), both blessed with stunning shorelines and bacchanalian fêtes. There's also arty Ogunquit, ME (p221), rock-n-rolling Asbury Park, NJ (p120) and Rehoboth Beach , DE (p268), a seasonal DC satellite.

Mid-Atlantic Gayborhoods

Washington, DC's LGBTIQ+ residents colonized DuPont Circle in the 1970s. These days, queer locals also live around Logan Circle and Capitol Hill. Scan local LGBTIQ+ publication *Washington Blade* for city insight. Philadelphia refers to a slice of Midtown Village as the Gayborhood – the 13th St corridor, sprinkled with LGBTIQ+ bars and businesses.

LGBTIQ+ Resources

Everywhere is Queer *(everywhereisqueer.com)* Download the app to find LGBTIQ owned businesses.

MisterB&B *(misterbnb.com)* Book lodging directly from members of the LGBTIQ+ community and allies.

LGBT National Help Center *(lgbthotline.org)* Counseling and information for people of all ages.

QUEER SOUTHERN CITIES

Atlanta is the LGBTIQ+ epicenter of the South, and Midtown's Peachtree St is its main artery. Most of New Orleans' LGBTIQ+ bars congregate around Bourbon St near St Anne, known as the Lavender Line. Visit during September's **Southern Decadence** *(southerndecadence.com)*, when queer crowds go wild. Despite Florida legislation, Miami's South Beach is super gay-friendly and nearby Wilton Manors has one of America's highest percentages of gay residents.

CLOCKWISE FROM TOP LEFT: PHALEXAVILES/SHUTTERSTOCK, NITO/SHUTTERSTOCK

Accessible Travel

Navigating the Eastern USA with physical or cognitive impairments can be tricky – and rewarding. Cities tend to be more accessible, though plenty of state beaches and national parks are heeding the call for inclusion. Always call ahead to confirm that hotels, restaurants and activities provide necessary accommodations.

RESOURCES

AccessibleGO *(accessiblego.com)* Community reviews and accessibility details on hotels, flights and more.

Wheelchair Getaways *(wheelchairgetaways.com)* Rent accessible vans across the nation.

Be My Eyes *(bemyeyes.com)* Volunteers help blind and visually impaired travelers navigate their environment through AI and live video.

America the Beautiful pass *(nps.gov/planyourvisit/passes.htm)* Disabled US citizens get entrance fees waived at federal recreation sites and national parks.

Hidden Disabilities Sunflower Program

Not all disabilities are visible. Wearing a Hidden Disabilities Sunflower lanyard *(hdsunflower.com/us)* helps signal to staff at participating airports and train stations that you may need extra assistance.

Airport

US airlines must legally provide disabled travelers guided assistance while boarding, deplaning or connecting to other flights. Contact your airline's special assistance phone line to ensure additional requests can be met.

Accommodations

US hotels constructed after 1993 must include accessibility features for people with disabilities: bathtubs with grab bars and a seat, roll-in showers with a seat, and communication equipment for those with hearing and vision impairments.

Roll on the Beach

Many Florida beaches are wheelchair-accessible. Plan ahead: *visitflorida.com/travel-ideas/articles/wheelchair-accessible-beaches.*

Subway vs Bus

City subway networks range from accessible dreams (Washington, DC) to limited-mobility nightmares (NYC). When in doubt, take the bus, often equipped with wheelchair lifts and designated wheelchair seating. Amtrak trains are generally accessible.

ACCESSIBLE ALL-STARS

Orlando, Disney World (p467) provides disability-friendly accommodations. In Washington, DC most of the 17 Smithsonian museums offer tactical or visual-description tours and sign language interpretation.

Outdoors for All

Most national and state parks offer accessible adventures. Standouts include **Letchworth State Park** (New York, p115), home of the Autism Nature Trail, and **Acadia National Park** (Maine, p228), where power-wheelchair users zoom around gravel carriage roads. Find more accessible attractions at *nps.gov.*

A STAGE FOR EVERYONE

NYC's Broadway theaters (and major theaters from Boston to Chicago) provide wheelchair seating (limited) and free assistive devices for captioning and audio description. Reserve ahead. TDF's Autism Friendly Performances adapt shows for sensory-sensitive audiences.

Nuts & Bolts

OPENING HOURS

Opening hours remain consistent year-round in big cities, but vary in rural areas based on seasons. Shorter hours may apply during low seasons, when some venues close completely.

Banks 9am–6pm Monday–Friday. Some also 9am–noon Saturday.

Cafes 7am–4pm in small towns; to 7pm in large cities.

Restaurants Breakfast around 7am–11am, lunch noon–3pm and dinner 5pm–10pm. Weekend brunch 10am–4pm.

Bars Normally 5pm–2am; to 1am in smaller cities; to 4am in places like NYC.

Clubs 10pm–2am; to 4am in NYC.

Shops 10am–7pm weekdays, 11am–8pm Saturday. Hours vary Sunday.

Grocery stores 8am–9pm.

Internet

Mobile coverage is reliable in cities but spotty in rural areas. Many establishments offer wi-fi access.

Toilets

Free restrooms can often be found in malls, libraries, transportation hubs, gas stations, and government-run parks and beaches.

GOOD TO KNOW

Time zones
Eastern Standard Time (GMT/UTC -5) and Central Standard Time (GMT/UTC -6)

Country calling code +1

Emergency number 911

Population
207.8 million

Electricity

Type A and B 120V/60Hz

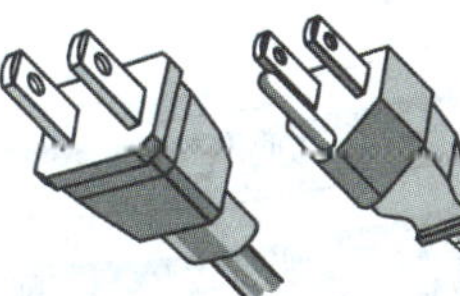

PUBLIC HOLIDAYS

The Eastern USA observes over a dozen public holidays. Banks, schools and government offices (including post offices) close, and while many businesses remain open, hours are subject to change. Expect peak hotel prices and packed venues; plan travel around these dates well in advance.

New Year's Day January 1

Martin Luther King Jr Day Third Monday in January

Presidents' Day Third Monday in February

Memorial Day Last Monday in May

Independence Day July 4

Labor Day First Monday in September

Indigenous Peoples' Day (aka Columbus Day) Second Monday in October

Veterans Day November 11

Thanksgiving Fourth Thursday in November

Christmas Day December 25

STORYBOOK

Our writers delve deep into different aspects of life in Eastern USA

A History of Eastern USA in 15 Places

Stitching together 400-plus years of history exposes a country amid transformation.

John Garry

p598

Introducing Eastern USA

These states might be 'United' in name, but the differences run deep.

John Garry

p602

How the US Got Its Groove

American music found its voice around the Eastern USA.

John Garry

p604

Southern Barbecue

Georgia and the Carolinas take barbecues extremely seriously.

Emily Matchar

p606

Birthplace of the Revolution

It started with a financial disagreement, which grew into a revolution, which grew into a new nation.

Mara Voorhees

p608

The Cherokee

The Cherokee are still living in mountainous, forested communities in the far west of North Carolina.

Regis St Louis

p611

The Birth of America's Summer Vacation

Summer is more than a season – it's the most exciting time of year.

John Garry

p614

US Capitol (p246)

BILL PERRY/SHUTTERSTOCK

A HISTORY OF EASTERN USA IN 15 PLACES

The origin story of the USA starts here – on land shaped by Indigenous inhabitants, redrawn by determined colonists, fractured by bloody wars and reimagined by industrialists. Stitching together 400-plus years of history exposes a country amid transformation – on a complex, contradictory, never-ending quest for liberty. By John Garry

THE EAST COAST stretches over 2000 miles from Maine to Florida, with rivers linking the port towns to the nation's interior. These boat-friendly waterways eventually became gateways to America, giving rise to cities shaped by the exchange of the goods and ideas that passed through.

When European colonizers began exploring the coast in the 16th and 17th centuries, the land thrived under Indigenous stewardship. The Iroquois Confederacy (or Haudenosaunee) lived around the Great Lakes, the Wampanoag Confederacy settled around Massachusetts, and Lenape communities spread along the Atlantic Ocean from southern New York to northern Delaware. Algonquian-speaking tribes thrived near Chesapeake Bay, while the Cherokee lived across Southern Appalachia, and the Muscogee (Creek) congregated in regions stretching to the Gulf Coast.

Over the next few centuries, these sovereign nations – among others – nearly vanished as a new nation spread across the continent. British, Dutch, French and Spanish forces vied for control until the end of the American Revolution. Since then, this region has seen it all: civil war, economic collapses, natural disasters and terrorist attacks. The Eastern USA is where millions of immigrants entered the US and social movements exploded, challenging the reality behind America's promise that all are 'created equal.' Get ready to sail through the nation's history – it's a bumpy ride.

1. Ocmulgee Mounds

INDIGENOUS BEGINNINGS

In the forests near Macon, GA, grass-covered mounds rise from the earth – remnants of an advanced Mississippian society that flourished here around 900 CE. About 1000 people lived among these ceremonial earthworks, part of an Indigenous presence that spanned over 12,000 years. That lineage was violently disrupted by the Indian Removal Act of 1830, which forcibly relocated the Muscogee Nation from their ancestral homeland to Oklahoma. The journey, now dubbed the Trail of Tears, displaced multiple southeastern tribes and claimed an estimated 10,000 lives. Today, this sacred landscape is poised to become the nation's next national park.

For more on the Ocmulgee Mounds, see page 374

2. Jamestown National Historic Site

LAYING THE FOUNDATION

When the British established an American settlement at Jamestown, VA, in 1607, it wasn't clear its inhabitants would survive. Sickness, starvation and clashes with the indigenous Powhatan Confederacy plagued its inhabitants. Nevertheless, the colony flourished: the new arrivals planted seeds for the Protestant religion to prosper, and in 1619, introduced British America's first representative government, a precursor to US democracy. That same year, the colony received a boatload of over 20 enslaved Africans – the beginning of an evil institution that lasted two centuries, forging a framework for racial inequality that reverberates around the nation today. The Archaearium archaeology museum in Williamsburg is dedicated to America's first English colony, with thousands of artifacts on display.

For more on Jamestown, visit the Archaearium, page 290

3. Plimoth Patuxet Museum

REFRAMING AMERICAN MYTHOLOGY

In 1620, religious separatists aboard the *Mayflower* arrived from England to present-day Massachusetts. The colony that the Pilgrims established became an enduring symbol of American principles: they sought religious freedom, created the first written agreement for self-governance in North America and celebrated the 'first Thanksgiving' with the Indigenous Wampanoag. But this rosy historical interpretation, long mythologized from the Pilgrims' point of view, casts the newcomers as moral beacons while disregarding the conflict they fueled. In 2020, the site of the colony changed its name from the Plimoth Plantation to the Plimoth Patuxet Museum – incorporating the Wampanoag place name to present a more accurate, inclusive account of the site's past.

For more information on the Plimoth Patuxet Museum, see page 175

4. International African American Museum

ROOTS OF SLAVERY

Historians believe roughly 90% of African Americans have ancestral ties to Gadsden's Wharf – a dock in Charleston, SC, constructed by enslaved hands in 1772. Until 1808, this site played a tragic role in the transatlantic slave trade, where an estimated 100,000 men, women and children were stolen from their homelands and forced into bondage on US soil. For 200 years, there was little acknowledgment of the site's central role in Black history – until the International African American Museum opened in 2023, memorializing the people held here in chains while facing an uncertain future.

For more on the International African American Museum, see page 336

5. Independence Hall

FORMING A NEW NATION

The United States took its first small step inside Philadelphia's steepled Georgian civic center in 1776 as the Second Continental Congress signed the Declaration of Independence – a condemnation of British tyranny and a manifesto of American ideals, proclaiming 'all men are created equal.' Eleven years later, it took a giant leap when the government signed the US Constitution inside the same room. Like the Declaration's unmet promises, the building's history is rife with contradictions: between 1850 and 1854, African American freedom seekers accused of being 'fugitive slaves' were put on trial inside Independence Hall and, in some cases, forced back into bondage.

For more on Independence Hall, see page 134

6. Gettysburg

CIVIL WAR TRAGEDY

Over 50,000 soldiers lost their lives during the 1863 Battle of Gettysburg – a three-day snapshot of the Civil War's brutality and the bloodiest conflict in American history. Between 1861 and 1865, the US fractured in two along the Mason–Dixon line, a Maryland–Pennsylvania boundary symbolizing the ideological split between the agrarian, slave-holding South and the industrial, abolitionist North. The fratricidal fighting ultimately ended slavery and claimed over 620,000 lives. Its haunting memory is palpable among these meadows and monuments, where Lincoln declared in the battle's aftermath, 'This nation, under God, shall have a new birth of freedom.'

For more on Gettysburg, see page 144

Ocmulgee Mounds (p374)

7. Ellis Island

AMERICA'S IMMIGRANT ORIGINS

America owes its image as an international melting pot to NYC's Ellis Island: between 1892 and 1954, roughly 12 million immigrants entered the US at this site. Hopefuls who passed through the island's 'Golden Gate' went on to make significant cultural contributions to the nation, with a who's who of notable New Yorkers including anarchist Emma Goldman, filmmaker Elia Kazan and songwriter Irving Berlin, who penned 'God Bless America.' Today, over 100 million Americans can trace their ancestry to this immigration depot, where newcomers once waded through a conveyor belt of exams to gain admittance and build a new life.

For more on Ellis Island, see page 64

8. Ford Piquette Avenue Plant

THE US GOES MOBILE

The automobile age officially revved its engine when Henry Ford introduced the Model T at the Ford Piquette Avenue Plant in 1908. Unlike its predecessors, which were playthings for the rich, Ford's invention was operationally fool-proof and affordable, allowing middle-class Americans to trade in their horses for horsepower. Detroit, the Model T's birthplace, became Motor City, fueled by Ford's assembly-line empire. In the coming decades, train use declined, cars became king and the American landscape was redrawn in their image.

For more on the Ford Piquette Avenue Plant, see page 541

9. Shenandoah National Park

CONSERVATION AND DISPLACEMENT

Virginia's wild west epitomizes the costs and benefits of preservation. After establishing Shenandoah in 1935, the US employed around 5000 workers from the Civilian Conservation Corps to develop the land – part of a New Deal project that helped young Americans find work during the Great Depression. The 200,000-acre park now protects over 50 mammal species and 1400 types of plants. But hike the park's trails and you'll notice abandoned barns and forgotten cemeteries. To create Shenandoah, over 2000 residents were displaced under 'eminent domain' – the act of seizing private property for public use, a practice disproportionately impacting and economically undercutting poor residents of the United States.

For more on Shenandoah National Park, see page 292

10. Lincoln Memorial

FREEDOM FIGHTERS

America's aspirational quest for equality takes the form of a temple along the western side of the National Mall in Washington, DC, where 36 Doric columns surround a 19ft marble-clad Abraham Lincoln. Lincoln's statue has witnessed countless presidential inaugurations, concerts and demonstrations since its completion in 1922 – though none echo louder through history than Dr Martin Luther King Jr's 'I Have a Dream' speech, delivered in 1963, 18 steps below President Lincoln's stone feet. King's call for racial justice, delivered a century after Lincoln signed the Emancipation Proclamation, paved the way for landmark legislation, including the Civil Rights Act of 1964.

For more on the Lincoln Memorial, see page 250

11. Stonewall Inn

EPICENTER OF LGBTIQ+ LIBERATION

Going to a gay bar in 1960s NYC came with potential consequences, including police raids and arrests – which is exactly what officers planned to inflict on attendees during a routine shakedown at the Stonewall Inn on June 28, 1969. But visitors to this Greenwich Village pub – mostly marginalized members of the LGBTIQ+ community, including gender-non-conforming drag queens and people of color – decided to revolt. There are contradictory accounts about who threw the first mythic brick at police and how long the uprising lasted, but one thing is certain: the events at Stonewall galvanized LGBTIQ+ people worldwide to fight for their rights.

For more on the Stonewall Inn, see page 76

12. One World Trade Center

A SKYLINE ALTERED, A NATION TRANSFORMED

Soaring 1776ft into the sky like a phoenix, One World Trade Center is a testament to American strength and New York's unwavering spirit. Opened in 2014, the glassy skyscraper overlooks the site where the Twin Towers stood until September 11, 2001,

Ellis Island (p64)
PAUL THOMAS CURRY/SHUTTERSTOCK

when two planes hijacked by operatives of the terrorist group Al Qaeda flew into the buildings. A third plane hit the Pentagon outside Washington, DC, and a fourth crashed in Shanksville, PA. Nearly 3000 people died. A somber memorial beneath the skyscraper honors those whose lives were lost.

For more on One World Trade Center, see page 61

13. City Park

FIGHTING TO STAY AFLOAT

City Park is the manicured green lung of New Orleans, with gardens and waterways spread across 1300 acres, all anchored by a magnificent art museum – a symbol of Louisiana's resilience. In 2005, the green space spent 20 days submerged by up to 8ft of toxic floodwater – a catastrophic consequence of Hurricane Katrina and negligent engineering. Poorly maintained levees, meant to protect the below-sea-level city, failed during the storm – which claimed more than 1800 lives and amounted to over $110 billion in damages. New flood-protection systems aim to thwart the next natural disaster, a growing inevitability as rising sea levels threaten the Eastern USA.

For more on City Park, see page 419

14. New River Gorge National Park & Preserve

NATURE'S RECLAMATION

'New' might seem like a misnomer for North America's oldest river, which some geologists estimate to be 320 million years old. Its prehistoric stones have seen Cherokee tribes come and go, followed by railroads and coal mining towns, nearly 50 of which erupted along the waterway in West Virginia in the late 1800s to mine for 'black gold.' But in 2020, this 70,000-acre expanse became the newest national park in the US – where coal-fueled ghost towns have been reclaimed by green vines, and forests once logged are now fully regrown. It's hopeful headway for a nation working to heal its industrial scars.

For more on New River Gorge National Park & Preserve, see page 300

15. US Capitol Building

POLITICAL UPHEAVAL

On January 6, 2021, the US Capitol Building – a symbol of democracy in Washington, DC – became the site of a violent insurrection. Thousands of Donald Trump supporters stormed the building in an attempt to overturn a presidential election Trump falsely claimed was stolen. Though Joe Biden was sworn in as president a few weeks later, the riot exposed America's ideological fault lines. In the years since, the nation has experienced legislative whiplash. Trump regained the presidency in 2024, winning by a 1.5% margin, and the US remains politically polarized. As infighting continues, one thing seems certain: the nation's dramatic days are far from over.

For more on the US Capitol Building, see page 246

INTRODUCING EASTERN USA

These states might be 'United' in name, but the differences run deeper than Kentucky's Mammoth Cave. Personalities and politics are as varied as the coastlines, mountains and skyscrapers. JOHN GARRY introduces the people of the region.

TEMPERAMENTAL AND UNINHIBITED – that's how demographers labeled the Northeast and Mid-Atlantic in a 2013 study published in the *Journal of Personality and Social Psychology*, which makes me want to say, in a thick 'New Yawk' accent, 'You talkin' to me?' That's my gut response as a die-hard New Yorker – reactionary and confrontational. And those words, originally ad-libbed by Robert de Niro as a Manhattan cabby in Martin Scorsese's *Taxi Driver*, only reinforce the results.

Researchers suggest people in these regions are 'reserved, aloof, impulsive, irritable and inquisitive' – the product of living in cramped quarters around the nation's most populous metropole.

Known for being agreeable and extroverted, people from the Midwest and the South earn a different label: 'friendly and conventional.' It helps explain the 'Thank you, Ma'am' of Southern hospitality and the firm handshake associated with Midwestern charm.

But personality is only part of the picture.

In the 19th century, seismic political shifts sparked the Civil War, splitting the East Coast between the Confederate, slave-holding South and the Union North. You can still feel its tremors: South Carolina's statehouse flew a Confederate flag until 2015, and it's still common to spot the controversial star-studded symbol decorating lawns outside the region's progressive enclaves.

Today, the sociopolitical seams are drawn at ballot boxes instead of battlefields, defined by conservative 'red' and liberal 'blue' states. In the last presidential election, 16 of the 29 eastern United States voted red – predominantly in the South and Midwest. Every New England state, plus its coastal neighbors down to Virginia, swung blue, along with Illinois and Minnesota.

Within each state, the smattering of color-coded voting blocks sometimes looks like a Jackson Pollock painting. The rift isn't always geographic – it often highlights urban-rural divides.

Washington, DC – according to US Census data, one of the nation's wealthiest, most diverse cities – is reliably liberal. Mississippi – the nation's poorest state, where most residents live in rural areas – remains a conservative stalwart. When it comes to race, pastoral Maine is 90% white. In skyscraper-stacked Chicago, the percentage of Black, Latinx and white residents is nearly equal. The subject of race in each state can be explosive, a consequence of old wounds unhealed.

Then there are the dialects: New England's 'you guys' is the South's 'y'all'. You'll likely hear Spanish when traveling through Miami, where 70% of the population is Latinx. In NYC, you'll hear a bit of everything in that thick 'New Yawk' accent. It's the sound of America's melting pot, seasoned by Irish, Italians, Puerto Ricans, Jamaicans, eastern Europeans and whatever group arrives next. This is the land of immigrants, after all.

America's Melting Pot

Between 1840 and 1919, 90% of immigrant arrivals in the US came from Europe. Since 1965, roughly 50% of all immigrants have come from Latin America. Immigrants make up roughly 20% of the population of Florida, New Jersey and New York.

Pictured clockwise from top left: Pride Parade, New York City; Chicago; New Orleans Jazz & Heritage Festival; Miami

CLOCKWISE FROM TOP LEFT: RBLFMR/SHUTTERSTOCK, XAVIERARNAU/GETTY IMAGES, ADAM MCCULLOUGH/SHUTTERSTOCK, ANDRESR/GETTY IMAGES

I LIVE ON THE EAST COAST

I was born in the Catskills – where white-tailed deer outnumber people – and was refined in NYC over the past 15 years. Like many New Yorkers, I'm a transplant, though my family roots stretch back several generations. My great-grandmother immigrated to America aboard the RMS *Titanic* (a 3rd-class passenger; she survived). She was one of the estimated 4.5 million Irish people who arrived in the US between 1820 and 1930. She planted herself in Manhattan, but like many New Yorkers, spent summers in the Catskills, where my parents fell in love and raised a family. I now reside in Brooklyn with my partner, whose Jewish Ukrainian grandfather found refuge in the country during Russia's early 20th-century pogroms. We're two of NYC's 700,000 LGBTIQ+ residents – the largest queer population in the nation. I see our lineage all over the city: in Irish pubs; Jewish delis; gay bars like Julius', where trailblazers fought for equality; and in the stories of NYC's modern immigrants, numbering over three million people.

HOW THE US GOT ITS GROOVE

American music found its voice around the Eastern USA, where sounds forged by Black communities migrated, collided and became the nation's soundtrack. By John Garry

IN 1991, WHITNEY Houston walked onto the field at the Super Bowl in Tampa and sang about 'the land of the free' in what would become a legendary rendition of 'The Star-Spangled Banner' – the notoriously tough-to-sing US national anthem.

In her voice, what's often a rigid military march becomes something looser and lyrical, echoing sounds of gospel and jazz. The notes on the page may look immovable, but Whitney's performance is untethered. It embodies the musical sound of America.

Problematic Patriotism

The origins of 'The Star-Spangled Banner' are colored with complications. Francis Scott Key (a lawyer, not a lyricist) penned the poem in 1814 after witnessing Great Britain's 25-hour bombardment of Baltimore's Fort McHenry during the War of 1812. A third verse, regularly omitted, contains a line that many interpret as an endorsement of slavery. It doesn't help that Key, who waxed about the 'land of the free,' was a slaveholder.

Pictured clockwise from top left: Louis Armstrong (p414); Big Bill Broonzy; Elvis Presley (p349); Whitney Houston

Then there's the melody – initially written as a drinking song by Englishman John Stafford Smith around 1775 and reformatted with Key's lyrics in the 19th century.

It's a curious choice for a national anthem, officially adopted in 1931: written by a man who defended slavery, set to a tune borrowed from the country America fought to escape – and a far cry from the nation's homegrown sound.

New American Rhythms

Long before Whitney belted in Tampa, a root of American music sprang up from Southern plantations. From 1619 to 1865, enslaved Africans forced to labor in cotton fields found a small slice of sovereignty in song. Music became an act of resistance, layered with sounds they carried across the Atlantic and passed down through generations. Traditions of call-and-response blended with spiritual tunes, emanating from a need for emotional release.

In the Mississippi Delta, that sound blossomed into the blues – a melancholic style characterized by soulful 'blue' notes and used by singers to express anguish in musical soliloquy. Black musician WC Handy, dubbed 'Father of the Blues,' helped popularize the genre with his 1912 hit 'Memphis Blues,' launching its commercial craze.

More distinct styles took shape in New Orleans around Congo Sq, where enslaved African Americans gathered on Sundays – their sole break from forced labor – to make music. West African syncopation and Caribbean beats fused with American church melodies and complex European chords, accompanied by banjos, drums and horns. These vibrant jam sessions laid the foundation for ragtime, notable for its 'ragged' African rhythms. When those syncopations blended with the soulful structure of blues in the late 19th and early 20th centuries, another revolutionary sound emerged: jazz.

If classical music was a stately, rehearsed speech brought here by Europeans, jazz was an improvisational conversation among friends, unbound by formality – the sound of unchained melodies ready to run.

Great Music Migration

By the early 20th century, African Americans were on the move – and so was their music. Between the 1910s and 1970s, an estimated six million Black people left the South for greener pastures, attempting to escape racial violence and explore economic opportunities in the Midwest and Northeast. In 1922, New Orleans jazz star Louis Armstrong trumpeted his way to Chicago before hopping to NYC. Mississippi-born Big Bill Broonzy brought the blues to Chicago around the same time, followed a decade later by Muddy Waters, who plugged in his guitar to electrify crowds.

This 'Great Migration' spawned a cultural revolution, most famous in NYC's Harlem but no less resplendent across the country. Cabarets and nightclubs from Detroit's Paradise Valley to Chicago's South Side fizzed with creativity like an uncorked jeroboam, flooding American cities with new music.

Musical Transformations

By the time Muddy Waters wrote 'The Blues Had a Baby and They Named It Rock and Roll' in 1977, rock-and-roll king Elvis Presley had already shaken Memphis with his gyrating hips and was in the final year of his life. Rock splintered into punk, played by the Ramones at NYC's CBGB, their grunge and metal descendants waiting in the wings.

The sounds of rhythm and blues blended with Black gospel to create soul in the 1950s, and by 1972, Berry Gordy's Motown had left Detroit for Los Angeles. Disco hit its high note in the 1970s, formed from soul and jazz, a precursor to the EDM scenes in Chicago and Detroit. Hip-hop was already riding high in the Bronx.

Country music – descended from Irish fiddle tunes, English folk ballads, German polkas, Mexican conjunto and more – became so steeped in white Southern identity that its bluesy bona fides were often overlooked. But early guitarists borrowed blues scales – and banjo rhythms, especially in bluegrass, trace to West African instruments like the *akonting*.

African American influence is the uncredited bass line beneath so many styles of music. The deeper you listen, the clearer it becomes – especially when a rare voice shaped by American melodies reimagines a classic. A percussive groove here, a soulful riff there, and suddenly, the past is present again.

'The land of the free' is a complicated lyric, not always in tune with the country it describes. But in 1991, Whitney made it work – a reminder that American 'freedom' was first found through song.

CLOCKWISE FROM TOP LEFT: NEW YORK DAILY NEWS ARCHIVE/GETTY IMAGES, EVERETT COLLECTION INC/ALAMY, RONALD C MODRA/GETTY IMAGES, GEORGE ROSE/GETTY IMAGES

SOUTHERN BARBECUE

Georgia and the Carolinas – especially North Carolina – take barbecue extremely seriously. By Emily Matchar

FIRST, SOME TERMS. In this region 'barbecue' is a noun, and it means pork. 'Barbecue', 'BBQ' and 'Bar-b-q' are all acceptable variations. What kind of pork? Well, that depends on where you're from – more on that later. A 'pit master' is the person who cooks the meat; they're the boss. Ready?

History

As an 18th-century Virginian once sniped, 'the inhabitants of North Carolina devour so much swine's flesh, that it fills them full of gross humours.' Rude, but probably true. North Carolinians have always liked their pork, which was probably introduced by early Spanish settlers. Settlers began smoking the meat over flames, likely inspired by Native American cooking methods. At some point vinegar sauce was added, possibly as a cheap imitation of Caribbean citrus juices. Whatever the origin, it helped disguise any spoilage. Over time the tang became the point.

East Versus West

The barbecue that originated in the eastern part of North Carolina began to migrate westward, and as it did, it changed. The whole hog doused in vinegar sauce gave way to pork shoulder with a slightly sweeter, ketchup-infused sauce, likely inspired by German settlers. Today this distinction is

Clockwise from top left: Smoked brisket; Pork barbecue sandwich with coleslaw, pickles and okra; BBQ pitmaster; Pulled pork burger

called 'eastern versus western' or 'eastern versus Lexington-style'. The latter refers to the city of Lexington, just west of North Carolina's center, geographically, which calls itself 'The Barbecue Capital of the World'. Order eastern-style and expect pulled or chopped whole-hog meat in a tangy sauce without a hint of ketchup. Order western-style and you'll get shoulder in a milder reddish sauce. All jokes about barbecue 'wars' aside, most people probably like both styles.

How to Order

When eating at a barbecue joint, you generally have a choice between a sandwich or plate. A sandwich means a round bun with meat and coleslaw. A plate means a mountain of meat with your choice of sides – slaw, collard greens, beans, mac 'n' cheese – and cornbread or a crispy golden pile of hush puppies. Hush puppies, you say? Fried balls of cornmeal batter. The name? Nobody knows. Another common barbecue side is Brunswick stew, a thick tomato-based soup with lima beans, corn, okra and meat, usually chicken. You may be asked if you want your 'cue pulled or sliced. Pulled means thicker strands of meat, while sliced is very soft and fine. To wash it down, the standard drink is extremely sweet iced tea, though these days you can ask for unsweetened without funny looks. For dessert, it's banana pudding (vanilla pudding with sliced bananas, vanilla wafer cookies and whipped cream).

Where There's Smoke

Purists say decent barbecue has to – must – be smoked over burning wood. The fragrant woodsmoke infuses into the meat as it cooks, giving it that unique flavor and succulence. But barbecue must be cooked 'low and slow' – at low temperatures for a long time, easily half a day or more. That means restaurants that use wood must employ an overnight pit master. As a result, most places now use gas or electric cookers. Will you notice the difference? Probably not. But better try both types just to be sure!

What About South Carolina? And Georgia?

South Carolina claims its own barbecue tradition. It has much in common with North Carolina's – pork, smoked, pulled or sliced. The main distinction is the use of mustard-based sauce, especially common in the central part of the state. Sometimes called 'Carolina gold', the sauce was likely developed under the influence of French and/or German settlers. South Carolina also offers the vinegar and ketchup sauces of North Carolina. Georgia has less of a unique barbecue style. You'll find Carolina-style barbecue, as well as items such as ribs and smoked brisket that are popular in places like Texas.

Where to Eat Barbecue

Some barbecue-lovers swear by certain markers of authenticity in a proper barbecue restaurant – a greasy lunch counter, a pile of wood out back, a parking lot full of pickups, a pit master in overalls. But there are enough nontraditional but delicious 'cue joints to mean that's not entirely fair. One way to choose: look at the Historic North Carolina BBQ Trail map (find it on visitnc.com), which lists the best-loved and most venerable establishments. Or just ask a local about their favorite spot.

Pig Pickin'

If you should happen to wrangle an invite to a pig pickin' – or spot a sign for a charity one – do not hesitate. A pig pickin' is a gathering where an entire hog is roasted, usually in an oil-drum cooker, and set out for guests to 'pick' their own meat. It's a festive occasion – a pig pickin' is often held at wedding receptions or July 4 celebrations, or to raise money for churches, schools or fire departments. Expect sides including deviled eggs, macaroni salad and baked beans. If you're extra lucky, someone might bring a pig pickin' cake – a vanilla cake with mandarin oranges, pineapple and whipped cream.

NC Barbecue Festivals

Lexington, NC, the aforementioned Barbecue Capital of the World, hosts a fall festival (thebarbecuefestival.com) in celebration of porky goodness. It's a real zoo, with hundreds of vendors, multiple stages with music, kids' games, pig-themed sculptures and more. Recent years have seen as many as 200,000 visitors. Though Charlotte, NC, is not known for its own barbecue tradition, it also has a barbecue festival *(carolinabbqfest.org)*, this one in spring, honoring eastern whole-hog style.

CLOCKWISE FROM TOP LEFT: JOSHUA RESNICK/SHUTTERSTOCK, LITTLE HAND IMAGES/GETTY IMAGES,SHARKSHOCK/SHUTTERSTOCK, HLPHOTO/SHUTTERSTOCK

Boston Tea Party Ships & Museum (p172)
JACLYN VERNAC/SHUTTERSTOCK

BIRTHPLACE OF THE REVOLUTION

It started with a financial disagreement (of sorts), which grew into a revolution, which grew into a new nation. By Mara Vorhees

THE AMERICAN FIGHT for independence from Britain began in Boston, when some local merchants got in a huff about unfair tax policies. Import duties and trade restrictions were having a huge negative effect on the economy in this busy port city, and the colonists protested. When the crown responded to local resistance by limiting colonial autonomy, the patriots of Massachusetts had had enough.

Taxation Without Representation

In the mid-18th century, the demands of empire kept Britain at war. The American colonists were drawn into the fighting in the French-Indian War. Despite their victory, all the colonists gained was a tax bill from the king. Covetous of New England's maritime wealth, the crown pronounced a series of Navigation Acts, restricting colonial trade. Boston merchants were defiant, conducting business as usual, except now it was on the sly.

The issue of taxation brought the clash between king and colony to a head. In the 1760s, the British parliament passed the Stamp Act and the Townshend Acts, which placed greater financial burdens on the colonists. With each new tax and toll, resentment intensified, as exhibited by vocal protests and violent mobs. The acts of defiance were defended by respectable lawyer John Adams, who cited the Magna Carta's principle of 'no taxation without representation.'

To each act of rebellion, the British throne responded with increasingly severe measures, eventually dispatching Redcoat regiments known as 'regulars' to restore order, suspending all local political power.

Sons of Liberty

Under siege on the street, unrepentant Bostonians went underground. The Sons of Liberty, a clandestine network of patriots, stirred up public resistance to British policy and harassed the king's loyalists. They were led by some well-known townsmen, including esteemed surgeon Dr Joseph Warren, upper-class merchant John Hancock, skilled silversmith Paul Revere and bankrupt brewer Sam Adams. Branded as treasonous rebels by the king, the Sons of Liberty became more radical and popular as the imperial grip tightened.

The resented Redcoat presence did not extinguish, but rather inflamed, local passions. In March 1770, a motley street gang provoked British regulars with slurs and snowballs until the troops fired into the crowd, killing five and wounding six. John Adams successfully defended the British troops, who were found to be acting in self-defense. The Sons of Liberty, however, scored a propaganda coup with their depictions of the Boston Massacre, as the incident came to be called.

Tempest in a Teapot

In May 1773, the British parliament passed the Tea Act, granting a trade monopoly to the politically influential but financially troubled East India Company. In December, three tea-bearing vessels arrived in Boston Harbor, but colonial merchants refused the shipments to protest the disadvantageous trade policy. When the ships tried to depart, Governor Hutchinson demanded their cargo be unloaded.

At a meeting in the Old South Church, the Sons of Liberty decided to take matters

BOSTON TEA PARTY
★ SHIPS & MUSEUM ★
Old South Meeting House
Green Dragon Tavern
Old State House
Castle William
Lexington
Cambridge
Faneuil Hall
Concord
Salem

into their own hands. Disguised as Mohawk indigenous people, they descended on the waterfront, boarded the ships and dumped 90,000lb of taxable tea into the harbor.

The king's retribution was swift. Legislation was rushed through parliament to punish Boston, 'the center of rebellious commotion in America, the ringleader in every riot.' With a series of laws dubbed the Intolerable Acts, the port was blockaded and the city placed under military rule. The Sons of Liberty spread the news of this latest outrage down the seaboard. The cause of Boston was becoming the cause of all the colonies: American independence versus British tyranny.

THE SONS OF LIBERTY DECIDED TO TAKE MATTERS INTO THEIR OWN HANDS. DISGUISED AS MOHAWK INDIGENOUS PEOPLE, THEY DESCENDED ON THE WATERFRONT, BOARDED THE SHIPS AND DUMPED 90,000LB OF TAXABLE TEA INTO THE HARBOR

Bunker Hill (p165)

SEAN PAVONE/SHUTTERSTOCK

The Shot Heard Round the World

Until now, all but the most pugnacious of patriots would have been satisfied with colonial economic autonomy and political representation, but the king's coercive tactics aroused indignation and acrimony. Both sides were spoiling for a fight.

British general Thomas Gage was sent over with 4000 troops and a fleet of warships. Local townsfolk and yeoman farmers organized themselves into Minutemen groups, citizen militias that could mobilize in a minute. They drilled on town commons and stockpiled weapons in secret stores.

In April 1775, Gage saw an opportunity to break colonial resistance. Acting on a tip from a local informant, he dispatched 700 troops on the road west to arrest fugitives Sam Adams and John Hancock and to seize a hidden stash of gunpowder. Bostonians had their own informants, including Gage's wife, who tipped off Joseph Warren on the troop movement.

Word was then passed to the Old North Church sexton to hang two signal lanterns in the steeple. Revere got the signal and quietly slipped across the river into Charlestown, where he mounted Brown Beauty and galloped into the night to alert the Minutemen.

At daybreak, the confrontation finally occurred. 'Here once the embattled farmers stood,' Ralph Waldo Emerson later wrote, 'and fired the shot heard round the world.' Imperial troops skirmished with Minutemen on Lexington Green and at the Old North Bridge in Concord. By midmorning, more militia had arrived and chased the bloodied Redcoats back to Boston in ignominious defeat. The inevitable had arrived: the war for independence.

From Bunker Hill to Dorchester Heights

Boston figured prominently in the early phase of the American Revolution. In June 1775, its citizens inflicted a hurtful blow on British morale at the Battle of Bunker Hill. The British took the hill after three tries, but their losses were greater than expected. Fighting on the front line, Warren was killed by a musket shot to the head in the final British charge. A few weeks later, George Washington assumed command of the ragged Continental Army in Cambridge.

Britain's military occupation of the city continued until March 1776, when Washington mounted captured British cannons on Dorchester Heights and trained them on the British fleet in Boston Harbor. Rather than see the king's expensive warships sent to the bottom, the British evacuated the city, trashing and looting as they went. Boston was liberated.

THE CHEROKEE

Where did the Cherokee go? They're still here, living in mountainous, forested communities in the far west of North Carolina. By Regis St Louis

THE CHEROKEE HAVE overcome many challenges since the loss of over 99% of their homeland in the 19th century. At the edge of the Smoky Mountains, the Qualla Boundary is a nation within a nation. It's home to the Eastern Band of the Cherokee Indians, who carry on age-old traditions that connect them to their ancestral land.

The Eastern Cherokee

Every schoolchild in America learns about President Andrew Jackson's genocidal Indian removal policy, which saw the Cherokee and other tribes evicted from their homeland in the late 1830s. Their weeks-long journey on foot became known as the Trail of Tears, a forced march of over 16,000 men, women and children. Between 25% and 50% would die along the way from exposure, starvation and disease. Once in the newly demarcated 'Indian Territory' of present-day Oklahoma, they would find a harsh, arid land quite different from the lush mountain valleys they'd left behind.

Less well known is the story of those who stayed. Hundreds of Cherokee hid out in the mountains, later joined by others who had managed to return to their homeland from Oklahoma. By 1850 some 1000 members were living in a small pocket of western North Carolina – a fraction of the 40,000 sq miles of former Cherokee territory that reached into Georgia, the Carolinas and five other states. Over the next few decades the group worked tirelessly to buy land back from the federal government. In the late 1860s the US acknowledged the right of the tribe (now officially known as the Eastern Band of the Cherokee Indians, a group independent from the Cherokee Nation of Oklahoma) to own and control lands. Today eastern Cherokee holdings encompass 57,000 acres of the Qualla Boundary, a tribally run community of seven municipalities located about an hour west of Asheville.

For much of the 20th century the tribe faced the same struggles as many Native communities around the country: there was rampant discrimination, along with a dire lack of economic opportunities, particularly after the collapse of the timber industry in the 1920s. New Deal programs in the 1930s provided jobs in building and conservation, and the creation of the Great Smoky Mountains National Park (p346) in 1934 brought a stream of visitors into the area, in turn creating tourism potential. Outsiders came seeking Indians, and some residents played to the stereotype, donning feathered headdresses and setting up tipis, neither of which are part of

Cherokee heritage. Dreamcatchers, fringed vests and other kitsch items were sold at roadside stands. It was a role not everyone felt comfortable with, but it provided income to the tribe.

Celebrating Cherokee Traditions

In the meantime, Cherokee continued making traditional crafts, including wood carvings, pottery, beadwork and baskets. Elaborate river-cane baskets are among the most emblematic symbols of Cherokee culture, with unearthed fragments of baskets dating back to the 15th century. In 1946 a group of 60 Cherokee artists and artisans established what would become the Qualla Arts & Crafts Mutual (p342), the nation's oldest Native American cooperative. It served as a place to sell high-quality crafts, ensuring the survival of age-old traditions. Today its membership has grown to over 350 artisans.

In 1948 the Cherokee opened a log-cabin museum with displays on Cherokee history and crafts. One of the oldest continually operated tribal museums in the US, it has grown over the years to become a major repository of Cherokee artifacts. In 2023 the museum began a multiyear renovation, sparked by a reevaluation of its role in the community. 'The old exhibit was not necessarily written by Native historians,' says Anna Chandler, the museum's manager of communications. 'The big focus of updating the main gallery is telling the Cherokee story from a Cherokee perspective.' The museum has been renamed the Museum of the Cherokee People (p340) – rather than the outdated 'Museum of the Cherokee Indian' – as a way to emphasize that 'this is a place to make tribal members feel welcome,' in Chandler's words. 'It's also a way to signal to visitors that Native people are not of the past. It places Cherokee people in the present day. We also worked really closely with the Cherokee Speakers Council to determine the Cherokee name of the museum. It's not a direct translation, but it's along the lines of "We are all Cherokee and it all belongs to us." That ownership, that community buy-in was really critical in rebranding, reintroducing and welcoming the community to be part of this new direction.'

Reinvestigating the past has led to other developments as well. In 2024 Clingmans Dome, the highest point in Great Smoky Mountains National Park, was renamed Kuwohi, its former Cherokee name, which means 'mulberry place'.

Investing in the Future & the Past

For much of the 20th century tourism provided a boost to the Cherokee economy, but business was always seasonal. Hard times arrived from November to March, when tourist numbers were low. Poverty rates never dipped below double digits, and sometimes they reached as high as 50%. In the 1990s the tribal council authorized a new kind of tourism that could provide steady revenue year-round. Opening in 1997, Harrah's Cherokee Casino Resort transformed the fortunes of the community. Now over four million visitors come to the resort each year, and annual earnings from its hotel rooms, entertainment venues and gambling halls are a staggering $400 million. Gambling revenue has been plowed back into the community, with millions of dollars of investment in schools, healthcare facilities and cultural attractions (including the Cherokee museum). The Cherokee's 16,000 individual tribal members also benefit, receiving annual payouts currently amounting to around $14,000 per person, which has helped lift many out of generational poverty. Since the 1990s the tribe has also invested in buying back Cherokee land – reclaiming ancestral places stolen from them in the 19th century. Among its most significant purchases is Kituwah (Mother Town), a sacred 309-acre site that's considered to be the place of origin for all Cherokee.

Cherokee dancer (p328)

RUNNING WHIRLWIND/ALAMY

Lake George (p111)
DEBRA MILLET/SHUTTERSTOCK

THE BIRTH OF AMERICA'S SUMMER VACATION

A series of 19th-century stories about New York's wild Adirondacks became a prototype for the modern guidebook and a passport to freedom. By John Garry

FOR MANY WATERFRONT destinations throughout the Mid-Atlantic, summer is more than a season – it's the most exciting time of year. Populations boom with vacationers who leave behind their cities and look forward to letting loose. The tradition may seem old hat, but it's relatively new. These are its origins.

Summer Arrives

Memorial Day sets off an East Coast alarm bell. Tiny waterfront towns that hibernated from October through April spring back to life by the last Monday of May. Summer has arrived. Vacationers are coming.

The wake-up call is particularly pronounced in Lake George – an Adirondack Mountains village where the population can swell from roughly 1000 to 50,000 throughout summer. When it comes to preparing for the incoming deluge, Lake George is a well-oiled machine. Mini-golf courses polish their fiberglass sculptures and fudge shops set out chunks of sweet treats. Marinas fill up their rental boats with gas. Campgrounds clean up winter's debris.

The entire region simmers with the splendor of summer vacation until Labor Day, when the season's enchantment disappears. But for those few precious months, the Adirondacks ace the art of escapism. This is, after all, where the American vacation was born.

Rise of the Vacation Class

In the early 19th century, traveling for leisure was a privilege reserved for the rich. In New York, the well-heeled went to spa towns like Saratoga Springs, where 'taking the waters' supposedly cured various ailments, while newlyweds traveled to Niagara Falls to sojourn with the sublime. But the average American had no concept of 'vacation'. The word wasn't even used in common parlance.

All that changed after the Civil War. Rapid industrialization transformed America's demographics: urban factories gave rise to an affluent middle class, and Puritan prejudice against 'idle hands' was countered with arguments about relaxation's benefits.

With time to kill and money to burn, the number of Americans traveling for rest and recreation began growing, aided by railroads. The nation was becoming an open book. The only thing nascent travelers needed was a guide.

America's Proto-Travel Guide

In the mid-1860s, a young clergyman named William HH Murray took his first trip to the Adirondacks – a vast wilderness known mostly by indigenous inhabitants and rugged outdoorsmen. Murray fell in love with the landscape and began writing about his off-the-radar adventures. By 1869, he published a book – *Adventures in the Wilderness; or, Camp-Life in the Adirondacks.*

Much like the poetic ponderings of his academic contemporaries Henry David Thoreau and Ralph Waldo Emerson, Murray persuasively preached the physical and spiritual benefits of connecting with nature. He argued that the pine-scented mountains could be the antidote to urban ailments, writing, 'no portion of our country surpasses, if indeed any equals, in health-giving qualities, the Adirondack Wilderness.'

His writing was simple and straightforward, and laid out plenty of practical information. This easy-to-follow advice – what to pack, where to stay, who to hire as a guide, how much money to spend – gave novice nature lovers confidence to rough it in the woods. Murray also attempted to democratize the Adirondack experience by appealing to a group often left out of outdoor exploration – women. A section of the guide focused solely on what they should wear. He noted that 'none enjoy the experiences more than ladies, and certain it is that none are more benefited by it.'

While critical reviews of Murray's work were mixed, the public ate it up. Within months, New York's mountains erupted with stampedes of urbanites, who streamed in from NYC, Boston and beyond, clutching Murray's words like their wilderness Bible.

But the summer of '69 wasn't exactly the Edenic destination Murray described. Locusts of black flies left visitors bug-bitten and bloody. Rain came down in torrents. Lodges became overwhelmed. Untrained wilderness guides led groups astray. Even with Murray's instructions, travelers were ill-prepared. Critics of Murray's disgruntled disciples derided them as 'Murray's Fools.'

Still, many readers remained undeterred. Some even waxed poetic about their experiences. Journalist and lecturer Kate Field, who spent that summer camping with three pioneering female companions among the mountains, summed up the region's unflagging magnetism best: 'The moral of the Adirondacks is freedom.'

Signs of Overtourism

The promise of freedom continued luring masses to the Adirondacks in 1870, and as crowds multiplied, businesses sprang up to meet their demands. By the end of the century, hotels, railroads, steamboats and wagon roads dotted the wilds, ready to make a buck off the bucket-list destination.

NYC blue bloods like the Vanderbilts and Rockefellers joined their ranks, purchasing private lakeside properties where they could 'vacate' the city's heat for cool mountain air. Their sprawling estates became the sites of 'Great Camps' – Gilded Age fortresses constructed with logs, covered in tree bark and decorated with taxidermy.

At the same time, local farming and logging reached its feverish peak. In 1885, maps commissioned by New York State's legislature showed that an estimated 27.8% of what's now Adirondack Park had been cleared. Murray's work presented a paradox, a dilemma plaguing sites from Machu Picchu to Venice today: extolling the virtues of the pristine Adirondacks inadvertently played a role in their decay.

Paradise Found

Thanks to state legislation and environmental activism, fortunately the story of the Adirondacks doesn't end in destruction. By 1885 New York's governor established a law ensuring the Adirondacks would be 'forever kept as wild forest lands.'

As America marched into the 20th century and the nation's final frontiers vanished, no destination would quite match what Murray described in 1869. Still, plenty of other East Coast utopias emerged as getaway hot spots. New Jersey's Atlantic City and Brooklyn's Coney Island became blue-collar escapes for work-weary travelers. Jewish summer resorts took root in New York's Catskills. African Americans found relaxation at Maryland's Highland Beach. The country's first gay and lesbian summer community spread its wings in Cherry Grove.

More travel guides soon filled the shelves of bookstores while Murray's musings faded into obscurity, but an idea he planted permanently lodged itself in the American psyche: now and then, everyone deserves a vacation.

INDEX

- Acadia National Park 228-30
- accessible travel 594
- accommodations 586
- activities 42-3, *see also individual activities*
  - Atlanta BeltLine's Eastside Trail 373
  - Blue Spring State Park 466
  - Dante Fascell Visitor Center 448
  - Orlando Wetlands Park 468
  - Raft One 356
  - Sheltowee Trace Adventure Resort 365
  - Skyline Park 373
- Adirondacks, the 109, 111-13
- Alabama 380-8, **381**
- Alexandria 296
- Ali, Muhammad 360
- alligators 444, 447
- Amherst 182
- Amish 143-4
- amusement parks
  - Adventure Landing Jacksonville Beach 476
  - Aquatica 470
  - Buffalo Heritage Carousel 117
  - Carousel Gardens 418
  - Cedar Point 532
  - Centennial Wheel 501
  - Deno's Wonder Wheel Park 97
  - Glen Echo Park 203
  - Greenway Carousel 158
  - Jane's Carousel 95
  - Luna Park 97
  - Orlando Eye 466
  - Roger at the Pier 278
  - SkyView Ferris wheel 370
  - SkyWheel 341
  - Slide Hill 59
  - Trimper Rides 278
  - Universal Orlando Resort™ 469
  - Walt Disney World® 467
  - Water Works Park 484
- animals 46, 577, *see also individual species*
- Ann Arbor 543
- Annapolis 274
- Antietam National Battlefield 283
- Apostle Islands 562-3
- aquariums
  - Echo Leahy Center for Lake Champlain 204
  - Florida Aquarium 484
  - Georgia Aquarium 368-9
  - Greater Cleveland Aquarium 527, 529
  - Mystic Aquarium 199
  - National Aquarium 279
  - New England Aquarium 159
  - Save the Bay's Hamilton Family Aquarium 190
  - SeaWorld 470
  - Shedd Aquarium 507
  - Tennessee Aquarium 355
  - Witt Stephens Jr Nature Center 401
  - Woods Hole Science Aquarium 178
- architecture
  - Buffalo 116
  - Cape May 122
  - Chicago 499, 501
  - Columbus 523
  - Lewes 270-1
  - Marina City 501
  - Newport 192
- Arkansas 397-406, **398**
- Arlington 295-6
- Asbury Park 124-5
- Asheville 325-6
- Assateague Island 278-9
- Athens 374
- Atlanta 367-74, **368**, **370**, **371**
- ATMs 582
- Auburn 520
- Aurora 115

B

- B&Bs 586
- bald eagles 143
- Baltimore 279-83, **280**, **282**
- Bar Harbor 228-30
- barbecue 606-7
- Bardstown 361
- baseball 171, 204, 254, 265, 281, 540
- Basie, Count 464
- basketball 540
- beaches 614
  - 12th Street Beach 508
  - Amsterdam Beach 103
  - Anne's Beach 454
  - Atlantic Beach 478
  - Bethany Beach 270
  - Boneyard Beach 478
  - Bradford Beach 556
  - Cape Hatteras National Seashore 318-19
  - Castle Island 172
  - Clearwater Beach 487
  - Cocoa Beach 474
  - Ditch Plains Beach 99
  - Edgewater Park Beach 529
  - Edisto Beach State Park 340
  - flag safety 592
  - Folly Beach 340
  - Fort Lauderdale Beach 456
  - Gansevoort Peninsula 78-9
  - Gunnison Beach 126
  - Hammonasset Beach State Park 197
  - Harbor Heights Beach 473
  - Higgs Beach 454
  - Jacksonville Beach 476, 478
  - Jacobs Beach 197
  - Kiawah Beachwater Park 340
  - Kirk Park Beach 103
  - Long Point Beach 181
  - Margaret T Burroughs Beach 508
  - Meyers Beach 563
  - Mid-Beach, Miami 432, 435
  - Million Dollar Beach 111
  - Montauk Beach 103
  - Montrose Beach 508
  - Myrtle Beach 341
  - Neptune Beach 478
  - North Avenue Beach 508
  - North Beach, Miami 435
  - North Beach, Savannah 376
  - Oak Street Beach 508
  - Rehoboth Beach 268-9
  - Sombrero Beach 454
  - South Beach, Miami 432
  - South Edison Beach 103
  - Springer's Point Preserve 319
  - St Pete Beach 487
- Beacon 105
- Beacon Hill 166-7
- Beaufort 316-17, 340
- Bennington 213
- Bentonville 405
- Berkeley Springs 305
- Berkshires, the 184-5
- bird-watching 319, 449
  - Anhinga Trail 447
  - Audubon Bird Sanctuary 388
  - Cape May Bird Observatory 122
  - Cape May Point State Park 123
  - Delaware River 143
  - Montrose Point Bird Sanctuary 499
  - Shark Valley 444
  - Wekiwa Springs State Park 466
- Birmingham 384-5, **385**
- Biscayne Bay 437
- Black Broadway 256-7
- Blackwater National Wildlife Refuge
- Blowing Rock 327
- Blue Ridge Parkway 48, 292
- blues 171, 349, 391, 392, 393, 503
  - Rainey, Gertrude 'Ma' 375
  - Sun Studio 347
- boat rides 124
  - Acadian Boat Tours 229
  - Adventure Harbor Tours 339
  - Apostle Islands Cruises 562-3
  - Balmy Days Cruises 225
  - Burlington Community Boathouse 204

boat rides *continued*
Cajun Country Swamp Tours 423
Cap'n Fish's Cruises 225
Chelsea Piers 87
Community Boating 168
Creole Queen 411
FR Smith & Sons 111-12
Heritage of Biscayne cruise 448
Island Queen Cruises 437
Jungle Queen Riverboat 459
Lake George Steamboat Company 112
Lucky Catch Cruises 223
Lulu Lobster Boat 229
Maine Kayak 225
Minnie-Ha-Ha 112
Portland Schooner Company 223
Rent a Boat Fort Lauderdale 459
Robbie's Marina 452
Schooner Woodwind 274
Schuylkill Banks 136
Spirit of Buffalo 117
Steamboat Natchez 411
Thriller Miami Speedboat Adventures 437
Watermark 274
Whistling Man Schooner Company 204
bodegas 91
books 37, 77, 302, 327
Boothbay Harbor 225
border crossings 582
Boston 158-75, **160-1**, **162**, **170**
accommodations 232
children, travel with 172
drinking & nightlife 169
entertainment 168, 171
food 166, 167, 168, 169, 171, 173
history 164-5, 167-8, 172, 173-5
tours 163, 164-5
travel within Boston 158, 169
Boundary Waters 575, 577
Brandywine Valley 139
Brevard 327-8
breweries 40, 543-4
18th Ward Brewing 96
Aslin Brewery 148
Avondale Brewing Company 385
beer bus 373
Bold Monk Brewing Co 373
Bookhouse Brewing 527
Brooklyn Brewery 95-6
Burial 326
Cincinnati's Brewing Heritage Trail 529
Fire Maker Brewing Company 373
Founders Brewing Co 544
Great Lakes Brewing Company 527
Grimm Artisanal Ales 96
Hansa Brewery 527
Harmony Brewing Company 544
Highland Brewing Co 325
Hop Lot Brewing Company 548
Lakefront Brewery 553-4, 555
Miller Brewing Company 553
Mitten Brewing Company 544
Monday Night Brewing 373
New Holland Brewing Pub on 8th 547
Scratch Brewing 515
Sierra Nevada 326
South Slope Brewing District 326
Talea 96
Vivant Brewery 544
Warped Wing Brewing Company 535
Wicked Weed 326
bridges
Aerial Lift Bridge 572
Bartonsville 213
Brooklyn Bridge 59-61
Cornish-Windsor Bridge 213
Endless Bridge 569
Fisher Railroad Bridge 213
John A Roebling Suspension Bridge 530
Montgomery 213
New River Gorge Bridge 300
Nichols Bridgeway 498
Old Steel Railroad Bridge 484
Purple People Bridge 530
Three-in-a-Row Bridges 213
Brown County 523
Brunswick 379
Bryson City 328
budget 583, 585, 586, 589
Buffalo 116
Bunyan, Paul 572, 573
Burlington 204-5

cable cars 113
camping 586
canoeing, *see* kayaking & canoeing
Cape Lookout National Seashore 317
Cape May 122-3
Capitol Hill 246-7
Capone, Al 138
Carrboro 325
cathedrals, *see* churches & cathedrals
Catskills, the 108-12
caves 363, 406, 524, 534, 547, 560
cemeteries 295-6, 319, 336, 412, 513, 543, 567
Central Park 92-3
Chanhassen 570
Chapel Hill 323
Charleston 299, 334-40, **335**, **338**
Charlevoix 544
Charlotte 321-2
Chattanooga 354-6
Cherokee 328, 611-13
Cherry Grove 103
Chicago 496-507, **497**, **500**, **502**, **504**, **505**, **507**, **508**
accommodations 578
children, travel with 503
drinking 501, 503, 504, 505
entertainment 502-3, 504, 506
food 496, 498, 500, 502, 506, 508
shopping 506
travel within Chicago 496
churches & cathedrals
Basilica of St Patrick's Old Cathedral 72
Cathedral Basilica of St Augustine 479
Cathedral Basilica of the Immaculate Conception 387-8
Dexter Avenue King Memorial Baptist Church 387
Dexter Avenue King Memorial Church 385
First Christian Church 523
Santuario Nacional de Nuestra Señora de la Caridad 443
Washington National Cathedral 260, 262
Cincinnati 529-30
Cleveland 526-7, 529
climate 34-5, 592
Clinton, Bill 397-9
clothing 36
Cocoa Village 474-5
Columbia 342
Columbus 530-1
Coney Island 96-7
Connecticut 193-201, **194**
Cooper-Young 349
coral 452
Coral Gables 442
Corolla 320-1
costs 583, 585, 586, 589
country music 125, 351
credit cards 585
crocodiles 447
culture 602-3
Adena 535
Amish 533-4
Cajun 422
Caribbean 409
Cherokee 328, 611-13
contemporary 252, 254
Creole 423
Grand Village of the Natchez Indians 396
Gullah 340
Gullah-Geechee 336, 338, 378, 342
Hopewell 535
Jewish 616
Mohican 184
Oconaluftee Indian Village 328
Shakers 185
Tibetan 522
Vermilionville 422
Wampanoag 178
Cumberland 283-4
Cumberland Island 379
Cuyahoga Valley National Park 528
cycling & cycling tours 43, *see also* mountain biking
Arkansas River Trail 401
Assateague Outfitters 279
Bentonville Bike Fest 401
Bike Zone Rentals 178
Brad's Bike Rental 223

Map Pages **000**

C&O Canal 284, 304
Charles River Esplanade 168
Corner Cycle 178
Crest Bike Rental 124
D & R Canal trail 129
Elroy-Sparta State Bike Trail 557
Georgetown-Lewes Trail 270
Grand Traverse Bike Tours 547
Indy Cultural Trail 519-20
Kingdom Trails 212
Lakefront Trail 507-8
Local Motion 204
Minuteman Bikeway 174
Mon River Trail 304
Monon Trail 519
Mt Nebo 401
Pine Creek Rail Trail 145
Province Lands Trail 181
Pure Energy Cycling & Java House 129
Riverfront Wilmington 265
Shining Sea Bikeway 178
Slaughter Pen 405
Summer Feet Cycling 223
Swamp Rabbit Trail 343
Washington Crossing State Park 129

Darwin Twine Ball 572
Dayton 534-5
Dean, James 522
Dearborn 541-2
Delaware 263-71, **264**
Detroit 537-41, **538**
disabilities, travelers with, *see* accessible travel
distilleries 572
diving 449
dolphins 123, 124, 340, 481
Door County 560-1
Douglass, Frederick 280
Dover 268
Doylestown 140-1
drinking 588, *see also individual locations*
driving & driving tours 48-9
6A 103
Blue Hill Peninsula 226-7, **227**
Blue Ridge Parkway 48, 292
Cherohala Skyway 356
Corolla Outback Adventures 321
Eastern Shore 277, **277**
Fayette Station Rd 300
Great River Road 559, **559**
Green Mountain 207
Heritage Trail 453, **453**
Highway 61 49, 573
Kancamagus Highway 220
Long Trail 207
M-22, the 547-8
Mt Washington Auto Road 219-20
Natchez Trace Parkway 48, 396
Overseas Hwy 49, 453
Route 66 514, **514**
Smugglers Notch 207
Stagecoach Trail 515
Vermont's Scenic Drive 100, 210-11, **211**
Western Catskills 110, **110**
Duluth 572
dunes 544, 545, 560
Durham 323, 324
Dylan, Bob 575

East Burke 212
electricity 595
Ellington, Duke 257, 464
Ellis Island 64-5
Empire State Building 80, 82
entertainment 16-17, *see also individual locations*, music, nightlife
Essex 197-8
etiquette 36
events, *see* festivals & events
Everglades & Biscayne National Park 444-9, **445**

Fairhope 388
Fairmount 522
Falmouth 178-9
family travel 43, 276, 587
Broadway at the Beach 341
Castle Island 172
Chinatown Fair Family Fun Center 72
City Putt 418
Diver Ed's Dive-In Theater 229
Glazer Children's Museum 484
Harry Potter Shop 503
House on the Rock 558
Maggie Daley Park 503
Market Common 341
Martin's Park 172
Ole Covered Wagon ride 145
Orlando Science Center 470
Planet Word 252
South Beach Park 476
Storyland 418
Topgolf 341
Faulkner, William 393
Fayetteville 301, 402-3, 405
Fenway-Kenmore 169, 171
ferries 583
Battery Maritime Building 59
Casco Bay Lines 223
Fulton Ferry Landing 91
Isle Royale Ferries 574
Madeline Island Ferry 563
Queen City Bike Ferry 117
Rock Island Ferry 561
Sandy Hook 125
Sayville Ferry 103
Washington Island Ferry 561
festivals & events 18, 35, 39
Abbey Road on the River 518
Adams Morgan Day 255
Annapolis Boat Show 279
ArtPrize 546
Atlantic City Air Show 125
Baltimore Pride 279
Barefoot Country Music Festival 125
Battle of Gettysburg Anniversary 145
Bean Fest & Championship Outhouse Races 401
Bentonia Blues Festival 393
Bentonville Bike Fest 401
Bentonville Film Festival 401
Bill Monroe's Bluegrass Festival 518
Blink 530
Bockfest Cincinnati 530
Bowen's Wharf Seafood Festival 192
Bright Lights 393
Cleveland Kurentovanje 530
Clifford Brown Jazz Festival 265
Cow Chip Throw 560
Deal Island Skipjack Race 279
Dedication Day 145
Double Decker Arts Festival 393
Feast of San Gennaro 69
First Friday Art Walk 388
Fourth of July 378
German Fest 555
Gettysburg Bluegrass Festival 145
Gettysburg Festival of Races 145
Great Lakes Surf Festival 546
Greater Florida Pride Parade & Festival 459
Hot Springs Documentary Film Festival 401
IngenuityFest 530
Irish Fest 555
James Dean Festival 522
Johnny Appleseed Festival 518
Juke Joint Festival 392, 393
Kentucky Bourbon Festival 361
Kentucky Derby Festival 360
King Biscuit Blues Festival 393
Kunta Kinte Heritage Festival 279
Little 500 518
Luminary Loppet 569
Macy's Thanksgiving Day Parade 97
Maine Lobster Festival 225
Maryland Crab Cake Festival 279
Maryland Renaissance Festival 279
Mermaid Parade 97
Movement 546
National Apple Harvest Festival 145
National Cherry Blossom Festival 249-50
National Cherry Festival 546
New Orleans Jazz & Heritage Festival 409
New Orleans Mardi Gras 407, 409
New Year's Eve 97
Newport Folk Festival 192
Newport Jazz Festival 192
Newport Oyster Festival 192
Newport Pride 192
NYC Pride March 97
Oktoberfest Zinzinnati 530
Ozark Folk Festival 401
Panoply 382
Parke County Covered Bridge Festival 518
Pirate Fest 378
Polish Fest 555
PrideFest 555

festivals & events *continued*
Red, White & Blueberry Festival 125
Remembrance Day 145
RollerCade 542
SCAD Sand Arts Festival 378
Shadfest 125
Smithsonian Folklife Festival 251
South 9th Street Italian Market Festival 137-8
St Paul Winter Carnival 569
Summerfest 555
Tanglewood Music Festival 184
Trout Parade 112
Tulip Time 546
Tybee Island Beach Bum Parade 378
Tybee Turtle Trot 378
Village Halloween Parade 97
Walktober 201
WaterFire 188
Watermen Appreciation Day 279
Woodstock Music & Art Fair 109
films 37, 269, 384, 401, 468, 522
Finger Lakes 113-15
Fire Island 103-4
Fire Island Pines 103
fishing 112, 124, 125, 225, 320, 452, 478
Fishtown 548
Fitzgerald, Ella 464
Fitzgerald, F Scott 570-1
Florence 182
Florida 426-89, **428-9**
accommodations 488-9
driving tour 453, **453**
itineraries 430-1
navigation 428-9
Florida Keys & Key West 450-5, **451**
Florida, Northeast 476-81
Florida, Southeast 456-63
food 38-41, 588, 589, *see also individual locations*
barbecue 606-7
cheese 562
food trucks 159, 162, 368
gumbo 419
football 385, 374, 532, 540
Ford, Henry 539
Fort Lauderdale 456-61, **457**
Franconia 220
Frankfort 362-3
Franklin, Aretha 383
Fredericksburg 296
Freedom Trail 164-5
Frost, Robert 205-6, 220

Galena 513, 515
galleries, *see* museums & galleries
gay travelers, *see* LGBTIQ+ travelers
Gaye, Marvin 539
geology 46
Georgia 366-79, **367**
Georgian Coast 376, 378
Gettysburg 144
gorges 382
Governors Island 58-9
Grand Central Terminal 83-4
Grand Marais 574-5
Grand Rapids 543-4
Great Lakes 491-579, **492-3**
accommodations 578-9
driving tours 514, 559, **514, 559**
festivals 494-5
itineraries 494-5
navigation 492-3
Great Smoky Mountains National Park 329-32, 355
Green Bay 561-2
Greensboro 323
Greensboro Sit-Ins 322
Greenville 342-3
Guilford 197

H

Harpers Ferry 304
Hartford 199-200
Harvard University 163, **162**
Havre de Grace 274
health 592
Heidelberg Project 539
Hemingway, Ernest 511, 544
Hibbing 575
High Line 77-8
highlights 10-21
Highway 61 49
hiking 42-3, *see also* walking
Alum Cove 406
Appalachian Mountain Club 218
Autism Nature Trail 115
Bear Lake Trail 447
Benton Falls Trail 356
Big Bluff & the Goat Trail 406
Blood Mountain 374
Brasstown Bald 374
Breakneck Ridge 107
Buck Mountain 111
Bull Hill 107
Cadillac North Ridge Trailhead 228
Cane Creek Canyon 382
Cascadilla Gorge 114
Christian Point Trail 447
Coler Mountain 405
Currituck Banks Maritime Forest Trai 320
Dogwood Trail 320
Endless Wall Trail 300
Falls Viewing Platform 108
Freedom Trail 320
Garden of the Gods 515
Glen Burney Falls Trail 327
Gorge Trail 115
Graham Creek Nature Preserve 388
Green Mountain Club 208
Gunflint Trail 575
Hawksbill Crag 406
Hell Brook Trail 208
Hocking Hills 534
Ice Age Trai 557
Indian Head 111
John Pennekamp Coral Reef State Park 450, 452
Kitty Hawk Woods 320
Knob, The 178
Lansing River Trail 542
Lincoln Woods Trail 220
Long Trail 208
Long Trail South 208
Looking Glass Rock 328
Mammoth Cave National Park 363
Marquette 551
Maryland Heights Trail 304
Mon River Trail 304
Monument Mountain 184-5
Mt Beacon 107
Mt Katahdin 230-1
Mt Nebo 401-2
Mt Tom State Reservation 182
Mt Washington 218
Nags Head Woods Preserve 320
Oak Leaf Trail 557
Ohiopyle State Park 149
Old Rag Mountain 293
Pine Creek Rail Trail 145
Pisgah National Forest 328
Prospect Mountain 111
Province Lands Trail 181
Quoddy Head State Park 230
Rainbow Lake Wilderness Area 356-7
Red Mountain Park 384
Shawnee National Forest 515
Shelby Bottoms 354
Skinner State Park 182
Storm King Mountain 107
Sunset Ridge Trail 208
Superior Hiking Trail 574
Walkway over the Hudson 107
White Mountains 220
historic buildings & sites, *see also* notable buildings
16th Street Baptist Church 384
AG Gaston Motel 384
Aiken-Rhett House 336
Bachman-Wilson House 405
Beaufort Historic Site 316
Bolivar Heights Battlefield 304
Boscobel House & Gardens 106
Cahokia Mounds State Historic Site 515
Capitol Hill 246-7
Castillo de San Marcos 481
Castle Williams 59
Chatham Manor 296
Clayton House 148
Clinton Presidential Center 397-9
College of William & Mary 289
Dexter Avenue King Memorial Baptist Church 385, 387
Dia Bridgehampton 104
Dover Green 268
Eastern State Penitentiary 138
Embassy Row 259
Emlen Physick Estate 122
Fisher Building 540
Flannery O'Connor Childhood Home 376
Fort Condé 388
Fort Jay 59
Fort Mackinac 548, 551
Fort Matanzas 481
Fort Morgan State Historic Site 388

Map Pages **000**

Fort Moultrie 339
Fort Raleigh National Historic Site 319
Fort Sumter 339
Freedmen's Colony 319
George Floyd Square 567
Gettysburg National Military Park 144
Guardian Building 540
Heurich House 259
Highland 290
Historic Corolla Park 320-1
Historic St Mary's City 274
Hopewell Culture National Historical Park 535
Independence National Historical Park 134-5
John Brown's Fort 304
Judd Foundation 72
Kane Manor Inn 145
Kelly Ingram Park 384
Kenmore 296
Kentuck Knob 149
Kykuit 106
Larz Anderson House 259
Laura Plantation 421
Little Rock Central High School National Historic Site 402
Mansion on O Street 259
Martin Luther King Jr National Historical Park 369
Mary Washington House 296
Mayflower Hotel 259
Melrose Estate 396
Mercer-Williams House 376
Minute Man National Historical Park 174
Mission Nombre de Dios 481
Monticello 290
Ocmulgee Mounds 374-5
Olana 107
Old Salem 323
Old State Capitol 362
Old Swedes Historic Site 265-6
Old Town Alexandria 296
Owens-Thomas House & Slave Quarters 376
Pabst Mansion 556
Park Avenue Armory 87
Plant Riverside District 376
Point Park 356
Poverty Point 423
Reconstruction Era National Historical Park 340
Rookery 501
SC Johnson Administration Building & Research Tower 556
Sloss 384
Star-Spangled Banner Flag House 283
Stonewall Inn 76
Taliesin 558
Tennessee State Capitol 351
Thomas Cole National Historic Site 106-7
Tribune Tower 501
United Nations 84
Unity Temple 511
Valley Forge National Historic Park 140
Vicksburg 394
Vicksburg National Military Park 395
Whalehead Club 321
Whitney Plantation 421
William Johnson House 396
Wingspread 556
Wrigley Building 501
Wormsloe State Historic Site 378
history 12-13
Black Heritage Trail 216, 218
Brooklyn 96
City Park 601
Ellis Island 600
Fort Hancock 125
Gettysburg 599
Independence Hall 599
International African American Museum 599
Jamestown National Historic Site 598
Lincoln Memorial 600
National Archives 251-2
New River Gorge National Park & Preserve 601
Ocmulgee Mounds 598
One World Trade Center 600
Plimoth Patuxet Museum 599
Portsmouth 216
Shenandoah National Park 600
Stonewall Inn 600
US Capitol Building 601
horse racing
Churchill Downs 360
Keeneland 362
Kentucky Derby 360
horseback riding 363, 365
horses, wild
Corolla Wild Horse Fund 321
Cumberland Island 379
hostels 586
Hot Springs National Park 400
Hudson Valley 104-7
Hudson Yards 78
Hull Rust Mine Viewpoint 575
Huntsville 380, 382
hurricanes 592
Hwy 61 391

ice skating 117
Illinois 509-15, **510**
independence, fight for 608-10
Independence National Historical Park 134-5
Indian Key 452
Indiana 516-24, **517**
Indiana Dunes National Park 521
Indianapolis 518-20
islands
Assateague Island 278-9
Cape Lookout National Seashore 317-18
Coney Island 96-7
Fenwick Island 270
Fire Island 103
Governors Island 58-9
Isle of Palms 340
Jekyll Island 379
Kiawah 340
Little Island 79
Long Beach Island 125
Madeline Island 563
Nantucket Island 181
Northerly Island 499
Peaks Island 223
Roanoke Island 319-20
Sullivan's Island 340
Tybee Island 376, 378
Isle Royale National Park 549
itineraries 24-33, **25**, **27**, **28-9**, **31**, **33**, *see also individual locations*

J

Jackson 393-4
Jackson, Michael 539
Jacksonville 476-8, **477**
jazz 124, 411-12
Baker's Keyboard Lounge 539
Blues Alley 260
Campbell 84
Cliff Bell's 539
Clifford Brown Jazz Festival 265
Green Mill 504
National Jazz Museum 90
New Orleans Jazz & Heritage Festival 409
Newport Jazz Festival 192
Smalls 80
Wally's Cafe 168
Jefferson, Thomas 250, 290, 292
Jekyll Island 379

Kalamazoo 542
kayaking & canoeing
Adventures of Mammoth Cave 363
Apostle Islands National Lakeshore 562
Assateague Outfitters 279
Assawoman Bay 270
Beaufort Paddle 317
BFLO Harbor Kayak 117
Buffalo National River 406
Cache Bayou Outfitters 515
Champagne's Swamp Tours 423
Coastal Expeditions 339-40
Community Sailing Center 205
Daicey Pond 231
Gorge Underground 364
Hidden River Outfitters 136
Jones Lagoon 449
Key Bridge Boathouse 262
Kittatinny Canoes 142
Lake Champlain Paddlers' Trail 205
Lake George Kayak Co 111
Maine Island Kayak Co 223
Maine State Sea Kayak 229
Manhattan Community Boathouse 86
Manhattan Kayak Co 86
Paddle for Pints 548
Paddle TC 548
Peninsula Kayak Company 560
Providence Kayak Co 188
Saco Bound 219

kayaking & canoeing *continued*
Thompson Boat Center 262
Wekiwa Springs Adventures 466
Wheel Fun Rentals 569
Keller, Helen 383
Kelleys Island 532-3
Kennedy, John F 240, 541
Kennedy Space Center 471
Kentucky 358-65, **359**
Kentucky Derby 360
Kermit the Frog 391
Key West, *see* Florida Keys & Key West
King, Martin Luther Jr 249, 384, 385, 387
Knoxville 357

Lafayette 422-3
Lake Champlain 204-5
Lake George 111-12
Lake Harriet 569
Lake of the Isles 569
Lake Placid 112-13
Lake Pontchartrain 422
Lake Willoughby 206
lakes
Bde Maka Ska 569
Bear Lake 447
Cedar Lake 569
Finger Lakes 113-15
Lake Champlain 204
Lake George 111-12
Lake Harriet 569
Lake of the Isles 569
Lake Placid 112-13
Lake Pontchartrain 422
Lake Willoughby 206
Rainbow Lake 356-7
Lambertville 129
Lancaster 143-4
language 37
Lansing 542-3
Last Green Valley 201
Laurel Highlands 148-9
leaf peeping 206
LEGOLAND 468, 470
Leland 548
Lenox 184
Letchworth State Park 115
Lexington 361-2
libraries 167
LGBTIQ+ travelers 593
Northalsted Pride 505-6
Pride Center 459
Wilton Drive 459
lighthouses
Au Sable Point Light Station 550
Cape Henry Lighthouse 294
Cape May Lighthouse 122
Currituck Beach Lighthouse 321
Grand Marais Lighthouse 575
Hereford Lighthouse 124
Montauk Point Lighthouse 98
Ocracoke Lighthouse 319
Sandy Hook Lighthouse 125
Tybee Island Light Station 376, 378
West Quoddy Head Lighthouse 230
Lincoln, Abraham 511, 513, 524, 541
Litchfield County 201
Little Italy 69
Little Rock 397-402, **399**
Logan 534
Long Beach Island 125
Long Island 98-9, 103-4, **102**
Louisiana 420-3, **421**
Louisville 360
Lowcountry 338

Mackinac Island 548, 551
Macon 374-5
Madison 197, 524, 556-8
Madison, James 293
Madison Square Garden 84
Maine 221-31, **222**
Mammoth Cave National Park 363
mangroves 449, 487
marijuana 592
marinas 190
markets
17th Street Market 287
Art Garden 415
Assembly Food Hall 353
Carrboro Farmers Market 325
Central Market 143
Charleston City Market 336
Chelsea Market 76-7
Dane County Farmers Market 557
Dupont Circle Farmers Market 259
Eastern Market 539, 254
Essex Market 73
Findlay Market 529
Golden Nugget Antique Flea Market 129
Grand Central Market 84
Krog Street Market 373
Litchfield Hills Farm Fresh Market 201
Malcolm Shabazz Harlem Market 91
Milwaukee Public Market 556
Nashville Farmers Market 351
Novo Asian Food Hall 146
Ottenheimer Market Hall 401
Ponce City Market 373
Reading Terminal Market 136-7
Riverfront Market 265
South 9th Street Italian Market 137
Time Out Market 95
Weaver Street Market 325
West Side Market 527
Wholey Fish Market 146
Winter Park Farmers' Market 468
Marley, Bob 265
Marquette 551
marshes, salt 198, 319
Martin Luther King Jr National Historical Park 369
Maryland 272-84, **273**
children, travel with 276
driving tour 277, **277**
Massachusetts 176-86, **177**
Memphis 347-51, **348**
Mercer, Henry 140
Merck Forest 212
Metromover 435
Metropolitan Museum of Art 88-9
Miami 432-43, **433**, **436**, **438**, **440**, **441**
accommodations 488
drinking 437, 442
food 435, 436, 438, 439, 440
shopping 439
travel within Miami 432
walking tour 434, **434**
Michigan 536-51, **537**
Michigan's Wine Country 547
Middlebury 205-6
Mill Mountain Star 292
Milford 268
Millionaire's Row 437
Milwaukee 552-6, **554**
Minneapolis 564-8, **566**, **568**
Minnesota 564-77, **565**
Mississippi 389-96, **390**
Mississippi Delta 391-2
Mobile 387-8
mobile payments 585
money 585
Montgomery 385-7
Montpelier 209, 212
monuments & memorials
Freedom Monument Sculpture Park 386
Indiana War Memorial 519
Korean War Veterans Memorial 250
Lincoln Memorial 250
Make Way for Ducklings 166
Martin Luther King Jr Memorial 249
Mary Tyler Moore Statue 572
National Memorial for Peace & Justice 386
National WWII Memorial 250
Paul Bunyan Statue 572
Pilgrim Monument 179
Stonewall National Monument 76
Vietnam Veterans Memorial 251
Vulcan 384
Washington Monument 244, 248
moonshine 357
Morgan, Zackquill 303
Morgantown 303-4
mosquitoes 574
motels 586
Moundville Archaeological Park 387
Mount Vernon 297
mountain biking 403, 557, *see also* cycling & cycling tours
mountains
Adirondack Mountain Reserve 111
Adirondacks, the 616
Blood Mountain 374
Buck Mountain 111
Cadillac Mountain 228
Coler Mountain 405
Grandfather Mountain 327
Lookout Mountain 355-6
Monument Mountain 184
Mt Greylock 185
Mt Katahdin 230-1
Mt Magazine 402
Mt Mansfield 208

Map Pages **000**

Mt Nebo 401-2
Old Rag Mountain 293
Ozark Mountains 406
Prospect Mountain 111
White Mountains 220
Mt Washington 218-20
murals
Crossroads of America mural 284
Krog Street Tunnel 373
Lincoln Street Art Park 537-8
Little Five Points 371, 372
Prince 564-5
Summit of the Americas 439
Vicksburg Riverfront Murals 395
Wynwood Walls 437, 439
museums & galleries
Abbe Museum 228
Addison/Ripley Fine Art 260
AKC Museum of the Dog 84
Alabama Music Hall of Fame 383
Allegany Museum 283-4
Amazeum 405
Amazing World of Dr Seuss 182
American Art Museum 252
American Civil War Museum 287
American Folk Art Museum 90
American Museum of Natural History 90
American Visionary Art Museum 281
American Writers Museum 498
America's Black Holocaust Museum 556
Andy Warhol Museum 148
Arab American National Museum 543
Art Deco Museum 435
Art Institute of Chicago 497-8
Art Omi 106
Asheville Art Museum 325
Asia Society & Museum 87
Atlanta History Center 373-4
Attic Gallery 394
Auburn Cord Duesenberg Automobile Museum 520
Automotive Hall of Fame 542
B&O Railroad Museum 281
Backstreet Cultural Museum 412
Baltimore Museum of Art 281
Baltimore Museum of Industry 281
Barnes Foundation 138
Bass, the 435
BB King Museum 391
Bechtler Museum of Modern Art 322
Bennington museum 213
Bethel Woods Center for the Arts 109
Big Duck 104
Biltmore 326
Birmingham Civil Rights Institute 384
Bobblehead Hall of Fame & Museum 556
Boscobel House & Gardens 106
Boston Children's Museum 172
Boston Fire Museum 172
Boston Tea Party Ships & Museum 172
Branch Museum of Architecture & Design 287
Broad Art Museum 543
Buffalo AKG Art Museum 117
Buffalo History Museum 117
Buffalo Transportation Pierce-Arrow Museum 117
Burchfield Penney Art Center 117
Cabildo 409
Capital City Museum 362
Carnegie Museums of Pittsburgh 148
Carrie Haddad's 105
Catfish Row Museum 395
Catskill Fly Fishing Center & Museum 112
Charleston Museum 334
Charlestown Navy Yard 173
Chazen Museum of Art 557
Chicago Children's Museum 503
Chicago Cultural Center 507
Chihuly Collection 487
Children's Museum of Indianapolis 518-19
Cincinnati Art Museum 530
Cincinnati Museum Center 529
City Reliquary 95
Clay Center for the Arts & Sciences 299
Cleveland Museum of Art 527
Columbus Museum of Art 531
Cooper-Hewitt Smithsonian Design Museum 87
Corning Museum of Glass 115
Country Music Hall of Fame & Museum 351
Crystal Bridges Museum 405
Cumberland Visitor Center & Museum 284
Delaware Children's Museum 265
Delaware History Museum 266
Delta Blues Museum 391-2
Detroit Institute of Arts 537
Dexter Parsonage Museum 387
Dia Beacon 104
Dia Bridgehampton 104
Dia Chelsea 80
Discovery World at Pier Wisconsin 556
Down Creek Gallery 318
Drawing Center 63
Eastern Shore Art Center 388
Eastern State Penitentiary 138-9
Edgar Allan Poe National Historic Site 138
Eiteljorg Museum 519-20
Electromagnetic Pinball Museum & Restoration 190
Eric Carle Museum of Picture Book Art 182
Evergreen Museum 281
Fairhope Museum of History 388
Field Museum 506-7
Flatwoods Monster Museum 302
Ford Piquette Avenue Plant 541
Fountain of Youth Archaeological Park 481
Frank Lloyd Wright Home & Studio 511
Franklinton Fridays 531
Frazier History Museum 360
Frick Art Museum 148
Frick Collection 90
Gagosian 80
Gallery Article 15 260
Gallier House Museum 411
Gateway to the Blues Museum 391
Georgia Museum of Art 374
German Village 530
Gettysburg National Military Park 144
Gilmore Car Museum 542
Grand Portage National Monument 573-4
Grand Rapids African American Museum & Archives 543
Grand Rapids Public Museum 543
Graveyard of the Atlantic Museum 318-19
Great Lakes Shipwreck Museum 543
Greyhound Bus Museum 572
Griffin Museum of Science & Industry 498
Hancock Shaker Village 185
Harley-Davidson Museum 555
Harvey B Gantt Center 322
Hatteras Island Ocean Center 319
Havre de Grace Decoy Museum 274
Heinz History Center 146
Helen Keller Birthplace 383
Henry Ford Museum of American Innovation 541-2
Henry Whitfield State Museum 197
High Line Nine 80
High Museum of Art 371
Highway 61 Blues Museum 391
Hill Center 254
Hirshhorn Museum 249
Historic Jamestown Archaearium 290
Historic New Orleans Collection 409
Historic Patuxet Homesit 175
History Museum of Mobile 388

museums & galleries *continued*
Hunter Museum of American Art 355
Huntsville Museum of Art 382
Imagine Museum 487
Indianapolis Museum of Art 519
Insect Asylum 498
Institute of Contemporary Art 172
International African American Museum 336
International Center of Photography 73
International Civil Rights Center & Museum 323
International Spy Museum 254
International Tennis Hall of Fame 190
Intrepid Sea, Air & Space Museum 86
James Museum of Western & Wildlife Art 487
Jay Etkin Gallery 349
Jepson Center 376
Jewish Museum 87
Jewish Museum of Florida-FIU 435
Jewish Museum of Maryland 281
Jimmy Carter Presidential Library & Museum 374
John Brown Wax Museum 304
Johnny Cash Museum 351
Juliette Gordon Low Birthplace Museum 376
Kalmar Nyckel Shipyard 265
Kentucky Historical Society 362
Kentucky Horse Park 361
Kentucky Military History Museum 362
Knoxville Museum of Art 357
KuBe Art Center 106
Kurt Vonnegut Museum & Library 520
Kykuit 106
Lake Placid Olympic Museum 112
Legacy Museum 386
Leslie-Lohman Museum of Art 63
Life-Saving Station Museum 278
Little Traverse History Museum 544
Living Sharks Museum 190
LongHouse Reserve 104
Louisiana Children's Museum 418
Louisville Slugger Museum & Factory 360
Lower Mississippi River Museum 394
Lucy Clark Gallery 327
Mackinac Art Museum 551
Magazzino Italian Art 106
Mark Twain House & Museum 199
Mattress Factory 148
Mayflower II 175
Memphis Brooks Museum of Art 350
Memphis Rock 'n' Soul Museum 347
Mercer Museum 141
Merchant's House Museum 72
Merry-Go-Round Museum 532
Metropolitan Museum of Art 88-9
Miami Museum of Art & Design 438
Milford Museum 268
Milwaukee Art Museum 555
Minneapolis Institute of Art 567
Mint Museum Uptown 321-2
Mississippi Civil Rights Museum 393
Mitchell Center for African American Heritage 266
Monongalia Arts Center 303
Mosaic Jekyll Island Museum 379
Motown Museum 539
Museum at Bethel Woods 109
Museum at Eldridge Street 71
Museum of African American History 167-8
Museum of Broadway 82
Museum of Contemporary Art 498
Museum of Contemporary Art Detroit 537
Museum of Contemporary Photography 507
Museum of Discovery 401
Museum of East Tennessee History 357
Museum of Fine Arts 169
Museum of Illusions 252, 498
Museum of Mississippi History 393-4
Museum of Modern Art 83
Museum of Native American History 405
Museum of the American Arts & Crafts Movement 487
Museum of the Cherokee People 328
Museum of the City of New York 87
Mütter Museum 138
Mystic Seaport Museum 198
Museum of Science & Industry 484
Natchez Museum of African American Culture & History 396
National Air & Space Museum 249
National Auto & Truck Museum 520
National Building Museum 252
National Center for Civil & Human Right 367
National Children's Museum 252
National Civil Rights Museum 347
National Constitution Center 130, 132
National Gallery of Art 249
National Great Blacks in Wax Museum 281
National Jazz Museum 90-1
National Maritime Museum of the Gulf 388
National Museum of African American History & Culture 241
National Museum of African Art 248
National Museum of Asian Art 248
National Museum of Mexican Art 507
National Museum of Natural History 241
National Museum of the American Indian 248-9
National Museum of the US Air Force 535
National Museum of Women in the Arts 252
National Mustard Museum 558
National Portrait Gallery 252
National September 11 Memorial Museum 61
National Underground Railroad Freedom Center 530
National WWII Museum 417
Neue Galerie 87
New Museum 73
New Orleans Museum of Art 419
New Orleans Pharmacy Museum 409
Newport Art Museum 190
Newport Car Museum 190
New York Earth Room 63
New-York Historical Society 90
Nicholas Roerich Museum 90
Nichols House Museum 166
Ocracoke Preservation Museum 319
Old Slave Mart Museum 335
Old State House Museum 401
Oldest Wooden School House Museum & Gardens 479
Opus 40 109
Orange County Regional History Center 470
Oscar Getz Museum of Bourbon History 361
Otherworld 531
Pace Gallery 80
Paula Cooper Gallery 80
Peggy Notebaert Nature Museum 503
Penn Center 340
Pennsylvania Academy of the Fine Arts 138
Pérez Art Museum Miami 437
Philadelphia Museum of Art 132
Phillips Collection 259

Map Pages **000**

Pin Point Heritage
Museum 378
Planet Word 252
Plimoth Grist Mill 175
Plimoth Patuxet
Museum 175
Poe Museum 289
Pollock-Krasner
House 104
Portland Museum of
Art 223
Presbytère 409
Princeton University Art
Museum 126
Provincetown
Museum 180
Reginald F Lewis
Museum 281
Rehoboth Art
League 269
Renwick Gallery 240-1
RE Olds Transportation
Museum 543
RISD Museum of Art 188
River Arts District 326
River Gallery 354-5
Rivers of Steel 148
Rock & Roll Hall of Fame
& Museum 526
Roanoke Island Festival
Park 319-20
Rodin Museum 138
Romero Britto Fine Art
Gallery 435
Rosa Parks Museum 387
Rubell Museum 252
Sag Harbor Whaling &
Historical Museum 103
Sailing Museum &
National Sailing Hall of
Fame 190
Sandwich Glass
Museum 178
Science Museum of
Virginia 287
Short North Arts
District 531
Smith Robertson
Museum 394
Solomon R Guggenheim
Museum 87
Sorrel Weed House 376
Spam Museum 572
Stax Museum of
American Soul Music
347, 349
Storm King Art Center
104-5
Strawbery Banke
Museum 216
Studebaker National
Museum 520
Studio Museum in
Harlem 91
Tampa Bay History
Center 484
Tampa Museum of
Art 484
Telfair Academy 376
Tenement Museum 69
Tennessee State
Museum 351
Torpedo Factory Art
Center 296
Transformer
Station 527
University of Michigan
Museum of Art 543
University of Michigan
Museum of Natural
History 543
University of Mississippi
Museum 393
US Space & Rocket
Center 382
USS Alabama 388
USS Cairo Museum 395
USS Constitution
Museum 173
Vermont Historical
Society Museum 212
Vicksburg Civil War
Museum 394
Village Craftsmen 318
Virginia Museum of Fine
Arts 287
Virginia Musical
Museum 289
Vizcaya Museum &
Gardens 443
Wadsworth
Atheneum 200
Wadsworth-Longfellow
House 223
Walmart Museum 405
Walters Art Museum 281
Washington Printmakers
Gallery 260
Weisman Art
Museum 567
Wells'Built Museum 464
West Virginia Bigfoot
Museum 302
Wexner Center for the
Arts 531
Whaling Museum 181
Whitney Museum of
American Art 73, 76
Wolfsonian-FIU 435
World of Coca-Cola 308
World's Only Mothman
Museum 302
Wright Brothers National
Memorial 320
Ybor City Museum State
Park 484
Zwaanendael Museum
270
mushrooms 140
music 37, 604-5, *see also individual genres*
Abbey Road on the
River 518
Apollo Theater 91
Armory 569
Armstrong Park 414
Asheville Music
Hall 325
Balcony Music Club 411
BB King's 349
Berklee Performance
Center 171
Blue Moon Saloon 422
Blues Highway 391
Boston Symphony
Orchestra: 171
Bowery Ballroom 73
Bright Lights 393
Bunker's Music Bar &
Grill 569
Clematis by Night 463
Clematis Social 463
Detroit 540
Double Decker Arts
Festival 393
Empty Bottle 504
Fame Studios 383
Fanny's House of
Music 354
Graceland 349
Grey Eagle 325
Ground Zero 392
Haw River
Ballroom 325
Hideout 504
Highland Brewing
Co 325
House of Blues 411
Jack of the Wood
Pub 325
Lafayette's Music
Room 349
Lake Harriet Band
Shell 569
Magic Stick 539
Metro 504
Museum at Bethel
Woods 109
Music Box Village
412, 414
Musket's Music
Station 363
New England
Conservatory 171
Orange Peel 325
Overton Park
Shell 350
Pour House 339
Preservation Hall 411-12
Princeton Record
Exchange 126
Pritzker Pavilion 499
Radio City Music
Hall 84
Red Room at Cafe 939 171
Refinery 339
Respectable Street 463
Robert's Western World
353-4
Royal American 339
Rum Boogie & Blues
Hall 349
Ryman Auditorium 351
Salt Shed 504
Saturn 384-5
Spazio 463
Tootsie's Orchid
Lounge 353
Wild Bill's 349
Wildwood's Honky
Tonk 123
Myrtle Beach 341
Mystic 198-9

N

Nantucket Island 181
Nashville 351-4, **352, 353**
Natchez 395-6
National Archives 251-2
National Mall 248
national parks & reserves
46-7, *see also* parks &
gardens, state parks &
reserves
Acadia National Park
228-30
Biscayne National
Park 448
Cherokee National
Forest 356
Congaree National
Park 344
Cuyahoga Valley
National Park 528
Daniel Boone National
Forest 365
Everglades National Park
446, 448
Great Smoky Mountains
National Park
329-32, 355
Hot Springs National
Park 400
Indiana Dunes National
Park 521
Isle Royale National
Park 549
Mammoth Cave National
Park 363
New River Gorge
National Park and
Preserve 300
Ocmulgee Mounds 374-5
Voyageurs National
Park 576

New England 153-233, **154-5**
accommodations 232-3
climate 156
driving tours 183, 210-11, 226-7, **183**, **211**, **227**
itineraries 156-7
navigation 154-5
New Hampshire 214-20, **215**
New Haven 195-7, **196**
New Hope 141-2
New Jersey 120-9, **54-5**, **121**
accommodations 151
activities 56-7
itineraries 56-7
navigation 54-5
New Orleans 407-19, **408**, **413**, **416**, **417**
accommodations 425
children, travel with 418
drinking 412, 414, 415, 418
entertainment 411-12
festivals & events 407, 409
food 409, 411, 414, 415, 417, 418, 419
shopping 418
travel within New Orleans 407
walking tours 410, **410**
New River Gorge 300-1
New York City 58-97, **60**, **64**, **66**, **70**, **74**, **81**, **85**, **94**
accommodations 150
drinking 63, 68, 72, 76, 77, 83, 87, 95-6
entertainment 67, 73, 80, 82-3
festivals & events 97
food 61, 63, 67, 69, 71, 73, 76-7, 79, 87, 90, 91, 97
shopping 61, 67-8, 71-2, 78
travel within New York City 58
walking tour 62, **62**
New York State 98-119, **54-5**, **100-1**
accommodations 150
activities 56-7
driving tour 110, **110**
itineraries 56-7
navigation 54-5
Newport 190-2, **191**
Niagara Falls 118-19
nightlife 589
Noir Collective 325, 326
Norfolk 294
North Carolina 314-32, **315**
North Shore 573-5
Northport 548
notable buildings, *see also* historic buildings & sites
520 W 28th St 78
Skyspace 405
St Regis Chicago 501
Sunsphere 357

Oak Park 509, 511
Ocean City 278
Ocracoke 319
offbeat 19
Ohio 525-35, **526**
Ohio Amish Country 533-4
Ohio City 527
Okefenokee National Wildlife Refuge 375
opening hours 595
Orlando & Walt Disney World® 464-70, **465**
Outer Banks 318-21
Overseas Hwy 49, 453
Oxford 392-3
oysters 67
Ozark Mountains 406

parks & gardens, *see also* national parks & reserves, state parks & reserves
Airlie Gardens 316
Alfred Caldwell Lily Pool 499
Atlanta Botanical Garden 372
Audubon Park 419
Battle Green 173-4
Bayfront Park 435, 437
Beacon Park 541
Belle Isle Park 541
Bluff View Art District 354
Bonnet House Museum & Gardens 459
Boston Common 162
Brickell Key Park 437
Brookgreen Gardens 341
Brooklyn Bridge Park 91, 95
Bryant Park 84, 86
Burlington Greenway 204
Campus Martius Park 541
Centennial Olympic Park 370
Centennial Park 354, 484
Central Park 92-3
Charles River Esplanade 168
Cheekwood 354
City Park 419
Columbus Park 63, 67
Concrete Park 558
Curry Hammock 454
Curtis Hixon Waterfront Park 484
Delaware Botanic Gardens 271
Delaware Park 116
Dequindre Cut Greenway 541
Dr Evermor's Sculpture Park 558
East Rock Park 195
Elizabeth Street Garden 68
Formal Gardens 350
Fort Lauderdale Beach Park 456
Fort Zachary Taylor Park 454
Grant Park 499
Harry P Leu Gardens 468
Historic Fourth Ward Park 373
Hudson River Park 78-9
Huntsville Botanical Garden 382
Institute Woods 127
Jetty Park 473
Labyrinth 158
Lincoln Park 499
Longwood Gardens 139
Lurie Garden 499
Margaret Pace Park 437
Martin's Park 172
Maurice A Ferré Park 437
Máximo Gómez Park 439
Mill Ruins Park 569
Millennium Park 498-9
Minneapolis Sculpture Garden 567
Minute Man National Historical Park 174
Morey's Piers 123
New Orleans Botanical Garden 419
Nichols Arboretum 543
Overton Park 350
Philadelphia's Magic Gardens 139
Piedmont Park 372
Pilgrims' First Landing Park 179-80
Point Park 356
Polk Bros Park 501
Public Garden 162, 166
Railroad Park 384
Rose Kennedy Greenway 158-9
Sarah P Duke Gardens 323
Saxapahaw Island Park 325
Schuylkill Banks 132, 136
Spohr Gardens 178
State Botanical Garden of Georgia 374
Storm King Art Center 104-5
Sunken Forest 103
Sydney & Walda Besthoff Sculpture Garden 419
Tubman Garrett Riverfront Park 265
Umpachenee Falls Park 184
Underline 437
United States National Arboretum 255, 259
Valley Forge National Historic Park 140
Veldheer Tulip Gardens 546
Virginia B Fairbanks Art & Nature Park 519
Vizcaya Museum & Gardens 443
Warner Parks 354
Washington Square Park 79-80
Water Works Park 482, 484
Watson Island Park 437
Wild Gardens of Acadia 229
Windmill Island Garden 546
Women's Rights National Historical Park 115
Parks, Rosa 385, 387, 541-2
Peacham 213
Pennsylvania 130-49, **54-5**, **131**
accommodations 151
activities 56-7
itineraries 56-7
navigation 54-5
Pennsylvania Wilds 144-5
Petoskey 544
petroglyphs 533
Philadelphia 130, 132-8, **133**
pickles 146
Pictured Rocks National Lakeshore 550
Pittsburgh 146-8, **147**
Pittsfield 185
planetariums 507
planning 36-7
Plantation Country 421

Map Pages **000**

Plymouth 174-5
Poconos, the 142-3
podcasts 37, 47
Point Pleasant 301-2
Porcupine Mountains 551
Portland 223-5
Portsmouth 216-18
Portuguese man o' war 458
Presley, Elvis 349
Prince 564-5, 570
Princeton 126-9, **127**
Prohibition 123
Providence 188-9, **189**
Provincetown 179-81
public holidays 595

Racine 556
rafting 356
rail tours 328, 355-6
Rainbow Lake Wilderness Area 356-7
Red River Gorge 363, 364
Rehoboth Beach 268-9
responsible travel 590-1
Rhode Island 186-92, **187**
Richmond 287-9, **288**
road trips, *see* driving & driving tours
rock-climbing 219, 229, 355, 511
Rockefellers, the 616
Rockland 225
roller-skating 542
Ross, Diana 539

safe travel 592
sailing 225
sales tax 585
sandboarding 320
Sandusky 531-2
Sandwich 178-9
Sandy Hook 125-6
Savannah 376, 377
Saxapahaw 325
seals 124, 190, 229
Seaport District 172
Sequoyah 320
Shawnee Hills 515
Shenandoah National Park 292-3
Shoals, the 382-3
shopping, *see individual locations*
skiing 112-13, 206, 208, 219, 305, 547
skyscrapers
  Edge 82
  Empire State Building 80, 82
  Freedom Tower 435, 438
  One World Trade Center 61
  Sun Dial Restaurant & View 370-1
  Top of the Rock 82
  Top of the World 279
  Willis Tower 501
Slater, Kelly 475
Sleeping Bear Dunes National Lakeshore 545
snorkeling 356, 449, 452
snow storms 592
snowmobiling 547
soccer 254
SoHo 61, 63
sound studios
  Muscle Shoals Sound Studios 383
  Sun Studio 347
South Bend 520, 522
South Carolina 333-44, **334**
South, the 309-425, **310-11**
  accommodations 424-5
  events 312-13
  itineraries 312-13
  navigation 310-11
Southwest Florida 482-7
Space Coast 471-5, **472**
spas 59, 72, 184, 305, 371
Spring Green 558
Springfield 182, 511, 513
Springsteen, Bruce 125
St Augustine 478-81, **480**
St Charles Avenue Streetcar 418
St Helena & Hunting Islands 340-1
St Mary's City 274, 276
St Paul 570-1
St Pete Pier 485
St Petersburg 485-7, **486**
stadiums 252
stargazing 534
state parks & reserves, *see also* national parks & reserves, parks & gardens
  Assateague State Park 278-9
  Bash Bish Falls State Park 184
  Berkeley Springs State Park 305
  Bicentennial Capitol Mall State Park 351
  Big Bay State Park 565
  Big Talbot Island State Park 478
  Blue Spring State Park 466
  Brown County State Park 523
  Buttermilk Falls State Park 114
  Camp Hero State Park 98-9
  Cape May Point State Park 123
  Cheesequake State Park 129
  Clark State Forest 520
  Clifty Falls State Park 520
  Crater of Diamonds State Park 402
  Cumberland Falls State Resort Park 365
  Daniel Boone National Forest 365
  Delaware Seashore State Park 270
  Devil's Den State Park 406
  DuPont State Fores 327-8
  Edisto Beach State Park 340
  Falls of the Ohio State Park 520
  First State Heritage Park 268
  Gooseberry Falls State Park 573
  Grand Haven State Park 551
  Grandfather Mountain State Park 327
  Gulf State Park 388
  Hammonasset Beach State Park 197
  High Point State Park 129
  Hither Hills State Park 103
  Holland State Park 551
  Hueston Woods State Park 534
  Hugh Taylor Birch State Park 458
  Hunting Island State Park 340-1
  Indian River Lagoon State Park 474
  Jekyll Island State Park 379
  Jockey's Ridge State Park 320
  John Bryan State Park 534
  John Pennekamp Coral Reef State Park 450, 452
  Judge CR Magney State Park 573
  Kelleys Island State Park 533
  Kittatinny Valley State Park 129
  Lake Guntersville State Park 382
  Leonard Harrison State Park 144-5
  Letchworth State Park 115
  Lignumvitae Key Botanical State Park 452, 454
  Ludington State Park 551
  Malabar Farm State Park 534
  Matthiessen 511
  Mohican-Memorial State Forest 534
  Montauk Point State Park 98
  Monte Sano State Park 382
  Mounds State Park 520
  Mt Tom State Reservation 182
  Myrtle Beach State Park 341
  Natural Bridge State Resort Park 364
  Newport State Park 560
  Norvin Green State Forest 129
  Oak Mountain State Park 384
  Ohiopyle State Park 149
  Old Forest State Natural Area 350
  Peninsula State Park 560
  Petit Jean 401
  Petoskey State Park 551
  Point Lookout State Park 276
  Porcupine Mountains 551
  Princeton Battlefield State Park 127
  Quoddy Head State Park 230
  Robert H Treman State Park 114
  Sebastian Inlet State Park 474
  Shadmoor State Park 104
  Skinner State Park 182
  South Bass Island State Park 534
  Starved Rock 511
  Tahquamenon Falls State Park 551
  Tallulah Gorge State Park 374
  Temperance River State Park 573
  Turkey Run State Park 520
  Underhill State Park 208-9
  Unicoi State Park & Lodge 374
  Vogel State Park 374
  Washington Crossing State Park 129

state parks & reserves *continued*
Watkins Glen State Park 114
Wekiwa Springs State Park 466
Wharton State Forest 129
White Pines Forest 511
White River State Park 519, 520
Statue of Liberty 64-5
Stiltsville 449
Stowe 206-9
Sturbridge 181-2
sunsets 561
supper clubs 563
surfing 99, 126, 294, 473
Sussex County 269-71
sustainability 590-1
Sutton 302
Suttons Bay 548
sweetgrass baskets 343

Tampa 482-5, **483**
Tampa Bay 482-7
temples 128
Tennessee 345-57, **346**
theaters
54 Below 83
Alabama Theatre 384
American Players Theatre 558
Apollo Theater 91
Atlantic Theater Company 80
Broadway tickets 83
Bucks County Playhouse 141-2
Chicago Theatre 506
Chopin Theatre 506
Clayton Theatre 269
Clear Space Theatre Company 269
Comedy Cellar 80
Den Theatre 503
Drama Book Shop 82
Frank Bradley's 132
GableStage 442
Goodman Theatre 506
Guthrie Theater 569
Historic Ritz Theatre 379
Howard Theatre 256
iO Theater 503
Jungle Theater 569
Lincoln Center 90
Lincoln Theatre 257
Lucille Lortel Theatre 80
Lyric 384
Metrograph 72
Metropolitan Theatre 303
Milton Theatre 269
Miracle Theatre 254
National Theatre 252
Neo-Futurist Theater 506
Paramount Theater 290
Playhouse Square 527
Playwrights Horizons 82-3
Public Theater 67
Sag Harbor Cinema 103
Second City 503
Shakespeare Theatre Company 252
Slipper Room 73
Steppenwolf Theatre 506
Studio Theatre 255
TheaterSquared 403
University Theater 402-3
Village Vanguard 80
Walton Arts Center 403
Warner Theatre 252
Woolly Mammoth Theatre Company 252
theme parks, *see* amusement parks
ticks 592
Times Square 84, 86
tipping 585
tornadoes 592
train travel 584
transportation, public 583
travel costs 583
travel with children, *see* family travel
travel seasons 34-5, *see also individual locations*
travel to/from Eastern USA 582
travel within Eastern USA 583
Traverse City 548
Tremont 529
Triangle, the 323
Tri-Peaks Region 401-2
tubing 142, 219, 268, 304, 342

U

Universal Orlando Resort™ 469
universities
Duke University 323
Harvard University 163, **162**
Howard University 256
Michigan State University 543
University of Arkansas 402-3
University of Georgia 374
University of Michigan 543
University of North Carolina 323
University of Notre Dame 522
University of Virginia 290
USS Constitution 173

vacations 614-16
Valley Forge 140
Vanderbilts, the 616
Venus Flytraps 316
Vermont 202-13, **203**
views 82
vinyl
Bossa N' Roll Records 468
Dr Music Records 388
Goner Records 349
Reckless Records 506
Virginia 285-98, **286**
visas 582
voodoo 409
Voyageurs National Park 576

walking, *see also* hiking
Bailey Woods Trail 393
Bridge Walk 300
Castle Island 172
Clinton Presidential Park Bridge 399
Freedom Trail 164
Gordons Pond Trail 270
Natchez Bluff River Trail 396
Navy Pier 501
Riverfront Park 354
Riverfront Wilmington 265
Robert Frost Interpretive Trail 205
Sabbaday Brook Trail 220
St Anthony Falls Heritage Trail 569
walking tours
Annapolis 275, **275**
Art Deco 434, **434**
Brandywine Valley's Estates 267, **267**
Charleston 337, **337**
Durham 324, **324**
Eureka Springs 404, **404**
French Quarter 410, **410**
Old Port 224, **224**
Portsmouth 217, **217**
Savannah's Squares 377, **377**
Wharf DC 245, **245**
Wright Sights 512, **512**
Walt Disney World® 467
Washington, DC 240-62, **241**, **244**, **251**, **253**, **258**, **261**
accommodations 306
children, travel with 252
drinking 260
entertainment 240, 252, 254, 255
festivals & events 249-50, 255
food 244, 249, 250, 251, 253, 254, 255, 259, 260, 262
shopping 260
travel within Washington, DC 240
walking tour 245, **245**
Washington, DC & the Capital Region 234-307, **236-7**
accommodations 306-7
itineraries 238-9
navigation 236-7
weather 238-9
waterfalls
Bastion Falls 108
Benton Falls Trail 356
Cathedral Falls 300
Cedar Falls 534
Cumberland Falls 364, 365
Dingmans Falls 143
Eagles Falls 365
Glen Burney Falls Trail 327
Glory Hole Falls 406
Hemmed-in Hollow Falls 406
Ithaca Falls 114
Kaaterskill Falls 108
Minnehaha Falls 569-70
Niagara Falls 118-19
Rainbow Lake Wilderness Area 356-7
Ruby Falls 356
Sabbaday Falls 220
Taughannock Falls 113
Waters, Muddy 502
watersports 43, *see also individual watersports*
weather 34-5, *see also individual locations*
West Palm Beach 461-3, **462**

Map Pages **000**

West Virginia 298-305, **299**
whales 123, 180-1, 225
whiskey 360, 361, 363
White House, the 242-3
White Mountains 220
whitewater rafting 231, 322, 328
wi-fi 582
wildlife sanctuaries & zoos
  Archie Carr National Wildlife Refuge 474
  Audubon Bird Sanctuary 388
  Audubon Zoo 419
  Bon Secour National Wildlife Refuge 388
  Central Florida Zoo & Botanic Gardens 470
  Chincoteague National Wildlife Refuge 294-5
  Cypress Creek National Wildlife Refuge 515
  Du Pont Environmental Education Center 265
  Duke Lemur Center 323
  Lincoln Park Zoo 503
  Manatee Lagoon 463
  Memphis Zoo 350
  Merritt Island National Wildlife Refuge 474
  Montrose Point Bird Sanctuary 499
  Okefenokee National Wildlife Refuge 375
  Pelican Island National Wildlife Refuge 463
  Potter Park Zoo 543
  Prime Hook National Wildlife Refuge 270
  Rachel Carson National Wildlife Refuge 316-17
  Smithsonian's National Zoo 255
  Stellwagen Bank National Marine Sanctuary 181
  Zoo Tampa at Lowry Park 484
Wildwood 123-4
Williamsburg 289-90
Wilmington 265-7, 316, **266**
wineries
  Bishop Estate Vineyard & Winery 141
  Blenheim Vineyards 290
  Blue Sky Vineyard 515
  Central Virginia Wine Tours 290
  Chaddsford Winery 141
  Forge Cellars 114
  Grand Central City Winery 84
  Hawk Haven 122
  Heart & Hands Wine Co's 114
  Jefferson Vineyards 292
  King Family Vineyards 292
  Lake Michigan Shore Wine Trail 547
  Lakewood Vineyards 114
  Leelanau Peninsula Wine Trail 547
  New Jersey Wine Grower's Association 122
  Old Mission Peninsula Wine Trail 547
  Penns Woods Winery 141
  Pippin Hill 292
  Seaside Seabird Sanctuary 487
  Shawnee Hills Wine Trail 515
  Six Eighty Cellars 114
  Va La Vineyards 141
  Wycombe Vineyards 141
Winston-Salem 323
Wisconsin 552-63, **553**
Wisconsin Dells 558
Wonder, Stevie 539
Woods Hole 178
Wright brothers 320, 534-5
Wright, Frank Lloyd 509, 511

Ybor City 484-5

ziplining 112, 219, 304, 328, 356
zoos, *see* wildlife sanctuaries & zoos

NOTES

"That first time we visited Shark Valley (p444) in the Everglades with gators sunning alongside the bike path as we coasted by."

JESSE SCOTT

"Whenever I see Manhattan's skyline from the Brooklyn Bridge (p59), I fall in love with NYC all over again."

JOHN GARRY

FROM LEFT: IONFOKUS/GETYY IMAGES, ROBERTO LA ROSA/SHUTTERSTOCK

Mapping data sources:
© Lonely Planet
© OpenStreetMap http://openstreetmap.org/copyright

THIS BOOK

Destination Editor Caroline Trefler

Production Editor Robin Yule

Image Editor Virginia Moreno

Cartographer Rachel Imeson

Coordinating Editor Andrea Dobbin

Assisting Editors Andrew Bain, Shauna Daly, Natalie Howard, Karyn Noble

Cover Researcher Kat Marsh

Thanks Michelle Bennett, Melanie Dankel, Helen Koehne, Kellie Langdon, Ailbhe MacMahon, Saralinda Turner, Clifton Wilkinson

Paper in this book is certified against the Forest Stewardship Council™ standards. FSC™ promotes environmentally responsible, socially beneficial and economically viable management of the world's forests.

Published by Lonely Planet Global Limited
CRN 554153
7th edition – Feb 2026
ISBN 978 1 83758 421 5

10 9 8 7 6 5 4 3 2 1
Printed in Malaysia